ACCOUNTING
THE BASIS FOR BUSINESS DECISIONS

Fifth Canadian Edition

Walter B. Meigs, Ph.D., C.P.A.
University of Southern California

Robert F. Meigs, D.B.A.
San Diego State University

Wai P. Lam, Ph.D., C.A.
University of Windsor

McGraw-Hill Ryerson Limited

Toronto Montreal Auckland Bogotá Cairo
Caracas Hamburg Lisbon London Madrid
Mexico Milan New Delhi Panama Paris
San Juan São Paulo Singapore Sydney Tokyo

ACCOUNTING
The Basis for Business Decisions
Fifth Canadian Edition

Copyright © McGraw-Hill Ryerson Limited, 1988, 1985, 1981, 1976, 1973, 1964. Adapted from ACCOUNTING: THE BASIS FOR BUSINESS DECISIONS written by Walter B. Meigs and Robert F. Meigs. Copyright © 1987, 1984, 1981, 1977, 1972, 1967, 1962 by McGraw-Hill Inc. All rights reserved. No part of this publication may be reproduced, stored in a data base or retrieval system, or transmitted in any form or by any means, electronic, mechanical, photocopying, recording, or otherwise, without prior written permission of McGraw-Hill Ryerson Limited.

ISBN 0-07-549524-4

1 2 3 4 5 6 7 8 9 10   D   7 6 5 4 3 2 1 0 9 8

Printed and bound in Canada

Cover and Book Design by Daniel Kewley

Canadian Cataloguing in Publication Data
  Meigs, Walter B., date–
    Accounting: the basis for business decisions

  5th Canadian ed.
  Includes index.
  ISBN 0-07-549524-4

  1. Accounting. I. Meigs, Robert F. II. Lam, Wai P.,
  date–   . III. Title.

HF5635.M45 1988   657'.044   C87-094950-0

CONTENTS

PART 5 CORPORATIONS

PART 7   MANAGERIAL ACCOUNTING: COST ACCOUNTING SYSTEMS

ACKNOWLEDGEMENTS

I would like to express my sincere thanks to the users of the preceding editions who offered helpful suggestions for this edition.

I am indebted to a number of individuals who thoroughly reviewed, either in part or as a whole, the text, along with the problems and solutions, and to those who provided valuable advice. They are: Don C. Cherry, Dalhousie University; Terry Litovitz, University of Toronto; Gordon Farrell, British Columbia Institute of Technology; Jim Macri, Clarkson Gordon; John A. Willes, Queen's University; Dan Partridge, Mount Allison University; Brenda Mallouk, University of Toronto; Ross Johnston, University of Windsor; Glen Ladouceur, Peat Marwick; Sam Garofalo, Confederation College; Esther Deutsch, Ryerson Polytechnical Institute; and Rich Newburg, Centennial College.

I am especially appreciative of the assistance and advice of Jackie Kaiser and Marilyn Nice of McGraw-Hill Ryerson Limited.

My special thanks go to Sandy Berlasty, University of Windsor, for her assistance in typing part of the manuscript, especially the chapter on statement of changes in financial position.

Finally, my family members — Jean, Angela, Lambert, and Gloria — also deserve a great deal of appreciation for their assistance in typing, editing, and proofreading the manuscript of the text, solutions, and supplements, as well as for their patience and understanding in accommodating this academic endeavour.

Wai P. Lam

PREFACE

A new edition provides authors with an opportunity to add new material, to condense the coverage of topics that have declined in relative importance, to reorganize portions of the book to improve instructional efficiency, and to refine and polish the treatment of basic subject matter. We have tried to do all these things in this fifth Canadian edition, the most extensive revision in the history of the text.

The environment of accounting is changing fast, and the shift toward computers and the increasing public interest in income tax policies and in financial reporting affect the goals and content of an introductory text in accounting. In order to function intelligently as a citizen as well as in the business community, every individual needs more than ever before an understanding of basic accounting concepts. Our goal is to present accounting as an essential part of the decision-making process for the voter, the taxpayer, the government official, the business manager, and the investor.

This edition, like the preceding one, is designed for use in the first university level course in accounting. In this course, instructors often recognize three groups of students: those who stand at the threshold of preparation for a career in accounting, students of business administration who need a thorough understanding of accounting as an important element of the total business information system, and students from a variety of other disciplines who will find the ability to use and interpret accounting information a valuable accomplishment. During the process of revision, we have tried to keep in mind the needs and interests of all three groups.

NEW FEATURES IN THIS EDITION

IN THE TEXT:

1 A short preview of each chapter, introducing students to both the educational goals and the technical content of the chapter.

2 Chapter learning objectives integrated into the text material through marginal notations and summaries at the end of each chapter.

3 Introductory chapters explaining the steps in the accounting cycle as applied to manual and to computer-based accounting systems.

4 Introductory level coverage of the new Statement of Changes in Financial Position, focussing on both the preparation and interpretation of this statement.

5 Coverage of the tax reform of 1987, including its effects upon individuals and corporations, effective 1988.

6 Over 120 new exercises and problems. In addition, the vast majority of the exercises and problems carried forward from the prior edition have been revised.

7 In each chapter, a new first exercise emphasizing accounting terminology. This exercise is coordinated with similar exercises in the *Test Bank* and the *Study Guide*.

8 A new type of problem material — Business Decision Cases — emphasizing the use and interpretation of accounting information in interesting yet practical business situations. These cases are more numerous and more varied than similar problems in past editions.

9 A new appendix in which students are asked to analyze the recent financial statements of a large well-known company.

10 Increased use of real business examples — termed Cases in Point — to illustrate key accounting concepts and business practices.

11 Increased emphasis upon accounting theory and generally accepted accounting principles throughout the text.

12 Increased emphasis upon the relationship of many accounting practices to the need for achieving adequate internal control.

13 Careful shortening of the text, which now contains 26 chapters rather than 28.

NEW ITEMS IN THE SUPPLEMENTAL PACKAGE:

1 *The Instructor's Guide*, which contains suggested course coverage and assignment materials as well as comments and observations by the authors. Included in this guide is the printed Canadian *Test Bank and Answers to the Test Bank*. A computerized version of this Test Bank is available free to adopters for use with the IBM-PC or Apple.

2 An expanded set of *Visual Classroom Displays,* now in colour and with multiple overlays.

3 A brand-new Canadian Problem Supplement available free to instructors.

4 A variety of software items, including a number of spreadsheet applications, traditional computerized practice sets, and the innovative *CYMA/McGraw-Hill General Ledger Software and Applications*.

FEATURES CARRIED FORWARD FROM PRIOR EDITIONS

Special qualities that are carried forward from prior editions include:
1 Depth of coverage. Topics are covered in a depth that will qualify the student for subsequent course work in accounting.
2 Accuracy in all problem material and solutions. All problems, solutions, and examination materials have been developed and tested first-hand by the authors in their own classes for introductory accounting students. This personal attention to accuracy is supplemented by independent testing by other accounting faculty.
3 Perspective — careful effort throughout the text and problems to utilize current and realistic prices, interest rates, and earnings levels.
4 People-oriented problems which depict the complex decisions that must be made by men and women acting as managers, investors, and in other roles.
5 Abundant problem material, including review questions, exercises, two sets of problems, and Business Decision Cases. In addition, each chapter contains a glossary of key terms and many chapters include a demonstration problem to assist students in developing skill in analyzing and solving accounting problems.
6 The concept of present value, presented in clear and understandable terms, integrated into discussions of the valuation of assets and liabilities.
7 Careful integration into the text and problem material of recent accounting developments and legal requirements in Canada and those in the United States that are relevant to the Canadian environment.
8 The most comprehensive package of supplementary materials available for any accounting textbook.
9 Checklist of key figures for problems and Business Decision Cases included on the inside cover pages of the textbook.

NEW AND EXTENSIVELY REVISED CHAPTERS

Many new topics are discussed in this fifth Canadian edition. For example, the first four chapters, presenting the basic accounting cycle, now explain the accounting procedures applied in computer-based accounting systems as well as those used in manual systems. Chapter 3, "Measuring Business Income," also includes new discussions of the accounting principles of realization (recognition) and matching. In addition, Chapter 4 has been extensively revised to explain more clearly and more thoroughly the nature and mechanics of adjusting entries.

Chapter 5, "Merchandising Transactions and Internal Control," condenses into one chapter material previously discussed in two chapters. Chapter 6, on accounting systems, has been revised to provide up-to-date coverage of computer-based accounting systems. Emphasis is placed upon means of achieving internal control in the computer environment.

In prior editions, we covered receivables and payables in a single chapter. We found that this approach was confusing to some students, so receivables and payables now are discussed in two separate chapters. Chapter 8 covers receivables, including a new discussion of notes receivable with interest included in the face amount. We have moved the discussion of notes payable to Chapter 11, our new chapter on current liabilities.

Chapter 10 condenses our coverage of plant assets, for which we previously used two chapters. An all-new Chapter 11 covers in one place the various types of current liabilities, including accounts payable, notes payable, and payrolls.

We moved the chapter on partnerships (Chapter 12) to precede the chapter on accounting principles (Chapter 13). This change, along with our new 26-chapter format, enables us to emphasize unincorporated businesses in the first semester and still end the semester with a review of generally accepted accounting principles. The second semester begins with a four-chapter unit on accounting issues relating primarily to corporations.

In Chapter 17, our coverage of consolidated financial statements has been shortened and updated to focus upon the recent wave of takeovers and acquisitions.

Many people view the tax reform of 1987 as a significant change in the history of tax law. Our extensively revised chapter on income taxes, Chapter 18, presents this new material in a clear and understandable manner.

Perhaps the most significant change in financial reporting in many years is the requirement that businesses now prepare a statement of changes in financial position on a cash and cash equivalent basis as a third major financial statement. Chapter 19 introduces and explains this new financial statement. The emphasis is not only on the preparation but also on the *uses* and *interpretation* of this statement.

Chapter 20, "Analysis and Interpretation of Financial Statements," is now followed by a new appendix, "Financial Statements of a Large Company: A Case Study." This appendix affords students an opportunity to apply the analytical techniques discussed in the chapter to the recent financial statements of a well-known company.

Two significant changes have been made in our managerial accounting chapters. First, Chapter 21 has been extensively revised to clarify the objectives and structure of a responsibility accounting system. Second, the chapter on cost-volume-profit analysis (now Chapter 24) has been moved to precede the chapter on budgeting and standard costs. This new sequence provides students with a better understanding of cost behaviour when we introduce the concepts of budgeting and establishing standard costs.

In summary, this edition is the most extensive revision we have ever prepared. In addition to changes in chapter content, there are many new pedagogical features, such as chapter previews, many more actual business examples, summaries of chapter learning objectives, and terminology exercises. Also, this edition includes over 120 new exercises, problems, and Business Decision Cases.

SUPPLEMENTARY MATERIALS

A distinguishing characteristic of this textbook is the wide variety of supplementary learning and teaching aids for students and instructors.

FOR STUDENTS

1 *A self-study guide* The *Study Guide* enables students to measure their progress by immediate feedback. This self-study guide includes an outline of the most important points in each chapter, an abundance of objective questions, and several short exercises for each chapter. In the back of the self-study guide are answers to questions and solutions to exercises to help students evaluate their understanding of the subject. The Study Guide will also be useful in classroom discussions and for review by students before examinations.

2 *Working papers* Partially completed working papers are available for all Group A and Group B problems, and for all Business Decision Cases. These working papers save time, because much of the data ''given'' in a problem has already been entered on the working paper. In addition, the working papers often provide guidance in organizing the solutions. The following sets of accounting work sheets are available:
Group A Problems, Chapters 1 through 15
Group A Problems, Chapters 14 through 26
Group B Problems, Chapters 1 through 15
Group B Problems, Chapters 14 through 26
All packages include working papers for the Business Decision Cases and any appendixes relating to the chapters.

3 *Accounting applications* Accounting applications are simulations of various accounting activities. This fifth Canadian edition offers the following manual accounting applications:

a *Big Screen Systems* A practice set designed to pull together the steps in the accounting cycle. This application is much shorter than in prior editions, because the student now steps in to the role of chief accountant in the middle of the month. Requires about 6 to 8 hours.

b *Valley Building Materials, Inc.* A narrative practice set involving a corporate entity and designed for use *after Chapter 16,* this item includes payrolls, capital stock transactions, and other transactions not included in the earlier applications.

SUPPLEMENTS FOR INSTRUCTORS

1 *Solutions manual* A comprehensive manual containing answers to all review questions, exercises, Group A and Group B problems, and Business Decision Cases in the text, along with complete answers to the two manual practice sets.

In the development of problem material for this book, special attention has been given to the inclusion of problems of varying length and difficulty. By referring to the time estimates, difficulty ratings, and problem descriptions in the *Solutions Manual,* instructors can choose problems that best fit the level, scope, and emphasis of the course they are offering.

2 *An instructor's guide* This separate manual includes, in the first part, the following three sections for each chapter of the textbook:

  a A brief topical outline of the chapter listing in logical sequence the topics the authors like to discuss in class.

  b An assignment guide correlating specific exercises and problems with various topics covered in the chapter.

  c Comments and observations.

The ''Comments and observations'' sections indicate the authors' personal views as to relative importance of topics and identify topics with which some students have difficulty. Specific exercises and problems are recommended to demonstrate certain points. Some of these sections include ''Asides,'' introducing real-world situations (not included in the text) that are useful in classroom discussions.

   Also included in the Instructor's Guide are sample assignment schedules, ideas for using each element of the supplemental package, and the *Test Bank* and *Answers for the Test Bank.*

   This new and enlarged test bank, which includes an abundance of true-false questions, multiple-choice questions, and short exercises organized on a chapter-by-chapter basis, is a valuable resource for instructors who prepare their own examinations. In its new format, this is one of the largest test banks ever to accompany any accounting textbook. And it's fully Canadian.

   The test bank is also available in two computer-based formats: *EXAMINER* for mainframe systems, and *MicroEXAMINER* for IBM or Apple personal computers. MicroEXAMINER now allows instructors to edit examination questions, as well as to add material to the test bank.

3 *Transparencies of solutions to exercises, problems, and cases* This visual aid enables instructors to display by overhead projector the complete solution to every numerical exercise, problem, and Business Decision Case in the text. The transparencies now use a bold typeface for greater clarity.

4 *Visual Classroom Displays* A large number of special teaching transparencies provide illustrations not shown in the textbook. The transparencies now use two colours and multiple overlays, enabling instructors to develop illustrations on a step-by-step basis.

OTHER SUPPLEMENTS

There are a number of *American supplementary materials* available for Canadian adopters. These materials, which can be used with very little or no Canadian adaptation, include:

1 *Accounting applications*

MANUAL

  a *Remington Restaurant Supply.* An alternative to Big Screen Systems.

  b *Echo Paint Co.,* by Richard A. Wright. This application, designed for use after Chapter 6, uses *cheques, invoices, and other business documents,* in lieu of a narrative of transactions. A highly realistic simulation, it is new to this edition.

c *Executive Woodcraft Company,* by Ronald W. Hilton. Emphasizing the flow of costs through a *cost accounting system,* this application also includes optional modules on cost-volume-profit analysis, budgeting, and special order analysis. It is new to this edition.

COMPUTER-BASED

a *CȲMA/McGraw-Hill* An educational version of a leading *general ledger software* package. The two narrative accounting applications, *Remington Restaurant Supply* and *Big Screen Systems,* are provided for use with this software. However, the software is extremely flexible; it may be used to work most accounting cycle problems, and to maintain personal accounting records or those of a small business.

b *Echo Paint Co.,* by Richard A. Wright and Educational Computer Systems, Inc. This computer-based version of the Echo Paint Co. application introduces students to business documents and the use of personal computers by simulating the activities of a computerized small business. The computer program is "tutorial" — that is, it identifies any errors made by the student and provides guidance in correcting them.

c *Valley Building Materials, Inc.* This computer-based application is designed for use after Chapter 16 of the text. It is based upon the American manual application, Valley Building Materials, Inc., but utilizes the personal computer. In addition, the application includes a number of "help screens," which identify and explain any student mistakes.

2 *Accounting/Lotus Connection,* by E. James Meddaugh. A supplement which enables students to apply Lotus 1-2-3 to a wide variety of accounting problems, which are included in the supplement. A separate solutions manual is available to instructors. Note: Users must have access to Lotus 1-2-3.

3 *Accounting/Spreadsheet Connection,* also by E. James Meddaugh. Same as above, except that it can utilize Lotus 1-2-3 *or clones,* such as VP Planner. Package includes VP Planner system disk.

4 Four separate sets of *achievement tests* and *comprehensive examinations.* Sets A and B each consist of six 50-minute achievement tests, each covering *three* chapters, and two comprehensive examinations covering the first and second halves of the textbook. The A and B sets are parallel, differing only in the sequence of questions and in quantitative problem data. The two sets of parallel tests may be used in the same classroom to ensure that no student sits next to someone taking an identical examination, or may be alternated from one semester to the next.

Sets C and D each include eight 50-minute achievement tests, each covering *four* chapters, and two 1 hour and 40 minute comprehensive examinations. The C and D sets parallel one another, differing only in the sequence of questions and in quantitative problem data.

5 An additional computerized test bank for the introductory accounting course.

1

THE ACCOUNTING CYCLE

In these first four chapters, the continuing example of Roberts Real Estate Company is used to illustrate the concepts of double-entry accrual accounting for a small, service-type business. Accounting for a merchandising concern will be introduced in Part 2.

CHAPTER

1

ACCOUNTING: THE
LANGUAGE OF BUSINESS

CHAPTER PREVIEW

This introductory chapter explores the nature of accounting information and the
environment in which it is developed and used. We emphasize the uses of accounting
reports, such as the financial statements, the services performed by accountants,
and the institutions that influence accounting practice. A basic financial statement — the balance sheet — is illustrated and discussed. We explain the nature of
assets, liabilities, and owner's equity; and why a balance sheet always "balances."
Attention is focussed upon the set of standards called "generally accepted accounting principles." Specific accounting principles introduced in Chapter 1 include
the concept of the business entity, the cost principle, objectivity, and the going-
concern assumption. We also introduce Roberts Real Estate, a company used as
a continuing example throughout the first four chapters. Three forms of business
organization are discussed.

After studying this chapter you should be able to meet these Learning Objectives:

1 **Define accounting and explain the purpose of accounting.**

2 **Explain the phrase "generally accepted accounting principles."**

3 **Describe the accounting profession and public, private, and government
accounting.**

4 **Explain the role of the CICA in the development of accounting standards.**

5 **State two basic financial objectives of every profit-oriented business.**

6 **Describe a balance sheet; define assets, liabilities, and owner's equity.**

7 **Discuss the accounting principles involved in asset valuation.**

8 **Indicate the effects of various transactions upon the balance sheet.**

9 **Describe the three forms of business organization.**

WHAT IS ACCOUNTING?

1 Define accounting and explain the purpose of accounting.

Accounting is the process of recording, measuring, classifying, summarizing, communicating, and interpreting economic activity. Some people mistakenly think of accounting as a highly technical field that can be understood only by professional accountants. Actually, nearly everyone practises accounting in one form or another on an almost daily basis. Whether you are preparing a household budget, balancing your cheque book, preparing your income tax return, or running a large business, you are working with accounting concepts and accounting information.

Accounting has often been called the "language of business." People in the business world — owners, managers, bankers, stockbrokers, investors — all use accounting terms and concepts to describe the resources and the activities of every business, large and small.

We live in an era of accountability. Although accounting has made its most dramatic progress in the field of business, the accounting function is vital to every unit of our society. An individual may be required to account for his or her income and to file an income tax return. Often an individual must supply personal accounting information in order to finance the purchase of a car or home, to qualify for a university or college scholarship, to secure a credit card, or to obtain a bank loan. Large corporations are accountable to their shareholders, to governmental agencies, and to the public. The federal government, the provinces, the cities, the school boards all must use accounting as a basis for controlling their resources and measuring their accomplishments. Accounting is equally essential to the successful operation of a business, a university, a fraternity, a social program, or a city.

In every election the voters must make decisions at the ballot box on issues involving accounting concepts. Therefore, some knowledge of accounting is needed by all citizens if they are to act intelligently in meeting the challenges of our society. This book will help you develop your knowledge of accounting and your ability to use accounting information in making economic and political decisions.

The purpose and nature of accounting information

The underlying purpose of accounting is to provide financial information about an economic entity. In this book the economic entity that we will be concentrating upon is a business enterprise. Financial information about a business is needed by managerial decision makers to help them plan and control the activities of the organization. Financial information is also needed by *outsiders* — owners, creditors, potential investors, the government, and the public — who have supplied money to the business or who have some other interest in the business that will be served by information about its financial position and operating results. Developing and communicating this information is the role of the business organization's *accounting system.*

Creating accounting information

An accounting system consists of the methods, procedures, and devices used by an organization or entity to keep track of its financial activities and to summarize these activities in a manner useful to decision makers. To accomplish these objectives, an accounting system may make use of computers and video displays as well as handwritten records and reports printed on paper. In fact, the accounting system for any sizable business is likely to include all these records and devices. Regardless of whether the accounting system is simple or sophisticated, three basic steps must be performed with data concerning financial or economic activities — the data must be *recorded*, *classified*, and *summarized*.

Step 1 — recording financial activity   The first function of an accounting system is to create a systematic record of the daily business activity, in terms of money. For example, goods and services are purchased and sold, credit is extended to customers, debts are incurred, and cash is received and paid out. These *transactions* are typical of business events that can be *measured* and expressed *in monetary terms,* and must be *entered in accounting records.* The mere statement of an intent to buy goods or services in the future does not represent a transaction. The term *transaction* refers to a completed action rather than to an expected or possible future action.

The recording of a transaction may be performed in many ways, such as writing with a pen or pencil, entering data through a computer keyboard, or passing machine-readable price tags over an optical scanner.

Of course, not all business events can be objectively measured and described in monetary terms. Therefore, we do not record in the accounting records such events as the death of a key executive or a threat by a labour union to call a strike.

Step 2 — classifying data   A complete record of all business activities usually amounts to a huge volume of data — too large and diverse to be useful to decision makers such as managers and investors. Therefore, the data must be classified into related groups or categories of transactions. For example, grouping together those transactions in which cash is received or paid out is a logical step in developing useful information about the cash position of a business.

Step 3 — summarizing the data   To be useful to decision makers, accounting data generally must be highly summarized. A complete listing of the sales transactions of a company such as Sears, for example, would be too long for anyone to read. The employees responsible for ordering merchandise need sales information summarized by product. Store managers will want sales information summarized by department, while Sears' top management will want sales information summarized by store. Outsiders, such as the company's shareholders and creditors, probably will be most interested in a single sales figure that represents the total sales of the entire company.

These three steps we have described — recording, classifying, and summarizing — are the means of creating accounting information. However, the accounting process includes more than the *creating* of information. It also involves *communicating* this information to interested parties and *interpreting* accounting information to help in the making of specific business decisions.

Often we will want to compare the financial statements of Company A with those of Company B. From this comparison, we can determine which company is the more profitable, which is financially stronger, and which offers the better chance of future success. We can benefit personally by making this kind of analysis of a company we are considering investing in — or going to work for.

Communicating accounting information — Who uses accounting reports?

An accounting system must provide information to managers and also to a number of outsiders who have an interest in the financial activities of the business enterprise. The major types of accounting reports that are developed by the accounting system of a business enterprise and the parties receiving the information generated by the accounting system are illustrated in the following diagram:

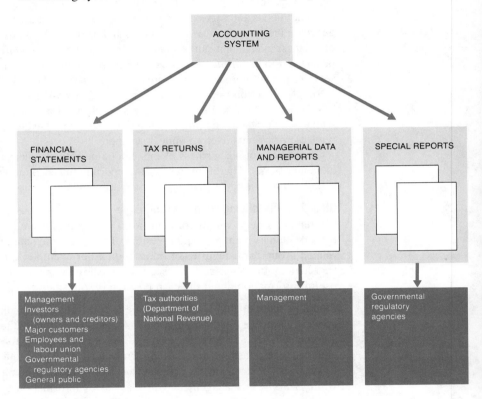

Accounting information is user-oriented

The persons receiving accounting reports are termed the **users** of accounting information. The type of information that a specific user will require depends upon the kinds of decisions that person must make. For example, managers need detailed information about daily operating costs for the purpose of controlling the operations of the business and setting reasonable selling prices. Outsiders, on the other hand, usually need summarized information concerning resources on hand and information on operating results for the past year to make investment decisions, to compute income taxes, or to make regulatory decisions.

Since the information needs of various users differ, it follows that the accounting system of a business entity must be able to provide various types of accounting reports. The information in these reports must be presented in accordance with certain "ground rules" and assumptions, so that users of the reports will be able to interpret the information properly. For example, if a report indicates that a business owns land with an accounting value of $90,000, what does this dollar amount represent? Is it the original cost of the land to the business, the current market value of the land, or the assessed value for purposes of levying property taxes? Obviously the user of any accounting report needs to understand the standards and assumptions that have been used in preparing the report. In turn, the standards employed in the preparation of an accounting report must relate to the information needs of the user.

Financial statements   Among the most important and most widely used of all accounting reports are financial statements. *Financial statements* are the main source of financial information to persons *outside* the business organization and also are useful to management. These statements are very concise, summarizing in a few pages the activities of a business for a specified period of time, such as a month or a year. They show the *financial position* of the business at the end of the time period and also the *operating results* by which the business arrived at this financial position.

The basic purpose of financial statements is to assist decision makers in evaluating the financial strength, profitability, and future prospects of a business. Thus, managers, investors, major customers, and labour all have a direct interest in these reports. Every large corporation prepares annual financial statements that are distributed to all shareholders of the business. In addition, these statements may be filed with various governmental agencies and become a matter of public record.

2 Explain the phrase "generally accepted accounting principles."

Generally accepted accounting principles (GAAP)   The accounting standards and concepts used in the preparation of financial statements are called *generally accepted accounting principles.* Some of these principles have been established by official standard-setting bodies such as the Canadian Institute of Chartered Accountants, while others have simply gained acceptance through wide-spread use. The various ideas, concepts, and accounting methods that make up generally accepted accounting principles continually change and evolve in response to changes in the business environment.

There is no comprehensive list of generally accepted accounting principles, yet accountants and users of financial statements must know which accounting concepts are acceptable and which are not. Helping you to develop an awareness of the accounting principles and concepts that are "generally accepted" is one of the major objectives of this textbook.

Developing accounting information in conformity with generally accepted accounting principles is called *financial accounting,* because this information summarizes the financial position and operating results of a business entity. In the first part of this book we will emphasize financial accounting concepts rather than income tax rules, reports to regulatory agencies, or internal reports to management. As we shall see, financial accounting concepts apply to all types and sizes of business organizations.

Income tax returns   The Department of National Revenue for Taxation (commonly known as Revenue Canada, Taxation) requires businesses and individuals to file annual income tax returns designed to measure taxable income. *Taxable income* is a legal concept defined by laws. Since government uses the income tax laws to achieve various social objectives as well as to finance its spending, income tax laws are frequently modified or changed. Thus the rules used in preparing income tax returns may vary from one year to the next. In general, however, there is a close parallel between income tax laws and financial accounting concepts.

Managerial data and reports   Management needs much detailed accounting data (in addition to financial statements) for use in planning and controlling the daily operations of the business. Management also needs information for long-range planning and for major decisions such as the introduction of a new product or the modernizing of an older plant. Accounting information provided to managers need not be presented in accordance with generally accepted accounting principles. Rather, it should be tailored to meet the managers' specific information needs.

Reports to regulatory agencies   The activities of many business enterprises are regulated by governmental agencies. These regulatory agencies often require special types of accounting information specifically tailored to their needs. For example, when making a decision whether to allow a rate increase by an electric company, a utilities commission might request information about the cost to the company of producing electricity and the company's need to accumulate funds to provide service to outlying areas. In large part, however, reports to regulatory agencies are based upon generally accepted accounting principles.

Using accounting information   Accounting extends beyond the process of creating records and reports. The ultimate objective of accounting is the *use* of this information, its analysis and interpretation. Accountants are concerned with the significance of the figures they produce. They look for relationships between business events and financial results; they study the effect of various alternatives, such as buying or leasing a new store building; and they search for significant trends that suggest what may happen in the future.

If managers, investors, creditors, and government officials are to make effective use of accounting information, they too must have some understanding of how the figures were put together and what they mean. An important part of this understanding is to recognize clearly the limitations of accounting reports. A business manager or other decision maker who lacks an understanding of accounting may not appreciate the extent to which accounting information is based upon *estimates* rather than upon precisely accurate measurements.

The distinction between accounting and bookkeeping

Persons with little knowledge of accounting may fail to understand the difference between accounting and bookkeeping. *Bookkeeping* means the recording of transactions, the record-making phase of accounting. The recording of transaction tends to be mechanical and repetitive; it is only a small part of the field of accounting and probably the simplest part. *Accounting* includes not only the maintenance of accounting records, but also the design of efficient accounting systems, the performance of audits, the development of forecasts, income tax work, and the interpretation of accounting information. A person might become a reasonably proficient bookkeeper in a few weeks or months; however, to become a professional accountant requires several years of study and experience.

3   Describe the accounting profession and public, private, and government accounting.

The accounting profession and the work of accountants

There are a number of professional accounting organizations in Canada that provide education and training leading to a certificate in accountancy. The education, training, and examination requirements vary considerably among these professional organizations. The members of these organizations tend to specialize in a given sub-area of their discipline, just as do lawyers and members of other professions. In terms of career opportunities, the field of accounting may be divided into three broad areas: (1) public accounting, (2) private accounting, and (3) governmental accounting.

The accounting profession

In Canada, there are three major professional accounting organizations: the provincial Institutes (in Quebec, Order) of Chartered Accountants, Societies of Management Accountants (formerly, the Societies of Industrial Accountants), and Certified General Accountants' Association (in Quebec, Professional Corporation). The national organizations of these three accounting bodies are the Canadian Institute of Chartered Accountants, the Society of Management Accountants of Canada, and the Certified General Accountants Association of Canada. Members of these organizations receive their respective professional designations as chartered accountants (CAs), certified management accountants (CMAs), and certified general accountants (CGAs). The Institutes of Chartered Accountants place more emphasis on public accounting, the Societies of Management Accountants are primarily interested in management or private accounting, and the Certified General Accountants are interested in private as well as public accounting.

Public accounting

Public accounting firms are organizations that offer a variety of accounting services to the public. These firms vary in size from one-person practices to large, international organizations with several thousand professional accountants.

Most of the people in public accounting are *chartered accountants (CAs).* Thus, public accounting firms often are called *CA firms.* The specific requirements regarding the right to practise public accounting vary among provinces. In some provinces, such as Ontario and Nova Scotia, only chartered accountants have the automatic privilege to practise public accounting. In other provinces, such as Alberta and British Columbia, the practice of public accounting is either open to anyone or open only to members of the professional accounting organizations.

The primary services offered by CA firms include auditing, income tax services, management advisory services, and small business services.

Auditing   The principal function of public accountants is auditing. How do people outside of a business — creditors, investors, government officials, and other interested parties — know that the financial statements prepared by a company's management are fair and reliable? In large part, these outsiders rely upon *audits* performed by a public accounting firm that is *independent* of the company issuing the financial statements.

An audit is a thorough investigation, in which the public accountants study the company's accounting records and gather other evidence regarding every item in the financial statements. This investigation enables the public accounting firm to express its professional *opinion* as to the fairness and reliability of the financial statements. Notice that the auditors are independent professionals, not employees of the company issuing the financial statements. Thus, the public accountants put their professional reputation on the line when they issue an opinion on a company's financial statements.

Audited financial statements have developed an excellent track record for fairness and reliability. Therefore, persons outside the business, such as bankers and investors, attach great importance to the audited financial statements and the auditor's report.

Large corporations, such as those listed on the Toronto Stock Exchange, have their financial statements audited each year. These audited statements are then sent to the companies' shareholders and creditors, and also are made available to the public. Only a large public accounting firm can audit a large corporation like Canadian Pacific Limited.

The largest public accounting firms and a few of their audit clients in recent years are listed below.

FIRM	SELECTED AUDIT CLIENTS
Clarkson Gordon	Provigo, Dome Petroleum, Canada Packers
Coopers & Lybrand	McCain Foods, Indal, General Foods
Deloitte Haskins & Sells	Imasco, General Motors, Woodward's
Peat Marwick	TransCanada Pipelines, Hudson's Bay, Bramalea
Price Waterhouse	Canadian Pacific, IBM, Alcan Aluminium
Thorne Ernst & Whinney	Air Canada, George Weston, Union Carbide
Touche Ross	Bell Canada, Chrysler, Ivaco

Income tax services   An important element of decision making by business executives is consideration of the income tax consequences of each alternative course of action. The public accountant is often called upon for "tax planning," which will show how a future transaction such as the acquisition of new equipment may be arranged in a manner that will hold income taxes to a legally minimum amount. The public accountant is also frequently retained to prepare the income tax returns. To render tax services, the public accountant must have extensive knowledge of tax statutes, regulations, and court decisions, as well as a thorough knowledge of accounting.

Management advisory services   Many public accounting firms offer their clients a wide range of management consulting services. For example, a public accounting firm might be engaged to study the feasibility of installing a computer-based accounting system, of introducing a new product line, or of merging with another company. The fact that business executives often seek their public accountants' advice on a wide range of problems illustrates the relevance of accounting information to virtually all business decisions.

Small business services   Most public accounting firms provide a variety of services specially suited to the needs of small businesses. These services may include, for example, compiling monthly financial statements, developing budgets or forecasts of future operations, or assisting the client in hiring accounting personnel or in obtaining a bank loan.

Private accounting

In contrast to the accountant in public practice who serves many clients, an accountant in private industry is employed by a single enterprise. The chief accounting officer of a medium-sized or large business is usually called the *controller,* in recognition of the fact that one of the primary uses of accounting data is to aid in controlling business operations. The controller manages the work of the accounting staff. He or she is also a part of the top management team charged with the task of running the business, setting its objectives, and seeing that these objectives are met.

The accountants in a private business, large or small, must record transactions and prepare periodic financial statements from accounting records. Within this area of general accounting, a number of specialized phases of accounting have developed. Among the more important of these are:

Design of accounting systems   Although the same basic accounting principles are applicable to all types of business, each enterprise requires an individually tailored *financial information system.* This system includes accounting forms, records, instruction manuals, flow charts, computer programs, and reports to fit the particular needs of the business. Designing an accounting system and putting it into operation constitute a specialized phase of accounting.

Cost accounting   Knowing the cost of a particular product is vital to the efficient management of a business. For example, an automobile manufacturer needs to know the cost of each type of car produced. Knowing the cost of each manufacturing process (such as painting an automobile) or the cost of any business operation (such as an employee training program) is also essential to making sound business decisions. The phase of accounting particularly concerned with collecting and interpreting cost data is called *cost accounting.*

Financial forecasting   A financial forecast (or budget) is a plan of financial operations for some future period expressed in monetary terms. By using a forecast, management is able to make comparisons between *planned operations* and *actual results achieved.* A forecast is thus an attempt to preview operating results before the actual transactions have taken place. A forecast is a particularly valuable tool for the controller because it provides each division of the business with a specific goal, and because it gives management a means of measuring the efficiency of performance throughout the company.

Income tax accounting   As income taxes have increased in importance and the determination of taxable income has become more complex, both internal accountants and independent public accountants have devoted more time to problems of taxation. Although many companies rely largely on public accounting firms for tax planning and the preparation of income tax returns, large companies also maintain their own tax departments.

Internal auditing   Most large corporations maintain staffs of *internal auditors* with the responsibility of evaluating the efficiency of operations and determining whether company policies are being followed consistently in all divisions of the corporation. The internal auditor, in contrast to the independent auditor (public accountant), is not responsible for determining the overall fairness of the company's annual financial statements.

Management accounting   Keep in mind that the accounting system provides information for both external and internal use. The external reporting function has already been touched upon in our discussion of a public accounting firm's independent audit of annual financial statements. The *internal* reporting function of an accounting system gives managers information needed for daily operations and also for long-range planning. Developing the types of information most relevant to specific managerial decisions and interpreting that information are called *management accounting* or *managerial accounting.* This topic is emphasized in the final chapters of this book.

Management accounting utilizes the techniques of both cost accounting and forecasting to achieve its goal of helping executives formulate both short-range and long-range plans, to measure success in carrying out these plans, to identify problems requiring executive attention, and to choose among alternative methods of attaining company objectives. At every organizational level of a company, specific problems arise for which accounting is needed to help define the problem, identify alternative courses of action, and make a choice among these alternatives.

Governmental accounting

Government officials rely on financial information to help them direct the affairs of their agencies just as do the executives of corporations. Many governmental accounting problems are similar to those applicable to private industry. In other respects, however, accounting for governmental affairs requires a somewhat different approach because the objective of earning a profit is absent from public affairs. Every agency of government at every level (federal, provincial, and local) must have accountants in order to carry out its responsibilities. Universities, hospitals, churches, and other not-for-profit institutions also follow a pattern of accounting that is similar to governmental accounting.

Professional accountants and top corporate executives

While most professional accountants devote their career in public, private, and government accounting, many have become top corporate executives. The chairpersons, presidents, and directors of many large and well-known Canadian corporations have a professional accounting designation.

 Top corporate executives with a professional accounting designation currently with very large and well-known Canadian corporations include: Claude Taylor, CMA, chairman of Air Canada; William Bradford, FCGA, president and CEO (chief executive officer) of North American Life Assurance; Kenneth Benson, CA, chairman and CEO of British Columbia Forest Products; Laurant Beaudoin, FCA, chairman and CEO of Bombardier; Rhys T. Eyton, CA, chairman and CEO of Canadian Airlines International; Lorne Lodge, FCA, chairman of IBM Canada; Paul Ivanier, CA, president and CEO of Ivaco; Melvin Hawkrigg, FCA, chairman of London Life; Donald Campbell, FCA, chairman of Maclean Hunter; James Black, FCA,

chairman of Molson; Judson Sinclair, CA, chairman of Moore; Gordon Cummings, CMA, president and CEO of National Sea Products; Adam Zimmerman, FCA, president of Noranda; Jean Perron, CGA, president of Normick Perron; John Cleghorn, CA, president of Royal Bank; and Gordon Grey, FCA, chairman of Royal LePage. Also, those who hold multiple corporate directorships (since listing all the corporations will be lengthy, only two are mentioned) include: J.W. (Jack) Adams, FCA (Canada Trust, F.W. Woolworth), Lloyd Barber, Ph.D, CA, president of University of Regina (Bank of Nova Scotia, Canadian Pacific), Marcel Belanger, FCA (Bell Canada Enterprises, Hudson's Bay), Warren Chippindale, FCA (Alcan Aluminium, Bell Canada Enterprises), and John H. Moore, FCA (London Life, Cadillac Fairview).

4 Explain the role of the CICA in the development of accounting standards.

Development of accounting standards — the Canadian Institute of Chartered Accountants

Research to develop accounting principles and practices that will keep pace with changes in the economic and political environment is a major activity of professional accountants and accounting educators. In Canada, the Canadian Institute of Chartered Accountants (CICA) is the most prominent and influential in the development and improvement of financial reporting and accounting practices. The CICA, through its Accounting Standards Committee, has issued a significant number of recommendations on accounting standards. The recommendations are contained in the *CICA Handbook* and are considered as generally accepted accounting principles. Both the Canada Business Corporations Act and the provincial securities commissions have recognized the *CICA Handbook* accounting recommendations as generally accepted accounting principles. The CICA is a self-regulated body and *not* a government agency.

It is important to note that accounting is not a closed system or a fixed set of rules, but is a constantly evolving body of knowledge. As we explore accounting principles and related practices in this book, you will become aware of certain problems and conflicts for which fully satisfactory answers are yet to be developed. The need for further research is apparent despite the fact that present-day accounting practices and standards of financial reporting are by far the best achieved to date.

Development of accounting standards in the United States — the FASB

In the United States, four groups that have been influential in the improvement of financial reporting and accounting practices are the Financial Accounting Standards Board (FASB), the American Institute of Certified Public Accountants, the Securities and Exchange Commission, and the American Accounting Association.

In addition to conducting extensive research, the FASB issues *Statements of Financial Accounting Standards,* which represent authoritative expressions of generally accepted accounting principles in the United States.

Profitability and solvency: basic financial objectives

5 State two basic financial objectives of every profit-oriented business.

The management of every business must keep foremost in its thinking two basic or primary objectives. The first is to earn a profit. The second is to stay solvent, that is, to have on hand sufficient cash to pay debts as they fall due. Profits and solvency, of course, are not the only objectives of business managers. There are many others, such as providing jobs for people, protecting the environment, creating new and improved products, and providing more goods and services at a lower cost. It is clear, however, that a business cannot hope to accomplish these objectives unless it meets the two basic tests of survival — operating profitably and staying solvent.

A business is a collection of resources committed by an individual or group of individuals, who hope that the investment will increase in value. Investment in any given business, however, is only one of a number of alternative investments available. If a business does not earn as great a profit as might be obtained from alternative investments, its owners will be well-advised to sell or terminate the business and invest elsewhere. A business that continually operates at a loss will eventually exhaust its resources and be forced out of existence. Therefore, in order to operate successfully and to survive, the owners or managers of an enterprise must direct the business in such a way that it will earn a reasonable profit.

Business concerns that have sufficient cash to pay their debts promptly are said to be *solvent.* In contrast, a company that finds itself unable to meet its obligations as they fall due is called *insolvent.* Solvency must be ranked as a basic objective of any enterprise, because a business that becomes insolvent may be forced by its creditors to stop operations and end its existence.

Accounting as the basis for business decisions

How do business executives know whether a company is earning profits or incurring losses? How do they know whether the company is solvent or insolvent, and whether it probably will be solvent, say, a month from today? The answer to both these questions in one word is *accounting.* Accounting is the process by which the profitability and solvency of a company can be measured. Accounting also provides information needed as a basis for making business decisions that will enable management to guide the company on a profitable and solvent course.

For specific examples of these decisions, consider the following questions. What prices should the firm set on its products? If production is increased, what effect will this have on the cost of each unit produced? Will it be necessary to borrow from the bank? How much will costs increase if a pension plan is established for employees? Is it more profitable to produce and sell product A or product B? Shall a given part be made or be bought from suppliers? Should an investment be made in new equipment? All these issues call for decisions that should depend, in part at least, upon accounting information. It might be reasonable to turn the question around and ask: What business decisions could be made intelligently *without* the use of accounting information? Examples would be hard to find.

In large-scale business undertakings such as the manufacture of automobiles or the operation of nationwide chains of retail stores, the top executives cannot possibly have close physical contact with and knowledge of the details of operations. Consequently, these executives must depend to an even greater extent than the small business owner upon information provided by the accounting system.

We have already stressed that accounting is a means of measuring and interpreting the results of business transactions and of communicating financial information. In addition, the accounting system must provide the decision maker with *predictive information* for making important business decisions in a changing world.

Internal control

The topic of internal control goes hand-in-hand with the study of accounting. We have stressed that business decisions of all types are based at least in part upon accounting information. Management needs assurance that the accounting information it receives is accurate and reliable. This assurance comes from the company's *system of internal control.*

A system of internal control consists of all the measures taken by an organization for the purpose of (1) protecting its resources against waste, fraud, and inefficiency; (2) ensuring accuracy and reliability in accounting and operating data; (3) securing compliance with company policies; and (4) evaluating the level of performance in all divisions of the company. In short, a system of internal control includes all of the measures designed to assure management that the entire business operates according to plan.

In performing an audit of financial statements, public accountants always study and evaluate the company's system of internal control. The stronger the system of internal control, the more confidence the public accountants can place in the reliability of the financial statements and accounting records.

A basic principle of internal control is that no one person should handle all phases of a transaction from beginning to end. When business operations are so organized that two or more employees are required to participate in every transaction, the possibility of fraud and error is reduced as the work of one employee gives assurance of the accuracy of the work of another. The principal reason for many business documents and accounting procedures is to achieve strong internal control. Therefore, we shall discuss various internal control concepts and requirements throughout our study of accounting.

FINANCIAL STATEMENTS: THE STARTING POINT IN THE STUDY OF ACCOUNTING

The preparation of financial statements is not the first step in the accounting process, but it is a convenient point to begin the study of accounting. The financial statements are the means of conveying to management and to interested outsiders a concise picture of the profitability and financial position of the business. Since these financial statements are in a sense the end product of the accounting process, the student who acquires a clear understanding of the content and meaning of financial statements will be in an excellent position to appreciate the purpose of the earlier steps of recording and classifying business transactions.

The two most widely used financial statements are the *balance sheet* and the *income statement.*[1] Together, these two statements (perhaps a page each in length) summarize all the information contained in the hundreds or thousands of pages comprising the detailed accounting records of a business. In this introductory chapter and in Chapter 2, we shall explore the nature of the balance sheet, or statement of financial position, as it is sometimes called. Once we have become familiar with the form and arrangement of the balance sheet and with the meaning of technical terms

---

[1] A third financial statement, called a *statement of changes in financial position*, will be discussed later.

such as *assets, liabilities,* and *owner's equity,* it will be easy to read and understand a report on the financial position of a business as it is for an architect to read the blueprints of a proposed building. (We shall discuss the income statement in Chapter 3.)

The balance sheet

6 Describe a balance sheet; define assets, liabilities, and owner's equity.

The purpose of a balance sheet is to show the financial position of a business *at a particular date.* Every business prepares a balance sheet at the end of the year, and most companies prepare one at the end of each month. A balance sheet consists of a listing of the assets and liabilities of a business and of the owner's equity. The following balance sheet portrays the financial position of Vagabond Travel Agency at December 31.

BALANCE SHEET SHOWS
FINANCIAL POSITION
AT A SPECIFIC DATE

VAGABOND TRAVEL AGENCY
Balance Sheet
December 31, 19___

ASSETS		LIABILITIES & OWNER'S EQUITY	
Cash	$ 7,500	Liabilities:	
Notes receivable	8,000	Notes payable	$ 52,000
Accounts receivable	57,000	Accounts payable	15,000
Supplies	1,500	Salaries payable	3,000
Land	40,000	Total liabilities	$ 70,000
Building	44,000	Owner's equity:	
Office equipment	12,000	Terry Crane, capital	100,000
Total	$170,000	Total	$170,000

Note that the balance sheet sets forth in its heading three items: (1) the name of the business, (2) the name of the financial statement "Balance Sheet," and (3) the date of the balance sheet. Below the heading is the body of the balance sheet, which consists of three distinct sections: assets, liabilities, and owner's equity. The remainder of this chapter is largely devoted to making clear the nature of these three sections.

Another point to note about the form of a balance sheet is that cash is always the first asset listed; it is followed by notes receivable, accounts receivable, supplies, and any other assets that will soon be converted into cash or consumed in operations. Following these items are the more permanent assets, such as land, buildings, and equipment.

The liabilities of a business are always listed before the owner's equity. Each liability (such as notes payable, accounts payable, and salaries payable) should be listed separately, followed by a total figure for liabilities.

The concept of the business entity

Generally accepted accounting principles require that a set of financial statements describe the affairs of a *specific* business entity. This concept is often called the *entity principle.*

A *business entity* is an economic unit that engages in *identifiable business activities.* The business entity is regarded as being *separate from the personal affairs of its owner.* For example, Vagabond is an economic unit operating as a travel agency. Its owner, Terry Crane, may have a personal bank account, a home, a car, and even another business, such as a cattle ranch. These items are not involved in the travel agency business, and should not appear in Vagabond's financial statements.

If the owner were to intermingle his or her personal affairs with the transactions of a business, the resulting financial statements would be misleading and would fail to describe clearly the activities of the business entity.

Assets

Assets are economic resources that are owned by a business and are expected to benefit future operations. Assets may have definite physical form such as buildings, machinery, or merchandise. On the other hand, some assets exist not in physical or tangible form, but in the form of valuable legal claims or rights; examples are accounts receivable (amounts due from customers), investments in government bonds, and patent rights.

One of the most basic and at the same time most controversial problems in accounting is determining the dollar values for the various assets of a business. At present, generally accepted accounting principles call for the valuation of assets in a balance sheet at *cost*, rather than at current market values. The specific accounting principles supporting cost as the basis for asset valuation are discussed in the following paragraphs.

7   Discuss the accounting principles involved in asset valuation.

The cost principle   Assets such as land, buildings, and equipment are typical of the many economic resources that will be used in producing income for the business. The prevailing accounting view is that such assets should be recorded at their cost. When we say that an asset is shown in the balance sheet at its ***historical cost***, we mean the dollar amount originally paid to acquire the asset; this amount may be very different from what we would have to pay today to replace it.

For example, let us assume that a business buys a tract of land for use as a building site, paying $100,000 in cash. The amount to be entered in the accounting records as the value of the asset will be the cost of $100,000. If we assume a booming real estate market, a fair estimate of the sales value of the land 10 years later might be $250,000. Although the market price or economic value of the land has risen greatly, the accounting value as shown in the accounting records and on the balance sheet would continue unchanged at the cost of $100,000. This policy of accounting for assets at their acquisition cost is often referred to as the ***cost principle*** of accounting.

In reading a balance sheet, it is important to bear in mind that the dollar amounts listed do not necessarily indicate the prices at which the assets could be sold, nor the prices at which they could be replaced. One useful generalization to be drawn from this discussion is that a balance sheet does ***not*** necessarily show ''how much a business is worth.''

The going-concern assumption   It is appropriate to ask *why* accountants do not change the recorded values of assets to correspond with changing market prices for these properties. One reason is that the land and building being used to house the business were acquired for ***use*** and not for resale; in fact, these assets cannot be sold without disrupting the business. The balance sheet of a business is prepared on the assumption that the business is a continuing enterprise, a ''going concern.'' Consequently, the present estimated prices at which the land and buildings could be sold are of less importance than if these properties were intended for sale.

The objectivity principle   Another reason for using cost rather than current market values in accounting for assets is the need for a definite, factual basis for valuation. The cost for land, buildings, and many other assets purchased for cash can be rather definitely determined. Accountants use the term *objective* to describe asset valuations that are factual and can be verified by independent experts. For example, if land is shown on the balance sheet at cost, any public accountant who performed an audit of the business would be able to find objective evidence that the land was actually valued at the cost incurred in acquiring it. Estimated market values, on the other hand, for assets such as buildings and specialized machinery are not factual and objective. Market values are constantly changing and estimates of the prices at which assets could be sold are largely a matter of personal opinion. Of course at the date an asset is acquired, the cost and market value are usually the same because the buyer would not pay more than the asset was worth and the seller would not take less than current market value. The bargaining process which results in the sale of an asset serves to establish both the current market value of the property and the cost to the buyer. With the passage of time, however, the current market value of assets is likely to differ considerably from the cost recorded in the owner's accounting records.

Accounting for inflation   Severe worldwide inflation in recent years has raised serious doubts as to the adequacy of the conventional cost basis in accounting for assets. When inflation becomes very severe, historical cost values for assets simply lose their relevance as a basis for making business decisions. Proposals for adjusting recorded dollar amounts to reflect changes in the value of the dollar, as shown by a general price index, have been considered for many years. However, stronger interest is being shown at present in balance sheets that would show assets at *current appraised values* or *replacement costs* rather than at historical cost.

The British government has experimented extensively with the revision of corporate accounting to reflect inflation. The British approach proposes that year-end balance sheets show assets at their current value rather than at historical or original cost. Many companies in the Netherlands are now using some form of current-value accounting. In the United States, the Financial Accounting Standards Board requires that large corporations disclose the *current replacement cost* of certain assets as *supplementary information* to conventional cost-based financial statements. In Canada, Section 4510 of the *CICA Handbook*, ''Reporting the Effects of Changing Prices,'' requires large publicly owned corporations to disclose certain current-cost and general inflation information as supplementary information to the annual historical cost financial statements.

Accounting concepts are not as exact and unchanging as many persons assume. To serve the needs of a fast-changing economy, accounting concepts and methods must also undergo continuous evolutionary change. As of today, however, the cost basis of valuing assets is still the generally accepted method.

Liabilities

Liabilities are debts. All business concerns have liabilities; even the largest and most successful companies find it convenient to purchase merchandise and supplies on credit rather than to pay cash at the time of each purchase. The liability arising from the purchase of goods or services on credit is called an *account payable,* and the person or company to whom the account payable is owed is called a *creditor.*

A business concern frequently finds it desirable to borrow money as a means of supplementing the funds invested by the owner, thus enabling the business to expand more rapidly. The borrowed funds may, for example, be used to buy merchandise that can be sold at a profit to the firm's customers. Or, the borrowed money might be used to buy new and more efficient machinery, thus enabling the company to turn out a larger volume of products at lower cost. When a business borrows money for any reason, a liability is incurred and the lender becomes a creditor of the business. The form of the liability when money is borrowed is usually a *note payable,* a formal written promise to pay a certain amount of money, plus interest, at a definite future time.

An *account payable,* as contrasted with a *note payable,* does not involve the issuance of a formal written promise to the creditor, and it usually does not call for payment of interest. When a business has both notes payable and accounts payable, the two types of liabilities are shown separately in the balance sheet, with notes payable usually listed first. A figure showing the total of the liabilities should also be inserted, as shown by the illustrated balance sheet on page 16.

The creditors have claims against the assets of the business, usually not against any particular asset but against the assets in general. The claims of the creditors are liabilities of the business and have priority over the claims of owners. Creditors are entitled to be paid in full even if such payment should exhaust the assets of the business, leaving nothing for the owner.

Owner's Equity

The owner's equity in a business represents the resources invested by the owner; it is equal to the total assets minus the liabilities. The equity of the owner is a *residual claim* because the claims of the creditors legally come first. If you are the owner of a business, you are entitled to whatever remains after the claims of the creditors are fully satisfied.

For example, using the data from the illustrated balance sheet of Vagabond Travel Agency:

Vagabond Travel Agency has total assets of $170,000
And total liabilities amounting to   70,000
Therefore, the owner's equity must equal $100,000

Suppose that the Vagabond Travel Agency borrows $10,000 from a bank. After recording the additional asset of $10,000 cash and recording the new liability of $10,000 owed to the bank, we would have the following:

Vagabond Travel Agency now has total assets of $180,000
And total liabilities are now   80,000
Therefore, the owner's equity still is equal to $100,000

It is apparent that the total assets of the business were increased by the act of borrowing money from a bank, but the increase in assets was exactly offset by an increase in liabilities, and the owner's equity remained unchanged. The owner's equity in a business *is not increased* by borrowing from banks or other creditors.

Increases in owner's equity   If you begin a small business of your own, you will probably invest cash and possibly some other assets to get the business started. Later, as the business makes payments for rent, office equipment, advertising, salaries to employees, and other items, you may find it necessary to supply additional cash to the business. Hopefully, before long, the business will become self-sustaining. Whenever, as owner of the business, you transfer cash or other personally owned assets to the business entity, your ownership equity will increase. In summary, the owner's equity in a business comes from two sources:

1 *Investment* by the owner
2 *Earnings* from profitable operation of the business

Only the first of these two sources of owner's equity is considered in this chapter. The second source, an increase in owner's equity through earnings of the business, will be discussed in Chapter 3.

Decreases in owner's equity   If you are the owner of a sole or single proprietorship, you have the right to withdraw cash or other assets from the business at any time. Since you are strongly interested in seeing the business succeed, you will probably not make withdrawals that would handicap the business entity in operating efficiently. Once the business achieves momentum and financial strength, you may choose to make substantial withdrawals. Withdrawals are most often made by writing a cheque drawn on the company's bank account and payable to the owner. However, other types of withdrawals also occur, such as taking office equipment out of the business for personal use by the owner, or by causing cash belonging to the business to be used to pay a personal debt of the owner. Every withdrawal by the owner reduces the total assets of the business and reduces the owner's equity. In summary, decreases in the owner's equity in a business are caused in two ways:

1 *Withdrawals* of cash or other assets by the owner
2 *Losses* from unprofitable operation of the business

Only the first of these two causes of decreases in owner's equity is emphasized in this chapter. The second cause, a decrease in owner's equity through operating at a loss, will be considered in Chapter 3.

The accounting equation

A fundamental characteristic of every balance sheet is that the total figure for assets always equals the total figure for liabilities and owner's equity. This agreement or balance of total assets with the total of liabilities plus owner's equity is one reason for calling this statement of financial position a *balance sheet*. But *why* do total assets equal the total of liabilities and owner's equity? The answer can be given in one short paragraph as follows.

The dollar totals on the two sides of the balance sheet are always equal because these two sides are merely two views of the same business resources. The listing of assets shows us *what resources* the business owns; the listing of liabilities and owner's equity tells us *who supplied these resources* to the business and how much each group supplied. Everything that a business owns has been supplied to it by the creditors or by the owner. Therefore, the total claims of the creditors plus the claim of the owner equal the total assets of the business.

The equality of assets on the one hand and of the claims of the creditors and the owner on the other hand is expressed in the equation:

FUNDAMENTAL ACCOUNTING EQUATION

$$
\begin{array}{ccccc}
\text{Assets} & = & \text{Liabilities} & + & \text{Owner's Equity} \\
\$170{,}000 & = & \$70{,}000 & + & \$100{,}000
\end{array}
$$

The amounts listed in the equation were taken from the balance sheet illustrated on page 16. A balance sheet is simply a detailed statement of this equation. To illustrate this relationship, compare the balance sheet of Vagabond Travel Agency with the above equation.

To emphasize that the equity of the owner is a residual element, secondary to the claims of creditors, it is often helpful to transpose the terms of the equation, as follows:

ALTERNATIVE FORM OF EQUATION

$$
\begin{array}{ccccc}
\text{Assets} & - & \text{Liabilities} & = & \text{Owner's Equity} \\
\$170{,}000 & - & \$70{,}000 & = & \$100{,}000
\end{array}
$$

Every business transaction, no matter how simple or how complex, can be expressed in terms of its effect on the accounting equation. A thorough understanding of the equation and some practice in using it are essential to the student of accounting.

Regardless of whether a business grows or contracts, this equality between the assets and the claims against the assets is always maintained. Any increase in the amount of total assets is necessarily accompanied by an equal increase on the other side of the equation, that is, by an increase in either the liabilities or the owner's equity. Any decrease in total assets is necessarily accompanied by a corresponding decrease in liabilities or owner's equity. The continuing equality of the two sides of the balance sheet can best be illustrated by taking a brand-new business as an example and observing the effects of various transactions upon its balance sheet.

Effects of business transactions upon the balance sheet

8   Indicate the effects of various transactions upon the balance sheet.

Assume that James Roberts, a licensed real estate broker, decided to start a real estate business of his own, to be known as Roberts Real Estate Company. The planned operations of the new business call for obtaining listings of houses being offered for sale by owners, advertising these houses, and showing them to prospective buyers. The listing agreement signed with each owner provides that Roberts Real Estate Company shall receive at the time of sale a commission equal to 6% of the sales price of the property.

The new business was begun on September 1, when Roberts deposited $180,000 in a bank account in the name of the business, Roberts Real Estate Company. The initial balance sheet of the new business then appeared as follows:

BEGINNING BALANCE SHEET OF A NEW BUSINESS

ROBERTS REAL ESTATE COMPANY
Balance Sheet
September 1, 19___

ASSETS		**OWNER'S EQUITY**	
Cash	$180,000	James Roberts, capital .	$180,000

Observe that the equity of the owner in the assets is designated on the balance sheet by the caption, James Roberts, capital. The word *capital* is the traditional accounting term used in describing the equity of the proprietor in the assets of the business.

Purchase of an asset for cash The next transaction entered into by Roberts Real Estate Company was the purchase of land suitable as a site for an office. The price for the land was $141,000 and payment was made in cash on September 3. The effect of this transaction on the balance sheet was twofold: first, cash was decreased by the amount paid out; and second, a new asset, Land, was acquired. After this exchange of cash for land, the balance sheet appeared as follows:

BALANCE SHEET TOTALS
UNCHANGED BY
PURCHASE OF LAND
FOR CASH

ROBERTS REAL ESTATE COMPANY
Balance Sheet
September 3, 19___

ASSETS		OWNER'S EQUITY	
Cash	$ 39,000	James Roberts, capital	$180,000
Land	141,000		
Total	$180,000	Total owner's equity	$180,000

Purchase of an asset for cash and on credit On September 5 an opportunity arose to buy from Kent Company a complete office building, which had to be moved to permit the construction of a freeway. A price of $36,000 was agreed upon, which included the cost of moving the building and installing it upon the Roberts Company's lot. As the building was in excellent condition and would have cost approximately $80,000 to build, Roberts considered this a very fortunate purchase.

The terms provided for an immediate cash payment of $15,000 and payment of the balance of $21,000 within 90 days. Cash was decreased $15,000, but a new asset, Building, was recorded at cost in the amount of $36,000. Total assets were thus increased by $21,000 but the total of liabilities and owner's equity was also increased as a result of recording the $21,000 account payable as a liability. After this transaction had been recorded, the balance sheet appeared as follows. Remember that cash is always the first asset listed in a balance sheet.

TOTALS INCREASED
EQUALLY BY PURCHASE
ON CREDIT

ROBERTS REAL ESTATE COMPANY
Balance Sheet
September 5, 19___

ASSETS		LIABILITIES & OWNER'S EQUITY	
Cash	$ 24,000	Liabilities:	
Land	141,000	Accounts payable	$ 21,000
Building	36,000	Owner's equity:	
		James Roberts, capital	180,000
Total	$201,000	Total	$201,000

Note that the building appears in the balance sheet at $36,000, its cost to Roberts Real Estate Company. The estimate of $80,000 as the probable cost to construct such a building is irrelevant. Even if someone should offer to buy the building from the Roberts Company for $80,000 or more, this offer, if refused, would have no bearing on the balance sheet. Accounting records are intended to provide a historical record of *costs actually incurred*; therefore, the $36,000 price at which the building was purchased is the amount to be recorded.

Sale of an asset on credit   After the office building had been moved to the Roberts Company's lot, Roberts decided that the lot was much larger than was needed. The adjoining business, Carter's Drugstore, wanted more room for a parking area so, on September 10, Roberts Company sold the unused part of the lot to Carter's Drugstore for a price of $11,000. Since the sales price was computed at the same amount per metre as Roberts Company had paid for the land, there was neither a profit nor a loss on the sale. No down payment was required but it was agreed that the full price would be paid within three months. By this transaction a new asset, Accounts Receivable, was acquired, but the asset Land was decreased by the same amount; consequently there was no change in the amount of total assets. After this transaction, the balance sheet appeared as follows.

NO CHANGE IN TOTALS
BY SALE OF LAND
AT COST

ROBERTS REAL ESTATE COMPANY
Balance Sheet
September 10, 19___

ASSETS		LIABILITIES & OWNER'S EQUITY	
Cash	$ 24,000	Liabilities:	
Accounts receivable	11,000	Accounts payable	$ 21,000
Land	130,000	Owner's equity:	
Building	36,000	James Roberts, capital	180,000
Total	$201,000	Total	$201,000

In the illustration thus far, Roberts Real Estate Company has an account receivable from only one debtor, and an account payable to only one creditor. As the business grows, the number of debtors and creditors will increase, but the Accounts Receivable and Accounts Payable designations will continue to be used. The additional records necessary to show the amount receivable from each individual debtor and the amount owing to each individual creditor will be explained in Chapter 6.

Purchase of an asset on credit   A complete set of office furniture and equipment was purchased on credit from General Equipment, Inc., on September 14 for $5,400. As the result of this transaction the business owned a new asset, Office Equipment, but it had also incurred a new liability in the form of Accounts Payable. The increase in total assets was exactly offset by the increase in liabilities. After this transaction the balance sheet appeared as follows:

ROBERTS REAL ESTATE COMPANY
Balance Sheet
September 14, 19___

ASSETS		LIABILITIES & OWNER'S EQUITY	
Cash	$ 24,000	Liabilities:	
Accounts receivable	11,000	Accounts payable	$ 26,400
Land	130,000	Owner's equity:	
Building	36,000	James Roberts, capital	180,000
Office equipment	5,400		
Total	$206,400	Total	$206,400

Collection of an account receivable   On September 20, cash in the amount of $1,500 was received as partial settlement of the account receivable from Carter's Drugstore. This transaction caused cash to increase and the accounts receivable to decrease by an equal amount. In essence, this transaction was merely the exchange of one asset for another of equal value. Consequently, there was no change in the amount of total assets. After this transaction, the balance sheet appeared as follows.

ROBERTS REAL ESTATE COMPANY
Balance Sheet
September 20, 19___

ASSETS		LIABILITIES & OWNER'S EQUITY	
Cash	$ 25,500	Liabilities:	
Accounts receivable	9,500	Accounts payable	$ 26,400
Land	130,000	Owner's: equity:	
Building	36,000	James Roberts, capital	180,000
Office equipment	5,400		
Total	$206,400	Total	$206,400

Payment of a liability   On September 30, Roberts Real Estate Company paid $3,000 in cash to General Equipment, Inc. This payment caused a decrease in cash and an equal decrease in liabilities. Therefore the balance sheet totals were still in balance. After this transaction, the balance sheet appeared as follows:

ROBERTS REAL ESTATE COMPANY
Balance Sheet
September 30, 19___

ASSETS		LIABILITIES & OWNER'S EQUITY	
Cash	$ 22,500	Liabilities:	
Accounts receivable	9,500	Accounts payable	$ 23,400
Land	130,000	Owner's: equity:	
Building	36,000	James Roberts, capital	180,000
Office equipment	5,400		
Total	$203,400	Total	$203,400

The transactions that have been illustrated for the month of September were merely preliminary to the formal opening for business of Roberts Real Estate Company on October 1. Since we have assumed that the business earned no commissions and incurred no expenses during September, the owner's equity at September 30 is shown in the above balance sheet at $180,000, unchanged from the original investment by Roberts on September 1. September was a month devoted exclusively to organizing the business and not to regular operations. In succeeding chapters we shall continue the example of Roberts Real Estate Company by illustrating operating transactions and considering how the net income of the business is determined.

Effect of business transactions upon the accounting equation

A balance sheet is merely a detailed expression of the accounting equation, Assets = Liabilities + Owner's Equity. To emphasize the relationship between the accounting equation and the balance sheet, let us now repeat the September transactions of Roberts Real Estate Company to show the effect of each transaction upon the accounting equation. Briefly restated, the seven transactions were as follows:

Sept. **1** Began the business by depositing $180,000 in a company bank account.
3 Purchased land for $141,000 cash.
5 Purchased a building for $36,000, paying $15,000 cash and incurring a liability of $21,000.
10 Sold part of the land at a price equal to cost of $11,000, collectible within three months.
14 Purchased office equipment on credit for $5,400.
20 Received $1,500 cash as partial collection of the $11,000 account receivable.
30 Paid $3,000 on accounts payable.

	CASH	+	ACCOUNTS RECEIVABLE	+	LAND	+	BUILDING	+	OFFICE EQUIP- MENT	=	ACCOUNTS PAYABLE	+	JAMES ROBERTS, CAPITAL
					ASSETS					= LIABIL- ITIES		+ OWNER'S EQUITY	
Sept. 1	+ $180,000		-0-		-0-		-0-		-0-		-0-		+ $180,000
Sept. 3	− 141,000				+ $141,000								
Balances	$39,000		-0-		$141,000		-0-		-0-		-0-		$180,000
Sept. 5	− 15,000						+ $36,000				+ $21,000		
Balances	$24,000		-0-		$141,000		$36,000		-0-		$21,000		$180,000
Sept. 10			+ $11,000		− 11,000								
Balances	$24,000		$11,000		$130,000		$36,000		-0-		$21,000		$180,000
Sept. 14									+ $5,400		+ 5,400		
Balances	$24,000		$11,000		$130,000		$36,000		$5,400		$26,400		$180,000
Sept. 20	+ 1,500		− 1,500										
Balances	$25,500		$9,500		$130,000		$36,000		$5,400		$26,400		$180,000
Sept. 30	− 3,000										− 3,000		
Balances	$22,500	+	$9,500	+	$130,000	+	$36,000	+	$5,400	=	$23,400	+	$180,000

The table on page 25 shows the effects of each of the September transactions on the accounting equation. The final line in the table corresponds to the amounts in the balance sheet at the end of September. Note that the equality of the two sides of the equation was maintained throughout the recording of the transactions.

FORMS OF BUSINESS ORGANIZATION

9   Describe the three forms of business organization.

A business enterprise may be organized as a *sole* or *single proprietorship*, a *partnership*, or a *corporation*.

Sole or single proprietorships

A business owned by one person is called a *sole* or single proprietorship. Often the owner also acts as the manager. Roberts Real Estate Company, the company used in our illustration, is a sole proprietorship owned by James Roberts. This form of business organization is common for small retail stores, farms, service businesses, and professional practices in law, medicine, and public accounting. In fact, the sole proprietorship is by far the most common form of business organization in our economy.

From an accounting viewpoint, a sole proprietorship is regarded as a business entity *separate from the other affairs of its owner.* From a legal viewpoint, however, the business and its owner are not regarded as separate entities. Thus, *the owner is personally liable* for the debts of the business. If the business becomes insolvent, creditors can force the owner to sell his or her personal assets to pay the business debts.

Partnerships

A business owned by two or more persons voluntarily associated as partners is called a partnership. Partnerships, like sole proprietorships, are widely used for small businesses and professional practices. As in the case of a sole proprietorship, a partnership is not legally an entity separate from its owners. Consequently, a partner is personally liable for the debts of the partnership. From an accounting standpoint, however, a partnership is a business entity separate from the personal activities of the partners.

Corporations

A corporation is a *legal entity,* having an existence separate and distinct from that of its owners. In the eyes of the law, a corporation is an "artifical person," with many of the rights and responsibilities of a real person. For example, a corporation may own assets in its own name and is responsible for its own debts.

The owners of a corporation are called *shareholders,* and their ownership is evidenced by shares of *capital stock.* The extent of an individual's ownership of a corporation is determined by the number of shares of stock that he or she owns. Shareholders are free to sell some or all of their shares to another investor at any time. Therefore, the ownership of a corporation is *easily transferable.*

A major advantage of the corporation is that the shareholders are *not personally liable* for the debts of the business. If a corporation becomes insolvent, creditors have claims only against the assets of the corporation. Thus, a shareholder can lose no more than the amount that he or she has invested in a corporation.

Transferability of ownership and limited personal liability make the corporation an ideal vehicle for bringing together large amounts of ownership capital from many individual owners. In fact, some corporations have more than a million shareholders. Thus, most large businesses are organized as corporations.

Balance sheets for the three types of organizations

Assets and liabilities are presented in the same manner in the balance sheets of each type of business organization. Some differences arise, however, in the presentation of owners' equity.

Roberts Real Estate Company was a sole proprietorship, owned by one person. Therefore, the owner's equity section of the balance sheet included only one item: the equity of the proprietor, James Roberts. If the business were a partnership of two or more persons, we would use the caption *Partners' Equity* instead of Owner's Equity and would list under that caption the amount of each partner's equity. If the business were organized as a corporation, the caption used in the balance sheet would be *Shareholders' Equity.* It is not customary in a corporation's balance sheet to show separately the equity of each shareholder. The equity of all the shareholders as a group is shown, and this ownership equity is divided into two amounts: (1) *Capital Stock,* the amount of the owners' original investment, and (2) *Retained Earnings,* the amount of profits (or losses) accumulated since the formation of the business.

These three methods of showing ownership equity in the balance sheet are illustrated below.

EQUITY OF THE OWNER, OF PARTNERS, AND OF SHAREHOLDERS

FOR A SOLE PROPRIETORSHIP

Owner's equity:
Dale Nelson, capital . . . . $ 50,000

FOR A PARTNERSHIP

Partners' equity:
Pamela Barnes, capital $40,000
Scott Davis, capital 35,000
Total capital . . . . $ 75,000

FOR A CORPORATION

Shareholders' equity:
Capital stock $1,000,000
Retained earnings 278,000
Total capital $1,278,000

The preceding illustration of the ownership equity of a corporation shows that $1 million of capital was invested in the corporation by shareholders, and that through profitable operation of the business an additional $278,000 of earned capital has been accumulated. The corporation has chosen to retain this $278,000 in the business rather than to distribute these earnings to the shareholders as *dividends.* The total earnings of the corporation may have been considerably more than $278,000, because any earnings that were paid to shareholders as dividends would not appear on the balance sheet. The term *retained earnings* describes only the earnings that were *not* paid out in the form of dividends. Although shareholders naturally like to receive dividends, resources resulted from retained earnings in the business may enable the corporation to acquire additional operating properties, to expand the scope of operations, and thereby to enjoy larger future earnings.

Generally accepted accounting principles apply to all three forms of business organization. In the first several chapters of this book, our study of basic accounting concepts will use as a model the sole proprietorship, which is the simplest and most common form of business organization.

USE OF FINANCIAL STATEMENTS BY OUTSIDERS

Through careful study of financial statements, it is possible for the outsider with a knowledge of accounting to obtain a fairly complete understanding of the financial position of the business and to become aware of significant changes that have occurred since the date of the preceding balance sheet. Bear in mind, however, that financial statements have limitations. As stated earlier, only those factors that can be reduced to monetary terms appear in the balance sheet.

Let us consider for a moment some important business factors that are not set forth in financial statements. Perhaps a new competing store has just opened for business across the street; the prospect for intensified competition in the future will not be described in the balance sheet. As another example, the health, experience, and managerial skills of the key people in the management group may be extremely important to the success of a business, but these qualities cannot be measured and expressed in dollars in the balance sheet.

Bankers and other creditors

Bankers who have loaned money to a business concern or who are considering making such a loan will be vitally interested in the balance sheet of the business. By studying the amount and kinds of assets in relation to the amount and payment dates of the liabilities, a banker can form an opinion as to the ability of the business to pay its debts promptly. The banker gives particular attention to the amount of cash and of other assets (such as accounts receivable) that will soon be converted into cash and then compares the amount of these assets with the amount of liabilities falling due in the near future. The banker is also interested in the amount of the owner's equity, as this ownership capital serves as a protecting buffer between the banker and any losses that may befall the business.

Another important group making constant use of balance sheets consists of the credit managers of manufacturing and wholesaling firms, who must decide whether prospective customers are to be allowed to buy merchandise on credit. The credit manager, like the banker, studies the balance sheets of customers and prospective customers for the purpose of estimating their debt-paying ability. Credit agencies such as Dun & Bradstreet make a business of obtaining financial statements from virtually all business concerns and appraising their debt-paying ability. The conclusions reached by these credit agencies are available to business concerns willing to pay for credit reports about prospective customers.

Owners

The financial statements of corporations listed on the stock exchanges are eagerly awaited by millions of shareholders, most of whom are not part of management and thus must rely mainly on the financial statements for their investment decisions. A favourable set of financial statements may cause the market price of the company's stock to rise dramatically; an unfavourable set of financial statements may cause the "bottom to fall out" of the market price. Current dependable financial statements are one of the essential ingredients for successful investment in securities. Of course, financial statements are equally important in sole proprietorships and partnerships. The financial statements tell the owners just how successful their business has been and summarize in concise form its present financial position.

Others interested in financial information

In addition to owners, managers, bankers, and merchandise creditors, other groups making use of accounting data include financial analysts, governmental agencies, employees, investors, and writers for business periodicals.

The purpose of this discussion is to show the extent to which a modern industrial society depends upon accounting. Even more important, however, is a clear understanding at the outset of your study that accounting does not exist just for the sake of keeping a record or in order to fill out income tax returns. These are but auxiliary functions. If you gain an understanding of accounting concepts, you will have acquired an analytical skill essential to the field of professional management. The prime and vital *purpose of accounting* is to aid decision makers in choosing among alternative courses of action.

END-OF-CHAPTER REVIEW

SUMMARY OF CHAPTER LEARNING OBJECTIVES

1 Define accounting and explain the purpose of accounting.

Accounting is the process of recording, measuring, classifying, summarizing, communicating, and interpreting economic activity. The purpose of accounting is to develop financial information about an economic entity and communicate this information to decision makers.

2 Explain the phrase, "generally accepted accounting principles."

Generally accepted accounting principles are the concepts, principles, and "ground rules" used in the preparation of financial statements.

3 Describe the accounting profession and public, private, and government accounting.

The accounting profession consists of three accounting organizations — the chartered accountants, the certified management accountants, and the certified general accountants. Public accountants offer a variety of accounting services to the public for a fee. These services include auditing, income tax services, management advisory services, and small business services. Private accountants, in contrast to public accountants, work for a single company. Their responsibilities include designing accounting systems, cost accounting, financial forecasting, tax work, and internal auditing. Accountants also work for governmental agencies. These governmental accountants perform functions similar to those of private accountants, and also such special functions as auditing income tax returns. Many professional accountants have become top corporate executives, such as chairpersons and presidents of large corporations.

4 Explain the role of the CICA in the development of accounting standards.

The CICA's Accounting Standards Committee issues recommendations in the *CICA Handbook*, which is a collection of authoritative expressions of generally accepted accounting principles. The CICA is a part of the private sector, not a governmental agency.

5 State two basic financial objectives of every profit-oriented business.

Two basic financial objectives of every profit-oriented business are (1) operating profitably, and (2) remaining solvent.

6 Describe a balance sheet; define assets, liabilities, and owner's equity.

A balance sheet is a financial statement showing the assets, liabilities, and owner's equity in a specific business entity. Assets are economic resources owned by the business; liabilities are the debts or financial obligations of the business; and owner's equity is the owner's *residual interest* in the business (equal to the excess of assets over liabilities).

7 Discuss the accounting principles involved in asset valuation.

Most assets are valued in accordance with the *cost principle*. This generally accepted accounting principle indicates that the valuation of assets in a balance sheet should be based upon historical cost, not upon current market value. Two other accounting principles supporting the valuation of assets at cost are the *going-concern assumption* and the *objectivity principle*.

8 Indicate the effects of various transactions upon the balance sheet.

A transaction that increases total assets also must increase either total liabilities or owner's equity. Similarly, a transaction that decreases total assets must decrease either total liabilities or owner's equity. Some transactions increase one asset while decreasing another; such transactions do not change the total amounts of assets, liabilities, or owner's equity.

9 Describe the three forms of business organization.

The three forms of business organization are sole proprietorship, partnership, and corporation. A proprietorship has one owner; partnership and corporation have two or more owners. Owners of proprietorship and partnerships are personally liable for the debts of their business while the shareholders of corporation are liable to the extent of their investments in the business.

KEY TERMS INTRODUCED OR EMPHASIZED IN CHAPTER 1

Accounting Accounting is the process of recording, measuring, classifying, summarizing, communicating, and interpreting economic activity.

Accounting equation Assets equal liabilities plus owner's equity. A = L + OE.

Accounting Standards Committee A committee of the CICA that is responsible for issuing recommendations with respect to matters of accounting practice. The committee's recommendations, which are contained in the *CICA Handbook,* are recognized as an authoritative source of generally accepted accounting principles.

Accounting system The methods, procedures, and devices used by an entity to keep track of its financial activities and to summarize these activities in a manner useful to decision makers.

Assets Economic resources owned by a business, which are expected to benefit future operations.

Auditing The principal activity of a public accountant. Consists of an independent examination of the accounting records and other evidence relating to a business to support the expression of an impartial expert opinion about the fairness and reliability of the financial statements.

Balance sheet A financial statement that shows the financial position of a business entity by summarizing the assets, liabilities, and owner's equity at a specific date.

Business entity An economic unit that enters into business transactions that must be recorded, summarized, and reported. The entity is regarded as *separate from its owner or owners.*

Canadian Institute of Chartered Accountants (CICA) The national organization of chartered accountants (CAs) that carries on extensive research and is influential in developing and improving accounting standards and practices.

Capital Stock Transferable units of ownership in a corporation.

Corporation A business organized as a separate legal entity, with ownership divided into transferable shares of capital stock.

Cost principle A widely used policy of accounting for assets at their original cost to the business.

Financial Accounting Standards Board (FASB) An independent group in the United States that conducts research in accounting and issues authoritative statements as to proper accounting principles and methods for reporting financial information.

Financial statements Reports that summarize the financial position and operating results of a business (balance sheet and income statement).

Generally accepted accounting principles (GAAP) The accounting concepts, measurement techniques, and standards of presentation used in financial statements. Examples include the cost principle, the going-concern assumption, and the objectivity principle.

Going-concern assumption An assumption by accountants that a business will continue to operate indefinitely unless specific evidence to the contrary exists, as, for example, impending bankruptcy.

Internal control All measures used by a business to guard against errors, waste, and fraud; to assure the reliability of accounting data; and to promote compliance with all company policies.

Liabilities Debts or obligation of a business. The claims of creditors against the assets of a business.

Objectivity principle It relates to factual evidence that can be verified by independent experts.

Owner's equity The excess of assets over liabilities. The amount of an owner's net investment in a business plus profits from successful operations that have been retained in the business.

Partnership A business owned by two or more persons voluntarily associated as partners.

Sole (single) proprietorship An unincorporated business owned by one person.

Solvency Having enough money to pay debts as they fall due.

DEMONSTRATION PROBLEM FOR YOUR REVIEW

The accounting data (listed alphabetically) for Crystal Auto Wash at August 31, 19___, follow. The figure for Cash is not given but it can be determined when all the available information is assembled in the form of a balance sheet.

Accounts payable	$ 9,000	Land	$40,000
Accounts receivable	800	Machinery & equipment . . .	25,000
Building	35,000	Notes payable	49,000
Cash	?	Salaries payable	3,000
Don Johnson, capital	44,400	Supplies	400

Instructions   Prepare a balance sheet at August 31, 19___.

SOLUTION TO DEMONSTRATION PROBLEM

CRYSTAL AUTO WASH
Balance Sheet
August 31, 19___

ASSETS		LIABILITIES & OWNER'S EQUITY	
Cash	$ 4,200	Liabilities:	
Accounts receivable	800	Notes payable	$ 49,000
Supplies	400	Accounts payable	9,000
Land	40,000	Salaries payable	3,000
Building	35,000	Total liabilities	$ 61,000
Machinery & equipment . .	25,000	Owner's equity:	
		Don Johnson, capital . .	44,400
Total	$105,400	Total	$105,400

ASSIGNMENT MATERIAL

REVIEW QUESTIONS

1 In broad, general terms, what is the purpose of accounting?

2 Why is a knowledge of accounting terms and concepts useful to persons other than professional accountants?

3 What is meant by the term *business transaction*?

4 What are financial statements and how do they relate to the accounting system?

5 Explain briefly why each of the following groups is interested in the financial statements of a business:

a Creditors

b Potential investors

c Labour unions

6 The following questions relate to the term, *generally accepted accounting principles:*

  a What type of accounting reports should be prepared in conformity with these principles?

  b Why is it important for these principles to be widely recognized?

  c Where do these principles come from?

  d List two examples of generally accepted accounting principles that relate to the valuation of assets.

7 Distinguish between *accounting* and *bookkeeping.*

8 What is the principal function of public accounting firms? What other services are commonly rendered by such firms?

9 Private accounting includes a number of subfields or specialized phases, of which cost accounting is one. Name four other such specialized phases of private accounting.

10 Is the CICA's Accounting Standards Committee a government agency? What is its role in the development of accounting standards?

11 One basic objective of every business is to operate profitably. What other basic objective must be met for a business to survive? Explain.

12 Not all the significant happenings in the life of a business can be measured and expressed in monetary terms and entered in the accounting records. Identify two or more significant events affecting a business that could not be satisfactorily measured and entered in its accounting records.

13 Information available from the accounting records provides a basis for making many business decisions. List five examples of business decisions requiring the use of accounting information.

14 What are the purposes of a company's system of internal control?

15 State briefly the purpose of a balance sheet.

16 Define assets. List five examples.

17 Define liabilities. List two examples.

18 Ray Company was offered $300,000 cash for the land and buildings occupied by the business. These assets had been acquired five years ago at a price of $200,000. Ray Company refused the offer, but is inclined to increase the land and buildings to a total valuation of $300,000 in the balance sheet in order to show more accurately ''how much the business is worth.'' Do you agree? Explain.

19 Explain briefly the concept of the *business entity.*

20 State the accounting equation in two alternative forms.

21 The owner's equity in a business arises from what two sources?

22 Why are the total assets shown on a balance sheet always equal to the total of the liabilities and the owner's equity?

23 Can a business transaction cause one asset to increase or decrease without affecting any other asset, liability, or the owner's equity?

24 If a transaction causes total liabilities to decrease but does not affect the owner's equity, what change, if any, will occur to total assets?

25 Give examples of transactions that would:

   a Cause one asset to increase and another asset to decrease without any effect on the liabilities or owner's equity.

   b Cause both total assets and total liabilities to increase without any effect on the owner's equity.

26 Assume that a business becomes insolvent. Can the owner (or owners) of the business be held personally liable for the debts of the business? Give separate answers assuming that the business is organized as (a) a sole or single proprietorship, (b) a partnership, or (c) a corporation.

27 Marigold Corporation has retained earnings of $2 million. Does this mean that the corporation is solvent? Explain.

EXERCiSES

Exercise 1-1
Accounting terminology

Listed below are nine technical accounting terms introduced in this chapter:

Audit	GAAP	Owner's equity
Corporation	Internal control	Sole proprietorship
CICA	Liabilities	Solvent

Each of the following statements may (or may not) describe one of these technical terms. For each statement, indicate the accounting term described, or answer ''None'' if the statement does not correctly describe any of the terms.

a The most common form of business organization in the economy.

b The ''ground rules'' for presenting accounting information in financial statements.

c A residual amount equal to total assets minus total liabilities.

d The organization that issues authoritative expressions of generally accepted accounting principles.

e A system of measures designed to assure management that all aspects of a business are operating according to plan.

f Unable to pay debts as they come due.

g An investigation conducted for the purpose of expressing a professional opinion upon the fairness and reliability of a set of financial statements.

Exercise 1-2
Preparing a balance sheet

The following balance sheet of Seafood Galley is incorrect because of improper headings and the misplacement of several accounts. Prepare a corrected balance sheet.

SEAFOOD GALLEY
March 31, 19___

ASSETS		OWNER'S EQUITY	
Lloyd Bridges, capital	$ 66,200	Accounts receivable	$ 37,800
Cash	10,900	Notes payable	75,400
Building	48,000	Supplies	1,400
Automobiles	16,500	Land	27,000
Total assets	$141,600	Total owner's equity	$141,600

Exercise 1-3
Preparing a balance sheet

The items included in the balance sheet of Hart Company at December 31, 19___, are listed below in random order. You are to prepare a balance sheet (including a complete heading). Arrange the assets in the sequence shown in the balance sheet illustrated on page 16 and include a figure for total liabilities. You must compute the amount for Jennifer Hart, capital.

Land	$95,000	Office equipment	$ 3,400
Accounts payable	14,600	Building	70,000
Accounts receivable	18,900	Cash	12,100
Jennifer Hart, capital	?	Notes payable	70,000

Exercise 1-4
Using the accounting equation

Compute the missing amount in each of the following:

	ASSETS	LIABILITIES	OWNER'S EQUITY
a	$195,000	$114,000	?
b	?	69,000	$ 50,000
c	410,000	?	202,000

Exercise 1-5
Using the accounting equation

a The assets of Atom Company total $235,000 and the owner's equity amounts to $70,000. What is the amount of the liabilities?

b The owners' equity of Party Game Corp. appears on the balance sheet as $95,000 and is equal to one-third the amount of total assets. What is the amount of liabilities?

c The assets of Hot Line Phones amounted to $75,000 on December 31, 1988 but increased to $105,000 by December 31, 1989. During this same period, liabilities increased by $25,000. The owner's equity at December 31, 1988 amounted to $50,000. What was the amount of owner's equity at December 31, 1989? Explain the basis for your answer.

Exercise 1-6
Effects of business transactions

For each of the following categories, state concisely a transaction that will have the required effect on elements of the accounting equation.

a Increase an asset and increase a liability.

b Decrease an asset and decrease a liability.

c Increase one asset and decrease another asset.

d Increase an asset and increase owner's equity.

e Increase one asset, decrease another asset, and increase a liability.

Exercise 1-7
Effects of business transactions

Several business transactions of Pizza Parlor are listed below.

a The owner invested cash in the business.

b Purchased a pizza oven for cash.

c Purchased a delivery truck at a price of $12,000, terms $1,500 cash and the balance payable in 24 equal monthly instalments.

d Paid a liability.

e Borrowed money from a bank.

f Sold land for cash at a price equal to its cost.

g Sold land for cash at a price in excess of its cost.

h Sold land for cash at a price less than its cost.

i Collected an account receivable.

Indicate the effects of each of these transactions upon the *total* amounts of the company's assets, liabilities, and owner's equity. Organize your answer in tabular form, using the following column headings and the symbols + for increase, − for decrease, and NE for no effect. The answer for transaction (**a**) is provided as an example:

TRANSACTION	ASSETS	LIABILITIES	OWNER'S EQUITY
(a)	+	NE	+

PROBLEMS

Group A

Problem 1A-1
Preparing a balance sheet; determining owner's equity

Listed below in random order are the items to be included in the balance sheet of Sun Basin Lodge at October 31, 19___. You are to prepare a balance sheet at October 31, using a sequence for assets similar to that in the illustrated balance sheet on page 16. Include a proper heading and a figure for total liabilities. The amount for John Chapman, capital, must be computed. Remember that the figure for total assets should appear on the same line as the amount for the total liabilities and owner's equity.

Notes payable	$91,000	Accounts receivable	$ 3,150
Land	58,000	Ski tow equipment	48,500
John Chapman, capital	?	Office equipment	1,225
Cash	2,225	Accounts payable	18,600
Buildings	86,000		

Problem 1A-2
Preparing a balance sheet; effects of a change in assets

HERE COMES TIGER! is the name of a travelling circus owned by Tiger Hays. The ledger accounts of the business at June 30 are listed in alphabetical order.

Accounts payable	$ 17,400	Notes receivable	$ 2,400
Accounts receivable	8,900	Props and equipment	39,720
Animals	56,040	Salaries payable	6,500
Cages	16,420	Tents	42,000
Cash	22,400	Tiger Hayes, capital	?
Costumes	11,280	Trucks	41,650
Notes payable	120,000	Wagons	28,910

Instructions

a Prepare a balance sheet by using these items and computing the amount of the owner's capital. Organize you balance sheet similar to the one illustrated on page 16. (After "Accounts Receivable," you may list the remaining assets in any order.) Include a proper balance sheet heading.

b Assume that late in the evening of June 30, after your balance sheet had been prepared, a fire destroyed one of the tents, which had cost $11,200. The tent was not insured. Explain what changes would be required in your June 30 balance sheet to reflect the loss of this asset.

Problem 1A-3
Explaining effects of
business transactions

Five selected transactions of Canyon Company are summarized in the table below. The effect of each transaction upon the accounting equation is shown, and also the new balance of each item in the equation. For each of the transactions (a) through (e), you are to write a sentence explaining the nature of the transaction.

	CASH	+	ACCOUNTS RECEIVABLE	+	LAND	+	BUILDING	+	OFFICE EQUIP- MENT	=	ACCOUNTS PAYABLE	+	J. DAY, CAPITAL
					ASSETS					=	LIABIL- ITIES	+	OWNER'S EQUITY
Balances	$3,000		$9,000		$35,000		$55,000		$3,000		$12,000		$93,000
(a)	+ 1,500		− 1,500										
Balances	$4,500		$7,500		$35,000		$55,000		$3,000		$12,000		$93,000
(b)									+ 800		+ 800		
Balances	$4,500		$7,500		$35,000		$55,000		$3,800		$12,800		$93,000
(c)	− 1,200										− 1,200		
Balances	$3,300		$7,500		$35,000		$55,000		$3,800		$11,600		$93,000
(d)	− 300								+ 900		+ 600		
Balances	$3,000		$7,500		$35,000		$55,000		$4,700		$12,200		$93,000
(e)	+ 5,000												+ 5,000
Balances	$8,000	+	$7,500	+	$35,000	+	$55,000	+	$4,700	=	$12,200	+	$98,000

Problem 1A-4
Recording effects of
business transactions

Travel Connection was organized on September 1 and completed the following transactions within a short time.

(1) K. Bell deposited $25,000 of personal funds in a bank account in the name of the new company.

(2) Purchased land and a building for a total price of $80,000, of which $30,000 was the value of the land and $50,000 was the value of the building. Paid $20,000 in cash and signed a note payable for the remaining $60,000.

(3) Bought office equipment on credit for $7,500 (30-day open account).

(4) Obtained a bank loan in the amount of $8,000. Signed a note payable.

(5) Paid $6,000 of the accounts payable.

(6) K. Bell invested an additional $3,000 of personal funds in the business by depositing cash in the company bank account.

Instructions

Construct a tabular arrangement of the accounting equation as illustrated on page 25. The column headings should be as follows:

CASH	+	LAND	+	BUILDING	+	OFFICE EQUIP- MENT	=	NOTES PAYABLE	+	ACCOUNTS PAYABLE	+	K. BELL, CAPITAL
		ASSETS					=		LIABILITIES		+	OWNER'S EQUITY

Use a separate line of the table to show the effects of each transaction on the assets, liabilities, and owner's equity. Identify each transaction by number along the left margin of the table. Show totals for all columns after transaction **(2)** and after each subsequent transaction.

Problem 1A-5
Preparing a balance
sheet; effects of
business transactions

The following is a list of the balance sheet items of Green Insurance Agency at May 31, 19___.

Accounts payable	$12,100	Cash	$?
Office equipment	7,200	Notes payable	30,000
J. Green, capital	76,900	Accounts receivable	15,400
Land	48,000	Building	46,000

Shortly after the above balance sheet date, the following transactions occurred.

June 1 One-half of the land owned by Green Insurance Agency was sold at a price of $24,000, which was equal to its cost. A down payment of $5,000 cash was received on this date along with a note receivable from the buyer for the remaining $19,000. The note is due in 60 days and does not bear interest.

2 Accounts payable of $2,300 were paid in cash.

Instructions

a Prepare a balance sheet at May 31, 19___.

b Prepare a balance sheet at June 2, after completion of the transactions described.

Problem 1A-6
Preparing a balance
sheet; discussion
and application of
accounting principles

Melonie Austin, owner and manager of Old Town Playhouse, needs to obtain a bank loan to finance the production of the company's next play. As part of the loan application, Austin was asked to prepare a balance sheet for the business. She prepared the following balance sheet, which is arranged correctly, but contains several errors with respect to certain accounting principles.

OLD TOWN PLAYHOUSE
Balance Sheet
September 30, 19___

ASSETS		LIABILITIES & OWNER'S EQUITY	
Cash	$ 18,600	Liabilities:	
Accounts receivable	156,200	Accounts payable	$ 4,600
Props and costumes	1,800	Salaries payable	28,200
Theatre building	13,500	Total liabilities	$32,800
Lighting equipment	8,500	Owner's equity:	
Automobile	12,000	Melonie Austin, capital	10,000
Total	$210,600	Total	$42,800

In discussions with Austin and by reviewing the accounting records of Old Town Playhouse, you discover the following facts:

(1) The amount of cash, $18,600, includes $12,000 in the company's bank account, $2,100 on hand in the company's safe, and $4,500 in Austin's personal savings account.

(2) Accounts receivable include $6,200 owed to the business by Artistic Tours. The remaining $150,000 is Austin's estimate of future ticket sales from September 30 through the end of the year (December 31).

(3) Austin explains that the props and costumes were purchased several days ago for $14,800. The business paid $1,800 of this amount in cash and issued a note payable to Actors' Supply Co. for the remainder of the purchase price ($13,000). As this note will not be paid until January of next year, it was not included among the company's liabilities.

(4) Old Town Playhouse rents the theatre building from Kievits International at a rate of $1,500 per month. The $13,500 represents the rent paid through September 30 of the current year. Kievits International acquired the building seven years ago at a cost of $126,000.

(5) The lighting equipment was purchased on September 26 at a cost of $8,500, but the stage manager says that it isn't worth a dime.

(6) The automobile is Austin's classic 1955 Porsche, which she purchased two years ago for $9,600. She recently saw a similar car advertised for sale at $12,000. She does not use the car in the business, but it has a personalized licence plate that reads "PLAHOUS."

(7) The accounts payable include business debts of $3,700 and the $900 balance of Austin's personal Visa card.

(8) Salaries payable includes $25,000 offered to Mario Dane to play the lead role in a new play opening next December and also $3,200 still owed to stage hands for work done through September 30.

(9) When Austin founded Old Town Playhouse four years ago, she invested $10,000 in the business. She has shown this amount as her owner's equity in order to comply with the cost principle. However, Live Theatre Inc., has offered to buy her business for $30,000, and she believes that perhaps the owner's equity should be changed to this amount.

Instructions   **a** Prepare a corrected balance sheet for Old Town Playhouse at September 30, 19___.

b For each of the nine numbered items above, explain your reasoning in deciding whether or not to include the items in the balance sheet and in determining the proper dollar valuation.

Group B

Problem 1B-1
Preparing a balance sheet; determine owner's equity

Prepare a balance sheet for the Bear Creek Chalet as of June 30, 19___, from the following random list of balance sheet items. Use a similar sequence for assets as in the illustrated balance sheet on page 16. Include a proper heading and a figure for total liabilities. The figure for Karen Monday, capital, must be computed.

Accounts payable	$12,500	Snowmobiles	$ 8,200
Karen Monday, capital	?	Notes payable	90,000
Building	52,000	Equipment	25,000
Accounts receivable	11,250	Land	65,000
Cash	9,750		

Problem 1B-2
Preparing a balance sheet; effect of a change in assets

Following, in random order, is a list of balance sheet items for Ruby Red Farms at September 30, 19___.

Land	$325,000	Fences & gates	$18,650
Barns and sheds	43,500	Irrigation system	11,180
Notes payable	295,000	Cash	9,045
Accounts receivable	12,425	Livestock	67,100
Citrus trees	42,600	Farm machinery	23,872
Accounts payable	42,830	Walter Berkeley, capital	?
Property taxes payable	4,675	Wages payable	1,010

Instructions　**a** Prepare a balance sheet by using these items and computing the amount for Walter Berkeley's capital. Use a sequence of assets similar to that illustrated on page 15. (After "Barns and sheds," you may list the remaining assets in any order.) Include a proper heading for your balance sheet.

b Assume that immediately after this September 30 balance sheet was prepared, a tornado completely destroyed one of the barns. The barn had a cost of $18,400, and was not insured against this type of disaster. Explain what changes would be required in your September 30 balance sheet to reflect the loss of this barn.

Problem 1B-3
Explaining effects of business transactions

Five transactions of Barrel Company are summarized in the table below with each transaction identified by a number. The effect of each transaction upon the accounting equation is shown, and also the new balance of each item in the equation. For each of the transactions (**a**) through (**e**), you are to write a sentence explaining the nature of the transaction.

	ASSETS					=	LIABIL-ITIES	+	OWNER'S EQUITY
	CASH	+ ACCOUNTS RECEIVABLE	+ LAND	+ BUILDING	+ OFFICE EQUIP-MENT	=	ACCOUNTS PAYABLE	+	T. LEE, CAPITAL
Balances	$4,000	$7,000	$29,000	$50,000	$7,000		$8,000		$89,000
(a)					+700		+700		
Balances	$4,000	$7,000	$29,000	$50,000	$7,700		$8,700		$89,000
(b)	+800	−800							
Balances	$4,800	$6,200	$29,000	$50,000	$7,700		$8,700		$89,000
(c)	−2,600						−2,600		
Balances	$2,200	$6,200	$29,000	$50,000	$7,700		$6,100		$89,000
(d)	−300				+1,300		+1,000		
Balances	$1,900	$6,200	$29,000	$50,000	$9,000		$7,100		$89,000
(e)	+1,500								+1,500
Balances	$3,400 +	$6,200 +	$29,000 +	$50,000 +	$9,000 =		$7,100 +		$90,500

Problem 1B-4
Recording effects of business transactions

The following items making up the balance sheet of Blue Sky Country at June 30 are listed in tabular form similiar to the illustration of the accounting equation on page 25.

	ASSETS				=	LIABILITIES	+	OWNER'S EQUITY
	CASH	+ ACCOUNTS RECEIVABLE	+ AUTOMOBILES +	OFFICE EQUIP-MENT	=	NOTES PAYABLE +	ACCOUNTS PAYABLE +	D. HALL, CAPITAL
Balances	$6,500	$58,400	$8,000	$3,800		$20,000	$25,200	$31,500

During a short period after June 30, Blue Sky country had the following transactions.

(1) Paid $1,200 of accounts payable.

(2) Collected $4,000 of accounts receivable.

(3) Bought office equipment at a cost of $5,700. Paid cash.

(4) Borrowed $10,000 from a bank. Signed a note payable for that amount.

(5) Purchased an automobile for $10,500. Paid $3,000 cash and signed a note payable for the balance of $7,500.

Instructions   You are to construct a table similar to the one illustrated in Problem 1B-3. First, list the June 30 balances of assets, liabilities, and owner's equity in the preceding tabular form. Next, complete the table using a separate line for each numbered transaction. Show the totals (balances) for all columns after each transaction.

Problem 1B-5
Preparing a balance sheet; effects of business transactions

The balance sheet items for Gremlin Auto Wash (arranged in alphabetical order) were as follows at August 1, 19___:

Accounts payable	$ 4,000	Land	$40,000
Accounts receivable	300	Notes payable	46,000
Building	20,000	Supplies	2,800
Cash	4,600	Susan Young, capital	?
Equipment	26,000		

During the next two days, the following transactions occurred:

Aug. 2   Young invested an additional $15,000 cash in the business. The accounts payable were paid in full. (No payment was made on the notes payable.)

3   Equipment was purchased at a cost of $9,000 to be paid within 10 days. Supplies were purchased for $500 cash from another car-washing concern, which was going out of business. These supplies would have cost $900 if purchased through normal channels.

Instructions   **a** Prepare a balance sheet at August 1, 19___.
b Prepare a balance sheet at August 3, 19___.

Problem 1B-6
Preparing a balance sheet; discussion and application of accounting principles

Vancouver Scripts is a service-type enterprise in the entertainment field, and its owner, Brad Jones, has only a limited knowledge of accounting. Jones prepared the following balance sheet, which, although arranged satisfactorily, contains certain errors with respect to certain accounting principles.

VANCOUVER SCRIPTS
Balance Sheet
November 30, 19___

ASSETS		LIABILITIES & OWNER'S EQUITY	
Cash	$ 940	Liabilities:	
Notes receivable	2,900	Notes payable	$ 67,000
Accounts receivable	2,465	Accounts payable	29,800
Land	70,000	Total liabilities	$ 96,800
Building	54,326	Owner's equity:	
Office furniture	6,848	Brad Jones, capital	63,080
Other assets	22,401		
Total	$159,880	Total	$159,880

By talking with Jones and inspecting the accounting records, you find the following:

(1) One of the notes receivable in the amount of $700 is an IOU, which Jones received in a poker game about two years ago. The IOU bears only the initials B.K. and Jones does not know the name or address of the maker.

(2) Office furniture <u>includes</u> an antique desk purchased November 29 of the current year at a cost of $2,100. Jones explains that no payment is due for the desk until January and therefore this debt is not included among the liabilities.

(3) Also included in the amount for office furniture is a typewriter that cost $525 but is not on hand, because Jones gave it to a son as a birthday present.

(4) The "Other assets" of $22,401 represents the total amount of income taxes Jones has paid over a period of years. Jones believes the income tax law to be unconstitutional, and a friend who attends law school will help Jones recover the taxes paid as soon as he completes his legal education.

(5) The land had cost $34,000, but was increased to $70,000 when a friend of Jones offered to pay that much for it if Jones would move the building off the lot.

Instructions   **a** Prepare a corrected balance sheet at November 30, 19___.

b For each of the five numbered items, use a separate numbered paragraph to explain whether the treatment followed by Jones is in accord with generally accepted accounting principles.

BUSINESS DECISION CASES

Case 1-1
Using a balance sheet
and other information
in business decisions

Adams Company and Baker Company are in the same line of business and both were recently organized, so it may be assumed that the recorded costs for assets are close to current market values. Balance sheets for the two companies are as follows:

ADAMS COMPANY
Balance Sheet
July 31, 19___

ASSETS		LIABILITIES & OWNER'S EQUITY	
Cash	$ 18,000	Liabilities:	
Accounts receivable	26,000	Notes payable	
Land	37,200	(due in 60 days)	$ 12,400
Building	38,000	Accounts payable	9,600
Office equipment	1,200	Total liabilities	$ 22,000
		Owner's equity:	
		Ed Adams, capital	98,400
Total	$120,400	Total	$120,400

BAKER COMPANY
Balance Sheet
July 31, 19___

ASSETS		LIABILITIES & OWNER'S EQUITY	
Cash	$ 4,800	Liabilities:	
Accounts receivable	9,600	Notes payable	
Land	96,000	(due in 60 days)	$ 22,400
Building	60,000	Accounts payable	43,200
Office equipment	12,000	Total liabilities	$ 65,600
		Owner's equity:	
		Jill Baker, Capital	116,800
Total	$182,400	Total	$182,400

Instructions   **a** Assume that you are a banker and that each company has applied to you for a 90-day loan of $12,000. Which is the more favourable prospect? Explain fully.

b Assume that you are an investor considering the purchase of one or both of the companies. Both Ed Adams and Jill Baker have indicated to you that they would consider selling their respective businesses. In either transaction you would assume the existing liabilities. For which business would you pay the higher price? Explain fully. (It is recognized that for either decision, additional information would be useful, but you are to reach your decisions on the basis of the information available.)

c Assume that Jill Baker has much greater personal assets than Ed Adams and that, while both Baker and Adams have other business operations, the total profits from all the other unrelated business operations are far greater for Baker than Adams. Would such assumptions change your answers to part (**a**) and (**b**)? Explain fully.

Case 1-2
Preparing a balance sheet for a corporation; discussion of accounting principles

Linda Shields and Mark Ryan own all the capital stock of Property Management Corporation. Both shareholders also work full time in the business. The company performs management services for apartment house owners, including finding tenants, collecting rents, and doing maintenance and repair work.

When the business was organized early this year, Shields and Ryan invested a total of $50,000 to acquire the capital stock. At December 31, a partial list of the corporation's balance sheet items included cash of $15,700, office equipment of $6,100, accounts payable of $16,100, and income taxes payable of $2,900. Additional information on financial position and operations appears in the following six numbered paragraphs.

(1) Earlier this year the corporation purchased an office building from Shields at a price of $42,000 for the land and $67,000 for the building. Shields had acquired the property several years ago at a cost of $25,000 for the land and $50,000 for the building. At December 31, Shields and Ryan estimated that the land was worth $47,000 and the building was worth $70,000. The corporation owes Shields a $49,000 note payable in connection with the purchase of the property.

(2) While working, Shields drives her own automobile, which cost $12,600. Ryan uses a car owned by the corporation, which cost $10,200.

(3) One of the apartment houses managed by the company is owned by Ryan. Ryan's cost was $100,000 for the land and $190,000 for the building.

(4) Company records show a $1,900 account receivable from Ryan and $23,400 accounts receivable from other clients.

(5) Shields has a $20,000 bank account in the same bank used by the corporation. She explains that if the corporation should run out of cash, it may use that $20,000 and repay her later.

(6) Company records have not been properly maintained, and the amount of retained earnings is not known. (You can compute this amount as a final step in preparing the balance sheet).

Instructions   **a** Prepare a balance sheet for the business entity Property Management Corporation at December 31, 19___.

b For each of the preceding notes numbered (**1**) through (**5**), explain your reasoning in deciding whether or not to include the items on the balance sheet and in determining the proper dollar valuation.

RECORDING CHANGES IN FINANCIAL POSITION

CHAPTER PREVIEW

This chapter has two major objectives. The first is to introduce the principles of double-entry accounting. The second is to illustrate the accounting cycle — the procedures used by a business to record, classify, and summarize the effects of business transactions in its accounting records. The activities of Roberts Real Estate Company, which were described in Chapter 1, are now recorded in the company's general journal and posted to the general ledger accounts. The preparation of a trial balance also is illustrated, and the uses and limitations of the trial balance are discussed. The chapter concludes by comparing the accounting procedures applied in manual accounting systems with those in computer-based systems.

After studying this chapter you should be able to meet these Learning Objectives:

1 Describe a ledger account and a ledger.

2 State the rules of debit and credit for balance sheet accounts.

3 Explain the double-entry system of accounting.

4 Explain the purpose of a journal and its relationship to the ledger.

5 Prepare journal entries to record common business transactions.

6 Post information from the journal to ledger accounts.

7 Prepare a trial balance and explain its uses and limitations.

8 Describe the basic steps of the accounting cycle in both manual and computer-based accounting systems.

The role of accounting records

Many business concerns have several hundred or even several thousand business transactions each day. It would not be practical to prepare a separate balance sheet after each transaction, and it is quite unnecessary to do so. Instead, the many individual transactions are recorded in the accounting records, and, at the end of the month or other accounting period, a balance sheet is prepared for these records. In this chapter, we shall see how business transactions are analyzed, entered in the accounting records, and classified for use in preparing a balance sheet. In later chapters, we shall also see that the accounting records contain the data necessary to prepare an income statement, income tax returns, and other financial reports.

THE LEDGER

1 Describe a ledger account and a ledger.

An accounting system includes a separate record for each item that appears in the balance sheet. For example, a separate record is kept for the asset cash, showing all the increases and decreases in cash, which result from the many transactions in which cash is received or paid. A similar record is kept for every other asset, for every liability, and for owner's equity. The form of record used to record increases and decreases in a single balance sheet item is called an ***account,*** or sometimes a ***ledger account.*** All these separate accounts are usually kept in a loose-leaf binder, and the entire group of accounts is called a ***ledger.***

Many businesses use computers for maintaining accounting records, and store data on magnetic discs rather than in ledgers. However, an understanding of accounting concepts is most easily acquired by study of a manual accounting system. The knowledge gained by working with manual accounting records is readily transferable to any type of automated accounting system. For these reasons, we shall use standard written accounting records such as ledger accounts in our study of basic accounting concepts. These written records continue to be used by a great many businesses, but for our purposes they should be viewed as conceptual devices rather than as physical components of an accounting system.

The use of ledger accounts

A ledger account is a means of accumulating in one place all the information about changes in a specific asset, a liability, or owner's equity. For example, a ledger account for the asset cash provides a record of the amount of cash receipts, cash payments, and the current cash balance. By maintaining a Cash account, management can keep track of the amount of cash available for meeting payrolls and for making current purchases of assets or services. This record of cash is also useful in planning future operations and in advance planning of applications for bank loans.

In its simplest form, an account has only three elements: (1) a title, consisting of the name of the particular asset, liability, or owner's equity; (2) a left side, which is called the ***debit*** side; and (3) a right side, which is called the ***credit*** side. This form of account, illustrated below, is called a **T account** because of its resemblance to the letter T. More complete forms of accounts will be illustrated later.

T ACCOUNT: A LEDGER
ACCOUNT IN SIMPLIFIED
FORM

TITLE OF ACCOUNT

Left or debit side	Right or credit side

Debit and credit entries

An amount recorded on the left or debit side of an account is called a **debit** or a **debit entry;** an amount entered on the right or credit side is called a **credit,** or a **credit entry.** Accountants also use the words debit and credit as verbs. The act of recording a debit in an account is called **debiting** the account; the recording of a credit is called **crediting** the account.

Students beginning a course in accounting often have erroneous notions about the meanings of the terms debit and credit. For example, to some people unacquainted with accounting, the word credit may carry a more favourable connotation than does the word debit. Such connotations have no validity in the field of accounting. Accountants use **debit** to mean an entry on the left-hand side of an account and **credit** to mean an entry on the right-hand side. Thus, debit and credit simply mean left and right, without any hidden or subtle implications.

To illustrate the recording of debits and credits in an account, let us go back to the cash transactions of Roberts Real Estate Company as illustrated in Chapter 1. When these cash transactions are recorded in an account, the receipts are listed in vertical order on the debit side of the account and the payments are listed on the credit side. The dates of the transactions may also be listed, as is indicated in the following illustration:

CASH TRANSACTIONS
ENTERED IN LEDGER
ACCOUNT

CASH

Sept. 1		180,000	Sept. 3	141,000
Sept. 20	22,500	1,500	Sept. 5	15,000
		181,500	Sept. 30	3,000
				159,000

Note that the total of the cash receipts, $181,500, is in small-size figures so that it will not be mistaken for a debit entry. The total of the cash payments (credits), amounting to $159,000, is also in small-size figures to distinguish it from the credit entries. These **footings,** or memorandum totals, are merely a convenient step in determining the amount of cash on hand at the end of the month. The difference in dollars between the total debits and the total credits in an account is called the **balance.** If the debits exceed the credits the account has a **debit balance;** if the credits exceed the debits the account has a **credit balance.** In the illustrated Cash account, the debit total of $181,500 is larger than the credit total of $159,000; therefore, the account has a debit balance. By subtracting the credits from the debits ($181,500 −

$159,000), we determine that the balance of the Cash account is $22,500. This debit balance is noted on the debit (left) side of the account. The balance of the Cash account represents the amount of cash owned by the business on September 30; in a balance sheet prepared at this date, cash in the amount of $22,500 would be listed as an asset.

2 State the rules of debit and credit for balance sheet accounts.

Debit balances in asset accounts   In the preceding illustration of a cash account, increases were recorded on the left or debit side of the account and decreases were recorded on the right or credit side. The increases were greater than the decreases and the result was a debit balance in the account.

All asset accounts normally have debit balances; in fact, the ownership of cash, land, or any other asset indicates that the increases (debits) to that asset have been greater than the decreases (credits). It is hard to imagine an account for an asset such as land having a credit balance, as this would indicate that the business had disposed of more land than it had acquired and had reached the impossible position of having a negative amount of land.

The fact that assets are located on the left side of the balance sheet is a convenient means of remembering the rule that an increase in an asset is recorded on the *left* (debit) side of the account, and also that an asset account normally has a debit (*left-hand*) balance.

ASSET ACCOUNTS
NORMALLY HAVE
DEBIT BALANCES

ANY ASSET ACCOUNT

(Debit) Increase	(Credit) Decrease

Credit balances in liability and owner's equity accounts   Increases in liability and owner's equity accounts are recorded by credit entries and decreases in these accounts are recorded by debits. The relationship between entries in these accounts and their position on the balance sheet may be summed up as follows: (1) liabilities and owner's equity belong on the *right* side of the balance sheet; (2) an increase in a liability or an owner's equity account is recorded on the *right* (credit) side of the account; and (3) liability and owner's equity accounts normally have credit (*right-hand*) balances.

LIABILITY AND OWNER'S
EQUITY ACCOUNTS
NORMALLY HAVE CREDIT
BALANCES

**ANY LIABILITY ACCOUNT
OR OWNER'S EQUITY ACCOUNT**

(Debit) Decrease	(Credit) Increase

The diagram on page 48 emphasizes again the relationship between the position of an account in the balance sheet and the method of recording an increase or decrease in the account. The accounts used are those previously shown in the balance sheet prepared for Robert Real Estate Company at the bottom of page 24.

DIAGRAM OF BALANCE
SHEET ACCOUNTS

BALANCE SHEET ACCOUNTS

(Left side of balance sheet) Assets	=	(Right side of balance sheet) Liabilities + Owner's Equity

CASH		ACCOUNTS PAYABLE	
(Debit) Increase	(Credit) Decrease	(Debit) Decrease	(Credit) Increase

ACCOUNTS RECEIVABLE		JAMES ROBERTS, CAPITAL	
(Debit) Increase	(Credit) Decrease	(Debit) Decrease	(Credit) Increase

LAND	
(Debit) Increase	(Credit) Decrease

BUILDING	
(Debit) Increase	(Credit) Decrease

OFFICE EQUIPMENT	
(Debit) Increase	(Credit) Decrease

Concise statement of the rules of debit and credit   The rules of debit and credit, which have been explained and illustrated in the preceding sections, may be concisely summarized as follows:

RULES OF DEBIT AND
CREDIT

ASSET ACCOUNTS	LIABILITY & OWNER'S EQUITY ACCOUNTS
Increases are recorded by debits Decreases are recorded by credits	Increases are recorded by credits Decreases are recorded by debits

3   Explain the double-entry system of accounting.

Double entry accounting: the equality of debits and credits   The rules of debit and credit are designed so that *equal amounts of debit and credit entries are needed to record every business transaction.* Assume, for example, that a company purchases land for $50,000. If the land were purchased for cash, the Land account would be debited for $50,000, and the Cash account would be credited for the same amount. If the land were purchased by issuing a note payable, the Land account would be debited and the liability account, Notes Payable, would be credited. If the land were purchased by paying $10,000 cash and issuing a note payable for the remaining $40,000, the transaction would be recorded as follows: debit Land, $50,000; credit Cash, $10,000; credit Notes Payable, $40,000. Notice that in each case, *equal dollar amounts* of debit and credit entries are needed to record the transaction.

The need for equal amounts of debit and credit entries to record every business transaction is called the *double-entry* system of accounting. The double-entry system is used by virtually every business organization, regardless of whether the company's accounting records are maintained manually or by computer.

Since every transaction is recorded by equal amounts of debits and credits, it follows that the total of all debit entries in the ledger is equal to the total of all credit entries. Later in this chapter, we shall see that this equality of debits and credits enables us to locate many types of errors that might be made while maintaining accounting records.

Recording transactions in ledger accounts: illustration

The procedure for recording transactions in ledger accounts will be illustrated by using the September transactions of Roberts Real Estate Company. Each transaction will first be analyzed in terms of increases and decreases in assets, liabilities, and owner's equity. Then we shall follow the rules of debit and credit in entering these increases and decreases in T accounts. Asset accounts will be shown on the left side of the page; liability and owner's equity accounts on the right side. For convenience in following the transactions into the ledger accounts, the letter used to identify a given transaction will also appear opposite the debit and credit entries for that transaction. This use of identifying letters is for illustrative purposes only and is not used in actual accounting practice.

Transaction (a)   Roberts invested $180,000 cash in the business on September 1.

RECORDING AN
INVESTMENT IN THE
BUSINESS

ANALYSIS	RULE	ENTRY
The asset Cash was increased	Increases in assets are recorded by debits	Debit: Cash, $180,000
The owner's equity was increased	Increases in owner's equity are recorded by credits	Credit: James Roberts, Capital, $180,000

CASH		JAMES ROBERTS, CAPITAL	
Sept. 1 (a) 180,000			Sept. 1 (a) 180,000

Transaction (b)   On September 3, Roberts Real Estate Company purchased land for cash in the amount of $141,000.

ANALYSIS	RULE	ENTRY
The asset Land was increased	Increases in assets are recorded by debits	Debit: Land, $141,000
The asset Cash was decreased	Decreases in assets are recorded by credits	Credit: Cash, $141,000

CASH

Sept. 1	180,000	Sept. 3	(b) 141,000

LAND

Sept. 3 (b) 141,000	

Transaction (c)   On September 5, Roberts Real Estate Company purchased a building from Kent Company at a total price of $36,000. The terms of the purchase required a cash payment of $15,000 with the remainder of $21,000 payable within 90 days.

ANALYSIS	RULE	ENTRY
A new asset, Building, was acquired	Increases in assets are recorded by debits	Debit: Building, $36,000
The asset Cash was decreased	Decreases in assets are recorded by credits	Credit: Cash, $15,000
A new liability, Accounts Payable, was incurred	Increases in liabilities are recorded by credits	Credit: Accounts Payable, $21,000

CASH

Sept. 1	180,000	Sept. 3	141,000
		Sept. 5 (c)	15,000

ACCOUNTS PAYABLE

Sept. 5	(c) 21,000

BUILDING

Sept. 5 (c) 36,000	

Transaction (d)   On September 10, Roberts Real Estate Company sold a portion of its land on credit to Carter's Drugstore for a price of $11,000. The land was sold at its cost, so there was no gain or loss on the transaction.

SALE OF LAND ON
CREDIT (NO GAIN
OR LOSS)

ANALYSIS	RULE	ENTRY
A new asset, Accounts Receivable, was acquired	Increases in assets are recorded by debits	Debit: Accounts Receivable, $11,000
The asset Land was decreased	Decreases in assets are recorded by credits	Credit: Land, $11,000

ACCOUNTS RECEIVABLE

Sept. 10 (d) 11,000	

LAND

Sept. 3 141,000	Sept. 10 (d) 11,000

Transaction (e)   On September 14, Roberts Real Estate Company purchased office equipment on credit from General Equipment, Inc., in the amount of $5,400.

PURCHASE OF AN
ASSET ON CREDIT

ANALYSIS	RULE	ENTRY
A new asset, Office Equipment, was acquired	Increases in assets are recorded by debits	Debit: Office Equipment, $5,400
A new liability, Accounts Payable, was incurred	Increases in liabilities are recorded by credits	Credit: Accounts Payable, $5,400

OFFICE EQUIPMENT		ACCOUNTS PAYABLE	
Sept. 14 (e) 5,400		Sept. 5 21,000	
		Sept. 14 (e) 5,400	

Transaction (f)   On September 20, cash of $1,500 was received as partial collection of the account receivable from Carter's Drugstore.

COLLECTION OF AN
ACCOUNT RECEIVABLE

ANALYSIS	RULE	ENTRY
The asset Cash was increased	Increases in assets are recorded by debits	Debit: Cash, $1,500
The assets Accounts Receivable was decreased	Decreases in assets are recorded by credits	Credit: Accounts Receivable, $1,500

CASH

Sept. 1	180,000	Sept. 3	141,000
Sept. 20 (f)	1,500	Sept. 5	15,000

ACCOUNTS RECEIVABLE

Sept. 10	11,000	Sept. 20	(f) 1,500

Transaction (g)   A cash payment of $3,000 was made on September 30 in partial settlement of the amount owing to General Equipment, Inc.

PAYMENT OF LIABILITY

ANALYSIS	RULE	ENTRY
The liability Accounts Payable was decreased	Decreases in liabilities are recorded by debits	Debit: Accounts Payable, $3,000
The asset Cash was decreased	Decreases in assets are recorded by credits	Credit: Cash, $3,000

CASH

Sept. 1	180,000	Sept. 3	141,000
Sept. 20	1,500	Sept. 5	15,000
		Sept. 30 (g)	3,000

ACCOUNTS PAYABLE

Sept. 30	(g) 3,000	Sept. 5	21,000
		Sept. 14	5,400

Running balance form of ledger account

The T form of account used thus far is very convenient for illustrative purposes. Details are avoided and we can concentrate on basic ideas. T accounts are also often used in advanced accounting courses and by professional accountants for preliminary analysis of a transaction. In other words the simplicity of the T account provides a

LEDGER ACCOUNT WITH
A BALANCE COLUMN

		CASH				Account No. 1
DATE	EXPLANATION	REF	DEBIT	CREDIT	BALANCE	
19—						
Sept. 1			180,000 00		180,000 00	
3				141,000 00	39,000 00	
5				15,000 00	24,000 00	
20			1,500 00		25,500 00	
30				3,000 00	22,500 00	

concise conceptual picture of the elements of a business transaction. In formal accounting records, however, more information is needed, and the T account is replaced in many manual accounting systems by a ledger account with special rulings, such as the illustration of the Cash account for Roberts Real Estate Company shown at the bottom of page 52.

The *Date* column shows the date of the transaction — which is not necessarily the same as the date the entry is made in the account. The *Explanation* column is needed only for unusual items, and in many companies it is seldom used. The *Ref* (Reference) column is used to list the page number of the journal in which the transaction is recorded, thus making it possible to trace ledger entries back to their source (a journal). The use of a *journal* is explained later in this chapter. In the *Balance* column of the account, the new balance is entered each time the account is debited or credited. Thus the current balance of the account can always be observed at a glance.

Although we will make extensive use of this three-column running balance form of account in later chapters, there will also be many situations in which we shall continue to use T accounts to achieve simplicity in illustrating accounting principles and procedures.

The "normal" balance of an account

The running balance form of ledger account does not indicate specifically whether the balance of the account is a debit or credit balance. However, this causes no difficulty because we know that asset accounts normally have debit balances and that accounts for liabilities and owner's equity normally have credit balances.

The balance of any account normally results from recording more increases than decreases. In asset accounts, increases are recorded as debits, so asset accounts normally have debit balances. In liability and owner's equity accounts, increases are recorded as credits, so these accounts normally have credit balances.

Occasionally an asset account may temporarily acquire a credit balance, either as a result of an accounting error or because of an unusual transaction. For example, an account receivable may acquire a credit balance because of overpayment by a customer. However, a credit balance in the Building account could be created only by an accounting error.

Sequence and numbering of ledger accounts

Accounts are usually arranged in the ledger in *financial statement order*, that is, assets first, followed by liabilities, owner's equity, revenue, and expenses. The number of accounts needed by a business will depend upon its size, the nature of its operations, and the extent to which management and regulatory agencies want detailed classification of information. An identification number is assigned to each account. A *chart of accounts* is a listing of the account titles and account numbers being used by a given business.

In the following list of accounts, certain numbers have not been assigned; these numbers are held in reserve so that additional accounts can be inserted in the ledger in proper sequence whenever such accounts become necessary. In this illustration, the numbers from 1 to 29 are used exclusively for asset accounts; numbers from 30 to 49 are reserved for liabilities; numbers in the 50s signify owner's equity accounts; numbers in the 60 represent revenue accounts and numbers from 70 to 99 designate expense accounts. The balance sheet accounts with which we are concerned in this chapter are numbered as shown in the following brief chart of accounts:

SYSTEM FOR NUMBERING
LEDGER ACCOUNTS

ACCOUNT TITLE	ACCOUNT NO.
Assets:	
Cash	1
Accounts Receivable	4
Land	20
Building	22
Office Equipment	25
Liabilities:	
Accounts Payable	32
Owner's Equity:	
James Roberts, Capital	50

In large businesses with hundreds or thousands of accounts, a more elaborate numbering system is used. Some companies use an eight- or ten-digit number for each ledger account; each of the digits carries special significance as to the classification of the account.

Sequence of asset accounts   At this point we need to give further attention to the sequence of accounts within the asset group. As shown in all the balance sheets illustrated thus far, cash is always listed first. It is followed by notes receivable, accounts receivable, and supplies. Next come the relatively permanent assets used in the business (often called *plant assets*). Of this group, land is listed first and followed by buildings. After these two items, any order is acceptable for other assets used in the business, such as automobiles, furniture and fixtures, computers, office equipment, store equipment, etc.

THE JOURNAL

4   Explain the purpose of a journal and its relationship to the ledger.

In our preceding discussion, we recorded business transactions directly in the company's ledger accounts. We did this in order to stress the effects of business transactions upon the individual asset, liability, and owner's equity accounts appearing in the company's balance sheet. In an actual accounting system, however, the information about each business transaction is initially recorded in an accounting record called the *journal*. After the transaction has been recorded in the journal, the debit and credit changes in the individual accounts are entered in the ledger. Since the journal is the accounting record in which transactions are *first recorded*, it is sometimes called the *book of original entry*.

The journal is a chronological (day-by-day) record of each business transaction. The information about each transaction that should be recorded in the journal is the date of the transaction, the debit and credit changes in specific ledger accounts, and a brief explanation of the transaction. At convenient intervals, the debit and credit amounts recorded in the journal are transferred to the accounts in the ledger. The updated ledger accounts, in turn, serve as the basis for preparing the balance sheet and other financial statements.

Why use a journal?

Since it is technically possible to record transactions directly in the ledger, why bother to maintain a journal? The answer is that the unit of organization for the journal is the *transaction,* whereas the unit of organization for the ledger is the *account.* By having both a journal and a ledger, we achieve several advantages that would not be possible if transactions were recorded directly in ledger accounts:

1 **The journal shows all information about a transaction in one place and also provides an explanation of the transaction**   In a journal entry, the debits and credits for a given transaction are recorded together, but when the transaction is recorded in the ledger, the debits and credits are entered in different accounts. Since a ledger may contain hundreds of accounts, it would be very difficult to locate all the facts about a particular transaction by looking in the ledger. The journal is the record that shows the complete story of a transaction in one entry.

2 **The journal provides a chronological record of all the events in the life of a business**   If we want to look up the facts about a transaction of some months or years back, all we need is the date of the transaction in order to locate it in the journal.

3 **The use of a journal helps to prevent errors**   If transactions were recorded directly in the ledger, it would be very easy to make errors such as omitting the debit or the credit, or entering the debit twice or the credit twice. Such errors are not likely to be made in the journal, since the off-setting debits and credits appear together for each transaction.

The general journal: illustration of entries

5 Prepare journal entries to record common business transactions.

Many businesses maintain several types of journals. The nature of operations and the volume of transactions in the particular business determine the number and type of journals needed. The simplest type of journal is called a *general journal* and is shown on page 56. It has only two money columns, one for debits and the other for credits; it may be used for all types of transactions.

The process of recording a transaction in a journal is called *journalizing* the transaction. To illustrate the use of the general journal, we shall now journalize the September transactions of Roberts Real Estate Company, which have been discussed previously.

Efficient use of a general journal requires two things: (1) ability to analyze the effect of a transaction upon assets, liabilities, and owner's equity; and (2) familiarity with the standard form and arrangement of journal entries. Our primary interest is in the analytical phase of journalizing; the procedural steps can be learned quickly by observing the following points in the illustration of journal entries:

1 The year, month, and day of the first entry on the page are written in the date column. The year and month need not be repeated for subsequent entries until a new page or a new month is begun.

2 The name of the account to be debited is written on the first line of the entry and is customarily placed at the extreme left next to the date column. The amount of the debit is entered on the same line in the *left-hand* money column.

SEPTEMBER JOURNAL ENTRIES FOR ROBERTS REAL ESTATE COMPANY

			GENERAL JOURNAL			Page	
DATE		ACCOUNT TITLES AND EXPLANATION	LP	DEBIT		CREDIT	
19—							
Sept.	1	Cash	1	1 80000			
		James Roberts, Capital	50			1 80000	
		Invested cash in the business.					
	3	Land	20	1 41000			
		Cash	1			1 41000	
		Purchased land for office site.					
	5	Building	22	36000			
		Cash	1			15000	
		Accounts Payable	32			21000	
		Purchased building to be moved to our lot. Paid part cash; balance payable within 90 days to Kent Company					
	10	Accounts Receivable	4	11000			
		Land	20			11000	
		Sold the unused part of our lot at cost to Carter's Drugstore. Due within 3 months					
	14	Office Equipment	25	5400			
		Accounts Payable	32			5400	
		Purchased equipment on credit from General Equipment, Inc.					
	20	Cash	1	1500			
		Accounts Receivable	4			1500	
		Collected part of receivable from Carter's Drugstore.					
	30	Accounts Payable	32	3000			
		Cash	1			3000	
		Made partial payment of the liability to General Equipment, Inc.					

3 The name of the account to be credited is entered on the line below the debit entry and is *indented,* that is, placed about one centimetre (or one-half of an inch) to the right of the date column. The amount credited is entered on the same line in the *right-hand* money column.

4 A brief explanation of the transaction is usually begun on the line immediately below the last account credited. The explanation is not indented.

5 A blank line should be left after each entry. This spacing causes each journal entry to stand out clearly as a separate unit and makes the journal easier to read.

6 An entry that includes more than one debit or more than one credit (such as the entry on September 5) is called a *compound journal entry.* Regardless of how many debits or credits are contained in a compound journal entry, *all the debits* are entered *before any credits* are listed.

7 The LP (ledger page) column just to the left of the debit money column is left blank at the time of making the journal entry. When the debits and credits are later transferred to ledger accounts, the numbers of the ledger accounts will be listed in this column to provide a convenient cross reference with the ledger.

In journalizing transactions, remember that the *exact title* of the ledger accounts to be debited and credited should be used. For example, in recording the purchase of office equipment for cash, *do not* make a journal entry debiting ''Office Equipment Purchased'' and crediting ''Cash Paid Out.'' There are no ledger accounts with such titles. The proper journal entry would consist of a debit to *Office Equipment* and a credit to *Cash*.

A familiarity with the general journal form of describing transactions is just as essential to the study of accounting as a familiarity with plus and minus signs is to the study of mathematics. The journal entry is a *tool* for *analyzing* and *describing* the impact of various transactions upon a business entity. The ability to describe a transaction in journal entry form requires an understanding of the nature of the transaction and its effects upon the financial position of the business.

Posting

6   Post information from the journal to ledger accounts.

The process of transferring the debits and credits from the general journal to the proper ledger accounts is called *posting.* Each amount listed in the debit column of the journal is posted by entering it on the debit side of an account in the ledger, and each amount listed in the credit column of the journal is posted to the credit side of a ledger account.

The mechanics of posting may vary somewhat with the preferences of the individual. The following sequence is commonly used:

1 Locate in the ledger the first account named in the journal entry.

2 Enter in the debit column of the ledger account the amount of the debit as shown in the journal.

3 Enter the date of the transaction in the ledger account.

4 Enter in the reference column of the ledger account the number of the journal page from which the entry is being posted.

5 The recording of the debit in the ledger account is now complete; as evidence of this fact, return to the journal and enter in the LP column the number of the ledger account to which the debit was posted.

6 Repeat the posting process described in the preceding five steps for the credit side of the journal entry.

Illustration of posting   To illustrate the posting process, the journal entry for the first transaction of Roberts Real Estate Company is repeated at this point along with the two ledger accounts affected by this entry.

Journal

	GENERAL JOURNAL				Page *1*
DATE	ACCOUNT TITLES AND EXPLANATION	LP	DEBIT		CREDIT
19—					
Sept. 1	*Cash*	*1*	*180000 00*		
	James Roberts, Capital	*50*			*180000 00*
	Invested cash in the business				

Ledger

	CASH				Account No. *1*
DATE	EXPLANATION	REF	DEBIT	CREDIT	BALANCE
19—					
Sept. 1		*1*	*180000 00*		*180000 00*

	JAMES ROBERTS, CAPITAL				Account No. *50*
DATE	EXPLANATION	REF	DEBIT	CREDIT	BALANCE
19—					
Sept. 1		*1*		*180000 00*	*180000 00*

Note that the Ref (Reference) column of each of the two ledger accounts illustrated contains the number 1, indicating that the posting was made from page 1 of the journal. Entering the journal page number in the ledger account and listing the ledger account number in the LP column in the journal provide a *cross reference* between these two records. It is often necessary to refer to the journal entry in order to obtain more information about an amount listed in a ledger account. A cross reference between the ledger and journal is therefore essential to efficient use of the records. Another advantage gained from entering in the journal the number of the ledger account to which a posting has been made is to provide evidence throughout the posting work as to which items have been posted. Otherwise, any interruption in the posting might leave some doubt as to which entries had been posted.

Journalizing and posting by hand is a useful method for the study of accounting, both for problem assignments and for examinations. The manual approach is also followed in many small businesses. One shortcoming is the opportunity for error that exists whenever information is being copied from one record to another. In businesses having a large volume of transactions, the posting of ledger accounts is performed automatically by computer, which speeds up the work and reduces errors.

Ledger accounts after posting

After all the September transactions have been posted, the ledger of Roberts Real Estate Company appears as shown below and on page 60. The accounts are arranged in the ledger in the same order as in the balance sheet, that is, assets first, followed by liabilities and owner's equity.

To conserve space in this illustration, several ledger accounts appear on a single page. In actual practice, however, each account occupies a separate page in the ledger.

LEDGER SHOWING
SEPTEMBER
TRANSACTIONS

CASH					Account No. 1
DATE	EXPLANATION	REF	DEBIT	CREDIT	BALANCE
19—					
Sept. 1		1	180 000 00		180 000 00
3		1		141 000 00	39 000 00
5		1		15 000 00	24 000 00
20		1	1 500 00		25 500 00
30		1		3 000 00	22 500 00

ACCOUNTS RECEIVABLE					Account No. 4
DATE	EXPLANATION	REF	DEBIT	CREDIT	BALANCE
19—					
Sept. 10		1	11 000 00		11 000 00
20		1		1 500 00	9 500 00

LAND — Account No. 20

DATE	EXPLANATION	REF	DEBIT	CREDIT	BALANCE
19—					
Sept. 3		1	141 000 00		141 000 00
10		1		11 000 00	130 000 00

BUILDING — Account No. 22

DATE	EXPLANATION	REF	DEBIT	CREDIT	BALANCE
19—					
Sept. 5		1	36 000 00		36 000 00

OFFICE EQUIPMENT — Account No. 25

DATE	EXPLANATION	REF	DEBIT	CREDIT	BALANCE
19—					
Sept. 14		1	5 400 00		5 400 00

ACCOUNTS PAYABLE — Account No. 32

DATE	EXPLANATION	REF	DEBIT	CREDIT	BALANCE
19—					
Sept. 5		1		21 000 00	21 000 00
14		1		5 400 00	26 400 00
30		1	3 000 00		23 400 00

JAMES ROBERTS, CAPITAL — Account No. 50

DATE	EXPLANATION	REF	DEBIT	CREDIT	BALANCE
19—					
Sept. 1		1		180 000 00	180 000 00

THE TRIAL BALANCE

7   Prepare a trial balance and . . .

Since equal dollar amounts of debits and credits are entered in the accounts for every transaction recorded, the sum of all the debits in the ledger must be equal to the sum of all the credits. If the computation of account balances has been accurate, it follows that the total of the accounts with debit balances must be equal to the total of the accounts with credit balances.

Before using the account balances to prepare a balance sheet, it is desirable to *prove* that the total of accounts with debit balances is in fact equal to the total of accounts with credit balances. This proof of the equality of debit and credit balances is called a *trial balance.* A trial balance is a two-column schedule listing the names and balances of all the accounts *in the order in which they appear in the ledger;* the debit balances are listed in the left-hand column and the credit balances in the right-hand column. The totals of the two columns should agree. A trial balance taken from the ledger of Roberts Real Estate Company follows:

TRIAL BALANCE AT
MONTH-END PROVES
LEDGER IS IN BALANCE

ROBERTS REAL ESTATE COMPANY
Trial Balance
September 30, 19___

Cash	$ 22,500	
Accounts receivable	9,500	
Land	130,000	
Building	36,000	
Office equipment	5,400	
Accounts payable		$ 23,400
James Roberts, capital		180,000
	$203,400	$203,400

Uses and limitations of the trial balance

. . . explain its uses and limitations.

The trial balance provides proof that the ledger is in balance. The agreement of the debit and credit totals of the trial balance gives assurance that:

1 Equal debits and credits have been recorded for all transactions.
2 The debit or credit balance of each account has been correctly computed.
3 The addition of the account balances in the trial balance has been correctly performed.

Suppose that the debit and credit totals of the trial balance do not agree. This situation indicates that one or more errors have been made. Typical of such errors are (1) the posting of a debit as a credit, or vice versa; (2) arithmetic mistakes in balancing accounts; (3) clerical errors in copying account balances into the trial balance; (4) listing a debit balance in the credit column of the trial balance, or vice versa; and (5) errors in addition of the trial balance.

The preparation of a trial balance does not prove that transactions have been correctly analyzed and recorded in the proper accounts. If, for example, a receipt of cash were erroneously recorded by debiting the Land account instead of the Cash account, the trial balance would still balance. Also, if a transaction were completely omitted from the ledger, the error would not be disclosed by the trial balance. In brief, *the trial balance proves only one aspect of the ledger, and that is the equality of debits and credits.*

Despite these limitations, the trial balance is a useful device. It not only provides assurance that the ledger is in balance, but it also serves as a convenient stepping stone for the preparation of financial statements. As explained in Chapter 1, the balance sheet is a formal statement showing the financial position of the business, intended for distribution to managers, owners, bankers, and various outsiders. The trial balance, on the other hand, is merely a working paper, useful to the accountant but not intended for distribution to others. The balance sheet and other financial statements can be prepared more conveniently from the trial balance than directly from the ledger, especially if there are a great many ledger accounts.

Locating errors

In the illustration given, the trial balance was in balance. Every accounting student soon discovers in working problems, however, that errors are easily made that prevent trial balances from balancing. The lack of balance may be the result of a single error or a combination of several errors. An error may have been made in adding the trial balance columns or in copying the balances from the ledger accounts. If the preparation of the trial balance has been accurate, then the error may lie in the accounting records, either in the journal or in the ledger accounts. What is the most efficient approach to locating the error or errors? There is no single technique that will give the best results every time, but the following procedures, done in sequence, will often save considerable time and effort in locating errors.

1　Prove the addition of the trial balance columns by adding these columns in the opposite direction from that previously followed.
2　If the error does not lie in addition, next determine the exact amount by which the schedule is out of balance. The amount of the discrepancy is often a clue to the source of the error. If the discrepancy is *divisible by 9,* this suggests either a *transposition error* or a *slide.* For example, assume that the Cash account has a balance of $2,175, but in copying the balance into the trial balance the figures are *transposed* and written as $2,157. The resulting error is $18, and like all transposition errors is divisible by 9. Another common error is the slide, or incorrect placement of the decimal point, as when $2,175.00 is copied as $21.75. The resulting discrepancy in the trial balance will also be an amount divisible by 9.

To illustrate another method of using the amount of a discrepancy as a clue to locating the error, assume that the Office Equipment account has a *debit* balance of $420, but that is erroneously listed in the *credit* column of the trial balance. This will cause a discrepancy of two times $420, or $840, in the trial balance totals. Since such errors as recording a debit in a credit column are not uncommon, it is advisable, after determining the discrepancy in the trial balance totals, to scan the columns for an amount equal to exactly *one-half* of the discrepancy. It is also advisable to look over the transactions for an item of the exact amount of the discrepancy. An error may have been made by recording the debit side of the transaction and forgetting to enter the credit side.

3 Compare the amounts in the trial balance with the balances in the ledger. Make sure that each ledger account balance has been included in the correct column of the trial balance.

4 Recompute the balance of each ledger account.

5 Trace all postings from the journal to the ledger accounts. As this is done, place a check mark in the journal and in the ledger after each figure verified. When the operation is completed, look through the journal and the ledger for unchecked amounts. In tracing postings, be alert not only for errors in amount but also for debits entered as credits, or vice versa.

Dollar signs

Dollar signs are not used in journals or ledgers. Some accountants use dollar signs in trial balances; some do not. In this book, dollar signs are used in trial balances. Dollar signs should always be used in the balance sheet, the income statement, and other formal financial reports. In the balance sheet, for example, a dollar sign is placed by the first amount in each column and also by the final amount or total. Many accountants also place a dollar sign by each subtotal or other amount listed below an underlining. In the published financial statements of large corportations, the use of dollar signs is often limited to the first and last figures in a column.

When dollar amounts are being entered in the columnar paper used in journals and ledgers, commas and decimal points are not needed. On unruled paper, commas and decimal points should be used. Most of the problems and illustrations in this book are in even dollar amounts. In such cases the cents column can be left blank, or, if desired, zeros or dashes may be used.

8 Describe the basic steps of the accounting cycle in both manual and computer-based accounting systems.

THE ACCOUNTING CYCLE: AN INTRODUCTION

The sequence of accounting procedures used to record, classify, and summarize accounting information is often termed the ***accounting cycle.*** The accounting cycle begins with the initial recording of business transactions and concludes with the preparation of formal financial statements summarizing the effects of these transactions upon the assets, liabilities, and owners' equity of the business. The term "cycle" indicates that these procedures must be repeated continuously to enable the business to prepare new, up-to-date financial statements at reasonable intervals.

At this point, we have illustrated a complete accounting cycle as it relates to the preparation of a balance sheet for a service-type business with a manual accounting system. The accounting procedures discussed to this point may be summarized as follows:

1 Record transactions in the journal As each business transaction occurs, it is entered in the journal, thus creating a chronological record of events. This procedure completes the recording step in the accounting cycle.

2 Post to ledger accounts The debit and credit changes in account balances are posted from the journal to the ledger. This procedure classifies the effects of the business transactions in terms of specific asset, liability, and owner's equity accounts.

3 Prepare a trial balance   A trial balance proves the equality of the debit and credit entries in the ledger. The purpose of this procedure is to verify the accuracy of the posting process and the computation of ledger account balances.

4 Prepare financial statements   At this point, we have discussed only one financial statement — the balance sheet. This statement shows the financial position of the business at a specific date. The preparation of financial statements summarizes the effects of business transactions occurring through the date of the statements and completes the accounting cycle.

In the next section of this chapter, and throughout this textbook, we shall extend our discussion to include computer-based accounting systems. In Chapters 3 and 4, we shall expand the accounting cycle to include the measurement of business income and the preparation of an income statement.

Manual and computer-based systems: a comparison

In our preceding discussion, we have assumed the use of a manual accounting system, in which all the accounting procedures are performed manually by the company's accounting personnel. The reader may wonder about the relevance of such a discussion in an era when even many small businesses use computer-based accounting systems. However, the concepts and procedures involved in the operation of manual and computer-based accounting systems are *essentially the same.* The differences are largely a question of whether specific procedures require human attention, or whether they can be performed automatically by machine.

Computers can be programmed to perform mechanical tasks with great speed and accuracy. For example, they can be programmed to read data, to perform mathematical computations, and to rearrange data into any desired format. However, computers cannot think. Therefore, they are not able to *analyze* business transactions. Without human guidance, computers cannot determine which events should be recorded in the accounting records, or which accounts should be debited and credited to properly record an event. With these abilities and limitations in mind, we will explore the effects of computer-based systems upon the basic accounting cycle.

Recording business transactions   The recording of transactions requires two steps. First, the transaction must be *analyzed* to determine whether it should be recorded in the accounting records and, if so, which accounts should be debited and credited and for what dollar amounts. Second, the transaction must be *physically entered* (recorded) in the accounting system. As computers do not know which transactions should be recorded, or how to record them properly, these two functions must be performed by accounting personnel in both manual and computerized systems.

Differences do exist, however, in the manner in which data are physically entered into manual and computer-based systems. In manual systems, the data are entered in the form of handwritten journal entries. In a computer-based system, the data will be entered through a keyboard, an optical scanner, or other input device. Also, data entered into a computer-based system need *not* be arranged in the format of a journal entry. The data usually are entered into a *data base,* instead of a journal.

What is a data base?   A data base is a warehouse of information stored within a computer system. The purpose of the data base is to allow information that will be used for several different purposes to be entered into the computer system *only once.* Data are originally entered into the data base. Then, as data are needed, the computer refers to the data base, selects the appropriate data, and arranges them in the desired format.

   The information that must be entered into the data base is the same as that contained in a journal entry — the date, the accounts to be debited and credited, the dollar amounts, and an explanation of the transaction. However, this information need not be arranged in the format of a journal entry. For example, in a data base, accounts usually are identified by number, rather than by title. Also, abbreviations such as "D" or "C" are used to indicate whether an account should be debited or credited. Once information has been entered in the data base, the computer can arrange this information into any desired format, such as journal entries, ledger accounts, and financial statements.

Posting to ledger accounts   Posting merely transfers existing information from one accounting record to another—a function that can be easily performed by a computer. In a computer-based system, data posted to the ledger accounts come directly from the data base, rather than from the journal.

Preparation of a trial balance   Preparation of a trial balance involves three steps: (1) determining the balances of ledger accounts, (2) arranging the account balances in the format of a trial balance, and (3) adding up the trial balance columns and comparing the column totals. All these functions involve information already contained in the data base and can be performed by the computer.

Preparation of financial statements   The preparation of a balance sheet is similar to the preparation of a trial balance and can be readily performed by the computer. The preparation of an income statement involves additional procedures, which will be discussed in Chapter 3.

Summary   Computers can eliminate the need for copying and rearranging information that already has been entered into the system. They also can perform mathematical computations. In short, computers eliminate most of the "paper work" involved in the operation of an accounting system. However, they *do not* eliminate the need for accounting personnel who can analyze business transactions and explain these events in conformity with generally accepted accounting principles.

   The differences in manual and computer-based systems with respect to the accounting procedures discussed in this chapter are summarized graphically in the flowcharts shown on page 66. Functions that are performed by accounting personnel are shown in colour; tasks that can be performed automatically by the computer are shown in black.

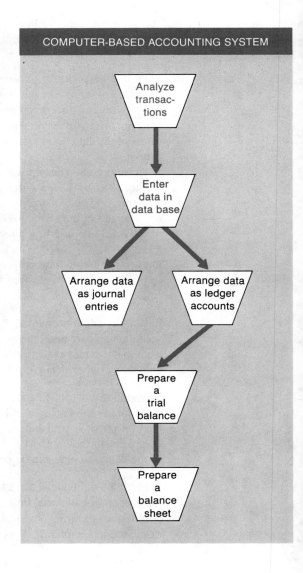

END-OF-CHAPTER REVIEW

SUMMARY OF CHAPTER LEARNING OBJECTIVES

1 Describe a ledger account and a ledger.

A ledger account is a device for recording the increases or decreases in one financial statement item, such as a particular asset, a type of liability, or owner's equity. The ledger is an accounting record that includes all the ledger accounts — that is, a separate account for each item included in the company's financial statements.

2 State the rules of debit and credit for balance sheet accounts.

Increases in assets are recorded by debits and decreases are recorded by credits. Increases in liabilities and in owner's equity are recorded by credits and decreases are recorded by debits. Notice that the debit and credit rules are related to an account's *location in the balance sheet*. If the account appears on the *left-hand side* of the balance sheet (asset accounts), increases in the account balance are recorded by *left-side entries* (debits). If the account appears on the *right-hand side* of the balance sheet (liability and owner's equity accounts), increases are recorded by *right-side entries* (credits).

3 Explain the double-entry system of accounting.

The double-entry system of accounting takes its name from the fact that every business transaction is recorded by *two sets of entries:* (1) debit entries to one or more accounts, and (2) credit entries to one or more accounts. In recording any transaction, the total dollar amount of the debit entries must equal the total dollar amount of the credit entries.

4 Explain the purpose of a journal and its relationship to the ledger.

The journal, or book of original entry, is the accounting record in which business transactions are initially recorded. The entry in the journal shows which ledger accounts have increased as a result of the transaction, and which have decreased. After the effects of the transaction have been recorded in the journal, the changes in the individual ledger accounts are then posted to the ledger.

5 Prepare journal entries to record common business transactions.

The effects of business transactions upon the assets, liabilities, or owner's equity of a business are recorded in the journal. Each journal entry includes the date of the transaction, the names of the ledger accounts affected, the dollar amounts of the changes in these accounts, and a brief explanation of the transaction.

6 Post information from the journal to ledger accounts.

The posting process transfers the information concerning changes in specific account balances from the journal into the ledger.

7 Prepare a trial balance and explain its uses and limitations.

In a trial balance, separate debit and credit columns are used to list the balances of the individual ledger accounts. The two columns are then totalled to prove the equality of the debit and credit balances. This process then provides assurance that (1) the total of the debits posted to the ledger is equal to the total of the credits, and (2) the balances of the individual ledger accounts were correctly computed. While a trial balance proves the equality of debit and credit entries in the ledger, it does *not* detect such errors as failure to record a business transaction, improper analysis of the accounts affected by the transaction, or the posting of debit or credit entries to the wrong accounts.

8 Describe the basic steps of the accounting cycle in both manual and computer-based accounting systems.

At this stage of our study, the steps in any accounting system are: (1) record transactions in a journal, (2) post the information to the ledger accounts, (3) prepare a trial balance, and (4) prepare financial statements. In a manual accounting system, all four steps are performed by accounting personnel. In a computer-based system, steps (2), (3), and (4) are performed automatically by the computer.

KEY TERMS INTRODUCED OR EMPHASIZED IN CHAPTER 2

Account (or **ledger account**) A record used to summarize all increases and decreases in a particular asset, such as Cash, or any other type of asset, liability, owners' equity, revenue, or expense.

Accounting cycle The sequence of accounting procedures applied in recording, classifying, and summarizing accounting information. The cycle begins with the occurrence of business transactions and concludes with the preparation of financial statements. This concept will be expanded in later chapters.

Chart of accounts A listing of the ledger account titles and numbers being used by a given business.

Credit An amount entered on the right-hand side of an account. A credit is used to record a decrease in an asset and an increase in a liability or owners' equity.

Credit balance The balance of an account in which the total amount of credits exceeds the total amount of debits.

Data base A storage centre of information within a computer-based accounting system. The idea behind a data base is that data intended for a variety of uses may be entered into the computer system only once, at which time the information is stored in the data base. Then, as the information is needed, the computer can retrieve it from the data base and arrange it in the desired format.

Debit An amount entered on the left-hand side of an account. A debit is used to record an increase in an asset and a decrease in a liability or in owner's equity.

Debit balance The balance of an account in which the total amount of debits exceeds the total amount of credits.

Double-entry system In recording transactions, the total dollar amount of debits must equal the total dollar amount of credits.

Financial statement order The usual sequence of accounts in a ledger; that is, assets first, followed by liabilities, owner's equity, revenue, and expenses.

Footing The total of amounts in a column.

Journal A chronological record of transactions, showing for each transaction the debits and credits to be entered in specific ledger accounts. The simplest type of journal is called a general journal.

Journalizing The process of recording a transaction in a journal. To journalize means to prepare an entry in a journal.

Ledger A loose-leaf book, file, or other record containing all the separate accounts of a business.

Posting The process of transferring information from the journal to individual accounts in the ledger.

Trial balance A two-column schedule listing the names and the debit or credit balances of all accounts in the ledger.

DEMONSTRATION PROBLEM FOR YOUR REVIEW

Stadium Parking was organized on July 2 to operate a parking lot near a new sports arena. The following transactions occurred during July prior to the company beginning its regular business operations.

July 2 Martin Taylor opened a bank account in the name of the business with a deposit of $65,000 cash.

July 3 Purchased land to be used as the parking lot for a total price of $140,000. A cash down payment of $28,000 was made and a note payable was issued for the balance of the purchase price.

July 5 Purchased a small portable building for $24,000 cash. The purchase price included installation of the building on the parking lot.

July 12 Purchased office equipment on credit from Suzuki & Co. for $3,000.

July 28 Paid $2,000 of the amount owed to Suzuki & Co.

The account titles and account numbers used by Auto Parks, Inc., to record these transactions are

Cash	1	Notes payable	30
Land	20	Accounts payable	32
Building	22	Martin Taylor, capital	50
Office equipment	25		

Instructions **a** Prepare journal entries for the month of July.

b Post to ledger accounts of the three-column running balance form.

c Prepare a trial balance at July 31.

SOLUTION TO DEMONSTRATION PROBLEM

a   General Journal   Page 1

DATE		ACCOUNT TITLES AND EXPLANATION	LP	DEBIT	CREDIT
19__					
July	2	Cash	1	65,000	
		Martin Taylor, Capital	50		65,000
		Owner invested cash to begin business.			
	3	Land	20	140,000	
		Cash	1		28,000
		Notes Payable	30		112,000
		Purchased land. Paid part cash and issued a note payable for the balance.			
	5	Building	22	24,000	
		Cash	1		24,000
		Purchased a small portable building for cash.			
	12	Office Equipment	25	3,000	
		Accounts Payable	32		3,000
		Purchased office equipment on credit from Suzuki & Co.			
	28	Accounts Payable	32	2,000	
		Cash	1		2,000
		Paid part of account payable to Suzuki & Co.			

b

	CASH			Account No. 1

DATE	EXPLANATION	REF	DEBIT	CREDIT	BALANCE
19—					
July 2		1	65000		65000
3		1		28000	37000
5		1		24000	13000
28		1		2000	11000

	LAND			Account No. 20

DATE	EXPLANATION	REF	DEBIT	CREDIT	BALANCE
19—					
July 3		1	140000		140000

	BUILDING			Account No. 22

DATE	EXPLANATION	REF	DEBIT	CREDIT	BALANCE
19—					
July 5		1	24000		24000

	OFFICE EQUIPMENT			Account No. 25

DATE	EXPLANATION	REF	DEBIT	CREDIT	BALANCE
19—					
July 12		1	3000		3000

NOTES PAYABLE						Account No. 30
DATE	EXPLANATION	REF	DEBIT	CREDIT	BALANCE	
19—						
July 3		1		1 1 2 0 0 0	1 1 2 0 0 0	

ACCOUNTS PAYABLE						Account No. 32
DATE	EXPLANATION	REF	DEBIT	CREDIT	BALANCE	
19—						
July 12		1		3 0 0 0	3 0 0 0	
28		1	2 0 0 0		1 0 0 0	

MARTIN TAYLOR, CAPITAL						Account No. 50
DATE	EXPLANATION	REF	DEBIT	CREDIT	BALANCE	
19—						
July 2		1		6 5 0 0 0	6 5 0 0 0	

c

STADIUM PARKING
Trial Balance
July 31, 19____

	DEBIT	CREDIT
Cash	$ 11,000	
Land	140,000	
Building	24,000	
Office equipment	3,000	
Notes payable		$112,000
Accounts payable		1,000
Martin Taylor, capital		65,000
	$178,000	$178,000

ASSIGNMENT MATERIAL

REVIEW QUESTIONS

1 In its simplest form, an account has only three elements or basic parts. What are these three elements?

2 What relationship exists between the position of an account on the balance sheet and the rules for recording increases in that account?

3 State briefly the rules of debit and credit as applied to asset accounts. As applied to liability and owner's equity accounts.

4 Is it true that favourable events or transactions are recorded by credits and unfavourable events by debits? Explain.

5 Does the term *debit* mean increase and the term *credit* mean decrease? Explain.

6 What requirement is imposed by the double-entry system in the recording of any business transaction?

7 Explain precisely what is meant by each of the following phrases. Whenever appropriate, indicate whether the left or right side of an account is affected and whether an increase or decrease is indicated.

   a A debit of $200 to the Cash account

   b Credit balance

   c Credit side of an account

   d A debit of $600 to Accounts Payable

   e Debit balance

   f A credit of $50 to Accounts Payable

   g A debit to the Land account

8 For each of the following transactions, indicate whether the account in parentheses should be debited or credited, and give the reason for your answer.

   a Purchased a copying machine on credit, promising to make payment in full within 30 days. (Accounts Payable)

   b Purchased land for cash. (Cash)

   c Sold an old, unneeded typewriter on 30-day credit. (Office Equipment)

   d Obtained a loan of $30,000 from a bank. (Cash)

   e James Brown began the business of Brown Sporting Goods Shop by depositing $20,000 cash in a bank account in the name of the business. (James Brown, Capital)

9 For each of the following accounts, state whether it is an asset, or a liability, or owner's equity; also state whether it would normally have a debit or a credit balance; (a) Office Equipment, (b) John Williams, Capital, (c) Accounts Receivable, (d) Accounts Payable, (e) Cash, (f) Notes Payable, (g) Land.

10 List the following four items in a logical sequence to illustrate the flow of accounting information through a manual accounting system:

a Information entered in journal

b Financial statements prepared from ledger

c Occurrence of a business transaction

d Debits and credits posted from journal to ledger

11 Why is a journal sometimes called the *book of original entry?*

12 Compare and contrast a *journal* and a *ledger.*

13 Which step in the recording of transactions requires greater understanding of accounting principles: (a) the entering of transactions in the journal, or (b) the posting of entries to ledger accounts?

14 What is a *compound journal entry?*

15 What purposes are served by a trial balance?

16 In preparing a trial balance, an accounting student listed the balance of the Office Equipment account in the credit column. This account had a balance of $2,450. What would be the amount of the discrepancy in the trial balance totals? Explain.

17 Are dollar signs used in journal entries? In ledger accounts? In trial balances? In financial statements?

18 A student beginning the study of accounting prepared a trial balance in which two unusual features appeared. The Buildings account showed a credit balance of $20,000, and the Accounts Payable account a debit balance of $100. Considering each of these two abnormal balances separately, state whether the condition was the result of an error in the records or could have resulted from proper recording of an unusual transaction.

19 Since it is possible to record the effects of business transactions directly in ledger accounts, why is it desirable for a business to maintain a journal?

20 List the procedures in the *accounting cycle* as described in this chapter.

21 What is a *data base?* How does a data base relate to the preparation of journal entries and ledger accounts in a computer-based system?

EXERCISES

Exercise 2-1
Accounting terminology

Listed below are nine technical accounting terms introduced in this chapter:

Account	Debit	Ledger
Credit	Double-entry	Posting
Data base	Journal	Trial balance

Each of the following statements may (or may not) describe one of these technical terms. For each statement, indicate the accounting term described, or answer ''none'' if the statement does not correctly describe any of the terms.

a An entry on the right-hand side of a ledger account.

b The accounting record in which transactions are initially recorded in a manual accounting system.

c Information stored in a computer-based accounting system that can be arranged into any desired format.

d A device that will detect the failure to record a business transaction in the accounting records.

e The accounting record from which a trial balance is prepared.

f The system of accounting in which every business transaction is recorded by an equal dollar amount of debit and credit entries.

Exercise 2-2
Analysis of transactions; double-entry accounting

Analyze separately each of the following transactions using the format illustrated at the end of the exercise. In each situation, explain the debit portion of the transaction before the credit portion.

a On May 1, Linda McKaig organized McKaig Software by opening a bank account in the company name with a deposit of $90,000 cash.

b On May 3, land was acquired for $55,000 cash.

c On May 5, a prefabricated building was purchased at a cost of $45,000 from Custom Company. A cash down payment of 20,000 was made and it was agreed that the balance should be paid in full within 30 days.

d On May 8, office equipment was purchased on credit from Taylor Office Supply Co. at a price of $8,500. The amount payable was to be paid within 60 days.

e On May 31, a partial payment of $3,500 was made on the liability to Taylor Office Supply Co.

Note: The type of analysis to be made is shown by the following illustration, using transaction (a) as an example.

a **(1)** The asset Cash was increased. Increases in assets are recorded by debits. Debit Cash, $90,000.

(2) The owner's equity was increased. Increases in owner's equity are recorded by credits. Credit Linda McKaig, Capital, $90,000.

Excercise 2-3
Using ledger accounts

Enter the following transactions in T accounts drawn on ordinary notebook paper. Enter the dates and amounts and label each debit and credit with the letter identifying the transaction. Prepare a trial balance at June 30.

a On June 10, Dan King opened a bank account in the name of his new business, King Realty Company, by making a deposit of $75,000 cash.

b On June 13, purchased land and an office building at a total price of $160,000, of which $120,000 was applicable to the land and $40,000 to the building. A cash payment of $50,000 was made and a note payable was issued for the balance.

c On June 20, office equipment was purchased at a cost of $8,400. A cash down payment of $2,800 was made, and it was agreed that the balance should be paid within 30 days.

d On June 30, paid $2,800 of the $5,600 liability arising from the purchase of office equipment on June 20.

Exercise 2-4
Effects of debits and credits on ledger account balances

The first five transactions of a newly organized company appear in the following T accounts.

CASH		OFFICE EQUIPMENT		ACCOUNTS PAYABLE	
(1) 57,500	(2) 42,500	(3) 11,250		(5) 6,250	(3) 11,250
	(4) 2,500				
	(5) 6,250				

LAND	DELIVERY TRUCK	BOB LOVE, CAPITAL
(2) 30,000	(4) 10,000	(1) 57,500

BUILDING	NOTES PAYABLE
(2) 45,000	(2) 32,500
	(4) 7,500

For each of the six transactions in turn, indicate the type of accounts affected (asset, liability, or owner's equity) and whether the account was increased or decreased. Arrange your answers in the form illustrated for transaction (1), shown here as an example.

	ACCOUNT(S) DEBITED		ACCOUNTS(S) CREDITED	
TRANSACTION	TYPE OF ACCOUNTS(S)	INCREASE OR DECREASE	TYPE OF ACCOUNT(S)	INCREASE OR DECREASE
(1)	Asset	Increase	Owner's equity	Increase

Exercise 2-5
Recording transactions in a journal

Enter the following transactions in the two-column journal of Cameron Sporting Goods. Include a brief explanation of the transaction as part of each journal entry.

Nov. 1 The owner, Bruce Cameron, invested an additional $40,000 cash in the business.

Nov. 3 Purchased an adjacent vacant lot for use as parking space. The price was $98,800, of which $28,800 was paid in cash; a note payable was issued for the balance.

Nov. 12 Collected an account receivable of $4,800 from a customer, Gene Krieger.

Nov. 17 Acquired office equipment from Tower Company for $7,600 cash.

Nov. 21 Issued a cheque for $864 in full payment of an account payable to Hampton Supply Co.

Nov. 28 Borrowed $35,000 cash from the bank by signing a 90-day note payable.

Exercise 2-6
Relationship between journal entries and ledger accounts

Transactions are recorded first in a journal and then posted to ledger accounts. In this exercise, however, your understanding of the relationship between journal and ledger is tested by asking you to study some ledger accounts and determine the journal entries that were probably made by the company's accountant to produce these ledger entries. The following accounts show the first six transactions of the South Pacific Travel Agency. Prepare a journal entry (include written explanation) for each transaction.

CASH				OFFICE EQUIPMENT		
Sept. 1	75,000	Sept. 3	20,000	Sept. 6	20,000	Sept. 15	5,000
Sept. 29	2,300	Sept. 25	15,000				

ACCOUNTS RECEIVABLE				NOTES PAYABLE		
Sept. 15	5,000	Sept. 29	2,300			Sept. 3	100,000

LAND		ACCOUNTS PAYABLE		
Sept. 3	72,000	Sept. 25	15,000	Sept. 6	20,000

BUILDING		RON LINDSEY, CAPITAL	
Sept. 3	48,000		Sept. 1	75,000

Exercise 2-7
Preparing a trial balance

Using the information in the ledger accounts presented in Exercise 2-6, prepare a trial balance for the South Pacific Travel Agency at September 30, 19___.

Exercise 2-8
Effects of errors upon a trial balance

The trial balance prepared by Field Company at September 30 was not in balance. In searching for the error, an employee discovered that a transaction for the purchase of a typewriter on credit for $610 had been recorded by a *debit* of $610 to the Office Equipment account and a *debit* of $610 to Accounts Payable. The credit column of the incorrect trial balance had a total of $92,600.

In answering each of the following five questions, explain briefly the reasons underlying your answer and state the dollar amount of the error if any.

a Was the Office Equipment account overstated, understated, or correctly stated in the trial balance?

b Was the total of the debit column of the trial balance ovestated, understated, or correctly stated?

c Was the Accounts Payable account overstated, or correctly stated in the trial balance?

d Was the total of the credit column of the trial balance overstated, understated or correctly stated?

e How much was the total of the debit column of the trial balance before correction of the error?

Exercise 2-9
Uses and limitations of a trial balance

Some of the following errors would cause the debit and credit columns of the trial balance to have unequal totals. For each of the four paragraphs, write a statement explaining with reasons whether the error would cause unequal totals in the trial balance. Each paragraph is to be considered independently of the others.

a A $540 payment for a new typewriter was recorded by a debit to Office Equipment of $54 and a credit to Cash of $54.

b A payment of $400 to a creditor was recorded by a debit to Accounts Payable of $400 and a credit to Cash of $40.

c An account receivable in the amount of $800 was collected in full. The collection was recorded by a debit to Cash for $800 and a debit to Accounts Payable for $800.

d An account payable was paid by issuing a cheque for $350. The payment was recorded by debiting Accounts Payable $350 and crediting Accounts Receivable $350.

Exercise 2-10
Steps in the accounting cycle; computerized accounting systems

Various steps and decisions involved in the accounting cycle are described in the following seven lettered statements. Indicate which of these procedures are mechanical functions that can be performed by machine in a computerized accounting system, and which require the judgment of people familiar with accounting principles and concepts.

(a) Decide whether or not events should be recorded in the accounting records.

(b) Determine which ledger accounts should be debited and credited to describe specific business transactions.

(c) Arrange recorded data in the format of journal entries.

(d) Arrange recorded data in the format of ledger accounts.

(e) Prepare a trial balance.

(f) Prepare financial statements (a balance sheet).

(g) Evaluate the debt-paying ability of one company relative to another.

PROBLEMS

Group A

Problem 2A-1
Analyzing transactions and preparing journal entries

Yoko Toyoda is the owner of Perfect Portraits, a photography studio. A few of the company's July business transactions are described as follows:

(1) On July 2, collected cash of $700 from accounts receivable.

(2) On July 7, purchased photographic equipment for $2,175, paying $500 in cash and charging the remainder on the company's 30-day account at Camera Supply Co.

(3) On July 9, returned to Camera Supply Co. $200 of photographic equipment that did not work properly. The return of this equipment reduced by $200 the amount owed to Camera Supply Co.

(4) On July 25, Yoko Toyoda made an additional investment in Perfect Portraits by depositing $2,500 cash in the company bank account.

(5) On July 31, paid the remaining $1,475 owed to Camera Supply Co.

Instructions

a Prepare an analysis of each of the above transactions. The form of analysis to be used is as follows, using transaction (1) as an example.

  1(a) The asset Cash was increased. Increases in assets are recorded by debits. Debit Cash, $700.

  (b) The asset Accounts Receivable was decreased. Decreases in assets are recorded by credits. Credit Accounts Receivable, $700.

b Prepare journal entries, including explanations, for the above transactions.

Problem 2A-2
Preparing a trial balance and a balance sheet

Robert Dash & Associates is an investment advisory service. The account balances at November 30 are shown by the following alphabetical list:

Accounts payable	$ 4,800	Notes payable	$145,000
Accounts receivable	16,700	Notes receivable	2,400
Automobiles	12,600	Office furniture	12,900
Building	110,000	Office supplies	850
Cash	17,650	Property taxes payable	1,060
Computer	18,800	Robert Dash, capital	129,650
Computer software	5,450	Salaries payable	3,740
Land	85,000	Technical library	1,900

Instructions

a Prepare a trial balance with the accounts arranged in financial statement order. Include a proper heading for your trial balance.

b Prepare a balance sheet. Include a subtotal for total liabilities.

Problem 2A-3
Recording transactions in a journal

Susan Cole, a chartered accountant, resigned from her position with a large CA firm in order to begin her own public accounting practice. The business transactions during September while the new venture was being organized are listed below.

Sept. 1 Cole opened a bank account in the name of her firm, Susan Cole, Chartered Accountant, by depositing $32,000, which she had saved over a period of years.

Sept. 10 Purchased a small office building located on a large lot for a total price of $91,200, of which $48,000 was applicable to the land and $43,200 to the building. A cash payment of $18,240 was made and a note payable was issued for the balance of the purchase price.

Sept. 15 Purchased a micro-computer system from Computer Stores, Inc., for $8,680 cash.

Sept. 19 Purchased office furniture, filing cabinets, and a typewriter from Davidson Office Supply Co. at a cost of $3,960. A cash down payment of $720 was made, the balance to be paid in three equal instalments due September 28, October 28, and November 28. The purchase was on open account and did not require signing of a promissory note.

Sept. 26 A $240 monitor in the micro-computer system purchased on September 15 stopped working. The monitor was returned to Computer Stores, Inc., which promised to refund the $240 within five days.

Sept. 28 Paid Davidson Office Supply Co. $1,080 cash as the first instalment due on the account payable for office equipment.

Sept. 30 Received $240 cash from Computer Stores, Inc., in full settlement of the account receivable created on September 26.

Instructions

Prepare journal entries to record the above transactions. Select the appropriate account titles from the following chart of accounts:

Cash	Office equipment
Accounts receivable	Notes payable
Land	Accounts payable
Building	Susan Cole, capital

Problem 2A-4
Posting to ledger accounts; preparing a trial balance and a balance sheet

Tom Morgan is a veterinarian. In January, he began organizing his own animal hospital, to be known as Animal Care Centre. Morgan has prepared the journal entries on page 79 to record all January business transactions. He has not posted these entries to ledger accounts. The ledger account numbers to be used are: Cash, 1; Office Supplies, 10; Land, 20; Building, 25; Medical Equipment, 27; Notes Payable, 30; Accounts Payable, 31; and Tom Morgan, Capital, 50.

Instructions

a Post the journal entries to ledger accounts of the three-column running balance form.

b Prepare a trial balance at January 31 from the ledger accounts completed in part **a**.

c Prepare a balance sheet at January 31, 19___.

General Journal

Jan.	2	Cash	60,000	
		Tom Morgan, Capital		60,000
		Investment in business by owner.		
	4	Land	45,000	
		Building	115,000	
		Cash		40,000
		Notes Payable		120,000
		Purchased land and building.		
	7	Medical Equipment	7,480	
		Accounts Payable		7,480
		Bought equipment on credit from		
		Medco. Inc.		
	8	Office Supplies	590	
		Accounts Payable		590
		Bought supplies from Miller Supply.		
	13	Accounts Payable	1,400	
		Medical Equipment		1,400
		Returned defective medical equipment		
		to Medco, Inc., for credit on Account.		
	18	Accounts Payable	590	
		Cash		590
		Made payment of liability to Miller Supply.		

Problem 2A-5
Preparing journal entries, posting, and preparing a trial balance

Ann Ryan, a licensed real estate broker, on October 1 began the organization of her own business to be known as Ryan Land Company. The following events occurred during October:

Oct. 2 Ann Ryan opened a bank account in the name of the business by depositing personal savings of $25,000.

Oct. 6 Purchased land and a small office building at a total price of $97,500 of which $64,000 was applicable to land and $33,500 to the building. The terms of the purchase required a cash payment of $19,500 and the issuance of a note payable for $78,000.

Oct. 15 Sold one-quarter of the land at its cost of $16,000 to a neighbouring business, Village Medical Clinic, which wanted to expand its parking lot. No down payment was required; Village Medical Clinic issued a note promising payment of the $16,000 in a series of five monthly instalments of $3,200 each, beginning October 30 (ignore interest). As the land was sold at the same price per square metre as Ryan Land Company had paid to acquire it, no gain or loss results on this transaction.

Oct. 20 Purchased office equipment on credit from Buffington Company in the amount of $5,280.

Oct. 30 Paid $3,440 as partial settlement of the liability to Buffington Company.

Oct. 31 Received the first $3,200 monthly instalment on the note receivable from Village Medical Clinic.

The account titles and account numbers to be used are:

Cash	1	Notes payable	30
Notes receivable	5	Accounts payable	32
Land	21	Ann Ryan, capital	50
Building	23		
Office equipment	26		

Instructions

a Prepare journal entries for the month of October.

b Post to ledger accounts of the three-column running balance form.

c Prepare a trial balance at October 31, 19___.

Problem 2A-6
Preparing journal entries, posting, and preparing a trial balance

After playing several seasons of professional football, George Harris had saved enough money to start a business, to be called Number One Auto Rental. The transactions during March while the new business was being organized are listed below:

Mar. 1 George Harris invested $140,000 cash in the business by making a deposit in a bank account in the name of the new company.

Mar. 3 The new company purchased land and a building at a cost of $120,000, of which $72,000 was regarded as applicable to the land and $48,000 to the building. The transaction involved a cash payment of $41,500 and the issuance of a note payable for $78,500.

Mar. 5 Purchased 10 new automobiles at $17,200 each from Fleet Sales Limited. Paid $40,000 cash, and agreed to pay $32,000 by March 31 and the remaining balance by April 15. The liability is viewed as an account payable.

Mar. 7 Sold an automobile at cost to Harris' father-in-law, Howard Facey, who paid $2,400 in cash and agreed to pay the balance within 30 days.

Mar. 8 One of the automobiles was found to be defective and was returned to Fleet Sales Limited. The amount payable to this creditor was thereby reduced by $17,200.

Mar. 20 Purchased office equipment at a cost of $4,000 cash.

Mar. 31 Issued a cheque for $32,000 in partial payment of the liability to Fleet Sales Limited.

The account titles and the account numbers used by the company are as follows:

Cash	10	Automobiles	22
Accounts receivable	11	Notes payable	31
Land	16	Accounts payable	32
Building	17	George Harris, capital	50
Office equipment	20		

Instructions

a Journalize the March transactions.

b Post to ledger accounts. Use the running balance form of ledger account.

c Prepare a trial balance at March 31.

Group B

Problem 2B-1
Analyzing transactions
and preparing journal
entries

The Tool Shed was organized to rent trailers, tools, and other equipment to its customers. The organization of the business began on May 1 and the following transactions occurred in May before the company began regular operations on June 1.

(1) On May 1, Robert Caldwell opened a bank account in the name of his new company with a deposit of $80,000 cash.

(2) On May 3, The Tool Shed bought land for use in its operations at a total cost of $75,000. A cash down payment of $15,000 was made, and a note payable (payable within 90 days without interest) was issued for the balance.

(3) On May 5, a movable building was purchased for $36,000 cash and installed on the lot.

(4) On May 10, equipment was purchased on credit from Ace Tool Company at a cost of $14,100. The account payable was to be paid within 30 days. (The asset account is entitled Rental Equipment.)

(5) On May 31, a cash payment of $20,000 was made in partial settlement of the note payable issued on May 3.

Instructions

a Prepare an analysis of each of the preceding transactions. The form of analysis to be used is as follows, using transaction (**1**) above as an example.

1(a) The asset Cash was increased. Increases in assets are recorded by debits. Debit Cash, $70,000.

(b) The owner's equity was increased. Increases in owner's equity are recorded by credits. Credit Robert Caldwell, Capital, $70,000.

b Prepare journal entries for the five transactions. Include an explanation as a part of each journal entry.

Problem 2B-2
Preparing a trial
balance and balance
sheet

The ledger accounts of Cheviot Hills Golf Club at September 30 are shown below in an alphabetical listing.

Accounts payable	$ 5,340	Lighting equipment	$ 52,900
Accounts receivable	1,300	Maintenance equipment	36,500
Building	64,200	Notes payable	390,000
Carol Martin, capital	264,060	Notes receivable	24,000
Cash	14,960	Office equipment	1,420
Fences	23,600	Office supplies	490
Golf carts	28,000	Sprinkler system	50,000
Land	375,000	Taxes payable	12,970

Instructions

a Prepare a trial balance with the ledger accounts arranged in the usual financial statement order. Include a proper heading.

b Prepare a balance sheet at September 30, 19___. Include a subtotal showing total liabilities.

Problem 2B-3
Recording transactions
in a journal

In May, Juan Ramirez, a physician, decided to open his own medical practice. During May, the new business engaged in the following transactions:

May 4 Ramirez opened a bank account in the name of his medical practice, Juan Ramirez, M.D., by depositing $30,000 cash.

May 16 Purchased a small medical office. The purchase price was $95,400, which included land valued at $50,000 and a building valued at $45,400. A cash down payment was made for $21,000, and a note payable was issued for the balance of the purchase price.

May 19   Purchased office furniture on account from Modern Office Co., $2,340.

May 22   Purchased medical supplies for cash from Denton Labs, $1,630.

May 23   Returned to Denton Labs $225 of the medical supplies purchased yesterday as these items were not exactly what Remirez had ordered. Denton Labs agreed to refund the $225 within 10 days.

May 30   Made an $1,170 partial payment on the account payable to Modern Office Co.

May 31   Received the $225 refund from Denton Labs for the supplies returned on May 23.

Instructions   Prepare journal entries to record the preceding transactions. Select the appropriate account titles from the following chart of accounts:

Cash	Land	Notes payable
Accounts receivable	Building	Accounts payable
Medical supplies	Office furniture	Juan Ramirez, capital

Problem 2B-4
Posting to ledger accounts; preparing a trial balance and a balance sheet

After several seasons of professional tennis competition, Chris Farr had saved enough money to start her own tennis school, to be known as Winners' Tennis College. During July, while organizing the business, Farr prepared the journal entries on page 83 to record all July transactions. She has not posted these entries to ledger accounts. The ledger account numbers to be used are: Cash 1, Office Supplies 9, Land 20, Tennis Courts 22, Tennis Equipment 25, Notes Payable 30, Accounts Payable 31, and Chris Farr, Capital 50.

Instructions   **a** Post the journal entries to ledger accounts of the three-column running balance form.

b Prepare a trial balance at July 31 from the ledger accounts completed in part **a**.

c Prepare a balance sheet at July 31, 19___.

Problem 2B-5
Preparing journal entries, posting, and preparing a trial balance

Coast Property Management was started on November 1 by Donald Klein to provide managerial services for the owners of apartment buildings. The organizational period extended throughout November and included the following transactions.

Nov.   1   Klein opened a bank account in the name of the business with a deposit of $27,000 cash.

Nov.   4   Purchased land and an office building for a price of $135,000, of which $75,000 was considered applicable to the land and $60,000 attributable to the building. A cash down payment of $25,000 was made and a note payable for $110,000 was issued for the balance of the purchase price.

Nov.   7   Purchased office equipment on credit from Harvard Office Equipment, $4,400.

Nov.   9   A typewriter (cost $560), which was part of the November 7 purchase of office equipment, proved defective and was returned for credit to Harvard Office Equipment.

Nov.   17   Sold one-third of the land acquired on November 4 to Regent Pharmacy at a price of $25,000. This price is equal to Coast Property's cost for this portion of the land, so there is no gain or loss on this transaction. Coast Property received a $5,000 cash

General Journal   Page 1

July	2	Cash	30,000	
		Chris Farr, Capital		30,000
		Investment in business by owner.		
	3	Land	28,400	
		Tennis Courts	75,000	
		Cash		20,000
		Notes Payable		83,400
		Purchased land and tennis courts.		
	6	Tennis Equipment	1,680	
		Accounts Payable		1,680
		Bought equipment on credit from		
		Rackets, Inc.		
	7	Office Supplies	315	
		Accounts Payable		315
		Bought supplies from Miller Supply.		
	12	Tennis Equipment	725	
		Accounts Payable		725
		Bought equipment from Rackets, Inc.		
	17	Accounts Payable	315	
		Cash		315
		Made payment of liability to Miller Supply.		
	22	Accounts Payable	725	
		Cash		725
		Made payment of liability to Rackets, Inc.		
		for purchase of July 12.		

down payment from Regent Pharmacy and a note receivable in the amount of $20,000, due in four monthly instalments of $5,000 each, beginning on November 30 (ignore interest).

Nov. 28 Paid $1,600 in partial settlement of the liability to Harvard Office Equipment.

Nov. 30 Received cash of $5,000 as partial collection of the note receivable from Regent Pharmacy.

The account titles and account numbers to be used are

Cash	1	Office equipment	25
Notes receivable	5	Notes payable	31
Land	21	Accounts payable	32
Building	23	Donald Klein, capital	51

Instructions   **a** Prepare journal entries for the month of November.

b Post to ledger accounts of the three-column running balance form.

c Prepare a trial balance at November 30.

Problem 2B-6
Preparing journal
entries, posting, and
preparing a trial
balance

Educational TV was organized in February 19___, to operate as a local television station. The account titles and numbers used by the business are as follows:

Cash	1	Telecasting equipment	24
Accounts receivable	5	Film library	25
Supplies	9	Notes payable	31
Land	21	Accounts payable	32
Building	22	Alice Wilson, capital	51
Transmitter	23		

The transactions for February were as follows:

Feb. 1 Alice Wilson deposited $300,000 cash in a bank account in the name of the business, Educational TV.

Feb. 2 Educational TV purchased the land, buildings, and telecasting equipment previously used by a local television station that had gone bankrupt. The total purchase price was $250,000, of which $100,000 was attributable to the land, $80,000 to the building, and the remainder to the telecasting equipment. The terms of the purchase required a cash payment of $160,000 and the issuance of a note payable for the balance.

Feb. 5 Purchased a transmitter at a cost of $200,000 from AC Mfg. Co., making a cash down payment of $56,000. The balance, in the form of a note payable, was to be paid in monthly instalments of $12,000, beginning February 15. (Interest expense is to be ignored.)

Feb. 9 Purchased a film library at a cost of $32,000 from Modern Film Productions, making a down payment of $15,000 cash, with the balance on account payable in 30 days.

Feb. 12 Bought supplies costing $3,000, paying cash.

Feb. 15 Paid $12,000 to AC Mfg. Co. as the first monthly payment on the note payable created on February 5. (Interest expense is to be ignored.)

Feb. 25 Sold part of the film library to City Community College; cost was $7,000 and the selling price also was $7,000. City Community College agreed to pay the full amount in 30 days.

Instructions **a** Prepare journal entries for the month of February.

b Post to ledger accounts of the three-column running balance form.

c Prepare a trial balance at February 28, 19___.

BUSINESS DECISION CASES

Case 2-1
Computer-based
accounting systems

John Moore is planning to create a computer-based accounting system for small businesses. His system will be developed from a data base program and will be suitable for use on personal computers.

The idea underlying data base software is that data needed for a variety of uses is entered into the data base only once. The computer is programmed to arrange this data into any number of desired formats. In the case of Moore's accounting system, the company's accounting personnel must enter the relevant information about each business transaction into the data base. The program that Moore plans to write will then enable the computer operator to have the information arranged by the computer into the formats of (1) journal entries (with written explanations), (2) three-column running balance form ledger accounts, (3) a trial balance, and (4) a balance sheet.

Instructions

a Identify the relevant information about each business transaction that the company's accounting personnel must enter into the data base to enable Moore's program to prepare the four types of accounting records and statements described above.

b As described in this chapter, the accounting cycle includes the steps of (1) analyzing and recording business transactions, (2) posting the debit and credit amounts to ledger accounts, (3) preparing a trial balance, and (4) preparing financial statements (at this stage, only a balance sheet). Indicate which of these functions can be performed automatically by Moore's computer program and which must still be performed by the company's accounting personnel.

Case 2-2
Preparing balance
sheets and an
introduction to
measuring income

David Ray, a college student with several summers' experience as a guide on canoe camping trips, decided to go into business for himself. On June 1, Ray organized Birchbark Canoe Trails by depositing $1,800 of personal savings in a bank account in the name of the business. Also on June 1, the business borrowed an additional $3,000 cash from John Ray (David's father) by issuing a three-year note payable. To help the business get started, John Ray agreed that no interest would be charged on the loan. The following transactions were also carried out by the business on June 1:

(1) Bought a number of canoes at a total cost of $5,100; paid $2,000 cash and agreed to pay the balance within 60 days.

(2) Bought camping equipment at a cost of $4,400 payable in 60 days.

(3) Bought supplies for cash, $700.

After the close of the season on September 10, Ray asked another student, Sharon Lee, who had taken a course in accounting, to help determine the financial position of the business.

The only record Ray had maintained was a cheque book with memorandum notes written on the cheque stubs. From this source Lee discovered that Ray had invested an additional $1,400 of savings in the business on July 2, and also that the accounts payable arising from the purchase of the canoes and camping equipment had been paid in full. A bank statement received from the bank on September 10 showed a balance on deposit of $2,910.

Ray informed Lee that all cash received by the business had been deposited in the bank and all bills had been paid by cheque immediately upon receipt; consequently, as of September 10 all bills for the season had been paid. However, nothing had been paid on the note payable.

The canoes and camping equipment were all in excellent condition at the end of the season and Ray planned to resume operations the following summer. In fact he had already accepted reservations from many customers who wished to return.

Lee felt that some consideration should be given to the wear and tear on the canoes and equipment but she agreed with Ray that for the present purpose the canoes and equipment should be listed in the balance sheet at the original cost. The supplies remaining on hand had cost $80 and Ray felt that these supplies could be used next summer.

Lee suggested that two balance sheets be prepared, one to show the condition of the business on June 1 and the other showing the condition on September 10. She also recommended to Ray that a complete set of accounting records be established.

Instructions   **a** Use the information in the first paragraph (including the three numbered transactions) as a basis for preparing a balance sheet dated June 1.

b Prepare a balance sheet at September 10. (Because of the incomplete information available, it is not possible to determine the amount of cash at September 10 by adding cash receipts and deducting cash payments throughout the season. The amount on deposit as reported by the bank at September 10 is to be regarded as the total cash belonging to the business at that date.)

c By comparing the two balance sheets, compute the change in owner's equity. Explain the sources of this change in owner's equity and state whether you consider the business to be successful. Also comment on the cash position at the beginning and end of the season. Has the cash position improved significantly? Explain.

CHAPTER

3

MEASURING
BUSINESS
INCOME

CHAPTER PREVIEW

In Chapter 3 our coverage of the accounting cycle is expanded to include the measurement of business income. Attention is focused on the accounting concepts of revenue, expense, net income, and owner's equity. Two important accounting principles are introduced — the realization (recognition) principle and the matching principle. The continuing example of Roberts Real Estate Company is then used to show how a business records revenue and expense transactions and prepares an income statement. As Roberts Real Estate Company owns depreciable assets, the concept of depreciation is introduced, and the recording of depreciation expense is illustrated. The procedures for closing the revenue and expense accounts at the end of the accounting period also are illustrated and explained. In summary, this chapter introduces and illustrates the basic concepts of accrual accounting.

After studying this chapter you should be able to meet these Learning Objectives:

1 Explain the nature of net income, revenue, and expenses.

2 Relate the realization (recognition) principle and the matching principle to the recording of revenue and expenses.

3 Apply the rules of debit and credit to revenue and expense transactions.

4 Define and record depreciation expense.

5 Prepare an income statement and explain its relationship to the balance sheet.

6 Prepare closing entries.

7 Describe the sequence of procedures in the accounting cycle.

8 Distinguish between the accrual basis and the cash basis of accounting.

In this chapter you will be introduced to the challenge of measuring business income. Some people mistakenly assume that measuring business income is a matter of simple arithmetic. In fact, no topic in accounting is more complex and controversial than measuring the net income of a specific business for a specific time period such as a month or a year. We will be concerned with one aspect or another of measuring and reporting income throughout this book.

The earning of net income, or profits, is a major goal of almost every business enterprise, large or small. *Net income* is the *increase in the owner's equity resulting from operation of the business.* This increase usually is accompanied by an increase in total assets. The opposite of net income, a decrease in owner's equity resulting from operation of the business, is termed a *net loss.* If you were to organize a small business of your own, you would do so with the hope and expectation that the business would operate at a profit (net income), thereby increasing your ownership equity. Individuals who invest in the capital stock of large corporations also expect the business to earn a profit that will increase the value of their investment.

The resources generated by profitable operation may be retained in the business to finance expansion, or they may be withdrawn by the owner or owners. Some of the largest corporations have become large by retaining their profits in the business and using these profits to finance growth. If profits are retained in the business, a company may be in a better position to acquire new plant and equipment, to carry on research leading to new and better products, and to extend sales operations into new territories.

1   Explain the nature of net income, revenue, and expenses.

Net income

Since the drive for profits underlies the very existence of business organizations, it follows that a most important function of an accounting system is to provide information about the profitability of a business. Before we can measure the profits of a business, we need to establish a sharp, clear meaning for *profits.* Economists often define profits as the amount by which an entity becomes *better off* during a period of time. Unfortunately, how much "better off" an entity has become is largely a matter of personal opinion and cannot be measured *objectively* enough to provide a useful definition for accountants.

For this reason, accountants usually look to actual business transactions to provide objective evidence that a business has been profitable or unprofitable. For example, if an item that cost a business $60 is sold for $100 cash, we have objective evidence that the business has earned a profit of $40. Since business managers and economists use the word *profits* in somewhat different senses, accountants prefer to use the alternative term *net income* and to define this term very carefully. *Net income is the excess of the price of goods sold and services rendered over the cost of goods and services used up during a given time period.* At this point, we shall adopt the technical accounting term *net income* in preference to the less precise term *profits.*

To determine net income, it is necessary to measure for a given time period (1) the price of goods sold and services rendered and (2) the cost of goods and services used up. The technical accounting terms for these items comprising net income are *revenue* and *expenses.* Therefore, we may state that *net income equals revenue minus expenses,* as shown in the following *income statement:*

ROBERTS REAL ESTATE COMPANY
Income Statement
For the Month Ended October 31, 19__

Revenue:		
Sales commissions earned		$10,640
Expenses:		
Advertising expense	$ 630	
Salaries expense	7,100	
Telephone expense	144	
Depreciation expense: building	150	
Depreciation expense: office equipment	45	8,069
Net income		$ 2,571

We will show how this income statement is developed from the accounting records of Roberts Real Estate Company later in this chapter. For the moment, however, this illustration will assist us in discussing some of the basic concepts involved in measuring business income.

Income must be related to a specified period of time   Notice that our sample income statement covers a *period* of time — namely, the month of October. A balance sheet shows the financial position of a business at a *particular date.* An income statement, on the other hand, shows the results of business operations over a span of time. We cannot intelligently evaluate net income unless it is associated with a specific time period. For example, if an executive says, "My business earns a net income of $10,000," the profitability of the business is unclear. Does it earn $10,000 per week, per month, or per year?

 The late J. Paul Getty, one of the world's first billion-aires, was once interviewed by a group of business students. One of the students asked Getty to estimate the amount of his income. As the student had not specified a time period, Getty decided to have some fun with his audience and responded, "About $11,000 . . ." He paused long enough to allow the group to express surprise over this seemingly low amount, and then completed his sentence, ". . . an hour." Incidentally, $11,000 per hour (24 hours per day) amounts to about $100 million per year.

Every business prepares an annual income statement, and most businesses prepare quarterly and monthly income statements as well. The period of time covered by an income statement is termed the company's *accounting period.* This period may be a month, a quarter of a year, a year, or any other specified period of time.

A 12-month accounting period used by an entity is called its *fiscal year.* The fiscal year used by most companies coincides with the calendar year and ends on December 31. However, some businesses elect to use a fiscal year that ends on some other date. It may be convenient for the business to end its fiscal year during a slack season rather than during a time of peak business activity. The fiscal year of the federal government, for example, begins on April 1 and ends 12 months later on March 31.

Let us now explore the meaning of the accounting terms *revenue* and *expenses*.

Revenue

Revenue is the price of goods sold and services rendered during a given accounting period. When a business renders services to its customers or delivers merchandise to them, it either receives immediate payment in cash or acquires an account receivable that will be collected and thereby become cash within a short time. The revenue for any given period is equal to the inflow of cash and receivables from sales made in that period. For any single transaction, the amount of revenue is a measurement of the asset values received from the customer.

Revenue causes an increase in owner's equity. The inflow of cash and receivables from customers increases the total assets of the company; on the other side of the accounting equation, the liabilities do not change, but owner's equity is increased to match the increase in total assets. Thus revenue is the gross increase in owner's equity resulting from business activities.

Various terms are used to describe different types of revenue; for example, the revenue earned by a real estate broker might be called *Sales Commissions Earned,* or alternatively, *Commissions Revenue.* In the professional practice of lawyers, physicians, dentists, and CAs, the revenue is called *Fees Earned.* A business that sells merchandise rather than services will use the term *Sales* to describe the revenue earned. Another type of revenue is *Interest Earned,* which means the amount received as interest on notes receivable, bank deposits, government bonds, or other securities.

2   Relate the realization (recognition) principle and the matching principle to the recording of revenue and expenses.

When to record revenue: the realization (recognition) principle   When is revenue recorded in the accounting records? For example, assume that on May 24, a real estate company signs a contract to represent a client in selling the client's personal residence. The contract entitles the real estate company to a commission equal to 6% of the selling price, due 30 days after the date of sale. On June 10, the real estate company sells the house at a price of $100,000, thereby earning a $6,000 commission ($100,000 × 6%), to be received on July 10. When should the company record this $6,000 commission revenue — in May, June, or July?

The company should record this revenue on June 10 — the day it *rendered the service* of selling the client's house. As the company will not collect this commission until July, it must also record an account receivable on June 10. In July, when this receivable is collected, the company must not record revenue a second time. Collecting an account receivable increases one asset, Cash, and decreases another asset, Accounts Receivable. Thus, collecting an account receivable *does not increase owner's equity* and does not represent revenue.

Our answer illustrates a generally accepted accounting principle called the *realization (recognition) principle.* This principle states that a business should record revenue at the time *services are rendered to customers* or *goods sold are delivered to customers.*[1] In short, revenue is recorded when it is *earned,* without regard as to when the cash is received.

---

[1] CICA, *CICA Handbook* (Toronto), paragraphs 3400.06–.08, 3400.11.

Expenses

Expenses are the cost of the goods and services used up in the process of earning revenue. Examples include the cost of employees' salaries, advertising, rent, utilities, and the gradual wearing-out (depreciation) of such assets as buildings, automobiles, and office equipment. All these costs are necessary to attract and service customers and thereby earn revenue. Expenses are often called the "costs of doing business," that is, the cost of the various activities necessary to carry on a business.

An expense always causes a decrease in owner's equity. The related changes in the accounting equation can be either (1) a decrease in assets, or (2) an increase in liabilities. An expense reduces assets if payment occurs at the time that the expense is recorded or if payment has been made in advance. If the expense will not be paid until later, as, for example, the purchase of advertising services on account, the recording of the expense will be accompanied by an increase in liabilities.

When to record expenses: the matching principle   A significant relationship exists between revenue and expenses. Expenses are incurred for the *purpose of producing revenue.* In measuring net income for a period, revenue should be offset by *all expenses incurred in producing that revenue.* This concept of offsetting expenses against revenue on a basis of "cause and effect" is called the *matching principle.*

Timing is an important factor in matching (offsetting) revenue with the related expenses. For example, in preparing monthly income statements, it is important to offset this month's expenses against this month's revenue. We should not offset this month's expenses against last month's revenue, because there is no cause and effect relationship between the two.

To illustrate the matching principle, assume that the salaries earned by sales personnel waiting on customers during July are not paid until early August. In which month should these salaries be regarded as an expense? The answer is July, because this is the month in which the sales personnel's services *helped to produce revenue.*

We previously explained that revenue and cash receipts are not one and the same thing. Similarly, expenses and cash payments are not identical. The cash payment for an expense may occur before, after, or in the same period that an expense helps to produce revenue. In deciding when to record an expense, the critical question is *"In what period will this expenditure help to produce revenue?"* not "When will the cash payment occur?"

Expenditures benefiting more than one accounting period   Many expenditures made by a business benefit two or more accounting periods. Fire insurance policies, for example, usually cover a period of 12 months. If a company prepares monthly income statements, a portion of the cost of such a policy should be allocated to insurance expense each month that the policy is in force. In this case, apportionment of the cost of the policy by months is an easy matter. If the 12-month policy costs $240, for example, the insurance expense for each month amounts to $20 (240 cost ÷ 12 months).

Not all transactions can be so precisely divided by accounting periods. The purchase of a building, furniture and fixtures, machinery, a typewriter, or an automobile provides benefits to the business over all the years in which such an asset is used. No one can determine in advance exactly how many years of service will be received from such long-lived assets. Nevertheless, in measuring the net income of a business for a period of one year or less, the accountant must *estimate* what portion of the cost of the building and other long-lived assets is applicable to the current year. Since the allocations of these costs are estimates rather than precise measurements, it follows that income statements should be regarded as useful *approximations* of net income rather than as absolutely exact measurements.

For some expenditures, such as those for advertising or employee training programs, it is not possible to estimate objectively the number of accounting periods over which revenue is likely to be produced. In such cases, generally accepted accounting principles require that the expenditure be charged *immediately to expense.* This treatment is based upon the accounting principles of *objectivity* and *conservatism.* Accountants require *objective evidence* that an expenditure will produce revenue in future periods before they will view the expenditure as creating an asset. When this objective evidence does not exist, they follow the conservative practice of recording the expenditure as an expense. *Conservatism,* in this context, means applying the accounting treatment that results in the *lowest* (most conservative) estimate of net income for the current period.

Withdrawals by the owner

The owner of an unincorporated business (James Roberts, in our continuing example) invests money in the enterprise and devotes all or part of his time to its affairs in the hope that the business will earn a net income. The owner does not earn interest on the money invested nor a salary for personal services. His incentive, rather than interest or salary, is the increase in owner's equity that will result if the business earns a net income.

An owner of an unincorporated business usually makes withdrawals of cash from time to time for personal use. These withdrawals are in anticipation of net income and are not regarded as an expense of the business. The withdrawal of cash by the owner is like an expense in one respect; it reduces the owner's equity. However, expenses are incurred for the purpose of generating revenue, and a withdrawal of cash by the owner does not have this purpose. From time to time the owner may also make additional investments in the business. Investments and withdrawals of cash by the owner may be thought of as exact opposites: investments do not represent revenue; withdrawals do not represent expenses. Investments and withdrawals of cash affect *only balance sheet accounts* and are *not reported in the income statement.*

Since a withdrawal of cash reduces the owner's equity, it *could be* recorded by debiting the owner's capital account (James Roberts, Capital, in our example). However, a clearer record is created if a separate *drawing account* (James Roberts, Drawing) is debited to record all amounts withdrawn.

Debits to the owner's drawing account are required for any of the following transactions:

1 Withdrawals of cash.
2 Withdrawals of other assets. The owner of a clothing store, for example, may, if he or she so chooses, withdraw merchandise for personal use. The amount of the

debit to the drawing account would be for the cost of the goods which were withdrawn.

3 Payment of the owner's personal bills out of company funds.

The disposition of the drawing account when financial statements are prepared will be illustrated later in this chapter.

Debit and credit rules for revenue and expense

3   Apply the rules of debit and credit to revenue and expense transactions.

We have stressed that revenue increases owner's equity and that expenses decrease owner's equity. The debit and credit rules for recording revenue and expenses in the ledger accounts are a natural extension of the rules for recording changes in owner's equity. The rules previously stated for recording increases and decreases in owner's equity were as follows:

> *Increases* in owner's equity are recorded by *credits*.
> *Decreases* in owner's equity are recorded by *debits*.

This rule is now extended to cover revenue and expense accounts:

> Revenue *increases* owner's equity; therefore revenue is recorded by a *credit*.
> Expenses *decrease* owner's equity; therefore expenses are recorded by *debits*.

Ledger accounts for revenue and expenses

During the course of an accounting period, a great many revenue and expense transactions occur in the average business. To classify and summarize these numerous transactions, a separate ledger account is maintained for each major type of revenue and expense. For example, almost every business maintains accounts for advertising expense, telephone expense, and salaries expense. At the end of the period, all the advertising expenses appear as debits in the Advertising Expense account. The debit balance of this account represents the total advertising expense of the period and is listed as one of the expense items in the income statement.

Revenue accounts are usually much less numerous than expense accounts. A small business such as Roberts Real Estate Company in our continuing illustration may have only one or two types of revenue, such as commissions earned from arranging sales of real estate, and fees earned from managing properties in behalf of clients. In a business of this type, the revenue accounts might be called Sales Commissions Earned and Management Fees Earned.

Recording revenue and expense transactions: an illustration

The organization of Roberts Real Estate Company during September has already been described. The illustration is now continued for October, during which the company earned commissions by selling several residences for its clients. Bear in mind that the company does not own any residential property; it merely acts as a broker or agent for clients wishing to sell their houses. A commission of 6% of the sales price of the house is charged for this service. During October the company not only earned commissions but also incurred a number of expenses.

Note that each illustrated transaction that affects an income statement account also affects a balance sheet account. This pattern is consistent with our previous discussion of revenue and expenses. In recording revenue transactions, we debit the assets received and credit a revenue account. In recording expense transactions, we debit an expense account and credit the asset Cash, or a liability account if payment is to be made later. The transactions for October were as follows:

Oct. 1 Paid $360 for publication of newspaper advertising describing various houses offered for sale.

ADVERTISING EXPENSE
INCURRED AND PAID

ANALYSIS	RULE	ENTRY
The cost of advertising is an expense	Expenses decrease the owner's equity and are recorded by debits	Debit: Advertising Expense, $360
The asset Cash was decreased	Decreases in assets are recorded by credits	Credit: Cash, $360

Oct. 6 Earned and collected a commission of $2,250 by selling a residence previously listed by a client.

REVENUE EARNED
AND COLLECTED

ANALYSIS	RULE	ENTRY
The asset Cash was increased	Increases in assets are recorded by debits	Debit: Cash, $2,250
Revenue was earned	Revenue increases the owner's equity and is recorded by a credit	Credit: Sales Commissions Earned, $2,250

Oct. 16 Newspaper advertising was purchased at a price of $270, payment to be made within 30 days.

ADVERTISING EXPENSE
INCURRED; TO BE
PAID LATER

ANALYSIS	RULE	ENTRY
The cost of advertising is an expense	Expenses decrease the owner's equity and are recorded by debits	Debit: Advertising Expense, $270
An account payable, a liability, was incurred	Increases in liabilities are recorded by credits	Credit: Accounts Payable, $270

Oct. 20 A commission of $8,390 was earned by selling a client's residence. The sales agreement provided that the commission would be received in 60 days.

ANALYSIS	RULE	ENTRY
An asset in the form of an account receivable was acquired	Increases in assets are recorded by debits	Debit: Accounts Receivable, $8,390
Revenue was earned	Revenue increases the owner's equity and is recorded by a credit	Credit: Sales Commissions Earned, $8,390

Oct. 31 Paid salaries of $7,100 to employees for services rendered during October.

SALARIES EXPENSE
INCURRED AND PAID

ANALYSIS	RULE	ENTRY
Salaries of employees are an expense	Expenses decrease the owner's equity and are recorded by debits	Debit: Salaries Expense, $7,100
The asset Cash was decreased	Decreases in assets are recorded by credits	Credit: Cash, $7,100

Oct. 31 A telephone bill for October amounting to $144 was received. Payment was required by November 10.

TELEPHONE EXPENSE
INCURRED, TO BE PAID
LATER

ANALYSIS	RULE	ENTRY
The cost of telephone service is an expense	Expenses decrease the owner's equity and are recorded by debits	Debit: Telephone Expense, $144
An account payable, a liability, was incurred	Increases in liabilities are recorded by credits	Credit: Accounts Payable, $144

Oct. 31 Roberts withdrew $1,800 for personal use.

WITHDRAWAL OF CASH
BY OWNER

ANALYSIS	RULE	ENTRY
Withdrawal of assets by the owner decreases the owner's equity	Decreases in owner's equity are recorded by debits	Debit: James Roberts, Drawing, $1,800
The asset Cash was decreased	Decreases in assets are recorded by credits	Credit: Cash, $1,800

The journal entries to record the October transactions are shown on page 96.

General Journal

Page 2

DATE		ACCOUNT TITLES AND EXPLANATION	LP	DEBIT	CREDIT
19__					
Oct.	1	Advertising Expense	70	360	
		Cash	1		360
		Paid for newspaper advertising.			
	6	Cash	1	2,250	
		Sales Commissions Earned	60		2,250
		Earned and collected commission by selling residence for client.			
	16	Advertising Expense	70	270	
		Accounts Payable	32		270
		Purchased newspaper advertising; payable in 30 days.			
	20	Accounts Receivable	4	8,390	
		Sales Commissions Earned	60		8,390
		Earned commission by selling residence for client; commission to be received in 60 days.			
	31	Salaries Expense	72	7,100	
		Cash	1		7,100
		Paid salaries for October.			
	31	Telephone Expense	74	144	
		Accounts Payable	32		144
		To record liability for October telephone service.			
	31	James Roberts, Drawing	51	1,800	
		Cash	1		1,800
		Withdrawal of cash by owner.			

The column headings at the top of the illustrated journal page (*Date, Account Titles and Explanations, LP, Debit,* and *Credit*) are seldom used in practice. They are included here as an instructional guide but will be omitted from some of the later illustrations of journal entries.

The ledger

The ledger of Roberts Real Estate Company after the October transactions have been posted is illustrated beginning on page 97. The accounts appear in financial statement order. To conserve space in this illustration, several ledger accounts appear on a single page; in actual practice, however, each account occupies a separate page in the ledger.

CASH — Account No. 1

DATE		EXPLANATION	REF	DEBIT	CREDIT	BALANCE
19—						
Sept.	1		1	180 000 00		180 000 00
	3		1		141 000 00	39 000 00
	5		1		15 000 00	24 000 00
	20		1	1 500 00		25 500 00
	30		1		3 000 00	22 500 00
Oct.	1		2		360 00	22 140 00
	6		2	2 250 00		24 390 00
	31		2		7 100 00	17 290 00
	31		2		1 800 00	15 490 00

ACCOUNTS RECEIVABLE — Account No. 4

DATE		EXPLANATION	REF	DEBIT	CREDIT	BALANCE
19—						
Sept.	10		1	11 000 00		11 000 00
	20		1		1 500 00	9 500 00
Oct.	20		2	8 390 00		17 890 00

LAND — Account No. 20

DATE		EXPLANATION	REF	DEBIT	CREDIT	BALANCE
19—						
Sept.	3		1	141 000 00		141 000 00
	10		1		11 000 00	130 000 00

BUILDING — Account No. 22

DATE		EXPLANATION	REF	DEBIT	CREDIT	BALANCE
19—						
Sept.	5		1	36 000 00		36 000 00

OFFICE EQUIPMENT					Account No. 25
DATE	EXPLANATION	REF	DEBIT	CREDIT	BALANCE
19—					
Sept. 14		1	5 4 0 0 00		5 4 0 0 00

ACCOUNTS PAYABLE					Account No. 32
DATE	EXPLANATION	REF	DEBIT	CREDIT	BALANCE
19—					
Sept. 5		1		21 0 0 00	21 0 0 00
14		1		5 4 0 00	26 4 0 00
30		1	3 0 0 00		23 4 0 00
Oct. 16		2		2 7 0 00	23 6 7 0 00
31		2		1 4 4 00	23 8 1 4 00

JAMES ROBERTS, CAPITAL					Account No. 50
DATE	EXPLANATION	REF	DEBIT	CREDIT	BALANCE
19—					
Sept. 1		1		1 80 00 00	1 80 00 00

JAMES ROBERTS, DRAWING					Account No. 51
DATE	EXPLANATION	REF	DEBIT	CREDIT	BALANCE
19—					
Oct. 31		2	1 8 0 0 00		1 8 0 0 00

	SALES COMMISSIONS EARNED					Account No. 60
DATE	EXPLANATION	REF	DEBIT	CREDIT	BALANCE	
19—						
Oct. 6		2		2250 00	2250 00	
20		2		8390 00	10640 00	

	ADVERTISING EXPENSE					Account No. 70
DATE	EXPLANATION	REF	DEBIT	CREDIT	BALANCE	
19—						
Oct. 1		2	360 00		360 00	
16		2	270 00		630 00	

	SALARIES EXPENSE					Account No. 72
DATE	EXPLANATION	REF	DEBIT	CREDIT	BALANCE	
19—						
Oct. 31		2	7100 00		7100 00	

	TELEPHONE EXPENSE					Account No. 74
DATE	EXPLANATION	REF	DEBIT	CREDIT	BALANCE	
19—						
Oct. 31		2	144 00		144 00	

Sequence of accounts in the ledger

Accounts are located in the ledger in financial statement order; that is, the balance sheet accounts first (assets, liabilities, and owner's equity) followed by the income statement accounts (revenue and expenses). The sequence of accounts within these five groups is shown by the following list.

BALANCE SHEET ACCOUNTS	INCOME STATEMENT ACCOUNTS

Assets:

01 Cash
02 Marketable securities
03 Notes receivable
04 Accounts receivable
08 Inventory (discussed in
        Chapter 5)
10 Office supplies (and unexpired
        insurance, prepaid rent, and
        other prepaid expenses
        discussed in Chapter 4)
20 Land
22 Buildings
25 Office equipment

Liabilities:

30 Notes payable
32 Accounts payable
34 Salaries payable (and other
        short-term liabilities
        discussed in Chapter 4)

Owner's Equity:

50 Terry Smith, capital
51 Terry Smith, drawing

Revenue:

60 Commissions earned (fees
        earned, rent earned, sales,
        etc.)

Expenses: (No standard sequence
    of listing exists for expense
    accounts.)
70 Advertising
72 Salaries
74 Telephone
76 Depreciation

Why are ledger accounts arranged in financial statement order?

Remember that a trial balance is prepared by listing the ledger account balances shown in the ledger, working from the first ledger account to the last. Therefore, if the accounts are located in the ledger in *financial statement order,* the same sequence will naturally be followed in the trial balance, and this arrangement will make it easier to prepare the balance sheet and income statement from the trial balance. Also, this standard arrangement of accounts will make it easier to locate any account in the ledger.

Notice that an *account number* has been assigned to each account. The number assigned to a particular account depends upon the account's location in the ledger and will not be the same from one company to the next. In a manual accounting system, these account numbers are entered in the *LP* column of the journal to show that an entry has been posted. In a computer-based system, accounts often are identified only by number, thus eliminating the need for the computer operator to enter the entire account title. In addition, the account numbers enable the computer to determine in which financial statement an account should be listed.

The trial balance

A trial balance prepared from the ledger accounts of Roberts Real Estate Company follows:

ROBERTS REAL ESTATE COMPANY
Trial Balance
October 31, 19___

Cash	$ 15,490	
Accounts receivable	17,890	
Land	130,000	
Building	36,000	
Office equipment	5,400	
Accounts payable		$ 23,814
James Roberts, capital		180,000
James Roberts, drawing	1,800	
Sales commissions earned		10,640
Advertising expense	630	
Salaries expense	7,100	
Telephone expense	144	
	$214,454	$214,454

This trial balance proves the equality of the debit and credit entries in the company's ledger. Notice that the trial balance contains income statement accounts as well as balance sheet accounts.

ADJUSTING ENTRY FOR DEPRECIATION EXPENSE

4   Define and record depreciation expense.

The preceding trial balance includes all the expenses arising from the October business transactions, but it does not include any *depreciation expense.* Our definition of expense is the *cost of goods and services used up in the process of obtaining revenue.* Some of the goods used up are purchased in advance and used up gradually over a long period of time. Buildings and office equipment, for example, are used up over a period of years. Each year, a portion of the usefulness of these assets expires, and a portion of their total cost should be recognized as *depreciation expense.* The term *depreciation* means the *systematic allocation of the cost of an asset to expense* over the accounting periods making up the asset's useful life.

Depreciation expense does not require monthly cash outlays; in effect, it is usually *paid in advance* when the related asset is originally acquired. Nevertheless, depreciation is an inevitable and continuing expense. Failure to record depreciation would result in *understating* total expenses of the period and consequently *overstating* the net income.

Building   The office building purchased by Roberts Real Estate Company at a cost of $36,000 is estimated to have a useful life of 20 years. The purpose of the $36,000 expenditure was to provide a place in which to carry on the business and thereby to obtain revenue. After 20 years of use the building is expected to be worthless and the original cost of $36,000 will have been entirely consumed. In effect, the company has purchased 20 years of "housing services" at a total cost of $36,000. A portion of this cost expires during each year of use of the building. If we assume that each year's operations should bear an equal share of the total cost (straight-line depreciation), the annual depreciation expense will amount to $1/20$ of $36,000, or $1,800. On a monthly basis, depreciation expense is $150 ($36,000 cost ÷ 240 months). There are alternative methods of spreading the cost of a depreciable asset over its useful life, some of which will be considered in Chapter 10.

The journal entry to record depreciation of the building during October is as shown below:

RECORDING DEPRECIATION OF THE BUILDING

General Journal   Page 2

DATE		ACCOUNT TITLES AND EXPLANATION	LP	DEBIT	CREDIT
19__					
Oct	31	Depreciation Expense: Building	76	150	
		Accumulated Depreciation: Building .	23		150
		To record depreciation for October.			
		Cost of $36,000 ÷ 240 months = $150			
		a month.			

The depreciation expense account will appear in the income statement for October along with the other expenses of salaries, advertising, and telephone. The Accumulated Depreciation: Building account will appear in the balance sheet as a deduction from the Building account, as shown by the following illustration of a partial balance sheet:

SHOWING ACCUMULATED DEPRECIATION IN THE BALANCE SHEET

ROBERTS REAL ESTATE COMPANY
Partial Balance Sheet
October 31, 19__

Building (at cost) $36,000
Less: Accumulated depreciation 150 $35,850

The end result of crediting the Accumulated Depreciation: Building account is much the same as if the credit had been made to the Building account; that is, the net amount shown on the balance sheet for the building is reduced from $36,000 to $35,850. Although the credit side of a depreciation entry *could* be made directly to the asset account, it is customary and more efficient to record such credits in a separate account entitled Accumulated Depreciation. The original cost of the asset and the total amount of depreciation recorded over the years can more easily be determined from the ledger when separate accounts are maintained for the asset and for the accumulated depreciation.

Accumulated Depreciation: Building is an example of a *contra-asset account,* because it has a credit balance and is offset against an asset account (Building) to produce the proper balance sheet amount for the asset.

Office equipment   Depreciation on the office equipment of Roberts Real Estate Company must also be recorded at the end of October. This equipment cost $5,400 and is assumed to have a useful life of 10 years. Monthly depreciation expense on the straight-line basis is, therefore, $45, computed by dividing the cost of $5,400 by the useful life of 120 months. The journal entry is as follows:

RECORDING
DEPRECIATION OF
OFFICE EQUIPMENT

		General Journal			Page 2
DATE		ACCOUNT TITLES AND EXPLANATION	LP	DEBIT	CREDIT
19__					
Oct	31	Depreciation Expense: Office Equipment .	78	45	
		Accumulated Depreciation:			
		Office Equipment	26		45
		To record depreciation for October. Cost			
		of $5,400 ÷ 120 months = $45 a month.			

No depreciation was recorded on the building and office equipment for September, the month in which these assets were acquired, because regular operations did not begin until October. Generally, depreciation is not recognized until the business begins active operation and the assets are *placed in use.*

The journal entry by which depreciation is recorded at the end of the month is called an *adjusting entry.* The adjustment of certain asset accounts and related expense accounts is a necessary step at the end of each accounting period so that the information presented in the financial statements will be as accurate and complete as possible. In the next chapter, adjusting entries will be shown for some items in addition to depreciation.

The adjusted trial balance

After all the necessary adjusting entries have been journalized and posted, an *adjusted trial balance* is prepared to prove that the ledger is still in balance. It also provides a complete listing of the account balances to be used in preparing the financial statements. The following adjusted trial balance differs from the trial balance shown on page 101 because it includes accounts for depreciation expense and accumulated depreciation.

ADJUSTED TRIAL
BALANCE

ROBERTS REAL ESTATE COMPANY
Adjusted Trial Balance
October 31, 19__

Cash	$ 15,490	
Accounts receivable	17,890	
Land	130,000	
Building	36,000	
Accumulated depreciation: building		$ 150
Office equipment	5,400	
Accumulated depreciation: office equipment		45
Accounts payable		23,814
James Roberts, capital		180,000
James Roberts, drawing	1,800	
Sales commissions earned		10,640
Advertising expense	630	
Salaries expense	7,100	
Telephone expense	144	
Depreciation expense: building	150	
Depreciation expense: office equipment	45	
	$214,649	$214,649

FINANCIAL STATEMENTS

Now that Roberts Real Estate Company has been operating for a month, managers and outside parties will want to know more about the company than just its financial position. They will want to know the results of operations — whether the month's activities have been profitable or unprofitable. To provide this additional information, we will prepare a more complete set of financial statements, consisting of an income statement and a balance sheet.[2]

The income statement

5   Prepare an income statement and explain its relationship to the balance sheet.

When we measure the net income earned by a business we are measuring its economic performance — its success or failure as a business enterprise. The owner, managers, and major creditors are anxious to see the latest available income statement and thereby to judge how well the company is doing. If the business is organized as a corporation, the shareholders and prospective investors also will be keenly interested in each successive income statement. The October income statement for Roberts Real Estate Company appears as follows:

INCOME STATEMENT SHOWING RESULTS OF OPERATIONS FOR OCTOBER

ROBERTS REAL ESTATE COMPANY
Income Statement
For the Month Ended October 31, 19___

Revenue:		
Sales commissions earned		$10,640
Expenses:		
Advertising expense	$ 630	
Salaries expense	7,100	
Telephone expense	144	
Depreciation expense: building	150	
Depreciation expense: office equipment	45	8,069
Net Income		$ 2,571

This income statement consists of the last six accounts in the adjusted trial balance. It shows that the revenue during October exceeded the expenses of the month, thus producing a net income of $2,571. Bear in mind, however, that our measurement of net income is not absolutely accurate or precise, because of the assumptions and estimates in the accounting process.

An income statement has certain limitations. Remember that the amounts shown for depreciation expense are based upon *estimates* of the useful lives of the company's building and office equipment. Also, the income statement includes only those events that have been *evidenced by business transactions.* Perhaps during October, Roberts Real Estate Company has made contact with many people who are right on the verge of buying or selling homes. Good business contacts are an important step toward profitable operations. However, such contacts are not reflected in the income statement because their value cannot be measured *objectively* until actual transac-

---

[2] A complete set of financial statements also includes a statement of changes in financial position, which will be discussed in Chapter 19 after further discussion of corporation accounting.

tions take place. Despite these limitations, the income statement is of vital importance and indicates that the new business has been profitable during its first month of operation.

Alternative titles for the income statement include *earnings statement* (or *statement of earnings*), *statement of operations,* and *profit and loss statement.* However, *income statement and statement of earnings are* the most popular terms for this important financial statement.[3] In summary, we can say that an income statement is used to summarize the *operating results* of a business by matching the revenue earned during a given time period with the expenses incurred in obtaining that revenue.

The balance sheet

In preparing a balance sheet for Roberts Real Estate at October 31, we can obtain the balances of the asset, liability, and owner's equity accounts from the adjusted trial balance on page 103. Previous illustrations of balance sheets have been arranged in *account form,* that is, with the assets on the left side of the page and the liabilities and owner's equity on the right side. The following balance sheet is shown in *report form,* that is, with the liabilities and owner's equity sections listed below rather than to the right of the asset section. Both the account form and the report form are widely used, with the latter being more popular.[4]

BALANCE SHEET AT
OCTOBER 31:
REPORT FORM

ROBERTS REAL ESTATE COMPANY
Balance Sheet
October 31, 19___

ASSETS

Cash		$ 15,490
Accounts receivable		17,890
Land		130,000
Building	$36,000	
Less: Accumulated depreciation	150	35,850
Office equipment	$ 5,400	
Less: Accumulated depreciation	45	5,355
Total assets		$204,585

LIABILITIES & OWNER'S EQUITY

Liabilities		
Accounts payable		$ 23,814
Owner's equity:		
James Roberts, capital, Oct. 1, 19___	$180,000	
Net income for October	2,571	
Subtotal	$182,571	
Less: Withdrawals	1,800	
James Roberts, capital, Oct. 31, 19___		180,771
Total liabilities & owner's equity		$204,585

[3] CICA, *Financial Reporting in Canada,* Seventeenth Edition (Toronto, 1987), p. 153.

[4] Ibid., p. 83.

Alternative titles for the balance sheet include *statement of financial position* and *statement of financial condition*. However, the title "balance sheet" is by far the most popular.[5]

Net income — a change in owner's equity

A set of financial statements becomes easier to understand if we recognize how the income statement and balance sheet are related. This relationship is illustrated in the owner's equity section of the Roberts Real Estate Company balance sheet. The original owner's equity of $180,000 was *increased* by reason of the $2,571 net income earned during October, making a total owner's equity of $182,571. This equity was *decreased*, however, by the owner's withdrawal of $1,800 in cash at the end of October, leaving a final balance of $180,771.

We have now seen the two common ways in which owner's equity may be increased: (1) investments of cash or other assets by the owner, and (2) operating the business at a net income. There also are two ways in which the owner's equity may be decreased: (1) withdrawal of assets by the owner, and (2) operating the business at a net loss.

Preparing the owner's equity section of a balance sheet   For a balance sheet to "balance," the amount shown as owner's equity must be the owner's equity at the *end* of the accounting period. The practice of also showing owner's equity at the beginning of the period, along with the changes in owner's equity, is an optional procedure. It is equally acceptable to show only the final amount of the owner's equity ($180,771 in our example).

In the assignment material following Chapter 3, we will ask you to show the changes in owner's equity in the equity section of the balance sheet. Our purpose is to stress that net income is *an increase in owner's equity,* not an asset owned by the business. In later chapters, however, we will adopt the shorter practice of showing in our balance sheet only the amount of owner's equity at the end of the period.

6   Prepare closing entries.

CLOSING THE ACCOUNTS

The accounts for revenue, expenses, and drawings are *temporary proprietorship accounts* used during the accounting period to classify and accumulate certain changes affecting the owner's equity. At the end of the period, we want to transfer the net effect of these various increases and decreases into the owner's capital account. We also want to reduce the balances of the temporary proprietorship accounts to *zero,* so that these accounts will be ready for measuring the revenue, expenses, and drawings of the next accounting period. These objectives are accomplished by the use of *closing entries.*

Revenue and expense accounts are *closed* at the end of each accounting period by *transferring their balances* to a summary account called *Income Summary.* When the credit balances of the revenue accounts and the debit balances of the expense

---

[5] Ibid.

accounts have been transferred into one summary account, the balance of this Income Summary will be the *net income* or *net loss* for the period. If the revenue (credit balances) exceeds the expenses (debit balances), the Income Summary account will have a credit balance representing net income. Conversely, if expenses exceed revenue, the Income Summary will have a debit balance representing net loss. This is consistent with the rule that increases in owner's equity are recorded by credits and decreases are recorded by debits.

As previously explained, all debits and credits in the ledger are posted from the journal; therefore, the closing of revenue and expense accounts requires the making of journal entries and the. posting of these journal entries to ledger accounts. A journal entry made for the purpose of closing a revenue or expense account by transferring its balance to the Income Summary account is called a *closing entry.*

A principal purpose of the year-end process of closing the revenue and expense accounts is to reduce their balances to zero. Since the revenue and expense accounts provide information for the income statement of *a given accounting period,* it is essential that these accounts have *zero balances* at the beginning of each new period. Closing the accounts "wipes the slate clean" and prepares the accounts for recording the revenue and expenses of the next accounting period.

It is common practice to close the accounts only once a year, but for illustration, we shall now demonstrate the closing of the accounts of Roberts Real Estate Company at October 31 after one month's operation.

Closing entries for revenue accounts   Revenue accounts have credit balances. Closing a revenue account, therefore, means transferring its credit balance to the Income Summary account. This transfer is accomplished by a journal entry debiting the revenue account in an amount equal to its credit balance, with an offsetting credit to the Income Summary account. The debit portion of this closing entry returns the balance of the revenue account to zero; the credit portion transfers the former balance of the revenue account into the Income Summary account. The only revenue account of Roberts Real Estate Company is Sales Commission Earned, which had a credit balance of $10,640 at October 31. The closing entry is as follows:

CLOSING A REVENUE
ACCOUNT

General Journal   Page 3

DATE		ACCOUNT TITLES AND EXPLANATION	LP	DEBIT	CREDIT
19__ Oct	31	Sales Commissions Earned	60	10,640	
		Income Summary	53		10,640
		To close the Sales Commissions Earned			
		account.			

After this closing entry has been posted, the two accounts affected will appear as shown at the top of page 108. A few details of account structure have been omitted to simplify the illustration; a directional arrow has been added to show the transfer of the $10,640 balance of the revenue account into the Income Summary account.

			Sales Commissions Earned		60				Income Summary		53

DATE		EXP.	REF	DEBIT	CREDIT	BALANCE	DATE		EXP.	REF	DEBIT	CREDIT	BALANCE
Oct	6		2		2,250	2,250	Oct	31		3		10,640	10,640
	20		2		8,390	10,640							
	31	To close	3	10,640		-0-							

Closing entries for expense accounts

Expense accounts have debit balances. Closing an expense account means transferring its debit balance to the Income Summary account. The journal entry to close an expense account, therefore, consists of a credit to the expense account in an amount equal to its debit balance, with an offsetting debit to the Income Summary account.

There are five expense accounts in the ledger of Roberts Real Estate Company. Five separate journal entries could be made to close these five expense accounts, but the use of one *compound journal entry* is an easier, time-saving method of closing all five expense accounts. A compound journal entry is an entry that includes debits to more than one account or credits to more than one account.

CLOSING THE VARIOUS EXPENSE ACCOUNTS BY USE OF A COMPOUND JOURNAL ENTRY

		General Journal			Page 3
DATE		ACCOUNT TITLES AND EXPLANATION	LP	DEBIT	CREDIT
19__					
Oct	31	Income Summary	53	8,069	
		Advertising Expense	70		630
		Salaries Expense	72		7,100
		Telephone Expense	74		144
		Depreciation Expense: Building	76		150
		Depreciation Expense:			
		Office Equipment	78		45
		To close the expense accounts.			

After this closing entry has been posted, the Income Summary account has a credit balance of $2,571, and the five expense accounts have zero balances, as shown on page 109.

Closing the Income Summary account

The five expense accounts have now been closed and the total amount of $8,069 formerly contained in these accounts appears in the debit column of the Income Summary account. The commissions of $10,640 earned during October appear in the credit column of the Income Summary account. Since the credit entry of $10,640 representing October revenue is larger than the debit of $8,069 representing October expenses, the account has a credit balance of $2,571 — the net income for October.

INCOME SUMMARY   Account No. 53

DATE		EXPLANATION	REF	DEBIT	CREDIT	BALANCE
19__						
Oct	31		3		10,640	10,640
	31		3	8,069		2,571

ADVERTISING EXPENSE   Account No. 70

DATE		EXPLANATION	REF	DEBIT	CREDIT	BALANCE
19__						
Oct	2		2	360		360
	16		2	270		630
	31	To close	3		630	-0-

SALARIES EXPENSE   Account No. 72

DATE		EXPLANATION	REF	DEBIT	CREDIT	BALANCE
19__						
Oct	31		2	7,100		7,100
	31	To close	3		7,100	-0-

TELEPHONE EXPENSE   Account No. 74

DATE		EXPLANATION	REF	DEBIT	CREDIT	BALANCE
19__						
Oct	31		2	144		144
	31	To close	3		144	-0-

DEPRECIATION EXPENSE: BUILDING   Account No. 76

DATE		EXPLANATION	REF	DEBIT	CREDIT	BALANCE
19__						
Oct	31		2	150		150
	31	To close	3		150	-0-

DEPRECIATION EXPENSE: OFFICE EQUIPMENT   Account No. 78

DATE		EXPLANATION	REF	DEBIT	CREDIT	BALANCE
19__						
Oct	31		2	45		45
	31	To close	3		45	-0-

The net income of $2,571 earned during October causes the owner's equity to increase. The ***credit*** balance of the Income Summary account is, therefore, transferred to the owner's capital account by the following closing entry.

	General Journal			Page 3

DATE		ACCOUNT TITLES AND EXPLANATION	LP	DEBIT	CREDIT
19__ Oct	31	Income Summary	53	2,571	
		James Roberts, Capital	50		2,571
		To close the Income Summary account for October by transferring the net income to the owner's capital account.			

After this closing entry has been posted, the Income Summary account has a zero balance, and the net income for October will appear as an increase (or credit entry) in the owner's capital account as shown below:

		INCOME SUMMARY			Account No. 53	
19__ Oct	31	Revenue	3		10,640	10,640
	31	Expenses	3	8,069		2,571
	31	To close	3	2,571		-0-

		JAMES ROBERTS, CAPITAL			Account No. 50	
19__ Sept	1	Investment by owner	1		180,000	180,000
Oct	31	Net income for October	3		2,571	182,571

In our illustration the business has operated profitably with revenue in excess of expenses. Not every business is so fortunate: if the expenses of a business are larger than its revenue, the Income Summary account will have a ***debit*** balance, representing a ***net loss*** for the accounting period. In that case, the closing of the Income Summary account requires a debit to the owner's capital account and an offsetting credit to the Income Summary account. The owner's equity will, of course, be reduced by the amount of the loss debited to the capital account.

Note that the Income Summary account is used only at the end of the period when the accounts are being closed. The Income Summary account has no entries and no balance except during the process of closing the accounts at the end of the accounting period.

Closing the owner's drawing account

As explained earlier in this chapter, withdrawals of cash or other assets by the owner are not considered as an expense of the business and, therefore, are not a factor in determining the net income for the period. Since drawings by the owner do not constitute an expense, the owner's drawing account is closed not into the Income Summary account but directly to the owner's capital account. The following journal entry serves to close the drawing account in the ledger of Roberts Real Estate Company at October 31.

DRAWING ACCOUNT IS CLOSED TO OWNER'S CAPITAL ACCOUNT

General Journal   Page 3

DATE		ACCOUNT TITLES AND EXPLANATION	LP	DEBIT	CREDIT
19__					
Oct	31	James Roberts, Capital	50	1,800	
		James Roberts, Drawing	51		1,800
		To close the owner's drawing account.			

After this closing entry has been posted, the drawing account will have a zero balance, and the amount withdrawn by Roberts during October will appear as a deduction or debit entry in the capital account, as shown below:

ONE ACCOUNT NOW SHOWS TOTAL EQUITY OF OWNER

JAMES ROBERTS, DRAWING   Account No. 51

19__					
Oct	31	Withdrawal	2	1,800	1,800
	31	To close	3		1,800	-0-

JAMES ROBERTS, CAPITAL   Account No. 50

19__						
Sept	1	Investment by owner	1		180,000	180,000
Oct	31	Net income for October	3		2,571	182,571
	31	From owner's drawing account	3	1,800		180,771

Summary of the closing process

Let us now summarize the process of closing the accounts.

1 Close the various *revenue* accounts by transferring their balances into the Income Summary account.
2 Close the various *expense* accounts by transferring their balances into the Income Summary account.
3 Close the *Income Summary account* by transferring its balance into the owner's capital account.
4 Close the owner's *drawing* account into the owner's capital account. (The balance of the owner's capital account in the ledger will now be the same as the amount of owner's equity appearing in the balance sheet.)

The closing of the accounts may be illustrated graphically by use of T accounts as follows:

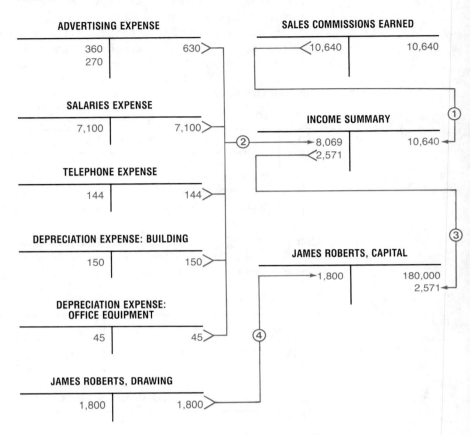

After-closing trial balance

After the revenue and expense accounts have been closed, it is desirable to prepare an *after-closing trial balance,* which will consist of balance sheet accounts *only.* There is always the possibility that an error in posting the closing entries may have upset the equality of debits and credits in the ledger. The after-closing trial balance is prepared from the ledger. It gives assurance that the accounts are in balance and ready for the recording of the transactions of the new accounting period. The after-closing trial balance of Roberts Real Estate Company is shown at the top of page 113.

Sequence of procedures in the accounting cycle

7   Describe the sequence of procedures in the accounting cycle.

The accounting procedures described to this point may be summarized in eight steps, as follows:

1   **Journalize transactions**   Enter all transactions in the general journal, thus creating a chronological record of events.

ROBERTS REAL ESTATE COMPANY
After-Closing Trial Balance
October 31, 19___

Cash	$ 15,490	
Accounts receivable	17,890	
Land	130,000	
Building	36,000	
Accumulated depreciation: building		$ 150
Office equipment	5,400	
Accumulated depreciation: office equipment		45
Accounts payable		23,814
James Roberts, capital		180,771
	$204,780	$204,780

2 Post to ledger accounts Post debits and credits from the general journal to the proper ledger accounts, thus creating a record classified by accounts.

3 Prepare a trial balance Prove the equality of debits and credits in the ledger.

4 Make end-of-period adjustments Draft adjusting entries in the general journal, and post to ledger accounts. Thus far we have illustrated only one type of adjustment: the recording of depreciation at the end of the period.

5 Prepare an adjusted trial balance Prove again the equality of debits and credits in the ledger.

6 Prepare financial statements An income statement is needed to show the results of operation for the period. A balance sheet is needed to show the financial position of the business at the end of the period.

7 Journalize and post closing entries The closing entries clear the revenue, expense, and drawing accounts, making them ready for recording the events of the next accounting period. The closing entries also transfer the net income or loss of the completed period to the owner's capital account.

8 Prepare an after-closing trial balance This step ensures that the ledger remains in balance after posting of the closing entries.

These eight procedures represent a complete accounting cycle. In Chapter 4, however, we shall see that the preparation of a *work sheet* will enable us to consolidate several of these procedures.

Accounting procedures in a computer-based system

The sequence of procedures performed in computer-based systems is essentially the same as in manual systems. Of course, the computer is programmed to perform a number of these steps automatically. In the preceding list, procedures 1 and 4 both involve the analysis of business transactions and judgmental decisions as to accounts to be debited and credited and the dollar amounts. These two steps in the accounting cycle require human judgment, regardless of whether the data is processed manually or by computer. As mentioned in Chapter 2, a computer-based system may call for recording transactions first in a data base, rather than in a journal. The computer then arranges the data into the format of journal entries, ledger accounts, trial balances, and financial statements.

Procedures such as posting and the preparation of trial balances and financial statements merely involve the *rearrangement* of recorded data and may easily be performed by computer. The preparation of closing entries also is a mechanical task, involving the transfer of recorded data from one ledger account to another. Thus, closing entries may be performed automatically in a computer-based system.

Accrual basis of accounting versus cash basis of accounting

8   Distinguish between the accrual basis and the cash basis of accounting.

A business that recognizes revenue in the period in which it is earned and that deducts in the same period the expenses incurred in generating this revenue is using the *accrual basis of accounting.* Because the accrual basis stresses the matching or offsetting of revenue and related expenses, it gives a realistic picture of the profitability of a business in each accounting period.

The alternative to the accrual basis of accounting is the *cash basis*. Under cash basis accounting, revenue is not recorded until received in cash; expenses are assigned to the period in which cash payment is made. Most business concerns use the accrual method of accounting, but individuals and some professionals (such as physicians and lawyers) maintain their accounting records on a cash basis.

The cash basis of accounting does not give a good picture of profitability. For example, it ignores uncollected revenue that has been earned and expenses that have been incurred but not paid. Throughout this book we shall be working with the accrual basis of accounting, except for that portion of Chapter 18 dealing with the income tax returns of individuals.

END-OF-CHAPTER REVIEW

SUMMARY OF CHAPTER LEARNING OBJECTIVES

1 Explain the nature of net income, revenue, and expenses.

Net income is the increase in owner's equity that results from the profitable operation of a business during an accounting period. The net income of an accounting period also is equal to revenue minus expenses. Revenue is the price of goods sold or services rendered during the accounting period. Expenses are the cost of goods or services used up in the process of earning revenue.

2 Relate the realization (recognition) principle and the matching principle to the recording of revenue and expenses.

Revenue should be recorded in the accounting records when it is realized. In this context, "realized" means "earned." In short, revenue is recognized when goods are sold or when services are rendered to customers. The matching principle indicates that expenses should be offset against revenue on a basis of cause and effect. That is, an expense should be recorded in the accounting records when the related good or service is consumed in the process of earning revenue.

3 Apply the rules of debit and credit to revenue and expense transactions.

Revenue increases owner's equity; therefore, revenue is recorded by a credit. Expenses decrease owner's equity; therefore, expenses are recorded by debits.

4 Define and record depreciation expense.

The term *depreciation* refers to the systematic allocation of the cost of a long-lived asset (such as equipment or a building) to expense over the asset's useful life. Depreciation is recorded by an entry debiting *Depreciation Expense* and crediting the contra-asset account, *Accumulated Depreciation.*

5 Prepare an income statement and explain its relationship to the balance sheet.

An income statement shows the revenue and expenses of a business during a specified accounting period. Expenses are offset (match) against revenue to produce a measurement of net income for the period. Net income, as measured in the income statement, explains an important change in the amount of owner's equity from one balance sheet to the next. (In addition to net income, the amount of owner's equity may be affected by withdrawals or additional investments by the owner.)

6 Prepare closing entries.

Closing entries serve two basic purposes. The first is to return the balances of the temporary proprietorship accounts (revenue, expenses, and drawing) to zero so that they may be used to measure the activities of the next accounting period. The second purpose of closing entries is to update the balance of the owner's capital account for the changes in owner's equity originally recorded in the temporary proprietorship accounts. Four closing entries generally are needed: (1) close the revenue accounts into the Income Summary account, (2) close the expense accounts into the Income Summary account, (3) close the balance of the Income Summary account (representing net income or net loss) into the owner's capital account, and (4) close the owner's drawing account into the owner's capital account.

7 Describe the sequence of procedures in the accounting cycle.

The accounting procedures in the accounting cycle may be summarized as follows: (1) journalize transactions, (2) post to ledger accounts, (3) prepare a trial balance, (4) make end-of-period adjustments, (5) prepare an adjusted trial balance, (6) prepare financial statements, (7) journalize and post closing entries, and (8) prepare an after-closing trial balance.

8 Distinguish between the accrual basis and the cash basis of accounting.

Under accrual accounting, revenue is recognized when it is earned and expenses are recognized in the period in which they are incurred in the effort to generate revenue. Under the cash basis, on the other hand, revenue is recognized when cash is received and expenses are recognized when cash payments are made. The accrual basis gives a better measurement of profitability than does the cash basis, because the accrual basis associates the recognition of income with the underlying earning process.

KEY TERMS INTRODUCED OR EMPHASIZED IN CHAPTER 3

Accounting period The span of time covered by an income statement. One year is the accounting period for much financial reporting, but financial statements are also prepared by companies for each quarter of the year and also for each month.

Accrual basis of accounting Calls for recording revenue in the period in which it is earned and recording expenses in the period in which they are incurred. The effect of events on the business is recognized as services are rendered or consumed rather than when cash is received or paid.

Accumulated depreciation A contra-asset shown as a deduction from the related asset account in the balance sheet. Depreciation taken throughout the useful life of an asset is accumulated in this account.

Adjusted trial balance A listing of all ledger account balances after the amounts have been changed to include the adjusting entries made at the end of the period.

Adjusting entries Entries required at the end of the period to update the accounts before financial statements are prepared. Adjusting entries serve to apportion transactions properly between the accounting periods affected and to record any revenue earned or expenses incurred that have not been recorded prior to the end of the period.

After-closing trial balance A trial balance prepared after all closing entries have been made and posted. Consists only of accounts for assets, liabilities, and owner's equity.

Cash basis of accounting Revenue is recorded when received in cash and expenses are recorded in the period in which cash payment is made. Does not lead to a logical measurement of income.

Closing entries Journal entries made at the end of the period for the purpose of closing temporary proprietorship accounts (revenue, expense, and drawing accounts) and transferring balances to the owner's capital account.

Conservatism The traditional accounting practice of resolving uncertainty by choosing the solution that leads to the lower (more conservative) amount of income being recognized in the current accounting period. This concept is designed to avoid overstatement of financial strength or earnings.

Contra-asset account An account with a credit balance that is offset against or deducted from an asset account to produce the proper balance sheet amount for the asset.

Depreciation The systematic allocation of the cost of an asset to expense during the periods of its useful life.

Drawing account The account used to record the withdrawals of cash or other assets by the owner. Closed at the end of the period by transferring its balance to the owner's capital account.

Expenses The cost of the goods and services used up in the process of obtaining revenue.

Fiscal year Any 12-month accounting period adopted by a business.

Income statement A report used to evaluate the performance of a business by matching its revenue and related expenses for a particular accounting period. Shows the net income or net loss.

Income Summary account The summary account in the ledger to which revenue and expense accounts are closed at the end of the period. The balance (credit balance for a net income, debit balance for a net loss) is transferred to the owner's capital account.

Matching principle The revenue earned during an accounting period is matched (offset) with the expenses incurred in generating this revenue.

Net income An increase in owner's equity resulting from profitable operations. Also, the excess of revenue earned over the related expenses for a given period.

Realization (recognition) principle The generally accepted accounting principle that determines when revenue should be recorded in the accounting records. Revenue is realized when services are rendered to customers or when goods sold are delivered to customers.

Revenue The price of goods sold and services rendered by a business.

DEMONSTRATION PROBLEM FOR YOUR REVIEW

Lane Insurance Agency began business on April 1, 19___. Assume that the accounts are closed and financial statements prepared each month. The company occupies rented office space but owns office equipment estimated to have a useful life of 10 years from date of acquisition, April 1. The trial balance for Lane Insurance Agency at June 30, 19___, is shown below.

Cash	$ 1,275	
Accounts receivable	605	
Office equipment	6,000	
Accumulated depreciation: office equipment		$ 100
Accounts payable		1,260
Richard Lane, capital, May 31, 19___		6,500
Richard Lane, drawing	1,000	
Commissions earned		3,710
Advertising expense	500	
Rent expense	370	
Telephone expense	120	
Salaries expense	1,700	
	$11,570	$11,570

Instructions

a Prepare the adjusting journal entry to record depreciation of the office equipment for the month of June.

b Prepare an adjusted trial balance at June 30, 19___.

c Prepare an income statement for the month ended June 30, 19___, and a balance sheet in report form at June 30, 19___. In the owner's equity section of the balance sheet, show the changes in the owner's capital account during the period.

SOLUTION TO DEMONSTRATION PROBLEM

a Adjusting journal entry:

Depreciation Expense: Office Equipment	50	
Accumulated Depreciation: Office Equipment		50

To record depreciation for June ($6,000 ÷ 120 months).

b

LANE INSURANCE AGENCY
Adjusted Trial Balance
June 30, 19___

Cash	$ 1,275	
Accounts receivable	605	
Office equipment	6,000	
Accumulated depreciation: office equipment		$ 150
Accounts payable		1,260
Richard Lane, capital		6,500
Richard Lane, drawings	1,000	
Commissions earned		3,710
Advertising expense	500	
Rent expense	370	
Telephone expense	120	
Salaries expense	1,700	
Depreciation expense: office equipment	50	
	$11,620	$11,620

c

LANE INSURANCE AGENCY
Income Statement
For the Month Ended June 30, 19___

Commissions earned		$3,710
Expenses:		
Advertising expense	500	
Rent expense	370	
Telephone expense	120	
Salaries expense	1,700	
Depreciation expense: office equipment	50	2,740
Net income		$ 970

LANE INSURANCE AGENCY
Balance Sheet
June 30, 19___

ASSETS

Cash		$1,275
Accounts receivable		605
Office equipment	$6,000	
Less: Accumulated depreciation	150	5,850
Total assets		$7,730

LIABILITIES & OWNER'S EQUITY

Liabilities:		
Accounts payable		$1,260
Owner's equity:		
Richard Lane, capital, May 31, 19___	$6,500	
Net income for June	970	
Subtotal	$7,470	
Less: Withdrawals	1,000	
Richard Lane, capital, June 30, 19___		6,470
Total liabilities & owner's equity		$7,730

ASSIGNMENT MATERIAL

REVIEW QUESTIONS

1 What is the meaning of the term *revenue*? Does the receipt of cash by a business indicate that revenue has been earned? Explain.

2 What is the meaning of the term *expenses*? Does the payment of cash by a business indicate that an expense has been incurred? Explain.

3 Explain the effect of operating profitably upon the *balance sheet* of a business entity.

4 A service enterprise performs services in the amount of $500 for a customer in May and receives payment in June. In which month is the $500 of revenue recognized? What is the journal entry to be made in May and the entry to be made in June?

5 When do accountants consider revenue to be realized? What basic question about recording revenue in accounting records is answered by the *realization (recognition) principle?*

6 Late in March, Classic Auto Painters purchased paint on account, with payment due in 60 days. The company used the paint to paint customers' cars during the first three weeks of April. Late in May, the company paid the paint store from which the paint had been purchased. In which month should Classic Auto Painters recognize the cost of this paint as expense? What generally accepted accounting principle determines the answer to this question?

7 John Haley, owner of Haley Company, regularly withdraws cash from the business. Should these drawings by the owner be considered as an expense of the business? Explain.

8 Explain the rules of debit and credit with respect to transactions recorded in revenue and expense accounts.

9 Supply the appropriate term (debit or credit) to complete the following statements.
   a The owner's equity account, Income Summary account, and revenue accounts are increased by _____ entries.
   b Asset accounts and expense accounts are increased by _____ entries.
   c Liability accounts and owner's equity accounts are decreased by _____ entries.

10 Supply the appropriate term (debit or credit) to complete the following statements.
   a When a business is operating *profitably*, the journal entry to close the Income Summary account will consist of a _____ to that account and a _____ to the owner's capital account.
   b When a business is operating at a *loss*, the journal entry to close the Income Summary account will consist of a _____ to that account and a _____ to the owner's capital account.
   c The journal entry to close the owner's drawing account consists of a _____ to that account and a _____ to the owner's capital account.

11 How does *depreciation expense* differ from other operating expenses?

12 Assume that a business acquires a delivery truck at a cost of $9,600. Estimated life of the truck is four years. State the amount of depreciation expense per year and per month. Give the adjusting entry to record depreciation on the truck at the end of the first month, and explain where the accounts involved would appear in the financial statements.

13 All ledger accounts belong in one of the following five groups: asset, liability, owner's equity, revenue, and expense. For each of the following accounts, state the group in which it belongs. Also indicate whether the normal balance would be a debit or credit.
   a Fees Earned
   b Notes Payable
   c Telephone Expense
   d Susan Nelson, Drawing
   e Building
   f Depreciation Expense
   g Accumulated Depreciation: Building

14 Does a well-prepared income statement provide an exact measurement of net income for the period, or does it represent merely an approximation of net income? Explain.

15 Which of the following accounts should be closed by a debit to Income Summary and a credit to the account listed?

Donald Harris, Drawing   Salaries Expense
Fees Earned   Accounts Payable
Advertising Expense   Depreciation Expense
Accounts Receivable   Accumulated Depreciation

16 Supply the appropriate terms to complete the following statements. _____ and _____ accounts are closed at the end of each accounting period by transferring their balances to a summary account called _____ _____. A _____ balance in this summary account represents net income for the period; a _____ balance represents a net loss for the period.

17 Which of the ten accounts listed below are affected by closing entries at the end of the accounting period?

Cash   Patricia Miller, Drawing
Fees Earned   Patricia Miller, Capital
Income Summary   Accumulated Depreciation
Accounts Payable   Accounts Receivable
Telephone Expense   Depreciation Expense

18 How does the accrual basis of accounting differ from the cash basis of accounting? Which gives a more accurate picture of the profitability of a business? Explain.

EXERCISES

Exercise 3-1
Accounting terminology

Listed below are twelve technical accounting terms introduced in this chapter:

Accounting period   Depreciation   Net income
Accrual basis of accounting Expenses   Realization
Cash basis of accounting   Income statement   Revenue
Closing entries   Matching   Withdrawals

Each of the following statements may (or may not) describe one of these technical terms. For each statement, indicate the accounting term described, or answer ''None'' if the statement does not correctly describe any of the terms.

a The generally accepted accounting principle used in determining when to recognize revenue.

b Recognizing revenue when it is earned and expenses when the related goods or services are used in the effort to obtain revenue.

c The systematic allocation of the cost of a long-lived asset, such as a building or equipment, to expense over the useful life of the asset.

d The procedures for transferring the balances of the revenue, expense, and owner's drawing account into the owner's capital account.

e The cost of goods and services used up in the process of earning revenue.

f The span of time covered by an income statement.

g An increase is owner's equity as a result of earning revenue and incurring expenses.

h A decrease in owner's equity not reported in the income statement.

i The generally accepted accounting principle used in determining when expenses should be offset against revenue.

Exercise 3-2
Heading of an income statement

On October 12, the accountant for Sunray Appliance Company prepared an income statement for the fiscal year ended September 30, 1989. The accountant used the following heading on this financial statement:

SUNRAY CO.
Income Statement
October 12, 1989

Instructions

a Identify any errors in this heading.

b Prepare a corrected heading.

Exercise 3-3
When is revenue realized?

The following transactions were carried out during the month of June by K. Davis and Company, a firm of real estate brokers. For each of the five transactions, you are to state whether the transaction represented revenue to the firm during the month of June. Give reasons for your decision in each case.

a Collected cash of $2,400 from an account receivable. The receivable originated in May from services rendered to a client.

b Arranged a sale of an apartment building owned by a client. The commission for making the sale was $14,400, but this amount will not be received until August 20.

c Davis invested an additional $6,400 cash in the business.

d Borrowed $12,800 from Century Bank to be repaid in three months.

e Earned $63 interest on a company bank account during the month of June. No withdrawals were made from this account in June.

Exercise 3-4
When are expenses incurred?

During May the Columbus Company carried out the following transactions. Which of these transactions represented expenses in May? Explain.

a Purchased a copying machine for $2,750 cash.

b Paid $192 for gasoline purchases for a delivery truck during May.

c Paid $1,280 salary to an employee for time worked during May.

d Paid a lawyer $560 for legal services rendered in April.

e The owner withdrew $1,600 from the business for personal use.

Exercise 3-5
Relationship between net income and owner's equity

Total assets and total liabilities of Rivero-West Agency as shown by the balance sheets at the beginning and end of the year were as follows:

	BEGINNING OF YEAR	END OF YEAR
Assets	$280,000	$390,000
Liabilities	110,000	160,000

Instructions

Compute the net income or net loss from operations for the year in each of the following independent cases.

a The owner made no withdrawals during the year and no additional investments.

b The owner made no withdrawals during the year but made an additional capital investment of $50,000.

c The owner made withdrawals of $20,000 during the year but made no additional investments.

d The owner made withdrawals of $10,000 during the year and made an additional capital investment of $25,000.

Exercise 3-6
**Relationship between
net income and
owner's equity**

Supply the missing figure in the following independent cases:

a Owner's equity at beginning of year $130,000
Net income for the year . . . .   -?-
Owner's drawings during the year   32,000
Owner's equity at end of year   145,500

b Owner's equity at beginning of year   91,200
Net income for the year   28,500
Owner's drawings during the year . . . .   -?-
Owner's equity at end of year   99,700

c Owner's equity at beginning of year . . . .   -?-
Net income for the year   189,400
Owner's drawings during the year   106,000
Owner's equity at end of year   532,900

d Owner's equity at beginning of year   74,000
Additional investment by owner during the year   10,000
Net income for the year   17,500
Owner's drawings during the year   12,000
Owner's equity at end of year . . . .   -?-

e Owner's equity at beginning of year   362,500
Additional investment by owner during the year   85,000
Net income for the year . . . .   -?-
Owner's drawings during the year   30,000
Owner's equity at end of year   469,100

Exercise 3-7
**Preparing journal
entries to record
revenue, expense, and
drawings transactions**

Shown below are selected transactions of the law firm of Emmons & Associates. You are to prepare journal entries to record the transactions in the firm's accounting records. The firm closes its accounts at the end of each calendar year.

Mar. 19 Drafted a prenuptial agreement for C.J. McCall. Sent McCall an invoice for $750, requesting payment within 30 days. (The appropriate revenue account is entitled Legal Fees Earned.)

May 31 Received a bill from Lawyer's Delivery Service for process service during the month of May, $1,150. Payment due by June 10. (The appropriate expense account is entitled Process Service Expense.)

Aug. 7 Ralph Emmons, owner of the law firm, withdrew $15,000 cash for personal purposes.

Dec. 31 Made a year-end adjusting entry to record depreciation expense on the firm's law library, $2,700.

Exercise 3-8
**Preparing closing
entries**

During the absence of the regular accountant of Lawn Care Co., a new employee, Ralph Jones, prepared the closing entries from the ledger accounts for the current year. Jones had very little understanding of accounting and the closing entries he prepared were not satisfactory in several respects. The entries by Jones were:

Entry 1
Lawn service revenue   78,000
Accumulated Depreciation   8,000
Accounts Payable   27,000
    Income Summary   113,000
To close accounts with credit balances.

Entry 2

Income Summary	73,000	
Salaries Expense		56,000
J. Mallory, Drawing		11,000
Advertising Expense		4,000
Depreciation Expense		2,000

To close accounts with debit balances.

Entry 3

J. Mallory, Capital	40,000	
Income Summary		40,000

To close Income Summary account.

Instructions   **a** Identify any errors that Jones made.

b Prepare four correct closing entries, following the pattern illustrated on pages 107-112.

PROBLEMS

Group A

Problem 3A-1
Preparing journal entries

Air Wolfe provides transportation by helicopter for skiers, backpackers, and others to remote mountainous areas. Among the ledger accounts used by the company are the following:

Cash	Advertising expense
Accounts payable	Fuel expense
Amy Wolfe, capital	Rent expense
Amy Wolfe, drawing	Repair & maintenance expense
Passenger fare revenue	Salaries expense

Some of the January transactions of Air Wolfe are listed below.

Jan. 3 Paid $1,600 rent for the building for January.

Jan. 4 Placed advertising in local newspapers for publication during January. The agreed price of $520 was payable within 10 days after the end of the month.

Jan. 15 Cash receipts from passengers for the first half of January amounted to $9,470.

Jan. 16 Amy Wolfe, the owner, withdrew $3,000 cash for personal use.

Jan. 16 Paid salaries to employees for services rendered in first half of January, $5,265.

Jan. 29 Received a bill for fuel used from Western Oil Co., amounting to $1,930, and payable by February 10.

Jan. 31 Paid $1,642 to Stevens Aircraft for repair and maintenance work during January.

Instructions   Prepare a journal entry (including an explanation) for each of the above transactions.

Problem 3A-2
Analyzing transactions for preparing journal entries

Garwood Marine is a boat repair shop. During August its transactions included the following:

(1) On August 1, paid rent for the month of August, $4,000.

(2) On August 3, at request of Rock Insurance, Inc., made repairs on boat of Charles Jones. Sent bill for $680 for services rendered to Rock Insurance, Inc.

(3) On August 9, made repairs to boat of J.R. Riley and collected in full the charge of $575.

(4) On August 14, placed advertisement in *Daily Star* to be published in issue of August 20 at cost of $95, payment to be made within 30 days.

(5) On August 25, received a cheque for $680 from Rock Insurance, Inc., representing collection of the receivable of August 3.

(6) On August 31, Wallace Garwood, owner of Garwood Marine, withdrew $3,500 from the business for personal use.

(7) On August 31, salaries of $800 were paid.

Instructions   **a** Write an analysis of each transaction. An example of the type of analysis desired is as follows:

(1)(a) Rent is an operating expense. Expenses are recorded by debits. Debit Rent Expense, $4,000.

(b) The asset Cash was decreased. Decreases in assets are recorded by credits. Credit Cash, $4,000.

b Prepare a journal entry (including explanation) for each of the above transactions.

Problem 3A-3
Preparing closing
entries

Family Fun Park is a miniature golf course. At year-end, the company prepared the following adjusted trial balance:

FAMILY FUN PARK
Adjusted Trial Balance
December 31, 19___

Cash	$ 13,500	
Accounts receivable	2,800	
Buildings	60,000	
Accumulated depreciation: buildings		$ 18,000
Golf course structures	30,000	
Accumulated depreciation: golf course structures		10,000
Roy Garcia, capital		72,000
Roy Garcia, drawing	25,000	
Admissions revenue		182,000
Advertising expense	15,000	
Rent expense	36,000	
Repairs expense	5,200	
Salaries expense	79,000	
Light & power expense	4,500	
Depreciation expense: buildings	6,000	
Depreciation expense: golf course structures	5,000	
	$282,000	$282,000

Instructions   **a** Prepare journal entries to close the accounts. Use four entries: (1) to close the revenue account, (2) to close the expense accounts, (3) to close the Income Summary account, and (4) to close the owner's drawing account.

b Assume that in the following year, Family Fun Park again had $182,000 of admissions revenue, but that expenses increased to $197,000. Assuming that the revenue account and all the expense accounts had been closed into the Income Summary account at December 31, prepare a journal entry to close the Income Summary account.

Problem 3A-4
Preparing financial
statements and
closing entries

Adams Engineering prepares financial statements and closes its accounts at the end of each calendar year. The following adjusted trial balance was prepared at December 31 of the most recent year.

ADAMS ENGINEERING
Adjusted Trial Balance
December 31, 19___

Cash	$ 8,250	
Notes receivable	9,100	
Accounts receivable	47,450	
Land	140,000	
Building	90,000	
Accumulated depreciation: building		$ 23,200
Office equipment	4,000	
Accumulated depreciation: office equipment		1,600
Notes payable		100,000
Accounts payable		16,200
Sally Adams, capital		132,300
Sally Adams, drawing	24,000	
Consulting fees earned		157,000
Advertising expense	22,500	
Insurance expense	2,800	
Utilities expense	2,600	
Salaries expense	76,200	
Depreciation expense: building	3,000	
Depreciation expense: office equipment	400	
	$430,300	$430,300

Instructions

a Prepare an income statement for the year ended December 31.

b Prepare a balance sheet in report form at December 31. In the owner's equity section, show the changes in the owner's capital during the year.

c Prepare closing entries at December 31. Use four entries.

Problem 3A-5
Preparing journal
entries, posting, and
preparing a trial
balance

Metro Park was organized on March 1 for the purpose of operating an automobile parking lot. Included in the company's ledger are the following ledger accounts and their identification numbers.

Cash	11	Heather Young, drawing	42
Land	21	Parking fees earned	51
Notes payable	31	Advertising expense	61
Accounts payable	32	Utilities expense	63
Heather Young, capital	41	Salaries expense	65

The business was organized and operations were begun during the month of March. Transactions during March were as follows:

Mar. 1 Heather Young deposited $50,000 cash in a bank account in the name of the business.

Mar. 5 Purchased land for $160,000, of which $40,000 was paid in cash. A short-term note payable was issued for the balance of $120,000.

Mar. 6 An arrangement was made with the Century Club to provide parking privileges for its customers. Century Club agreed to pay $1,200 monthly, payable in advance. Cash was collected for the month of March.

Mar. 7 Arranged with Times Printing company for a regular advertisement in the *Times* at a monthly cost of $390. Paid for advertising during March by cheque, $390.

Mar. 15 Parking receipts for the first half of the month were $1,836, exclusive of the monthly fee from Century Club.

Mar. 31 Received bill for light and power from Pacific Power Limited in the amount of $78, to be paid by April 10.

Mar. 31 Paid $2,720 to employees for services rendered during the month. (Payroll taxes are to be ignored.)

Mar. 31 Parking receipts for the second half of the month amounted to $5,338.

Mar. 31 Young withdrew $2,000 for personal use.

Mar. 31 Paid $5,000 cash on the note payable incurred with the purchase of land. (You are to ignore any interest on the note.)

Instructions

a Journalize the March transactions.

b Post to ledger accounts. Enter ledger account numbers in the LP column of the journal as the posting work is done.

c Prepare a trial balance at March 31.

Problem 3A-6
End-of-period
adjusting and closing
procedures; preparing
financial statements
and after-closing
trial balance

Home Repair is a new business that began operations on July 2. The company follows a policy of closing its accounts and preparing financial statements at the end of each month. A trial balance at September 30 follows:

HOME REPAIR
Trial Balance
September 30, 19___

Cash	$ 2,500	
Accounts receivable	1,500	
Land	29,400	
Building	50,400	
Accumulated depreciation: building		$ 336
Repair equipment	7,500	
Accumulated depreciation: repair equipment		250
Notes payable		28,000
Accounts payable		1,594
Paul Klein, capital		58,800
Paul Klein, drawing	1,400	
Repair service revenue		8,520
Advertising expense	150	
Repair parts expense	700	
Utilities expense	170	
Wages expense	3,780	
	$97,500	$97,500

Note that the trial balance includes two assets subject to depreciation: the building and the repair equipment. The accumulated depreciation accounts in the trial balance show the total depreciation for only July and August; the depreciation for September has not yet been recorded.

Instructions

a Prepare adjusting entries at September 30 to record depreciation. Use one entry to record depreciation on the building and a second entry to record depreciation on the repair equipment. The amounts of depreciation for September are $168 on the building and $125 on the repair equipment.

b Prepare an *adjusted* trial balance at September 30.

c Prepare an income statement for the month ended September 30 and a balance sheet in report form. In the owner's equity section of the balance sheet, show the change in capital resulting from September operations.

d Prepare journal entries to close the accounts. Use four entries: (1) to close the revenue account, (2) to close the expense accounts, (3) to close the Income Summary account, and (4) to close the owner's drawing account.

e Prepare an after-closing trial balance.

Problem 3A-7
Complete accounting cycle

John Ryan organized Freeway Express on June 1, 19___, to provide long-distance moving of household furniture. During June the following transactions occurred:

June 1 Ryan deposited $270,000 cash in a bank account in the name of the business, Freeway Express.

June 3 Purchased land and building for a total price of $156,000, of which $60,000 was applicable to the land, and $96,000 to the building. Paid cash for full amount.

June 5 Purchased three trucks from Dawson Motors at a cost of $40,000 each. A cash down payment of $50,000 was made, the balance to be paid by July 22.

June 6 Purchased office equipment for cash, $4,800.

June 6 Moved furniture for Mr. and Mrs. David Hart from Vancouver to Calgary for $2,500. Collected $1,000 in cash, balance due within 30 days.

June 11 Moved furniture for various clients for $11,800. Collected $4,400 in cash, balance due within 30 days.

June 15 Paid salaries to employees for first half of the month, $5,000.

June 24 Moved furniture for various clients for a total of $6,480. Cash collected in full.

June 30 Salaries expense for the second half of month of $5,800 was paid.

June 30 Received a gasoline bill for the month of June from Atlantic Oil Company in the amount of $6,200, to be paid before July 10.

June 30 Received bill of $300 for repair work on trucks during June by Century Motor Company. Payment due in 10 days.

June 30 The owner, John Ryan, withdrew $1,500 cash for personal use.

Ryan estimated a useful life of 20 years for the building, 4 years for the trucks, and 10 years for the office equipment.

The account titles to be used and the account numbers are as illustrated at the top of page 128.

Cash	1	John Ryan, capital	50
Accounts receivable	3	John Ryan, drawing	51
Land	5	Income summary	60
Building	7	Moving service revenue	62
Accumulated depreciation:		Salaries expense	70
building	8	Gasoline expense	72
Trucks	10	Repairs expense	74
Accumulated depreciation:		Depreciation expense:	
trucks	11	building	76
Office equipment	13	Depreciation expense:	
Accumulated depreciation:		trucks	78
office equipment	14	Depreciation expense:	
Accounts payable	30	office equipment	80

Instructions

a Prepare journal entries. (Number journal pages and enter the proper journal page number in the "Ref" column of the ledger accounts as each debit or credit is posted.)

b Post to ledger accounts. (As each journal entry is posted to the ledger, enter the identification number of the ledger account debited or credited in the "LP" column of the journal. This will show that the amount has been posted and will provide a cross reference between journal and ledger.)

c Prepare a trial balance as of June 30, 19___.

d Prepare adjusting entries for depreciation during June and post to ledger accounts.

e Prepare an adjusted trial balance.

f Prepare an income statement for June, and a balance sheet at June 30, in report form. Show the changes in the owner's capital account in the equity section of the balance sheet.

g Prepare closing entries and post to ledger accounts.

h Prepare an after-closing trial balance.

Group B

Problem 3B-1
Preparing journal
entries

Bay Plumbers performs repair work on both a cash and credit basis. Credit customers are required to pay within 30 days from date of billing. The ledger accounts used by the company include:

Cash	David Cohen, drawing
Accounts receivable	Repair service revenue
Tools	Advertising expense
Notes payable	Rent expense
Accounts payable	Salaries expense

Among the September transactions were the following:

Sept. 1 Performed repair work for Arden Hardware, a credit customer. Sent bill for $1,322.

Sept. 2 Paid rent for September, $750.

Sept. 3 Purchased tools with estimated life of 10 years for $1,275 cash.

Sept. 10 Performed repairs for Harris Drugs ad collected in full the charge of $565.

Sept. 15 Newspaper advertising to appear on September 18 was arranged at a cost of $275. Received bill from *Tribune* requiring payment within 30 days.

Sept. 18 Received payment in full of the $1,322 account receivable from Arden Hardware for our services on September 1.

Sept. 20 David Cohen, owner of Bay Plumbers, withdrew $1,100 cash from the business for personal use.

Sept. 30 Paid salaries of $3,425 to employees for services rendered during September.

Instructions Prepare a journal entry (including explanation) for each of the above transactions.

Problem 3B-2
Analyzing transactions
and preparing journal
entries

The July transactions of Auto Haus, an automobile repair shop, included the following:

(1) On July 2, paid rent for the month of July, $2,400.

(2) On July 3, at request of National Insurance, Inc., made repairs on car of Stanley West. Sent bill for $610 for services rendered to National Insurance, Inc.

(3) On July 9, made repairs to car of H.F. Smith and collected in full the charge of $430.

(4) On July 14, placed advertisement in *Windsor Star* to be published in issue of July 16 at cost of $150, payment to be made within 30 days.

(5) On July 25, received a cheque for $610 from National Insurance, Inc., representing collection of the receivable of July 3.

(6) On July 31, the owner, Hans Klauder, withdrew $3,600 cash for personal use.

(7) On July 31, obtained a loan from bank. Received $15,000 cash and signed a note payable for that amount.

Instructions

a Write an analysis of each transaction. An example of the type of analysis desired is as follows for transaction (1) above.

(1)(a) Rent is an operating expense. Expenses are recorded by debits. Debit Rent Expense, $2,400.

(b) The asset Cash was decreased. Decreases in assets are recorded by credits. Credit Cash, $2,400.

b Prepare a journal entry (including explanation) for each of the above transactions.

Problem 3B-3
Preparing closing
entries

An adjusted trial balance for Martin Insurance Agency at December 31 appears below.

MARTIN INSURANCE AGENCY
Adjusted Trial Balance
December 31, 19___

Cash	$ 10,200	
Accounts receivable	20,000	
Office equipment	15,000	
Accumulated depreciation: office equipment		$ 3,000
Accounts payable		6,000
Linda Martin, capital		19,700
Linda Martin, drawing	18,000	
Commissions earned		185,000
Advertising expense	36,500	
Rent expense	32,000	
Salaries expense	64,500	
Utilities expense	16,000	
Depreciation expense: office equipment	1,500	
	$213,700	$213,700

Instructions   **a** Prepare journal entries to close the accounts. Use four entries: (1) to close the revenue account, (2) to close the expense accounts, (3) to close the Income Summary account, and (4) to close the owner's drawing account.

b Does the amount of net income or net loss appear in the closing entries? Explain fully.

Problem 3B-4
Preparing financial
statements and
closing entries

Celebrity Agency closes its accounts and prepares financial statements at the end of each calendar year. The following adjusted trial balance was prepared at December 31 of the most recent year.

CELEBRITY AGENCY
Adjusted Trial Balance
December 31, 19___

Cash	$ 7,300	
Notes receivable	6,000	
Accounts receivable	12,800	
Land	120,000	
Building	100,000	
Accumulated depreciation: building		$ 12,000
Office equipment	14,000	
Accumulated depreciation: office equipment		8,600
Notes payable		80,000
Accounts payable		18,200
Halley St. James, capital		143,300
Halley St. James, drawing	25,000	
Commissions earned		89,500
Advertising expense	12,500	
Insurance expense	3,600	
Utilities expense	3,800	
Salaries expense	41,200	
Depreciation expense: building	4,000	
Depreciation expense: office equipment	1,400	
	$351,600	$351,600

Instructions   **a** Prepare an income statement for the year ended December 31.

b Prepare a balance sheet in report form at December 31. In the owner's equity section, show the changes in the owner's capital during the year.

c Prepare closing entries at December 31. Use four entries.

Problem 3B-5
Preparing journal
entries, posting, and
preparing a trial
balance

During the month of June, John Lane organized and began to operate an air taxi service to provide air transportation from a major city to a number of small towns not served by scheduled airlines. Transactions during the month of June were as follows:

June 1 John Lane deposited $55,000 cash in a bank account in the name of the business, Lane Air Service.

June 2 Purchased an aircraft for $225,000 paying $45,000 in cash and issuing a note payable for $180,000.

June 4 Paid $2,500 cash to rent a building for June.

June 10 Cash receipts from passenger fares revenue for the first 10 days amounted to $3,320.

June 14 Paid $1,850 to Ace Aircraft Co. for maintenance and repair services.

June 15 Paid $5,880 salaries to employees for services rendered during first half of June.

June 20 Cash receipts from passenger fares revenue for the second 10 days amounted to $7,800.

June 30 Cash receipts from passenger fares revenue for the last 10 days of June amounted to $9,100.

June 30 Paid $6,000 salaries to employees for services rendered during the second half of June.

June 30 Lane withdrew $2,000 from business for personal use.

June 30 Received a fuel bill from Phillips Oil Limited amounting to $4,540 to be paid before July 10.

The account titles and numbers used by Lane Air Service are as follows:

Cash	1	Passenger fares revenue	51
Aircraft	15	Maintenance expense	61
Notes payable	31	Fuel expense	62
Accounts payable	32	Salaries expense	63
John Lane, capital	41	Rent expense	64
John Lane, drawing	42		

Instructions   Based on the foregoing transactions:

a Prepare journal entries. (Number journal pages to permit cross reference to ledger.)

b Post to ledger accounts. (Number ledger accounts to permit cross reference to journal.) Enter ledger account numbers in the LP column of the journal as the posting work is done.

c Prepare a trial balance at June 30, 19___.

Problem 3B-6
End-of-period
adjusting and closing
procedures; preparing
financial statements
and after-closing
trial balance

The operations of Sunset Realty consist of obtaining listings of houses being offered for sale by owners, advertising these houses, and showing them to prospective buyers. The company earns revenue in the form of commissions. The building and office equipment used in the business were acquired on January 2 of the current year and were immediately placed in use. Useful life of the building was estimated to be 30 years and that of the office equipment 5 years. The company closes its accounts monthly; on March 31 of the current year, the trial balance is as shown at the top of page 132.

Instructions   From the trial balance and supplementary data given, prepare the following as of March 31, 19___.

a Adjusting entries for depreciation during March of building and of office equipment.

b Adjusted trial balance.

c Income statement for the month of March and a balance sheet at March 31 in report form. In the owner's equity section of the balance sheet, show the changes in owner's capital during March.

d Closing entries.

e After-closing trial balance.

SUNSET REALTY
Trial Balance
March 31, 19___

	DEBIT	CREDIT
Cash	6,500	
Accounts receivable	5,000	
Land	25,000	
Building	72,000	
Accumulated depreciation: building		$ 400
Office equipment	24,000	
Accumulated depreciation: office equipment		800
Notes payable		81,000
Accounts payable		10,000
Ellen Norton, capital		37,800
Ellen Norton, drawing	2,000	
Commissions earned		20,000
Advertising expense	900	
Automobile rental expense	700	
Salaries expense	13,300	
Telephone expense	600	
	$150,000	$150,000

Problem 3B-7
Complete accounting cycle

April Stein, M.D., after completing her medical education, established her own practice on May 1. The following transactions occurred during the first month.

May 1 Stein opened a bank account in the name of the practice, April Stein M.D., by making a deposit of $12,000.

May 1 Paid office rent for May, $1,700.

May 2 Purchased office equipment for cash, $7,200.

May 3 Purchased medical instruments from Niles Instruments, Inc., at a cost of $9,000. A cash down payment of $1,000 was made and a note payable was issued for the remaining $8,000.

May 4 Retained by Metro Hospital to be on call for emergency service at a monthly fee of $400. The fee for May was collected in cash.

May 15 Excluding the retainer of May 4, fees earned during the first 15 days of the month amounted to $1,600, of which $600 was in cash and $1,000 was in accounts receivable.

May 15 Paid Mary Hester, R.N., her salary for the first half of May, $1,000.

May 16 Dr. Stein withdrew $975 for personal use.

May 19 Treated Michael Tracy at Metro Hospital's emergency for minor injuries received in an accident.

May 27 Treated Cynthia Knight (a foreign student without medical insurance), who paid $25 cash for an office visit and who agreed to pay $35 on June 1 for laboratory medical tests completed May 27.

May 31 Excluding the treatment of Cynthia Knight on May 27, fees earned during the last half of month amounted to $4,000, of which $1,100 was in cash and $2,900 was in accounts receivable.

May 31 Paid Mary Hester, R.N., $1,000 salary for the second half of month.

May 31 Received a bill from McGraw Medical Supplies in the amount of $640 representing the amount of medical supplies used during May.

May 31 Paid utilities for the month, $300.

Other information   Dr. Stein estimated the useful life of medical instruments at 3 years and of office equipment at 5 years. The account titles to be used and the account numbers are as follows:

Cash	10	April Stein, drawing	41
Accounts receivable	13	Income summary	45
Medical instruments	20	Fees earned	49
Accumulated depreciation:		Medical supplies expense	50
medical instruments	21	Rent expense	51
Office equipment	22	Salaries expense	52
Accumulated depreciation:		Utilities expense	53
office equipment	23	Depreciation expense:	
Notes payable	30	medical instruments	54
Accounts payable	31	Depreciation expense:	
April Stein, capital	40	office equipment	55

Instructions **a** Journalize the above transactions. (Number journal pages to permit cross-reference to ledger.)

b Post to ledger accounts. (Use running balance form of ledger account. Number ledger accounts to permit cross reference to journal.)

c Prepare a trial balance at May 31, 19___.

d Prepare adjusting entries to record depreciation for the month of May and post to ledger accounts.

e Prepare an adjusted trial balance.

f Prepare an income statement and a balance sheet in report form.

g Prepare closing entries and post to ledger accounts.

h Prepare an after-closing trial balance.

BUSINESS DECISION CASES

Case 3-1
Accrual accounting;
relationship of
depreciation expense
to cash outlays

The Dark Room is a business that develops film within one hour, using a large and expensive developing machine. The business is organized as a sole proprietorship and operates in rented quarters in a large shopping centre. Sharon Douglas, owner of The Dark Room, plans to retire and has offered the business for sale. A typical monthly income statement for The Dark Room appears at the top of page 134.

Revenue is received in cash at the time that film is developed. The wages, rent, supplies, and miscellaneous expenses are all paid in cash on a monthly basis. Douglas explains that the developing machine, which is 12 months old and is fully paid for, is being depreciated over a period of five years. She is using this estimated useful life because she believes that faster and more efficient machines will probably be available at that time. However, if the business does not purchase a new machine, the existing machine should last for 10 years or more.

Revenue:		
Fees earned		$8,900
Operating expenses:		
Wages	$1,600	
Rent	1,850	
Supplies	920	
Depreciation: developing machine	1,510	
Miscellaneous	460	6,340
Net income		$2,560

Dave Berg, a friend of yours, is negotiating with Douglas to buy The Dark Room. Berg does not have enough money to pay the entire purchase price in cash. However, Douglas has offered to accept a note payable from Berg for a substantial portion of the purchase price. The note would call for 18 monthly payments in the amount of $2,500, which would pay off the remainder of the purchase price as well as the interest charges on the note. Douglas points out that these monthly payments can be made "out of the monthly earnings of the business."

Berg comes to you for advice. He feels that the sales price asked by Douglas is very reasonable, and that the owner-financing makes this an excellent opportunity. However, he is worried about turning over $2,500 of the business's earnings to Douglas each month. Berg states, "This arrangement will only leave me with about $60 each month. I figure that my family and I need to take about $1,200 out of this business each month just to meet our living expenses." Also, Berg is concerned about the depreciation expense. He does not understand when or to whom the depreciation expense must be paid, or how long this expense will continue.

Instructions

a Explain to Berg the nature of depreciation expense, including when this expense is paid and what effect, if any, it has upon monthly cash expenditures.

b Advise Berg as to how much cash the business will generate each month. Will this amount enable Berg to pay $2,500 per month to the former owner and still withdraw $1,200 per month to meet his personal living expenses?

c Caution Berg about the need to replace the developing machine. Briefly discuss when this expenditure might occur and how much control, if any, Berg has over the timing and dollar amount of this expenditure.

Case 3-2
Accrual accounting; relationship of revenue to cash receipts

Nancy Jo Hoover, owner of a small business called Imports from India, has accepted a salaried position overseas and is trying to interest you in buying the business. Hoover describes the operating results of the business as follows: "The business has been in existence for only 18 months, but the growth trend is very impressive. Just look at these figures."

	CASH COLLECTIONS FROM CUSTOMERS
First six-month period	$120,000
Second six-month period	160,000
Third six-month period	180,000

"I think you'll agree those figures show real growth," Hoover concluded.

You then asked Hoover whether sales were made only for cash or on both a cash and credit basis. She replied as follows:

"At first we sold both for cash and on open account. In the first six months we made total sales of $200,000 and 70% of those sales were made on credit. We had $80,000 of accounts receivable at the end of the first six-month period.

"During the second six-month period, we tried to discourage selling on credit because of the extra paper work involved and the time required to follow up on slow-paying customers. Our sales on credit in that second six-month period amounted to $70,000, and our total accounts receivable were down to $60,000 at the end of that period.

"During the third six-month period we made sales only for cash. Although we prefer to operate on a cash basis only, we did very well at collecting receivables. We collected in full from ever customer to whom we ever sold on credit and we don't have a dollar of accounts receivable at this time."

Instructions   **a** To assist you in evaluating the performance of Imports from India, prepare a schedule comparing cash collections and sales data for each of the three 6-month periods under review. Use the following column headings:

	(1) SALES ON CREDIT	(2) COLLECTIONS ON ACCOUNTS RECEIVABLE	(3) ENDING BALANCE OF ACCOUNTS RECEIVABLE	(4) SALES FOR CASH (5) − (2)	(5) TOTAL CASH COLLECTIONS FROM CUSTOMERS	(6) TOTAL SALES (1) + (4)
First six months ...					$120,000	
Second six months .					160,000	
Third six months ...					280,000	

b Based upon your analysis in part **a**, do you consider Hoover's explanation of the "growth trend" of cash collections to be a well-founded portrayal of the progress of the business? Explain fully any criticism you may have of Hoover's line of reasoning.

COMPLETION OF THE ACCOUNTING CYCLE

CHAPTER PREVIEW

In Chapter 4 we complete our coverage of the accounting cycle for a service-type business. Emphasis is placed upon steps performed at the end of the cycle, including adjusting entries, preparation of a work sheet, and reversing entries. The continuing example of Roberts Real Estate Company is used to illustrate and explain the four basic types of adjusting entries and the preparation of a work sheet. The discussion of reversing entries emphasizes the optional nature of this final step in the accounting cycle. As in our earlier chapters on the accounting cycle, the procedures employed in computer-based accounting systems are compared with those in manual systems.

After studying this chapter you should be able to meet these Learning Objectives:

1 Explain how accounting periods of equal length are useful in evaluating the income of a business.

2 State the purpose of adjusting entries and explain how these entries are related to the concepts of accrual accounting.

3 Describe the four basic types of adjusting entries.

4 Prepare a work sheet and discuss its usefulness.

5 Describe the steps in the accounting cycle.

6 Explain when and why reversing entries may be used.

Accounting periods and financial statements

For the purpose of measuring net income and preparing financial statements, the life of a business is divided into accounting periods of equal length. Because accounting periods are equal in length, we can compare the income of the current period with that of prior periods to see if our operating results are improving or declining.

1 Explain how accounting periods of equal length are useful in evaluating the income of a business.

As explained in Chapter 3, the *accounting period* means the span of time covered by an income statement. The usual accounting period for which complete financial statements are prepared and distributed to investors, bankers, and governmental agencies is one year. However, most businesses also prepare quarterly and monthly financial statements so that management will be currently informed on the profitability of the business from month to month.

Transactions affecting more than one accounting period

Dividing the life of a business into relatively short accounting periods creates the need for *adjusting entries* at the end of each period. Some transactions affect the revenue or expense of only one accounting period. Adjusting entries are *not* required for these types of transactions. Adjusting entries are required, however, for those transactions that affect the revenue or expenses of *more than one accounting period.* For example, assume that a company that prepares monthly financial statements purchases a one-year insurance policy at a cost of $1,200. Clearly, the entire $1,200 does not represent the insurance expense of the current month. Rather, it is the insurance expense for *12* months; only $1/12$ of this cost, or $100, should be recognized as expense in each month covered by the policy. The allocation of this $1,200 cost to expense in 12 separate accounting periods is accomplished by making an adjusting entry at the end of each period.

ADJUSTING ENTRIES: A CLOSER LOOK

2 State the purpose of adjusting entries and explain how these entries are related to the concepts of accrual accounting.

The purpose of adjusting entries is to record certain revenue and expenses that are not properly measured in the course of recording daily business transactions. Thus, adjusting entries help in achieving the goals of accrual accounting — recording revenue when it is *earned* and recording expenses when the related goods and services are *used.* In Chapter 3, the concept of adjusting entries was introduced when Roberts Real Estate Company recorded depreciation for the month of October. Adjusting entries are necessary to record depreciation expense, because buildings and equipment are purchased in a single accounting period but are used over many periods. Some portion of the cost of these assets should be allocated to expense in each period of the asset's estimated life. In this chapter, we will see that the use of adjusting entries is not limited to recording depreciation expense. Adjusting entries are needed *whenever transactions affect the revenue or expense of more than one accounting period.*

Types of adjusting entries

A business may need to make a dozen or more adjusting entries at the end of each accounting period. The exact number of adjustments will depend upon the nature of

3 Describe the four basic types of adjusting entries.

the company's business activities. However, all adjusting entries fall into one of four general categories:

1 Entries to apportion recorded costs   A cost that will benefit more than one accounting period usually is recorded by debiting an asset account. In each period that benefits from the use of this asset, an adjusting entry is made to allocate a portion of the asset's cost to expense.

2 Entries to apportion unearned revenue   A business may collect in advance for services to be rendered to customers in future accounting periods. In the period in which services are rendered, an adjusting entry is made to record the portion of the revenue earned during the period.

3 Entries to record unrecorded expenses   An expense may be incurred in the current accounting period even though no bill has yet been received and payment will not occur until a future period. Such unrecorded expenses are recorded by an adjusting entry made at the end of the accounting period.

4 Entries to record unrecorded revenue   Revenue may be earned during the current period, but not yet billed to customers or recorded in the accounting records. Such unrecorded revenue is recorded by making an adjusting entry at the end of the period.

Characteristics of adjusting entries

It will be helpful to keep in mind two important characteristics of all adjusting entries. First, every adjusting entry *involves the recognition of either revenue or expense.* Revenue and expenses represent changes in owner's equity. However, owner's equity cannot change by itself; there also must be a corresponding change in either assets or liabilities. *Thus, every adjusting entry affects both an income statement account* (revenue or expense) *and a balance sheet account* (asset or liability).

Second, adjusting entries are based upon the concepts of accrual accounting, *not upon monthly bills or month-end transactions.* No one sends us a bill saying, "Depreciation expense on your building amounts to $500 this month." Yet, we must be aware of the need to estimate and record depreciation expense if we are to measure net income properly for the period. Making adjusting entries requires a greater understanding of accrual accounting concepts than does the recording of routine business transactions. In many businesses, the adjusting entries are made by the company's controller or by a professional accountant, rather than by the regular accounting staff.

To demonstrate the various types of adjusting entries, the illustration of Roberts Real Estate Company will be continued for November. We shall consider in detail only those November transactions that require adjusting entries at the end of the month.

Apportioning recorded costs

When a business makes an expenditure that will benefit more than one accounting period, the amount usually is debited to an asset account. At the end of each period benefiting from this expenditure, an adjusting entry is made to transfer an appropriate portion of the cost from the asset account to an expense account. This adjusting entry reflects the fact that part of the asset has been used up — or become expense — during the current accounting period.

An adjusting entry to apportion a recorded cost consists of a debit to an expense account and a credit to an asset account (or a contra-asset account). Examples of these adjustments include the entries to record depreciation expense and to apportion the costs of *prepaid expenses.*

Prepaid expenses   Payments in advance are often made for such items as insurance, rent, and office supplies. If the advance payment (or prepayment) will benefit more than just the current accounting period, the cost *represents an asset* rather than an expense. The cost of this asset will be allocated to expense in the accounting periods in which the services or the supplies are used. In summary, *prepaid expenses are assets;* they become expenses only as the goods or services are used up.

Insurance   To illustrate these concepts, assume that on November 1, Roberts Real Estate Company paid $600 for a one-year fire insurance policy covering the building. This expenditure was debited to an asset account by the following journal entry:

EXPENDITURE FOR
INSURANCE POLICY
RECORDED AS ASSET

Unexpired Insurance   600
   Cash   600
Purchased a one-year fire insurance policy.

Since this expenditure of $600 will protect the company against fire loss for one year, the insurance expense applicable to each month's operations is $1/12$ of the annual expense, or $50. In order that the accounting records for November show insurance expense of $50, the following *adjusting entry* is required at November 30:

ADJUSTING ENTRY,
PORTION OF ASSET
EXPIRES (BECOMES
EXPENSE)

Insurance Expense   50
   Unexpired Insurance   50
To record insurance expense for November.

This adjusting entry serves two purposes: (1) it apportions the proper amount of insurance expense to November operations and (2) it reduces the asset account to $550 so that the correct amount of unexpired insurance will appear in the balance sheet at November 30.

What would be the effect on the income statement for November if the above adjustment were not made? The expenses would be understated by $50 and consequently the net income would be overstated by $50. The balance sheet also would be affected by failure to make the adjustment: the assets would be overstated by $50 and so would the owner's equity. The overstatement of the owner's equity would result from the overstated amount of net income transferred to the owner's equity account when the accounts were closed at November 30.

Office supplies   On November 2, Roberts Real Estate Company purchased enough stationery and other office supplies to last for several months. The cost of the supplies was $720, and this amount was debited to an asset account by the following journal entry:

Office Supplies	720	
Cash		720
Purchased office supplies.		

No entries were made during November to record the day-to-day usage of office supplies, but on November 30 a count was made of the supplies still on hand. This physical count showed unused supplies with a cost of $500. Thus, supplies costing $220 were used during November. On the basis of the November 30 count, an adjusting entry is made debiting an expense account $220 (the cost of supplies consumed during November), and reducing the asset account by $220. The *adjusting entry* follows:

Office Supplies Expense	220	
Office Supplies		220
To record consumption of office supplies in November.		

After this entry is posted, the asset account, Office Supplies, will have a balance of $500, representing the cost of office supplies on hand at November 30. The Office Supplies account will appear in the balance sheet as an asset; the Office Supplies Expense account will be shown in the income statement.

How would failure to make this adjustment affect the financial statements? In the income statement for November, the expenses would be understated by $220 and the net income overstated by the same amount. Since the overstated amount for net income in November would be transferred into the owner's equity account in the process of closing the accounts, the owner's equity section of the balance sheet would be overstated by $220. Assets also would be overstated because Office Supplies would be listed at $220 too much.

Recording prepayments directly in the expense accounts   In our illustration, payments for insurance and office supplies, which are expected to provide benefits for more than one accounting period, are recorded by debiting an asset account, such as Unexpired Insurance or Office Supplies. However, some companies follow an alternative practice of debiting these prepayments directly to an expense account such as Insurance Expense. At the end of the period, the adjusting entry would then consist of a debit to Unexpired Insurance and a credit to Insurance Expense for the portion of the insurance cost *that has not yet expired.*

This alternative method leads to the same results in the balance sheet and income statement as does the method used in our illustration. Under both procedures, the cost of benefits consumed in the current period is treated as an expense, and the cost of benefits applicable to future periods is carried forward in the balance sheet as an asset.

In this text and in the end-of-chapter problem material, we will follow the practice of recording prepayments in *asset accounts* and then making adjusting entries to transfer these costs to expense accounts as the assets expire.

Depreciation of building   The recording of depreciation expense at the end of an accounting period provides another example of an adjusting entry that *apportions a recorded cost.* The November 30 adjusting entry to record depreciation of the building used by Roberts Real Estate Company is exactly the same as the October 31 *adjusting entry* explained in Chapter 3.

<table>
<tr><td>ADJUSTING ENTRY.
COST OF BUILDING IS
GRADUALLY CONVERTED
TO EXPENSE</td><td>Depreciation Expense: Building .... 150</td><td></td></tr>
<tr><td></td><td>   Accumulated Depreciation: Building ....</td><td>150</td></tr>
<tr><td></td><td>To record depreciation for November.</td><td></td></tr>
</table>

This allocation of depreciation expense to November operations is based on the following facts: the building cost $36,000 and is estimated to have a useful life of 20 years (240 months). Using the straight-line method of depreciation, the portion of the original cost that expires each month is $1/240$ of $36,000, or $150.

The Accumulated Depreciation: Building account now has a credit balance of $300 as a result of the October and November credits of $150 each. The book value of the building is $35,700; that is, the original cost of $36,000 minus the accumulated depreciation of $300. The term *book value* means the net amount at which an asset is shown in the accounting records, as distinguished from its market value. *Carrying value* is an alternative term, with the same meaning as book value.

Depreciation of office equipment   The November 30 adjusting entry to record depreciation of the office equipment is the same as the *adjusting entry* for depreciation a month earlier, as shown in Chapter 3.

<table>
<tr><td>ADJUSTING ENTRY, COST
OF OFFICE EQUIPMENT
GRADUALLY CONVERTED
TO EXPENSE</td><td>Depreciation Expense: Office Equipment .... 45</td><td></td></tr>
<tr><td></td><td>   Accumulated Depreciation: Office Equipment ....</td><td>45</td></tr>
<tr><td></td><td>To record depreciation for November.</td><td></td></tr>
</table>

The original cost of the office equipment was $5,400, and the estimated useful life was 10 years (120 months). Depreciation each month under the straight-line method is therefore $1/120$ of $5,400, or $45.

What is the book value of the office equipment at this point? The original cost of $5,400, minus accumulated depreciation of $90 for two months, leaves a book value of $5,310.

Apportioning unearned revenue

In some instances, customers may *pay in advance* for services to be rendered in later accounting periods. For example, a football team collects much of its revenue in advance through the sale of season tickets. Health clubs collect in advance by selling long-term membership contracts. Airlines sell many of their tickets well in advance of a scheduled flight.

For accounting purposes, amounts collected in advance *do not represent revenue,* because these amounts have *not yet been earned.* Amounts collected from customers in advance are recorded by debiting the Cash account and crediting an *unearned revenue* account. Unearned revenue also may be called *deferred revenue.*

When a company collects money in advance from its customers, it has an *obligation* to render services in the future. Therefore, the balance of an unearned revenue account is considered to be a liability; *it appears in the liability section of the balance sheet, not in the income statement.* Unearned revenue differs from other liabilities because it usually will be settled by rendering services, rather than by making payment in cash. In short, it will be *worked off* rather than *paid off*. Of course if the business is unable to render the service, it must discharge this liability by refunding money to its customers.

 One of the largest liabilities in the balance sheet of Air Canada is "Advance ticket sales." This account, with a balance of approximately $190 million, represents unearned revenue resulting from the sale of tickets for future flights. Most of this unearned revenue will be earned as the future flights occur. Some customers, however, will change their plans and will return their tickets to Air Canada for a cash refund.

When the company renders the services for which customers have paid in advance, it is working off its liability to these customers and is earning the revenue. At the end of the accounting period in which the revenue is earned, an *adjusting entry* is made to transfer an appropriate amount from the unearned revenue account to a revenue account. This adjusting entry consists of a debit to a liability account (unearned revenue) and a credit to a revenue account.

To illustrate these concepts, assume that on November 1, Roberts Real Estate Company agreed to act as manager of some rental properties for a monthly fee of $300. The owner of the properties, Frank Day, was leaving the country on an extended trip and therefore paid the company for six months' service in advance. The journal entry to record the transaction on November 1 was

MANAGEMENT FEE COLLECTED BUT NOT YET EARNED	Cash	1,800
	Unearned Management Fees	1,800
	Collected in advance six months' fees for management of properties owned by Frank Day.	

Remember that Unearned Management Fees is a *liability* account, not a revenue account. This management fee will be earned gradually over a period of six months as Roberts Real Estate Company performs the required services. At the end of each monthly accounting period, the company will make an adjusting entry transferring $1/6$ of this management fee, or $300 from the unearned revenue account to a revenue account. The first in this series of monthly transfers will be made on November 30 by the following *adjusting entry:*

ADJUSTING ENTRY TO RECOGNIZE EARNING OF A PART OF MANAGEMENT FEE	Unearned Management Fees	300
	Management Fees Earned	300
	Fee earned by managing Frank Day property during November.	

After this entry has been posted, the Unearned Management Fees account will have a $1,500 credit balance. This balance represents the company's obligation to render $1,500 worth of services over the next five months and will appear in the liability section of the company's balance sheet. The Management Fees Earned account will be shown as revenue in the November income statement.

Recording advance collections directly in the revenue accounts   We have stressed that amounts collected from customers in advance represent liabilities, not revenue. However, some companies follow an accounting policy of crediting these advance collections directly to a revenue account. This treatment is based upon the expectation that the revenue will be earned prior to the end of the current accounting period. If the revenue is not earned by the end of the period, an adjusting entry is required. This adjusting entry will consist of a debit to the revenue account and a credit to the unearned revenue account for the portion of the advance payments *not yet earned.* This alternative accounting practice leads to the same results as does the method used in our Roberts Real Estate Company illustration.

In this text, we will follow the practice of crediting advance payments from customers to an *unearned revenue account.*

Recording unrecorded expenses

We have already discussed adjusting entries that apportion recorded costs. Such entries recognize expenses stemming from *past* transactions. Hence, the adjusting entry apportions a cost that has already been recorded in the accounting records.

We will now describe another type of adjusting entry that also recognizes expenses incurred during the current accounting period. This type of adjusting entry recognizes expenses that will be paid in *future* transactions; thus, no cost has yet been recorded in the accounting records. Salaries of employees and interest on borrowed money are common examples of expenses that accumulate from day to day, but that usually are not recorded until they are paid. These expenses are said to *accrue* over time, that is, to grow or to accumulate. At the end of the accounting period, an adjusting entry should be made to record any expenses that have accrued, but that have not yet been recorded. Since these expenses will be paid at a future date, the adjusting entry consists of a debit to an expense account and a credit to a liability account. We shall now use the example of Roberts Real Estate Company to illustrate this type of adjusting entry.

Accrual of interest   On November 1, Roberts Real Estate Company borrowed the sum of $3,000 from a bank. Banks require every borrower to sign a *promissory note,* that is, a formal, written promise to repay the amount borrowed plus interest at an agreed future date. (Various forms of notes in common use and the accounting problems involved will be discussed more fully in Chapter 11.) The note signed by Roberts, with certain details omitted, is shown at the top of page 144.

The note payable is a liability of Roberts Real Estate Company, similar to an account payable but different in that a formal written promise to pay is required and interest is charged on the amount borrowed. A Notes Payable account is credited when the note is issued; the Notes Payable account will be debited three months later when the note is paid. Interest accrues throughout the life of the note payable, but it is

$3,000   Windsor, Ontario   November 1, 19____

Three months _____ after date _____ I _____ promise to pay

to the order of _____ National Bank _____

_____ ---Three thousand and no/100--- _____ dollars

for value received, with interest at _____ 12 percent per year _____

Roberts Real Estate Company

By *James Roberts*

not payable until the note matures on February 1. To the bank making the loan, the note signed by Roberts is an asset, a note receivable. The revenue earned by banks consists largely of interest charged to borrowers.

The journal entry made on November 1 to record the borrowing of $3,000 from the bank was as follows:

Cash   3,000
    Notes Payable   3,000
Obtained from bank three-month loan with interest at 12% a year.

Three months later, Roberts Real Estate Company must pay the bank $3,090, representing repayment of the $3,000 note payable plus $90 interest ($3,000 $\times$ .12 $\times$ $^3/_{12}$).[1] The $90 is the total interest expense for the three months. Although no payment will be made for three months, one-third of the interest expense ($30) is ***incurred*** each month, in the chart on page 145.

The following ***adjusting entry*** is made at November 30 to charge November operations with one month's interest expense and also to record the amount of interest owed to the bank at the end of November.

Interest Expense   30
    Interest Payable   30
To record interest expense accrued during November on note payable
($3,000 $\times$ 12% $\times$ $^1/_{12}$).

The debit balance in the Interest Expense account will appear in the November income statement; the credit balances in the Interest Payable and Notes Payable accounts will be shown in the balance sheet as liabilities. These two liability accounts will remain in the records until the maturity date of the loan, at which time a cash

[1] To simplify the interest calculation for demonstration purposes, the months rather than the days are used and thus the three days of grace for a note payable are not considered.

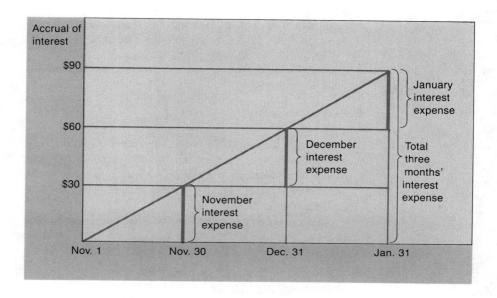

payment to the bank will wipe out both the Notes Payable account and the Interest Payable account.

Accrual of salary   On November 20, Roberts hired Carl Nelson as a part-time salesperson whose duties were to work evenings calling on property owners to secure listings of property for sale or rent. The agreed salary was $225 for a five-evening week, payable each Friday; payment for the first week was made on Friday, November 24. Personal income taxes and other taxes relating to payroll are ignored in this illustration.

Assume that the last day of the accounting period, November 30, fell on Thursday. Nelson had worked four evenings since being paid the preceding Friday and therefore had earned $180 ($4/5 \times 225). In order that this $180 of November salary expense be reflected in the accounts before the financial statements are prepared, an **_adjusting entry_** is necessary at November 30.

ADJUSTING ENTRY FOR
SALARIES EXPENSE
INCURRED BUT UNPAID
AT NOVEMBER 30

Salaries Expense	180	
Salaries Payable		180

To record salary expense and related liability to salesperson for last four evenings' work in November.

The debit balance in the Salaries Expense account will appear as an expense in the November income statement; the credit balance of $180 in the Salaries Payable account is the amount owing to the salesperson for work performed during the last four days of November and will appear among the liabilities in the balance sheet at November 30.

The next regular payday for Nelson will be Friday, December 1, which is the first day of the new accounting period. Since the accounts were adjusted and closed on November 30, all the revenue and expense accounts have zero balances at the beginning of business on December 1. The payment of a week's salary to Nelson will be recorded by the following entry on December 1:

PAYMENT OF SALARY
OVERLAPPING TWO
ACCOUNTING PERIODS

Salaries Payable	180	
Salaries Expense	45	
Cash		225

Paid weekly salary to salesperson.

Note that the net result of the November 30 accrual entry has been to split the salesperson's weekly salary expense between November and December. Four days of the work week in November, so four days' pay, or $180, was recognized as November expense. One day of the work week fell in December so $45 was recorded as December expense.

No accrual entry is necessary for other salaries in Roberts Real Estate Company because everyone except Nelson is paid regularly on the last working day of the month.

Recording unrecorded revenue

A business may earn revenue during the current accounting period but might not bill the customer until a future accounting period. This situation is likely to occur if additional services will be performed for the same customer, in which case the bill might not be prepared until all services are completed. Any revenue that has been **earned but not recorded** during the current accounting period should be recorded at the end of the period by means of an adjusting entry. This adjusting entry consists of a debit to an account receivable and a credit to the appropriate revenue account. The term **accrued revenue** often is used to describe revenue that has been earned during the period but that has **not been recorded** prior to the making of adjusting entries.

To illustrate this type of adjusting entry, assume that on November 16, Roberts Real Estate Company entered into a management agreement with Angela Clayton, the owner of two small office buildings. The company agreed to manage the Clayton properties for a fee of $240 a month, payable on the fifteenth of each month. No entry is made in the accounting records at the time of signing a contract, because no services have yet been rendered and no change has occurred in assets or liabilities. The managerial duties are to begin immediately, but the first monthly fee will not be received until December 15. The following **adjusting entry** is therefore necessary at November 30:

ADJUSTING ENTRY FOR
FEES EARNED BUT NOT
YET BILLED

Management Fees Receivable	120	
Management Fees Earned		120

To record accrued revenue from services rendered to Angela Clayton during November.

The debit balance in the Management Fees Receivable account will be shown in the balance sheet as an asset. The credit balance of the Management Fees Earned account, including earnings for both the Frank Day and the Angela Clayton contracts, will appear in the November income statement.

The collection of the first monthly fee from Clayton will occur in the next accounting period (December 15, to be exact). Of this $240 cash receipt, half represents collection of the asset account, Management Fees Receivable, created at November 30 by the adjusting entry. The other half of the $240 cash receipt represents revenue earned during December; this should be credited to the December revenue account for Management Fees Earned. The entry on December 15 is as follows:

MANAGEMENT FEE
APPLICABLE TO TWO
ACCOUNTING PERIODS

Cash	240	
Management Fees Receivable		120
Management Fees Earned		120

Collected commission from Angela Clayton for month ended December 15.

The net result of the November 30 accrual entry has been to divide the revenue from managing the Clayton properties between November and December in accordance with the timing of the services rendered.

Adjusting entries and the accrual basis of accounting

Adjusting entries help make accrual basis accounting work successfully. By preparing adjusting entries, we can recognize revenue in the accounting period in which it is *earned* and also recognize any unrecorded expenses that helped to *produce that revenue*. For example, the adjusting entry to record revenue that has been earned but not yet recorded helps achieve our goal of including in the income statement all the revenue *realized* during the accounting period. The adjusting entries that recognize expenses help to achieve the *matching principle* — that is, offsetting revenues with all the expenses incurred in generating that revenue.

THE WORK SHEET

4 Prepare a work sheet and discuss its usefulness.

The work necessary at the end of an accounting period includes construction of a trial balance, journalizing and posting of adjusting entries, preparation of financial statements, and journalizing and posting of closing entries. So many details are involved in these end-of-period procedures that it is easy to make errors. If these errors are recorded in the journal and in the ledger accounts, considerable time and effort can be wasted in correcting them. Both the journal and the ledger are formal, permanent records. One way of avoiding errors in the permanent accounting records and also of simplifying the work to be done at the end of the period is to use a *work sheet.*

In a manual accounting system, a work sheet is a large columnar sheet of paper, especially designed to arrange in a convenient systematic form all of the accounting data required at the end of the period. The work sheet is not a part of the permanent accounting records; it is prepared in pencil by accountants for their own convenience. If an error is made on the work sheet, it may be erased and corrected much more easily than an error in the formal accounting records. Furthermore, the work sheet is so designed as to minimize errors by automatically bringing to light many types of discrepancies that otherwise might be entered in the journal and posted to the ledger accounts. Dollar signs, decimal points, and commas are not used with the amounts

TRIAL BALANCE
IS ENTERED IN
FIRST PAIR OF
COLUMNS ON
WORK SHEET

ROBERTS REAL ESTATE COMPANY
Work Sheet
For the Month Ended November 30, 19___

	TRIAL BALANCE		ADJUSTMENTS		ADJUSTED TRIAL BALANCE		INCOME STATEMENT		BALANCE SHEET	
	DR	CR	DR	CR	DR	CR	DR	CR	DR	CR
Cash	21,740									
Accounts receivable	16,990									
Unexpired insurance	600									
Office supplies	720									
Land	130,000									
Building	36,000									
Accumulated depreciation: building		150								
Office equipment	5,400									
Accumulated depreciation: office equip.		45								
Notes payable		3,000								
Accounts payable		23,595								
Unearned management fees		1,800								
James Roberts, capital		180,771								
James Roberts, drawing	1,500									
Sales commissions earned		15,484								
Advertising expense	1,275									
Salaries expense	9,425									
Telephone expense	1,195									
	224,845	224,845								

entered on the worksheets, although commas are shown on this example. A work sheet for Roberts Real Estate appears on page 148.

The work sheet may be thought of as a testing ground on which the ledger accounts are adjusted, balanced, and arranged in the general form of financial statements. The satisfactory completion of a work sheet provides considerable assurance that all the details of the end-of-period accounting procedures have been properly brought together. After this point has been established, the work sheet then serves as the source from which the formal financial statements are prepared and the adjusting and closing entries are made in the journal.

Preparing the work sheet

Notice that the heading of the work sheet illustrated for Roberts Real Estate consists of three parts: (1) the name of the business, (2) the title *Work Sheet,* and (3) the period of time covered. The body of the work sheet contains five pairs of money columns, each pair consisting of a debit and a credit column. The procedures to be followed in preparing a work sheet will now be illustrated in five simple steps.

1 Enter the ledger account balances in the Trial Balance columns   The titles and balances of the ledger accounts at November 30 are copied into the Trial Balance columns of the work sheet, as illustrated on page 148.[2] In practice these amounts may be taken directly from the ledger. It would be a duplication of work to prepare a trial balance as a separate schedule and then to copy this information into the work sheet. As soon as the account balances have been listed on the work sheet, these two columns should be added and the totals entered.

2 Enter the adjustments in the Adjustments columns   The required adjustments for Roberts Real Estate Company have been explained earlier in this chapter; these same adjustments are now entered in the Adjustments columns of the work sheet. (See page 150.)

As a cross reference, the debit and credit parts of each adjustment are keyed together by placing a key letter to the left of each amount. For example, the adjustment debiting Insurance Expense and crediting Unexpired Insurance is identified by the key letter (a). The use of the key letters makes it easy to match a debit entry in the Adjustments columns with its related credit. The identifying letters also key the debit and credit entries in the Adjustments columns to the brief explanations which appear at the bottom of the work sheet.

The titles of any accounts debited or credited in the adjusting entries but *not listed* in the trial balance should be written on the work sheet below the trial balance. For example, Insurance Expense does not appear in the trial balance; therefore it should be written on the first available line below the trial balance totals. After all the adjustment debits and credits have been entered in the Adjustments columns, this pair of columns must be totalled. Proving the equality of debit and credit totals helps to detect any arithmetical errors and to prevent them from being carried over into other columns of the work sheet.

---

[2] The November balances of the ledger accounts reflect all transactions that occurred in the month, even though only those transactions that require adjusting entries have been presented so that we can concentrate on the demonstration of adjustments and work sheet.

EXPLANATORY
FOOTNOTES KEYED
TO ADJUSTMENTS

ROBERTS REAL ESTATE COMPANY
Work Sheet
For the Month Ended November 30, 19___

	TRIAL BALANCE DR	TRIAL BALANCE CR	ADJUSTMENTS* DR	ADJUSTMENTS* CR	ADJUSTED TRIAL BALANCE DR	ADJUSTED TRIAL BALANCE CR	INCOME STATEMENT DR	INCOME STATEMENT CR	BALANCE SHEET DR	BALANCE SHEET CR
Cash	21,740									
Accounts receivable	16,990									
Unexpired insurance	600			(a) 50						
Office supplies	720			(b) 220						
Land	130,000									
Building	36,000									
Accumulated depreciation: building		150		(c) 150						
Office equipment	5,400									
Accumulated depreciation: office equip.		45		(d) 45						
Notes payable		3,000								
Accounts payable		23,595								
Unearned management fees		1,800	(e) 300							
James Roberts, capital		180,771								
James Roberts, drawing	1,500									
Sales commissions earned		15,484								
Advertising expense	1,275									
Salaries expense	9,425		(g) 180							
Telephone expense	1,195									
	224,845	224,845								
Insurance expense			(a) 50							
Office supplies expense			(b) 220							
Depreciation expense: building			(c) 150							
Depreciation expense: office equip.			(d) 45							
Management fees earned				(e) 300 (h) 120						
Interest expense			(f) 30							
Interest payable				(f) 30						
Salaries payable				(g) 180						
Management fees receivable			(h) 120							
			1,095	1,095						

*Adjustments:
(a) Portion of insurance cost which expired during November.
(b) Office supplies used during November.
(c) Depreciation of building during November.
(d) Depreciation of office equipment during November.
(e) Earned one-sixth of the fee collected in advance on the Day properties.
(f) Interest expense accrued during November on note payable ($3,000 × 12% × $1/12$).
(g) Salesperson's salary for last four days of November.
(h) Management fee accrued on Clayton contract in November.

3 Enter the account balances as adjusted in the Adjusted Trial Balance columns
The work sheet as it appears after completion of the Adjusted Trial Balance columns
is illustrated on page 152. Each account balance in the first pair of columns is combined with the adjustment, if any, in the second pair of columns, and the combined
amount is entered in the Adjusted Trial Balance columns. This process of combining
the items on each line throughout the first four columns of the work sheet requires
horizontal addition or subtraction. It is called "cross footing," in contrast to the
addition of items in a vertical column, which is called "footing" the column.

For example, the Office Supplies account has a debit balance of $720 in the Trial
Balance columns. This $720 debit amount is combined with the $220 credit appearing on the same line in the Adjustments column; the combination of a $720 debit with
a $220 credit produces an adjusted debit amount of $500 in the Adjusted Trial
Balance debit column. As another example, consider the Office Supplies Expense
account. This account had no balance in the Trial Balance columns but shows a $220
debit in the Adjustments debit column. The combination of a zero starting balance
and $220 debit adjustment produces a $220 debit amount in the Adjusted Trial
Balance.

Many of the accounts in the trial balance are not affected by the adjustments made
at the end of the month; the balances of these accounts (such as Cash, Land,
Building, or Notes Payable in the illustrated work sheet) are entered in the Adjusted
Trial Balance columns in exactly the same amounts as shown in the Trial Balance
columns. After all the accounts have been extended into the Adjusted Trial Balance
columns, this pair of columns is totalled to prove that no arithmetical errors have
been made up to this point.

**4 Extend each amount in the Adjusted Trial Balance columns into the Income State-
ment columns or into the Balance Sheet columns**   Assets, liabilities, and the owner's
capital and drawing accounts are extended to the Balance Sheet columns; revenue
and expense accounts are extended to the Income Statement columns.

The process of extending amounts horizontally across the work sheet begins with
the account at the top of the work sheet — usually Cash. The cash figure is extended
to the Balance Sheet debit column. Then the accountant goes down the work sheet
line by line, extending each account balance to the appropriate Income Statement or
Balance Sheet column. The likelihood of error is much less when each account is
extended in the order of its appearance on the work sheet, than if accounts are
extended in random order. The work sheet as it appears after completion of this sort-
ing process is illustrated on page 153. Note that each amount in the Adjusted Trial
Balance columns is extended to one *and only one* of the four remaining columns.

**5 Total the Income Statement columns and the Balance Sheet columns. Enter the
net income or net loss as a balancing figure in both pairs of columns, and again
compute column totals**   The work sheet as it appears after this final step is shown on
page 154.

The net income or net loss for the period is determined by computing the difference
between the totals of the two Income Statement columns. In the illustrated work
sheet, the credit column total is the larger and the excess represents net income as
shown at the top of page 155.

ENTER THE ADJUSTED
AMOUNTS IN COLUMNS 5
AND 6 OF WORK SHEET

ROBERTS REAL ESTATE COMPANY
Work Sheet
For the Month Ended November 30, 19____

	TRIAL BALANCE		ADJUSTMENTS*		ADJUSTED TRIAL BALANCE		INCOME STATEMENT		BALANCE SHEET	
	DR	CR	DR	CR	DR	CR	DR	CR	DR	CR
Cash	21,740				21,740					
Accounts receivable	16,990				16,990					
Unexpired insurance	600			(a) 50	550					
Office supplies	720			(b) 220	500					
Land	130,000				130,000					
Building	36,000				36,000					
Accumulated depreciation: building		150		(c) 150		300				
Office equipment	5,400				5,400					
Accumulated depreciation: office equip.		45		(d) 45		90				
Notes payable		3,000				3,000				
Accounts payable		23,595				23,595					
Unearned management fees		1,800	(e) 300			1,500				
James Roberts, capital		180,771				180,771				
James Roberts, drawing	1,500				1,500					
Sales commissions earned		15,484				15,484				
Advertising expense	1,275				1,275					
Salaries expense	9,425		(g) 180		9,605					
Telephone expense	1,195				1,195					
	224,845	224,845								
Insurance expense			(a) 50		50					
Office supplies expense			(b) 220		220					
Depreciation expense: building			(c) 150		150					
Depreciation expense: office equip.			(d) 45		45					
Management fees earned				(e) 300 (h) 120		420				
Interest expense			(f) 30		30					
Interest payable				(f) 30		30				
Salaries payable				(g) 180		180				
Management fees receivable			(h) 120		120					
			1,095	1,095	225,370	225,370				

*Explanatory notes relating to adjustments are the same as on page 150.

EXTEND EACH ADJUSTED
AMOUNT TO COLUMNS
FOR INCOME STATEMENT
OR BALANCE SHEET

ROBERTS REAL ESTATE COMPANY
Work Sheet
For the Month Ended November 30, 19___

	TRIAL BALANCE		ADJUSTMENTS*		ADJUSTED TRIAL BALANCE		INCOME STATEMENT		BALANCE SHEET	
	DR	CR	DR	CR	DR	CR	DR	CR	DR	CR
Cash	21,740				21,740				21,740	
Accounts receivable	16,990				16,990				16,990	
Unexpired insurance	600			(a) 50	550				550	
Office supplies	720			(b) 220	500				500	
Land	130,000				130,000				130,000	
Building	36,000				36,000				36,000	
Accumulated depreciation: building		150		(c) 150		300				300
Office equipment	5,400				5,400				5,400	
Accumulated depreciation: office equip.		45		(d) 45		90				90
Notes payable		3,000				3,000				3,000
Accounts payable		23,595				23,595				23,595
Unearned management fees		1,800	(e) 300			1,500				1,500
James Roberts, capital		180,771				180,771				180,771
James Roberts, drawing	1,500				1,500				1,500	
Sales commissions earned		15,484				15,484		15,484		
Advertising expense	1,275				1,275		1,275			
Salaries expense	9,425		(g) 180		9,605		9,605			
Telephone expense	1,195				1,195		1,195			
	224,845	224,845								
Insurance expense			(a) 50		50		50			
Office supplies expense			(b) 220		220		220			
Depreciation expense: building			(c) 150		150		150			
Depreciation expense: office equip.			(d) 45		45		45			
Management fees earned				(e) 300 (h) 120		420		420		
Interest expense			(f) 30		30		30			
Interest payable				(f) 30		30				30
Salaries payable				(g) 180		180				180
Management fees receivable			(h) 120		120				120	
			1,095	1,095	225,370	225,370				

*Explanatory notes relating to adjustments are the same as on page 150.

COMPLETED
WORK SHEET

ROBERTS REAL ESTATE COMPANY
Work Sheet
For the Month Ended November 30, 19___

	TRIAL BALANCE DR	TRIAL BALANCE CR	ADJUSTMENTS* DR	ADJUSTMENTS* CR	ADJUSTED TRIAL BALANCE DR	ADJUSTED TRIAL BALANCE CR	INCOME STATEMENT DR	INCOME STATEMENT CR	BALANCE SHEET DR	BALANCE SHEET CR
Cash	21,740				21,740				21,740	
Accounts receivable	16,990				16,990				16,990	
Unexpired insurance	600			(a) 50	550				550	
Office supplies	720			(b) 220	500				500	
Land	130,000				130,000				130,000	
Building	36,000				36,000				36,000	
Accumulated depreciation: building		150		(c) 150		300				300
Office equipment	5,400				5,400				5,400	
Accumulated depreciation: office equip.		45		(d) 45		90				90
Notes payable		3,000				3,000				3,000
Accounts payable		23,595				23,595				23,595
Unearned management fees		1,800	(e) 300			1,500				1,500
James Roberts, capital		180,771				180,771				180,771
James Roberts, drawing	1,500				1,500				1,500	
Sales commissions earned		15,484				15,484		15,484		
Advertising expense	1,275				1,275		1,275			
Salaries expense	9,425		(g) 180		9,605		9,605			
Telephone expense	1,195				1,195		1,195			
	224,845	224,845								
Insurance expense			(a) 50		50		50			
Office supplies expense			(b) 220		220		220			
Depreciation expense: building			(c) 150		150		150			
Depreciation expense: office equip.			(d) 45		45		45			
Management fees earned				(e) 300 (h) 120		420		420		
Interest expense			(f) 30		30		30			
Interest payable				(f) 30		30				30
Salaries payable				(g) 180		180				180
Management fees receivable			(h) 120		120				120	
			1,095	1,095	225,370	225,370	12,570	15,904	212,800	209,466
Net Income							3,334			3,334
							15,904	15,904	212,800	212,800

Income Statement credit column total (revenue) $15,904
Income Statement debit column total (expenses)   12,570
Difference: net income for period . . . . $ 3,334

Note on the work sheet that the net income of $3,334 is entered in the Income Statement *debit* column as a balancing figure and also on the same line as a balancing figure in the Balance Sheet *credit* column. The caption *Net Income* is written in the space for account titles to identify and explain this item. New totals are then computed for both the Income Statement columns and the Balance Sheet columns. Each pair of columns is now in balance.

The reason for entering the net income of $3,334 in the Balance Sheet credit column is that the net income accumulated during the period in the revenue and expense accounts causes an increase in the owner's equity. If the balance sheet columns did not have equal totals after the net income had been recorded in the credit column, the lack of agreement would indicate that an error has been made in the work sheet.

Let us assume for a moment that the month's operations had produced a *net loss* rather than a *net income*. In that case the Income Statement debit column would exceed the credit column. The excess of the debits (expenses) over the credits (revenue) would have to be entered in the *credit column* in order to bring the two Income Statement columns into balance. The incurring of a net loss would decrease the owner's equity; therefore, the net loss would be entered as a balancing figure in the Balance Sheet *debit column*. The Balance Sheet columns would then have equal totals.

Self-balancing nature of the work sheet   Why does the entering of the net income or net loss in one of the Balance Sheet columns bring this pair of columns into balance? The answer is short and simple. All the accounts in the Balance Sheet columns have November 30 balances with the exception of the owner's capital account, which still shows the October 31 balance. By bringing in the current month's net income as an addition to the October 31 capital, the capital account is brought up to date as of November 30 (except for the drawing account, which is later closed to the capital account). The Balance Sheet columns now prove the familiar proposition that assets are equal to the total of liabilities and owner's equity.

Uses for the work sheet

Preparing financial statements   Preparing the formal financial statements from the work sheet is an easy step. All the information needed for both the income statement and the balance sheet has already been sorted and arranged in convenient form in the work sheet. For example, compare the amounts in the income statement at the top of page 156 with the amounts listed in the Income Statement columns of the completed work sheet.

Notice that in our November 30 work sheet, the owner's capital account still contains its November 1 balance of $180,771. This is because all the changes in owner's equity occurring in the month were recorded in the *temporary* proprietorship accounts (the revenue, expense, and drawing accounts), rather than in the owner's

DATA TAKEN FROM
INCOME STATEMENT
COLUMNS OF WORK
SHEET

ROBERTS REAL ESTATE COMPANY
Income Statement
For the Month Ended November 30, 19___

Revenue:		
Sales commissions earned		$15,484
Management fees earned		420
Total revenue		$15,904
Expenses:		
Advertising	$1,275	
Salaries	9,605	
Telephone	1,195	
Insurance	50	
Office supplies	220	
Depreciation: building	150	
Depreciation: office equipment	45	
Interest	30	
Total expenses		12,570
Net income		$ 3,334

capital account. In the ledger, the owner's capital account will be brought up-to-date when the November closing entries are recorded and posted.

The work sheet provides us with all the information we need to compute the amount of owner's equity at November 30. During November, owner's equity was increased by the earning of net income ($3,334) and decreased by the withdrawal of assets by the owner ($1,500). Previously, we have used the owner's equity section of the balance sheet to show these changes in the owner's capital account. An alternative is to show these changes in a separate financial statement, called a *statement of owner's equity.* When this separate statement is prepared, only the *ending balance* of the owner's capital account is shown in the balance sheet.

A statement of owner's equity covers the same span of time as does the income statement. The November statement of owner's equity for Roberts Real Estate Company is shown below:

NET INCOME EXCEEDED
WITHDRAWALS BY
OWNER

ROBERTS REAL ESTATE COMPANY
Statement of Owner's Equity
For the Month Ended November 30, 19___

James Roberts, capital, Nov. 1, 19___	$180,771
Add: Net income for November	3,334
Subtotal	$184,105
Less: Withdrawals	1,500
James Roberts, capital, Nov. 30, 19___	$182,605

Finally, the November 30 balance sheet for Roberts Real Estate contains the amounts for assets and liabilities listed in the Balance Sheet columns of the work sheet, along with the new balance of owner's equity as shown on page 157.

ROBERTS REAL ESTATE COMPANY
Balance Sheet
November 30, 19___

ASSETS

Cash		$ 21,740
Accounts receivable		16,990
Management fees receivable		120
Unexpired insurance		550
Office supplies		500
Land		130,000
Building	$36,000	
Less: Accumulated depreciation	300	35,700
Office equipment	$ 5,400	
Less: Accumulated depreciation	90	5,310
Total assets		$210,910

LIABILITIES & OWNER'S EQUITY

Liabilities:	
Notes payable	$ 3,000
Accounts payable	23,595
Interest payable	30
Salaries payable	180
Unearned management fees	1,500
Total liabilities	$ 28,305
Owner's equity:	
James Roberts, capital	182,605
Total liabilities & owner's equity	$210,910

Recording adjusting entries in the accounting records   After the financial statements have been prepared from the work sheet at the end of the period, adjusting journal entries are prepared to bring the ledger accounts into agreement with the financial statements. This is an easy step because the adjustments have already been computed on the work sheet. The amounts appearing in the Adjustments columns of the work sheet and the related explanations at the bottom of the work sheet provide all the necessary information for the adjusting entries, as shown in the following illustration. These adjusting entries are first entered in the journal and then posted to the ledger accounts.

General Journal   Page 5

DATE		ACCOUNT TITLES AND EXPLANATION	LP	DEBIT	CREDIT
19___					
Nov	30	Insurance Expense		50	
		Unexpired Insurance			50
		Insurance expense for November.			

General Journal   Page 5

DATE		ACCOUNT TITLES AND EXPLANATION	LP	DEBIT	CREDIT
19__					
Nov	30	Office Supplies Expense		220	
		Office Supplies			220
		Office supplies used during November.			
	30	Depreciation Expense: Building		150	
		Accumulated Depreciation: Building .			150
		Depreciation for November			
		($36,000 ÷ 240 = $150).			
	30	Depreciation Expense: Office Equipment .		45	
		Accumulated Depreciation:			
		Office Equipment			45
		Depreciation for November			
		($5,400 ÷ 120 = $45).			
	30	Unearned Management Fees		300	
		Management Fees Earned			300
		Earned one-sixth of fee collected in			
		advance for management of the			
		properties owned by Frank Day.			
	30	Interest Expense		30	
		Interest Payable			30
		Interest expense accrued during			
		November on note payable			
		($3,000 × 12% × 1/12)			
	30	Salaries Expense		180	
		Salaries Payable			180
		To record expense and related liability			
		to salesperson for last four evenings'			
		work in November.			
	30	Management Fees Receivable		120	
		Management Fees Earned			120
		To record the receivable and related			
		revenue earned for managing			
		properties owned by Angela Clayton.			

Recording closing entries When the financial statements have been prepared, the revenue and expense accounts have served their purpose for the current period and should be closed. These accounts then will have zero balances and will be ready for the recording of revenue and expenses during the next fiscal period. The completed work sheet provides in convenient form all the information needed to make the closing entries. The preparation of closing entries from the work sheet may be summarized as follows:

1 To close the accounts listed in the Income Statement credit column, debit the revenue accounts and credit Income Summary.

2 To close the accounts listed in the Income Statement debit column, debit Income Summary and credit the expense accounts.

3 To close the Income Summary account, transfer the balancing figure in the Income Statement columns of the work sheet ($3,334 in the illustration) to the owner's capital account. A net income is transferred by debiting Income Summary and crediting the capital account; a net loss is transferred by debiting the capital account and crediting Income Summary.

4 To close the owner's drawing account, debit the capital account and credit the drawing account. Note on the work sheet that the account, James Roberts, Drawing, is extended from the Adjusted Trial Balance debit column to the Balance Sheet debit column. It does not appear in the Income Statement columns because a withdrawal of cash by the owner is not regarded as an expense of the business.

The closing entries at November 30 are shown as follows:

CLOSING ENTRIES
DERIVED FROM
WORK SHEET

General Journal   Page 6

DATE		ACCOUNT TITLES AND EXPLANATION	LP	DEBIT	CREDIT
19__					
Nov	30	Sales Commission Earned		15,484	
		Management Fees Earned		420	
		Income Summary			15,904
		To close the revenue accounts.			
	30	Income Summary		12,570	
		Advertising Expense			1,275
		Salaries Expense			9,605
		Telephone Expense			1,195
		Insurance Expense			50
		Office Supplies Expense			220
		Depreciation Expense: Building			150
		Depreciation Expense:			
		Office Equipment			45
		Interest Expense			30
		To close the expense accounts.			
	30	Income Summary		3,334	
		James Roberts, Capital			3,334
		To close the Income Summary account.			
	30	James Roberts, Capital		1,500	
		James Roberts, Drawing			1,500
		To close the owner's drawing account.			

Work sheets in computer-based systems   The "work sheet" in a computer-based accounting system usually consists of a display on the monitor screen rather than a sheet of columnar paper. Spreadsheet programs, such as SuperCalc, Lotus, and Framework are ideally suited to preparing a work sheet in a computerized accounting system.

Most of the steps involved in preparing a work sheet are mechanical and can be performed automatically in a computer-based system. Thus, the work sheet can be prepared faster and more easily than in a manual system. A trial balance, for example, is merely a listing of the ledger account balances, and can be prepared instantly by computer. Entering the adjustments, on the other hand, requires human judgment and analysis. Someone familiar with generally accepted accounting principles and with the unrecorded business activities of the company must decide what adjustments are necessary and must enter the adjustment data. Once the adjustments have been entered, the computer can instantly complete the work sheet. When the accountant is satisfied that the adjustments shown in the work sheet are correct, the adjusting and closing entries can be entered in the formal accounting records with the touch of a button.

5 Describe the steps in the accounting cycle.

The accounting cycle

As stated at the beginning of this chapter, the life of a business is divided into accounting periods of equal length. In each period we repeat a standard sequence of accounting procedures beginning with the journalizing of transactions and concluding with an after-closing trial balance.

Because the work sheet includes the trial balance, the adjusting entries in preliminary form, and an adjusted trial balance, the use of a work sheet will modify the sequence of procedures given in Chapter 3, as follows:

1 **Journalize transactions**   Analyze business transactions as they occur and record them promptly in a journal.
2 **Post to ledger accounts**   Transfer debits and credits from journal entries to ledger accounts.
3 **Prepare a work sheet**   Begin with a trial balance of the ledger, enter all necessary adjustments, sort the adjusted account balances between income statement accounts and balance sheet accounts, and determine the net income or net loss.
4 **Prepare financial statements**   Utilize the information in the work sheet to prepare an income statement, a statement of owner's equity, and a balance sheet.
5 **Adjust and close the accounts**   Using the information in the work sheet as a guide, enter the adjusting entries in the journal. Post these entries to ledger accounts. Prepare and post journal entries to close the revenue and expense accounts into the Income Summary account and to transfer the net income or net loss to the owner's capital account. Also prepare and post a journal entry to close the owner's drawing account into the owner's capital account.
6 **Prepare an after-closing trial balance**   Prove that equality of debit and credit balances in the ledger has not been upset by the adjusting and closing procedures.

The preceding sequence of accounting procedures constitutes a complete accounting process. The regular repetition of this standardized set of procedures in each accounting period is often referred to as the *accounting cycle.* The procedures of a complete accounting cycle are illustrated below. The white symbols indicate the accounting procedures; the shaded gray symbols represent accounting records, schedules, and statements.

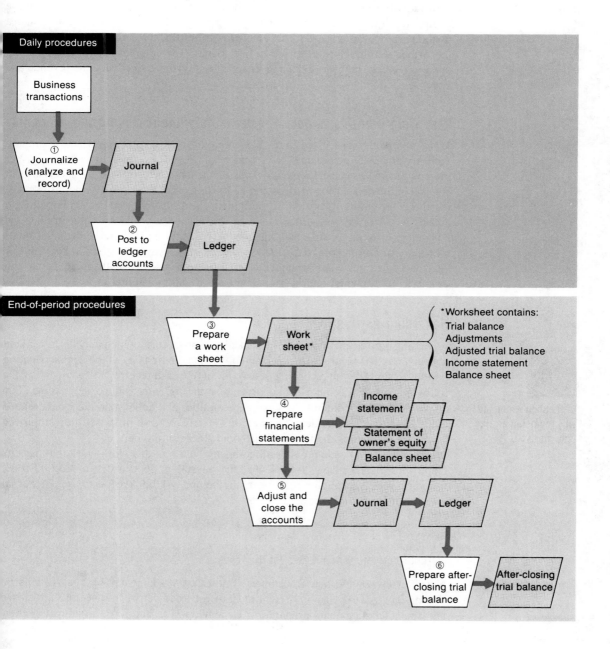

Note that the preparing of financial statements (Step 4) comes before entering adjusting and closing entries in the journal and posting these entries to the ledger (Step 5). This sequence reflects the fact that *management wants the financial statements as soon as possible.* Once the work sheet is complete, all information required for the financial statements is available. Top priority then goes to preparation of the financial statements.

In most business concerns the accounts are closed only once a year; for these companies the accounting cycle is one year in length. For purposes of illustration in a textbook, however, it is often convenient to assume that the entire accounting cycle is performed within the time period of one month. The completion of the accounting cycle is the occasion for preparing financial statements and closing the revenue and expense accounts.

Preparing monthly financial statements without closing the accounts

Many companies that close their accounts only once a year nevertheless prepare *monthly* financial statements for managerial use. These monthly statements are prepared from work sheets, but the adjustments indicated on the work sheets are not entered in the accounting records and no closing entries are made. Under this plan, the time-consuming operation of journalizing and posting adjustments and closing entries is performed only at the end of the fiscal year, but the company has the advantage of monthly financial statements. Monthly and quarterly financial statements are often referred to as *interim statements,* because they are in between the year-end statements. The annual or year-end statements are usually audited by a firm of public accountants; interim statements are usually unaudited.

Reversing entries

6 Explain when and why reversing entries may be used.

Reversing entries are an optional bookkeeping procedure, which may be carried out at year-end (these entries are dated and posted on the first day of the next accounting period) to simplify the recording of certain routine cash receipts and payments in the following period. As the name suggests, a *reversing entry* is the exact reverse of an adjusting entry. It contains the same account titles and dollar amounts as the related adjusting entry, but the debits and credits are the reverse of those in the adjusting entry and the date is the first day of the next accounting period.

Let us use as an example a small company on a five-day work week that pays its employees each Friday. Assume that the payroll is $600 a day or $3,000 for a five-day week. Throughout the year, the company's bookkeeper makes a journal entry each Friday as follows:

REGULAR WEEKLY
ENTRY FOR PAYROLL

Salaries expense	3,000	
Cash		3,000

To record payment of salaries for the week.

Next, let us assume that December 31, the last working day of Year 1, falls on Wednesday. All expenses of Year 1 must be recorded before the accounts are closed and financial statements prepared at December 31. Therefore, an adjusting entry must be made to record the salaries expense and the related liability to employees for the three days they have worked since the last payday. The adjusting entry for $1,800 (computed as 3 × $600 daily salary expense) is shown below:

Dec. 31 Salaries Expense 1,800
          Salaries Payable 1,800
          To record salaries expense and the related liability to
          employees for last three days worked in December.

The closing of the accounts on December 31 will reduce the Salaries Expense account to zero, but the liability account, Salaries Payable, will remain open with its $1,800 credit balance at the beginning of the new year. On the next regular payday, Friday, January 2, the company's bookkeeper can record the $3,000 payroll by a debit of $1,800 to Salaries Payable, a debit of $1,200 to Salaries Expense, and a credit of $3,000 to Cash. However, splitting the debit side of the entry in this manner ($1,800 to the liability account and $1,200 to expense) requires more understanding and alertness for the bookkeeper than if the entry were identical with the other 51 payroll entries made during the year.

By making a *reversing entry* as of the first day of the new accounting period, we can simplify the recording of routine transactions and avoid the need for the company's bookkeeper to refer to prior adjusting entries for guidance. The reversing entry for the $1,800 year-end accrual of salaries would be dated January 1, Year 2, and would probably be made under the direction of the accountant responsible for the year-end closing of the accounts and preparation of financial statements. The entry would be as follows:

Jan. 1 Salaries Payable 1,800
          Salaries Expense 1,800
          To reverse the accrual of salaries made on Dec. 31, Year 1.

This reversing entry closes the Salaries Payable account by transferring the $1,800 liability to the credit side of the Salaries Expense account. Thus, the Salaries Expense account begins the new year with an abnormal credit balance of $1,800. On Friday, January 2, the normal payroll entry for $3,000 will be made to the same accounts as on every other Friday during the year.

Jan. 2 Salaries Expense 3,000
          Cash 3,000
          Paid salaries for week ended Jan. 2, Year 2.

After this January 2 entry has been posted, the ledger account for Salaries Expense will show a debit balance of $1,200, the result of this $3,000 debit and the $1,800 credit from the reversing entry on January 1. The amount of $1,200 is the correct expense for the two workdays of the new year at $600 a day. The results, of course, are *exactly the same* as if no reversing entry had been used and the company's bookkeeper had split the debit side of the January 2 payroll entry between Salaries Payable and Salaries Expense.

The ledger accounts for Salaries Expense and for Salaries Payable are shown below to illustrate the effect of posting the adjusting entry and the reversing entry.

SALARIES EXPENSE			DEBIT	CREDIT	BALANCE	Account No.
YEAR 1			DEBIT	CREDIT	BALANCE	
Various	(51 weekly entries of $3,000)				153000	
Dec. 31	Adjusting entry (3 days @ $600)		1800		154800	
31	To close at year-end			154800	—0—	
Year 2						
Jan. 1	Reversing entry			1800	1800 cr.	
2	Weekly payroll		3000		1200	

SALARIES PAYABLE			DEBIT	CREDIT	BALANCE	Account No.
YEAR 1			DEBIT	CREDIT	BALANCE	
Dec. 31	Adjusting entry (3 days @ $600)			1800	1800	
Year 2						
Jan. 1	Reversing entry		1800		—0—	

Which adjusting entries should be reversed? Even when a company follows a policy of making reversing entries, *not all adjusting entries should be reversed.* Only those adjustments that *create an account receivable or a short-term liability* should be reversed. These adjustments will be followed by cash receipts or cash payments within the near future. Reversing these adjusting entries will enable the company's bookkeeper to record the upcoming cash transactions in a routine manner.

An adjusting entry that apportions an amount recorded in the past *should not be reversed.* Thus we do *not* reverse the adjusting entries that apportion recorded costs (such as depreciation), or that record the earning of revenue collected in advance.

In summary, reversing entries may be made for those adjusting entries that record *unrecorded expenses* or *unrecorded revenue.* Reversing entries are *not* made for adjustments that apportion recorded costs or recorded revenue.

Reversing entries in a computer-based system   Reversing entries do not require any analysis of transactions. Rather, they merely involve reversing the debit and credit amounts of specific adjusting entries. The adjusting entries to be reversed can be identified by a simple rule — namely, reverse those adjustments that increase accounts receivable or short-term liabilities. Thus, a computer may be programmed to prepare reversing entries automatically.

Finally, remember that reversing entries are *optional.* They are intended to simplify the accounting process, but they are *not essential* in the application of generally accepted accounting principles or in the preparation of financial statements.

END-OF-CHAPTER REVIEW

SUMMARY OF CHAPTER LEARNING OBJECTIVES

1 Explain how accounting periods of equal length are useful in evaluating the income of a business.

The net income of a business is measured for a specified period of time, termed the accounting period. When accounting periods are of equal length, we can compare the income of the current period with that of prior periods to see if operating results are improving or declining.

2 State the purpose of adjusting entries and explain how these entries are related to the concepts of accrual accounting.

The purpose of adjusting entries is to record certain revenue and expenses that are not properly measured in the course of recording daily business transactions. Adjusting entries help to achieve the basic goals of accrual accounting — recognizing revenue when it is earned, and recognizing expenses when the goods or services are used.

3 Describe the four basic types of adjusting entries.

The four basic types of adjusting entries are entries to: (1) apportion recorded costs, (2) apportion unearned revenue, (3) record unrecorded expenses, and (4) record unrecorded revenue.

4 Prepare a work sheet and discuss its usefulness.

A work sheet is a "testing ground" on which the ledger accounts are adjusted, balanced, and arranged in the format of financial statements. A work sheet consists of a trial balance, the end-of-period adjusting entries, an adjusted trial balance, and columns showing the ledger accounts arranged as an income statement and balance sheet. The completed work sheet is used as the basis for preparing financial statements and for recording adjusting and closing entries in the formal accounting records.

5 Describe the steps in the accounting cycle.

When a work sheet is prepared, the steps in the accounting cycle may be summarized as follows: (1) journalize transactions, (2) post to ledger accounts, (3) prepare a work sheet, (4) prepare financial statements, (5) adjust and close the accounts, and (6) prepare an after-closing trial balance.

6 Explain when and why reversing entries may be used.

Reversing entries are an optional bookkeeping procedure that may be applied at the end of the accounting period to simplify the recording of routine cash receipts and payments in the following accounting period. When reversing entries are used, they should be made for any adjusting entry that creates an account receivable or a short-term liability. In short, they should be made for any adjusting entry that accrues either revenue or expense.

KEY TERMS INTRODUCED OR EMPHASIZED IN CHAPTER 4

Accounting cycle The sequence of accounting procedures performed during an accounting period. The procedures include journalizing transactions, posting, preparation of a work sheet and financial statements, adjusting and closing the accounts, and preparation of an after-closing trial balance.

Accrued expenses Expenses such as salaries of employees and interest on notes payable that have been accumulating day-by-day, but are unrecorded and unpaid at the end of the period. Also called *unrecorded expenses.*

Accrued revenue Revenue that has been earned during the accounting period but has not been recorded or collected prior to the closing date. Also called *unrecorded revenue.*

Book value The net amount at which an asset is shown in accounting records. For depreciable assets, book value equals cost minus accumulated depreciation. Also called *carrying value.*

Carrying value See book value.

Deferred revenue See unearned revenue.

Interim statements Financial statements prepared at intervals of less than one year. Usually quarterly and monthly statements.

Prepaid expenses Advance payments for such expenses as rent and insurance. The portion that has not been used up at the end of the accounting period is included in the balance sheet as an asset.

Promissory note A formal written promise to repay an amount borrowed plus interest at a future date.

Reversing entries An optional year-end bookkeeping technique consisting of the reversal on the first day of the new accounting period of those year-end adjusting entries that accrue expenses or revenue and thus will be followed by later cash payments or receipts. Purpose is to permit company personnel to record routine transactions in a standard manner without referring to prior adjusting entries.

Unearned revenue An obligation to render services or deliver goods in the future because of receipt of advance payment.

Unrecorded expenses See accrued expenses.

Unrecorded revenue See accrued revenue.

Work sheet A large columnar sheet designed to arrange in convenient form all the accounting data required at the end of the period. Facilitates preparation of financial statements and the work of adjusting and closing the accounts.

DEMONSTRATION PROBLEM FOR YOUR REVIEW

Reed Geophysical Company adjusts and closes its accounts at the end of the calendar year. At December 31, 19___, the following trial balance was prepared from the ledger:

REED GEOPHYSICAL COMPANY
Trial Balance
December 31, 19___

Cash	$ 12,540	
Prepaid rent	3,300	
Prepaid dues and subscriptions	960	
Supplies	1,300	
Equipment	20,000	
Accumulated depreciation: equipment		$ 1,200
Notes payable		5,000
Unearned consulting fees		35,650
Glen Reed, capital		17,040
Glen Reed, drawing	27,000	
Consulting fees earned		90,860
Salaries expense	66,900	
Telephone expense	2,550	
Rent expense	11,000	
Miscellaneous expense	4,200	
	$149,750	$149,750

Other data

(a) For the first 11 months of the year, office rent had been charged to the Rent Expense account at a rate of $1,000 per month. On December 1, however, the company signed a new rental agreement and paid three months' rent in advance at a rate of $1,100 per month. This advance payment was debited to the Prepaid Rent account.

(b) Dues and subscriptions expired during the year in the total amount of $710.

(c) A count of supplies on hand was made at December 31; the cost of the unused supplies was $450.

(d) The useful life of the equipment has been estimated at 10 years from date of acquisition.

(e) Accrued interest on notes payable amounted to $100 at year-end.

(f) Consulting services valued at $32,550 were rendered during the year for clients who had made payment in advance.

(g) It is the custom of the firm to bill clients only when consulting work is completed or, in the case of prolonged engagements, at six-month intervals. At December 31, engineering services valued at $3,000 had been rendered to clients but not yet billed. No advance payments had been received from these clients.

(h) Salaries earned by employees but not yet paid amounted to $2,200 at December 31.

Instructions   Prepare a work sheet for the year ended December 31, 19___.

SOLUTION TO DEMONSTRATION PROBLEM

The work sheet required in the solution to the demonstration problem is to be found on page 168.

REED GEOPHYSICAL COMPANY
Work Sheet
For the Year Ended December 31, 19____

	TRIAL BALANCE		ADJUSTMENTS*		ADJUSTED TRIAL BALANCE		INCOME STATEMENT		BALANCE SHEET	
	DR	CR	DR	CR	DR	CR	DR	CR	DR	CR
Cash	12,540				12,540				12,540	
Prepaid rent	3,300			(a) 1,100	2,200				2,200	
Prepaid dues and subscriptions	960			(b) 710	250				250	
Supplies	1,300			(c) 850	450				450	
Equipment	20,000				20,000				20,000	
Accumulated depreciation: equipment		1,200		(d) 2,000		3,200				3,200
Notes payable		5,000				5,000				5,000
Unearned consulting fees		35,650	(f) 32,550			3,100				3,100
Glen Reed, capital		17,040				17,040				17,040
Glen Reed, drawing	27,000				27,000				27,000	
Consulting fees earned		90,860		(f) 32,550 (g) 3,000		126,410		126,410		
	149,750	149,750								
Salaries expense	66,900		(h) 2,200		69,100		69,100			
Telephone expense	2,550				2,550		2,550			
Rent expense	11,000		(a) 1,100		12,100		12,100			
Miscellaneous expense	4,200				4,200		4,200			
Dues and subscriptions expense			(b) 710		710		710			
Supplies expense			(c) 850		850		850			
Depreciation expense: equipment			(d) 2,000		2,000		2,000			
Interest expense			(e) 100		100		100			
Interest payable				(e) 100		100				100
Consulting fees receivable			(g) 3,000		3,000				3,000	
Salaries payable				(h) 2,200		2,200				2,200
			42,510	42,510	157,050	157,050	91,610	126,410	65,440	30,640
Net Income							34,800			34,800
							126,410	126,410	65,440	65,440

*Adjustments:
(a) Rent expense for December.
(b) Dues and subscriptions expense for year.
(c) Supplies used for year ($1,300 – $450 = $850).
(d) Depreciation expense for year.
(e) Accrued interest on notes payable
(f) Consulting services performed for clients who paid in advance.
(g) Services rendered but not billed.
(h) Salaries earned but not paid.

ASSIGNMENT MATERIAL

REVIEW QUESTIONS

1 What is the purpose of making adjusting entries? Your answer should relate adjusting entries to the goals of accrual accounting.

2 Do all transactions involving revenue or expenses require adjusting entries at the end of the accounting period? If not, what is the distinguishing characteristic of those transactions that do require adjusting entries?

3 Do adjusting entries affect income statement accounts, balance sheet accounts, or both? Explain.

4 Why does the recording of adjusting entries require a better understanding of the concepts of accrual accounting than does the recording of routine revenue and expense transactions occurring throughout the period?

5 Why does the purchase of a one-year insurance policy four months ago give rise to insurance expense in the current month?

6 If services have been rendered during the current accounting period but no revenue has been recorded and no bill has been sent to the customers, why is an adjusting entry needed? What types of accounts should be debited and credited by this entry?

7 What is meant by the term *unearned revenue?* Where should an unearned revenue account appear in the financial statements? As the work is done, what happens to the balance of an unearned revenue account?

8 At the end of the current year, the adjusted trial balance of the Midas Company showed the following account balances, among others:

Building, $31,600
Depreciation Expense: Building, $1,580
Accumulated Depreciation: Building, $11,060

Assuming that straight-line depreciation has been used, what length of time do these facts suggest that the Midas Company has owned the building?

9 The weekly payroll for employees of Ryan Company, which works a five-day week, amounts to $5,000. All employees are paid up-to-date at the close of business each Friday. If December 31 falls on Tuesday, what year-end adjusting entry is needed?

10 The Marvin Company purchased a one-year fire insurance policy on August 1 and debited the entire cost of $540 to Unexpired Insurance. The accounts were not adjusted or closed until the end of the year. Give the adjusting entry at December 31, the year-end date.

11 Office supplies on hand in the Melville Company amounted to $642 at the beginning of the year. During the year additional office supplies were purchased at a cost of $1,561 and charged to the asset account. At the end of the year a physical count showed that supplies on hand amounted to $812. Give the adjusting entry needed at December 31, the year-end date.

12 At year-end the adjusting entry to reduce the Unexpired Insurance account by the amount of insurance premium applicable to the current period was accidentally omitted. Which items in the income statement will be in error? Will these items be overstated or understated? Which items in the balance sheet will be in error? Will they be overstated or understated?

13 What is the purpose of a work sheet?

14 In performing the regular end-of-period accounting procedures, does the preparation of the work sheet precede or follow the posting of adjusting entries to ledger accounts? Why?

15 Assume that when the income statement columns of a work sheet are first totalled, the total of the debit column exceeds the total of the credit column by $60,000. Explain how the amount of net income (or net loss) should be entered in the work sheet columns.

16 Does the ending balance of the owner's capital account appear in the work sheet? Explain.

17 Can each step in the preparation of a work sheet be performed automatically in a computer-based accounting system? Explain.

18 List in order the procedures comprising the accounting cycle when a work sheet is used.

19 Is a work sheet ever prepared when there is no intention of closing the accounts?

20 The weekly payroll of Stevens Company, which has a five-day work week, amounts to $15,000 and employees are paid up-to-date every Friday. On January 1 of the current year, the Salaries Expense account showed a credit balance of $9,000. Explain the nature of the accounting entry or entries that probably led to this balance.

21 Four general types of adjusting entries were discussed in this chapter. If reversing entries are made, which of these types of adjusting entries should be reversed? Why?

EXERCISES

Exercise 4-1
Accounting terminology

Listed below are nine technical accounting terms introduced in this chapter:

Accrued expense	Interim statements	Statement of owner's equity
Accrued revenue	Prepaid expense	Unearned revenue
Adjusting entries	Reversing entries	Work sheet

Each of the following statements may (or may not) describe one of these technical terms. For each statement, indicate the accounting term described, or answer "None" if the statement does not correctly describe any of the terms.

a Entries made during the accounting period to correct errors found in the accounting records.

b Interest expense that has been incurred, but has not yet been paid or recorded.

c A liability to customers who have made advance payments for services to be rendered in a future accounting period.

d An optional bookkeeping procedure designed to simplify the recording of routine cash transactions in the upcoming accounting period.

e A device for working out the end-of-period accounting procedures before adjusting and closing entries are entered into the formal accounting records.

f Entries needed to achieve the goals of accrual accounting when transactions affect the revenue or expenses of more than one accounting period.

Exercise 4-2
Effects of adjusting entries

Armored Transport, Inc., provides armored car services to businesses throughout the city. The company has a one-month accounting period. On June 30, adjusting entries were made to record:

a Depreciation expense for the month.

b Revenue earned during the month that has not yet been billed to customers.

c Salaries payable to company personnel that have accrued since the last payday in June.

d The portion of the company's prepaid insurance policies that has expired during June.

e Earning a portion of the amount collected in advance from Rocky Mountain Bank for armored car services.

f Interest expense that has accrued during June.

Indicate the effect of each of these adjusting entries upon the major elements of the company's financial statements — that is, upon revenue, expenses, net income, assets, liabilities, and owners' equity. Organize your answer in tabular form, using the column headings shown below and the symbols + for increase, − for decrease, and NE for no effect. The answer for adjusting entry (a) is provided as an example.

ADJUSTING ENTRY	INCOME STATEMENT			BALANCE SHEET		
	REVENUE	EXPENSES	NET INCOME	ASSETS	LIABILITIES	OWNERS' EQUITY
a	NE	+	−	−	NE	−

Exercise 4-3
Preparing adjusting entries for recorded costs and recorded revenue

The Outlaws, a professional football team, prepare financial statements on a monthly basis. Football season begins in August, but in July the team engaged in the following transactions:

a Paid $1,050,000 to Rainy City as advance rent for use of Rainy City Stadium for the five-month period from August 1 through December 31. This payment was debited to the asset account, Prepaid Rent.

b Collected $2,080,000 cash from sales of season tickets for the team's eight home games. This amount was credited to Unearned Ticket Revenue.

During the month of August, The Outlaws played one home game and two games on the road. Their record was two wins, one loss.

Instructions

Prepare the two adjusting entries required at August 31 to apportion this recorded cost and recorded revenue.

Exercise 4-4
Preparing adjusting entries for unrecorded revenue and expenses

The law firm of Barlow & Cloud prepares its financial statements on an annual basis at December 31. Among the situations requiring year-end adjusting entries were the following:

a Salaries to staff lawyers are paid on the fifteenth day of each month. Salaries accrued since December 15 amount to $14,300 and have not yet been recorded.

b The firm is defending R.H. Dominelli in a civil law suit. The agreed upon legal fees are $2,000 per day while the trial is in progress. The trial has been in progress for nine days during December and is not expected to end until late January. No legal fees have yet been billed to Dominelli.

Instructions

Prepare the two adjusting entries required at December 31 to record the accrued salaries expense and the accrued legal fees revenue.

Exercise 4-5
Adjusting entry and subsequent business transaction

On Friday of each week, Lake Company pays its sales personnel weekly salaries amounting to $60,000 for a five-day work week.

a Draft the necessary adjusting entry at year-end, assuming that December 31 falls on Wednesday.

b Also draft the journal entry for the payment by Lake Company of a week's salaries to its sales personnel on Friday, January 2, the first payday of the new year. (Assume that the company does not use reversing entries.)

Exercise 4-6
Preparing various adjusting entries

Hill Corporation adjusts and closes its accounts at the end of the calendar year. Prepare the necessary adjusting entries at December 31 based on the following information.

a A bank loan had been obtained on September 1. Accrued interest on the loan at December 31 amounts to $4,800. No interest expense has yet been recorded.

b Depreciation of office equipment is based on an estimated life of five years. The balance in the Office Equipment account is $25,000; no change has occurred in the account during the year.

c Interest receivable on government bonds owned at December 31 amounts to $2,300. This accrued interest revenue has not been recorded.

d On December 31, an agreement was signed to lease a truck for 12 months beginning January 1 at a rate of 35 cents a kilometre. Usage is expected to be 2,000 kilometres per month and the contract specifies a minimum payment equivalent to 18,000 kilometres a year.

e The company's policy is to pay all employees up-to-date each Friday. Since December 31 fell on Monday, there was a liability to employees at December 31 for one day's pay amounting to $2,800.

Exercise 4-7
Relationship of adjusting entries to business transactions

Among the ledger accounts used by Glenwood Speedway are the following: Prepaid Rent, Rent Expense, Unearned Admissions Revenue, Admissions Revenue, Prepaid Printing, Printing Expense, Concessions Receivable, and Concessions Revenue. For each of the following items, write first the journal entry (if one is needed) to record the external transaction and second the adjusting entry, if any, required on May 31, the end of the fiscal year.

a On May 1, borrowed $200,000 cash from National Bank by issuing a 12% note payable due in three months.

b On May 1, paid rent for six months beginning May 1 at $25,000 per month.

c On May 2, sold season tickets for a total of $700,000 cash. The season includes 70 racing days: 20 in May, 25 in June, and 25 in July.

d On May 4, an agreement was reached with Snack-Bars, Inc., allowing that company to sell refreshments at the track in return for 10% of the gross receipts for refreshment sales.

e On May 6, schedules for the 20 racing days in May and the first 10 racing days in June were printed and paid for at a cost of $9,000.

f On May 31, Snack-Bars, Inc., reported that the gross receipts from refreshments sales in May had been $145,000 and that the 10% owed to Glenwood Speedway would be remitted on June 10.

Exercise 4-8
Preparing closing entries from a work sheet

Using the information contained in the work sheet illustrated on page 168, prepare the four year-end closing entries for Reed Geophysical Company.

Exercise 4-9
Preparing reversing entries

Milo Company closes its accounts at the end of each calendar year. The company operates on a five-day work week and pays its employees up-to-date each Friday. The weekly payroll is regularly $5,000. On Wednesday, December 31, Year 1, an adjusting entry was made to accrue $3,000 salaries expense for the three days worked since the last payday. The company *did not* make a reversing entry. On Friday, January 2, Year 2, the regular weekly payroll of $5,000 was paid and recorded by the usual entry debiting Salaries Expense $5,000 and crediting Cash $5,000.

Were Milo Company's accounting records correct for Year 1? For Year 2? Explain two alternatives the company might have followed with respect to payroll at year-end. One of the alternatives should include a reversing entry.

PROBLEMS

Group A

Problem 4A-1
Preparing adjusting entries

East Beach Motel adjusts and closes its accounts once a year on December 31. Most guests of the motel pay at the time they check out, and the amounts collected are credited to Rental Revenue. A few guests pay in advance for rooms and these amounts are credited to Unearned Rental Revenue at the time of receipt. The following information is available as a source for preparing adjusting entries at December 31.

(a) A one-year bank loan in the amount of $80,000 had been obtained on November 1. No interest has been paid and no interest expense has been recorded. The interest accrued at December 31 is $1,600.

(b) On December 16, a suite of rooms was rented to a corporation for six months at a monthly rental of $3,200. The entire six months' rent of $19,200 was collected in advance and credited to Unearned Rental Revenue. At December 31, the amount of $1,600, representing one-half month's rent, was considered to be earned and the remainder of $17,600 was considered to be unearned.

(c) As of December 31 the motel has earned $18,090 rental revenue from current guests who will not be billed until they are ready to check out.

(d) Salaries earned by employees at December 31 but not yet paid amount to $11,640.

(e) Depreciation on the motel for the year ended December 31 was $51,250.

(f) Depreciation on a station wagon owned by the motel was based on a four-year life. The station wagon had been purchased new on September 1 of the current year at a cost of $12,600. Depreciation for four months should be recorded at December 31.

(g) On December 31, East Beach Motel entered into an agreement to host the National Building Suppliers Convention in June of next year. The motel expects to earn rental revenue of at least $30,000 from the convention.

Instructions

For each of the above numbered paragraphs, draft a separate adjusting journal entry (including explanation), if the information indicates that an adjusting entry is needed.

Problem 4A-2
Preparing adjusting entries from a trial balance

On January 1, 19___, Dale Cole organized Executive Parking Service to operate a valet parking service in the garage of a large office building. The business rents the garage from the owner of the building. The company makes adjusting and closing entries at the end of each month. Shown on page 174 is a trial balance and other information needed in making adjusting entries at January 31.

Other data

(a) The monthly insurance expense amounted to $2,100.

(b) The amount of office supplies on hand, based on a physical count on January 31, was $150.

(c) No interest had as yet been paid or recorded on the note payable; as of January 31 accrued interest amounted to $90.

EXECUTIVE PARKING SERVICE
Trial Balance
January 31, 19___

Cash	$11,330	
Unexpired insurance	12,600	
Office supplies	400	
Office equipment	10,500	
Notes payable		$ 9,000
Unearned parking fees		14,740
Dale Cole, capital		12,500
Dale Cole, drawing	2,450	
Parking fees earned		18,750
Rent expense	12,000	
Utilities expense	890	
Salaries expense	4,820	
	$54,990	$54,990

(d) Depreciation on the office equipment amounted to $175.

(e) Many businesses in the office building have made advance payments to cover several months' parking privileges for their executives and employees. These advance payments had been credited to the Unearned Parking Fees account. At January 31, it was determined that $3,210 of these advance payments had been earned.

(f) Security Bank, one of the tenants in the building, agreed to pay $2,000 per month for the use of 10 ground floor parking spaces for bank customers. The $2,000 fee for January is due on February 10 and has not yet been recorded.

(g) Salaries earned by employees but not paid amounted to $1,240 at January 31.

Instructions   You are to use the above trial balance and other information as a basis for preparing the adjusting entries (with explanations) needed at January 31.

Problem 4A-3
Preparing adjusting
entries and an adjusted
trial balance

James Ryan operates a private investigating business called Action Investigations. Some clients are required to pay in advance for Ryan's services, while others are billed after the services have been rendered. Advance payments are credited to an account entitled Unearned Retainer Fees, which represents unearned revenue. Action Investigations adjusts and closes its accounts each month. At May 31, the trial balance appeared as shown on page 175.

Other data   (a) The monthly rent was $600.

(b) Office supplies on hand May 31 amounted to $900.

(c) The office equipment was purchased on January 1. The useful life was estimated at five years.

(d) Fees of $4,000 were earned during the month by performing services for clients who had paid in advance.

(e) Investigative services rendered during the month but not yet collected or billed to clients amounted to $1,200.

(f) Salaries earned by employees during the month but not yet paid amounted to $1,300.

Instructions   a Prepare adjusting entries.

b Prepare an adjusted trial balance. Accounts not appearing in the trial balance but used in the adjusting entries should be listed in the proper sequence in the adjusted trial balance. For

ACTION INVESTIGATIONS
Trial Balance
May 31, 19___

Cash	$20,000	
Prepaid rent	3,000	
Office supplies	1,100	
Office equipment	10,800	
Accumulated depreciation: office equipment		$ 400
Accounts payable		2,000
Unearned retainer fees		19,000
James Ryan, capital		16,000
James Ryan, drawing	700	
Fees earned		13,000
Telephone expense	800	
Travel expense	1,000	
Salaries expense	13,000	
	$50,400	$50,400

example. Professional Fees Receivable should be listed among the assets, and Rent Expense should be listed among the expense accounts.

Problem 4A-4
Preparing adjusting entries and financial statements

In August 19___, Sherri DeLong, a lawyer, opened her own law practice, to be known as the Law Office of Sherri DeLong. The business adjusts and closes its accounts at the end of each month. The following trial balance was prepared at August 31, 19___, after one month of operations:

LAW OFFICE OF SHERRI DELONG
Trial Balance
August 3, 19___

Cash	$ 1,500	
Fees receivable	-0-	
Prepaid office rent	6,400	
Office supplies	600	
Office equipment	7,800	
Accumulated depreciation: office equipment		$ -0-
Notes payable		8,000
Interest payable		-0-
Salaries payable		-0-
Unearned retainer fees		5,710
Sherri DeLong, capital		6,000
Sherri DeLong, drawing	2,000	
Legal fees earned		890
Salaries expense	1,340	
Miscellaneous expense	960	
Office rent expense	-0-	
Office supplies expense	-0-	
Depreciation expense: office equipment	-0-	
Interest expense	-0-	
	$20,600	$20,600

Other data

(a) The law practice rents an office at a monthly rate of $1,600. On August 1, four months' rent was paid in advance and charged to the Prepaid Rent Account.

(b) Office supplies on hand at August 31 amounted to $200.

(c) The office equipment was purchased on August 1 and is being depreciated over an estimated useful life of 10 years.

(d) No interest has yet been paid on the note payable. Accrued interest at August 31 amounts to $100.

(e) Salaries earned by the staff but not yet paid amounted to $470 at August 31.

(f) Many clients are asked to make an advance payment for the legal services to be rendered in future months. These advance payments are credited to the Unearned Retainer Fees account. During August, $3,450 of these advances were earned by the business.

(g) Some clients are not billed until all services relating to their matter have been rendered. As of August 31, services priced at $1,140 had been rendered to these clients but had not yet been recorded in the accounting records.

Instructions

a Prepare adjusting entries as of August 31.

b Prepare an adjusted trial balance. (Note: Follow the same sequence of accounts as shown in the trial balance.)

c Prepare an income statement for the month ended August 31, a statement of owner's equity, and a balance sheet.

Problem 4A-5
Format of a work sheet

Rolling Hills Golf Course obtains revenue from greens fees and also from a contract with a concessionaire who sells refreshments on the premises. The books are closed at the end of each calendar year; at December 31 the data for adjustments were compiled and a work sheet

	TRIAL BALANCE		ADJUSTMENTS*	
	DR	CR	DR	CR
Cash	9,100			
Unexpired insurance	2,100			(a) 700
Prepaid advertising	1,000			(b) 300
Land	375,000			
Equipment	48,000			
Accumulated depreciation:				
equipment		8,000		(f) 4,000
Notes payable		110,000		
Unearned revenue from				
concessions		7,500	(d) 5,000	
Howard Catts, capital		268,000		
Howard Catts, drawing	15,000			
Revenue from greens fees		174,500		
Advertising expense	5,500		(b) 300	
Water expense	10,400			
Salaries expense	78,900		(e) 1,100	
Repairs and maintenance				
expense	17,500			
Miscellaneous expense	5,500			
	568,000	568,000		

	TRIAL BALANCE		ADJUSTMENTS*	
	DR	CR	DR	CR
Insurance expense			(a) 700	
Interest expense			(c) 400	
Interest payable				(c) 400
Revenue from concessions				(d) 5,000
Salaries payable . . . . : . .				(e) 1,100
Depreciation expense:				
equipment			(f) 4,000	
			11,500	11,500

*Adjustments:
(a) $700 insurance expired during year.
(b) $300 prepaid advertising expired at end of year.
(c) $400 accrued interest on notes payable.
(d) $5,000 concession revenue earned during year.
(e) $1,100 of salaries earned but unpaid at Dec. 31, 19___.
(f) $4,000 depreciation expense for year.

was prepared. The first four columns of the work sheet contained the above account balances and adjustments.

Instructions   Prepare a 10-column work sheet utilizing the trial balance and adjusting data provided. Include at the bottom of the work sheet a brief explanation keyed to each adjusting entry.

Problem 4A-6
Preparing a work sheet   Hillside Stadium adjusts and closes its accounts at the end of each month. Following are a trial balance and supplementary information needed for adjusting the accounts at September 30.

HILLSIDE STADIUM
Trial Balance
September 30, 19___

Cash	$ 65,000	
Prepaid advertising	15,000	
Unexpired insurance	60,000	
Land	375,000	
Building	378,000	
Accumulated depreciation: building		$ 33,600
Equipment	90,000	
Accumulated depreciation: equipment		48,000
Notes payable		470,000
Accounts payable		8,500
Anne Day, capital		376,000
Anne Day, drawing	10,100	
Revenue from admissions		87,000
Salaries expense	21,250	
Light and power expense	8,750	
	$1,023,100	$1,023,100

Other data   (a) During September, $12,000 of Prepaid Advertising expense was used up.

(b) Of the $60,000 in Unexpired Insurance, the amount of $20,000 became insurance expense during September.

(c) Depreciation expense on the building, $1,050 in September; on the equipment, $1,500.

(d) Interest accrued on notes payable at September 30, $4,700.

(e) Hillside Stadium's share of revenue from concessions for September, as reported by concessionaire, $8,000. No entry has yet been made for this revenue. Collection is expected within 10 days.

(f) At September 30, the salaries earned by employees amounted to $4,000.

Instructions   Prepare a 10-column work sheet using the trial balance and adjusting data provided. Include at the bottom of the work sheet a brief explanation keyed to each adjusting entry.

Problem 4A-7
Preparing a work
sheet, financial
statements, and
adjusting and closing
entries

Trade Winds Airlines provides passenger and freight service among some Pacific islands. The accounts are adjusted and closed each month. At June 30 the trial balance that follows was prepared from the ledger.

TRADE WINDS AIRLINES
Trial Balance
June 30, 19___

Cash	$ 38,000	
Prepaid rent	9,600	
Unexpired insurance	21,000	
Prepaid maintenance service	22,500	
Spare parts	57,000	
Airplanes	864,000	
Accumulated depreciation: airplanes		$ 108,000
Notes payable		600,000
Unearned passenger revenue		60,000
Steve Morgan, capital		231,050
Steve Morgan, drawing	12,000	
Passenger revenue earned		110,950
Fuel expense	13,800	
Salaries expense	66,700	
Advertising expense	5,400	
	$1,110,000	$1,110,000

Other data   (a) Monthly rent amounted to $3,200, reducing the Prepaid Rent account to $6,400.

(b) Insurance expense for June was $2,400.

(c) All necessary maintenance work was provided by Ryan Air Service at a fixed charge of $7,500 a month. Service for three months had been paid for in advance on June 1.

(d) Spare parts used in connection with maintenance work amounted to $3,750 during the month.

(e) Depreciation of the airplanes for the month of June was $7,200.

(f) The Chamber of Commerce had purchased *2,000 special tickets for $60,000.* Note that the special price per ticket was $30. Each ticket allowed the holder one flight. During the month 400 of these *special price tickets* had been used by the holders.

(g) Salaries earned by employees but not paid amounted to $3,300 at June 30.

(h) Interest accrued on notes payable at June 30 amounted to $7,000.

Instructions

a Prepare a work sheet for the month ended June 30, 19___.

b Prepare an income statement, a statement of owner's equity, and a balance sheet.

c Prepare adjusting and closing journal entries.

Problem 4A-8
Use of reversing
entries

Financial Press maintains its accounts on the basis of a fiscal year ending June 30. The company works a five-day week and pays its employees up-to-date each Friday. Weekly salaries have been averaging $15,000. At the fiscal year-end, the following events occured relating to salaries.

May 27 (Friday) Paid regular weekly salaries of $15,000.

May 31 (Tuesday) Prepared an adjusting entry for accrued salaries of $6,000.

June 1 (Wednesday) Prepared a reversing entry for accrued salaries.

June 3 (Friday) Paid regular weekly salaries of $15,000.

Instructions

a Prepare journal entries (with explanations) for the four above events relating to salaries.

b How much of the $15,000 in salaries paid on June 3 represents a June expense?

c Assume that no reversing entry had been made by Financial Press; prepare the journal entry for payment of salaries on June 3.

Group B

Problem 4B-1
Preparing adjusting
entries

The accounting records of Timberline Lodge are maintained on the basis of monthly accounting period. The following facts are to be used for making adjusting entries at April 30.

(a) A three-month bank loan in the amount of $300,000 had been obtained on April 1. No interest has yet been paid or recorded. Interest accrued at April 30 is $3,000.

(b) Salaries earned by employees but not yet recorded or paid amounted to $9,900,

(c) Depreciation expense on the buildings for the month ended April 30 amounted to $12,000.

(d) A one-year fire insurance policy had been purchased on April 1. The premium of $1,800 for the entire life of the policy had been paid on April 1 and recorded as Unexpired Insurance.

(e) A portion of the land owned had been leased on April 16 of the current year to a service station operator at a yearly rental rate of $12,000. One year's rent was collected in advance at the date of the lease and credited to Unearned Rental Revenue.

(f) A bus to carry guests to and from the airport had been rented beginning early on April 19 from Truck Rentals, Inc., at a daily rate of $60. No rental payment had yet been made. (The bus has been rented for 12 days in April.)

(g) The company signed an agreement on April 30 to lease a truck from Ace Motors for a period of one year beginning May 1 at a rate of 30 cents a kilometre and with a clause providing for a minimum monthly charge of $400.

(h) Among the assets owned by Timberline Lodge were government bonds. Accrued interest on the bonds at April 30 was computed to be $2,925. None of the interest has yet been recorded.

Instructions

For each of the above paragraphs that warrants adjustment of the accounts, you are to prepare an adjusting journal entry. Include an explanation as part of each entry.

Problem 4B-2
Preparing adjusting entries from a trial balance

Gary Smith organized Safe Storage on Janaury 1 for the purpose of leasing a large vacant building and renting space in this building to others for storage of industrial materials. The accounting policies of the company call for making adjusting entries and closing the accounts each month. Shown below is a trial balance and other information for use in preparing adjusting entries at January 31.

SAFE STORAGE
Trial Balance
January 31, 19___

Cash	$12,400	
Unexpired insurance	4,800	
Office supplies	450	
Office equipment	7,200	
Notes payable		$ 3,000
Unearned storage fees		6,900
Gary Smith, capital		10,850
Gary Smith, drawing	450	
Storage fees earned		11,650
Rent expense	3,500	
Utilities expense	780	
Salaries expense	2,820	
	$32,400	$32,400

Other data

(a) The monthly insurance expense amounted to $400.

(b) The amount of office supplies on hand, based on a physical count on January 31, was $200.

(c) A $3,000 one-year note payable was signed on January 1. Interest accrued at January 31 was $30.

(d) The useful life of office equipment was estimated at five years.

(e) Clients leasing large amounts of space were given a discount rate if they paid several months rent in advance. These advance payments were credited to Unearned Storage Fees. At January 31, $3,260 of these unearned storage fees had been earned by Safe Storage.

(f) Several clients neglected to send in storage fees amounting to $330 for the month of January. These amounts have not been recorded but are considered collectible.

(g) Salaries earned by employees but not yet recorded or paid amounted to $640.

Instructions

Based on the above trial balance and other information, prepare the adjusting entries (with explanations) needed at January 31.

Problem 4B-3
Preparing adjusting entries and an adjusted trial balance

Valley Advisory Service was organized on June 1, 19___, to provide investment counselling to investors in securities. Some customers pay in advance on a subscription basis; others are billed after services are rendered. Assume that the company's accounts are adjusted and closed each month. The trial balance at October 31 follows:

VALLEY ADVISORY SERVICE
Trial Balance
October 31, 19___

Cash	$12,400	
Accounts receivable	4,600	
Prepaid rent	2,200	
Office supplies	800	
Office equipment	18,000	
Accumulated depreciation: office equipment		$ 1,200
Accounts payable		4,100
Unearned revenue		6,000
Tom Marshall, capital		24,300
Tom Marshall, drawing	2,000	
Fees earned		14,000
Telephone expense	900	
Travel expense	1,700	
Salaries expense	7,000	
	$49,600	$49,600

Other data   **(a)** The monthly rent expense was $1,100.

(b) Office supplies on hand October 31 amounted to $300, as shown by a physical count.

(c) The office equipment was purchased on June 1. The useful life was estimated at five years.

(d) During October, the business earned $1,500 from clients who had paid in advance. These advance payments had been credited to the Unearned Revenue account.

(e) Investment advisory services rendered during the month but not yet billed amounted to $3,300.

(f) Salaries earned by employees during the month but not yet recorded or paid amounted to $2,400.

Instructions   **a** Prepare adjusting entries at October 31.

b Prepare an adjusted trial balance. (Place the liability account, Salaries Payable, to follow Accounts Payable.)

Problem 4B-4
Preparing adjusting entries, adjusted trial balance, and financial statements

Wiley organized a drafting firm on June 1. At June 30, before the accounts were adjusted and closed for the first time, a trial balance was prepared as illustrated at the top of page 182.

Other data   **(a)** The business rents an office at a monthly rate of $1,500. On June 1, the first three months' rent was paid in advance and was charged to Prepaid Office Rent.

(b) Drafting supplies on hand on June 30 amounted to $500.

(c) Drafting equipment was purchased on June 1. The useful life was estimated at five years.

(d) Accrued interest on notes payable was $50 as of June 30.

BLUEPRINTS, ETC.
Trial Balance
June 30, 19___

Cash	$ 8,450	
Drafting fees receivable	7,200	
Prepaid office rent	4,500	
Drafting supplies	1,200	
Drafting equipment	6,600	
Accumulated depreciation: drafting equipment		$ -0-
Notes payable		10,000
Interest payable		-0-
Salaries payable		-0-
Unearned fees		3,000
Marsha Wiley, capital		14,150
Marsha Wiley, drawing	1,800	
Fees earned		19,000
Salaries expense	16,200	
Miscellaneous expense	200	
Office rent expense	-0-	
Drafting supplies expense	-0-	
Depreciation expense: drafting equipment	-0-	
Interest expense	-0-	
	$46,150	$46,150

(e) On June 10, the company received a $3,000 advance payment for services to be rendered to Arrow Development Co. This amount had been credited to the Unearned Fees account. As of June 30, $900 of these fees had been earned.

(f) Services rendered and chargeable to other clients amounted to $3,700 as of June 30. No entries had yet been made to record the revneue earned by performing services for these clients.

(g) Salaries earned by staff personnel but not yet recorded or paid amounted to $1,500 on June 30.

Instructions

a Prepare adjusting entries as of June 30.

b Prepare an adjusted trial balance. (*Note:* Follow the same sequence of accounts as shown in the trial balance given in the problem.)

c Prepare an income statement for the month ended June 30, a statement of owner's equity, and a balance sheet.

Problem 4B-5
Format of work sheet

The four-column schedule on page 183 represents the first four columns of a 10-column work sheet to be prepared for Pacific TV Repair Service for the month ended April 30, 19___. (The completed Adjustment columns have been included to minimize the detail work involved.) These adjustments were derived from the following information available at April 30.

(a) Monthly rent expense, $900.

(b) Insurance expense for the month, $100.

(c) Advertising expense for the month, $120.

(d) Cost of supplies on hand, based on physical count on April 30, $435.

(e) Depreciation expense on equipment, $130 per month.

(f) Accrued interest on notes payable, $80.

(g) Salaries earned by employees but not yet recorded or paid, $500.

(h) Services amounting to $400 were rendered during April for customers who had paid in advance. This portion of the Unearned Revenue account should be regarded as earned as of April 30.

PACIFIC TV REPAIR SERVICE
Work Sheet
For the Month Ended April 30, 19___

	TRIAL BALANCE DR	TRIAL BALANCE CR	ADJUSTMENTS DR	ADJUSTMENTS CR
Cash	10,000			
Prepaid rent	1,800			(a) 900
Unexpired insurance	600			(b) 100
Prepaid advertising	360			(c) 120
Supplies	630			(d) 195
Equipment	11,700			
Accumulated depreciation: equipment		3,120		(e) 130
Notes payable		8,000		
Unearned revenue		1,200	(h) 400	
B.R. Miller, capital		11,600		
B.R. Miller, drawing	1,500			
Revenue from services		4,635		(h) 400
Salaries expense	1,965		(g) 500	
	28,555	28,555		
Rent expense			(a) 900	
Insurance expense			(b) 100	
Advertising expense			(c) 120	
Supplies expense			(d) 195	
Depreciation expense: equipment			(e) 130	
Interest expense			(f) 80	
Interest payable				(f) 80
Salaries payable				(g) 500
			2,425	2,425

Instructions   Prepare a 10-column work sheet utilizing the trial balance and adjusting data provided. Include at the bottom of the work sheet a brief explanation keyed to each adjusting entry.

Problem 4B-6
Preparing a work sheet   Southern Cross Flying Service provides air service for visitors to a famous island resort. The company follows the policy of adjusting and closing its accounts each month. At June 30, the trial balance on page 184 was prepared from the ledger.

SOUTHERN CROSS FLYING SERVICE
Trial Balance
June 30, 19___

Cash	$ 21,000	
Prepaid rent	10,500	
Unexpired insurance	20,000	
Prepaid maintenance service	21,000	
Spare parts	14,000	
Airplanes	648,000	
Accumulated depreciation: airplanes		$ 97,200
Notes payable		400,000
Unearned passenger revenue		52,000
Ellen Rice, capital		168,900
Ellen Rice, drawing	11,500	
Passenger revenue earned		140,800
Fuel expense	18,800	
Salaries expense	86,700	
Advertising expense	7,400	
	$858,900	$858,900

Other data

(a) Monthly rent amounted to $3,500.

(b) Insurance expense for June was $4,000.

(c) All necessary maintenance work was provided by Ryan Air Service at a fixed charge of $7,000 a month. Service for three months had been paid for in advance on June 1.

(d) Spare parts used in connection with maintenance work amounted to $3,750 during the month.

(e) Depreciation of the airplanes for the month of June was $5,400.

(f) The amount shown as unearned passenger revenue represents tickets sold to customers in advance of the scheduled flight. During June, $13,700 of the tickets were presented by customers and earned by the airline.

(g) Salaries earned by employees but not recorded or paid amounted to $3,300 at June 30.

(h) Interest accrued on notes payable at June 30 amounted to $4,000.

Instructions   Prepare a 10-column work sheet using the trial balance and adjusting data provided. Include at the bottom of the work sheet a brief explanation keyed to each adjusting entry.

Problem 4B-7
Preparing a work sheet and financial statements   Oceanside Cinema closes its accounts each month. At November 30, the trial balance shown at the top of page 185 and other information outlined below were available for adjusting and closing the accounts.

Other data

(a) Advertising expense for the month, $3,750.

(b) Film rental expense for the month, $16,850.

(c) Depreciation expense on building, $700 per month; on projection equipment, $600 per month.

(d) Accrued interest on notes payable, $1,650.

(e) The company's share of revenue from concessions for November, as reported by concessionaire, $3,250. Payment should be received by December 6.

(f) Salaries earned by employees but not paid, $1,500.

OCEANSIDE CINEMA
Trial Balance
November 30, 19___

Cash	$ 27,000	
Prepaid advertising	5,200	
Prepaid film rental	26,000	
Land	80,000	
Building	168,000	
Accumulated depreciation: building		$ 10,500
Projection equipment	36,000	
Accumulated depreciation: projection equipment		3,000
Notes payable		190,000
Accounts payable		4,400
L.B. Jones, capital		116,400
L.B. Jones, drawing	4,250	
Revenue from admissions		33,950
Salaries expense	8,700	
Light and power expense	3,100	
	$358,250	$358,250

Instructions   Prepare:

a A work sheet for the month ended November 30

b An income statement

c A statement of owner's equity

d A balance sheet

Problem 4B-8
Use of reversing entries

The following events relating to salaries occurred in Valley Centre near December 31, the end of the fiscal year.

Dec. 28 (Friday) Recorded payment of regular weekly salaries of $6,000.

Dec. 31 (Monday) Prepared an adjusting entry for accrued salaries of $1,200.

Jan. 1 (Tuesday) Made a reversing entry for accrued salaries.

Jan. 4 (Friday) Recorded payment of regular weekly salaries of $6,000.

Instructions   **a** Prepare journal entries (with explanations) for the four events relating to salaries.

b How much of the $6,000 in salaries paid on January 4 represents a January expense? Explain.

c Assume that no reversing entry was made by the company; prepare the journal entry for payment of salaries on January 4.

BUSINESS DECISION CASES

Case 4-1
Computer-based accounting systems

In Case 2-1, John Moore used data base software to design a simple accounting system for use on personal computers. Moore's first system prepared only a balance sheet; he is now ready to design an enhanced system that will perform all of the steps in the accounting cycle and will produce a complete set of financial statements. This enhanced system also will utilize data base software.

The idea underlying data base software is that data intended for a variety of different uses must be entered into the data base only once. The computer can then arrange these data into any number of desired formats. It can also combine data and perform mathematical computations using data in the data base.

In Moore's new accounting system, the computer will arrange the data into the following formats: (1) journal entries (with explanations) for all transactions, (2) 3-column running balance ledger accounts, (3) a 10-column work sheet, (4) a complete set of financial statements, (5) journal entries for all adjusting and closing entries, (6) an after-closing trial balance, and (7) reversing entries. As each of these records and statements is prepared, any totals or subtotals in the record are included automatically in the data base. For example, when ledger accounts are updated, the new account balances become part of the data base.

Instructions   In Chapter 4, the steps of the accounting cycle were described as follows: (a) journalize transactions, (b) post to ledger accounts, (c) prepare a work sheet, (d) prepare financial statements, (e) adjust and close the accounts, (f) prepare an after-closing trial balance, and (g) prepare reversing entries. For each step in this cycle, briefly describe the types of data used in performing the step. Indicate whether this data is already contained in the data base, or whether the computer operator must enter data to enable the computer to perform the step.

Case 4-2
Accrual accounting
compared to cash
basis

Sam Reed is interested in buying Foxie's, an aerobic dance studio. He has come to you for help in interpreting the company's financial statements and to seek your advice about purchasing the business.

Foxie's has been in operation for one year. The business is a sole proprietorship owned by Pam Austin. Foxie's rents the building in which it operates, as well as all of its exercise equipment. As virtually all of the company's business transactions involve cash receipts or cash payments, Austin has maintained the accounting records on a cash basis. She has prepared the following income statement and balance sheet from these cash basis records at year-end:

Income Statement

Revenue:		
Membership fees	$150,000	
Membership dues	30,000	$180,000
Expenses:		
Rent	$ 18,000	
Wages	52,000	
Advertising	20,000	
Miscellaneous	15,000	105,000
Net income		$ 75,000

Balance Sheet

ASSETS

Cash	$ 25,000

LIABILITIES & OWNER' EQUITY

Pam Austin, capital	$ 25,000

Austin is offering to sell Foxie's for the balance of her capital account — $25,000. Reed is very enthusiastic and states, "How can I go wrong? I'll be paying $25,000 to buy $25,000 cash, and I'll be getting a very profitable business that generates large amounts of cash in the deal."

In a meeting with you and Reed, Austin makes the following statement: "This business has been very good to me. In the first year of operations, I've been able to withdraw $50,000 in cash. Yet the business is still quite solvent — it has lots of cash and no debts."

You ask Austin to explain the difference between membership fees and membership dues. She responds, "Foxie's is an exclusive club. We cater only to members. This year, we sold 500 five-year memberships. Each membership requires the customer to pay $300 cash in advance and to pay dues of $10 per month for five years. I credited the advance payments to the Membership Fees account and credited the $10 monthly payments to Membership Dues. Thus, all the revenue is hard cash — no 'paper profits' like you see in so many businesses."

You then enquire as to when these five-year memberships were sold. Austin responds, "On the average, these memberships are only six months old. No members have dropped out, so Foxie's should continue receiving dues from these people for another four and one-half years, thus assuring future profitability. Another beneficial factor is that the company hasn't sold any new memberships in the last several months. Therefore, I think that the company could discontinue its advertising and further increase future profitability. Since further advertising may not produce any new members, the $3,000 television commercial for early next year, for which I have paid, is really worthless and I have included it in the $20,000 advertising expense of this year."

Instructions   **a** The financial statements of Foxie's were prepared on the cash basis of accounting, not the accrual basis. Prepare a revised income statement and balance sheet applying the concepts of accrual accounting.

b Assume that none of the 500 members drop out of Foxie's during the next year, and that the business sells no new memberships. What would be the amount of the company's expected cash receipts? Assuming that advertising expense is discontinued but that other expenses remain the same, what would be the expected amount of cash payments for the coming year?

c Use the information in your analysis in parts **a** and **b** to draft a letter to Reed advising him on the wisdom of purchasing Foxie's for $25,000. Specifically address the issues of whether the business (1) is profitable, (2) has no debts, and (3) is likely to generate sufficient cash to enable the owner to make large cash withdrawals during the coming year.

2

MERCHANDISING CONCERNS, INTERNAL CONTROL, AND ACCOUNTING SYSTEMS

This next part consists of two chapters. In Chapter 5 we explain the accounting concepts applicable to merchandising companies and discuss means of achieving internal control over purchases and sales of merchandise. In Chapter 6 we explore some of the ways that an accounting system may be modified to handle efficiently a large volume of transactions.

5 MERCHANDISING TRANSACTIONS AND INTERNAL CONTROL

6 ACCOUNTING SYSTEMS: MANUAL AND COMPUTER-BASED

MERCHANDISING TRANSACTIONS AND INTERNAL CONTROL

CHAPTER PREVIEW

In this chapter our discussion of the accounting cycle is expanded to include merchandising concerns — those businesses that sell goods rather than services. We illustrate and explain various types of merchandising transactions, the computation of net sales and the cost of goods sold, a work sheet and closing entries for a merchandising company, classified financial statements, and the computation of the current ratio and working capital. Both the perpetual and periodic inventory systems are described. In addition, this chapter introduces the important topic of internal control, with emphasis upon control procedures relating to purchases and sales of merchandise.

After studying this chapter you should be able to meet these Learning Objectives:

1. Account for purchases and sales of merchandise.

2. Determine the cost of goods sold by the periodic inventory system.

3. Prepare a work sheet and closing entries for a merchandising company.

4. Prepare a classified balance sheet and either a single-step or multiple-step income statement.

5. Explain the purpose of the current ratio and the meaning of working capital.

6. Explain the nature and importance of a system of internal control.

7. Explain how purchase orders, invoices, receiving reports, and other business documents are used to maintain internal control over merchandise transactions.

8. Explain the advantage of recording purchase invoices by the net price method.

MERCHANDISING COMPANIES

The preceding four chapters have illustrated step by step the complete accounting cycle for businesses rendering personal services. Service-type companies represent an important part of our economy. They include, for example, airlines, railroads, hotels, insurance companies, ski resorts, hospitals, and professional sports teams. These enterprises earn revenue by rendering services to their customers. The net income of a service-type business is equal to the excess of revenue over the operating expenses incurred.

In contrast to the service-type businesses, merchandising companies, both wholesalers and retailers, earn revenue by selling goods or merchandise. The term *merchandise* refers to goods acquired for resale to customers. Selling merchandise introduces a new and major cost of doing business — the cost to the company of the merchandise being resold to customers. This cost is termed the *cost of goods sold* and is so important that it is shown separately from operating expenses in the income statement of a merchandising company. Thus, the net income of a merchandising company is the excess of revenue over the *sum* of (1) the cost of goods sold and (2) the operating expenses of the business. These relationships are illustrated in the following highly condensed income statement of a merchandising concern:

CORNER STORE
Income Statement
For the Year Ended December 31, 19___

Net sales	$1,000,000
Less: Cost of goods sold	700,000
Gross profit on sales	$ 300,000
Less: Operating expenses	250,000
Net income	$ 50,000

In this simplified example of an income statement, Corner Store sold for $1,000,000 goods that cost $700,000. Thus the store earned a $300,000 gross profit on sales. Operating expenses, such as store rent and salaries, are subtracted from the gross profit to produce net income of $50,000.

Notice that the cost of goods sold is deducted from revenue to arrive at a subtotal called *gross profit.* If a merchandising business is to succeed or even survive, it must sell its goods at prices higher than it pays to the vendors or suppliers from whom it buys. Gross profit represents the difference between the selling price of merchandise sold during the period and the cost paid by the business to acquire that merchandise. Management and investors are both interested in the amount of gross profit, because it must exceed the company's operating expenses if the business is to earn any net income. If gross profit is less than the operating expenses, the business will incur a net loss. If the level of gross profit is unsatisfactory, management will consider such actions as changing sales prices or selling a different line of merchandise.

Revenue from sales

Revenue earned by selling merchandise is credited to a revenue account entitled **Sales.** The figure shown in our illustrated income statement, however, is the **net sales** for the accounting period. The term net sales means total sales revenue **minus** sales returns and allowances, and sales discounts. To illustrate this concept, let us now illustrate the sales section of Corner Store's income statement in greater detail:

CORNER STORE
Partial Income Statement
For the Year Ended December 31, 19___

Sales		$1,012,000
Less: Sales returns and allowances	$8,000	
Sales discounts	4,000	12,000
Net sales		$1,000,000

1   Account for purchases and sales of merchandise.

The $1,012,000 figure labelled "sales" in the partial income statement is sometimes called **gross sales.** This amount represents the total of both cash and credit sales made during the year. When a business sells merchandise to its customers, it either receives immediate payment in cash or acquires an account receivable to be collected at a later date. Cash sales are rung up on cash registers as the transactions occur. At the end of the day, the total shown on all the company's cash registers represents total cash sales for the day and is recorded by a journal entry, as follows:

JOURNAL ENTRY FOR CASH SALES

Cash	900	
Sales		900
To record the sale of merchandise for cash.		

For a sale of merchandise on credit, a typical journal entry would be

JOURNAL ENTRY FOR SALE ON CREDIT

Accounts Receivable	500	
Sales		500
Sold merchandise on credit to Kay's Gift Shop; payment due within 30 days.		

Sales revenue is earned in the period in which the merchandise is **delivered to the customer,** even though payment may not be received for a month or more after the sale. Consequently, the revenue earned in a given accounting period may differ considerably from the cash receipts of that period.

The amount and trend of sales are watched very closely by management, investors, and others interested in the progress of a company. A rising volume of sales is evidence of growth and suggests the probability of an increase in earnings. A declining trend in sales, on the other hand, is often the first signal of reduced earnings and of financial difficulties ahead. The amount of sales for each year is compared with the sales of the preceding year; the sales of each month may be compared with the sales of the preceding month and also with the corresponding month of the preceding year. These comparisons bring to light significant trends in the volume of sales.

Sales returns and allowances

Most merchandising companies allow customers to obtain a refund or credit by returning merchandise that is found to be unsatisfactory. When customers find that merchandise purchased has minor defects, they may agree to keep such merchandise if an allowance is made on the sales price. Refunds and allowances have the effect of reversing previously recorded sales and reducing the amount of revenue earned by the business. The journal entry to record sales returns and allowances is shown below:

JOURNAL ENTRY FOR
SALES RETURNS AND
ALLOWANCES

Sales Returns and Allowances	100	
Cash (or Accounts Receivable)		100
Made refund for merchandise returned by customer.		

At the end of the accounting period, the amount accumulated in the Sales Returns and Allowances account will be shown in the income statement as a deduction from sales, as illustrated earlier, thus, the Sales Returns and Allowances account is called a *contra-revenue* account.

Why use a separate Sales Returns and Allowances account rather than recording refunds by directly debiting the Sales account? The answer is that using a separate contra-revenue account enables management to see both the total amount of sales and the amount of sales returns and allowances. The relationship between these two amounts gives management an indication of customer satisfaction with the merchandise.

Credit terms

For all sales of merchandise on credit, the terms of payment should be clearly stated, so that buyer and seller can avoid any misunderstanding as to the time and amount of the required payment. One common example of credit terms is "net 30 days" or "n/30," meaning that the net amount of the invoice or bill is due in 30 days. Another common form of credit terms is "10 e.o.m.," meaning payment is due 10 days after the end of the month in which the sale occurred.

Sales discounts

Manufacturers and wholesalers often sell goods on credit terms of 30 to 60 days or more, but offer a discount for earlier payment. For example, the credit terms may be "2% 10 days, net 30 days." These terms mean that the authorized credit period is 30 days, but that the customer company may deduct 2% of the amount of the invoice if it makes payment within 10 days. On the invoice, these terms would appear in the abbreviated form "2/10, n/30"; this expression is read, "2, 10, net 30." The 10-day period during which the discount is available is called the *discount period*. Because a sales discount provides an incentive to the customer to make an early cash payment, it is also referred to as a **cash discount.**

For example, assume that Adams Company on November 3 sells merchandise for $1,000 on credit to Zipco, Inc., terms 2/10, n/30. At the time of the sale, the seller does not know if the customer will take advantage of the discount by paying within the discount period; therefore, Adams Company records the sale at the full price by the following entry:

```
Nov.  3 Accounts Receivable ...............................  1,000
           Sales  ......................................            1,000
           To record sale to Zipco, Inc., terms 2/10, n/30.
```

The customer now has a choice between saving $20 by paying within the discount period, or waiting a full 30 days and paying the full price. If Zipco makes the payment on or before November 13, it is entitled to deduct 2% of $1,000 or $20, and settle the obligation for $980. If Zipco decides to forgo the discount, it may postpone payment an additional 20 days until December 3 but must then pay $1,000.

Assuming that payment is made by Zipco on November 13, the last day of the discount period, the entry by Adams Company to record collection of the receivable is

JOURNAL ENTRY FOR
SALES DISCOUNTS

```
Nov. 13 Cash .........................................   980
           Sales Discounts ...................................    20
               Accounts Receivable ..........................         1,000
           Collected from Zipco, Inc., for our sale of Nov. 3, less 2%
           cash discount.
```

If a customer returns a portion of the merchandise before making payment, the discount applies only to the portion of the goods kept by the customer. In the above example, if Zipco had returned $300 worth of goods out of the $1,000 purchase, the discount would have been applicable only to the $700 portion of the order that the customer kept.

Sales Discounts in a contra-revenue account. In the income statement, sales discounts are deducted from gross sales revenue along with any sales returns and allowances. This treatment was illustrated in the partial income statement presented earlier.

Cost of goods sold

The cost of the merchandise sold during the year appears in the income statement as a deduction from the net sales of the year. The merchandise that is **available for sale but not sold** during the year constitutes the **inventory** of merchandise on hand at the end of the year. This inventory is included in the year-end balance sheet as an asset.

How can management determine, at the end of a year, a month, or other accounting period, the quantity and the cost of the goods remaining on hand? How can management determine the cost of the goods sold during the period? These amounts must be determined before either a balance sheet or an income statement can be prepared. In fact, the determination of inventory value and of the cost of goods sold may be the most important single step in measuring the profitability of a business. The two alternative approaches to the determination of inventory and of cost of goods sold are called the *perpetual inventory system* and the *periodic inventory system.*

The perpetual inventory system

Automobile dealers and television stores sell merchandise of **high unit value** and make a relatively small number of sales each day. Because sales transactions are few and of substantial amount, it is easy to look up the cost of the individual automobile or television set being sold. Thus a cost figure can be recorded as the **cost of goods sold** for each sales transaction. Under this system, the records show the cost of each article in stock. Units added to inventory and units removed for delivery to customers are recorded on a daily basis — hence the name **perpetual inventory system.** When financial statements are to be prepared, the total cost of goods sold during the accounting period is easily determined by adding the costs recorded from day to day for the units sold.

The perpetual inventory system will be discussed in Chapter 8; at present we are concentrating upon the **periodic inventory system** used by many companies dealing in merchandise of low unit value.

The periodic inventory system

2   Determine the cost of goods sold by the periodic inventory system.

In a business selling a variety of merchandise with low unit prices, the periodic inventory system may be more suitable than attempting to maintain perpetual inventory records of all items in stock. A business such as a drugstore may sell a customer a bottle of aspirin, a candy bar, and a tube of toothpaste. It is not practical to look up in the records at the time of each sale the cost of such small items. Instead, stores that deal in merchandise of low unit value usually wait until the end of the accounting period to determine the cost of goods sold. To do this, the store must have information on three things: (1) the beginning inventory, (2) the cost of goods purchased during the period, and (3) the ending inventory or cost of goods unsold and on hand at the end of the period. This information enables the store to compute the cost of goods sold during the period as shown below:

COMPUTING COST OF GOODS SOLD

Inventory at beginning of year	$ 50,000
Purchases	250,000
Cost of goods available for sale	$300,000
Less: Inventory at end of year	60,000
Cost of goods sold	$240,000

In this example the store had $50,000 of merchandise at the beginning of the year. During the year it purchased an additional $250,000 worth of merchandise. Thus it had available for sale merchandise costing $300,000. By the end of the year all but $60,000 worth of merchandise had been sold. Consequently, the cost of the goods sold during the year must have been $240,000.

In more general terms, we can say that every merchandising business has *available for sale* during an accounting period the merchandise on hand at the beginning of the period *plus* the merchandise purchased during the period. If all these goods were sold during the period, there would be no ending inventory, and cost of goods sold would be equal to the cost of goods available for sale. Normally, however, some goods remain unsold at the end of the period; *cost of goods sold is then equal to the cost of goods available for sale minus the ending inventory of unsold goods.*

The cost of goods sold is an important concept that requires careful attention. To gain a thorough understanding of this concept, we need to consider the nature of the accounts used in determining the cost of goods sold.

Beginning inventory and ending inventory

An inventory of merchandise consists of the goods on hand and available for sale to customers. The goods on hand at the beginning of an accounting period are called the *beginning inventory;* the goods on hand at the end of the period are called the *ending inventory.* Since a new accounting period begins as soon as the old one ends, the *ending inventory of one accounting period is the beginning inventory of the following period.*

A business using the periodic inventory system will determine the amount of the ending inventory by taking a physical inventory. Taking inventory includes three steps. First, all items of merchandise in the store and stockrooms are counted; second, the quantity of each item is multiplied by the cost per unit; and third, the costs of the various kinds of merchandise are added together to get a total cost figure for all goods on hand.

The cost figure for ending inventory appears as an asset in the balance sheet and as a deduction in the cost of goods sold section of the income statement. It is brought into the accounting records by *a closing entry debiting Inventory and crediting Income Summary.* (This entry will be illustrated and explained more fully later in this chapter.) After the ending inventory has been recorded in the ledger, the Inventory account remains unchanged throughout the next accounting period. It represents both the ending inventory of the completed accounting period and the beginning inventory of the following period. Keep in mind that the Inventory account is not debited or credited as goods are purchased or sold. The balance in the Inventory account during the years shows the amount of goods on hand at the beginning of the current period.

Cost of merchandise purchased for resale

Under the periodic inventory system, the cost of merchandise purchased for resale is recorded by debiting an account called Purchases, as shown below:

```
Nov. 3  Purchases ...................................  10,000
            Accounts Payable ...........................          10,000
        Purchased merchandise from ABC Supply Co. Credit
        terms 2/10, n/30.
```

The Purchases account *is used only for merchandise acquired for resale;* assets acquired for use in the business (such as a delivery truck, a typewriter, or office supplies) are recorded by debiting the appropriate asset account, not the Purchases account. The Purchases account does not indicate whether the purchased goods have been sold or are still on hand.

At the end of the accounting period, the balance accumulated in the Purchases account represents the total cost of merchandise purchased during the period. This amount is used in preparing the income statement. The Purchases account has then served its purpose and it is closed to the Income Summary account. Since the Purchases account is closed at the end of each period, it has a zero balance at the beginning of each succeeding period.

Purchase discounts   As explained earlier, manufacturers and wholesalers frequently grant a cash discount to customers who will pay promptly for goods purchased on credit. The selling company regards a cash discount as a *sales discount;* the buying company calls the discount a *purchase discount.*

If the $10,000 purchase of November 3 shown on page 197 is paid for on or before November 13, the last day of the discount period, the purchasing company will save 2% of the price of the merchandise, or $200, as shown by the following entry:

JOURNAL ENTRY FOR
PURCHASE DISCOUNTS

Nov. 13	Accounts Payable	10,000	
	Purchase Discounts		200
	Cash		9,800

Paid ABC Supply Co. for purchase of Nov. 3, less 2% cash discount.

The effect of the discount was to reduce the cost of the merchandise to the buying company. The credit balance of the Purchase Discounts account should therefore be deducted in the income statement from the debit balance of the Purchases account.

If the buying company chooses to postpone payment rather than take the discount, it will have the use of $9,800 for an additional 20 days. However, the extra $200 expense is a high penalty to incur for the use of $9,800 for 20 days. (A 20-day period is approximately $1/18$ of a year; 18 times 2% amounts to 36%.[1]) Although interest rates vary widely, most businesses are able to borrow money from banks at an annual interest rate of 20% or less. Well-managed businesses, therefore, generally pay all invoices within the discount period even though this policy necessitates borrowing from banks in order to have the necessary cash available.

Purchase returns and allowances   When merchandise purchased from suppliers is found to be unsatisfactory, the goods may be returned, or a request may be made for an allowance on the price. A return of goods to the supplier is recorded as follows:

JOURNAL ENTRY FOR
RETURN OF GOODS TO
SUPPLIER

Accounts Payable	1,200	
Purchase Returns and Allowances		1,200

To reduce liability to Jet Supply Co. by the cost of goods returned for credit.

---

[1] A more accurate estimate of interest expense on an annual basis can be obtained as follows: ($200 × 18) ÷ $9800 = 36.7%.

It is preferable to credit Purchase Returns and Allowances when merchandise is returned to a supplier rather than crediting the Purchases account directly. The accounts then show both the total amount of purchases and the amount of purchases that required adjustment or return. Management is interested in the percentage relationship between goods purchased and goods returned, because the returning of merchandise for credit is an expensive, time-consuming process. Excessive returns suggest inefficiency in the operation of the purchasing department and a need to find more dependable suppliers.

The Transportation-in account

The cost of merchandise acquired for resale logically includes any transportation charges necessary to bring the goods to the purchaser's place of business. A separate ledger account is used to accumulate transportation charges on merchandise purchased. The journal entry to record transportation charges on inbound shipments of merchandise is as follows:

JOURNALIZING
TRANSPORTATION
CHARGES ON PURCHASES
OF MERCHANDISE

```
Transportation-in .........................................  125
    Cash (or Accounts Payable) ...............................        125
Freight charges on merchandise purchased from Miller Brothers.
```

Since transportation charges are part of the **delivered cost** of merchandise purchased, the Transportation-in (also called Freight-in) account is combined with the Purchases account in the income statement to determine the cost of goods available for sale.

Transportation charges on inbound shipments of merchandise from suppliers must not be confused with transportation charges on outbound shipments of goods to customers. Freight charges and other expenses incurred in making deliveries to customers are regarded as selling expenses; these outlays are debited to a separate account entitled Delivery Expense and are not included in the cost of goods sold.

F.O.B. shipping point and F.O.B. destination

The agreement between the buyer and seller (supplier) of merchandise includes a provision as to which party shall bear the cost of transporting the goods. The term *F.O.B. shipping point* means that the seller will place the merchandise "free on board" the railroad cars or other means of transport, and that the buyer must pay transportation charges from that point. In most merchandise transactions involving wholesalers or manufacturers, the buyer bears the transportation cost. Sometimes, however, as a matter of convenience, the seller prepays the freight and includes this cost in the amount billed to the buyer. *F.O.B. destination* means that the seller agrees to bear the freight cost.

Inventory theft and other losses

Under the periodic inventory system, it is assumed that all goods available for sale during the year are either sold or are on hand at year-end for the ending inventory. As a result of this assumption, the cost of merchandise lost because of shoplifting, employee theft, or spoilage will be included automatically in cost of goods sold. For example, assume that a store has goods available for sale that cost $600,000. Assume that shoplifters steal $10,000 worth of goods and that the ending inventory is $100,000. (If the thefts had not occurred, the ending inventory would have been $10,000 larger.) The cost of goods sold is computed at $500,000 by subtracting the $100,000 ending inventory from the $600,000 cost of goods available for sale. The theft loss is thus not shown separately in the income statement. In reality, cost of goods *sold* was $490,000, and cost of goods *stolen* was $10,000.

Although the periodic inventory system causes inventory losses to be included automatically in cost of goods sold, accountants have devised a method of estimating losses of merchandise from theft. This method is explained in Chapter 9.

Income statement for a merchandising company

To bring together the various concepts discussed thus far in the chapter, we need to look at a classified income statement for a merchandising business. The income statement of Olympic Sporting Goods shown on the next page has three major sections: (1) a revenue section, (2) a cost of goods sold section, and (3) an operating expenses section. We have already discussed the various accounts used in the first two sections. Note that the amount of *gross profit on sales,* $240,000, is determined by subtracting the cost of goods sold from net sales.

Gross profit rate: a key statistic   Managers, owners, bankers, and others seeking to evaluate the health of a merchandising business often compute the gross profit as a percentage of net sales. For Olympic Sporting Goods, the gross profit amounts to 40% of net sales (gross profit, $240,000 divided by net sales, $600,000, equals 40%). This percentage is called the *gross profit rate.*

By computing the gross profit rate of a business for several years in a row, the user of financial statements gains insight into whether business is improving or declining. A rising gross profit rate is a sign of financial strength, indicating strong demand for the company's products. A falling gross profit rate, on the other hand, may indicate that the business is having to cut prices in order to sell its products, or that it is unable to pass cost increases on to its customers.

Of course, the gross profit rate will vary among different companies and different industries. Users of financial statements may compare the gross profit rate of one company to that of other companies in the same industry, or to the gross profit rate of the same company in prior years. In most merchandising companies, the rate of gross profit usually varies between 30% and 50% of net sales.

Classifications of operating expenses   The operating expenses in the third major section of the income statement are classified either as *selling expenses* or as *general and administratie expenses.* Selling expenses include all expenses of storing and displaying merchandise for sale, advertising, sales salaries, and delivering goods to customers. General and administrative expenses include the expenses of the general offices, accounting department, personnel office, and credit and collection departments.

In many companies, certain expenses, such as depreciation of the building, need to be divided, part to selling expense and part to general and administrative expenses. Olympic Sporting Goods divided its $8,000 of depreciation expense by allocating $6,000 to selling expenses and $2,000 to general and administrative expenses. This allocation can conveniently be made when the income statement is prepared from the

OLYMPIC SPORTING GOODS
Income Statement
For the Year Ending December 31, 19___

Sales			$617,000
Less: Sales returns and allowances		$ 12,000	
Sales discounts		5,000	17,000
Net Sales			$600,000
Cost of goods sold:			
Inventory, Jan. 1		$ 60,000	
Purchases	$367,000		
Less: Purchases returns and			
allowances	$6,700		
Purchase discounts	3,300	10,000	
Net purchases		$357,000	
Add: Transportation-in		13,000	
Cost of goods purchased		370,000	
Cost of goods available for sale		$430,000	
Less: Inventory, Dec. 31		70,000	
Cost of goods sold			360,000
Gross profit on sales			$240,000
Operating expenses:			
Selling expenses:			
Sales salaries		$ 74,000	
Advertising		29,000	
Delivery service		10,700	
Depreciation		6,000	
Total selling expenses		$119,700	
General & administrative expenses:			
Office salaries		$ 57,000	
Utilities		3,100	
Depreciation		2,000	
Total general & administrative expenses		62,100	
Total operating expenses			181,800
Income from operations			$ 58,200
Interest expense			8,200
Net income			$ 50,000

THIS INCOME STATEMENT CONSISTS OF THREE MAJOR SECTIONS

NONOPERATING ITEMS CAN BE A FOURTH SECTION

work sheet; thus no additional ledger accounts are required. The account for utilities expense, $3,100, was not divided because management did not consider the amount large enough to warrant such treatment.

Nonoperating items   Some expenses, such as interest expense, are not directly related to operating activities. These *nonoperating* expenses may be listed separately in the income statement after the subtotal *income from operations*. Interest is not considered an operating expense because it stems from the manner in which assets are financed, not from the daily operating activities of the business.

If nonoperating expenses are listed separately, **nonoperating revenue** (such as interest earned) also should be listed in this section of the income statement. Other nonoperating items include income or loss from investments, gains or losses arising from lawsuits, and (for corporations only) income taxes expense.

Classifying operating expenses into subcategories and showing nonoperating items separately assists management and others in identifying those areas within the business that are operating efficiently and those that are incurring excessive costs.

Appraising the adequacy of net income   The net income of Olympic Sporting Goods for the current year amounted to $50,000. Should this be viewed as excellent, fair, or poor performance for a business of this size?

In evaluating the net income of an unincorporated business, it is important to remember that no "salary" has been deducted for the value of the personal services rendered to the business by the owner. The reason for omitting the owner's "salary" from the expenses of the business is that the owner could set this salary at any desired level. An unrealistic owner's salary, whether too high or too low, would lessen the usefulness of the income statement as a device for measuring the earning power of the business.

In addition, the owner may have a considerable amount of money invested in the business in the form of owner's equity. As no interest expense is recorded on equity investments, the income statement ignores the amount of the owner's financial investment in the business.

Finally, the net income of a business should be adequate to compensate the owner for taking significant risks. There are no guarantees that a business will earn an adequate net income in future years. In fact, losses might occur that could wipe out some or all of the owner's investment.

In summary, the net income of an unincorporated business should be sufficient to compensate the owner for three factors: (1) personal services rendered to the business, (2) the amount of capital invested, and (3) the degree of risk taken. Using these criteria, let us appraise the adequacy of the $50,000 net income of Olympic Sporting Goods.

Assume that Robert Riley, the owner of the company, works full time in the business. Also assume that if he were not running his own business, he could earn a salary of $35,000 per year managing a similar store. In addition, Riley had $115,000 invested in Olympic Sporting Goods at the beginning of the year. If this money had been invested to stocks and bonds, we might assume that Riley would have earned investment income of, say, $12,000. Thus, the two factors of the owner's personal services and financial investment indicate a need for the company to earn at least $47,000 per year to be considered successful. As the business actually earned $50,000, a $3,000 "cushion" is left to compensate Riley for the risks involved in running his own business. Whether or not $3,000 is adequate compensation for these risks depends upon the degree of risk involved in this type of business activity, and Riley's personal attitude toward risk taking.

Of course, some people simply enjoy owning their own business. Such people might rather own their own business even if they could earn more money by working for someone else. These people are said to derive **_psychic income_** from ''being their own boss.'' Psychic income is personal satisfaction, which cannot be objectively measured in terms of dollars and cents.

Work sheet for a merchandising business

3   Prepare a work sheet and closing entries for a merchandising company.

A merchandising company, like the service business discussed in Chapter 4, uses a work sheet at the end of the period to organize the information needed to prepare financial statements and to adjust and close the accounts. The new elements in the work sheet for Olympic Sporting Goods on the following page are the beginning inventory, the ending inventory, and the other merchandising accounts. These new accounts are shown in black to help focus your attention on their treatment.

Trial balance columns   The Trial Balance columns were prepared by listing the ledger account balances at December 31. Notice that the Inventory account in the Trial Balance debit column shows a balance of $60,000, the cost of merchandise on hand at the end of the **_prior year._** No entries were made in the Inventory account during the current year despite the various purchases and sales of merchandise. The significance of the Inventory account in the trial balance is that it shows the amount of merchandise with which Olympic Sporting Goods began operations on Janaury 1 of the current year.

Adjustment columns and Adjusted Trial Balance columns   The merchandising accounts usually do not require adjustment. Their balances are carried directly from the Trial Balance columns to the Adjusted Trial Balance columns.

In our illustration, the only adjustment needed at December 31 is the entry to record depreciation expense. Salaries to employees and interest on the note payable were paid on December 31, so no adjusting entries were needed for these items.

Income Statement columns   The accounts that will appear in a company's income statement are the ones to be carried from the Adjusted Trial Balance columns to the Income Statement columns of the work sheet. These are the revenue accounts, cost of goods sold accounts, and operating expense accounts.

Recording the ending inventory on the work sheet   The key point to be observed in this work sheet is the method of recording the **_ending inventory._** On December 31, Riley and his assistants took a physical inventory of all merchandise on hand. The entire inventory, priced at cost, amounted to $70,000. This ending inventory, dated December 31, does not appear in the trial balance totals. The amount of $70,000 is listed in the Income Statement credit column and also in the Balance Sheet debit column. By entering the ending inventory in the Income Statement **_credit_** column, we are in effect **_deducting_** it from the total of the beginning inventory, the purchases, and the transportation-in, all of which are extended from the trial balance to the Income statement **_debit_** column.

One of the functions of the Income Statement columns is to bring together all the accounts involved in determining the cost of goods sold. The accounts with debit balances are the beginning Inventory, Purchases, and Transportation-in; these accounts total $440,000. Against this total the three credit items of Purchase Returns and Allowances, $6,700, Purchase Discounts, $3,300, and ending Inventory, $70,000,

OLYMPIC SPORTING GOODS
Work Sheet
For the Year Ended December 31, 19____

	TRIAL BALANCE DR	TRIAL BALANCE CR	ADJUSTMENTS* DR	ADJUSTMENTS* CR	ADJUSTED TRIAL BALANCE DR	ADJUSTED TRIAL BALANCE CR	INCOME STATEMENT DR	INCOME STATEMENT CR	BALANCE SHEET DR	BALANCE SHEET CR
Cash	14,500				14,500				14,500	
Accounts receivable	43,500				43,500				43,500	
Inventory, Jan. 1	60,000				60,000		60,000			
Land	52,000				52,000				52,000	
Building	160,000				160,000				160,000	
Accumulated depreciation: building		56,000		(a) 8,000		64,000				64,000
Notes payable		82,000				82,000				82,000
Accounts payable		55,000				55,000				55,000
Robert Riley, capital		115,000				115,000				115,000
Robert Riley, drawing	26,000				26,000				26,000	
Sales		617,000				617,000		617,000		
Sales returns and allowances	12,000				12,000		12,000			
Sales discounts	5,000				5,000		5,000			
Purchases	367,000				367,000		367,000			
Purchase returns and allowances		6,700				6,700		6,700		
Purchase discounts		3,300				3,300		3,300		
Transportation-in	13,000				13,000		13,000			
Sales salaries	74,000				74,000		74,000			
Advertising expense	29,000				29,000		29,000			
Delivery service expense	10,700				10,700		10,700			
Office salaries	57,000				57,000		57,000			
Utilities expense	3,100				3,100		3,100			
Interest expense	8,200				8,200		8,200			
	935,000	935,000								
Depreciation expense: building			(a) 8,000		8,000		8,000			
			8,000	8,000	943,000	943,000				
Inventory, Dec. 31								70,000	70,000	
							647,000	697,000	366,000	316,000
Net Income							50,000			50,000
							697,000	697,000	366,000	366,000

NOTE THE TREATMENT OF THE BEGINNING INVENTORY

NOTE THE TREATMENT OF THE ENDING INVENTORY

*Adjustment: (a) Depreciation of building during the year.

are offset. The three accounts with debit balances exceed in total the three credit balances by an amount of $360,000; this amount is the cost of goods sold, as shown in the income statement on page 201.

The ending inventory is also entered in the Balance Sheet debit column of the work sheet, because this inventory of merchandise on December 31 will appear as an asset in the year-end balance sheet.

Completing the work sheet   When all the accounts on the work sheet have been extended into the Income Statement or Balance Sheet columns, the final four columns are totalled. The net income is computed, and the work sheet completed in the same manner as illustrated in Chapter 4 for a service business.

Financial statements

The work to be done at the end of the period is much the same for a merchandising business as for a service-type firm. First, the work sheet is completed; then, financial statements are prepared from the data in the work sheet; next, the adjusting and closing entries are entered in the journal and posted to the ledger accounts; and finally, an after-closing trial balance is prepared.[2] This completes the periodic accounting cycle.

Income statement   The income statement on page 201 was prepared from the Olympic Sporting Goods work sheet. Note particularly the arrangement of items in the cost of goods sold section of the income statement; this portion of the income statement shows in summary form most of the essential accounting concepts covered in this chapter.

Statement of owner's equity   The statement of owner's equity shows the increase in owner's equity from the year's net income and the decrease from the owner's withdrawals during the year. Note that the final amount in the statement of owner's equity also appears in the balance sheet as the new balance of the owner's capital account.

WHICH FIGURE FOR OWNER'S EQUITY WILL APPEAR IN THE BALANCE SHEET?

OLYMPIC SPORTING GOODS
Statement of Owner's Equity
For the Year Ended December 31, 19___

Robert Riley, capital, Jan. 1	$115,000
Add: Net income for the year	50,000
Subtotal	$165,000
Less: Withdrawals	26,000
Robert Riley, capital, Dec. 31	$139,000

Balance sheet   In studying the balance sheet on page 206, note that all items are taken from the Balance Sheet columns of the work sheet, but that the amount for Robert Riley, Capital is the December 31 balance of $139,000, computed as shown in the preceding statement of owner's equity.

[2] The journalizing of the adjusting entry for Olympic Sporting Goods is not illustrated here because this entry is similar to those demonstrated in previous chapters.

OLYMPIC SPORTING GOODS
Balance Sheet
December 31, 19___

ASSETS

Cash		$ 14,500
Accounts receivable		43,500
Inventory		70,000
Land		52,000
Building	$160,000	
Less: Accumulated depreciation	64,000	96,000
Total assets		$276,000

LIABILITIES & OWNER'S EQUITY

Liabilities:		
Notes payable		$ 82,000
Accounts payable		55,000
Total liabilities		$137,000
Owner's equity:		
Robert Riley, capital		139,000
Total liabilities & owner's equity		$276,000

Closing entries

The entries used in closing revenue and expense accounts have been explained in preceding chapters. The only new elements in this illustration of closing entries for a merchandising business are the entries showing the *elimination* of the beginning inventory and the *recording* of the ending inventory. The beginning inventory is cleared out of the Inventory account by a debit to Income Summary and a credit to Inventory. A separate entry could be made for this purpose, but we can save time by making one compound entry that will debit the Income Summary account with the balance of the beginning inventory and with the balances of all temporary proprietorship accounts having debit balances.

The *temporary proprietorship accounts* include all the accounts appearing in the income statement. As the name suggests, the temporary proprietorship accounts are used to temporarily accumulate the increases and decreases in the proprietor's equity resulting from operation of the business. The entry to close out the beginning inventory and temporary proprietorship accounts with debit balances is shown at the top of page 207. (For emphasis, the accounts unique to a merchandising business are shown in black.)

The preceding closing entry closes all the operating expense accounts, as well as the accounts used to accumulate the cost of goods sold. It also closes the accounts for Sales Returns and Allowances and for Sales Discounts. After this first closing entry, the Inventory account has a zero balance. Therefore, it is time to record in this account the new inventory of $70,000 determined by count at December 31.

To bring the ending inventory into the accounting records after the stock-taking on December 31, we could make a separate entry debiting Inventory and crediting the Income Summary account. It is more convenient, however, to combine this step with

CLEARING OUT BEGINNING INVENTORY AND CLOSING TEMPORARY PROPRIETORSHIP ACCOUNTS WITH DEBIT BALANCES

Dec. 31	Income Summary	647,000	
	Inventory (Jan. 1)		60,000
	Sales Returns and Allowances		12,000
	Sales Discounts		5,000
	Purchases		367,000
	Transportation-in		13,000
	Sales Salaries		74,000
	Advertising Expense		29,000
	Delivery Service		10,700
	Office Salaries		57,000
	Utilities Expense		3,100
	Interest Expense		8,200
	Depreciation Expense: Building		8,000
	To close out the beginning inventory and the temporary proprietorship accounts with debit balances.		

the closing of the Sales account and any other temporary proprietorship accounts having credit balances, as illustrated in the following closing entry:

RECORDING ENDING INVENTORY AND CLOSING TEMPORARY PROPRIETORSHIP ACCOUNTS WITH CREDIT BALANCES

Dec. 31	Inventory (Dec. 31)	70,000	
	Sales	617,000	
	Purchase Returns and Allowances	6,700	
	Purchase Discounts	3,300	
	Income Summary		697,000
	To record the ending inventory and to close all temporary proprietorship accounts with credit balances.		

The remaining closing entries serve to transfer the balance of the Income Summary account to the owner's capital account and to close the drawing account, as follows:

CLOSING THE INCOME SUMMARY ACCOUNT AND OWNER'S DRAWING ACCOUNT

Dec. 31	Income Summary	50,000	
	Robert Riley, Capital		50,000
	To close the Income Summary account.		

Dec. 31	Robert Riley, Capital	26,000	
	Robert Riley, Drawing		26,000
	To close the drawing account.		

After the preceding four closing entries have been posted to the ledger, the only ledger accounts left with dollar balances will be balance sheet accounts. An after-closing trial balance should be prepared to prove that the ledger is in balance after the year-end entries to adjust and close the accounts have been recorded.

Sales taxes

Sales taxes are levied by various provinces on certain retail sales. Sales taxes actually are imposed upon the consumer, not upon the seller. However, the seller must collect the tax, file tax returns at times specified by law, and remit the taxes collected on all reported sales.

For cash sales, sales tax is collected from the customer at the time of the sales transaction. For credit sales, the sales tax is included in the amount charged to the customer's account. The liability to the governmental unit for sales taxes may be recorded at the time the sale is made as shown in the following journal entry:

SALES TAX RECORDED
AT TIME OF SALE

Accounts Receivable (or Cash)	1,050	
Sales Tax Payable		50
Sales		1,000
To record sales of $1,000 subject to 5% sales tax.		

This approach requires a separate credit entry to the Sales Tax Payable account for each sale. At first glance, this may seem to require an excessive amount of bookkeeping. However, today's electronic cash registers can be programmed to record automatically the sales tax liability at the time of each sale.

An alternative approach to sales taxes   Instead of recording the sales tax liability at the time of sale, some businesses prefer to credit the Sales account with the entire amount collected, including the sales tax, and to make an adjustment at the end of each period to reflect sales tax payable. For example, suppose that the total recorded sales for the period under this method were $315,000. Since the Sales account includes both the sales price and the sales tax (say, 5%), it is apparent that $315,000 is *105%* of the actual sales figure. Actual sales are $300,000 (computed $315,000 ÷ 1.05) and the amount of sales tax due is $15,000. (Proof: 5% of $300,000 = $15,000.) The entry to record the liability for sales taxes would be

SALES TAX RECORDED AS
ADJUSTMENT OF SALES

Sales	15,000	
Sales Tax Payable		15,000
To remove sales taxes of 5% on $300,000 of sales from the Sales account, and reflect as a liability.		

This second approach is widely used in businesses that do not use electronic devices for recording each sales transaction.

If some of the products being sold are not subject to sales tax, the business must keep separate records of taxable and nontaxable sales.

Classified financial statements

4 Prepare a classified balance sheet and either a single-step or multiple-step income statement.

The financial statements illustrated up to this point have been rather short and simple because of the limited number of accounts used in these introductory chapters. Now let us look briefly at a more comprehensive balance sheet for a merchandising business.

In the balance sheet of Graham Company illustrated on the next page, the assets are classified into three groups: (1) current assets, (2) plant and equipment, and (3) other assets. The liabilities are classified into two types: (1) current liabilities and (2) long-term liabilities. This classification of assets and liabilities is virtually a standard one throughout Canadian business.

GRAHAM COMPANY
Balance Sheet
December 31, 19___

ASSETS

Current assets:
Cash		$ 25,000
Marketable securities		13,000
Notes receivable		30,000
Accounts receivable		70,000
Inventory		100,000
Prepaid expenses		12,000
Total current assets		$250,000

Plant and equipment:
Land		$60,000	
Building	$140,000		
Less: Accumulated depreciation	56,000	84,000	
Store equipment	$ 24,000		
Less: Accumulated depreciation	18,000	6,000	
Delivery equipment	$ 19,000		
Less: Accumulated depreciation	10,000	9,000	
Total plant and equipment			159,000

Other assets:
Land (future building site)	125,000
Total assets	$534,000

LIABILITIES & OWNER'S EQUITY

Current liabilities:
Notes payable (due in 6 months)	$ 15,000
Accounts payable	59,900
Salaries payable	14,100
Unearned revenue	11,000
Total current liabilities	$100,000

Long-term liabilities:
Mortgage payable (due in 10 years)	181,000
Total liabilities	$281,000

Owner's equity:
George Graham, capital	253,000
Total liabilities & owner's equity	$534,000

The purpose of balance sheet classification

The purpose underlying a standard classification of assets and liabilities is to aid management, owners, creditors, and other interested persons in understanding the financial position of the business. Standard practices as to the order and arrangement of a balance sheet are a means of saving the time of the reader and of giving a clearer picture of the company's financial position.

Current assets   Current assets include cash, government bonds and other market-able securities, receivables, inventories, and prepaid expenses. To qualify for inclusion in the current asset category, an asset must be capable of being converted into cash within a relatively short period without interfering with the normal operation of the business. The period is usually one year, but it may be longer for businesses having an operating cycle in excess of one year.

The term *operating cycle* means the average time period between the purchase of merchandise and the conversion of this merchandise back into cash. The series of transactions comprising a complete cycle often runs as follows: (1) purchase of merchandise, (2) sale of the merchandise on credit, (3) collection of the account receivable from the customer. The word *cycle* suggests the circular flow of capital from cash to inventory to receivables and back into cash again. This cycle of trans-actions in a merchandising business is portrayed in the following diagram:

THE OPERATING CYCLE
REPEATS CONTINUOUSLY

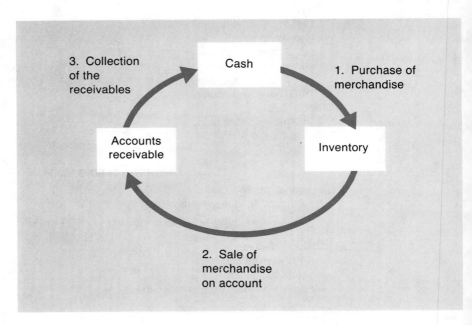

In a business handling fast-moving merchandise (a supermarket, for example) the operating cycle may be completed in a few weeks; for most merchandising businesses the operating cycle requires several months but less than a year.

The sequence in which current assets are listed depends upon their liquidity; the closer an asset is to becoming cash the higher is its liquidity. The total amount of a company's current assets and the relative amount of each type give some indication of the company's short-run, debt-paying ability.

Current liabilities   Liailities that must be paid within one year or the operating cycle (whichever is longer) are called *current liabilities.* Among the more common types of current liabilities are notes payable, accounts payable, taxes payable, salaries payable, interest payable, and unearned revenue. Notes payable are usually listed first, followed by accounts payable; any sequence of listing is acceptable for other current liabilities.

Settlement of most types of current liabilities requires writing a cheque to the creditor; in other words, use of the current asset cash. A somewhat different procedure for settlement is followed for the current liability of unearned revenue. As explained in Chapter 4, unearned revenue is a liability that arises when money is received from customers in advance for goods or services to be delivered in the future. To meet such obligations usually will require using up current assets either through delivering merchandise to the customer or making payments to employees or others to provide the agreed services.

The key point to recognize is the relationship between current liabilities and current assets. Current liabilities must be paid in the near future and current assets must be available to make these payments. Comparison of the amount of current liabilities with the amount of current assets is an important step in evaluating the ability of a company to pay its debts in the near future.

5 Explain the purpose of the current ratio and the meaning of working capital.

Current ratio   Many bankers and other users of financial statements believe that for a business to qualify as a good credit risk, the total current assets should be about twice as large as the total current liabilities. In studying a balance sheet, a banker or other creditor will compute the **current ratio** by dividing total current assets by total current liabilities. The current ratio is a convenient measure of the short-run debt-paying ability of a business.

In the illustrated balance sheet of Graham Company, the current assets of $250,000 are two and one-half times as great as the current liabilities of $100,000; the current ratio is therefore $2^1/_2$ to 1, which would generally be regarded as a strong current position. The current assets could shrink substantially and still be sufficient for payment of the current liabilities. Although a strong current ratio is desirable, an extremely high current ratio (such as 4 to 1 or more) may signify that a company is holding too much of its resources in cash, marketable securities, and other current assets and is not pursuing opportunities for growth as aggressively as it might.

Working capital   The excess of current assets over current liabilities is called *working capital;* the relative amount of working capital is another indication of short-term financial strength. In the illustrated balance sheet of Graham Company, working capital is $150,000, computed by subtracting the current liabilities of $100,000 from the current assets of $250,000. The importance of *solvency* (ability to meet debts as they fall due) was emphasized in Chapter 1. Ample working capital permits a company to meet its short-term obligations, to qualify for favourable credit terms, and to take advantage of opportunities quickly. Many companies have been forced to suspend business because of inadequate working capital, even though total assets were much larger than total liabilities.

Classification and format of income statements

There are two common forms of income statements: the *multiple-step income statement* and the *single-step income statement.* The multiple-step statement is more convenient in illustrating accounting principles and has been used consistently in our illustrations thus far. The income statement for Olympic Sporting Goods on page 201 is in multiple-step form. It is also a **classified** income statement because the various items of expense are classified into significant groups. The single-step form of income statement is illustrated at the bottom of this page.

Multiple-step income statement   The multiple-step income statement is so named because of the series of steps in which costs and expenses are deducted from revenue. As a first step, the cost of goods sold is subtracted from net sales to produce a subtotal for gross profit on sales. As a second step, operating expenses are deducted to obtain another subtotal called income from operations. As a final step, nonoperating revenue is added and nonoperating expenses are deducted to arrive at net income.

Variations may exist in the format of multiple-step income statements. For example, if a business has no nonoperating items, the subtotal for income from operations will not appear. Also, management may elect not to classify operating expenses into subcategories such as selling expenses and general and administrative expenses.

The multiple-step income statement is noted for its numerous sections and significant subtotals. These sections and subtotals assist managers in identifying important trends in various types of business activities. Therefore, the multiple-step format is widely used in small businesses and for the monthly (interim) income statements used by the managers of large businesses.

Single-step income statement   The income statements prepared by large corporations for distribution to thousands of shareholders often are greatly condensed because the public presumably is more interested in a concise report than in the details of operations. The single-step form of income statement takes its name from the fact that the total of all expenses (including the cost of goods sold) is deducted from total revenue in a single step. All types of revenue, such as sales, interest earned, and rent revenue, are added together to show the total revenue. Then all expenses are grouped together and deducted in one step without developing subtotals. A condensed income statement in single-step form is shown below for National Corporation, a large merchandising company.

CONDENSED SINGLE-
STEP INCOME
STATEMENT

NATIONAL CORPORATION
Income Statement
For the Year Ended December 31, 19___

Revenue:		
Net sales		$90,000,000
Interest earned		1,800,000
Total revenue		$91,800,000
Expenses:		
Cost of goods sold	$60,000,000	
Selling expenses	10,200,000	
General & administrative expenses	9,750,000	
Interest expense	4,200,000	
Income taxes expense	3,150,000	
Total expenses		87,300,000
Net income		$ 4,500,000

Use of the single-step income statement has become more common in recent years, perhaps because it is relatively simple and easy to read. It stresses the total relationship between revenue and expenses in the determination of net income. A disadvantage of this format is that useful concepts such as the gross profit on sales are not readily apparent.

THE SYSTEM OF INTERNAL CONTROL
The meaning and purpose of internal control

6   Explain the nature and importance of a system of internal control.

In this section we shall round out our discussion of a merchandising business by considering the *system of internal control* by which management maintains control over the purchasing, receiving, storing, and selling of merchandise. Strong internal controls are needed not only for purchases and sales transactions, but for all other types of transactions as well. In fact, the concept of internal control affects all the assets of a business, all liabilities, the revenue and expenses, and every aspect of operations. The purpose of internal control is to *provide assurance that the entire business operates in accordance with management's plans and policies.*

As defined in Chapter 1, the system of internal control includes all the measures taken by an organization for the propose of (1) protecting its resources against waste, fraud, and inefficency; (2) ensuring accuracy and reliability in accounting and operating data; (3) securing compliance with company policies; and (4) evaluating the level of performance in all divisions of the company.

Many people think of internal control as a means of safeguarding cash and preventing fraud. Although internal control is an important factor in protecting assets and preventing fraud, this is only a part of its role. Remember that business decisions are based on accounting data. A primary objective of the system of internal control is to ensure the *reliability* of the accounting data used in making decisions.

Administrative controls and accounting controls   Internal control procedures fall into two major classes: administrative controls and accounting controls. *Administrative controls* are measures that increase operational efficiency and compliance with policies in all parts of the organization. For example, an administrative control may be a requirement that travelling salespersons submit reports showing the number of calls made on customers each day. Another example is a directive requiring airline pilots to have an annual medical examination. These internal administrative controls have no direct bearing on the reliability of the financial statements. Consequently, administrative controls are not of direct interest to accountants and external (independent) auditors.

Internal accounting controls are measures that relate to protection of assets and to the reliability of accounting and financial reports. An example is the requirement that a person whose duties involve handling cash shall not also maintain accounting records. More broadly stated, the accounting function must be kept separate from the custody of assets. Another *accounting control* is the requirement that cheques, purchase orders, and other documents be serially numbered. Still another example is the rule that a person who orders merchandise and supplies should not be the one to receive them and should not sign cheques to pay for them.

GUIDELINES TO ACHIEVING STRONG INTERNAL CONTROL

Organization plan to establish responsibility for every function

An organization plan should indicate clearly the departments or persons responsible for such functions as purchasing, receiving incoming shipments, maintaining accounting records, approving credit to customers, and preparing the payroll. When an individual or department is assigned responsibility for a function, authority to make decisions should also be granted. The lines of authority and responsibility can be shown on an *organization chart*, as illustrated on the next page.

Control of transactions

If management is to direct the activities of a business according to plan, every transaction should go through four steps: It should be *authorized, approved, executed,* and *recorded.* For example, consider the sale of merchandise on credit. The top management of the company may *authorize* the sale of merchandise on credit to customers who meet certain standards. The manager of the credit and collection department may *approve* a sale of given dollar amount to a particular customer. The sales transaction is *executed* by preparing a sales invoice and delivering the merchandise to the credit customer. The sales transaction is *recorded* in the accounting department by debiting Accounts Receivable and crediting Sales.

Consider for a moment the losses that would probably be incurred if this internal control of transactions did not exist. Assume, for example, that all employees in a store were free to sell on credit any amount of merchandise to any customer, and responsibility for recording the sales transactions was not fixed on any one person or department. The result no doubt would be many unrecorded sales; of those sales transactions that were recorded, many would involve uncollectible receivables.

Subdivision of duties strengthens internal control

The subdivision of duties within a company should be designed so that *no one person or department handles a transaction completely from beginning to end.* When duties are divided in this manner, the work of one employee serves to verify that of another and any errors that occur tend to be detected promptly.

To illustrate the development of internal control through subdivision of duties, let us review the procedures for a sale of merchandise on account by a wholesaler. The sales department of the company is responsible for securing the order from the customer; the credit department must approve the customer's credit before the order is filled; the stock room assembles the goods ordered; the shipping department packs and ships the goods; and the accounting department records the transaction. Each department receives written evidence of the action of the other departments and reviews the documents describing the transaction to see that the actions taken correspond in all details. The shipping department, for instance, does not release the merchandise until after the credit department has approved the customer as a credit risk. The accounting department does not record the sale until it has received documentary evidence that (1) the goods were ordered, (2) the extension of credit was approved, and (3) the merchandise was shipped to the customer.

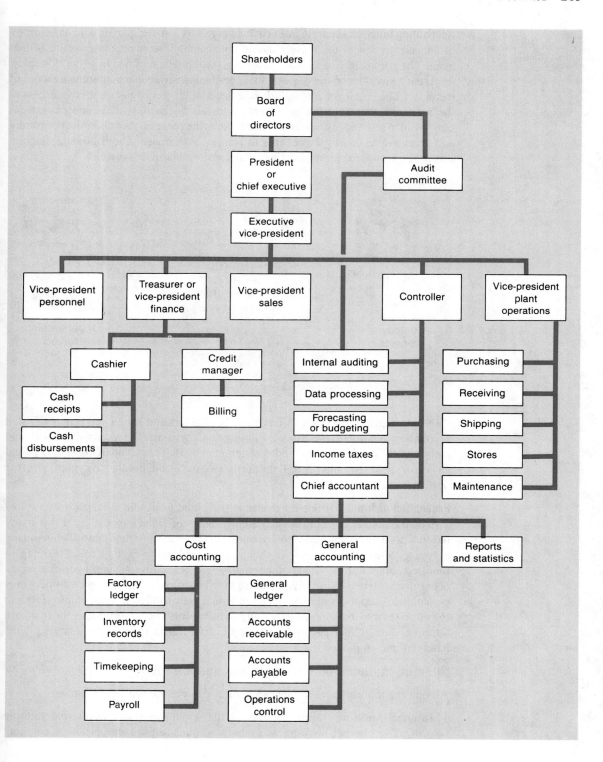

Accounting function separate from custody of assets   An employee who has custody of an asset or access to an asset should not maintain the accounting record of that asset. The person having custody of an asset will not be inclined to waste it, steal it, or give it away if he or she is aware that another employee is maintaining a record of the asset. The employee maintaining the accounting record does not have access to the asset and therefore has no incentive to falsify the record. If one person has custody of assets and also maintains the accounting records, there is both opportunity and incentive to falsify the records to conceal a shortage. The following diagram illustrates how separation of duties creates strong internal control.

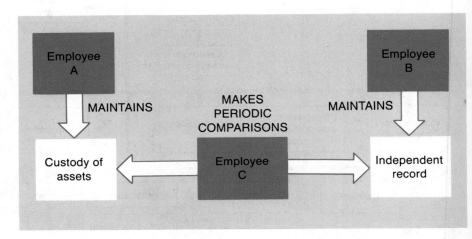

In this diagram Employee A has custody of assets and Employee B maintains an accounting record of the assets. Employee C periodically counts the assets and compares the count with the record maintained by B. This comparison should reveal any errors made by either A or B unless the two have collaborated to conceal an error or a fraud.

Prevention of fraud   If one employee is permitted to handle all aspects of a trans-action, the danger of fraud is increased. Studies of fraud cases suggest that many individuals may be tempted into dishonest acts if given complete control of company property. Most of these persons, however, would not engage in fraud if doing so required collaboration with another employee. Losses through employee dishonesty occur in a variety of ways: merchandise may be stolen; payments by customers may be withheld; suppliers may be overpaid with a view to kickbacks to employees; and lower prices may be allowed to favoured customers. The opportunities for fraud are almost endless if all aspects of a sale or purchase transaction are concentrated in the hands of one employee.

Specific methods of achieving internal control

Among the more important internal control devices are the following:

1 Internal auditing   Virtually every large organization has an internal auditing staff. The internal auditors study both administrative controls and accounting controls in all units of the organization and prepare reports to top management on their findings.

2 Financial forecasts   A plan of operations is prepared each year setting goals for each division of the business, as, for example, the expected volume of sales, amounts of expenses, and future cash balances. Actual results are compared with forecasted amounts month by month. This comparison strengthens control because variations from planned results are investigated promptly.

3 Serially numbered documents   Documents such as cheques, purchase orders, and sales invoices should be serially numbered. If a document is misplaced or concealed, the break in the sequence of numbers will call attention to the discrepancy.

4 Competent personnel   Even the best-designed system of internal control will not work well unless the people using it are competent. Competence and integrity of employees are in part developed through training programs, but they also are related to the policies for selection of personnel, and the adequacy of supervision.

Limitations and cost of internal control

Although internal control is highly effective in increasing the reliability of accounting data and in protecting against fraud, no system of internal control is foolproof. Two or more dishonest employees working in collusion can defeat the system — temporarily. Carelessness by employees and misunderstanding of instructions can cause a breakdown in controls. Finally, the question of cost of controls cannot be ignored. Too elaborate a system of internal contral may entail greater expense than is justified by the protection gained. For this reason, a system of internal control must be tailored to meet the needs of an individual business.

INTERNAL CONTROLS OVER THE PURCHASE AND SALE OF MERCHANDISE

Business documents and procedures

7   Explain how purchase orders, invoices, receiving reports, and other business documents are used to maintain internal control over merchandise transactions.

Carefully designed business documents and procedures for using them are necessary to ensure that all transactions are properly authorized, approved, executed, and recorded. Some of the more important of these business documents and the procedures related to them are shown in the following table.

BUSINESS DOCUMENT	INITIATED BY	SENT TO

Purchase requisition
  Issued when quantity
  of goods on hand falls
  below established
  reorder point
	Departmental sales
	managers or inventory
	control department
		Purchasing department

Purchase order
  Specifies prices,
  quantities, and method
  of transportation
	Purchasing department	Original to selling company
		(vendor, supplier), copies
		to buyer's accounting,
		receiving, and finance
		departments

BUSINESS DOCUMENT	INITIATED BY	SENT TO
Invoice Confirms that goods have been shipped and requests payment	Seller (supplier)	Accounting department of buying company
Receiving report Based on count and inspection of goods received	Receiving department of buying company	Original to accounting department, copies to purchasing department and to department requisitioning goods
Invoice approval form	Accounting department of buying company	Finance department to support issuance of cheque. Returned to accounting department with carbon copy of cheque.

Purchase orders

In many businesses and especially in large organizations, the buying company uses its own purchase order forms. A purchase order of Fairway Pro Shop issued to Adams Manufacturing Company is illustrated as follows:

SERIALLY NUMBERED
PURCHASE ORDER

PURCHASE ORDER

Order No. 999

FAIRWAY PRO SHOP
10 Fairway Avenue, Toronto, Ontario

To: Adams Manufacturing Company   Date Nov. 10, 19____

19 Union Street   Ship via Jones Truck Co.

Calgary, Alberta   Terms: 2/10, n/30

Please enter our order for the following:

Quantity	Description	Price	Total
15 sets	Model S irons	$120.00	$1,800.00
50 dozen	X3Y Shur-Par golf balls	14.00	700.00
			$2,500.00

Fairway Pro Shop

By D. D. McCarthy

Several copies of a purchase order are usually prepared. The original is sent to the supplier; it constitutes an authorization to deliver the merchandise and to submit a bill based on the prices listed.

The issuance of a purchase order does not call for any entries in the accounting records of either the prospective buyer or seller. The company that receives an order does not consider that a sale has been made *until the merchandise is delivered.* At that point ownership of the goods changes, and both buyer and seller should make accounting entries to record the transaction.

Invoices

When a manufacturer or wholesaler receives an order for its products, it takes two actions. One is to ship the goods to the customer and the other is to send the customer an invoice. By the act of shipping the merchandise, the seller is giving up ownership of one type of asset, inventory; by issuing the invoice the seller is recording ownership of another form of asset, an account receivable.

An invoice contains a description of the goods being sold, the quantities, prices, credit terms, and method of shipment. The following illustration shows an invoice issued by Adams Manufacturing Company in response to the previously illustrated purchase order from Fairway Pro Shop.

INVOICE IS BASIS FOR
ACCOUNTING ENTRY

INVOICE

ADAMS MANUFACTURING COMPANY
19 Union Street
Calgary, Alberta

Sold to: Fairway Pro Shop   Invoice no. 782

10 Fairway Avenue   Invoice Date Nov. 15, 19____

Toronto, Ontario   Your order no. 999

Shipped to Same   Date shipped Nov. 15, 19____

Terms 2/10, n/30   Shipped via Jones Truck Co.

Quantity	Description	Price	Amount
15 sets	Model S irons	$120.00	$1,800.00
50 dozen	X3Y Shur-Par golf balls	14.00	700.00
			$2,500.00

From the viewpoint of the seller, an invoice is a *sales invoice;* from the buyer's viewpoint it is a *purchase invoice.* The invoice is the basis for an entry in the accounting records of both the seller and the buyer because it evidences the transfer of ownership of goods. At the time of issuing the invoice, the selling company makes an entry debiting Accounts Receivable and crediting Sales. The buying company, however, does not record the invoice as a liability until after verifying the following aspects of the transaction:

1 The invoice agrees with the purchase order as to prices, quantities, and other provisions.
2 The invoice is arithmetically correct in all extensions of price times quantity and in the addition of amounts.
3 The goods covered by the invoice have been received and are in satisfactory condition.

Evidence that the merchandise has been received in good condition must be obtained from the receiving department. It is the function of the receiving department to receive all incoming goods, to inspect them as to quality and condition, and to determine the quantities received by counting, measuring, or weighing. The receiving department should prepare a serially numbered report for each shipment received; one copy of this *receiving report* is sent to the accounting department for use in verifying the invoice.

The verification of the invoice in the accounting department is accomplished by comparing the purchase order, the invoice, and the receiving report. Comparison of these documents establishes that the merchandise described in the invoice was actually ordered, has been received in good condition, and was billed at the prices specified in the purchase order.

When these verification procedures have been completed, the invoice is recorded as a liability by an entry debiting the Purchases account and crediting Accounts Payable.

Debit and credit memoranda (debit memos, credit memos)

If merchandise purchased on account is unsatisfactory and is to be returned to the supplier (or if a price reduction is agreed upon), a *debit memorandum* may be prepared by the purchasing company and sent to the supplier. The debit memorandum informs the supplier that his or her account is being debited (reduced) by the buyer and explains the circumstances.

The supplier upon being informed of the return of damaged merchandise (or having agreed to a reduction in price) will issue a *credit memorandum* as evidence that the account receivable from the purchaser is being credited (reduced) by the supplier.

Notice that issuing a credit memorandum has the same effect upon a customer's account as does receiving payment for the customer—that is, the account receivable is credited (reduced). Thus, it is important that an employee with authority to issue credit memoranda *not be allowed to handle cash receipts from customers.* If both of these duties were assigned to the same employee, that person could abstract some of the cash collected from customers and conceal this theft by issuing credit memoranda.

8 Explain the advantage of recording purchase invoices by the net price method.

Recording purchase invoices at net price

Most well-managed companies have a firm policy of taking all purchase discounts offered. The recording of purchase invoices at their gross amount and making payment of a reduced amount within the discount period was described earlier in this chapter. Some companies that regularly take advantage of all available purchase discounts prefer the alternative method of recording purchase invoices at the *net amount* after discount rather than at the gross amount. If the amount that the buyer intends to pay is the invoice amount minus a cash discount, why not record this net amount as the liability at the time the invoice is received? For example, if Fairway Pro Shop receives a $10,000 purchase invoice from Gator Sportswear bearing terms of 2/10, n/30, the entry could be

ENTRY FOR PURCHASE:
NET PRICE METHOD

Nov. 3 Purchases	9,800	
Accounts Payable		9,800
To record purchase invoice from Gator Sportswear less 2% cash discount available.		

Assuming that the invoice is paid within 10 days, the entry for the payment is as follows:

ENTRY FOR PAYMENT:
NET PRICE METHOD

Nov. 13 Accounts Payable	9,800	
Cash		9,800
To record payment of $10,000 invoice from Gator Sportswear less 2% cash discount.		

Through oversight or carelessness, the purchasing company occasionally may fail to make payment of an invoice within the 10-day discount period. If such a delay occurred in paying the invoice from Gator Sportswear, the full amount of the invoice would have to be paid rather than the recorded liability of $9,800. The journal entry to record the late payment on, say, December 3, is as follows:

ENTRY FOR PAYMENT
AFTER DISCOUNT PERIOD:
NET PRICE METHOD

Dec. 3 Accounts Payable	9,800	
Purchase Discounts Lost	200	
Cash		10,000
To record payment of invoice and loss of discount by delaying payment beyond the discount period.		

Under this method the cost of goods purchased is properly recorded at $9,800, and the additional payment of $200 caused by failure to pay the invoice promptly is placed in a special expense account designed to attract the attention of management. The gross price (gross amount) method of recording invoices described earlier in this chapter shows the amount of purchase discounts *taken* each period; the *net price (net amount) method* now under discussion shows the amount of purchase discounts *lost* each period. The latter method has the advantage of drawing the attention of management to a breakdown in internal control. The fact that a purchase discount has been taken does not require attention by management, but a discount lost because of inefficiency in processing accounts payable does call for managerial investigation.

Under the net price method, inefficiency and delay in paying invoices is not concealed by including the lost discount in the cost of merchandise purchased. The purchases are stated at the net price available if all discounts had been taken; any purchase discounts lost are shown separately in the income statement as an operating expense.

END-OF-CHAPTER REVIEW

SUMMARY OF CHAPTER LEARNING OBJECTIVES

1 Account for purchases and sales of merchandise.

Sales of merchandise are credited to the Sales revenue account. Sales returns and allowances and sales discounts are debited to contra-revenue accounts. Purchases of merchandise are debited to the Purchases account. Purchase returns and allowances and purchase discounts are credited to accounts that are deducted from the balance of the Purchases account in the income statement.

2 Determine the cost of goods sold by the periodic inventory system.

Under the periodic inventory system, the cost of goods sold is equal to the beginning inventory, plus net purchases (including transportation-in), minus the ending inventory.

3 Prepare a work sheet and closing entries for a merchandising company.

A work sheet for a merchandising business is much like the work sheet for a service-type business. The basic difference is the addition of beginning and ending inventories. The beginning inventory appears in the Trial Balance debit column and is extended into the Income Statement debit column. The ending inventory is entered in the Income Statement credit column and in the Balance Sheet debit column.

At the end of the period, the beginning inventory is closed along with the expense accounts. The ending inventory is recorded by debiting the Inventory account and crediting the Income Summary account. This entry may be combined with the entry to close the revenue accounts.

4 Prepare a classified balance sheet and either a single-step or a multiple-step income statement.

In a classified balance sheet, assets are subdivided into the categories of *current assets, plant and equipment,* and *other assets.* Liabilities are classified as *current liabilities* (those due within one year or an operating cycle), or *long-term liabilities.*

In a multiple-step income statement, the cost of goods sold is deducted from net sales to provide the subtotal, gross profit. Operating expenses then are deducted to arrive at income from operations. As a final step, nonoperating items are added or subtracted to arrive at net income. In a single step-income statement all revenue items are combined, and then all expenses are combined and deducted from total revenue in a single step.

5 Explain the purpose of the current ratio and the meaning of working capital.

The purpose of the current ratio (current assets divided by current liabilities) is to provide the users of financial statements with a quick indication of the solvency of a business.

Working capital is the excess of current assets over current liabilities. This measurement indicates the amount of uncommitted liquid resources on hand.

6 Explain the nature and importance of a system of internal control.

A system of internal control includes all measures to (1) protect assets from waste, fraud, or inefficient use, (2) ensure the reliability of accounting data, (3) obtain compliance with company policies, and (4) evaluate performance. In short, the system of internal control attempts to keep the entire business organization operating in accordance with management's plans and policies.

7 Explain how purchase orders, invoices, receiving reports, and other business documents are used to maintain internal control over merchandise transactions.

A basic principle of internal control is that no one employee or department should handle all aspects of a business transaction. The business documents described above provide written evidence (documentation) of the procedures performed by each department participating in a transaction. The contents of these documents should agree, thus confirming the details of the transaction. Hence, the work of each department verifies the work of the others.

8 Explain the advantage of recording purchase invoices by the net price method.

When purchases are recorded at the net amount, purchase discounts *lost* are recorded in a separate account and are promptly brought to management's attention. When purchases are recorded at the gross amount, only those discounts *taken* are recorded in the accounting records. Thus, discounts passed up are concealed in the cost of purchases, rather than being highlighted.

KEY TERMS INTRODUCED OR EMPHASIZED IN CHAPTER 5

Cost of goods sold   A computation appearing as a separate item or section of an income statement showing the cost of goods sold during the period. Computed by adding net delivered cost of merchandise purchases to beginning inventory to obtain cost of goods available for sale, and then deducting from this total the amount of the ending inventory. Usually equal to between 50% and 70% of net sales.

Credit memorandum   A document issued to show a reduction in the amount owed by a customer because of goods returned, a defect in the goods or services provided, or an error.

Current assets   Cash and other assets that can be converted into cash within one year or the operating cycle (whichever is longer) without interfering with the normal operation of the business.

Current ratio   Current assets divided by current liabilities. A measure of short-run debt-paying ability.

Gross profit on sales   Revenue from sales minus cost of goods sold.

Internal control   All measures used by a business to guard against errors, waste, or fraud and to assure the reliability of accounting data. Designed to aid in the efficient operation of a business and to encourage compliance with company policies.

Invoice   An itemized statement of goods being bought or sold. Shows quantities, prices, and credit terms. Serves as the basis for an entry in the accounting records of both seller and buyer because it evidences the transfer of ownership of goods.

Multiple-step income statement   An income statement in which cost of goods sold and expenses are subtracted from revenue in a series of steps, thus producing significant subtotals prior to net income.

Net price method   A policy of recording purchase invoices at amounts net of (reduced by) cash discounts.

Operating cycle   The average time period from the purchase of merchandise to its sale and conversion back into cash.

Net sales Gross sales revenue minus sales returns and allowances and minus sales discounts.

Periodic inventory system A system of accounting for merchandise in which inventory at the balance sheet date is determined by counting and pricing the goods on hand. Cost of goods sold is computed by subtracting the ending inventory from the cost of goods available for sale.

Perpetual inventory system A system of accounting for merchandise that provides a continuous record showing the quantity and cost of all goods on hand.

Psychic income A feeling of personal satisfaction derived from taking a certain course of action. Psychic income is not measured in accounting records and does not appear in an income statement. However, it often influences a decision maker's actions.

Purchase order A serially numbered document sent by the purchasing department of a business to a supplier or vendor for the purpose of ordering materials or services.

Receiving report An internal form prepared by the receiving department for each incoming shipment showing the quantity and condition of goods received.

Single-step income statement An income statement in which the cost of goods sold and all expenses are combined and deducted from total revenue in a single step to determine net income.

Working capital Current assets minus current liabilities. Another measure of short-run debt-paying ability.

DEMONSTRATION PROBLEM FOR YOUR REVIEW

Village Supply completed the following merchandising transactions during May. The company's policy calls for taking advantage of all cash discounts available to it from suppliers; purchase invoices are recorded at the *net amount* (the net price method). In making sales, the company grants credit terms of 2/10, n/30, and strictly enforces the 10-day limitation. The amounts listed as cash sales below are net of sales discounts.

May 3 Sold merchandise to Rich Company for cash, $32,880.

May 16 Sold merchandise on account to Riverside Company, $14,820.

May 16 Purchased merchandise from Hilton Supply Company, $18,900; terms 2/10, n/30.

May 17 Paid transportation charges on goods received from Hilton Supply Company, $726.

May 18 Issued credit memorandum No. 102 to Riverside Company for allowance on damaged goods, $420.

May 24 Purchased merchandise from Pete Construction Co., $17,100; terms 1/10, n/30.

May 25 Returned defective goods with invoice price of $900 to Pete Construction Co., accompanied by debit memorandum No. 122.

May 26 Received cash from Riverside Company in full payment of account.

May 26 Paid Hilton Supply Company account in full.

Instructions
a Journalize the above transactions.
b Prepare a partial income statement for May showing sales and cost of goods sold (in detail), and gross profit on sales. Assume the inventory at April 30 to be $11,400 and the inventory at May 31 to be $13,920.
c What is the amount of the account payable to Pete Construction Co. at May 31? What would be the amount of this liability at May 31 if the company followed a policy of recording purchase invoices at the gross amount?

SOLUTION TO DEMONSTRATION PROBLEM

a

General Journal

May	3	Cash	32,880	
		Sales		32,880
		To record the sales of merchandise for cash.		
	16	Accounts Receivable	14,820	
		Sales		14,820
		To record sale to Riverside Company		
	16	Purchases	18,522	
		Accounts Payable		18,522
		To record $18,900 purchase invoice from Hilton Supply Company less 2% cash discount available (terms 2/10, n/30).		
	17	Transportation-in	726	
		Cash		726
		Paid transportation charges on goods purchased from Hilton Supply Company.		
	18	Sales Returns & Allowances	420	
		Accounts Receivable		420
		Issue credit memo No. 102 to customer, Riverside Company for damaged goods.		
	24	Purchases	16,929	
		Accounts Payable		16,929
		To record $17,100 purchase invoice from Pete Construction Co., less 1% cash discount available (terms 1/10, n/30).		
	25	Accounts Payable	891	
		Purchase Returns & Allowances		891
		To reduce liability to Pete Construction Co., for net amount of defective goods returned. Invoice price $900 − 1% discount = $891 recorded liability. Debit memo No. 122.		
	26	Cash	14,112	
		Sales Discounts	288	
		Accounts Receivable		14,400
		Collected from Riverside Company for our May 16 sale, $14,820 − allowance of $420 and 2% discount on balance of $14,400.		
	26	Accounts Payable	18,522	
		Cash		18,522
		Paid $18,900 purchase invoice from Hilton Supply Company less 2% discount.		

b

VILLAGE SUPPLY
Partial Income Statement
For the Month Ended May 31, 19___

Sales			$47,700
Less: Sales returns & allowances		$ 420	
Sales discounts		288	708
Net sales			$46,992
Cost of goods sold:			
Inventory, Apr. 30, 19___			$11,400
Purchases	$35,451		
Transportation-in	726		
Delivered cost of purchases	$36,177		
Less: Purchase returns & allowances	891		
Net purchases		35,286	
Cost of goods available for sale		$46,686	
Less: Inventory, May 31, 19___		13,920	
Cost of goods sold			32,766
Gross profit on sales			$14,226

c Account payable (net), $16,038; account payable (gross), $16,200. Computed as $16,038 ÷ .99 = $16,200, or $17,100 purchases − $900 return = $16,200.

ASSIGNMENT MATERIAL

REVIEW QUESTIONS

1 During the current year, Green Bay Company made all sales of merchandise at prices in excess of cost. Will the business necessarily report a net income for the year? Explain.

2 The income statement for Stereo West showed gross profit on sales of $144,000, operating expenses of $130,000, and cost of goods sold of $216,000. What was the amount of net sales?

3 Valley Mart during its first year of operations had cost of goods sold of $480,000 and a gross profit equal to 40% of sales. What was the dollar amount of net sales for the year?

4 Is the normal balance of the Sales Returns and Allowances account a debit or a credit? Is the normal balance of the Purchase Returns and Allowances account a debit or a credit?

5 Supply the proper terms to complete the following statements:

a Net sales − cost of goods sold = _?_

b Beginning inventory + purchases − purchase returns and allowances − purchase discounts + transportation-in = _?_

c Cost of goods sold + ending inventory = _?_

d Cost of goods sold + gross profit on sales = _?_

e Net income + operating expenses = _?_

6 During the current year, Davis Corporation purchased merchandise costing $200,000. State the cost of goods sold under each of the following alternative assumptions:

a No beginning inventory; ending inventory $40,000

b Beginning inventory $60,000; no ending inventory

c Beginning inventory $58,000; ending inventory $78,000

d Beginning inventory $90,000; ending inventory $67,000

7 Zenith Company uses the periodic inventory system and maintains its accounting records on a calendar-year basis. Does the beginning or the ending inventory figure appear in the trial balance prepared from the ledger on December 31?

8 Compute the amount of cost of goods sold, given the following account balances: beginning inventory $40,000, purchases $84,000, purchase returns and allowances $4,500, purchase discounts $1,500, transportation-in $1,000, and ending inventory $36,000.

9 In which columns of the work sheet for a merchandising company does the ending inventory appear?

10 State briefly the difference between the *perpetual* inventory system and the *periodic* inventory system.

11 When the periodic inventory system is in use, how is the amount of inventory determined at the end of the period?

12 What is the purpose of a closing entry consisting of a debit to the Income Summary account and a credit to the Inventory account?

13 Tireco is a retail store in a province that imposes a 5% sales tax. Would you expect to find an account entitled Sales Tax Expense and another account entitled Sales Tax Payable in Tireco's ledger? Explain your answer.

14 Explain the terms *current assets, current liabilities,* and *current ratio.*

15 Madison Corporation has current assets of $540,000 and current liabilities of $300,000. Compute the current ratio and the amount of working capital.

16 Barnes Imports has a current ratio of 3 to 1 and working capital of $60,000. What are the amounts of current assets and current liabilities?

17 What is the purpose of a system of internal control? List four specific objectives that the measures included in a system of internal control are designed to achieve.

18 Suggest a control device to protect a business against the loss or nondelivery of invoices, purchase orders, and other documents that are routed from one department to another.

19 Criticize the following statement: "In our company we get things done by requiring that a person who initiates a transaction follow it through in all particulars. For example, an employee who issues a purchase order is held responsible for inspecting the merchandise upon arrival, approving the invoice, and preparing the cheque in payment of the purchase. If any error is made, we know definitely whom to blame."

20 Explain why the operations and custodianship functions should be separate from the accounting function.

21 A system of internal control is often said to include two major types of controls: administrative controls and accounting controls. Explain the nature of each group and give an example of each.

22 How does a single-step income statement differ from a multiple-step income statement?

23 Company A sells merchandise to Company B on credit and two days later agrees that B can return a portion of the merchandise. B does so. Should the document issued by Company A to Company B be a debit memorandum or a credit memorandum? Explain your reasoning.

24 Name three business documents needed by the accounting department to verify that a purchase of merchandise has occurred and that payment of the related liability should be made.

EXERCISES

Exercise 5-1
Accounting
terminology

Listed below are nine technical accounting terms introduced in this chapter:

Cost of goods available for sale	Gross profit on sales	System of internal control
Cost of goods sold	Inventory	Working capital
Current ratio	Periodic inventory system	
	Perpetual inventory system	

Each of the following statements may (or may not) describe one of these technical terms. For each statement, indicate the accounting term described, or answer "None" if the statement does not correctly describe any of the terms.

a Goods acquired and held for sale to customers.

b Current assets minus current liabilities.

c Accounting procedures that involve taking a physical inventory in order to determine the amount of inventory and the cost of goods sold.

d Net sales minus the cost of goods sold.

e Beginning inventory plus the delivered cost of net purchases.

f Measures intended to make all aspects of a business operate in accordance with management's plans and policies.

g A policy of recording purchase invoices at amounts net of available cash discounts.

Exercise 5-2
Accounting for
purchases and sales
of merchandise

Delta Traders sold merchandise to Denver Suppliers for $84,000 terms 2/10, n/30. Denver Suppliers paid for the merchandise within the discount period. Both companies record invoices at the gross amounts.

a Give the journal entries by Delta Traders to record the sale and the subsequent collection

b Give the journal entries by Denver Suppliers to record the purchase and the subsequent payment.

Exercise 5-3
Relationships among
merchandising
accounts

Some of the items in the income statement of Traders' Market are listed below.

Net sales	$400,000
Gross profit on sales	160,000
Beginning inventory	30,000
Purchase discounts	1,000
Purchase returns & allowances	4,000
Transportation-in	6,000
Operating expenses	80,000
Purchases	250,000

Use the appropriate items from this list as a basis for computing (a) the cost of goods sold, (b) the cost of goods available for sale, and (c) the ending inventory.

Exercise 5-4
Income statement relationships in a merchandising business

This exercise stresses the sequence and relationship of items in a multiple-step income statement for a merchandising business. Each of the five horizontal lines in the table represents a separate set of income statement items. You are to copy the table and fill in the missing amounts. A net loss in the right-hand column is to be indicated by placing brackets before and after the amount, as for example, in line **e** (25,000).

	NET SALES	BEGIN-NING INVENTORY	NET PURCHASES	ENDING INVENTORY	COST OF GOODS SOLD	GROSS PROFIT	EXPENSES	NET INCOME OR (LOSS)
a	200,000	54,000	130,000	44,000	?	60,000	70,000	?
b	500,000	60,000	340,000	?	330,000	?	?	25,000
c	600,000	120,000	?	85,000	390,000	210,000	165,000	?
d	800,000	?	500,000	150,000	?	260,000	205,000	?
e	?	230,000	?	255,000	660,000	240,000	?	(25,000)

Exercise 5-5
Preparing closing entries from a worksheet

The accountant for Village Ski Shop prepared a work sheet at December 31, 1989. Shown below are the Income Statement columns from that work sheet. During 1989, Alice Tsui, owner of Village Ski Shop, withdrew assets of $22,000 from the business. Using this information, prepare four separate journal entries to close the accounts at December 31. Use the sequence of closing entries illustrated in this chapter.

	INCOME STATEMENT	
	DEBIT	CREDIT
Inventory, Jan. 1, 1989	90,000	
Sales		420,350
Sales returns & allowances	8,700	
Sales discounts	2,650	
Purchases	275,000	
Purchase returns & allowances		3,200
Purchase discounts		5,100
Transportation-in	4,300	
Selling expenses	48,000	
General and administrative expenses	36,000	
Interest expense	7,000	
Inventory, Dec. 31, 1989		81,000
	471,650	509,650
Net income	38,000	
	509,650	509,650

Exercise 5-6
Multiple-step and single-step income statements

Use the data from the Village Ski Shop work sheet in Exercise 5-5 to prepare:
a A multiple-step income statement in as much detail as the work sheet data will allow.
b A single-step income statement in condensed form. "Condensed form" means that net sales and the cost of goods sold will each be shown as a single amount, without showing the individual account balances that are used to compute these subtotals.

Exercise 5-7
Single-step income statement

Prepare a single-step income statement for the year ended December 31, 19___, for Angloria Corporation by selecting the appropriate items from the following list:

Accounts receivable	$ 18,000
Accumulated depreciation — equipment	15,000
Net sales	800,000
Cost of goods sold	620,000
Interest earned	30,000
Rental income	16,000
General and administrative expenses	60,000
Selling expenses	50,000
Income taxes expense	46,000
Inventory, December 31, 19___	120,000
Purchases	660,000
Inventory, January 1, 19___	80,000

Exercise 5-8
Accounting for sales taxes

Christine's Shoe Store operates in an area in which a 5% sales tax is levied on all products handled by the store. On cash sales, the salesclerks include the sales tax in the amount collected from the customer and ring up the entire amount on the cash register without recording separately the tax liability. On credit sales, the customer is charged for the list price of the merchandise plus 5%, and the entire amount is debited to Accounts Receivable and credited to the Sales account. On sales of less than one dollar, the tax collected is rounded to the nearest cent.

Sales tax is remitted to the government monthly. At March 31 the Sales account showed a balance of $214,830 for the month ended March 31.

a What amount of sales tax is owed at March 31?

b Give the journal entry to record the sales tax liability on the books.

Exercise 5-9
Computing current ratio and working capital

The balance sheet of Hunt Company contained the following items, among others:

Cash	$ 39,600
Accounts receivable	158,000
Inventory	206,400
Store equipment (net)	192,000
Other assets	28,800
Mortgage payable (due in three years)	48,000
Notes payable (due in 10 days)	19,200
Accounts payable	142,400
Bob Hunt, capital	220,800

Instructions

a From the preceding information compute the amount of current assets and the amount of current liabilities.

b How much working capital does Hunt Company have?

c Compute the current ratio.

Exercise 5-10
Recording purchases by the alternative methods

Taft Company received purchase invoices during July totalling $44,000, all of which carried credit terms of 2/10, n/30. It was the company's regular policy to take advantage of all available cash discounts, but because of employee vacations during July, there was confusion and delay in making payments to suppliers, and none of the July invoices was paid within the discount period.

a What was the amount of the additional cost incurred by Taft Company as a result of the company's failure to take the available purchase discounts?

b Explain briefly two alternative ways in which Taft Company's amount of purchases might be presented in the July income statement.

c What method of recording purchase invoices can you suggest that would call to the attention of the Taft Company management the inefficiency of operations in July?

PROBLEMS

Group A

Problem 5A-1
Recording merchandising transactions

Runners' World deals in a wide variety of low-priced merchandise and uses the periodic inventory system. Purchases are recorded at the full (gross) invoice price. Shown below is a partial list of the transactions occurring during May.

May 2 Purchased merchandise (running shoes) on credit from MinuteMan Shoes, $9,600. Terms, 2/10, n/30.

May 3 Paid freight charges of $45 on the shipment of merchandise purchased from Minute-Man Shoes.

May 4 Upon unpacking the shipment from MinuteMan, discovered that some of the shoes were the wrong style. Returned these shoes, which cost $400, to MinuteMan and received full credit.

May 9 Sold merchandise on account to Desert Spa Hotel, $4,100. Terms, 2/10, n/30.

May 11 Paid $22 freight charges on the outbound shipment to Desert Spa Hotel.

May 12 Paid MinuteMan Shoes within the discount period the remaining amount owed for the May 2 purchase.

May 16 Sold merchandise on account to Holiday Sportswear, $2,755. Terms, 2/10, n/30.

May 19 Received cheque from Desert Spa Hotel within the discount period in full settlement of the May 9 sale.

May 21 Holiday Sportswear returned $650 of the merchandise it had purchased on May 16. Runners' World has a policy of accepting all merchandise returns within 30 days of the date of sale without question. Full credit was given to Holiday for the returned merchandise.

Instructions

Prepare journal entries to record each of these transactions in the accounting records of Runners' World. Include a written explanation for each journal entry.

Problem 5A-2
Preparing closing entries and an income statement

The following accounts relate to the income of Leather Bandit for the three-month period ended March 31, 19___:

Sales	$250,000	Transportation-in	$ 1,700
Sales returns &		Inventory, Jan. 1, 19___	97,000
allowances	5,000	Inventory, Mar. 31, 19___	102,700
Sales discounts	3,700	Operating expenses	72,400
Purchases	160,000	Interest expense	3,400
Purchase returns			
& allowances	2,500		
Purchase discounts	3,200		

Instructions

a Compute the amount of net sales for the three-month period.

b Compute the cost of goods sold.

c Prepare a *condensed* multiple-step income statement. Show both net sales and the cost of goods sold as "one-line items," without showing the accounts used to compute these amounts. Interest expense should be shown after determining Income from Operations.

d Prepare closing entries for the three-month period ended March 31. Only three closing entries are required, as the owner, Francisco Martinez, did not withdraw any assets during the period.

Problem 5A-3
Preparing a work sheet and adjusting and closing entries

Fitness Products is a small company maintaining its accounts on a calendar-year basis and using a periodic inventory system. A four-column schedule consisting of the first four columns of a 10-column work sheet appears below.

FITNESS PRODUCTS
Work Sheet
For the Year Ended December 31, 19___

	TRIAL BALANCE		ADJUSTMENTS	
	DEBIT	CREDIT	DEBIT	CREDIT
Cash	7,600			
Accounts receivable	39,500			
Inventory, Jan. 1	60,000			
Unexpired insurance	4,400			(b) 3,400
Store equipment	22,000			
Accumulated depreciation:				
Store equipment		5,700		(a) 1,900
Accounts payable		40,400		
Mark Allen, capital		88,400		
Mark Allen, drawing	20,000			
Sales		529,000		
Sales returns & allowances	21,000			
Sales discounts	8,000			
Purchases	368,000			
Purchase returns & allowances . .		18,000		
Purchase discounts		6,000		
Transportation-in	12,000			
Advertising expense	32,000			
Rent expense	25,000			
Salaries expense	68,000			
	687,500	687,500		
Depreciation expense			(a) 1,900	
Insurance expense			(b) 3,400	
			5,300	5,300

The completed Adjustments columns have been included in the work sheet to minimize the detail work involved. These adjustments were derived from the following information available at December 31.

(a) Depreciation expense for the year on store equipment, $1,900.

(b) Insurance premiums expired during the year, $3,400.

A physical inventory taken at December 31 showed the ending inventory to be $66,000.

Instructions

a Prepare a 10-column work sheet. Include at the bottom of the work sheet a legend consisting of a brief explanation keyed to each adjusting entry.

b Prepare the two journal entries needed to adjust the accounts at December 31.

c Prepare the necessary journal entries to close the accounts on December 31.

Problem 5A-4
Preparing a work sheet, financial statements, and adjusting and closing entries

Shown below is a trial balance prepared from the ledger of Wilson Marine Supply at December 31, 19___. The accounts are maintained on a calendar-year basis and are adjusted and closed annually.

WILSON MARINE SUPPLY
Trial Balance
December 31, 19___

Cash	$ 16,300	
Accounts receivable	49,200	
Inventory, Jan. 1, 19___	62,000	
Unexpired insurance	1,800	
Office supplies	800	
Land	17,000	
Building	60,000	
Accumulated depreciation: building		$ 2,400
Equipment	16,000	
Accumulated depreciation: equipment		4,800
Accounts payable		47,900
Jane Wilson, capital		99,500
Jane Wilson, drawing	18,000	
Sales		326,000
Sales returns & allowances	4,100	
Sales discounts	1,100	
Purchases	192,000	
Purchase returns & allowances		2,000
Purchase discounts		1,600
Transportation-in	4,800	
Salaries and wages expense	40,000	
Property taxes expense	1,100	
	$484,200	$484,200

Other data

(a) Examination of policies showed $600 *unexpired* insurance on December 31.

(b) Supplies on hand at December 31 were estimated to amount to $300.

(c) The building is being depreciated over a 25-year useful life. The equipment is being depreciated over a 10-year useful life.

(d) Accrued salaries as of December 31 were $5,000.

(e) Inventory of merchandise on December 31 was $44,600.

Instructions a Prepare a 10-column work sheet at December 31, 19___.

b Prepare an income statement, a statement of owner's equity, and a classified balance sheet

c Prepare adjusting entries.

d Prepare closing entries.

Problem 5A-5
**Computing current
ratio and working
capital; evaluating
solvency**

Some of the year-end ledger account balances of V. Boyer's Warehouse are listed below.

Delivery equipment	$ 26,000
Interest payable	7,180
Advance payments from customers	3,320
Notes payable (due in 90 days)	62,000
Marketable securities	25,700
Accounts receivable	90,500
Accounts payable	37,340
Interest receivable	200
Inventory	87,400
Accumulated depreciation: delivery equipment	13,155
Salaries payable	2,560
Cash	21,000
Land	95,000
Furniture & fixtures	11,200
Mortgage payable (due in 20 years)	115,000
Buildings	306,500

Instructions a Prepare a partial balance sheet for V. Boyer's Warehouse consisting of the current asset section and the current liability section **only**. Select the appropriate items from the above list.

b Compute the current ratio and the amount of working capital. Explain how each of these measurements is computed. State with reasons whether you consider the company to be in a strong or weak current position.

Problem 5A-6
**Internal control
measures**

Following are eight possible errors that might occur in a merchandising business. List th letter (*a* through *h*) designating each of these errors. Beside each letter, place the numbe indicating the internal control measure that would prevent this type of error from occurring If none of the specified control measures would effectively prevent the error, place "0" afte the letter.

Possible Errors

a The cashier conceals the embezzlement of cash by reducing the balance of the Cash account

b Management is unaware that the company often fails to pay its bills in time to take advan tage of the cash discounts offered by its suppliers.

c Paid a supplier for goods that were never received.

d The purchasing department ordered goods from one supplier when a better price could hav been obtained by ordering from another supplier.

e Paid an invoice in which the supplier had accidentally doubled the price of the merchandise

f Paid a supplier for goods that were delivered, but that were never ordered.

g Purchased merchandise that turned out not to be popular with customers.

h Several sales invoices were misplaced and the accounts receivable department is therefore unaware of the unrecorded credit sales.

Internal Control Measures

1 Use of serially numbered documents

2 Comparison of purchase invoice with the receiving report

3 Comparison of purchase invoice with the purchase order

4 Separation of the accounting function from custody of assets

5 Separation of the responsibilities for approving and recording transactions

6 Use of the net price method of recording purchases

0 None of the above control procedures can effectively prevent this error from occurring.

Problem 5A-7
Recording purchases
by the net price
method

The following transactions were completed by Data Tech during November, the first month of operation. The company uses the periodic inventory method and records purchase invoices at the *net amount* (net price method).

Nov. 1 Purchased merchandise from Hayes Company, $9,000; terms 2/10, n/30.

Nov. 7 Purchased merchandise from Joseph Corporation, $12,000; terms 2/10, n/30.

Nov. 8 Merchandise having a gross price of $1,200, purchased from Hayes Company, was found to be defective. It was returned to the seller, accompanied by debit memorandum No. 382.

Nov. 17 Paid Joseph Corporation's invoice of November 7, less cash discount.

Nov. 24 Purchased merchandise from Joseph Corporation, $7,600; terms 2/10, n/30.

Nov. 30 Paid Hayes Company's invoice of November 1, taking into consideration the return of goods on November 8.

Assume that the merchandise inventory on November 1 was $31,980; on November 30, $40,000.

Instructions

a Journalize the above transactions, recording invoices at the *net amount.*

b Prepare the cost of goods sold section of the income statement.

c Based upon these November transactions, what is the amount of accounts payable at the end of November? What would the amount of accounts payable be at the end of November if Data Tech followed the policy of recording purchase invoices at the gross amount?

Group B

Problem 5B-1
Journalizing
merchandising
transactions

The General Store uses the periodic inventory system and records its purchases at the gross invoice price. Following is a partial list of the transactions occurring during May:

May 1 Sold merchandise for cash in the amount of $1,700.

May 2 Purchased merchandise on credit from Five-Folk Suppliers, $18,000. Terms, 2/10, n/30.

May 2 Paid inbound transportation charges on merchandise purchased from Five-Folk Suppliers, $600.

May 6 Purchased office equipment for use in business on credit from Steele Company, $2,777. Terms, net 30 days.

May 9 Sold merchandise on account to Trent Construction Company, $13,960. Terms, net 30 days.

May 10 Paid transportation charges on shipment to customer, Trent Construction Company, $80.

May 12 Paid Five-Folk Suppliers within discount period for purchase made on May 2.

May 12 Purchased merchandise for cash, $324.

May 12 Returned defective office equipment, which cost $540, to Steele Company for credit.

May 16 Sold merchandise on account to S.W. Hardy, $6,100. Terms 2/10, n/30.

May 17 Granted a $100 allowance to S.W. Hardy on merchandise delivered on May 16, because of minor defects discovered in the merchandise.

May 23 Agreed to cancel the account receivable from Trent Construction Company (May 9) in exchange for their services in erecting on our property a garage needed in our operation. Construction of garage completed today.

May 26 Received cheque from S.W. Hardy within discount period in settlement of transaction of May 16. Customer took discount applicable to remaining balance after $100 allowance on May 17.

May 28 Paid balance due Steele Company.

Instructions Prepare a separate journal entry (including an explanation) for each of the above transactions.

Problem 5B-2
Preparing closing entries and an income statement

The following accounts relate to the income of Apache Station for the three-month period ended June 30, 19___:

Sales	$500,000	Transportation-in	$ 900
Sales returns &		Inventory, Apr. 1, 19___	170,000
allowances	15,000	Inventory, June 30, 19___	164,100
Sales discounts	7,800	Operating expenses	121,400
Purchases	310,000	Interest income	4,200
Purchase returns &			
allowances	4,500		
Purchase discounts	6,200		

Instructions **a** Compute the amount of net sales for the three-month period.

b Compute the cost of goods sold.

c Prepare a *condensed* multiple-step income statement. Show both net sales and the cost of goods sold as "one-line items," without showing the accounts used to compute these amounts.

d Prepare closing entries for the three-month period ended June 30. Only three closing entries are required, as the owner, Lillian Larson, did not withdraw any assets during the period

Problem 5B-3
Preparing a work sheet and adjusting and closing entries

A four-column schedule consisting of the first four columns of a 10-column work sheet for Foreign Auto Parts follows:

FOREIGN AUTO PARTS
Work Sheet
For the Year Ended December 31, 19___

	TRIAL BALANCE		ADJUSTMENTS	
	DEBIT	CREDIT	DEBIT	CREDIT
Cash	18,500			
Accounts receivable	56,000			
Inventory, Jan. 1	75,000			
Prepaid advertising	3,500			(b) 2,400
Fixtures	25,000			
Accumulated depreciation:				
fixtures		7,500		(a) 2,500
Accounts payable		65,000		
John Dawes, capital		75,900		
John Dawes, drawing	22,000			
Sales		640,000		
Sales returns & allowances	27,000			
Sales discounts	8,000			
Purchases	384,000			
Purchase returns & allowances . .		12,600		
Purchase discounts		6,000		
Transportation-in	10,000			
Delivery expense	48,000			
Rent expense	36,000			
Salaries expense	94,000			
	807,000	807,000		
Depreciation expense: fixtures . . .			(a) 2,500	
Advertising expense			(b) 2,400	
			4,900	4,900

The company uses the periodic inventory system and maintains its accounting records on a calendar-year basis. The completed Adjustments columns have been included in the work sheet to minimize the detail work involved. These adjustments were derived from the following information available at December 31:

(a) Depreciation expense for the year on fixtures, $2,500.

(b) Advertising used up during the year, $2,400.

A physical inventory taken at December 31 showed the ending inventory to be $69,100.

Instructions   **a** Prepare a 10-column work sheet. Include at the bottom of the work sheet a legend consisting of a brief explanation keyed to each adjusting entry.

b Prepare the two journal entries to adjust the accounts at December 31.

c Prepare the necessary journal entries to close the accounts on December 31.

Problem 5B-4
Preparing a work sheet,
financial statements,
and adjusting and
closing entries

The trial balance below was prepared from the ledger of Jessop's Boots & Saddles at December 31. The company maintains its accounts on a calendar-year basis and closes the accounts only once a year. The periodic inventory system is in use.

JESSOP'S BOOTS & SADDLES
Trial Balance
December 31, 19___

Cash	$ 15,000	
Accounts receivable	76,000	
Inventory, Jan. 1	140,000	
Unexpired insurance	4,000	
Office supplies	1,800	
Land	35,000	
Buildings	100,000	
Accumulated depreciation: buildings		$ 40,000
Notes payable		80,000
Accounts payable		60,000
Tom Jessop, capital		119,800
Tom Jessop, drawing	26,000	
Sales		633,000
Sales returns and allowances	42,000	
Sales discounts	16,000	
Purchases	381,000	
Purchase returns and allowances		23,000
Purchase discounts		8,000
Transportation-in	10,000	
Advertising expense	25,000	
Salaries expense	85,000	
Utilities expense	7,000	
	$963,800	$963,800

Other data

(a) Insurance expired during the year amounted to $2,500.

(b) The buildings are being depreciated over a 25-year life.

(c) Office supplies unused and on hand at year-end amounted to $800.

(d) A physical inventory of merchandise at December 31, showed goods on hand of $120,000.

Instructions

a Prepare a 10-column work sheet at December 31.

b Prepare an income statement, a statement of owner's equity, and a *classified* balance sheet. The operating expenses need not be subdivided.

c Prepare adjusting entries and closing entries.

Problem 5B-5
Computing current
ratio and working
capital; evaluating
solvency

Some of the year-end ledger account balances of Diet Frozen Dinners are listed below.

Inventory	$184,100
Accumulated depreciation: delivery equipment	6,300
Salaries payable	2,560
Cash	17,210
Land	95,000
Furniture & fixtures	11,200

Mortgage payable (due in 20 years)	249,600
Anne Redgrave, capital	212,320
Delivery equipment	31,500
Interest payable	1,600
Advance payments from customers	5,760
Notes payable (due in 90 days)	20,000
Marketable securities	24,000
Accounts receivable	90,540
Accounts payable	75,430
Interest receivable	200

Instructions

a Prepare a partial balance sheet for Diet Frozen Dinners consisting of the current asset section and the current liability section *only.* Select the appropriate items from the above list.

b Compute the current ratio and the amount of working capital. Explain how each of these measurements is computed. State with reasons whether you consider the company to be in a strong or weak current position.

Problem 5B-6
Internal control:
a short case study

At the Uptown Theatre, the cashier is located in a box office at the front of the building. The cashier receives cash from customers and operates a ticket machine that ejects serially numbered tickets. The serial number appears on each end of the ticket. The tickets come from the printer in large rolls that fit into the ticket machine and are removed at the end of each cashier's working period.

After purchasing a ticket from the cashier, in order to be admitted to the theatre a customer must hand the ticket to an attendant stationed some ten metres from the box office at the entrance to the theatre lobby. The attendant tears the ticket in half and returns the ticket stub to the customer. The other half of the ticket is dropped by the attendant into a locked box.

Intstructions

a Describe the internal controls present in Uptown Theatre's method of handling cash receipts.

b What steps should be taken regularly by the theatre manager or other supervisor to make these internal controls work most effectively?

c Assume that the cashier and the attendant decided to collaborate in an effort to abstract cash receipts. What action might they take?

d On the assumption made in *c* of collaboration between the cashier and the attendant, what features of the control procedures would be most likely to disclose the embezzlement?

Problem 5B-7
Recording purchases at
the net price method

Rancho Furniture completed the following transaction relating to the purchase of merchandise during August, the first month of operation. It is the policy of the company to record all purchase invoices at the *net amount* and to pay invoices within the discount period.

Aug. 1 Purchased merchandise from Carolina Corporation, invoice price, $21,000; terms 2/10, n/30.

Aug. 8 Purchased merchandise from Thomas Company, $36,000; terms 2/10, n/30.

Aug. 8 Merchandise with an invoice price of $3,000 purchased from Carolina Corporation on August 1 was found to be defective. It was returned to the supplier accompanied by debit memorandum No. 118, reducing the liability.

Aug. 18 Paid Thomas Company's invoice of August 8, less cash discount.

Aug. 25 Purchased merchandise from Thomas Company, $22,800; terms 2/10, n/30.

Aug. 30 Paid Carolina Corporation's invoice of August 1, taking into consideration the return of defective goods on August 8.

The inventory of merchandise on August 1 was $79,400; on August 31, $87,800.

Instructions
a Journalize the above transactions.

b Prepare the cost of goods sold section of the income statement.

c What is the amount of the account payable to Thomas Company at the end of August? What would be the amount of this account payable if Rancho Furniture followed the policy of recording purchase invoices at the gross amount?

BUSINESS DECISION CASES

Case 5-1
The Baker Street
Diversion

Printing Made Easy sells a variety of printers for use with personal computers. Last April Arthur Doyle, the company's purchasing agent, discovered a weakness in internal control and engaged in a scheme to steal printers. Doyle issued a purchase order for 20 printers to one of the company's regular suppliers, but included a typewritten note requesting that the printers be delivered to 221B Baker Street, Doyle's home address.

The supplier shipped the printers to Baker Street and sent a sales invoice to Printing Made Easy. When the invoice arrived, an accounting clerk carefully complied with company policy and compared the invoice with a copy of the purchase order. After noting agreement between these documents as to quantities, prices, and model numbers, the clerk recorded the transaction in the accounting records and authorized payment of the invoice.

Instructions

What is the weakness in internal control discovered by the purchasing agent to enable him to commit this theft? What changes would you recommend in the company's internal documentation and invoice approval procedures to prevent such problems in the future?

Case 5-2
Using a balance sheet
to evaluate solvency

Megan DeLong, an experienced engineer, is considering buying Eastern Engineering Company at year-end from its current owner, Jack Peterson. Eastern Engineering Company, a sole proprietorship, has been a profitable business, earning about $70,000 to $75,000 each year. DeLong is certain she could operate the business just as profitably. The principal activity of the business has been the performance of engineering studies for government agencies interested in the development of air and water pollution control programs.

Peterson has agreed to sell the business for "what he has in it" — namely, $200,000. DeLong comes to you with the balance sheet of Eastern Engineering Company, which follows, and asks your advice about buying the business.

EASTERN ENGINEERING COMPANY
Balance Sheet
December 31, 19___

ASSETS		LIABILITIES & OWNER'S EQUITY	
Cash	$ 40,500	Notes payable	$ 60,000
Government contract		Accounts payable	20,600
receivable	110,000	Wages payable	5,400
Other contracts receivable	21,500	J. Peterson, capital	200,000
Equipment			
(net of depreciation)	76,000		
Patents	38,000	Total liabilities & owner's	
Total assets	$286,000	equity	$286,000

DeLong immediately points out, as evidence of the firm's solvency, that the current ratio for Eastern Engineering is 2 to 1. In discussing the specific items on the balance sheet, you find that the patents were recently purchased by Eastern, and DeLong believes them to be worth their $38,000 cost. The notes payable liability consists of one note to the manufacturer of the equipment owned by Eastern, which Peterson had incurred five years ago to finance the purchase of the equipment. The note becomes payable, however, in February of the coming year. The accounts payable all will become due within 30 to 60 days.

Since DeLong does not have enough cash to buy Peterson's equity in the business, she is considering the following terms of purchase: (1) Peterson will withdraw all the cash from the business, thus reducing his equity to $159,500, (2) Peterson will also keep the $110,000 receivable from the government, leaving his equity in the business at $49,500, and (3) by borrowing heavily, DeLong thinks she can raise $49,500 in cash, which she will pay to Peterson for his remaining equity. DeLong will assume the existing liabilities of the business.

Instructions   **a** Prepare a classified balance sheet for Eastern Engineering Company as it would appear immediately after DeLong acquired the business, assuming that the purchase is carried out immediately on the proposed terms.

b Compute the current ratio and the working capital position of Eastern Engineering Company after DeLong's purchase of the business.

c Write a memorandum to DeLong explaining what problems she might encounter if she purchases the business as planned.

ACCOUNTING SYSTEMS: MANUAL AND COMPUTER-BASED

CHAPTER PREVIEW

In this chapter we address the problem of streamlining an accounting system to handle efficiently a large volume of transactions. Special journals are illustrated and explained, with emphasis upon how such journals reduce the time and effort involved in recording and posting transactions. The use of subsidiary ledger accounts is explained, along with the relationship between a subsidiary ledger and the related controlling account in the general ledger. Computer-based accounting systems also are described, including the use of point-of-sale terminals to record business transactions. Attention is focussed upon achieving strong internal control in computer-based systems.

After studying this chapter you should be able to meet these Learning Objectives:

1 Explain the nature of special journals and the reasons for their use.

2 Use special journals to record sales on credit, purchases on account, and cash transactions.

3 Explain the usefulness of a subsidiary ledger and its relationship to a controlling account in the general ledger.

4 Post entries in special journals to the general ledger and subsidiary ledgers.

5 Discuss accounting applications of computers and means of achieving internal control in computer-based accounting systems.

Streamlining the accounting process

An accounting system consists of the business documents, journals, ledgers, procedures, and internal controls needed to produce reliable financial statements and other accounting reports. Accounting systems in common use range from simple systems in which accounting records are maintained by hand to sophisticated systems in which accounting records are maintained on magnetic disks. The accounting system used in any given company should be tailored to the size and to the information needs of the company.

In the early chapters of an introductory accounting book, basic accounting principles can be discussed most conveniently in terms of a small business with only a few customers and suppliers. This simplified model of a business has been used in preceding chapters to demonstrate the analysis and recording of the more common types of business transactions.

The recording procedures illustrated thus far call for recording each transaction by an entry in the general journal, and then posting each debit and credit from the general journal to the proper account in the ledger. We must now face the practical problem of streamlining and speeding up this basic accounting system so that the accounting department can keep pace with the rapid flow of transactions in a modern business.

MANUAL ACCOUNTING SYSTEMS

Two devices used in streamlining an accounting system are *special journals* and *subsidiary ledgers.* These specialized accounting records are most easily illustrated in a manual accounting system. However, both special journals and subsidiary ledgers also are used in computer-based accounting systems.

Special journals

Explain the nature f special journals nd the reasons for eir use.

We have seen that any type of business transaction can be recorded in a general journal. A *special journal,* however, is an accounting record designed to handle the recording of *only one type* of business transaction. In order to record *all* types of business transactions, a business usually needs several special journals, as well as a general journal.

Why use a separate special journal to record a particular type of business transaction? The answer is that transactions may be recorded *much more quickly* in a journal that is specially designed for recording that particular type of transaction. Also, as we shall see later in this chapter, the amount of time spent posting transaction data may be greatly reduced. Finally, the use of special journals permits the work of recording transactions to be divided among several employees. Each special journal may be maintained by a different person.

The savings of time and effort are greatest when a separate special journal is designed to record each type of business transaction that *occurs frequently.* In most businesses, the great majority of transactions (perhaps 90 to 95%) fall into four types. These four types of transactions and the four corresponding special journals are listed on the next page.

TYPE OF TRANSACTION	NAME OF SPECIAL JOURNAL
Sales of merchandise on credit	Sales journal
Purchases of merchandise on credit	Purchases journal
Receipts of cash	Cash receipts journal
Payments of cash	Cash payments journal

In addition to these special journals, a general journal still must be used to record those transactions that *do not fit* into any of the special journals. The general journal has been illustrated in preceding chapters. The adjective *"general"* is used to distinguish this multipurpose journal from the special journals. We will now discuss the four special journals mentioned above, along with the related concept of subsidiary ledgers. The general journal also will be illustrated.

Sales journal

2 Use special journals to record sales on credit, purchases on account, and cash transactions.

Shown below is a *sales journal* containing entries for *all sales on credit (on account)* made during November by the Seaside Company. Whenever merchandise is sold on credit, several copies of a sales invoice are prepared. The information listed on a sales invoice usually includes the date of the sale, the serial number of the invoice, the customer's name, the amount of the sale, and the credit terms. One copy of the sales invoice is used by the seller as the basis for entry in the sales journal.

ENTRIES FOR SALES
ON CREDIT DURING
NOVEMBER

Sales Journal   Page 1

TE		ACCOUNT DEBITED	INVOICE NO.	✓	AMOUNT
19__					
Nov	2	Jill Adams	301	✓	450
	4	Harold Black	302	✓	1,000
	5	Robert Cross	303	✓	975
	11	H.R. Davis	304	✓	620
	18	C.D. Early	305	✓	900
	23	Mary Frost	306	✓	400
	29	D.H. Gray	307	✓	11,850
					16,195
					(5) (41)

Notice that the illustrated sales journal contains special columns for recording each of these aspects of the sales transaction, except the credit terms. If it is the practice of the business to offer different credit terms to different customers, a column may be inserted in the sales journal to show the terms of sale. In this illustration it is assumed that all sales are made on terms of 2/10, n/30; consequently, there is no need to write the credit terms as part of each entry. It is important to remember that *only sales on credit are entered in the sales journal.* When merchandise is sold for cash, the transaction is recorded in a *cash receipts* journal, which is illustrated later in this chapter.

Advantages of the sales journal   Note that each of the seven sales transactions is recorded on a single line. Each entry consists of a debit to a customer's account; the offsetting credit to the Sales account is understood without being written, because sales on account are the only transactions recorded in this special journal.

An entry in a sales journal need not include an explanation; if more information about the transaction is desired it can be obtained by referring to the file copy of the sales invoice. The invoice number is listed in the sales journal as part of each entry. The one-line entry in the sales journal requires much less writing than would be necessary to record a sales transaction in the general journal. Since there may be several hundred or several thousand sales transactions each month, the time saved in recording transactions in this streamlined manner becomes quite important.

Every entry in the sales journal represents a debit to a customer's account. Charges to customers' accounts should be posted daily so that each customer's account will always be up-to-date and available for use in making decisions relating to collections and to the further extension of credit. A check mark (✓) is placed in the sales journal opposite each amount posted to a customer's account, to indicate that the posting has been made.

Another advantage of the special journal for sales is the great saving of time in posting credits to the Sales account. Remember that every amount entered in the sales journal represents a credit to Sales. In the illustrated sales journal, there are seven transactions (and in practice there might be 7,000). Instead of posting a separate credit to the Sales account for each sales transaction, we can wait until the end of the month and make *one posting* to the Sales account for the *total* of the amounts recorded in the sales journal.

In the illustrated sales journal for November, the sales on account totalled $16,195. On November 30 this amount is posted as a credit to the Sales account, and the ledger account number for Sales (41) is entered under the total figure in the sales journal to show that the posting operation has been performed. The total sales figure is also posted as a debit to ledger account No. 5, Accounts Receivable. To make clear the reason for this posting to Accounts Receivable, an explanation of the nature of controlling accounts and subsidiary ledgers is necessary.

Controlling accounts and subsidiary ledgers

3   Explain the usefulness of a subsidiary ledger and its relationship to a controlling account in the general ledger.

In preceding chapters all transactions involving accounts receivable from customers have been posted to a single account entitled Accounts Receivable. Under this procedure, however, it is not easy to look up the amount receivable from a given customer. In practice, a business selling goods on credit *maintains a separate account receivable for each customer.* If there are 4,000 customers, this would require a ledger with 4,000 accounts receivable, in addition to the accounts for other assets, and for liabilities, owner's equity, revenue, and expenses. Such a ledger would be cumbersome and unwieldy. Also, the trial balance prepared from such a large ledger would be a very long one. If the trial balance showed the ledger to be out of balance, the task of locating the error or errors would be most difficult. All these factors indicate that it is not desirable to have too many accounts in one ledger. Fortunately, a simple solution is available; this solution is to divide the ledger into several separate ledgers.

In a business that has a large number of customers and a large number of creditors, it is customary to divide the ledger into three separate ledgers. All the accounts with *customers* are placed in alphabetical order in a separate ledger, called the ***accounts receivable ledger.*** All the accounts with ***creditors*** are arranged alphabetically in another ledger called the ***accounts payable ledger.*** Both of these ledgers are known as ***subsidiary ledgers,*** because they support and are controlled by the general ledger.

After placing the accounts receivable from customers in one subsidiary ledger and the accounts payable to creditors in a second subsidiary ledger, we have left in the original ledger all the revenue and expense accounts and also all the balance sheet

RELATIONSHIP OF
SUBSIDIARY LEDGERS
TO CONTROLLING
ACCOUNTS IN GENERAL
LEDGER

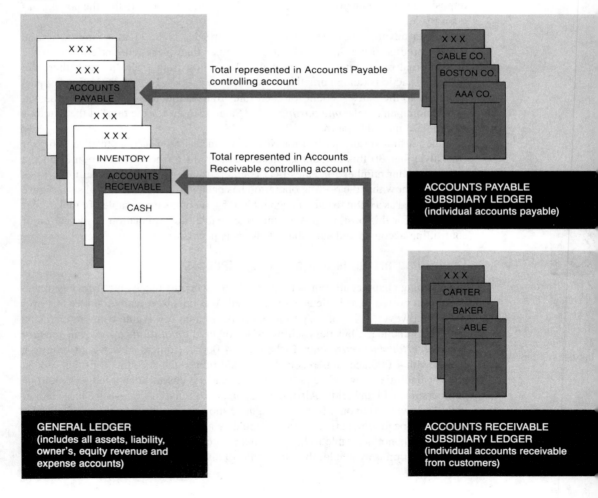

accounts except those with individual customers and individual creditors. This ledger is called the *general ledger,* to distinguish it from the subsidiary ledgers.

When the numerous individual accounts receivable from customers are placed in a subsidiary ledger, an account entitled Accounts Receivable continues to be maintained in the general ledger. This account shows the *total amount due from all customers;* in other words, this single *controlling account* in the general ledger represents the numerous customers' accounts which make up the subsidiary ledger. The general ledger is still in balance because the controlling account, Accounts Receivable, has a balance equal to the total of the individual customers' accounts. Agreement of the controlling account with the sum of the accounts receivable in the subsidiary ledger also provides assurance of accuracy in the subsidiary ledger.

A controlling account entitled Accounts Payable is also kept in the general ledger in place of the numerous accounts with creditors that form the accounts payable subsidiary ledger. Because the two controlling accounts represent the total amounts receivable from customers and payable to creditors, a trial balance can be prepared from the general ledger alone. The illustration on page 246 shows the relationship of the subsidiary ledgers to the controlling accounts in the general ledger.

4 Post entries in special journals to the general ledger and subsidiary ledgers.

Posting to subsidiary ledgers and to controlling accounts   To illustrate the posting of subsidiary ledgers and of controlling accounts, let us refer again to the sales journal illustrated earlier. Each debit to a customer's account is posted currently during the month from the sales journal to the customer's account in the accounts receivable ledger. The accounts in this subsidiary ledger are usually kept in alphabetical order and are not numbered. When a posting is made to a customer's account, a check mark (✓) is placed in the sales journal as evidence that the posting has been made to the subsidiary ledger.

At month-end the sales journal is totalled. The total amount of sales for the month, $16,195, is posted as a credit to the Sales account and also as a debit to the controlling account, Accounts Receivable, in the general ledger. The controlling account will, therefore, equal the total of all the customers' accounts in the subsidiary ledger.

The diagram on page 248 shows the day-to-day posting of individual entries from the sales journal to the subsidiary ledger. The diagram also shows the month-end posting of the total of the sales journal to the two general ledger accounts affected, Accounts Receivable and Sales. Note that the amount of the monthly debit to the controlling account is equal to the sum of the debits posted to the subsidiary ledger.

Purchases journal

The handling of purchase transactions when a purchases journal is used follows a pattern quite similar to the one described for the sales journal.

The purchases journal shown includes *all purchases of merchandise on credit* during the month by the Seaside Company. The date of each purchase invoice is shown in a separate column, because the cash discount period begins on this date. It is the company's policy to record purchase invoices at their gross amount. The five entries for purchases are posted as they occur during the month as credits to the creditors' accounts in the subsidiary ledger for accounts payable. As each posting is completed a check mark (✓) is placed in the purchases journal.

SUBSIDIARY LEDGER
POSTED DAILY; GENERAL
LEDGER POSTED
MONTHLY

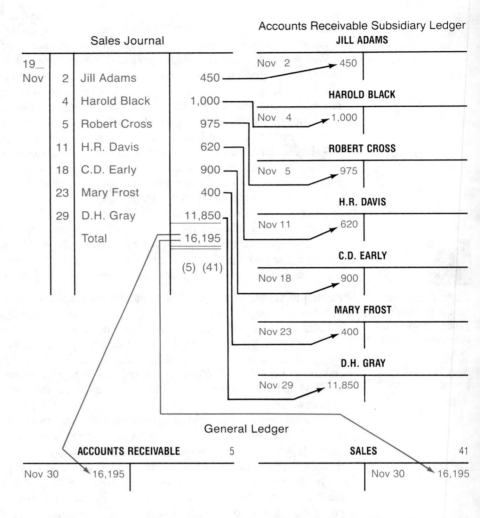

At the end of the month the purchases journal is totalled and ruled as shown in the illustration at the top of page 249. The total figure, $7,250, is posted to two general ledger accounts as shown at the bottom of page 249.

1 As a debit to the Purchases account
2 As a credit to the Accounts Payable controlling account

The account numbers for Purchases (50) and for Accounts Payable (21) are then placed in parentheses below the column total of the purchases journal to show that the posting has been made.

Under the particular system being described, the only transactions recorded in the purchases journal are *purchases of merchandise on credit.* The term *merchandise* means goods acquired for resale to customers. If merchandise is purchased for cash rather than on credit, the transaction should be recorded in the *cash payments journal,* not in the purchases journal.

ENTRIES FOR PURCHASES
ON CREDIT DURING
NOVEMBER

		Purchases Journal			Page 1
DATE		ACCOUNT CREDITED	INVOICE DATE	✓	AMOUNT
19__			19__		
Nov	2	Ace Supply Co. (net 30)	Nov 2	✓	3,325
	4	Barker & Bright (2/10, n/20)	4	✓	700
	10	Canning & Sons (net 30)	9	✓	500
	17	Davis Co. (2/10, n/30)	16	✓	900
	27	Excelsior, Inc. (net 30)	25	✓	1,825
					7,250
					(50) (21)

The following diagram shows the day-to-day posting of individual entries from the
purchases journal to the accounts with creditors in the subsidiary ledger for accounts
payable. The diagram also shows how the column total of the purchases journal is
posted at the end of the month to the general ledger accounts, Purchases and Accounts
Payable. One objective of this diagram is to emphasize that the amount of the monthly
credit to the controlling account is equal to the sum of the credits posted to the subsidiary ledger.

SUBSIDIARY LEDGER
POSTED DAILY; GENERAL
LEDGER POSTED
MONTHLY

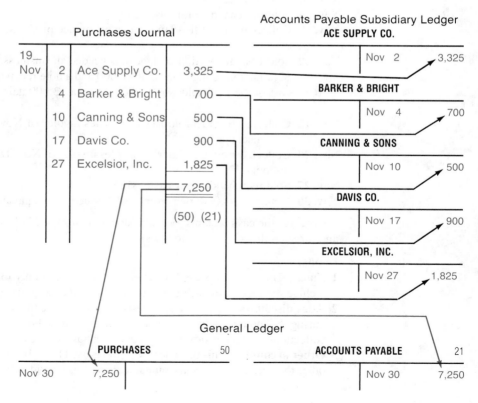

When assets other than merchandise are being acquired, as, for example, a delivery truck or an office desk for use in the business, the journal to be used depends upon whether a cash payment is made. If assets of this type are purchased for cash, the transaction is entered in the cash payments journal; if the transaction is on credit, the general journal is used. The purchases journal is not used to record the acquisition of these assets because the total of this journal is posted to the Purchases account, which is used in determining the cost of goods sold.

Cash receipts journal

All transactions involving the receipt of cash are recorded in the cash receipts journal. One common example is the sale of merchandise for cash. As each cash sale is made, it is rung up on a cash register. At the end of the day the total of the cash sales is computed by striking the total key on the register. This total is entered in the cash receipts journal, which therefore contains one entry for the total cash sales of the day. For other types of cash receipts, such as the collection of accounts receivable from customers, a separate journal entry may be made for each transaction.

The cash receipts journal illustrated on page 252 contains entries for all of the November transactions of the Seaside Company that involved the receipt of cash. These transactions are listed below:

Nov. 1 R.B. Jones invested $75,000 cash to establish the Seaside Company.

Nov. 4 Sold merchandise for cash, $300.

Nov. 5 Sold merchandise for cash, $400.

Nov. 8 Collected from Jill Adams for sales invoice of Nov. 2, $450 less 2% cash discount.

Nov. 10 Sold a small portion of land not needed in business for a total price of $7,000, consisting of cash of $1,000 and a note receivable for $6,000. The cost of the land sold was $5,000; thus, a $2,000 gain was realized on the sale.

Nov. 12 Collected from Harold Black for sales invoice of Nov. 4, $1,000 less 2% cash discount.

Nov. 20 Collected from C.D. Early for sales invoice of Nov. 18, $900 less 2% cash discount.

Nov. 27 Sold merchandise for cash, $125.

Nov. 30 Obtained $4,000 loan from bank. Issued a note payable in that amount.

Note that the cash receipts journal illustrated on page 252 has three debit columns and three credit columns as follows:

Debits:

1 Cash   This column is used for every entry, because only those transactions that include the receipt of cash are entered in this special journal.

2 Sales discounts   This column is used to accumulate the sales discounts allowed during the month. Only one line of the cash receipts book is required to record a collection from a customer who takes advantage of a cash discount.

3 Other accounts   This third debit column is used for debits to any and all accounts other than cash and sales discounts, and space is provided for writing in the name of the account. For example, the entry of November 10 in the illustrated cash receipts journal shows that cash and a note receivable were obtained when land was sold. The amount of cash received, $1,000, is entered in the Cash debit column; the account title Notes Receivable is written in the Other Accounts debit column along with the amount of the debit to this account, $6,000. These two debits are offset by credit entries to Land, $5,000, and to Gain on Sale of Land, $2,000, in the Other Accounts credit column.

Credits:

1 Accounts receivable   This column is used to list the credits to customers' accounts as receivables are collected. The name of the customer is written in the space entitled Account Credited to the left of the Accounts Receivable column.

2 Sales   The existence of this column will save posting by permitting the accumulation of all sales for cash during the month and the posting of the column total at the end of the month as a credit to the Sales account.

3 Other accounts   This column is used for credits to any and all accounts other than Accounts Receivable and Sales. In some instances, a transaction may require credits to two accounts. Such cases are handled by using two lines of the special journal, as illustrated by the transaction of November 10, which required credits to both the Land account and to Gain on Sale of Land.

Posting the cash receipts journal   It is convenient to think of the posting of a cash receipts journal as being divided into two phases. The first phase consists of the daily posting of individual amounts throughout the month; the second phase consists of the posting of column totals at the end of the month.

Posting during the month   Daily posting of the Accounts Receivable credit column is desirable. Each amount is posted to an individual customer's account in the accounts receivable subsidiary ledger. A check mark (✓) is placed in the cash receipts journal alongside each item posted to a customer's account to show that the posting operation has been performed. When debits and credits to customers' accounts are posted daily, the current status of each customer's account is available for use in making decisions as to further granting of credit and as a guide to collection efforts on past-due accounts.

The debits and credits in the Other Accounts sections of the cash receipts journal may be posted daily or at convenient intervals during the month. If this portion of the posting work is done on a current basis, less detail-work will be left for the busy period at the end of the month. As the postings of individual items are made, the number of the general ledger account debited or credited is entered in the LP column of the cash receipts journal opposite the item posted. Evidence is thus provided in the special journal as to which items have been posted.

Posting column totals at month end   At the end of the month, the cash receipts journal is ruled as shown in the illustration on page 252. Before posting any of the column totals, it is first important to prove that *the sum of the debit column totals is equal to the sum of the credit column totals.*

INCLUDES ALL
TRANSACTIONS
INVOLVING RECEIPT
OF CASH

Cash Receipts Journal

Page 1

| | | DEBITS | | | | | | CREDITS | | | | |
| | | | | OTHER ACCOUNTS | | | | ACCOUNTS RECEIVABLE | | | OTHER ACCOUNTS | |
DATE	EXPLANATION	CASH	SALES DISCOUNTS	NAME	LP	AMOUNT	ACCOUNT CREDITED	✓	AMOUNT	SALES	LP	AMOUNT
19— Nov 1	Investment by owner	75,000					R.B. Jones, Capital				30	75,000
4	Cash sales	300								300		
5	Cash sales	400								400		
8	Invoice Nov. 2, less 2%	441	9				Jill Adams	✓	450			
10	Sale of land	1,000		Notes Receivable	3	6,000	Land				11	5,000
							Gain on Sale of Land				40	2,000
12	Invoice Nov. 4, less 2%	980	20				Harold Black	✓	1,000			
20	Invoice Nov. 18, less 2%	882	18				C.D. Early	✓	900			
27	Cash sales	125								125		
30	Obtained bank loan	4,000					Notes Payable				20	4,000
		83,128	47			6,000			2,350	825		86,000
		(1)	(43)			(X)			(5)	(41)		(X)

After the totals of the cash receipts journal have been crossfooted, the following column totals are posted:

1 Cash debit column. Posted as a debit to the Cash account.
2 Sales Discounts debit column. Posted as a debit to the Sales Discounts account.
3 Accounts Receivable credit column. Posted as a credit to the controlling account, Accounts Receivable.
4 Sales credit column. Posted as a credit to the Sales account.

As each column total is posted to the appropriate account in the general ledger, the ledger account number is entered in parentheses just below the column total in the special journal. This notation shows that the column total has been posted and also indicates the account to which the posting was made. The totals of the Other Accounts columns in both the debit and credit sections of the special journal are not posted, because the amounts listed in the column affect various general ledger accounts and have already been posted as individual items. The symbol (X) is placed below the totals of these two columns to indicate that no posting for these totals is made.

Cash payments journal

Another widely used special journal is the cash payments journal, sometimes called the cash disbursements journal, in which *all payments of cash* are recorded. Among the more common of these transactions are payments of accounts payable to creditors, payment of operating expenses, and cash purchases of merchandise.

The cash payments journal illustrated on the following page contains entries for all November transactions of the Seaside Company that required the payment of cash. These transactions are:

Nov. 1 Paid rent on store building for November, $800.
Nov. 2 Purchased merchandise for cash, $500.
Nov. 8 Paid Barker & Bright for invoice of Nov. 4, $700 less 2%.
Nov. 9 Bought land, $65,000, and building, $35,000, for future use in business. Paid cash of $70,000 and signed a promissory note for the balance of $30,000. (Land and building were acquired in a single transaction.)
Nov. 17 Paid salaries, $3,600.
Nov. 26 Paid Davis Co. for invoice of Nov. 16, $900 less 2%.
Nov. 27 Purchased merchandise for cash, $400.
Nov. 28 Purchased merchandise for cash, $650.
Nov. 29 Paid for newspaper advertising, $50.
Nov. 29 Paid for one-year insurance policy, $720.

Note in the illustrated cash payments journal that the three credit columns are located to the left of the three debit columns; any sequence of columns is satisfactory in a special journal as long as the column headings clearly distinguish debits from credits. The Cash column is often placed first in both the cash receipts journal and the cash payments journal because it is the column used in every transaction.

Good internal control over cash disbursements requires that all payments be made by cheque. The cheques are serially numbered and as each transaction is entered in the cash payments journal, the cheque number is listed in a special column provided

INCLUDES ALL
TRANSACTIONS
INVOLVING PAYMENT
OF CASH

Cash Payments Journal

| | | | | CREDITS | | | | | | DEBITS | | | | |
DATE	CH. NO.		EXPLANATION	CASH	PURCHASE DISCOUNTS	OTHER ACCOUNTS NAME	LP	AMOUNT	ACCOUNT DEBITED	ACCOUNTS PAYABLE ✓	AMOUNT	PUR-CHASES	LP	OTHER ACCOUNTS AMOUNT
19__ Nov	1	1	Paid November rent	800					Store Rent expense				54	800
	2	2	Purchased merchandise	500								500		
8	3	8	Invoice of Nov. 4., less 2%	686	14				Barker & Bright	✓	700			
9	4	9	Bought land and building	70,000		Notes payable	20	30,000	Land				11	65,000
									Building				12	35,000
17	5	17	Paid salaries	3,600					Salaries Expense				53	3,600
26	6	26	Invoice of Nov. 16 less 2%	882	18				Davis Co.	✓	900			
27	7	27	Purchased merchandise	400								400		
28	8	28	Purchased merchandise	650								650		
29	9	29	Newspaper advertisement	50					Advertising Expense				55	50
29	10	29	One-year insurance policy	720					Unexpired Insurance				6	720
				78,288	32			30,000			1,600	1,550		105,170
				(1)	(52)			(X)			(21)	(50)		(X)

just to the right of the date column. An unbroken sequence of cheque numbers in this column gives assurance that every cheque issued has been recorded in the accounting records.

Posting the cash payments journal   The posting of the cash payments journal falls into the same two phases already described for the cash receipts journal. The first phase consists of the daily posting of entries in the Accounts Payable debit column to the individual accounts of creditors in the accounts payable subsidiary ledger. Check marks (✓) are entered opposite these items to show that the posting has been made. If a creditor telephones to inquire about any aspect of his account, information on all purchases and payments made to date is readily available in the accounts payable subsidiary ledger.

The individual debit and credit entries in the Other Accounts columns of the cash payment journal may be posted daily or at convenient intervals during the month. As the postings of these individual items are made, the number of the general ledger account debited or credited is entered in the LP column of the cash payments journal opposite the item posted.

The second phase of posting the cash payments journal is performed at the end of the month. When all the transactions of the month have been journalized, the cash payments journal is ruled as shown in our illustration, and the six money columns are totalled. The equality of debits and credits is then proved before posting.

After the totals of the cash payments journal have been proved to be in balance, the totals of the columns for Cash, Purchase Discounts, Accounts Payable, and Purchases are posted to the corresponding accounts in the general ledger. The numbers of the accounts to which these postings are made are listed in parentheses just below the respective column totals in the cash payments journal. The totals of the Other Accounts columns in both the debit and credit sections of this special journal are not to be posted, and the symbol (X) is placed below the totals of these two columns to indicate that no posting of these totals is required.

The general journal

When all transactions involving cash or the purchase and sale of merchandise are recorded in special journals, only a few types of transactions remain to be entered in the general journal. Examples include the declaration of dividends, the purchase or sale of plant and equipment on credit, the return of merchandise for credit to a supplier, and the return of merchandise by customers for credit to their accounts. The general journal is also used for adjusting and closing entries at the end of the accounting period.

The following transactions of the Seaside Company during November could not conveniently be handled in any of the four special journals and were therefore entered in the general journal.

Nov. 25 A customer, Mary Frost, returned for credit $50 worth of merchandise that had been sold to her on Nov. 23.

Nov. 28 The Seaside Company returned to a supplier, Excelsior, Inc., for credit $300 worth of the merchandise purchased on Nov. 27.

Nov. 29 Purchased for use in the business office equipment costing $1,225. Agreed to make payment within 30 days to XYZ Equipment Co.

General Journal   Page 1

DATE		ACCOUNT TITLES AND EXPLANATION	LP	DR	CR
19__					
Nov	25	Sales Returns and Allowances	42	50	
		Accounts Receivable, Mary Frost . .	5/✓		50
		Allowed credit to customer for return of			
		merchandise from sale of Nov. 23.			
	28	Accounts Payable, Excelsior, Inc.	21/✓	300	
		Purchase Returns and Allowances .	51		300
		Returned to supplier for credit a portion			
		of merchandise purchased on Nov. 27.			
	29	Office Equipment	14	1,225	
		Accounts Payable, XYZ Equipment			
		Co.	21/✓		1,225
		Purchased office equipment on 30-day			
		credit.			

Each of the preceding three entries includes a debit or credit to a controlling account (Accounts Receivable or Accounts Payable) and also identifies by name a particular creditor or customer. When a ***controlling account*** is debited or credited by a general journal entry, the debit or credit must be posted *twice:* one posting to the controlling account in the ***general ledger*** and another posting to a customer's account or a creditor's account in a ***subsidiary ledger.*** This double posting is necessary to keep the controlling account in agreement with the subsidiary ledger.

For example, in the illustrated entry of November 25 for the return of merchandise by a customer, the credit part of the entry is posted twice:

1 To the Accounts Receivable controlling account in the general ledger; this posting is evidenced by listing the account number (5) in the LP column of the general ledger.

2 To the account of Mary Frost in the subsidiary ledger for accounts receivable; this posting is indicated by the check mark (✓) placed in the LP column of the general journal.

Showing the source of postings in ledger accounts

When a general journal and several special journals are in use, the ledger accounts should indicate the book of original entry from which each debit and credit was posted. An identifying symbol is placed opposite each entry in the reference column of the account. The symbols used in this text are as follows:

S1 meaning page 1 of the Sales Journal
P1 meaning page 1 of the Purchases Journal

CR1 meaning page 1 of the Cash Receipts Journal
CP1 meaning page 1 of the Cash Payments Journal
J1 meaning page 1 of the General Journal

Subsidiary ledger accounts

The following illustration shows a customer's account in a subsidiary ledger for accounts receivable.

SUBSIDIARY LEDGER:
ACCOUNT RECEIVABLE

Name of Customer

DATE			REF	DEBIT	CREDIT	BALANCE
19__						
July	2		S1	400		400
	20		S3	200		600
Aug	4		CR7		400	200
	15		S6	120		320

The advantage of this three-column form of account is that it shows at a glance the present balance receivable from the customer. The current amount of a customer's account is often needed as a guide to collection activities, or as a basis for granting additional credit. In studying the preceding illustration, note also that the Reference column shows the source of each debit and credit.

Accounts appearing in the accounts receivable subsidiary ledger are assumed to have debit balances. If one of these customers' accounts should acquire a credit balance by overpayment or for any other reason, the word *credit* should be written after the amount in the Balance column.

The same three-column form of account is also generally used for creditors' accounts in an accounts payable subsidiary ledger, as indicated by the following illustration:

SUBSIDIARY LEDGER:
ACCOUNT PAYABLE

Name of Creditor

DATE			REF	DEBIT	CREDIT	BALANCE
19__						
July	10		P1		625	625
	25		P2		100	725
Aug	8		CP4	725		0
	12		P3		250	250

Accounts in the accounts payable subsidiary ledger normally have credit balances. If, by reason of payment in advance or accidental overpayment, one of these accounts should acquire a debit balance, the word *debit* should be written after the amount in the Balance column.

As previously stated, both the accounts receivable and accounts payable subsidiary ledgers are customarily arranged in alphabetical order and account numbers are not used. This arrangement permits unlimited expansion of the subsidiary ledgers, as accounts with new customers and creditors can be inserted in proper alphabetical sequence.

Ledger accounts

The general ledger   The general ledger accounts of the Seaside Company illustrated next indicate the source of postings from the various books of original entry. The subsidiary ledger accounts appear on pages 260–262. To gain a clear understanding of the procedures for posting special journals, you should trace each entry in the illustrated special journals to the general ledger accounts and also to the subsidiary ledger accounts where appropriate. The general ledger accounts are shown in T-account form in order to distinguish them more emphatically from the accounts in the subsidiary ledgers.

Note that the Cash account contains only one debit entry and one credit entry, although there were many cash transactions during the month. The one debit, $83,128, represents the total cash received during the month and was posted from the cash receipts journal on November 30. Similarly, the one credit entry of $78,288 was posted on November 30 from the cash payments journal and represents the total of all cash payments made during the month.

GENERAL LEDGER
ACCOUNTS

CASH 1

19__ Nov	30		CR1	83,128	19__ Nov	30		CP1	78,288

NOTES RECEIVABLE 3

19__ Nov	10		CR1	6,000					

ACCOUNTS RECEIVABLE 5

19__ Nov	30		S1	16,195	19__ Nov	25		J1	50
						30		CR1	2,350

UNEXPIRED INSURANCE 6

19__ Nov	29		CP1	720					

LAND 11

19__ Nov	9		CP1	65,000	19__ Nov	10		CR1	5,000

BUILDING   12

19__									
Nov	9		CP1	35,000					

OFFICE EQUIPMENT   14

19__									
Nov	29		J1	1,225					

NOTES PAYABLE   20

					19__				
					Nov	9		CP1	30,000
						30		CR1	4,000

ACCOUNTS PAYABLE   21

19__					19__				
Nov	28		J1	300	Nov	29		J1	1,225
	30		CP1	1,600		30		P1	7,250

R.B. JONES, CAPITAL   30

					19__				
					Nov	1		CR1	75,000

GAIN ON SALE OF LAND   40

					19__				
					Nov	10		CR1	2,000

SALES   41

					19__				
					Nov	30		CR1	825
						30		S1	16,195

SALES RETURNS AND ALLOWANCES   42

19__									
Nov	25		J1	50					

SALES DISCOUNTS   43

19__										
Nov	30		CR1	47						

PURCHASES   50

19__										
Nov	30		CR1	1,550						
	30		P1	7,250						

PURCHASE RETURNS AND ALLOWANCES   51

					19__					
					Nov	28		J1	300	

PURCHASE DISCOUNTS   52

					19__					
					Nov	30		CP1	32	

SALARIES EXPENSE   53

19__										
Nov	17		CP1	3,600						

STORE RENT EXPENSE   54

19__										
Nov	1		CP1	800						

ADVERTISING EXPENSE   55

19__										
Nov	29		CP1	50						

Accounts receivable ledger   The subsidiary ledger for accounts receivable appears as follows after the posting of the various journals has been completed.

CUSTOMERS' ACCOUNTS

JILL ADAMS

19__										
Nov	2				S1	450		450
	8				CR1		450	0

HAROLD BLACK

19__							
Nov	4		S1	1,000		1,000
	12		CR1		1,000	0

ROBERT CROSS

19__						
Nov	5		S1	975		975

H.R. DAVIS

19__						
Nov	11		S1	620		620

C.D. EARLY

19__						
Nov	18		S1	900		900
	20		CR1		900	0

MARY FROST

19__						
Nov	23		S1	400		400
	25		J1		50	350

D.H. GRAY

19__						
Nov	29		S1	11,850		11,850

Accounts payable ledger   The accounts with creditors in the accounts payable subsidiary ledger are as follows:

ACE SUPPLY CO.

19__						
Nov	2		P1		3,325	3,325

BARKER & BRIGHT

19__						
Nov	4		P1		700	700
	8		CP1	700		0

CANNING & SONS

19__						
Nov	10		P1		500	500

DAVIS CO.

19__						
Nov	17		P1		900	900
	26		CP1	900		0

EXCELSIOR, INC.

19__						
Nov	27		P1		1,825	1,825
	28		J1	300		1,525

XYZ EQUIPMENT CO.

19__						
Nov	29		J1		1,225	1,225

Reconciling subsidiary ledgers and controlling accounts

At the end of each accounting period, the equality of debits and credits in the general ledger is established by preparation of a trial balance, as illustrated in preceding chapters. When controlling accounts and subsidiary ledgers are in use, it is also necessary to determine that each subsidiary ledger is in agreement with its controlling account. This process is termed *reconciling* the subsidiary ledger with the controlling account.

The first step in reconciling a subsidiary ledger with its controlling account is to prepare a schedule of the balances of the accounts in the subsidiary ledger. The total of this schedule then is compared with the balance of the controlling account. The Seaside Company's trial balance and schedules (also called trial balances) of accounts receivable and accounts payable appear on page 263. Notice that the totals of the accounts receivable and accounts payable ledger schedules agree with the balance of the related controlling accounts.

Reconciling subsidiary ledgers with their controlling accounts is an important internal control procedure and should be performed at least once a month. This procedure may disclose such errors in the subsidiary ledger as failure to post transactions, transposition or slide errors, or mathematical errors in determining the balances of specific accounts receivable or accounts payable. However, this procedure will *not* disclose an entry that was posted to the wrong account within the subsidiary ledger.

GENERAL LEDGER
TRIAL BALANCE

SEASIDE COMPANY
Trial Balance
November 30, 19___

Cash	$ 4,840	
Notes receivable	6,000	
Accounts receivable (see schedule below)	13,795	
Unexpired insurance	720	
Land	60,000	
Building	35,000	
Office equipment	1,225	
Notes payable		$ 34,000
Accounts payable (see schedule below)		6,575
R.B. Jones, Capital		75,000
Gain on sale of land		2,000
Sales		17,020
Sales returns and allowances	50	
Sales discounts	47	
Purchases	8,800	
Purchase returns and allowances		300
Purchase discounts		32
Salaries expense	3,600	
Store rent expense	800	
Advertising expense	50	
	$134,927	$134,927

SUBSIDIARY LEDGERS
IN BALANCE WITH
CONTROL ACCOUNTS

Schedule of Accounts Receivable
November 30, 19___

Robert Cross	$ 975
H.R. Davis	620
Mary Frost	350
D.H. Gray	11,850
Total (per balance of controlling account)	$13,795

Schedule of Accounts Payable
November 30, 19___

Ace Supply Co.	$3,325
Canning & Sons	500
Excelsior, Inc.	1,525
XYZ Equipment Co.	1,225
Total (per balance of controlling account)	$6,575

Variations in special journals

The number of columns to be included in each special journal and the number of special journals to be used will depend upon the nature of the particular business and especially upon the volume of the various kinds of transactions. For example, the desirability of including a Sales Discounts column in the cash receipts journal depends upon whether a business offers discounts to its customers for prompt payment.

A retail store may find that customers frequently return merchandise for credit. To record efficiently this large volume of sales returns, the store may establish a special sales returns and allowances journal. A special purchase returns and allowances journal may also be desirable if returns of goods to suppliers occur frequently.

Special journals should be regarded as labour-saving devices that may be designed with any number of columns appropriate to the needs of the particular business. A business will usually benefit by establishing a special journal for any type of transaction that *occurs quite frequently.*

Direct posting from invoices

In many business concerns the efficiency of data processing is increased by posting sales invoices directly to the customers' accounts in the accounts receivable ledger rather than copying sales invoices into a sales journal and then posting to accounts in the subsidiary ledger. If the sales invoices are *serially numbered,* a file or binder of duplicate sales invoices arranged in numerical order may take the place of a formal sales journal. By accounting for each *serial number,* it is possible to be certain that all sales invoices are included. At the end of the month, the invoices are totalled on a calculator, and a general journal entry is made debiting the Accounts Receivable controlling account and crediting Sales for the total of the month's sales invoices.

Direct posting may also be used in recording purchase invoices. As soon as purchases invoices have been verified and approved, credits to the creditors' accounts in the accounts payable ledger may be posted directly from the purchase invoices.

The trend toward direct posting from invoices to subsidiary ledgers is mentioned here as further evidence that accounting records and procedures can be designed in a variety of ways to meet the individual needs of different business concerns.

Unit record for each transaction

Our discussion has thus far been limited to a manual accounting system. One of the points we have emphasized is that an *immediate record* should be made of every business transaction. This initial record of each transaction need not be an entry in the accounting records. Rather, the transaction often is first recorded on a *business document* or form, such as an invoice, a cheque stub, or a cash register receipt. This concept of making an *individual record* of each transaction is an important one in every type of accounting system. Regardless of whether accounting records are maintained by hand or by electronic equipment, the *documentation* of each transaction is an essential step in the accounting process.

COMPUTER-BASED ACCOUNTING SYSTEMS

The concepts of special journals and subsidiary ledgers apply to computer-based accounting systems as well as manual systems. In fact, special journals and subsidiary ledgers are far easier to maintain in computerized systems. We have stressed that one of the purposes of special journals is to reduce the amount of time involved in writing journal entries and posting to ledger accounts. In a computer-based system, the accountant need only enter the data needed for the computer to prepare journal entries. All the writing and all the posting to general ledger and subsidiary ledger accounts is then handled by machine (according to the instructions in the computer program) with no further human effort.

Advantages of computer-based systems

The primary advantage of the computer is its incredible speed. The time needed for a computer to post a transaction or determine an account balance is but a few millionths of a second. This speed creates several advantages over manual accounting systems, including the following:

1 **Large amounts of data can be processed quickly and efficiently** Large businesses may engage in tens of thousands of transactions per day. In processing such a large volume of data, computers can save vast amounts of time in each step of the accounting process, including the recording of transactions, posting to ledger accounts, and preparing of accounting records, schedules, and reports.

    For example, a large department store makes thousands of credit sales each day. To process these transactions manually would require a huge bookkeeping staff. Through devices such as *point-of-sale terminals* (electronic cash registers), a computer can process these transactions automatically as the salesperson rings up the sale.

2 **Account balances can be kept up-to-date** The speed with which data can be processed by a computer enables businesses to keep subsidiary ledger accounts, perpetual inventory records, and most general ledger accounts continually up-to-date.

3 **Additional information can be developed at virtually no additional cost** Earlier we illustrated the type of sales journal that might be prepared in a manual accounting system. A similar journal can be maintained in a computerized system. However, the computer can also rearrange this information to show daily sales totals for each sales department, for each salesperson, and for specific products. Time and cost considerations often make the preparation of such supplementary information impractical in a manual accounting system.

4 **Instant feedback can be available as transactions are taking place** In *online, real-time (OLRT)* computer systems, the employee executing a transaction can have a terminal which is in direct communication with the computer. Thus, the employee has immediate access to accounting information useful in executing the current transaction.

 The electronic cash registers now found in many department stores are point-of-sale terminals in direct communication with the store's computer system. When a salesperson makes a credit sale to a customer who is using a store credit card, the salesperson enters the credit card number into the terminal. The computer compares this number to a list of cancelled or stolen credit cards and also determines whether the current sales transaction would cause the customer's account balance to exceed a predetermined credit limit. If one of these procedures indicates that credit should not be extended to the customer, the computer notifies the salesperson not to make the credit sale.

5 Additional internal control procedures are possible in a computer-based system Approval of each credit sale, described in the preceding *Case in point,* is but one example of an internal control procedure that makes use of the unique capabilities of the computer. Such a control procedure may not be practical in a manual system, especially if the accounts receivable subsidiary ledger is not kept continually up-to-date.

Internal control and the computer

5 Discuss accounting applications of computers and means of achieving internal control in computer-based accounting systems.

Computer hardware itself is highly reliable and the possibility of errors caused by computer malfunction is very small. However, the use of reliable equipment does not entirely eliminate the possibility of errors in accounting records. Human beings create the information that is entered into the computer, and human beings make mistakes. In addition, the computer program may contain errors and, therefore, may process certain transactions improperly. Finally, there is the risk of improper human intervention — someone tampering with the computer programs or the computer-based records for the purpose of deliberately falsifying accounting information.

Thus internal control is just as important in a computer-based system as in a manual accounting system. We shall now discuss some of the most important internal control concepts for computer-based accounting systems.

Organizational controls

We have stressed the need for separation of duties as a means of achieving internal control. This concept is equally important in manual and computer-based accounting systems. An employee with custody of assets should not also have access to accounting records. If these duties are assigned to the same employee, this person has the opportunity to conceal a shortage of assets by falsifying the accounting records.

Separation of duties is also necessary among a company's computer department personnel. The purpose of such separation is to ensure that *no one person is in a position to make unauthorized changes* in programs or computer-based records. Thus, all programs should be tested by someone *other than* the programmer who wrote the program. In addition, the responsibilities for *programming* and actual *operation* of the computer should be assigned to different employees. Several computer-based frauds have occurred when programmers were also responsible for daily computer operations. An individual with this combination of duties is in a position to use the computer to make unauthorized changes in programs. As an additional precaution, the computer should create a *log* of all instructions given to the machine by the computer operator. This record should be reviewed daily by a computer department control group to determine that the operator has not made any unauthorized changes in programs or files.

 One recent computer fraud in a large company was linked to a well-publicized change in income tax rates. Knowing that employees expected a change in the amount of income tax withheld from their paycheques, a computer programmer wrote a new payroll program which overstated by a few dollars the income tax withheld from each employee. The program then added

these excess withholdings to the programmer's own paycheque. As a large labour force was involved, the dollar amount of this fraud was quite substantial.

This fraud would not have been possible if the new payroll program had been carefully tested by other employees.

Security controls

The purpose of security controls is to safeguard computer-based records, computer programs, and computer equipment against damage, theft, or unauthorized use. It is essential that only authorized personnel have access to computer programs and accounting records. When programs or records can be accessed from a computer terminal, the user of the terminal should be required to enter *secret passwords* to gain access to the system. The computer should issue a warning to the computer department control group if repeated attempts are made to gain access to the system using incorrect passwords. Computer facilities, programs, and records should be safely locked up after working hours.

 A consultant for a large bank was able to use the bank's electronic funds transfer system to transfer $10 million of the bank's money to his own account at another bank. The consultant had noticed that the "secret" passwords necessary to make wire transfers were posted on the wall beside a computer terminal.

The fraud remained undetected for eight days. In the meantime, the consultant transferred the money to a Swiss bank account and then converted it into diamonds. He might never have been caught except that he returned home and tried to sell some of the diamonds.

Input controls

Input controls are precautions taken to ensure that the data being entered into the computer are correct. Input controls vary, depending upon whether transactions are being entered into the system as they occur (*online, real-time*), or whether they are processed periodically in large groups or *batches.*

In an online, real-time (*OLRT*) system, input controls include such concepts as identification numbers and passwords to identify authorized users. In addition, the terminals used for recording specific types of transactions should have only *limited access* to the computer-based records. For example, the point-of-sale terminals in retail department stores are used to record cash sales and credit sales. Therefore, the only entries that need to be made from these terminals are debits to the Cash and Accounts Receivable accounts and credits to the Sales account. These terminals should not have access to other accounts or records.

Another input control in an OLRT system is the use of *machine-readable input.* For example, many items in supermarkets are labelled with machine-readable codes. The cashier passes this merchandise over an optical scanner, which identifies the merchandise to the computer. The computer then determines the price of the item from a master price list and displays this amount for both the cashier and the customer to see. This automatic entry procedure virtually eliminates errors in recording the sales price of merchandise.

Often transactions are processed in periodic batches, rather than as they occur. The preparation of a payroll at the end of each pay period is a common example of *batch processing*. Advance preparation of *control totals* can be an effective input control when data is processed in a batch. A control total represents the total dollar amount of all transactions sent to the computer department for processing. The computer will add up the total dollar amount of all data processed and print this total as part of the computer output. The predetermined control total may then be compared to the total printed by the computer. This comparison will show whether any data has been added or lost within the computer department, and also will bring to light such items as transposition errors.

Program controls

Program controls are error-detecting measures built into the computer program. An example of a program control is a *limit test,* which compares every item of data processed by the computer to a specified dollar limit. In the event an amount exceeds the dollar limit, the computer does not process that item and prints out an error report. A limit test is particularly effective in such computer applications as preparing paycheques, when it is known that none of the paycheques should be for more than a specified amount, such as $1,000.

Another example of a program control is an *item count*. The total number of data items to be processed by the computer is determined, and that total is entered as part of the input to the computer. The computer then counts the number of items it processes, and if this number differs from the predetermined total, an error report is printed. This item count ensures that all the data are actually processed by the computer.

Accounting applications of the computer

The use of electronic data processing equipment is possible for virtually every phase of accounting operations. A public accounting firm, in conducting an annual audit, may use the computer as an audit tool. For this purpose the auditors may employ specially written computer programs to aid in their work of sampling and analyzing data to determine the fairness of the financial statements.

The most common application of the computer, however, is to process large masses of accounting data relating to routine repetitive operations such as recording retail sales, maintaining perpetual inventory records, preparing payroll, and posting to ledger accounts.

Retail sales — accounts receivable and inventory records   The point-of-sale terminals now prominent in many retail establishments greatly reduce the work involved in accounting for sales transactions. Many of these terminals use an optical scanner or other electronic device to "read" magnetically coded labels attached to the merchandise. As the merchandise is passed over the optical scanner, the code is sent instantaneously to the computer. From the code number, the computer is able to identify the item being sold, record the amount of the sale, and transfer the cost of the item from the Inventory account to the Cost of Goods Sold account. If the transaction is a credit sale, the salesclerk enters the customer's credit card number in the electronic register. This number enables the computer to update instantly the customer's account in the subsidiary ledger.

Note that all of the accounting is done automatically as the salesclerk rings up the sale. Thus any number of transactions can be recorded and posted with virtually no manual work. At the end of each day, the computer prints a complete sales journal along with up-to-date balances for the general ledger and subsidiary ledger accounts relating to sales transactions.

Payrolls   The preparation of payrolls requires many computations, preparation of paycheques, reports to governmental agencies, and updating of various detailed accounting records. Most of these functions are well-suited to computers. In fact, the first use made of computers in the business community was in processing payrolls. (Accounting for payrolls is discussed in Chapter 11.)

Computer-based journals and ledgers   As mentioned earlier in this chapter, computers also may be used to maintain the journals and ledgers and to prepare financial statements. Transactions and end-of-period adjustments still must be analyzed by persons possessing a knowledge of accounting principles. However, after these transactions have been analyzed and prepared in computer input form, the computer can be used to print the journals, post to the ledger accounts, and print the financial statements and other financial reports. The advantage of maintaining accounting records by computer is that the possibility of mathematical errors is greatly reduced, and the speed of the computer permits the records to be kept continuously up-to-date.

Other accounting applications of computers include forecasting the profit possibilities inherent in alternative courses of action, analyzing gross profit margins by department or by product line, and determining future cash requirements long in advance. Recent developments of accounting applications of the computer provide much more information about business operations than was available to management in the past.

END-OF-CHAPTER REVIEW

SUMMARY OF CHAPTER LEARNING OBJECTIVES

1 Explain the nature of special journals and the reasons for their use.

Special journals are accounting records designed for efficiently journalizing a particular type of business transaction. The reasons for using special journals are (1) to divide the task of recording business transactions among several different employees, and (2) to minimize the amount of work involved in recording and posting business transactions that occur with great frequency.

2 Use special journals to record sales on credit, purchases on account, and cash transactions.

All sales on credit are recorded in the sales journal, and all purchases of merchandise on account are recorded in the purchases journal. Both of these types of transactions affect only two ledger accounts. All transactions involving the receipt of cash are recorded in the cash receipts journal, and all transactions requiring cash payments are recorded in the cash payments journal.

3 Explain the usefulness of a subsidiary ledger and its relationship to a controlling account in the general ledger.

A subsidiary ledger provides detailed information about the individual items that comprise the balance of a general ledger account. Consider, for example, the general ledger account entitled Accounts Receivable. This account shows the total amount of a company's accounts receivables from all its customers. While this total figure is useful in preparing financial statements, it does not show the amounts owed by specific individuals. Thus, it does not provide the information needed to send monthly statements to individual customers. The accounts receivable subsidiary ledger, on the other hand, includes a separate account showing the name and amount receivable from each customer. A subsidiary ledger also is maintained for accounts payable, so that the business will have a record of the amount owed to each individual creditor.

The sum of the account balances in a subsidiary ledger is equal to the balance of the related controlling account in the general ledger.

4 Post entries in special journals to the general ledger and subsidiary ledgers.

Only the entries in the "Other accounts" columns of the two cash journals should be posted immediately to the general ledger. For all other postings to general ledger accounts, we periodically total the various money columns in the special journals and post only the column totals. These column totals may include the effects of hundreds of individual transactions. Therefore, the use of special journals greatly reduces the number of postings to general ledger accounts. Postings to subsidiary ledger accounts, however, should be made promptly upon the journalizing of each transaction.

5 Discuss accounting applications of computers and means of achieving internal control in computer-based accounting systems.

The incredible speed with which information is processed in a computer-based accounting system offers numerous advantages, including (1) processing large amounts of data quickly and efficiently, (2) keeping account balances up-to-date, (3) developing additional data at virtually no additional cost, and (4) providing instant "feedback" as transactions are taking place.

Internal control is equally important in manual and computer-based accounting systems. A computer-based system requires adequate organizational controls, security controls, input controls, and program controls.

KEY TERMS INTRODUCED OR EMPHASIZED IN CHAPTER 6

Accounts payable ledger A subsidiary ledger containing an account with each supplier or vendor. The total of the ledger agrees with the general ledger controlling account, Accounts Payable.

Accounts receivable ledger A subsidiary ledger containing an account with each credit customer. The total of the ledger agrees with the general ledger controlling account, Accounts Receivable.

Batch processing A method of data processing in which transactions are accumulated into groups for processing at periodic intervals, rather than being processed as the transactions occur. Batch processing is widely used for such applications as payrolls. Contrasts with *online, real-time processing.*

Cash payments journal A special journal used to record all payments of cash.

Cash receipts journal A special journal used to record all receipts of cash.

Controlling account A general ledger account that is supported by detailed information in a subsidiary ledger.

Input controls Internal control measures to ensure accuracy of data entered into a computer (such as control totals, the total dollar amount of documents to be processed).

Online, real-time (OLRT) processing Using terminals in direct communication with the computer to process transactions instantaneously as they occur. Airline reservation systems, teller terminals at banks, and point-of-sale terminals at retail stores are examples of OLRT systems. Contrasts with *batch processing*.

Organizational controls Internal control procedures to ensure a proper delegation and segregation of duties among employees (for example, an asset custodian should not be allowed to have access to accounting records).

Point-of-sale terminal Electronic cash registers used for *online, real-time processing* of sales transactions. Widely used in large retail stores.

Program controls Error-detecting measures built into a computer program (such as a limit test setting a maximum dollar amount, or item counts specifying the number of items to be processed).

Purchases journal A special journal used exclusively to record purchases of merchandise on credit.

Sales journal A special journal used exclusively to record sales of merchandise on credit.

Security controls Internal control procedures designed to protect computer programs, records, and equipment against theft, damage, and unauthorized use.

Subsidiary ledger A supplementary record used to provide detailed information for a control account in the general ledger. The total of accounts in a subsidiary ledger equals the balance of the related control account in the general ledger.

DEMONSTRATION PROBLEM FOR YOUR REVIEW

The Signal Corporation began operations on November 1, 19___. The chart of accounts used by the company included the following accounts, among others:

Cash	10	Purchases	60
Marketable securities	15	Purchase returns & allowances	62
Office supplies	18	Purchase discounts	64
Notes payable	30	Salaries expense	70
Accounts payable	32	Utilities expense	71

November transactions relating to the purchase of merchandise and to accounts payable follow, along with selected other transactions.

Nov. 1 Purchased merchandise from Moss Co. for $3,000. Invoice dated today; terms 2/10, n/30.

Nov. 3 Received shipment of merchandise from Wilmer Co. and invoice dated November 2 for $7,600; terms 2/10, n/30.

Nov. 6 Purchased merchandise from Archer Company at cost of $5,600. Invoice dated November 5, terms 2/10, n/30.

Nov. 9 Purchased marketable securities for $1,200, cheque No. 1.

Nov. 10 Issued cheque No. 2 to Moss Co. in settlement of invoice dated November 1, less discount.

Nov. 12 Received shipment of merchandise from Cory Corporation and an invoice dated November 11 in amount of $7,100; terms net 30 days.

Nov. 14 Issued cheque No. 3 to Archer Company in settlement of invoice of November 5.

Nov. 16 Paid for office supplies of $110, cheque No. 4.

Nov. 17 Purchased merchandise for cash, $950, cheque No. 5.

Nov. 19 Purchased merchandise from Klein Co. for $11,500. Invoice dated November 18; terms 1/10, n/30.

Nov. 21 Purchased merchandise from Belmont Company for $8,400. Invoice dated November 20; terms 1/10, n/30.

Nov. 24 Purchased merchandise for cash, $375, cheque No. 6.

Nov. 26 Purchased merchandise from Brooker Co. for $6,500. Invoice dated today; terms 1/10, n/30.

Nov. 28 Paid utilities, $150, cheque No.7.

Nov. 30 Paid salaries for November, $2,900, cheque No. 8.

Nov. 30 Issued cheque No. 9 for $2,600 to Wilmer Co. and a 12%, 90-day promissory note for $5,000 in settlement of invoice dated November 2.

Instructions

a Record the transactions in the appropriate journals. Use a single-column purchases journal and a six-column cash payments journal. Record purchases at gross amount.

b Indicate how postings would be made by placing ledger account numbers and check marks in the appropriate columns of the journals.

c Prepare a schedule of accounts payable at November 30 to prove that the subsidiary ledger is in balance with the controlling account.

SOLUTION TO DEMONSTRATION PROBLEM

a & b   Purchases Journal   Page 1

DATE		ACCOUNT CREDITED	INVOICE DATE		✓	AMOUNT
19__			19__			
Nov	1	Moss Co. (2/10, n/30)	Nov	1	✓	3,000
	3	Wilmer Co. (2/10, n/30)		2	✓	7,600
	6	Archer Company (2/10, n/30)		5	✓	5,600
	12	Cory Corporation (net 30)		11	✓	7,100
	19	Klein Co. (1/10, n/30)		18	✓	11,500
	21	Belmont Company (1/10, n/30)		20	✓	8,400
	26	Brooker Co. (1/10, n/30)		26	✓	6,500
						$49,700
						(60) (32)

See page 273 for the Cash Payments Journal.

a & b

Cash Payments Journal

| | | | CREDITS | | | | | | DEBITS | | | | |
DATE	CH. NO.	EXPLANATION	CASH	PURCHASE DISCOUNTS	OTHER ACCOUNTS NAME	LP	AMOUNT	ACCOUNT DEBITED	ACCOUNTS PAYABLE ✓	AMOUNT	PURCHASES	OTHER ACCOUNTS LP	AMOUNT
19_ Nov 9	1	Bought securities	1,200					Marketable Securities				15	1,200
10	2	Invoice, Nov. 1, less 2%	2,940	60				Moss Co.	✓	3,000			
14	3	Invoice Nov. 5, less 2%	5,488	112				Archer Company	✓	5,600			
16	4	Purchased office supplies	110					Office Supplies				18	110
17	5	Cash purchases	950								950		
24	6	Cash purchases	375								375		
28	7	Paid utilities	150					Utilities Expense				71	150
30	8	Paid salaries	2,900					Salaries Expense				70	2,900
30	9	Invoice, Nov. 2, note issued for unpaid balance	2,600		Notes Payable	30	5,000	Wilmer Co.	✓	7,600			
			16,713	172			5,000			16,200	1,325		4,360
			(10)	(64)			(X)			(32)	(60)		(X)

c

SIGNAL CORPORATION
Schedule of Accounts Payable
November 30, 19___

Belmont Company	$ 8,400
Brooker Co.	6,500
Cory Corporation	7,100
Klein Co.	11,500
Total (per general ledger controlling account)	$33,500

ASSIGNMENT MATERIAL

REVIEW QUESTIONS

1 What advantages are offered by the use of special journals?

2 Arrow Company uses a general journal and four special journals: (1) sales journal, (2) purchases journal, (3) cash receipts journal, and (4) cash payments journal. Which journal should the company use to record (a) cash sales, (b) depreciation expense, and (c) credit sales? Explain the reasoning underlying your answer.

3 The column total of one of the four special journals described in this chapter is posted at month-end to two general ledger accounts. One of these two accounts is Accounts Payable. What is the name of the special journal? What account is debited and what account is credited with this total?

4 Pine Hill General Store makes about 500 sales on account each month, using only a two-column general journal to record these transactions. What would be the extent of the work saved by using a sales journal?

5 When accounts receivable and accounts payable are kept in subsidiary ledgers, will the general ledger continue to be a self-balancing ledger with equal debits and credits? Explain.

6 Explain how, why, and when the cash receipts journal and cash payments journal are crossfooted.

7 During November the sales on credit made by the Hardy Company actually amounted to $41,625, but an error of $1,000 was made in totalling the amount column of the sales journal. When and how will the error be discovered?

8 For a large modern department store, such as a Sears or Zellers, is it necessary to maintain a manual single-column sales journal? Explain.

9 Briefly describe some of the advantages of processing accounting information by computer rather than manually.

10 Explain several factors that may cause accounting information processed by a computer to be in error.

11 What is the purpose of subdividing duties among the personnel of a company's computer department?

12 A computer usually maintains a log of all instructions given to the computer by the computer operator while data is being processed. What use should be made of this log? Explain.

13 Explain the purpose of *security controls* in a computer-based accounting system.

14 Explain the meaning of the term *input control* and give an example.

15 Explain the meaning of the term *program control* and give an example.

16 Distinguish between *online, real-time* processing and *batch* processing.

17 In processing the monthly payroll by computer, the gross pay of one employee was accidentally recorded as $1,238 instead of $1,283. Will this error most likely be brought to light by a limit test, an item count, or a control total? Explain.

EXERCISES

**Exercise 6-1
Accounting
terminology**

Listed below are nine technical accounting terms introduced in this chapter:

Control total	Online, real-time	Security controls
Controlling account	Organizational controls	Special journal
Input controls	Reconciling	Subsidiary ledger

Each of the following statements may (or may not) describe one of these technical terms. For each statement, indicate the accounting term described, or answer "None" if the statement does not correctly describe any of the terms.

a An accounting record used to record in an efficient manner a specific type of business transaction that occurs frequently.

b Measures to ensure that data entered into a computer-based accounting system are correct.

c The total dollar amount of all of the transactions in a single batch that has been sent to the computer department for processing.

d The process of determining agreement between the balance of a controlling account and the sum of the account balances in the related subsidiary ledger.

e Measures intended to provide assurance that no one person is in a position to make unauthorized changes in computer programs or in computer-based records.

f A form of data processing that gives the employee participating in a transaction immediate access to accounting information that may be useful in executing that transaction.

g A group of accounts that in total equal the balance of a controlling account in the general ledger.

**Exercise 6-2
Recording transactions
in special journals**

Medical Supply Co. uses a cash receipts journal, a cash payments journal, a sales journal, a purchases journal, and a general journal. Indicate which journal should be used to record each of the following transactions.

a Payment of property taxes

b Purchase of office equipment on credit

c Sale of merchandise on credit

d Sale of merchandise for cash

e Cash refund to a customer who returned merchandise

f Return of merchandise to a supplier for credit

g Adjusting entry to record depreciation

h Purchase of delivery truck for cash

i Purchase of merchandise on account

j Return of merchandise by a customer company for credit to its account

Exercise 6-3
Posting from special journals

Island Company, a merchandising concern, uses a cash receipts journal, a cash payments journal, a sales journal, a purchases journal, and a general journal.

a In which of the five journals would you expect to find the smallest number of transactions recorded?

b At the end of the accounting period, the total of the sales journal should be posted to what account or accounts? As a debit or credit?

c At the end of the accounting period, the total of the purchases journal should be posted to what account or accounts? As a debit or credit?

d Name two subsidiary ledgers which would probably be used in conjunction with the journals listed above. Identify the journals from which postings would regularly be made to each of the two subsidiary ledgers.

e In which of the five journals would adjusting and closing entries be made?

Exercise 6-4
Posting from special journals

The accounting system used by Adams Company includes a general journal and also four special journals for cash receipts, cash payments, sales, and purchases of merchandise. On January 31, after all January posting had been completed, the Accounts Receivable controlling account in the general ledger had a debit balance of $160,000, and the Accounts Payable controlling account had a credit balance of $48,000.

The February transactions recorded in the four special journals can be summarized as follows:

Sales journal	Total transactions, $96,000
Purchases journal	Total transactions, $56,000
Cash receipts journal	Accounts Receivable column total, $76,800 (credit)
Cash payments journal	Accounts Payable column total, $67,200 (debit)

a What posting would be made of the $76,800 total of the Accounts Receivable column in the cash receipts journal at February 28?

b What posting would be made of the $96,000 total of the sales journal at February 28?

c What posting would be made of the $56,000 total of the purchases journal at February 28?

d What posting would be made of the $67,200 total of the Accounts Payable column in the cash payments journal at February 28?

e Based on the above information, state the balances of the Accounts Receivable controlling account and the Accounts Payable controlling account in the general ledger after completion of posting at February 28.

Exercise 6-5
Using subsidiary ledgers

Pacific Products uses a sales journal to record all sales of merchandise on credit. During July the transactions in this journal were as follows:

Sales Journal

DATE		ACCOUNT DEBITED	INVOICE NO.	AMOUNT
July	6	Robert Baker	437	3,600
	15	Minden Company	438	8,610
	17	Pell & Warden	439	1,029
	26	Stonewall Corporation	440	17,500
	27	Robert Baker	441	3,000
				33,739

Entries in the general journal during July include one for the return of merchandise by a customer, as follows:

July	18	Sales Returns and Allowances		500	
		Accounts Receivable, Minden Company			500
		Allowed credit to customer for return of merchandise from sale of July 15.			

a Prepare a subsidiary ledger for accounts receivable by opening a T account for each of the four customers listed above. Post the entries in the sales journal to these individual customers' accounts. From the general journal, post the credit to the account of Minden Company.

b Prepare a general ledger account in T form as follows: a controlling account for Accounts Receivable, a Sales account, and a Sales Returns and Allowances account. Post to these accounts the appropriate entries from the sales journal and general journal.

c Prepare a schedule of accounts receivable at July 31 to prove that this subsidiary ledger is in agreement with its controlling account.

Exercise 6-6
Locating errors in special journals and subsidiary ledgers

Keystone Company maintains a manual accounting system with the four special journals and general journal described in this chapter. During September, the following errors were made. For each of the errors you are to explain how and when the error will be brought to light.

a Incorrectly added the debit entries in a customer's account in the accounts receivable subsidiary ledger as $950 when it should have been $550.

b A purchase of merchandise on credit from Rex Company in the amount of $1,000 was erroneously entered in the purchases journal as a $100 purchase.

c Recorded correctly in the sales journal a $400 sale of merchandise on credit but posted the transaction to the customer's account in the subsidiary ledger as a $40 sale.

Exercise 6-7
Posting directly from invoices

Trendline Graphics, a wholesaler, follows the practice of posting customers' accounts in the accounts receivable subsidiary ledger directly from duplicate copies of sales invoices rather than copying the invoices into a sales journal. Credit memos also are posted directly to customers' accounts. At month-end, a general journal entry is made for the total of sales invoices issued during the month, and another general journal entry is used to record the total of the credit memos issued.

During January, the company issued 389 sales invoices totalling $116,420. Also during January, 27 credit memos were issued in the total amount of $2,160. You are to prepare the two general journal entries needed at January 31.

Exercise 6-8
Internal control in
a computer-based
system

Mission Stores uses electronic registers to record its sales transactions. All merchandise bears a magnetic code number which can be read by an optical scanner. When merchandise is sold, the salesclerk passes each item over the scanner. The computer reads the code number, determines the price of the item from a master price list, and displays the price on a screen for the customer to see. After each item has been passed over the scanner, the computer displays the total amount of the sale and records the transaction in the company's accounting records.

If the transaction is a credit sale, the salesclerk enters the customer's credit card number into the register. The computer checks the customer's credit status and updates the accounts receivable subsidiary ledger.

Items **a** through **d** describe problems that may arise in a retailing business that uses manual cash registers and accounting records. Explain how the electronic registers used by Mission Stores will help reduce or eliminate these problems. If the electronic registers will not help to eliminate the problems, explain why not.

a A salesclerk is unaware of a recent change in the price of a particular item.

b Merchandise is stolen by a shoplifter.

c A salesclerk fails to record a cash sale and keeps the cash received from the customer.

d A customer buys merchandise on account using a stolen Mission Stores credit card.

PROBLEMS

Group A

Problem 6A-1
Relationship between
subsidiary ledgers and
controlling accounts

Tyrolian Products sells skis and ski clothing. The company uses journals and ledgers similar to those illustrated in Chapter 6. At November 30, the subsidiary ledger for accounts receivable included accounts with individual customers as shown on the next page. Note that these accounts include postings from three different journals.

The purpose of this problem is to show the relationship between a controlling account and a subsidiary ledger. By studying the four subsidiary ledger accounts, you can determine what amounts should appear in the controlling account. (In actual practice, of course, both the controlling account and the subsidiary ledger would be completed by posting amounts from the various journals.)

Instructions

You are to make the necessary entries in the general ledger controlling account, Accounts Receivable, for the month of November. Use a three-column, running balance form of ledger account. (Remember that a controlling account is posted on a daily basis for transactions recorded in the general journal, but is posted only at the end of the month for the **monthly** **totals** of special journals such as the sales journal and the cash receipts journal.)

Include in the controlling account the balance at October 31, the transactions from the general journal during November in chronological order, and the running balance of the

NORDIC SPORTSWEAR

DATE		EXPLANATION	REF	DEBIT	CREDIT	BALANCE
19—						
Oct.	31	Balance				12400
Nov.	10		J1		630	11770
	11		S4	8000		19770
	30		CR2		11770	8000

OLLIE'S SKI SHOP

DATE	EXPLANATION	REF	DEBIT	CREDIT	BALANCE
19 –					
Nov. 4		S4	281 60		281 60
29		S4	76 80		358 40
29		CR2		281 60	76 80

PACIFIC SPORTS CENTRE

DATE	EXPLANATION	REF	DEBIT	CREDIT	BALANCE
19 –					
Nov. 3		S4	22 40		22 40
9		S4	41 60		64 00
27		CR2		22 40	41 60

QUALITY STORES, INC.

DATE	EXPLANATION	REF	DEBIT	CREDIT	BALANCE
19 –					
Oct. 31	Balance				207 36
Nov. 8		CR1		128 00	79 36
8		J1		25 60	53 76
28		CR2		53 76	–0–

account after each entry. Finally, make one posting for all sales on credit during November and one posting for all cash collections from credit customers during November. For each amount entered in the Accounts Receivable controlling account, the date and source (name of journal and journal page) should be listed. Use the symbols shown on pages 256 and 257 to identify the various journals.

Problem 6A-2
Special journals and
posting procedures

Among the ledger accounts used by Creek Drug Store are the following:

Cash	10	Accounts payable	30
Office supplies	18	Purchases	50
Land	20	Purchase returns & allowances	52
Building	22	Purchase discounts	53
Notes payable	28	Salaries expense	60

The August transactions relating to the purchase of merchandise for resale and to accounts payable follow, along with selected other transactions. It is Creek Drug's policy to record purchase invoices at their gross amount.

Aug. 1 Purchased merchandise from Medco Labs at a cost of $8,470. Invoice dated today; terms 2/10, n/30.

Aug. 4 Purchased merchandise from Ameri Products for $19,300. Invoice dated August 3; terms 2/10, n/30.

Aug. 5 Returned for credit to Medco Labs defective merchandise having a list price of $1,220.

Aug. 6 Received shipment of merchandise from Tricor Corporation and their invoice dated August 5 in amount of $14,560. Terms net 30 days.

Aug. 8 Purchased merchandise from Vita-Life, Inc., $24,480. Invoice dated today with terms 1/10, n/60.

Aug. 10 Purchased merchandise from King Corporation, $30,000. Invoice dated August 9; terms 2/10, n/30.

Aug. 10 Issued cheque No. 101 for $7,105 to Medco Labs in settlement of balance resulting from purchase of August 1 and purchase return of August 5.

Aug. 11 Issued cheque No. 102 for $18,914 to Ameri Products in payment of August 3 invoice, less 2%.

Aug. 18 Issued cheque No. 103 for $29,400 to King Corporation in settlement of invoice dated August 9, less 2% discount.

Aug. 20 Purchased merchandise for $1,080, cheque No. 104.

Aug. 21 Bought land and building for $208,800. Land was worth $64,800, and building, $144,000. Paid cash of $36,000 (cheque No. 105) and signed a promissory note for the balance of $172,800.

Aug. 23 Purchased merchandise for $900, cheque No. 106.

Aug. 26 Purchased merchandise from Ralston Company for $32,400. Invoice dated August 26, terms 2/10, n/30.

Aug. 28 Paid for office supplies of $270, cheque No. 107.

Aug. 29 Purchased merchandise for $1,890, cheque No. 108.

Aug. 31 Paid salaries for August, $17,920, cheque No. 109.

Instructions

a Record the transactions in the appropriate journals. Use a single-column purchases journal, a six-column cash payments journal, and a two-column general journal. Foot and rule the special journals. Make all postings to the proper general ledger accounts and to the accounts payable subsidiary ledger.

b Prepare a schedule of accounts payable at August 31 to prove that the subsidiary ledger is in balance with the controlling account for accounts payable.

Problem 6A-3
Using special journals
to record cash
transactions

Backpacker & Co. uses an accounting system that includes multicolumn special journals for cash receipts and cash payments. These journals are similar to those illustrated in this chapter. However, the cheque number column is not required for the cash payments journal. All the cash transactions during April are described in the following:

Apr. 1 Cash sales of merchandise, $6,207.

Apr. 1 Paid inbound freight charges on merchandise from Watkins Company, $473.

Apr. 2 Cash purchase of merchandise, $7,114.

Apr. 2 Paid Spalding Company invoice, $2,700 less 1% discount.

Apr. 4 Purchased furniture and fixtures, $5,120, making a down payment of $1,280 and issuing a note payable for the balance.

Apr. 5 Received $960 cash as partial collection of our $3,840 invoice to National Co. Also received a note receivable for the $2,880 balance of this invoice.

Apr. 6 Paid Newcomb Company invoice, $4,500 less 2% discount.

Apr. 7 Paid note due today, $9,600, plus interest amounting to $192.

Apr. 10 The owner, D.B. Cooper, invested additional cash of $32,000 in the business.

Apr. 12 Cash sales of merchandise, $4,243.

Apr. 15 Paid April rent, $2,080.

Apr. 18 Cash purchase of merchandise, $4,640.

Apr. 19 Paid gas and oil bill, $176, for automobile belonging to Mrs. D.B. Cooper. (Car is not used in the business.)

Apr. 20 Received $1,960 cash in full settlement of our $2,000 invoice to Mesa Company after allowing 2% discount.

Apr. 21 Paid account payable to Mammoth Co., $5,200 less 2% discount.

Apr. 23 Paid sales commissions of $2,528 to sales staff.

Apr. 30 Received payment in full settlement of our $5,500 invoice to Presley Company, less 2% discount.

Apr. 30 Paid monthly salaries, $9,000.

Instructions   **a** Enter the above transactions in the cash receipts journal and the cash payments journal.

b Foot and rule the journals.

Problem 6A-4
Using special journals: a comprehensive problem

Town Trader began operations on May 1. The chart of accounts used by the company included the following accounts, among others:

Cash	10	Sales	50
Accounts receivable	15	Sales returns & allowances	52
Unexpired insurance	19	Sales discounts	54
Land	20	Purchases	60
Building	21	Purchase returns & allowances	62
Notes payable	30	Purchase discounts	64
Accounts payable	32	Transportation-in	66
Mortgage payable	36	Salaries expense	72
Susan James, capital	40	Interest expense	83

The company offers terms of 2/10, n/30 on all sales of merchandise on credit. Record credit purchases at gross amount. The transactions during May were as follows:

May 1 The owner, Susan James, deposited $81,000 in a bank account under the name, Town Trader.

May 4 Purchased land and building, paying $40,000 cash and signing a mortgage for the balance of $60,000. Estimated value of the land was $45,000.

May 5 Purchased merchandise from Lakeview Company, $12,000. Invoice dated today; terms 2/10, n/30.

May 6 Sold merchandise on credit to Brad Parks, $6,800, invoice No. 1.

May 7 Sold merchandise for cash, $1,300.

May 9 Paid $220 for a one-year fire insurance policy.

May 10 Paid freight charges of $177 on purchase from Lakeview Company.

May 12 Sold merchandise on credit to ABC Corporation, $8,800, invoice No. 2.

May 13 Purchased merchandise for cash, $2,556.

May 15 Received payment from Brad Parks. Invoice No. 1, dated May 6, less 2% discount.

May 15 Paid Lakeview Company invoice of May 5, less discount.

May 16 Issued credit memorandum No. 1 to ABC Corporation, $800, for goods returned today by ABC Corporation.

May 18 Purchased merchandise from Baker Company, $6,000. Invoice dated today; terms 2/10, n/30.

May 20 A portion of merchandise purchased from Baker Company was found to be substandard. After discussion with the vendor, a price reduction of $200 was agreed upon and a credit memo for this amount was received from Baker Company.

May 22 Received payment from ABC Corporation. Invoice No. 2, less return of merchandise on May 16 and discount on balance.

May 23 Purchased merchandise from Lakeview Company, $7,560. Invoice dated today; terms 2/10, n/60.

May 27 Sold merchandise for cash, $927.

May 28 Borrowed $15,400 from bank, issuing a note payable as evidence of indebtedness.

May 28 Paid Baker Company invoice of May 18, less allowance and discount.

May 30 Paid first instalment on mortgage, $900. This payment included interest of $600, and reduced the mortgage liability by $300.

May 30 Purchased merchandise for cash, $1,656.

May 31 Paid monthly salaries of $6,000.

May 31 Sold merchandise on credit to Frank Sullivan, $4,950, invoice No. 3.

Instructions **a** Enter the May transactions in the following journals:
Two-column general journal
One-column sales journal
One-column purchases journal
Six-column cash receipts journal
Six-column cash payments journal (the cheque number column is not required).

b Foot and rule all special journals.

c Show how posting would be made by placing the ledger account numbers and check marks in the appropriate columns of the journals. This instruction includes placing ledger account numbers in the LP columns as well as under the totals for the month.

Problem 6A-5
Using special
journals: a second
comprehensive
problem

Sand Castle Company uses the following accounts (among others) in recording transactions:

Cash	10	Sales returns & allowances	62
Notes receivable	14	Sales discounts	64
Accounts receivable	16	Purchases	70
Supplies	17	Purchase returns & allowances	72
Unexpired insurance	18	Purchase discounts	74
Equipment	26	Transportation-in	76
Notes payable	30	Salaries expense	80
Accounts payable	32	Gain on sale of equipment	90
Mortgage payable	40	Interest expense	92
Sales	60		

For customers to whom Sand Castle sells on open account, the credit terms are 2/10, n/30. The November transactions of Sand Castle Company were as follows:

Nov. 2 Purchased merchandise on account from Durapave, Inc., $28,000. Invoice was dated today with terms of 2/10, n/30.

Nov. 3 Sold merchandise on credit to Ace Contractors, $16,000, invoice No. 428.

Nov. 4 Purchased supplies for cash, $1,875.

Nov. 5 Sold merchandise for cash, $6,000.

Nov. 7 Paid Durapave, Inc., $30,000, representing October purchase. No discount was allowed by Durapave, Inc., on this purchase.

Nov. 10 Purchased merchandise from Tool Company, $32,500. Invoice dated November 9 with terms of 1/10, n/30.

Nov. 10 Collected from Ace Contractors for invoice No. 428 for $16,000, less 2% discount, and for October sales of $20,800 on which the discount had lapsed.

Nov. 12 Sold merchandise on credit to Rex Company, $21,750, invoice No. 429.

Nov. 14 Paid freight charges of $2,050 on goods purchased November 10 from Tool Company.

Nov. 14 Sold equipment for $22,000, receiving cash of $1,500 and a note receivable for the balance. Equipment had been acquired recently at a cost of $20,000 for use in the business, but because of a change in plans, it was never used.

Nov. 15 Issued credit memorandum No. 38 upon return of $1,000 of merchandise by our customer, Rex Company.

Nov. 18 Paid for one-year fire insurance policy, $1,425.

Nov. 18 Purchased merchandise for cash, $7,625.

Nov. 19 Paid the Tool Company invoice dated November 9, less the 1% discount.

Nov. 20 Sold merchandise on account to Vincent Co., $13,650, invoice No. 430.

Nov. 22 Purchased merchandise for cash, $4,050.

Nov. 22 Sold merchandise for cash, $4,675.

Nov. 22 Received payment from Rex Company for invoice No. 429. Customer made deduction for credit memorandum No. 38 issued November 15, and a 2% discount.

Nov. 23 Sold merchandise on account to Waite, Inc., $9,950, invoice No. 431.

Nov. 25 Purchased merchandise from Smith Company, $26,500. Invoice dated November 24 with terms of 2/10, n/60.

Nov. 26 Issued debit memorandum No. 42 for $2,125 to Smith Company because of shortage in merchandise delivered to us as compared with their invoice of November 24.

Nov. 27 Purchased equipment having a list price of $60,000. Paid $10,000 down and signed a promissory note for the balance of $50,000.

Nov. 30 Paid monthly salaries of $14,800 for services rendered by employees during November.

Nov. 30 Paid monthly instalment on mortgage, $3,000 of which $1,020 was interest expense.

Instructions   **a**   Record the November transactions in the following journals:
General journal — two columns
Sales journal — one column
Purchases journal — one column
Cash receipts journal — six columns
Cash payments journal — six columns (cheque number column is not required)

b   Foot and rule all special journals and show how postings would be made by placing ledger account numbers and check marks in the appropriate columns of the journals.

Problem 6A-6
Internal control
measures — emphasis
upon computer-based
systems

Shown below are eight possible errors or problems that might occur in a business. Also listed are several internal control measures. List the letter (**a** through **h**) designating each possible error. Beside this letter, place the number indicating the internal control procedure that should prevent this type of problem from occurring. If none of the specified internal control measures would effectively prevent the problem, place an "0" opposite the letter. Unless stated otherwise, assume that a computer-based accounting system is in use.

Possible Errors or
Problems

a A salesclerk rings up a sale at an incorrect price.

b In preparing the monthly payroll, a factory worker's wages of $900 for the two-week pay period are accidentally entered into the computer as $9,000.

c A shoplifter steals merchandise while the sales clerk is busy with another customer.

d A credit sale is posted to the wrong account in the accounts receivable subsidiary ledger.

e The cashier of a business conceals a theft of cash by adjusting the balance of the Cash account in the company's computer-based accounting records.

f Through oversight, a credit sale is never posted from the sales journal to the accounts receivable subsidiary ledger. (Assume that a manual accounting system is in use.)

g A department store salesclerk unknowingly makes a credit sale to a customer who is using a store credit card that has been reported stolen.

h While running the program to prepare the monthly payroll, a computer operator inserts data causing the machine to prepare paycheques for five fictitious employees.

Internal Control Measures

1 The computer prepares a report with separate daily sales totals for each salesperson.

2 Subsidiary ledgers are periodically compared to the balances of the controlling accounts in the general ledger.

3 Employees with custody of assets do not have access to accounting records.

4 All merchandise has a magnetically coded label that can be read automatically by a device attached to the electronic cash register. This code identifies to the computer the merchandise being sold.

5 Credit cards issued by the store have magnetic codes that can be read automatically by a device attached to the electronic cash register. Credit approval and posting to customers' accounts are handled by computer.

6 An item count.

7 A limit test.

0 None of the above control measures effectively prevents this type of error from occurring.

Group B

Problem 6B-1
Relationship between subsidiary ledgers and controlling accounts

The accounting system used by Furniture Warehouse includes a general journal and four special journals for daily recording of transactions. Information recorded in these journals is posted to a general ledger and two subsidiary ledgers: one of the subsidiary ledgers contains accounts receivable and the other accounts payable. All three ledgers are in the three-column, running balance form. At September 30, the subsidiary ledger for accounts payable contained the accounts with creditors beginning below and continuing on page 286. Note that postings to these accounts have been made from three different journals.

RALEIGH PRODUCTS, INC.

DATE		EXPLANATION	REF	DEBIT	CREDIT	BALANCE
19—						
Sept.	1		P1		1 6 0 0 0	1 6 0 0 0
	20		P1		1 2 8 0 0	2 8 8 0 0
	21	Returned Mdse.	J2	8 0 0		2 8 0 0 0
	28		CP3	1 5 2 0 0		1 2 8 0 0

SUPERIOR FURNITURE CO.

DATE		EXPLANATION	REF	DEBIT	CREDIT	BALANCE
19—						
Sept.	22		P1		1 3 7 6 0	1 3 7 6 0

TRADITIONAL INTERIORS

DATE		EXPLANATION	REF	DEBIT	CREDIT	BALANCE
19–						
Aug.	31	Balance				960
Sept.	15		CP3	960		–0–
	16		PI		3000	3000
	20		PI		4800	7800

ULTRA DESIGNS, INC.

DATE		EXPLANATION	REF	DEBIT	CREDIT	BALANCE
19–						
Aug.	31	Balance				35200
Sept.	5	Returned Mdse.	J2	1920		33280
	20		CP3	24000		9280
	25		PI		1600	10880

Instructions You are to prepare the general ledger controlling account, Accounts Payable, corresponding to the above subsidiary ledger accounts for the month of September. Use a three-column running balance form of ledger account. (Remember that a controlling account is posted on a daily basis for transactions recorded in the general journal, but is posted only at the end of the month for the ***monthly totals*** of special journals such as the purchases journal and the cash payments journal.)

Enter in the controlling account the beginning balance at August 31, the transactions from the general journal during September in chronological order, and the running balance of the account after each entry. Finally, make one posting for all purchases of merchandise on credit during September and one posting for all cash payments to suppliers during September. For each entry in the controlling account, show the date and source (journal and page number) of the item. Use the symbols shown on pages 256 and 257 to identify the individual journals.

Problem 6B-2
Using special journals and showing posting references

The accounting records of Video Games, a wholesale distributor of packaged software for computer games, include a general journal, four special journals, a general ledger, and two subsidiary ledgers. The chart of accounts includes the following accounts, among others.

Cash	10	Sales	50
Notes receivable	15	Sales returns & allowances	52
Accounts receivable	17	Sales discounts	54
Notes payable	30	Purchase returns & allowances . .	62
Accounts payable	32		

Transactions in June involving the sale of merchandise and the receipt of cash are shown below.

June 1 Sold merchandise to The Game Store for cash, $472.

June 4 Sold merchandise to Bravo Company, $8,500. Invoice No. 618; terms 2/10, n/30.

June 5 Received cash refund of $1,088 for merchandise returned to a supplier.

June 8 Sold merchandise to Micro Stores for $4,320. Invoice No. 619; terms 2/10, n/30.

June 11 Received $2,310 cash as partial collection of a $6,310 account receivable from Olympus Corporation. Also received a note receivable for the $4,000 remaining balance due.

June 13 Received cheque from Bravo Company in settlement of invoice dated June 4, less discount.

June 16 Sold merchandise to Books, Etc. for $4,040. Invoice No. 620; terms 2/10, n/30.

June 16 Returned $960 of merchandise to supplier, Software Co., for reduction of account payable.

June 20 Sold merchandise to Graphics, Inc., for $7,000. Invoice No. 621; terms 2/10, n/30.

June 21 Books, Etc. returned for credit $640 of merchandise purchased on June 16.

June 23 Borrowed $24,000 cash from a local bank, signing a six-month note payable.

June 25 Received $3,332 from Books, Etc., in full settlement of invoice dated June 16, less return on June 21 and 2% discount.

June 30 Collected from Graphics, Inc., amount of invoice dated June 20, less 2% discount.

June 30 Received a 60-day note receivable for $4,320 from Micro Stores in settlement of invoice dated June 8.

Instructions Record the above transactions in the appropriate journals. Use a single-column sales journal, a six-column cash receipts journal, and a two-column general journal. Foot and rule the special journals and indicate how postings would be made by placing ledger account numbers and check marks in the appropriate columns of the journals.

Problem 6B-3
Using special journals
to record cash
transactions

Lopez Plaza uses multicolumn cash receipts and cash payments journals similar to those illustrated in this chapter. The cash activities for the month of May are presented as follows.

May 1 The owner, R.J. Lopez, invested additional cash of $45,000 in the business.

May 2 Paid May rent, $3,600.

May 2 Cash sales of merchandise, $12,300.

May 4 Purchased fixtures, $10,500, making a down payment of $1,500 and issuing a note payable for the balance.

May 9 Received $2,100 cash as partial collection of $6,300 account receivable from Bee Co. Also received a note receivable for the $4,200 balance due.

May 12 Paid Dallas Co. invoice, $9,000 less 2%.

May 15 Received $3,822 cash in settlement of our invoice to Bing Company for $3,900, less 2%.

May 19 Cash purchase of merchandise, $7,200.

May 23 Paid instalment on note payable due today, $1,440, of which $702 represented interest expense.

May 25 Cash sales of merchandise, $8,045.

May 25 Paid Post Company invoice, $9,900 less 2%.

May 28 Cash purchase of merchandise, $6,450.

May 30 Received cash in settlement of Baker Company invoice, $7,800, less 2%.

May 31 Paid monthly salaries, $28,034.

Instructions   Enter the above transactions in a six-column journal for cash receipts and a six-column journal for cash payments (cheque number column is not required). Compute column totals and rule the journals. Determine the equality of debits and credits in column totals.

Problem 6B-4
Using special journals:
a comprehensive
problem

Skyline Associates began operations in October. The following ledger accounts are used in recording the company's October transactions:

Cash	2	Sales	50
Accounts receivable	6	Sales returns & allowances	52
Unexpired insurance	10	Sales discounts	54
Land	20	Purchases	60
Building	22	Purchases returns & allowances	62
Notes payable	30	Purchase discounts	64
Accounts payable	32	Transportation-in	66
Mortgage payable	38	Salaries expense	72
James Cloud, capital	40	Interest expense	83

The transactions for the month of October follow. All credit sales by Skyline Associates carry terms of 2/10, n/30. Record credit purchases at gross amount.

Oct. 1 James Cloud deposited $120,000 cash in a bank account in the name of the new business, Skyline Associates.

Oct. 3 Purchased land and building on contract, paying $90,000 cash and signing a mortgage for the remaining balance of $285,000. Estimated value of the land was $165,000.

Oct. 6 Purchased merchandise from Fast Company, $18,300. Invoice dated today; terms 2/10, n/30.

Oct. 7 Sold merchandise on credit to W.B. Allen, $9,000, invoice No. 1.

Oct. 7 Sold merchandise for cash, $2,220.

Oct. 7 Paid $810 for a one-year fire insurance policy.

Oct. 9 Paid freight charges of $615 on Fast Company purchase of Oct. 6.

Oct. 11 Sold merchandise on credit to Connors Company, $14,700, invoice No. 2.

Oct. 13 Purchased merchandise for cash, $4,260.

Oct. 15 Received payment in full from W.B. Allen; invoice No. 1, dated Oct. 7, less 2% discount.

Oct. 16 Issued credit memorandum No. 1 to Connors Company, $1,200 for goods returned today. See our sale of Oct. 11 to Connors.

Oct. 16 Paid Fast Company invoice of Oct. 6, less discount.

Oct. 18 Purchased merchandise from Hope Corporation, $11,100. Invoice dated today; terms 2/10, n/30.

Oct. 20 A portion of merchandise purchased from Hope Corporation was found to be unsatisfactory. After discussion with the vendor, a price reduction of $300 was agreed upon and debit memorandum No. 1 was issued in that amount.

Oct. 21 Received payment in full from Connors Company. Invoice No. 2, dated Oct. 11, less returns and discounts.

Oct. 25 Purchased merchandise from Fast Company, $12,600. Invoice dated today; terms 2/10, n/30.

Oct. 26 Sold merchandise for cash, $1,545.

Oct. 28 Borrowed $19,000 from the bank, issuing a note payable as evidence of indebtedness.

Oct. 28 Paid Hope Corporation invoice dated Oct. 18, less Oct. 20 adjustment of $300 and discount.

Oct. 30 Paid first instalment on mortgage, $3,300. This payment included interest of $2,070.

Oct. 30 Purchased merchandise for cash, $760.

Oct. 31 Paid monthly salaries of $16,345.

Oct. 31 Sold merchandise on credit to J. Jones, $8,250, invoice No. 3.

Instructions Enter the October transactions in the following journals:
Two-column general journal
One-column sales journal
One-column purchases journal
Six-column cash receipts journal
Six-column cash payments journal (cheque number column is not required)
Foot and rule all special journals and show how postings would be made by placing ledger account numbers and check marks in the appropriate columns of the journals.

Problem 6B-5
Using special
journals: a second
comprehensive
problem

The transactions of AutoMart during April were as follows:

Apr. 1 Sold merchandise for cash, $4,000.

Apr. 2 Purchased supplies for cash, $350.

Apr. 3 Sold merchandise to Filmore Company, $9,200, Invoice No. 428; terms 2/10, n/30.

Apr. 4 Purchased merchandise on account from Dunlop Co., $12,000. Invoice was dated today with terms of 2/10, n/30. Record invoice at gross amount.

Apr. 9 Paid the Dunlop Co., invoice dated April 4.

Apr. 10 Purchased merchandise from Burton Company, $11,700. Invoice dated April 9 with terms of 1/10, n/30.

Apr. 11 Collected from Filmore Company for invoice No. 428, dated April 3.

Apr. 12 Sold merchandise to Payless, Inc., $7,360. Invoice No. 429; terms 2/10, n/30.

Apr. 13 Paid freight charges of $740 on goods purchased from Burton Company.

Apr. 14 Sold land for $90,000, receiving cash of $20,000 and a note receivable for the balance. The land had been acquired at a cost of $75,000 for use in the business, but due to a change of plans it was no longer needed.

Apr. 16 Issued credit memorandum No. 68 in favour of Payless, Inc., upon their return of $360 of merchandise.

Apr. 17 Paid for one-year fire insurance policy, $1,400.

Apr. 18 Purchased merchandise for cash, $2,700.

Apr. 19 Paid the Burton Company invoice dated April 9.

Apr. 20 Sold merchandise on account to Peat Brothers, $7,000. Invoice No. 430. Required customer to sign a 30-day, non-interest-bearing note. (Record this sale in the Sales Journal by a charge to Accounts Receivable, then transfer from Accounts Receivable to Notes Receivable by means of an entry in the general journal.)

Apr. 20 Purchased merchandise for cash, $1,500.

Apr. 21 Sold merchandise for cash, $1,800.

Apr. 21 Received payment from Payless, Inc., for invoice No. 429. Customer made deduction for credit memorandum No. 68 issued April 16 and took 2% discount.

Apr. 25 Purchased merchandise from Amber Company, $9,500. Invoice dated April 24, with terms 2/10, n/60.

Apr. 26 Issued debit memorandum No. 42 to Amber Company in connection with merchandise returned today to Amber amounting to $300.

Apr. 29 Purchased equipment having a list price of $21,600. Paid $3,600 down and signed a promissory note for the balance of $18,000.

Apr. 30 Paid monthly salaries of $15,300 for services rendered by employees during April.

Apr. 30 Paid monthly instalment on mortgage, $2,260, of which $1,370 was interest.

The following ledger accounts are used by AutoMart.

Cash	10	C. Irwin, drawing	52
Notes receivable	14	Sales	60
Accounts receivable	16	Sales returns & allowances	62
Supplies	17	Sales discounts	64
Unexpired insurance	18	Purchases	70
Land	20	Purchase returns & allowances	72
Equipment	26	Purchase discounts	74
Accumulated depreciation:		Transportation-in	76
equipment	28	Salaries expense	80
Notes payable	30	Depreciation expense:	
Accounts payable	32	equipment	88
Mortgage payable	40	Gain on sale of land	90
C. Irwin, capital	50	Interest expense	92

Instructions   **a** Record the April transactions in the following journals:
General journal — two columns
Sales journal — one column
Purchases journal — one column
Cash receipts journal — six columns
Cash payments journal — six columns (cheque number column is not required)

b Foot and rule all special journals.

c Show how postings would be made by placing ledger account numbers and check marks in the appropriate columns of the journals.

**Problem 6B-6
Internal control
measures — emphasis
upon computer-based
systems**

The lettered paragraphs that follow describe eight possible errors or problems that might occur in a retail business. Also listed are seven internal control measures. List the letter (**a** through **h**) designating the errors or problems. Beside each letter, place the number indicating the internal control measure that should prevent this type of problem from occurring. If none of the specified internal control measures would effectively prevent the problem, place a ``0'' opposite the letter. Unless stated otherwise, assume that a computer-based accounting system is in use.

**Possible Errors or
Problems**

a A salesclerk unknowingly makes a credit sale to a customer whose account has already reached the customer's prearranged credit limit.

b While running the program to prepare the weekly payroll, a computer operator inserts data causing the machine to prepare paycheques for two fictitious employees.

c Certain merchandise proves to be so unpopular with customers that it cannot be sold except at a price well below its original cost.

d A salesclerk rings up a sale at an incorrect price.

e A salesclerk uses a point-of-sale terminal to improperly reduce the balance of a friend's account in the company's accounts receivable records.

f One of the salesclerks is quite lazy and leaves most of the work of serving customers to the other salesclerks in the department.

g A customer is never billed because through oversight the credit sale was never posted from the sales journal to the accounts receivable subsidiary ledger. (Assume that a manual accounting system is in use.)

h A shoplifter steals merchandise while the salesclerk is busy with another customer.

**Internal Control
Measures**

1 Limiting the types of transactions that can be processed from point-of-sale terminals to cash sales and credit sales.

2 All merchandise has a magnetically coded label that can be read automatically by a device attached to the electronic cash register. This code identifies to the computer the merchandise being sold.

3 Credit cards issued by the store have magnetic codes that can be read automatically by a device attached to the electronic cash register. Credit approval and posting to customer's accounts are handled by the computer.

4 Subsidiary ledger accounts are periodically reconciled to the balance of the controlling account in the general ledger.

5 The computer prepares a report with separate daily sales totals for each salesperson.

6 A limit test.

7 An item count.

0 None of the above control measures would effectively prevent this type of error from occurring.

BUSINESS DECISION CASES

Case 6-1
Designing a special
journal and explaining
its use

Leisure Clothing is a mail-order company that sells clothes to the public at discount prices. Recently Leisure Clothing initiated a new policy allowing a 10-day free trial on all clothes bought from the company. At the end of the 10-day period, the customer may either pay cash for the purchase or return the goods to Leisure Clothing. The new policy caused such a large boost in sales that, even after considering the many sales returns, the policy appeared quite profitable.

The accounting system of Leisure Clothing includes a sales journal, purchases journal, cash receipts journal, cash payments journal, and general journal. As an internal control procedure, an officer of the company reviews and initials every entry in the general journal before the amounts are posted to the ledger accounts. Since the 10-day free trial policy has been in effect, hundreds of entries recording sales returns have been entered in the general journal each week. Each of these entries has been reviewed and initialled by an officer of the company, and the amounts have been posted to Sales Returns and Allowances and to the Accounts Receivable controlling account in the general ledger, and also to the customer's account in the accounts receivable subsidiary ledger.

Since these sales return entries are so numerous, it has been suggested that a special journal be designed to handle them. This could not only save time in journalizing and posting the entries, but also eliminate the time-consuming individual review of each of these repetitious entries by an officer of the company.

Instructions

a How many amounts are entered in the general journal to describe a single sales return transaction? Are these amounts the same?

b Explain why these sales return transactions are suited to the use of a special journal. Explain in detail how many money columns the special journal should have, and what postings would have to be done either at the time of the transaction or at the end of the period.

c Assume that there were 3,000 sales returns during the month. How many postings would have to be made during the month if these transactions were entered in the general journal? How many postings would have to be made if the special journal you designed in **b** were used? (Assume a one-month accounting period.)

Case 6-2
Designing a special
journal and recording
transactions

At Valley Savings, tellers use computer terminals to record transactions with customers. All cash receipts fall into one of the three categories of transaction described below:

Transaction
code

1 Deposits into savings accounts (debit Cash, credit the liability account, Savings Deposits).

2 Deposits into chequing accounts (debit Cash, credit the liability account, Demand Deposits).

3 Loan payments collected (debit Cash; credit Notes Receivable for the portion of the payment applied to the principal amount owed, and credit Interest Revenue for any interest charges included in the payment).

To record the receipt of cash from a customer, the teller enters the following information into the computer terminal:

1 A three-digit teller identification number.

2 The transaction code (1, 2, or 3) indicating the nature of the transaction.

3 The customer's six-digit account number or loan number.

4 The dollar amount received.

Using this information, the computer records the transactions and updates all general ledger and subsidiary ledger accounts. The computer automatically records the date of each transaction. For loan payments received from customers, the computer automatically determines the portion of the payment representing interest revenue and the portion representing a reduction in notes receivables.

Instructions   **a** On a sheet of blank paper, design the special journal that might be printed by Valley Savings' computer listing the cash receipts recorded by the company's tellers. Your journal should have columns to show the date, teller identification number, a brief description of the transaction (in place of the transaction code), all dollar amounts debited or credited to various ledger accounts, the customer's account number or loan number, and all posting references to subsidiary ledger accounts.

You may use the cash receipts journal illustrated in this chapter as a model. However, you will have to make numerous changes in the number of columns and in column headings to accommodate the special needs of Valley Savings.

b Enter the following three transactions in your journal. Each transaction is dated August 19.
  (1) Teller No. 012 receives $1,800 for deposit into savings account No. 222222.
  (2) Teller No. 004 receives $720 for deposit into chequing account No. 666666.
  (3) Teller No. 007 receives $641 as a monthly payment on loan No. 999999. (The computer determines that $606 of this payment represents interest revenue and the remaining $35 reduces the note receivable from the customer.)

3

ACCOUNTING
FOR
ASSETS

The manner in which a business records and values its assets affects both the balance sheet and the income statement. By studying the accounting principles involved in asset valuation, we will learn much about the content and limitations of financial statements.

7

THE CONTROL OF CASH TRANSACTIONS

CHAPTER PREVIEW

Our chapter title suggests that internal control is especially needed to prevent fraud and theft relating to cash transactions. This is true because cash is useful to every business and to every individual. Cash is high in value, but light in weight and small in bulk—hence a fortune can be transported in a briefcase. The threat of fraud and the related theft of cash are increased by the fact that currency bears no identifying data that can prove legal ownership. In this chapter, we emphasize that adequate internal control over cash transactions requires that each day's cash receipts be deposited intact in the bank and that all payments be made by cheque. We also illustrate and explain the use of regular monthly bank reconciliations, a petty cash fund, and a voucher system as means of achieving internal control over cash transactions.

After studying this chapter you should be able to meet these Learning Objectives:

1 **Describe the balance sheet presentation of cash and explain the objectives of cash management.**

2 **State the major steps in achieving internal control over cash transactions.**

3 **Prepare a bank reconciliation and explain its purpose.**

4 **Describe the operation of a petty cash fund.**

5 **Explain how a voucher system can be used to establish strong internal control over cash payments.**

Accountants define cash as money on deposit in banks and any items that banks will accept for immediate deposit. These items include not only coins and paper money, but also cheques and money orders. On the other hand, notes receivable, IOUs, and postdated cheques are not accepted for immediate deposit and are not included in our definition of cash.

Reporting cash in the balance sheet

1   Describe the balance sheet presentation of cash and explain the objectives of cash management.

In the balance sheet, cash is listed first among the current assets, because it is the most current and liquid of all assets. The banker, credit manager, or investor who studies a balance sheet critically is always interested in the total amount of cash as compared with other balance sheet items, such as accounts payable. These outside users of a company's financial statements are not interested, however, in such details as the number of separate bank accounts, or in the distinction between cash on hand and cash in banks. A business that carries chequing accounts with several banks will maintain a separate ledger account for each bank account. On the balance sheet, however, the entire amount of cash on hand and cash on deposit with the several banks will be shown as a single amount. One objective in preparing financial statements is to keep them short, concise, and easy to read.

Some bank accounts are restricted as to their use, so that they are not available for making payments to meet normal operating needs of the business. An example (discussed in Chapter 16) is a bond sinking fund, consisting of cash being accumulated by a corporation for the specific purpose of paying off bonded indebtedness at a future date and not available for any other use. A bank account located in a foreign country may also be restricted if monetary regulations prevent the transfer of funds between the two countries. Restricted bank accounts are not regarded as current assets because they are not available for use in paying current liabilities.

Management responsibilities relating to cash

Efficient management of cash includes policies that will

1   Provide accurate accounting for cash receipts, cash payments, and cash balance
2   Prevent losses from fraud or theft
3   Maintain a sufficient amount of cash at all times to make necessary payments plus a reasonable balance for emergencies
4   Prevent unnecessarily large amounts of cash from being held idle in bank accounts that produce little or no revenue

Internal control over cash is sometimes regarded merely as a means of preventing fraud or theft. A good system of internal control, however, will also aid in achieving management's other objectives of accurate accounting for cash transactions and the maintenance of adequate but not excessive cash balances.

Basic requirements for internal control over cash

2   State the major steps in achieving internal control over cash transactions.

Cash is more susceptible to theft than any other asset. Furthermore, a large portion of the total transactions of a business involve the receipt or payment of cash. For both these reasons, internal control over cash is of great importance to management and also to the employees of a business. If a cash shortage arises in a small business in which internal controls are weak or nonexistent, every employee is under suspicion. Perhaps no one employee can be proved guilty of the theft, but neither can any employee prove his or her innocence.

On the other hand, if internal controls over cash are adequate, theft without detection is virtually impossible except through the collusion of two or more employees. To achieve internal control over cash or any other group of assets requires first of all that *the custody of assets be clearly separated from the recording of transactions.* Secondly, the recording function should be subdivided among employees, so that the work of one person is verified by that of another. This *subdivision of duties* ensures the accurate accounting for cash; it also discourages fraud, because collusion among employees would be necessary to conceal it. Internal control is more easily achieved in large companies than in small companies, because extensive subdivision of duties is more feasible in the larger business.

The major steps in establishing internal controls over cash include the following:

1 Separate the function of handling cash from the maintenance of accounting records. Employees who handle cash should not have access to the accounting records, and accounting personnel should not have access to cash.
2 Prepare a control listing of cash receipts at the time and place the money is received. For cash sales, this listing may be a cash register tape, created by ringing up each sale on a cash register. For cheques received through the mail, a control listing of incoming cheques should be prepared by the employee assigned to open the mail.
3 Require that all cash receipts be deposited intact daily in the bank.
4 Make all payments by cheque. The only exception should be for small payments to be made in cash from a petty cash fund. Payments should never be made out of cash receipts. Cheques should never be drawn payable to Cash. A cheque drawn to a named payee requires endorsement by the payee on the back of the cheque before it can be cashed or deposited. This endorsement provides permanent evidence identifying the person who received the funds. On the other hand, a cheque payable to Cash can be deposited or cashed by anyone.
5 Require that the validity and amount of every expenditure be verified before a cheque is issued in payment.
6 Separate the function of approving expenditures from the function of signing cheques.

The application of these principles in building an adequate system of internal control over cash can best be illustrated by considering separately the topics of cash receipts and cash payments. A company may supplement its system of internal control by obtaining a fidelity bond from an insurance company. Under a fidelity bond, the insurance company agrees to reimburse an employer for *proven* losses resulting from fraud or embezzlement by bonded employees.

Cash receipts

Cash receipts consist of two major types: cash received over the counter at the time of a sale and cash (mostly cheques) received through the mail as collections on accounts receivable.

Use of cash registers   Cash received over the counter at the time of a sale should be rung up on a cash register, *so located that the customer will see the amount recorded.* Since the customer presumably will not pay more than the amount shown on the register, the use of cash registers provides assurance that an immediate record is made of all cash sales. Most businesses require that salesclerks ring up a sale before wrapping the merchandise. The cash register should have a locked-in tape on which it prints the amount of each sale and the total sales for the day. In many large stores, every cash register (point-of-sale terminal) is linked directly to a computer and each cash sales transaction immediately becomes part of the accounting records.

We have stressed that good internal control requires that the custody of cash be separated from the recording of cash transactions. This separation of cash handling from record keeping is evident in proper use of cash registers. The salesclerk who rings up the sale has access to the money in the cash register but not to the locked-in tape with the record of sales transactions. When the salesclerk ends a workday, he or she will count the cash in the register and turn it in to the cashier's office. Both the salesclerk and the cashier have access to cash; therefore, neither of them should have access to the locked-in tape in the cash register. A representative of the accounting department will remove the tape from the cash register, compare the total amount shown on the tape with the amount turned in to the cashier, and make an entry in the cash receipts journal to record cash sales.

Through this subdivision of duties, we have achieved the goal of safeguarding cash receipts by separating cash handling from the making of entries in the accounting records. The salesclerk and the cashier cannot abstract cash without detection because they do not have access to the cash register tape on which the total cash receipts are shown. The accounting department representative who removes the cash register tape and makes the accounting entry does not have access to cash. To repeat: internal control to safeguard cash requires that the custody of cash be clearly separated from the function of maintaining an accounting record of cash.

Many large supermarkets have achieved faster checkout lines and stronger internal control by using electronic scanning equipment to read and record the price of all groceries passing the checkout counters. (The electronic scanning equipment or point-of-sale terminal replaces the traditional cash register.) All 12,000 or so grocery items on the shelves bear a product code, consisting of a pattern of thick and thin vertical bars. At the checkout counter, the code on each item is read by a scanning laser. The code is sent instantaneously to a computer that locates the price and description of the item and flashes that information on a display panel in view of the customer and the checkout clerk. After all of the items have been passed through the scanner, the display panel shows the total amount of the sale. The clerk then enters the amount of cash received from the customer, and the display panel shows the amount of change that the customer should receive.

This system has many advantages. Not only is an immediate record made of all cash receipts, but the risk of errors in pricing merchandise or in making change is greatly reduced. This system also improves inventory control by giving management continuous information on what is being sold moment by moment, classified by product and by manufacturer. Comparison of these sales records with records of purchases will direct attention to any losses from theft or shoplifting.

Use of prenumbered sales tickets   Another means of establishing internal control over cash sales is by writing out a prenumbered sales ticket in duplicate at the time of each sale. The original is given to the customer and the carbon copy is retained. Prenumbered sales tickets are often used in businesses such as restaurants in which one central cashier rings up the sales made by all salespeople.

At the end of the day, an employee computes the total sales figure from these sales tickets and also makes sure that no tickets are missing from the series. This total sales figure is then compared with the cash register tape total and the total cash receipts.

Cash received through the mail   The procedures for handling cheques and currency received through the mail are also based on the internal control principle that two or more employees should participate in every transaction.

The first step is for the mailroom clerk to prepare daily a list of all amounts received. This list should be prepared in triplicate and should show the name of each sender, the amount, and the reason for the payment. One copy of this daily list is sent with the money to the cashier. A second copy is sent to the accounting department and the third copy is retained by the mailroom clerk. The cashier deposits at the bank the total money received and the accounting department employee enters the amount received in the accounting records. At month-end, the bank account will be reconciled by a fourth employee whose duties do not permit access to cash. (Reconciling the bank account is explained later in this chapter.)

With this subdivision of duties, the concealment of errors or fraud in handling cash receipts is impossible without collusion among employees. The mailroom clerk must list all cash received or customers will challenge the balance in their monthly statements. The cashier must deposit all money received or the bank balance will not reconcile with the cash balance shown by the accounting records. The employee in the accounting department does not have access to cash, nor does the person who prepares the bank reconciliation. These procedures create strong internal control by providing for participation of two or more employees in each cash receipt transaction. These procedures also strengthen internal control by providing for immediate recording of every cash receipt, by separating the function of cash handling from that of maintaining acounting records, and by causing the work of one employee to serve as proof of the accuracy of the work of others. The plan we have described is typical, but its precise form will vary from one company to the next, depending upon such factors as the number of employees, volume of transactions, and extent of automation.

Cash over and short   In handling over-the-counter cash receipts, a few errors in making change will inevitably occur. These errors will cause a cash shortage or overage at the end of the day, when the cash is counted and compared with the reading on the cash register.

For example, assume that the total cash sales for the day amount to $500 as recorded by the cash register, but that the cash in the drawer when counted amounts to only $490. The following entry would be made to record the day's sales and the cash shortage of $10.

Cash	490	
Cash Over and Short	10	
Sales		500

The account entitled Cash Over and Short is debited with shortages and credited with overages. If the cash shortages during an entire accounting period are in excess of the cash overages, the Cash Over and Short accounts will have a debit balance and will be shown as miscellaneous *expense* in the income statement. On the other hand, if the overages exceed the shortages, the Cash Over and Short account will show a credit balance at the end of the period and should be treated as an item of miscellaneous *revenue.*

Subdivision of duties   Employees who handle cash receipts should *not have access to the accounting records.* This combination of duties might enable the employee to alter the accounting records and thereby conceal a cash shortage. For example, assume that an employee who serves as both the cashier and bookkeeper of a small business removes $200 from the day's cash sales receipts. The employee could conceal this theft by simply recording the day's cash sales at $200 less than the actual amount. Thus, the balance of the Cash account will not exceed the amount of cash on hand after the theft.

Employees who handle cash receipts also should *not have authority to issue credit memoranda for sales returns.* This combination of duties might enable the employee to conceal cash shortages by issuing fictitious credit memoranda. Assume, for example, that an employee with these responsibilities collects $100 cash from a customer as payment of the customer's account. The employee mght remove this cash and issue a $100 credit memorandum, indicating that the customer had returned the merchandise instead of paying off the account. The credit memoranda would cause the customer's account to be credited. However, the offsetting debit would be to the Sales Returns and Allowances account, not to the Cash account. Thus, the books would remain in balance, the customer would receive credit for the abstracted payment, and there would be no record of cash having been received.

Cash payments

To maintain an adequate system of internal control, it is essential that each day's cash receipts be deposited intact in the bank, and that *all cash payments be made by cheque.* Many of the largest and most spectacular fraud cases have been carried out through payment of fictitious invoices. Consequently, strong control over cash payments or disbursements is just as important, perhaps even more important, than internal control over cash receipts. Cheques should be prenumbered by the printer and issued in numerical sequence. Any spoiled cheques should be marked "VOID" and filed in sequence in the paid cheque file. Thus, every cheque number in the series can be accounted for, and every cash payment to a supplier or other creditor can be traced to a paid cheque.

The approval of invoices for payment is a function to be clearly separated from the issuance of cheques to make such payment. Every transaction requiring a cash disbursement should be verified and approved before payment is made. The official designated to **sign cheques** should not be given authority to **approve invoices** for payment or to make entries in the accounting records. Each cheque presented to a company official for signature should be accompanied by an approved invoice and supporting documents showing that the transaction has been fully verified and that payment is justified. When the cheque is signed, the invoice and supporting documents should be perforated or stamped ''Paid'' to eliminate any possibility of their being presented later in support of another cheque. If these rules are followed, it is almost impossible for a fraudulent cash disbursement to be concealed without the collusion of two or more persons.

In large companies which issue hundreds or thousands of cheques daily, it is not practical for a company official to sign each cheque manually. Instead, cheque-signing machines with various built-in control devices are used. This automation of the cheque-signing function does not weaken the system of internal control if attention is given to proper use of the machine and to control of the cheques both before and after they pass through the cheque-signing machine.

 A large construction company issued a great many cheques every day but paid little attention to internal controls over its cash payments. Stacks of unissued cheques were kept in an unlocked supply closet along with Styrofoam coffee cups. Because the number of cheques issued was too great for the treasurer to sign them manually, a cheque-signing machine was used. This machine, after signing the cheques, ejected them into a box equipped with a lock. In spite of warnings from the company's CA firm, company officials found that it was "too inconvenient" to keep the box locked. The company also failed to make any use of the cheque-counting device built into the cheque-signing machine. Although the company maintained very large amounts on deposit in chequing accounts, it did not bother to reconcile bank statements for weeks or months at a time.

These weaknesses in internal control led to a crisis when an employee was given a three-week-old bank statement and a bundle of paid cheques and told to prepare a bank reconciliation. The employee found that the bundle of paid cheques accompanying the bank statement was incomplete. No paid cheques were on hand to support over $700,000 of charges deducted on the bank statement. Further investigation revealed that over $1 million in unauthorized and unrecorded cheques had been paid from the corporation's bank accounts. These cheques had been issued out of serial number sequence and had been run through the company cheque-signing machine. It was never determined who had carried out the theft and the money was not recovered.

BANK CHEQUING (CURRENT) ACCOUNTS

Opening a bank account

Prepare a bank reconciliation and explain its purpose.

Virtually every business has one or more bank chequing (current) accounts, which are opened and maintained in much the same way as a personal chequing account. To open a personal chequing account, you deposit money at a bank and provide the bank with identification data, such as a social insurance number and a driver's licence.

For either a personal or a business chequing account, the bank requires the new depositer to sign a signature card, with his or her name signed exactly as it will be written in signing cheques. If two persons are to be authorized to sign cheques on the account, each must sign the signature card. The signature card is kept on file by the bank, so that any cheque bearing a signature not familiar to bank employees may be compared with the depositor's signature card. When a corporation opens a bank account, the board of directors will pass a resolution designating the officers or employees authorized to sign cheques. A copy of the resolution is given to the bank.

Bank Deposit Ticket

Parkview Company
109 Parkview Road
Toronto, Ontario M5K 1B9

2 90080 44480 2 38484

15 × 1	15	00
10 × 2	20	00
3 × 5	15	00
2 × 10	20	00
2 × 20	40	00
× 50		
× 100		
COIN	2	00
SUB-TOTAL TELLER	112	00
VISA		
U.S. CHEQUES		
TOTAL CHEQUES (BROUGHT FORWARD)	911	77
SUB-TOTAL ▶		
U.S. EXCHANGE (PLUS/MINUS)		
GRAND TOTAL ▶	1,023	77

CURRENT ACCOUNT DEPOSIT

Front side of deposit ticket

NATIONAL BANK
260 Bland Street
Toronto, Ontario M4W 1G5

Date _July 12_ , 19 _8X_

PARTICULARS	AMOUNT	
	36	47
	12	02
	155	15
	100	00
	41	25
	15	00
	90	00
	10	47
	8	25
	37	69
	84	50
	98	00
	68	47
	50	00
	104	50
TOTAL CHEQUES (CARRY FORWARD)	911	77

CURRENT ACCOUNT DEPOSIT

Reverse side of deposit ticket

The bank provides the depositor with a book of cheques and deposit tickets (slips), each cheque imprinted with the depositor's name, address, and telephone number if desired. An identification number assigned by the bank to this new chequing account is also printed on each cheque and each deposit ticket in magnetic ink so that transactions can be processed by computer. The cost of printing cheques is charged to the depositor. Cheques printed for a bank customer are serially numbered by the printer, an important internal control measure in accounting for all cheques used.

Making deposits

The depositor fills out a *deposit ticket* (usually in duplicate) for each deposit. The deposit ticket on page 304 illustrates a listing of each cheque deposited. Space is also provided for listing the amounts of coin and currency deposited. A bank teller stamps or signs the duplicate deposit ticket and returns it to the depositor. By keeping a file of duplicate deposit tickets, the depositor has *documentary evidence* of the amount of money turned over to the bank. From the viewpoint of maintaining strong internal control over cash receipts, such evidence is most important. Comparison of the duplicate deposit tickets with the cash receipts journal provides proof that the cashier or other employee has complied with company policy by making daily deposits of all cash received.

Writing cheques

A cheque is a written order signed by the depositor instructing the bank to pay a specified amount of money to a designated person or organization, as shown below.

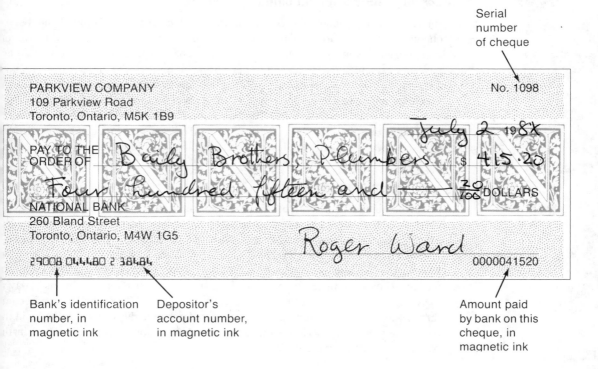

Serial number of cheque

PARKVIEW COMPANY
109 Parkview Road
Toronto, Ontario, M5K 1B9

No. 1098

PAY TO THE ORDER OF   Baily Brothers, Plumbers $ 415.20

July 2 198X

Four hundred fifteen and 20/100 DOLLARS

NATIONAL BANK
260 Bland Street
Toronto, Ontario, M4W 1G5

Roger Ward

⑄9008 044480 2 38484   0000041520

Bank's identification number, in magnetic ink

Depositor's account number, in magnetic ink

Amount paid by bank on this cheque, in magnetic ink

The three parties to a cheque are (1) the *maker* (or drawer) who signs the cheque; (2) the *bank* on which the cheque is written; and (3) the *payee,* the person to whom the cheque is payable.

The manager of a business needs to know on a daily basis the amount in the bank chequing account. In a small business, this running balance may be maintained on the cheque book stubs. The depositor should record on the cheque book stubs the amount of each cheque written and the amount of each deposit. The balance of cash on deposit is entered after each transaction. At the end of the month after the Cash account in the ledger has been posted with the monthly totals from the cash receipts journal and the cash payments journal, the balance of the ledger account, Cash, should agree with the month-end balance shown on the cheque book stubs.

Stop payment orders　Like other documents, cheques are sometimes lost or stolen. The maker of a lost or stolen cheque should immediately issue a *stop payment order* to the bank, identifying the missing cheque by serial number and amount. Since a cheque itself is an order by the depositor instructing the bank to make a certain payment, a stop payment order is merely a reversal of the original order. After issuing a stop payment order for a missing cheque, the maker can cancel the original cheque in the record of cash payments and issue a replacement cheque.

If the bank should by accident pay a cheque after a stop payment has been filed by the depositor, this improper payment could not be deducted from the depositor's account. The bank would have to recover from the person who cashed the cheque or bear the loss itself.

Earning interest on chequing accounts

Interest-bearing chequing accounts permitting the writing of a small number of cheques per month are available to individuals and also to corporations. However, most businesses must write a large number of cheques, and banks generally do not pay interest on business accounts permitting unlimited cheque writing. To take advantage of the interest revenue opportunities now available, many business concerns maintain one or more regular accounts for daily use along with an interest-bearing account in which surplus funds are deposited. Transfers between the two accounts are made as required to ensure interest is earned on funds not immediately needed for operating purposes. Any interest earned on a bank account will be listed on the bank statement at month-end.

The bank statement

Each month the bank will provide the depositer with a statement of his or her account, accompanied by the cheques paid and charged to the account during the month. The following bank statement shows the balance on deposit at the beginning of the month, the deposits, the cheques paid, any other debits and credits during the month, and the new balance at the end of the month. (To keep the illustration short we have shown a limited number of deposits rather than one for each business day in the month. It may be assumed that all cash received by Parkview Company came through the mail and that no cash was received on some days.) Certain items in the bank statement of Parkview Company need explanation and are discussed in the paragraphs following the illustration.

NATIONAL BANK
260 Bland Street Toronto, Ontario M4W 1G5

238484

IN ACCOUNT WITH	Parkview Company
	109 Parkview Road
	Toronto, Ontario M5K 1B9

UNDER YOUR AGREEMENT WITH THE BANK, THIS STATEMENT WILL BE CONSIDERED CORRECT EXCEPT AS TO ERRORS OR OMISSIONS OF WHICH YOU NOTIFY THE BANK WITHIN 10 DAYS AFTER IT IS DELIVERED OR MAILED TO YOU

PLEASE NOTIFY THE BANK OF ANY CHANGE OF ADDRESS.

CHEQUES AND DEBITS			CREDITS AND DEPOSITS	DATE	BALANCE
		BALANCE BROUGHT FORWARD ▶		June 30, 198X	5,029.30
			300.00	7-2	5,329.30
1,100.00			1,250.00	7-2	5,479.30
415.20	10.00			7-3	5,054.10
1,025.00	90.00	36.50	1,185.10	7-5	5,087.70
			60.00	7-7	5,147.70
96.00	400.00			7-10	4,651.70
1,376.57			1,023.77	7-12	4,298.90
425.00				7-15	3,873.90
2,095.75			2,200.00	7-18	3,978.15
85.00			101.19	7-21	3,994.34
1,150.27			1,083.25	7-24	3,927.32
50.25DM			500.00CM	7-30	4,377.07
12.00SC			635.10	7-31	5,000.17

NO. OF DEBIT	TOTAL AMOUNT — DEBITS	NO. OF CREDITS	TOTAL AMOUNT — CREDITS
15	8,367.54	10	8,338.41

EXPLANATION OF CHARACTERS

CC CERTIFIED CHEQUE	D DISCOUNT	EX EXCHANGE	OD OVERDRAFT
CL COLLECTION	DM DEBIT MEMO	IN INTEREST	RI RETURNED ITEM
CM CREDIT MEMO	EC ERROR CORRECTED	LT TOTAL SEVERAL CHEQUES	SC SERVICE CHARGE

NSF cheques   Bank deposits made by a business include cheques received from customers. Occasionally a customer's cheque may "bounce"; that is, the bank on which the cheque is drawn may refuse payment. The most common cause for such refusal is that the customer's bank balance is less than the amount of the cheque. For example, on July 24 Parkview Company received a cheque for $50.25 from J.B. Ball, and the cheque was included in the bank deposit made on that day. The

Ball cheque was returned to National Bank by the bank on which it was drawn marked NSF (Not Sufficient Funds), indicating that Ball did not have a sufficient balance on deposit to cover the cheque. National Bank therefore charged the NSF cheque against Parview Company's account as shown by the July 30 debit of $50.25. (The symbol DM alongside this entry stands for Debit Memorandum.)

After getting the NSF cheque back from the bank, Parkview Company should remove this cheque from the cash classification by a journal entry debiting an account receivable from J.B. Ball and crediting Cash. The NSF cheque is thus regarded as a receivable until it is collected directly from the maker and redeposited or is determined to be worthless.

Bank service charges   Under the date of July 31 on the illustrated bank statement is a debit for $12, accompanied by the symbol SC. This symbol means Service Charge, a charge made by the bank to cover the expense of handling the account. The amount of the service charge is generally based upon such considerations as the average balance of the account and the number of cheques and deposits. Banks do not usually impose a service charge on large chequing accounts. However, a service charge is shown here for the purpose of illustrating its use. When the bank sends the monthly statement and paid cheques to the depositor, it will include debit memoranda for service charges and any other charges not represented by cheques.

Miscellaneous charges and credit   Other charges that may appear on the bank statement include rental fees for safe deposit boxes, charges for printing cheques, collection charges on notes left with the bank for collection, and interest charges on borrowings from the bank. Miscellaneous credits may include interest earned, collections on notes receivable, and corrections of errors.

Reconciling the bank account

The purpose of reconciling the bank account is to assure that the bank and the depositor are in agreement on the amount of money on deposit. Remember that both the bank and the depositor are maintaining independent records of the deposits, the cheques, and the running balance of the bank account. Once a month the accountant prepares a *bank reconciliation* to verify that these two independent sets of records are in agreement.

The balance shown on the monthly statement received from the bank will usually not agree with the balance of cash shown by the depositor's accounting records. Certain transactions recorded by the depositor will not yet have been recorded by the bank. The most common examples are

1 Outstanding cheques. These are cheques written by the depositor and deducted from the Cash account on the depositor's records. Such cheques have been mailed or delivered to the payees but not yet presented to the bank for payment.
2 Deposits in transit. Deposits mailed to the bank are usually not received by the bank and not entered on the bank's records until a day or two later than the entry on the depositor's accounting records. Also, deposits made at the bank after a certain time (e.g., 4 p.m.) will not be recorded by the bank until the next day.

Transactions that may appear on the bank statement but that have not yet been recorded by the depositor include:

1 Service charges
2 Charges for NSF cheques
3 Credits for interest earned
4 Miscellaneous bank charges and credits

In some cases the bank reconciliation will be complete after such items as outstanding cheques, deposits in transit, and miscellaneous bank charges and credits have been taken into account. Other cases may require the correction of errors by the bank or errors by the depositor to complete the reconciliation. When a company maintains accounts in several banks, one possible type of error is to record a cheque drawn on one bank as a payment from another bank account. Similar errors may occur in recording deposits.

Specific steps in preparing a bank reconciliation

Preparing a bank reconciliation means determining those items that make up the difference between the balance appearing on the bank statement and the balance of cash according to the depositor's records. By listing and studying these discrepancies, it is possible to determine the correct figure for cash owned. This is the amount that should appear on the balance sheet. Specific steps to be taken in preparing a bank reconciliation are as follows:

1 Compare the deposits listed on the bank statement with the deposits shown in the company's records. Place check marks in the company's cash records and on the bank statement beside the items that agree. Any unchecked item in the company's records of deposits will be deposits not yet recorded by the bank, and should be added to the balance reported by the bank. Determine that any deposits in transit listed in last month's reconciliation are included as deposits in the current month's bank statement.

2 Arrange the paid cheques in sequence by serial numbers and compare each cheque with the corresponding entry in the cash payments journal. (In the case of personal bank accounts for which the only record maintained is the cheque book, compare each paid cheque with the cheque stub.) Place a check mark in the depositor's cash payments journal opposite each entry for which a paid cheque has been returned by the bank. The unchecked entries should be listed in the bank reconciliation as *outstanding cheques to be deducted from the balance reported by the bank.* Determine whether the cheques listed as outstanding in the bank reconciliation for the preceding month have been returned by the bank this month. If not, such cheques should be listed as outstanding in the current reconciliation.

3 Deduct from the balance per the depositor's records any debit memoranda issued by the bank that have not been recorded by the depositor. In the illustrated bank reconciliation on page 311, examples are the NSF cheque for $50.25 and the $12 service charge.

4 Add to the balance per the depositor's records any credit memoranda issued by the bank that have not been recorded by the depositor. An example in the illustrated

bank reconciliation is the credit of $500 collected by the bank in behalf of Parkview Company. Any interest credited to the account by the bank must be added to the balance per the depositor's records.

5 Determine that the *adjusted* balance of the depositor's records is equal to the *adjusted* balance of the bank statement, as in the illustration on page 311.

6 Prepare journal entries for any items on the bank statement that have not yet been recorded in the depositor's accounts.

Illustration of bank reconciliation   The July bank statement prepared by the bank for Parkview Company was illustrated on page 307. This statement shows a balance of cash on deposit at July 31 of $5,000.17. We shall assume that Parkview Company's records at July 31 show a bank balance of $4,182.57. Our purpose in preparing the bank reconciliation is to identify the items that make up the difference of $817.60 and to determine the correct cash balance.

Assume that the specific steps to be taken in preparing a bank reconciliation have been carried out and that the following reconciling items have been discovered:

1 A deposit of $310.90 mailed to the bank on July 31 does not appear on the bank statement.

2 A credit memorandum issued by the bank on July 30 in the amount of $500 was returned with the July bank statement and appears in the Deposits column of that statement. This credit represents the proceeds of a note receivable left with the bank by Parkview Company for the purpose of collection. The collection of the note has not yet been recorded by Parkview Company.

3 Four cheques issued in July or prior months have not yet been paid by the bank. These are as follows:

CHEQUE NO.	DATE	AMOUNT
801	June 15	$100.00
888	July 24	10.25
890	July 27	402.50
891	July 30	205.00

4 A debit memorandum issued by the bank on July 31 for a $12 service charge was enclosed with the July bank statement.

5 Cheque No. 875 was issued July 20 in the amount of $85 but was erroneously listed on the cheque stub and in the cash payments journal as $58. The cheque, in payment of telephone service, was paid by the bank, returned with the July bank statement, and correctly listed on the bank statement as an $85 charge to the account. The Cash account is overstated because of this $27 error ($85 − $58)

6 No entry has as yet been made in Parkview Company's accounts to reflect the bank's action on July 30 of charging against the account the NSF cheque for $50.25 drawn by J.B. Ball.

The July 31 bank reconciliation for Parkview Company is shown on page 311. The adjusted balance of $4,593.32 is the amount of cash owned by Parkview Company and is, therefore, the amount that should appear as cash in the July 31 balance sheet.

PARKVIEW COMPANY
Bank Reconciliation
July 31, 19___

Balance per depositor's records, July 31, 19___		$4,182.57
Add: Note receivable collected for us by bank		500.00
		$4,682.57
Deduct: Service charge	$ 12.00	
NSF cheque of J.B. Ball	50.25	
Error on cheque No. 875	27.00	89.25
Adjusted balance		$4,593.32

Balance per bank statement, July 31, 19___		$5,000.17
Add: Deposit of July 31 not recorded by bank		310.90
		$5,311.07
Deduct: Outstanding cheques:		
No. 801	$100.00	
No. 888	10.25	
No. 890	402.50	
No. 891	205.00	717.75
Adjusted balance (as above)		$4,593.32

Note that the adjusted balance of cash differs from both the bank statement and the depositor's records. This difference exists because neither set of records is up-to-date as of July 31, and also because of the existence of an error in Parkview's records.

Adjusting the records after the reconciliation   To make Parkview Company's records up-to-date and accurate, four journal entries affecting the Cash account are necessary for the four items that make up the difference between the $4,182.57 balance per the depositor's records and the adjusted balance of $4,593.32. These four reconciling items call for the following entries:

Cash	500.00	
Notes Receivable		500.00
To record the collection of a note receivable for us by the bank.		

Miscellaneous Expense	12.00	
Cash		12.00
To record the service charge by the bank.		

Accounts Receivable, J.B. Ball	50.25	
Cash		50.25
To record as a receivable from J.B. Ball the amount of the NSF cheque returned to us by the bank.		

Telephone Expense	27.00	
Cash		27.00
To correct the error by which cheque No. 875 for an $85 payment for telephone service was recorded as $58 ($85 − $58 = $27).		

Instead of making four separate journal entries affecting the Cash account, one compound journal entry can be made to record all four of the above items.

Treatment of old outstanding cheques

Some cheques may remain outstanding for several months; in fact, a few may never be presented for payment. Internal control is weakened if cheques are allowed to remain outstanding indefinitely. The list of outstanding cheques should be reviewed regularly and stop payment orders should be issued for cheques outstanding for more than a reasonable period of time (three months is often the limit for this purpose). Otherwise, old outstanding cheques could be omitted to cover up an understatement of cash in a bank account. Also, it is quite inefficient to list these old cheques in a bank reconciliation each month over a long period of time.

Petty Cash

4 Describe the operation of a petty cash fund.

As previously emphasized, adequate internal control over cash requires that all cash received be deposited in the bank and all disbursements be made by cheque. However, every business finds it convenient to have a small amount of cash on hand with which to make some minor expenditures. Examples include postage due, taxi fares, and small emergency purchases of office supplies. Internal control over these small cash payments can best be achieved through a petty cash fund. To issue cheques for such items would be inconvenient, time-consuming, and expensive in relation to the amounts involved.

Establishing the petty cash fund   To create a petty cash fund, a cheque is written payable to Petty Cash for a round amount such as $100 or $200, which will cover the small expenditures to be paid in cash for a period of two or three weeks. This cheque is cashed and the money kept on hand in a petty cash box or drawer in the office.

The entry for the issuance of the cheque is:

CREATING THE PETTY
CASH FUND

| Petty Cash . . . . | 200 | |
| Cash . . . . | | 200 |

To establish a petty cash fund.

Making disbursements from the petty cash fund   As cash payments are made out of the petty cash box, the custodian of the fund is required to fill out a *petty cash receipt* or *voucher* for each expenditure. A petty cash receipt shows the date, the amount paid, the purpose of the expenditure, and the signature of the person receiving the money, as shown on page 313. A petty cash receipt should be prepared for every payment made from the fund. The petty cash box should, therefore, always contain cash and/or receipts totalling the exact amount of the fund.

The petty cash custodian should be informed that occasional surprise counts of the fund will be made and that he or she is personally responsible for the fund being intact at all times. Careless handling of petty cash has often been a first step toward large thefts; consequently, misuse of petty cash funds should not be tolerated.

Replenishing the petty cash fund   Assume that a petty cash fund of $200 was established on June 1 and that payments totalling $174.95 were made from the fund during the next two weeks. Since the $200 originally placed in the fund is nearly exhausted, the fund should be replenished. To replenish a petty cash fund means to

PETTY CASH RECEIPT		
No. __299__		Date __Nov. 6, 19__
For __Postage__		
Charge to __Postage Expense__		Amount
		4 | 13
Received by		Approved by
J. R. West		*K. H.*

replace the amount of money that has been spent, thus restoring the fund to its original amount. A cheque is drawn payable to Petty Cash for the exact amount of the expenditures, $174.95. This cheque is cashed and the money placed in the petty cash box. The petty cash receipts (vouchers) totalling that amount are perforated to prevent their reuse and filed in support of the replenishment cheque. The journal entry to record the issuance of the cheque will debit the expense accounts indicated by inspection of the vouchers, as follows:

REPLENISHMENT OF
PETTY CASH FUND

Office Supplies Expense	80.60	
Transportation-in	16.00	
Postage Expense	45.25	
Miscellaneous Expense	33.10	
Cash		174.95

To replenish the petty cash fund.

Note that *expense accounts* are debited each time the fund is replenished. The Petty Cash account is debited only when the fund is first established. There ordinarily will be no further entries in the Petty Cash account after the fund is established, unless the fund is discontinued or a decision is made to change its size from the original $200 amount.

The petty cash fund is usually replenished at the end of an accounting period, even though the fund is not running low, so that all vouchers in the fund are charged to expense accounts before these accounts are closed and financial statements prepared.

The voucher system

5   Explain how a voucher system can be used to establish strong internal control over cash payments.

One widely used method of establishing control over cash payments is the voucher system. The basic idea of this system is that every transaction that will result in a cash payment must be verified, approved in writing, and recorded before a cheque is issued. A written authorization called a *voucher* is prepared for every transaction that will require a cash payment, regardless of whether the transaction is for payment of an expense, purchase of merchandise or a plant asset, or for payment of a liability. Vouchers are serially numbered so that the loss or misplacement of a voucher would immediately be apparent.

To demonstrate the internal control inherent in a voucher system, consider the way a voucher is used in verifying an invoice received from a supplier. A serially numbered voucher is attached to each incoming invoice. The voucher (as illustrated on page 315) has spaces for listing the data from the invoice and showing the ledger accounts to be debited and credited in recording the transaction. Space is also provided for approval signatures for each step in the verification and approval process. A completed voucher provides a description of the transaction and also of the work performed in verifying the liability and approving the cash disbursement.

One purpose in preparing a voucher is to assure that the supplier's invoice is in agreement with our purchase order and our receiving report. The voucher provides an answer to such important questions as:

1 Are the goods and services charged to us on the supplier's invoice in accordance with our previously issued purchase order?
2 Have we received in good condition the quantities shown on the invoice?
3 Are all prices, computations, discounts, and credit terms on the invoice accurate?

If the answer to these questions is Yes, the invoice should be paid. The voucher provides written evidence that we ordered and received the goods or services we are being asked to pay for.

The Vouchers Payable account   When a voucher system is installed, a ledger account called Vouchers Payable replaces the Accounts Payable controlling account which we have used previously. Every voucher is credited to the Vouchers Payable account. For example, a voucher describing the purchase of merchandise will consist of a debit to Purchases and credit to Vouchers Payable. A voucher covering the acquisition of a plant asset will debit a plant asset account such as Office Equipment and credit Vouchers Payable. When an expense such as salaries, rent, or advertising is incurred, the voucher recording the expense will debit the appropriate expense account and credit Vouchers Payable. In the preparation of a balance sheet, however, most companies prefer to show the liability for Vouchers Payable under the more widely understood title of Accounts Payable.

Preparing a voucher   Strong control over payment of invoices from suppliers is one of the advantages of a voucher system. A voucher is prepared by filling in the appropriate blanks with information taken from the invoice, such as the invoice date, invoice number, amount, and the creditor's name and address. The voucher with the seller's invoice attached is then sent to the employees responsible for verifying the extensions and footings on the invoice and for comparing prices, quantities, and terms with those specified in the purchase order and receiving report. When completion of the verification process has been evidenced by approval signatures of the persons performing these steps, the voucher and supporting documents are sent to an employee of the accounting department, who indicates on the voucher the accounts to be debited and credited.

The voucher is now reviewed by an accounting supervisor to provide assurance that the verification procedures have been satisfactorily completed and that the liability is a proper one. In a company using a manual accounting system, the approved voucher will then be entered in a journal called a *voucher register*.

Illustration of a Voucher — Front and Back

Use of voucher ensures verification of invoice

BROADHILL CORPORATION
Regina, Saskatchewan

Voucher no. _241_ ←———— Serial number

Pay to _Black Company_
3160 Main Street
Halifax, Nova Scotia

Date _May 1, 19—_
Date due _May 10, 19—_

Date of invoice _April 30, 19—_   Gross amount $ _1,000.00_
Invoice number _847_   Less: Cash discount   _20.00_
Credit terms _2/10, n 30_   Net amount $ _980.00_

Approval

	Dates	Approved by
Extensions and footings verified	May 1, 19—	RG
Prices in agreement with purchase order	May 1, 19—	RG
Quantities in agreement with receiving report	May 1, 19—	RG
Credit terms in agreement with purchase order	May 1, 19—	RG
Account distribution & recording approved	William Cross	
Approved for payment	Judith Davis	

Verification procedures

Accounting supervisor

←———— Approved for payment

Reverse side of voucher

Voucher no. _241_

Account distribution

	Amount
Purchases	$ 1,000.00
Transportation-in	
Repairs	
Heat, light, and power	
Advertising	
Delivery expense	
Misc. general expense	
Telephone	
Sales salaries	
Office salaries	

Accounts debited

Date _May 1, 19—_

Date due _May 10, 19—_

Payee _Black Company_
3160 Main Street
Halifax, Nova Scotia

Amount of invoice $ 1,000.00
Less: Cash discount   20.00
Net amount $ 980.00

Paid by cheque no _632_
Date of cheque _May 10, 19—_

Account credited ———→ Credit vouchers payable   Amount of cheque $ 980.00

(total) 1,000.00   Entered in voucher register by _A.S._

Account distribution by _K.R.D._

The voucher register

The voucher register shown below replaces the purchases journal described in Chapter 6. It may be thought of as an expanded purchases journal with additional debit columns for various types of expense and asset accounts.

In comparing the voucher register with a purchases journal, it should be emphasized that the purchases journal is used *only* to record purchases of merchandise on account. The voucher register, on the other hand, is used to record *all types of expenditures:* for plant and equipment, for the payment of notes payable, for expenses, and for payroll as well as for purchases of merchandise. Every entry in the voucher register will consist of a credit to Vouchers Payable, but the debits may affect various asset and expense accounts. Occasionally the entry may require a debit to a liability account; as for example, when a voucher is prepared to authorize the issuance of a cheque to pay an existing mortgage or note payable.

Each voucher is entered in the voucher register in numerical order as soon as it is prepared and approved. When payment is made, the number and date of the cheque are entered in the columns provided for this purpose. The total amount of unpaid vouchers may be determined from the register at any time merely by listing the "open" items, that is, vouchers for which no entry has yet been made in the Payment columns. The total of the unpaid vouchers appearing in the voucher register should agree with the total of the vouchers in the unpaid vouchers file at the same date.

The procedures for posting from the voucher register to the general ledger are similar to those previously described for other special journals. The letters VR are placed in the Reference column of a ledger account to show that the posting came from the voucher register.

Voucher Register

| VOUCHER NO. | DATE (19__) | | CREDITOR | PAYMENT | | VOUCHERS PAYABLE CR | PUR-CHASES, DR | TRANSPOR-TATION-IN, DR |
				DATE (19__)	CHEQUE NO.			
241	May	1	Black Company	May	10	632	1,000	1,000	
242		2	Midwest Freight		3	627	50		50
243		4	Ames Company		4	628	125		
244		5	Royal Bank		5	629	8,080		
245		5	Rathco, Inc.		6	631	1,200	1,200	
246		5	Midwest Freight		6	630	110		110
286		30	O.K. Supply Co.				70		
287		30	J. Jones		30	665	210		
288		30	Black Company				1,176	1,176	
289		31	Petty Cash		31	666	90		55
290		31	Payroll		31	667	1,865		
							25,875	9,220	640
							(21)	(151)	(152)

The balance of the general ledger account, Vouchers Payable, should be reconciled at the end of the month with the total of the unpaid vouchers shown in the voucher register and also with the total of the vouchers in the unpaid vouchers file.

Paying the voucher within the discount period   After the voucher has been entered in the voucher register, it is placed (with the supporting documents attached) in a tickler file according to the date of required payment. When the payment date arrives, an employee in the accounting department removes the voucher from the unpaid file, draws a cheque for signature by the treasurer, and records payment of the voucher in the cheque register (discussed in the following section of this chapter). The unsigned cheque and the supporting voucher are now sent to the treasurer or other designated official in the finance department. The treasurer reviews the voucher, especially the approval signatures, and signs the cheque. Thus, the invoice is *approved for payment* in the accounting department, but the actual cash disbursement is made by the finance department. *No one person or department is in a position both to approve invoices for payment and to issue signed cheques.*

Once the cheque has been signed, the treasurer should mail it directly to the creditor. The voucher and all supporting documents are then perforated with a PAID stamp and forwarded to the accounting department, which will note payment of the voucher in the voucher register and file the paid voucher. The purpose of perforating the voucher and supporting documents is to prevent these same documents being used again in support of a duplicate payment. The operation of a voucher system is illustrated in the flow chart on page 318. Notes have been made on the illustration identifying the most important internal control features in the system.

ADVER- TISING EXPENSE DR	OFFICE SUPPLIES DR	REPAIRS EXPENSE DR	SALARIES EXPENSE DR	OTHER GENERAL LEDGER ACCOUNTS			
				ACCOUNT NAME	LP	DEBIT	CREDIT
		125		Notes Payable	20	8,000	
				Interest Expense	179	80	
	70	210					
	15			Misc. Expense	185	20	
			1,865				
510	470	335	3,800			10,900	
(161)	(14)	(174)	(124)			(x)	

OPERATION OF A VOUCHER SYSTEM

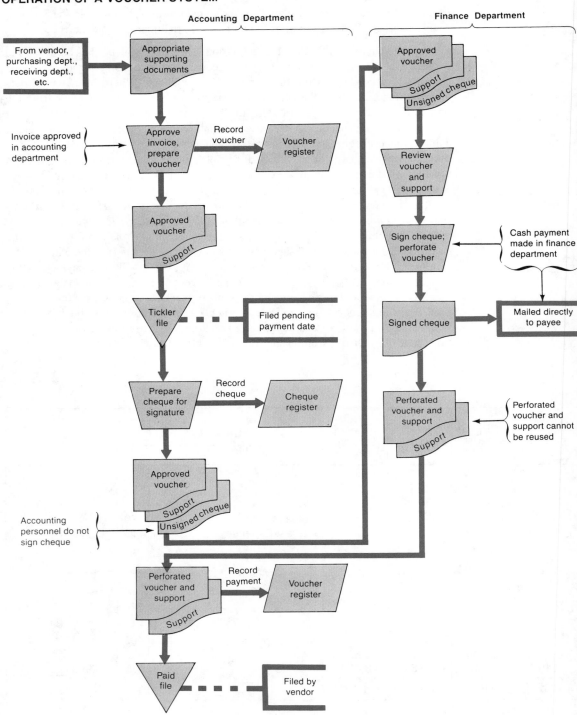

The cheque register

A cheque register is merely a simplified version of the cash payments journal illustrated in Chapter 6. When a voucher system is in use, *cheques are issued only in payment of approved and recorded vouchers.* Consequently, every cheque issued is recorded by a debit to Vouchers Payable and a credit to Cash. The cheque register therefore contains a special column for debits to Vouchers Payable and a Cash credit column. The only other money column needed in this compact record is for credits to Purchase Discounts when invoices are paid within the cash discount period. In this illustration we are assuming that the company records purchase invoices at the gross amount. (If a company follows the policy of recording purchase invoices at the net amount, the column for Purchase Discounts would be omitted, because the discounts would be deducted before recording the vouchers.) Following is a cheque register with entries corresponding to the payments listed in the voucher register presented earlier.

Cheque Register

CHEQUE NO.	DATE 19__		PAYEE	VOUCHER NO.	VOUCHERS PAYABLE, DEBIT	PURCHASE DISCOUNTS, CREDIT	CASH, CREDIT
627	May	3	Midwest Freight	242	50		50
628		4	Ames Company	243	125		125
629		5	Royal Bank	244	8,080		8,080
630		6	Midwest Freight	246	110		110
631		6	Rathco, Inc.	245	1,200		1,200
632		10	Black Company	241	1,000	20	980
665		30	J. Jones	287	210		210
666		31	Petty Cash	289	90		90
667		31	Payroll	290	1,865		1,865
					23,660	240	23,420
					(21)	(153)	(1)

To record the payment of a voucher, an entry is made in the cheque register, and a notation of the cheque number and date is placed on the appropriate line in the voucher register. At the end of the month the column totals of the cheque register are posted as for other special journals; this posting consists of a debit to the Vouchers Payable account for the total of the vouchers paid during the month, a credit to the Purchase Discounts account, and a credit to the Cash account. The symbol ChR is placed in the ledger accounts to indicate that a posting came from the cheque register.

The voucher register as a subsidiary ledger   When a voucher system is in use, there is no need to maintain an accounts payable subsidiary ledger such as the one described in Chapter 6.

Each line of the voucher register represents a liability account with an individual creditor. This liability account comes into existence when an invoice is received and a voucher is prepared and recorded, describing the amount owed under the terms of that invoice. When a voucher is paid, the cheque number and date are entered on the line for that voucher to show that the liability is ended. Inspection of the voucher register reveals which items have not been paid. A list of unpaid vouchers corresponds to a list of unpaid liabilities. The voucher register thus serves a dual purpose; it is primarily a journal, but it also serves as the equivalent of a subsidiary ledger of liability accounts.

Electronic funds transfer system (EFTS)

Our discussion of cash transactions and bank accounts would be incomplete without mention of the many new systems for transferring funds electronically rather than by delivery of physical documents. In the banking field, for example, automated clearing houses may eliminate the need for banks to exchange bundles of customers' cheques some day. If you pay your telephone bill by a cheque written on Bank A, the telephone company traditionally has deposited your cheque in its bank (Bank B). Bank B would then deliver your cheque and others like it to Bank A in order to collect. At the same time Bank A would be presenting a bundle of cheques deposited with it but drawn on Bank B. In reality, many banks, not just Bank A and Bank B, would be involved in this "clearing house" activity. Since the number of cheques written each day is in the millions, this exchange of paper represents a great opportunity for saving through electronic transfer of funds. Electronic equipment now exists that enables banks to transfer funds from the account of one depositor to the account of another without all this cumbersome exchange of paper.

Many other applications of electronic funds transfer are now in use. For example, a company may pay all its employees (if they agree) by delivering payroll information to its bank on magnetic tape or disk. The bank's computer debits the employer's account and credits the bank account of each employee without any paper changing hands.

The further development of electronic funds transfer systems seems to be impeded more by government regulations, legislative barriers, and public attitudes than by lack of technology. A considerable portion of the public appears to be reluctant to move into a "chequeless society." However, the federal government has been successful in persuading a great number of people receiving monthly Canada pension payments to have their bank accounts credited monthly by EFTS rather than to receive and deposit their pension cheques.

END-OF-CHAPTER REVIEW

SUMMARY OF CHAPTER LEARNING OBJECTIVES

1 Describe the balance sheet presentation of cash and explain the objectives of cash management.

Cash is listed first among the current assets and includes cash in banks and on hand. The objectives of cash management are accurate accounting for all cash transactions, the prevention of cash fraud or loss, and the maintenance of adequate but not excessive cash balances.

2 State the major steps in achieving internal control over cash transactions.

The major steps in achieving internal control over cash transactions are: (1) to separate cash handling from the accounting function, (2) to prepare a control listing of all cash received through the mail and from over-the-counter cash sales, (3) to deposit all cash receipts in the bank daily, (4) to make all payments by cheque, (5) to verify every expenditure before issuing a cheque in payment, and (6) to separate the function of approving payments from the function of signing cheques.

3 Prepare a bank reconciliation and explain its purpose.

The balance of cash shown on the month-end bank statement usually will differ from the amount of cash shown in the depositor's ledger. The difference is caused by items that have been recorded by either the depositor or the bank, but not recorded by both. Examples are outstanding cheques and deposits in transit. The bank reconciliation adjusts the cash balance per the books and the cash balance per the bank statement for any unrecorded items, and thus produces the correct amount of cash to be shown in the balance sheet at the end of the month.

The purpose of a bank reconciliation is to achieve the control inherent in the maintenance of two independent records of cash transactions; one record maintained by the depositor and the other by the bank. When these two records are reconciled (brought into agreement), we gain assurance of a correct accounting for cash transactions.

4 Describe the operation of a petty cash fund.

A petty cash fund represents an exception to the general rule of making all payments by cheque. A few small payments, such as postage due and taxi fares, can be made more conveniently through a petty cash fund than by the time-consuming and expensive process of issuing a cheque. The petty cash fund is established by writing and cashing a cheque payable to Petty Cash. For each cash payment from the fund, a petty cash voucher is placed in the fund. When the cash in the fund runs low, it is replenished by a cheque for the amount of vouchers in the fund. The debits are to expense accounts and the credit is to cash.

5 Explain how a voucher system can be used to establish strong internal control over cash payments.

A voucher system requires that every transaction that will result in a cash payment must be verified, approved in writing, and recorded before a cheque is issued. A voucher is a serially numbered document attached to each incoming invoice. The voucher has spaces for listing data from the invoice, the receiving report, and the purchase order. It also provides space for approval signatures for each step in verification. The vouchers are entered in a book of original entry called a voucher register. Cheques are recorded in a cheque register, which replaces the cash payments journal.

KEY TERMS INTRODUCED OR EMPHASIZED IN CHAPTER 7

Bank reconciliation An analysis that explains the difference between the balance of cash shown on the bank statement and the balance of cash shown on the depositor's records.

Cash Currency, coins, cheques, money orders, and any other medium of exchange that a bank will accept for deposit.

Cash over and short A ledger account used to accumulate the cash overages and shortages resulting from errors in making change.

Cheque register A simplified version of the cash payments journal used for recording cash payments when a voucher system is in use.

Deposit ticket A form filled out by the depositor listing the cheques and currency being deposited. Each cheque is listed separately.

Deposits in transit Cash receipts that have been entered in the depositor's accounting records and mailed to the bank or left in the bank's night depository, but that reached the bank too late to be included in the current monthly bank statement.

Electronic funds transfer system The electronic transfer of funds from the bank account of one depositor to the account of another without the delivery of cheques. Many related applications are in use to reduce paper work in cash transactions.

NSF cheque A customer's cheque that was deposited but returned because of a lack of funds (Not Sufficient Funds) in the account on which the cheque was drawn.

Outstanding cheques Cheques issued by a business to suppliers, employees, or other payees but not yet presented to the bank for payment.

Petty cash fund A small amount of cash set aside for making minor cash payments for which writing of cheques is not practicable.

Voucher A written authorization used in approving a transaction for recording and payment.

Voucher register A book of original entry used to record vouchers that have been approved for payment.

Voucher system An accounting system designed to provide strong internal control over cash disbursements. Requires that every transaction that will result in a cash payment be verified, approved, and recorded before a cheque is prepared.

DEMONSTRATION PROBLEM FOR YOUR REVIEW

The following information is available in reconciling the bank statement for the White River Company on November 30, 19___.

(1) The ledger account for Cash showed a balance at November 30 of $12,761.94. The bank statement at November 30 indicated a balance of $9,734.70.

(2) The November 30 cash receipts of $5,846.20 had been left in the bank's night depository on that date and did not appear among the deposits on the November bank statement.

(3) The paid cheques returned with the November bank statement disclosed two errors in the company's cash records. Cheque No. 936 for $504.00 had been erroneously recorded as $50.40 in the cash payments journal, and cheque No. 942 for $245.50 has been recorded as $254.50. Cheque No. 936 was issued in payment of advertising expense and cheque No. 942 was for the acquisition of office equipment.

(4) Included with the November bank statement was an NSF cheque for $220 signed by a customer, J. Wilson. This amount had been charged against the bank account on November 30.

(5) Of the cheques issued in November, the following were not included among the paid cheques returned by the bank:

CHEQUE NO.	AMOUNT	CHEQUE NO.	AMOUNT
924	$136.25	944	$ 95.00
940	105.00	945	716.15
941	11.46	946	60.00
943	826.70		

(6) A service charge for $340 by the bank had been made in error against the White River Company account.

(7) A non-interest-bearing note receivable for $1,890 owned by the White River Company had been left with the bank for collection. On November 30 the company received a memorandum from the bank indicating that the note had been collected and credited to the company's account after deduction of a $5 collection charge. No entry has been made by the company to record collection of the note.

(8) A debit memorandum for $12 was enclosed with the paid cheques at November 30. This charge covered the printing of chequebooks bearing the White River Company name and address.

Instructions   **a** Prepare a bank reconciliation at November 30.

b Prepare journal entries required at November 30 to bring the company's records up-to-date.

SOLUTION TO DEMONSTRATION PROBLEM

a

WHITE RIVER COMPANY
Bank Reconciliation
November 30, 19___

Balance per depositor's records, Nov. 30			$12,761.94
Add: Error in recording cheque No. 942			
for office equipment:			
Recorded as	$ 254.50		
Correct amount	245.50	$ 9.00	
Note receivable collected by bank	$1,890.00		
Less: collection charge	5.00	1,885.00	1,894.00
			$14,655.94
Less: Error in recording cheque No. 936			
for advertising expense:			
Correct amount	$ 504.00		
Recorded as	50.40	$ 453.60	
NSF cheque, J. Wilson		220.00	
Charge by bank for printing cheques		12.00	685.60
Adjusted balance			$13,970.34
Balance per bank statement, Nov. 30			$ 9,734.70
Add: Deposit of Nov. 30 not recorded by bank		$5,846.20	
Service charge made by bank in error		340.00	6,186.20
Subtotal			$15,920.90
Less: Outstanding cheques on Nov. 30:			
No. 924		$ 136.25	
No. 940		105.00	
No. 941		11.46	
No. 943		826.70	
No. 944		95.00	
No. 945		716.15	
No. 946		60.00	1,950.56
Adjusted balance (as above)			$13,970.34

b Journal entries required at November 30 to bring the company's records up-to-date.

```
19___
Nov. 30  Cash ....................................  1,894.00
           Miscellaneous Expense .....................     5.00
              Office Equipment .......................            9.00
              Notes Receivable ......................         1,890.00
           To record increase in Cash account as
           indicated by bank reconciliation.


Nov. 30  Advertising Expense .......................    453.60
           Miscellaneous Expense .....................     12.00
           Accounts Receivable, J. Wilson ..............    220.00
              Cash ..................................           685.60
           To record decreases in Cash account as
           indicated by bank reconciliation.
```

ASSIGNMENT MATERIAL

REVIEW QUESTIONS

1 Among the various assets owned by a business, cash is probably the one for which strong internal control is most urgently needed. What specific attributes of cash cause this special need for internal control?

2 The accountant's work in verifying the amount of cash which should appear in a balance sheet is aided by the existence of two independent records of the deposits, the cheques, and the balance of cash. Identify these two independent records of cash transactions.

3 Does the expression "efficient management of cash" mean anything more than procedures to prevent losses from fraud or theft? Explain.

4 If a company has accounts in three banks, should it maintain a separate ledger account for each? Should the company's balance sheet show the amount on deposit in each of the three accounts as a separate item? Explain.

5 Mention some principles to be observed by a business in establishing strong internal control over cash receipts.

6 Explain how internal control over cash transactions is strengthened by compliance with the following rule: "Deposit each day's cash receipts intact in the bank, and make all disbursements by cheque."

7 List two items often encountered in reconciling a bank account that may cause cash per the bank statement to be larger than the balance of cash shown in the accounts.

8 In the reconciliation of a bank account, what reconciling items necessitate a journal entry in the depositor's accounting records?

9 Pico Stationery Shop has for years maintained a petty cash fund of $75, which is replenished twice a month.

a How many debit entries would you expect to find in the Petty Cash account each year?

b When would expenditures from the petty cash fund be entered in the ledger accounts?

10 A cheque for $455 issued in payment of an account payable was erroneously listed in the cash payments journal as $545. The error was discovered early in the following month when the paid cheque was returned by the bank. What corrective action is needed?

11 It is standard accounting practice to treat as cash all cheques received from customers. When a customer's cheque is received, recorded, and deposited, but later returned by the bank marked NSF, what accounting entry or entries would be appropriate?

12 Ringo Store sells only for cash and records all sales on cash registers before delivering merchandise to the customers. On a given day the cash count at the close of business indicated $10.25 less cash than was shown by the totals on the cash register tapes. In what account would this cash shortage be recorded? Would the account be debited or credited?

13 Name three internal control practices relating to cash that would be practicable even in a small business having little opportunity for division of duties.

14 With respect to a *voucher system,* what is meant by the terms *voucher, voucher register,* and *cheque register?*

15 Randall Company uses a voucher system to control its cash disbursements. With respect to a purchase of merchandise, what three documents would need to be examined to verify that the voucher should be approved?

16 Assume that a company using a general journal, a cash receipts journal, a cash payments journal, a sales journal, and a purchases journal decides to adopt a voucher system. Which of the five journals would be changed or replaced? Explain.

17 On January 10 Susan Jones wrote a cheque for $500 and mailed it to Joe Smith in payment of a debt. On January 25, Smith called and asked to be paid, stating that no cheque had been received. Jones placed a stop payment order with her bank and wrote another cheque that she delivered personally to Smith.

a What information should Jones have given the bank in connection with the stop payment order in order that the bank could guard against paying the first cheque?

b In preparing a bank reconciliation at January 31, should Jones include on the outstanding cheque list the cheque on which payment had been stopped? Explain.

c If the first cheque was presented to the bank by a third person on February 15 and was cashed by the bank despite the existence of the stop payment order, would the loss fall on Jones, Smith, or the bank?

18 What information usually appears on a bank statement?

19 Evaluate the following statement. "The purpose of preparing a bank reconciliation is to determine which of two independent records of cash is correct. If both records are incorrect, the reconciliation cannot be completed."

20 Suggest an internal control procedure to prevent the documents supporting a paid voucher from being resubmitted later in support of another cash disbursement.

EXERCISES

Exercise 7-1
Accounting
terminology

Listed below are nine technical accounting terms introduced in this chapter:

Bank reconciliation	Cheque register	Voucher
Cash management	NSF cheques	Voucher register
Cash over and short	Petty cash fund	Voucher system

Each of the following statements may (or may not) describe one of these technical terms. For each statement, indicate the accounting term described, or answer ''None'' if the statement does not correctly describe any of the terms.

a Includes measures to prevent the maintenance of excessively large balances in non-interest-bearing bank accounts.

b A special journal used to record the payment of vouchers in a voucher system.

c A system used for making small cash disbursements that do not justify the procedures involved in issuing a cheque.

d Cheques issued by a business that have not yet been presented for payment.

e The account in which errors in making change to cash customers would be recorded.

f A sequence of procedures for assuring that every potential expenditure has been reviewed and approved before a cheque is issued.

Exercise 7-2
Internal control over
cash receipts

All the cash receipts of Steel Products consist of cheques received through the mail. The incoming mail is opened either by the cashier or by the employee maintaining the accounts receivable subsidiary ledger, depending on who has time available. The company does not prepare a list of cash receipts before they are entered in the accounts. The controller of Steel Products stresses the need for flexibility in assignment of duties to the 20 employees comprising the office staff in order to keep all employees busy and achieve maximum economy of operation.

Instructions

a Criticize the existing procedures for Steel Products' handling of cash receipts from the standpoint of internal control.

b Explain how the daily preparation of a list of cheques received through the mail would strengthen the company's internal control over cash.

Exercise 7-3
Internal control:
identifying strength
and weakness

Some of the following practices are suggestive of strength in internal controls; others are suggestive of weakness. Identify each of the eight practices with the term Strength or Weakness. Give reasons for your answers.

a After the monthly bank reconciliation has been prepared, any difference between the adjusted balance per the depositor's records and the adjusted balance per the bank statement is entered in the Cash Over and Short account.

b Cheques for expenditures of less than $50 are drawn payable to ''Cash,'' rather than specifically identifying the payee.

c Vouchers and all supporting documents are perforated with a ''PAID'' stamp before being sent to the finance department for review and signing of cheques.

d Cheques received through the mail are recorded daily by the person maintaining accounts receivable records.

e All cash receipts are deposited daily.

f All payments under $200 are made through a petty cash fund.

g Any difference between a day's over-the-counter cash receipts and the day's total shown by the cash register is added to or removed from petty cash.

h Each invoice from a supplier is processed individually through a voucher system; no accounts payable subsidiary ledger is maintained.

Exercise 7-4
Subdivision of duties

Certain subdivisions of duties are highly desirable for the purpose of achieving a reasonable degree of internal control. For each of the following five responsibilities, explain whether or not assigning the duty to an employee who also handles cash receipts would represent a significant weakness in internal control. Briefly explain your reasoning.

a Responsibility for issuing credit memoranda for sales returns.

b Responsibility for preparing a control listing of all cash collections.

c Responsibility for preparing monthly bank reconciliations.

d Responsibility for executing both cash and credit sales transactions.

e Responsibility for maintaining the general ledger.

Exercise 7-5
Bank reconciliation

The following information relating to the bank chequing account is available for Data Centre at July 31:

a	Balance per depositor's records at July 31	$8,671.25
b	Balance per bank statement at July 31	9,893.15
c	Outstanding cheques	2,102.50
d	Deposit in transit	872.60
e	Service charge by bank	8.00

Prepare a bank reconciliation for Data Centre at July 31.

Exercise 7-6
Reconciling items

In reconciling the bank account of Lane Company, the accountant had to deal with the following six items.

(1) Outstanding cheques

(2) Bank service charges.

(3) Cheque No. 502 was issued in the correct amount of $350 and paid by the bank in that amount, but had been incorrectly recorded in Lane Company's cash payments journal as $530.

(4) Collection by bank of note receivable left with bank by Lane Company for collection and credit to Lane Company's account.

(5) Customers' cheques deposited by Lane Company but returned by bank marked NSF.

(6) Deposit in transit.

You are to classify each of the above six items under one of the following headings: (a) an addition to the balance per the bank statement; (b) a deduction from the balance per the bank statement; (c) an addition to the balance per the depositor's records; (d) a deduction from the balance per the depositor's records.

Exercise 7-7
Adjusting the cash account

The bank statement received by Target Company for the month ended November 30 showed a balance of $42,000 and included a $180 credit for interest earned by Target Company on the bank account during November. All cheques issued by Target were returned with the bank statement except for 10 cheques totalling $6,400 which had been issued on the last day of November. A deposit of $3,200 mailed by Target to the bank on November 30 did not appear on the bank statement.

Instructions   **a** What amount should appear as cash on Target Company's balance sheet at November 30? Show computations.

b What amount of cash was shown by Target Company's records before any month-end adjustments were made?

Exercise 7-8
Bank reconciliation and adjusting entries

The following information relates to the cash position of Whipstock, Inc., at September 30.

(1) At September 30, cash per the accounting records was $5,815; cash per the bank statement was $5,327.

(2) Cash receipts of $1,451 on September 30 were not deposited until October 1.

(3) The following memoranda accompanied the bank statement;

(a) A debit memo for service charges for the month of September, $8.

(b) A debit memo attached to a $200 cheque drawn by Susan Scott, marked NSF.

(4) The following cheques had been issued but were not included among the paid cheques returned by the bank; No. 921 for $326, No. 924 for $684, and No. 925 for $161.

Instructions   **a** Prepare a bank reconciliation as of September 30.

b Prepare the necessary adjusting journal entries.

Exercise 7-9
Petty Cash

Three-Par, Inc., established a petty cash fund of $200 on December 1. At December 31, the end of the company's fiscal year, the fund contained the following:

Currency and coins	$ 78.82
Expense vouchers:	
Taxi fares (debit Travel Expense)	34.90
Office supplies expense	46.28
Contributions to Boy Scouts and others	40.00
Total	$200.00

Prepare journal entries in general journal form to record the establishment of the petty cash fund on December 1 and its replenishment on December 31.

Exercise 7-10
Voucher system

Tonopah Trail uses a voucher system. The following transactions occurred early this month: (a) voucher No. 110 prepared to establish a petty cash fund of $200; (b) cheque No. 650 issued in payment of voucher No. 110; (c) voucher No. 111 prepared to purchase merchandise from Vegas Associates at a cost of $12,000; (d) cheque No. 651 issued in payment of voucher No. 111; (e) voucher No. 112 prepared to purchase office equipment at cost of $4,000 from Wood Interiors; (f) cheque No. 652 issued in payment of voucher No. 112; (g) voucher No. 113 prepared to replenish the petty cash fund which contained $30 cash, and receipts for postage $88, travel expense $65, and contributions expense $17; (h) cheque No. 653 issued in payment of voucher No. 113. Cheque cashed and proceeds placed in petty cash fund.

You are to record the transactions in *general journal form* (without explanations). Also indicate after each entry the journal (or book of original entry) in which in actual practice the transactions would be recorded. For example, your treatment of transaction (a) should be as follows:

(a) Petty Cash	200	
Vouchers Payable		200
(Voucher register)		

PROBLEMS

Group A

Problem 7A-1
Internal control procedures

Listed below are nine errors or problems that might occur in the processing of cash transactions. Also shown is a list of internal control procedures.

Possible Errors or Problems

a An employee steals the cash collected from a customer for an account receivable and conceals this theft by issuing a credit memorandum indicating that the customer returned the merchandise.

b The same voucher was circulated through the system twice, causing the supplier to be paid twice for the same invoice.

c Without fear of detection, the cashier sometimes abstracts cash forwarded to him from the mailroom or the sales department instead of depositing these receipts in the company's bank account.

d A purchase invoice was paid even though the merchandise was never received.

e A salesclerk often rings up a sale at less than the actual sales price and then removes the additional cash collected from the customer.

f The cashier conceals a shortage of cash by making an entry in the general ledger debiting Miscellaneous Expense and crediting Cash.

g A salesclerk occasionally makes an error in the amount of change given to a customer.

h The employee designated to sign cheques is able to steal blank cheques and issue them for unauthorized purposes without fear of detection.

i All cash received during the last four days is lost in a burglary on Thursday night.

Internal Control Procedures

1 Monthly reconciliation of bank statements to accounting records.

2 Use of a Cash Over and Short account.

3 Adequate subdivision of duties.

4 Use of prenumbered sales tickets.

5 Depositing each day's cash receipts intact in the bank.

6 Use of electronic cash registers equipped with optical scanners to read magnetically coded labels on merchandise.

7 Immediate preparation of a control listing when cash is received, and the comparison of this listing to bank deposits.

8 Cancellation of paid vouchers.

9 Requirement that a voucher be prepared as advance authorization of every cash disbursement.

0 None of the above control procedures can effectively prevent this type of error from occurring.

Instructions

List the letters (**a** through **i**) designating each possible error or problem. Beside this letter, place the number indicating the internal control procedure that should prevent this type of error or problem from occurring. If none of the specified internal control procedures would effectively prevent the error, place a "0" opposite the letter.

Problem 7A-2
Preparing a bank reconciliation

At November 30, West Coast Imports has available the following data concerning its bank account:

(1) At November 30, cash per the accounting records was $42,482; per bank statement, $37,758.

(2) The cash receipts of $6,244 on November 30 were deposited but not recorded by the bank until December 1.

(3) Included on the bank statement was a credit for $167 interest earned on this account during November.

(4) Two cheques were outstanding at November 30: No. 921 for $964 and No. 925 for $1,085.

(5) Enclosed with the bank statement were two debit memoranda for the following items:
  (a) Service charge for November, $14.
  (b) A $700 cheque of customer Frank Miller, marked NSF.

(6) Cheque No. 920 for $168 in payment for purchases was recorded incorrectly as $186.

Instructions

a Prepare a bank reconciliation at November 30.

b Prepare three adjusting entries (in general journal form) based on the bank reconciliation.

Problem 7A-3
Operating a Petty Cash Fund

In order to handle small cash disbursements in an efficient manner, Whitehall Company established a petty cash fund on July 10. The company does not use a voucher system. The following events relating to petty cash occurred in July.

July 10 A cheque for $300 drawn payable to Petty Cash was issued and cashed to establish the fund.

July 31 At month-end a count of the fund disclosed the following:

Office supplies expense	$50.40
Postage expense	69.00
Travel expense	49.38
Miscellaneous expense	50.62
Currency and coin remaining in the fund	80.60

July 31 A cheque was issued to replenish the petty cash fund.

Instructions

a Prepare an entry in general journal form to record the establishment of the petty cash fund on July 10.

b Prepare an entry to record the replenishment of the petty cash fund on July 31.

c Net income for Whitehall Company in July was $6,785.20. What amount of net income would have appeared in the July income statement if the company had not replenished the petty cash fund on July 31?

Problem 7A-4
A more comprehensive bank reconciliation

The cash transactions and cash balances of Norfleet Farm for July were as follows:

(1) The ledger account for Cash showed a balance at July 31 of $16,766.95.

(2) The July bank statement showed a closing balance of $18,928.12.

(3) The cash received on July 31 amounted to $4,017.15. It was left at the bank in the night depository chute after banking hours on July 31 and was therefore not recorded by the bank on the July statement.

(4) Also included with the July bank statement was a debit memorandum from the bank for $7.65 representing service charges for July.

(5) A credit memorandum enclosed with the July bank statement indicated that a non-interest-bearing note receivable for $4,545 from Rene Manes, left with the bank for collection, had been collected and the proceeds credited to the account of Norfleet Farm.

(6) Comparison of the paid cheques returned by the bank with the entries in the cash payments journal revealed that cheque No. 821 for $835.02 issued July 15 in payment for office equipment had been erroneously entered in the cash payments journal as $853.02.

(7) Examination of the paid cheques also revealed that three cheques, all issued in July, had not yet been paid by the bank: No. 811 for $861.12; No. 814 for $640.80; No. 823 for $301.05.

(8) Included with the July bank statement was a $180 cheque drawn by Howard Williams, a customer of Norfleet Farm. This cheque was marked NSF. It had been included in the deposit of July 27 but had been charged back against the company's account on July 31.

Instructions   **a**   Prepare a bank reconciliation for Norfleet Farm at July 31.

  b   Prepare journal entries (in general journal form) to adjust the accounts at July 31. Assume that the accounts have not been closed.

  c   State the amount of cash that should appear on the balance sheet at July 31.

Problem 7A-5
Weak internal control
and a fraudulent
bank reconciliation

Bayview Company, a successful small business, had never given much consideration to internal control concepts and the internal controls over cash transactions were not adequate. Betty Jones, the cashier-bookkeeper, handled cash receipts, made small disbursements from the cash receipts, maintained accounting records, and prepared the monthly reconciliations of the bank account.

The bank statement for the month ended April 30 showed a balance on deposit of $29,500. The outstanding cheques were as follows: No. 6052 for $431.16, No. 6173 for $366.00, No. 6174 for $530.61, No. 7611 for $316.13, No. 7613 for $614.04, and No. 7622 for $310.01. The balance of cash shown by the company's ledger account for Cash was $34,824.96, which included the cash on hand.

Recognizing the weakness existing in internal control over cash transactions, Jones removed all the cash on hand in excess of $6,365.14, and then prepared the following reconciliation in an effort to conceal this theft. In studying this reconciliation, you should take nothing for granted and keep in mind that Jones is trying to mislead anyone who reviews her work.

Balance per accounting records, Apr. 30		$34,824.96
Add: Outstanding cheques:		
No. 7611	$316.13	
No. 7613	614.04	
No. 7622	310.01	1,040.18
		$35,865.14
Deduct: Cash on hand		6,365.14
Balance per bank statement, Apr. 30		$29,500.00

Instructions   **a**   Determine how much cash Jones took. Prepare a bank reconciliation in a form which shows the difference between the correct (adjusted) balances per the accounting records and per the bank statement. The difference is the amount of undeposited cash that should be on hand. Comparison of the undeposited cash that should be on hand with the actual amount on hand will indicate the amount of the cash shortage.

b Explain how Jones attempted to conceal her theft in the improper bank reconciliation shown above. Your explanation may be in the form of a list of dollar amounts that add up to the total dollar amount stolen by Jones.

c Suggest some specific internal control measures for Bayview Company.

Problem 7A-6
Using bank statement and records to prepare bank reconciliation

At August 31, the balance of the Cash account in the ledger of Maui Shark was exactly equal to the ending balance shown on the bank statement. Since the two sets of records were in agreement at August 31, no bank reconciliation was needed at that date.

Cash Receipts			Cash Payments			
DATE		CASH DR	DATE		CH. NO.	CASH CR
Sept	1	72.80	Sept	1	65	130.00
	3	361.00		1	66	90.00
	6	280.00		1	67	35.48
	8	510.00		2	68	31.15
	10	205.60		4	69	60.00
	13	180.14		4	70	70.00
	15	345.00		5	71	515.00
	18	427.50		8	72	62.50
	20	90.00		9	73	13.30
	22	360.00		10	74	28.00
	27	625.00		13	75	650.00
	28	130.25		19	76	125.06
	29	280.50		19	77	40.00
	30	690.50		19	78	85.00
		4,558.29		20	79	24.10
				21	80	38.60
				22	81	65.00
				22	82	162.40
				23	83	150.00
				26	84	15.00
				28	85	270.00
				28	86	105.20
				28	87	225.00
				28	88	355.00
				30	89	25.00
				30	90	45.00
				30	91	255.00
						3,670.79

The cash receipts journal and the cash payments journal maintained by Maui Shark showed transactions during September as listed. On October 1, Maui Shark received from its bank a bank statement covering the month of September. Enclosed with the bank statement were 23 cheques paid by the bank during September and a $14.25 debit memorandum for service charges. The September bank statement appears on page 333.

BANK STATEMENT

Maui Shark
Lahaina, B.C.

The First National Bank

Cheques			Deposits	Date	Balance
				Aug. 31	7,658.75
31.15	35.48	130.00	72.80	Sept. 2	7,534.92
60.00			361.00	Sept. 5	7,835.92
70.00	515.00		280.00	Sept. 7	7,530.92
90.00				Sept. 8	7,440.92
13.30	62.50		510.00	Sept. 9	7,875.12
28.00			205.60	Sept. 12	8,052.72
650.00			180.14	Sept. 14	7,582.86
			345.00	Sept. 16	7,927.86
85.00			427.50	Sept. 19	8,270.36
24.10	125.06			Sept. 20	8,121.20
40.00			90.00	Sept. 21	8,171.20
162.40	65.00		360.00	Sept. 23	8,303.80
15.00			625.00	Sept. 27	8,913.80
355.00	270.00	225.00	130.25	Sept. 29	8,194.05
255.00	25.00	14.25SC	280.50	Sept. 30	8,180.30

Instructions

a Compute the amount of cash at September 30 according to the depositor's records.

b Prepare a bank reconciliation at September 30.

c Prepare a general journal entry to adjust the Cash account at September 30, based on information contained in the bank reconciliation in part b.

**Problem 7A-7
Using a voucher
system to control
cash payments**

(Problem 7A-7 can be worked most conveniently when the partially filled-in work sheets accompanying the text are being used.) Lakeport Traders uses a voucher system to control its cash payments. The voucher register and cheque register are similar to those illustrated in this chapter. At November 30 the following vouchers were in the unpaid file:

DATE DUE	VOUCHER NO.	PAYEE	DATE OF INVOICE	AMOUNT	TERMS
Dec. 2	912	Stein Co.	Nov. 2	$ 6,500	n/30
Dec. 4	923	Four Corners	Nov. 24	10,000	2/10, n/30

The following vouchers were prepared during December:

DATE	VOUCHER NO.	PAYEE	AMOUNT	TERMS	ACCOUNT DISTRIBUTION
Dec. 1	928	Post Seven	$ 8,000	2/10, n/30	Purchases
4	929	Expressline	450	cash	Transportation-in
9	930	Village Store	210	n/30	Office Supplies
12	931	Classic Office	3,800	n/30	Office Equipment
14	932	Ozark, Inc.	12,000	2/10, n/30	Purchases
15	933	Expressline	625	cash	Transportation-in
17	934	Pacific Bank	21,900		Notes Payable, $20,000 Interest Expense, $1,900
22	935	Torino, Inc.	4,000	2/10, n/30	Purchases
22	936	Herald	650	n/30	Advertising Expense
24	937	Gulf Supply	310	n/30	Office Supplies
31	938	Payroll	14,600	cash	Salaries Expense
31	939	Petty Cash	167	cash	Office Supplies, $19 Advertising, $40 Transportation-in, $18 Postage Expense, $90

During December the following cheques were issued:

DATE	CHEQUE NO.	PAYEE	VOUCHER NO.	AMOUNT
Dec. 2	401	Stein Co.	912	$ 6,500
4	402	Four Corners	923	9,800
4	403	Expressline	929	450
11	404	Post Seven	928	7,840
15	405	Expressline	933	625
17	406	Pacific Bank	934	21,900
24	407	Ozark, Inc.	932	11,760
31	408	Payroll	938	14,600
31	409	Petty Cash	939	167

Instructions   **a** Record the $16,500 of unpaid vouchers at November 30 in the general ledger liability account for Vouchers Payable, account No. 21.

b Enter individually the 12 December vouchers in a voucher register similar to the one illustrated in this chapter.

c Enter the nine December cheques in a cheque register similar to the one illustrated in this chapter. The date of each cheque and its serial number also should be listed in the appropriate columns of the voucher register.

d Compute month-end totals of both the voucher register and the cheque register. Make the appropriate posting of totals to the Vouchers Payable ledger account mentioned in **a** above. Also prepare a schedule of unpaid vouchers at December 31.

Group B

Problem 7B-1
Internal control procedures
Listed at the top of page 335 are nine errors or problems that might occur in the processing of cash transactions. Immediately following these errors or problems is a separate list of internal control procedures.

Possible Errors or Problems

a In serving customers who do not appear to be attentive, a salesclerk often rings up a sale at less than the actual sales amount and then removes the additional cash collected from the customer.

b John Davis, who has prepared bank reconciliations for Marlo Corporation for several years, has noticed that some cheques issued by the company are never presented for payment. Davis, therefore, has formed the habit of dropping any cheques outstanding for more than six months from the outstanding chequelist and removing a corresponding amount of cash from the cash receipts. These actions taken together have left the ledger account for cash in agreement with the adjusted bank balance and have enriched Davis substantially.

c A voucher was presented for payment the second time, causing the supplier to be paid twice for the same invoice.

d Lisa Miller, an employee of Plaza Home Repairs, frequently has trouble in getting the bank reconciliation to balance. If the book balance is more than the bank balance, she writes a cheque payable to Cash and cashes it. If the book balance is less than the bank balance, she makes an accounting entry debiting Cash and crediting Cash Over and Short.

e Without fear of detection, the cashier sometimes abstracts cash forwarded to him from the mailroom or the sales department instead of depositing these receipts in the company's bank account.

f The monthly bank reconciliation continually shows a difference between the adjusted bank balance and the adjusted book balance because the cashier regularly deposits actual cash receipts but the debits to the Cash account reflect cash register readings that differ by the amount of errors in making change in cash sales transactions.

g All cash received from Monday through Thursday was lost in a burglary on Thursday night.

h A salesclerk occasionally makes an error in the amount of change given to a customer.

i The official designated to sign cheques is able to steal blank cheques and issue them for unauthorized purposes without fear of detection.

Internal Control Procedures

1 Periodic reconciliation of bank statements to accounting records.

2 Use of a Cash Over and Short account.

3 Adequate subdivision of duties.

4 Use of prenumbered sales tickets.

5 Depositing each day's cash receipts intact in the bank.

6 Use of electronic cash registers equipped with optical scanners to read magnetically coded labels on merchandise.

7 Immediate preparation of a control listing when cash is received, and the comparison of this listing to bank deposits.

8 Cancellation of paid vouchers.

9 Requirement that a voucher be prepared as advance authorization of every cash disbursement.

0 None of the above control procedures can effectively prevent this type of error from occurring.

Instructions List the letters (**a** through **i**) designating each possible error or problem. Beside this letter, place the number indicating the internal control procedure that should prevent this type of error or problem from occurring. If none of the specified internal control procedures would effectively prevent the error, place a ''0'' opposite the letter.

Problem 7B-2
Preparing a bank reconciliation

Prepare a bank reconciliation for Grayco at July 31, 19___, from the information listed below.

(1) Cash per the accounting records at July 31 amounted to $35,409; the bank statement at this date showed a balance of $32,251.

(2) The cash receipts of $5,464 on July 31 were mailed to the bank but not received by the bank during July.

(3) The paid cheques returned by the bank included a stolen cheque for $882 that had been paid in error by the bank after Grayco had issued a stop payment order to the bank. Note that the bank was at fault.

(4) The following memoranda accompanied the bank statement:
(a) A debit memo of $13 for service charges for July.
(b) A debit memo attached to a $680 cheque of a customer, Albert Davis, marked NSF.

(5) The following cheques had been issued by Grayco but were not included among the paid cheques returned by the bank: No. 167 for $1,369, No. 174 for $844, and No. 179 for $676.

(6) The bank charged $8 for collecting the company's note receivable of $1,000.

Problem 7B-3
Operating a petty cash fund

Santa Rosa Winery maintains a petty cash fund to control small cash payments. The company does not use a voucher system. Following are the transactions involving the establishment of the fund and its replenishment at September 30, the end of the company's fiscal year:

Sept. 12 A cheque for $360 was issued and cashed to establish a petty cash fund.

Sept. 30 A count of the fund showed currency and coin of $96.11 remaining on hand. Petty cash vouchers in the fund were as follows:

Office supplies expense	$100.43
Postage expense	73.92
Telephone and telegraph expense	23.10
Miscellaneous expense	66.44

Sept. 30 Although the fund had not been used fully, management wished to replenish the fund before the accounts were closed for the fiscal year. A cheque was therefore issued and cashed on this date in the amount necessary to replenish the fund.

Instructions

a Prepare journal entries in general journal form to record the establishment of the fund on September 12 and its replenishment on September 30.

b What would have been the effect, if any, on net income for the fiscal year ended September 30 if the company had forgotten to replenish the fund on September 30? Explain.

Problem 7B-4
Another bank reconciliation

The information needed to prepare a bank reconciliation and the related adjusting entries for Wicked Pony at March 31 is listed as follows:

(1) Cash balance per the accounting records of Wicked Pony, $18,100.

(2) The bank statement showed a balance of $22,134.27 at March 31.

(3) Accompanying the bank statement was a debit memorandum relating to a cheque for $186 from a customer, D. Jones. The cheque was returned by the bank and stamped NSF.

(4) Cheques outstanding as of March 31 were as follows: No. 84 for $1,841.02; No. 88 for $1,323.00; No. 89 for $16.26.

(5) Also accompanying the bank statement was a debit memorandum for $44.80 for safe deposit box rent; the bank had erroneously charged this item to the account of Wicked Pony.

(6) On March 29, the bank collected a non-interest-bearing note for Wicked Pony. The note was for $2,963; the bank charged a collection fee of $8.40.

(7) A deposit of $2,008.50 was in transit; it had been mailed to the bank on March 31.

(8) In recording a $160 cheque received on account from a customer, Ross Company, the accountant for Wicked Pony erroneously listed the collection in the cash receipts journal as $16. The cheque appeared correctly among the deposits on the March bank statement.

(9) The bank service charge for March amounted to $5.31; a debit memo in this amount was returned with the bank statement.

Instructions
a Prepare a bank reconciliation at March 31.
b Prepare the necessary journal entries.
c What amount of cash should appear on the company's March 31 balance sheet?

Problem 7B-5
Weak internal control and a fraudulent bank reconciliation

The owners of Ivory Products had never given much thought to internal control concepts and the internal controls over cash transactions were weak. John Lee, the cashier-bookkeeper, handled cash receipts, made small disbursements from the cash receipts, maintained accounting records, and prepared the monthly reconciliations of the bank account.

At April 30, the statement received from the bank showed a balance on deposit of $30,510. The outstanding cheques were as follows; No. 7062 for $371.16, No. 7183 for $306.00, No. 7284 for $470.61, No. 8621 for $415.34, No. 8623 for $713.80, and No. 8632 for $111.04. The balance of cash shown by the company's ledger account for Cash was $35,474.96, which included the cash on hand. The bank statement for April showed a credit of $360 arising from the collection of a note left with the bank; the company's accounts did not include an entry to record this collection.

Recognizing the weakness existing in internal control over cash transactions, Lee removed all the cash on hand in excess of $6,025.14, and then prepared the reconciliation shown below in an attempt to conceal this theft.

Balance per accounting records, Apr. 30		$35,474.96
Add: Outstanding cheques:		
No. 8621	$415.34	
No. 8623	713.80	
No. 8632	111.04	1,060.18
		$36,535.14
Less: Cash on hand		6,025.14
Balance per bank statement, Apr. 30		$30,510.00
Less: Unrecorded credit		360.00
True cash, Apr. 30		$30,150.00

Instructions **a** Determine how much cash Lee took. Prepare a bank reconciliation in a form that shows the difference between the adjusted balance per the accounting records and the adjusted bank balance. The difference is the amount of undeposited cash which should be on hand.

b Explain how Lee attempted to conceal his theft in the preceding improper bank reconciliation. Your explanation may be in the form of a list of dollar amounts that add up to the total cash stolen by Lee.

c Suggest some specific internal control devices for Ivory Products.

Problem 7B-6
Using bank statement
and records to prepare
bank reconciliation

The Cash account in the ledger of Southern Cross at October 31 was equal to the ending balance on the October bank statement. Because the bank statement and the accounting records were in agreement, no bank reconciliation was needed at October 31.

Cash Receipts				Cash Payments			
DATE			**CASH DR**	**DATE**		**CH. NO.**	**CASH CR**
Nov.	2		82.80	Nov.	1	65	148.00
	4		351.00		1	66	90.00
	6		280.00		1	67	25.48
	8		500.00		2	68	23.15
	10		215.60		4	69	60.00
	13		280.14		4	70	80.00
	15		245.00		5	71	505.00
	17		327.50		9	72	62.50
	20		190.00		10	73	18.30
	22		360.00		10	74	23.00
	26		625.00		13	75	650.00
	28		150.25		19	76	25.06
	29		260.50		19	77	40.00
	30		315.25		19	78	85.00
			4,183.04		20	79	124.10
					21	80	48.60
					22	81	65.00
					22	82	162.40
					23	83	100.00
					26	84	15.00
					28	85	290.00
					28	86	125.20
					28	87	225.00
					28	88	335.00
					29	89	45.00
					29	90	65.00
					30	91	135.00
							3,570.79

The cash receipts journal and cash payments journal showed transactions during November as listed. On December 2, Southern Cross received a bank statement covering the month of November. Enclosed were 23 cheques paid by the bank during November and a $16.50 debit memorandum for service charges. The bank statement appears on the next page.

BANK STATEMENT

Southern Cross
Windsor, Ontario

The Canadian Bank

Cheques			Deposits	Date	Balance
				Oct. 31	7,658.75
23.15	25.48	148.00	82.80	Nov. 3	7,544.92
60.00			351.00	Nov. 5	7,835.92
80.00	505.00		280.00	Nov. 7	7,530.92
90.00				Nov. 8	7,440.92
62.50			500.00	Nov. 9	7,878.42
23.00	18.30		215.60	Nov. 12	8,052.72
650.00			280.14	Nov. 14	7,682.86
			245.00	Nov. 16	7,927.86
85.00			327.50	Nov. 19	8,170.36
124.10	25.06			Nov. 20	8,021.20
40.00			190.00	Nov. 21	8,171.20
162.40	65.00		360.00	Nov. 23	8,303.80
15.00			625.00	Nov. 27	8,913.80
335.00	290.00	225.00	150.25	Nov. 29	8,214.05
135.00	45.00	16.50SC	260.50	Nov. 30	8,278.05

Instructions

a Compute the amount of cash at November 30 according to the depositor's records.

b Prepare a bank reconciliation at November 30.

c Prepare a general journal entry to adjust the Cash account at November 30, based on information contained in the bank reconciliation in part **b**.

**Problem 7B-7
Using a voucher
system to control
cash payments**

(Problem 7B-7 can be worked most conveniently when the partially filled-in work sheets accompanying the text are being used.)

The voucher system used by Clinton Centre includes a voucher register and a cheque register similar to those illustrated in this chapter. At September 30, the following vouchers were in the unpaid file.

DATE DUE	VOUCHER NO.	CREDITOR	DATE OF INVOICE	AMOUNT	TERMS
Oct. 3	438	Brown Co.	Sept. 3	$1,800	n/30
Oct. 6	460	Gray, Inc.	Sept. 26	5,000	2/10, n/30

During October the following vouchers were prepared:

DATE	VOUCHER NO.	PAYEE	AMOUNT	TERMS	ACCOUNT DISTRIBUTION
Oct. 1	462	Ames Co.	$ 8,000	2/10, n/30	Purchases
7	463	Rapid Freight	1,300	cash	Transportation-in
10	464	Steel Desk	2,650	n/30	Office Equipment
12	465	Barco	5,600	2/10, n/30	Purchases
13	466	Rapid Freight	250	cash	Transportation-in
15	467	First Bank	11,400		Notes Payable $10,000 Interest Expense $1,400
17	468	Bell Co.	325	cash	Office Supplies
18	469	Ames Co.	1,000	2/10, n/30	Purchases
20	470	Tribune	280	cash	Advertising
25	471	Clip Co.	210	n/30	Office Supplies
29	472	AAA Service	550	n/30	Repairs
31	473	Payroll	12,000	cash	Salaries Expense

The following cheques were issued during October:

DATE	CHEQUE NO.	PAYEE	VOUCHER NO.	AMOUNT
Oct. 3	601	Brown Co.	438	$ 1,800
6	602	Gray, Inc.	460	4,900
7	603	Rapid Freight	463	1,300
11	604	Ames Co.	462	7,840
13	605	Rapid Freight	466	250
15	606	First Bank	467	11,400
17	607	Bell Co.	468	325
20	608	Tribune	470	280
22	609	Barco	465	5,488
28	610	Ames Co.	469	980
31	611	Payroll	473	12,000

Instructions   a Record the $6,800 of unpaid vouchers at September 30 in the general ledger liability account for Vouchers Payable, account No. 21.

b Enter individually the 12 October vouchers in a voucher register similar to the one illustrated in this chapter.

c Enter the 11 October cheques in a cheque register similar to the one illustrated in this chapter. The date of each cheque and its serial number also should be listed in the appropriate columns of the voucher register for each voucher paid.

d Compute month-end totals of both the voucher register and the cheque register. Make the appropriate posting of totals to the general ledger account for Vouchers Payable, account No. 21. Prepare a list of unpaid vouchers at October 31. The total of this schedule should agree with the balance of the Vouchers Payable account in the general ledger.

BUSINESS DECISION CASES

Case 7-1
Internal control — a short case study

J.K. Panther, a trusted employee of Bluestem Products, found himself in personal financial difficulties and decided to "borrow" (steal) $3,000 from the company and to conceal his theft.

As a first step, Panther removed $3,000 in currency from the cash register. This amount represented the bulk of the cash received in over-the-counter sales during the three business days since the last bank deposit. Panther then removed a $3,000 cheque from the day's incoming mail; this cheque had been mailed in by a customer, Michael Adams, in full payment of his account. Panther made no entry in the cash receipts journal for the $3,000 collection from Adams but deposited the cheque in Bluestem Products' bank account in place of the $3,000 over-the-counter cash receipts he had stolen.

In order to keep Adams from protesting when his month-end statement reached him, Panther made a general journal entry debiting Sales Returns and Allowances and crediting Accounts Receivable — Michael Adams. Panther posted this entry to the two general ledger accounts affected and also to Adams's account in the subsidiary ledger for accounts receivable.

Instructions

a Did these actions by Panther cause the general ledger to be out of balance or the subsidiary ledger to disagree with the controlling account? Explain.

b Assume that Bluestem Products prepares financial statements at the end of the month without discovering the theft. Would any items in the balance sheet or the income statement be in error? Explain.

c Several weaknesses in internal control apparently exist in Bluestem Products. Indicate three specific changes needed to strengthen internal control over cash receipts.

Case 7-2
Internal control — a challenging case study

June Davis inherited a highly successful business, Bluestem Products, shortly after her twenty-second birthday and took over the active management of the business. A portion of the company's business consisted of over-the-counter sales for cash, but most sales were on credit and were shipped by truck. Davis had no knowledge of internal control practices and relied implicitly upon the bookkeeper-cashier, J.K. Panther, in all matters relating to cash and accounting records. Panther, who had been with the company for many years, maintained the accounting records and prepared all financial statements with the help of two assistants, made bank deposits, signed cheques, and prepared bank reconciliations.

The monthly income statements submitted to Davis by Panther showed a very satisfactory rate of net income; however, the amount of cash in the bank declined steadily during the first 18 months after Davis took over the business. To meet the company's weakening cash position, a bank loan was obtained and a few months later when the cash position again grew critical, the loan was increased.

On April 1, two years after Davis assumed the management of the company, Panther suddenly left town, leaving no forwarding address. Davis was immediately deluged with claims of creditors who stated their accounts were several months past due and that Panther had promised all debts would be paid by April 1. The bank telephoned to notify Davis that the company's account was overdrawn and that a number of cheques had just been presented for payment.

In an effort to get together some cash to meet this emergency, Davis called on two of the largest customers of the company, to whom substantial sales on account had recently been made, and asked if they could pay their accounts at once. Both customers informed her that their accounts were paid in full. They produced paid cheques to substantiate their payments and explained that Panther had offered them reduced prices on merchandise if they would pay within 24 hours after delivery.

To keep the business from insolvency, Davis agreed to sell at a bargain price a half interest in the company. The sale was made to Helen Smith, who had had considerable experience in the industry. One condition for the sale was that Smith should become the general manager of the business. The cash investment by Smith for her half interest was sufficient for the company to meet the demands on it and continue operations.

Immediately after Smith entered the business, she launched an investigation of Panther's activities. During the course of this investigation the following irregularities were disclosed:

(1) During the last few months of Panther's employment with the company, bank deposits were much smaller than the cash receipts. Panther had abstracted most of the receipts and substituted for them a number of worthless cheques bearing fictitious signatures. These cheques had been accumulated in an envelope marked "Cash Receipts — For Deposit Only."

(2) Numerous legitimate sales of merchandise on account had been charged to fictitious customers. When the actual customer later made payment for the goods, Panther abstracted the cheque or cash and made no entry. The account receivable with the fictitious customer remained in the records.

(3) When cheques were received from customers in payment of their accounts, Panther had frequently recorded the transaction by debiting an expense account and crediting Accounts Receivable. In such cases Panther had removed from the cash receipts an equivalent amount of currency, thus substituting the cheque for the currency and causing the bank deposit to agree with the recorded cash receipts.

(4) More than $3,000 a month had been stolen from petty cash. Fraudulent petty cash vouchers, most of them charged to the Purchases account, had been created to conceal these thefts and to support the cheques cashed to replenish the petty cash fund.

(5) For many sales made over the counter, Panther had recorded lesser amounts on the cash register or had not rung up any amount. He had abstracted the funds received but not recorded.

(6) To produce income statements that showed profitable operations, Panther had recorded many fictitious sales. The recorded accounts receivable included many from nonexistent customers.

(7) In preparing bank reconciliations, Panther had omitted many outstanding cheques, thus concealing the fact that the cash in the bank was less than the amount shown by the ledger.

(8) Inventory had been recorded at inflated amounts in order to increase reported profits from the business.

Instructions **a** For each of the numbered paragraphs, describe one or more internal control procedures you would recommend to prevent the occurrence of such fraud.

b Apart from specific internal controls over cash and other accounts, what general precaution could June Davis have taken to assure herself that the accounting records were properly maintained and the company's financial statements complete and dependable? Explain fully.

RECEIVABLES

CHAPTER PREVIEW

When a business sells goods or services on credit, it does so in the belief that the customer will make payment in accordance with the terms of sale. This confidence in the collectibility of receivables is the basis for showing accounts receivable and notes receivable as assets in the balance sheet and for including credit sales as revenue in the income statement. Along with our overall confidence in receivables, however, is a recognition that a few customers will fail to pay as agreed. Making sales on credit inevitably leads to some credit losses. In this chapter, we explore methods of measuring the expense of uncollectible accounts and reflecting this expense in the financial statements. We also consider various forms of notes receivable and the calculation of interest. In the final pages of the chapter, we show how the concept of present value is applied to long-term notes receivable.

After studying this chapter you should be able to meet these Learning Objectives:

1 Explain the nature and financial statement presentation of uncollectible accounts and apply the balance sheet approach and the income statement approach to estimating these accounts.

2 Account for the write-off of uncollectible accounts receivable and for any later recoveries.

3 Compare the allowance method and the direct charge-off method of accounting for uncollectible accounts.

4 Account for credit card sales.

5 Explain the uses of promissory notes and the nature of interest.

6 Account for the receipt of notes, accrual of interest, collection or default, and the discounting of notes receivable.

7 Account for notes receivable with the interest charges included in the face amount.

8 Discuss the concept of present value in accounting for long-term notes receivable.

One of the key factors underlying the tremendous expansion of our economy ha
been the trend toward selling all types of goods and services on credit. The automc
bile industry has long been the classic example of the use of retail credit to achiev
the efficiencies of large-scale output. Today, however, in nearly every field of reta
trade it appears that sales and profits can be increased by granting customers th
privilege of making payment a month or more after the date of sale. The sales c
manufacturers and wholesalers are made on credit to an even greater extent than i
retail trade.

ACCOUNTS RECEIVABLE

The credit department

**1 Explain the nature
and financial statement
presentation of
uncollectible accounts
and apply the balance
sheet approach and the
income statement
approach to estimating
these accounts.**

No business concern wants to sell on credit to a customer who will prove unable c
unwilling to pay his or her account. Consequently, most business organizations hav
a credit department that investigates the credit worthiness of each prospective custome
If the prospective customer is a business concern, its financial statements will b
obtained and analyzed to determine its financial strength and the trend of operatin
results. The credit department naturally prefers to rely upon financial statements tha
have been audited by public accountants.

Regardless of whether the prospective customer is a business concern or an individua
consumer, the investigation by the credit department will probably include the obtainin
of a credit report from a local credit agency or from a national credit-rating institutio
such as Dun & Bradstreet. A credit agency compiles credit data on individuals an
business concerns and distributes this information to its clients. Most companies tha
make numerous sales on credit find it worthwhile to subscribe to the services of on
or more credit agencies.

Uncollectible accounts

A business that sells its goods or services on credit will inevitably find that some o
its accounts receivable are uncollectible. Regardless of how thoroughly the credi
department investigates prospective customers, some uncollectible accounts wil
arise as a result of errors in judgment or because of unexpected developments. I
fact, a limited amount of uncollectible accounts (bad debts) is evidence of a soun
credit policy. If the credit department should become too cautious and conservativ
in rating customers, it might avoid all credit losses but, in so doing, lose profitabl
business by rejecting many acceptable customers.

Reflecting uncollectible accounts in the financial statements

In measuring business income, one of the most fundamental principles of accountin
is that *revenue must be matched with the expenses incurred in generating tha
revenue.*

Uncollectible accounts expense (also called bad debts expense) is caused by sellin
goods on credit to customers who fail to pay their bills; such expenses, therefore, ar
incurred in the year in which the sales are made, even though the accounts receivabl
are not determined to be uncollectible until the following year. An account receivabl
that originates from a sale on credit in Year 1 and is determined to be uncollectibl

sometime during Year 2 represents an expense of Year 1. Unless each year's uncollectible accounts expense is *estimated* and *reflected* in the year-end balance sheet and income statement, these financial statements will show a distorted picture of earnings and of financial position.

To illustrate, let us assume that Arlington Corporation began business on January 1, 1988, and made most of its sales on credit throughout the year. At December 31, 1988, accounts receivable amounted to $200,000. On this date the management reviewed the status of the accounts receivable, giving particular study to accounts which were past due. This review indicated that the collectible portion of the $200,000 of accounts receivable amounted to approximately $190,000. In other words, management estimated that uncollectible accounts for the first year of operations amounted to $10,000. The following adjusting entry should be made at December 31:

PROVISION FOR
UNCOLLECTIBLE
ACCOUNTS

Uncollectible Accounts Expense	10,000	
Allowance for Doubtful Accounts		10,000
To record the estimated uncollectible accounts expense		
for 1988, the first year of operation.		

The Uncollectible Accounts Expense account created by the debit part of this entry is closed into the Income Summary account in the same manner as any other expense account. The Allowance for Doubtful Accounts that was credited in the above journal entry will appear in the balance sheet as a deduction from the face amount of the accounts receivable. It serves to reduce the accounts receivable to their *realizable value* in the balance sheet, as shown by the following illustration:

ARLINGTON CORPORATION
Partial Balance Sheet
December 31, 1988

HOW MUCH IS THE
ESTIMATED REALIZABLE
VALUE OF THE ACCOUNTS
RECEIVABLE?

Current assets:		
Cash		$ 75,000
Accounts receivable	$200,000	
Less: Allowance for doubtful accounts	10,000	190,000

The Allowance for Doubtful Accounts

There is no way of telling in advance which accounts receivable will be collected and which ones will prove to be worthless. It is therefore not possible to credit the account of any particular customer to reflect our overall estimate of the year's credit losses. Neither is it possible to credit the Accounts Receivable controlling account in the general ledger. If the Accounts Receivable controlling account were to be credited with the estimated amount of doubtful accounts, this controlling account would no longer be in balance with the total of the numerous customers' accounts in the subsidiary ledger. The only practical alternative, therefore, is to credit a separate account called *Allowance for Doubtful Accounts* with the amount estimated to be uncollectible.

The Allowance for Doubtful Accounts often is described as a *contra-asset* account or a *valuation* account. Both of these terms indicate that the Allowance for Doubtful Accounts has a credit balance, which is offset against the asset Accounts Receivable to produce the balance sheet value for this asset.

Estimating uncollectible accounts

Before the accounts are closed and financial statements are prepared at the end of the accounting period, an estimate of the expected amount of uncollectible accounts should be made. This estimate will usually be based upon past experience and modified in accordance with current business conditions. Losses from uncollectible receivables tend to be greater during periods of recession than in periods of growth and prosperity. Because the allowance for doubtful accounts is necessarily an estimate and not a precise calculation, the factor of personal judgment may play a considerable part in determining the size of this valuation account.

Conservatism as a factor in valuing accounts receivable   The larger the allowance established for doubtful accounts, the lower the net valuation of accounts receivable will be. Some accountants and some business executives tend to favour the most conservative valuation of assets that logically can be supported. *Conservatism* in the preparation of a balance sheet implies a tendency to resolve uncertainties in the valuation of assets by reporting assets at the lower end of the range of reasonable values.

The valuation of assets at conservative amounts is a long-standing tradition in accounting, stemming from the days when creditors were the major users of financial statements. From the viewpoint of bankers and others who use financial statements as a basis for granting loans, conservatism in valuing assets has long been regarded as a desirable policy.

Assume that the balance sheet of Company A presents optimistic, exaggerated values for the assets owned. Assume also that this ''unconservative'' balance sheet is submitted to a banker in support of an application for a loan. The banker studies the balance sheet and makes a loan to Company A in reliance upon the values listed. Later the banker finds it impossible to collect the loan and also finds that the assets upon which the loan was based had been greatly overstated in the balance sheet. The banker will undoubtedly consider the overly optimistic character of Company A's balance sheet as partially responsible for the loss incurred by the bank. Experiences of this type have led creditors as a group to stress the desirability of conservatism in the valuation of assets.

In considering the argument for balance sheet conservatism, it is important to recognize that the income statement also is affected by the estimate made of uncollectible accounts. The act of providing a relatively large allowance for doubtful accounts involves a correspondingly heavy charge to expense. Setting asset values at a minimum in the balance sheet has the related effect of stating the current year's net income at a minimum amount.

Two approaches of estimating uncollectible accounts

Two alternative approaches or methods are widely used in making the annual estimate of uncollectible accounts. One is based on an aging (or analysis) of accounts receivable;

the other is based on a percentage of net credit sales. These two approaches or methods are explained in the following.

Estimating uncollectible accounts by aging the accounts receivable One method consists of adjusting the valuation account to a new balance equal to the estimated uncollectible portion of the existing accounts receivable. This method is referred to as the ***balance sheet*** approach and is based upon an ***aging of the accounts receivable.*** The adjusting entry takes into consideration the existing balance in the Allowance for Doubtful Accounts. A past-due account receivable is always viewed with some suspicion. The fact that a receivable is past due suggests that the customer is either unable or unwilling to pay. The analysis of accounts receivable by age is known as aging the accounts, as illustrated by the following schedule.

F YOU WERE CREDIT MANAGER, WHAT USE WOULD YOU MAKE OF THIS ANALYSIS?

Analysis of Accounts Receivable by Age
December 31, 19___

CUSTOMER	TOTAL	NOT YET DUE	1–30 DAYS PAST DUE	31–60 DAYS PAST DUE	61–90 DAYS PAST DUE	OVER 90 DAYS PAST DUE
A.B. Adams	$ 500	$ 500				
B.L. Baker	150			$ 150		
R.D. Carl	800	800				
H.V. Davis	900				$ 800	$ 100
R.M. Evans	400	400				
Others	32,250	16,300	$10,000	4,200	200	1,550
Totals	$35,000	$18,000	$10,000	$4,350	$1,000	$1,650
Percentage . . .	100	51	29	12	3	5

This analysis of accounts receivable gives management a useful picture of the status of collections and the probabilities of credit losses. Almost half the total accounts receivable are past due. The question "How long past due?" is pertinent, and is answered by the bottom line of the aging analysis. About 29% of the total receivables are past due from 1 to 30 days; another 12% are past due from 31 to 60 days; about 3% are past due from 61 to 90 days; and 5% of the total receivables consist of accounts past due more than three months. If an analysis of this type is prepared at the end of each month, management will be informed continuously on the trend of collections and can take appropriate action to ease or to tighten credit policy. Moreover, a yardstick is available to measure the performance of the persons responsible for collection activities.

The longer past due an account receivable becomes, the greater the likelihood that it will not be collected in full. In recognition of this fact, the analysis of receivables by age groups can be used as a stepping-stone in determining a reasonable amount to add to the Allowance for Doubtful Accounts. To determine this amount, we estimate the percentage of uncollectible accounts for each age group of accounts receivable. This percentage, when applied to the dollar amount in each age group, gives the estimated uncollectible portion for each group. By adding together the estimated uncollectible accounts for all the age groups, the required balance in the Allowance for Doubtful Accounts is determined. The following schedule lists the group totals from the preceding illustration and shows how the estimated total uncollectible accounts is computed.

Accounts Receivable by Age Groups

	AMOUNT	PERCENTAGE CONSIDERED UNCOLLECTIBLE	ESTIMATED UNCOLLECTIBLE ACCOUNTS
Not yet due	$18,000	1	$ 180
1–30 days past due	10,000	3	300
31–60 days past due	4,350	10	435
61–90 days past due	1,000	20	200
Over 90 days past due	1,650	50	825
Totals	$35,000		$1,940

This summary indicates that an allowance for doubtful accounts of $1,940 is required. Before making the adjusting entry, it is necessary to consider the existing balance in the allowance account. If the Allowance for Doubtful Accounts currently has a credit balance of, say, $500, the adjusting entry should be for $1,440 in order to bring the account up to the required balance of $1,940. This entry is as follows:

Uncollectible Accounts Expense 1,440
   Allowance for Doubtful Accounts   1,440
To increase the valuation account to the estimated required
total of $1,940 computed as follows:
   Present credit balance of valuation account . . . . $ 500
   Current provision for doubtful accounts   1,440
   New credit balance in valuation account $1,940

On the other hand, if the Allowance for Doubtful Accounts contained a *debit* balance of $500 before adjustment, the adjusting entry would be made in the amount of $2,440 ($1,940 + $500) in order to create the desired credit balance of $1,940. (The circumstances that can lead to a temporary debit balance in the Allowance for Doubtful Accounts will be explained later in this chapter.)

Estimating uncollectible accounts as a percentage of net sales   An alternative method preferred by some companies consists of computing the charge to uncollectible accounts expense as a percentage of the net sales for the year. The question to be answered is not "How large a valuation allowance is needed to reduce our receivables to realizable value?" Instead, the question is stated as "How much uncollectible accounts *expense* is associated with this year's volume of sales?" This method may be regarded as the *income statement* approach to estimating uncollectible accounts.

As an example, assume that for several years the expense of uncollectible accounts has averaged 1% of net sales (sales minus returns and allowances and sales discounts). At the end of the current year, before adjusting entries, the following account balances appear in the ledger:

	DR	CR
Sales		$1,260,000
Sales returns and allowances	$40,000	
Sales discounts	20,000	
Allowance for doubtful accounts		1,500

The *net sales* of the current year amount to $1,200,000; 1% of this amount is $12,000. The existing balance in the Allowance for Doubtful Accounts *should be ignored in computing the amount of the adjusting entry,* because the percentage of net sales method stresses the *relationship between uncollectible accounts expense and net sales* rather than the valuation of receivables at the balance sheet date. The entry is

PROVISION FOR UNCOLLECTIBLE ACCOUNTS BASED ON PERCENTAGE OF NET SALES

Uncollectible Accounts Expense	12,000	
Allowance for Doubtful Accounts		12,000
To record uncollectible accounts expense of 1% of the year's		
net sales (.01 × $1,200,000).		

If a company makes both cash sales and credit sales, it is better to *exclude the cash sales* from consideration and to compute the percentage relationship of uncollectible accounts expense to credit sales only.

This approach of estimating uncollectible accounts receivable as a percentage of credit sales is easier to apply than the method of aging accounts receivable. The aging of receivables, however, tends to give a more reliable estimate of uncollectible accounts because of the consideration given to the age and collectibility of the specific accounts receivable at the balance sheet date. Some companies use the income statement approach for preparing monthly financial statements and internal reports but use the balance sheet method for preparing annual financial statements.

Writing off an uncollectible account receivable

2 Account for the write-off of uncollectible accounts receivable and for any later recoveries.

Whenever an account receivable from a specific customer is determined to be uncollectible, it no longer qualifies as an asset and should be written off. To *write off* an account receivable is to reduce the balance of the customer's account to zero. The journal entry to accomplish this consists of a credit to the Accounts Receivable controlling account in the general ledger (and to the customer's account in the subsidiary ledger), and an offsetting debit to the Allowance for Doubtful Accounts.

Referring again to the example of Arlington Corporation as shown earlier, the ledger accounts were as follows after the adjusting entry for estimated uncollectible accounts had been made on December 31, 1988:

Accounts receivable	$200,000
Less: Allowance for doubtful accounts	10,000

Next let us assume that on January 27, 1989, customer William Brown became bankrupt and the account receivable from him in the amount of $1,000 was determined to be worthless. The following entry should be made by Arlington Corporation:

Allowance for Doubtful Accounts	1,000	
Accounts Receivable, William Brown		1,000

To write off the receivable from William Brown as uncollectible.

The important thing to note in this entry is that the debit is made to the *Allowance for Doubtful Accounts* and *not* to the Uncollectible Accounts Expense account. The estimated expense of credit losses is charged to the Uncollectible Accounts Expense account at the end of each accounting period. When a particular account receivable is later determined to be worthless and is written off, this action does not represent an additional expense but merely confirms our previous estimate of the expense. If the Uncollectible Accounts Expense account were first charged with *estimated* credit losses and then later charged with *proven* credit losses, we would be double counting the actual uncollectible accounts expense.

After the entry writing off William Brown's account has been posted, the Accounts Receivable controlling account and the Allowance for Doubtful Accounts appear as follows:

ACCOUNTS RECEIVABLE

1988		1989	
Dec. 31	200,000	Jan. 27 (Brown write-off)	1,000

ALLOWANCE FOR DOUBTFUL ACCOUNTS

1989		1988	
Jan. 27 (Brown write-off)	1,000	Dec. 31	10,000

Note that the *net* amount of the accounts receivable was unchanged by writing off William Brown's account against the Allowance for Doubtful Accounts. The write-off reduced the asset account and the allowance account by the same amount.

BEFORE THE WRITE-OFF		AFTER THE WRITE-OFF	
Accounts receivable	$200,000	Accounts receivable	$199,000
Less: Allowance for		Less: Allowance for	
doubtful accounts . .	10,000	doubtful accounts . .	9,000
Net value of receivables . . .	$190,000	Net value of receivables . . .	$190,000

The fact that writing off a worthless receivable against the Allowance for Doubtful Accounts does not change the net carrying value of accounts receivable shows that no expense is entered in the accounting records when an account receivable is written off. This example bears out the point stressed earlier in the chapter. *Credit losses belong in the period in which the sale is made, not in a later period in which the account receivable is discovered to be uncollectible.*

Write-offs seldom agree with previous estimates   The total amount of accounts receivable actually written off will seldom, if ever, be exactly equal to the estimated amount previously credited to the Allowance for Doubtful Accounts.

If the amounts written off as uncollectible turn out to be less than the estimated amount, the Allowance for Doubtful Accounts will continue to show a credit balance. If the amounts written off as uncollectible are greater than the estimated amount, the Allowance for Doubtful Accounts will acquire a *temporary debit balance,* which will be eliminated by the adjustment at the end of the period.

Recovery of an account receivable previously written off

Occasionally a receivable that has been written off as worthless will later be collected in full or in part. Such collections are often referred to as *recoveries* of uncollectible accounts or bad debts. Collection of an account receivable previously written off is evidence that the write-off was an error; the receivable should therefore be reinstated as an asset.

Let us assume, for example, that a past-due account receivable in the amount of $400 from J.B. Barker was written off by the following entry:

ARKER ACCOUNT
ONSIDERED
NCOLLECTIBLE

Allowance for Doubtful Accounts	400	
Accounts Receivable, J.B. Barker		400
To write off the receivable from J.B. Barker as uncollectible.		

At some later date the customer, J.B. Barker, pays the account in full. The entry to restore Barker's account will be

ARKER ACCOUNT
EINSTATED

Accounts Receivable, J.B. Barker	400	
Allowance for Doubtful Accounts		400
To reinstate as an asset an account receivable previously written off.		

A separate entry will be made in the cash receipts journal to record the collection from Barker. This entry will debit Cash and credit Accounts Receivable, J.B. Barker.

Compare the allowance method and the direct charge-off method of accounting or uncollectible ccounts.

Direct charge-off method

Some companies do not use a valuation allowance for accounts receivable. Instead of making year-end adjusting entries to record uncollectible accounts expense on the basis of estimates, these companies recognize no uncollectible accounts expense until specific receivables are determined to be worthless. This method makes no attempt to match revenue and related expenses. Uncollectible accounts expense is recorded in the period in which individual accounts receivable are determined to be worthless rather than in the period in which the sales were made.

When a particular customer's account is determined to be uncollectible, it is written off directly to Uncollectible Accounts Expense by an entry like the following:

Uncollectible Accounts Expense	250	
Accounts Receivable, Bell Products		250
To write off the receivable from Bell Products as uncollectible.		

When the direct charge-off method is in use, the accounts receivable will be listed in the balance sheet at their gross amount, and *no valuation allowance* will be used. The receivables, therefore, are not stated at their probable realizable value. In some situations, however, use of the direct charge-off method is reasonable. If a company makes most of its sales for cash, the amount of its accounts receivable will be small in relation to other assets. The expense from uncollectible accounts should also be small. Consequently, the direct charge-off method is acceptable because its use does not have a *material* effect on the reported net income. Another situation in which the direct charge-off method works satisfactorily is in a company that sells all or most of its output to a few large companies that are financially strong. In this setting there may be no basis for estimating credit losses.

From the standpoint of accounting theory, however, the allowance method (using either the balance sheet or income statement approach) is better, for it enables expenses to be *matched with the related revenue* and thus aids in making a logical measurement of net income, and a proper presentation of assets in the balance sheet.

Credit card sales

4   Account for credit card sales.

Many retailing businesses avoid the risk of uncollectible accounts by making credit sales to customers who use well-known credit cards, such as American Express, Visa, and MasterCard. A customer who makes a purchase using one of these cards must sign a multiple-copy form, which includes a *credit card draft*. A credit card draft is similar to a cheque that is drawn upon the funds of the credit card company rather than upon the personal bank account of the customer. The credit card company promptly pays cash to the merchant to redeem these drafts. At the end of each month the credit card company bills the credit card holder for all the drafts it has redeemed during the month. If the credit card holder fails to pay the amount owed, it is the credit card company that sustains the loss.

By making sales through credit card companies, merchants receive cash more quickly from credit sales and avoid uncollectible accounts expense. Also, the merchant avoids the expenses of investigating customers' credit, maintaining an accounts receivable subsidiary ledger, and making collections from customers.

Bank credit cards   Some widely used credit cards (such as Visa, American Express and Master Card) are issued by banks and trust companies. When the credit card company is a bank or a trust company, the retailing business may deposit the signed credit card drafts directly in its chequing account, along with the currency and personal cheques received from customers. Since banks and trust companies accept these credit card drafts for immediate deposit, sales to customers using bank credit cards are recorded as *cash sales*.

In exchange for handling the credit card drafts, the bank or trust company makes monthly service charge which usually runs between 1.69% and 5% of the amount of the drafts deposited by the merchant during the month. This monthly service charge is deducted from the merchant's chequing account and appears with other service charges in the merchant's monthly statement issued by the banks or trust companies.

Other credit cards   When customers use nonbank credit cards (such as Diners Club), the retailing business cannot deposit the credit card drafts directly in its bank account. Instead of debiting Cash, the merchant records an account receivable from the credit card company. Periodically, the credit card drafts are mailed to the credit card company, which then sends a cheque to the merchant. Credit card companies however, do not redeem the drafts at the full sales price. The agreement between the credit card company and the merchant usually allows the credit card company to take a discount of between 3½ and 5% when redeeming the drafts.

To illustrate the procedures in accounting for these credit card sales, assume that Bradshaw Camera Shop sells a camera for $200 to a customer who uses a Quick Charge credit card. The entry would be

RECEIVABLE IS FROM THE
CREDIT CARD COMPANY

```
Accounts Receivable, Quick Charge Co. ........................  200
    Sales .........................................................          200
To record sale to customer using Quick Charge credit card.
```

At the end of the week, Bradshaw Camera Shop mails credit card drafts totalling $1,200 to Quick Charge Co., which redeems the drafts after deducting a 5% discount. When payment is received by Bradshaw, the entry is

```
Cash .........................................................  1,140
Credit Card Discount Expense ...........................     60
    Accounts Receivable, Quick Charge Co. .................         1,200
To record collection of account receivable from Quick
Charge Co., less 5% discount.
```

The expense account, Credit Card Discount Expense, should be included among the selling expenses in the income statement of Bradshaw Camera Shop.

From a theoretical viewpoint, one might argue that the credit card discount expense should be recorded at the date of sale rather than at the date of collection. In this case, the sale of the camera for $200 would have been recorded by debiting Credit Card Discount Expense for $10 and Accounts Receivable, Quick Charge Co. for $190. Although this procedure would be theoretically preferable in terms of matching revenue with related expenses, it requires computing the discount expense separately for each sales transaction. For this reason it is common practice to record the discount expense at the date of collection. Since the discount expense is small and collection usually occurs shortly after the date of sale, the difference between the two methods does not have a material effect upon the financial statements. However, if the amount of accounts receivable is substantial at year-end date, an adjusting entry to recognize the credit card discount expense can be made at that date.

Credit balances in accounts receivable

Customers' accounts in the accounts receivable subsidiary ledger normally have debit balances, but occasionally a customer's account will acquire a credit balance. This may occur because the customer overpays, pays in advance, or returns merchandise previously paid for. Any credit balances in the accounts receivable subsidiary ledger should be accompanied by the notation "Cr" to distinguish them from accounts with normal debit balances.

Suppose that the Accounts Receivable controlling account in the general ledger has a debit balance of $9,000, representing the following individual accounts with customers in the subsidiary ledger:

49 accounts with debit balance totalling	$10,000
1 account with a credit balance	1,000
Net debit balance of 50 customers' accounts	$ 9,000

One of the basic rules in preparing financial statements is that assets and liabilities should be shown at their gross amounts rather than being netted against each other. Accordingly, the amount that should appear as accounts receivable in the balance sheet is not the $9,000 balance of the controlling account, but the $10,000 total of the receivables with debit balances. The account with the $1,000 *credit balance is a liability* and should be shown as such rather than being concealed as an offset against an asset. The balance sheet presentation should be as follows:

Current assets:		Current liabilities:	
Accounts receivable	$10,000	Credit balances in customers'	
		accounts	$1,000

Analysis of accounts receivable

What dollar amount of accounts receivable would be reasonable for a business making annual credit sales of $1,200,000? Comparison of the average amount of accounts receivable with the sales on credit during the period indicates how long it takes to convert receivables into cash. For example, if annual credit sales of $1,200,000 are made at a uniform rate throughout the year and the accounts receivable at year-end amount to $200,000, we can see at a glance that the receivables represent one-sixth of the year's sales, or about 60 days of uncollected sales. Management naturally wants to make efficient use of the available capital in the business, and therefore is interested in a rapid ''turnover'' of accounts receivable. If the credit terms offered by the business in this example were, say, 30 days net, the existence of receivables equal to 60 days' sales would warrant investigation. The analysis of receivables is considered more fully in Chapter 20.

5   Explain the uses of promissory notes and the nature of interest.

NOTES RECEIVABLE

The importance of notes receivable varies greatly by type of business, depending on the kind of product, sales price, and credit terms. In many lines of business, notes receivable are acquired every day and constitute an important part of total assets. In other types of business, notes receivable are infrequent. Business concerns that sell high-priced durable goods such as automobiles and farm equipment regularly accept notes receivable from their customers. General retailers, such as Sears and Zellers, sell huge amounts of merchandise on the instalment plan, calling for a series of payments over a period of perhaps 24 months or more. (Instalment sales are discussed later in this chapter.) Notes receivable also are obtained by many companies in settlement of past-due accounts receivable. Settlements of this type aid the debtor by extending the time for payment and also aid the creditor because the note receivable can readily be turned into cash by endorsing the note and selling it to a bank or finance company.

Notes receivable are the largest and most important kind of asset for nearly every bank. Interest earned on notes receivable is a bank's largest and most important type of revenue. Consequently, the collectibility of the notes receivable owned by a bank is the key factor in determining the success or failure of that bank. In recent years, many of the largest banks (for example, Bank of Montreal and Royal Bank) have made huge loans in other countries. Great difficulty is now being encountered by the banks in collecting interest on these notes. If the notes and the related interest receivable should become uncollectible, the financial health of the banking system could be seriously threatened. For example, loans from the six Canadian chartered banks to less-developed countries currently amount to about $25 billion and the allowance for losses for these loans stands at around $3 billion, and additional allowance is anticipated.

Definition of a promissory note

A promissory note is an unconditional promise in writing to pay on demand or at a specified future date a definite sum of money.

The person who signs the note and thereby promises to pay is called the **maker** of the note. The person to whom payment is to be made is called the **payee** of the note. In the illustration below, G.L. Smith is the maker of the note and A.B. Davis is the payee.

SIMPLIFIED FORM OF PROMISSORY NOTE

$1,000	London, Ontario	July 10, 19__

One month ____ after date ____ I ____ promise to pay

to the order of ____ A.B. Davis ____

-----One thousand and no/100----- ____ dollars

payable at ____ Canadian National Bank ____

for value received, with interest at ____ 12% per annum ____

G.L. Smith

From the viewpoint of the maker, G.L. Smith, the illustrated note is a liability and is recorded by crediting the Notes Payable account. However, from the viewpoint of the payee, A.B. Davis, this same note is an asset and is recorded by debiting the Notes Receivable account. The maker of a note expects to pay cash at the maturity date; the payee expects to receive cash at that date.

Nature of Interest

Interest is a charge made for the use of money. A borrower incurs interest expense. A lender earns interest revenue. When you encounter notes payable in a company's financial statements, you know that the company is borrowing and you should expect to find interest expense. When you encounter notes receivable, you should expect interest revenue.

Computing interest   A formula used in computing interest is as follows:

Principle × Rate of Interest × Time = Interest

(Often expressed as P × R × T = I)

Interest rates are usually stated on an annual basis. For example, the interest on a $10,000, one-year, 12% note is computed as follows:

$10,000 × 0.12 × 1 = $1,200

If the term of the note were only four months instead of a year, the interest charge would be $400, computed as follows:

$10,000 × 0.12 × $4/12$ = $400

If the term of the note is expressed in days, the exact number of days must be used in computing the interest. *The day on which a note is dated is not included; the day on which a note falls due is included.* Thus, a note dated today and maturing tomorrow involves only one day's interest. To stress concepts rather than precise calculations, it is convenient to assume a *360-day year* and to *disregard the three days of grace*[1]. Thus, interest computations will be based on a 360-day year and without the three days of grace for both the illustrations and the assignment questions, exercises, problems, and cases in this chapter.

Suppose, for example, that a 60-day, 12% note for $10,000 is drawn on June 10. The interest charge could be computed as follows:

$10,000 × 0.12 × $60/360$ = $200

The principal of the note ($10,000) plus the interest ($200) equals $10,200 and this amount (the *maturity value*) will be payable on August 9. The computation of days to maturity is as follows:

Days remaining in June (30 − 10; date of origin is not included)	20
Days in July	31
Days in August to maturity date (date of payment is included)	9
Total days called for by note	60

Prevailing interest rates   Interest rates, like the prices of goods and services, are always in a process of change. The Bank of Canada has a policy of deliberately causing interest rates to rise or fall in an effort to keep the economy running at a reasonable level of activity. In the early 1980s, the Bank of Canada combatted inflation by raising interest rates to record levels (20% and more). Then, as both

---

[1] All notes, other than notes payable on demand, are legally due and payable three days after the due date indicated on the notes. These extra three days are called the three days of grace. Thus, a 60-day note drawn on June 10 and payable on August 9 is legally due and payable on August 12.

inflation and business activity declined, the Bank of Canada reduced interest rates by more than half in an effort to stimulate business activity and increase employment.

The rate of interest you receive by depositing money in a savings account at a bank or a trust company depends in part on the length of time you agree to leave the deposit untouched. The lowest interest rate (presently 5% to 6% a year) applies to a passbook account, which gives you the right to withdraw all or part of your deposit at any time. However, you can earn a higher rate of interest (presently 7% to 8% a year) if you agree to leave your money on deposit for, say, a year or more.

If you had obtained a long-term mortgage loan on a residence at the time this book was going to press, you would now be paying between 10 and 12% as an annual interest rate. A business obtaining a loan from a bank may pay between 9% and 15% a year. Early in the 1980s interest rates were roughly double the rates that prevailed a few years earlier. By the mid-1980s, rates were down again to pre-1980 levels.

The interest rate that banks charge on loans to the largest and strongest corporations is called the *prime rate*. Smaller companies and those not in a strong financial position may have to pay several percentage points more than the prime rate in order to obtain a bank loan.

Many retail stores charge interest on instalment accounts at $1\frac{1}{2}\%$ a month, which is equivalent to 18% a year. Keep in mind that interest rates vary widely depending upon the nature of the loan and the financial strength of the borrower — and upon the fiscal policy of the federal government.

Accounting for notes receivable

Account for the
ceipt of notes,
crual of interest,
llection or default,
d the discounting of
tes receivable.

All notes receivable are usually posted to a single account in the general ledger. Entries in the Notes Receivable account may conveniently be identified by writing the name of the maker of the note in the Explanation column on each line used to record the receipt or collection of a note receivable. A subsidiary ledger is not essential because the notes themselves are the equivalent of a subsidiary ledger and provide any necessary information as to maturity, interest rates, collateral pledged, and other details. The amount debited to Notes Receivable is always the *face amount* of the note, regardless of whether or not the note bears interest. When an interest-bearing note is collected, the amount of cash received will be larger than the face amount of the note if the interest charge is not included in the face amount of the note. (Notes receivable with interest included in the face amount will be discussed later in this chapter.) The interest collected is credited to an Interest Revenue account and the face amount of the note is credited to the Notes Receivable account.

Illustrative entries   Assume that a 12%, 90-day note receivable is acquired from a customer, Marvin White, in settlement of an existing account receivable of $30,000. The entry for acquisition of the note is as follows:

TE RECEIVED TO
PLACE ACCOUNT
CEIVABLE

Dec. 1	Notes Receivable	30,000	
	Accounts Receivable, Marvin White		30,000
	Accepted 12%, 90-day note in settlement of		
	account receivable.		

At December 31, the end of the company's fiscal year, the interest earned to date on notes receivable should be accrued by an adjusting entry as follows:

Dec. 31	Interest Receivable	300	
	Interest Revenue		300
	To accrue interest for the month of December on Marvin White note. ($30,000 × 12% × $^1/_{12}$ = $300).		

On March 1 (90 days after the date of the note), the note matures. The entry to record collection of the note will be:

Mar. 1	Cash	30,900	
	Notes Receivable		30,000
	Interest Receivable		300
	Interest Revenue		600
	Collected 12%, 90-day note from Marvin White. ($30,000 × 12% × $^3/_{12}$ = $900 interest, of which $600 was earned in current year).		

The preceding three entries show that interest is being earned throughout the life of the note and that the interest should be apportioned between years on a time basis. The revenue of each year will then include the interest actually earned in that year.

If the maker of a note defaults   A note receivable which cannot be collected at maturity is said to have been *defaulted* by the maker. Immediately after the default of a note, an entry should be made by the holder to transfer the amount due from the Notes Receivable account to an account receivable from the debtor.

Assuming that a 60-day, 12% note receivable for $1,000 from Robert Jones is not collected at maturity, the following entry would be made:

Accounts Receivable, Robert Jones	1,020	
Notes Receivable		1,000
Interest Revenue		20
To record default by Robert Jones of a 12%, 60-day note.		

The interest earned on the note is recorded as a credit to Interest Revenue and is also included in the account receivable from the maker. The interest receivable on a defaulted note is just as valid a claim against the maker as is the principal of the note if the principal is collectible, then presumably the interest too can be collected.

The transfer of past-due notes receivable into Accounts Receivable accomplishes two things. First, the Notes Receivable account is limited to current notes not yet matured and is, therefore, regarded as a highly liquid type of asset. Second, the account receivable ledger card will show that a note has been defaulted and will present a complete picture of all transactions with the customer.

Renewal of a note receivable   Sometimes the two parties to a note agree that the note shall be renewed rather than paid at the maturity date. In this situation a new note should be prepared and the old one cancelled. If the old note does not bear interest, the entry could be made as shown at the top of page 359.

Since this entry causes no change in the balance of the Notes Receivable account, a question may arise as to whether the entry is necessary. The renewal of a note is an

RENEWAL OF NOTE SHOULD BE RECORDED	Notes Receivable	10,000	
	Notes Receivable		10,000
	A 60-day, non-interest-bearing note from Bell Company renewed today with new 60-day, 14% note.		

important transaction requiring managerial attention; a general journal entry is needed to record the action taken by management and to provide a permanent record of the transaction. If journal entries were not made to record the renewal of notes, confusion might arise as to whether some of the notes included in the balance of the Notes Receivable account were current or defaulted.

Discounting notes receivable

Many business concerns that obtain notes receivable from their customers prefer to sell the notes to a financial institution such as a bank for cash rather than to hold them until maturity. Selling a note receivable to a bank or finance company is often called *discounting* a note receivable. The holder of the note endorses the back of the note (as in endorsing a cheque) and delivers the note to the bank. The bank expects to collect the *maturity value* (principal plus interest) from the maker of the note at the maturity date, but if the maker fails to pay, the bank can demand payment from the endorser.

When a business endorses a note and turns it over to a bank for cash, the business (as endorser) is contingently liable to the bank. A *contingent liability* is a potential liability which either will develop into a full-fledged liability or will be eliminated entirely by a future event. The future event in the case of a discounted note receivable is the payment (or default) of the note by the maker. If the maker pays, the contingent liability of the endorser is thereby ended. If the maker fails to pay, the contingent liability of the endorser becomes a real liability. In either case the period of contingent liability ends at the maturity date of the note.

The discounting of notes receivable with a bank may be regarded by a company as an alternative to borrowing by issuing its own note payable. To issue its own note payable to the bank would create a liability; to obtain cash by discounting a note receivable creates only a contingent liability. However, such a contingent liability should be disclosed in a footnote to financial statements.

Computing the proceeds The amount of cash obtained from the bank by discounting a note receivable is called the *proceeds* of the note. We can compute the proceeds in three simple steps.

1 Compute the maturity value of the note. (Principal plus interest payable at maturity.)
2 Compute the discount charged by the bank. (Multiply the discount rate charged by the bank by the maturity value of the note for the time period the bank must hold the note. This time period runs from the date of discounting to the date the note is due.)
3 Deduct the discount from the maturity value of the note. The result is the cash received from discounting the note.

To illustrate, assume that on July 2 Retail Sales Company receives a 75-day, 12% note for $8,000 from Raymond Kelly. The note will mature on September 15 (29 days in July, 31 days in August, and 15 days in September). On July 17, Retail

Sales Company discounts this note receivable with its bank, which charges a discount rate of 15% a year. How much cash will Retail Sales Company receive? The computation is as follows:

Face of the note	$8,000
Add: Interest for 75 days from date of note to maturity	
($8,000 × .12 × $^{75}/_{360}$)	200
Maturity value	$8,200
Less: Bank discount at 15% for the discount period of 60 days	
(July 17 to Sept. 15) ($8,200 × .15 × $^{60}/_{360}$)	205
Proceeds (cash received from bank)	$7,995

[handwritten margin note: Don't include Interest from maker!]

[handwritten margin note: not]

The entry for the transaction (in general journal form) is as follows:

Cash	7,995	
Interest Expense	5	
Notes Receivable		8,000

Discounted Raymond Kelly note at bank at 15% annual interest rate. Maturity value $8,200 minus $205 discount equals proceeds of $7,995.

In this illustration, the cash of $7,995 received from the bank was less than the $8,000 face amount of the note. The proceeds received from discounting a note may be *either more or less* than the face amount of the note, depending upon the interest rates and time periods involved. The difference between the face amount of the note being discounted and the cash proceeds is usually recorded as either Interest Expense or Interest Revenue. If the proceeds are less than the face value, the difference is debited to Interest Expense. However, if the proceeds exceed the face value of the note, the difference is credited to Interest Revenue.

Discounted note receivable paid by maker   Before the maturity date of the discounted note, the bank will notify the maker, Raymond Kelly, that it is holding the note. Kelly will therefore make payment directly to the bank. In this case, Retail Sales Company's contingent liability as an endorser is ended and no entry is needed.

Discounted note receivable defaulted by maker   If Kelly should be unable to pay the note at maturity, the bank will give notice of the default to the endorser, Retail Sales Company, which immediately becomes obligated to pay, and will make the following entry to record the payment.

Accounts Receivable, Raymond Kelly	8,200	
Cash		8,200

To record payment to bank of maturity value of discounted Kelly note, defaulted by maker.

Under these assumptions Retail Sales Company's contingent liability to the bank has become a real liability and has been discharged by a cash payment. Retail Sales Company now has an account receivable from the maker of the defaulted note for the amount that it was compelled to pay to the bank.

Notes receivable with interest included in the face amount

In our discussion to this point, we have used notes receivable with the interest rate *stated separately*. We now want to compare this form of note with an alternative form in which the interest charge is *included in the face amount* of the note. For example, assume that Genetic Services has a $10,000 account receivable from a customer, Biolab. The customer is short of cash and wants to postpone payment, so Genetic Services agrees to accept a six-month promissory note from Biolab with interest at the rate of 12% a year to replace the $10,000 account receivable. The interest for six months will amount to $600 and the total amount to be received at maturity will be $10,000 principal plus $600 interest, or $10,600 altogether.

If the note is drawn with interest stated separately, as in the first illustration as follows, the wording will be ". . . Biolab promises to pay to Genetic Services the sum of $10,000 with interest at the rate of 12% a year."

THIS NOTE IS FOR THE PRINCIPAL AMOUNT WITH INTEREST STATED SEPARATELY

Ottawa, Ontario	November 1, 19__

Six months after this date Biolab

promises to pay to Genetic Services the sum of $ 10,000

with interest at the rate of 12% a year.

Signed *George Harris*

Title Treasurer, Biolab

If the alternative form of note is used, the $600 interest will be included in the face amount and the note will appear as shown:

INTEREST IS INCLUDED IN FACE AMOUNT OF THIS NOTE

Ottawa, Ontario	November 1, 19__

Six months after this date Biolab

promises to pay to Genetic Services the sum of $ 10,600

Signed *George Harris*

Title Treasurer, Biolab

Notice that the face amount of the note ($10,600) is greater than the $10,000 account receivable that it replaces. However, the value of the note receivable at November 1 is only $10,000; the other $600 included in the face amount of the note represents *unearned* interest. As this interest is earned over the life of the note, the value of the note will rise to $10,600 at maturity.

The journal entry by Genetic Services at November 1 to record the acquisition of the note will be as follows:

INTEREST INCLUDED IN FACE OF NOTE

Notes Receivable	10,600	
Discount on Notes Receivable		600
Accounts Receivable		10,000

Obtained from Biolab a six-month note with interest at 12% included in the face amount.

The asset account, Notes Receivable, was debited with the full face amount of the note ($10,600). It is, therefore, necessary to credit a contra-asset, Discount on Notes Receivable, for the $600 of unearned interest included in the face amount of the note. The Discount on Notes Receivable will appear in the balance sheet as a deduction from Notes Receivable. In our illustration, the amounts in the balance sheet will be Notes Receivable, $10,600 minus Discount on Notes Receivable, $600, or a net asset value of $10,000 on November 1.

Discount on notes receivable   The $600 balance of the account Discount on Notes Receivable at November 1 represents *unearned interest.* As the interest is earned over the life of the note, the amount in the discount account will be gradually transferred into Interest Revenue. Thus, at the maturity date of the note, Discount on Notes Receivable will have a zero balance and the value of the note receivable will have increased to $10,600. The process of transferring the amount in the Discount on Notes Receivable account into the Interest Revenue account is called *amortization* of the discount.

Amortization of the discount   The discount on short-term notes receivable usually is amortized by the straight-line method, which allocates the same amount of discount to interest revenue for each month of the note's life.[2] Thus, the $600 discount on the Biolab note will be transferred from Discount on Notes Receivable into Interest Revenue at the rate of $100 per month ($600 ÷ 6 months).

Adjusting entries should be made to amortize the discount at the end of the year and at the date the note matures. At December 31, Year 1, Genetic Services will make the following adjusting entry to recognize the two months' interest revenue earned since November 1.

AMORTIZATION OF DISCOUNT

Discount on Notes Receivable	200	
Interest Revenue		200

To record interest revenue earned to end-of-year on six-month note dated Nov. 1 ($600 discount × 2/6).

---

[2] When an interest charge is included in the face amount of a long-term note, the effective interest method of amortizing the discount is often used instead of the straight-line method. The effective interest method of amortization is introduced later in this chapter and discussed more fully in Chapter 16.

At December 31, the net valuation of the note receivable will appear in the balance sheet of Genetic Services as shown below:

ASSET SHOWN NET OF
DISCOUNT

Current assets:
Notes receivable $10,600
Less: Discount on notes receivable 400 $10,200

The net asset valuation of $10,200 consists of the $10,000 principal amount receivable from Biolab plus the $200 interest that has accrued since November 1.

When the note matures on May 1 the next year, Genetic Services will recognize the $400 interest revenue earned since year-end and will collect $10,600 from Biolab. The entry is:

TWO-THIRDS OF
INTEREST APPLICABLE
TO SECOND YEAR

Cash 10,600
Discount on Notes Receivable 400
    Interest Revenue 400
    Notes Receivable 10,600
To record collection of six-month note due today and to recognize interest revenue earned since year-end ($10,000 × 12% × $^4/_{12}$ = $400).

Comparison of the two forms of notes receivable

We have illustrated two alternative methods which Genetic Services could use in accounting for its $10,000 receivable, depending upon the form of the note. Journal entries for both methods, along with the resulting balance sheet presentations of the asset at November 1 and December 31, are summarized on the next page. Notice that both methods result in Genetic Services recognizing the same amount of interest revenue and the same asset valuation in the balance sheet. The form of the note does not change the economic substance of the transaction.

The concept of present value

8 Discuss the concept of present value in accounting for long-term notes receivable.

Assume that you receive three offers for an automobile you are trying to sell. One offer is for $4,000 cash; the second offer is a one-year note for $4,100; and the third offer is a two-year note for $4,250. Assume also that the offers are from financially responsible persons. Which of the three is the best offer?

We can make this decision by using the concept of present value. This concept is based upon the "time value" of money—the idea that an amount of money received today is equivalent to a larger amount of money that will not be received until some time in the future. Money available today can be invested to earn interest and thereby become equivalent to a larger amount in the future. The more distant the future cash receipt, the smaller its *present value.*

If we apply this present value concept to decide among the three offers for the automobile, it is apparent that the $4,000 cash is the best offer. Assume that the current rate of interest on a bank savings account is 8% a year. The amount of $4,000 invested today would grow to $4,320 within one year. Turning to the third offer, if we invest $4,000 today for a two-year period at an annual interest rate of 8%, our investment will grow to about $4,666 within the two years. We can conclude,

COMPARISON OF THE TWO FORMS OF NOTES RECEIVABLE

NOTE WRITTEN FOR $10,000 PLUS 12% INTEREST

ENTRY TO RECORD ACQUISITION OF NOTES ON NOV. 1

Notes Receivable	10,000	
Accounts Receivable		10,000

PARTIAL BALANCE SHEET AT NOV. 1

Current assets:
Notes Receivable	$10,000

ADJUSTING ENTRY AT DEC. 31

Interest Receivable	200	
Interest Revenue		200

PARTIAL BALANCE SHEET AT DEC. 31

Current assets:
Notes Receivable	$10,000	
Interest Receivable	200	$10,200

ENTRY TO RECORD COLLECTION OF NOTE ON MAY 1

Cash	10,600	
Notes Receivable		10,000
Interest Receivable		200
Interest Revenue		400

NOTE WRITTEN WITH INTEREST INCLUDED IN FACE AMOUNT

ENTRY TO RECORD ACQUISITION OF NOTES ON NOV. 1

Notes Receivable	10,600	
Discount on Notes Receivable		600
Accounts Receivable		10,000

PARTIAL BALANCE SHEET AT NOV. 1

Current assets:
Notes Receivable	$10,600	
Less: Discount on Notes Receivable	600	$10,000

ADJUSTING ENTRY AT DEC. 31

Discount on Notes Receivable	200	
Interest Revenue		200

PARTIAL BALANCE SHEET AT DEC. 31

Current assets:
Notes Receivable	$10,600	
Less: Discount on Notes Receivable	400	$10,200

ENTRY TO RECORD COLLECTION OF NOTE ON MAY 1

Cash	10,600	
Discount on Notes Receivable	400	
Interest Revenue		400
Notes Receivable		10,600

therefore, that the two offers in the form of notes are not attractive. They offer us far less than the going rate of interest to wait for a future cash receipt.

Interest rates are not always apparent   If you lend cash and accept a long-term note, you can easily determine whether an interest charge is included in the face amount of the note. For example, if you lend $9,000 and receive a note for $10,000, you know that an interest charge of $1,000 has been included in the face amount of the note. However, if you receive a $10,000 note in exchange for noncash assets, such as land or machinery, the amount of interest (if any) included in the face amount of the note may be less apparent.

If a realistic rate of interest is stated separately in a long-term note, we may assume that no interest charge is included in the face amount. If no interest rate is stated, however, or if the stated interest rate is unrealistically low (such as 2% a year), a portion of the face amount of the note must be assumed to represent an interest charge. The note should be valued at its ***present value*** rather than at the face amount.

When a note does not call for the payment of interest, the present value of the note is less than its face amount, because the face amount of the note will not be received until the maturity date. The difference between the present value of a note and its face amount should be viewed as an interest charge included in the face amount. Often we can determine the present value of a note by the fair market value of the asset acquired when the note is issued. As an alternative, we can compute the present value by using the mathematical techniques illustrated in Appendix A following Chapter 16.

The ***effective rate of interest*** associated with a note is that interest rate that will cause the note's present value to increase to the full maturity value of the note by the due date.

An illustration of notes recorded at present value

To illustrate the use of present value in transactions involving long-term notes receivable, let us assume that on September 1, Tru-Tool, Inc., sells equipment to Everts Company and accepts as payment a one-year note in the face amount of $230,000 with no mention of an interest rate. It is not logical to assume that Tru-Tool, Inc., would extend credit for one year without charging any interest. Therefore, some portion of the $230,000 face amount of the note should be regarded as a charge for interest.

Let us assume that the regular sales price of the equipment sold in this transaction is $200,000. In this case the present value of the note is apparently $200,000, and the remaining $30,000 of the face amount represents a charge for interest. The rate of interest which will cause the $200,000 present value of the note to increase to the $230,000 maturity value in one year is 15%. Thus, the face amount of the note actually includes an interest charge computed at the effective interest rate of 15%.

The selling company, Tru-Tool, Inc., should use the present value of the note in determining the amount of revenue to be recognized from the sale. The $30,000 interest charge included in the face amount of the note receivable from Everts Company represents ***unearned interest*** to Tru-Tool, Inc., and is ***not part of the sales price of the equipment.*** If Tru-Tool, Inc., were to treat the entire face amount of the note receivable as the sales price of the equipment, the result would be to overstate sales revenue and notes receivable by $30,000, and also to understate interest revenue by this amount over the life of the note. Tru-Tool, Inc., should record the sale at the present value of the note received, as follows:

<table>
<tr><td>PRESENT VALUE OF
THIS NOTE RECEIVABLE
IS $200,000</td><td>Notes Receivable ....</td><td>230,000</td><td></td></tr>
<tr><td></td><td>Discount on Notes Receivable ....</td><td></td><td>30,000</td></tr>
<tr><td></td><td>Sales ....</td><td></td><td>200,000</td></tr>
</table>

Sold equipment to Everts Company and received a one-year note with a 15% interest charge included in the face amount.

As the $30,000 interest is earned over the life of the note, this amount will be transferred into Interest Revenue. At December 31, Tru-Tool, Inc., will have earned four months' interest revenue and will make the following entry.

<table>
<tr><td>PRESENT VALUE HAS
INCREASED $10,000
BY DEC. 31</td><td>Discount on Notes Receivable ....</td><td>10,000</td><td></td></tr>
<tr><td></td><td>Interest Revenue ....</td><td></td><td>10,000</td></tr>
</table>

To record interest earned from Sept. 1 through Dec. 31 on Everts Company note ($200,000 × 15% × $^4/_{12}$).

On September 1 of the following year, when the note receivable is collected from Everts Company, the required entry will be

<table>
<tr><td>PRESENT VALUE HAS
RISEN TO $230,000
BY MATURITY DATE</td><td>Cash ....</td><td>230,000</td><td></td></tr>
<tr><td></td><td>Discount on Notes Receivable ....</td><td>20,000</td><td></td></tr>
<tr><td></td><td>Interest Revenue ....</td><td></td><td>20,000</td></tr>
<tr><td></td><td>Notes Receivable ....</td><td></td><td>230,000</td></tr>
</table>

To record collection of Everts Company note and to recognize interest earned since year-end.

In an earlier era of accounting practice, failure to use the concept of present value in recording transactions involving long-term notes sometimes resulted in large overstatements of assets and sales revenue, especially by real estate development companies. In recognition of this problem, the Financial Accounting Standards Board in the United States now requires the use of present value in recording transactions involving *long-term* notes receivable or payable that do not bear reasonable stated rates of interest.[3] In Canada, there are no similar pronouncements by the CICA in this area.

When a note is issued for a short period of time, any interest charge included in its face amount is likely to be relatively small. Therefore, the use of present value is not required in recording normal transactions with customers or suppliers involving notes due in less than one year. Notes given or received in such transactions that do not specify an interest rate may be considered non-interest-bearing.

Instalment receivables

Another application of present value is found in the recording of *instalment sales*. Many retailing businesses sell merchandise on instalment sales plans, which permit

---

[3] *APB Opinion No. 21*, "Interest on Receivables and Payable," AICPA (New York: 1971).

customers to pay for their credit purchases through a series of monthly payments. The importance of instalment sales is emphasized by many recent balance sheets of large companies, which show receivables in millions of dollars, nearly all of which call for collection in monthly instalments.

When merchandise is sold on an instalment plan, substantial interest charges are usually added to the "cash selling price" of the product in determining the total dollar amount to be collected in the series of instalment payments. The amount of sales revenue recognized at the time of sale, however, is limited to the *present value* of these instalment payments. In most cases, the present value of these future payments is equal to the regular sales price of the merchandise. The portion of the instalment account receivable that represents unearned finance charges is credited to the contra-asset account, Discount on Instalment Receivables. The balance of this contra-asset account is then amortized into Interest Revenue over the length of the collection period.

Although the collection period for an instalment receivable often runs as long as 24 to 36 months, such receivables are regarded as current assets if they correspond to customary credit terms of the industry.[4] In published balance sheets, the Discount on Instalment Receivables is often called Deferred Interest Income or Unearned Finance Charges. A typical balance sheet presentation of instalment accounts receivable follows:

Trade accounts receivable:

Accounts receivable	$ 75,040,000
Instalment contracts receivable, including $31,000,000 due after one year but not exceeding two years	52,640,000
	$127,680,000
Less: Deferred interest income ($8,070,000) and allowance for doubtful accounts ($1,872,000)	9,942,000
Total trade accounts and notes receivable	$117,738,000

END-OF-CHAPTER REVIEW

SUMMARY OF CHAPTER LEARNING OBJECTIVES

1 Explain the nature and financial statement presentation of uncollectible accounts and apply the balance sheet approach and the income statement approach to estimating these accounts.

Uncollectible accounts are the inevitable result of making sales on credit. Thus, the uncollectible accounts expense is presented in the income statement and the allowance for doubtful account is deducted from accounts receivable in the balance sheet.

Under the balance sheet approach, we arrange the year-end accounts receivable into age groups and estimate the uncollectible portion. Then, we adjust the allowance account to equal this estimate.

[4] CICA, *CICA Handbook* (Toronto), paragraph 3020.02.

Under the income statement approach, we compute the amount of the adjusting entry for uncollectible accounts as a percentage of the year's net sales. This approach leaves out of consideration any existing balance in the allowance account.

2 Account for the write-off of uncollectible accounts receivable and for any later recoveries.

When an account receivable from a specific customer is determined to be uncollectible, it no longer qualifies as an asset and should be written off. The journal entry for the write-off consists of a debit to Allowance for Doubtful Accounts and a credit to Accounts Receivable.

Occasionally a receivable that has been written off as worthless will later be collected. Such collections are called recoveries of uncollectible accounts or bad debts. Two accounting entries are needed: (1) to reinstate the receivable by debiting Accounts Receivable and crediting the Allowance for Doubtful Accounts, and (2) to record the collection by debiting Cash and crediting Accounts Receivable.

3 Compare the allowance method and the direct charge-off method of accounting for uncollectible accounts.

The allowance method is theoretically preferable because it applies the matching principle to revenue and to the expenses incurred in producing that revenue. Thus, uncollectible accounts or bad debts associated with the year's sales are recognized as expenses of the period in which the sales were made. However, some companies (for which uncollectible accounts are not material) use the direct charge-off method. Under this method, no uncollectible accounts expense is recognized until specific receivables are determined to be worthless.

4 Account for credit card sales.

Many retail businesses avoid the risk of uncollectible accounts by making credit sales to customers who present well-known bank credit cards, such as Visa and MasterCard. The credit card drafts received by a merchant are deposited at the bank for immediate credit, hence are the equivalent of cash sales. For nonbank credit cards, such as Diners' Club, the merchant collects directly from the credit card company, which deducts a service charge.

5 Explain the uses of promissory notes and the nature of interest.

A promissory note is an unconditional promise to pay on demand or at a specified future date a fixed sum of money. Companies that sell high-priced durable goods, such as farm machinery, regularly accept notes receivable from their customers. Sales of all types of merchandise on the instalment plan also usually involve the use of notes. In addition, notes receivable are obtained by companies in settlement of past-due accounts receivable.

Notes receivable usually bear interest, computed at an annual rate by the formula "Principal × Rate × Time = Interest." Interest is a charge for the use of money. Annual rates have varied widely in recent years with the prime rate rising to about 20% and then declining to its present level of about 10%.

6 Account for the receipt of notes, accrual of interest, collection or default, and the discounting of notes receivable.

Notes receivable are recorded at their face amount. Interest revenue is recognized as earned at the end of the accounting period and at the maturity of the note. If the maker defaults, the principal of the note and the interest earned are transferred to an account receivable pending collection or write-off. Notes receivable are often discounted or sold to a financial institution such as a bank for cash. The amount received (proceeds) is equal to the maturity value of the note minus the discount charged by the bank. A contingent liability to the bank exists until the note matures, which means that the person discounting the note must pay the bank if the maker of the note should default.

7 Account for notes receivable with the interest charges included in the face amount.

A note may be drawn with the interest included in the face amount, as an alternative to stating the interest separately. Such notes are recorded at the face amount and the interest is credited to Discount on Notes Receivable. The discount represents unearned interest and is amortized to Interest Revenue over the life of the note.

8 Discuss the concept of present value in accounting for long-term notes receivable.

An amount of money received today is equivalent to a larger amount of money to be received at a future date. If a long-term note receivable does not include a reasonable stated rate of interest, the present value of the note is less than its face amount. The entry to record the note will include a debit to Notes Receivable for the face amount and a credit to Discount on Notes Receivable for the difference between the face amount and the present value. The discount is earned over the life of the note and transferred to Interest Revenue. The carrying value of the note rises gradually to reach the face amount by the maturity date.

KEY TERMS INTRODUCED OR EMPHASIZED IN CHAPTER 8

Aging the accounts receivable The process of classifying accounts receivable by age groups such as current, past due 1–30 days, past due 31–60 days, etc. A step in estimating the uncollectible portion of the accounts receivable.

Allowance for Doubtful Accounts A valuation account or contra account relating to accounts receivable and showing the portion of the receivables estimated to be uncollectible.

Contingent liability A potential liability that either will develop into a full-fledged liability or will be eliminated entirely by a future event.

Contra-asset account A ledger account that is deducted from or offset against a related asset account in the financial statements, for example, Allowance for Doubtful Accounts and Discount on Notes Receivable.

Default Failure to pay interest or principal of a promissory note at the due date.

Direct charge-off method A method of accounting for uncollectible receivables in which no expense is recognized until individual accounts are determined to be worthless. At that point the account receivable is written off with an offsetting debit to uncollectible accounts expense. Fails to match revenue and related expenses.

Discount on Notes Receivable A contra-asset account representing any unearned interest included in the face amount of a note receivable. Over the life of the note, the balance of the Discount on Notes Receivable account is amortized into Interest Revenue.

Discounting notes receivable Selling a note receivable prior to its maturity date.

Effective interest rate The rate of interest that will cause the present value of a note to increase to the maturity value by the maturity date.

Interest A charge made for the use of money. The formula for computing interest is Principal $\times$ Rate of interest $\times$ Time = Interest ($P \times R \times T = I$).

Maker (of a note) A person or entity who issues a promissory note.

Maturity date The date on which a note becomes due and payable.

Maturity value The value of a note at its maturity date, consisting of principal plus interest.

Payee The person named in a promissory note to whom payment is to be made (the creditor).

Present value of a future cash receipt The amount of money that an informed investor would pay today for the right to receive that future cash receipt. The present value is always less than the future amount, because money available today can be invested to earn interest and thereby become equivalent to a larger amount in the future.

Proceeds The amount received from selling a note receivable prior to its maturity. Maturity value minus discount equals proceeds.

Three days of grace The extra three days added to the due date on all notes, other than the demand notes, to determine the legal date on which the note is due and payable. To stress concepts and for the ease of interest computation, these three days of grace are disregarded in this chapter.

DEMONSTRATION PROBLEM FOR YOUR REVIEW

The Monastery, Inc., sells custom wood furniture to decorators and the general public. Selected transactions relating to the company's receivables for the month of August follow. The company uses the allowance method in accounting for uncollectible accounts.

Aug. 8 A $420 account receivable from S. Wilson was determined to be worthless and was written off.

Aug. 11 Received a 60-day note from StyleCraft Co. in settlement of $3,600 open account. Interest computed at the effective rate of 8% was included in the face amount of the note.

Aug. 13 Sold merchandise to Century Interiors and received a $15,000, 60-day, 8% note dated August 13.

Aug. 20 Received full payment from J. Porter of a $4,500, 60-day, 12% note dated June 21. Accrued interest receivable of $30 had been recorded in prior months.

Aug. 23 Discounted the Century Interiors note dated August 13 at the bank. The bank discount rate of 9% was applied to the maturity value of the note for the 50 days remaining to maturity.

Aug. 25 An account receivable of $325 from G. Davis had been written off in June; full payment was unexpectedly received from Davis.

Aug. 29 Sales to ExtraCash credit card customers during August amounted to $14,800. (Summarize all credit card sales in one entry. ExtraCash Inc. is a credit card company.)

Aug. 30 Collected cash from ExtraCash Inc. for the August credit card sales, less a 5% discount charged by ExtraCash.

Aug. 31 As a result of substantial write-offs, the Allowance for Doubtful Accounts has a debit balance of $320. Aging of the accounts receivable indicates that the allowance account should have a $1,200 credit balance at the end of August.

Instructions Prepare journal entries to record the transactions listed above and to make any adjusting entry necessary at August 31, 19___.

SOLUTION TO DEMONSTRATION PROBLEM

General Journal

19___			
Aug. 8	Allowance for Doubtful Accounts	420	
	Accounts Receivable, S. Wilson		420
	Wrote off uncollectible account from S. Wilson.		

Aug. 11	Notes Receivable	3,648	
	Discount on Notes Receivable		48
	Accounts Receivable, StyleCraft Co.		3,600

Received 60-day note with interest at effective rate
of 8% included in face amount in settlement of open
account.

13	Note Receivable, Century Interiors	15,000	
	Sales		15,000

Sale of merchandise for a 60-day, 8% note.

20	Cash	4,590	
	Notes Receivable		4,500
	Interest Receivable		30
	Interest Revenue		60

Collected note from J. Porter, including $90 interest.

23	Cash	15,010	
	Notes Receivable		15,000
	Interest Revenue		10

Discounted Century Interiors' note at bank, proceeds
computed as follows: Maturity value $15,200 − bank
charge of $190 ($15,200 × .09 × $^{50}/_{360}$) = $15,010.

25	Account Receivable, G. Davis	325	
	Allowance for Doubtful Accounts		325

To reinstate Davis receivable previously written off.

25	Cash	325	
	Accounts Receivable, G. Davis		325

To record collection of Davis account.

29	Accounts Receivable, ExtraCash Inc.	14,800	
	Sales		14,800

To record credit card sales for August.

30	Cash	14,060	
	Credit Card Discount Expense	740	
	Accounts Receivable, ExtraCash Inc.		14,800

Collected August credit card sales invoices, less 5%.

31	Uncollectible Accounts Expense	1,520	
	Allowance for Doubtful Accounts		1,520

To provide for estimated uncollectibles as follows:

Balance required	$1,200
Present balance (debit)	320
Required increase in allowance	$1,520

31	Discount on Notes Receivable . . . . :	16	
	Interest Revenue		16

To record interest earned through Aug. 31 on StyleCraft
note receivable ($48 discount × $^{20}/_{60}$ = $16).

ASSIGNMENT MATERIAL

Note to Students: Answers to Review Questions, Exercises, and Problems regarding the computations of maturity date and interest on notes receivable are based on a 360-day year and without the three days of grace so as to stress concept and to avoid cumbersome computations.

REVIEW QUESTIONS

1 Jones Company, a retailer, makes most of its sales on credit. In the first 10 years of operation, the company incurred some bad debts or uncollectible accounts expense each year. Does this record indicate that the company's credit policies are in need of change?

2 Company A and Company B are virtually identical in size and nature of operations, but Company A is more conservative in valuing accounts receivable. Will this greater emphasis on conservatism cause A to report higher or lower net income than Company B? Assume that you are a banker considering identical loan applications from A and B and you know of the more conservative policy followed by A. In which set of financial statements would you feel more confidence? Explain.

3 Adams Company determines at year-end that its Allowance for Doubtful Accounts should be increased by $6,500. Give the adjusting entry to carry out this decision.

4 In making the annual adjusting entry for uncollectible accounts, a company may utilize a *balance sheet approach* to make the estimate or it may use an *income statement approach*. Explain these two alternative approaches.

5 At the end of its first year in business, Baxter Laboratories had accounts receivable totalling $148,500. After careful analysis of the individual accounts, the credit manager estimated that $146,100 would ultimately be collected. Give the journal entry required to reflect this estimate in the accounts.

6 In February of its second year of operations, Baxter Laboratories (Question 5 above) learned of the failure of a customer, Sterling Corporation, which owed Baxter $800. Nothing could be collected. Give the journal entry to recognize the uncollectibility of the receivable from Sterling Corporation.

7 Bell Company, which uses the allowance method of accounting for uncollectible accounts, wrote off as uncollectible a $1,200 receivable from Dailey Company. Several months later, Dailey Company obtained new long-term financing and promptly paid all its old debts in full. Give the journal entry or entries (in general journal form) which Bell Company should make to record this recovery of $1,200.

8 What is the direct charge-off method of handling credit losses as opposed to the allowance method? What is its principal shortcoming?

9 Morgan Corporation has decided to write off its account receivable from Brill Company because the latter has entered bankruptcy. What general ledger accounts should be debited and credited, assuming that the allowance method is in use? What general ledger accounts should be debited and credited if the direct charge-off method is in use?

10 Mill Company, which has accounts receivable of $309,600 and an allowance for doubtful accounts of $3,600, decides to write off as worthless a past-due account receivable for $1,500 from J.D. North. What effect will the write-off have upon total current assets? Upon net income for the period? Explain.

11 Describe a procedure by which management could be informed each month of the status of collections and the overall quality of the accounts receivable on hand.

12 What are the advantages to a retailer of making credit sales only to customers who use nationally recognized credit cards?

13 Alta Mine Co., a restaurant that had always made cash sales only, adopted a new policy of honouring several nationally known credit cards. Sales did not increase, but many of Alta Mine Co.'s regular customers began charging dinner bills on the credit cards. Has the new policy been beneficial to Alta Mine Co.? Explain.

14 Determine the maturity date of the following notes (disregard the three days of grace):

a A three-month note dated March 10

b A 30-day note dated August 15

c A 90-day note dated July 2

15 X Company acquires a 9%, 60-day note receivable from a customer, Robert Waters, in settlement of an existing account receivable of $4,000. Give the journal entry to record acquisition of the note and the journal entry to record its collection at maturity. Use a 360-day year and disregard the three days of grace in computing interest.

16 Williams Gear sold merchandise to Dayco in exchange for a one-year note receivable. The note was drawn with a face amount of $13,310, *including* a 10% interest charge. Compute the amount of sales revenue to be recognized by Williams Gear.

17 Maxline Stores sells merchandise with a sales price of $1,260 on an instalment plan requiring 12 monthly payments of $120 each. How much revenue will this sale ultimately generate for Maxline Stores? Explain the nature of this revenue and when it should be recognized in the accounting records.

18 With reference to Question 17 above, make the journal entries required in the accounting records of Maxline Stores to record:

a Sale of the merchandise on the instalment plan.

b Collection of the first monthly instalment payment. (Assume that an equal portion of the discount is amortized at the time that each instalment payment is received.)

EXERCISES

Exercise 8-1
Accounting
terminology

Listed below are nine technical accounting terms introduced in this chapter:

Amortization	Aging schedule	Discounting a note receivable
Default	Contingent liability	Writing off receivables
Conservatism	Present value concept	Direct Charge-off method

Each of the following statements may (or may not) describe one of these technical terms. For each statement, indicate the accounting term described, or answer "None" if the statement does not correctly describe any of the terms.

a Resolving uncertainties in the valuation of assets by reporting assets at the lower end of the range of reasonable values.

b Sale of a note receivable to a bank rather than holding the note to maturity.

c Unearned interest revenue applicable to future periods.

d Recognition of credit losses only when specific accounts receivable are determined to be worthless.

e Systematic allocation of a discount on notes receivable to interest revenue.

f Failure to make payment of principal or interest per the terms of a promissory note.

g The obligation of the endorser of a discounted note receivable to make payment if the maker fails to pay at the due date.

Exercise 8-2
Balance sheet
approach

At year-end, Clayton Corporation had accounts receivable totalling $294,000. The company uses the balance sheet approach to estimate uncollectible accounts expense. An aging analysis of the receivables showed an estimated loss of $7,320. You are to draft the year-end adjusting entries for uncollectible accounts under each of the following independent assumptions:

a The Allowance for Doubtful Accounts had a credit balance of $5,280.

b The Allowance for Doubtful Accounts had a debit balance of $1,776.

Exercise 8-3
Income statement
approach

Meadow Corporation uses the income statement approach to estimate uncollectible accounts. At December 31 the company had accounts receivable of $150,000 and a credit balance of $1,050 in the Allowance for Doubtful Accounts. On this date, the controller estimated that bad debts expense would amount to one-half of 1% of the $900,000 of net sales made during the year. This estimate was entered in the accounts by an adjusting entry at December 31. On January 14, an account receivable of $825 from J.R. Baker was determined to be uncollectible and was written off. However, on July 5, Baker inherited some property and immediately paid the $825 past-due account. You are to prepare four entries in general journal form to record the above events.

Exercise 8-4
Both approaches

Lincoln Corporation's unadjusted trial balance at year-end included the following accounts:

	DEBIT	CREDIT
Sales (75% represent credit sales)		$1,152,000
Accounts receivable	$288,000	
Allowance for doubtful accounts		2,184

Compute the uncollectible accounts expense for the current year, assuming that uncollectible accounts expense is determined as follows:

a Income statement approach, 1% of total sales.

b Income statement approach, 1½% of credit sales.

c Balance sheet approach. The estimate based on an aging of accounts receivable is that an allowance of $12,000 will be adequate.

Exercise 8-5
Credit balances in
accounts receivable

Basin Company has accounts receivable from 100 customers in its accounts receivable subsidiary ledger. The controlling account in the general ledger shows a debit balance of $930,000. The subsidiary ledger shows that 99 of the customers' accounts have debit balances and that one customer has a credit balance of $45,000. How should these facts be shown in the balance sheet? Explain the reason for the treatment you recommend.

Exercise 8-6
Write-off of
uncollectible account

Star Company follows the income statement approach to estimating uncollectible accounts expense. For several years the company has computed the charge to uncollectible accounts expense as 1% of net sales. All sales are made on credit. The following data appear in the accounting records at December 31, Year 9, before adjustments.

	DEBIT	CREDIT
Sales		$5,360,000
Sales Returns & Allowances	$200,000	
Sales Discounts	160,000	
Allowance for Doubtful Accounts		7,600

On January 12, Year 10, the company wrote off a $4,800 account receivable from John Brown which was determined to be uncollectible.

Prepare journal entries in general journal form to record the estimated uncollectible accounts expense at December 31, Year 9, and the write-off of the Brown receivable on January 12, Year 10.

Exercise 8-7
Write-offs and
recoveries

The balance sheet of Barco. Inc., at the end of last year included the following items:

Notes receivable from customers	$ 36,000
Interest on notes receivable	720
Accounts receivable	151,200
Less: Allowance for doubtful accounts	3,600

You are to record the following events of the current year in general journal entries:

a Accounts receivable of $3,456 are written off as uncollectible. *acumulado.*

b A customer's note for $990 on which interest of $54 has been accrued in the accounts is deemed uncollectible, and both balances are written off against the Allowance for Doubtful Accounts.

considerado

c An account receivable for $468 previously written off is collected.

d Aging of accounts receivable at the end of the current year indicates a need for a $5,400 allowance to cover possible failure to collect accounts currently outstanding. (Consider the effect of entries for **a, b,** and **c** on the amount of the Allowance for Doubtful Accounts.)

Exercise 8-8
Discounting notes
receivable

Three notes receivable, each in the amount of $60,000, were discounted by Micro, Inc., at its bank on May 10. The bank charged a discount rate of 12% per year, applied to the maturity value.

DATE OF NOTE	ANNUAL INTEREST RATE, %	LIFE OF NOTE
Note A — Apr. 10	12	3 months
Note B — Mar. 31	9	60 days
Note C — Mar. 11	16	90 days

From the above date, compute the proceeds of each note. Remember that all interest rates quoted are annual rates. In making interest calculations, assume a 360-day year and disregard the three days of grace. Answers should be rounded to the nearest cent wherever necessary.

Exercise 8-9
Two forms of notes receivable

Chapel Associates on November 1 made a loan of $300,000 to a supplier, Southern Comet. The agreement provided for repayment of the $300,000 in six months plus interest at an annual rate of 12%. (Remember that interest is stated at an annual rate.)

Show two different presentations of the note receivable from Southern Comet on Chapel Associates' December 31 balance sheet, assuming that the note was drawn as follows:

a For $300,000 with interest stated separately and payable at maturity.

b With the total interest charge included in the face amount of the note.

Exercise 8-10
Interest included in face amount of note

Dale Motors, an automobile dealer, sold three trucks to Zorro Truck Lines on April 1, Year 1, for a total price of $68,000. Under the terms of the sale, Dale Motors received $20,000 cash and a promissory note due in full 18 months later. The face amount of the note was $53,760, which included interest on the note for the 18 months.

Prepare entries (in general journal form) for Dale Motors relating to this sales transaction and to the note for the fiscal year ended **September 30.** Include the adjusting entry needed to record interest earned to September 30.

PROBLEMS

Group A

Problem 8A-1
Estimating uncollectible accounts; write-offs

Hiawatha Corporation maintains an allowance account to reduce accounts receivable to realizable value. An analysis of the accounts receivable at year-end produced the following age groups:

(1) Not yet due	$162,000
(2) 1–30 days past due	90,000
(3) 31–60 days past due	39,000
(4) 61–90 days past due	9,000
(5) Over 90 days past due	15,000
Total accounts receivable	$315,000

In reliance upon its past experience with collections, the company estimated the percentages probably uncollectible for the above five age groups to be as follows: Group 1, 1%; Group 2, 4%; Group 3, 10%; Group 4, 30%; and Group 5, 50%.

Prior to adjustment at December 31 (the year-end date), the Allowance for Doubtful Accounts showed a credit balance of $5,400.

Instructions

a Compute the estimated amount of uncollectible accounts based on the above classification by age groups.

b Prepare the adjusting entry needed to bring the Allowance for Doubtful Accounts to the proper amount.

c Assume that on January 10 of the following year, Hiawatha Corporation learned that an account receivable that had originated on September 1 in the amount of $5,000 was worthless because of the bankruptcy of the customer, Bart Company. Prepare the journal entry required on January 10 to write off this account receivable.

Problem 8A-2
Estimating uncollectible accounts

The balance sheet of Offshore Services at December 31 last year showed accounts receivable of $705,600 and an allowance for doubtful accounts of $36,000. During January of the current year, transactions affecting accounts receivable occurred as follows:

(1) Sales on account $515,000
(2) Sales returns & allowances 10,300
(3) Cash collections from customers (no cash discounts) 510,000
(4) Account receivable from Lasers, Inc., written off as worthless 12,900

After a careful aging and analysis of all customers' accounts at January 31, it was decided that the allowance for doubtful accounts should be adjusted to a balance of $35,600 in order to reflect accounts receivable at net realizable value in the January 31 balance sheet.

Instructions

a Give the entry in general journal form for each of the four numbered items above and the adjusting entry at January 31 to provide for uncollectible accounts.

b Show the amounts of accounts receivable and the allowance for doubtful accounts as they would appear in a partial balance sheet at January 31.

c Assume that three months after the receivable from Lasers, Inc., had been written off as worthless, Lasers, Inc., won a large award in the settlement of patent litigation and immediately paid the $12,900 debt to Offshore Services. Prepare the journal entry or entries (in general journal form) to reflect this recovery of a receivable previously written off.

Problem 8A-3
Estimating
uncollectible accounts

Colours Etc., owned by Ann Nelson, sells paper novelty goods to retail stores. All sales are made on credit and each month the company has estimated its uncollectible accounts expense as a percentage of net sales. The percentage used has been ½ of 1% of net sales. However, it appears that this provision has been inadequate because the Allowance for Doubtful Accounts has a debit balance of $3,900 at December 31 prior to making the monthly provision. Nelson has therefore decided to change the method of estimating uncollectible accounts expense and to rely upon an analysis of the age and character of the accounts receivable at the end of each month.

At December 31, the accounts receivable totalled $260,000. This total amount included past-due accounts in the amount of $46,000. None of these past-due accounts was considered worthless; all accounts regarded as worthless had been written off as rapidly as they were determined to be uncollectible. After careful investigation of the $46,000 of past-due accounts at December 31, Nelson decided that the probable loss contained therein was 10%. In addition she decided to provide for a loss of 1% of the current accounts receivable.

Instructions

a Compute the estimated amount of uncollectible accounts applicable to the $260,000 of accounts receivable at December 31, based on the analysis by the owner.

b Prepare the journal entry necessary to carry out the change in company policy with respect to providing for uncollectible accounts expense.

Problem 8A-4
Note receivable:
entries for collection
and for default

Plaza North sells a variety of merchandise to retail stores on open account, but insists that any customer who fails to pay an invoice when due must replace it with an interest-bearing note. The company adjusts and closes its accounts at December 31. Among the transactions relating to notes receivable were the following:

Nov. 1 Received from a customer (Hill Stores) a 14%, six-month note for $18,000 in settlement of an account receivable due today.

May 1 Collected in full the 14%, six-month note receivable from Hill Stores, including interest.

Instructions

a Prepare journal entries (in general journal form) to record: (1) the receipt of the note on November 1; (2) the adjustment for interest on December 31; and (3) collection of principal and interest on May 1. Assume that the company does not use reversing entries and disregard the three days of grace.

b Assume that instead of paying the note on May 1, the customer (Hill Stores) had defaulted. Give the journal entry by Plaza North to record the default. Assume that Hill Stores has sufficient resources that the note eventually will be collected. Disregard the three days of grace.

Problem 8A-5
Accounting for
notes receivable:
a comprehensive
problem

On December 1, 19___, the accounting records of Oak Tree Corporation showed the following information on receivables. (In calculating interest, the company's policy is to assume a 360-day year and to disregard the three days of grace.)

Notes receivable:

Jill Barnes, 10% 45-day note dated Nov. 4	$18,000
C.D. Dawson, 12%, 90-day note dated Dec. 1	16,000
Total	$34,000

Accounts receivable:

Judi Morgan	$ 7,275
T.J. Peppercorn	6,700
R.T. Greenberg	9,000
Total	$22,975

Instalment contracts receivable:

Jay Dallas (monthly payment $450)	$ 8,550
Unearned interest on instalment contracts:	
Applicable to Jay Dallas contract	$ 1,140

During the month of Dcember selected transactions affecting receivables were as follows:

Dec. 7 T.J. Peppercorn paid $700 on account and gave a 30-day, 10% note to cover the $6,000 balance.

Dec. 12 Received a 60-day, 12% note from Judi Morgan in full settlement of her account.

Dec. 19 Jill Barnes wrote that she would be unable to pay the note due today and enclosed a cheque for the interest due along with a new 30-day, 10% note replacing the old note. No accrued interest had been recorded in November.

Dec. 28 Discounted the Judi Morgan note at the bank and received proceeds of $7,288.

Dec. 31 Received the monthly payment on the Jay Dallas instalment contract. The payment of $450 includes $60 of interest earned during December. The interest charges included in the face amount of the instalment contract had originally been credited to the contra-asset account, Unearned Interest on Instalment Contracts.

Instructions

a Prepare five journal entries (in general journal form) for the five December transactions listed above.

b Prepare an adjusting entry at December 31 to accrue interest on the three notes receivable on hand (the Peppercorn, Barnes, and Dawson notes). Include in the explanation portion of the adjusting entry the computations to determine the accrued interest on each of the three notes.

c Prepare a partial balance sheet for Oak Tree Corporation at December 31 showing under the heading of current assets the notes receivable, accounts receivable, instalment contracts receivable, unearned interest on instalment contracts, and interest receivable. Also add a footnote to disclose the amount of the contingent liability for the discounted note receivable.

Problem 8A-6
Long-term note
receivable with
interest included
in face amount

On April 1, 1988, Monitor Corporation sold merchandise to West Supply Co. in exchange for a note receivable due in *one year*. The note was drawn in the face amount of $58,240, which included the principal amount and an interest charge. In its December 31, 1988, balance sheet, Monitor Corporation correctly presented the note receivable as follows:

Note receivable, due Mar. 31, 1989 . . . . $58,240
Less: Discount on note receivable 1,560 $56,680

Instructions

a Determine the monthly interest revenue earned by Monitor Corporation from this note receivable.

b Compute the amount of interest revenue recognized by Monitor Corporation from the note during 1988.

c Compute the amount of sales revenue recognized by Monitor Corporation on April 1, 1988, when this note was received.

d Compute the effective annual rate of interest (stated as a percentage) represented by the interest charge originally included in the face amount of the note.

e Prepare all journal entries relating to this note in the accounting records of Monitor Corporation for 1988 and 1989. Assume that adjusting entries are made only at December 31, and that the note was collected on the maturity date.

Group B

Problem 8B-1
Estimating
uncollectible
accounts; write-offs

Best Products' year-end aging of the accounts receivable produced the following classification:

(1) Not yet due . . . . $ 74,000
(2) 1–30 days past due 30,000
(3) 31–60 days past due 13,000
(4) 61–90 days past due 3,000
(5) Over 90 days past due 5,000
    Total $125,000

On the basis of past experience, the company estimated the percentages probably uncollectible for the above five age groups to be as follows: Group 1, 1%; Group 2, 3%; Group 3, 10%; Group 4, 20%; and Group 5, 50%.

The Allowance for Doubtful Accounts before adjustment at December 31 (year-end date) showed a credit balance of $1,800.

Instructions

a Compute the estimated amount of uncollectible accounts based on the above classification by age groups.

b Prepare the adjusting entry needed to bring the Allowance for Doubtful Accounts to the proper amount.

c Assume that on February 1 of the following year, Best Products learned that an account receivable which had originated on October 10 in the amount of $1,900 was worthless because of the bankruptcy of the customer, Mesa Company. Prepare the journal entry required on January 10 to write off this account.

Problem 8B-2
Estimating
uncollectible accounts

At December 31 of last year, the balance sheet of Sandpoint, Inc., included $280,000 in accounts receivable and an allowance for doubtful accounts with a credit balance of $14,000. The following summary shows the totals of certain types of transactions occurring during January of the current year.

(1) Sales on account	$190,000
(2) Sales returns & allowances	3,600
(3) Cash collections from customers (no cash discounts)	170,000
(4) Account receivable from Dan King written off as worthless following the failure of his business	4,000

At January 31, after a careful aging and analysis of all customers' accounts, the company decided that the allowance for doubtful accounts should be adjusted to the amount of $16,000 in order to reflect accounts receivable at net realizable value in the January 31 balance sheet.

Instructions

a Give the appropriate entry in general journal form for each of the four numbered items above and the adjusting entry at January 31 to provide for uncollectible accounts.

b Show the amounts of accounts receivable and the allowance for doubtful accounts as they would appear in a partial balance sheet at January 31.

c Assume that six months after the receivable from Dan King had been written off as worthless, he won $120,000 in a lottery and immediately paid the $4,000 owed to Sandpoint, Inc. Give the journal entry or entries to reflect this collection in Sandpoint, Inc.'s accounts. (Use general journal form.)

Problem 8B-3
Estimating
uncollectible accounts

Snowwhite, Inc., owned by Linda Snow, had for the past three years been engaged in selling small toys to retail stores. Sales are made on credit and each month the company has estimated its uncollectible accounts expense as a percentage of net sales. The percentage used has been 1% of net sales. However, it appears that this provision has been inadequate because the Allowance for Doubtful Accounts has a debit balance of $2,700 at May 31 prior to making the monthly provision. Snow has therefore decided to change the method of estimating uncollectible accounts expense and to rely upon an analysis of the age and character of the accounts receivable at the end of each month.

At May 31, the end of the company's fiscal year, the accounts receivable totalled $180,000. This total amount included past-due accounts in the amount of $38,000. None of these past-due accounts was considered hopeless because accounts regarded as worthless had been written off immediately. After a careful review of the past-due accounts at May 31, Linda Snow decided that the probable loss contained therein was 10%. In addition, she should anticipate a loss of 1% of the current accounts receivable.

Instructions

a Compute the probable uncollectible accounts expense applicable to the accounts receivable at May 31, based on the analysis by the owner.

b Prepare the journal entry necessary to carry out the change in company policy with respect to providing for uncollectible accounts expense.

Problem 8B-4
Note receivable:
entries for collection
and for default

Hanover Mills sells merchandise to retail stores on 30-day credit, but insists that any customer who fails to pay an invoice when due must replace it with an interest-bearing note. The company adjusts and closes its accounts at December 31. Among the transactions relating to notes receivable were the following.

Oct. 1 Received from a customer (Jones Brothers) a 12%, 6-month note for $10,000 in settlement of an account receivable due today.

Apr. 1 Collected in full the 12%, 6-month note receivable from Jones Brothers, including interest.

Instructions

a Prepare journal entries (in general journal form) to record: (1) the receipt of the note on October 1; (2) the adjustment for interest on December 31; and (3) collection of principal and interest on April 1. Assume that the company does not use reversing entries. Disregard the three days of grace.

b Assume that instead of paying the note on April 1, the customer (Jones Brothers) had defaulted. Give the journal entry by Hanover Mills to record the default. Assume that Jones Brothers has sufficient resources that the note will eventually be collected. Disregard the three days of grace.

Problem 8B-5
Accounting for notes receivable: a comprehensive problem

The following information concerning the receivables of the Bunker Corporation appeared in the accounts on December 1, 19___. The company uses a 360-day year for all interest calculations. Disregard the three days of interest.

Accounts receivable:

C.L. Laurence	$ 2,425
E.D. Nemson	3,870
C.A. Shively	6,200
Total	$12,495

Notes receivable:

A.P. Marra, 8%, 45-day note, dated Nov. 4	$ 6,000
C.M. Hines, 9%, 90-day note, dated Nov. 30	4,000
Total	$10,000

Instalment contracts receivable:

M. Moyers (monthly payment $150)	$ 2,850

Unearned interest on instalment contracts:

Applicable to M. Moyers contract	$ 386

During the month of December, the following additional transactions took place:

Dec. 7 E.D. Nemson paid $870 on account and gave a 30-day, 8% note to cover the balance.

Dec. 12 Received a 60-day, 8% note from C.L. Laurence in full settlement of his account.

Dec. 19 A.P. Marra wrote that he would be unable to pay the note due today and included a cheque to cover the interest due and a new 30-day, 7% note renewing the old note. No accrued interest has been recorded in prior months.

Dec. 28 Discounted the C.L. Laurence note at the bank. The proceeds on the note amounted to $2,434.

Dec. 31 Received the monthly payment on the M. Moyers contract. The payment of $150 includes $20 of interest revenue earned during December. The interest charges included in the face amount of the instalment contract had originally been credited to the contra-asset account, Unearned Interest on Instalment Contracts.

Instructions   **a** Prepare five journal entries (in general journal form) for the five December transactions listed above.

b Prepare an adjusting entry at December 31 to accrue interest receivable on the three notes receivable on hand (the Nemson, Marra, and Hines notes). Include in the explanation portion of the adjusting entry the computations to determine the accrued interest on each of the three notes.

c Prepare a partial balance sheet for Bunker Corporation at December 31 showing under the heading of current assets the notes receivable, accounts receivable, instalment contracts receivable, unearned interest on instalment contracts, and interest receivable. Also add a footnote to disclose the amount of the contingent liability for the discounted note receivable.

Problem 8B-6
Long-term note receivable with interest included in face amount

On May 1, 1989, Merrimac Corporation sold merchandise to West Supply Co. in exchange for a note receivable due in *one year.* The note was drawn in the face amount of $47,300, which included the principal amount and an interest charge. In its January 31, 1990, balance sheet, Merrimac Corporation correctly presented the note receivable as follows:

Note receivable, due April 30, 1990	$47,300	
Less: Discount on note receivable	825	$46,475

Instructions   **a** Determine the monthly interest revenue earned by Merrimac Corporation from this note receivable.

b Compute the amount of interest revenue recognized by Merrimac Corporation from the note for the year ended January 31, 1990.

c Compute the amount of sales revenue recognized by Merrimac Corporation on May 1, 1989, when this note was received.

d Compute the effective annual rate of interest (stated as a percentage) represented by the interest charge originally included in the face amount of the note.

e Prepare all journal entries relating to this note in the accounting records of Merrimac Corporation. Assume that adjusting entries are made only at January 31, 1990, and that the note was collected on the maturity date.

BUSINESS DECISION CASES

Case 8-1
How did he do it?

Allan Carter was a long-time employee in the accounting department of Marston Company. Carter's responsibilities included the following:

(1) Maintain the accounts receivable subsidiary ledger.

(2) Prepare vouchers for cash disbursements. The voucher and supporting documents were forwarded to John Marston, owner of the company.

(3) Compute depreciation on all plant assets.

(4) Authorize all sales returns and allowances given to credit customers and prepare the related credit memoranda. The credit memoranda were forwarded to Howard Smith, who maintains the company's journals and general ledger.

John Marston personally performs the following procedures in an effort to achieve strong internal control:

(1) Prepare monthly bank reconciliations.

(2) Prepare monthly trial balances from the general ledger and reconcile the accounts receivable controlling account with the subsidiary ledger.

(3) Prepare from the subsidiary ledger all monthly statements sent to customers and investigate any complaints from customers about inaccuracies in these statements.

(4) Review all vouchers and supporting documents before signing cheques for cash disbursements.

Carter became terminally ill and retired. Shortly thereafter, he died. However, he left a letter confessing that over a period of years he had embezzled over $300,000 from Marston Company. As part of his scheme, he had managed to obtain both a bank account and a post office box in the name of Marston Company. He had then contacted customers whose accounts were overdue and offered them a 20% discount if they would make payment within five days. He instructed them to send their payments to the post office box. When the payments arrived, he deposited them in his "Marston Company" bank account. Carter stated in his letter that he had acted alone, and that no other company employees knew of his dishonest actions.

Marston cannot believe that Carter committed this theft without the knowledge and assistance of Howard Smith, who maintained the journals and the general ledger. Marston reasoned that Carter must have credited the customers' accounts in the accounts receivable subsidiary ledger, because no customers had complained about not receiving credit for their payments. Smith must also have recorded these credits in the general ledger, or Marston would have discovered the problem by reconciling the subsidiary ledger with the controlling account. Finally, Smith must have debited some other account in the general ledger to keep the ledger in balance. Thus, Marston is about to bring criminal charges against Smith.

Instructions

a Explain how Carter might have committed this theft without Smith's knowledge and without being detected by Marston's control procedures. (Assume that Carter had no personal access to the journals or general ledger.)

b Which of the duties assigned to Carter should not have been assigned to an employee responsible for maintaining accounts receivable? Would internal control be strengthened if this duty were assigned to the company's cashier? Explain.

Case 8-2
Instalment sales, timing of interest revenue, and credit policy

Record House and Concert Sound are two companies engaged in selling stereo equipment to the public. Both companies sell equipment at a price 50% greater than cost. Customers may pay cash, purchase on 30-day accounts, or make instalment payments over a 36-month period. The instalment receivables include a three-year interest charge (which amounts to 30% of the sales price) in the face amount of the contract. Condensed income statements prepared by the companies for their first year of operations follow:

	RECORD HOUSE	CONCERT SOUND
Sales	$387,000	$288,000
Cost of goods sold	210,000	192,000
Gross profit on sales	$177,000	$ 96,000
Operating expenses	63,000	60,000
Operating income	$114,000	$ 36,000
Interest revenue	-0-	10,800
Net income	$114,000	$ 46,800

When Record House makes a sale of stereo equipment on the instalment plan it immediately credits the Sales account with the face amount of the instalment receivable. In other words, the interest charges are included in sales revenue at the time of the sale. The interest charges included in Record House's instalment receivables originating in the first year amount to $72,000, of which $59,100 is unearned at the end of the first year. Record House uses the direct charge-off method to recognize uncollectible accounts expense. During the year, accounts receivable of $2,100 were written off as uncollectible, but no entry was made for $37,200 of accounts estimated to be uncollectible at year-end.

Concert Sound records sales revenue equal to the present value of its instalment receivables and recognizes the interest *earned during the year* as interest revenue. Concert Sound provides for uncollectible accounts by the allowance method. The company recognized uncollectible accounts expense of $11,100 during the year and this amount appeared to be adequate.

Instructions

a Prepare a condensed income statement for Record House for the year, using the same methods of accounting for instalment sales and uncollectible accounts as were used by Concert Sound. The income statement you prepare should contain the same seven items shown in the above income statements. Provide footnotes showing the computations you made in revising the amount of sales and any other figures you decide to change.

b Compare the income statement you have prepared in part **a** to the one originally prepared by Record House. Which income statement do you believe better reflects the results of the company's operations during the year? Explain.

c What do you believe to be the key factor responsible for making one of these companies more profitable than the other? What corrective action would you recommend be taken by the less profitable company to improve future performance?

CHAPTER

9

INVENTORIES

CHAPTER PREVIEW

Our first goal in Chapter 9 is to show that determining the valuation of inventory also establishes the cost of goods sold. Thus, the validity of both the balance sheet and the income statement rest on accuracy in the valuation of inventory. A second goal is to stress that inventory is valued at cost, but that several alternative methods are available to measure cost. Four methods (specific identification, average cost, fifo, and lifo) are illustrated and evaluated. Also, the lower-of-cost-and-market rule is discussed. Both the gross profit method and the retail method are introduced as examples of estimating inventory. The chapter concludes by indicating the significance of internal control over inventories and the advantages offered by use of the perpetual inventory system whenever feasible.

After studying this chapter you should be able to meet these Learning Objectives:

1 Explain what goods should be included in inventory.

2 Describe the effects of an inventory error on the income statements of the current year and the following year.

3 Determine the cost of inventory by using (1) specific identification, (2) average cost, (3) fifo, and (4) lifo. Discuss the merits and shortcomings of these methods.

4 Define inventory profits and explain why some accountants consider these profits fictitious.

5 Explain the lower-of-cost-and-market rule.

6 Estimate ending inventory by the gross profit method and by the retail method.

7 Explain how a perpetual inventory system operates.

In the previous chapters we have illustrated how the amount of inventory on hand a year-end is recorded in the accounts. Remember that the inventory figure appears i both the balance sheet and the income statement. In the balance sheet, inventory i often the largest current asset. In the income statement, the ending inventory i subtracted from the cost of goods *available* for sale to determine the *cost of good sold* during the period.

In our previous discussions, the dollar amount of the ending inventory was give with only a brief explanation as to how this amount was determined. The basis for th valuation of inventory, as for most other types of assets, is cost (if the market value i lower, then this lower value should be used, as discussed later.) We are now ready t explore the concept of *cost* as applied to inventories of merchandise.

Inventory defined

1   Explain what goods should be included in inventory.

One of the largest assets in a retail store or in a wholesale business is the inventory c merchandise. The sale of this merchandise at prices in excess of cost is the majo source of revenue. For a merchandising company, *the inventory consists of a. goods owned and held for sale in the regular course of business.* Merchandise hel for sale will normally be converted into cash within less than a year's time and i therefore regarded as a current asset. In the balance sheet, inventory is liste immediately after accounts receivable, because, with the exception of cash sales, it i just one step further removed from conversion into cash than are the account receivable.

In manufacturing businesses there are three major types of inventories: *ra materials, goods in process of manufacture,* and *finished goods.* All three classe of inventories are included in the current asset section of the balance sheet.

To expand our definition of inventory to fit manufacturing companies as well a merchandising companies, we can say that inventory means the aggregate of thos items of tangible property that are held for sale in the ordinary course of business, c are in process of production for such sale, or are to be currently consumed in th production of goods or services to be available for sale.[1]

Periodic inventory system versus perpetual inventory system

The distinction between a periodic inventory system and a perpetual inventor system was explained earlier in Chapter 5. To summarize briefly, a periodic syste of inventory accounting requires that acquisitions of merchandise be recorded b debits to a Purchases account. At the date of a sales transaction, no entry is made t record the cost of the goods sold. Under the periodic inventory system, the Inventor account is brought up to date only at the end of the accounting period when all th goods on hand are counted and priced.

The periodic inventory system is likely to be used by a business that sells a variet of merchandise with low unit prices, such as a drugstore or hardware store. T maintain perpetual inventory records in such a business would ordinarily be to time-consuming and expensive.

Companies that sell products of high unit value such as automobiles and televisic sets usually maintain a perpetual inventory system that shows at all times the amour

[1] CICA, *Terminology for Accountants*, Third Edition (Toronto 1983), p. 81.

of inventory on hand. As merchandise is acquired, its cost is added to an inventory account; as goods are sold, their cost is transferred out of inventory and into a cost of goods sold account. This continuous updating of the inventory account explains the name *perpetual* inventory system. Of course, the quantity in the inventory account should be verified by a physical count of inventory, at least once a year.

In the early part of this chapter we will use the periodic inventory system as a point of reference; in the latter part we will emphasize perpetual inventories.

Inventory valuation and the measurement of income

In measuring the gross profit on sales earned during an accounting period, we subtract the *cost of goods sold* from the total *sales* of the period. The figure for sales is easily accumulated from the daily record of sales transactions, but in many businesses no day-to-day record is maintained showing the cost of goods sold.[2] The figure representing the cost of goods sold during an entire accounting period is computed at the end of the period by separating the *cost of goods available for sale* into two elements:

1 The cost of the goods sold
2 The cost of the goods not sold, which therefore comprise the ending inventory

This idea, with which you are already quite familiar, may be concisely stated in the form of an equation as follows:

FINDING COST OF GOODS SOLD

Beg inventory + purchases

Cost of Goods Available for Sale − **Ending Inventory** = **Cost of Goods Sold**

Determining the amount of the ending inventory is the key step in establishing the cost of goods sold. In separating the *cost of goods available for sale* into its components of *goods sold* and *goods not sold,* we are just as much interested in establishing the proper amount for cost of goods sold as in determining a proper figure for inventory. Throughout this chapter you should bear in mind that the procedures for determining the amount of the ending inventory are also the means for determining the cost of goods sold. The valuation of inventory and the determination of the cost of goods sold are in effect the two sides of a single coin.

The Canadian Institute of Chartered Accountants has summarized this relationship between inventory valuation and the measurement of income: "The method selected for determining cost should be one which results in the fairest matching of costs against revenues regardless of whether or not the method corresponds to the physical flow of goods."[3] The expression "matching of costs against revenues" means determining what portion of the cost of goods available for sale should be deducted from the revenue of the current period and what portion should be carried forward (as inventory) to be matched against the revenue of the following period.

---

[2] As explained in Chapter 5, a company that maintains perpetual inventory records will have a day-to-day record of the cost of goods sold and of goods in inventory. Our present discussion, however, is based on the assumption that the periodic system of inventory is being used.

[3] CICA, *CICA Handbook* (Toronto), paragraph 3030-09.

Importance of an accurate valuation of inventory

The most important current assets in the balance sheets of most companies are cash, accounts receivable, and inventory. Of these three, the inventory of merchandise is usually much the largest. Because of the relatively large size of this asset, an error in the valuation of inventory may cause a material mis-statement of financial position and of net income. An error of 20% in valuing the inventory may have as much effect on the financial statements as would the complete omission of the asset cash.

An error in inventory will of course lead to other erroneous figures in the balance sheet, such as the total current assets, total assets, owner's equity, and the total liabilities and owner's equity. The error will also affect key figures in the income statement, such as the cost of goods sold, the gross profit on sales, and the net income for the period. Finally, it is important to recognize that *the ending inventory of one year is also the beginning inventory of the following year.* Consequently, the income statement of the second year will also be in error by the full amount of the original error in inventory valuation.

2 Describe the effects of an inventory error on the income statements of the current year and the following year.

Effects of an error in valuing inventory: illustration   Assume that on December 31, 1988, the inventory of the Hillside Company is actually $100,000 but, through an accidental error, it is recorded as $90,000. The effects of this $10,000 error on the income statement for 1988 are indicated in the first of the following illustrations, showing two income statements side by side. The left-hand set of figures shows the inventory of December 31 at the *proper value of $100,000* and represents a correct income statement for 1988. The right-hand set of figures represents an incorrect income statement, because the ending inventory is *erroneously listed as $90,000.* Note the differences between the two income statements with respect to net income, gross profit on sales, and cost of goods sold. Income taxes have been omitted in this illustration because it relates to an unincorporated business.

EFFECTS OF ERROR IN
INVENTORY

HILLSIDE COMPANY
Income Statement
For the Year Ended December 31, 1988

	WITH CORRECT ENDING INVENTORY		WITH INCORRECT ENDING INVENTORY	
Sales		$240,000		$240,000
Cost of goods sold:				
Beginning inventory, Jan. 1, 1988	$ 75,000		$ 75,000	
Purchases	210,000		210,000	
Cost of goods available for sale	$285,000		$285,000	
Less: Ending inventory, Dec. 31, 1988	100,000		90,000	
Cost of goods sold		185,000		195,000
Gross profit on sales		$ 55,000		$ 45,000
Operating expenses		30,000		30,000
Net income		$ 25,000		$ 15,000

This illustration shows that an understatement of $10,000 in the ending inventory caused an understatement of $10,000 in the net income for 1988. Next, consider the effect of this error on the income statement of the following year. The ending inventory of 1988 is, of course, the beginning inventory of 1989. The preceding illustration is now continued to show side by side a correct income statement and an incorrect statement for 1989. The *ending* inventory of $120,000 for 1989 is the same in both statements and is to be considered correct. Note that the $10,000 error in the beginning inventory of the right-hand statement causes an error in the cost of goods available for sale, in cost of goods sold, in gross profit, and in net income for 1989.

EFFECTS ON SUCCEEDING
YEAR

HILLSIDE COMPANY
Income Statement
For the Year Ended December 31, 1989

	WITH CORRECT BEGINNING INVENTORY		WITH INCORRECT BEGINNING INVENTORY	
Sales		$265,000		$265,000
Cost of goods sold:				
Beginning inventory,				
Jan. 1, 1989	$100,000		$ 90,000	
Purchases	230,000		230,000	
Cost of goods available				
for sale	$330,000		$320,000	
Less: Ending inventory,				
Dec. 31, 1989	120,000		120,000	
Cost of goods sold		210,000		200,000
Gross profit on sales		$ 55,000		$ 65,000
Operating expenses		33,000		33,000
Net income		$ 22,000		$ 32,000

Counterbalancing errors   The illustrated income statements for 1988 and 1989 show that an understatement of the ending inventory in 1988 caused an understatement of net income in that year and an offsetting overstatement of net income for 1989. Over a period of two years the effects of an inventory error on net income will *counterbalance,* and the total net income for the two years together will be the same as if the error had not occurred. Since the error in reported net income for the first year is exactly offset by the error in reported net income for the second year, it might be argued that an inventory error has no serious consequences. Such an argument is not sound, for it disregards the fact that accurate yearly figures for net income are a primary objective of the accounting process. Moreover, many actions by management and many decisions by creditors and owners are based upon *trends* indicated in the financial statements for two or more years. Note that the inventory error has made the 1989 net income appear to be more than twice as large as the 1988 net income, when in fact *less* net income was earned in 1989 than in 1988. Anyone relying on the erroneous financial statements would be greatly misled as to the trend of Hillside Company's earnings.

To produce dependable financial statements, inventory must be accurately determined at the end of each accounting period. The counterbalancing effect of the inventory error by the Hillside Company is shown in the following illustration.

COUNTERBALANCING
EFFECT ON NET INCOME

	WITH INVENTORY CORRECTLY STATED	WITH INVENTORY AT DEC. 31 1988, UNDERSTATED	
		REPORTED NET INCOME WILL BE	REPORTED NET INCOME WILL BE OVERSTATED (UNDERSTATED)
Net income for 1988	$25,000	$15,000	$(10,000)
Net income for 1989	22,000	32,000	10,000
Total net income for two years	$47,000	$47,000	$ –0–

Relation of inventory errors to net income   The effects of errors in inventory upon net income may be summarized as follows:

1 When the *ending* inventory is understated, the net income for the period will be understated.

2 When the *ending* inventory is overstated, the net income for the period will be overstated.

3 When the *beginning* inventory is understated, the net income for the period will be overstated.

4 When the *beginning* inventory is overstated, the net income for the period will be understated.

Although single errors in inventory that counterbalance over two years are not uncommon, they are only part of the picture. Some companies (usually small and unaudited) intentionally understate their ending inventory year after year for the purpose of evading income taxes. This type of fraud is discussed further at a later point in this chapter.

Taking a physical inventory

At the end of each accounting period the ledger accounts will show up-to-date balances for most of the assets. For inventory, however, the balance in the ledger account represents the *beginning* inventory, because no entry has been made in the Inventory account since the end of the preceding period. All purchases of merchandise during the present period have been recorded in the Purchases account. The ending inventory does not appear anywhere in the ledger accounts; it must be determined by a physical count of merchandise on hand at the end of the accounting period.

Establishing a balance sheet valuation for the ending inventory requires two steps: (1) determining the quantity of each kind of merchandise on hand, and (2) multiplying the quantity by the cost per unit. The first step is called *taking the inventory;* the second is called *pricing the inventory.* Taking inventory, or more precisely, taking a physical inventory, means making a systematic count of all merchandise on hand.

In most merchandising businesses the taking of a physical inventory is a year-end event. In some lines of business an inventory may be taken at the close of each month. It is common practice to take inventory after regular business hours or on Sunday. By taking the inventory while business operations are suspended, a more accurate count is possible than if goods were being sold or received while the count was in process.

Planning the physical inventory   Unless the taking of a physical inventory is carefully planned and supervised, serious errors are apt to occur that will invalidate the results of the count. To prevent such errors as the double counting of items, the omission of goods from the count, and other quantitative errors, it is desirable to plan the inventory so that the work of one person serves as a check on the accuracy of another.

There are various methods of counting merchandise. One of the simplest procedures is carried out by the use of two-member teams. One member of the team counts and calls the description and quantity of each item. The other person lists the descriptions and quantities on an inventory sheet. (In some situations a tape recorder is useful in recording quantities counted.) When all goods have been counted and listed, the items on the inventory sheet are priced at cost, and the unit prices are multiplied by the quantities to determine the valuation of the inventory.

Goods in transit   Do goods in transit belong in the inventory of the seller or of the buyer? If the selling company makes delivery of the merchandise in its own trucks, the merchandise remains its property while in transit. If the goods are shipped by rail, air, or other public carrier, the question of ownership of the goods while in transit depends upon whether the public carrier is acting as the agent of the seller or of the buyer. If the terms of the shipment are *F.O.B.* (free on board) *shipping point,* title passes at the point of shipment and the goods are the property of the buyer while in transit. If the terms of the shipment are *F.O.B. destination,* title does not pass until the shipment reaches the destination, and the goods belong to the seller while in transit. In deciding whether goods in transit at year-end should be included in inventory, it is therefore necessary to refer to the terms of the agreement with vendors (suppliers) and customers.

At the end of the year a company may have received numerous orders from customers, for which goods have been segregated and packed but not yet shipped. These goods generally should be included in inventory. An exception to this rule is found occasionally when the goods have been prepared for shipment but are being held for later delivery at the request of the customer.

Passage of title to merchandise   The debit to Accounts Receivable and the offsetting credit to the Sales account should be made *when title to the goods passes to the customer.* It would obviously be improper to set up an account receivable and at the same time to include the goods in question in inventory. Great care is necessary at year-end to ensure, when the terms are F.O.B. shipping point, that all last-minute shipments to customers are recorded as sales of the current year and, on the other hand, that no customer's order is recorded as a sale until the date the goods are shipped. Sometimes, in an effort to meet sales quotas, companies have recorded sales on the last day of the accounting period, when in fact the merchandise was not shipped until early in the next period. Such practices lead to an overstatement of the year's earnings and are not in accordance with generally accepted principles of accounting.

Merchandise in inventory is valued at *cost,* whereas accounts receivable are stated at the *sales price* of the merchandise sold. Consequently, the recording of a sale prior to delivery of the goods results in an unjustified increase in the total assets of the company. The increase will equal the difference between the cost and the selling price of the goods in question. The amount of the increase will also be reflected in the income statement, where it will show up as additional earnings. An unscrupulous company, which wanted to make its financial statements present a more favourable picture than actually existed, might do so by treating year-end orders from customers as sales even though the goods were not yet shipped.

Pricing the inventory

One of the most interesting and widely discussed problems in accounting is the pricing of inventory. Even those business executives who have little knowledge of accounting are usually interested in the various methods of pricing inventory, because inventory valuation may have a significant effect upon reported net income.

Accounting for inventories involves determination of cost and of current fair value or replacement cost or net realizable value. An understanding of the meaning of the term *cost* as applied to inventories is a first essential in dealing with the overall problem of inventory valuation.

Cost basis of inventory valuation

Cost of an inventory item may be defined as its "laid-down" cost. For example, the "laid-down" cost for merchandise purchased for sale or raw materials purchased for production is the invoice cost plus customs and excise duties and freight and cartage.[4] In other words, cost means in principle the sum of the applicable and necessary expenditures and charges incurred, directly or indirectly, in bringing an inventory item to its existing condition and location. A number of interesting questions arise in determining the *cost* of inventory. For example, should any expenditures other than the invoice price of purchased goods always be considered as part of inventory cost? Another provocative question — if identical items of merchandise are purchased at different prices during the year, which of these purchase prices represents the cost of the items remaining in inventory at year-end? We will now address these and other questions involved in determining the cost of inventory.

Inclusion of additional incidental costs in inventory — a question of materiality   From a theoretical point of view, the cost of an item of inventory includes the invoice price, minus any discount, plus all expenditures necessary to place the article in the proper location and condition for sale. Among these additional incidental costs are import duties, transportation-in, storage, insurance of goods being shipped or stored, and costs of receiving and inspecting the goods.

In determining the cost of the ending inventory, some companies add to the net invoice price of the goods a reasonable share of the charges for transportation-in incurred during the year. However, in other lines of business, it is customary and

---

[4] Ibid., paragraph 3030-02.

logical to price the year-end inventory *without* adding transportation-in or any other incidental costs because these charges *are not material in amount.* Although this practice results in a slight understatement of inventory cost, the understatement is so small that it does not affect the usefulness or reliability of the financial statements. Thus, the omission of transportation and other incidental charges from the cost of inventory often may be justified by the factors of convenience and economy. Accounting textbooks stress theoretical concepts of cost and income determination. The student of accounting should be aware, however, that in many business situations a close *approximation* of cost will serve the purpose at hand. The extra work involved in developing more precise accounting data must be weighed against the benefits that will result.

To sum up, we can say that in theory a portion of all the incidental costs of acquiring goods should be assigned to each item in the year-end inventory. However, the expense of computing cost in such a precise manner would usually outweigh the benefits to be derived. Consequently, these incidental costs relating to the acquisition of merchandise are usually treated as expense of the period in which incurred, rather than being carried forward to another accounting period by inclusion in the balance sheet amount for inventory. Thus, the accounting principle of *materiality* may at times take priority over the principle of *matching costs and revenue.*

Inventory valuation methods

3   Determine the cost of inventory by using (1) specific identification, (2) average cost, (3) fifo, and (4) lifo. Discuss the merits and shortcomings of these methods.

The prices of many kinds of merchandise are subject to frequent change. When *identical* lots of merchandise are purchased at various dates during the year, each lot may be acquired at a different cost price.

To illustrate the several alternative methods in common use for determining which purchase prices apply to the identical units remaining in inventory at the end of the period, assume the data shown in the following schedule.

	NUMBER OF UNITS	COST PER UNIT	TOTAL COST
Beginning inventory	100	$ 80	$ 8,000
First purchase (Mar. 1)	50	90	4,500
Second purchase (July 2)	50	100	5,000
Third purchase (Oct. 1)	50	120	6,000
Fourth purchase (Dec. 1)	50	130	6,500
Available for sale	300		$30,000
Units sold	180		
Units in ending inventory	120		

This schedule shows that 180 units were sold during the year and that 120 identical units are on hand at year-end to make up the ending inventory. In order to establish a dollar amount for cost of goods sold and for the ending inventory, we must make an assumption as to which units were sold and which units remain on hand at the end of the year. There are several acceptable assumptions on this point; four of the most common will be considered. Each assumption made as to the cost of the units in the ending inventory leads to a different method of pricing inventory and to different amounts in the financial statements. The four assumptions (and inventory valuation methods) to be considered are known as (1) specific identification, (2) average cost, (3) first-in, first-out (fifo) and (4) last-in, first-out (lifo).

Although each of these four methods will produce a different answer as to the cost of goods sold and the cost of the ending inventory, the valuation of inventory in each case is said to be at "cost." In other words, *these methods represent alternative definitions of inventory cost.*

Specific identification method   The specific identification method is best suited to inventories of high-priced, low-volume items. If each item in inventory is different from all others, as in the case of valuable paintings, custom jewelry, estate homes, and most other types of real estate, the specific identification method is clearly the logical choice. This type of inventory presents quite different problems from an inventory composed of large quantities of identical items.

If the units in the ending inventory can be identified as coming from specific purchases, they *may* be priced at the amounts listed on the purchase invoices. Continuing the example already presented, if the ending inventory of 120 units can be identified as, say, 50 units from the purchase of March 1, 40 units from the purchase of July 2, and 30 units from the purchase of December 1, the cost of the ending inventory may be computed as follows:

<table>
<tr><td>SPECIFIC IDENTIFICATION
METHOD AND . . .</td><td>50 units from the purchase of Mar. 1 @ $90 . . . .</td><td>$ 4,500</td></tr>
<tr><td></td><td>40 units from the purchase of July 2 @ $100 . . . .</td><td>4,000</td></tr>
<tr><td></td><td>30 units from the purchase of Dec. 1 @ $130 . . . .</td><td>3,900</td></tr>
<tr><td></td><td>Ending inventory (specific identification) . . . .</td><td>$12,400</td></tr>
</table>

The cost of goods sold during the period is determined by subtracting the ending inventory from the cost of goods available for sale.

<table>
<tr><td>. . . COST OF GOODS
SOLD COMPUTATION</td><td>Cost of goods available for sale . . . .</td><td>$30,000</td></tr>
<tr><td></td><td>Less: Ending inventory . . . .</td><td>12,400</td></tr>
<tr><td></td><td>Cost of goods sold (specific identification method) . . . .</td><td>$17,600</td></tr>
</table>

The specific identification method has an intuitive appeal because it assigns actual purchase costs to the specific units purchased. For decision-making purposes, however, this approach does not always provide the most useful accounting information for a company handling a large volume of identical units.

As a simple example, assume that a coal dealer purchased 100 tonnes of coal at $60 a tonne and a short time later made a second purchase of 100 tonnes of the same grade of coal at $80 a tonne. The two purchases are in separate piles and it is a matter of indifference as to which pile is used in making sales to customers. Assume that the dealer makes a retail sale of one tonne of coal at a price of $100. In measuring the gross profit on the sale, which cost figure should be used, $60 or $80? To insist that the cost depended on which of the two identical piles of coal was used in filling the delivery truck is an argument of questionable logic.

A situation in which the specific identification method is more likely to give meaningful results is in the purchase and sale of such high-priced articles as boats, automobiles, and jewelry.

Average cost method   Average cost is computed by dividing the total cost of goods available for sale by the number of units available for sale. This computation gives a *weighted average unit cost,* which is then applied to the units in the ending inventory.

AVERAGE COST METHOD
AND . . .

Cost of goods available for sale	$30,000
Number of units available for sale	300
Average unit cost	$ 100
Ending inventory (at average cost, 120 units @ $100)	$12,000

Note that this method, when compared with the specific identification method, leads to a different amount for cost of goods sold as well as a different amount for the ending inventory.

. . . COST OF GOODS
SOLD COMPUTATION

Cost of goods available for sale	$30,000
Less: Ending inventory	12,000
Cost of goods sold (average cost method)	$18,000

When the average cost method is used, the cost figure of $12,000 determined for the ending inventory is influenced by all the various prices paid during the year. The price paid early in the year may carry as much weight in pricing the ending inventory as a price paid at the end of the year. A common criticism of the average cost method of pricing inventory is that it attaches no more significance to current prices than to prices that prevailed several months earlier.

First-in, first-out method   The first-in, first-out method, which is often referred to as *fifo,* is based on the assumption that the first merchandise acquired is the first merchandise sold. In other words, each sale is made out of the *oldest* goods in stock; *the ending inventory therefore consists of the most recently acquired goods.* The fifo method of determining inventory cost may be adopted by any business, regardless of whether or not the physical flow of merchandise actually corresponds to this assumption of selling the oldest units in stock. Using the same data as in the preceding illustrations, the 120 units in the ending inventory would be regarded as consisting of the most recently acquired goods as follows:

FIRST-IN, FIRST-OUT
METHOD AND . . .

50 units from the Dec. 1 purchase @ $130	$ 6,500
50 units from the Oct. 1 purchase @ $120	6,000
20 units from the July 2 purchase @ $100	2,000
Ending inventory, 120 units (at fifo cost)	$14,500

During a period of *rising prices* the first-in, first-out method will result in a larger amount ($14,500) being assigned as the cost of the ending inventory than would be assigned under the average cost method. When a relatively large amount is allocated as cost of the ending inventory, a relatively small amount will remain as cost of goods sold, as indicated by the following calculation:

. . . COST OF GOODS
SOLD COMPUTATION

Cost of goods available for sale	$30,000
Less: Ending inventory	14,500
Cost of goods sold (first-in, first-out method)	$15,500

It may be argued in support of the first-in, first-out method that the inventory valuation reflects recent costs and is therefore a realistic value in the light of conditions prevailing at the balance sheet date.

Last-in, first-out method   The last-in, first-out method, commonly known as *lifo,* is one of the most interesting methods of pricing inventories. The title of this method suggests that the most recently acquired goods are sold first, and that *the ending inventory consists of "old" goods acquired in the earliest purchases.* Although this assumption is not in accord with the physical movement of merchandise in most businesses, there is a strong logical argument to support the lifo method.

For the purpose of measuring income, the *flow of costs* may be more significant than the physical flow of merchandise. Supporters of the lifo method contend that the measurement of income should be based upon *current* market conditions. Therefore, current sales revenue should be offset by the *current* cost of the merchandise sold. Under the *lifo* method, the costs assigned to the cost of goods sold are relatively current, because they stem from the most recent purchases. Under the *fifo* method, on the other hand, the cost of goods sold is based on "older" costs.

Using the same data as in the preceding illustrations, the 120 units in the ending inventory would be priced as if they were the oldest goods available for sale during the period, as follows:

LAST-IN, FIRST-OUT
METHOD AND . . .

100 units from the beginning inventory @ $80	$8,000
20 units from the purchase of Mar. 1 @ $90	1,800
Ending inventory, 120 units (at lifo cost)	$9,800

Note that the lifo cost of the ending inventory ($9,800) is very much lower than the fifo cost ($14,500) of ending inventory in the preceding example. Since a relatively small part of the cost of goods available for sale is assigned to ending inventory, it follows that a relatively large portion must have been assigned to cost of goods sold, as shown by the following computation:

. . . COST OF GOODS
SOLD COMPUTATION

Cost of goods available for sale	$30,000
Less: Ending inventory	9,800
Cost of goods sold (last-in, first-out method)	$20,200

Comparison of the alternative methods of pricing inventory   We have now illustrated four common methods of pricing inventory at cost; the specific identification method, the average cost method, the first-in, first-out method, and the last-in, first-out method. By way of contrasting the results obtained from the four methods illustrated, especially during a period of rapid price increases, let us summarize the amounts computed for ending inventory, cost of goods sold, and gross profit on sales under each of the four methods. Assume that sales for the period amounted to $27,500.

FOUR METHODS OF
DETERMINING
INVENTORY COST
COMPARED

	SPECIFIC IDENTIFI- CATION METHOD	AVERAGE COST METHOD	FIRST-IN, FIRST- OUT METHOD	LAST-IN, FIRST- OUT METHOD
Sales	$27,500	$27,500	$27,500	$27,500
Cost of goods sold:				
Beginning inventory	$ 8,000	$ 8,000	$ 8,000	$ 8,000
Purchases	22,000	22,000	22,000	22,000
Cost of goods available for sale	$30,000	$30,000	$30,000	$30,000
Less: Ending inventory	12,400	12,000	14,500	9,800
Cost of goods sold	$17,600	$18,000	$15,500	$20,200
Gross profit on sales	$ 9,900	$ 9,500	$12,000	$ 7,300

This comparison of the four methods makes it apparent that during periods of *rising prices,* the use of lifo will result in lower reported profits than would be the case under the other methods of inventory valuation.

During a period of *declining prices,* the use of lifo will cause the reporting of relatively large profits as compared with fifo, which will hold reported profits to a minimum. Therefore, the choice of an inventory pricing method may significantly affect the amount of income reported during prolonged periods of changing price levels.

Which method of inventory valuation is best? All four of the inventory methods described are regarded as acceptable accounting practices.[5] No one method of inventory valuation can be considered as the "correct" or the "best" method. In the selection of a method, consideration should be given to the probable effect upon the balance sheet, upon the income statement, and upon such business decisions as the establishment of selling prices for goods.

The specific identification method has the advantage of portraying the actual physical flow of merchandise. However, this method permits manipulation of income by selecting which items to deliver in filling a sales order. Also, the specific identification method may lead to faulty pricing decisions by implying that identical items of merchandise have different economic values.

Identical items will have the same accounting values only under the average cost method. Assume for example that a hardware store sells a given size nail for 65 cents per kilogram. The hardware store buys the nails in 100 kg quantities at different times at prices ranging from 40 to 50 cents per kilogram. Several hundred kilograms of nails are always on hand, stored in a large bin. The average cost method properly recognizes that when a customer buys a kilogram of nails it is not necessary to know

[5] According to the CICA's *Financial Reporting in Canada*, Seventeenth Edition (Toronto, 1987), page 91, the most common methods of valuing inventory at cost are first-in, first-out and average cost, with last-in, first-out as a distant third and specific identification as a distant fourth.

exactly which nails the customer happened to select from the bin in order to measure the gross profit on the sale.

A shortcoming in the average cost method is that changes in current replacement costs of inventory are concealed because these costs are averaged with older costs. As a result of this averaging, the reported gross profit may not reflect current market conditions. This problem is illustrated in the discussion of *inventory profits* later in this chapter.

The inflation of recent years is a strong argument for the use of the lifo method. When prices are rising drastically, the most significant cost data to use as a guide to sales policies are probably the *current replacement costs* of the goods being sold. The lifo method of inventory valuation comes closer than any of the other methods described to measuring net income in the light of current selling prices and replacement costs.

On the other hand, the use of lifo during a period of rising prices is apt to produce a balance sheet figure for inventory that is far below the current replacement cost of the goods on hand. The fifo method of inventory valuation will lead to a balance sheet valuation of inventory more in line with current replacement costs.

Some business concerns that adopted lifo many years ago now show a balance sheet figure for inventory that is less than half the present replacement cost of the goods in stock. An inventory valuation method that gives significant figures for the income statement may thus produce misleading amounts for the balance sheet, whereas a method that produces a realistic figure for inventory on the balance sheet may provide less realistic data for the income statement.

The search for the "best" method of inventory valuation is rendered difficult because the inventory figure is used in both the balance sheet and the income statement, and these two financial statements are intended for different purposes. In the income statement the function of the inventory figure is to permit a matching of costs and revenue. In the balance sheet the inventory and the other current assets are regarded as a measure of the company's ability to meet its current debts. For this purpose a valuation of inventory in line with current replacement cost or net realizable value (estimated selling price less estimated costs of completion and sale) would appear to be more significant.

Consistency in the valuation of inventory

The *principle of consistency* is one of the basic concepts underlying reliable financial statements. This principle means that once a company has adopted a particular accounting method, that company should follow that method consistently rather than switch methods from one year to the next. Consider the consequences if we were to ignore the principle of consistency in accounting for inventories. A company could cause its net income for any given year to increase or decrease merely by changing its method of inventory valuation. The principle of consistency does not mean that every company in an industry must use the same accounting method; it does mean that a given company should not switch year after year from one accounting method to another.

Bear in mind that a company has considerable latitude in selecting a method of inventory valuation best suited to its needs. The principle of consistency comes into play after a given method has been selected. We have already illustrated in the example on page 397 how different methods can produce differences in reported income. Consequently, a change from one inventory method to another will usually cause reported income to change significantly in the year in which the change is made. Frequent switching of methods would make the income statements undependable as a means of portraying trends in operating results. Because of the principle of consistency, the user of financial statements is able to assume that the company has followed the same accounting methods it used in the preceding year. Thus, the value of financial statements is increased because they enable the user to make reliable comparisons of the results achieved from year to year.

The principle of consistency does not mean that a business can *never* change its method of inventory valuation. A business may change its method when circumstances warrant such a change.[6] When a change is made, both the reasons for the change and the effects of the change upon reported net income should be *disclosed fully* in the footnotes accompanying the financial statements. *Adequate disclosure* of all information necessary for the proper interpretation of financial statements is another basic principle of accounting. Even when the same method of inventory pricing is being followed consistently, the financial statements should include a disclosure of the pricing method in use.

The environment of inflation

We have previously discussed the relationship between the valuation of assets in the balance sheet and the recognition of costs and expenses in the income statement. As

HISTORICAL COSTS APPEAR IN BOTH BALANCE SHEET AND INCOME STATEMENT

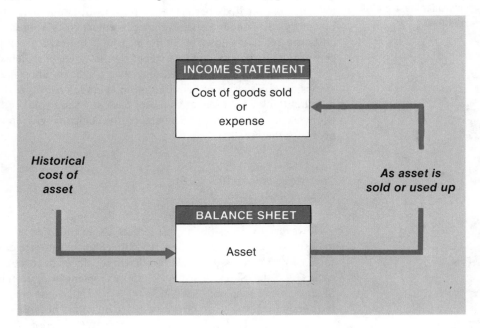

6 CICA, *CICA Handbook* (Toronto), paragraph 3030.01.

assets are sold or used up, their cost is removed from the balance sheet and recognized in the income statement as a cost or expense. In the case of inventory, the cost of units sold is transferred from the balance sheet to the income statement as cost of goods sold. In the case of depreciable assets, such as a building, the cost is gradually transferred to the income statement as depreciation expense. This flow of costs is illustrated in the chart on page 399.

A period of sustained inflation causes some distortion in financial statements that are based upon historical costs. Rising price levels may cause assets to be valued in the balance sheets at amounts substantially below their current replacement cost. Similarly, the cost assigned to the income statement as these assets are sold or used up tends to understate the cost to the business of replacing these assets.

The inflationary policies and high income taxes of recent years have stimulated the interest of business management in the choice of inventory methods. Although the rate of inflation slowed significantly in the early 1980s, most business executives and government officials expect the trend of rising prices to continue. In other words, an environment of inflation has come to be considered as normal in many sectors of the economy. The lifo method of inventory valuation causes reported net income to reflect the increasing cost of replacing the merchandise sold during the year. Therefore, the existence of inflation is an argument for the lifo method of inventory valuation.

Inventory profits

4 Define inventory profits and explain why some accountants consider these profits fictitious.

Many accountants believe that the use of fifo or of average cost during a period of inflation results in the reporting of overstated profits and consequently in the payment of excessive income taxes. Profits are overstated under both the fifo and average cost methods because the gross profit is computed by subtracting "old" inventory costs rather than current replacement costs from sales revenue. These old costs are relatively low, resulting in a high reported gross profit. However, the company must pay the higher current cost in order to replenish its inventory.

To illustrate this concept, assume that TV Sales Shop has an inventory of 20 television sets that were acquired at an average cost of $270. During the current month, 10 television sets are sold for cash at a sales price of $350 each. Using the average cost method to value inventory, the company will report the following gross profit for the month:

Sales (10 × $350)	$3,500
Cost of goods sold (10 × $270)	2,700
Gross profit on sales	$ 800

However, TV Sales Shop must replace its inventory of television sets to continue in business. Because of inflation, TV Sales Shop can no longer buy 10 television sets for $2,700. Let us assume that the current replacement cost of television sets is $325 each; TV Sales Shop must pay $3,250 to replenish its inventory. Thus, TV Sales Shop is able to keep only $250 ($3,500 − $3,250) of the reported $800 gross profit; the remaining $550 has to be reinvested in inventory because of the increasing cost of television sets. This $550 would be considered a fictitious profit, or an ***inventory profit,*** by many accountants and business executives.

The inventory profit included in the reported net income of a business may be computed by deducting the cost of goods shown in the income statement from the *replacement cost* (computed at the date of sale) of these goods.

In periods of rapid inflation, a significant portion of the reported net income of companies using fifo or average cost actually may be inventory profits. The net income of companies using lifo will include much less inventory profit because lifo causes more current costs to be included in the cost of goods sold.

Disclosing the effects of inflation

In an effort to compensate for the distortions in financial statements caused by inflation and changing prices, the accounting profession in a number of countries, including Canada and the United States, has recommended that large public corporations present in their annual reports supplementary information on the effects of inflation and changing prices.

In Canada, the CICA Accounting Standards Committee recommended in *Section 4510* of the *CICA Handbook*, "Reporting the Effects of Changing Prices," certain components of both constant-dollar (inflation) accounting and current-cost (specific price) accounting as *supplementary information* to be disclosed by large publicly owned corporations in their *annual* reports, together with conventional historical cost financial statements. Corporations are subject to the requirements of *Section 4510* if they have total assets (after the related accumulated depreciation, depletion, and amortization) of $350 million or more, or if inventories and property, plant and equipment (before the related accumulated depreciation, depletion, and amortization) total $50 million or more.

The recommended supplementary information to be disclosed in the annual reports includes:

1 The *current cost* amounts of (a) *cost of goods sold,* and depreciation, depletion, and amortization expenses, (b) *inventory,* and property, plant, and equipment at the end of the period, and (c) net assets at the end of the period.
2 The changes in the *current cost* amounts of *inventory* and property, plant, and equipment during the period.
3 The amount of the changes in the current costs of inventory and property, plant, and equipment during the period *attributable to the effects of inflation* (that is, the change in the general price level or the purchasing power of the dollar).
4 The amount of the gain or loss in the purchasing power (due to the effect of inflation), resulting from holding net monetary items (the excess of monetary liabilities over monetary assets or vice versa) during the period.[7]

The objective of the CICA recommendations is to provide information about the effects on an enterprise's financial position and operating results that are caused by (1) changes in prices of specific goods and services purchased, produced, and used, and (2) changes in the general purchasing power of the monetary unit in which transactions are measured.[8] Thus, *Section 4510* of the *CICA Handbook* is concerned

[7] CICA, *CICA Handbook*, paragraphs 4510.17, 4510.18, and 4510.24.
[8] Ibid., paragraph 4510.04.

with both the concepts of specific price level changes (that is, current-cost account-ing) and general price level changes (that is, inflation or constant-dollar accounting).

In the United States, *Statement No. 33* of the Financial Accounting Standards Board (FASB), "Financial Reporting and Changing Prices," also requires large corporations to disclose the extent to which historical costs appearing in both the balance sheet and in the income statement understate current price levels. These disclosures can be in a footnote to the historical cost-based financial statements or in a special set of supplementary financial statements. One requirement of *Statement No. 33* is that large corporations disclose what it would cost to *replace* their inventories at year-end and what their cost of goods sold would be if computed by using the ***current replacement cost*** at the date of sale. In late 1986, FASB issued statement 89, making these disclosures voluntary rather than mandatory.

Note that the disclosure of the effects of inflation and changing prices recommended by the CICA does not replace historical cost as a basis of accounting. Such disclosure serves only as supplementary information to the historical-cost financial statements.

It should be noted also that the recommendations of *Section 4510* do not carry the same force of compliance by business enterprises as other recommendations of the *CICA Handbook* because the former are related to supplementary information in the annual report and are not necessarily part of the annual financial statements. Consequently, these recommendations are essentially voluntary in nature. The extent to which business enterprises adopt these recommendations will depend largely on whether the enterprises are convinced that the benefits exceed the cost involved in providing the supplementary information. The most recent survey showed that only a small number of business enterprises, ranging from 43 to 62 (or about 16% to 19%) of the 275 to 323 enterprises included in the survey, complied with the CICA recommendations during the first three years, and the number was declining.[9]

In issuing *Section 4510* in December 1982, the Accounting Standards Committee of CICA acknowledged that it represented a first step in the search for the most mean-ingful presentation of the effects of inflation and changing prices on a business enterprise and that business enterprises should be "encouraged to experiment with the disclosure of other assets and liabilities and related expenses measured on a current cost basis."[10] The committee committed itself to a comprehensive review of *Section 4510* within five years of its release and to make such appropriate revisions as considered necessary. Thus, such a comprehensive review would be forthcoming soon.

5 Explain the lower-of-cost-and-market rule.

The lower-of-cost-and-market rule (LCM)

Although cost is the primary basis for valuation of inventories, circumstances may arise under which inventory may properly be valued at less than its cost. If the *utility* of the inventory has fallen below cost because of a decline in the price level, a loss has occurred. This loss may appropriately be recognized as a loss of the current

---

[9] CICA, *Reporting the Effects of Changing Prices — A Report on the Third Year's Experience with Section 4510 of the CICA Handbook* (Toronto, October, 1986), p. 3. See also *Financial Reporting In Canada* 17th ed, p. 79.
[10] CICA, *CICA Handbook*, paragraph 4510.08.

period by reducing the accounting value of the inventory from cost to a lower level designated as *market*. The word market as used in this context usually means *current replacement cost* or *net realizable value*.[11] For a merchandising company, current replacement cost is the amount the concern would have to pay at the present time for the goods in question, purchased in the customary quantities through the usual sources of supply and including transportation-in. Net realizable value, as noted earlier, is "the estimated selling price in the ordinary course of business less estimated costs of completion and sale" such as selling expenses in a merchandising company.[12] To avoid misunderstanding, many companies are disclosing both the cost method and the market method, such as "the lower of first-in, first-out and replacement cost," or "the lower of the average cost and net realizable value."

In the early days of accounting, when the principal users of financial statements were creditors and attention was concentrated upon the balance sheet, *conservatism* was a dominant consideration in asset valuation. The lower-of-cost-and-market rule was then considered justifiable because it tended to produce a "safe" or minimum value for inventory. The rule was widely applied for a time without regard for the possibility that although replacement costs had declined, there might be no corresponding and immediate decline in selling prices.

As the significance of the income statement has increased, considerable dissatisfaction with the lower-of-cost-and-market (replacement cost) rule has developed. If ending inventory is written down from cost to a lower replacement cost figure but the merchandise is sold during the next period at the usual selling prices, the effect of the write-down will have been to reflect a fictitious loss in the first period and an exaggerated profit in the second period. Selling prices do not always drop when replacement prices decline. Even if selling prices do follow replacement prices downward, they may not decline by a proportionate amount.

Because of these objections, the lower-of-cost-and-market rule of using replacement cost as market should be modified according to the circumstances. For example, if the inventory can probably be sold at prices that will yield a *normal profit,* the inventory should be carried at cost even though current replacement cost is lower. Assume that merchandise is purchased for $1,000 with the intention of reselling it to customers for $1,500. The replacement cost then declines from $1,000 to $800, but it is believed that the merchandise can still be sold to customers for $1,450. In other words, the normal anticipated profit has shrunk by $50. The carrying value of the inventory could then be written down from $1,000 to $950. There is no justification for reducing the inventory to the replacement cost of $800 under these circumstances.

Another example for modifying the lower-of-cost-and-market replacement cost rule is that inventory should never be carried at an amount greater than *net realizable value.* Assume that because of unstable market conditions, it is believed that goods acquired at a cost of $5,000 and having a current replacement cost of $4,500 will probably have to be sold for no more than $5,200 and that the selling expenses

---

[11] Of the 270 companies surveyed by CICA, 93% used the lower-of-cost-and-market rule for inventory valuation. The most common "market methods" for inventory valuation are net realizable value and replacement cost. See CICA *Financial Reporting in Canada*, op. cit., pp. 90 and 91.
[12] CICA, *CICA Terminology for Accountants*, p. 96.

involved will amount to $1,200. The inventory should then be reduced to a carrying value (net realizable value) of $4,000, which is less than current replacement cost.

Application of the lower-of-cost-and-market rule The lower-of-cost-and-market for inventory is often computed by determining the cost and the market figures for each item in inventory and using the lower of the two amounts in every case. If, for example, item A cost $100 and replacement cost is $90, the item should be priced at $90. If item B cost $200 and replacement cost is $225, this item should be priced at $200. The total cost of the two items is $300 and total replacement cost is $315, but the total inventory value determined by applying the lower-of-cost-and-market rule to each item in inventory is only $290. This application of the lower-of-cost-and-market rule is illustrated by the following tabulation:

PRICING INVENTORY AT LOWER-OF-COST-AND-MARKET

Application of Lower-of-Cost-and-Market Rule, Item-by-Item Method

		UNIT COST		TOTAL COST		LOWER OF COST AND MARKET
ITEM	QUANTITY	COST	MARKET	COST	MARKET	
A	10	$100	$ 90	$ 1,000	$ 900	$ 900
B	8	200	225	1,600	1,800	1,600
C	50	50	60	2,500	3,000	2,500
D	80	90	70	7,200	5,600	5,600
Totals				$12,300	$11,300	$10,600

If the lower-of-cost-and-market rule is applied item by item, the carrying value of the above inventory would be $10,600. However, an alternative and less rigorous version of the lower-of-cost-and-market rule calls for applying it to the total of the entire inventory rather than to the individual items. If the above inventory is to be valued by applying the lower-of-cost-and-market rule to the total of the inventory, the balance sheet amount for inventory is determined merely by comparing the total cost of $12,300 with the total market value of $11,300 and using the lower of the two figures. Still another alternative method of using the lower-of-cost-and-market concept is to apply it to categories of the inventory rather than item by item. Each of these alternative methods of applying the lower-of-cost-and-market rule is acceptable in current accounting practice, although once a method has been selected it should be followed consistently from year to year.

Estimating ending inventory and cost of goods sold

6 Estimate ending inventory by the gross profit method and by the retail method.

When the periodic inventory system is being used, a physical inventory must be taken to determine the amount of the ending inventory. However, business managers need monthly financial statements in order to manage a business efficiently. To prepare these monthly financial statements, we need to know the amount of inventory at the end of each month. However, the taking of a physical inventory is too time-consuming and costly a job to be performed every month. Most companies take a physical inventory only once a year. For monthly or quarterly financial statements, these companies use an estimated amount for the ending inventory. One method of *estimating* inventories is the **gross profit method;** another method is called the **retail inventory method.**

Gross profit method

The gross profit method is a quick, simple technique for estimating inventories that can be used in almost all types and sizes of business. In using the gross profit method, we assume that the rate of gross profit earned in the preceding year will remain the same for the current year. (Some companies prefer to use an average of the gross profit rates of recent years.) When we know the rate of gross profit, we can divide the dollar amount of net sales into two elements: (1) the gross profit and (2) the cost of goods sold. We view net sales as 100%. If gross profit, for example, is 40%, the cost of goods sold must be 60%. In other words, the cost of goods sold percentage (cost percentage) is determined by deducting the gross profit percentage from 100%.

When the gross profit percentage is known, the ending inventory can be estimated by the following procedures:

1 Determine the *cost of goods available for sale* from the general ledger records of beginning inventory and net purchases.
2 Estimate the *cost of goods sold* by multiplying the net sales by the cost percentage.
3 Deduct the *cost of goods sold* from the *cost of goods available for sale* to find the estimated ending inventory.

To illustrate, assume that Metro Hardware has a beginning inventory of $50,000 on January 1. During the month of January, net purchases amount to $20,000 and net sales total $30,000. Assume that the company's normal gross profit rate is 40% of net sales; it follows that the cost percentage is 60%. Using these facts, the inventory on January 31 may be estimated as follows:

STEP 1 . . .	Goods available for sale:	
	Beginning inventory, Jan. 1	$50,000
	Net purchases	20,000
	Cost of goods available for sale	$70,000
STEP 2 . . .	Deduct: Estimated cost of goods sold:	
	Net sales $30,000	
	Cost percentage (100% − 40%) 60%	
	Estimated cost of goods sold	18,000
STEP 3 . . .	Estimated ending inventory, Jan. 31	$52,000

The gross profit method of estimating inventory has several uses apart from the preparation of monthly financial statements. If an inventory is destroyed by fire, the company must determine the amount of the inventory on hand at the date of the fire in order to file an insurance claim. The most convenient way to determine this inventory amount is often the gross profit method.

The gross profit method is also used at year-end after the taking of a physical inventory to confirm the overall reasonableness of the amount determined by the counting and pricing process.

The retail method of estimating ending inventory

The retail method of inventory is widely used by department stores and other types of retail business. To use the retail inventory method, a store must maintain records showing the beginning inventory *at cost* and *at retail*. The term ''at retail'' means the marked selling prices of all items in the store. The records also must show the purchases during the period both *at cost* and *at retail.* The only other information needed is the net sales for the month. The amount of net sales, it should be noted, is equal to the amount recorded in the Sales revenue account during the period minus sales returns only. Sales discounts and sales allowances are excluded so as *not* to inflate the ending inventory at retail selling price.

The records described above enable us to know the amount of goods available for sale, stated both at cost and at retail selling prices. (As you know, goods available for sale are the total of beginning inventory and net purchases.) With this information all we need to do is deduct the net sales for the month from the retail sales value of the goods available for sale. The result will be the ending inventory at retail selling price. A final step is to convert the ending inventory at retail selling price to a cost basis by multiplying it by the *cost percentage.* The cost percentage is the *ratio of cost to selling price for the current period.* To compute the cost percentage, divide the cost of goods available for sale by the retail sales value of these goods. The end result of these procedures is that we have an estimated cost value for inventory without going through the extensive work of taking a physical inventory.

The following illustration shows the calculation of an ending inventory of $280,000 by the retail inventory method.

ESTIMATING INVENTORY FOR MONTHLY FINANCIAL STATEMENTS	COST PRICE	RETAIL SELLING PRICE
Goods available for sale:		
Beginning inventory	$415,000	$ 560,000
Net purchases	285,000	440,000
Goods available for sale	$700,000	$1,000,000
Cost percentage: $700,000 ÷ $1,000,000 = 70%		
Deduct: Net sales at retail		600,000
Ending inventory at retail selling price		$ 400,000
Ending inventory at cost ($400,000 × 70%)	$280,000	

Reducing a physical inventory to cost by the retail method   A second use for the retail inventory method is to aid in the completion of the annual physical inventory. Goods on sale in retail stores have price tags attached, showing retail prices. When the annual physical inventory is taken, it is more convenient to list the retail price from the price tags than to look up purchase invoices to find the unit cost of each item in the store. The total of the inventory at retail selling price is then reduced to cost by applying the cost percentage, that is, the ratio between cost and selling price during the current period. The illustration on page 407 shows a year-end physical inventory amounting to $235,400 at retail selling price. This amount is reduced to a cost basis of $141,240 by applying the cost percentage of 60%.

In this illustration we have shown the calculation of inventory by the retail inventory method without going into the complications that would arise from markups and markdowns in the original retail selling prices. Such changes in price are considered in advanced accounting courses.

	COST PRICE	RETAIL SELLING PRICE
Goods available for sale:		
Beginning inventory	$131,000	$220,000
Net purchases	49,000	80,000
Goods available for sale	$180,000	$300,000

Cost percentage: $180,000 ÷ $300,000 = 60%
Ending inventory at retail selling price

(per physical inventory)		$235,400
Ending inventory at cost ($235,400 × 60%)	$141,240	

Although the inventory amount is an estimate, experience has shown this retail inventory method to be a reliable one. An inventory amount established in this manner is acceptable in audited financial statements.

Internal control

Inventories are usually the largest current asset of a merchandising or manufacturing business. Furthermore, the very nature of inventories makes them subject to theft and to major errors and misstatement. The large dollar amounts involved, coupled with the rapid turnover of inventory items, and the variety of alternative valuation methods, make it possible for a major shortage to occur in inventories without attracting immediate attention. Thus, the accountant's approach to inventories should stress an awareness of the possibility of large intentional errors as well as major accidental errors in establishing inventory quantities and amounts. If one or more members of a company's management is determined to evade income taxes, to conceal shortages arising from fraud, or to mislead absentee owners, inventories constitute the most likely area for such fraudulent action to take place.

To provide the strong internal control procedures needed to protect inventories, the various physical functions involved in acquiring and handling merchandise should be assigned to separate departments. These functions may include purchasing, receiving, storing, issuing, and shipping the items which comprise the inventory. Thus, the organizational structure of a company should include a purchasing department with exclusive authority to make all purchases. All merchandise received by the company should be cleared through a receiving department. This department will count the merchandise received, detect any damaged items, issue a receiving report to the accounts payable department and other departments, and transmit the merchandise to the stores department.

In addition to the protection afforded by extensive subdivision of duties, another important approach to assuring reliability in the amounts reported as inventory and cost of goods sold is an annual audit by a public accounting firm. Every independent audit includes firsthand observation of the annual taking of a physical inventory. Such observation by a competent outsider provides assurance that the goods on hand are carefully counted and priced, thus leading to valid amounts for inventory and cost of goods sold in the financial statements. In addition, the independent auditors will study and test the system of internal control.

Many small companies have too few employees to permit the extensive subdivision of duties described above. Moreover, these small concerns usually are unwilling to incur the cost of an annual audit by a public accounting firm. Under these circumstances, the amounts shown in the financial statements (especially inventory, cost of goods sold, gross profit, and net income) should be viewed with caution by absentee owners, bankers, creditors, and other outsiders.

Perpetual inventory system

7 Explain how a perpetual inventory system operates.

Companies that deal in merchandise of high unit cost, such as automobiles, television sets, or expensive jewelry, find a perpetual inventory system worthwhile and efficient. Since inventory is often one of the largest assets in a business and has a rapid rate of turnover, strong internal control is especially important. A perpetual inventory system, if properly designed and operated, can provide the strongest possible internal control over the inventory of merchandise. The key feature of a perpetual inventory system is that the records show continuously the amount of inventory on hand and the cost of goods sold. Companies with computer-based accounting records including point-of-sale terminals are in a good position to carry on continuous updating of inventory records.

Internal control and perpetual inventory systems

A perpetual inventory system has the potential of providing excellent internal control. However, the fact that perpetual inventory records are in use does not automatically guarantee strong internal control. Such basic internal control concepts as the subdivision of duties, the control of documents by serial numbers, and separation of the accounting function from the custody of assets are essential elements with either the perpetual or periodic inventory systems.

Par-Flite, a manufacturer of golf equipment, maintained an inventory of several thousand sets of golf clubs. The clubs were kept in a storeroom with barred windows and doors under the supervision of John Adams. Adams was also responsible for maintaining detailed perpetual inventory records of the golf clubs in the storeroom. Another employee acquired an unauthorized key to the storeroom and began stealing large numbers of clubs. Adams discovered that the quantities on hand did not agree with the perpetual records he maintained. Afraid that his records would be criticized as highly inaccurate, he made numerous changes in the records so they would agree with quantities of golf clubs on hand. The theft of clubs continued and large losses were sustained before the inventory shortage came to the attention of management.

If the person maintaining records had not also been responsible for physical custody of the merchandise, there would have been no incentive or opportunity to conceal a shortage by falsifying the records. Satisfactory internal control over inventories requires that the accounting function be separate from the custody of assets. Frequent comparison of quantities of merchandise on hand with the quantities shown by the perpetual inventory records should be made by employees who do not have responsibility either for custody of assets or for maintenance of records.

Perpetual inventory records

The information required for a perpetual system can be processed electronically or manually. In a manual system a subsidiary record card, as shown in the following illustration, is used for each type of merchandise on hand. If the company has 100 different kinds of products in stock, then 100 inventory record cards will make up the subsidiary inventory record. Following is an inventory record card for item XL-2000.

On this card, the quantity and cost of units received will be listed at the date of receipt; the quantity and cost of units sold will be recorded at the date of sale; and after each purchase or sales transaction, the balance remaining on hand will be shown. This running balance will be shown in number of units, cost per unit, and total dollar amount.

PERPETUAL INVENTORY
RECORD CARD

Item	XL-2000						Maximum	20	
Location	Storeroom 2						Minimum	8	

	PURCHASED			SOLD			BALANCE		
Date	Units	Unit cost	Total	Units	Unit cost	Total	Units	Unit cost	Balance
Jan. 1							12	$50.00	$600.00
7				2	$50.00	$100.00	10	50.00	500.00
9	10	$55.00	$550.00				10	50.00	
							10	55.00	1,050.00
12				8	50.00	400.00	2	50.00	
							10	55.00	650.00
31				2	50.00	100.00			
				1	55.00	55.00	9	55.00	495.00

The information on the illustrated inventory record shows that the first-in, first-out basis of pricing the inventory is being used. After the sale of two units on January 7, the remaining inventory consisted of 10 units at a cost of $50 each. The purchase on January 9 of 10 units carried a unit cost of $55, rather than $50, hence must be accounted for separately. The balance on hand after the January 9 purchase appears on two lines: 10 units at $50 and 10 units at $55. When 8 units were sold on January 12, they were treated as coming from the oldest stock on hand and therefore had a cost of $50 each. The balance remaining on hand then consisted of 2 units at $50 and 10 units at $55. When 3 units were sold on January 31, the cost consisted of 2 units at $50 and one unit at $55. The ending inventory of 9 units consists of the most recently acquired units with a cost of $55 each.

Perpetual inventory records may also be maintained on a last-in, first-out basis or on an average cost basis, but these systems involve some complexities that are considered in advanced accounting courses.

Control over the amount invested in inventory can be strengthened by listing on each inventory card the maximum and minimum quantities that should be kept in stock. By maintaining quantities within these limits, over-stocking and out-of-stock situations can be avoided.

General ledger entries for a perpetual inventory system   The general ledger controlling account entitled *Inventory* is continuously (perpetually) updated when a perpetual inventory system is in use. This Inventory account controls the many subsidiary record cards discussed above. A continuously updated Cost of Goods Sold account is also maintained in the general ledger.

The purchase of merchandise by a company using a perpetual inventory system requires a journal entry affecting general ledger controlling accounts as follows:

Inventory   1,500
    Accounts Payable, Lake Company   1,500
To record purchase of merchandise on credit.

This purchase transaction would also be recorded in the subsidiary ledger (the perpetual inventory cards) showing the quantity of each kind of merchandise purchased. The $1,500 purchase from Lake Company might affect only one or perhaps a dozen of the subsidiary records, depending on how many types of merchandise were included in this purchase transaction.

For every sales transaction, we can determine the cost of the goods sold by referring to the appropriate perpetual inventory card record. Therefore, at the time of a sale, we can record both the amount of the selling price and the *cost* of the goods sold, as illustrated in the following pair of related entries.

Accounts Receivable, J. Williams   140
    Sales   140
To record the sale of merchandise on credit.

Cost of Goods Sold   100
    Inventory   100
To record the cost of goods sold and the related decrease in inventory.

To avoid making a large number of entries in the general journal, a special column can be entered in the sales journal to show the cost of the goods involved in each sales transaction. At the end of the month the total of this "Cost" column can be posted as a debit to Cost of Goods Sold and a credit to Inventory.

A company maintaining perpetual inventory records will also conduct a physical count of all merchandise once a year and compare the amount of the physical inventory with the perpetual inventory records. An adjusting entry can be made to bring the inventory records into agreement with the physical inventory. For example, if shoplifting or other factors have caused an inventory shortage, the adjusting entry will consist of a debit to the loss account, Inventory Shortage, and a credit to Inventory.

When a perpetual inventory system is in use, the Inventory account is increased by purchases of merchandise. It is decreased by the cost of goods sold, by purchase returns and allowances, and by purchase discounts. At the end of the year the dollar balances of all the subsidiary inventory record cards should be added to see that the total is in agreement with the general ledger controlling account. The only adjustment necessary at year-end will be to correct the Inventory controlling account and the subsidiary records for any discrepancies indicated by the taking of a physical inventory.

The advantages of a perpetual inventory system as indicated in the preceding discussion include:

1 Stronger internal control. By comparing the physical inventory with the perpetual records, management will be made aware of any shortages or errors and can take corrective action.

2 A physical inventory can be taken at dates other than year-end, or it can be taken for different products or different departments at various dates during the year, since the perpetual records always show the amounts that *should* be on hand.

3 Quarterly or monthly financial statements can be prepared more readily because of the availability of dollar amounts for inventory and cost of goods sold in the accounting records.

END-OF-CHAPTER REVIEW

SUMMARY OF CHAPTER LEARNING OBJECTIVES

1 Explain what goods should be included in inventory.

For a merchandising company, the inventory consists of all goods owned and held for sale in the regular course of business.

2 Describe the effects of inventory error on the income statements of the current year and the following year.

The ending inventory of one year is also the beginning inventory of the next year. Therefore, an error in the year-end inventory affects the income statements of two successive years. For example, an overstatement of ending inventory will cause an overstatement of net income this year and a counterbalancing understatement of net income next year.

3 Determine the cost of inventory by using (1) specific identification, (2) average cost, (3) fifo, and (4) lifo. Discuss the merits and shortcomings of these methods.

When identical units of merchandise are purchased at various prices during the year, one of four assumptions is made as to which units were sold and which units remain on hand at year-end. The four assumptions (and inventory valuation methods) are (1) specific identification, (2) average cost, (3) first-in, first-out (fifo), and (4) last-in, first-out (lifo). The *specific identification method* is suitable for high-priced items, but not for a large volume of low priced merchandise. *Average cost* is computed by dividing total cost of goods available for sale by the number of units available for sale. This method utilizes both current costs and price which prevailed several months earlier. The *first-in, first-out (fifo) method* assumes that the first merchandise acquired is the first merchandise sold. The ending inventory, therefore consists of the most recently acquired goods priced at recent prices. This method gives realistic inventory amount in the balance sheet. The *last-in, first-out (lifo)* method assume that the most recently acquired goods are sold first. Therefore, the ending inventory consist of "old" goods acquired in the earlier purchases and priced at prices that prevailed in the past During periods of inflation, the lifo method results in lower reported profits and lower ending inventory than the other methods.

4 Define inventory profits and explain why some accountants consider these profits fictitious

The use of fifo or average cost during periods of inflation results in reporting higher profit than would be reported under lifo. Some accountants believe that current replacement cost rather than "old" inventory costs should be subtracted from sales revenue in computing gross profit. These accountants believe that using fifo or average costs during periods of inflation leads to "fictitious inventory profits," because these methods do not recognize that units sold must be replaced in inventory at today's higher prices.

5 Explain the lower-of-cost-and-market rule.

The word *market* in this context generally means current replacement cost or net realizable value. The rule indicates that if market value at year-end is less than the cost of inventory, the lower value should be used.

6 Estimate ending inventory by the gross profit method and by the retail method.

Estimating inventory by the gross profit method or by the retail method is useful to corroborate year-end inventories established by physical count. These estimating methods also permit the preparation of monthly financial statements without taking monthly physical inventories Also, these methods are useful in estimating losses of inventory from fire or theft. Under the gross profit method, the cost of goods sold is computed by deducting the estimated gross profit margin from sales. The cost of goods sold is then deducted from cost of goods available for sale to determine ending inventory. With the retail method, the inventory is computed at retail price and then converted to a cost basis by multiplying it by the cost percentage. The cost percentage is the ratio of cost to selling price for the current period.

7 Explain how a perpetual inventory system operates.

Under a perpetual inventory sytem, the records are continuously updated as purchases and sales are made. Thus the records show at all times the amount of inventory on hand and the cost of goods sold in the current accounting period. A perpetual inventory system provide stronger internal control than does the periodic inventory system illustrated in earlier chapters. However, a perpetual inventory system may not be suitable for a business having a large volume of transactions in low-price items.

KEY TERMS INTRODUCED OR EMPHASIZED IN CHAPTER 9

Average cost method A method of inventory valuation. Weighted-average unit cost is computed by dividing the total cost of goods available for sale by the number of identical units available for sale.

Consistency in inventory valuation An accounting standard that calls for the use of the same method of inventory pricing from year to year, with full disclosure of the effects of any change in method. Intended to make financial statements comparable.

First-in, first-out (fifo) method A method of computing the cost of inventory and the cost of goods sold based on the assumption that the first merchandise acquired is the first merchandise sold, and that the ending inventory consists of the most recently acquired goods.

F.O.B. destination A term meaning the seller bears the cost of shipping goods to the buyer's location. Title to the goods remains with the seller while the goods are in transit.

F.O.B. shipping point The buyer of goods bears the cost of transportation from the seller's location to the buyer's location. Title to the goods passes at the point of shipment and the goods are the property of the buyer while in transit.

Gross profit method A method of estimating the cost of the ending inventory based on the assumption that the rate of gross profit remains approximately the same from year to year.

Inventory profits The amount by which the cost of replacing goods sold (computed at the date of sale) exceeds the reported cost of goods sold. Many accountants consider inventory profits to be a "fictitious" profit, because this amount usually must be reinvested in inventories and therefore is not available for distribution to shareholders.

Last-in, first-out (lifo) method A method of computing the cost of goods sold by use of the prices paid for the most recently acquired units. Ending inventory is valued on the basis of prices paid for the units first acquired.

Lower-of-cost-and-market method A method of inventory pricing in which goods are valued at the lower of original cost (e.g., fifo or average) and market (e.g., replacement cost or net realizable value.)

Net realizable value The estimated selling price in the ordinary course of business less estimated costs of completion and sale.

Perpetual inventory system Provides a continuous (perpetual) running record of the goods on hand. As goods are sold their cost is transferred to a Cost of Goods Sold account.

Physical inventory A systematic count of all goods on hand, followed by the application of unit prices to the quantities counted and development of a dollar value for ending inventory.

Retail method A method of estimating inventory in a retail store based on the assumption that the cost of goods on hand bears the same percentage relationship to retail prices as does the cost of all goods available for sale to the original retail prices. Inventory is first priced at retail and then converted to cost by application of a cost-to-retail percentage.

Specific identification method A method of pricing inventory by identifying the units in the ending inventory as coming from specific purchases.

DEMONSTRATION PROBLEM FOR YOUR REVIEW

Information relating to the inventory quantities, purchases, and sales of a certain type of capacitor by Morton Electronics during Year 6 is shown as follows:

	NUMBER OF UNITS	COST PER UNIT	TOTAL COST
Inventory, Jan. 1, Year 6	400	$2.80	$1,120
First purchase (Mar. 15)	515	3.00	1,545
Second purchase (June 6)	620	3.50	2,170
Third purchase (Sept. 20)	480	4.20	2,016
Fourth purchase (Dec. 31)	385	4.60	1,771
Goods available for sale	2,400		$8,622
Units sold during Year 6	1,860		
Inventory, Dec. 31, Year 6	540		

Instructions   Compute the cost of the December 31, Year 6, inventory and the cost of goods sold for th[e] capacitors in Year 6 using:

a The first-in, first-out method (fifo)

b The last-in, first-out method (lifo)

c The average cost method

SOLUTION TO DEMONSTRATION PROBLEM

a Fifo method

Inventory:

385 units from the Dec. 31 purchase @ $4.60	$1,77[ ]
155 units from the Sept. 20 purchase @ $4.20	65[ ]
Ending inventory, 540 units (at fifo cost)	$2,42[ ]

Cost of goods sold:

Cost of goods available for sale	$8,62[ ]
Less: Ending inventory (fifo)	2,42[ ]
Cost of goods sold (fifo)	$6,20[ ]

b Lifo method

Inventory:

400 units from beginning inventory @ $2.80	$1,12[ ]
140 units from the Mar. 15 purchase @ $3.00	42[ ]
Ending inventory, 540 units (at lifo cost)	$1,54[ ]

Cost of goods sold:

Cost of goods available for sale	$8,62[ ]
Less: Ending inventory (lifo)	1,54[ ]
Cost of goods sold (lifo)	$7,08[ ]

c Average cost method

Inventory:

Cost of goods available for sale	$ 8,62[ ]
Number of units available for sale	2,40[ ]
Average cost per unit ($8,622 ÷ 2,400 units)	$3.592[ ]
Ending inventory (at average cost, 540 units × $3.5925)	$ 1,94[ ]

Cost of goods sold:

Cost of goods available for sale	$8,62[ ]
Less: Ending inventory (average cost)	1,94[ ]
Cost of goods sold (average cost)	$6,68[ ]

Alternative computation of cost of goods sold:

Cost of goods sold (1,860 units at $3.5925)	$6,68[ ]

ASSIGNMENT MATERIAL

REVIEW QUESTIONS

1 Which of the seven items in the following list are used in computing the *cost of goods available for sale?*

a Ending inventory

b Sales

c Beginning inventory

d Purchases

e Transportation-in

f Purchase returns and allowances

g Delivery expense

2 Through an error in counting of merchandise at December 31, 1988, the Trophy Company overstated the amount of goods on hand by $8,000. Assuming that the error was not discovered, what was the effect upon net income for 1988? Upon owner's equity at December 31, 1988? Upon net income for 1989? Upon owner's equity at December 31, 1989?

3 Is the establishment of an appropriate valuation for the merchandise inventory at the end of the year more important in producing a dependable income statement, or in producing a dependable balance sheet?

4 Explain the meaning of the term *physical inventory.*

5 Near the end of December, Hadley Company received a large order from a major customer. The work of packing the goods for shipment was begun at once but could not be completed before the close of business on December 31. Since a written order from the customer was on hand and the goods were nearly all packed and ready for shipment, Hadley felt that this merchandise should not be included in the physical inventory taken on December 31. Do you agree? What is probably the reason behind Hadley's opinion?

6 During a prolonged period of rising prices, will the fifo or lifo method of inventory valuation result in higher reported profits?

7 Throughout several years of strongly rising prices, Company A used the lifo method of inventory valuation and Company B used the fifo method. In which company would the balance sheet figure for inventory be closer to current replacement cost of the merchandise on hand? Why?

8 You are making a detailed analysis of the financial statements and accounting records of two companies in the same industry, Adams Company and Bar Company. Price levels have been rising steadily for several years. In the course of your investigation, you observe that the inventory value shown on the Adams Company balance sheet is quite close to the current replacement cost of the merchandise on hand. However, for Bar Company, the carrying value of the inventory is far below current replacement cost. What method of inventory valuation is probably used by Adams Company? By Bar Company? If we assume that the two companies are identical except for the inventory valuation method used, which company has probably been reporting higher net income in recent years?

9 Why do some accountants consider the net income reported by businesses during a period of rising prices to be overstated?

10 Assume that a business uses the first-in, first-out method of accounting for inventories during a prolonged period of inflation and that the business pays dividends equal to the amount of reported net income. Suggest a problem that may arise in continued successful operation of the business. What does this situation have to do with "inventory profits"?

11 The *CICA Handbook* requires large corporations to disclose the current cost of their inventories and to disclose what their cost of goods sold would be if computed by using current costs. Do you think this policy indicates that corporate profits have tended to be overstated or understated in recent years? Explain.

12 Explain the meaning of the term *market* as used in the expression "lower-of-cost-and-market."

13 One of the items in the inventory of Grayline Stores is marked for sale at $125. The purchase invoice shows the item cost $95, but a newly issued price list from the manufacturer shows the present replacement cost to be $90. What inventory valuation should be assigned to this item if Grayline Stores follows the lower-of-cost-and-market rule?

14 Explain the usefulness of the *gross profit method* of estimating inventories.

15 A store using the *retail inventory method* takes its physical inventory by applying current retail selling prices as marked on the merchandise to the quantities counted. Does this procedure indicate that the inventory will appear in the financial statements at retail selling price? Explain.

16 Estimate the ending inventory by the gross profit method, given the following data: beginning inventory $40,000, net purchases $100,000, net sales $106,667, average gross profit rate 25% of net sales.

17 Summarize the difference between the *periodic system* and the *perpetual system* of accounting for inventory. Which system would usually cost more to maintain? Which system would be most practicable for a restaurant, a retail drugstore, a new car dealer?

18 Identify each of the four statements that follow as true or false. Also, give a brief explanation. In the accounting records of a company using a perpetual inventory system:
a The Inventory account will ordinarily remain unchanged until the end of an accounting period.
b The Cost of Goods Sold account is debited with the sales price of merchandise sold.
c The Inventory account and the Cost of Goods Sold account will both normally have debit balances.
d The Inventory account and the Cost of Goods Sold account will normally have equal but offsetting balances.

19 A large art gallery has in inventory several hundred paintings. No two are alike. The least expensive is priced at more than $1,000 and the higher priced items carry prices of $100,000 or more. Which of the four methods of inventory valuation discussed in this chapter would you consider to be most appropriate for this business? Give reasons for your answer.

EXERCISES

Exercise 9-1
Accounting
terminology

In the following list are nine technical accounting terms introduced in this chapter:

Inventory profits	Lifo method	Average cost method
Retail method	Fifo method	Gross profit method
Lower-of-cost-and-market method	Periodic inventory system	Perpetual inventory system

Each of the following statements may (or may not) describe one of these technical terms. For each statement, indicate the accounting term described, or answer "None" if the statement does not correctly describe any of the terms.

a Procedures that provide a continuous running record of the inventory on hand and the cost of goods sold.

b The difference between the amount reported in the income statement as the cost of goods sold and the amount that a business actually must pay to replace goods sold.

c A pricing method in which inventory appears in the balance sheet at expected sales price, rather than at cost.

d A pricing method in which the oldest goods on hand are assumed to be the first ones sold.

e The pricing method most appropriate for an inventory of unique items, such as oil paintings or custom jewelry.

f The pricing method most likely to report lower net income during a period of rising prices.

g A method for estimating inventory and the cost of goods sold that does not require recording purchases at two separate amounts.

Exercise 9-2
Effects of errors in
inventory valuation

The condensed income statements prepared by Chapel Company for two successive years follow:

	1989	1988
Sales	$1,000,000	$960,000
Cost of goods sold	586,400	609,600
Gross profit on sales	$ 413,600	$350,400
Operating expenses	307,000	298,000
Net income	$ 106,600	$ 52,400

The inventory at the end of 1988 was understated by $33,600, but the error was not discovered until after the accounts had been closed and financial statements prepared at the end of 1989. The balance sheets for the two years showed owner's equity of $142,800 at the end of 1988 and $173,600 at the end of 1989.

Compute the correct net income figures for 1988 and 1989 and the gross profit percentage for each year based on corrected data. What correction, if any, should be made in owner's equity at the end of 1988 and at the end of 1989?

Exercise 9-3
F.O.B. shipping point
and F.O.B. destination

Fraser Company had two large shipments of merchandise in transit at December 31. One was a $90,000 inbound shipment of merchandise (shipped December 28, F.O.B. shipping point), which arrived at the Fraser receiving dock on January 2. The other shipment was a $55,000 outbound shipment of merchandise to a customer, which was shipped and billed by Fraser on December 30 (terms F.O.B. shipping point) and reached the customer on January 3.

In taking a physical inventory on December 31, Fraser counted all goods on hand and priced the inventory on the basis of average cost. The total amount was $480,000. In developing this figure, Fraser gave no consideration to goods in transit.

What amount should appear as inventory on the company's balance sheet at December 31? Explain. If you indicate an amount other than $480,000, state what asset or liability other than inventory would also be changed in amount.

Exercise 9-4
Lifo, fifo, and average cost

The records of Barker, Inc., showed the beginning inventory balance of Item T12 on January 1 and the purchases of this item during the current year to be as follows:

Jan. 1	Beginning inventory	1,000 units @ $10.00	$ 10,000
Feb. 23	Purchase	3,200 units @ $11.00	35,200
Apr. 20	Purchase	2,000 units @ $11.20	22,400
May 4	Purchase	2,000 units @ $11.60	23,200
Nov. 30	Purchase	800 units @ $12.50	10,000
Totals	....	9,000 units	$100,800

At December 31 the ending inventory consisted of 1,200 units.

Determine the cost of the ending inventory, based on each of the following methods of inventory valuation:

a Average cost

b First-in, first-out

c Last-in, first-out

Exercise 9-5
Lifo, fifo, and average cost

One of the products sold by National Plumbing Supply is a 2 cm brass gate valve. The company purchases these valves several times during the year and sells the item daily. The inventory quantities, purchases, and sales for the year are summarized as follows:

	NUMBER OF UNITS	COST PER UNIT	TOTAL COST
Beginning inventory (Jan. 1)	9,100	$4.00	$ 36,400
First purchase (Feb. 20)	20,000	4.10	82,000
Second purchase (May 10)	30,000	4.25	127,500
Third purchase (Aug. 24)	50,000	4.60	230,000
Fourth purchase (Nov. 30)	10,900	5.00	54,500
Goods available for sale	120,000		$530,400
Units sold during the year	105,000		
Ending inventory (Dec. 31)	15,000		

Compute the cost of the ending inventory of gate valves, using the following inventory valuation methods:

a First-in, first-out

b Last-in, first-out

c Average cost

Exercise 9-6
Discussion of inventory
profits

Olympic Bicycle Shop uses the first-in, first-out method of inventory valuation. At the end of the current year the shop had exactly the same number of bicycles in stock as at the beginning of the year, and the same proportion of each model. However, the year had been one of severe inflation and the cost of the ending inventory was shown in the accounts at $36,000 whereas the cost of the beginning inventory had been only $24,000. The net income reported by the shop for the year was $27,000. Comment on the validity of the reported net income and indicate what adjustment might be reasonable to give the owner of this business a realistic picture of the results of the year's operations.

Exercise 9-7
Applying the LCM rule

Pullman Company has compiled the following information concerning items in its inventory at December 31:

		UNIT COST	
ITEM	QUANTITY	COST (FIFO)	MARKET
A	200	$ 46	$ 50
B	70	160	136
C	62	100	110
D	81	280	290

Determine the total inventory value to appear on Pullman Company's balance sheet under the lower-of-cost-and-market rule, assuming (a) that the rule is applied to inventory as a whole and (b) that the rule is applied on an item-by-item basis.

Exercise 9-8
Estimating inventory by
the gross profit method

When Bob Long arrived at his store on the morning of January 29, he found empty shelves and display racks; thieves had broken in during the night and stolen the entire inventory. Long's accounting records showed that he had $84,000 inventory on January 1 (cost value). From January 1 to January 29, he had made net sales of $100,000 and net purchases of $64,800. The gross profit during the past several years had consistently averaged 30% of sales. Long wishes to file an insurance claim for the theft loss. You are to use the gross profit method to estimate the cost of his inventory at the time of the theft. Show computations.

Exercise 9-9
Estimating inventory
by the retail method

Vagabond Shop wishes to determine the approximate month-end inventory using data from the accounting records without taking a physical count of merchandise on hand. From the following information, estimate the cost of the September 30 inventory by the *retail method* of inventory valuation.

	COST PRICE	RETAIL SELLING PRICE
Inventory of merchandise, Aug. 31	$529,600	$800,000
Purchases (net) during September	340,800	480,000
Sales (net) during September		454,000

Exercise 9-10
Using the perpetual
inventory system

Fitness Equipment Corporation uses a *perpetual inventory system.* On January 1, the Inventory account had a balance of $36,200. During the first few days of January the following transactions occurred.

Jan. 2 Purchased merchandise on credit from Bell Company for $7,400.

Jan. 3 Sold merchandise for cash, $4,500. The cost of this merchandise was $2,700.

a Prepare entries in general journal form to record the above transactions.

b What was the balance of the Inventory account at the close of business January 3?

PROBLEMS

Group A

Problem 9A-1
Inventory errors:
effect on earnings

Three years after organizing Pacific Screen, the owners decided to offer the business for sale as a going concern. The income statements of the business for the last three years include the following key figures.

	1989	1988	1987
Net sales	$540,000	$520,000	$500,000
Cost of goods sold	356,400	348,800	345,000
Gross profit on sales	$183,600	$171,200	$155,000
Gross profit percentage	34%	33%*	31%

*Rounded to the nearest full percentage point.

In discussions with prospective buyers, the owners are emphasizing the rising trends of gross profit and gross profit percentage as very favourable factors.

Assume that you are retained by a prospective purchaser of the business to make an investigation of the fairness and reliability of Pacific Screen's accounting records and financial statements. You find everything in order except for the following: (1) An arithmetical error in the computation of inventory at the end of 1987 had caused a $10,000 understatement in that inventory; and (2) a duplication of figures in the computation of inventory at the end of 1988 had caused an overstatement of $27,000 in that inventory. The company uses the periodic inventory system and these errors had not been brought to light prior to your investigation.

Instructions

a Prepare a revised three-year schedule along the lines of the preceding illustration.

b Comment on the trend of gross profit and gross profit percentage before and after the revision.

Problem 9A-2
Fifo, lifo, average
cost

Much of the revenue earned by Motor Flow, Inc., comes from the sale of a specialized type of valve. During the year, the inventory quantities, purchases, and sales of this valve were as follows:

	NUMBER OF UNITS	COST PER UNIT	TOTAL COST
Inventory, Jan. 1	8,000	$5.89	$ 47,12
First purchase (Mar. 15)	10,300	6.20	63,86
Second purchase (June 6)	12,400	6.60	81,84
Third purchase (Sept. 20)	9,600	6.80	65,28
Fourth purchase (Dec. 31)	7,700	7.00	53,90
Goods available for sale	48,000		$312,00
Units sold during the year	37,200		
Inventory, Dec. 31	10,800		

Instructions   **a** Compute the cost of the December 31 inventory and the cost of goods sold for the valves during the year using:

(1) The first-in, first-out method

(2) The last-in, first-out method

(3) The average-cost method

b Which of the three inventory pricing methods provides the most realistic balance sheet valuation of inventory in light of the current replacement cost of the valves? Does this same method also produce the most realistic measure of income in light of the costs being incurred by Motor Flow to replace the valves when they are sold? Explain.

Problem 9A-3
More on fifo, lifo,
and average cost
and income statement

Micro Ring specializes in the sale of a single product. During the year, 106,000 units were sold for a total price of $800,000. The inventory at January 1 consisted of 9,100 units valued at cost of $36,400. Purchases during the year were as follows: 20,000 units @ $4.10; 30,000 units @ $4.25; 50,000 units @ $4.60; and 10,900 units @ $5.00.

Instructions   **a** Compute the December 31 inventory using:

(1) The first-in, first-out method

(2) The last-in, first-out method

(3) The average cost method

b Prepare partial income statements for each of the above three methods of pricing inventory. The income statements are to be carried only to the determination of gross profit on sales.

c Assuming that the three inventory pricing methods are acceptable for income tax purposes, which would be most advantageous from an income tax standpoint during a period of rising prices? Comment on the significance of the inventory figure under the method you recommend with respect to current replacement cost.

Problem 9A-4
A more efficient
method for pricing
inventory

The inventory of Station One, a retail store, consists of a wide range of articles of low unit price. The selling price of each item is plainly marked on the merchandise. At each year-end, the company has taken a physical count of goods on hand and has priced these goods at cost by looking up individual purchase invoices to determine the unit cost of each item in stock. Stevens, the store manager, is anxious to find a more economical method of assigning dollar values to the year-end inventory, explaining that it takes much more time to price the inventory than to count the merchandise on hand.

By analyzing the accounting records you are able to determine that net purchases of merchandise in the year totalled $1,330,000; the retail selling price of this merchandise was $1,750,000. At the end of the year a physical inventory showed goods on hand priced to sell at $375,000. This represented a considerable increase over the inventory of a year earlier. At December 31 a year ago, the inventory on hand had appeared in the balance sheet at cost of $170,000, although it had a retail value of $250,000.

Instructions   **a** Outline a plan whereby the inventory can be computed without the necessity of looking up individual purchase invoices. List step by step the procedures to be followed.

b Compute the cost of the inventory at December 31 of the current year, using the method described in **a**.

c Explain how the inventory method you have described can be modified for the preparation of monthly financial statements when no physical count of inventory is taken.

Problem 9A-5
Entries for perpetual
inventory

Satellite Trackers sells satellite tracking systems for receiving television broadcasts from satellites in outer space. At December 31 last year, the company's inventory amounted to $22,000. During the first week of January this year, the company made only one purchase and one sale. These transactions were as follows:

Jan. 3 Sold one tracking system costing $11,200 to Mystery Mountain Resort for cash, $18,900.

Jan. 6 Purchased merchandise on account from Yamaha, $9,600. Terms, net 30 days.

Instructions

a Prepare journal entries to record these transactions, assuming that Satellite Trackers uses the perpetual inventory system. Use separate entries to record the sale and the cost of goods sold for the sale on January 3.

b Compute the balance of the Inventory account on January 7.

c Prepare journal entries to record the two transactions, assuming that Satellite Trackers uses the periodic inventory system.

d Compute the cost of goods sold for the first week of January, assuming use of a periodic inventory system. Use your answer to part **b** as the ending inventory.

e Which inventory system do you believe a company such as Satellite Trackers would probably use? Explain your reasoning.

Problem 9A-6
Perpetual inventory records in a small business

A perpetual inventory system is used by Rural Robot. This system includes a perpetual inventory record card for each of the 60 types of products the company keeps in stock. The following transactions show the purchases and sales of one of these products (XK3) during September.

Sept.	1	Balance on hand, 50 units, cost $60 each	$3,000
Sept.	4	Purchase, 20 units, cost $65 each	1,300
Sept.	8	Sale, 35 units, sales price $100 each	3,500
Sept.	9	Purchase, 40 units, cost $65 each	2,600
Sept.	20	Sale, 60 units, sales price $100 each	6,000
Sept.	25	Purchase, 40 units, cost $70 each	2,800
Sept.	30	Sale, 5 units, sales price $110 each	550

Instructions

a Record the beginning inventory, the purchases, the cost of goods sold, and the running balance on an inventory record card like the one illustrated in this chapter. Use the first-in first-out method.

b Assume that all sales were made on credit. Compute the total sales and total cost of goods sold of product XK3 for September. Prepare an entry in general journal form to record these sales and a second entry to record the cost of goods sold for September.

c Compute the gross profit on sales of product XK3 for the month of September.

Problem 9A-7
Determine corrected income statements and owner's equity

Income statements prepared by Tin Lohung Tile for 1989 and 1990 are as follows:

	1990	1989
Net sales	$630,000	$594,000
Cost of goods sold:		
Beginning inventory	$227,736	$216,000
Net purchases	384,264	368,393
Cost of goods available for sale	$612,000	$584,393
Ending inventory	234,000	227,736
Cost of goods sold	$378,000	$356,657
Gross profit on sales	$252,000	$237,343
Expenses	90,000	81,000
Net income	$162,000	$156,343

The owner's equity as shown in the company's balance sheet was as follows: December 31, 1988, $180,000; December 31, 1989, $336,343; and December 31, 1990, $498,343.

Early in 1991, Y.T. Chan, accountant for Tin Lohung Tile, made a review of the documents and procedures used in taking the physical inventory at December 31 for both 1989 and 1990. His investigation disclosed the two questionable items listed below:

(1) Merchandise shipped to a customer on December 31, 1989, F.O.B. shipping point, was included in the physical inventory taken that date. The cost of the merchandise was $2,620 and the sales price was $3,280. Because of the press of year-end work, the sales invoice was not prepared until January 6, 1990. On that date the sale was recorded as a January transaction by entry in the sales journal, and the sales invoice was mailed to the customer.

(2) Merchandise costing $6,156, which had been received on December 31, 1989, had been included in the inventory taken on that date, although the purchase was not recorded until January 8, 1990, when the vendor's invoice arrived. The invoice was then recorded in the purchases journal as a January transaction.

Instructions   **a** Prepare corrected income statements for the years ended December 31, 1989 and 1990. (You may find it helpful to set up T accounts for Sales, 1989, and Sales, 1990; Purchases, 1989, and Purchases, 1990; and Inventory, December 31, 1989.)

b Compute corrected amounts for owner's equity at December 31, 1989 and 1990. (No withdrawals were made by the owner during these two years.)

GROUP B

Problem 9B-1
Impact of inventory errors on trend of earnings

The owners of Midnight Venture are offering the business for sale as a going concern. The income statements of the business for the last three years include the following key figures.

	1989	1988	1987
Net sales	$430,000	$425,000	$400,000
Cost of goods sold	240,800	243,000	240,000
Gross profit on sales	$189,200	$182,000	$160,000
Gross profit percentage	44%	43%*	40%

*Rounded to nearest full percentage point.

In discussions with prospective buyers, the owners are emphasizing the rising trends of gross profit and gross profit percentage as very favourable factors.

Assume that you are retained by a prospective purchaser of the business to make an investigation of the fairness and reliability of Midnight Venture's accounting records and financial statements. You find everything in order except for the following: (1) The inventory was understated by $12,000 at the end of 1987 and (2) it was overstated by $21,500 at the end of 1989. The company uses the periodic inventory system and these errors had not been brought to light prior to your investigation.

Instructions   **a** Prepare a revised three-year schedule along the lines of the one in the preceding illustration.

b Comment on the trend of gross profit and gross profit percentage before and after the revision.

Problem 9B-2
Comparison of fifo, lifo, and average cost methods

One of the popular products carried by Outrider is a new speaker unit. The inventory quantities, purchases, and sales of this unit for the current year are summarized.

	NUMBER OF UNITS	COST PER UNIT	TOTAL COST
Inventory, Jan. 1	900	$10.00	$ 9,000
First purchase (Apr. 3)	1,180	10.20	12,036
Second purchase (July 7)	800	10.35	8,280
Third purchase (Oct. 22)	620	10.70	6,634
Fourth purchase (Dec. 15)	1,000	10.85	10,850
Goods available for sale	4,500		$46,800
Units sold during the year	3,200		
Inventory, Dec. 31	1,300		

Instructions

a Compute the cost of the December 31 inventory and the cost of goods sold for the new speaker units in the current year using:
(1) The first-in, first-out method
(2) The last-in, first-out method
(3) The average cost method

b Which of the three inventory pricing methods provides the most realistic balance sheet valuation of inventory in light of the current replacement cost of the speaker units? Does this same method also produce the most realistic measure of income in light of the costs being incurred by Outrider to replace the speakers when they are sold? Explain.

Problem 9B-3
Fifo, lifo, average cost; income statement

Audio Meter achieved total sales revenue of $930,000 for the current year. The company sells only one product. The beginning inventory at January 1 of the current year consisted of 15,000 units valued at cost of $112,500. Purchases during the year were as follows: 20,000 units at $7.75; 28,500 units at $8.00; 21,000 units at $8.30; and 15,500 units at $8.40. The ending inventory at December 31 consisted of 22,500 units.

Instructions

a Compute the dollar amount of the year-end (December 31) inventory using:
(1) The first-in, first-out method
(2) The last-in, first-out method
(3) The average cost method

b Prepare partial income statements for each of the above three methods of pricing inventory. The income statements are to be carried only to the determination of gross profit on sales

c Assuming that the three inventory pricing methods are acceptable for income tax purposes, which would be most advantageous from an income tax standpoint during a period of rising prices? Comment on the significance of the inventory figure under the method you recommend with respect to current replacement cost.

Problem 9B-4
Retail inventory method

Rose Garden, a retail business, had net sales during January of $32,600. Purchases of merchandise from suppliers during January amounted to $20,620. Of these January purchases, invoices totalling $13,620 were paid during the month; the remaining January invoices totalling $7,000 were still unpaid at January 31. The merchandise purchased during January had a retail sales value of $29,500.

On January 1 the merchandise on hand represented a cost of $21,200 as determined by the year-end physical inventory. The retail sales value of this inventory was $32,000. The retail selling price was plainly marked on every item of merchandise in the store.

At January 31 the manager of Rose Garden wished to estimate the cost of inventory on hand without taking time to count the merchandise and look up the cost prices as shown on purchase invoices.

Instructions
a Use the retail inventory method to estimate the cost of the inventory at January 31.

b What effect, if any, does the fact that January purchase invoices in the amount of $7,000 were unpaid at January 31 have upon the determination of the amount of inventory at January 31?

Problem 9B-5
Entries for perpetual inventory

Halley's Space Scope sells state-of-the-art telescopes to individuals and organizations interested in study of the solar system. At December 31, the end of the fiscal year, the company's inventory amounted to $90,000. During the first part of January, the company made only one purchase and one sale. These transactions were as follows:

Jan. 5 Sold one telescope costing $28,000 to Eastern University for cash, $40,000.

Jan. 8 Purchased merchandise on account from Solar Optics, $18,500. Terms, net 30 days.

Instructions
a Prepare journal entries to record these transactions, assuming that Halley's Space Scope uses the perpetual inventory system. Use separate entries to record the sale and the cost of goods sold for the sale on January 5.

b Compute the balance of the Inventory account on January 9.

c Prepare journal entries to record the two transactions, assuming that Halley's Space Scope uses the periodic inventory system.

d Compute the cost of goods sold for the first part of January, assuming use of a periodic inventory system. Use your answer to part b as the ending inventory.

e Which inventory system do you believe a company such as Halley's Space Scope would probably use? Explain your reasoning.

Problem 9B-6
Perpetual inventory records in a small business

A perpetual inventory system is used by Black Hawk, Inc., and an inventory record card is maintained for each type of product in stock. The following transactions show beginning inventory, purchases, and sales of Product KR9 for the month of May.

May 1 Balance on hand, 20 units, cost $40 each $800
May 5 Sale, 8 units, sales price $60 each 480
May 6 Purchase, 20 units, cost $45 each 900
May 21 Sale, 10 units, sales price $60 each 600
May 31 Sale, 15 units, sales price $65 each 975

Instructions
a Record the beginning inventory, the purchases, the cost of goods sold, and the running balance on an inventory record card like the one illustrated in this chapter. Use the first-in, first-out method.

b Assume that all sales were made on credit. Compute the total sales and the total cost of goods sold of product KR9 for May. Prepare an entry in general journal form to record these sales and a second entry to record the cost of goods sold for the month of May.

c Compute the gross profit on sales of product KR9 for the month of May.

Problem 9B-7
Determine corrected income statements and owner's equity

The owner's equity as shown in the balance sheets prepared by Village Supply for the last three years was as follows: December 31, 1988, $560,000; December 31, 1989, $676,500; and December 31, 1990, $787,800.

The income statements for Years 1989 and 1990 were as follows:

	1990	1989
Net sales	$879,500	$835,500
Cost of goods sold:		
Beginning inventory	$123,400	$110,200
Net purchases	540,200	501,200
Cost of goods available for sale	$663,600	$611,400
Ending inventory	140,600	123,400
Cost of goods sold	$523,000	$488,000
Gross profit on sales	$356,500	$347,500
Expenses	245,200	231,000
Net income	$111,300	$116,500

Samuel Peterson, accountant for Village Supply, decided early in 1991 to make a review of the documents and procedures used in taking the physical inventory at December 31, 1989 and 1990. His investigation revealed the following two questionable items:

(1) Merchandise shipped to a customer on December 31, 1989, F.O.B shipping point, was included in the physical inventory at December 31, 1989. The cost of the merchandise was $2,720 and the sales price was $4,580. Because of the press of year-end work, the sales invoice was not prepared until January 8, 1990. On that date the sale was recorded as a January, 1990, transaction in the sales journal, and the invoice was mailed to the customer.

(2) Merchandise with a cost of $12,260 that had been received on December 31, 1989, had been included in the inventory taken on that date, although the purchase was not recorded until January 8, 1990, when the vendor's invoice arrived. The invoice was then recorded in the purchases journal as a January transaction.

Instructions   a Prepare corrected income statements for the periods ended December 31, 1989 and 1990. (You may find it helpful to set up T accounts for Sales, 1989, and Sales, 1990; Purchases, 1989, and Purchases, 1990; and Inventory, December 31, 1989.)

b Compute corrected amounts for owner's equity at December 31, Years 1989 and 1990. (No withdrawals were made by the owner during these two years.)

BUSINESS DECISION CASES

Case 9-1
Have I got a deal
for you!

You are the sales manager of Continental Motors, an automobile dealership specializing in European imports. Among the automobiles in Continental Motors' showroom are two Italian sports cars, which are identical in every respect except for colour; one is red and the other white. The red car had been ordered last February, at a cost of $13,300. The white car had been ordered early last March, but because of a revaluation of the Italian lira relative to the dollar, the white car had cost only $12,000. Both cars arrived on the same boat and had just been delivered to your showroom. Since the cars were identical except for colour and both colours were equally popular, you had listed both cars at the same suggested retail price, $18,000.

Smiley Miles, one of your best salesmen, comes into your office with a proposal. He has a customer in the showroom who wants to buy the red car for $18,000. However, when Miles pulled the inventory card on the red car to see what options were included, he happened to notice the inventory card of the white car. Continental Motors, like most automobile dealerships, uses the specific identification method to value inventory. Consequently, Miles noticed that the red car had cost $13,300, while the white one had cost Continental Motors only $12,000. This gave Miles the idea for the following proposal.

"Have I got a deal for you! If I sell the red car for $18,000, Continental Motors makes a gross profit of $4,700. But if you'll let me discount that white car $500, I think I can get my customer to buy that one instead. If I sell the white car for $17,500, the gross profit will be $5,500, so Continental Motors is $800 better off than if I sell the red car for $18,000. Since I came up with this plan, I feel I should get part of the benefit, so Continental Motors should split the extra $800 with me. That way, I'll get an extra $400 commission, and the company still makes $400 more than if I sell the red car."

Instructions

a Prepare a schedule which shows the total revenue, cost of goods sold, and gross profit to Continental Motors if **both** cars are sold for $18,000 each.

b Prepare a schedule showing the revenue, cost of goods sold, and gross profit to Continental Motors if both cars are sold but Miles's plan is adopted and the white car is sold for $17,500. Assume the red car is sold for $18,000. To simplify comparison of this schedule to the one prepared in part **a**, include the extra $400 commission to Miles in the cost of goods sold of the part **b** schedule.

c State your decision whether or not to accept Miles's proposal, and explain to Miles why the proposal either would or would not be to the advantage of Continental Motors.

Case 9-2
Inventory: Attracting attention!

Carla Wilson is an auditor with the Revenue Canada. She has been assigned to audit the income tax return of The French Connection, a corporation engaged in selling imported bicycles by mail order. Selected figures from the company's income tax return are as follows:

Sales	$1,200,000
Beginning inventory	30,000
Purchases	885,000
Ending inventory	15,000
Cost of goods sold	900,000
Gross profit	300,000

As Wilson examined these figures, she began to suspect that the income reported by The French Connection had been understated. She sent a letter to the company to arrange a date for performing the tax audit. As part of her preliminary investigation, Wilson then telephoned The French Connection, inquiring what types of bicycles the company had available for immediate delivery. The salesclerk told her that the French Connection had in stock three makes of French bicycles and three lines of Italian bicycles.

Wilson's letter about the tax audit was received by Greg Thomas, the president and owner of The French Connection. The letter made Thomas quite nervous, because over the last five years he had understated the income reported in the company's income tax returns by a total of $100,000. Thomas hurriedly began making his own preparations for the tax audit. These preparations included renting an empty building a few blocks from The French Connection.

When Wilson arrived at The French Connection, she was met by Thomas. Wilson introduced herself and asked to see the company's accounting records. As Thomas was showing her to the company's accounting office, they passed through the bicycle warehouse. Much of the large warehouse was empty, but along one wall were about 50 bicycles. Each had the name "LeMond" written on the frame in bright red letters.

Thomas explained, "Milo LeMond is the finest bicycle maker in all of France. We have the largest selection of his bicycles in the country."

Wilson asked if the company had more bicycles at another location.

Thomas replied, "No. This is our entire inventory. We stock about 50 bikes. After all, these bikes cost us about $300 each. One of the secrets of success in the mail-order business is not tying up a lot of money in big inventory. We've cut way back on our inventory over the years —helps keep our costs down.''

Wilson's suspicions had been confirmed. She now knew that The French Connection had substantially understated its income. Of course, she would still have to find out by just how much. She felt a little sorry for Thomas. Not only would his company have to face additional taxes and a stiff penalty, but he might be in for a jail sentence. Wilson was sure that the company's understatement of income was no accident—it was a deliberate act of tax evasion, which Thomas was now trying desperately to conceal.

Instructions   **a** What was it about the figures in The French Connection's income tax return that originally made Wilson suspicious that the company might have understated its income?

b What happened to confirm Wilson's suspicions? Why does she believe that the understatement of income was a deliberate act which Thomas is now attempting to conceal?

c Assume that The French Connection correctly reported all its revenue in its income tax returns. How do you think that Thomas caused the company's income to be understated year after year?

d What do you think Thomas has in the building he rented? Be as specific as possible.

PLANT AND EQUIPMENT, DEPRECIATION, AND INTANGIBLE ASSETS

CHAPTER PREVIEW

In the first part of Chapter 10, our goal is to define plant and equipment and to explain the principles for determining its cost. Once cost has been recorded, the next step is to allocate this cost of plant and equipment over the years of its use by means of a depreciation program. Various methods of depreciation are then presented such as, for example, straight-line, units-of-output, declining-balance, and sum-of-the-years'-digits methods. Also, the accounting for the sale and trade-in of plant and equipment is discussed. The final part of the chapter deals with the accounting treatment of natural resources and intangible assets.

After studying this chapter you should be able to meet these Learning Objectives:

1 **Determine the cost of plant assets.**

2 **Distinguish between capital expenditures and revenue expenditures.**

3 **Explain the relationship between depreciation and the matching principle.**

4 **Compute depreciation by the straight-line, units-of-output, declining-balance, and sum-of-the-years'-digits methods.**

5 **Explain why depreciation based upon historical costs may cause an overstatement of net income.**

6 **Record the sale, trade-in, or scrapping of a plant asset.**

7 **Account for the depletion of natural resources.**

8 **Explain the nature of goodwill and indicate when this asset should appear in the accounting records.**

PLANT AND EQUIPMENT

The term *plant and equipment* is used to describe long-lived assets acquired for use in the operation of the business and not intended for resale to customers. Among the more common examples are land, buildings, machinery, furniture and fixtures, office equipment, and automobiles. A delivery truck in the showroom of an automobile dealer is inventory; when this same truck is sold to a drugstore for use in making deliveries to customers, it becomes a unit of plant and equipment.

The term *fixed assets* has long been used in accounting literature to describe all types of plant and equipment and is still used in the published financial statements of large corporations. *Plant and equipment*, however, appears to be a more descriptive term. Another alternative title used on many corporation balance sheets is *property, plant, and equipment.*

Plant and equipment — a stream of services

It is convenient to think of a plant asset as a stream of services to be received by the owner over a period of years. Ownership of a delivery truck, for example, may provide about 200,000 km of transportation. The cost of the delivery truck is customarily entered in a plant and equipment account entitled Delivery Truck, which in essence represents a stream of many years of transportation service. Similarly, a building may be regarded as a stream of many years of housing services. As the years go by, these services are utilized by the business and the cost of the plant asset gradually is transferred into depreciation expense.

An awareness of the similarity between plant assets and prepaid expenses is essential to an understanding of the accounting process by which the cost of plant assets is allocated to the accounting periods in which the benefits of ownership are received.

Major categories of plant and equipment

Plant and equipment items are often classified into the following groups:

1 Tangible plant assets. The term *tangible* denotes physical substance, as exemplified by land, a building, or a machine. This category may be subdivided into two distinct classifications:
   a Plant property subject to depreciation; included are plant assets of limited useful life such as buildings and office equipment.
   b Land. The only plant asset not subject to depreciation is land, which has an unlimited term of existence.
2 Intangible assets. The term *intangible assets* describes assets that are used in the operation of the business but have no physical substance, and are noncurrent. Examples include patents, copyrights, trademarks, franchises, and goodwill. Current assets such as accounts receivable or prepaid rent are not included in the intangible classification, even though they lack physical substance.

Determining the cost of plant and equipment

1 Determine the cost of plant assets.

The cost of plant and equipment includes all expenditure reasonable and necessary in acquiring the asset and placing it in a position and condition for use in the operations of the business. Only **reasonable** and **necessary** expenditures should be included. For example, if the company's truck driver receives a traffic ticket while hauling a new machine to the plant, the traffic fine is **not** part of the cost of the new machine. If the machine is dropped and damaged while being unloaded, the cost of repairing the damage should be recognized as expense in the current period and should **not** be added to the cost of the machine.

Cost is most easily determined when an asset is purchased for cash. The cost of the asset is then equal to the cash outlay necessary in acquiring the asset plus any expenditures for freight, insurance while in transit, installation, trial runs, and any other costs necessary to make **the asset ready for use.** If plant assets are **purchased** on the instalment plan or by issuance of notes payable, the interest element or carrying charge should be recorded as interest expense and **not** as part of the cost of the plant assets. However, if a company **constructs** a plant asset for its own use, interest costs incurred **during the construction period** are viewed as part of the cost of the asset.[1]

This principle of including in the cost of a plant asset all the incidental charges necessary to put the asset in use is illustrated by the following example. A factory in Windsor orders a machine from a tool manufacturer at a list price of $10,000, with a $200 cash discount. Sales tax of $600 must be paid, also freight charges of $1,250. Transportation from the railroad station to the factory costs $150, and installation labour amounts to $400. The cost of the machine to be entered in the Machinery account is computed as follows:

ITEMS INCLUDED IN COST OF MACHINE

Price of machine	$10,000
Sales tax	600
Freight	1,250
Transportation from railroad station to factory	150
Installation labour	400
	$12,400
Less: Cash discount	200
Cost of machine	$12,200

Why should all the incidental charges relating to the acquisition of a machine be included in its cost? Why not treat these incidental charges as expenses of the period in which the machine is acquired?

The answer is to be found in the basic accounting principle of **matching costs and revenue.** The benefits of owning the machine will be received over a span of years, 10 years, for example. During those 10 years the operation of the machine will contribute to revenue. Consequently, the total costs of the machine should be recorded in the accounts as an asset and allocated against the revenue of the 10 years. All costs incurred in acquiring the machine are costs of the services to be received from using the machine.

Land   When land is purchased, various incidental costs are generally incurred, in addition to the purchase price. These additional costs may include commissions to

[1] While the CICA has no pronouncement in this area, the FASB in the United States has issued *FASB Statement No. 34*, "Capitalization of Interest Costs" (Stamford, Conn.: 1979).

real estate brokers, land transfer tax, legal fees for examining the title, delinquent taxes paid by the purchaser, and fees for surveying, draining, clearing, and grading the property. All these expenditures become part of the cost of the land.

Apportionment of a lump-sum purchase   Separate ledger accounts are necessary for land and buildings, because buildings are subject to depreciation and land is not. The treatment of land as a nondepreciable asset is based on the premise that land used as a building site has an unlimited life. When land and building are purchased for a lump sum, the purchase price must be apportioned between the land and the building. An appraisal may be necessary for this purpose. Assume, for example, that land and a building are purchased for a bargain price of $400,000. The apportionment of this cost on the basis of an appraisal may be made as follows:

APPORTIONING COST BETWEEN LAND AND BUILDING

	VALUE PER APPRAISAL	PERCENTAGE OF TOTAL	APPORTIONMENT OF COST
Land	$200,000	40%	$160,000
Building	300,000	60%	240,000
Total	$500,000	100%	$400,000

Sometimes a tract of land purchased as a building site has on it an old building that is not suitable for the buyer's use. The Land account should be charged with the entire purchase price *plus any costs incurred in tearing down or removing the building.* Proceeds received from sale of the materials salvaged from the old building are recorded as a credit in the Land account.

Land improvements   Improvements to real estate such as driveways, fences, parking lots, landscaping and sprinkler systems have a limited life and are therefore subject to depreciation. For this reason they should be recorded not in the Land account but in a separate account entitled Land Improvements.

Buildings   Old buildings are sometimes purchased with the intention of repairing them prior to placing them in use. Repairs made under these circumstances are charged to the Buildings account. After the building has been placed in use, ordinary repairs are considered as maintenance expense when incurred.

Capital expenditures and revenue expenditures

2   Distinguish between capital expenditures and revenue expenditures.

Expenditures for the purchase or expansion of plant assets are called *capital expenditures* and are recorded in asset accounts. Expenditures for ordinary repairs, maintenance, fuel, and other items necessary to the ownership and use of plant and equipment are called *revenue expenditures* and are recorded by debits to expense accounts. The charge to an expense account is based on the assumption that the benefits from the expenditure will be used up in the current period, and the cost should therefore be deducted from the revenue of the current period in determining the net income.

A business may purchase many items that will benefit several accounting periods, but that have a relatively low cost. Examples of such items include auto batteries, wastebaskets, and pencil sharpeners. Such items are theoretically capital expenditures, but if they are recorded as assets in the accounting records it will be necessary to compute and record the related depreciation expense in future periods. We have mentioned previously the idea that the extra work involved in developing more precise accounting information should be weighed against the benefits that result. Thus, for reasons of convenience and economy, expenditures that are *not material* in dollar amount are treated in the accounting records as expenses of the current period. In brief, *any material expenditure that will benefit several accounting periods is considered a capital expenditure. Any expenditure that will benefit only the current period or that is not material in amount is treated as a revenue expenditure.*

Many companies develop formal policy statements defining capital and revenue expenditures as a guide toward consistent accounting practice from year to year. These policy statements often set a minimum dollar limit for a capital expenditure (such as $100 or $200).

Effect of errors in distinguishing between capital and revenue expenditures   Because a capital expenditure is recorded by debiting an asset account, the transaction has no immediate effect upon net income. However, the depreciation of the amount entered in the asset account will be reflected as an expense in future periods. A revenue expenditure, on the other hand, is recorded by debiting an expense account and therefore represents an immediate deduction from earnings in the current period.

Assume that the cost of a new delivery truck is erroneously debited to the Repairs Expense account. The result will be to overstate repairs expense, thereby understating the current year's net income. If the error is not corrected, the net income of subsequent years will be overstated because no depreciation expense will be recognized during the years in which the truck is used.

On the other hand, assume that ordinary truck repairs are erroneously debited to the asset account, Delivery Truck. The result will be to understate repairs expense, thereby overstating the current year's net income. If the error is not corrected, the net income of future years will be understated because of excessive depreciation charges based upon the inflated balance of the Delivery Truck account.

These examples indicate that a careful distinction between capital and revenue expenditures is essential to attainment of one of the most fundamental objectives of accounting — the determination of net income for each year of operation of a business.

During an annual audit of Bowden Limited, a CA firm was reviewing entries in the general journal. An entry that caught the attention of Carol Jones, CA, consisted of a debit to Office Furniture and a credit to Notes Payable for $52,000. Upon investigation, Jones learned that the transaction involved a hand-carved clock acquired from James Burns, the former president of Bowden. Burns's hobby for many years had been the building of hand-carved clocks. At a retirement banquet honouring Burns, Bowden had awarded him a $52,000 bonus, represented by the company's short-term note payable. At the same banquet, Burns had presented Bowden with one of his clocks.

Further investigation by Jones indicated that the commercial value of the clock was about $400. Jones therefore advised the company to transfer the $52,000 expenditure out of the Office Furniture account and into Executive Compensation Expense.

3   Explain the relationship between depreciation and the matching principle.

DEPRECIATION
Allocating the cost of plant and equipment over the years of use

Plant assets, with the exception of land, are of use to a company for only a limited number of years, and the cost of each plant asset is allocated as expense among the years in which it is used. Accountants use the term *depreciation* to describe this gradual conversion of the cost of a plant asset into expense. Depreciation, as the term is used in accounting, does not mean the decrease in market value of a plant asset over a period of time. *Depreciation means the allocation of the cost of a plant asset to expense in the periods in which services are received from the asset.*

When a delivery truck is purchased, its cost is first recorded as an asset. This cost becomes expense over a period of years through the accounting process of depreciation. On the other hand, when gasoline is purchased for the truck, the price paid for each tankful is immediately recorded as expense. In theory, both oulays (for the truck and for a tank of gas) represent the acquisition of assets. However, since it is reasonable to assume that a tankful of gasoline will be consumed in the accounting period in which it is purchased, we record the outlay for gasoline as an expense immediately. It is important to recognize, however, that *both the outlay for the truck and the payment for the gasoline become expense in the period or periods in which each renders services.*

Depreciation differs from most expenses in that it does not require a cash payment at or near the time it is recorded. The entry to record depreciation (a debit to Depreciation Expense and a credit to Accumulated Depreciation) has no effect on current assets or current liabilities. However, when depreciable assets wear out, a large cash payment must be made immediately or over a period of time in order to replace them.

A separate Depreciation Expense account and a separate Accumulated Depreciation account are generally maintained for each group of depreciable assets such as factory buildings, delivery equipment, and office equipment so that a proper allocation of depreciation expense can be made between functional areas of activity such as sales and manufacturing.

Depreciation not a process of valuation

Accounting records do not purport to show the constantly fluctuating market values of plant and equipment. Occasionally the market value of a building may rise substantially over a period of years because of a change in the price level, or for other reasons. Depreciation is continued, however, regardless of the increase in market value. The accountant recognizes that the building will render useful services for only a limited number of years, and that its full cost must be allocated as expense of those years regardless of fluctuations in market value.

Cost — Accum dep.

The **book value** or **carrying value** of a plant asset is its cost minus the related accumulated depreciation. Plant assets are shown in the balance sheet at their book values, representing the portion of their cost that will be allocated to expense in future periods. Accumulated depreciation represents the portion of the assets' cost that has already been recognized as expense.

Accumulated depreciation does not consist of cash

Many readers of financial statements who have not studied accounting mistakenly believe that accumulated depreciation accounts represent money accumulated for the purpose of buying new equipment when the present equipment wears out. Perhaps the best way to combat such mistaken notions is to emphasize that a credit balance in an accumulated depreciation account represents the **expired cost** of assets acquired in the past. The amounts credited to the accumulated depreciation account could, as an alternative, have been credited directly to the plant and equipment account. An accumulated depreciation account has a **credit** balance; it does not represent an asset; and it cannot be used in any way to pay for new equipment. To pay for a new plant asset requires cash; the total amount of cash owned by a company is shown by the asset account for cash.

Causes of depreciation

The two major causes of depreciation are physical deterioration and obsolescence.

Physical deterioration   Physical deterioration of a plant asset results from use, and also from exposure to sun, wind, and other climatic factors. When a plant asset has been carefully maintained, it is not uncommon for the owner to claim that the asset is as ''good as new.'' Such statements are not literally true. Although a good repair policy may greatly lengthen the useful life of a machine, every machine eventually reaches the point at which it must be discarded. In brief, the making of repairs does not lessen the need for recognition of depreciation.

Obsolescence   The term **obsolescence** means the process of becoming out of date or obsolete. An airplane, for example, may become obsolete even though it is in excellent physical condition; it becomes obsolete because better planes of superior design and performance have become available.

The usefulness of plant assets may also be reduced because the rapid growth of a company renders such assets inadequate. **Inadequacy** of a plant asset may necessitate replacement with a larger unit even though the asset is in good physical condition. Obsolescence and inadequacy are often closely associated; both relate to the opportunity for economical and efficient use of an asset rather than to its physical condition.

Methods of computing depreciation

4 Compute depreciation by the straight-line, units-of-output, declining-balance, and sum-of-the-year's-digits methods.

There are several alternative methods of computing depreciation. A business need not use the same method of depreciation for all its various assets. For example, a company may use straight-line depreciation on some assets and a declining-balance method for other assets. Furthermore, the methods used for computing depreciation expense in financial statements **may differ** from the methods used in the preparation of the company's income tax return.

Straight-line method   The simplest and most widely used method of computing depreciation is the straight-line method.[2] This method was described in Chapter 3 and has been used repeatedly in problems throughout this book. Under the straight-line method, an equal portion of the cost of the asset is allocated to each period of use; consequently, this method is most appropriate when usage of an asset is fairly uniform from year to year.

The computation of the periodic charge for depreciation is made by deducting the estimated *residual* or *salvage value* from the cost of the asset and dividing the remaining *depreciable cost* by the years of estimated useful life. For example, if a delivery truck has a cost of $20,000, a residual value of $2,000, and an estimated useful life of four years, the annual computation of depreciation expense will be as follows:

$$\frac{\text{Cost} - \text{Residual Value}}{\text{Years of Useful Life}} = \frac{\$20,000 - \$2,000}{4} = \$4,500$$

This same depreciation computation is shown in tabular form as follows:

COMPUTING
DEPRECIATION BY
STRAIGHT-LINE METHOD

Cost of the depreciable asset	$20,000
Less: Estimated residual value (amount to be realized by sale of asset when it is retired from use)	2,000
Total amount to be depreciated (depreciable cost)	$18,000
Estimated useful life	4 years
Depreciation expense each year ($18,000 ÷ 4)	$ 4,500

The following schedule summarizes the accumulation of depreciation over the useful life of the asset. The amount to be depreciated is $18,000 (cost of $20,000, minus estimated residual value of $2,000).

CONSTANT ANNUAL
DEPRECIATION EXPENSE

Depreciation Schedule: Straight-Line Method

YEAR	COMPUTATION	DEPRECIATION EXPENSE	ACCUMULATED DEPRECIATION	BOOK VALUE
				$20,000
First	(¼ × $18,000)	$ 4,500	$ 4,500	15,500
Second	(¼ × $18,000)	4,500	9,000	11,000
Third	(¼ × $18,000)	4,500	13,500	6,500
Fourth	(¼ × $18,000)	4,500	18,000	2,000
		$18,000		

Depreciation rates for various types of assets can conveniently be stated as percentages. In the above example the asset had an estimated life of four years, so the depreciation expense each year was ¹/₄ of the depreciable amount. The fraction ''¹/₄'' is of course

[2] CICA, *Financial Reporting in Canada*, Seventeenth Edition (Toronto, 1987), p. 157. The straight-line method was used by 248 of the 293 companies surveyed; 112 of these 248 companies also used either the diminishing (declining) balance or unit-of-production (output) method.

equivalent to an annual rate of 25%. Similarly, a 10-year life indicates a depreciation rate of $^1/_{10}$, or 10%, and an 8-year life a depreciation rate of $^1/_8$, or $12^1/_2$%.

In the preceding illustration we assumed that the company maintained its accounts on a calendar-year basis and that the asset was acquired on January 1, the beginning of the accounting period. If the asset had been acquired sometime during the year, on October 1 for example, it would have been in use for only three months, or $^3/_{12}$ of a year. Consequently, the depreciation to be recorded at December 31 would be only $^3/_{12}$ of $4,500, or $1,125. Stated more precisely, the depreciation expense in this situation is computed as follows: 25% × $18,000 × $^3/_{12}$ = $1,125.

In practice, the possibility of residual value is sometimes ignored and the annual depreciation charge computed by dividing the total cost of the asset by the number of years of estimated useful life. This practice may be justified in those cases in which residual value is not material and is difficult to estimate accurately.

Units-of-output (production) method   For certain kinds of assets, more equitable allocation of the cost can be obtained by dividing the cost (minus salvage value, if significant) by the estimated units of output or production rather than by the estimated years of useful life. A truck line or bus company, for example, might compute depreciation on its vehicles by a kilometre basis. If we assume that the delivery truck in our example has an estimated useful life of 200,000 km, the depreciation rate per kilometre of operation is 9 cents ($18,000 ÷ 200,000). This calculation of the depreciation rate may be stated as follows:

$$\frac{\text{Cost} - \text{Residual Value}}{\text{Estimated Units of Output (kilometres)}} = \frac{\text{Depreciation per}}{\text{Unit of Output (kilometre)}}$$

or

$$\frac{\$20,000 - \$2,000}{200,000 \text{ km}} = \$0.09 \text{ depreciation per kilometre}$$

At the end of each year, the amount of depreciation to be recorded would be determined by multiplying the 9-cent rate by the number of kilometres the truck had operated during the year. This method is suitable only when the total units of output of the asset over its entire useful life can be estimated with reasonable accuracy.

Accelerated depreciation methods   The term *accelerated depreciation* means recognition of relatively large amounts of depreciation in the early years of use and reduced amounts in the later years. Many types of plant and equipment are most efficient when new and therefore provide more and better services in the early years of useful life. If we assume that the benefits derived from owning an asset are greatest in the early years when the asset is relatively new, then the amount of the asset's cost that we allocate as depreciation expense should be greatest in these same early years. This is consistent with the basic accounting concept of matching costs with related revenue. Accelerated depreciation methods are widely used in income tax returns because they reduce the current year's tax burden by recognizing a relatively large amount of depreciation expense.

Declining-balance (diminishing-balance) method   One of the accelerated deprecia-tion methods that allocates a large portion of the cost of an asset to the early years of its useful life is called the *declining-balance method.* Within this method, a number of percentage can be used. One of the common methods is called *double-declining-balance.* This method consists of doubling the straight-line depreciation rate and applying this doubled rate to the undepreciated cost (book value) of the asset.

To illustrate, consider our example of the $20,000 delivery truck. The estimated useful life of the truck is four years; therefore, the depreciation rate under the straight-line method would be 25%. To depreciate the automobile by the double-declining-balance method, we double the straight-line rate of 25% and apply the doubled rate of 50% to the book value. Depreciation expense in the first year would then amount to $10,000. In the second year the depreciation expense would drop to $5,000, computed at 50% of the remaining book value of $10,000. In the third year depreciation would be $2,500, and in the fourth year only $1,250. The following table shows the computation of each year's depreciation expense by the declining-balance method.

ACCELERATED
DEPRECIATION: DOUBLE-
DECLINING-BALANCE

Depreciation Schedule: Double-Declining-Balance Method

YEAR	COMPUTATION	DEPRECIATION EXPENSE	ACCUMULATED DEPRECIATION	BOOK VALUE
				$20,000
First	(50% × $20,000)	$10,000	$10,000	10,000
Second	(50% × $10,000)	5,000	15,000	5,000
Third	(50% × $ 5,000)	2,500	17,500	2,500
Fourth	(50% × $ 2,500)	1,250	18,750	1,250

Notice that the estimated residual value of the delivery truck did not enter into the computation of depreciation expense by the declining-balance method such as the double-declining illustrated above. This is because the declining-balance method provides an "automatic" residual value. As long as each year's depreciation expense is equal to only a portion of the undepreciated cost of the asset, the asset will never be entirely written off. However, if the asset has a significant residual value, depreciation should *stop at this point.* Since our delivery truck has an estimated residual value of $2,000, the depreciation expense for the fourth year should be limited to $500 rather than the $1,250 computed in the table. By limiting the last year's depreciation expense in this manner, the book value of the truck at the end of the fourth year will be equal to its $2,000 estimated residual value.

If the asset in the above illustration had been acquired on October 1 rather than on January 1, depreciation for only three months would be recorded in the first year. The computation would be 50% × $20,000 × $^{3}/_{12}$, or $2,500. For the next calendar year the calculation would be 50% × ($20,000 − $2,500), or $8,750.

Sum-of-the-years'-digits method   This is another method of allocating a large por-tion of the cost of an asset to the early years of its use. The depreciation rate to be used is a fraction, of which the numerator is the remaining years of useful life (as of the beginning of the year) and the denominator is the sum of the years of useful life. Consider again the example of the delivery truck costing $20,000 having an estimated life of four years and an estimated residual value of $2,000. Since the asset has an estimated life of four years, the denominator of the fraction will be 10, computed as follows:[3] $1 + 2 + 3 + 4 = 10$. For the first year, the depreciation will be $4/10 \times (\$20,000 - \$2,000)$, or $7,200. (Notice that we reduced the cost of the truck by the estimated residual value in determining the amount to be depreciated.) For the second year, the depreciation will be $3/10 \times \$18,000$, or $5,400; in the third year $2/10 \times \$18,000$, or $3,600; and in the fourth year, $1/10 \times \$18,000$, or $1,800. In tabular form, this depreciation program will appear as follows:

ACCELERATED
DEPRECIATION: SUM
OF THE YEARS' DIGITS

Depreciation Schedule: Sum-of-the-Years'-Digits Method

YEAR	COMPUTATION	DEPRECIATION EXPENSE	ACCUMULATED DEPRECIATION	BOOK VALUE
				$20,000
First	($4/10 \times \$18,000$)	$ 7,200	$ 7,200	12,800
Second	($3/10 \times \$18,000$)	5,400	12,600	7,400
Third	($2/10 \times \$18,000$)	3,600	16,200	3,800
Fourth	($1/10 \times \$18,000$)	1,800	18,000	2,000
		$18,000		

Assume that the asset being depreciated by the sum-of-the-years'-digits method was acquired on October 1 and the company maintains its accounts on a calendar-year basis. Since the asset was in use for only three months during the first accounting period, the depreciation to be recorded in this first period will be for only $3/12$ of a full year, that is, $3/12 \times \$7,200$, or $1,800. For the second accounting period the depreciation computation will be:

$9/12 \times (4/10 \times \$18,000)$ $5,400
$3/12 \times (3/10 \times \$18,000)$ 1,350
Depreciation expense, second period $6,750

A similar pattern of allocation will be followed for each accounting period of the asset's life.

Depreciation for fractional periods When an asset is acquired in the middle of an accounting period, it is not necessary to compute depreciation expense to the nearest day or week. In fact, such a computation would give a misleading impression of great precision. Since depreciation is based upon an estimated useful life of many

[3] Alternatively, the denominator may be computed by using the formula $n\left(\dfrac{n+1}{2}\right)$, where n is the useful life of the asset. According to this formula, the sum of the years' digits for an asset with a four-year life is computed as follows: $4\left(\dfrac{4+1}{2}\right) = 4(2.5) = 10$. Similarly, the sum of the years' digits for an asset with a 10-year life would be computed as follows: $10\left(\dfrac{10+1}{2}\right) = 10(5.5) = 55$.

years, the depreciation applicable to any one year is only an approximation at best.

One widely used method of computing depreciation for part of a year is to round the calculation to the nearest whole month. Thus, if an asset is acquired on July 12, depreciation is computed for the six months beginning July 1. If an asset is acquired on July 16 (or any date in the latter half of July), depreciation is recorded for only five months (August through December) in the current calendar year.

Another acceptable approach, called the *half-year convention,* is to record six months' depreciation on all assets acquired during the year. This approach is based upon the assumption that the actual purchase dates will "average out" to approximately midyear. The half-year convention is widely used for assets such as office equipment, automobiles, and machinery.

The half-year convention enables us to treat similar assets acquired at different dates during the year as a single group. For example, assume that an insurance company purchases hundreds of typewriters throughout the current year at a total cost of $600,000. The company depreciates typewriters by the straight-line method, assuming a five-year life and no residual value. Using the half-year convention, the depreciation expense on all of the typewriters purchased during the year may be computed as follows: $600,000 ÷ 5 years × $^{6}/_{12}$ = $60,000. If we did not use the half-year convention, depreciation would have to be computed separately for typewriters that had been purchased in different months.

Revision of depreciation rates

Depreciation rates are based on estimates of the useful life of assets. These estimates of useful life are seldom precise and sometimes are grossly in error. Consequently, the annual depreciation expense based on the estimated useful life may be either excessive or inadequate. What action should be taken when, after a few years of using a plant asset, it is decided that the asset actually is going to last for a considerably longer or shorter period than was originally estimated? When either of these situations arises, a revised estimate of useful life should be made and the periodic depreciation expense decreased or increased accordingly.

The acceptable procedure for correcting the depreciation program is to *spread the remaining undepreciated cost of the asset over the years of remaining useful life.*[4] This correction affects only the amount of depreciation expense that will be recorded in the *current and future periods.* The financial statements of past periods are *not* revised to reflect changes in the estimated useful lives of depreciable assets. However, it is desirable to disclose the nature and effect of such a change.

To illustrate, assume that a company acquires a $10,000 asset that is estimated to have a 10-year useful life and no residual value. Under the straight-line method, the annual depreciation expense is $1,000. At the end of the sixth year, accumulated depreciation amounts to $6,000, and the asset has an undepreciated cost (or book value) of $4,000.

At the beginning of the seventh year, it is decided that the asset will last for eight more years. The revised estimate of useful life is, therefore, a total of 14 years. The

---

[4] CICA, *CICA Handbook* (Toronto), paragraph 1506.24.

depreciation expense to be recognized for the seventh year and for each of the remaining years is $500, computed as follows:

Undepreciated cost at end of sixth year ($10,000 – $6,000)	$4,000
Revised estimate of remaining years of useful life	8 years
Revised amount of annual depreciation expense ($4,000 ÷ 8)	$ 500

Consistency in the use of depreciation methods

As previously stated, a company may use different depreciation methods to depreciate different assets. However, once a depreciation method has been selected for a particular asset, the accounting principle of consistency requires that this method be used throughout the asset's useful life. In short, a company should not change its method of depreciating an asset from year to year. However, a company may change its method of depreciating certain assets if good reasons exist to support the change. Such changes in accounting methods should be adequately disclosed in the company's financial statements.

Inflation and depreciation

5 Explain why depreciation based upon historical costs may cause an overstatement of net income.

The valuation of plant and equipment on a cost basis and the computation of depreciation in terms of cost will work very well during periods of stable price levels. However, the substantial rise in the price level in recent years has led many government officials and business executives to suggest that a more realistic measurement of net income could be achieved by basing depreciation on the *current cost*, for example, *estimated current replacement cost,* of plant assets rather than on the original cost of the assets presently in use.

As a specific illustration, assume that a manufacturing company purchased machinery in 1980 at a cost of $1,000,000. Estimated useful life was 10 years and straight-line depreciation was used. During this 10-year period the price level rose sharply. By 1990 the machinery purchased in 1980 was fully depreciated; it was scrapped and replaced by new machinery in 1990. Although the new machines were not significantly different from the old, they cost $3,000,000, or three times as much as the old machinery. Many accountants would argue that the depreciation expense for the 10 years was in reality $3,000,000, because this was the outlay required for new machinery if the company was merely to "stay even" in its productive facilities. It also may be argued that net income is *overstated* during a period of rising prices if depreciation is based on the lower plant costs of some years ago.

Historical cost versus replacement cost

The above criticism of depreciation accounting based on the historical cost of assets is a convincing one. (*Historical cost* means the cost actually incurred by a company in acquiring an asset.) However, this criticism does not mean that business is on the verge of abandoning the cost principle in accounting for assets and computing depreciation. To substitute estimated current replacement cost for the historical cost of plant and equipment would create many new difficulties and a great deal of confusion. For many assets, current replacement cost cannot be determined easily or with precision. For example, the current cost of replacing a steel mill with its great variety of complex, made-to-order machinery would involve making many assumptions and unprovable estimates. Or, as another example, consider the difficulty of estimating the replacement cost of a large tract of timber or of a gold mine.

Another difficulty in substituting replacement cost for historical cost of plant assets would be that the whole process of establishing estimated cost data would presumably need to be repeated each year. In contrast, historical cost (which we presently use as the basis of accounting for plant and equipment) is determined at the time of acquiring an asset and remains unchanged throughout the useful life of the asset.

These difficulties connected with the possible adoption of replacement cost as a basis of accounting for assets do not mean that such a change cannot or should not be attempted. However, these difficulties do explain to a great extent why business has continued to use historical cost as a primary basis of accounting for assets even during continued inflation.

Disclosure of current cost

Persistent inflation has led to criticism that traditional financial statements do not portray adequately the effects of rising prices on earnings and on certain assets. In response, the accounting profession in a number of countries, including Canada and the United States, has recommended that large public corporations present in their *annual* reports *supplementary* information on the effects of changing prices.

In Canada, *Section 4510* of the *CICA Handbook*, "Reporting the Effects of Changing Prices," recommends that large public corporations disclose in their annual reports, as supplementary information, *the current cost* (replacement or reproduction cost) of plant and equipment as well as the depreciation, depletion, and amortization expenses on a current cost basis. Also, as mentioned in Chapter 9, the changes in the current costs of plant and equipment during the period should be disclosed. Note that the recommended disclosures are intended as *supplementary* information and *do not replace* the historical-cost financial statements.

In the United States, the Financial Accounting Standards Board issued *Statement No. 33*, "Financial Reporting and Changing Prices," which requires large corporations to disclose the estimated current replacement cost of plant and equipment. Also required to be disclosed is depreciation expense based on the replacement cost of the assets. The disclosure can be made in a footnote to the financial statements or as a supplementary section accompanying the financial statements. As mentioned in Chapter 9, the FASB has made such disclosure voluntary rather than mandatory.

6   Record the sale, trade-in, or scrapping of a plant asset.

DISPOSAL OF PLANT AND EQUIPMENT

When depreciable assets are disposed of at any date other than the end of the fiscal year, an entry should be made to record depreciation for the *fraction of the year* ending with the date of disposal. If the half-year convention is in use, six months' depreciation should be recorded on all assets disposed of during the year. In the following illustrations of the disposal of items of plant and equipment, it is assumed that any necessary entries for fractional-period depreciation have been recorded.

As units of plant and equipment wear out or become obsolete, they must be scrapped, sold, or traded in on new equipment. Upon the disposal or retirement of a depreciable asset, the cost of the property is removed from the asset account, and the accumulated depreciation is removed from the related contra-asset account. Assume, for example, that office equipment purchased 10 years ago at a cost of $5,000 has been fully depreciated and is no longer useful. The entry to record the scrapping of the worthless equipment is as follows:

SCRAPPING FULLY
DEPRECIATED ASSET

| Accumulated Depreciation: Office Equipment . . . . | 5,000 | |
| Office Equipment . . . . | | 5,000 |

To remove from the accounts the cost and the accumulated depreciation on fully depreciated office equipment now being scrapped. No salvage value.

Once an asset has been fully depreciated, no more depreciation should be recorded on it, even though the property is in good condition and is continued in use. The objective of depreciation is to spread the *cost* of an asset over the *estimated* period of its usefulness; in no case can depreciation expense be greater than the amount paid for the asset. When a fully depreciated asset is continued in use beyond the original estimate of useful life, the asset account and the Accumulated Depreciation account should remain in the accounting records without further entries until the asset is retired.

Gains and losses on disposal of plant and equipment

Since the residual value and useful life of plant assets are only estimates, it is not uncommon for plant assets to be sold at a price that differs from their book value at the date of disposal. When plant assets are sold, any gain or loss on the disposal is computed by comparing the *book value with the amount received from the sale.* A sales price in excess of the book value produces a gain; a sales price below the book value produces a loss. These gains or losses, if material in amount, should be shown separately in the income statement in computing the income from operations.

Disposal at a price above book value   Assume that a machine that cost $10,000 and has a book value of $2,000 is sold for $3,000. The journal entry to record this disposal is as follows:

GAIN ON DISPOSAL OF
PLANT ASSET

Cash	3,000	
Accumulated Depreciation: Machinery	8,000	
Machinery		10,000
Gain on Disposal of Plant Assets		1,000

To record sale of machinery at a price above book value.

Disposal at a price below book value   Now assume that the same machine is sold for $500. The journal entry in this case would be as follows:

Cash	500	
Accumulated Depreciation: Machinery	8,000	
Loss on Disposal of Plant Assets	1,500	
Machinery		10,000
To record sale of machinery at a price below book value.		

The disposal of a depreciable asset at a price equal to book value would result in neither a gain nor a loss. The entry for such a transaction would consist of a debit to Cash for the amount received, a debit to Accumulated Depreciation for the balance accumulated, and a credit to the asset account for the original cost.

Trading in used assets on new

Certain types of depreciable assets, such as automobiles and office equipment, are customarily traded in on new assets of the same kind. The trade-in allowance granted by the dealer may differ materially from the book value of the old asset. If the dealer grants a trade-in allowance in excess of the book value of the asset being traded in, there is the suggestion of a gain being realized on the exchange. The evidence of a gain is not conclusive, however, because the list price of the new asset may purposely have been set higher than a realistic cash price to permit the offering of inflated trade-in allowances.

Because trade-in allowances often do not indicate the real market value of the old asset, it would be a reasonable and prudent accounting practice to recognize *no gain when a depreciable asset is traded in on another similar asset*. Thus, the cost of the new asset is considered to be the sum of (1) the book value of the old asset traded in, plus (2) the additional amount paid or to be paid in acquiring the new asset.

To illustrate the handling of an exchange transaction in this manner, asume that a delivery truck is acquired at a cost of $8,000. The truck is depreciated on the straight-line basis with the assumption of a five-year life and no salvage value. Annual depreciation expense is $8,000 ÷ 5, or $1,600. After four years of use, the truck is traded in on a new model having a list price of $10,000. The truck dealer grants a trade-in allowance of $2,400 for the old truck; the additional amount to be paid to acquire the new truck is, therefore, $7,600 ($10,000 list price minus $2,400 trade-in allowance). The *cost basis* of the new truck is computed as follows:

Cost of old truck	$8,000
Less: Accumulated depreciation ($1,600 × 4)	6,400
Book value of old truck	$1,600
Add: Cash payment for new truck (list price, $10,000 − $2,400	
trade-in allowance)	7,600
Cost basis of new truck	$9,200

The trade-in allowance and the list price of the new truck are not recorded in the accounts; their only function lies in determining the amount that the purchaser must pay in addition to turning in the old truck. The journal entry for this exchange transaction is as follows:

ENTRY FOR TRADE-IN

Delivery Truck (new)	9,200	
Accumulated Depreciation: Delivery Truck (old)	6,400	
Delivery Truck (old)		8,000
Cash		7,600

To remove from the accounts the cost of old truck and
accumulated depreciation thereon, and to record new truck at
cost equal to book value of old truck traded in plus cash paid.

Although the $2,400 trade-in allowance granted by the dealer exceeded the $1,600 book value of the old truck, notice that no gain is recognized on the disposal of the old truck. A gain may result from the outright sale of a depreciable asset, but not from trading that asset in upon a new but similar asset.

Although a reasonable and prudent accounting practice would not permit recognition of a gain on a trade-in, it does permit recognition of a *loss*. For example, assume that a company received a trade-in allowance of only $10,000 for old machinery that had a book value of $100,000 ($400,000 cost − $300,000 accumulated depreciation) and paid $590,000 cash. The price of the new machine was $600,000. A journal entry illustrating this situation follows:

NOTICE RECOGNITION
OF LOSS ON TRADE-IN

Machinery (new)	600,000	
Accumulated Depreciation: Machinery (old)	300,000	
Loss on Trade-in of Plant Assets	90,000	
Machinery (old)		400,000
Cash		590,000

To recognize a loss on trade-in of machinery.

The reasoning in requiring recognition of the loss is that a trade-in allowance substantially below an asset's book value indicates that the depreciation expense relating to this asset has been understated in prior years.

old machine = 400,000   new machine = 600,000
accum dep = 300,000   trade in = 10,000
NBV   100,000   Pay   590,000

NATURAL RESOURCES

Accounting for natural resources

7   Account for the
depletion of
natural resources.

Mining properties, oil and gas reserves, and tracts of standing timber are leading examples of natural resources or "wasting assets." The distinguishing characteristics of these assets are that they are physically consumed and converted into inventory. Theoretically, a coal mine might be regarded as an underground "inventory" of coal; however, such an "inventory" is certainly not a current asset. In the balance sheet, mining property and other natural resources are classified as property, plant, and equipment.

We have explained that plant assets such as buildings and equipment depreciate because of physical deterioration or obsolescence. A mine or an oil reserve does not "depreciate" for these reasons, but it is gradually *depleted* as the natural resource is removed from the ground. Once all of the coal has been removed from a coal mine, for example, the mine is "fully depleted" and will be abandoned or sold for its residual value.

To illustrate the depletion of a natural resource, assume that Rainbow Minerals pays $10,500,000 to acquire the Red Valley Mine, which is believed to contain 10 million tonnes of coal. The residual value of the mine after all of the coal is removed is estimated to be $500,000. The depletion that will occur over the life of the mine is the original cost minus the residual value, or $10,000,000. This depletion will occur at the rate of *$1 per tonne* ($10,000,000 ÷ 10 million tonnes) as the coal is removed from the mine. If we assume that 2 million tonnes are mined during the first year of operations, the entry to record the depletion of the mine would be as follows:

RECORDING DEPLETION

Depletion of Coal Deposits	2,000,000	
Accumulated Depletion: Red Valley Mine		2,000,000
To record depletion of the Red Valley Mine for the		
year; 2,000,000 tonnes mined @ $1 per tonne.		

Accumulated Depletion is a contra-asset account similar to the Accumulated Depreciation account; it represents the portion of the mine which has been used up (depleted) to date. In Rainbow Mineral's balance sheet, the Red Valley Mine now appears as follows:

Property, Plant, & Equipment:		
Mining properties: Red Valley Mine	$10,500,000	
Less: Accumulated depletion	2,000,000	$8,500,000

The Depletion of Coal Deposits account may be viewed as similar to the Purchases account of a merchandising business. This account is added to any other mining costs and any beginning inventory of coal to arrive at the cost of goods (coal) available for sale. If all of the coal has been sold by year-end, these costs are deducted from revenue as the cost of goods sold. If some of the coal is still on hand at year-end, a portion of these costs should be assigned to the ending inventory of coal, which is a current asset.

Depreciation of buildings and equipment closely related to natural resources   Buildings and equipment installed at a mine or drilling site may be useful only at that particular location. Consequently, such assets should be depreciated over their normal useful lives, or over the life of the natural resource, *whichever is shorter.* Often depreciation on such assets is computed using the units-of-output method, thus relating the depreciation expense to the rate at which units of the natural resource are removed.

INTANGIBLE ASSETS

Characteristics

As the word *intangible* suggests, assets in this classification have no physical substance. Leading examples are goodwill, patents, trademarks, and copyrights. Intangible assets are classified in the balance sheet as a separate section entitled intangible assets (or sometimes under other assets or deferred charges), following plant assets. However, not all assets that lack physical substance are regarded as intangible assets. An account receivable, for example, or a short-term prepayment is of nonphysical nature but is classified as a current asset and is not regarded as an intangible. In brief, *intangible assets are assets that are used in the operation of the business but that have no physical substance and are noncurrent.*

The basis of valuation for intangible assets is cost. In some companies, certain intangible assets such as trademarks may be of great importance but may have been acquired without the incurring of any cost. An intangible asset should appear in the balance sheet *only* if a cost of acquisition or development has been incurred.

Operating expenses versus intangible assets

For an expenditure to qualify as an intangible asset, there must be reasonable evidence of future benefits. Many expenditures offer some prospects of yielding benefits in subsequent years, but the existence and life-span of these benefits is so uncertain that most companies treat these expenditures as operating expenses. Examples are the expenditures for intensive advertising campaigns to introduce new products, and the expense of training employees to work with new types of machinery or office equipment. There is little doubt that some benefits from these outlays continue beyond the current period, but because of the uncertain duration of the benefits, it is almost universal practice to treat expenditures of this nature as expense of the current period. Another reason for charging these outlays to expense is the practical difficulty of separating them from the recurring expenses of current operations.

Amortization

The term *amortization* is used to describe the write-off to expense of the cost of an intangible asset over its useful life. The usual accounting entry for amortization consists of a debit to Amortization Expense and a credit to the intangible asset account. There is no theoretical objection to crediting an accumulated amortization account rather than the intangible asset account, but this method is seldom encountered in practice.

Although it is difficult to estimate the useful life of an intangible such as a trademark, it is highly probable that such an asset will not contribute to future earnings on a permanent basis. The cost of the intangible asset should, therefore, be deducted from revenue during the years in which it may be expected to aid in producing revenue. Under the current accounting practices, the maximum period for amortization of an intangible asset would not exceed 40 years.[5] The straight-line method of amortization is generally used for intangible assets.

Goodwill

8   Explain the nature of goodwill and indicate when this asset should appear in the accounting records.

Business executives used the term *goodwill* in a variety of meanings before it became part of accounting terminology. One of the most common meanings of goodwill in a non-accounting sense concerns the benefits derived from a favourable reputation among customers. To accountants, however, goodwill has a very specific meaning not necessarily limited to customer relations. It means the *present value of future*

---

[5] While CICA is silent in this area, in the United States *APB Opinion No. 17*, ''Intangible Assets,'' AICPA (New York: 1970), para. 29, supports this position. However, *CICA Handbook* paragraph 1580.58 recommends that goodwill should be amortized on a straight-line basis over its useful life, which should not exceed 40 years.

earnings in excess of the normal return on net identifiable assets. Above-average earnings may arise not only from favourable customer relations but also from such factors as superior management and manufacturing efficiency.

The phrase *normal return on net identifiable assets* requires explanation. Net assets means the owner's equity in a business, or assets minus liabilities. Goodwill, however, is not an *identifiable* asset. The existence of goodwill is implied by the ability of a business to earn an above-average return; however, the cause and precise dollar value of goodwill are largely matters of personal opinion. Therefore, *net identifiable assets* means all assets *except goodwill,* minus liabilities. A *normal return* on net identifiable assets is the rate of return which investors demand in a particular industry to justify their buying a business at the *fair market value* of its net identifiable assets. A business has goodwill when investors will pay a higher price because the business earns more than the normal rate of return.

Assume that two businesses in the same line of trade are offered for sale and that the normal return on the fair market value of net identifiable assets in this industry is 15% a year. The relative earning power of the two companies during the past five years is shown as follows:

	COMPANY X	COMPANY Y
Fair market value of net identifiable assets	$1,000,000	$1,000,000
Normal rate of return on net assets	15%	15%
Average net income for past five years	$ 150,000	$ 190,000
Normal earnings, computed as 15% of net identifiable assets	150,000	150,000
Earnings in excess of normal	$ –0–	$ 40,000

An investor would be willing to pay $1,000,000 to buy Company X, because Company X earns the normal 15% return that justifies the fair market value of its net identifiable assets. Although Company Y has the same amount of net identifiable assets, an investor would be willing to pay *more* for Company Y than for Company X because Company Y has a record of superior earnings that will presumably continue for some time in the future. The extra amount that a buyer would pay to purchase Company Y represents the value of Company Y's goodwill.

Estimating goodwill   How much will an investor pay for goodwill? Above-average earnings in past years are of significance to prospective purchasers only if they believe that these earnings will continue after they acquire the business. Investors' appraisals of goodwill, therefore, will vary with their estimates of the future earning power of the business. Very few businesses, however, are able to maintain above-average earnings for more than a few years. Consequently, the purchaser of a business will usually limit any amount paid for goodwill to not more than four or five times the amount by which annual earnings exceed normal earnings.

Arriving at a fair value for the goodwill of a going business is a difficult and subjective process. Any estimate of goodwill is in large part a matter of personal opinion. The following are several methods that a prospective purchaser might use in estimating a value for goodwill:

1 Negotiated agreement between buyer and seller of the business may be reached on the amount of goodwill. For example, it might be agreed that the fair market value of net identifiable assets is $1,000,000 and that the total purchase price for the business will be $1,180,000 thus providing a $180,000 payment for goodwill.

2 Goodwill may be determined as a multiple of the amount by which average annual earnings exceed normal earnings. Referring to our example involving Company Y, a prospective buyer may be willing to pay four times the amount by which average earnings exceed normal earnings, indicating a value of $160,000 (4 × $40,000) for goodwill. The purchase price of the business, therefore, would be $1,160,000.

The multiple applied to the excess annual earnings will vary widely from perhaps 1 to 10. An investor who pays four times the excess earnings for goodwill must, of course, expect these earnings to continue for at least four years so as to recover the amount that is paid for the goodwill.

3 Goodwill may be estimated by *capitalizing* the amount by which average earnings exceed normal earnings. Capitalizing an earnings stream means dividing those earnings by the investor's required rate of return. The result is the maximum amount which the investor could pay for the earnings and have them represent the required rate of return on the investment. To illustrate, assume that the prospective buyer decides to capitalize the $40,000 annual excess earnings of Company Y at a rate of 20%. This approach results in a $200,000 estimate ($40,000 ÷ .20 = $200,000) for the value of goodwill. (Note that $40,000 per year represents a 20% return on a $200,000 investment.)

A weakness in the capitalization method is that *no provision is made for the recovery* of the investment for the goodwill. If the prospective buyer is to earn a 20% return on the $200,000 investment in goodwill, either the excess earnings must continue *forever* (an unlikely assumption) or the buyer must be able to recover the $200,000 investment at a later date by selling the business at a price above the fair market value of net identifiable assets.

Recording goodwill in the accounting records   Goodwill is recorded in the accounting records *only when it is purchased;* this situation usually occurs only when a business is purchased in its entirety (or in a business combination in which a company acquires control of another, goodwill is recognized in the consolidated balance sheet only.) After the fair market values of all identifiable assets have been recorded in the accounting records of the new owners, any additional amount paid for the business may properly be debited to an asset account entitled Goodwill. This intangible asset must then be amortized over a period not to exceed 40 years, although a much shorter amortization period usually is appropriate.[6]

Many businesses have never purchased goodwill but have generated it internally through developing good customer relations, superior management, or other factors which result in above-average earnings. Because there is no objective means of determining the dollar value of goodwill unless the business is sold, internally developed goodwill is *not recorded* in the accounting records. Thus, goodwill may be a very important asset of a successful business but may not even appear in the company's balance sheet.

[6] CICA, *CICA Handbook* (Toronto), paragraph 1580.58.

Patents

A patent is an exclusive right granted by the federal government for manufacture, use, and sale of a particular product. The purpose of this exclusive grant is to encourage the invention of new machines and processes. When a company acquires a patent by purchase from the inventor or other holder, the purchase price should be recorded by debiting the intangible asset account Patents.

Patents are granted for a period of 17 years from the date of issue, and the period of amortization must not exceed that period. However, if the patent is likely to lose its usefulness in less than 17 years, amortization should be based on the shorter period of estimated useful life. Assume that a patent is purchased from the inventor at a cost of $100,000, after five years of the legal life have expired. The remaining *legal* life is, therefore, 12 years, but if the estimated *useful* life is only four years, amortization should be based on this shorter period. The entry to be made to record the annual amortization expense would be:

ENTRY FOR
AMORTIZATION
OF PATENT

Amortization Expense: Patents	25,000	
Patents		25,000
To amortize cost of patent on a straight-line basis and estimated life of four years.		

Trademarks and trade names

Coca Cola's distinctive bottle is an example of a trademark known around the world. A trademark is a word, symbol, or design that identifies a product or group of products and affords a measure of protection to the owner whether or not registration has occurred. However, registration of a trademark in Canada serves as evidence of ownership and facilitates a higher degree of protection. Registration has a term of 15 years but may be renewed indefinitely for further terms of 15 years.

A trade name is the name under which a business is carried on whether or not it is the legally incorporated name of the business. If a trade name is used as a trademark, it may be registered as a trademark.

The costs of developing a trademark or trade name often consist of advertising campaigns, which should be treated as expense when incurred. If a trademark or trade name is purchased, however, the cost may be substantial. Such cost should be capitalized and amortized to expense over a reasonable period of time, which generally would not be more than 40 years. If the use of the trademark is discontinued or its contribution to earnings becomes doubtful, any unamortized cost should be written off immediately.

Franchises

A franchise is a right granted by a company or a governmental unit to conduct certain type of business in a specific geographical area. An example of a franchise is the right to operate a McDonald's restaurant in a specific neighbourhood. The cost of franchises varies greatly and often may be quite substantial. When the cost of franchise is small, it may be charged immediately to expense or amortized over short period such as five years. When the cost is substantial, amortization should be based upon the life of the franchise.

Copyrights

A copyright is an exclusive right granted by the federal government to protect the production and sale of literary or artistic materials for the life of the creator plus 50 years. The cost of obtaining a copyright in some cases is minor and therefore is chargeable to expense when paid. Only when a copyright is purchased will the expenditure be material enough to warrant its being capitalized and spread over the useful life. The revenue from copyrights is usually limited to only a few years, and the purchase cost should, of course, be amortized over the years in which the revenue is expected.

Other intangibles and deferred charges

Many other types of intangible assets are found in the published balance sheets of large corporations. Some examples are formulas, processes, name lists, and film rights.

Intangibles, particularly those with limited lives, are sometimes classified as "deferred charges" in the balance sheet. A *deferred charge* is an expenditure that is expected to yield benefits for several accounting periods, and should be amortized over its estimated useful life. Included in this category are such items as bond issuance costs, plant rearrangement and moving costs, start-up costs, and organization costs. The distinction between intangibles and deferred charges is not an important one; both represent a "stream of services" in the form of long-term prepayments awaiting allocation to those accounting periods in which the services will be consumed.

Research and development (R&D) costs

The spending of millions of dollars a year on research and development leading to all kinds of new products is a striking characteristic of modern industry. In the past, some companies treated all research and development costs as expense in the year incurred; other companies in the same industry recorded these costs as intangible assets to be amortized over future years. This diversity of practice prevented the financial statements of different companies from being comparable.

The lack of uniformity in accounting for R&D was ended when the *CICA Handbook* recommended that all research and development costs be charged to expense when incurred except when the *development costs* have met the following specific criteria: (1) the product is clearly defined and the attributable costs can be identified, (2) the product is technically and commercially feasible and adequate resources are available to complete the project, and (3) the future benefits of the product could be considered as reasonably certain and the enterprise intends to sell or use the product.[7] Those development costs that have met *all* these criteria should be *deferred* to future periods. The amortization of these deferred development costs should be on a systematic and rational basis so as to result in a fair matching of such costs with related benefits.[8] In the United States, however, the FASB requires that all research and development costs be charged to expense when incurred.[9]

---

[7] CICA, *CICA Handbook*, (Toronto), paragraphs 3450.20 and 3450.21.
[8] Ibid., paragraphs 3450.26, 3450.27, and 3450.28.
[9] *FASB Statement No. 2*, "Accounting for Research and Development Costs" (Stamford, Conn.: 1974), paragraph 12.

END-OF-CHAPTER REVIEW

SUMMARY OF CHAPTER LEARNING OBJECTIVES

1 Determine the cost of plant assets.

Plant assets are long-lived assets acquired for use in the business and not for resale to customers. The matching principle of accounting requires that we include in the plant and equipment accounts those costs which will provide services over a period of years. During these years, the use of the plant assets contributes to the earning of revenue. The cost of a plant asset includes all expenditures reasonable and necessary in acquiring the asset and placing it in a position and condition for use in the operations of the business.

2 Distinguish between capital expenditures and revenue expenditures.

Capital expenditures include any material expenditure that will benefit several accounting periods. Revenue expenditures are expenditures that benefit only the current period or that are not material in amount.

3 Explain the relationship between depreciation and the matching principle.

Depreciation is the allocation of the cost of a plant asset to expense in the periods in which services are received from the asset. Plant assets enable a business to earn revenue; therefore the cost of the asset becomes expense over the years in which the asset generates revenue.

4 Compute depreciation by the straight-line, units-of-output, declining-balance, and sum-of-the-years'-digits methods.

The straight-line method is a simple and widely used method of computing depreciation. It allocates an equal portion of the cost of an asset to each period of use. The units-of-output method assigns an equal portion of the cost to each unit produced. Accelerated methods of depreciation mean recognizing relatively large amounts of depreciation in the early years of use and reduced amounts in later years. The accelerated methods are based in part upon the assumption that plant and equipment provide greater economic benefits in the early years. The declining-balance method and the sum-of-the-years'-digits method are widely used types of accelerated depreciation.

5 Explain why depreciation based upon historical costs may cause an overstatement of net income.

During sustained inflation, net income tends to be overstated if depreciation is based upon historical cost. The depreciation expense over the life of the asset is less than the cost of replacing the asset when it must be retired. Depreciation expense must be as much as replacement cost if a company is merely to "stay even" in its productive facilities. Large corporations are required to disclose as supplementary information what depreciation expense would be if based on current cost (e.g., replacement cost.)

6 Record the sale, trade-in, or scrapping of a plant asset.

When plant assets are disposed of, depreciation should be recorded to the date of disposal. The cost is then removed from the Asset account and the total recorded depreciation is removed from the Accumulated Depreciation account. The sale of a plant asset at a price above or below book value results in a gain or loss to be reported in the income statement. For exchange of similar assets (trade-ins), it would be a reasonable and prudent accounting practice to recognize a loss but not a gain.

7 Account for the depletion of natural resources.

Natural resources (or wasting assets) include mines, oil fields, and standing timber. Their cost is converted into inventory as the resource is mined, pumped, or cut. This allocation of the cost of a natural resource to inventories is called depletion. The depletion rate per unit extracted equals the cost of the resource divided by the estimated number of units it contains.

8 Explain the nature of goodwill and indicate when this asset should appear in the accounting records.

Goodwill is the present value of future earnings in excess of the normal return on net identifiable assets. A business has goodwill only if it earns more than the normal rate of return for the industry. Goodwill is recorded in the accounts only when an investor buys an entire company and pays a price higher than the fair market value of the net identifiable assets.

KEY TERMS INTRODUCED OR EMPHASIZED IN CHAPTER 10

Accelerated depreciation Methods of depreciation that call for recognition of relatively large amounts of depreciation in the early years of an asset's useful life and relatively small amounts in the later years.

Amortization The systematic write-off to expense of the cost of an intangible asset over the periods of its economic usefulness.

Book value The cost of a plant asset minus the total recorded depreciation, as shown by the Accumulated Depreciation account. The remaining undepreciated cost is also known as *carrying value.*

Capital expenditure A cost incurred to acquire a long-lived asset. An expenditure that will benefit several accounting periods.

Declining-balance depreciation An accelerated method of depreciation in which a rate (e.g., a multiple of the straight-line rate) is applied each year to the *undepreciated cost* of the asset.

Deferred charge An expenditure expected to yield benefits for several accounting periods and therefore capitalized and written off during the periods benefited.

Depletion Allocating the cost of a natural resource to the units removed as the resource is mined, pumped, cut, or otherwise consumed.

Depreciation The systematic allocation of the cost of an asset to expense over the years of its estimated useful life.

Goodwill The present value of expected future earnings of a business in excess of the earnings normally realized in the industry. Recorded when a business entity is purchased at a price in excess of the fair value of its net identifiable assets (excluding goodwill) less liabilities.

Half-year convention The practice of taking six months' depreciation in the year of acquisition and the year of disposition, rather than computing depreciation for partial periods to the nearest month. The half-year convention generally is *not* used for assets that are purchased very infrequently during the year, e.g., buildings.

Intangible assets Those assets that are used in the operation of a business but that have no physical substance and are noncurrent.

Natural resources Mines, oil fields, standing timber, and similar assets that are physically consumed and converted into inventory.

Net identifiable assets Total of all assets *except goodwill* minus liabilities.

Replacement cost The estimated cost of replacing an asset at the current balance sheet date. Disclosure of such data is required of large public companies.

Residual (salvage) value The portion of an asset's cost expected to be recovered through sale or trade-in of the asset at the end of its useful life.

Revenue expenditure Any expenditure that will benefit only the current accounting period.

Straight-line depreciation A method of depreciation that allocates the cost of an asset (minus any residual value) equally to each year of its useful life.

Sum-of-years'-digits depreciation An accelerated method of depreciation. The depreciable cost is multiplied each year by a fraction of which the numerator is the remaining years of useful life (as of the beginning of the current year) and the denominator is the sum of the years of useful life.

Units-of-output depreciation A depreciation method in which cost (minus residual value) is divided by the estimated units of lifetime output. The unit depreciation cost is multiplied by the actual units of output each year to compute the annual depreciation expense.

DEMONSTRATION PROBLEM FOR YOUR REVIEW

The ledger of Cypress Company contained an account entitled Property, which had been used to record a variety of expenditures. At the end of the year, the Property account contained the following entries:

Debit entries:

Jan.	10	Purchase for cash of building site	$200,000
Feb.	4	Cost of removing old building from site	8,000
Sept.	30	Paid contract price for new building completed today	560,000
Sept.	30	Insurance, inspection fees, and other costs directly	
		related to construction of new building	18,000
		Total debits	$786,000

Credit entries:

Feb.	4	Proceeds from sale of salvaged material from		
		demolition of old building	$ 3,000	
Dec.	31	Depreciation for the year computed at 4% of		
		balance in Property account ($783,000). Debit		
		was to Depreciation Expense	31,320	
		Total credits		34,320
Dec.	31	Balance in Property account at year-end		$751,680

Instructions

a List the errors made in the application of accounting principles or practices by Cypress Company.

b Prepare a compound correcting journal entry at December 31, assuming that the estimated life of the new building is 25 years and that depreciation is to be recognized for three months of the current year using the straight-line method. The accounts have not been closed for the year.

SOLUTION TO DEMONSTRATION PROBLEM

a Errors in accounting principles or practices were:

    (1) Including land (a nondepreciable asset) in the same account with building (a depreciable asset)

(2) Using the total of land and building as a base for applying the depreciation rate on building
(3) Recording a full year's depreciation on a new building that was in use only the last three months of the year
(4) Crediting the depreciation for the period directly to an asset account (Property) rather than to a contra-asset account (Accumulated Depreciation: Building)

Correcting Journal Entry

Dec. 31	Land	205,000	
	Building	578,000 ✓	
	Property		751,680
	Accumulated Depreciation: Building		5,780 ✓
	Depreciation Expense		25,540

To correct the accounts reflecting land, building, and depreciation in accordance with the computations shown in the following schedule:

	LAND	BUILDING
Amount paid to acquire building site	$200,000	
Cost of removing old building from site	8,000	
Less: proceeds from salvaged materials	(3,000)	
Contract price for new building		$560,000
Insurance, inspection fees, and other costs		
directly related to construction of new building		18,000
Totals	$205,000	$578,000

Depreciation: $578,000 \times 4\% \times {}^{3}/_{12} = \$5,780$

Correction of depreciation expense: $31,320 - $5,780 = $25,540

ASSIGNMENT MATERIAL

REVIEW QUESTIONS

1 Which of the following characteristics would prevent an item from being included in the classification of plant and equipment? (a) Intangible, (b) limited life, (c) unlimited life, (d) held for sale in the regular course of business, (e) not capable of rendering benefits to the business in the future.

2 The following expenditures were incurred in connection with a large new machine acquired by a metals manufacturing company. Identify those that should be included in the cost of the asset. (a) Freight charges, (b) sales tax on the machine, (c) payment to a passing motorist whose car was damaged by the equipment used in unloading the machine, (d) wages of employees for time spent in installing and testing the machine before it was placed in service, (e) wages of employees assigned to lubrication and minor adjustments of machine one year after it was placed in service.

3 What is the distinction between a *capital expenditure* and a *revenue expenditure?*

4 If a capital expenditure is erroneously treated as a revenue expenditure, will the net income of the current year be overstated or understated? Will this error have any effect upon the net income reported in future years? Explain.

5 Which of the following statements best describes the nature of depreciation?

a Regular reduction of asset value to correspond to the decline in market value as the asset ages.

b A process of correlating the carrying value of an asset with its gradual decline in physical efficiency.

c Allocation of cost in a manner that will ensure that plant and equipment items are not carried on the balance sheet at amounts in excess of net realizable value.

d Allocation of the cost of a plant asset to the periods in which services are received from the asset.

6 Should depreciation continue to be recorded on a building when ample evidence exists that the current market value is greater than original cost and that the rising trend of market values is continuing? Explain.

7 Criticize the following quotation:

"We shall have no difficulty in paying for new plant assets needed during the coming year because our estimated outlays for new equipment amount to only $80,000, and we have more than twice that amount in our accumulated depreciation account at present."

8 A factory machine acquired at a cost of $94,200 was to be depreciated by the sum-of-the-years'-digits method over an estimated life of eight years. Residual salvage value was estimated to be $15,000. State the amount of depreciation during the first year and during the eighth year.

9 After 4 years of using a machine acquired at a cost of $15,000, Chunmoon Construction Limited determined that the original estimated life of 10 years had been too short and that a total useful life of 12 years was a more reasonable estimate. Explain briefly the method that should be used to revise the depreciation program, assuming that straight-line depreciation has been used. Assume that the revision is made after recording depreciation and closing the accounts at the end of 4 years of use of the machine.

10 Give some reasons why a company may change its depreciation policy for financial reporting purposes from an accelerated depreciation method to the straight-line method.

11 Explain two approaches to computing depreciation for the fractional period in the year in which an asset is purchased. (Neither of your approaches should require the computation of depreciation to the nearest day or week.)

12 Explain what is meant by the following quotation: "In periods of rising prices companies do not recognize adequate depreciation expense, and reported corporate net income is substantially overstated."

13 Century Company traded in its old computer on a new model. The trade-in allowance for the old computer is greater than its book value. Should Century Company recognize a gain on the exchange in determining its net income for financial reporting? Explain.

14 Newton Products purchased for $2 million a franchise making it the exclusive distributor of Gold Creek Beer in three Atlantic provinces. This franchise has an unlimited legal life and may be sold by Newton Products to any buyer who meets with Gold Creek Beer's approval. The accountant at Newton Products believes that this franchise is a permanent asset, which should appear in the company's balance sheet indefinitely at $2 million, unless it is sold. Is this treatment in conformity with reasonable and prudent accounting practices?

15 Lead Hill Corporation recognizes $1 depletion for each tonne of ore mined. During the current year the company mined 600,000 tonnes but sold only 500,000 tonnes, as it was attempting to build up inventories in anticipation of a possible strike by employees. How much depletion should be deducted from revenue of the current year?

16 Define *intangible assets*. Would an account receivable arising from a sale of merchandise under terms of 2/10, n/30 qualify as an intangible asset under your definition?

17 Over what period of time should the cost of various types of intangible assets be amortized by regular charges against revenue? (Your answer should be in the form of a principle or guideline rather than a specific number of years.) What method of amortization is generally used?

18 Several years ago March Metals purchased for $120,000 a well-known trademark for padlocks and other security products. After using the trademark for three years, March Metals discontinued it altogether when the company withdrew from the lock business and concentrated on the manufacture of aircraft parts. Amortization of the trademark at the rate of $3,000 a year is being continued on the basis of a 40-year life, which the owner of March Metals says is required by reasonable and prudent accounting standards. Do you agree? Explain.

19 Under what circumstances should *goodwill* be recorded in the accounts?

20 In reviewing the financial statements of Digital Products Co. Ltd. with a view to investing in the company's stock, you notice that net tangible assets total $1 million, that goodwill is listed at $400,000, and that average earnings for the past five years have been $50,000 a year. How would these relationships influence your thinking about the company?

EXERCISES

**Exercise 10-1
Accounting
terminology**

Listed below are nine technical accounting terms introduced in this chapter:

Amortization	Double-declining-balance	Intangible asset
Revenue expenditure	Replacement cost of plant	Book value
Accumulated depletion	Research & development	Goodwill

Each of the following statements may (or may not) describe one of these technical terms. For each statement, indicate the accounting term described, or answer "None" if the statement does not correctly describe any of the terms.

a A depreciation method which often consists of doubling the straight-line rate and applying this doubled rate to the undepreciated cost of the asset.

b Subject of supplementary disclosure required in the financial statements of large public corporations.

c The cost of a plant asset minus the total recorded depreciation on the asset.

d A material expenditure that will benefit several accounting periods.

e The systematic allocation to expense of the cost of an intangible asset.

f The portion of the cost of a natural resource which has been consumed or used up.

g A type of asset usually found only in the financial statements of a company that has purchased another business in its entirety.

h Noncurrent assets lacking in physical substance.

Exercise 10-2
Identifying costs to
be capitalized

Lane Corporation purchased machinery with a list price of $54,000. The vendor's invoice included sales tax of $2,646. Lane paid the invoice within the discount period and received a cash discount of $1,100. Lane also paid inbound transportation charges of $645 on the new machines as well as labour costs of $1,140 to install the machines in various locations. During the process of unloading and installation, one of the machines fell from a loading platform and was damaged. The repairs required on the damaged machine cost $3,270.

After the machines had been in operation for three months, they were thoroughly cleaned and lubricated at a cost of $390. You are to prepare a list of the amounts that should be capitalized by debit to the Machinery account. Show the total cost of the new machines.

Exercise 10-3
Distinguishing capital
expenditures from
revenue expenditures

Identify the following expenditures as capital expenditures or revenue expenditures:

a Purchased new battery at a cost of $40 for two-year-old delivery truck.

b Installed an escalator at a cost of $12,500 in a three-story building that had previously been used for some years without elevators or escalators.

c Purchased a pencil sharpener at a cost of $3.50.

d Immediately after acquiring a new delivery truck at a cost of $11,800, paid $615 to have the name of the store and other advertising material painted on the truck.

e Painted delivery truck at a cost of $175 after two years of use.

f Original life of the delivery truck had been estimated as four years and straight-line depreciation of 25% yearly had been recognized. After three years' use, however, it was decided to recondition the truck thoroughly, including a new engine and transmission, at a cost of $4,000. By making this expenditure it was believed that the useful life of the truck would be extended from the original estimate of four years to a total of six years.

Exercise 10-4
Units-of-output method

During the current year, Airport Auto Rentals purchased 60 new automobiles at a cost of $11,200 per car. The cars will be sold to a wholesaler at an estimated $5,700 each as soon as they have been driven 100,000 km. Airport Auto Rentals computes depreciation expense on its automobiles by the units-of-output method, based upon kilometres.

Instructions

a Compute the amount of depreciation to be recognized for each kilometre that a rental automobile is driven.

b Assuming that the 60 rental cars are driven a total of 2,650,000 km during the current year, compute the total amount of depreciation expense that Airport Auto Rentals should recognize on this fleet of cars for the year.

Exercise 10-5
Double-declining-
balance method

Machinery with an estimated useful life of five years was acquired by VPI Industries at a cost of $55,000. The estimated residual value of the machinery is $6,000. Compute the annual depreciation on this machinery for each of the five years using the double-declining-balance method.

Exercise 10-6
Trade-in and cost
basis

Rex Company traded in an old machine on a similar new one. The original cost of the old machine was $30,000 and the accumulated depreciation was $24,000. The list price of the new machine was $40,000 and the trade-in allowance was $8,000. What amount must Rex pay? Compute the indicated gain or loss (regardless of whether it should be recorded in the accounts). Compute the cost of the new machine.

Exercise 10-7
Depreciation for
fractional years

On June 3, Standard Tire Company purchased equipment at a cost of $300,000. The useful life of the equipment was estimated at six years and the residual value at $30,000. Compute the depreciation expense to be recognized in each calendar year during the life of the equipment under each of the following methods:

a Straight-line (round computations for a partial year to the nearest full month)

b Straight-line (use the half-year convention)

Exercise 10-8
Disposal of equipment
by sale, trade-in, or as
scrap

A tractor that cost $25,000 had an estimated useful life of five years and an estimated salvage value of $5,000. Straight-line depreciation was used. Give the entry (in general journal form) required by each of the following alternative assumptions:

a The tractor was sold for cash of $15,000 after two years' use.

b The tractor was traded in after three years on another tractor with a list price of $36,000. Trade-in allowance was $14,600.

c The tractor was scrapped after four years' use. Since scrap dealers were unwilling to pay anything for the tractor, it was given to a scrap dealer for his services in removing it.

Exercise 10-9
Depletion: recording
and reporting

Midwest Mining Company purchased the Black Hills Mine for $3,800,000 cash. The mine was estimated to contain 2 million tonnes of ore and have a residual value of $800,000.

During the first year of mining operations at the Black Hills Mine, 400,000 tonnes of ore were mined, of which 300,000 tonnes were sold.

a Prepare a journal entry to record depletion of the Black Hills Mine during the year.

b Show how the mine and accumulated depletion would appear in Midwest Mining Company's balance sheet after the first year of operations.

c Will the entire balance of the account debited in part a be deducted from revenue in determining the income for the year? Explain.

Exercise 10-10
Estimating goodwill

During the past several years the annual net income of Goldtone Appliance has averaged $270,000. At the present time the company is being offered for sale. The fair market value of its net assets (total assets minus all liabilities) is $1,500,000.

An investor negotiating to buy the company offers to pay an amount equal to the fair market value for the net assets and to assume all liabilities. In addition, the investor is willing to pay for goodwill an amount equal to net earnings in excess of 15% on net assets, capitalized at a rate of 25%.

On the basis of this agreement, what price is the investor offering for Goldtone Appliance?

PROBLEMS

Group A

Problem 10A-1
Determining cost of
plant assets

West Coast Printing, a newly organized corporation, purchased printing equipment having a price of $176,000 from a manufacturer in Winnipeg. Included on the seller's invoice was an additional amount of $12,074 for sales tax. West Coast Printing paid the invoice within the discount period and received a discount of $3,600. Other payments relating to the acquisition of the equipment were a freight bill of $2,600 and a labour cost for installing the equipment of $4,200. During the installation process, an accident caused damages to the equipment which was repaired at a cost of $6,300. As soon as the equipment was in place, West Coast printing obtained insurance on it for a premium of $1,800. All the items described above were charged to the Printing Equipment account. No entry for depreciation has yet been made and the accounts have not yet been closed.

Instructions

a Prepare a list of the expenditures that should have been capitalized by debiting the Printing Equipment account. Show the correct total cost for this asset.

b Prepare one compound journal entry to correct the error or errors by the company in recording these transactions.

c In one sentence state the accounting principle or concept that indicates the nature of expenditures properly included in the cost of equipment. (Do not list individual types of expenditure.)

Problem 10A-2
Three depreciation methods

New machinery was acquired by Video Corporation at a cost of $300,000. Useful life of the machinery was estimated to be 5 years, with residual salvage value of $36,000.

Instructions

Compute the annual depreciation expense throughout the five-year life of the machinery under each of the following methods of depreciation:

a Straight-line

b Sum-of-the-years'-digits

c Double-declining-balance.

Problem 10A-3
Trade-in of plant assets; a comprehensive problem

Hartman Editorial Services has entered into the following two transactions involving trade-ins of plant assets:

(1) A truck that had cost $12,000 was traded in on a new truck with a list price of $16,800. The trade-in allowance on the old truck was $4,500, and the remaining $12,300 was paid in cash. At the date of the trade-in, the old truck had been fully depreciated to its estimated residual value of $2,000.

(2) A word processor with a cost of $6,700 was traded in on a new word processor with a list price of $7,900. The trade-in allowance was $500, with the remaining $7,400 cost being paid in cash. At the date of this transaction, the accumulated depreciation on the old word processor amounted to $3,200.

Instructions

a Prepare journal entries to record each of these exchange transactions. (The asset accounts used for trucks and for word processors are entitled Vehicles and Office Equipment, respectively.)

b Compute the depreciation expense that Hartman Editorial Services will recognize on each of the newly acquired assets in the year of acquisition. Assume that each asset will be depreciated over 5 years using the straight-line method, with an estimated residual value of $2,000, and with use of the half-year convention.

Problem 10A-4
Methods of depreciation and their effects on net income

On October 4, Year 1, Farm Fresh Foods purchased equipment at a cost of $62,000. The equipment was estimated to have a useful life of 6 years and a residual value of $20,000. The manager of Farm Fresh Foods is trying to decide upon the appropriate depreciation method for this equipment and wants to see how various methods will affect the company's net income.

Instructions

a Compute the depreciation for each calendar year in which depreciation would be recognized using each of the following methods:
(1) Straight-line, with depreciation for fractional periods rounded to the nearest full month.
(2) Sum-of-the-years'-digits, using the half-year convention.

b After reviewing your schedule, the manager asks the following questions. Write a brief reply to each question, explaining the reasons for your answer.

(1) Are both methods acceptable for financial reporting purposes?

(2) Which method would result in the company's reporting the highest net income during the next three years (Years 1, 2, and 3)? Briefly explain.

(3) Which method would enable the company to show a trend of net income growth during the life of the equipment? Briefly explain.

Problem 10A-5
Acquisition and
disposal of plant
asset; depreciation
and revision of
depreciation

On February 18, 1988, Offshore Salvage Co. purchased a salvage barge for $127,500 cash. At this date, management estimated that the barge would have a useful life of 10 years and a residual value of $15,000. Offshore Salvage Co. adjusts and closes its books at the end of each calendar year. All items of plant and equipment are depreciated by the straight-line method, with the half-year convention applied in the years of acquisition and disposal.

Late in 1990, management decided that the barge was receiving very heavy use and that its estimated useful life should be revised from 10 years to 6 years. No change was made in the estimated residual value. The change in the estimated useful life was made prior to recording depreciation for 1990.

On August 11, 1991, the barge was damaged during a salvage operation. Rather than attempt to repair it, Offshore sold it to another salvage company for $60,000 cash.

Instructions

Prepare journal entries to record the purchase of the barge, depreciation during each of the four years, and the sale of the barge on August 11, 1991.

Problem 10A-6
Depletion of a mine

Early in 1988, Global Minerals began operation at its Wedding Bells Mine. The mine had been acquired several years earlier at a cost of $6,900,000. The mine is expected to contain 3 million tonnes of ore and to have a residual value of $1,500,000. Before beginning mining operations, the company installed equipment costing $2,700,000 at the mine. This equipment will have no economic usefulness once the mine is depleted.

Ore removed from the Wedding Bells Mine amounted to 500,000 tonnes in 1988 and 682,000 tonnes in 1989.

Instructions

a Compute the per-tonne depletion rate of the mine and the per-tonne depreciation rate of the mining equipment.

b Make the year-end adjusting entries at December 31, 1988, and December 31, 1989, to record depletion of the mine and the related depreciation. (Use separate entries to record depletion of the mine and depreciation of the equipment.)

c Show how the Wedding Bells Mine should appear in Global's balance sheet at the end of 1989. (Use "Ore Deposits: Wedding Bells Mine" as the title of the asset account; show accumulated depletion but do not include the equipment.)

Problem 10A-7
Intangible assets or
operating expense:
GAAP

During the current year Magnum Industries incurred the following expenditures, which should be recorded either as operating expenses of the current year, or as intangible assets.

a Expenditure to acquire a franchise as one of four Canadian distributors of an Italian automobile. The franchise expires in 49 years.

b Incurred research and development costs in an effort to produce a 200,000 km tire. At year-end, the project looks promising. If successful, the product will be patented for 17 years, but should contribute to revenue for at least 20 years.

c Purchased a patent on a fuel-saving device. The patent has a remaining legal life of 13 years, but Magnum Industries expects to produce and sell the device for a period of 5 years.

d Expenditures to advertise a new product. The product is patented and is expected to contribute to company revenue for the entire 17-year life of the patent.

e Expenditures for management training programs. The average manager stays with the company for a period of 9½ years, but attends a management training program every two years.

Instructions   Explain whether each of the above expenditures should be recorded as an operating expense of the current year or as an intangible asset. If you view the expenditure as creating an intangible asset, indicate the number of years over which the asset should be amortized. Explain your reasoning.

Group B

Problem 10B-1
Determining cost of plant assets

Hall Drilling, a newly organized corporation, purchased equipment for use in its business. The equipment had a price of $224,000. Included on the seller's invoice was an additional amount of $13,171 for sales tax. Hall Drilling paid the invoice within the discount period and received a discount of $4,480. Incidental costs incurred relating to the acquisition of the equipment were a freight charge of $2,200 and labour costs for installing the equipment of $4,800. During the installation process, an accident caused damages to the equipment; the damages were repaired at a cost of $3,000. As soon as the equipment was in place, the company obtained insurance on it for a premium of $2,200. All the above described items were entered in the Equipment account. No entry for depreciation has yet been made and the accounts have not yet been closed.

Instructions   **a** Prepare a list of the expenditures that should be included in the Equipment account. Show the correct total cost of this asset.

b Prepare one compound journal entry to correct the error or errors made by the company in recording these transactions.

c In one sentence state an accounting principle or concept that indicates the nature of expenditures properly included in the cost of equipment. (Do not list individual types of expenditure.)

Problem 10B-2
Three depreciation methods

Trident Company purchased new equipment with an estimated useful life of 5 years. Cost of the equipment was $200,000 and the residual salvage value was estimated to be $23,000.

Instructions   Compute the annual depreciation expense throughout the five-year life of the equipment under each of the following methods of depreciation:

a Straight-line

b Sum-of-the-years'-digits

c Double-declining-balance.

Problem 10B-3
Trade-in of a plant asset

On May 1, Clinton Corporation traded in old machinery on the purchase of new machinery priced at $191,000. The terms of the transaction may be summarized as follows:

Price of new machinery		$191,000
Trade-in allowance for old machinery	$ 21,000	
Cash paid	60,000	
Note payable issued (12%, one year)	110,000	$191,000

The machinery traded in had an original cost of $180,000 and had been depreciated at the rate of $18,000 a year. Residual value had been ignored on the grounds of not being material

Accumulated depreciation amounted to $144,000 at December 31 prior to the year of the exchange. No depreciation had been recorded between the annual closing of the accounts on December 31 and the exchange for the new machinery on May 1.

Instructions   **a** Prepare a journal entry to record depreciation to the nearest month for the fractional period ended May 1.

b Prepare a journal entry to record the acquisition of the new machine on May 1.

Problem 10B-4
Methods of depreciation
and their effects on
net income

Jade Palace purchased equipment on July 29, Year 2, at a cost of $83,000. The equipment was expected to have a residual value of $20,000 after a useful life of six years.

Instructions   **a** Compute the depreciation for each calendar year in which depreciation would be recognized using each of the following methods:

(1) Straight-line, with depreciation for fractional years rounded to the nearest full month.

(2) Sum-of-the-years'-digits, using the half-year convention.

b The manager of Jade Palace is trying to decide which depreciation method to use in the company's financial statements and asks the following questions. Write a brief reply to each question and explain the reasons for your answer.

(1) Are both methods acceptable for financial statement purposes?

(2) Which method would enable the business to report the largest amount of net income during the next couple of years?

(3) Which method would enable the company to show a trend of growth in net income during the life of the equipment?

Problem 10B-5
Acquisition and
disposal of plant
asset; depreciation
and revision of
depreciation

Moonfung Associates adjusts and closes its accounts at the end of each calendar year and uses the straight-line method of depreciation on all its plant and equipment. On January 9, 1988, machinery was purchased for cash at a cost of $19,000. Useful life was estimated to be 10 years and residual value $3,000.

Three years later in December, 1990, after steady use of the machinery, the company decided that because of rapid technological change, the estimated total useful life should be revised from 10 years to 7 years. No change was made in the estimate of residual value. The revised estimate of useful life was decided upon prior to recording depreciation for the period ended December 31, 1990.

On June 22, 1991, Moonfung Associates decided to lease new, more efficient machinery; consequently, the machinery described above was sold on this date for $10,280 cash.

Instructions   Prepare journal entries to record the purchase of the machinery, the recording of depreciation for each of the 4 years, and the disposal of the machinery on June 22, 1991. Depreciation in the year of acquisition and in the year of disposal should be rounded to the nearest full month.

Problem 10B-6
Depletion of an oil
field

On March 17, 1988, Wildcat Oil Company began operations at its Southfork Oil Field. The oil field had been acquired several years earlier at a cost of $11.6 million. The field is estimated to contain 4 million barrels of oil and to have a residual value of $2 million after all the oil has been pumped out. Equipment costing $480,000 was purchased for use at the Southfork Field. This equipment will have no economic usefulness once Southfork is depleted.

Wildcat Oil also built a pipeline at a cost of $2,880,000 to serve the Southfork Field. Although this pipeline is physically capable of being used for many years, its economic usefulness is limited to the productive life of the Southfork Field and there is no residual value.

Production at the Southfork Field amounted to 420,000 barrels in 1988 and 510,000 barrels in 1989.

Instructions   **a** Compute the per-barrel depletion rate of the oil field and the per-barrel depreciation rates of the equipment and the pipeline.

b Make the year-end adjusting entries required at December 31, 1988, and December 31, 1989, to record depletion of the oil field and the related depreciation. (Make separate entries to record depletion of the oil field, depreciation of the equipment, and depreciation of the pipeline.)

c Show how the Southfork Field should appear in Wildcat Oil's balance sheet at the end of 1989. (Use "Oil Reserves: Southfork Field" as the title of the asset account; show accumulated depletion, but do not include the equipment or pipeline.)

Problem 10B-7
Intangible assets or
operating expense:
GAAP

During the current year, Home Sales Corporation incurred the following expenditures, which should be recorded either as operating expenses of the current year or as intangible assets:

a Expenditures for the training of new employees. The average employee remains with the company for 14 years, but is retrained for a new position every 3 years.

b Purchased from another company the trademark to a household product. The trademark has an unlimited legal life, and the product is likely to contribute to revenue indefinitely.

c Incurred significant research and development costs to develop a dirt-resistant fibre. The company expects that the fibre would be patented, and that sales of the resulting products would contribute to revenue for at last 50 years.

d An expenditure to acquire the patent on a popular video game. The patent has a remaining legal life of 14 years, but Home Sales expects to produce and sell the game for only 3 years.

e Spent a large amount to sponsor a television mini-series about the French Revolution. The purpose in sponsoring the program was to make television viewers more aware of the company's name and its product lines.

Instructions   Explain whether each of the above expenditures should be recorded as an operating expense or an intangible asset. If you view the expenditure as an intangible asset, indicate the number of years over which the asset should be amortized. Explain your reasoning.

BUSINESS DECISION CASES

Case 10-1
Effects of depreciation
methods on reported
earnings

Samuel Slater is interested in buying a manufacturing business and has located two similar companies being offered for sale. Both companies are sole proprietorships that began operations three years ago, each with invested capital of $400,000. A considerable part of the assets in each company is represented by a building with an original cost of $100,000 and an estimated life of 40 years, and by machinery with an original cost of $200,000 and an estimated life of 20 years. Residual value is estimated at zero.

Bay Company uses straight-line depreciation and Cove Company uses declining-balance depreciation (double the straight-line rate). In all other respects the accounting policies of the two companies are quite similar. Neither company has borrowed from banks or incurred any indebtedness other than normal trade payables. The nature of products and other characteristics of operations are much the same for the two companies.

Audited financial statements for the three years show net income as follows:

YEAR	BAY COMPANY	COVE COMPANY
1	$ 62,000	$ 59,000
2	65,200	63,200
3	68,400	66,900
Totals	$195,600	$189,100

Slater asks your advice as to which company to buy. They are offered for sale at approximately the same price, and Slater is inclined to choose Bay Company because of its consistently higher earnings. On the other hand, the fact that Cove Company has more cash and a stronger working capital position is impressive. The audited financial statements show that withdrawals by the two owners have been approximately equal during the three-year life of each company.

Instructions   **a** Compute the depreciation recorded by each company in the first three years. Round off depreciation expense for each year to the nearest dollar.

b Write a memorandum to Slater advising which company in your judgment represents the more promising purchase. Give specific reasons to support your recommendation. Include a recomputation of the earnings of Cove Company by using straight-line depreciation in order to make its income statements comparable with those of Bay Company. Compare the earnings of the two companies year by year after such revision to a uniform basis.

Case 10-2
The best of three:
an investor's choice

Ruth Barnes, an experienced executive in retail store operation, is interested in buying an established business in the retail clothing field. She is now attempting to make a choice among three similar concerns that are available for purchase. All three companies have been in business for five years. The balance sheets presented by the three companies may be summarized as follows:

(handwritten: liquidity = 209,600   214,400   257,600)

ASSETS	COMPANY X	COMPANY Y	COMPANY Z
Cash	$ 24,000	$ 24,000	$ 40,000
Accounts receivable	185,600	190,400	217,600
Inventory	352,000	288,000	288,000
Plant assets (net)	110,400	128,000	80,000
Goodwill		4,800	
	$672,000	$635,200	$625,600

(handwritten: 656)

LIABILITIES & OWNER'S EQUITY			
Current liabilities	$284,800	$296,000	$320,000
Owner's equity	387,200	339,200	305,600
	$672,000	$635,200	$625,600

The average annual net earnings of the three businesses during the past five years has been as follows: Company X, $59,200; Company Y, $51,200; and Company Z, $54,400.

With the permission of the owners of the three businesses, Barnes arranged for a chartered accountant to examine the accounting records of the companies. This investigation disclosed the following information:

Accounts receivable   In Company X, no provision for uncollectible accounts had been made at any time, and no accounts receivable had been written off. Numerous past-due receivables were in the accounts, and the estimated uncollectible items that had accumulated during the past five years amounted to $16,000. In both Company Y and Company Z, the receivables appeared to be carried at net realizable value.   *(handwritten: COS is the most appropriate)*

Inventories   Company Y had adopted the first-in, first-out method of inventory valuation when first organized but had changed to the last-in, first-out method after one year. As a result of this change in method of accounting for inventories, the present balance sheet figure for inventories was approximately $32,000 less than replacement cost. The other two companies had used the first-in, first-out method continuously, and their present inventories were approximately equal to replacement cost. These replacement costs approximate fair market value.

Plant and equipment In each of the three companies, the plant assets included a building which had cost $80,000 and had an estimated useful life of 25 years with no residual scrap value. Company X had taken no depreciation on its building; Company Y had used straight-line depreciation at 4% annually; and Company Z had erroneously depreciated its building by applying a constant rate of 4% to the undepreciated balance. All plant assets other than buildings had been depreciated on a straight-line basis (correctly applied) in all companies. Barnes believed that the book value of the plant assets in all three companies would approximate fair market value if depreciation were computed uniformly on a straight-line basis.

Goodwill The item of goodwill, $4,800, on the balance sheet of Company Y represented the cost of a nonrecurring advertising campaign conducted during the first year of operation.

Barnes is willing to pay for net tangible assets (except cash) at adjusted book value that approximates fair market value, plus an amount for goodwill equal to three times the average annual net earnings in excess of 10% on the net tangible assets. Cash will not be included in the transfer of assets.

Instructions

a Prepare a revised summary of balance sheet data after correcting all errors made by the companies. In addition to correcting errors, make the necessary changes to apply straight-line depreciation and first-in, first-out inventory methods in all three companies. Round all amounts to the nearest dollar.

b Determine revised amounts for average annual net earnings of the three companies after taking into consideration the correction of errors and changes of method called for in a above.

c Determine the price which Barnes should offer for each of the businesses.

4

CURRENT LIABILITIES, PARTNERSHIPS, AND ACCOUNTING PRINCIPLES

Part 4 consists of three chapters. In Chapter 11 we deal with current liabilities; in Chapter 12 we discuss accounting for partnerships; and in Chapter 13 we review the accounting principles introduced in earlier chapters. Chapter 13 also includes the special topic of accounting for inflation.

CHAPTER 11

CHAPTER

CURRENT LIABILITIES AND PAYROLL ACCOUNTING

CHAPTER PREVIEW

In this chapter we concentrate on current liabilities, with special attention to notes payable. An important element of current liabilities arises from the payroll accounting system; consequently, the basic concepts of payroll accounting are discussed in the final section of this chapter. Long-term liabilities will be considered in Chapter 16.

After studying this chapter you should be able to meet these Learning Objectives:

1 Explain how the prompt recognition of liabilities relates to the matching principle of accounting.

2 Define current liabilities and explain how this classification is used in interpreting a balance sheet.

3 Account for the issuance of notes payable, the accrual of interest, and the payment of a note at maturity.

4 Explain the accounting treatment of notes payable that have interest included in the face amount.

5 Describe the basic separation of duties in a payroll system and explain how this plan contributes to strong internal control.

6 Account for a payroll, including computation of amounts to be withheld, and payroll taxes on the employer.

The nature of liabilities

Liabilities are obligations arising from past transactions and requiring the future payment of assets or future performance of services. We determine the dollar amount o a liability from the *cost principle*. In other words, we value the liability at the cost o the asset or service we receive in exchange for assuming the liability. For example assume that we make a $10,000 credit purchase of merchandise for our inventory terms net 30 days. We should immediately record a $10,000 liability, an amoun equal to the cost of the asset acquired.

To illustrate a transaction calling for the future performance of services, assume that a real estate firm receives cash of $2,400 as a fee to manage an apartmen building during the next six months. The real estate firm should immediately record a $2,400 liability (Unearned Management Fees). This liability will be discharged by rendering future services rather than by making a cash payment.

Liabilities of definite amount vs. estimated liabilities   Most liabilities are of definite dollar amount clearly stated by contract. Examples are accounts payable, note payable, dividends payable, sales taxes payable, accrued liabilities such as interes payable, and revenue collected in advance such as unearned management fees. Ou principal responsibility in accounting for these liabilities is to see that they are identified promptly as they come into existence and are properly recorded in the accounts.

Estimated liabilities have two key characteristics: the liability is known to exist but the precise dollar amount cannot be determined until a later date. A commo example is the liability of a manufacturer to honour a warranty on products sold. Fo instance, assume that a company manufactures and sells television sets that carry two-year warranty. To achieve the objective of offsetting current revenue with al related expenses, the liability for future warranty repairs on television sets sold during the current period should be estimated and recorded at the balance sheet date This estimate will be based upon the company's past experience.

Another common example of estimated liabilities is income tax on corporations. The income earned by a corporation is subject to tax by the federal and provincia governments. Because of the complexities and frequent changes in the income ta laws, a corporation often needs several weeks or months after the year-end to determine the precise amount of the income tax liability. If disputes arise between corporation and the tax authorities over the amount of the tax owed, the issue sometimes take years to resolve. However, income tax is a major expense of the yea in which income is earned. Consequently, the tax liability must be estimated. The estimated amount is entered in the accounts and appears in the financial statement both as an expense and as a liability.

Disclosure of contingent liabilities   In Chapter 8, we discussed the contingent liability that arises when a business discounts a note receivable to a bank. The busines endorses the note and thereby promises to pay the note if the maker fails to do so. The contingent liability created by discounting the note is a potential liability that wil become a full-fledged liability or will be eliminated altogether by a future event.

Lawsuits pending against a company pose the threat of a possible large liability coming into existence. Often it is impossible to estimate the outcome of the lawsuit but it is nevertheless important to disclose in the financial statements the status of th litigation. Otherwise, the user of the financial statements might be unaware of situations with possible major impact on the continued existence of the business.

Because contingent liabilities are potential liabilities rather than full-fledged liabilities, they are not included in the liability section of the balance sheet. However, these potential liabilities may affect the financial position of the business if future events cause them to become real liabilities. Therefore, contingent liabilities should be *disclosed in footnotes to the financial statements.* The contingent liability arising from the discounting of notes receivable could be disclosed by the following footnote:

Note 6: Contingencies

At December 31, 19___, the Company was contingently liable for notes receivable discounted with maturity values in the amount of $250,000.

The following are some examples of note disclosure of contingent liabilities from published financial statements.[1]

1   RANGER OIL LTD.

Contingencies

(a) The Company has guaranteed $3,548.000 of a bank loan to an affiliate.

(b) Discussions are currently being held with the U.K. taxation authorities with respect to the nature and timing of the tax deductibility of the SEDCO 714 capital costs. At this stage in the discussions, the necessity for revisions to the Company's tax provisions has not been established. Adjustments, if any, made with respect to this matter, would be accounted for as a prior period adjustment. Management believes the Company's tax returns, as filed, are substantially correct and that no adjustments are required.

2   DOME PETROLEUM LTD.

Contingencies

The Company has the following contingent liabilities:

(a) The Company is contingently liable for $225.0 million advanced to Dome Canada by the Arctic Petroleum Corporation of Japan.

(b) In 1983, Revenue Canada-Taxation issued reassessments to the Company disallowing the frontier exploration allowance claimed in 1980. Management believes that these amounts were validly claimed and intends to contest the issue. If the Company is not successful, a prior period adjustment will be made relating to 1980 which will increase the deficit and deferred income taxes by $44.3 million.

3   TÉLÉ-MÉTROPOLE INC.

Contingencies

A legal action in the amount of $3,150,000 was filed jointly against the Company and its subsidiary Télé-Métropole International Inc. This lawsuit relates to the endorsement by the Company of a surety-bond given by its subsidiary, in favor of the bank to guarantee the execution of certain obligations assumed by the producer of a film. It is not possible at this time to determine the amount, if any, that may eventually be claimed against the Company and its subsidiary. Any amount awarded as a result of these claims will be recorded as a prior year adjustment.

[1] CICA, *Financial Reporting in Canada*, 16th and 17th eds. (Toronto, 1985 and 1987), pp. 37–38, adapted.

Commitments   Contracts for future transactions are called commitments. They are not liabilities. However, commitments (contractual obligations) that are significant or material should be disclosed by footnotes to the financial statements.[2] For example, a professional baseball club may issue a three-year contract to a player at an annual salary of, say, $1 million. This is a commitment to pay for services to be rendered in the future. There is no obligation to make payment until the services are received. Because there is no present obligation, no liability exists. Other examples of commitments include a corporation's long-term employment contract with a key officer, a contract for construction of a new plant, and a contract to buy inventory over a period of years. The common quality of all these commitments is an intent to enter into transactions in the future. Keep in mind that financial statements should not be cluttered with footnotes on insignificant matters. Commitments are disclosed only if they are unusual in nature and material in amount, or if losses from the commitment are being incurred, as evidenced by the following examples from published financial statements of large Canadian corporations.[3]

1   THE ALGOMA STEEL CORP., LTD.

Commitments

(a) The Corporation, as a participant in the Tilden Mine joint venture, is entitled to receive its 30% share of production and is committed to pay its share of costs including minimum charges for principal and interest to cover the servicing of long term debt. The Corporation's share of such minimum charges was $31.5 million in 1986 and will average approximately $26.7 million annually during the next five years. The Corporation's share of long term debt at December 31, 1986 was $112.3 million (U.S. $81.3 million).

(b) The estimated amount required to complete approved capital projects is $45 million which includes $21 million for the new seamless tube mill. At December 31, 1986, contractual commitments amounted to $20 million in respect of these projects.

2   CANADIAN TIRE CORP., LTD.

Commitments

As at December 29 [of the current year], the corporation had commitments of $3,900,000 for the acquisition of property and equipment and the expansion of retail store facilities.

3   CRESTBROOK FOREST INDUSTRIES LTD.

Commitments

A large portion of the company's sales are in U.S. dollars and the company reduces its exposure to exchange fluctuations by entering into forward exchange contracts. These contracts aggregated U.S. $30,000,000 at December 31 [of the current year], at an average rate of Canadian $1.2363. One half of the contracts expire in each of [the next two years].

The company engages in a lumber hedging program whereby it reduces its exposure to lumber price fluctuations. At December 31 [of the current year], the company had hedged 34,710 MFBM at an average price of U.S. $171.59 per MFBM.

[2] CICA, *CICA Handbook* (Toronto), paragraph 3280.01.
[3] CICA, *Financial Reporting in Canada*, pp. 39–40, adapted.

4   LAWSON & JONES LTD.

Capital Commitment

The company has entered into agreements to purchase four major pieces of equipment for approximately $10,824,000. To December 31, 1984, advances of $1,726,000 have been made with payments of $5,266,000 due in 1985 and the remaining $3,832,000 due in semi-annual instalments from 1986 to 1989.

Timely recognition of liabilities

1 Explain how the prompt recognition of liabilities relates to the matching principle of accounting.

Correct timing in the recognition of liabilities is essential to producing dependable financial statements. An omission of a liability from the balance sheet is usually accompanied by the understatement of an expense in the income statement. For example, if an invoice for advertising expense is not recorded in the period it is received, liabilities will be understated and advertising expense will be understated. This understatement of expenses causes net income to be overstated along with the owner's equity. The essential rule is that *a liability must be recognized in the accounting period in which it comes into being.* For purchases of merchandise on credit, the recognition of the liability (as evidenced by the purchase order, purchase invoice, and receiving report) is a routine procedure subject to strong internal controls. However, the recognition of liabilities related to expenses, such as product warranty expense, professional fees, interest, and salaries owed at the end of the period, requires the use of adjusting entries and is more subject to errors and omissions.

The need for prompt recognition of all liabilities stems from the *matching principle* of accounting. This principle requires that we recognize in each period all the expenses incurred in producing the revenue of the period. For expenses that do not require payment until some time after they are incurred, we must record the expense when incurred and credit a liability account to show our obligation to make this later payment.

Current liabilities

2 Define current liabilities and explain how this classification is used in interpreting a balance sheet.

Current liabilities are obligations that must be paid within one year or within the operating cycle, whichever is longer. Another requirement for classification as a current liability is the expectation that the debt will be paid from current assets. Occasionally, a current liability may be replaced with a new short-term liability rather than being paid in cash. For example, a company short of cash may issue a short-term note payable to settle a past-due account payable. Liabilities that do not fall due within one year or within the operating cycle are classified as long-term liabilities.

The current liability classification parallels the current asset classification. As explained in Chapter 5, the amount of working capital (current assets less current liabilities) and the current ratio (current assets divided by current liabilities) are valuable indicators of a company's ability to pay its debts in the near future. In other words, these indicators help us to judge a company's liquidity or solvency.

Among the more common current liabilities are accounts payable, notes payable, dividends payable, current portion of long-term debt (such as this year's required payments on a long-term mortgage), sales taxes payable, accrued liabilities (such as interest payable), revenue collected in advance (such as unearned management fees), payroll liabilities, and estimated liabilities, including product warranty liability and corporate income taxes.

Accounts payable

Accounts payable are sometimes subdivided into trade accounts payable and other accounts payable. Trade accounts payable are short-term obligations to suppliers for purchases of merchandise. Other accounts payable include the liability for acquisition of assets such as office equipment and for any goods and services other than merchandise. We have previously discussed in Chapter 5 the guidelines for maintaining strong internal control over accounts payable. These guidelines include the locating of the purchasing function in a separate purchasing department and making payment only of liabilities that have been approved after comparison of invoice, purchase order, and receiving report. The voucher system is especially useful in providing assurance of the integrity of the system for approving and paying invoices.

NOTES PAYABLE

3   Account for the issuance of notes payable, the accrual of interest, and the payment of a note at maturity.

Notes payable are issued whenever bank loans are obtained. Other transactions that may give rise to notes payable include the purchase of real estate or costly equipment, the purchase of merchandise, and the substitution of a note for a past-due account payable.

Notes payable issued to banks

Assume that on November 1 Porter Company borrows $10,000 from its bank for a period of six months at an annual interest rate of 12%. Six months later on May 1 Porter Company will have to pay the bank the *principal* amount of $10,000 plus $600 interest ($10,000 $\times$ .12 $\times$ $^{6}/_{12}$.)[4] The owners of Porter Company have authorized John Caldwell, the company's treasurer, to sign notes payable issued by the company. The following note issued by Porter Company could read as shown (omitting a few minor details).

THIS NOTE IS FOR
THE PRINCIPAL AMOUNT
WITH INTEREST STATED
SEPARATELY

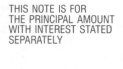

Halifax, Nova Scotia		November 1, 19___

Six months   after this date   Porter Company

promises to pay to Security Bank the sum of $ 10,000

with interest at the rate of   12%   per annum.

Signed   *John Caldwell*

Title   Treasurer

---

[4] As indicated in Chapter 8, a 360-day year is used and the three days of grace are disregarded in the computation of interest in order to focus on concepts rather than precise calculations.

The journal entry in Porter Company's accounting records for this borrowing is:

FACE AMOUNT OF NOTE

Cash 10,000
    Notes Payable   10,000
Borrowed $10,000 for six months at 12% interest per year.

Notice that no liability is recorded for the interest charges when the note is issued. At the date that money is borrowed, the borrower has a liability *only for the principal amount of the loan;* the liability for interest accrues day by day over the life of the loan. At December 31, two months' interest expense has been incurred, and the following year-end adjusting entry is made:

A LIABILITY FOR
INTEREST ACCRUES DAY
BY DAY

Interest Expense 200
    Interest Payable   200
To record interest expense incurred through year-end on 12%,
six-month note dated Nov. 1 ($10,000 × .12 × $^2/_{12}$ = $200).

If we assume that the company does not use reversing entries, the entry on May 1 when the note is paid will be:

PAYMENT OF PRINCIPAL
AND INTEREST

Notes Payable 10,000
Interest Payable   200
Interest Expense   400
    Cash   10,600
To record payment of 12%, six-month note on maturity date
and to recognize interest expense incurred since year-end
($10,000 × .12 × $^4/_{12}$ = $400).

Notes payable with interest charges included in the face amount

4 Explain the accounting treatment of notes payable that have interest included in the face amount.

THIS NOTE SHOWS
INTEREST INCLUDED IN
FACE AMOUNT OF NOTE

Instead of stating the interest rate separately as in the preceding illustration, the note payable issued by Porter Company could have been drawn to include the interest charge in the face amount of the note, as follows:

Halifax, Nova Scotia   November 1, 19__

Six months   after this date   Porter Company

promises to pay to Security Bank the sum of $ 10,600

Signed   *John Caldwell*

Title   Treasurer

Notice that the face amount of this note ($10,600) is greater than the $10,000 amount borrowed. Porter Company's liability at November 1 is only $10,000; the other $600 included in the face amount of the note represents *future interest charges.* As interest expense is incurred over the life of the note, Porter Company's liability will grow to $10,600, just as in the preceding illustration.

The entry to record Porter Company's $10,000 borrowing from the bank at November 1 will be as follows for this type of note payable:

INTEREST INCLUDED IN FACE OF NOTE		
Cash	10,000	
Discount on Notes Payable	600	
Notes Payable		10,600

Issued to bank a 12%, six-month note payable with interest charge included in the face amount of note.

The liability account, Notes Payable, was credited with the full face amount of the note ($10,600). It is therefore necessary to debit a *contra-liability* account, *Discount on Notes Payable,* for the future interest charges included in the face amount of the note. Discount on Notes Payable is shown in the balance sheet as a deduction from Notes Payable. In our illustration, the amounts in the balance sheet would be Notes Payable, $10,600, minus Discount on Notes Payable, $600, or a net liability of $10,000 at November 1.

Discount on Notes Payable   The balance of the account Discount on Notes Payable represents *interest charges applicable to future periods.* As this interest expense is incurred, the balance of the discount account gradually is transferred into the Interest Expense account. Thus, at the maturity date of the note, Discount on Notes Payable will have a zero balance, and the net liability will have increased to $10,600. The process of transferring the amount in the Discount on Notes Payable account into the Interest Expense account is called *amortization* of the discount.

Amortization of the discount   The discount on *short-term* notes payable usually is amortized by the straight-line method, which allocates the same amount of discount to interest expense for each month the note is outstanding.[5] Thus, the $600 discount on the Porter Company note payable will be transferred from Discount on Notes Payable into Interest Expense at the rate of $100 per month ($600 ÷ 6 months).

Adjusting entries should be made to amortize the discount at the end of the year and at the date the note matures. At December 31, Porter Company will make the following adjusting entry to recognize the two months' interest expense incurred since November 1:

AMORTIZATION OF DISCOUNT		
Interest Expense	200	
Discount on Notes Payable		200

To record interest expense incurred to end of year on 12%, six-month note dated Nov. 1 ($600 discount × $^2/_6$).

---

[5] When an interest charge is included in the face amount of a long-term note, the effective interest method of amortizing the discount is often used instead of the straight-line method. The effective interest method of amortization is discussed in Chapter 16.

Notice that the liability for accrued interest is recorded by crediting Discount on Notes Payable rather than Interest Payable. The credit to Discount on Notes Payable reduces the debit balance in this contra-liability account from $600 to $400, thereby increasing the *net liability* for notes payable by $200.

At December 31, Porter Company's net liability for the bank loan will appear in the balance sheet as shown in the following:

LIABILITY SHOWN NET
OF DISCOUNT

Current liabilities:
    Note payable $10,600
    Less: Discount on notes payable 400 $10,200

The net liability of $10,200 consists of the $10,000 principal amount of the debt plus the $200 interest that has accrued since November 1.

When the note matures on May 1, Porter Company will recognize the four months' interest expense incurred since year-end and will pay the bank $10,600. The entry is

TWO-THIRDS OF
INTEREST APPLICABLE
TO SECOND YEAR

Notes Payable   10,600
Interest Expense   400
    Discount on Notes Payable   400
    Cash   10,600
To record payment of six-month note due today and recognize interest expense incurred since year-end ($10,000 × 12% × $^4/_{12}$ = $400).

Comparison of the two forms of notes payable

We have illustrated two alternative methods that Porter Company could use in accounting for its $10,000 bank loan, depending upon the form of the note payable. The journal entries for both methods, along with the resulting balance sheet presentations of the liability at November 1 and December 31, are summarized on the next page. Notice that both methods result in Porter Company recognizing the same amount of interest expense and the same total liability in its balance sheet. The form of the note does not change the economic substance of the transaction.

PAYROLL ACCOUNTING

Labour costs and related payroll taxes constitute a large and constantly increasing portion of the total costs of operating most business organizations. In the commercial airlines, for example, labour costs often have represented 40% to 50% of total operating costs.

The task of accounting for payroll costs would be an important one simply because of the large amounts involved; however, it is further complicated by the government legislation that requires employers to maintain certain specific information in their payroll records not only for the business as a whole but also for each individual employee. Frequent reports of total wages and amounts withheld must be filed with government agencies. These reports are prepared by every employer and must be accompanied by payment to the government of the amounts withheld from employees and of the payroll taxes levied on the employer.

Comparison of the Two Forms of Notes Payable

NOTE WRITTEN FOR $10,000 PLUS 12% INTEREST

ENTRY TO RECORD BORROWING ON NOV. 1

Cash	10,000	
Notes Payable		10,000

PARTIAL BALANCE SHEET AT NOV. 1

Current liabilities:
Notes payable	$10,000

ADJUSTING ENTRY AT DEC. 31

Interest Expense	200	
Interest Payable		200

PARTIAL BALANCE SHEET AT DEC. 31

Current liabilities:
Notes payable	$10,000	
Interest payable	200	$10,200

ENTRY TO RECORD PAYMENT OF NOTE ON MAY 1

Notes Payable	10,000	
Interest Payable	200	
Interest Expense	400	
Cash		10,600

NOTE WRITTEN WITH INTEREST INCLUDED IN FACE AMOUNT

ENTRY TO RECORD BORROWING ON NOV. 1

Cash	10,000	
Discount on Notes Payable	600	
Notes Payable		10,600

PARTIAL BALANCE SHEET AT NOV. 1

Current liabilities:
Notes Payable	$10,600	
Less: Discount on notes payable	600	10,000

ADJUSTING ENTRY AT DEC. 31

Interest Expense	200	
Discount on Notes Payable		200

PARTIAL BALANCE SHEET AT DEC. 31

Current liabilities:
Notes payable	$10,600	
Less: Discount on notes payable	400	$10,200

ENTRY TO RECORD PAYMENT OF NOTE ON MAY 1

Notes Payable	10,600	
Interest Expense	400	
Discount on Notes Payable		400
Cash		10,600

A basic rule in most business organizations is that every employee must be paid on time, and the payment must be accompanied by a detailed explanation of the computations used in determining the net amount received by the employee. The payroll system must therefore be capable of processing the input data (such as employee names, social insurance numbers, hours worked, pay rates, overtime, and taxes) and producing a prompt and accurate output of paycheques, payroll records, withholding statements, and reports to government agencies. In addition, the payroll system must have built-in safeguards against overpayments to employees, the issuance of duplicate paycheques, payments to fictitious employees, and the continuance on the payroll of persons who have been terminated as employees.

Internal control over payrolls

Payroll fraud has a long history. Before the era of social insurance records and computers, payroll records were often handwritten and incomplete. Employees were commonly paid in cash and documentary evidence was scanty. Some specific characteristics of present-day payroll accounting make payroll fraud more difficult. These helpful factors include the required frequent filing of payroll data with the government, and the universal use of employer identification numbers and employees' social insurance numbers. For example, ''padding'' a payroll with fictitious names is more difficult when social insurance numbers must be on file for every employee, individual earnings records must be created, and reports must be submitted to the Revenue Canada, showing for every employee the gross earnings together with unemployment insurance and Canada Pension premiums and income tax withheld.

5 Describe the basic separation of duties in a payroll system and explain how this plan contributes to strong internal control.

However, neither automation of the accounting process nor extensive reporting of payroll data to government has caused payroll fraud to disappear. Satisfactory internal control over payrolls still requires separation and subdivision of duties. In an EDP system, this means clear separation of the functions of systems analysts, programmers, computer operators, and control group personnel.

In most organizations the payroll activities include the functions of (1) employing workers, (2) timekeeping, and (3) payroll preparation and record keeping, and (4) the distribution of pay to employees. Internal control will be strengthened if each of these functions is handled by a separate department.

Personnel (employment) department   The work of the personnel or employment department begins with interviewing and hiring job applicants. When a new employee is hired, the personnel department prepares records showing the date of employment, the authorized rate of pay, and payroll deductions. The personnel department sends a written notice to the payroll department to place the new employee on the payroll. Changes in pay rates and termination of employees will be recorded in personnel department records. When a person's employment is terminated, the personnel department should conduct an exit interview and notify the payroll department to remove the employee's name from the payroll.

Timekeeping   For employees paid by the hour, the time of arrival and departure should be punched on time cards. A new time card should be placed in the rack by the time clock at the beginning of each week or other pay period. Control procedures should exist to ensure that each employee punches his or her own time card and no other. The timekeeping function should be lodged in a separate department that will control the time cards and transmit these source documents to the payroll department.

The payroll department   The input of information to the payroll department consists of hours reported by the timekeeping department, and authorized names, pay rates, and payroll deductions received from the personnel department. The output of the payroll department includes (1) payroll cheques, (2) individual employee records of earnings and deductions, and (3) regular reports to the government showing the earnings of employees and taxes withheld.

Distribution of paycheques   The paycheques prepared in the payroll department are transmitted to the *paymaster,* who distributes them to the employees. The paymaster should not have responsibility for hiring or firing employees, timekeeping, or preparation of the payroll.

Paycheques for absent employees should never be turned over to other employees or to supervisors for delivery. Instead, the absent employee should later pick up the paycheque from the paymaster after presenting proper identification and signing a receipt. The distribution of paycheques by the paymaster provides assurance that paycheques will not continue to be issued to fictitious employees or employees who have been terminated.

The operation of a typical payroll system is illustrated on the flow chart at the top of page 481. Notes have been made indicating the major internal control points within the system.

There is seldom justification for paying employees in cash. The use of paycheques provides better evidence that payments were made only to existing employees at authorized rates. Even in companies with numerous small branches, it is imperative that branch managers *not* be authorized to combine such duties as hiring and firing employees with the preparation of payrolls, or the distribution of paycheques. Much better internal control can be achieved by lodging in the headquarters office the work outlined above relating to employment, pay rates, pay changes, deductions, terminations, payroll preparation, and distribution of paycheques.

Deductions from earnings of employees

6   Account for a payroll, including computation of amounts to be withheld, and payroll taxes on the employer.

The take-home pay of most employees is much less than the gross earnings. Major factors explaining this difference between the amount earned and the amount received are unemployment insurance premiums, Canada Pension Plan contributions, federal and provincial income taxes withheld, and other deductions. The unemployment insurance, Canada Pension Plan, and income taxes are administered by Revenue Canada, Taxation, and employers are required to report and remit to it the total amounts withheld plus their contributions on a twice-monthly or monthly basis, depending on the size of the amount involved.[6] These and other deductions are discussed in the following sections.

[6] The Province of Quebec administers and collects its provincial income tax and pension plan. Also, while the administration of the Unemployment Insurance Act is the joint responsibility of Revenue Canada, Taxation, and Employment and Immigration Canada, the coverage and collection provisions of this Act (and of the Canada Pension Plan Act) are administered by Revenue Canada, Taxation.

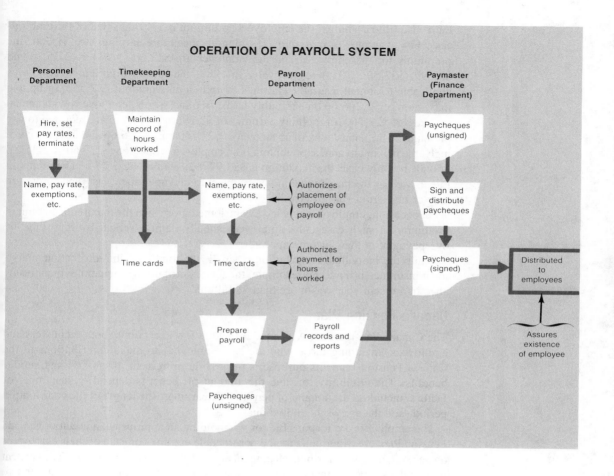

OPERATION OF A PAYROLL SYSTEM

Unemployment Insurance

Since its inception in 1940, the federal Unemployment Insurance Act has undergone significant changes. The current act requires, with a few exceptions, both employers and employees to contribute to unemployment insurance. The purpose of the act is to provide relief from financial hardships for those who are unemployed even though they are willing and able to work. The eligibility for, and the amount of, unemployment benefits depend on a number of factors, including past insurable earnings, length of insurable employment, and regional unemployment rate.

The employers are responsible for withholding an appropriate amount of unemployment insurance premium from their employees. The amount of premium withheld together with the premium contributed by the employer is remitted to Revenue Canada, Taxation. Employees are subject to unemployment insurance premium when they have cash earnings of 20% of the maximum weekly insurable earnings (this maximum amount changes annually, in 1987 it was $530) **or** when they have worked 15 hours a week. For the year 1987, the employees' premium is 2.35% of their insurable earnings; the employers' premium is 1.4 times that of the employees'. For example, if an employee's monthly insurable earnings are $1,000, the premiums for the employee and the employer are $23.50 (1,000 × 2.35%) and $32.90 ($23.50 × 1.4) respectively. In 1987, the rate of premium of 2.35% is applicable to annual insurable earnings of up to a maximum of $27,560, or up to a maximum of $2,296.66 on a monthly basis. In other words, employees with annual earnings of $27,560 (or monthly earnings of $2,296.66) or more are required to pay premium on the annual maximum amount of $27,560 (or $2,296.66 monthly). Accordingly, the maximum annual premium for an employee is $647.66 ($27,560 × 2.35%), or on a monthly basis the maximum is $53.97 ($2,296.66 × 2.35%).[7] The premium rate as well as the maximum amounts subject to unemployment insurance premium may change from year to year.

On occasion, employees may have contributed more than the maximum amount of premium. In such cases, the employees should claim a refund by reporting the overpayment in their income tax returns.

While the individual contribution is small, the total contribution for unemployment insurance is huge. For example, the total contribution of unemployment insurance in a recent year was more than $8 billion.

Canada Pension Plan

The Canada Pension Plan Act requires, with a few exceptions, both employers and employees, including those who are self-employed, to make contributions to the Canada Pension Plan. Its purpose is to provide retirement, disability, and similar benefits. The eligibility for, and the amount of, benefits depend on a number of factors, including the amount of pensionable earnings, the length of the contribution period, and the age of the indivdidual.

The employers are responsible for withholding an appropriate amount of Canada Pension Plan contribution from the pensionable earnings of each of their employees and are required to contribute an amount equal to that of the employees'. The amount withheld together with the amount contributed by the employers is remitted to Revenue Canada, Taxation. For the year 1987, the employees' contribution is 1.9% of the annual pensionable earnings, with the first $2,500 exempted, and the employers' contribution is the same as that of the employees'. For example, if an employee's annual pensionable earnings are $18,000, both the employee and the employer are required to contribute $294.50 each [($18,000 less $2,500 basic annual exemption) times 1.9%]. In 1987, the rate of contribution of 1.9% is applicable to annual pensionable earnings of over $2,500, up to a maximum of $23,400 (i.e., earnings of $25,900 less the $2,500 basic annual exemption). In other words, employees with annual pensionable earnings of $2,500 or less are not required to contribute, and employees with pensionable earnings of $25,900 or more are required to contribute on the maximum amount of $23,400. Accordingly, the maximum annual contribution for an employee is $444.60 ($23,400 × 1.9%).

Since contributions are made periodically, employees with annual earnings exceeding the maximum pensionable earnings may pay up the $444.60 maximum contribution

---

[7] Due to rounding, the monthly figures will add up to less than the annual figure of $647.66. Tables showing the proper premiums at various earning levels are provided by Revenue Canada, Taxation. These tables are for both unemployment insurance and Canada Pension Plan.

in the early part of the year. If an employee, for example, earns $48,000 a year, the monthly contribution is $72.04 ($4,000 less the monthly exemption of $208.33 at 1.9%), and the employee will have contributed $432.24 in the first six months and will only be required to contribute the balance of $12.36 in the seventh month.[8] The rate, and the amount subject to, Canada Pension Plan, may change from year to year. On occasion, an employee may have contributed more than the maximum amount. In such cases, the employee should claim a refund by reporting the overpayment in his or her income tax return.

The Canada Pension Plan applies to all provinces except the province of Quebec, which has its own similar pension plan. The two plans are closely coordinated so that contributing employees are protected wherever they may work in Canada.

The total contribution to Canada Pension Plan is very large; a recent year's contribution amounted to more than $4 billion.

Federal and provincial income taxes

Our pay-as-you-go system of income taxes requires employers to withhold a portion of the earnings of their employees. The amount withheld depends upon the amount of the earnings and upon the amount of income tax exemptions to which the employee is entitled. To er .r re that the proper amount of income tax is withheld, each employee is required to file with the employer a Tax Exemption Return, TD1 form, showing the total amount of exemptions, the Net Claim Code, and the supporting details. However, this return need not be filed by employees claiming the "basic personal exemption" only — i.e., claiming the minimum amount of exemption.

The illustration on the next page shows the relevant portions of the TD1 form for Philip Chanson, who claims a number of exemptions. There are other exemptions such as age, disability, etc., in the TD1 form. These and other aspects of income tax will be discussed in Chapter 18.

Based on the earnings and the amount of exemption, the employer can determine the income tax to be withheld from the employee by referring to the income tax deduction tables provided by Revenue Canada, Taxation. The amount withheld from employees is remitted to Revenue Canada, Taxation. This amount includes both the federal and provincial income taxes for all provinces except the province of Quebec, which collects its own income tax. Thus, employers in Quebec must withhold separate deductions for federal and Quebec income taxes.

Other deductions from employees' earnings

In addition to the compulsory deductions for unemployment insurance, Canada (or Quebec) Pension Plan, and income taxes, many other deductions are voluntarily authorized by employees. Union dues, insurance premiums, savings bond purchases, charitable contributions, retirement programs, and pension plans are examples of voluntary payroll deductions.

---

[8] The monthly exemption is arrived at by dividing the annual exemption of $2,500 by 12. The proper amounts of contributions can be obtained from the deduction tables provided by Revenue Canada, Taxation. Since the exemption has already been taken into account in these tables, there is no need to deduct the monthly or weekly exemption from the earnings. For example, if the monthly earnings plus taxable benefits, if any, are $1,000, look up the earnings' bracket between $999.65 and $1,000.17 to obtain the proper amount of contribution, which is $15.04.

Revenue Canada Taxation	Revenu Canada Impôt	TAX EXEMPTION RETURN - PART B DÉCLARATION D'EXEMPTION D'IMPÔT - PARTIE B	TD1 Rev. 1987

FAMILY NAME (Print) - *NOM DE FAMILLE (en majuscules)*
Chanson

ADDRESS - *ADRESSE*
80 Sleepy Hollow Road
Greenwich, Ontario N8E 3L8

USUAL FIRST NAME AND INITIALS - *PRÉNOM USUEL ET INITIALES*
Philip K.

FOR NON-RESIDENT ONLY - *RÉSERVÉ AUX NON-RÉSIDENTS*
COUNTRY OF PERMANENT RESIDENCE
PAYS DE LA RÉSIDENCE PERMANENTE

EMPLOYEE NO. - *NUMÉRO DE L'EMPLOYÉ*
101

SOCIAL INSURANCE NUMBER
NUMÉRO D'ASSURANCE SOCIALE
123 456 789

DATE OF BIRTH - *DATE DE NAISSANCE*

Day - *Jour*	Month - *Mois*	Year - *Année*
18	11	1938

Claim for Exemptions — *Exemptions demandées*

1. Basic Personal Exemption - *Exemption personnelle de base* ▶ 4,220.00

2. Claim only one of these two exemptions - *Demandez une seule des deux exemptions suivantes:*

2.1 **If Married and Supporting Spouse** - *Si vous êtes marié(e) et assurez le soutien de votre conjoint*
See Note 5 in Part A - *Voyez le numéro 5 de la Partie A*

☐ whose net income for the year will not exceed } 520   Claim - *Demandez* 3,700
dont le revenu net pour l'année ne dépassera pas

☐ whose net income for the year will exceed } 520 but not   4,220.00
dont le revenu net pour l'année dépassera sans dépasser

Less: spouse's net income - *Moins le revenu du conjoint*
Claim - *Demandez* ▶ **3,700 00**

---

3. Exemption for Dependant Children

See Note 7 in Part A, give details and claim according to:

(i) **under age 18** at December 31st and net income will not exceed $3,100 claim $560. If net income exceeds $3,100 but $4,220 claim $560 minus one half the amount in excess of $3,100.

(ii) **age 18 or over** at December 31st and net income will not exceed $1,820 claim $1,200. If net income exceeds $1,820 but not $4,220 claims $1,200 minus one half the amount in excess $1,820.

or (iii) **age 18 or over** at December 31st and **mentally or physically infirm** and net income will not exceed $2,770 claim $1,450. If net income exceeds $2,770 but not $4,220 claim $1,450 minus the amount in excess of $2,770.

3. Exemption pour enfants à charge

Voyez le numéro 7 de la Partie A, donnez les précisions demandées et demandez l'exemption selon ce qui suit:

(i) **moins de 18 ans** le 31 décembre. Si son revenu ne dépassera pas 3100$, demandez 560$. Si son revenu net se situera entre 3100$ et 4220$, demandez 560$, moins la moitié de la fraction qui dépasse 3100$.

(ii) **18 ans ou plus** le 31 décembre. Si son revenu net ne dépassera pas 1820$, demandez 1200$. Si son revenu net se situera entre 1820$ et 4220$, demandez 1200$, moins la moitié de la fraction qui dépasse 1820$.

ou (iii) **18 ans ou plus** le 31 décembre, mais l'enfant souffre **d'une incapacité physique ou mentale**. Si son revenu net ne dépassera pas 2770$, demandez 1450$. Si son revenu net se situera entre 2770$, et 4220$, demandez 1450$, moins la fraction qui dépasse 2770$.

Name of child (Attach list if space is insufficient) - *Nom de l'enfant (Faute d'espace annexez une liste)*	Estimated annual net Income - *Revenu net annuel estimatif*	Date of birth - *Date de naissance*			If over 21, state school attended *S il a plus de 21 ans, indiquez l'école fréquentée*		
		Day *Jour*	Month *Mois*	Year *Année*			
David	1,680	8	10	1968		▶ 1,200	00
Linda	2,800	6	12	1973		▶ 560	00

8. Total add items 1 to 7   **8. Total** Additionnez les montants 1 à 7 ▶ **9,680 00**

9. Deduct: Taxable Family Allowance Payments
(To be received in year for children claimed above.)
9. Soustraire: les allocations familiales imposables
(À recevoir au cours de l'année pour les enfants nommés ci-dessus.) ▶ **766 00**

10. Net Claim, item 8 less item 9
(Will not be less than $4,220. Enter this amount on reverse side of Part A.)
10. Demande nette, montant 8 moins montant 9
(Ne doit pas être inférieure à 4220$. Inscrivez ce montant au verso de la Partie A.) ▶ **8,914 00**

11. Enter the Net Claim Code as per the Table of Net Claim Codes contained in Part A. This code is not for the computer users but only for those employers/payers using the booklet "Tables - Income Tax Deductions at Source"
11. Inscrivez le code de demande nette, selon la Table des codes de demande nette qui se trouve à la Partie A. Ce code ne s'applique pas aux utilisateurs d'ordinateurs, mais seulement aux employeurs et aux payeurs qui utilisent les tables de retenues à la source d'impôt sur le revenu ▶ **9**

Table of Net Claim Codes 1987 *Table des codes de demande nette*

Net Claim - *Demande nette* Exceeding - Not exceeding *Excédant - N'excédant pas*	Net Claim Code *Code de demande nette*	Net Claim - *Demande nette* Exceeding - Not exceeding *Excédant - N'excédant pas*	Net Claim Code *Code de demande nette*
For use re: Tables 11 and 12 *Utilisation: Tables 11 et 12*	0	7,890 – 8,660	8
4,219 – 4,270	1	8,660 – 9,470	9
4,270 – 4,940	2	9,470 – 10,360	10
4,940 – 5,670	3	10,360 – 11,230	11
5,670 – 6,310	4	11,230 – 12,060	12
6,310 – 7,140	5	12,060 – 12,710	13
7,140 – 7,510	6	12,710 and up - *et plus*	X
7,510 – 7,890	7	No tax withholding required *Aucune retenue d'impôt requise*	E

Source: Revenue Canada Taxation. Reproduced with permission of the Minister of Supply and Services Canada.

Employer's responsibility for amounts withheld

In withholding amounts from an employee's earnings for either voluntary or involuntary deductions, the employer acts merely as a collection agent. The amounts withheld are paid to the designated organization, such as a government agency or labour union. The employer is also responsible for maintaining accounting records that will enable it to file required reports and make timely payments of the amounts withheld. From the employer's viewpoint, the amounts withheld from employees' earnings represent current liabilities.

Illustration: computation of employee's net pay

This illustration shows the deductions that typically may explain the difference between *gross earnings* for a pay period and the "take-home" pay, or net amount received by an employee. The deductions are in part based upon the amount of exemptions indicated in Philip Chanson's Tax Exemption Return. The pay period is for the month of June.

TOTAL EARNINGS
MINUS DEDUCTIONS
EQUALS TAKE-HOME
PAY

Gross earnings of employee Chanson for the month		$3,600.00
Deductions:		
Unemployment insurance	$ 53.97	
Canada Pension Plan	64.44	
Income tax	880.75	
Registered pension plan (assume 8%)	288.00	
Group insurance	32.84	
Total deductions from Chanson's earnings		1,320.00
Net take-home pay for the month for employee Chanson		$2,280.00

While the deductions of registered pension plan and group insurance are based on the agreement between Philip Chanson and his employer and thus do not require further clarification, the other three deductions do require some brief explanation. The unemployment insurance of $53.97 is the maximum monthly premium because Chanson's annual earnings exceed the maximum insurable annual earnings of $27,560. Thus, the premium is computed as: ($27,560 ÷ 12) × 2.35% = $53.97. The Canada Pension Plan contribution of $64.44 is computed by taking 1.9% of the pensionable earnings of $3,391.67 (i.e., $3,600 less the monthly exemption of $208.33). Since the maximum annual contribution is $444.60 and Chanson has thus far contributed $386.64 (6 months at $64.44), he will contribute only $57.96 in the month of July to make up the total of $444.60 and he will not be required to contribute any further. Consequently, Chanson's take-home pay will be more in those subsequent months, provided his monthly earnings remain at $3,600.

The income tax deduction of $880.75 is obtained from one of the income tax deduction tables published by Revenue Canada, Taxation, based on the monthly salary of $3,600 and the "net claim code" of 9 indicated in Chanson's TD1. These tables show the amounts to be deducted for employees at various earnings levels and for varying amounts of exemptions. A small section of an income tax deduction table appears at the top of page 486; the amount applicable to Philip Chanson in our illustration is circled. It should be noted that the amounts of income tax in the table are subject to frequent changes.

MONTHLY PAY Use appropriate bracket — PAIE PAR MOIS Utilisez le palier approprié	ONTARIO **MONTHLY TAX DEDUCTIONS** Basis — 12 Pay Periods per Year			**TABLE 5**				ON **RETENUES D'I** Base — 12 période		
	IF THE EMPLOYEE'S "NET CLAIM CODE" ON FORM TD1 IS — SI LE ·CODE DE DEMANDE NETTE· DE L'EMPLOYÉ SEL									
	1	**2**	**3**	**4**	**5**	**6**	**7**	**8**	**9**	**10**
	DEDUCT FROM EACH PAY — *RETENEZ SUR CHAQUE PAIE*									
3412.00 - 3451.99	973.95	961.70	939.40	917.55	910.05	875.00	863.05	844.70	819.55	792.45
3452.00 - 3491.99	989.25	977.00	954.70	932.85	925.35	890.30	878.35	860.00	834.85	807.75
3492.00 - 3531.99	1006.90	992.30	970.00	948.15	940.65	905.60	893.65	875.30	850.15	823.05
3532.00 - 3571.99	1025.25	1010.55	985.30	963.45	955.95	920.90	908.95	890.60	865.45	838.35
3572.00 - 3611.99	1043.60	1028.90	1002.10	978.75	971.25	936.20	924.25	905.90	880.75	853.65
3612.00 - 3651.99	1061.95	1047.25	1020.45	994.25	986.55	951.50	939.55	921.20	896.05	868.95
3652.00 - 3691.99	1080.35	1065.60	1038.85	1012.65	1003.65	966.80	954.85	936.50	911.35	884.25
3692.00 - 3731.99	1098.70	1083.95	1057.20	1031.00	1022.00	982.10	970.15	951.80	926.65	899.55
3732.00 - 3771.99	1117.05	1102.35	1075.55	1049.35	1040.35	998.30	985.45	967.10	941.95	914.85
3772.00 - 3811.99	1135.40	1120.70	1093.90	1067.70	1058.70	1016.65	1002.30	982.40	957.25	930.15

Source: Revenue Canada Taxation. Reproduced with permission of the Minister of Supply and Services Canada.

Payroll records and procedures

Although payroll records and procedures vary greatly according to the number of employees and the extent of automation in processing payroll data, there are a few fundamental steps common to payroll work in most organizations. One of these steps taken at the end of each pay period is the preparation of a *payroll register* showing for each employee the gross earnings, amounts withheld, and net pay. When the computation of the payroll register has been completed, the next step is to reflect the expense and the related liabilities in the ledger accounts. A general journal entry such as the following may be used to bring into the accounts the information summarized in the payroll register. (This entry does not include payroll taxes on the employer.)

JOURNAL ENTRY TO
RECORD PAYROLL

Sales Salaries Expense	5,800	
Office Salaries Expense	4,200	
Liability for Unemployment Insurance Withheld		235
Liability for Canada Pension Plan Withheld		166
Liability for Income Tax Withheld		1,479
Liability for Group Insurance Withheld		220
Salaries Payable		7,900

To record the payroll for the month.

The two debits to expense accounts indicate that the business has incurred salary expense of $10,000; however, only $7,900 of this amount will be paid to the employees on payday. The payment will be recorded by a debit to Salaries Payable and a credit to Cash. The remaining $2,100 (consisting of deductions for unemployment insurance, Canada Pension Plan, income tax and insurance premiums withheld) is lodged in liability accounts. Payment of these liabilities will be made at various later dates.

Statement of Remuneration Paid   Employers are required to furnish every employee with a Statement of Remuneration Paid (T4), as shown in the following illustration

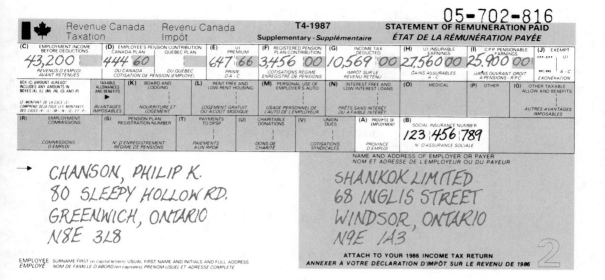

Source: Revenue Canada Taxation. Reproduced with permission of the Minister of Supply and Services Canada.

This statement shows the gross earnings for the calendar year and the amounts withheld for unemployment insurance, Canada Pension Plan, income tax, and registered pension plan. The employer is required to send a copy of this statement to Revenue Canada, Taxation, on or before the last day of February of the following year. When the employee files an income tax return, he or she must attach a copy (copy 2) of this statement.

Payroll taxes on the employer

As discussed earlier in this chapter, employers are required to contribute to unemployment insurance and Canada Pension Plan. These contributions are expenses to the business and are commonly called "payroll taxes expense."

Accounting entry for employer's payroll taxes   The entry to record the employer's payroll taxes is usually made at the same time the payroll is recorded. To illustrate, let us use again the $10,000 payroll first used on page 486 in the discussion of amounts withheld from employees; this time, however, we are illustrating taxes levied on the employer.

JOURNAL ENTRY TO
RECORD PAYROLL TAXES
ON EMPLOYER

Payroll Taxes Expense	495	
Unemployment Insurance Tax Payable		329
Canada Pension Plan Tax Payable		166
To record payroll taxes on employer for the month.		

Thus the total payroll expense for the employer is $10,495, which consists of wages of $10,000 and payroll taxes of $495.

Workers' Compensation   In addition to unemployment insurance and Canada Pension Plan, employers are required by *provincial* legislation to make a contribution to Workers' Compensation Board. The purpose of the provincial legislation is to provide compensation, including medical costs, to employees who have suffered injury from accidents arising out of and in the course of employment. The responsibility for contribution rests solely with the employers; thus, the employees are not required to contribute.

The amount of contribution is based on a number of factors, including the amount of the payroll, the nature of employment, and the accident-cost records. The employer should record the workers' compensation contribution as an expense to the business and recognize the liability when the assessment from the Workers' Compensation Board is received.

Distinction between employees and independent contractors

Every business obtains personal services from *employees* and also from *independent contractors.* The employer-employee relationship exists when the company paying for the services has a right to direct and supervise the person rendering the services. Independent contractors, on the other hand, are retained to perform a specific task and exercise their own judgment as to the best methods for performing the work. Examples of independent contractors include CAs engaged to perform an audit, lawyers retained to represent a company in a lawsuit, and a plumber called in to repair a broken pipe. The *fees* paid to independent contractors are not included in payroll records and are not subject to withholding or payroll taxes.

END-OF-CHAPTER REVIEW

SUMMARY OF CHAPTER LEARNING OBJECTIVES

1 Explain how the prompt recognition of liabilities relates to the matching principle of accounting.

The matching principle requires that we recognize all the expenses incurred in producing the revenue of the period. To record expenses that do not require payment until a later date, we recognize promptly our liability to make this later payment and also record the related expense.

2 Define current liabilities and explain how this classification is used in interpreting a balance sheet.

Current liabilities are debts to be paid out of current assets within one year or the operating cycle, whichever is longer. By computing the current ratio and the amount of working capital, we compare the current assets with current liabilities and form an opinion as to a company's short-term debt-paying ability.

3 Account for the issuance of notes payable, the accrual of interest, and the payment of a note at maturity.

Notes payable are issued to obtain bank loans and often for the purchase of real estate and high-cost equipment. The Notes Payable account is credited with the face amount of the note at the time of issuance and debited with the face amount when the note is paid at maturity. The interest may be stated separately or included in the face amount of the note. In either case the interest accrued at the end of each fiscal period should be recognized by use of adjusting entries. Interest is also recognized at the maturity of each note.

4 Explain the accounting treatment of notes payable that have interest included in the face amount.

The face amount of a note may include the principle amount of the debt plus future interest charges for the life of the note. The entry to record a note in this form includes a debit to Discount on Notes Payable for the future interest charges and a credit to Notes Payable for the face amount of the note. The discount is amortized over the life of the note by transfer to interest expense. Amortizing the discount causes the carrying value of the liability to rise gradually over the life of the note and to reach the face amount at maturity.

5 Describe the basic separation of duties in a payroll system and explain how this plan contributes to strong internal control.

The separation of duties needed to achieve strong internal control over payrolls includes placing in separate departments the functions of (a) personnel (employment), (b) timekeeping, (c) preparation of payroll cheques, records, and reports, and (d) distribution of paycheques. With this separation of duties, payroll fraud such as placing fictitious names on the payroll, overstating employees' earnings, or retaining employees' names on the payroll after their termination would be next to impossible without collusion between departments.

6 Account for a payroll, including computation of amounts to be withheld, and payroll taxes on the employer.

Accounting for a payroll includes computing the gross earnings for each employee, making the proper deductions for unemployment insurance and Canada Pension Plan withheld, income taxes withheld, and any other deductions authorized by employees. The employer's share of unemployment insurance and Canada Pension Plan must also be computed and recorded as expenses. The employer must maintain accounting records which will permit the filing of required reports and timely payment of both payroll taxes and amounts withheld from employees' cheques.

KEY TERMS INTRODUCED OR EMPHASIZED IN CHAPTER 11

Amortization of discount The process of systematically writing off to interest expense each period a portion of the discount on a note payable. Causes the carrying value of the liability to rise to the face value of the note by the maturity date.

Canada Pension Plan A national plan established by a federal act that requires both the employer and the employee to make contributions to the plan. Its purpose is to provide retirement, disability, and similar benefits.

Commitments Agreements to carry out future transactions. Not a liability because the transaction has not yet been performed, but should be disclosed in footnotes to the financial statements if the commitment is significant.

Contingent liability A potential liability that either will develop into a full-fledged liability or will be eliminated entirely by a future event.

Contra liability account A ledger account that is deducted from or offset against a related liability account in the balance sheet. For example, Discount on Notes Payable.

Discount on Notes Payable A contra liability account representing any interest charges applicable to future periods included in the face amount of a note payable. Over the life of the note, the balance of the Discount on Notes Payable account is amortized into Interest Expense.

Gross earnings Total amount earned by an employee before deductions such as unemployment insurance, Canada Pension Plan, income tax withheld, and any voluntary deductions.

Independent contractor A person or firm providing services to a company for a fee or commission. Not controlled or supervised by the client company. Not subject to payroll taxes.

Maturity value The value of a note at its maturity date, consisting of principal plus any interest payable at that date.

Note payable A liability evidenced by issuance of a formal written promise to pay a certain amount of money, usually with interest, at a future date.

Payroll A record listing the names of employees during a given pay period, the rates of pay, time worked, gross earnings, deductions for taxes and any other amounts withheld, and net pay.

Payroll register A form of payroll record showing for each pay period all payroll information for employees individually and in total.

Principal amount That portion of the maturity value of a note that is attributable to the amount borrowed or to the cost of the asset acquired when the note was issued, rather than being attributable to interest charges.

Statement of Remuneration Paid (T4) A form furnished by the employer to every employee that shows the gross earnings for the calendar year and the amounts withheld for unemployment insurance, Canada Pension Plan, income tax, and other items such as registered pension plan.

Tax Exemption Return (TD1) A form prepared and signed by the employee that shows the total amount of exemptions and the supporting details. It is used to determine the proper amount of income tax to be withheld from the employee's remuneration.

Unemployment insurance An insurance plan established by a federal act that imposes a premium contribution on both the employer and the employee. Its purpose is to provide relief from financial hardships for the unemployed.

Workers' Compensation A provincial legislation that requires the employer to make a contribution to the Workers' Compensation Board. Its purpose is to provide compensation to employees who have suffered injury from accidents arising out of and in the course of employment.

ASSIGNMENT MATERIAL

REVIEW QUESTIONS

1 Distinguish between:

   a Current and long-term liabilities

   b Estimated and contingent liabilities

2 Should commitments or contingent liabilities appear on a balance sheet? If so, in what part of the balance sheet?

3 Jonas Company issues a 90-day, 12% note payable to replace an account payable to Smith Supply Company in the amount of $8,000. Draft the journal entries (in general journal form) to record the issuance of the note payable and the payment of the note at the maturity date. (Disregard the three days of grace and use a 360-day year.)

4 Howard Benson applied to the City Bank for a loan of $20,000 for a period of three months. The loan was granted at an annual interest rate of 12%. Write a sentence illustrating the wording of the note signed by Benson if

a Interest is stated separately in the note.

b Interest is included in the face amount of the note.

5 With reference to Question **4** give the journal entry required on the books of Howard Benson for issuance of each of the two types of notes.

6 Sylmar Industries buys a substantial amount of equipment having an estimated service life of five years by issuing a two-year note payable. The note includes no mention of an interest charge. Explain the errors that will result in the future financial statements of Sylmar Industries if the equipment and related liability are recorded at the face value, rather than the present value, of the note.

7 The personnel department of Meadow Company failed to notify the payroll department that five hourly factory workers had been terminated at the end of the last pay period. Assuming a normal subdivision of duties regarding personnel, timekeeping, preparation of payroll, and distribution of paycheques, what control procedure will prevent the payroll department from preparing paycheques for these five employees in the current period?

8 That type of payroll fraud known as "padding" a payroll is a more difficult manoeuvre under today's payroll accounting practices than it was a generation or more ago. What present-day factors make the padding of payrolls a complex and more difficult type of fraud?

9 Name the deductions that employers are required to withhold from employees. What account or accounts would be credited with the amounts withheld?

10 Explain which of the following taxes relating to an employee's wages are borne by the employee and which by the employer:

a Workers' Compensation

b Unemployment insurance

c Canada Pension Plan

d Income taxes

11 Is the Salary Expense account equal to "take-home" pay or to gross earnings? Why?

12 Distinguish between an employee and an independent contractor. Why is this distinction important with respect to payroll accounting?

EXERCISES

**Exercise 11-1
Accounting
terminology**

Listed below are nine technical accounting terms introduced in this chapter:

Estimated liabilities	Payroll register	Maturity value of note
Unemployment insurance	Independent contractor	Contingent liabilities
Commitments	Canada Pension Plan	Discount on Notes Payable

Each of the following statements may (or may not) describe one of these technical terms. For each statement, indicate the accounting term described, or answer "None" if the statement does not correctly describe any of the terms.

a The principal amount of a promissory note plus any interest payable at the maturity date.

b A federal tax based on payrolls and imposed at a higher amount on employers than on employees.

c Legal obligations that are known to exist but for which the dollar amount is presently uncertain.

d Information presented in footnotes to financial statements concerning agreements to carry out certain transactions in the future.

e Interest charges included in the face amount of a note payable.

f An employee whose compensation is based on units of output rather than an hourly wage or a monthly salary.

g A federal tax based on payrolls and imposed equally on both employers and employees.

Exercise 11-2
Two forms for notes payable

Mavis Corporation on November 1 borrowed $100,000 from a local bank and agreed to repay that amount plus 12% interest (per year) at the end of six months. Show two different presentations of the liability to the bank on Mavis Corporation's December 31 balance sheet, assuming that the note payable to the bank was drawn as follows:

a For $100,000, with interest stated separately and payable at maturity

b With the total interest charge included in the face amount of the note

Exercise 11-3
Interest included in face amount of note payable

Ram Truck Lines bought three trucks from Scott Motors on April 1, 1988 for a total price of $204,000. Under the terms of the purchase, Ram Truck Lines paid $60,000 cash and issued a promissory note due in full 18 months later. The face amount of the note was $161,280, which included interest on the note for the 18 months.

Prepare all entries (in general journal form) for Ram Truck Lines relating to the purchase of the trucks and the note for the fiscal year ended December 31, 1988. Include the adjusting entries to record interest expense and depreciation expense to December 31. (The trucks are to be depreciated over an eight-year service life by the straight-line method. There is no estimated salvage value.)

Exercise 11-4
Internal control over payroll

A foreman in the factory of Barton Products, a large manufacturing company, discharged an employee but did not notify the personnel department of this action. The foreman then began forging the employee's signature on time cards. When giving out paycheques, the foreman diverted to his own use the paycheques drawn payable to the discharged worker. What internal control measure would be most effective in preventing this fraudulent activity?

Exercise 11-5
Determine Canada Pension Plan, unemployment insurance, and income tax deductions

Diane Hill was employed as a chemist throughout the year at Metal Industries. Her monthly salary was $3,600 during the first six months of the year; on July 1 her salary was increased to $3,800 monthly. Hill's TD1 form shows a net claim of $7,900 and a net claim code of 8. Assume that Canada Pension Plan contribution is 2% on the first $26,000 earned in a calendar year, with a $3,000 exemption, and that unemployment insurance is 2.4% on a maximum monthly insurable earning of $2,300.

Compute Diane Hill's deductions for Canada Pension Plan contribution, unemployment insurance, and income tax withheld, and her net pay for the month of June and for the month of July. (Refer to the withholding tables on page 486 to determine the amounts of income tax withheld.)

Exercise 11-6
Journal entries for payroll and payroll taxes

The payroll record of Miller Company for the month of January showed the following amounts for total earnings: sales employees, $8,800; office employees, $9,200. Amounts withheld consisted of unemployment insurance premium, $432, Canada Pension Plan, $342, and income tax, $3,280.

a Prepare a general journal entry to record the payroll. Do not include taxes on the employer.

b Prepare a general journal entry to record the payroll taxes expense to Miller Company relating to this payroll. Assume that the employer's rate for unemployment insurance is 1.4 times the employees' premium and that the employer's contribution to Canada Pension Plan is the same as the employees'.

Exercise 11-7
Employer's payroll taxes

The payroll of Fields Company may be summarized as follows:

Gross earnings of employees	$100,000
Employee earnings subject to unemployment insurance	90,000
Employee earnings subject to Canada Pension Plan	86,000

Assuming that the employer is required to contribute unemployment insurance at 1.4 times the employee's rate of 2.35% and to contribute 1.9% to Canada Pension Plan, compute the amount of Fields Company's payroll taxes expense for the year, showing separately the amount of each of the two taxes. (Note: Taxes on employees are not involved in this exercise.)

PROBLEMS

Group A

Problem 11A-1
Liabilities: their valuation and disclosure

The six events listed below occurred at Capitol Products on or near the end of the fiscal year, December 31.

a On December 15, signed a contract for purchase of 50,000 barrels of oil a month for the next 18 months at a price of $15 a barrel. As of December 31, the quoted market price per barrel for oil of this grade had declined to $13 a barrel.

b On December 31, discounted a $200,000 note receivable at a bank and received cash of $198,000. The note bears interest at 9% a year and has a total life of one year.

c On October 31, borrowed $500,000 from a bank and signed a 6-month note payable for $530,000 with interest included in the face amount.

d On December 31, purchased machinery at a price of $200,000 and signed a note payable due six months from today in the total amount of $210,000. Interest of $10,000 was included in the face amount of the note.

e On December 31, signed a two-year contract with a labour union providing for a 4% increase in wage rates each year. The increase in wages for the first year was estimated at $1,300,000.

f At December 31, the ledger account Salaries Payable had a balance of $220,000.

Instructions

For each of the six events, you are to indicate the dollar amount, if any, which should appear in the current liability section of the December 31 balance sheet. If any event does not affect current liabilities, indicate whether it should appear in the balance sheet, and the proper location and dollar amount.

Problem 11A-2
Current liabilities: journal entries

During the year ended December 31, Rockport Associates had a number of transactions relating to accounts payable and notes payable. Among these transactions the following were to be found:

Mar. 6 Purchased merchandise from A.B. Hayes on open account, $25,200.

Apr. 8 Informed A.B. Hayes that it was unable to make payment as previously agreed. Issued to Hayes a 14%, eight-month note to replace the open account payable.

Apr. 20 Borrowed $48,000 from Canadian National Bank today and signed a six-month, 16% note as evidence of indebtedness. The interest was added to the $48,000 amount borrowed and included in the face amount of the note.

May 15 Purchased merchandise from Birmingham, Incorporated, on 30-day open account, $19,200.

Oct. 20 Paid note (principal and interest) due today at Canadian National Bank.

Dec. 8 Paid note (principal and interest) due today to A.B. Hayes.

Instructions Prepare all necessary journal entries (in general journal form) to record the above transactions in the accounts of Rockport Associates. Show all supporting computations as part of the explanations of the journal entries. Adjusting entries are not required. (Disregard the three days of grace.)

Problem 11A-3
Notes payable;
accruing interest

During the fiscal year ended October 31, Dunleer Corporation carried out the following transactions involving notes payable.

June 6 Borrowed $11,200 from Tom Hutchins, issuing to him a 45-day, 12% note payable.

July 13 Purchased office equipment from Harper Company. The invoice amount was $16,800 and Harper Company agreed to accept as full payment a 12%, three-month note for the invoiced amount.

July 21 Paid the Hutchins note plus accrued interest.

Sept. 1 Borrowed $235,200 from National Bank at an interest rate of 12% per annum; signed a 90-day note with interest included in the face amount of the note.

Oct. 1 Purchased merchandise in the amount of $3,000 from Kramer Co. Gave in settlement a three-month note bearing interest at 14%.

Oct. 13 The $16,800 note payable to Harper Company matured today. Paid the interest accrued and issued a new 30-day, 12% note to replace the maturing note.

Instructions **a** Prepare journal entries (in general journal form) to record the above transactions. (Use a 360-day year and disregard the three days of grace in making the interest calculations.)

b Prepare the adjusting entries needed at October 31, prior to closing the accounts. Use one entry for the two notes on which interest is stated separately and a separate entry for the National Bank note in which interest is included in the face amount of the note.

Problem 11A-4
Notes payable: a
comprehensive
problem

The following transactions relating to notes payable were completed by Desktop Graphics during the three months ended June 30. (Use a 360-day year and disregard the three days of grace in computing interest.)

Apr. 1 Bought office equipment for use in the business from Stylecraft, Inc., for $39,000, making a $5,400 cash down payment and issuing a one-year note payable for the balance. The face amount of the note was $38,976, which included a 16% interest charge. Use one compound journal entry that includes Discount on Notes Payable.

Apr. 16 Paid $15,000 cash and issued a 90-day, 12%, $27,000 note to Hall Company in settlement of open account payable in the amount of $42,000.

Apr. 25 Purchased more office equipment from Bryan Hall Limited for $52,200, issuing a 60-day, 11% note payable in settlement.

May 11 Borrowed $216,000 from Manufacturers Bank, issuing a 90-day note payable as evidence of indebtedness. An interest charge computed at 15% per year was included in the face amount of the note.

June 15 Purchased merchandise on account from Phoenix Co., $54,000.

June 18 Issued a 60-day note bearing interest at 11% in settlement of the account payable to Phoenix Co.

June 24 Paid the 60-day, 11% note due to Bryan Hall Limited, which matured today.

Instructions

a Prepare journal entries (in general journal form) to record the listed transactions for the three months ended June 30.

b Prepare adjusting entries to record the interest expense on notes payable through June 30. Prepare one adjusting entry to record the accrued interest payable on the two notes for which interest is stated separately (the Hall Company note and the Phoenix Co. note). The other adjusting entry should record the amortization of discount on the two notes in which interest is included in the face amount (the Stylecraft, Inc., note and the Manufacturers Bank note).

c Prepare a partial balance sheet at June 30 reflecting the above transactions. Show Notes Payable to Bank as one item and Notes Payable: Other as a separate liability. Also include the interest payable in the current liability section of the balance sheet.

Problem 11A-5
Payroll fraud

Friendly Finance Limited makes small loans through a network of more than 100 branch offices in several provinces. A branch manager is in charge of each office and the number of employees under the manager's supervision is usually from four to seven. Each branch manager prepares a weekly payroll sheet, including his or her own salary. All employees are paid from cash on hand. The employees sign the payroll sheet signifying receipt of their salaries. Hours worked by hourly personnel are inserted in the payroll sheet from time cards prepared by the employees and approved by the manager.

The weekly payroll sheets are sent to the home office along with other accounting statements and reports. The home office compiles employee earnings records and prepares all government salary reports from the payroll sheets.

Salaries are established by home office job evaluation schedules. Salary adjustments, promotions, and transfers of full-time employees are approved by a home office salary committee based upon recommendations of branch managers and area supervisors. Branch managers advise the salary committee of new full-time employees and terminations. Part-time and temporary employees are hired without referral to the salary committee.

Instructions

You are to evaluate the company's payroll system, especially the internal control features, and then suggest five ways in which the branch managers might carry out payroll fraud.

Problem 11A-6
Determine income tax and payroll cost; entries for payroll

Gary Norton, an accountant employed by Land Corporation, earned $41,520 in the calendar year just ended. His salary was unchanged throughout the year and was paid monthly in the amount of $3,460. Norton's TD1 form shows a net claim of $7,630 and a net claim code of 7. The income tax withheld from Norton's monthly salary can be determined by reference to the deduction table on page 486. Assume that Canada Pension Plan is 1.9% on the first $25,900, with a $2,500 exemption, and that unemployment insurance is 2.35% on earnings up to $27,560. Also withheld from Norton's paycheques was a monthly deduction of $50 authorized by Norton for group insurance. Note that the total of this deduction for the year was $600.

Instructions   **a** Determine the amount of income tax withheld during the entire year from Norton's cheques.

b Prepare two general journal entries summarizing the payroll transactions with employee Norton for the entire year. (Do not show monthly amounts.) The first entry should summarize the gross pay and deductions for Norton but should not include payroll taxes on the employer. Ignore any payments of tax or insurance during the year and let the liability accounts show the totals for the year. Credit Cash for the amount paid to Norton.

In a second entry, record the payroll taxes on the employer for the entire year. Assume that the employer's rate for unemployment insurance is 1.4 times the employee's premium and that the employer's contribution to Canada Pension Plan is the same as the employee's. Again, ignore any payments of tax during the year and let the liability accounts show the totals for the year.

c Compute the total yearly cost (including taxes) to Land Corporation of having Norton on the payroll at an annual salary of $41,520.

Problem 11A-7
Entries for payroll
and payroll taxes;
determine total
payroll cost

The payroll records of Florenceville Company for the first week in January showed total salaries earned by employees of $15,000. This total included $9,000 of salaries to sales employees and $6,000 to office employees.

The amounts withheld from employee's pay consisted of unemployment insurance of $290, Canada Pension Plan of $210, income taxes of $2,800, and group insurance premiums of $140.

Instructions   **a** Prepare a general journal entry to summarize the preceding payroll and the deductions from the earnings of employees. Payroll taxes on the employer are not to be included in this entry.

b Prepare a general journal entry to summarize the payroll taxes on the employer associated with the above payroll. Assumed tax rates are as follows: unemployment insurance at 1.4 times employee's premium and Canada Pension Plan at the same rate as that of the employees'.

c What is the amount of the total payroll expense of Florenceville Company for the first week in January? Show computations.

Problem 11A-8
Determine payroll
taxes

The employees' earnings records of Dartmouth Ltd. at April 30 in the current year are as follows:

EMPLOYEE	CUMULA-TIVE EARNINGS	EMPLOYEE	CUMULA-TIVE EARNINGS
Arthur, D.S.	$14,322	Greer, C.K.	$26,167
Barnett, S.T.	27,868	Hamilton, A.J.	8,771
Darwin, E.G.	6,550	Monday, M.D.	17,328

Assume that the rate of unemployment insurance for employees is 2.35% and the rate for the employer is 1.4 times that of the employees. The maximum monthly insurable earnings for each employee is $2,296.66. The rate for Canada Pension Plan is assumed to be 1.9% for both the employees and the employer and the rate is applied to the employees' first $23,400 pensionable earnings (i.e., gross earnings of $25,900 less $2,500 exemption).

Instructions   **a** Prepare a schedule showing for each employee the cumulative earnings, the earnings subject to unemployment insurance and the earnings subject to Canada Pension Plan contribution for the year to date. Columnar headings for the schedule should be as shown at the top of page 497.

b Compute the total amounts of unemployment insurance and of Canada Pension deducted from the earnings of employees as a group for the year to date.

EMPLOYEE	CUMULATIVE EARNINGS	EARNINGS SUBJECT TO	
		UNEMPLOYMENT INSURANCE	CANADA PENSION PLAN

c Compute the total payroll taxes expense of Dartmouth Ltd. and the percentage of total payroll represented by payroll taxes expense.

Group B

Problem 11B-1
Liabilities: their
valuation and
disclosure

The following six events occurred at Midway Corporation at or near the fiscal year-end of March 31.

a On March 31, obtained a bank loan by signing a note payable promising to pay $100,000 principal, plus $9,000 interest (computed at 12% per year), all payable nine months from today.

b On March 31, purchased a tract of land for use in the business at a price of $300,000. Signed a note payable due nine months from today in the total amount of $324,750. The note constituted full payment for the land.

c A ledger account entitled Liability for Income Tax Withheld had a balance of $9,000 at March 31.

d On March 31, signed a contract with a labour union providing for annual 6% increases in wage rates for the next three years. It was estimated that the increase in the first year would amount to $2,000,000.

e On March 31, signed a contract with a supplier of raw materials to purchase 10,000 tonnes a month for 12 months at a price of $70 per tonne.

f On March 31, discounted a $100,000 note receivable at a bank and received cash of $104,000. The note had a total life of one year and carried an interest rate of 12%.

Instructions

For each of the six events, you are to indicate the dollar amount, if any, which should appear in the current liability section of the March 31 balance sheet. If an event does not affect current liabilities, indicate whether it should appear in the balance sheet, and the proper location and dollar amount.

Problem 11B-2
Notes payable;
adjusting entries
for interest

Arrowhead Corporation engaged in the following transactions involving notes payable during the fiscal year ended October 31. Use a 360-day year and disregard the three days of grace for all interest calculations.

June 6 Borrowed $6,000 from a long-time employee, C.W. Jones. Issued a 45-day, 12% note payable to Jones as evidence of the indebtedness.

July 13 Purchased office equipment from New Company. This invoice amount was $9,000 and the New Company agreed to accept as full payment a 14%, three-month note for the invoiced amount.

July 21 Paid the Jones note plus accrued interest.

Sept. 1 Borowed $126,000 from Security Bank at an interest rate of 16% per annum; signed a 90-day note with interest included in the face amount of the note.

Oct. 1 Purchased merchandise in the amount of $5,400 from Post Co. Gave in settlement a three-month note bearing interest at 14%.

Oct. 13 The $9,000 note payable to New Company matured today. Paid the interest accrued and issued a new 30-day, 14% note to replace the maturing note.

Instructions **a** Prepare journal entries (in general journal form) to record the preceding transactions.

b Prepare the adjusting entries needed at October 31, prior to closing the accounts. Use one adjusting entry to accrue interest on the two notes in which interest is stated separately (the Post Co. note and the New Company note). Use a separate adjusting entry to record interest expense accrued on the note with interest included in the face amount (the Security Bank note).

Problem 11B-3
Notes payable and
interest computations

During the fiscal year ending June 30 and shortly thereafter, Houston Centre had the following transactions relating to notes payable.

Feb. 6 Borrowed $10,000 from L.W. Smith and issued a 45-day, 16% note payable.

Mar. 12 Purchased delivery truck from E-Z Company. Issued a 12%, three-month note payable for $15,000, the full cost of the truck.

Mar. 23 Paid the note due today to L.W. Smith plus accrued interest.

May 1 Borrowed the amount of $200,000 for 90 days from Dominion Bank at an interest rate of 14% per year; signed a note payable with the interest included in the face amount of the note.

May 31 Purchased merchandise for $7,500 from Patten Co. Issued a 90-day note bearing interest at 16% annually.

June 12 The $15,000 note payable to E-Z Company matured today. Paid in cash the interest accrued and issued a new 30-day note bearing interest at 14% per annum to replace the maturing note. (Use one compound journal entry for this transaction.)

June 30 End of fiscal year.

July 12 Paid principal and interest of the 30-day, 14% note to E-Z Company dated June 12 which matured today.

July 30 Paid in full the 90-day note to Dominion Bank dated May 1 and maturing today.

Instructions **a** Prepare journal entries (in general journal form) to record the six transactions dated prior to June 30. All interest rates quoted are annual rates. Use a 360-day year and disregard the three days of grace for interest computations.

b Prepare two adjusting entries at June 30 relating to interest expense. The first entry should accrue interest on the two notes with interest stated separately (the note to Patten Company and the note to E-Z Company). The explanation should include computations showing the amount of interest accrued on each note. The second adjusting entry should record interest on the Dominon Bank note in which interest was included in the face amount.

c Prepare journal entries for the two transactions occurring in July.

Problem 11B-4
Notes payable:
a comprehensive
problem

During the three months ended November 30, Optics, Inc. had the following transactions relating to notes payable. Use a 360-day year and disregard the three days of grace in computing interest.

Sept. 1 Purchased equipment for use in the business from Eastern Gear, Inc., for $13,800, making an $1,800 cash down payment and issuing a one-year note payable for the balance. The face amount of the note was $13,440, which included a 12% interest charge. (Use one compound journal entry which includes discount on Notes Payable.)

Sept. 16 Gave $5,000 cash and a 90-day, 8% note to Lees Company in settlement of open account due today in the amount of $14,000.

Sept. 25 Purchased office equipment from ADM Company for $16,800, giving a 60-day, 9% note in settlement thereof.

Oct. 11 Borrowed $72,000 from Manufacturers Bank, giving a 90-day note as evidence of indebtedness. An interest charge computed at 17% per annum was included in the face amount of the note.

Nov. 15 Purchased merchandise on account from Toyshang Co., $18,000.

Nov. 18 Issued a 60-day note bearing interest at 9% in settlement of the Toyshang Co. account.

Nov. 24 Paid the 60-day, 9% note due to ADM Company, which matured today.

Instructions

a Prepare journal entries (in general journal form) to record the listed transactions for the three months ended November 30.

b Prepare adjusting entries to record the interest expense on notes payable through November 30. Prepare one adjusting entry to record the accrued interest on the two notes for which interest is stated separately (the Lees Company note and the Toyshang Co. note). The other adjusting entry should record the amortization of discount on the two notes in which interest is included in the face amount (the Eastern Gear, Inc., note and the Manufacturers Bank note).

c Prepare a partial balance sheet at November 30 reflecting the above transactions. Show Notes Payable to Bank as one item and Notes Payable: Other as a separate liability. Also include the interest payable in the current liability section of the balance sheet.

Problem 11B-5
Internal control
over payrolls

Char Burger, a chain of 10 drive-in hamburger stands, is a sole proprietorship owned by Betty Lee. Although Lee has other business interests, she devotes a portion of her time to management of the drive-in chain. A manager is employed at each of the 10 locations and the number of employees at each location varies from 6 to 12.

The manager of each unit prepares payroll sheets each week showing hours worked as reported by the employees on time cards which are approved by the manager. Each manager's salary is also listed on the weekly payroll. Upon completion of the payroll, the manager pays all employees and him- or herself in cash. Each employee acknowledges receipt of payment by signing the payroll sheet.

Employees at each branch are employed and terminated by the local managers, who also set wage rates. The salaries of the managers are authorized by Betty Lee.

Each week the payroll sheets are mailed by the managers to Lee, whose secretary prepares individual earnings records for each employee and compiles government reports from the weekly payroll sheets.

Instructions

a Write a paragraph evaluating the adequacy of internal controls over payrolls. State the specific practices, if any, which you think should be changed.

b List four specific ways in which payroll fraud could be carried on by the manager of any of the 10 drive-ins.

Problem 11B-6
Determine income
tax and payroll cost;
entries for payroll

Martin earns a salary of $45,600 per year from Peaktou Resort, payable at a rate of $3,800 per month. Assume that unemployment insurance is 2.35% on earnings of up to a maximum of $27,560 and that Canada Pension Plan is 1.9% on the maximum of $25,900, with a $2,500 exemption. Martin's TD1 form shows a net claim of $7,000 and a net claim code of 5. In addition, Martin has authorized the withholding of $70 per month throughout the year for group life insurance. Assume that the employer's contributions are — unemployment insurance, 1.4 times the employee's premium; Canada Pension Plan, same as the employee's.

Instructions   **a** Determine the amount of income tax withheld during the entire year from Martin's paycheques. (The amount of the monthly withholding can be determined from the withholding table on page 486.)

b Prepare entries (in general journal form) to summarize for the entire year (1) the amounts paid to and withheld from Martin, and (2) the payroll taxes upon Peaktou Resort relating to employee Martin. (In drafting these summary entries, ignore any payments of tax during the year and let the liability accounts show the total for the year. Credit Cash for the amount paid to Martin.)

c Compute the total cost to Peaktou Resort during the year, including payroll taxes, of having Martin on the payroll at a salary of $45,600.

Problem 11B-7
Entries for payroll
and payroll taxes;
determine total
payroll cost

During January, Kaiser, Inc., incurred weekly salaries expense of $16,200, classified as follows: $8,000 of salaries expense for the sales force and $8,200 salaries expense for office personnel.

Amounts withheld were $4,160 for income taxes, $180 for group insurance premiums, $250 for unemployment insurance, and $280 for Canada Pension Plan.

Instructions   **a** Prepare a general journal entry to record the payroll and the deductions from employees' earnings. Do not include payroll taxes on the employer in this journal entry.

b Prepare a general journal entry to record the payroll taxes on the employer as a result of the above payroll. Assumed tax rates are: unemployment insurance at 1.4 times the employees' premium and Canada Pension Plan at the same rate as that of the employees.

c What is the total weekly payroll expense of Kaiser, Inc., for January? Show computations.

Problem 11B-8
Determine payroll
taxes

The employees' earnings records of McCain Associates at March 31 in the current year are as follows:

EMPLOYEE	CUMULA-TIVE EARNINGS	EMPLOYEE	CUMULA-TIVE EARNINGS
Axler, C.F.	$ 8,593	Gamble, E.H.	$28,701
Cox, R.M.	6,121	Hart, P.W.	25,261
Ford, G.A.	3,530	Kelly, P.T.	29,890

Assume that the rate of unemployment insurance for employees is 2.35% and the rate for the employer is 1.4 times that of the employees. The maximum monthly insurable earnings for each employee is $2,296.66. The rate for Canada Pension Plan is assumed to be 1.9% for both the employees and the employer, and the rate is applied to the employees' first $23,400 pensionable earnings (i.e., gross earnings of $25,900 less $2,500 exemption).

Instructions   **a** Prepare a three-column schedule showing for each employee the following amounts: cumulative earnings (as given), earnings subject to unemployment insurance, and earnings subject to Canada Pension Plan.

b Some payroll taxes are levied on the employee and some on the employer. Use the information shown in **a** above to compute the payroll taxes deducted from the earnings of the employees as a group. (Income taxes are not involved in this problem.)

c Compute the total payroll taxes levied on the employer, McCain Associates, and the percentage of the total payroll represented by this payroll tax.

BUSINESS DECISION CASES

Case 11-1
Liabilities,
contingencies,
and commitments

Marian Rogers, a CA on the audit staff of a national public accounting firm, is in charge of the annual audit of Crystal Corporation, a successful medium-size client. On December 31, Rogers receives a telephone call from John Arnold, the controller of Crystal. Arnold explains that the company's board of directors has just signed two contractual arrangements with its former president, who has retired. The first agreement provides that Crystal will pay its ex-president $10,000 a month for five years if during that time he does not compete with the company in a rival business. The second agreement states that Crystal will pay the ex-president $8,000 per month for five years, for which he is to provide such advisory services as the company may request.

The controller asks Rogers if the year-end balance sheet would exclude $216,000 as a current liability to the ex-president and $864,000 as a long-term liability, or whether the total amount of $1,080,000 should be disclosed as a contingency in a note to the financial statements. The controller emphasized that these amounts were quite material in terms of the company's earnings and resources.

Instructions
Explain fully how you think Marian Rogers should respond to the questions raised by the controller.

Case 11-2
Internal control
over payrolls

The payroll procedures of Metals, Inc., a manufacturing concern with 80 factory employees, may be summarized as follows:

1 Applicants are interviewed and hired by Carl Olson, the factory superintendent. He obtains an employee's Tax Exemption Return (TD1) form from each new employee and writes on it the hourly rate of pay to be used. The superintendent gives this form to a payroll clerk as notice that a new employee has been added.

2 When hourly pay rate changes are made, the superintendent advises the payroll clerk verbally of the new rate for the employee(s) affected.

3 Blank time cards are kept in a box at the factory entrance. On Mondays each employee takes a time card, writes in his or her name, and makes pencil notations during the week of hours of arrival and departure. At the end of the week, the employee returns the card to the box.

4 The completed cards are taken from the box on Monday mornings. Two payroll clerks divide the cards alphabetically between them; compute the gross pay, deductions, and net pay; post the information to the employee's individual earnings records; and prepare and number the payroll cheques.

5 The payroll cheques are signed by the chief accountant and given to the superintendent, who distributes them to employees and holds those for any absent employees.

6 The payroll bank account is reconciled by the chief accountant, who also prepares the payroll tax reports.

Instructions
With the objective of improving the system of internal control over the hiring practices and payroll procedures of Metals, Inc., you are to recommend any basic changes needed in organization, equipment, forms, and procedures. Then list at least six specific hiring practices and payroll procedures that you believe should be instituted.

PARTNERSHIPS

CHAPTER PREVIEW

In prior chapters we have used the sole proprietorship as a model in our study of basic accounting concepts. In this chapter we focus on the partnership and the accounting issues related to this form of business organization. Among these topics are the maintenance of a separate capital account for each partner, the equitable division of partnership net income or net loss among the partners, the admission and the withdrawal of individual partners, and finally the liquidation of a partnership business.

After studying this chapter you should be able to meet these Learning Objectives:

1   Describe the basic characteristics of a partnership.

2   Discuss the advantages and disadvantages of the partnership as a form of business organization.

3   Distinguish between a regular partnership and a limited partnership.

4   Account for the formation of a partnership.

5   Divide the net income of a partnership among the partners.

6   Account for (a) the admission of a new partner, (b) the withdrawal of a partner, and (c) the liquidation of a partnership.

Three types of business organization are common to Canadian business: the sole proprietorship, the partnership, and the corporation. Partnerships are a popular form of organization because they provide a convenient, inexpensive means of combining the capital and the special abilities of two or more persons. The partnership form of organization is widely used in all types of small business and also in the professions. A partnership is often referred to as a *firm;* the name of the firm often includes the word ''company,'' as, for example, ''Adams, Barnes, and Company.''

In Canada, each province has its own partnership legislation. The provincial partnership legislation may consist of one or more acts; for example, British Columbia has a Partnership Act, while Ontario has three acts — a Partnerships Act, a Partnership Registration Act, and a Limited Partnerships Act. All provincial partnership legislation covers essentially the same ground and provides essentially the same fundamental rules on the nature, organization, and operation of partnerships.

What constitutes a partnership? The answer can be found in the partnerships act. The legal definition of a partnership is essentially the same in all provincial legislation, except for minor differences in wording. The Ontario Partnerships Act, for example, has the following definition:

> Partnership is the relation that subsists between persons carrying on a business in common with a view to profit, but the relation between the members of a company or association that is incorporated by or under the authority of any special or general Act in force in Ontario or elsewhere, or registered as a corporation under any such Act, is not a partnership within the meaning of this Act.

In this chapter, we shall concentrate on the significant features of and the accounting problems peculiar to a partnership.

Significant features of a partnership

Before taking up the accounting problems peculiar to partnerships, it will be helpful to consider briefly some of the distinctive characteristics of the partnership form of organization. These characteristics (such as limited life and unlimited liability) all stem from the concept that a partnership is not a separate legal entity in itself but merely a voluntary association of individuals.

1 Describe the basic characteristics of a partnership.

Ease of formation Generally, a partnership can be created with a minimum amount of formality. When two or more persons agree, orally or in writing, to carry on a business with a view to profit, such agreement constitutes a contract and a partnership is automatically created. The contract should be in writing in order to lessen the chances for misunderstanding and future disagreement. The voluntary aspect of a partnership agreement means that no one can be forced into a partnership or forced to continue as a partner.

Richard and Mike were friends and employees of the same large corporation. They became interested in forming a partnership to acquire a nearby small business being offered for sale for a down payment of $50,000. They felt that they could manage the business (which had two employees) in their spare time. Richard and Mike agreed that each would deposit $25,000 in a partnership bank account. There was no written agreement of partnership. Richard made his deposit from his personal savings; Mike had only $10,000 of his own but was able to obtain the other $15,000 from his brother-in-law, Joe, to whom he described the business with great enthusiasm. Mike then deposited $25,000 in the partnership bank account and the business was purchased. Richard had never met Joe and was not aware of his $15,000 investment.

A few months later, Joe became annoyed because he had received no return on his investment. He appeared suddenly at the business while Richard was there, stating that he was a partner and demanding to see the accounting records and the bank statements. Richard refused, and after an angry argument, Joe was forcibly ejected. The question of whether Joe was a "silent partner" caused bitter disagreement among all three of the principals. During this dispute, the business was forced to shut down because of lack of working capital. Richard, Mike, and Joe each retained a lawyer to seek damages from the others.

Although a partnership may be at times a somewhat unstable form of organization, a written agreement of partnership might have avoided the problems encountered by Richard and Mike — and by Joe.

Limited life   A partnership may be ended at any time by the death or withdrawal of any member of the firm. Other factors that may bring an end to a partnership include the bankruptcy or incapacity of a partner, the expiration of the period specified in the partnership contract, or the completion of the project for which the partnership was formed. The admission of a new partner or the retirement of an existing member means an end to the old partnership, although the business may be, and usually is, continued by the formation of a new partnership.

Mutual agency   Each partner acts as an agent of the partnership, with authority to enter into contracts for the purchase and sale of goods and services. The partnership is bound by the acts of any partner as long as these acts are within the scope of normal operations. The factor of mutual agency suggests the need for exercising great caution in the selection of a partner. To be in partnership with an irresponsible person or one lacking in integrity is an intolerable situation.

Unlimited liability   Each partner is personally responsible for all the debts of the firm. The lack of any ceiling on the liability of a partner may deter a wealthy person from entering a partnership.

A new member joining an existing partnership may or may not assume liability for debts incurred by the firm prior to his or her admission. A partner withdrawing from membership must give adequate public notice of withdrawal; otherwise the former partner may be held liable for partnership debts incurred subsequent to his or her withdrawal. The retiring partner remains liable for partnership debts existing at the time of withdrawal unless the creditors agree to a release of this obligation.

Co-ownership of partnership property and income   When a partner invests a building, inventory, or other property in a partnership, he or she does not retain any personal right to the assets contributed. The property becomes jointly owned by all partners. Each member of a partnership also has an ownership right in the income generated by the partnership.

2 Discuss the advantages and disadvantages of the partnership as a form of business organization.

Advantages and disadvantages of a partnership

Perhaps the most important advantage of most partnerships is the opportunity to bring together sufficient capital to carry on a business. The opportunity to combine special skills such as, for example, the specialized talents of an engineer and an accountant, may also induce individuals to join forces in a partnership. To form a partnership is much easier and less expensive than to organize a corporation. Members of a partnership enjoy more freedom from government regulation and more flexibility of action than do the owners of a corporation. The partners may withdraw funds and make business decisions of all types without the necessity of formal meetings or legalistic procedures.

Operating as a partnership *may* in some cases produce income tax advantages as compared with doing business as a corporation. The partnership itself is not a legal entity and does not have to pay income taxes as does a corporation, although the individual partners pay taxes on their respective shares of the firm's income.

Offsetting these advantages of a partnership are such serious disadvantages as limited life, unlimited liability (except for a limited partner in a limited partnership, as discussed in the following section), and mutual agency. Furthermore, if a business is to require a large amount of capital, the partnership is a less effective device for raising funds than is a corporation. Many persons who invest freely in common stocks of corporations are unwilling to enter a partnership because of the unlimited liability imposed on partners.

Limited partnerships

In recent years a number of businesses have been organized as "limited partnerships." This form of organization is widely used for businesses that provide tax sheltered income to investors, such as real estate syndications and mining ventures. However, limited partnerships are not appropriate for businesses in which the owners intend to be active managers.

3 Distinguish between a regular partnership and a limited partnership.

A limited partnership must have at least one *general partner* as well as one or more *limited partners.* The general partners are partners in the traditional sense, with unlimited liability for the debts of the business and the right to make managerial decisions. The limited partners, however, are basically *investors* rather than traditional partners. They have the right to participate in the income or earnings of the business, but their liability for losses is limited to the amount of their investment. Also, limited partners do not actively participate in management of the business. Thus, the concepts of unlimited liability and mutual agency apply only to the general partners in a limited partnership.

In this chapter, we emphasize the characteristics and accounting practices of conventional partnerships rather than limited partnerships. Limited partnerships are discussed in depth in courses on business law and income taxes.

The partnership contract

Although a partnership can be formed by an oral agreement, it is highly desirable that a written partnership agreement be prepared, summarizing the partners' mutual understanding on such points as:

1 Names of the partners, and the duties and rights of each

2 Amount to be invested by each partner including the procedure for valuing an noncash assets invested or withdrawn by partners

3 Methods of sharing net income (earnings) and losses

4 Withdrawals to be allowed each partner

5 Provision for liquidation. This part of the agreement may specify a method fo sharing a deficiency in a partner's capital account by other partners.

Partnership accounting

An adequate accounting system and an accurate measurement of income are neede by every business, but they are especially important in a partnership because the ne income is divided among two or more owners. Each partner needs current, accurat information on operations so that he or she can make intelligent decisions on suc questions as additional investments, expansion of the business, or sale of an interes in the partnership.

Rowe and Davis were partners in an automobile dealership and auto repair shop. Rowe was the active manager of the business, but Davis had supplied nearly all the capital. Aware that the firm was quite profitable, Rowe devised a scheme to become the sol owner by buying out his partner. In order to persuade Davis to sell his interest at a bargain price, Rowe deliberately began falsifying the accounting records and financial statements in a manner to understate the earnings of the business. Much of the revenue from auto repair work was not recorded at all; depreciation expense was overstated; ending inventories were understated; and the cost of new items of plant and equipment were charged to expense. The result was a series of monthly income statements that showed the business operating at a larger loss each month Faced with these discouraging financial statements, Davis became pessimistic ove the prospects for the business and was on the verge of selling his interest to Rowe at a price far below the balance in his capital account.

However, a friend suggested that before selling out, Davis should insist upon an audit of the business by a CA firm. An audit was performed and revealed that the business was in fact highly profitable. When confronted by Davis with the auditors' findings, Rowe withdrew from the partnership and Davis became the sole owner

Partnership accounting is similar to that in a sole proprietorship, except that separa capital and drawing accounts are maintained for each partner. A distinctive feature partnership accounting is that the net income of the business must be divided amor the partners in the manner specified by the partnership agreement.

Opening the accounts of a new partnership

4   Account for the formation of a partnership.

When a partner contributes assets other than cash, a question always arises as to th value of such assets. The valuations assigned to noncash assets should be their *fa market values* at the date of transfer to the partnership. The valuations assigned mu be agreed to by all partners.

To illustrate the opening entries for a newly formed partnership, assume that on January 1 Joan Blair and Richard Cross, who operate competing retail stores, decide to form a partnership by consolidating their two businesses. A capital account will be opened for each partner and credited with the agreed valuation of the *net assets* (total assets less total liabilities) that the partner contributes. The journal entries to open the accounts of the partnership of Blair and Cross are as follows:

ENTRIES FOR FORMATION OF PARTNERSHIP

Cash	40,000	
Accounts Receivable	60,000	
Inventory	90,000	
Accounts Payable		30,000
Joan Blair, Capital		160,000

To record the investment by Joan Blair in the partnership of Blair and Cross.

Cash	10,000	
Inventory	60,000	
Land	60,000	
Building	100,000	
Accounts Payable		70,000
Richard Cross, Capital		160,000

To record the investment by Richard Cross in the partnership of Blair and Cross.

The values assigned to assets in the accounts of the new partnership may be quite different from the amounts at which these assets were carried in the accounts of their previous owners. For example, the land contributed by Cross and valued at $60,000 might have appeared in his accounting records at a cost of $20,000. The building that he contributed was valued at $100,000 by the partnership, but it might have cost Cross only $80,000 some years ago and might have been depreciated on his records to a net value of $60,000. Assuming that market values of land and buildings had risen sharply while Cross owned this property, it is only fair to recognize the *current market value* of these assets at the time he transfers them to the partnership and to credit his capital account accordingly. Depreciation of the building in the partnership accounts will be based on the assigned value of $100,000 at the date of acquisition by the partnership.

Additional investments

Assume that after six months of operation the firm is in need of more cash, and the partners make an additional investment of $10,000 each on July 2. These additional investments are credited to the capital accounts as follows:

ENTRY FOR ADDITIONAL INVESTMENT

Cash	20,000	
Joan Blair, Capital		10,000
Richard Cross, Capital		10,000

To record additional investments.

Drawing accounts

The drawing account maintained for each partner serves the same purpose as th drawing account of the owner of a sole proprietorship. The transactions calling fo debits to the drawing accounts of partners may be summarized as follows:

1 Cash or other assets withdrawn by a partner
2 Payments from partnership funds of the personal debts of a partner
3 Partnership cash collected on behalf of the firm by a partner but retained by th partner personally

Credits to the drawing accounts are seldom encountered; one rather unusua transaction requiring such an entry may be the payment of a partnership liability by partner out of personal funds.

Loans from partners

Ordinarily any funds furnished to the firm by a partner are recorded by crediting tha partner's capital account. Occasionally, however, a partnership may be in need c funds but the partners do not wish to increase their capital investment in the busines: or perhaps one partner is willing to advance funds when the others are not. Unde these circumstances, the advance of funds may be designated as a loan from th partner and credited to a partner's loan account. Partnership liabilities to outside: always take precedence over any loans from partners.

Closing the accounts of a partnership at year-end

At the end of the accounting period, the balance in the Income Summary account i closed to the partners' capital accounts, in accordance with the income-sharin: provisions of the partnership contract. If the partnership contract does not mentio how net income is to be divided, the law assumes that the intention of the partner was for an *equal division* of net income and losses. If the partnership agreemer specifies a method of dividing net income but does not mention the possibility of nε losses, any net losses are divided in the proportions provided for sharing net income

In the previous illustration of the firm of Blair and Cross, an equal sharing of nε income was agreed upon. Assuming that a net income of $60,000 was realize during the first year of operations, the entry to close the Income Summary accour would be as follows:

CLOSING INCOME
SUMMARY: NET INCOME
SHARED EQUALLY

Income Summary	60,000	
Joan Blair, Capital		30,00
Richard Cross, Capital		30,00

To divide net income for the year in accordance with partnership
agreement to share it equally.

The next step in closing the accounts is to transfer the balance of each partner' drawing account to his capital account. Assuming that withdrawals during the yea amounted to $24,000 for Blair and $16,000 for Cross, the entry at December 3 (year-end date) to close the drawing accounts is as follows:

CLOSING THE DRAWING
ACCOUNTS TO CAPITAL
ACCOUNTS

Joan Blair, Capital	24,000	
Richard Cross, Capital	16,000	
Joan Blair, Drawing		24,000
Richard Cross, Drawing		16,000

To transfer debit balances in partners' drawing accounts to
their respective capital accounts.

Income statement for a partnership   The income statement for a partnership differs
from that of a sole proprietorship in only one respect: a final section may be added to
show the division of the net income between the partners, as illustrated for the firm
of Blair and Cross.

NOTE DISTRIBUTION
OF NET INCOME

BLAIR AND CROSS
Income Statement
For the Year Ended December 31, 19___

Sales			$600,000
Cost of goods sold:			
Inventory, Jan. 1	$150,000		
Purchases	460,000		
Cost of goods available for sale	$610,000		
Less: Inventory, Dec. 31	210,000		
Cost of goods sold		400,000	
Gross profit on sales		$200,000	
Operating expenses:			
Selling expenses	$100,000		
General & administrative expenses	40,000	140,000	
Net income		$ 60,000	
Division of net income:			
To Joan Blair (50%)	$ 30,000		
To Richard Cross (50%)	30,000	$ 60,000	

Statement of partners' capitals   The partners will usually want an explanation of the
change in their capital accounts from one year-end to the next. A supplementary
schedule called a *statement of partners' capitals* is prepared to show this information.

The balance sheet of Blair and Cross would show the capital balance for each
partner, as well as the total capital of $360,000.

CHANGES IN CAPITAL
ACCOUNTS DURING THE
YEAR

BLAIR AND CROSS
Statement of Partners' Capitals
For the Year Ended December 31, 19___

	BLAIR	CROSS	TOTAL
Balances, Jan. 1, 19___	$160,000	$160,000	$320,000
Add: Additional investments	10,000	10,000	20,000
Net income for the year	30,000	30,000	60,000
Subtotals	$200,000	$200,000	$400,000
Less: Drawings	24,000	16,000	40,000
Balances, Dec. 31, 19___	$176,000	$184,000	$360,000

Partnership income and income taxes

Partnerships are not required to pay income taxes   Partners must include their shares of the partnership net income (after certain technical adjustments) on their individual income tax returns. Partnership net income is thus taxable to the partners individually in the year in which it is earned. The income tax rules applicable to investment in a partnership are covered in advanced accounting courses.

Note that partners report and pay tax on their respective shares of the net income earned by the partnership during the year and *not* on the amounts which they have drawn out of the business during the year. *The net income of the partnership is taxable to the partners each year,* even though there may have been no withdrawals. This treatment is consistent with that accorded a sole proprietorship.

The nature of partnership net income

The net income earned by a partnership, like that of a sole proprietorship, may be regarded as consisting of three distinct elements: (1) compensation for the personal services rendered by the partners, (2) compensation (interest) for the use of invested capital, and (3) a reward for the entrepreneurial functions of risk taking. Recognition of these *three elements of partnership net income* will be helpful in forming an equitable plan for the division of net income.

If one partner devotes full time to the business while another does not participate actively, the income-sharing plan should give weight to this disparity in contributions of services. Any salaries authorized for partners *are regarded as a preliminary step in the division of net income, not as an expense of the business.* The partner is considered an owner, not an employee. The services that a partner renders to the firm are, therefore, considered to be rendered in anticipation of a share in net income, not in contemplation of a salary. The net income reported by a partnership cannot be compared directly with that earned by a corporation of similar size, because the corporation treats as expense any payments to owner-managers for personal services rendered.

In the solution of problems in this book, the student should *record withdrawals of assets by partners as debits to the partners' drawing accounts, regardless of whether or not the withdrawals are described as salaries.* Some alternative treatments of salaries of partners can be explored in advanced accounting courses.

In the preceding illustrations of the partnership of Blair and Cross, we assumed that the partners invested equal amounts of capital, rendered equal services, and divided net income equally. We are now ready to consider cases in which the partners invest unequal amounts of capital and services.

Dividing partnership net income among the partners

Partners can share net income or loss in any manner they decide upon; however most income-sharing agreements fall under one of the following types:

5   Divide the net income of a partnership among the partners.

1   A fixed ratio. The fixed ratio method has already been illustrated in the example of the Blair and Cross partnership, in which net income was shared equally, that is, 50% and 50%. Partners may agree upon any fixed ratio such as 60% and 40% or 70% and 30%.

2 Salaries to partners, with remaining net income or loss divided in a fixed ratio.

3 Interest on partners' capitals, with remaining net income or loss divided in a fixed ratio.

4 Salaries to partners, interest on partners' capitals, and remaining net income or loss divided in a fixed ratio.

All these methods of sharing partnership net income are intended to recognize differences in the personal services rendered by partners and in the amounts of capital invested in the firm. For example, if one partner invests twice as much capital as another, this needs to be considered in the plan for sharing income. If one partner works full time in the business and the other only half time, this difference can be compensated for by setting different salaries. Different salaries to partners are also reasonable when one partner is more experienced or has a special skill not possessed by other partners.

In the illustrations that follow, it is assumed that beginning capitals were Brooke Adams, $160,000, and Ben Barnes, $40,000. At year-end, the Income Summary account showed a credit balance of $96,000, representing the net income for the year before any partners' salaries or interest on capital.

Salaries to partners, with remainder in a fixed ratio Because partners often contribute different amounts of personal services, partnership agreements often provide for partners' salaries as a factor in the division of net income.

For example, assume that Adams and Barnes agree that Adams will be allowed an annual salary of $24,000 and Barnes an annual salary of $48,000. Any remaining profits are to be divided equally. It is agreed that the salaries will be withdrawn in cash each month and recorded by debits to the drawing accounts.[1] The authorized salaries total $72,000 a year; this amount represents a first step in the division of the year's net income and is therefore subtracted from the net income of $96,000. The remaining net income of $24,000 will be divided equally.

Division of Net Income

	ADAMS	BARNES	NET INCOME
Net income to be divided			$96,000
Salaries to partners	$24,000	$48,000	72,000
Remaining income after salaries			$24,000
Allocated in a fixed ratio:			
Adams (50%)	12,000		
Barnes (50%)		12,000	24,000
Total share to each partner	$36,000	$60,000	$ –0–

Under this agreement, Adams's share of the $96,000 net income amounts to $36,000 and Barnes's share amounts to $60,000. The entry to close the Income Summary account would be as illustrated at the top of the next page.

[1] Salaries may be used as a device for dividing partnership net income, even though the partners do not wish to make any withdrawals of cash whatsoever. In this illustration, however, it is assumed that cash is withdrawn by each partner in an amount equal to his authorized salary.

Income Summary	96,000	
Brooke Adams, Capital		36,000
Ben Barnes, Capital		60,000

To close the Income Summary account by crediting each
partner with his authorized salary and dividing the remaining
net income equally.

Interest on partners' capitals, with remainder in a fixed ratio   Next we shall assume
a business situation in which the partners spend very little time in the business and net
income depends primarily on the amount of money invested. The income-sharing
plan then might emphasize invested capital as a basis for the first step in allocating
net income.

For example, assume that Adams and Barnes agree that both partners are to be
allowed interest at 15% on their beginning capitals, with any remaining net income
or loss to be divided equally. Net income to be divided is $96,000 and the beginning
capitals are Adams, $160,000, and Barnes, $40,000, the same as in the preceding
illustration.

INCOME SHARING;
INTEREST ON CAPITALS
AND FIXED RATIO AS
BASIS

Division of Net Income

	ADAMS	BARNES	NET INCOME
Net income to be divided			$96,000
Interest on beginning capitals:			
Adams ($160,000 × 15%)	$24,000		
Barnes ($40,000 × 15%)		$ 6,000	
Total allocated as interest			30,000
Remaining income after interest on capitals			$66,000
Allocated in a fixed ratio:			
Adams (50%)	33,000		
Barnes (50%)		33,000	66,000
Total share to each partner	$57,000	$39,000	$ –0–

The entry to close the Income Summary account in this example would be:

Income Summary	96,000	
Brooke Adams, Capital		57,00C
Ben Barnes, Capital		39,00€

To close the Income Summary account by crediting each
partner with interest at 15% on beginning capital and
dividing the remaining net income equally.

Salaries, interest on capitals, and remainder in a fixed ratio   The preceding exampl‹
took into consideration the difference in amounts of capital provided by Adams an‹
Barnes but ignored any difference in personal services performed. In the next example
we shall assume that the partners agree to an income-sharing plan providing fo
salaries and for interest on beginning capitals. Salaries, as before, are authorized ‹
$24,000 for Adams and $48,000 for Barnes. Beginning capitals are $160,000 fo
Adams and $40,000 for Barnes. Partners are to be allowed interest at 10% on the›

beginning capital balances, and any net income or loss remaining after authorized salaries and interest allowances is to be divided equally.

INCOME SHARING; SALARIES, INTEREST, AND FIXED RATIO AS BASIS

Division of Net Income

	ADAMS	BARNES	NET INCOME
Net income to be divided			$96,000
Salaries to partners	$24,000	$48,000	72,000
Income after salaries			$24,000
Interest on beginning capitals:			
Adams ($160,000 × 10%)	16,000		
Barnes ($40,000 × 10%)		4,000	
Total allocated as interest			20,000
Remaining income after salaries and interest . . .			$ 4,000
Allocated in a fixed ratio:			
Adams (50%)	2,000		
Barnes (50%)		2,000	4,000
Total share to each partner	$42,000	$54,000	$ –0–

The journal entry to close the Income Summary account in this case will be:

Income Summary	96,000	
Brooke Adams, Capital		42,000
Ben Barnes, Capital		54,000

To close the Income Summary account by crediting each partner with authorized salary, interest at 10% on beginning capital, and dividing the remaining net income equally.

Authorized salaries and interest in excess of net income   In the preceding example the total of the authorized salaries and interest was $92,000 and the net income to be divided was $96,000. Suppose that the net income had been only $80,000; how should the division have been made?

If the partnership contract provides for salaries and interest on invested capital, these provisions are to be followed even though the net income for the year is *less* than the total of the authorized salaries and interest. If the net income of the firm of Adams and Barnes amounted to only $80,000, this amount would be distributed as follows:

AUTHORIZED SALARIES AND INTEREST MAY EXCEED NET INCOME

	ADAMS	BARNES	NET INCOME
Net income to be divided			$ 80,000
Salaries to partners	$24,000	$48,000	72,000
Income after salaries			$ 8,000
Interest on beginning capitals:			
Adams ($160,000 × 10%)	16,000		
Barnes ($40,000 × 10%)		4,000	
Total allocated as interest			20,000
Residual loss after salaries and interest			$(12,000)
Allocated in a fixed ratio:			
Adams (50%)	(6,000)		
Barnes (50%)		(6,000)	12,000
Total share to each partner	$34,000	$46,000	$ –0–

Notice that after allowing for the specified partners' salaries and interest on partners' capital, the partnership has a residual loss of $12,000. Since the partnership contract states that any residual net income or loss is to be divided equally between Adams and Barnes, the entry to close the Income Summary account will be as follows:

Income Summary	80,000	
Brooke Adams, Capital		34,00C
Ben Barnes, Capital		46,00C

To close the Income Summary account by crediting each partner with authorized salary and with interest on invested capital and by dividing the residual loss equally.

6 Account for (a) the admission of a new partner, (b) the withdrawal of a partner, and (c) the liquidation of a partnership.

Admission of a new partner

An individual may gain admission to an existing partnership in either of two ways (1) by buying an interest from one or more of the present partners, or (2) by makin; an investment in the partnership. When an incoming partner purchases an equity from a present member of the firm, the payment goes personally to the old partner, an there is no change in the assets or liabilities of the partnership. On the other hand, i the incoming partner acquires an equity by making an investment in the partnership the assets of the firm are increased by the amount paid in by the new partner.

By purchase of an interest   When a new partner buys an interest from a presen member of a partnership, the only change in the accounts will be a transfer from th capital account of the selling partner to the capital account of the incoming partne

Assume, for example, that L has an $80,000 equity in the partnership of L, M and N. Partner L arranges to sell his entire interest to X for $100,000 cash. Partner M and N agree to the admission of X, and the transaction is recorded in the partnershi accounts by the following entry:

INCOMING PARTNER
BUYS INTEREST FROM
PRESENT PARTNER

L, Capital	80,000	
X, Capital		80,0C

To record the transfer of L's equity to the incoming partner, X.

Note that the entry in the partnership accounts was for $80,000, the record amount of Partner L's equity. *The amount of this entry was not influenced by th price paid the retiring partner by the new member.* The payment of $100,000 fro X to L was a personal transaction between the two individuals; it did not affect th assets or liabilities of the partnership and therefore is not entered in the partnersh accounting records.

As a separate but related example, assume that X is to gain admission to the firm L,M, and N by purchasing one-fourth of the equity of each partner. The prese capital accounts are as follows: Partner L, $80,000; Partner M, $80,000; and Pa ner N, $80,000. The payments by the incoming partner X are to go to the o partners personally and not to the partnership. The only entry required is the followin

NO CHANGE IN TOTAL
CAPITAL

L, Capital	20,000	
M, Capital	20,000	
N, Capital	20,000	
X, Capital		60,000

To record admission of X to a one-fourth interest in the firm by purchase of one-fourth of the equity of each of the old partners.

By an investment in the firm   An incoming partner may acquire an equity by making an investment in the firm. In this case the payment by the new partner goes to the partnership and not to the partners as individuals; the investment therefore increases the partnership assets and also the total owners' equity of the firm. Assume that Ann Phillips and Judy Ryan are partners, each having a capital account of $100,000. They agree to admit Bart Smith to a one-half interest in the business upon his investment of $200,000 in cash. The entry to record the admission of Smith would be as follows:

INVESTMENT IN
BUSINESS BY NEW
PARTNER

Cash	200,000	
Bart Smith, Capital		200,000

To record the admission of Bart Smith to a one-half interest in the firm.

Although Smith has a one-half equity in the net assets of the new firm of Phillips, Ryan, and Smith, he is not necessarily entitled to receive one-half of the net income. Income sharing is a matter for agreement among the partners; if the new partnership contract contains no mention of income sharing, the assumption is that the three partners intended to share net income and losses equally.

Allowing a bonus to former partners   If an existing partnership has exceptionally high earnings year after year, the present partners may demand a *bonus* as a condition for admission of a new partner. In other words, to acquire an interest of, say, $80,000, the incoming partner may be required to invest $120,000 in the partnership. The excess investment of $40,000 may be regarded as a bonus to the old partners and credited to their capital accounts in the established ratio for income sharing.

To illustrate the recording of a bonus to the old partners, let us assume that Janet Rogers and Richard Steel are members of a highly successful partnership. As a result of profitable operations, the partners' capital accounts have doubled within a few years and presently stand at $100,000 each. David Taylor desires to join the firm and offers to invest $100,000 for a one-third interest. Rogers and Steel refuse this offer but extend a counter-offer to Taylor of $120,000 for a one-fourth interest in the capital of the firm and a one-fourth interest in income. Taylor accepts these terms because of his desire to share in the unusually large income of the business. The recording of Taylor's admission to the partnership is based on the following calculations:

CALCULATION OF BONUS
TO OLD PARTNERS

Net assets (owners' equity) of old partnership	$200,000
Cash investment by Taylor	120,000
Net assets (owners' equity) of new partnership	$320,000
Taylor's one-fourth interest	$ 80,000

To acquire an interest of $80,000 in the net assets of $320,000, Taylor has invested $120,000. His excess investment or bonus of $40,000 will be divided equally between Rogers and Steel, since their partnership agreement called for equal sharing of net income and losses.

The entry to record Taylor's admission to the partnership follows:

RECORDING BONUS TO OLD PARTNERS

Cash	120,000	
David Taylor, Capital		80,000
Janet Rogers, Capital		20,000
Richard Steel, Capital		20,000

To record admission of David Taylor as a partner with a one-fourth interest in capital and net income.

Allowing a bonus to new partner   An existing partnership may sometimes be very anxious to bring in a new partner who can bring needed cash to the firm. In other instances the new partner may possess special talents or may have advantageous business contacts that will add to the profitability of the partnership. Under either of these sets of circumstances, the old partners may be willing to offer the new member a bonus in the form of a capital account larger than the amount of the incoming partner's investment.

Assume, for example, that John Bryan and Merle Davis are equal partners, each having a capital account of $36,000. Since the firm is in desperate need of cash, they offer to admit Kay Grant to a one-third interest in the firm upon her investment of only $24,000 in cash. The amounts of the capital accounts for the three members of the new firm are computed as follows:

Total capital of old partnership:		
John Bryan, capital	$36,000	
Merle Davis, capital	36,000	$72,000
Cash invested by Kay Grant		24,000
Total capital of new three-member partnership		$96,000
Capital of each partner in the new firm:		
John Bryan ($96,000 × $1/3$)	$32,000	
Merle Davis ($96,000 × $1/3$)	32,000	
Kay Grant ($96,000 × $1/3$)	32,000	96,000

The journal entry illustrated below records the admission of Grant to a one-third interest in the business and also adjusts each capital account to the required level of $32,000.

ENTRY FOR BONUS TO NEW PARTNER

Cash	24,000	
John Bryan, Capital	4,000	
Merle Davis, Capital	4,000	
Kay Grant, Capital		32,000

To record admission of Grant to a one-third interest, and the allowance of a bonus to her.

Withdrawal of a partner

A partner may, with the consent of the other partners, sell his or her interest to an outsider. In this case the payment by the incoming partner goes directly to the withdrawing partner, and there is no change in the assets or liabilities of the partnership. The only entry required is to transfer the capital account of the withdrawing partner to an account with the new partner. This transaction is virtually the same as the one described on page 514 for the admission of a partner by purchase of an interest.

Next, let us change our assumptions slightly and say that Carol Coe, the withdrawing partner, has a $100,000 interest which she sells to her fellow partners, A and B, in equal amounts. A and B make the agreed payment to Coe from their personal funds, so again the partnership assets and liabilities are not changed. Regardless of the price agreed to for Coe's interest, the transaction can be handled in the partnership accounting records merely by transferring the $100,000 balance in Coe's capital account to the capital accounts of the other two partners.

NO CHANGE IN TOTAL
CAPITAL

Carol Coe, Capital	100,000	
A, Capital		50,000
B, Capital		50,000

To record the sale of Coe's interest in equal portions to A and B.

Payment to withdrawing partner from partnership assets   The withdrawing partner, Carol Coe, may be paid from partnership funds an amount equal to her capital account or a larger or smaller amount. If the partnership has been in business for several years during a period of inflation, it is probable that the assets, especially land, have market values higher than their cost as shown in the accounting records. A partner withdrawing from the firm naturally expects to receive an amount related to current market values; consequently, the settlement is likely to be an amount higher than her capital account. It is sometimes suggested that upon the withdrawal of a partner, the assets should be revalued upward (including the recognition of goodwill, if any) and the increase credited to the partners' capital accounts.[2] However, this would be a departure from the cost principle. Although the increase in market value of assets logically should be used in computing the amount to pay the withdrawing partner, it need not be recorded in the accounting records. Any excess payment to the withdrawing partner may be treated as a bonus to her that must be charged against the capital accounts of the continuing partners in the agreed ratio for sharing net income and losses, as illustrated below:

BONUS PAID TO
WITHDRAWING PARTNER

Carol Coe, Capital (retiring partner)	100,000	
A, Capital	20,000	
B, Capital	20,000	
Cash		140,000

To record the withdrawal of partner Coe, and payment of her capital account plus a bonus of $40,000.

---

[2] The issues regarding whether partnership assets should be revalued upon the admission, withdrawal, or retirement of a partner are covered in advanced accounting courses.

As a separate example, assume that Coe is to receive a settlement smaller than her capital account balance, because she agrees to take a loss in order to expedite the settlement. If Coe surrenders her $100,000 interest for $80,000, the entry will be:

<table>
<tr><td style="vertical-align: top;">PAYMENT TO
WITHDRAWING PARTNER
OF LESS THAN BOOK
EQUITY</td><td>Carol Coe, Capital 100,000
    Cash   80,000
    A, Capital   10,000
    B, Capital   10,000
To record the withdrawal of Coe, and settlement in full
for $20,000 less than the balance of her capital account.</td></tr>
</table>

Death of a partner

A partnership is dissolved by the death of any member. To determine the amount owing to the estate of the deceased partner, it is usually necessary to close the accounts and prepare financial statements. This serves to credit all partners with their individual shares of the net income earned during the fractional accounting period ending with the date of *dissolution.*

The partnership agreement may prescribe procedures for making settlement with the estate of a deceased partner. Such procedures often include an audit by public accountants, appraisal of assets, and computation of goodwill. If payment to the estate must be delayed, the amount owed should be carried in a liability account replacing the deceased partner's capital account.

Insurance on lives of partners   Members of a partnership often obtain life insurance policies that name the partnership as the beneficiary. Upon the death of a partner, the cash collected from the insurance company is used to pay the estate of the deceased partner. In the absence of insurance on the lives of partners, there might be insufficient cash available to pay the deceased partner's estate without disrupting the operation of the business.

Liquidation of a partnership

A partnership is terminated or dissolved whenever a new partner is added or an old partner withdraws. The termination or dissolution of a partnership, however, does not necessarily indicate that the business is to be discontinued. Often the business continues with scarcely any outward evidence of the change in membership of the firm. Termination of a partnership indicates a change in the membership of the firm which may or may not be followed by liquidation.

The process of breaking up and discontinuing a partnership business is called *liquidation.* Liquidation of a partnership spells an end to the business. If the business is to be discontinued, the assets will be sold, the liabilities paid, and the remaining cash distributed to the partners.

Sale of the business   The partnership of X, Y, and Z sells its business to the North Corporation. The balance sheet appears as follows:

PARTNERSHIP AT TIME
OF SALE

X, Y, AND Z
Balance Sheet
December 31, 19___

ASSETS		LIABILITIES & PARTNERS' EQUITY	
Cash	$ 50,000	Accounts payable	$100,000
Inventory	200,000	X, capital	140,000
Other assets	150,000	Y, capital	120,000
		Z, capital	40,000
Total	$400,000	Total	$400,000

The terms of sale provide that the partnership will retain the cash of $50,000 and will pay the liabilities of $100,000. The inventory and other assets will be sold to the North Corporation for a consideration of $230,000. The entries relating to the sale of the inventory and other assets are as follows:

ENTRIES FOR SALES
OF BUSINESS

Accounts Receivable, North Corporation	230,000	
Loss on Sale of Business	120,000	
Inventory		200,000
Other Assets		150,000
To record the sale of all assets other than cash to North Corporation.		

Cash	230,000	
Accounts Receivable, North Corporation		230,000
Collected the receivable from sale of assets.		

Division of the gain or loss from sale of the business   The gain or loss from the sale of the business must be divided among the partners in the agreed net income and loss sharing ratio *before* any cash is distributed to them. The amount of cash to which each partner is entitled in liquidation cannot be determined until each capital account has been increased or decreased by the proper share of the gain or loss on disposal of the assets. Assuming that X, Y, and Z share net income and losses equally, the entry to allocate the $120,000 loss on the sale of the business will be as follows:

ENTRY TO DIVIDE LOSS
ON SALE

X, Capital	40,000	
Y, Capital	40,000	
Z, Capital	40,000	
Loss on Sale of Business		120,000
To divide the loss on the sale of the business among the partners in the established ratio for sharing net income and losses.		

Distribution of cash   The balance sheet of X, Y, and Z appears at the top of page 520 after the loss on the sale of the assets has been entered in the partners' capital accounts:

X, Y, AND Z
Balance Sheet
(After the Sale of All Assets Except Cash)

ASSETS		LIABILITIES & PARTNERS' EQUITY	
Cash	$280,000	Accounts payable	$100,000
		X, capital	100,000
		Y, capital	80,000
		Z, capital	–0–
Total	$280,000	Total	$280,000

The creditors must be paid in full before cash is distributed to the partners. The sequence of entries will be as follows:

(1) PAY CREDITORS

Accounts Payable	100,000	
Cash		100,000
To pay the creditors in full.		

(2) PAY PARTNERS

X, Capital	100,000	
Y, Capital	80,000	
Cash		180,000

To complete liquidation of the business by distributing the remaining cash to the partners according to the balances in their capital accounts.

Note that the equal division of the $120,000 loss on the sale of the business reduced the capital account of Partner Z to zero; therefore, Z received nothing when the cash was distributed to the partners. This action is consistent with the original agreement of the partners to share net income and losses equally. In solving partnership liquidation problems, accounting students sometimes make the error of dividing the cash among the partners in the net income and loss sharing ratio. A net income and loss sharing ratio means just what the name indicates; it is a ratio for sharing net income and losses, *not a ratio for sharing cash or any other asset.* The amount of cash that a partner should receive in liquidation will be indicated by the balance in his or her capital account after the gain or loss from the disposal of assets has been divided among the partners in the agreed ratio for sharing net income and losses.

Treatment of debit balance in a capital account   To illustrate this situation, let us change our assumptions concerning the sale of the assets by the firm of X, Y, and Z and say that the loss incurred on the sale of assets was $144,000 rather than the $120,000 previously illustrated. Z's one-third share of a $144,000 loss would be $48,000, which would wipe out the $40,000 credit balance in his capital account and create an $8,000 debit balance. After the liabilities had been paid, a balance sheet for the partnership would appear as shown at the top of page 521.

To eliminate the debit balance in the capital account for Z, the partnership should collect from Z $8,000 in cash. If this collection is made, the capital balance for Z will become zero, and the cash on hand will be increased to $164,000, which is just enough to pay X and Y the balances shown by their capital accounts.

X, Y, AND Z
Balance Sheet
(After the Sale of All Assets Except Cash)

ASSETS		PARTNERS' EQUITY	
Cash	$156,000	X, capital	$ 92,000
		Y, capital	72,000
		Z, capital (deficiency)	(8,000)
Total	$156,000	Total	$156,000

If Z is unable to pay the $8,000 due to the firm, how should the $156,000 of cash on hand be divided between X and Y, whose capital accounts stand at $92,000 and $72,000 respectively? Failure of Z to pay in the debit balance means an additional loss to X and Y; according to the original partnership agreement, X and Y are to share net income and losses equally. Since partnership agreements generally specify that such a debit balance or deficiency be shared in the net income and loss ratio, let us assume that this was included in the liquidation provisions of the partnership agreement. Therefore, each must absorb $4,000 additional loss caused by Z's inability to pay the $8,000 due to the partnership. The $156,000 of cash on hand should be divided between X and Y in such a manner that the capital account of each will be paid down to $4,000, their respective shares of the additional loss. The journal entry to record this distribution of cash to X and Y is as follows:

X, Capital	88,000	
Y, Capital	68,000	
Cash		156,000

To divide the remaining cash by paying down the capital accounts of X and Y to a balance of $4,000 each, representing the division of Z's loss between them.

After this entry has been posted, the only accounts still open in the partnership records will be the capital accounts of the three partners. A trial balance of the ledger will appear as follows:

X, Y, AND Z
Trial Balance
(After Distribution of Cash)

X, capital		$4,000
Y, capital		4,000
Z, capital (deficiency)	$8,000	
	$8,000	$8,000

If Z is able later to pay in the $8,000 debit balance, X and Y will then receive the additional $4,000 each indicated by the credit balances in their accounts. However, if Z is definitely unable to pay the $8,000, these accounts should be closed.

The sharing of a debit balance may become a rather difficult issue if the partnership agreement is silent or the partners fail to agree on how such a debit balance is to be shared. Even though there are provisions on this issue in the partnership legislation, they are potentially subject to different interpretations. One interpretation was provided in the English case *Garner v. Murray* (1904), where it was ruled that the debit balance was to be shared among the other partners in the ratio of their capital account balances as at the date of liquidation. The reason was that the debit balance was considered a personal debt of one partner to the other partners rather than a business or operating loss. As a practical matter, however, the issue of how the debit balance should be shared rarely arises, apparently because partnership agreements generally specify a method for such a situation.

In solving the problems on partnership liquidation in this text, it is assumed that the partnership agreement specifies the sharing of a debit balance of a partner's capital account by other partners in the net income and loss ratio.

END-OF-CHAPTER REVIEW

SUMMARY OF CHAPTER LEARNING OBJECTIVES

1 Describe the basic characteristics of a partnership.

A partnership is a voluntary association of two or more persons who agree to combine their efforts and resources to carry on as co-owners a business for profit. Among the basic characteristics is the *ease of formation.* A partnership can be created merely by the action of two persons in agreeing to become partners. This agreement should be in writing, however, and should specify the capital contributions of each partner, the plan for sharing net income, and other aspects of operation. Another characteristic is the *limited life* of a partnership. The admission of a new partner, as well as the withdrawal or death of a partner, dissolves a partnership. Each partner has the right to act as agent for the firm (*mutual agency*) and each partner is *personally responsible* for all debts of the firm.

2 Discuss the advantages and disadvantages of the partnership as a form of business organization.

The advantages include the combining of the capital and the special skills of two or more persons, the ease of formation, and relative freedom from government regulation. The disadvantages are limited life, unlimited liability, and mutual agency.

3 Distinguish between a regular partnership and a limited partnership.

A limited partnership has two types of partners: (1) a general partner and (2) a number of limited partners. The general partner has the traditional role of a partner with unlimited liability for partnership debts and with managerial responsibility. The limited partners are basically investors; their liability for losses is limited to the amount of their investments, and they do not participate in management. Limited partnerships are commonly used for ventures that offer tax sheltered income to investors.

4 Account for the formation of a partnership.

When a partnership is formed by partners contributing cash and/or other assets to the firm, these investments are recorded by debiting asset accounts and crediting the partners' capital accounts. For noncash assets, the amount should be the *fair market value* at the date of transfer to the partnership. When two or more owners of going businesses become partners, the partnership usually assumes the liabilities. The capital accounts are credited with the value of the net assets (assets less total liabilities).

5 Divide the net income of a partnership among the partners.

The partnership agreement should specify how net income or loss is to be divided. If the agreement does not mention income-sharing, partners will share equally any amount of net income or loss. To recognize differences in the value and amount of personal services rendered by partners, it is common to provide salaries to partners as a step in sharing net income. To compensate for differences in the amounts of capital contributed, interest may be allowed on capital as a further step in sharing net income. Often both salaries and interest allowances are agreed upon, with any residual net income or loss to be divided in a fixed ratio.

6 Account for (a) the admission of a new partner, (b) the withdrawal of a partner, and (c) the liquidation of a partnership.

A new member may be admitted to an existing partnership in either of two ways: (1) by purchase of an interest from a present partner, or (2) by investing assets in the partnership. The purchase of an interest is a transaction between two individuals and is recorded by a transfer from the capital account of the selling partner to the capital account of the incoming partner. The alternative method, investment of assets in the firm by the incoming partner, increases total assets and owners' equity. It may involve a bonus to the old partners or to the new partner, depending on the terms of admitting the new partner.

To withdraw from a partnership, a partner may sell his or her interest. This is recorded by an entry transferring the capital account of the former partner to the new partner. As an alternative, the withdrawing partner may be paid from partnership assets.

Liquidation of a partnership means ending the business by selling the assets, paying creditors, and distributing remaining assets to the partners. Any gain or loss is divided in the agreed ratio. Insolvency of a partner may cause transfer of his or her share of a loss to the other partners.

KEY TERMS INTRODUCED OR EMPHASIZED IN CHAPTER 12

Dissolution (of a partnership) Termination of an existing partnership by any change in the personnel of the partners or by liquidating the business.

General partner A partner in a limited partnership who has the traditional rights and responsibilities of a partner, including mutual agency and unlimited personal liability for the debts of the business.

Limited partner A partner in a limited partnership who has the right to participate in income, but whose liability for losses is limited to the amount he or she has invested and who does not have the right to participate in management of the business. A limited partner's role is that of an investor rather than that of a traditional partner.

Limited partnership A partnership that has one or more *limited partners* as well as one or more *general partners*. Limited partnerships are used primarily to attract investment capital from the limited partners for such ventures as exploratory mining and real estate development.

Liquidation The process of breaking up and discontinuing a partnership, including the sale of assets, payment of creditors, and distribution of remaining assets to the partners.

Mutual agency Authority of each partner to act as agent for the partnership within its normal scope of operations and to enter into contracts which bind the partnership.

Partnership contract An agreement among partners on the formation and operation of the partnership. Usually includes such points as a plan for sharing income, amounts to be invested, and provision for liquidation.

Statement of partners' capitals A financial statement that shows for each partner and for the firm the amounts of beginning capitals, additional investments, net income, drawings, and ending capitals.

ASSIGNMENT MATERIAL

REVIEW QUESTIONS

1 Jane Miller is the proprietor of a small manufacturing business. She is considering the possibility of joining in partnership with Mary Bracken, whom she considers to be thoroughly competent and congenial. Prepare a brief statement outlining the advantages and disadvantages of the potential partnership to Miller.

2 Allen and Baker are considering forming a partnership. What do you think are the two most important factors for them to include in their partnership agreement?

3 What is meant by the term *mutual agency?*

4 A mining exploration business is managed by two experienced executives and is financed by 50 investors from throughout the country. To allow maximum income tax benefits to the investors, the business is organized as a partnership. Explain why this type of business would probably be a limited partnership rather than a regular partnership.

5 What factors should be considered in drawing up an agreement as to the way in which net income shall be shared by two or more partners?

6 Scott has land having a book value of $50,000 and a fair market value of $80,000 and a building having a book value of $70,000 and a fair market value of $60,000. The land and building become Scott's sole capital contribution to a partnership. What is Scott's capital balance in the new partnership? Why?

7 Is it possible that a partnership agreement containing interest and salary allowances as a step toward dividing net income could cause a partnership net loss to be distributed so that one partner's capital account would be decreased by more than the amount of the entire partnership net loss?

8 Partner John Young has a choice to make. He has been offered by his partners a choice between no salary allowance and a one-third share in the partnership net income or a salary of $16,000 per year and a one-quarter share of residual net income. Write a brief memorandum explaining the factors he should consider in reaching a decision.

9 Partner X withdraws $25,000 from a partnership during the year. When the financial statements are prepared at the end of the year, X's share of the partnership income is $15,000. Which amount must X report on his income tax return?

10 What factors should be considered when comparing the net income figure of a partnership to that of a corporation of similar size?

11 Explain the difference between being admitted to a partnership by (a) buying an interest from an existing partner and (b) making an investment in the partnership.

12 If C is going to be admitted to the partnership of A and B, why is it first necessary to determine the current fair market value of the assets of the partnership of A and B?

13 Shirley Bray and Carl Carter are partners who share net income and losses equally. The current balances in their capital accounts are: Bray, $50,000; Carter, $35,000. If Carter sells his interest in the firm to Deacon for $70,000 and Bray consents to the sale, what entry should be made in the partnership accounting records?

14 Describe how a *dissolution* of a partnership may differ from a *liquidation* of a partnership.

15 What measure can you suggest to prevent a partnership from having insufficient cash available to pay the estate of a deceased partner without disrupting the operation of the business?

16 Upon the death of Robert Bell, a partner in the firm of Bell, Cross, and Davis, Charles Bell, the son of Robert Bell, demanded that he replace his father as a member of the partnership. Can Charles Bell enforce this demand? Explain.

EXERCISES

Exercise 12-1
Accounting
terminology

Listed below are nine technical accounting terms introduced in this chapter:

Unlimited liability	Partnership contract	Dissolution of partnership
Liquidation	Fair market value	Interest on partners' capitals
General partner	Limited partner	Partnership net income

Each of the following statements may (or may not) describe one of these technical terms. For each statement, indicate the accounting term described, or answer "None" if the statement does not correctly describe any of the terms.

a Serves to identify partners, specify capital contributions, and establish income-sharing formula.

b The process of breaking up and discontinuing a partnership business.

c Amounts to be entered in asset accounts of a partnership to record the investment by partners of noncash assets.

d A method of dividing partnership net income to assure that a partner's share of net income will not be less than the prime rate of interest applied to his or her capital account.

e A characteristic of the partnership type of organization that causes many wealthy investors to choose investments in limited partnerships or corporations rather than in regular partnerships.

f Results from the retirement of a partner from the firm or the admission of a new partner.

g A partner whose financial responsibility does not exceed the amount of his or her investment and who does not actively participate in management.

h An income-sharing provision designed to compensate for differences in dollar amounts contributed by different partners.

Exercise 12-2
Formation of a partnership

A business owned by Megan Rogers was short of cash and Rogers therefore decided to form a partnership with Steve Wilson, who was able to contribute cash to the new partnership. The assets contributed by Rogers appeared as follows in the balance sheet of her business: cash, $500; accounts receivable, $28,900, with an allowance for doubtful accounts of $600; inventory, $36,000; and store equipment, $19,000. Rogers had recorded depreciation of $1,500 during her use of the store equipment in her sole proprietorship.

Rogers and Wilson agreed that the allowance for doubtful accounts was inadequate and should be $1,200. They also agreed that a fair value for the inventory was its replacement cost of $42,000 and that the fair value of the store equipment was $15,000. You are to open the partnership accounts by making a general journal entry to record the investment by Rogers.

Exercise 12-3
Partners' capital and drawing accounts

Explain briefly the effect of each of the following transactions on a partner's capital and drawing accounts:

a Partner borrows funds from the business.

b Partner collects a partnership account receivable while on vacation and uses the funds for personal purposes.

c Partner receives in cash the salary allowance provided in the partnership agreement.

d Partner takes home merchandise (cost $80, selling price $120) for personal use.

e Partner has loaned money to the partnership. The principal together with interest at 15% is now repaid to the partner in cash.

Exercise 12-4
Dividing partnership income

Redmond and Adams, both of whom are CAs, form a partnership, with Redmond investing $40,000 and Adams $30,000. They agree to share net income as follows:

(1) Interest at 15% on beginning capital balances.

(2) Salary allowances of $50,000 to Redmond and $40,000 to Adams.

(3) Any partnership net income in excess of the amount required to cover the interest and salary allowances, to be divided 60% to Redmond and 40% to Adams.

The partnership net income for the first year of operations amounted to $120,500 before interest and salary allowances. Show how this $120,500 should be divided between the two partners. Use a three-column schedule with a separate column for each partner and a total column. List on separate lines the amounts of interest, salaries, and the residual amount divided.

Exercise 12-5
Admission of a new partner

A and B are partners having capital balances of $60,000 and $32,000. They share net income equally. The partnership has been quite profitable and has an excellent reputation. A and B agree to admit C to a one-third interest in the partnership for an investment of $58,000. The assets of the business are not to be revalued. Explain how the bonus to the old partners is computed and prepare a general journal entry to record the admission of C.

Exercise 12-6
Withdrawal of a partner

The capital accounts of the XYZ partnership are as follows: X, $120,000; Y, $60,000; Z, $90,000. Net income is shared equally. Partner Y is withdrawing from the partnership and it is agreed that he shall be paid $80,000 for his interest because the earnings of the business are high in relation to the assets of the firm. Assuming that the excess of the settlement over the amount of Y's capital account is to be recorded as a bonus to Y, prepare a general journal entry to record Y's retirement from the firm.

Exercise 12-7
Liquidation of a
partnership

The CDE partnership is being liquidated. After all of the liabilities have been paid and all of the assets sold, the balances of the partners' capital accounts are as follows: C, $42,000 credit balance; D, $18,000 debit balance; E, $53,000 credit balance. The partners share net income equally.

a How should the available cash (the only remaining asset) be distributed if it is impossible to determine at this date whether D will be able to pay the $18,000 he owes the firm?

b Draft the journal entries to record a partial payment of $11,000 to the firm by D, and the subsequent distribution of this cash.

PROBLEMS

Group A

Problem 12A-1
Formation of a
partnership; closing
the Income Summary
account

The partnership of Avery and Kirk was formed on July 2, when George Avery and Dinah Kirk agreed to invest equal amounts and to share net income and losses equally. The investment by Avery consists of $40,000 cash and an inventory of merchandise valued at $56,000.

Kirk also is to contribute a total of $96,000. However, it is agreed that her contribution will consist of the following assets of her business along with the transfer to the partnership of her business liabilities. The agreed values of the various items as well as their carrying values on Kirk's records are listed below. Kirk also contributes enough cash to bring her capital account to $96,000.

	INVESTMENT BY KIRK	
	BALANCES ON KIRK'S RECORDS	AGREED VALUE
Accounts receivable	$89,600	$89,600
Allowance for doubtful accounts	3,840	8,000
Inventory	9,600	12,800
Office equipment (net)	12,800	9,000
Accounts payable	28,800	28,800

Instructions

a Draft entries (in general journal form) to record the investments of Avery and Kirk in the new partnership.

b Prepare the beginning balance sheet of the partnership (in report form) at the close of business July 2, reflecting the above transfers to the firm.

c On the following June 30 after one year of operation, the Income Summary account showed a credit balance of $78,000 and the Drawing account for each partner showed a debit balance of $32,000. Prepare journal entries to close the Income Summary account and the drawing accounts at June 30.

Problem 12A-2
Dividing partnership
income; financial
statements

The adjusted trial balance of Adams Company indicates the account balances at the end of the current year as illustrated at the top of page 528.

There were no changes in partners' capital accounts during the year. The inventory at the end of the year was $28,200. The partnership agreement provided that partners are to be allowed 10% interest on invested capital as of the beginning of the year and that the residual net income is to be divided equally.

	DEBIT	CREDIT
Cash	$ 32,620	
Accounts receivable (net)	81,000	
Inventory (beginning of year)	27,360	
Prepaid expenses	3,900	
Equipment	90,000	
Accumulated depreciation		$ 18,000
Notes payable		9,600
Accounts payable		38,520
Accrued expenses		2,880
Adams, capital		70,000
Adams, drawing	10,080	
Finley, capital		60,000
Finley, drawing	7,200	
Sales		648,960
Purchases	391,800	
Selling expenses	112,380	
Administrative expenses	91,620	
Totals	$847,960	$847,960

Instructions

a Prepare an income statement for the current year, using the appropriate accounts from the preceding list. At the bottom of the income statement, prepare a schedule showing the division of net income.

b Prepare a statement of partners' capitals for the current year.

c Prepare a balance sheet at the end of the current year.

Problem 12A-3
Various methods for dividing partnership net income

Elizabeth Dunn and Roberto Pascal, both real estate appraisers, formed a partnership, with Dunn investing $40,000 and Pascal investing $60,000. During the first year, the net income of the partnership amounted to $45,000.

Instructions

a Determine how the $45,000 net income would be divided under each of the following four independent assumptions as to the agreement for sharing net income and losses. Use schedules of the types illustrated in this chapter to show all steps in the division of net income between the partners.
(1) The partnership agreement does not mention income sharing.
(2) Interest at 15% to be allowed on beginning capital investments and balance to be divided equally.
(3) Salaries of $24,000 to Dunn and $20,000 to Pascal, balance to be divided equally.
(4) Salaries of $18,000 to Dunn and $26,000 to Pascal, interest at 15% to be allowed on beginning capital investments, balance to be divided equally.

b Prepare the journal entry to close the Income Summary account, using the division of net income developed in the last case (a, 4) above.

Problem 12A-4
Dividing partnership income and losses

Financial Planners has three partners — A, B, and C. During the current year their beginning capital balances were: A, $140,000; B, $100,000; and C, $60,000. The partnership agreement provides that partners shall receive salary allowances as follows: A, none; B, $50,000; and C, $38,000. The partners shall also be allowed 12% interest annually on their beginning capital balances. Residual net income or loss is to be divided: A, $1/2$; B, $1/3$; and C, $1/6$.

Instructions   Prepare separate schedules showing how income will be divided among the three partners in each of the following cases. The figure given in each case is the annual net income available for distribution among the partners.

  a Income of $502,000

  b Income of $73,000

  c Loss of $29,000

Problem 12A-5
Admission of a
new partner

A condensed balance sheet for the partnership of Modern Art Gallery, owned by Hale and Kent, at September 30 follows. On this date the two partners agreed to admit a new partner, Lee. Hale and Kent have been dividing net income in a ratio of 3:2 (that is, 60% and 40%), and this ratio will continue between the two of them after the admission of Lee. The new partnership will have a net income and loss sharing ratio of Lee, 50%; Hale, 30%; and Kent, 20%.

MODERN ART GALLERY
Balance Sheet
September 30

ASSETS		LIABILITIES & PARTNERS' EQUITY		
Current assets	$180,000	Liabilities		$160,000
Plant & equipment (net)	420,000	Partners' capitals:		
		Hale, capital .	$280,000	
		Kent, capital .	160,000	440,000
Total	$600,000	Total		$600,000

Instructions   Described in the following list are four different situations under which Lee might be admitted to partnership. Considering each independently, prepare the journal entries necessary to record the admission of Lee to the firm.

  a Lee purchases a one-half interest (50% of the entire ownership equity) in the partnership from Hale for $260,000. Payment is made to Hale as an individual.

  b Lee purchases one-half of Hale's interest and one-half of Kent's interest, paying Hale $168,000 and Kent $96,000.

  c Lee invests $300,000 in the partnership and receives a one-half interest in capital and net income. It is agreed that there will be no change in the valuation of the present net assets. (Bonus to Lee is charged against Hale and Kent in a 3:2 ratio.)

  d Lee invests $540,000 cash in the partnership and receives a one-half interest in capital and net income. The bonus to the old partners indicated by the amount of the investment by Lee for a one-half interest will be divided between Hale and Kent in the 3:2 ratio.

Problem 12A-6
Retirement of a
partner

In the partnership of World Travel Agency, the partners' capital accounts at the end of the current year were as follows: Roy Kim, $220,000; Susan John, $148,000; and Mark Ray, $60,000. The partnership agreement provides that net income will be shared 40% to Kim, 50% to John, and 10% to Ray. At this time Kim decides to retire from the firm.

Instructions   Following are descriptions of a number of independent situations involving the retirement of Kim. In each situation prepare the journal entries necessary to reflect the withdrawal of Kim from the firm.

  a Kim sells three-fourths of his interest to Ray for $208,000 and the other one-fourth to John for $64,000. The payments to Kim are made from the personal funds of Ray and John, not from the partnership.

b Kim accepts $90,000 in cash and a patent having a book value of $100,000 in full payment for his interest in the firm. This payment consists of a transfer of partnership assets to the retiring partner. The continuing partners agree that a revaluation of assets is not needed. The excess of Kim's capital account over the payment to him for withdrawal should be credited to the continuing partners ($5/6$ to John and $1/6$ to Ray).

c Kim receives $100,000 in cash and a 10-year, 12% note for $180,000 in full payment for his interest. Assets are not to be revalued. The bonus to Kim is to be charged against the capital accounts of the continuing partners ($5/6$ for John and $1/6$ for Ray).

Problem 12A-7
Liquidation of a partnership

The partnership of Talent Scouts has ended its operations and is in the process of liquidation. All assets except for cash and accounts receivable have already been sold. The task of collecting the accounts receivable is now to be carried out as rapidly as possible. The general ledger balances are as follows:

	DEBIT	CREDIT
Cash	$ 27,200	
Accounts receivable	116,800	
Allowance for doubtful accounts		$ 6,400
Liabilities		36,800
May, capital (net income-loss share 30%)		43,200
Nix, capital (net income-loss share 50%)		33,600
Peat, capital (net income-loss share 20%)		24,000

Instructions

For each of the two independent situations described, prepare journal entries to record the collection or sale of the receivables, the payment of liabilities, and the distribution of all remaining cash to the partners. Support all entries with adequate explanation; the entries for distribution of cash to the partners should have explanations showing how the amounts were determined.

a Collections of $66,400 are made on receivables, and the remainder are deemed uncollectible. Debit the uncollectible receivables in excess of the allowance to an account entitled Loss on Liquidation.

b Receivables are sold to a collection agency; the partnership receives in cash as a final settlement 30% of the gross amount of its receivables. The personal financial status of the partners is uncertain, but all available cash is to be distributed at this time. (Nix's deficiency will be charged to May and Peat in a 30:20 ratio.)

Group B

Problem 12B-1
Formation of a partnership

The partnership of Kelley and Reed was formed on January 1, when Tom Kelley and Pat Reed agreed to invest equal amounts and to share net income equally. The investment by Kelley consists of $44,000 cash and an inventory of merchandise valued at $76,000. Reed is also to contribute a total of $120,000. However, it is agreed that her contribution will consist of the following assets of her business along with the transfer to the partnership of her business liabilities. The agreed value of the various items as well as their carrying values on Reed's records are listed at the top of page 531. Reed also contributed enough cash to bring her capital account to $120,000.

Instructions

a Draft general journal entries to record the investments of Kelley and Reed in the new partnership.

	INVESTMENT BY REED	
	BALANCES ON REED'S RECORDS	AGREED VALUE
Accounts receivable	$117,600	$117,600
Allowance for doubtful accounts	5,040	8,500
Inventory	16,600	20,800
Office equipment (net)	16,800	19,500
Accounts payable	37,800	37,800

b Prepare the beginning balance sheet of the partnership (in report form) at the close of business January 1, reflecting the above transfers to the firm.

c On the following December 31 after one year of operations, the Income Summary account had a credit balance of $92,000 and the Drawing account for each partner showed a debit balance of $36,000. Prepare journal entries to close the Income Summary account and the drawing accounts at December 31.

Problem 12B-2
Dividing income;
statement of
partners' capitals

The adjusted trial balance of Design Associates indicates the following account balances at the end of the current year:

	DEBIT	CREDIT
Cash	$ 17,800	
Accounts receivable	105,200	
Allowance for doubtful accounts		$ 2,000
Inventory	27,700	
Showroom fixtures	32,400	
Accumulated depreciation		6,400
Notes payable		9,000
Accounts payable		38,000
Baylor, capital		70,000
Baylor, drawing	32,000	
Carter, capital		60,000
Carter, drawing	24,000	
Sales		648,000
Purchases	381,600	
Selling expenses	110,000	
Administrative expenses	102,700	
Totals	$833,400	$833,400

There were no changes in partners' capital accounts during the year. The company uses a periodic inventory system and the physical inventory at the end of the year was $28,500. The partnership agreement provided that partners are to be allowed 15% interest on invested capital as of the beginning of the year and that the residual net income is to be divided equally.

Instructions

a Prepare an income statement for the current year, using the appropriate accounts from the preceding list. At the bottom of the income statement, prepare a schedule showing the distribution of net income.

b Prepare a statement of partners' capitals for the current year.

c Prepare a balance sheet at the end of the current year.

Problem 12B-3
Sharing partnership net income: various methods

The partnership of Coast Associates was formed with Lewis investing $40,000 and Martin investing $60,000. During the first year, net income amounted to $55,000.

Instructions

a Determine how the $55,000 net income would be divided under each of the following three independent assumptions as to the agreement for sharing net income and losses. Use schedules of the type illustrated in this chapter to show all steps in the division of net income between the partners.

(1) Net income is to be divided in a fixed ratio: 40% to Lewis and 60% to Martin.

(2) Interest at 15% to be allowed on beginning capital investments and balance to be divided equally.

(3) Salaries of $18,000 to Lewis and $28,000 to Martin, interest at 15% to be allowed on beginning capital investments, balance to be divided equally.

b Prepare the journal entry to close the Income Summary account, using the division of net income developed in the last case (**a**, 3) above.

Problem 12B-4
Division of partnership income and of partnership loss

Research Consultants has three partners — L, M, and N. During the current year their capital balances were: L, $160,000; M, $90,000; and N, $50,000. The partnership agreement provides that partners shall receive salary allowances as follows: L, $8,000; M, $48,000; and C, $32,000. The partners shall also be allowed 12% interest annually on their capital balances. Residual net income or losses are to be divided: L, $1/2$; M, $1/3$; and N, $1/6$.

Instructions

Prepare separate schedules showing how income will be divided among the three partners in each of the following cases. The figure given in each case is the annual income available for distribution among the partners.

a Income of $490,000

b Income of $67,000

c Loss of $20,000

Problem 12B-5
A new partner joins the firm

Aspen Lodge is a partnership with a record of profitable operations. At the end of the current year the capital accounts of the three partners and the ratio for sharing net income and losses are as shown in the following schedule. At this date, it is agreed that a new partner, Wolfgang Ritter, is to be admitted to the firm.

	CAPITAL	NET-INCOME SHARING RATIO
Olga Svenson	$200,000	$5/8$
Jill Kidd	160,000	$1/4$
Miles Kohl	120,000	$1/8$

Instructions

For each of the following situations involving the admission of Ritter to the partnership, give the necessary journal entry to record his admission.

a Ritter purchases one-half of Kidd's interest in the firm, paying Kidd personally $95,000.

b Ritter buys a one-quarter interest in the firm for $140,000 by purchasing one-fourth of the present interest of each of the three partners. Ritter pays the three individuals directly.

c Ritter invests $240,000 cash in the firm and receives a one-quarter interest in capital and net income of the business. Give the necessary journal entries to record Ritter's admission as a partner and the division of the bonus to the old partners in their established ratio for net income sharing.

Problem 12B-6
Withdrawal of a partner

Century City Brokers is a partnership of three individuals. At the end of the current year, the firm had the following balance sheet.

CENTURY CITY BROKERS
Balance Sheet
December 31, 19___

ASSETS		LIABILITIES & PARTNERS' EQUITY		
Cash	$ 65,000	Liabilities		$ 99,000
Receivables	75,000	Partners' capitals:		
Inventory	160,000	Swartz, capital	$132,000	
Land	105,000	Cross, capital	90,000	
		Dart, capital	84,000	306,000
Total	$405,000	Total		$405,000

The partners share net income and losses in the ratio of 50% to Swartz, 30% to Cross, and 20% to Dart. It is agreed that Dart is to withdraw from the partnership on this date.

Instructions

Listed are a number of different assumptions involving the withdrawal of Dart from the firm. For each situation you are to prepare the general journal entry or entries needed to record Dart's withdrawal.

a Dart, with the permission of the other partners, gives his equity to his brother-in-law, Jones, who is accepted as a partner in the firm.

b Dart sells one-fourth of his interest to Cross for $24,000 cash and sells the other three-fourths to Swartz for $72,000 cash. The payments are made by Cross and Swartz personally and not by the partnership.

c Dart is paid $90,000 from partnership funds for his interest. The bonus indicated by this payment is charged against the continuing partners ($^5/_8$ against Swartz and $^3/_8$ against Cross).

d Dart is paid $60,000 cash and given inventory having a book value of $66,000. These assets come from the firm. The partners agree that no revaluation of assets will be made. (Ratio for sharing net income and losses between Swartz and Cross is 5:3.)

e The partners agree that land is worth $195,000 at present market prices. They do not wish to write up this asset in the accounts but believe that Dart is entitled to a settlement which includes his 20% interest in the increase in value. Dart is paid $48,000 in cash and given a two-year, 12% note for $54,000. The bonus should be charged against Swartz and Cross in the ratio of $^5/_8$ and $^3/_8$.

Problem 12B-7
Liquidation; insolvent partners

The December 31 balance sheet of Data Survey, a partnership, follows:

DATA SURVEY
Balance Sheet
December 31, 19___

ASSETS		LIABILITIES & PARTNERS' EQUITY		
Cash	$ 60,000	Liabilities		$120,000
Other assets	300,000	Partners' capitals:		
		Hand, capital	$100,000	
		Trent, capital	80,000	
		Dell, capital	60,000	240,000
Total	$360,000	Total		$360,000

In order to focus attention on the principles involved in liquidating a partnership, the balance sheet has been shortened by combining all assets other than cash under the caption of Other Assets.

Hand, Trent, and Dell share net income in a ratio of 3:2:1, respectively. At the date of the balance sheet the partners decided to liquidate the business.

Instructions   Prepare schedules showing how the liquidation of the partnership would affect the various balance sheet items and how the cash would be distributed for each of the four independent cases listed. Use six money columns in your schedules, as follows:

CASH	OTHER ASSETS	LIABILITIES	HAND, CAPITAL	TRENT, CAPITAL	DELL, CAPITAL

a Other assets are sold for $252,000.

b Other assets are sold for $96,000. All partners have personal assets and will contribute any necessary amounts to the partnership.

c Other assets are sold for $74,400. Trent has personal assets and will contribute any necessary amounts; Hand and Dell are both personally bankrupt. (Round the distribution of Hand's deficit to the nearest dollar.)

d Other assets are sold for $48,000. Dell is personally solvent and will contribute any amount for which he is liable. Hand and Trent both have personal debts in excess of their personal assets.

BUSINESS DECISION CASES

Case 12-1
Developing an equitable plan for dividing partnership income

Juan Ramirez and Robert Cole are considering forming a partnership to engage in the business of aerial photography. Ramirez is a licensed pilot, is currently earning $48,000 a year, and has $50,000 to invest in the partnership. Cole is a professional photographer who is currently earning $20,000 a year. He has recently inherited $70,000 that he plans to invest in the partnership.

Both partners will work full time in the business. After careful study, they have estimated that expenses are likely to exceed revenue by $10,000 during the first year of operations. In the second year, however, they expect the business to become profitable, with revenue exceeding expenses by an estimated $90,000. (Bear in mind that these estimates of expenses do not include any salaries or interest to the partners.) Under present market conditions, a fair rate of return on capital invested in this type of business is 20%.

Instructions   **a** On the basis of this information, prepare a brief description of the income-sharing agreement that you would recommend for Ramirez and Cole. Explain the basis for your proposal.

b Prepare a separate schedule for each of the next two years showing how the estimated amounts of net income would be divided between the two partners under your plan. (Assume that the original capital balances for both partners remain unchanged during the two-year period. This simplifying assumption allows you to ignore the changes that would normally occur in capital accounts as a result of divisions of net income, or from drawings or additional investments.)

c Write a brief statement explaining the differences in allocation of income to the two partners and defending the results indicated by your income-sharing proposal.

Case 12-2
An offer of partnership

Upon graduation from college, Ray Bradshaw began work as a staff assistant for a national CA firm. During the next few years, Bradshaw received his CA certificate and was promoted to the level of senior on the firm's audit staff.

At this time, Bradshaw received an offer from a small local CA firm, Ames and Bolt, to join that firm as a third partner. Both Ames and Bolt have been working much overtime and they would expect a similar workload from Bradshaw. Ames and Bolt draw salaries of $50,000 each and share residual net income equally. They offer Bradshaw a $50,000 salary plus one-third of residual net income. The offer provides for Bradshaw to receive a one-third equity in the firm and requires him to make a cash investment of $100,000. Balance sheet data for the firm of Ames and Bolt are as follows:

Current assets	$ 60,000	Current liabilities	$ 30,000
Property & equipment	240,000	Long-term liabilities	145,000
		Ames, Capital	62,500
		Bolt, Capital	62,500
Total	$300,000	Total	$300,000

Projected net income of the CA firm for the next four years is estimated as follows. These estimated earnings are before partners' salaries and are based on the assumption that Bradshaw joins the firm and makes possible an increased volume of business.

Year 1	$159,000	Year 2	$168,000
Year 3	$186,000	Year 4	$198,000

If Bradshaw decides to continue in his present position with the national CA firm rather than join the local firm, he estimates that his salary over the next four years will be as follows:

Year 1	$51,000	Year 2	$54,000
Year 3	$60,000	Year 4	$66,000

Instructions

a Assuming that Bradshaw accepts the offer from Ames and Bolt, determine the amount of his beginning capital and prepare the entry in the partnership accounts to record Bradshaw's admission to the firm.

b Compute the yearly amounts of Bradshaw's income from the partnership for the next four years. Compare these amounts with the salary that he will receive if he continues in his present employment and write a memo explaining the factors Bradshaw should consider in deciding whether to accept or decline the offer from Ames and Bolt.

c Assuming that Bradshaw declines the offer, suggest some alternatives that he might propose if he decides to present a counter-offer to Ames and Bolt.

CHAPTER

13

ACCOUNTING PRINCIPLES
AND CONCEPTS;
EFFECTS OF INFLATION

CHAPTER PREVIEW

Throughout this text we try to explain the theoretical roots of each new account-ing principle or standard as it first comes under consideration. In this chapter, our first objective is to look back and review some of the major ideas, concepts, and traditions that form the "ground rules" for financial reporting. Our second objective is to introduce methods of adjusting accounting information for the effects of inflation. We explain and illustrate how net income can be measured under the alternative assumptions of constant dollars and current costs. Emphasis is focussed upon the interpretation of income statements prepared under these assumptions.

After studying this chapter you should be able to meet these Learning Objectives:

1 Identify the major sources of generally accepted accounting principles.

2 Discuss the accounting principles, assumptions, and conventions presented on pages 538–546.

3 Define an audit and discuss the nature of the auditors' report.

4 Explain why the use of historical costs during periods of inflation may overstate income.

5 Distinguish between the constant dollar and current cost approaches to measuring net income. Prepare an income statement using either approach.

6 Use a price index to restate historical costs to an equivalent number of current dollars.

7 Explain why holding monetary items causes gains or losses in purchasing power.

8 Explain some of the key features of Section 4510 of the *CICA Handbook* on "Reporting the Effects of Changing Prices."

Need for recognized accounting standards

The basic objective of financial statements is to provide information about a business enterprise; information that will be useful in making economic decisions. Investors, managers, economists, bankers, labour leaders, and government administrators all rely upon financial statements and other accounting reports in making the decisions that shape our economy. Therefore, it is of vital importance that the information contained in financial statements be highly relevant, reliable, and clearly understood. Also, it is important for financial statements to be prepared in a manner that permits them to be compared fairly with prior years' statements and with financial statements of other companies. In short, we need a well-defined body of accounting principles or standards to guide accountants in preparing financial statements with the characteristics of *relevance, reliability, understandability,* and *comparability.*

Generally accepted accounting principles (GAAP)

The principles that constitute the ''ground rules'' for financial reporting are termed *generally accepted accounting principles.* Accounting principles are also referred to as *standards, assumptions, postulates, and concepts.* The various terms used to describe accounting principles indicate the many efforts that have been made to develop a satisfactory framework of accounting theory.[1] The efforts to construct a satisfactory body of accounting theory are still in process, because accounting theory must continually change with changes in the business environment and changes in the needs of financial statement users.

Accounting principles are not rooted in laws of nature, as are the laws of the physical sciences. Rather, accounting principles are developed in relation to what we consider to be the most important objectives of financial reporting. For example, in recent years accountants as well as business executives have recognized that part of the ''cost'' to society of conducting certain types of economic activity includes the pollution of air and water and other damage to the environment. Research is currently being undertaken to develop accounting principles for the identification and measurement of these ''social costs.''

1 Identify the major sources of generally accepted accounting principles.

Authoritative support for accounting principles

To qualify as ''generally accepted,'' an accounting principle must usually receive ''substantial authoritative support.'' The most influential authoritative group in Canada is the **Accounting Standards Committee (AcSC)** of the Canadian Institute of Chartered Accountants (CICA). The AcSC is responsible for the development and promulgation of accounting principles, and its recommendations are contained in the ''Accounting Recommendations'' section of the *CICA Handbook*. These recommendations are considered as generally accepted accounting principles (GAAP) by

---

[1] See, for example, in Canada, *Corporate Reporting: Its Future Evolution*, CICA (Toronto: 1980), in the United States, *Accounting Study No. 1*, ''The Basic Postulates of Accounting,'' AICPA (New York: 1961); *Accounting Research Study No. 3*, ''A Tentative Set of Broad Accounting Principles for Business Enterprises,'' AICPA (New York: 1962); and the series of *Statements of Financial Accounting Concepts* issued by the FASB.

the accounting profession, the administrators of provincial securities commissions, and a number of corporations acts, including the Canada Business Corporations Act.

The pronouncements of the American Institute of Certified Public Accountants (AICPA), the Financial Accounting Standards Board (FASB), and the Securities and Exchange Commission (SEC) in the United States also have significant influence on GAAP in Canada. This influence stems from a number of factors, the most important of which being: the quality of the pronouncements, the substantial involvement of American companies in Canadian commercial activity, and the need to comply, as required by SEC, with the American pronouncements by those Canadian corporations listed on the stock exchanges in the United States.

Other influential groups that engage in research to improve accounting principles in both Canada and the United States include the Certified General Accountants Association of Canada, the Society of Management Accountants of Canada, the Canadian Academic Accounting Association, and the American Accounting Association.

In addition to the above sources, ''substantial authoritative support'' may include widespread use of an accounting practice within a particular industry or general recognition of a practice in the accounting literature.

Because accounting principles must evolve with changes in the business environment, there is no complete list of generally accepted accounting principles. There is, however, a consensus among accountants and informed users of financial statements as to what these principles are. Most accounting principles are applicable to profit-making organizations of any size and form. We shall now discuss briefly the major principles that govern the accounting process and comment on some of the areas of controversy.

The accounting entity concept

2   Discuss the
accounting principles,
assumptions, and
conventions presented
on pages 538-546.

One of the basic principles of accounting is that information is compiled for a clearly defined accounting entity. An accounting entity is any *economic unit* that controls resources and engages in economic activities. An individual is an accounting entity. So is a business enterprise, whether organized as a proprietorship, partnership, or corporation. Governmental agencies are accounting entities, as are all nonprofit clubs and organizations. An accounting entity may also be defined as an identifiable economic unit *within a larger accounting entity.* For example, the Chevrolet Division of General Motors of Canada may be viewed as an accounting entity separate from GM's other activities.

The basic accounting equation, Assets = Liabilities + Owner's Equity, reflects the accounting entity concept since the elements of the equation relate *to the particular entity whose economic activity is being reported in the financial statements.* Although we have considerable flexibility in defining our accounting entity, we must be careful to use the *same definition* in the measurement of assets, liabilities, owner's equity, revenue, and expense. An income statement would not make sense, for example, if it included all the revenue of General Motors of Canada but listed only the expenses of the Chevrolet Division.

Although the entity concept appears straightforward, it can pose some judgmental allocation problems for accountants. Assume, for example, that we want to prepare an income statement for only the Chevrolet Division of General Motors. Also assume that a given plant facility is used in the production of Chevrolets, Pontiacs, and school buses. How much of the depreciation on this factory building should be regarded as an expense of the Chevrolet Division? We will discuss the solution to such problems in later chapters; however, the importance of the entity concept in developing meaningful financial information should be clear.

The going-concern assumption

An underlying assumption in accounting is that an accounting entity will continue in operation for a period of time sufficient to carry out its existing commitments. The assumption of continuity, especially in the case of corporations, is in accord with experience in our economic system. This assumption leads to the concept of the *going concern.* In general, the going-concern assumption justifies ignoring immediate liquidating values in presenting assets and liabilities in the balance sheet.

For example, suppose that a company has just purchased a three-year insurance policy for $5,000. If we assume that the business will continue in operation for three years or more, we will consider the $5,000 cost of the insurance as an asset that provides services (freedom from risk) to the business over a three-year period. On the other hand, if we assume that the business is likely to terminate in the near future, the insurance policy should be recorded at its cancellation value—the amount of cash which can be obtained from the insurance company as a refund on immediate cancellation of the policy, which may be, say, $4,500.

Although the assumption of a going concern is justified in most normal situations, it should be dropped when it is not in accord with the facts. For example, accountants are sometimes asked to prepare a statement of financial position for an enterprise that is about to liquidate. In this case the assumption of continuity is no longer valid and the accountant drops the going-concern assumption and reports assets at their current liquidating value and liabilities at the amount required to settle the debts immediately.

The time period principle

We assume an indefinite life for most accounting entities. But accountants are asked to measure operating progress and changes in economic position at relatively short time intervals during this indefinite life. Users of financial statements need periodic measurements for decision-making purposes.

The need for frequent measurements creates many of the accountant's most challenging problems. Dividing the life of an enterprise into time segments, such as a year or a quarter of a year, requires numerous estimates and assumptions. For example, estimates must be made of the useful lives of depreciable assets and assumptions must be made as to appropriate depreciation methods. Thus periodic measurements of net income and financial position are at best only informed estimates. The tentative nature of periodic measurements should be understood by those who rely on periodic accounting information.

The monetary principle

The monetary principle means that money is used as the basic measuring unit for financial reporting. Money is the common denominator in which accounting measurements are made and summarized. The dollar, or any other monetary unit, represents a unit of value; that is, it reflects ability to command goods and services. Implicit in the use of money as a measuring unit is the **assumption that the dollar is a stable unit of value,** just as the kilometre is a stable unit of distance and a hectare is a stable unit of area.

Having accepted money as a measuring unit, accountants freely combine dollar measures of economic transactions that occur at various times during the life of an accounting entity. They combine, for example, a $20,000 cost of equipment purchased in 1978 and the $40,000 cost of similar equipment purchased in 1988 and report the total as a $60,000 investment in equipment.

Unlike the kilometre and the hectare, which are stable units of distance and area, the dollar **is not a stable unit of value.** The prices of goods and services in our economy change over time. When the **general price level** (a phrase used to describe the average of all prices) increases, the value of money (that is, its ability to command goods and services) decreases.

Despite the steady erosion in the purchasing power of the dollar in Canada during the last 40 years, accountants have continued to prepare financial statements in which the value of the dollar is assumed to be stable. This unrealistic assumption is one of the reasons why financial statements are viewed by some critics as misleading. Accounting principles are currently evolving toward the preparation of supplementary accounting information for the changing value of the dollar and for current replacement costs. The adjustment of accounting information to reflect the effects of inflation will be discussed in a subsequent section of this chapter.

The objectivity principle

The term **objective** refers to measurements that are **unbiased** and subject to verification by independent experts. For example, the price established in an arm's-length transaction is an objective measure of exchange value at the time of the transaction. Exchange prices established in business transactions constitute much of the raw material from which accounting information is generated. Accountants rely on various kinds of evidence to support their financial measurements, but they seek always the most objective evidence available. Invoices, contracts, paid cheques, and physical counts of inventory are examples of objective evidence.

If a measurement is objective, 10 competent investigators who make the same measurement will come up with substantially identical results. However, 10 competent accountants who set out independently to measure the net income of a given business would **not** arrive at an identical result. Despite the goal of objectivity, it is not possible to insulate accounting information from opinion and personal judgment. The cost of a depreciable asset can be determined objectively but not the periodic depreciation expense. To measure the cost of the asset services that have been used up during a given period requires estimates of the residual value and service life of the asset and judgment as to the depreciation method that should be used. Such estimates and judgments can produce significant variations in net income.

Objectivity in accounting has its roots in the quest for reliability. Accountants want to make their economic measurements reliable and, at the same time, as relevant to decision makers as possible. Where to draw the line in the trade-off between **reliability** and **relevance** is one of the crucial issues in accounting theory. Thus, accountants are constantly faced with the necessity of compromising between what users of financial information would like to know and what it is possible to measure with a reasonable degree of reliability.

Asset valuation: the cost principle

Both the balance sheet and the income statement are affected by the cost principle. Assets are initially recorded in the accounts at cost, and no adjustment is made to this valuation in later periods, except to allocate a portion of the original cost to expense as the assets expire. At the time an asset is originally acquired, cost represents the "fair market value" of the goods or services exchanged, as evidenced by an arm's-length transaction. With the passage of time, however, the fair market value of such assets as land and buildings may change greatly from their historical cost. These later changes in fair market value generally have been ignored in the accounts, and the assets have continued to be valued in the balance sheet at historical cost (less the portion of that cost which has been allocated to expense).

Increasing numbers of professional accountants believe that current market value should be used as the basis for asset valuation rather than historical cost. These accountants argue that current values would result in a more meaningful balance sheet. Also, they claim that current values should be allocated to expense to represent fairly the cost to the entity of the goods or services consumed in the effort to generate revenue.

The cost principle is related to the principle of *objectivity.* Those who support the cost principle argue that it is important that users have confidence in financial statements, and this confidence can best be maintained if accountants recognize changes in assets and liabilities only on the basis of completed transactions. Objective evidence generally exists to support cost, but evidence supporting current values may be less readily available.

Measuring revenue: the realization (recognition) principle

When is revenue realized and thus recognized in the accounting records? Under the assumptions of accrual accounting, revenue should be recognized "when it is earned." However, the "earning" of revenue usually is an extended *economic process* and does not actually take place at a single point in time.

Some revenue, such as interest earned, is directly related to time periods. For this type of revenue, it is easy to determine how much revenue has been earned by computing how much of the earning process is complete. However, the earning process for sales revenue relates to *economic activity* rather than to a specific period of time. In a manufacturing business, for example, the earning process involves (1) acquisition of raw materials, (2) production of finished goods, (3) sale of the finished goods, and (4) collection of cash from credit customers.

In the manufacturing example, there is little objective evidence to indicate how much revenue has been earned during the first two stages of the earning process. Accountants therefore usually do not recognize revenue until the revenue has been *realized.* Section 3400 of the *CICA Handbook* stipulates these criteria for revenue realization or recognition: (1) the significant risks and rewards of ownership of goods have been transferred from the seller to the buyer or the services have been performed, (2) reasonable assurance exists regarding the measurement of the consideration from the sale of goods or service rendered, and the extent to which goods may be returned, and (3) ultimate collection of the consideration from the sale of goods or services rendered is reasonably assured.[2] Accordingly, revenue is realized when both of the following conditions are met: (1) the earning process is *essentially complete* and (2) *objective evidence* exists as to the amount of revenue earned.

In most cases, the realization principle indicates that revenue should be recognized *at the time goods are sold or services are rendered*.[3] At this point the business has essentially completed the earning process and the sales value of the goods or services can be measured objectively. At any time prior to sale, the ultimate sales value of the goods or services sold can only be estimated. After the sale, the only step that remains is to collect from the customer, and this is usually a relatively certain event.

In Chapter 3, we described a *cash basis* of income measurement whereby revenue is recognized only when cash is collected from customers and expenses are recorded only when cash is actually paid out. Cash basis accounting *does not conform* to generally accepted accounting principles, but it may be used by individuals in determining their *taxable* income. (Remember that the accounting methods used in income tax returns often differ from those used in financial statements.)

The instalment method   Under the instalment method, the seller recognizes the gross profit on sales gradually over an extended time span as the cash is actually collected from customers. If the gross profit rate on instalment sales is 30%, then out of every dollar collected on instalment receivables, the sum of 30 cents represents gross profit.

To illustrate, assume that on December 15, Year 1, a retailer sells for $400 a television set that cost $280, or 70% of the sale price. The terms of the sale call for a $100 cash down payment with the balance payable in 15 monthly instalments of $20 each, beginning on January 1, Year 2. (Interest charges are ignored in this illustration.) The collections of cash and recognition of profit under the instalment method are summarized as follows:

INSTALMENT METHOD
ILLUSTRATED

YEAR	CASH COLLECTED	− COST RECOVERY, 70%	= PROFIT EARNED, 30%
1	$100	$ 70	$ 30
2	240	168	72
3	60	42	18
Totals	$400	$280	$120

Since the instalment method delays the recognition of profit beyond the point of sale, there is little theoretical justification for its use. Under generally accepted accounting principles, use of the instalment method is permissible only when the amounts likely to be collected on instalment sales are so uncertain that no reasonable basis exists for estimating an allowance for doubtful accounts. However, this is usually a rare occurrence. Consequently, the instalment method is seldom used for financial reporting.

---

[2] CICA, *CICA Handbook* (Toronto), paragraphs 3400.06, 3400.07, and 3400.08.
[3] Ibid., paragraphs 3400.06, 3400.07, 3400.08, and 3400.11.

Percentage-of-completion   Under certain circumstances, accountants recognize income during the production process.[4] An example arises in the case of long-term construction contracts, such as the building of a dam over a period of 10 years.[5] Clearly the income statements of a company engaged in such a project would be of little use to managers or investors if no profit or loss were reported until the dam was finally completed. The accountant therefore estimates the portion of the dam completed during each accounting period, and recognizes the gross profit on the project *in proportion* to the work completed. This is known as the percentage-of-completion method of accounting for long-term contracts.

The percentage-of-completion method works as follows:

1 An estimate is made of the total costs to be incurred and the total profit to be earned over the life of the project.
2 Each period, an estimate is made of the portion of the total project completed during the period. This estimate is usually made by expressing the costs incurred during the period as a percentage of the estimated total cost of the project.
3 The percentage figure determined in step 2 is applied to the estimated total profit on the contract to compute the amount of profit applicable to the current accounting period.
4 No estimate is made of the percentage of work during the final period. In the period in which the project is completed, any remaining profit is recognized.

To illustrate, assume that Reed Construction Limited enters into a contract to build an irrigation canal at a price of $5,000,000. The canal will be built over a three-year period at an estimated total cost of $4,000,000. Therefore, the estimated total profit on the project is $1,000,000. The following schedule shows the actual costs incurred and the amount of profit to be recognized in each of the three years using the percentage-of-completion method:

PROFIT RECOGNIZED AS
WORK PROGRESSES

YEAR	(A) ACTUAL COSTS INCURRED	(B) PERCENTAGE OF WORK DONE IN YEAR (COLUMN A ÷ $4,000,000)	(C) PROFIT CONSIDERED EARNED ($1,000,000 × COLUMN B)
1	$ 600,000	15	$150,000
2	2,000,000	50	500,000
3	1,452,000	*	298,000 balance
Totals	$4,052,000		$948,000

*Balance required to complete the contract.

The percentage of the work completed during Year 1 was estimated by dividing the actual cost incurred in the year by the estimated total cost of the project ($600,000 ÷ $4,000,000 = 15%). Because 15% of the work was done in Year 1, 15% of the estimated total profit of $1,000,000 was considered earned in that year ($1,000,000 × 15% = $150,000). Costs incurred in Year 2 amounted to 50% of the estimated total

---

[4] Op. cit., *CICA Handbook*, paragraphs 3400.08 and 3400.14.
[5] According to the CICA's *Financial Reporting in Canada*, 17th ed., page 95, of the 24 companies reporting construction contracts, 17 used the percentage-of-completion method, 4 used the completed-contract method, and 3 used both methods.

costs ($2,000,000 ÷ $4,000,000 = 50%); thus, 50% of the estimated total profit was recognized in Year 2 ($1,000,000 × 50% = $500,000). Note that no percentage-of-work-completed figure was computed for Year 3. In Year 3, the total actual cost (including the cost overrun of $52,000) is known ($4,052,000), and the actual total profit on the contract is determined to be $948,000 ($5,000,000 − $4,052,000). Since profits of $650,000 were previously recognized in Years 1 and 2, the *remaining* profit ($948,000 − $650,000 = $298,000) must be recognized in Year 3.

Although an expected *profit* on a long-term construction contract is recognized in proportion to the work completed, a different treatment is accorded to an expected *loss*. If at the end of any accounting period it appears that a loss will be incurred on a contract in progress, the *entire loss should be recognized at once*.

The percentage-of-completion method should be used only when the total profit expected to be earned can be *reasonably estimated in advance*. If there are substantial uncertainties in the amount of profit that will ultimately be earned, no profit should be recognized until *production is completed*. This approach is often referred to as the *completed-contract method*. If the completed-contract method had been used in the preceding example, no profit would have been recognized in Years 1 and 2; the entire profit of $948,000 would be recorded in Year 3 when the contract was completed and actual costs known.

Measuring expenses: the matching principle

Revenue, the gross increase in net assets resulting from the production or sale of goods and services, is offset by expenses incurred in bringing the company's output to the point of sale. Examples of expenses relating to revenue are the cost of merchandise sold, the expiration of asset services, and out-of-pocket expenditures for operating costs. The measurement of expenses occurs in two stages: (1) measuring the *cost* of goods and services that will be consumed or expire in generating revenue and (2) determining *when* the goods and services acquired have contributed to revenue and their cost thus *becomes an expense*. The second aspect of the measurement process is often referred to as *matching costs and revenue* and is fundamental to the *accrual basis* of accounting.

Costs are matched with revenue in two major ways:

1 In relation to the product sold or service rendered   If goods or services can be related to the product or service that constitutes the output of the enterprise, its cost becomes an expense when the product is sold or the service rendered to customers. The cost of goods sold in a merchandising company is a good example of this type of expense. Similarly, a commission paid to a real estate salesperson by a real estate brokerage office is an expense directly related to the revenue generated by the salesperson.

2 In relation to the time period during which revenue is earned   Some costs incurred by businesses cannot be directly related to the product or service output of the company. Expired fire insurance, property taxes, depreciation on a building, the salary of the president of the company — all are examples of costs incurred in generating revenue that cannot be related to specific transactions. The accountant refers to this class of costs as *period costs*, and charges them to expense by associating them with the *period of time* during which they are incurred and presumably contribute to revenue, rather than by associating them with specific revenue-producing transactions.

The consistency principle

The principle of *consistency* implies that a particular accounting method, once adopted, will not be changed from period to period. This assumption is important because it assists users of financial statements in interpreting changes in financial position and changes in net income.

Consider the confusion that would result if a company ignored the principle of consistency and changed its method of depreciation every year. The company could cause its net income for any given year to increase or decrease merely by changing its depreciation method.

The principle of consistency does not mean that a company should *never* make a change in its accounting methods. In fact, a company *should* make a change if a proposed new accounting method will provide more useful information than does the method presently in use. But when a significant change in accounting methods does occur, the fact that a change has been made, and the dollar effects of the change, should be *fully disclosed* in the financial statements.

Consistency applies to a single accounting entity and increases the comparability of financial statements from period to period. Different companies, even those in the same industry, may follow different accounting methods. For this reason, it is important to determine the accounting methods used by companies whose financial statements are being compared.

The disclosure principle

Adequate disclosure means that all *material* and *relevant facts* concerning financial position, and the results of operations, *are communicated to users.* This can be accomplished either in the financial statements or in the notes accompanying the statements. Such disclosure should make the financial statements more useful and less subject to misinterpretation.

Adequate disclosure does not require that information be presented in great detail; it does require, however, that no important information be withheld. For example, if a company has been named as defendant in a large lawsuit, this information must be disclosed. Other examples of information that should be disclosed in financial statements include:

1 A summary of the accounting policies (for example, principles and methods) used in the preparation of the statements
2 Dollar effects of any changes in these accounting methods during the current period
3 Other significant events affecting financial position, including major new contracts for sales of goods or services, and pending legislation that may significantly affect operations
4 Identification of assets that have been pledged as collateral to secure loans
5 Terms of major borrowing arrangements and existence of large contingent liabilities
6 Contractual provisions relating to leasing arrangements, employee pension and bonus plans, and major proposed asset acquisitions

Even significant events that occur *after* the end of the accounting period but befor
the financial statements are issued may need to be disclosed.

Naturally, there are practical limits to the amount of disclosure that can be made i
financial statements and the accompanying notes. The key point to bear in mind i
that the supplementary information should be *relevant to the interpretation* of th
financial statements.

Materiality

The term *materiality* refers to the *relative importance* of an item or event. Accoun
tants are primarily concerned with significant information and are not overly concerne
with those items that have little effect on financial statements. For example, shoul
the cost of a pencil sharpener, a wastepaper basket, or a stapler be recorded in a
asset account and depreciated over its useful life? Even though more than one perio
will benefit from the use of such assets, the concept of *materiality* permits th
immediate recognition of the cost of these items as an expense.

We must recognize that the materiality of an item is a relative matter; what i
material for one business entity may not be material for another. Materiality of a
item may depend not only on its *amount* but also on its *nature*. In summary, we ca
state the following rule: *An item is material if there is a reasonable expectation tha
knowledge of it would influence the decisions of prudent users of financial statement.*

Conservatism as a guide in resolving uncertainties

We have previously referred to the use of *conservatism* in connection with th
measurement of net income and the reporting of accounts receivable and inventorie
in the balance sheet. Although the concept of conservatism may not qualify as a
accounting principle, it has long been a powerful influence upon asset valuation an
income determination. Conservatism is most useful when matters of judgment o
estimates are involved. Ideally, accountants should base their estimates on soun
logic and select those accounting methods that neither overstate nor understate th
facts. When some doubt exists about the valuation of an asset or the realization of
revenue or gain, however, accountants traditionally select the accounting option tha
produces a lower net income and less favourable financial position for the curren
period.

An example of conservatism is the traditional practice of pricing inventory at th
lower of cost and market. Decreases in the market value of the inventory are recog
nized as a part of the cost of goods sold in the current period, but increases in marke
value of inventory are ignored. Failure to apply conservatism when valuations ar
especially uncertain may produce misleading information and result in losses t
creditors and shareholders.

Auditors' opinion on published financial statements

**3   Define an audit and
discuss the nature of
the auditors' report.**

The annual financial statements of large corporations are used by great numbers o
shareholders, creditors, government regulators, and members of the general publi
What assurance do these people have that the information in these statements i
reliable and is presented in conformity with generally accepted accounting principles
The answer is that the annual financial statements of large corporations are *audite*
by independent public accountants.

An audit is a thorough investigation of every material item, dollar amount, and disclosure that appears in the financial statements. After completing the audit, the auditors express their opinion as to the *fairness* of the financial statements. This opinion is contained in the *auditors' report,* published with the statements in the company's annual report to its shareholders.

Considering the extensive investigation that precedes it, the audit opinion is surprisingly short. It usually consists of two brief paragraphs, unless the auditors comment on unusual features of the financial statements. The first paragraph describes the *scope* of the auditors' examination; the second states their *opinion* of the financial statements. A report by a public accounting firm might read as follows:

INDEPENDENT AUDITORS' REPORT

> We have examined the balance sheet of Canadian Oil Corporation as at December 31, 19___, and the statements of income, retained earnings, and changes in financial position for the year then ended. Our examination was made in accordance with generally accepted auditing standards and accordingly included such tests and other procedures as we considered necessary in the circumstances.
>
> *In our opinion,* these financial statements *present fairly* the financial position of Canadian Oil Corporation as at December 31, 19___, and the results of its operations and the changes in its financial position for the year then ended *in accordance with generally accepted accounting principles* applied on a basis *consistent with that of the preceding year.* [Emphasis supplied.]

Over many decades, audited financial statements have developed an excellent track record of reliability. Note, however, that the auditors *do not guarantee* the accuracy of financial statements; rather, they render their *professional opinion* as to the overall *fairness* of the statements. "Fairness," in this context, means that the financial statements are *not misleading.* However, just as a physician may make an error in the diagnosis of a particular patient, there is always a possibility that an auditor's opinion may be in error. The primary responsibility for the reliability of financial statements rests with the management of the issuing company, not with the independent auditors.

ACCOUNTING FOR THE EFFECTS OF INFLATION

Inflation may be defined either as an increase in the general price level or as a decrease in the purchasing power of the dollar. The *general price level* is the weighted average of the prices of all goods and services in the economy. Changes in the general price level are measured by a *general price index* with a base year assigned a value of 100. The index compares the level of current prices with that of the base year. Assume, for example, that Year 1 is the base year. If prices rise by 10% during Year 2, the price index at the end of Year 2 will be 110. At the end of Year 9 the price index might be 200, indicating that the general price level had doubled since Year 1.

The most widely recognized measure of the general price level in Canada is the Consumer Price Index for Canada (CPI), published by Statistics Canada. The base year of the Consumer Price Index is 1957. The CPI has increased considerably, indicating that prices (on the average) have risen substantially since 1957.

We often hear statements such as "Today's dollar is worth only 33 cents." The "worth" or "value" of a dollar lies in its ability to buy goods or services. This "value" is called **purchasing power.** The reciprocal of the general price index (100 divided by the current level of the index) represents the purchasing power of the dollar in the current year *relative to that in the base year.* For example, say the reciprocal of the CPI in May 1988, was 100 ÷ 400, or .25, therefore, we might say that $1 in 1988 was equivalent in purchasing power to about 25 cents in 1957.

What effect do material changes in general price levels, and thus changes in the value of money, have on accounting measures? By combining transactions measured in dollars of various years, the accountant in effect ignores changes in the size of the measuring unit. For example, suppose that a company purchases land for $200,000 and 10 years later sells this land for $400,000. Using the dollar as a measuring unit, we would recognize a gain of $200,000 ($400,000 sales price − $200,000 cost) on the sale of land. But if prices doubled during that 10-year period and the value of money was cut in half, we might say that the company was *no better off* as a result of buying and selling this land. The $400,000 received for the land after 10 years represents the same command over goods and services as $200,000 did when invested in the land 10 years earlier.

We have experienced persistent inflation in Canada for over 40 years; more importantly, the forces that have been built into our economic and political institutions almost guarantee that inflation will continue. The only question is how severe the inflationary trend will be. Our traditional accounting process is based upon the assumption of a stable dollar. This cost-based system works extremely well in periods of stable prices; it works reasonably well during prolonged but mild inflation but it loses virtually all meaning if inflation becomes extreme. One of the greatest challenges to the accounting profession today is to develop new accounting methods that will bring financial statements into accord with the economic reality of an inflationary environment.

4 Explain why the use of historical costs during periods of inflation may overstate income.

Income — fact or illusion?

Corporate income is watched closely by business managers, investors, and government officials. The trend of income plays a significant role in the allocation of the nation's investment resources, in levels of employment, and in national economic policy. As a result of the *stable monetary assumption,* however, a strong argument may be made that much of the corporate income reported today is an illusion.

In the measurement of business income, a distinction must be drawn between income and the recovery of costs. A business earns an income only when the value of goods sold and services rendered (revenue) *exceeds* the value of resources consumed in the earning process (costs and expenses). Accountants have traditionally assigned "values" to resources consumed in the earning process by using historical dollar amounts. Depreciation expense, for example, may be based upon prices paid to acquire assets 10 or 20 years ago.

When the general price level is rising rapidly, such historical costs may significantly understate the current economic value of the resources being consumed. If costs and expenses are understated, it follows that reported income is overstated. In other words, the stable monetary assumption may lead to reporting *illusory* income; much of the net income reported by business enterprises actually may be a return of costs.

 In a recent year, Exxon Corporation appeared to be one of the most profitable companies in the world, reporting net income of $4.2 billion. But when the giant oil company's income statement was adjusted for the effects of inflation, the income vanished — instead, there appeared a net loss of $296 million. What happened? Did Exxon operate at an income or a loss? The accounting concepts discussed in the following sections of this chapter should shed some light on these interesting questions.

Two approaches to "inflation accounting"

5 Distinguish between the constant dollar and current cost approaches to measuring net income. Prepare an income statement using either approach.

Two alternative approaches to modifying our accounting process to cope with inflation have received much attention. These two approaches are:

1 **Constant dollar accounting**   Under this approach, historical costs in the financial statements are adjusted to the *number of current dollars representing an equivalent amount of purchasing power.* Thus, all amounts are expressed in units (current dollars) of equal purchasing power. Since a general price index is used in restating the historical costs, constant dollar accounting shows the effects of changes in the *general* price level (general inflation). Constant dollar accounting is also called *general price level* accounting.

2 **Current cost accounting**   This method differs from constant dollar accounting in that assets and expenses are shown in the financial statements at the current cost to *replace* those specific resources. The *current replacement cost* of a specific asset may rise or fall at a different rate from the general price level. Thus, current cost accounting shows the effects of *specific price changes,* rather than changes in the general price level.

To illustrate these approaches to "inflation accounting," assume that in Year 1 you purchased 500 kg of sugar for $100 when the general price index was at 100. Early in Year 2, you sold the sugar for $108 when the general price index was at 110 and the replacement cost of 500 kg of sugar was $104. What is the amount of your income or loss on this transaction? The amount of income or loss determined under current accounting standards (unadjusted historical cost) and the two "inflation accounting" alternatives is shown as follows.

WHICH "COST" OF GOODS SOLD IS MOST REALISTIC?

	UNADJUSTED HISTORICAL COST	ADJUSTED FOR GENERAL INFLATION (CONSTANT DOLLARS)	ADJUSTED FOR CHANGES IN SPECIFIC PRICES (CURRENT COSTS)
Revenue	$108	$108	$108
Cost of goods sold	100	110	104
Income (loss)	$ 8	$ (2)	$ 4

Under each method, an amount is deducted from revenue to provide for recovery of cost. However, the value assigned to the "cost" of goods sold differs under each of the three approaches.

Unadjusted historical cost   This method is used in current accounting practice. The use of unadjusted historical cost is based upon the assumption that the dollar is a stable unit of measure. Income is determined by comparing sales revenue with the *historical cost* of the asset sold. In using this approach to income determination, accountants assume that a business is as well off when it has recovered its *original dollar investment,* and that it is better off whenever it recovers more than the original number of dollars invested in any given asset.

In our example of buying and selling sugar, the income figure of $8 shows *how many dollars* you came out ahead. However, this approach ignores the fact that Year 1 dollars and Year 2 dollars are *not equivalent in terms of purchasing power.* It also ignores the fact that the $100 deduction intended to provide for the recovery of cost is not sufficient to allow you to *replace* the 500 kg of sugar.

Constant dollar accounting   When financial statements are adjusted for changes in the general price level, historical amounts are restated as the number of current dollars *equivalent in purchasing power* to the historical cost. Income is determined by comparing revenue with the *amount of purchasing power* (stated in current dollars) originally invested.

The general price index tells us that $110 in Year 2 is equivalent in purchasing power to the $100 invested in sugar in Year 1. But you do not have $110 in Year 2; you received only $108 dollars from the sale of the sugar. Thus, you have sustained a *$2 loss in purchasing power.*

Current cost accounting   In current cost accounting, income is measured by comparing revenue with the *current replacement cost* of the assets consumed in the earning process. The logic of this approach lies in the concept of the going concern. What will you do with the $108 received from the sale of the sugar? If you are going to continue in the sugar business, you will have to buy more sugar. At current market prices, it will cost you $104 to replace 500 kg of sugar; the remaining $4, therefore, is designated as income.

Current cost accounting recognizes in the income statement the costs which a going concern actually has to pay to replace its expiring assets. The resulting income figure, therefore, closely parallels the maximum amount that a business could distribute to its owners and still be able to maintain the *present size and scale* of its operations.

Which approach measures income?   Which of these three approaches correctly measures income? The answer is that all three methods provide a valid measurement, but that each approach utilizes a different definition of "cost" and of "income." The real question confronting the accounting profession is, which of these alternative measures of income is the *most useful to decision makers?* This question is being considered very carefully by the CICA in Canada and the FASB and the SEC in the United States and other interested parties.

Disclosing the effects of inflation in financial statements

Perhaps the day will come when constant dollar or current cost information will replace the use of historical costs in financial statements. However, a change of this magnitude cannot be made without much planning and consideration of the possible consequences. Accounting information is used on a daily basis by millions of economic decision makers. A major change in the nature of this information is sure to affect the allocation of resources within our economy. Decision makers would have to learn to interpret the new information; capital would move out of some industries and into others; income tax laws and other government economic policies might change. In light of these considerations, careful experimentation with constant dollar and current cost information is needed before we abandon the use of historical costs as our basis for financial statements.

As an experimental step, the CICA in Canada and the FASB in the United States have issued pronouncements recommending large publicly owned corporations to include with their historical cost-based financial statements *supplementary* information in the annual reports showing certain constant dollar and current cost information.[6] Note that this information is supplementary to the conventional financial statements and is not a substitute for them. This action by the CICA and the FASB will introduce decision makers to certain constant dollar and current cost information on an experimental basis. So far this experimentation has not led to widespread use of constant dollar or current cost information, perhaps due to the slowdown in the rate of inflation in the past few years.[7]

The CICA's pronouncement, *CICA Handbook*, Section 4510, "Reporting the Effects of Changing Prices," will be highlighted in the final section of the chapter.

Illustration of constant dollar and current cost information

To illustrate applications of the constant dollar and current cost accounting discussed earlier, let us assume that the following supplementary information is required:

1 Net income measured in constant dollars.
2 The gain or loss in purchasing power that results from holding monetary assets or having monetary liabilities.
3 Net income on a current cost basis.

The format for making these disclosures is shown in the following illustration. (The three required disclosures are identified by the numbered arrows.)

WHICH INCOME FIGURE DO YOU THINK IS MOST REALISTIC?

SUPPLEMENT TO FINANCIAL STATEMENTS

FLATION COMPANY
Income Statement Adjusted for Changing Prices
For Year 10

	AS REPORTED IN THE UNADJUSTED HISTORICAL COST STATEMENTS	ADJUSTED FOR GENERAL INFLATION (CONSTANT DOLLARS)*	ADJUSTED FOR CHANGES IN SPECIFIC PRICES (CURRENT COSTS)
Net Sales	$600,000	$600,000	$600,000
Costs and expenses:			
Cost of goods sold	$360,000	$370,000	$391,500
Depreciation expense	60,000	80,000	90,000
Other expenses	130,000	130,000	130,000
Total	$550,000	$580,000	$611,500
Net income (loss)	$ 50,000	①⟶ $ 20,000	③⟶ $ (11,500)
Net gain from decline in purchasing power of net amounts owed		②⟶ $ 8,000	

Stated in dollars of average purchasing power during Year 10.

[6] In 1984, FASB dropped the requirement that companies include net income disclosure measured in constant dollars. In 1986, FASB made these supplementary disclosures voluntary.
[7] CICA, *Reporting the Effects of Changing Prices — A Report in the Third Year's Experience with Section 4510 of the CICA Handbook* (Toronto, October, 1986), p. 4. CICA, *Financial Reporting in Canada*, 17th ed., p. 79.

We shall now use the information in this illustration to demonstrate further the concepts of constant dollar and current cost accounting and to interpret these disclosures from the viewpoint of the financial statement user.

Net income measured in constant dollars

6 Use a price index to restate historical costs to an equivalent number of current dollars.

A basic problem with the use of historical costs for measuring income is that revenue and expenses may be stated in dollars having different amounts of purchasing power. Sales revenues, for example, are recorded in current-year dollars. Depreciation expense, on the other hand, is based upon dollars spent to acquire assets in past years. As previously emphasized, dollars in the current year and dollars of past years are not equivalent in terms of purchasing power.

In a constant dollar income statement, expenses based on "old" dollars are *restated* at the number of current dollars representing the equivalent amount of purchasing power. When all revenue and expenses are stated in units of similar purchasing power, we can see whether the business is gaining or losing in terms of the amount of purchasing power it controls.

To restate a historical amount in terms of an equivalent number of current dollars, we multiply the historical amount by the ratio of the current general price level to the historical general price level, as follows:

$$\text{Historical cost} \times \frac{\text{Average general price index for current period}}{\text{Index at date of historical cost}} = \begin{array}{l}\text{Equivalent number} \\ \text{of current dollars}\end{array}$$

For example, assume that land was purchased for $100,000 when the general price index stood at 100. If the general price index is now 170, we may find the number of current dollars equivalent to the purchasing power originally invested in the land by multiplying the $100,000 historical cost by *170/100.* The result, $170,000, represents the number of current dollars equivalent in purchasing power to the 100,000 historical dollars.

Price Index levels for our illustration   The following changes in the general price index are assumed in our Flation Company illustration:

DATE	PRICE INDEX
Beginning of Year 8 (acquisition date for depreciable assets)	150
End of Year 9	180
Average price level for Year 10*	200
End of Year 10	216
Rate of inflation for Year 10†	20%

*The "average" price level for the year is computed as a monthly average and need not lie exactly halfway between the price levels at the beginning and end of the year.
†The inflation rate is computed by dividing the increase in the price index over the year by the price index at the beginning of the year: (216 − 180) ÷ 180 = 20%.

In restating historical dollars to current dollars, we shall use the *average price level* for Year 10 (200) to represent the purchasing power of current dollars.[8]

[8] An acceptable alternative is to use the year-end price level to represent the purchasing power of current dollars. However, use of the year-end price level means that all income statement amounts, including revenue and expense transactions conducted during the current year, must be restated. For this reason, companies presenting constant dollar information often use the average price level for the current year

Not all amounts are restated   Compare the constant dollar and historical cost income statements of the Flation Company for Year 10. Note that only two items—depreciation expense and the cost of goods sold — have been restated in the constant dollar statement. Sales revenue and expenses other than depreciation consist of transactions occurring during the current year. Therefore, these amounts are *already* stated in current dollars. We need to adjust to current dollars only those expenses that are based on costs incurred in past years.

Restating the cost of goods sold   During Year 10, Flation Company sold merchandise with a historical cost of $360,000. Assume that $90,000 of these goods came from the beginning inventory, acquired at the end of Year 9 when the price level was 180; the remaining $270,000 of these goods were purchased during Year 10. The restatement of the cost of goods sold to average Year 10 dollars follows:

	HISTORICAL DOLLARS	CONVERSION RATIO	EQUIVALENT CURRENT DOLLARS
Beginning inventory	$ 90,000 ×	$200/180$ =	$100,000
Purchased in Year 10	270,000	* =	270,000
Cost of goods sold	$360,000		$370,000

*No adjustment necessary — amount already is stated in current dollars.

Restating depreciation expense   Assume that Flation Company's depreciation expense all relates to equipment purchased early in Year 8 when the price level was 150. The equipment cost $600,000 and is being depreciated over 10 years by the straight-line method. Since the average price level in Year 10 is 200, the purchasing power originally invested in this equipment is equivalent to $800,000 current dollars ($600,000 × 200/150 = $800,000). Thus, the amount of purchasing power expiring in Year 10, stated in current dollars, is $80,000 ($800,000 ÷ 10 years).

A shortcut approach is simply to restate the historical depreciation expense, as follows:

HISTORICAL DOLLARS	CONVERSION RATIO	EQUIVALENT CURRENT DOLLARS
$60,000	× 200/150 =	$80,000

Since depreciable assets are long-lived, the price level prevailing when the assets were acquired may be substantially different from the current price level. In such cases, the amount of depreciation expense recognized becomes one of the most significant differences between historical dollar and current dollar financial statements.

Interpreting the constant dollar income statement

The basic difference between historical dollar and constant dollar income statements is the unit of measure. Historical dollar income statements use the dollar as a basic unit of measure. The unit of measure in constant dollar income statements is the *purchasing power of the current dollar.*

A conventional income statement shows how many dollars were added to owner's equity from the operation of the business. Identifying a dollar increase in owner's equity as "income" implies that owners are better off when they recover more than the original number of dollars they invested. No attention is given to the fact that a greater number of dollars may still have less purchasing power than was originally invested.

A *constant dollar* income statement shows whether the *inflow of purchasing power* from current operations is larger or smaller than the *purchasing power consumed* in the effort to generate revenue. In short, the net income figure tells us whether the amount of purchasing power controlled by the business has increased or decreased as a result of operations.

Gains and losses in purchasing power

7 Explain why holding monetary items causes gains or losses in purchasing power.

Constant dollar accounting introduces a new consideration in measuring the effects of inflation upon a business: gains and losses in purchasing power from holding monetary items. *Monetary items* are those assets and liabilities representing claims to a *fixed number of dollars.* Examples of monetary assets are cash, notes receivable and accounts receivable; most liabilities are monetary, including notes payable and accounts payable.

Holding monetary assets during a period of rising prices results in a loss of purchasing power because the value of the money is falling. In contrast, owing money during a period of rising prices gives rise to a gain in purchasing power because debts may be repaid using dollars of less purchasing power than those originally borrowed.

To illustrate, assume that Flation Company held $30,000 in cash throughout Year 10, while the price level rose 20% (from 180 to 216). By the end of the year this $30,000 cash balance will have lost 20% of its purchasing power, as demonstrated by the following analysis:

Number of dollars needed at year-end to represent the same purchasing power as $30,000 at the beginning of the year ($30,000 × 216/180)	$36,000
Number of dollars actually held at year-end	30,000
Loss in purchasing power as a result of holding monetary assets	$ 6,000

(We can also compute this $6,000 loss simply by multiplying the amount of the monetary assets held throughout the year by the 20% inflation rate: $30,000 × 20% = $6,000.

A similar analysis is applied to any monetary liabilities. Assume, for example, that Flation Company has a $70,000 note payable outstanding throughout Year 10. The resulting gain in purchasing power is computed as follows:

Number of dollars at year-end representing the same purchasing power as $70,000 owed at beginning of year ($70,000 × $216/180$)	$84,000
Number of dollars actually owed at year-end	70,000
Gain in purchasing power as a result of owing a fixed number of dollars	$14,000

Accordingly, Flation Company has experienced an $8,000 net gain in purchasing power ($14,000 gain − $6,000 loss), because its monetary liabilities were greater than its monetary assets.[9] The disclosure of this net gain is illustrated in the supplementary information on page 551.

Interpreting the net gain or loss in purchasing power

In determining the change in the purchasing power represented by owner's equity, we must consider **both** the amount of constant dollar net income **and** the amount of any gain or loss resulting from monetary items. Thus, the purchasing power of the owner's equity in Flation Company increased by $28,000 during Year 10 ($20,000 net income + $8,000 gain in purchasing power from monetary items.).

The purchasing power gain from monetary items is shown separately from the determination of net income to emphasize the special nature of this gain. The income statement shows the purchasing power created or lost *as a result of business operations.* The $8,000 net gain in purchasing power, however, is caused entirely by the *effect of inflation* upon the purchasing power of monetary assets and liabilities. A business that owns monetary assets or owes money may have a purchasing power gain or loss even if it earns no revenue and incurs no expenses.

In evaluating the effect of inflation upon a particular business, we must consider the effect of inflation upon operations and its effects upon the monetary assets and liabilities of the business. If a business must maintain high levels of cash or accounts receivable from customers, we should recognize that inflation will continually erode the purchasing power of these assets. On the other hand, if a business is able to finance its operations with borrowed capital, inflation will benefit the company by allowing it to repay smaller amounts of purchasing power than it originally borrowed.

Net income on a current cost basis

Constant dollar accounting does not abandon historical costs as the basis for measurement but simply expresses these costs in terms of the current value of money. Current cost accounting, on the other hand, does represent a departure from the historical cost concept. The term ''current cost'' usually refers to the *current replacement cost* of assets. In a current cost income statement, expenses are stated at the estimated cost to *replace the specific assets* sold or used up. Thus, current cost accounting involves estimates of current market values, rather than adjustments to historical costs for changes in the general price level.

To determine the cost of goods sold on a current cost basis. All we need to know is (1) how many units of inventory were sold during the year, and (2) the average replacement cost of these units during Year 10. If Flation Company sold 145,000 units during the year, and the average replacement cost was $2.70 per unit, the cost of goods sold would be $391,500 on a current cost basis (145,000 units × $2.70). Note that the historical cost of units in the company's beginning inventory does not enter into the current cost computation.

---

[9] Some readers may notice that our net gain is stated in end-of-year 10 dollars. To be technically consistent with the other constant dollar data illustrated earlier, this net gain should be restated in dollars of average purchasing power for Year 10. The gain can be restated as follows: $8,000 × $^{200}/_{216}$ = $7,407. We have ignored this restatement because it is not material in dollar amount and is an unnecessary refinement for an introductory discussion.

Of course, the replacement cost of an asset may fluctuate during the year. Since a cost such as depreciation expense occurs continually *throughout* the year, current cost measurements are based on the *average* replacement cost during the year, not on the replacement cost at year-end.

To illustrate, assume that the replacement cost of Flation Company's equipment was estimated to be $850,000 at the beginning of Year 10 and $950,000 at year-end. Current cost depreciation expense should be based upon the $900,000 average replacement cost of the equipment during the year. Since the equipment has a 10-year life, the depreciation expense appearing in the current cost income statement (page 551) is $90,000 ($900,000 ÷ 10 years).

Interpreting a current cost income statement

A current cost income statement does *not* measure the flow of general purchasing power in and out of the business. Rather, it shows whether a company earns enough revenue to *replace* the goods and services used up in the effort to generate that revenue. The resulting net income figure closely parallels *distributable income*—the maximum amount that the business can distribute to its owners and still maintain the present size and scale of its operations.

Unfortunately, the financial statements of large corporations show that many companies in industries vital to our economy are reporting income measured on a historical cost basis but are incurring large *losses* according to their supplementary current cost disclosures. Companies in the steel industry and utilities industry provide excellent examples. What does this mean to an informed reader of financial statements? In short, it means that these companies do not earn sufficient revenue to maintain their productive capacity. In the long run, they must either obtain capital from other sources or scale down the size of their operations.

The CICA's recommendations on accounting for changing prices

8 Explain some of the key features of Section 4510 of the CICA Handbook on "Reporting the effects of changing prices."

In Section 4510 of the *CICA Handbook*, ''Reporting the Effects of Changing Prices,'' the CICA recommends that large publicly owned corporations disclose in their *annual* reports *certain* components of *constant dollar* and *current cost* accounting as *supplementary information.* It is important to note that this constant dollar and current cost information is a supplement to and *not* a replacement for the historical cost financial statements. Corporations are subject to the CICA recommendations if they have total assets (after the related accumulated depreciation, depletion, and amortization) of $350 million or more, or if inventories and property, plant, and equipment (before the related accumulated depreciation, depletion, and amortization total $50 million or more. These total amounts are the beginning balances of the historical cost financial statements.

The objective of the CICA recommendations is to provide information about the effect on an enterprise's financial position and operating results that are caused by (1) changes in prices of specific goods and services purchased, produced, and used and (2) changes in the general purchasing power of the monetary unit in which transactions are measured.[10] Thus, the CICA is concerned with both the concepts of

---

[10] CICA, *CICA Handbook* (Toronto), paragraph 4510.04.

specific price level changes (that is, current cost accounting) and general price level changes (that is, constant dollar accounting).

The following are some of the recommended disclosures to be included in annual reports as supplementary information:

1 The current cost amounts of (a) cost of goods sold and depreciation, depletion, and amortization expenses and (b) inventory and property, plant, and equipment at the end of the period.

2 The changes in the current cost amounts of inventory and property, plant, and equipment during the period.

3 The income (before extraordinary items, if any) after reflecting the current cost amounts of cost of goods sold and of depreciation, depletion, and amortization expenses of property, plant, and equipment, and the income taxes expense. This income amount is called *income on a current cost basis.*

4 The amount of the changes in the current costs of inventory and property, plant, and equipment during the period attributable to the effect of general inflation (that is, the change in the general price level or the purchasing power of the dollar).

5 The amount of the gain or loss in the purchasing power (due to the effect of general inflation) resulting from holding net monetary items (the excess of monetary liabilities over monetary assets or vice versa) during the period.

The recommended disclosure on the gains or loss in the purchasing power was illustrated in the Flation Company example. Similarly, the recommended disclosure of income on a current cost basis was illustrated in the Flation Company example. Further discussion on these and other recommended disclosures is covered in *Intermediate Accounting.*

In issuing Section 4510 in December 1982, the CICA's Accounting Standards Committee acknowledged that it represented a first step in the search for the most meaningful presentation of the effect of inflation on a business enterprise and that business enterprises should be ''encouraged to experiment with the disclosure of other assets and liabilities and related expenses measured on a current cost basis.''[11] The committee is committed to a comprehensive review of Section 4510 within five years of its release and to make such appropriate revisions as considered necessary. Accordingly, such review should be forthcoming soon.

It should be noted that the recommendations of Section 4510 do not carry the same force of compliance by business enterprises as other recommendations of the *CICA Handbook* because the former are related to supplementary information in the annual report and not necessarily part of the annual financial statements. Consequently, these recommendations are essentially voluntary in nature. The extent to which business enterprises adopt these recommendations will depend largely on whether the enterprises are convinced that the benefits exceed the cost involved in providing the supplementary information. As noted in Chapter 9, only a small number of business enterprises governed by Section 4510 complied with the recommended disclosures and the number is declining.[12] The reasons for such noncompliance

---

[11] Ibid., paragraph 4510.08.
[12] CICA, *Reporting the Effects of Changing Prices*, p. 3.

include the slowdown in the rate of inflation, the small differential between historical and current costs, the complexity of the recommendations, and the experimental nature of the recommendations.[13]

END-OF-CHAPTER REVIEW

SUMMARY OF CHAPTER LEARNING OBJECTIVES

1 Identify the major sources of generally accepted accounting principles.

The recommendations in the *CICA Handbook*, developed and promulgated by the CICA's Accounting Standards Committee, represent the most influential source of generally accepted accounting principles. In addition, some principles have become ''generally accepted'' as a result of widespread use.

2 Discuss the accounting principles, assumptions, and conventions presented on pages 538–546.

The principles and conventions discussed in this chapter include the concept of an accounting entity, the going-concern assumption, the time period principle, the monetary assumption, objectivity, the cost principle, the realization (recognition) principle, matching, consistency, disclosure, materiality, and conservatism. This is neither a complete nor an official listing of generally accepted accounting principles, but these are some of the most important concepts that underlie current accounting practice.

3 Define an audit and discuss the nature of the auditors' report.

An *audit* is an investigation conducted by a firm of public accountants to verify the content of a company's financial statements. After performing this investigation, the public accounting firm issues an *auditors' report* expressing the firm's professional opinion as to the fairness and completeness of these statements. Virtually all large corporations have their financial statements audited each year, and the auditors' report is made available both to investors and to the general public.

4 Explain why the use of historical costs during periods of inflation may overstate income.

Under current accounting practice, assets are recorded at cost; this cost then is allocated to expense as the assets are used up. Due to inflation, these historical costs may significantly understate the current economic value of the sources being consumed. If expenses are understated, it follows that income will be overstated.

5 Distinguish between the constant dollar and current cost approaches to measuring net income. Prepare an income statement using either approach.

Under *constant dollar* accounting, the historical costs of resources consumed during the current period are restated for changes in the *general* price level. Thus, a constant dollar income statement shows whether revenue is sufficient to recover the *purchasing power* consumed in the effort to generate that revenue. Under *current cost* accounting, the resources

[13] Ibid., p. 4.

consumed are shown at their current replacement cost. Thus, the income statement indicates whether revenue is sufficient to recover the *current market value* of the resources consumed so as to maintain the present size and scale of operations.

6 Use a price index to restate historical costs to an equivalent number of current dollars.

To restate a historical cost to an equivalent number of current dollars, the historical cost is multiplied by the ratio of the current general price level to the historical general price level.

7 Explain why holding monetary items causes gains or losses in purchasing power.

Monetary items are those assets and liabilities representing claims to a fixed number of dollars. Holding monetary assets during a period of inflation results in a loss of purchasing power because the value of money is falling. Owing money during a period of inflation results in a gain in purchasing power because debts may be repaid using dollars of less purchasing power than those originally borrowed.

8 Explain some of the key features of Section 4510 of the *CICA Handbook* on "Reporting the Effects of Changing Prices."

Section 4510 recommends that large public corporations disclose in their annual reports such supplementary information as purchasing power gain or loss, as well as cost of goods sold, depreciation, and income at current cost, and changes in current cost of inventory and property, plant and equipment.

KEY TERMS INTRODUCED OR EMPHASIZED IN CHAPTER 13

Auditors' report The report issued by a firm of public accountants after auditing the financial statements of a business. Expresses an opinion on the fairness of the financial statements and indicates the nature and limits of the responsibility being assumed by the independent auditors.

Conservatism A traditional practice of resolving uncertainties by choosing an asset valuation at the lower point of the range of reasonableness. Also refers to the policy of postponing recognition of revenue to a later date when a range of reasonable choice exists. Designed to avoid overstatement of financial strength and earnings.

Consistency An assumption that once a particular accounting method is adopted, it will not be changed from period to period. Intended to make financial statements of a given company comparable from year to year.

Constant dollar accounting The technique of expressing all financial statement amounts in dollars of equal purchasing power. This is accomplished by restating historical costs for subsequent changes in the general price level. Also called *general price level* (general inflation) *accounting.*

Cost principle The traditional, widely used policy of accounting for assets at their historical cost determined through arm's-length bargaining. Justified by the need for objective evidence to support the valuation of assets.

Current cost accounting The valuation of assets and measurements of income in terms of current replacement costs rather than historical costs. This approach to inflation accounting indicates the ability of a business to replace its physical capital (specific inventory and plant assets) as it is sold or used up.

Disclosure principle Financial statements should disclose all material and relevant information about the financial position and operating results of a business. The notes accompanying financial statements are an important means of disclosure.

Entity concept Any economic unit that controls economic resources and is accountable for these resources may be considered an accounting entity. The resources and the transactions of the entity are not to be intermingled with those of its owner or owners.

General price level The weighted-average price of all goods and services in the economy. Inflation may be defined as an increase in the general price level.

Generally accepted accounting principles Those accounting principles that have received substantial authoritative support, such as the accounting recommendations in the *CICA Handbook*. Often referred to by the acronym *GAAP*.

Going-concern assumption An assumption that a business entity will continue in operation indefinitely and thus will carry out its existing commitments.

Instalment method An accounting method that provides for recognition of realized profit on instalment contracts in proportion to cash collected.

Materiality The relative importance of an amount or item. An item that is not significant enough to influence the decisions of users of financial statements is considered as *not* material. The accounting treatment of immaterial items may be guided by convenience rather than by theoretical principles.

Monetary items Monetary items include assets representing claims to a *fixed number* of dollars (such as cash and receivables) and most liabilities. Holding monetary assets during a period of rising prices results in a loss in purchasing power; conversely, owing monetary liabilities results in a gain in purchasing power.

Monetary (stable-dollar) assumption In using money as a measuring unit and preparing financial statements expressed in dollars, accountants make the assumption that the dollar is a stable unit of measurement. This assumption is obviously faulty in an environment of continued inflation.

Objectivity (objective evidence) The valuation of assets and the measurement of income are to be based as much as possible on objective evidence, such as exchange prices in arm's-length transactions.

Percentage-of-completion method A method of accounting for long-term construction projects that recognizes revenue and profits in proportion to the work completed, based on an estimate of the portion of the project completed each accounting period.

Purchasing power The ability of money to buy goods and services. As the general price level rises, the purchasing power of the dollar declines.

Realization (recognition) principle The principle of recognizing revenue in the accounts only when the earning process is virtually complete, which is usually at the time of sale of goods or rendering service to customers.

ASSIGNMENT MATERIAL

REVIEW QUESTIONS

1 What is the basic objective of financial statements?

2 To qualify as "generally accepted," accounting principles must receive substantial authoritative support. Name the most influential group in Canada and three groups or organization.

in the United States that provide substantial authoritative support to accounting principles in Canada.

3 Explain what is meant by the expression "trade-off between *reliability* and *relevance*" in connection with the preparation of financial statements.

4 Barker Company has at the end of the current period an inventory of merchandise which cost $500,000. It would cost $600,000 to replace this inventory, and it is estimated that the goods will probably be sold for a total of $700,000. If the firm were to terminate operations immediately, the inventory could probably be sold for $480,000. Discuss the relative reliability and relevance of each of these dollar measurements of the ending inventory.

5 Why is it necessary for accountants to assume the existence of a clearly defined accounting entity?

6 If it appears that the going-concern assumption is no longer valid for a particular company, should the plant assets still be valued in the balance sheet at cost less accumulated depreciation? Explain.

7 "The matching of costs and revenue is the natural extension of the time period principle." Evaluate this statement.

8 Define *objectivity, consistency, materiality,* and *conservatism.*

9 Is the assumption that the dollar is a stable unit of measure realistic? What alternative procedures would you suggest?

10 a Why is it important that any change in accounting methods from one period to the next be disclosed?

  b Does the concept of consistency mean that all companies in a given industry follow similar accounting methods?

11 Briefly define the principle of *disclosure.* List five examples of information that should be disclosed in financial statements or in notes accompanying the statements.

12 Corporations are required to include in their financial statements a description of the accounting policies followed in the preparation of their financial statements. What advantages do you see in this practice?

13 A public accounting firm's standard audit report consists of two major paragraphs. Describe the essential content of each paragraph.

14 Define *monetary assets* and indicate whether a gain or loss results from the holding of such assets during a period of rising prices.

15 Why is it advantageous to be in debt during an inflationary period?

16 Evaluate the following statement: "During a period of rising prices, the conventional income statement overstates net income because the amount of depreciation recorded is less than the value of the service potential of assets consumed."

17 How does constant dollar accounting differ from current cost accounting? For which one would the Consumer Price Index be used?

18 Alpha Company sells pocket calculators that have been decreasing in cost while the general price level has been rising. Explain why Alpha Company's cost of goods sold on a constant dollar basis and on a current cost basis would be higher or lower than on a historical cost basis.

19 The latest financial statements of National Manufacturing Co. indicate that income measured in terms of constant dollars is much lower than income measured in historical dollars. What is the most probable explanation for this large difference?

20 What conclusion would you draw about a company that consistently shows large net losses when its income is measured on a current cost basis?

21 List the three supplementary disclosures discussed in this chapter. Which of them are required disclosures by the CICA?

EXERCISES

Exercise 13-1
Accounting
terminology

Listed below are nine technical accounting terms introduced in this chapter:

Purchasing power	Realization	Monetary items
Constant dollar	Objectivity	GAAP
Current cost	Materiality	Conservatism

Each of the following statements may (or may not) describe one of these technical terms. For each statement, indicate the accounting term described, or answer "None" if the statement does not correctly describe any of the terms.

a Accountants' tendency to resolve doubt by selecting the accounting options that tend to minimize the amount of net income reported in the current period.

b An approach to inflation accounting in which costs and expenses are restated for changes in the general price level.

c The recommendations issued by the CICA's Accounting Standards Committee.

d The value of a dollar, expressed in terms of its ability to buy goods and services.

e The accounting principle used in determining when revenue should be recorded in accounting records.

f Assets and liabilities that represent claims to a fixed number of dollars.

g An accounting concept that may justify departures from other accounting principles for purposes of convenience and economy.

Exercise 13-2
Accounting principles

Mystery Playhouse prepares monthly financial statements. At the beginning of its three-month summer season, the company has programs printed for each of its 48 upcoming performances. Under certain circumstances, either of the following accounting treatments of the costs of printing these programs would be acceptable. Justify both of the accounting treatments, using accounting principles discussed in this chapter.

a The cost of printing the programs is recorded as an asset and is allocated to expense in the month in which the programs are distributed to patrons attending performances.

b The entire cost of printing the programs is charged to expense when the invoice is received from the printer.

Exercise 13-3
Accounting principles

For each situation described, indicate the principle of accounting that is being violated. You may choose from the following principles:

Accounting entity	Materiality
Consistency	Objectivity
Disclosure	Realization
Matching	Stable monetary unit

a The bookkeeper for a large, metropolitan auto dealership depreciates metal wastebaskets over a period of five years.

b Upon completion of the construction of a condominium project that will soon be offered for sale, Townhome Developers increased the balance sheet valuation of the condominiums to their sales value and recognized the expected income on the project.

c Plans to dispose of a major segment of the business are not communicated to readers of the financial statements.

d The cost of expensive, custom-made machinery installed in an assembly line is charged to expense, because it is doubtful that the machinery would have any resale value if the assembly line were shut down.

e A small commuter airline recognizes no depreciation on its aircraft because the planes are maintained in "as good as new" condition.

Exercise 13-4
Profit recognition: instalment method

On September 15, 1988, Susan Moore sold a piece of property that cost her $56,000 for $80,000, net of commissions and other selling expenses. The terms of sale were as follows: down payment, $8,000; balance, $3,000 on the fifteenth day of each month for 24 months, starting October 15, 1988. Compute the gross profit to be recognized by Moore in 1988, 1989, and 1990 (a) on the **accrual basis** of accounting and (b) on the **instalment basis** of accounting. Moore uses a fiscal year ending December 31.

Exercise 13-5
Profit recognition: percentage-of-completion method

The Clinton Corporation recognizes the profit on a long-term construction project as work progresses. From the following information compute the profit that should be recognized each year, assuming that the original cost estimate on the contract was $6,000,000 and that the contract price is $7,500,000.

YEAR	COSTS INCURRED	PROFIT CONSIDERED REALIZED
1988	$1,800,000	$?
1989	3,000,000	?
1990	1,171,000	?
Total	$5,971,000	$1,529,000

Exercise 13-6
Effects of changing price levels

Empire Company paid $500,000 cash in 1986 to acquire land as a long-term investment. At this time, the general price level stood at 100. In 1990, the general price index stands at 140, but the price of land in the area in which Empire Company invested has doubled in value. Rental receipts for grazing and farming during the five-year period were sufficient to pay all carrying charges on the land.

Empire Company prepares a constant dollar income statement and discloses purchasing power gains and losses as supplementary information to its historical-cost-based financial statements.

a How much, if any, of a purchasing power gain or loss relating to the land will be included in the supplementary disclosures over the five-year period? (Assume the land is still owned at the end of 1990).

b Assume the land is sold in 1990 for $685,000. Compute the gain or loss on the sale on a basis of (1) historical cost and (2) constant dollars.

Exercise 13-7
Monetary items:
gains and losses
in purchasing power·

Three companies started business with $600,000 at the beginning of the current year when the general price index stood at 120. The First Company invested the money in a note receivable due in four years; the Second Company invested its cash in land; and the Third Company purchased a building for $1,800,000, assuming a liability for the unpaid balance of $1,200,000. The price level stood at 140 at the end of the year. Compute the purchasing power gain or loss on monetary items for each company during the year.

Exercise 13-8
Cost of goods sold
using constant dollars
and current costs

For the current year, PhotoMart computed the cost of goods sold for the Presto, its biggest-selling camera, as follows (historical cost, fifo basis):

	UNITS ×	UNIT COST =	TOTAL
From beginning inventory	400	$40.00	$16,000
From current year purchases	1,700	42.00	71,400
Cost of goods sold	2,100		$87,400

The beginning inventory of Presto cameras had been acquired when the general price index stood at 320. During the current year, the average level of the price index was 350, and the average replacement cost of a Presto was $42.

Compute the cost of goods sold for Presto cameras in the current year on:

a A constant dollar basis

b A current cost basis.

Exercise 13-9
Depreciation using
constant dollars and
current costs

Western Showcase purchased equipment for $300,000 in Year 3 when the general price index stood at 120. The company depreciates the equipment over 15 years by the straight-line method, with no estimated salvage value. In Year 7, the general price level is 180 and the estimated replacement cost of the equipment is $468,000.

Compute the amount of depreciation expense for Year 7 on:

a A historical cost basis

b A constant dollar basis

c A current cost basis

PROBLEMS

Group A

Problem 13A-1
Accounting principles

Paragraphs **a** through **e**, which can be found on page 565, describe accounting practices that *are in accord* with generally accepted accounting principles. From the list of accounting principles that are also shown on page 565, identify those principles that you believe justify or explain each described accounting practice. (Most of the practices are explained by a single principle; however, more than one principle may relate to a particular practice.) Briefly explain the relationship between the described accounting practice and the underlying accounting principle.

Accounting principles

time period (handwritten)

Consistency   Accounting entity
Materiality   Matching revenue with expense
Objectivity   Going-concern assumption
Realization   Adequate disclosure
Conservatism   Stable monetary unit

Accounting practices

a The purchase of a two-year fire insurance policy is recorded by debiting an asset account even though no refund will be received if the policy is cancelled.

b Hand tools with a small unit cost are charged to expense when purchased even though the individual tools have a useful life of several years.

c An airline records depreciation on its aircraft even though an excellent maintenance program keeps the planes in "as good as new" condition.

d A lawsuit filed against a company is described in footnotes to the company's financial statements even though the lawsuit was filed with the court shortly after the company's balance sheet date.

e A real estate developer carries an unsold inventory of condominiums in its accounting records at cost rather than at estimated sales value.

Problem 13A-2
Accounting principles

In each of the following situations indicate the accounting principle or concept, if any, that has been violated and explain briefly the nature of the violation. If you believe the treatment *is in accord with generally accepted accounting principles,* state this as your position and briefly defend it.

a Pearl Cove Hotel recognizes room rental revenue on the date that a reservation is received. For the summer season, many guests make reservations as much as a year in advance of their intended visit.

b In prior years Regal Corporation has used the declining-balance method of depreciation for both financial reporting purposes and for income tax purposes. In the current year, Regal began to use straight-line depreciation on all assets for financial reporting purposes, but continued to depreciate assets by the declining-balance method for income tax purposes.

c The liabilities of Ellis Construction Co. are substantially in excess of the company's assets. In order to present a more impressive balance sheet for the business, Roy Ellis, the owner of the company, included in the company's balance sheet such personal assets as his savings account, automobile, and real estate investments.

d On January 9, 1989, Gable Company's only plant was badly damaged by a tornado and will be closed for much of the coming year. No mention was made of this event in the financial statements for the year ended December 31, 1988, as the tornado occurred after year-end.

e Friday Production follows a policy of valuing its plant assets at liquidation values in the company's balance sheet. No depreciation is recorded on these assets. Instead, a loss is recognized if the liquidation values decline from one year to the next. If the liquidation values increase during the year, a gain is recognized.

Problem 13A-3
Alternative methods
of income recognition

Early in 1988, Roadbuilders, Inc., was notified that it was the successful bidder on the construction of a section of a highway. The bid price for the project was $24 million. Construction is to begin in 1988 and will take about 27 months to complete; the deadline for completion is in April of 1990.

The contract calls for payments of $6 million per year to Roadbuilders, Inc., for four years, beginning in 1988. (After the project is complete, the government will also pay a reasonable interest charge on the unpaid balance of the contract.) The company estimates that construction costs will total $16 million, of which $6 million will be incurred in 1988, $8 million in 1989, and $2 million in 1990.

The controller of the company, Joe Morgan, recognizes that there are a number of ways he might account for this contract. He might recognize income at the time the contract is completed (sales method), in April of 1990. Alternatively, he might recognize income during construction (percentage-of-completion method), in proportion to the percentage of the total cost incurred in each of the three years. Finally, he might recognize income in proportion to the percentage of the total contract price collected in instalment receipts during the four-year period (instalment method).

Instructions   **a** Prepare a schedule (in millions of dollars) showing the profit that would be recognized on this project in each of the next four years under each of the three accounting methods being considered by the controller. Assume that the timing and construction costs go according to plan. (Ignore the interest revenue relating to the unpaid balance of the contract.)

b Explain which accounting method you consider to be *most* appropriate in this situation. Also explain why you consider the other two methods less appropriate.

Problem 13A-4
Interpreting constant
dollar and current
cost disclosures

The following supplementary schedule appears with the financial statements of Lagerbier for the current year.

Income Statement Adjusted for Changing Prices
(in thousands of dollars)

	AS REPORTED IN THE UNADJUSTED HISTORICAL COST STATEMENTS	ADJUSTED FOR GENERAL INFLATION (CONSTANT DOLLARS)	ADJUSTED FOR CHANGES IN SPECIFIC PRICES (CURRENT COSTS)
Net sales	$600,000	$600,000	$600,000
Costs and expenses:			
Cost of goods sold	$400,000	$415,000	$410,000
Depreciation expense ..	50,000	65,000	95,000
Other expenses	110,000	110,000	110,000
Total	$560,000	$590,000	$615,000
Net Income (Loss)	$ 40,000	$ 10,000	$ (15,000)
Loss from decline in purchasing power of net monetary assets owned		$ 18,000	

Instructions   Explain the reasoning behind your answer to each of the following questions:

a Has the replacement cost of the company's inventory increased faster or more slowly than the general price level during the year?

b Has the replacement cost of the company's depreciable assets increased faster or more slowly than the general price level since these assets were acquired?

c Were the average monetary assets held by the company during the year greater or smaller than the average monetary liabilities owed?

d What was the total change in the purchasing power of the owner's equity in this business during the year?

e Assuming that this is a typical year, are the company's earnings sufficient to maintain the present size and scope of its operations on a long-term basis?

Problem 13A-5
Constant dollars and current costs: a comprehensive problem

Sandy Malone, the president of Sandstone Art Company, has asked you to prepare constant dollar and current cost income statements to supplement the company's financial statements. The company's accountant has provided you with the following data:

Income Statement — Historical Cost
For the Current Year

Net sales		$840,000
Costs and expenses:		
Cost of goods sold	$420,000	
Depreciation expense	60,000	
Other expenses	320,000	
Total costs and expenses		800,000
Net income		$ 40,000

Other Data

(1) Changes in the general price index during the current year were as follows:

	PRICE INDEX
Beginning of current year	120
Average for current year	130
End of current year	138
Rate of inflation [(138 − 120) ÷ 120]	15%

Amounts in the constant dollar income statement are to be expressed in current-year dollars of average purchasing power.

(2) The company sells a single product and uses the first-in, first-out method to compute the cost of goods sold. The historical cost of goods sold includes the following unit sales at the following costs:

	UNITS ×	AVERAGE UNIT COSTS =	TOTAL
From beginning inventory	10,000	$6.00	$ 60,000
From current-year purchases	56,250	6.40	360,000
Cost of goods sold	66,250	6.34	$420,000

The $60,000 beginning inventory was purchased when the general price index stood at 120. (It is not necessary to know total purchases or ending inventory for the current year.)

(3) The company's depreciable assets consist of equipment acquired five years ago when the price index stood at 75. The equipment cost $900,000 and is being depreciated over a 15-year life by the straight-line method with no estimated salvage value.

The estimated replacement cost of the equipment was $1,200,000 at the beginning of the current year and $1,260,000 at year-end.

(4) Throughout the current year, the company has owned monetary assets of $180,000 and has owed monetary liabilities of $320,000.

Instructions   Prepare a supplementary schedule in the format illustrated in this chapter. Include comparative income statements prepared on the bases of historical costs, constant dollars, and current costs. Also show the net gain or loss from holding monetary items. Include supporting computations for (1) cost of goods sold — constant dollar basis, (2) depreciation expense — constant dollar basis, (3) net gain or loss in purchasing power from holding monetary items, (4) cost of goods sold — current cost basis, and (5) depreciation expense — current cost basis.

Group B

Problem 13B-1
Accounting principles

Paragraphs **a** through **e** describe accounting practices that *are in accord* with generally accepted accounting principles. From the following list of accounting principles, identify those principles that you believe justify or explain each described accounting practice. (Most of the prescribed practices are explained by a single principle; however, more than one principle may relate to a given practice.) Briefly explain the relationship between the described accounting practice and the underlying accounting principle.

Accounting principles

Consistency	Accounting entity concept
Materiality	Matching revenue with expense
Objectivity	Going-concern assumption
Realization	Adequate disclosure
Conservatism	Stable monetary unit

Accounting practices   **a** If land costing $60,000 were sold for $65,000, a $5,000 gain would be reported regardless of inflation during the years that the land has been owned.

b When equipment is purchased an estimate is made of its useful life, and the equipment is then depreciated over this period.

c The personal assets of the owner of a sole proprietorship are not disclosed in the financial statements of the business, even when these personal assets are sufficient to assure payment of all the business's liabilities.

d In estimating the appropriate size of the allowance for doubtful accounts, most accountants would rather see this allowance be a little too large rather than a little too small.

e The methods used in the valuation of inventory and for the depreciation of plant assets are described in a footnote to the financial statements.

Problem 13B-2
Accounting principles

In each of the following situations indicate the accounting principle or concept, if any, that has been violated and explain briefly the nature of the violation. If you believe the treatment *is in accord with generally accepted accounting principles,* state this as your position and defend it.

a Holly Manufacturing purchased an expensive special-purpose machine with an estimated useful life of 10 years. Proper installation of the machine required that it be set in the concrete of the factory floor. Once the machine was installed, Holly's controller felt that it had no resale value, so he charged the entire cost of the machine to expense in the current period.

b Lee Oil Co. reported on its balance sheet as an intangible asset the total of all wages, supplies, depreciation on equipment, and other costs related to the drilling of a producing oil well and then amortized this asset as oil was produced from the well.

c A large lawsuit pending against Consumer Products Co. was not mentioned in the footnotes to the company's financial statements because the lawsuit had not actually been filed with the court until seven days after the end of the current year.

d Bob Standish is president of Dutchman Mines. During the current year, geologists and engineers revised upward the estimated amount of ore deposits on the company's property. Standish instructed the company's accountant to record goodwill of $2 million, representing the estimated value of unmined ore in excess of previous estimates. The offsetting credit was made to a revenue account.

e Aspen Airlines follows the practice of charging the purchase of hand tools with a unit cost of less than $50 to an expense account rather than to an asset account. The average life of these tools is about three years.

Problem 13B-3
Alternative methods
of income recognition

Yarmouth Boat Works builds custom sailboats. During the first year of operations, the company built four boats for Island Charter Company. The four boats had a total cost of $216,000 and were sold for a total price of $360,000, due on an instalment basis. Island Charter Company paid $120,000 of this sales price during the first year, plus an additional amount for interest charges.

At year-end, work is in progress on two other boats that are 40% complete. The contract price for these two boats totals $250,000 and costs incurred on these boats during the year total $60,000 (40% of estimated total costs of $150,000).

Instructions

Compute the gross profit for Yarmouth Boat Works during its first year of operations under each of the following assumptions. (Interest earned from Island Charter Company does not enter into the computation of gross profit.)

a The entire gross profit is recognized on the four boats completed and gross profit on the two boats under construction is recognized on a percentage-of-completion basis.

b Gross profit on the four boats completed is recognized on the instalment basis and no portion of the gross profit on the two boats under construction will be recognized until the boats are completed and delivered to customers, and cash is collected.

Problem 13B-4
Interpreting constant
dollar and current cost
disclosures

The annual report of Navigational Instruments for the current year includes the following supplementary schedule showing the effects of inflation upon the company:

Income Statement Adjusted for Changing Prices
(in thousands of dollars)

	AS REPORTED IN THE UNADJUSTED HISTORICAL COST STATEMENTS	ADJUSTED FOR GENERAL INFLATION (CONSTANT DOLLARS)	ADJUSTED FOR CHANGES IN SPECIFIC PRICES (CURRENT COSTS)
Net sales	$900,000	$900,000	$900,000
Costs and expenses:			
Cost of goods sold	$480,000	$490,000	$510,000
Depreciation expense ..	240,000	320,000	260,000
Other expenses	100,000	100,000	100,000
Total	$820,000	$910,000	$870,000
Net Income (Loss)	$ 80,000	$ (10,000)	$ 30,000
Gain from decline in purchasing power of net amounts owed		$ 24,000	

Instructions

Use the supplementary schedule to answer each of the following questions. Explain the reasoning behind your answers.

a Has the replacement cost of the company's inventory increased faster or more slowly than the general price index during the current year?

b Has the replacement cost of the company's depreciable assets increased faster or more slowly than the general price level since these assets were acquired?

c Were the average monetary assets held by the company during the year greater or smaller than the average monetary amounts owed?

d What was the total change in the purchasing power of the owner's equity in the business during the year?

e Assuming that this was a typical year, are the company's earnings sufficient to maintain the present size and scope of current operations on a long-term basis?

Problem 13B-5
Constant dollars and
current costs:
a comprehensive
problem

The accounting staff of Nashville Engineering has provided the following data to assist you in preparing constant dollar and current cost information to supplement the company's financial statements for the current year.

Income Statement — Historical Cost
For the Current Year

Net sales		$930,000
Costs and expenses:		
Cost of goods sold	$465,000	
Depreciation expense	80,000	
Other expenses	300,000	
Total costs and expenses		845,000
Net income		$ 85,000

Other data

(1) Changes in the general price level during the current year were as follows:

	PRICE INDEX
Beginning of year	140
Average for year	150
End of year	161
Rate of inflation [(161 − 140) ÷ 140]	15%

Amounts in the constant dollar income statement are to be stated in current-year dollars of average purchasing power.

(2) The company sells a single product and uses the first-in, first-out method to compute the cost of goods sold. The historical cost of goods sold included the following unit sales at the following costs:

	UNITS ×	AVERAGE UNIT COSTS =	TOTAL
From beginning inventory	14,000	$7.50	$105,000
From current-year purchases	40,000	9.00	360,000
Cost of goods sold	54,000	8.61	$465,000

The $105,000 beginning inventory was purchased when the general price index stood at 140.

(3) The company's depreciable assets consist of equipment acquired four years ago when the general price index stood at 80. The equipment cost $800,000 and is being depreciated over a 10-year life by the straight-line method with no estimated salvage value.

The estimated replacement cost of the equipment was $1,500,000 at the beginning of the current year and $1,580,000 at year-end.

(4) Throughout the current year, the company owned monetary assets of $165,000 and owed monetary liabilities of $300,000.

Instructions Prepare a supplementary schedule in the format illustrated in this chapter. Include comparative income statements prepared on the bases of historical cost, constant dollars, and current costs. Also show the net gain or loss resulting from monetary items. Show supporting computations for (1) cost of goods sold stated in constant dollars, (2) depreciation expense stated in constant dollars, (3) net gain or loss in purchasing power from monetary items, (4) cost of goods sold measured in current costs, and (5) depreciation expense measured in current costs.

BUSINESS DECISION CASES

Case 13-1
Income: now you see it . . . now you don't

Following is a supplementary schedule that appeared in a recent annual report of Chevon Oil Corporation (in millions of dollars):

	AS REPORTED IN THE HISTORICAL COST STATEMENTS	CURRENT COST
Revenues	$29,207	$29,207
Costs and Expenses		
Cost of products sold and operating expenses . . .	21,835	22,281
Depreciation, depletion and amortization	1,388	2,630
Taxes other than on income	2,469	2,469
Interest and debt expense	961	961
Provision for taxes on income	1,020	1,020
Net Income (Loss)	$ 1,534	$ (154)

Instructions Use this supplementary schedule to answer each of the following questions. Explain the reasoning behind your answers.

a Was Chevon's revenue sufficient to recover the original number of dollars invested in the goods and services consumed during the year?

b Was Chevon's revenue sufficient to replace the goods and services consumed in the effort to generate revenue during the year?

c What do you think is the principal reason for the large difference between the amounts of net income (or net loss) computed under the alternative measurement techniques of historical cost and current cost?

Case 13-2
Accounting principles and income measurement

For many years, Festival Films used the lifo method of inventory valuation and the declining-balance method of depreciation in measuring the net income of its mail-order business. In addition, the company charged off all costs of catalogues as incurred. In Year 10, the company changed its inventory pricing method to fifo, adopted the straight-line method of depreciation, and decided to charge off catalogue costs only as catalogues were distributed to potential customers.

The following information for the last three years is taken from the company's accounting records:

	YEAR 10	YEAR 9	YEAR 8
Sales (net)	$500,000	$400,000	$350,000
Purchases (net)	300,000	220,000	200,000
Ending inventory — fifo	50,000	45,000	40,000
Ending inventory — lifo	30,000	28,000	25,000
Depreciation — declining-balance method	27,500	30,000	35,000
Depreciation — straight-line method	20,000	20,000	20,000
Operating expenses other than depreciation . . .	120,500	93,000	80,000
Catalogue costs included in operating expenses but considered applicable to future revenue . . .	18,500	8,000	5,000
Net income as computed by Festival Films	100,000	60,000	37,000

At the end of Year 10, Festival Films prepared the following comparative income statement and presented it to a banker in connection with an application for a substantial long-term loan:

FESTIVAL FILMS
Comparative Income Statement
For Years Ended December 31

	YEAR 10	YEAR 9
Sales (net)	$500,000	$400,000
Cost of goods sold*	278,000	217,000
Gross profit on sales	$222,000	$183,000
Operating expenses	122,000	123,000
Net income	$100,000	$ 60,000

*Based on lifo inventory method in Year 9; inventory at end of Year 10 was valued on fifo basis.

The loan officer for the Pacific National Bank, where Festival Films has applied for the loan, asks you to help decide whether to lend the money to Festival Films.

Instructions **a** Prepare a more detailed comparative income statement for Years 9 and 10. For the cost of goods sold section, you should use the figures listed in the three-column schedule at the beginning of this problem to show as individual items the beginning inventory, net purchases, cost of goods available for sale, ending inventory, and cost of goods sold. In the section for operating expenses, show the depreciation expense separately from other operating expenses. Summary figures should be the same as those compiled by Festival Films.

   Criticize the detailed comparative income statement in terms of generally accepted accounting principles. Indicate the dollar effect on net income of any violations of accounting principles.

b Prepare two comparative income statements for Years 9 and 10. First, prepare a comparative statement on the same accounting basis as in prior years. Second, prepare a comparative income statement on the revised basis of accounting decided upon by the company.

c What good feature is common to both of the comparative income statements called for in **b** above? Comment on the trend of net income shown in each income statement in **b** above and also in the comparative income statement prepared by Festival Films.

CORPORATIONS

The next four chapters and an appendix focus on accounting issues that primarily affect corporations. Although sole proprietorships and partnerships are more numerous than corporations, it is the corporation that plays the dominant role in our economy. Corporations own more assets, earn more revenue, provide more jobs, and attract more investment capital than all other forms of business organization combined.

CORPORATIONS: ORGANIZATION AND SHAREHOLDERS' EQUITY

CHAPTER PREVIEW

This chapter begins our study of businesses organized as corporations. First, we describe the nature of a corporation, explain the concept of a "separate legal entity," and discuss the advantages and disadvantages of the corporate form of organization. Next, we focus attention upon the shareholders' equity section of a corporate balance sheet. Contributed capital is distinguished from retained earnings, and preferred stock is contrasted with common stock. Distinctions are drawn between the concepts of no-par value, par value, book value, and market value. Various shareholders' equity transactions are illustrated and explained, including the issuance of capital stock and the declaration and payment of cash dividends. Also covered are such topics as subscriptions to capital stock, accounting for donated capital, and the computation of book value per share.

After studying this chapter you should be able to meet these Learning Objectives:

1 Discuss the advantages and disadvantages of organizing a business as a corporation.

2 Explain the rights of shareholders and the roles of corporate directors and officers.

3 Describe the differences in the balance sheet presentation of the ownership equity in a corporation and in a sole proprietorship.

4 Discuss the nature and issuance of capital stock, focussing on no-par value capital stock.

5 Discuss the features of preferred stock and of common stock.

6 Account for subscriptions to capital stock and for donated capital.

7 Explain the meaning and significance of book value of common stock and its relationship to market value.

Who owns a corporation? The owners of a corporation are called *shareholders.*[1] Shareholders in a large corporation such as Canadian Pacific or Bell Canada Enterprises include thousands of men and women, as well as many pension funds, mutual investment funds, labour unions, banks, universities, and other organizations. Because a corporation can be used to pool the savings of any number of investors, it is an ideal means of obtaining the capital necessary for large-scale business activities.

Nearly all large businesses and many small ones are organized as corporations. There are still more sole proprietorships and partnerships than corporations, but in dollar volume of business activity, corporations hold an impressive lead. Because of the dominant role of the corporation in our economy, it is important for everyone interested in business, economics, or politics to have an understanding of corporations and their accounting practices.

What is a corporation?

A corporation is a *legal entity* having an existence separate and distinct from that of its owners. In the eyes of the law a corporation is an "artificial person," having many of the rights and responsibilities of a real person.

A corporation, as a separate legal entity, may own property in its own name. Thus, the assets of a corporation belong to the corporation itself, *not to the shareholders.* A corporation has legal status in court—that is, it may sue and be sued as if it were a person. As a legal entity, a corporation may enter into contracts, is responsible for its own debts, and pays income taxes on its earnings.

Advantages of the corporate form of organization

1   Discuss the advantages and disadvantages of organizing a business as a corporation.

The corporation offers a number of advantages not available in other forms of organization. Among these advantages are the following:

1 **No personal liability for shareholders**   Creditors of a corporation have a claim against the assets of the corporation, not against the personal property of the shareholders. Thus, the amount of money that shareholders risk by investing in a corporation is *limited to the amount of their investment.* To many investors, this is the most important advantage of the corporate form.

2 **Ease of accumulating capital**   Ownership of a corporation is evidenced by transferable *shares of capital stock.* The sale of corporate ownership in units of one or more shares permits both large and small investors to participate in ownership of the business. Some corporations have half a million or more individual shareholders. For this reason, large corporations are often said to be *publicly owned* or *broadly held.* Of course not all corporations are large. Many small businesses are organized as corporations and are owned by a limited number of shareholders. Such corporations are said to be *closely held.*

3 **Ownership shares are readily transferable**   Shares of capital stock may be sold by one investor to another without dissolving or disrupting the business organization.

[1] According to the CICA's *Financial Reporting in Canada*, 17th ed., 1987, pp. 137-138, the terms "shareholder," "shareholders' equity," and "capital stock" are far more commonly used than "stockholder," "stockholders' equity," and "share capital"; thus, the first three terms are used in this book.

The shares of most large corporations may be bought or sold by investors in organized markets, such as the **Toronto Stock Exchange.** Investments in these shares have the advantage of *liquidity,* because investors may easily convert their corporate ownership into cash by selling their capital stock.

4 Continuous existence   A corporation is a separate legal entity with a perpetual existence. The continuous life of the corporation despite changes in ownership is made possible by the issuance of transferable shares of capital stock. By way of contrast, a partnership is a relatively unstable form of organization that is dissolved by the death or retirement of any of its members. The continuity of the corporate entity is essential to most large-scale business activities.

5 Professional management   The shareholders own the corporation, but they do not manage it on a daily basis. To administer the affairs of the corporation, the shareholders must elect a **board of directors.** The directors, in turn, then hire a president and other corporate officers to manage the business. There is no mutual agency in a corporation; thus, an individual shareholder has no right to participate in the management of the business unless he or she has been hired as a corporate officer.

Disadvantages of the corporate form of organization

Among the disadvantages of the corporation are:

1 Heavy taxation   The income of a partnership or a sole proprietorship is taxable only as personal income to the owners of the business. The income of a corporation, on the other hand, is subject to income taxes that must be paid by the corporation. The combination of federal and provincial corporate income taxes often takes a major share of a corporation's before-tax income. If a corporation distributes its earnings to shareholders, the shareholders must pay personal income taxes on the amounts they receive. This practice of first taxing corporate income to the corporation and then taxing distributions of that income to the shareholders is sometimes called *double taxation.* However, this double taxation is minimized by the federal dividend tax credit claimed by the shareholders.

2 Greater regulation   A corporation comes into existence under the terms of federal or provincial laws and these same laws may provide for considerable regulation of the corporation's activities and disclosures. For example, the withdrawal of funds from a corporation is subject to certain limits set by law. Moreover, various securities acts administered by the provincial securities commissions require publicly owned corporations to make extensive disclosure of their affairs.

3 Separation of ownership and control   The separation of the functions of ownership and management may be an advantage in some cases but a disadvantage in others. On the whole, the excellent record of growth and earnings in most large corporations indicates that the separation of ownership and control has benefited rather than injured shareholders. In a few instances, however, a management group has chosen to operate a corporation for the benefit of insiders. The shareholders may find it difficult in such cases to take the concerted action necessary to oust the officers.

Income taxes in corporate financial statements

Since a corporation is a separate legal entity subject to taxes upon its income, the ledger of a corporation should include accounts for recording income taxes. No such accounts are needed for a business organized as a sole proprietorship or partnership.

Income taxes are based on a corporation's earnings. At year-end, before preparing financial statements, income taxes are recorded by an adjusting entry such as the following:

RECORDING CORPORATE
INCOME TAXES

Income Taxes Expense or Income Taxes	72,750	
Income Taxes Payable		72,750

To record the income taxes payable for the year ended
December 31.

The account debited in this entry, Income Taxes Expense (or Income Taxes), is an expense account and usually appears as the very last deduction in the income statement as follows:

FINAL STEP IN INCOME
STATEMENT

Income before income taxes	$200,000
Income taxes expense	72,750
Net income	$127,250

The liability account, Income Taxes Payable, will ordinarily be paid within a few months and should, therefore, appear in the current liability section of the balance sheet. More detailed discussion of a corporate income taxes is presented in Chapter 18.

Formation of a corporation

A corporation is created by obtaining a **certificate of incorporation** or **letters patent** or **memorandum of association** from the federal or provincial government where the company is to be incorporated. To obtain a certificate of incorporation, for example, an application called the **articles of incorporation** is submitted to the federal or provincial government. Once the certificate is obtained, the shareholders in the new corporation hold a meeting to elect **directors** and to pass **bylaws** as a guide to the company's affairs. The directors in turn hold a meeting at which officers of the corporation are appointed.

Organization costs   The formation of a corporation is a much more costly step than the organization of a partnership. The necessary costs include the payment of an incorporation fee to the federal or provincial government, the payment of fees to lawyers for their services in drawing up the articles of incorporation, payments to promotors, and a variety of other outlays necessary to bring the corporation into existence. These costs are charged to an asset account called Organization Costs. In the balance sheet, organization costs appear under the "Other assets" caption, as illustrated on page 597.

The incurring of these organization costs leads to the existence of the corporate entity; consequently, the benefits derived from these costs may be regarded as extending over the entire life of the corporation. Since the life of a corporation may continue indefinitely, one might argue that organization costs are an asset with an unlimited life. However, income tax rules permit one-half of the organization costs to be written off at an annual rate of 10%, based on the declining-balance method; consequently, most companies elect to write off organization costs in this manner. Accountants have been willing to accept this practice, because organization costs are not material in dollar amount. The accounting principle of *materiality* permits departures from theoretical concepts on the grounds of convenience if the practice in question will not cause any material distortion of net income or financial position.

2 Explain the rights of shareholders and the roles of corporate directors and officers.

Rights of shareholders   The ownership of capital stock in a corporation usually carries the following basic rights:

1 To vote for directors, and thereby to be represented in the management of the business. The approval of a majority of shareholders may also be required for such important corporate actions as mergers and acquisitions, the selection of independent auditors, the incurring of long-term debts, the establishment of stock option plans, or the splitting of capital stock into a larger number of shares.

When a corporation issues two classes of capital stock such as common stock and preferred stock, voting rights generally are granted only to the holders of common stock. These two different types of capital stock will be discussed in detail later in this chapter.

2 To share in income by receiving *dividends* declared by the board of directors. Shareholders in a corporation may not make withdrawals of company assets, as may an owner of an unincorporated business. However, the earnings of a profitable corporation may be distributed to shareholders in the form of cash dividends. The payment of a dividend always requires formal authorization by the board of directors.

3 To share in the distribution of assets if the corporation is liquidated. When a corporation ends its existence, the creditors of the corporation must first be paid in full; any remaining assets are divided among shareholders in proportion to the number of shares owned.

4 To subscribe for additional shares in the event that the corporation decides to increase the amount of stock outstanding. This *pre-emptive right* entitles shareholders to maintain their percentages of ownership in the company by subscribing, in proportion to their present shareholdings, to any additional shares issued. Under the Canada Business Corporations Act, a corporation may provide such pre-emptive right in its articles of incorporation if it so wishes.

Shareholders' meetings usually are held once a year. Each share of stock is entitled to one vote. In large corporations, these annual meetings are usually attended by relatively few persons, often by less than 1% of the shareholders. Prior to the meeting, the management group will request shareholders who do not plan to attend in person to send in *proxy statements* assigning their votes to the existing management. Through this use of the proxy system, management may secure the right to vote as much as, perhaps, 80% or more of the total outstanding shares.

Functions of the board of directors   The primary functions of the board of directors are to manage the corporation and to act in the best interest of the corporation. At this level, management may consist principally of formulating policies and reviewing acts of the officers. Specific duties of the directors include declaring dividends, setting the salaries of officers, reviewing the system of internal control with the internal auditors and with the company's external auditors, and authorizing important contracts of various kinds.

The extent of participation in management by the board of directors varies widely from one company to another. In recent years increasing importance has been attached to the inclusion of outside directors on the boards of large corporations. The term **outside directors** refers to individuals who are not officers of the company and who thus have a view independent of that of corporate officers.

Functions of corporate officers   Corporate officers are at the top level of the professional managers appointed by the board of directors to run the business. These officers usually include a president or chief executive officer (CEO), one or more vice-presidents, a controller, a treasurer, and a secretary. A vice-president is often made responsible for the sales function; other vice-presidents may be given responsibility for such important functions as personnel, finance, and production.

The responsibilities of the controller, treasurer, and secretary are most directly related to the accounting phase of business operation. The **controller,** or chief accounting officer, is responsible for the maintenance of adequate internal control and for the preparation of accounting records and financial statements. Such specialized activities as budgeting, tax planning, and preparation of tax returns are usually placed under the controller's jurisdiction. The **treasurer** has custody of the company's funds and is generally responsible for planning and controlling the company's cash position. The **secretary** represents the corporation in many contractual and legal matters and maintains minutes of the meetings of directors and shareholders. Another responsibility of the secretary is to coordinate the preparation of the annual report, which includes the financial statements and other information relating to corporate activities. In small corporations, one officer frequently acts as both secretary and

TYPICAL CORPORATE
ORGANIZATION

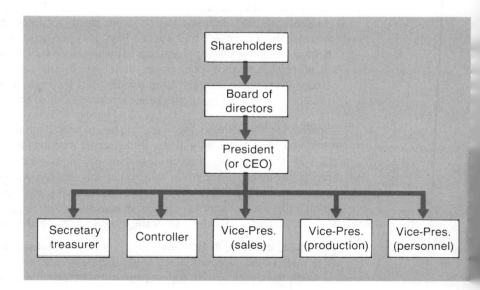

treasurer. The organization chart on page 580 indicates lines of authority extending from shareholders to the directors to the president and other officers.

Shareholders' equity

3 Describe the differences in the balance sheet presentation of the ownership equity in a corporation and in a sole proprietorship.

The sections of the balance sheet showing assets and liabilities are much the same for a corporation as for a sole proprietorship. The owner's equity section is the principal point of contrast. In the balance sheet of a corporation, the term *shareholders' equity* is used instead of owners' equity.

The owners' equity in a corporation, as in other types of business organizations, is equal to the assets of the business minus the liabilities. However, corporation laws require that the shareholders' equity section of a corporate balance sheet clearly indicate the *source* of the owners' equity. The two most basic sources of owners' equity are (1) investment by the shareholders (contributed capital), and (2) earnings from profitable operation of the business (retained earnings or earned capital).

When shareholders invest cash or other assets in the business, the corporation issues in exchange shares of capital stock as evidence of the shareholders' equity ownership. In the simplest case, capital invested by the shareholders is recorded in the corporation's accounting records by a credit to an account entitled *Capital Stock.* The capital contributed or paid in by shareholders is regarded as permanent capital not ordinarily subject to withdrawal.

The increase in shareholders' equity arising from profitable operations is called *retained earnings.* At the end of the year the balance of the Income Summary account is closed into the Retained Earnings account. For example, if net income for the year is $70,000, the closing entry will be as follows:

Income Summary   70,000
    Retained earnings   70,000
To close the Income Summary account by transferring the
year's net income into the Retained Earnings account.

If the company operates at a loss of, say, $25,000, the Income Summary account will have a debit balance. The account must then be credited to close it. The closing entry will be:

Retained Earnings   25,000
    Income Summary   25,000
To close the Income Summary account by transferring the
year's net loss into the Retained Earnings account.

If a corporation has sufficient cash, a distribution of income may be made to shareholders. Distributions of this nature are termed *dividends* and decrease both total assets and total shareholders' equity. Since dividends are regarded as distributions of retained earnings, the decrease in shareholders' equity is recorded in the Retained Earnings account. Thus, the amount of retained earnings at any balance sheet date represents the *accumulated earnings of the company since the date of incorporation, minus any losses, and minus all dividends distributed to shareholders.*

Some people mistakenly believe that retained earnings represents a fund of cash available to a corporation. *Retained earnings is not an asset; it is an element of shareholders' equity.* Although the amount of retained earnings indicates the portion of total assets that are *financed* by earnings (net income) retained by this corporation, it does *not* indicate the *form* in which these resources are currently held. The resources generated by retaining earnings may have been invested in land, buildings, equipment, or any other kind of asset. The total amount of cash owned by a corporation is shown by the balance of the Cash account, which appears in the asset section of the balance sheet.

Shareholders' equity on the balance sheet   For a corporation with $100,000 of capital stock and $40,000 of retained earnings, the shareholders' equity section of the balance sheet (omitting certain details) will appear as follows:

CONTRIBUTED CAPITAL
AND EARNED CAPITAL

Shareholders' equity:
Capital stock $100,000
Retained earnings 40,000 $140,000

If this same company had been unprofitable and had incurred losses aggregating $30,000 since its incorporation, the shareholders' equity section of the balance sheet would be as follows:

CONTRIBUTED CAPITAL
REDUCED BY LOSSES
INCURRED

Shareholders' equity:
Capital stock $100,000
Less: Deficit 30,000 $70,000

This second illustration tells us that $30,000 of the original $100,000 invested by shareholders has been lost. Note that the capital stock in both illustrations remains at the fixed amount of $100,000, the shareholders' original investment. The accumulated income or losses since the organization of the corporation are shown as *retained earnings* or as a *deficit* and are not intermingled with the contributed capital. The term *deficit* indicates a negative amount of retained earnings.

Cash dividends

The term *dividend,* when used by itself, is generally understood to mean a distribution of cash by a corporation to its shareholders. Dividends are stated as a specific amount per share of capital stock, as, for example, a dividend of $1 per share. The amount received by each shareholder is in proportion to the number of shares owned. A shareholder who owns 100 shares will receive a cheque for $100.

Dividends are paid only through action by the board of directors. The board has full discretion to declare a dividend or to refrain from doing so. Once the declaration of a dividend has been announced, the obligation to pay the dividend is a current liability of the corporation and cannot be rescinded.

Because a dividend is declared on one date by the board of directors and paid at a later date, two separate journal entries are necessary. To illustrate the entries for declaration and payment of a cash dividend, assume that a corporation declares a dividend of $1 a share on 100,000 shares of outstanding capital stock. The dividend is declared on December 15 and is payable on January 25. The two entries would be as follows:

Dec. 15	Retained Earnings	100,000	
	Dividends Payable		100,000
	To record declaration by the board of directors of a cash dividend of $1 per share on the 100,000 shares of capital stock outstanding.		
Jan. 25	Dividends Payable	100,000	
	Cash		100,000
	To record payment of the $1 per share dividend declared December 15 on the 100,000 shares of capital stock outstanding.		

The account **Dividends Payable,** which was credited at the date of declaring the dividend, is a current liability. If a company has more than one issue of capital stock (such as both common stock and preferred stock, or class A and class B), it may use a separate Dividends Payable account for each issue.

Some companies, in recording the declaration of a dividend, will debit an account entitled Dividends instead of debiting the Retained Earnings account. Whenever a Dividends account is used, a closing entry will be required at the end of the year to transfer the debit balance in the Dividends account into the Retained Earnings account. Under either method the end result is a reduction in retained earnings for the amount of the dividends declared.

What is capital stock?

4 Discuss the nature and issuance of capital stock, focussing on no-par value capital stock.

As previously mentioned, the caption *capital stock* in the balance sheet of a corporation represents the amount invested by the owners of the business. When the owners of a corporation invest cash or other assets in the business, the corporation issues capital stock as evidence of the investors' ownership equity.

The basic unit of capital stock is called a *share,* but a corporation may issue capital stock certificates in denominations of 1 share, 100 shares, or any other number. The total number of shares of capital stock outstanding at any given time represents 100% ownership of the corporation. *Outstanding* shares are those in the hands of shareholders. The number of shares owned by an individual investor determines the extent of his or her ownership of the corporation.

Assume, for example, that Star Corporation issues a total of 50,000 shares of capital stock to investors in exchange for cash. If we assume further that Susan Morgan acquires 5,000 shares of the 50,000 shares outstanding, we may say that she has a 10% interest in the corporation. Suppose that Morgan now sells 2,000 shares to Evans. The total number of shares outstanding remains unchanged at 50,000, although Morgan's percentage of ownership has declined to 6% and a new shareholder, Evans, has acquired a 4% interest in the corporation. The transfer of 2,000 shares from Morgan to Evans had *no effect* upon the corporation's assets, liabilities, or amount of capital stock outstanding. The only way in which this transfer of capital stock affects the corporation is that the record of shareholders must be revised to show the number of shares held by each owner.

Authorization and issuance of capital stock

While the articles of incorporation *may* specify the number of shares of capital stock that a corporation is authorized to issue, a corporation is *not required* to do so under the Canada Business Corporations Act. Thus, a corporation governed by the federal act does not have a limit on the maximum number of shares of capital stock it can issue unless it chooses to have one by stating such a limit in its articles of incorporation. The federal act does require, however, that the shares of capital stock of corporations be *without par or nominal value.* Provincial corporation legislation, such as the Ontario Business Corporations Act, parallels that of the federal act in these respects. On the other hand, certain provincial legislation still requires corporations to specify the maximum number of shares of capital stock they are authorized to issue and permits corporations to issue capital stock with a par value. Thus, some of the large corporations still have maximum number of authorized capital stock and par value capital stock.

 Provigo has 1,375,000 preferred shares authorized, with a par value of $25 each; Maritime Telegraph and Telephone has maximum authorized preferred and common stock, some with par value, and the premium on common stock (the excess of issue price over par value) is in excess of $38,000,000; Bow Valley Industries has 200 million shares of no-par common stock authorized, with only slightly over 40 million shares issued and outstanding.[2]

It should be noted that mere authorization of a capital stock issue (with or without a maximum limit) does not bring an asset into existence, nor does it give the corporation any capital. The obtaining of authorization from the federal or provincial government for a capital stock issue merely affords a legal opportunity to obtain assets through the sale of capital stock.

No-par value capital stock

Recent federal and provincial corporation legislation clearly indicates that no-par value capital stock will become increasingly common in Canada. The following are some of the important reasons for the emergence of the concept of no-par value capital stock:

1 It avoids the assignment of an arbitrary amount as par value that is subject to misunderstanding by investors. For example, issued capital stock traded on stock exchanges at below its par value may sometimes be interpreted as a bargain even though the stock is at its fair market value. Thus, no-par stock eliminates such an opportunity for misunderstanding. Of course, the market value of any stock fluctuates according to the changes in the investors' perception about the value of the business, not according to the par value.

---

[2] These three corporations ranked 10th, 242nd and 223rd respectively in *The Financial Post 500* largest corporations in the Summer, 1987 issue.

2 It provides a corporation with greater flexibility in the arrangement of its capital structure. For example, a corporation can split the existing no-par shares into a greater number of shares (as will be discussed in Chapter 15) without having to consider the effect on the par value. Also, no-par stock eliminates the problem of issuing stock at a discount, which generally is not allowed by law. Of course, since the par value is usually set at a very low amount, in reality the question of issuing stock at a discount seldom arises.

3 It eliminates the confusion and misunderstanding associated with the nature and meaning of such accounts as premium on capital stock, since no-par stock does not result in the establishment of these premium accounts.

Issuance of no-par value capital stock   When no-par value capital stock is issued, the entire proceeds on the issue are credited to the Capital Stock account. Assuming that 6,000 shares of no-par value capital stock are issued at a price of $10 each, the entry to record the issue is as follows:

ENTRY FOR NO-PAR
CAPITAL STOCK

Cash	60,000	
Capital Stock		60,000

Issued 6,000 shares of no-par capital stock at a price
of $10 a share.

The amount credited to the Capital Stock account represents the legal capital or the *stated capital*[3] — the amount that cannot be reduced except by (1) losses from business operations or (2) legal action taken by a majority vote of shareholders or permitted by the legislation governing the corporation.

The shareholders' equity section of the balance sheet is illustrated as follows (assuming an unlimited number of authorized shares and the existence of $26,000 in retained earnings in order to have a complete illustration).

Shareholders' equity:
  Capital stock, no-par value, authorized, an unlimited number
    of shares, issued and outstanding, 6,000 shares $60,000
  Retained earnings 26,000
    Total shareholders' equity $86,000

In certain cases, corporations with no-par value capital stock may be allowed to assign a stated value to its capital stock. When a corporation issues such capital stock with stated value, the amount to be credited to the Capital Stock account is limited to the stated value. Assuming that 8,000 no-par value shares with a stated value of $9 each are issued at a price of $11 each, the entry to record the issue would be:

Cash	88,000	
Capital Stock		72,000
Excess of Contributed Capital over Stated Value of		
Capital Stock		16,000

Issued 8,000 shares of no-par value capital stock at $11 each;
stated value per share was $9.

---

[3] "Stated capital" is the term used in the Canada Business Corporations Act and certain provincial corporations acts.

Par value capital stock

The par value of capital stock represents the arbitrary amount assigned by a corporation as its legal capital per share. It merely indicates the amount per share to be entered in the Capital Stock account; it is *not* an indication of its market value. Par value may be $1, $2, $5, per share, or any amount decided upon by the corporation. Generally, the par values of most corporations are very small.

Issuance of par value capital stock   When par value capital stock is issued, the Capital Stock account is credited with the par value of the shares sold. Assuming that 6,000 shares of $10 par value capital stock are issued at a price of $10 each, the entry would be:

ENTRY FOR PAR VALUE
CAPITAL STOCK

Cash	60,000	
Capital Stock		60,000
Issued 6,000 shares of $10 par value capital stock at their par value.		

When capital stock is sold for more than its par value, the Capital Stock account is credited with the par value of the shares issued, and a separate account, Premium on Capital Stock, is credited for the excess of selling price over par. If, for example, the issuance price is $15 rather than $10, as in the previous illustration, the entry for the 6,000 shares would be:

CAPITAL STOCK ISSUED
IN EXCESS OF PAR VALUE

Cash	90,000	
Capital Stock		60,000
Premium on Capital Stock		30,000
Issued 6,000 shares of $10 par value capital stock at a price of $15 a share.		

The premium (the amount in excess of par value) does not represent an income to the corporation. It is part of the invested capital, and it will be added to the capital stock on the balance sheet to show the total contributed capital.[4] The shareholders' equity section of the balance sheet is illustrated as follows. (An authorization for 800,000 shares and the existence of $10,000 in retained earnings are assumed in order to have a complete illustration.)

CORPORATION'S CAPITAL
CLASSIFIED BY SOURCE

Shareholders' equity:	
Capital stock, $10 par value, authorized, 800,000 shares,	
issued and outstanding, 6,000 shares	$ 60,000
Premium on capital stock	30,000
Total contributed capital	$ 90,000
Retained earnings	10,000
Total shareholders' equity	$100,000

---

[4] It is more appropriate to treat the premium on capital stock as part of the contributed capital than as part of contributed surplus, even though the latter is preferred by the *CICA Handbook*.

If capital stock is issued by a corporation for less than par, the account Discount on Capital Stock should be debited for the difference between the issuance price and the par value. The issuance of capital stock at a discount is not permitted under the federal and most provincial business corporations acts.

Preferred stock and common stock

5 Discuss the features of preferred stock and of common stock.

In order to appeal to as many investors as possible, a corporation may issue more than one class of capital stock. Under the Canada Business Corporations Act, a corporation may have more than one class of capital stock, provided that the rights, privileges, restrictions, and conditions of each class are set forth in the articles of incorporation and that at least one class of capital stock has the rights typically associated with what is traditionally known as "common stock." These rights are identical with the first three rights mentioned earlier, namely, (1) to vote at any meeting of shareholders of the corporation, (2) to receive any dividend declared by the corporation, and (3) to receive the remaining property of the corporation on dissolution. The federal act does not use the terms "common" and "preferred" to distinguish the different classes of capital stock. However, since the terms "preferred stock" and "common stock" have been widely used in practice and have been proven useful in distinguishing classes of capital stock, they will be used throughout this book.

The basic type of capital stock issued by every corporation is generally called common stock. Common stock has the three basic rights previously mentioned. Whenever these rights are modified, the term preferred stock (or sometimes Class B Common) is used to describe this second type of capital stock. Some corporations issue two or more classes of preferred stock, each class having certain distinctive features designed to interest a particular type of investor. In summary, every business corporation has common stock; a good many corporations also issue preferred stock; and some companies have two or more types of preferred stock.

Common stock may be regarded as the basic, residual element of ownership. It carries voting rights and, therefore, is the means of exercising control over the business. Common stock has unlimited possibilities of increase in value; during periods of business expansion the market prices of common stocks of some leading corporations may rise to many times their former values. On the other hand, common stocks lose value more rapidly than other types of securities when corporations encounter periods of unprofitable business.

The following shareholders' equity section illustrates the balance sheet presentation for a corporation having both preferred and common stock; note that the item of retained earnings is not apportioned between the two groups of shareholders.

BALANCE SHEET PRESENTATION OF SHAREHOLDERS' EQUITY

Shareholders' equity:

$12 cumulative preferred stock, no-par value, authorized, an unlimited number of shares, issued and outstanding, 50,000 shares	$ 5,000,000
Common stock, no-par value, authorized, an unlimited number of shares, issued and outstanding, 2,000,000 shares	10,000,000
Retained earnings	3,500,000
Total shareholders' equity	$18,500,000

Characteristics of preferred stock

Preferred stocks may have the following distinctive features:

1 Preferred as to dividends
2 Preferred as to assets in the event of the liquidation of the company
3 Callable (redeemable) at the option of the corporation
4 No voting power

Another very important feature is a clause permitting the **conversion** of preferred stock into common at the option of the holder. Preferred stocks vary widely with respect to the special rights and privileges granted. Careful study of the terms of the individual preferred stock contract is a necessary step in the evaluation of any preferred stock.

Stock preferred as to dividends   Stock preferred as to dividends is entitled to receive each year a dividend of specified amount before any dividend is paid on the common stock. The dividend is usually stated as a dollar amount per share, for example, $12 cumulative preferred stock, as shown in the preceding section. Some preferred stocks state the dividend preference as a **percentage of par value.** For example, a **9%** preferred stock with a par value of $100 per share would mean that $9 must be paid yearly on each share of preferred stock before any dividends are paid on the common stock.

The holders of preferred stock have no assurance that they will always receive the indicated dividend. A corporation is obligated to pay dividends to shareholders only when the board of directors declares a dividend. Dividends must be paid on preferred stock before anything is paid to the common shareholders, but if the corporation is not prospering, it may decide not to pay dividends on either preferred or common stock. For a corporation to pay dividends, income must be earned and cash must be available. However, preferred stocks in general offer **more assurance of regular dividend payments** than do common stocks.

Cumulative preferred stock   The dividend preference carried by most preferred stocks is a **cumulative** one. If all or any part of the regular dividend on the preferred stock is omitted in a given year, the amount omitted is said to be **in arrears** and must be paid in a subsequent year before any dividend can be paid on the common stock. Assume that a corporation was organized January 1, 1988, with 10,000 shares of $8 cumulative preferred stock and 50,000 shares of common stock. Dividends paid in 1988 were at the rate of $8 per share of preferred stock and $2 per share of common. In 1989, earnings declined sharply and the only dividend paid was $2 per share of the preferred stock. No dividends were paid in 1990. What is the status of the preferred stock at December 31, 1990? Dividends are in arrears in the amount of $14 a share ($6 omitted during 1989 and $8 omitted in 1990). On the entire issue of 10,000 shares of preferred stock, the dividends in arrears amount to $140,000.

Dividends in arrears **are not listed among the liabilities of a corporation, because no liability exists until a dividend is declared by the board of directors.** Nevertheless, the amount of any dividends in arrears on preferred stock is an important factor to investors and should always be **disclosed.** This disclosure is usually made by a note accompanying the balance sheet such as the following:

Note 6: Dividends in arrears

As of December 31, 1990, dividends on the $8 cumulative preferred stock were in arrears to the extent of $14 per share and amounted in total to $140,000.

In 1991, we shall assume that the company earned a large income and wished to pay dividends on both the preferred and common stocks. Before paying a dividend on the common, the corporation must pay the $140,000 in arrears on the cumulative preferred stock *plus* the regular $8 a share applicable to the current year. The preferred shareholders would, therefore, receive a total of $220,000 in dividends in 1991; the board of directors would then be free to declare dividends on the common stock.

For a *noncumulative* preferred stock, any unpaid or omitted dividend is lost forever. Because of this factor, investors view the noncumulative feature as an unfavourable element, and very few noncumulative preferred stocks are issued.

Stock preferred as to assets   Most preferred stocks carry a preference as to assets in the event of liquidation of the corporation. If the business is terminated, the preferred stock is entitled to payment in full of its par value or a higher stated liquidation value before any payment is made on the common stock. This priority also includes any dividends in arrears.

Callable or redeemable preferred stock   Preferred stocks often include a *call or redemption provision*. This provision grants the issuing corporation the right to repurchase the stock from the shareholders at a stipulated *call (redemption) price*. The call price is usually slightly higher than the par value or the issued price of the stock. For example, $100 par value preferred stock may be callable at $105 or $110 per share. In addition to paying the call price, a corporation that redeems its preferred stock must pay any dividends in arrears. A call provision gives a corporation flexibility in adjusting its financial structure, for example, by eliminating a preferred stock and replacing it with other securities if future growth of the company makes such change advantageous.

Convertible preferred stock   In order to add to the attractiveness of preferred stock as an investment, corporations sometimes offer a *conversion privilege* that entitles the preferred shareholders to exchange their shares for common stock in a stipulated ratio. If the corporation prospers, its common stock will probably rise in market value, and dividends on the common stock will probably increase. The investor who buys a convertible preferred stock rather than common stock has greater assurance of regular dividends. In addition, through the conversion privilege, the investor is assured of sharing in any substantial increase in value of the company's common stock.

As an example, assume that Remington Corporation issued a $9, no-par convertible preferred stock on January 2, at a price of $100 a share. Each share was convertible into four shares of the company's no-par value common stock at any time. The common stock had a market price of $20 a share on January 2, and an annual dividend of $1 a share was being paid. During the next few years, Remington Corporation's earnings increased, the dividend on the common stock was raised to an annual rate of $3, and the market price of the common stock rose to $40 a share. At this point the preferred stock would have a market value of *at least $160,* since it could be converted at any time into four shares of common stock with a market value of $40 each. In other words, the market value of a convertible preferred stock will tend to move in accordance with the price of the common.

When the dividend rate is increased on the common stock, some holders of the preferred stock may convert their holdings into common stock in order to obtain a higher cash return on their investments. If the holder of 100 shares of the preferred stock presented these shares for conversion, Remington Corporation would make the following journal entry:

CONVERSION OF
PREFERRED STOCK
INTO COMMON

$9 Convertible Preferred Stock	10,000	
Common Stock		10,000

To record the conversion of 100 shares of preferred stock
of no-par value into 400 shares of no-par value common stock.

Note that the issue price recorded for the 400 shares of common stock is based upon the carrying value of the preferred stock in the accounting records, not upon market prices at the date of conversion.

Participating clauses in preferred stock   Since participating preferred stocks are very seldom used, discussion of them will be brief. A fully participating preferred stock is one that, in addition to the regular specified dividend, is entitled to participate in some manner with the common stock in any additional dividends paid. For example, a $5 participating preferred stock would be entitled to receive $5 a share before the common stock received anything. After $5 a share had been paid to the preferred shareholders, a $5 dividend could be paid on the common stock. If the company desired to pay an additional dividend to the common, say, an extra $3 per share, the preferred stock would also be entitled to receive an extra $3 dividend. In brief, a fully participating preferred stock participates dollar for dollar with the common stock in any dividends paid in excess of the stated rate on the preferred stock.

It is important to remember that most preferred stocks are *not* participating. Although common stock dividends may increase year after year if the corporation prospers, the dividends on most preferred stocks are fixed in amount. A $6 preferred stock, unless it is participating, *will never pay an annual dividend in excess of $6.*

Market price of preferred stock

Investors buy preferred stocks primarily to receive the dividends that these stocks pay. But what happens to the market price of an $8 preferred stock, originally issued at a price of $100, if government policies and other factors cause long-term interest rates to rise to, say, 15 or 16%? If investments offering a return of 16% are readily available, investors will no longer pay $100 for a share of preferred stock that provides a dividend of only $8 per year. Thus, the market price of the preferred stock will fall to about half of its original issue price, or about $50 per share. At this market price, the stock offers a 16% return (called the *dividend yield*) to an investor purchasing the stock ($8 per year ÷ $50 = 16%). However, if the prevailing long-term interest rates should again decline to the 8% range, the market price of this preferred stock should quickly rise to approximately the issued price of $100.

In conclusion, the market price of preferred stock *varies inversely with interest rates.* As interest rates rise, preferred stock prices decline; as interest rates fall, preferred stock prices rise.

The underwriting of capital stock issues

When a large amount of capital stock is to be issued, the corporation will probably utilize the services of an investment dealer, frequently referred to as an *underwriter.* The underwriter guarantees the issuing corporation a specific price for the capital stock and makes a profit by selling the capital stock to the investing public at a higher price. The corporation records the issuance of the capital stock at the net amount received from the underwriter. The use of an underwriter assures the corporation that the entire capital stock issue will be sold without delay, and the entire amount of funds to be raised will be available on a specific date.

Market price of common stock

The preceding sections concerning the issuance of capital stock did not raise a question as to how the market price of capital stock was determined. The price which the corporation sets on a new issue of capital stock is based on several factors including (1) an appraisal of the company's expected future earnings, (2) the probable dividend rate per share, (3) the present financial position of the company, and (4) the current state of the investment market.

After the capital stock has been issued, the price at which it will be traded among investors will rise and fall in response to all the forces of the marketplace. The market price per share will tend to reflect the progress of the company, with primary emphasis being placed on earnings and dividends. At this point in our discussion, the significant fact to emphasize is that market price is not related to any par value, and that it tends to reflect investors' expectations of future earnings and dividends.

Stock issued for assets other than cash

Corporations generally sell their capital stock for cash and use the cash to buy the various types of assets needed in the business. Sometimes, however, a corporation may issue shares of its capital stock in a direct exchange for land, buildings, or other assets. Stock may also be issued in payment for services rendered by lawyers and promoters in the formation of the corporation.

When a corporation issues capital stock in exchange for services or for assets other than cash, the transaction should be recorded at the current *market value* of the goods or services received. Often, the best evidence as to the market value of these goods or services is the market value of the shares issued in exchange. For example, assume that a company issues 10,000 shares of its no-par value common stock in exchange for land. Competent appraisers may have differing opinions as to the market value of the land. But let us assume that the company's common stock is currently selling on a stock exchange for $90 per share. It is logical to say that the cost of the land to the company is $900,000, the market value of the shares issued in exchange.

Once the valuation has been decided, the entry to record the issuance of the stock in exchange for the land is as follows:

HOW WERE DOLLAR
AMOUNTS DETERMINED?

Land	900,000	
Common Stock		900,000

To record the issuance of 10,000 shares of no-par value common stock in exchange for land. Current market value of stock ($90 per share) used as basis for valuing the land.

Similarly, if 100 shares of the no-par value common stock with a market value of $90 per share are issued to lawyers and promoters for their services of $9,000 in the formation of the corporation, the entry to record the exchange is:

Organization costs	9,000	
Common Stock		9,000

To record the issuance of 100 shares of no-par value common stock in exchange for organization costs of $9,000.

As mentioned earlier, the fair market value of the assets such as land and building may also be used as a basis of valuation if it is proven to be more objective and reliable than the market value of the shares used in the exchange. The responsibility for the determination of market value rests with the board of directors of the corporation. Thus, the board must assess all available evidence to ensure that the most objective and reliable basis of valuation is used.

Subscriptions to capital stock

6   Account for subscriptions to capital stock and for donated capital.

Small corporations sometimes sell capital stock on a subscription plan, in which the investor agrees to pay the subscription price at a future date or in a series of instalments. When the subscription contract is signed, Stock Subscriptions Receivable is debited and Capital Stock Subscribed is credited. Later, as instalments are collected, the entry is a debit to Cash and a credit to Stock Subscriptions Receivable. When the entire subscription price has been collected, the stock certificates are issued. The issuance of the stock is recorded by debiting Capital Stock Subscribed and crediting Capital Stock. The following illustration demonstrates the accounting procedures for stock subscriptions.

In this example, 10,000 shares of no-par value capital stock are subscribed at a price of $15. Subscriptions for 6,000 of these shares are then collected in full. A partial payment is received on the other 4,000 shares.

The entry for the subscription is as follows:

Stock Subscriptions Receivable   150,000
    Capital Stock Subscribed   150,000
Received subscriptions for 10,000 shares of no-par value
stock at price of $15 a share.

When the subscriptions for 6,000 shares are collected in full, certificates for 6,000 shares will be issued. The following entries are made:

Cash   90,000
    Stock Subscriptions Receivable   90,000
Collected subscriptions in full for 6,000 shares at $15 each.

Capital Stock Subscribed   90,000
    Capital Stock   90,000
Issued certificates for 6,000 fully paid no-par value shares
issued at $15 each.

The subscriber to the remaining 4,000 shares paid only half of the amount of the subscription but promised to pay the remainder within a month. Stock certificates will not be issued until the subscription is collected in full, but the partial collection is recorded by the following entry:

Cash   30,000
    Stock Subscriptions Receivable   30,000
Collected partial payment on subscription for 4,000 shares.

From the corporation's point of view, Stock Subscriptions Receivable is a current asset, which ordinarily will be collected within a short time. If financial statements are prepared between the date of obtaining subscriptions and the date of issuing the stock, the Capital Stock Subscribed account is regarded as legal capital and will appear in the shareholders' equity section of the balance sheet.

Donated Capital

On occasion, a corporation may receive assets as a gift. To increase local employment, for example, some cities have given corporations the land upon which to build factories. When a corporation receives such a gift, both total assets and total shareholders' equity increase by the market value of the assets received. *No income is recognized when a gift is received;* the increase in shareholders' equity is regarded as contributed capital. The receipt of a gift is recorded by debiting the appropriate asset accounts and crediting an account entitled *Donated Capital.* Donated capital appears in the shareholders' equity section of the balance sheet, as illustrated on page 598.

For example, the entry to record the donation of land with a market value of $210,000 is as follows:

Land   210,000
    Donated Capital   210,000
To record the donation of land with a market value of $210,000.

Shareholder records in a corporation

A large corporation with shares listed on the Toronto Stock Exchange or other exchanges usually has millions of shares outstanding and several hundred thousand shareholders. Each day many shareholders sell their shares; the buyers of these shares become new members of the company's family of shareholders. An investor purchasing stock in a corporation receives a *stock certificate* from the company indicating the number of shares acquired. If the investor later sells these shares, this stock certificate must be surrendered to the corporation for cancellation before a new certificate is issued to the new owner of the shares.

A corporation must have an up-to-date record of the names and addresses of this constantly changing army of shareholders so that it can send dividend cheques, financial statements, and voting forms to the right people. Also, the corporation must make sure that old stock certificates are cancelled as new ones are issued so that no excess certificates become outstanding.

Shareholders' ledger   When there are numerous shareholders, it is not practical to include a separate account for each shareholder in the general ledger. Instead, a single controlling account entitled Capital Stock appears in the general ledger, and a subsidiary shareholders' ledger is maintained. This ledger contains a page for each individual shareholder. Entries in the shareholders' ledger are made in number of shares rather than in dollars. Thus, each shareholder's account shows the number of shares owned, and the dates of acquisitions and sales. This record enables the corporation to send each shareholder a single dividend, even though the shareholder may have acquired several stock certificates at different dates.

Stock transfer agent and stock registrar   Companies with shares traded on organized stock exchanges must engage an independent stock transfer agent and stock registrar to maintain their shareholder records and to control the issuance of stock certificates. These transfer agents and registrars usually are large banks or trust companies. When stock certificates are to be transferred from one owner to another, the old certificates are sent to the transfer agent, who cancels them, makes the necessary entries in the shareholders' ledger, and prepares a new certificate for the new owner of the shares. This new certificate then must be registered with the stock registrar before it represents valid and transferable ownership of stock in the corporation.

Small, closely held corporations generally do not use the services of independent registrars and transfer agents. In these companies, the shareholder records usually are maintained by the corporate secretary. To prevent the accidental or fraudulent issuance of an excessive number of stock certificates, even a small corporation should require that each certificate be signed by at least two designated corporate officers.

7 Explain the meaning and significance of the book value of common stock and its relationship to market value.

Book value per share of common stock

Because the equity of each shareholder in a corporation is determined by the number of shares he or she owns, an accounting measurement of interest to many shareholders is book value per share of common stock. Book value per share is equal to the **net assets** represented by one share of stock. The term **net assets** means total assets minus total liabilities; in other words, net assets are equal to total shareholders' equity. Thus in a corporation that has issued common stock only, the book value per share is computed by dividing total shareholders' equity by the number of shares outstanding.

For example, assume that a corporation has 4,000 shares of common stock outstanding and the shareholders' equity section of the balance sheet is as follows:

HOW MUCH IS BOOK VALUE PER SHARE?

Common stock, no-par value	$ 44,000
Retained earnings	76,000
Total shareholders' equity	$120,000

The book value per share is $30; it is computed by dividing the shareholders' equity of $120,000 by the 4,000 shares of outstanding stock. In computing book value, we are not concerned with the number of authorized shares but merely with the outstanding shares, because the total of the outstanding shares represents 100% of the shareholders' equity.

 Book value per share is regularly reported in such financial news media as *The Financial Post* and the *Financial Times*, and also in the annual reports of such large corporations as Dofasco Inc., Federal Industries Ltd., and Nova, an Alberta Corporation.

Book value when a company has both preferred and common stock Book value is usually computed only for common stock. If a company has both preferred and common stock outstanding, the computation of book value per share of common stock requires two steps. First, the redemption value or call price of the entire preferred stock issue, and any dividends in arrears, are deducted from total shareholders' equity. Second, the remaining amount of shareholders' equity is divided by the number of common shares outstanding to determine book value per common share. This procedure reflects the fact that the common shareholders are the residual owners of the corporate entity.

To illustrate, assume that the shareholders' equity of Video Limited at December 31 is as follows:

WO CLASSES OF STOCK

$8 preferred stock, no-par, callable at $110, issued and outstanding, 10,000 shares	$1,000,000
Common stock, no-par; issued and outstanding, 50,000 shares	1,250,000
Retained earnings	130,000
Total shareholders' equity	$2,380,000

Because of a weak cash position, Video Limited has paid no dividends during th
current year. As of December 31, dividends in arrears on the cumulative preferre
stock total $80,000.

All the equity belongs to the common shareholders, except the $1.1 million ca
price ($110 × 10,000 shares) applicable to the preferred stock and the $80,000 c
dividends in arrears on preferred stock. The calculation of book value per share c
common stock can therefore be made as follows:

Total shareholders' equity		$2,380,00(
Less: Equity of preferred shareholders:		
Call price of preferred stock	$1,100,000	
Dividends in arrears	80,000	1,180,00(
Equity of common shareholders		$1,200,00(
Number of common shares outstanding		50,00(
Book value per share of common stock		
($1,200,000 ÷ 50,000)		$2(

The concept of book value may be of vital importance in many contracts. Fc
example, a majority shareholder might obtain an option to purchase the shares of th
minority shareholders at book value at a specified future date. Many court cases hav
hinged on definitions of book value.

Book value is also used in judging the reasonableness of the market price of
stock. However, it must be used with great caution; the fact that a stock is selling a
less than its book value does not necessarily indicate a bargain. As stated in an earlie
section, current earnings, dividends per share, prospects for future earnings, an
current investment market conditions are usually more important factors affectin
market price than is book value.

Book value does *not* indicate the amount that the holder of a share of stock woul
receive if the corporation were to be dissolved. In liquidation, the assets woul
probably be sold at prices quite different from their carrying values in the accounts
and the shareholders' equity would go up or down accordingly.

Changes in book value   Many events cause the book value per share of commo
stock to change. For example, earning net income increases total shareholders
equity, thereby increasing book value per share. Net losses and the declaration c
dividends both reduce shareholders' equity and book value.

Another event that affects book value is the issuance of additional shares c
common stock at a price either above or below the present book value per share. T
illustrate, assume that a corporation has total shareholders' equity of $1,000,000, n
preferred stock, and 100,000 shares of common stock outstanding. The book valu
per share is $10 ($1,000,000 ÷ 100,000 shares). If the company issues an additiona
20,000 shares of common stock at $22 per share, total shareholders' equity wi
increase to $1,440,000 and the total outstanding common stock will be 120,00(
shares. Note that the book value per share is now $12 ($1,440,000 ÷ 120,00(
shares). Thus, the sale of additional common stock at a price above book valu

increases the average book value per share. Conversely, the sale of additional shares at a price below book value decreases the average book value per share.

Balance sheet for a corporation illustrated

A fairly complete balance sheet for a corporation is illustrated below and on page 598. Note the inclusion in this balance sheet of liabilities for income taxes payable and dividends payable. These liabilities do not appear in the balance sheet of unincorporated businesses. Note also that the caption for each capital stock account indicates the type of capital stock, and the number of shares issued. The caption for preferred stock also indicates the dividend rate, call price, and other important features.

Bear in mind that current practice includes many alternatives in the choice of terminology and the arrangement of items in financial statements. A set of financial statements of a public corporation is presented in the appendix following Chapter 20.

DEL MAR CORPORATION
Balance Sheet
December 31, 1989

ASSETS

Current assets:			
Cash			$ 305,600
Accounts receivable (net of allowance for doubtful accounts)			1,105,200
Stock subscriptions receivable: common			110,000
Inventories (lower of fifo cost and net realizable value)			1,300,800
Short-term prepayments			125,900
Total current assets			$2,947,500
Plant and equipment:			
Land — at cost		$ 900,000	
Buildings and equipment — at cost	$5,283,000		
Less: Accumulated depreciation	1,250,000	4,033,000	4,933,000
Other assets: Organization costs			14,000
Total assets			$7,894,500

LIABILITIES & SHAREHOLDERS' EQUITY

Current liabilities:	
Accounts payable	$ 998,100
Income taxes payable	324,300
Dividends payable	109,700
Interest payable	20,000
Total current liabilities	$1,452,100
Long-term liabilities:	
Bonds payable, 12%, due Oct. 1, 1999	1,000,000
Total liabilities	$2,452,100

Shareholders' equity:

Cumulative $8 preferred stock, no-par, callable at $104, authorized, an unlimited number of shares, issued and outstanding, 10,000 shares	$1,000,000	
Common stock, no-par, authorized, an unlimited number of shares, issued and outstanding, 600,000 shares	2,670,000	
Common stock subscribed, 20,000 shares	20,000	
Donated capital	210,000	
Total contributed capital	$3,900,000	
Retained earnings	1,542,400	
Total shareholders' equity		5,442,400
Total liabilities & shareholders' equity		$7,894,500

END-OF-CHAPTER REVIEW

SUMMARY OF CHAPTER LEARNING OBJECTIVES

1 Discuss the advantages and disadvantages of organizing a business as a corporation.

The primary advantages are: no personal liability of shareholders for the debts of the business, the transferability of ownership shares, continuity of existence, ability to hire professional management, and the relative ease of accumulating large amounts of capital. The primary disadvantages are: "double taxation" of earnings (in spite of the federal dividend tax credit claimed by shareholders) and greater governmental regulation.

2 Explain the rights of shareholders and the roles of corporate directors and officers.

Shareholders in a corporation normally have the right to elect the board of directors, to share in dividends declared by the directors, to share in the distribution of assets if the corporation is liquidated, and to subscribe to additional shares if the corporation decides to increase the number of shares outstanding.

The directors formulate company policies, review the actions of the corporate officers, and protect the interests of the company. Corporate officers are professional managers appointed by the board of directors to manage the business on a daily basis.

3 Describe the differences in the balance sheet presentation of the ownership equity in a corporation and in a sole proprietorship.

In the balance sheet of a sole proprietorship, the total amount of ownership equity appears in a single account, entitled, for example, J. Doe, Capital. In the balance sheet of a corporation, separate accounts are used to distinguish between contributed capital and earned capital. In the simplest case, this may be accomplished with two accounts: Capital Stock and Retained Earnings. Additional accounts are needed if the corporation has issued more than one type of capital stock or if stock with a par value is issued at a price above par value.

4 Discuss the nature and issuance of capital stock, focussing on no-par value capital stock.

Capital stock is evidence of ownership in a corporation. Capital stock is usually without par value, to avoid misunderstanding and to facilitate capital structure changes. When no-par capital stock is issued for cash, the transaction is recorded by debiting Cash, crediting Capital Stock for the amount received. If the stock is issued in exchange for assets other than cash, the transaction is recorded at either the fair market value of the shares issued or the fair market value of the assets received, whichever can be determined more objectively.

5 Discuss the features of preferred stock and of common stock.

Preferred stock has preference over common stock with respect to dividends and to distributions in the event of liquidation. This "preference" means that preferred shareholders must be paid in full before any payments are made to holders of common stock. The dividends on preferred stock usually are fixed in amount. In addition, the stock usually is callable at the option of the issuing corporation, and often has no voting rights. Preferred stocks sometimes have special features, such as being convertible into shares of common stock.

Common stock represents the true "residual ownership" of a corporation. These shares have voting rights. Also, the common stock dividend is not fixed in dollar amount — thus, it may increase or decrease based upon the company's performance.

6 Account for subscriptions to capital stock and for donated capital.

Stock subscriptions represent investors' promises to buy shares of stock at some future date at an agreed-upon price. When shares are subscribed, the corporation records a receivable and credits Capital Stock Subscribed. When the receivable is collected and the subscribed shares are issued, the balance of the Capital Stock Subscribed account is transferred to the regular Capital Stock account.

Assets donated to a corporation are recorded in the accounting records at their fair market value. The offsetting credit is to a shareholders' equity account, entitled Donated Capital.

7 Explain the meaning and significance of book value of common stock and its relationship to market value.

Book value is the amount of net assets represented by each share of common stock. Book value may be either higher or lower than the current market value; however, it may give an indication of the reasonableness of the current market price.

Market value is the current price at which shares of stock may be bought or sold. When a stock is traded on an organized stock exchange, the market price is quoted daily in the financial press. Market price is based upon a combination of factors, including investors' expectations of future earnings, dividend yield, interest rates, and alternative investment opportunities.

KEY TERMS INTRODUCED OR EMPHASIZED IN CHAPTER 14

Board of directors Persons elected by common shareholders to direct the affairs of a corporation.

Book value per share The shareholders' equity represented by each share of common stock, computed by dividing common shareholders' equity by the number of common shares outstanding.

Call (redemption) price The price to be paid by a corporation for each share of callable preferred stock if the corporation decides to call (redeem) the preferred stock.

Capital stock Transferable units of ownership in a corporation. A broad term that may refer to common stock, preferred stock, or both.

Closely held corporation A corporation owned by a small group of shareholders. The capital stock of closely held corporations is not traded on stock exchanges.

Common stock A type of capital stock which possesses the basic rights of ownership including the right to vote. Represents the residual element of ownership in a corporation.

Contributed capital The amounts invested in a corporation by its shareholders.

Corporation A business organized as a legal entity separate from its owners, with ownership divided into shares of transferable stock. Shareholders are not liable for debts of the corporation.

Deficit Accumulated losses incurred by a corporation. A negative amount of retained earnings.

Dividend A distribution of cash by a corporation to its shareholders.

No-par stock Stock without par value.

Organization costs Costs incurred to form a corporation.

Par value The legal capital and the face amount of a share of capital stock. Represents the minimum amount per share to be invested in the corporation when shares are originally issued.

Preferred stock A class of capital stock usually having preferences as to dividends and in the distribution of assets in event of liquidation.

Retained earnings That portion of shareholders' equity resulting from income earned and retained in the business. Retained earnings are increased by the earning of net income and are decreased by the incurring of net losses and by the declaration of dividends.

Stock certificate A document issued by a corporation (or its transfer agent) as evidence of the ownership of the number of shares stated on the certificate.

Stock registrar An independent fiscal agent retained by a corporation to provide assurance against overissuance of stock certificates.

Stock transfer agent A bank or trust company retained by a corporation to maintain its records of capital stock ownership and make transfers from one investor to another.

Shareholders' ledger A subsidiary record showing the number of shares owned by each shareholder.

Subscriptions to capital stock Formal promises to buy shares of stock from a corporation with payment at a later date. Stock certificates are delivered when full payment is received.

Underwriter An investment dealer who handles the sale of a corporation's stock to the public.

DEMONSTRATION PROBLEM FOR YOUR REVIEW

At the close of the current year, the shareholders' equity section of the Rockhurst Corporation's balance sheet appeared as follows:

Shareholders' equity:
$1.50 preferred stock, no-par value,
   authorized, an unlimited number of shares:
      Issued and outstanding, 432,000 shares $11,340,000
      Subscribed, 216,000 shares 5,670,000 $17,010,000
Common stock, no-par, authorized, an unlimited number of
   shares, issued and outstanding, 2,460,000 shares   19,926,000
Retained earnings (deficit) . . . .   (600,000)
   Total shareholders' equity $36,336,000

Among the assets of the corporation appears the following item: Subscriptions Receivable: Preferred, $1,123,200.

Instructions On the basis of this information, write a brief answer to the following questions, showing any necessary supporting computations.

a What was the average price per share received (including stock subscribed) by the corporation on its preferred stock?

b What was the average price per share received by the corporation on its common stock?

c What is the average amount per share that subscribers of preferred stock have yet to pay on their subscriptions?

d What is the total contributed capital including preferred stock subscribed?

e What is the total legal or stated capital of the capital stock including preferred stock subscribed?

SOLUTION TO DEMONSTRATION PROBLEM

a Preferred stock: Issued and outstanding $11,340,000
                  Subscribed   5,670,000
      Total contributed and subscribed $17,010,000
      Total shares (432,000 + 216,000)   648,000
      Average price per share ($17,010,000 ÷ 648,000) $26.25

b Common stock: issued and outstanding $19,926,000
      Total shares   2,460,000
      Average price per share ($19,926,000 ÷ 2,460,000) . . . . $ 8.10

c Subscriptions receivable, preferred . . . . $ 1,123,200
      Shares subscribed   216,000
      Average price per share ($1,123,200 ÷ 216,000) . . . . $ 5.20

d $36,936,000 (preferred $17,010,000 + common $19,926,000)

e $36,936,000 (preferred $17,010,000 + common $19,926,000)

ASSIGNMENT MATERIAL

REVIEW QUESTIONS

1 Why are large corporations often said to be *publicly owned?*

2 Distinguish between corporations and partnerships in terms of the following characteristics:
  a Owners' liability for debts of the business
  b Transferability of ownership interest
  c Continuity of existence
  d Taxation on income

3 Generally, what are the basic rights of the owner of a share of corporate capital stock? In what way are these basic rights commonly modified with respect to the owner of a share of preferred stock?

4 Explain the meaning of the term *double taxation* as it applies to corporate income.

5 Distinguish between *contributed capital* and *retained earnings* of a corporation. Why is such a distinction useful?

6 If the Retained Earnings account has a debit balance, how is it presented in the balance sheet and what is it called?

7 Explain the reasons for the emergence of the concept of no-par value capital stock in federal and provincial corporation legislation.

8 Explain the significance of *par value*. Does par value indicate the reasonable market price for a share of stock? Explain.

9 Describe the usual nature of the following features as they apply to a share of preferred stock: (a) cumulative, (b) convertible, and (c) callable (redeemable).

10 Why is noncumulative preferred stock considered a very unattractive form of investment?

11 When capital stock is issued by a corporation in exchange for assets other than cash, accountants face the problem of determining the dollar amount at which to record the transaction. Discuss the factors to be considered and explain their significance.

12 State the classification (asset, liability, shareholders' equity, revenue, or expense) of each of the following accounts:
   a Subscriptions receivable
   b Organization costs
   c Preferred stock
   d Retained earnings
   e Capital stock subscribed
   f Premium on common stock
   g Income taxes payable

13 A professional baseball team received as a gift from the city the land upon which to build a stadium. What effect, if any, will the receipt of this gift have upon the baseball team's balance sheet and income statement? Explain.

14 Explain the following terms:
   a Stock transfer agent
   b Shareholders' ledger
   c Underwriter
   d Stock registrar

15 What does *book value per share* of common stock represent? Does it represent the amount common shareholders would receive in the event of liquidation of the corporation? Explain briefly.

16 How is book value per share of common stock computed when a company has both preferred and common stock outstanding?

17 What would be the effect, if any, on book value per share of common stock as a result of each of the following independent events: (a) a corporation obtains a bank loan; (b) a dividend is declared (to be paid in the next accounting period); (c) additional shares of common stock are issued at a price above the current book value per share.

EXERCISES

Exercise 14-1
Accounting
terminology

Listed below are nine technical accounting terms introduced in this chapter:

Retained earnings	Book value	Common stock
Contributed capital	Market value	Preferred stock
Deficit	No-par value	Dividend in arrears

Each of the following statements may (or may not) describe one of these technical terms. For each statement, indicate the accounting term described, or answer "None" if the statement does not correctly describe any of the terms.

a The per share value quoted daily in the financial press for stocks traded on organized securities exchanges, such as the Toronto Stock Exchange.

b The type of capital stock most likely to increase in value as a corporation becomes increasingly profitable.

c An amount of cash on hand from which dividends may be paid to shareholders.

d The net assets represented by one share of capital stock.

e The entire proceeds from issuing common stock are considered as the legal capital.

f The type of capital stock for which the dividend usually is fixed in dollar amount.

g A distribution of cash by a corporation to its shareholders.

h That portion of owners' equity arising from the issuance of capital stock.

Exercise 14-2
Computing retained earnings

In 1988, its first year of operation, Plastic Pipe Corporation earned net income of $190,000 and paid dividends of $2.00 per share on its 70,000 outstanding shares of capital stock. In 1989, the corporation incurred a net loss of $85,000 and paid no dividends.

Instructions

a Prepare the journal entry to close the Income Summary account at December 31, 1989 (the year of the $85,000 net loss).

b Compute the amount of retained earnings or deficit that will appear in the company's balance sheet at December 31, 1989.

Exercise 14-3
Recording dividends

Showboat Corporation has only one issue of capital stock, consisting of 50,000 outstanding shares. The net income in the first year of operations was $106,000. No dividends were paid in the first year. On January 15 of the second year, a dividend of $1.30 per share was declared by the board of directors payable February 15.

Instructions

a Prepare the journal entry at December 31 of the first year to close the Income Summary account.

b Prepare the journal entries for declaration of the dividend on January 15 and payment of the dividend on February 15 of the second year.

Exercise 14-4
Preparing the shareholders' equity section of a balance sheet

Heritage Corporation was organized on July 2, 19___. The corporation was authorized to issue an unlimited number of shares of no-par value, $10 cumulative preferred stock, and an unlimited number of shares of no-par common stock.

Ten thousand shares of the preferred stock were issued at $100 and 170,000 shares of the common stock were sold for $31 per share. Prepare the shareholders' equity section immediately after the issuance of the securities but prior to operation of the company.

Exercise 14-5
Computing retained earnings

Wolfe Limited has outstanding two classes of no-par value stock: 5,000 shares of $8 cumulative preferred and 25,000 shares of common. The company had a $50,000 deficit at the beginning of the current year, and preferred dividends had not been paid for two years. During the current year, the company earned $300,000. What will be the balance in retained earnings at the end of the current year, if the company pays a dividend of $2 per share on the common stock?

Exercise 14-6
Analyzing
shareholders' equity

The shareholders's equity section of the balance sheet appeared as follows in a recent annual report of Kona Corporation:

Shareholders' equity:
  Capital stock:
    $5.50 cumulative preferred stock; no-par value, unlimited
      shares authorized, 180,000 shares issued and outstanding . . $ 18,000,000
    Common stock; no-par value, unlimited shares authorized,
      4,000,000 shares issued and outstanding   33,000,000
    Retained earnings   75,800,000
      Total shareholders' equity $126,800,000

Instructions

From this information compute answers to the following questions:

a What was the average issuance price per share of the preferred stock?

b What was the average issuance price of a share of common stock?

c What is the amount of the total legal capital and the amount of the total contributed capital?

d What is the total amount of the annual dividend requirement on the preferred stock issue?

e Total dividends of $5,200,000 were declared on the preferred and common stock during the year, and the balance in retained earnings at the *beginning* of the year had been $65,800,000. What was the amount of net income for the year?

Exercise 14-7
Computing book value

The information necessary to compute the net assets (shareholders' equity) and book value per share of common stock for Ringside Corporation follows:

$9 cumulative preferred stock, no-par (callable at $110), issued
  and outstanding, 2,000 shares $200,000
Common stock, no-par, issued and outstanding, 60,000 shares   752,800
Deficit   131,800
Dividends in arrears on preferred stock, 1 full year   16,000

Instructions

a Compute the amount of net assets (shareholders' equity).

b Compute the book value per share of common stock.

PROBLEMS

Group A

Problem 14A-1
Preparing the
shareholders' equity
section of a balance
sheet

Following are two separate cases requiring preparation of the shareholders' equity section of a corporate balance sheet.

a Early in 1987, Bell Corporation was formed with authorization to issue unlimited shares of no-par value common stock. Fifty thousand shares were issued at a price of $8 per share. The corporation reported a net loss of $82,000 for 1987 and a net loss of $25,000 in 1988. In 1989, net income was $70,000. No dividends were declared in any of the three years.

b Parker Industries was organized early in 1985 and authorized to issue an unlimited number of shares of no-par value common and 30,000 shares of cumulative preferred stock. All the preferred stock was issued at par and 120,000 shares of common stock were sold for $16 per share. The preferred stock was callable at 105% of its $100 par value and was entitled to dividends of 10% before any dividends were paid to common. During the first five years of its existence, the corporation earned a total of $3,200,000 and paid dividends of 50 cents per share each year on the common stock.

Instructions   For each of the independent situations described, prepare in good form the shareholders' equity section of the balance sheet as of December 31, 1989. Include a supporting schedule for each case showing your determination of the balance of retained earnings that should appear in the balance sheet.

Problem 14A-2
Shareholders' equity:
a short, comprehensive
problem

Early in the year Roger Gordon and several friends organized a corporation called Mobile Communications, Inc. The corporation was authorized to issue 50,000 shares of $100 par value, $10 cumulative preferred stock and an unlimited number of shares of no-par value common stock. The following transactions (among others) occurred during the year:

Jan. 6 Issued for cash 20,000 shares of common stock at $14 per share. The shares were issued to Gordon and 10 other investors.

Jan. 7 Issued an additional 500 shares of common stock to Gordon in exchange for his services in organizing the corporation. The shareholders agreed that these services were worth $7,000.

Jan. 12 Issued 2,500 shares of preferred stock for cash of $288,000.

June 4 Acquired land as a building site in exchange for 15,000 shares of common stock. In view of the appraised value of the land and the progress of the company, the directors agreed that the common stock was to be valued for purposes of this transaction at $15 per share.

Nov. 15 The first annual dividend of $10 per share was declared on the preferred stock to be paid December 20.

Dec. 20 Paid the cash dividend declared on November 15.

Dec. 31 After the revenue and expenses (except income taxes) were closed into the Income Summary account, that account showed a before-tax net income of $150,000. Income taxes were determined to be $43,500.

Instructions   **a** Prepare journal entries in general journal form to record the above transactions. Include entries at December 31 to (1) record the income tax liability; (2) close the Income Tax Expense account into the Income Summary account; and (3) close the Income Summary account.

b Prepare the shareholders' equity section of the Mobile Communications, Inc., balance sheet at December 31.

Problem 14A-3
Starting a new
corporation; includes
stock subscriptions

Pancho's Cantina is the best Mexican restaurant in town — maybe the best anywhere. For years, the restaurant was a sole proprietorship owned by Wayne Label. Many of Label's friends and customers had offered to invest in the business if he ever decided to open new locations. So, early this year, Label decided to expand the business. He formed a new corporation, called Pancho's Cantinas, Inc., which planned to issue stock and use the money received to open new Pancho's restaurants in various locations.

The new corporation is authorized to issue an unlimited number of shares of no-par value capital stock. In April the corporation entered into the following transactions:

Apr. 1 Received subscriptions from various investors for 25,000 shares of capital stock to be issued at a price of $20 per share.

Apr. 24 Received an invoice from a lawyer for $6,200 for services relating to the formation of the new corporation. This invoice is due in 30 days.

Apr. 28 Received $40,000 cash as full payment from Shirley Long, an investor who had sub-scribed to 2,000 shares of capital stock. A stock certificate was immediately issued to Long for 2,000 shares. (No payments have been received from the subscribers to the other 23,000 shares.)

Apr. 30 Issued 25,000 of capital stock to Label in exchange for the assets of the original Pancho's Cantina. These assets and their current market values on this date are listed as follows:

Inventory	$ 15,000
Land	145,000
Building	210,000
Equipment and fixtures	130,000

Apr. 30 Issued 100 shares of capital stock to Label in exchange for $2,000 cash, thus assuring Label voting control of the corporation even after the other investors pay for their subscribed shares.

The new corporation will begin operation of the original Pancho's Cantina on May 1. Therefore the corporation had no revenue or expenses relating to restaurant operations during April. No depreciation of plant assets or amortization of organization costs will be recognized until May when operations get under way.

Instructions
a Prepare journal entries to record the April transactions in the accounting records of the new corporation.

b Prepare a classified balance sheet for the corporation as of April 30, 19___.

Problem 14A-4
Analysis of
shareholders' equity

The year-end balance sheet of Jamestown Corporation includes the following shareholders' equity section (with certain details omitted):

Shareholders' equity:
$9.80 cumulative preferred stock, no-par value, callable at $110, authorized unlimited shares, issued and outstanding 18,000 shares	$ 1,800,000
Common stock, no-par value, authorized unlimited shares, issued and outstanding 420,000 shares	8,610,000
Donated capital	500,000
Retained earnings	6,400,000
Total shareholders' equity	$17,310,000

Instructions
On the basis of this information, answer the following questions and show any necessary supporting computations:

a What was the average issuance price of a share of preferred stock?

b What is the total dollar amount of the annual dividend requirement on preferred stock?

c What was the average issuance price of a share of common stock?

d What is the current book value per share of common stock?

e What is the total contributed capital?

f Total dividends of $1,011,000 were declared on the preferred and common stock during the year, and the balance of retained earnings at the beginning of the year was $5,184,000. What was the amount of net income for the year?

Problem 14A-5
Issuing stock for
assets other than cash

The following independent cases involve the issuance of capital stock in exchange for assets other than cash.

(1) DuPar Corporation, a successful, family-owned company, is in the process of acquiring a tract of land suitable for the construction of a factory. The DuPar Corporation has agreed to offer 26,000 shares of common stock in exchange for the land, which has an agreed fair market value of $650,000, based on two independent appraisals. DuPar Corporation stock is not traded on any stock exchange.

Instructions

Give the journal entry that should be made to record this transaction under each of the following assumptions:

a The stock has a no-par value.

b The stock has a $20 par value.

c The stock has no par, with a stated value of $5.

(2) Irwin Products, a well-established company, issued 3,800 shares of its $5 par value common stock in exchange for certain patents. The patents were entered in the accounts at $19,000. At this time, Irwin Products' common stock was quoted on the over-the-counter market at "25 bid and 27 asked"; that is, sellers were offering stock at $27 per share, and buyers were offering to buy at $25 per share.

Instructions

Comment on the company's treatment of this transaction. Write a brief statement explaining whether you agree or disagree, and why. What is the essential difference between the evidence available to the accountant as a basis for the record of DuPar Corporation and the evidence available for Irwin Products? If the common stock were without par value, would this have any effect on Irwin Products' treatment in this case?

Problem 14A-6
Shareholders' equity
section of a balance
sheet

Following are two independent cases requiring the preparation of the shareholders' equity section of a corporate balance sheet.

Case A In 1986, Allan Jones organized SunRay Corporation to manufacture solar panels. The corporation was authorized to issue unlimited shares of no-par value common stock and unlimited shares of $9 cumulative, no-par value, preferred stock. Five thousand preferred shares were issued at $100 and 20,000 shares of common stock were issued at $25 per share. During the first three years of its existence, SunRay Corporation earned a total of $410,000 and paid yearly dividends of $2.50 per share on the common stock, in addition to the regular dividends on the preferred stock. During 1989, however, the corporation incurred a loss of $230,000 and paid no dividends.

Case B Nancy Monroe organized Monroe Furniture, Inc., in January, 1986. The corporation issued at $16 per share 50,000 of its unlimited authorized shares of no-par common stock. On January 1, 1987, the company sold at $50 per share 10,000 of its unlimited authorized shares of no-par value, $4 cumulative preferred stock. On January 1, 1988, the company again needed money and issued 5,000 shares of its unlimited authorized shares of $9, no-par, cumulative preferred stock for a total of $518,000. The company suffered losses and paid no dividends during 1986 and 1987, reporting a deficit of $200,000 at the end of 1987. During 1988 and 1989 combined, the company earned a total of $800,000. Dividends of $1.50 per share were paid on common stock in 1988 and $3.00 per share in 1989.

Instructions

For each of the independent cases described above, prepare in good form the shareholders' equity section of the balance sheet at December 31, 1989. Include a supporting schedule for each case showing your determination of the balance of retained earnings or deficit at that date.

Group B

The following two cases are independent of each other. Each case provides the information necessary to prepare the shareholders' equity section of a corporate balance sheet.

Case A Baker Limited was organized early in 1988 with authorization to issue an unlimited number of shares of no-par value common stock. Twenty thousand shares were issued at a price of $12 per share. The operations of the company resulted in a net loss of $20,000 for 1988 and a net loss of $52,000 in 1989. In 1990 net income was $21,000. No dividends were declared during the three-year period.

Case B When Street Corporation was formed, authorization was obtained to issue an unlimited number of shares of no-par value common stock and 2,000 shares of $100 par value cumulative preferred stock. All the preferred stock was issued at par and 80,000 shares of the common stock were sold for $10 per share. The preferred stock was callable at $105 per share and was entitled to dividends of 9% before any dividends were paid to common. During the first five years of existence, the corporation earned a total of $560,000 and paid dividends of 20 cents per share each year on common stock.

For each of the two cases described prepare in good form the shareholders' equity section of the latest balance sheet. Include a supporting schedule for each case showing your determination of the balance of retained earnings that should appear in the balance sheet.

Jack Daniels organized Black Iron Corporation early in 1988. On January 9, the corporation issued to Daniels and other investors 50,000 of its unlimited authorized shares of no-par value common stock at a price of $14 per share.

After the revenue and expense accounts (except income tax expense) were closed into the Income Summary account at the end of the year, that account showed a before-tax net income of $124,000. Income taxes were determined to be $44,000. No dividends were paid during 1988.

On June 15, 1989, the board of directors declared a cash dividend of 60 cents per share, payable at July 31.

a Prepare the journal entries for 1988, to (1) record the issuance of the common stock, (2) record the income tax liability at December 31, (3) close the Income Tax Expense account into the Income Summary account, and (4) close the Income Summary account.

b Prepare the journal entries in 1989 for the declaration of the dividend on June 15 and payment of the dividend on July 31.

c Assuming the operations for 1989 resulted in a $19,700 net loss, prepare the journal entry to close the Income Summary account at December 31.

d Prepare the shareholders' equity section of the balance sheet at December 31, 1989. Include a supporting schedule showing your determination of retained earnings at that date.

Problem 14B-3
Issuance of capital
stock and stock
subscriptions

For several years, Linda Green has operated a successful business organized as a sole proprietorship. In order to raise the capital to operate on a larger scale, she decided to organize a new corporation to continue in the same line of business. In January, Green organized Far West Corporation, which was authorized to issue unlimited shares of no-par value common stock. During January, Far West Corporation completed the following transactions:

Jan. 19 Issued 10,000 shares of common stock to various investors for cash at $22 per share.

Jan. 28 Issued 30,000 shares of common stock to Green in exchange for assets with a current market value as follows:

Inventory	$120,000
Equipment	50,000
Building	260,000
Land	230,000

Jan. 29 Received an invoice from a lawyer for $7,000 for services relating to the formation of Far West Corporation. The invoice will be paid in 30 days.

Jan. 30 Received subscriptions for 5,000 shares of common stock at $22 per share; 1,000 of the shares were subscribed by Green and 9,000 were subscribed by other investors.

Jan. 31 Collected from Green the full amount of her subscription to 1,000 shares of common stock and issued a stock certificate for these shares. (No collection has yet been made from the subscribers to the other 4,000 shares.)

The corporation will begin operations in February; no revenue was earned and no expenses were incurred during January. No depreciation of plant assets and no amortization of organization cost will be recognized until February when operations get under way.

Instructions

a Prepare journal entries to record the transactions for January in the accounting records for Far West Corporation.

b Prepare a classified balance sheet for the corporation at January 31.

Problem 14B-4
Analyzing
shareholders' equity

Following is the shareholders' equity section of the balance sheet of Springfield Products at the end of the current year.

Shareholders' equity:
$2.75 preferred stock, $50 par value, authorized
   40,000 shares:

Issued and outstanding	$720,000	
Subscribed	360,000	$1,080,000
Common stock, no par, authorized unlimited shares:		
Issued and outstanding, 136,000 shares	$844,000	
Subscribed, 28,000 shares	140,000	984,000
Premium on preferred		108,000
Retained earnings (deficit)		(300,000)
Total shareholders' equity		$1,872,000

Among the assets of the corporation appear the following items: Stock Subscriptions Receivable: Preferred, $180,000; Stock Subscriptions Receivable: Common, $91,000.

Instructions On the basis of this information, write brief answers to the following questions, showing any necessary supporting computations.

a How many shares of preferred stock have been issued?

b How many shares of preferred stock have been subscribed?

c What was the average price per share received by the corporation on its preferred stock, including preferred stock subscribed?

d What was the average price per share received by the corporation on its common stock, including common stock subscribed?

e What is the average amount per share that subscribers of preferred stock have yet to pay on their subscriptions?

f What is the total contributed capital of Springfield Products?

g What is the average amount per share that common stock subscribers have already paid on their subscriptions?

Problem 14B-5
Computing book value
per share

SwitchMaster builds an excellent product, but the company is poorly managed. Maria Soto wants to acquire enough of the company's voting stock to elect a new board of directors that will hire new management. Soto has entered into contracts with several of SwitchMaster's shareholders to buy their common stock at a price equal to its book value at the end of 1990. Because SwitchMaster has issued both preferred and common stock, Soto is not certain how the book value per share of common stock should be computed. She has come to you for assistance and has provided you with the following information:

At the end of 1990, the total shareholders' equity of SwitchMaster is $1,200,000. The company was organized early in 1986 and immediately issued 5,000 shares of $8, no-par, preferred stock for $500,000 and 30,000 shares of no-par common stock. Except as explained below, there have been no changes in the number of shares outstanding.

Instructions

Compute for Soto the book value per share of common stock at the end of 1990 under each of the following *independent* assumptions:

a The preferred stock was redeemed by SwitchMaster in 1989 and only the common stock remains outstanding.

b All shares of preferred and common stock are still outstanding. The preferred stock is callable at $105 and there are no dividends in arrears.

c The preferred stock is cumulative and callable at $108. The company paid the full preferred dividend in 1986 and 1987 but has paid no dividends since.

d The preferred stock was convertible into common stock at a rate of four shares of common stock for each share of preferred. By the end of 1990, all 5,000 shares of preferred stock had been converted into common stock.

Problem 14B-6
Shareholders' equity:
two challenging cases

The following two independent cases presented require preparation of the shareholders' equity section of a corporate balance sheet.

Case A In 1987, Barbara Sterns organized Flowerland, Inc., a chain of retail nurseries. The corporation was authorized to issue unlimited shares of no-par value common stock and unlimited shares of $5 cumulative, $50 par value, preferred stock. Ten thousand shares of the preferred stock were issued for a total of $511,000 and 35,000 shares of common stock were issued at $20 per share. During the first three years of its existence, Flowerland, Inc., earned a total of $352,000 and paid yearly dividends of $1 per share on the common stock, in addition to the regular dividends on the preferred stock. During 1990, however, the corporation incurred a loss of $165,000 and paid no dividends.

Case B Tom Martinez organized Urban Transport Corporation in January, 1987. The corporation issued at $15 per share one-half of its 100,000 authorized shares of $5 par common stock. On January 2, 1988, the corporation sold at $100 for each of the 5,000 shares of $8, no-par value, cumulative preferred stock (with unlimited shares authorized). On January 2, 1989, the company again needed money and issued 5,000 shares of its unlimited authorized shares of $9, no-par, cumulative preferred stock for a total of $494,000. The company suffered losses in its first two years, reporting a deficit of $270,000 at the end of 1988. During 1989 and 1990 combined, the company earned a total of $950,000. Dividends of $1 per share were paid on common stocks in 1989 and $3.50 per share in 1990.

Instructions

For each of the independent cases described, prepare in good form the shareholders' equity section of the balance sheet at December 31, 1990. Include a supporting schedule for each case showing your determination of the balance sheet of retained earnings at that date.

BUSINESS DECISION CASES

Case 14-1
Factors affecting the market prices of preferred and common stocks

ADM Labs is a publicly owned company with several issues of capital stock outstanding. Over the past decade, the company has consistently earned modest income and has increased its common stock dividend annually by 5 or 10 cents per share. Recently the company introduced several new products, which you believe will cause future sales and earnings to increase dramatically. You also expect a gradual increase in long-term interest rates from their present level of about 11% to, perhaps, 12 or 12½%. Based upon these forecasts, explain whether you would expect to see the market prices of the following issues of ADM capital stock increase or decrease. Explain your reasoning in each answer.

a 10%, $100 par value, preferred stock (currently selling at $90 per share.)

b No-par value common stock (currently paying an annual dividend of $2.50 and selling at $40 per share).

c $7 no-par value, convertible preferred stock (currently selling at $119 per share).

Case 14-2
Whether or not to incorporate

Mario Valenti owns Valenti Ford, a successful automobile dealership. For 25 years, Valenti has operated the business as a sole proprietorship and has acted as both owner and manager. Now, he is 70 years old and is planning on retiring from active management. However, he wants the dealership to stay in the family; his long-term goal is to leave the business to his two children and five grandchildren.

Valenti is wondering whether or not he should incorporate his business. If he were to reorganize Valenti Ford as a corporation, he could then leave an appropriate number of shares of stock to each of his heirs. Otherwise, he could leave the entire business to his heirs to be operated as a partnership. In selecting the appropriate form of business entity, Valenti has formulated the following objectives:

1 *Ownership;* Valenti wants each of his two children to own 25% of the business and each of his five grandchildren to own 10%.

2 *Continuity of existence:* Valenti wants the business to continue indefinitely, even if one or more of the heirs should die or should no longer want to participate in ownership.

3 *Management:* When Valenti retires, he plans to give Joe Heinz, a long-time employee, responsibility for managing the business. Although Valenti wants to keep the ownership of the business in the family, he does not believe that any of his family members have the time or experience to manage the business on a daily basis. In fact, Valenti believes that two of his grandchildren simply have no "business sense," and he does not want them to participate in management.

4 *Income taxes:* Valenti wants to organize the business in a manner that will minimize income taxes to be paid by his heirs. He expects that all the earnings of the business will normally be distributed to its owners on an annual basis.

5 *Owners' liability:* Valenti recognizes that an automobile dealership might become liable for vast amounts of money, if, for example, improper repairs caused a customer's car to be involved in an accident. Although the business carries insurance, he wants to be sure that his heirs' equity in the business does not place their personal assets at risk in the event of business losses.

Instructions

a For each of the preceding five numbered paragraphs explain how the choice of business organization (partnership or corporation) relates to Valenti's stated objective.

b In light of your analysis in part **a**, above, would you recommend that Valenti reorganize Valenti Ford as a corporation, or leave the business unincorporated so that his heirs may operate it as a partnership?

15

CORPORATIONS: OPERATIONS, EARNINGS PER SHARE, AND DIVIDENDS

CHAPTER PREVIEW

Chapter 15 explores special topics relating primarily to the financial statements of large, publicly owned corporations. We illustrate how extraordinary events are presented in the income statement and how accounting changes are disclosed in financial statements. We also illustrate and explain the presentation of earnings per share, with emphasis upon the interpretation of the different per-share amounts. The remainder of the chapter explains the presentation of the statement of retained earnings and discusses a variety of transactions affecting shareholders' equity, including cash dividends, stock dividends, stock splits, prior period adjustments, and treasury stock transactions.

After studying this chapter you should be able to meet these Learning Objectives:

1   **Explain how predictive information and its relationship to the presentation of extraordinary items and accounting changes are presented in the income and other financial statements.**

2   **Compute earnings per share.**

3   **Distinguish between basic and fully diluted earnings per share.**

4   **Account for stock dividends and stock splits, and explain the probable effect of these transactions upon market price.**

5   **Define prior period adjustments and explain how they are presented in financial statements.**

6   **Prepare a statement of retained earnings.**

7   **Account for treasury stock transactions.**

The most important aspect of corporate financial reporting, in the view of most shareholders, is the determination of periodic net income. Both the market price of common stock and the amount of cash dividends per share depend to a considerable extent on the current level of earnings (net income). Even more important than the absolute amount of net income is the *trend* of earnings over time. Is net income increasing or decreasing from one year to the next? The common stocks of those companies that regularly achieve higher earnings year after year become the favourite securities of the investment community. Such stature helps greatly in raising new capital, in attracting and retaining highly competent management, and in many other ways.

In this chapter, we will see that the corporate income statement is organized to help investors to evaluate the trend of earnings and to associate total earnings with their ownership shares. In addition, we will explain the presentation of the statement of retained earnings and discuss transactions that may affect the amount of shareholders' equity and the market price of common stock, but that do not affect net income. Transactions of this nature include cash and stock dividends, stock splits, prior period adjustments, and treasury stock transactions.

Public misconceptions of the rate of corporate earnings

Numerous public opinion surveys indicate that many people mistakenly believe that corporate earnings generally amount to somewhere between 20% and 50% of sales. College and university students should be better informed, but the authors have found, from questioning students in classes at the beginning of the first course in accounting, that college students in guessing at the average rate of corporate earnings usually suggest far higher rates than actually exist. If you will look at the published annual reports of leading corporations, you will find that net income usually falls somewhere between 2% and 10% of sales. Remember that these financial statements have been audited by independent public accounting firms. For all manufacturing companies a representative rate of earnings in recent years has been around 4% to 5%. Of course, there are exceptions. This question of the rate of corporate earnings will be considered more fully in Chapter 20.

Developing predictive information in the income statement

Explain predictive information and its relationship to the presentation of extraordinary items and accounting changes in the income and other financial statements.

An income statement provides a great deal of useful information about the operation and performance of a company. An annual income statement, for example, reveals the rate of gross profit on sales, the net income for the year, the percentage of net income per dollar of sales, and the net income earned on each share of common stock. Thus, it can serve as a basis for evaluating a company's past as well as its future performance. To accomplish this dual objective, the income statement must not only reflect all activities of a company for a period but also must clearly distinguish, with adequate separate disclosure, the normal recurring operating activities from the unusual and nonrecurring events. In any business, unusual and nonrecurring events may occur that cause the current net income to be quite different from the net income we should expect the company to earn in the future. For example, the company may have realized a gain or loss in the current year from the disposal of a significant segment of its business or may have sustained large losses from an earthquake or some other significant event not typical of its normal business activities and no likely to recur in the near future.

How do we distinguish these unusual and nonrecurring events from the normal and recurring activities, and how should they be presented in the income statement These events are considered as *extraordinary items* and should be separately dis closed in the income statement, as discussed in the following section.

Extraordinary items

Extraordinary items are those gains, losses, and provisions for losses that have me all of the following criteria established by the Accounting Standards Committee o the CICA:

1 not typical of the normal business activities
2 not expected to occur regularly over a period of years
3 not considered as recurring factors in any evaluation of the ordinary operation[1]

Examples of extraordinary items include gains or losses resulting from the follow ing events:

1 the sale or abandonment of a plant or significant segment of the business or th sale of investments not acquired for resale
2 expropriation of properties by government or other regulatory bodies
3 earthquakes or floods[2]

These gains and losses are shown in the income statement under a separate headin called extraordinary items, after the income from normal operations. The nature an income tax effect of the gains or losses should be adequately disclosed. An illustration c an income statement with extraordinary items follows:

COASTAL CORPORATION
Income Statement
For the Year Ended December 31, 19___

Net sales		$10,000,00
Cost and expenses:		
Cost of goods sold	$6,000,000	
Selling	1,100,000	
General and administrative	700,000	
Write-off of obsolete inventory	200,000	
Income taxes (excluding tax effects of		
extraordinary loss)	800,000	8,800,00
Income before extraordinary item		$1,200,00
Extraordinary item: Loss from earthquake, net of		
reduction in income taxes of $200,000		300,00
Net income		$ 900,00

[1] CICA, *CICA Handbook*, (Toronto), paragraph 3480.05.
[2] CICA, *CICA Handbook*, (Toronto), paragraph 3480.04.

Sometimes, a gain or loss that is both abnormal in size and caused by unusual circumstances may result from normal business activities. Since such a gain or loss does not meet all the three criteria for extraordinary items, it should be shown in the income statement as part of the normal operations either as a separate item or by way of a note. This is to highlight the unusual nature of the gain or loss. An illustration of this type of gain or loss is the write-off of obsolete inventory shown in the preceding income statement. Examples of other unusual gains and losses that warrant separate disclosure but **not** as extraordinary items include:

1 losses and provision for losses with respect to bad debts;
2 adjustments with respect to contract prices
3 gains and losses from fluctuations of foreign exchange rates.[3]

The clear distinction and separate disclosure of extraordinary and unusual items from normal and recurring activities as illustrated in the preceding income statement provides a more informative basis to evaluate Coastal's current operating results and to predict its likely future performance. If the net income of $900,000 this year is substantially less than last year's, it may be attributed mainly to the losses from the extraordinary and the unusual items. Also, if the normal operating conditions remain unchanged next year, Coastal will likely be expected to earn income from its normal operations only, as the losses from obsolete inventory and the earthquake will not be incurred again. Thus, Coastal's current operating results can be more meaningfully evaluated and its future operations can be more reliably predicted.

Based on a survey of 300 companies, slightly less than one-half of them reported extraordinary items. Of the 131 instances of extraordinary items reported, the most common were gains and losses from sales of assets and discontinued operations.[4]

Accounting changes

Other matters having an effect on the trend of earnings include: (1) a change in an accounting policy, (2) a change in an accounting estimate, and (3) a correction of an error in prior period financial statements. These matters are covered by Section 1506, *''Accounting Changes,''* of the *CICA Handbook*. The recommendations of the *CICA Handbook* are highlighted in the following paragraphs.

Changes in accounting policy encompass changes in accounting principles as well as accounting methods used in the preparation of financial statements. As stated in Chapter 13 and other chapters, the consistent application of accounting principles and methods from one accounting period to another enhances the usefulness of financial statements on a comparative basis. Also, management may justify a change to another acceptable accounting principle on the grounds that it is more appropriate. For example, a change in determining inventory cost from a weighted-average to a first-in first-out method or a change in recognizing depreciation expense from a straight-line to a declining-balance method constitutes a change in accounting policy.

---

[3] CICA, *CICA Handbook*, (Toronto), paragraph 3480.11.
[4] CICA, *Financial Reporting in Canada*, 17th ed. (Toronto, 1987), pp. 185-186.

Since a change in accounting policy affects two or more accounting periods, Section 1506 of the *CICA Handbook* recommends that the effect of an accounting policy change be reflected on a ***retroactive*** basis with a ***restatement*** of those prior period financial statements affected by the change. Thus, each of those prior period financial statements presented on a comparative basis is to be restated to reflect the new accounting policy. In addition, the cumulative effect of the change on the periods preceding the earliest period included in the comparative financial statements is treated as an adjustment to the beginning balance of retained earnings of the earliest period.

Changes in accounting estimates include such items as a revision of the estimate of the amount of allowance for doubtful accounts or a revision of the estimate of a nine-year economic life of a depreciable asset to a six-year life. Since a change in an estimate is a result of ***new*** information, Section 1506 of the *CICA Handbook* recommends that the effect of such a change be accounted for in the period of change or in the period of change and the applicable future periods, depending on whether the change affects one or more periods. Thus, this differs from the treatment of a change in accounting policy in that a restatement of prior periods or a cumulative adjustment is ***not*** required.

Corrections of errors are required when errors are discovered in prior period financial statements. Errors may result from a mistake in computation, a misinterpretation or misrepresentation of information, an oversight of available information, or a misappropriation of assets.[5] Examples of corrections of errors include the discovery that inventories were materially overstated and depreciation expenses were substantially understated in prior period financial statements. Section 1506 of the *CICA Handbook* recommends that a correction of an error be accounted for ***retroactively*** and that the prior period financial statements presented for comparative purposes be ***restated***. In addition, it requires disclosure in the current period regarding: (1) a description of the error, (2) the effect of the correction of the error on the financial statements of the current and prior periods, and (3) the fact that the prior period financial statements presented for comparative purposes have been restated. The disclosure of the effect of the correction on such significant items as net income, earnings per share, and working capital also may be appropriate. These requirements for a correction of an error are logical because they make comparisons of performance of a business enterprise over a number of periods more meaningful and not misleading.

The chart at the top of page 617 summarizes the accounting and reporting requirements of Section 1506 of the *CICA Handbook*. It is interesting to note that both a change in an accounting policy and a correction of an error in prior period financial statements receive the same treatment — retroactive application and restatement. Such a treatment is also accorded to prior period adjustments as discussed later in this chapter. (Statement presentation is also almost identical, as illustrated for prior period adjustments on page 627.) Thus, although these two types of accounting changes do not have the four characteristics of a prior period adjustment, both of them are required to have the same retroactive application and restatement of prior period financial statements.

---

[5] CICA, *CICA Handbook*, (Toronto), paragraph 1506.25.

FINANCIAL STATEMENTS AFFECTED

TYPE OF ACCOUNTING CHANGE	INCOME	RETAINED EARNINGS	ACCOUNTING AND REPORTING REQUIREMENTS
1. Change in accounting policy	Prior period	Current and prior periods	Retroactive application and restatement
2. Change in accounting estimate	Current or current and future periods	Not applicable	Current or current and prospective application
3. Correction of error in prior period	Prior period	Current and prior periods	Retroactive application and restatement

The in-depth coverage of the topic of accounting changes is more appropriately covered in the intermediate accounting course.

Earnings per share (EPS)

2 Compute earnings per share.

Perhaps the most widely used of all accounting statistics is *earnings per share* of common stock. Everyone who buys or sells stock in a corporation needs to know the annual earnings per share. Stock market prices are quoted on a per-share basis. If you are considering investing in common stock of a corporation at a price of, say, $80 per share, you need to know the earnings per share and the annual dividend per share in order to decide whether this price is reasonable. In other words, how much earning power and how much dividend income would you be getting for each share you buy?

To compute earnings per share, the annual net income applicable to the common shareholders is divided by the average number of common shares outstanding. The concept of earnings per share applies *only to common stock;* preferred stock has no claim to earnings beyond the stipulated preferred stock dividends. (However, fully participating preferred stock is treated as "common stock" for earnings per share computations.)

Many financial analysts express the relationship between earnings per share and market price per share as a *price-earnings ratio* (p/e ratio). This ratio is computed by dividing the market price per share of common stock by the annual earnings per share.

Weighted-average number of shares outstanding   The simplest example of computing earnings per share is found when a company has issued only common stock and the number of shares outstanding has not changed during the year. In this situation, the net income for the year divided by the number of shares outstanding at year-end equals earnings per share.

In many companies, however, the number of shares of stock outstanding is changed one or more times during the year. When additional shares are issued in exchange for assets during the year, the computation of earnings per share is based upon the *weighted-average* number of shares outstanding.[6]

[6] When the number of shares outstanding changes as a result of a stock split or a stock dividend (discussed later in this chapter), the computation of the weighted-average number of shares outstanding should be adjusted *retroactively* to the beginning of the period, as if the shares had been outstanding for the whole period.

The weighted-average number of shares for the year is determined by multiplying the number of shares outstanding by the fraction of the year that said number of shares outstanding remained unchanged. For example, assume that 100,000 shares of common stock were outstanding during the first nine months of 1989 and 140,000 shares during the last three months. Assume also that the increase in shares outstanding resulted from the sale of 40,000 shares for cash. The weighted-average number of shares outstanding during 1989 would be 110,000, determined as follows:

100,000 shares × $^9/_{12}$ of a year	75,000
140,000 shares × $^3/_{12}$ of a year	35,000
Weighted-average number of common shares outstanding	110,000

This procedure gives more meaningful earnings per share data than if the total number of shares outstanding at the end of the year were used in the calculations. By using the weighted-average number of shares, we recognize that the proceeds from the sale of the 40,000 shares were available to generate only during the last three months of the year. The contribution to earnings made by 40,000 shares outstanding during one-fourth of the year is equivalent to that of 10,000 shares outstanding for a full year. In other words, the weighted-average number of shares outstanding consists of 100,000 shares outstanding during the entire year plus the 10,000-share full-year equivalent of the shares issued during the year.

Preferred dividends and earnings per share   When a company has preferred stock outstanding, the preferred shareholders participate in net income to the extent of the preferred stock dividends. To determine the earnings *applicable to the common stock,* we must first deduct from net inome the amount of any preferred stock dividends. To illustrate, let us assume that Tanner Corporation has 200,000 shares of common stock and 10,000 shares of $4 preferred stock outstanding throughout the year. Net income for the year totals $480,000. Earnings per share of common stock would be computed as follows:

Net income	$480,000
Less: Dividends on preferred stock (10,000 shares × $4)	40,000
Earnings applicable to common stock	$440,000
Weighted-average number of common shares outstanding	200,000
Earnings per share of common stock ($440,000 ÷ 200,000 shares)	$2.20

Presentation of earnings per share in the income statement

All publicly owned corporations are required to present earnings-per-share data in their income statements.[7] If an income statement includes income before extraordinary items, the per-share figure is shown for this amount as well as for net income.

---

[7] CICA, *CICA Handbook* (Toronto), paragraph 3500.06.

This additional per-share amount is computed by substituting the income before extraordinary items for the net income figure in the preceding calculation.

To illustrate all of the potential per-share computations, we will expand our Tanner Corporation example to include income before extraordinary items. The following condensed income statement is intended to illustrate the proper format for presenting earnings per share figures and to provide a review of the calculations.

TANNER CORPORATION
Income Statement
For the Year Ended December 31, 19___

Net sales	$8,000,000
Cost and expenses (detail omitted for illustrative purposes)	7,400,000
Income before extraordinary items	$ 600,000
Extraordinary item — loss from tornado damage, net of income taxes of $80,000	120,000
Net income	$480,000
Earnings per share of common stock:	
Earnings before extraordinary item	$2.80 [a]
Extraordinary loss	(.60)
Net earnings	$2.20 [b]

a ($600,000 − $40,000) ÷ 200,000 shares
b ($480,000 − $40,000) ÷ 200,000 shares

We have shown the per-share amount for the extraordinary loss to emphasize its effect on the final earnings-per-share amount. This is a desirable but not a required disclosure.[8] For illustration, we have also shown how two of the amounts for earnings per share were computed. These explanatory computations would not be included in an actual income statement.

Interpreting the different per-share amounts   To knowledgeable users of financial statements, each of these figures has a different significance. Earnings per share before extraordinary items represents the results of ordinary business activity. This figure is the most useful one for predicting future operating results. *Net earnings* per share, on the other hand, shows the overall operating results of the current year, including any extraordinary items.

Unfortunately the term *earnings per share* often is used without qualification in referring to various types of per-share data. When using per-share information, it is important to know exactly which per-share statistic is being presented. For example, the price-earnings ratios (market price divided by earnings per share) for common stocks listed on major stock exchanges are reported in the *Financial Post* and many other newspapers. Which earnings per share figures are used in computing these ratios? If a company reports an extraordinary gain or loss, the price-earnings ratio is computed using the per-share *earnings before the extraordinary item*. Otherwise, the ratio is based upon *net earnings* (net income) per share.

---

[8] Ibid., paragraph 3500.11.

3 Distinguish between basic and fully diluted earnings per share.

Basic and fully diluted earnings per share

Let us assume that a company has an outstanding issue of preferred stock that is convertible into shares of common stock at a rate of, say, two shares of common for each share of preferred. The conversion of this preferred stock would increase the number of common shares outstanding and might *dilute* (reduce) earnings per share. Any common shareholder interested in the trend of earnings per share will want to know what effect the conversion of the preferred stock would have upon this statistic.

To inform investors of the potential dilution that might occur, two figures are presented for each earnings-per-share statistic. The first figure, called *basic* earnings per share, is based upon the weighted-average number of common shares actually outstanding during the year. Thus, this figure ignores the potential dilution represented by the convertible preferred stock.[9] The second figure, called *fully diluted* earnings per share, shows the impact that conversion of the preferred stock would have upon basic earnings per share.

Basic earnings per share are computed in the same manner illustrated in our preceding example of Tanner Corporation. Fully diluted earnings per share, on the other hand, are computed on the assumption that all the preferred stock *had been converted into common stock at the beginnng of the current year.*[10] (The mechanics of computing fully diluted earnings per share are covered in the intermediate accounting course.)

It is important to remember that fully diluted earnings per share represent a *hypothetical case.* This statistic is computed even though the preferred stock actually was *not* converted during the year. The purpose of showing fully diluted earnings per share is to warn common shareholders what *could* have happened. When the difference between basic and fully diluted earnings per share becomes significant, investors should recognize the *risk* that future earnings per share may be reduced by conversions of other securities into common stock.

When a company reports both basic and fully diluted earnings per share, the price earnings ratio shown in newspapers is based upon the basic figure (and before extraordinary items).

Cash dividends

The prospect of receiving cash dividends is a principal reason for investing in the capital stocks of corporations. An increase or decrease in the established rate of dividends will usually cause an immediate rise or fall in the market price of the company's capital stock. Shareholders are keenly interested in prospects for future dividends and as a group are strongly in favour of more generous dividend payments. The board of directors, on the other hand, is primarily concerned with the long-run growth and financial strength of the corporation; it may prefer to restrict dividends to a minimum in order to conserve cash for purchase of plant and equipment or for

---

[9] If certain criteria are met, preferred shares are treated, for example, as "*common stock*" and are entered into the computation of basic earnings per share. This and other complex issues relating to earnings per share are discussed in Section 3500 of the *CICA Handbook* and in intermediate accounting texts.

[10] If the preferred stock had been issued during the current year, we would assume that it was converted into common stock on the date it was issued.

other needs of the company. Many of the so-called "growth companies" plough back into the business most of their earnings and pay only very small cash dividends.

The preceding discussion suggests three requirements for the payment of a cash dividend. These are:

1 Retained earnings   Since dividends represent a distribution of earnings to shareholders, the theoretical maximum for dividends is the total undistributed net income of the company, represented by the credit balance of the Retained Earnings account. As a practical matter, many corporations limit dividends to somewhere near 40% of annual net income, in the belief that a major portion of the net income must be retained in the business if the company is to grow and to keep pace with its competitors.

2 An adequate cash position   The fact that the company reports large earnings does not mean that it has a large amount of cash on hand. Cash generated by earnings may have been invested in new plant and equipment, or in paying off debts, or in acquiring a larger inventory. There is no necessary relationship between the balance in the Retained Earnings account and the balance in the Cash account. The traditional expression, "paying dividends out of retained earnings" is misleading. Cash dividends can be paid only "out of" cash.

3 Dividend action by the board of directors   Even though the company's net income is substantial and its cash position seemingly satisfactory, dividends are not paid automatically. A formal action by the board of directors is necessary to declare a dividend.

Dividend dates

Four significant dates are involved in the distribution of a dividend. These dates are:

1 Date of declaration   On the day on which the dividend is declared by the board of directors, a liability to make the payment comes into existence.

2 Date of record   The date of record always follows the date of declaration, usually by a period of two or four weeks, and is always stated in the dividend declaration. In order to be eligible to receive the dividend, a person must be listed as the owner of the stock on the date of record.

3 Ex-dividend date   The ex-dividend date is significant for investors in companies with stocks traded on the stock exchanges. To permit the compilation of the list of shareholders as of the record date, it is customary for the stock to go "ex-dividend" four business days before the date of record. A stock is said to be selling ex-dividend on the day that it loses the right to receive the latest declared dividend. A person who buys the stock before the ex-dividend date is entitled to receive the dividend; conversely, a shareholder who sells shares before the ex-dividend date does not receive the dividend.

4 Date of payment   The declaration of a dividend always includes announcement of the date of payment as well as the date of record. Usually the date of payment comes from two to four weeks after the date of record.

The journal entries to record the declaration and payment of a cash dividend were illustrated in Chapter 14 but are repeated here with emphasis on the date of declaration and date of payment.

| June 1 | Retained Earnings . . . . | 100,000 | |
| | Dividends Payable . . . . | | 100,000 |

To record declaration of a cash dividend of $1 per share on the 100,000 shares of common stock outstanding. Payable July 10 to shareholders of record on June 20.

| July 10 | Dividends Payable . . . . | 100,000 | |
| | Cash . . . . | | 100,000 |

To record payment of $1 per share dividend declared June 1 to shareholders of record on June 20.

As mentioned in Chapter 14, some companies record the declaration of a dividend by debiting a Dividends account instead of debiting Retained Earnings. In this case, a closing entry is required at the end of the year to transfer the debit balance of the Dividends account into the Retained Earnings account. Under either method, the balance of the Retained Earnings account ultimately is reduced by the amount of all dividends declared during the period.

Most dividends are paid in cash, but occasionally a dividend declaration calls for payment in assets other than cash. A large distillery once paid a dividend consisting of a bottle of whiskey for each share of capital stock. When a corporation goes out of existence (particularly a small corporation with only a few shareholders), it may choose to distribute noncash assets to its owners rather than to convert all its assets into cash.

Liquidating dividends

A *liquidating* dividend occurs when a corporation returns to shareholders all or part of their capital investment. Liquidating dividends are usually paid only when a corporation is going out of existence or is making a permanent reduction in the size of its operations. Normally dividends are paid as a result of profitable operations, and the recipients of a dividend are entitled to assume that the dividend represents a distribution of income unless they are specifically notified that the dividend is a return of invested capital.

Stock dividends

4   Account for stock dividends and stock splits, and explain the probable effect of these transactions upon market price.

Stock dividend is a term used to describe a distribution of additional shares of stock to a company's shareholders that is in direct proportion to their present holdings. In brief, the dividend is payable in *additional shares of stocks* rather than in cash. Most stock dividends consist of additional shares of common stock distributed to holders of common stock, and our discussion will be limited to this type of stock dividend.

A *cash* dividend reduces the assets of a corporation and reduces the shareholders' equity by the same amount. A *stock* dividend, on the other hand, causes no change in assets and no change in the *total* amount of the shareholders' equity. The only effect of a stock dividend on the accounts is to transfer a portion of the retained earnings into the Common Stock account (and, if there is par value and the value of the stock dividend per share is greater than the par value per share, an additional transfer into the Contributed Capital from Stock Dividends account is needed.) In other words, a stock dividend merely "reshuffles" the shareholders' equity accounts, increasing the permanent capital accounts and decreasing the Retained Earnings account. A shareholder who receives a stock dividend will own an increased number of shares, but his or her total ownership equity in the company will be *no larger than before.*

To illustrate this point, assume that a corporation with 2,000 shares of stock is owned equally by James Davis and Susan Miller, each owning 1,000 shares of stock. The corporation declares a stock dividend of 10% and distributes 200 additional shares (10% of 2,000 shares), with 100 shares going to each of the two shareholders. Davis and Miller now hold 1,100 shares apiece, but each still owns one-half of the business. The corporation had not changed; its assets and liabilities and its total shareholders' equity are exactly the same as before the dividend. From the shareholders' point of view, the ownership of 1,100 shares out of a total of 2,200 outstanding shares represents no more than did the ownership of 1,000 shares out of a total of 2,000 shares previously outstanding.

Assume that the market price of this stock was $110 per share prior to the stock dividend. Total market value of all the outstanding shares was, therefore, 2,000 times $110, or $220,000. What would be the market value per share and in total after the additional 200 dividend shares were issued? The 2,200 shares now outstanding should have the same total market value as the previously outstanding 2,000 shares, because the "pie" has merely been divided into more but smaller pieces. The price per share should have dropped from $110 to $100, and the aggregate market value of outstanding shares would consequently be computed as 2,200 shares times $100, or $220,000. Whether the market price per share will, in all cases, decrease in proportion to the change in number of outstanding shares is a completely different matter. The market prices of stocks listed on a stock exchange are influenced daily by many different factors.

Reasons for distribution of stock dividends   Many reasons have been given for the popularity of stock dividends; for example:

1 To conserve cash. When the trend of earnings is favourable but cash is needed for expansion, a stock dividend may be an appropriate device for "passing along the earnings" to shareholders without weakening the corporation's cash position.
2 To reduce the market price of corporation's stock to a more convenient trading range by increasing the number of shares outstanding. This objective is usually present in large stock dividends (25% to 100% or more).

Entries to record stock dividends   Assume that a corporation had the following shareholders' equity accounts on December 15, 1988, just prior to declaring a 10% stock dividend:

SHAREHOLDERS' EQUITY
BEFORE STOCK DIVIDEND

Shareholders' equity:
Common stock, no-par value, unlimited shares authorized,
    100,000 shares issued and outstanding $1,500,000
Retained earnings   2,000,000
    Total shareholders' equity $3,500,000

Assume also that the closing market price of the stock on December 15, 1988, was $30 a share. The company declares a 10% stock dividend, consisting of 10,000 common shares (10% × 100,000 = 10,000). The entry to record the *declaration* of the dividend is as follows:

STOCK DIVIDEND
DECLARED; NOTE USE OF
MARKET PRICE OF STOCK

1988
Dec. 15 Retained Earnings 300,000
          Stock Dividend to be Distributed   300,000
      To record declaration of a 10% stock dividend
      consisting of 10,000 shares of no-par value
      common stock. To be distributed on Feb. 9, 1989,
      to shareholders of record on Jan. 15, 1989.
      Amount of retained earnings transferred to
      permanent capital is based on market price
      of $30 a share on Dec. 15, 1988.

The Stock Dividend to Be Distributed account is *not a liability,* because there is no obligation to distribute cash or any other asset. If a balance sheet is prepared between the date of declaration of a stock dividend and the date of distribution of the shares, this account should be presented in the shareholders' equity section of the balance sheet.

The entry to record *distribution* of the dividend shares is as follows:

STOCK DIVIDEND
DISTRIBUTED

1989
Feb. 9 Stock Dividend to be Distributed 300,000
        Common Stock   300,000
      To record distribution of stock dividend of
      10,000 shares.

Note that the amount of retained earnings transferred to permanent capital accounts by the above entries is the *market value,* as indicated by the market price prevailing at the date of declaration. The reasoning behind this practice is simple: Since shareholders tend to measure the "worth" of a small stock dividend (say, 20% to 25% or less) in terms of the market value of the additional shares issued, then Retained Earnings should be reduced by this amount.

Large stock dividends (for example, those in excess of 20% to 25%), on the other hand, generally have the effect of proportionately reducing the market price of the stock. For example, a 100% stock dividend would reduce the market price by about 50%, because twice as many shares would be outstanding. A 100% stock dividend is very similar to the 2 for 1 *stock split* discussed in the following section of this chapter.

Stock splits

Most large corporations are interested in as wide as possible a distribution of their securities among the investing public. If the market price reaches very high levels, for example, $150 per share, the corporation may feel that, by splitting the stock 5 for 1 and thereby reducing the price to $30 per share, the number of shareholders may be increased. Much of the trading in securities occurs in 100-share lots and an extra commission is charged on smaller transactions. Many corporations have split their stock; some have done so several times. Generally the number of shareholders has increased noticeably after the stock has been split.

A stock split consists of increasing the number of outstanding shares and reducing the par value per share, if any, in proportion. For example, assume that a corporation has outstanding 1 million shares of $10 par value capital stock. The market price is $90 per share. The corporation now reduces the par value from $10 to $5 per share and increases the number of shares from 1 million to 2 million. When the capital stock has no par value, then the corporation simply increases its share from 1 to 2 million. This action would be called a 2 for 1 stock split. A shareholder who owned 100 shares of the capital stock before the split would own 200 shares after the split. Since the number of oustanding shares has been doubled without any change in affairs of the corporation, the market price will probably drop from $90 to approximately $45 a share.

A stock split does not change the balance of any ledger account; consequently, the transaction may be recorded merely by a memorandum notation in the general journal and in the Capital Stock account.

Distinction between stock splits and large stock dividends What is the difference between a 2 for 1 stock split and a 100% stock dividend? There is very little difference; both will double the number of outstanding shares without changing total shareholders' equity, and both will serve to cut the market price of the stock in half. The stock dividend, however, will cause a transfer from the Retained Earnings account to the Capital Stock or Common Stock account equal to the par value or the declared dollar amount for no-par value of the dividend shares, whereas the stock split does not change the dollar balance of any account.[11]

After an increase in the number of shares as a result of a stock split or stock dividend, earnings per share are computed in terms of the increased number of shares. In presenting five- or ten-year summaries, the earnings per share for earlier years are *retroactively revised* to reflect the increased number of shares currently outstanding and thus make the trend of earnings per share from year to year a valid comparison.

Retained earnings

Throughout this book, the term *retained earnings* is used to describe that portion of shareholders' equity derived from profitable operations. Retained earnings is a historical concept, representing the accumulated earnings (including prior period adjustments) minus dividends declared from the date of incorporation to the present.

---

[11] Canada Business Corporations Act, Section 41(2).

If we assume that there are no *prior period adjustments,* the major sources of entries in the Retained Earnings account will be (1) the periodic transfer of net income (or loss) from the Income Summary account and (2) the debits resulting from the declaration of dividends.

Prior period adjustments to the Retained Earnings account

5   Define prior period adjustments and explain how they are presented in financial statements.

Prior period adjustments are those gains or losses that have *all four* of the following characteristics:

1 are specifically identified with and directly related to the business activities of particular prior periods
2 are not attributable to economic events occurring subsequent to the date of the financial statements for such prior periods
3 depend primarily on decisions or determinations by persons other than management or owners
4 could not be reasonably estimated prior to such decisions or determinations[12]

Because of the restrictiveness of these characteristics, prior period adjustments are rare. The *CICA Handbook* provides only two examples:

1 nonrecurring adjustments or settlements of income taxes
2 settlements of claims resulting from litigation[13]

In contrast to extraordinary items described earlier in the chapter, *prior period adjustments* are excluded from the determination of net income for the current accounting period and are applied retroactively to the income of the related prior periods.[14] The financial statements affected by such an adjustment, when presented for comparative purposes, are to be *restated,* together with any related income tax effect. Also, the beginning balance of retained earnings for the periods subsequent to the period to which the adjustment relates should be *restated.* In the period where a prior period adjustment occurs, the following disclosures are required:

1 a description of the adjustment
2 its effects on the financial statements of the current and prior periods
3 the fact regarding the restatement of the financial statements of prior periods that are presented.[15]

Statement of retained earnings

6   Prepare a statement of retained earnings.

In addition to the balance sheet and the income statement, most corporations include a statement of retained earnings and a statement of changes in financial position in their annual reports to shareholders. (The latter statement will be illustrated in Chapter 19.) If a company is audited by a public accounting firm, all four of these basic financial statements are covered by the audit report. A simple example of a statement of retained earnings follows:

[12] CICA, *CICA Handbook,* paragraph 3600.03.
[13] Ibid., paragraph 3600.02.
[14] Ibid., paragraph 3600.06.
[15] Ibid., paragraph 3600.08.

SHORE LINE CORPORATION
Statement of Retained Earnings
For the Year Ended December 31, 1989

Retained earnings at beginning of year	$620,000
Net income for the year	280,000
Subtotal	$900,000
Less: Dividends	100,000
Retained earnings at end of year	$800,000

In the published annual reports of publicly owned corporations, the statement of retained earnings is usually presented in *comparative* form covering two years. This format and the treatment of a prior period adjustment are shown in the following illustration for Vista Corporation.

VISTA CORPORATION
Statement of Retained Earnings
For Years Ended December 31

	1989	1988
Retained earnings at beginning of year:		
As originally reported	$820,000	$780,000
Prior period adjustment — additional income taxes for 1985	(60,000)	(60,000)
As restated	$760,000	$720,000
Net income	160,000	110,000
Subtotal	$920,000	$830,000
Less: Cash dividends on common stock:		
$0.80 per share in 1989	80,000	
$0.70 per share in 1988		70,000
Retained earnings at end of year	$840,000	$760,000

The additional income taxes for 1985 were assessed by the tax authority and settled in 1989 and are shown as an adjustment to the beginning balance in retained earnings for both 1989 and 1988, since both beginning amounts were overstated. The statement of retained earnings thus provides a useful vehicle for the disclosure of prior period adjustments and for the explanation of all changes in retained earnings during the accounting period.

The statement of retained earnings may be combined with the income statement. This alternative form of presentation is used by some companies. Such a *combined statement of income and retained earnings* for Lacey Corporation is illustrated at the top of page 628.

The statement for Lacey Corporation emphasizes the close relationship of operating results and retained earnings. Some readers of financial statements, however, object to the fact that net income (or loss) is "buried" in the body of a combined statement of income and retained earnings rather than being prominently displayed as the final figure before reporting earnings per share.

LACEY CORPORATION
Combined Statement of Income and Retained Earnings
For Years Ended December 31

	1989	1988
Net sales	$2,900,000	$2,700,000
Cost of goods sold	1,730,000	1,650,000
Gross profit on sales	$1,170,000	$1,050,000
Operating expenses	620,000	590,000
Income before income taxes	$ 550,000	$ 460,000
Income taxes	260,000	214,000
Net income	$ 290,000	$ 246,000
Retained earnings at beginning of year	730,000	664,000
Subtotal	$1,020,000	$ 910,000
Dividends: $1 per share in 1989 and $0.90 per share in 1988	210,000	180,000
Retained earnings at end of year	$ 810,000	$ 730,000
Earnings per share of common stock	$1.38	$1.23

Appropriations and restrictions of retained earnings

A few corporations transfer a portion of their retained earnings into separate accounts called *appropriations* or *reserves*. The purpose of such appropriations or reserves is to indicate to users of financial statements that a portion of retained earnings is not available for the declaration of cash dividends. The limitation on cash dividends may be established voluntarily by the board of directors or it may be required by law or contract. An appropriation of retained earnings is recorded by a debit to Retained Earnings and a credit to the appropriation account such as Retained Earnings Appropriated for Contingencies. Appropriation accounts are still a part of total retained earnings.

When the restriction on retained earnings is no longer needed, the appropriation account is eliminated by transferring its balance back to the Retained Earnings account.

Instead of establishing appropriations of retained earnings, most corporations disclose restrictions on the declaration of cash dividends in notes accompanying the financial statements. For example, a company with total retained earnings of $10,000,000 might include the following note in its financial statements:

FOOTNOTE DISCLOSURE
OF RESTRICTIONS
PLACED ON RETAINED
EARNINGS

Note 7: Restriction of retained earnings

As of December 31, 1989, certain long-term debt agreements prohibited the declaration of cash dividends that would reduce the amount of retained earnings below $5,200,000. Retained earnings not so restricted amounted to $4,800,000.

Since the only purpose of appropriating retained earnings is to inform readers of the financial statements that a portion of the retained earnings is "reserved" for a specific purpose and is not available for declaration of cash dividends, this information can be conveyed more directly, with less danger of misunderstanding, by a note accompanying the financial statements.

Treasury stock

Corporations sometimes acquire shares of their own capital stock by purchase in the open market. Paying out cash to acquire shares will reduce the assets of the corporation and reduce the shareholders' equity by the same amount. One reason for such purchases is to have stock available to reissue to officers and employees under bonus plans. Other reasons may include a desire to increase the reported earnings per share or to support the current market price of the stock.

Treasury stock may be defined as shares of a corporation's own capital stock that have been issued and later *acquired by the issuing company,* but that have not been cancelled or permanently retired. Treasury shares may be issued again at any time. Shares of capital stock held in the treasury are not entitled to receive dividends, to vote, or to share in assets upon dissolution of the company. In the computation of earnings per share, shares held in the treasury are not regarded as outstanding shares.

A corporation may, under certain provincial legislation, acquire its own capital stock for the purpose of reissuing or cancelling it in the future. However, other legislation such as the Canada Business Corporations Act and the Ontario Business Corporations Act require that such acquired capital stock be cancelled or restored to the authorized but unissued status. Thus, corporations under such legislation are prohibited to have treasury stock. Also, corporation legislation does not permit a corporation to acquire its own capital stock when it is insolvent or if such an acquisition would render it insolvent.

7 Account for treasury stock transactions.

Recording purchases of treasury stock

Purchases of treasury stock should be recorded by debiting the Treasury Stock account with the cost of the stock. For example, if Torrey Corporation acquires 150 shares of its own no-par stock at a price of $100 per share, the entry is as follows:

TREASURY STOCK
RECORDED AT COST

Treasury Stock	15,000	
Cash		15,000
Purchased 150 shares of no-par treasury stock at $100 per share.		

Treasury stock not an asset   When treasury stock is purchased, the corporation is eliminating part of its shareholder's equity by paying off one or more shareholders. The purchase of treasury stock should be regarded as a *reduction of shareholders' equity,* not as the acquisition of an asset. For this reason, the Treasury Stock account should appear in the balance sheet *as a deduction in the shareholders' equity section.* The presentation of treasury stock in a corporate balance sheet is illustrated on page 631.

Reissuance of treasury stock

When treasury shares are reissued, the Treasury Stock account is credited for the cost of the shares reissued and Contributed Capital from Treasury Stock Transactions is debited or credited for any difference between *cost* and the reissue price. To illustrate, assume that 100 of the treasury shares acquired by Torrey Corporation at a cost of $100 per share are now reissued at a price of $115 per share. The entry to record the reissuance of these shares at a price above cost would be:

Cash	11,500	
Treasury Stock		10,000
Contributed Capital from Treasury Stock Transactions		1,500
Sold 100 shares of treasury stock, which cost $10,000, at a price of $115 per share.		

If treasury stock is reissued at a price below cost, contributed capital from previous treasury stock transactions of the same class is reduced (debited) by the excess of cost over the reissue price.[16] To illustrate, assume that Torrey Corporation reissues its remaining 50 shares of treasury stock (cost $100 per share) at a price of $90 per share. The entry would be:

Cash	4,500	
Contributed Capital from Treasury Stock Transactions	500	
Treasury Stock		5,000
Sold 50 shares of treasury stock, which cost $5,000, at a price of $90 each.		

If there is insufficient or no contributed capital from previous treasury stock transactions to cover the excess, the balance or the entire excess of the cost of the treasury shares over the reissue price may be recorded as a debit in the Retained Earnings account.[17]

No gain or loss on treasury stock transactions   Note that *no gain or loss is recognized on treasury stock transactions*, even when the shares are reissued at a price above or below cost. A corporation earns income by selling goods and services to outsiders, not by issuing or reissuing shares of its own capital stock. When treasury shares are reissued at a price above cost, the corporation receives from the new shareholder a larger amount of capital than that paid by the corporation for the treasury shares. Conversely, if treasury shares are reissued at a price below cost, the corporation ends up with less capital as a result of the purchase and reissuance of the shares. Thus, any changes in shareholders' equity resulting from treasury stock transactions are regarded as changes in *contributed capital* and are *not* included in the measurement of net income.

Restriction of retained earnings when treasury stock is acquired

If a corporation is to maintain its contributed capital intact, it must not pay out to its shareholders any more than it earns. As previously stated in the section dealing with

---

[16] CICA, *CICA Handbook* (Toronto), paragraph 3240.20.
[17] Ibid.

dividends, the amount of dividends to be paid must not exceed the corporation's accumulated earnings, or the corporation will be returning a portion of the shareholders' original investment to them.

The payment of cash dividends and the acquisition of treasury stock have a good deal in common. In both transactions, the corporation is disbursing cash to its shareholders. Of course, the dividend payment is spread out among all the shareholders, whereas the payment to purchase treasury stock may go to only a few shareholders, but this does not alter the fact that the corporation is turning over some of its assets to its owners. The total amount that a corporation may pay to its shareholders without reducing contributed capital is shown by the balance in the Retained Earnings account. Consequently, it is important that a corporation keep track of the total amount disbursed in payment for treasury stock and make sure that this amount plus any dividends paid does not exceed the company's accumulated earnings. This objective is conveniently accomplished by *restricting* the availability of retained earnings for dividends to the extent of the cost of treasury stock held at the balance sheet date. The restriction should be disclosed in a note accompanying the financial statements.

Illustration of shareholders' equity section

The following illustration of a shareholders' equity section of a balance sheet shows a fairly detailed classification, by source, of the various elements of corporate capital:

COMPARE WITH
PUBLISHED FINANCIAL
STATEMENTS

SHAREHOLDERS' EQUITY

Capital stock:
$9 preferred stock, no-par value, unlimited authorized shares, 1,000 shares issued and outstanding	$200,000	
Common stock, no-par value, unlimited authorized shares, issued 60,000 shares, of which 1,000 are held in treasury	540,000	
Common stock subscribed, 6,000 shares	30,000	$770,000
Contributed capital from treasury stock transactions		5,000
Total contributed capital		$775,000
Retained earnings (of which $12,000, an amount equal to the cost of treasury stock purchased, is unavailable for dividends)		162,000
		$937,000
Less: Treasury stock, common, 1,000 shares at cost		12,000
Total shareholders' equity		$925,000

The published financial statements of leading corporations indicate that there is no one standard arrangement for the various items making up the shareholders' equity section. Variations occur in the selection of titles, in the sequence of items, and in the extent of detailed classification. Many companies, in an effort to avoid excessive detail in the balance sheet, will combine several related ledger accounts into a single balance sheet item.

END-OF-CHAPTER REVIEW

SUMMARY OF CHAPTER LEARNING OBJECTIVES

1 Explain how predictive information and its relationship to the presentation of extraordinary items and accounting changes are presented in the income and other financial statements

The effects of any extraordinary items are shown in separate sections of the income statement after determination of the income (or loss) from ordinary activities, to enhance the predictive nature of the information in the income statement. Similarly, the proper presentation of accounting changes achieves the same objective.

2 Compute earnings per share.

Net earnings per share is computed by dividing the income applicable to the common stock by the weighted average number of common shares outstanding. If the income statement includes income before extraordinary items, per-share figures are shown for this amount as well as for net income.

3 Distinguish between basic and fully diluted earnings per share.

Fully diluted earnings per share must be computed only for companies that have outstanding securities convertible into shares of common stock. In such situations, the computation of basic earnings per share is based upon the number of common shares actually outstanding during the year. The computation of fully diluted earnings, however, is based upon the potential number of common shares outstanding if the various securities were converted into common shares. The purpose of showing fully diluted earnings is to warn investors of the extent to which conversions of securities could dilute basic earnings per share.

4 Account for stock dividends and stock splits, and explain the probable effect of these transactions upon market price.

Small stock dividends are recorded by transferring the market value of the additional shares to be issued from retained earnings to the appropriate capital accounts. A stock split, on the other hand, is recorded only by a memorandum entry indicating that the number of outstanding shares has been increased (and that the par value per share, if any, has been reduced proportionately). Both stock dividends and stock splits increase the number of shares outstanding but neither transaction changes total shareholders' equity. Therefore, both stock dividends and stock splits should reduce the market price per share in proportion to the number of additional shares issued.

5 Define prior period adjustments and explain how they are presented in financial statements.

A prior period adjustment is a rare event such as settlement of income taxes or lawsuits which causes an adjustment to the amount of net income reported in a prior year. As the income of the prior year has already been closed into retained earnings, the adjustment is accomplished by debiting or crediting the Retained Earnings account. Prior period adjustments appear in the statement of retained earnings, not in the income statement for the current period.

6 Prepare a statement of retained earnings.

A statement of retained earnings shows the changes in the balance of the Retained Earnings account during the period. In its simplest form, this financial statement shows the beginning balance of retained earnings, adds the net income for the period, subtracts any dividends declared, and thus computes the ending balance of retained earnings. Any prior period adjustments also are shown in this financial statement.

7 Account for treasury stock transactions.

Purchases of treasury stock are recorded by debiting a contra-equity account, entitled Treasury Stock. No gain or loss is recorded when the treasury shares are reissued at a price above or below cost. Rather, any difference between the reissuance price and the cost of the shares is debited or credited to a special contributed capital account, or in certain cases, debiting the retained earnings account.

KEY TERMS INTRODUCED OR EMPHASIZED IN CHAPTER 15

Basic earnings per share Net income applicable to the common stock divided by weighted-average number of common shares outstanding.

Changes in accounting estimates Include such items as a revision of the estimate of the amount of allowance for doubtful accounts or a revision of the estimate of a nine-year economic life of a depreciable asset to a six-year life.

Changes in accounting policy Encompass changes in accounting principles as well as accounting methods used in the preparation of financial statements.

Comparative financial statements Financial statements of the current year and the preceding year that are presented together to facilitate comparison.

Corrections of errors Required when errors are discovered in prior period financial statements. Such errors may result from a mistake in computation, a misinterpretation or misrepresentation of information, an oversight of available information, and a misappropriation of assets.

Date of record The date on which a person must be listed as a shareholder in order to be eligible to receive a dividend. Follows the date of declaration of a dividend by two or four weeks.

Earnings per share (EPS) Net income applicable to the common stock divided by the weighted-average number of common shares outstanding during the year.

Ex-dividend date A date generally four days prior to the date of record specified in a dividend declaration. A person buying a stock prior to the ex-dividend date also acquires the right to receive the dividend. The four-day interval permits the compilation of a list of shareholders as of the date of record.

Extraordinary items Transactions and events that are material in dollar amount, unusual in nature, and occur infrequently; for example, a large earthquake loss. Such items are shown separately in the income statement after the determination of Income before Extraordinary Items.

Fully diluted earnings per share Earnings per share computed under the assumption that all convertible securities had been converted into additional common shares at the beginning of the current year. The purpose of this hypothetical computation is to warn common shareholders of the risk that future earnings per share might be diluted by the conversion of other securities into common stock.

Price-earnings ratio Market price of a share of common stock divided by annual earnings per share.

Prior period adjustment An adjustment to the earnings reported in the financial statements of a prior year. Prior period adjustments are recorded directly in the Retained Earnings account and are not included in the income statement of the current period; examples, settlement of income taxes and litigations.

Restrictions of retained earnings Action by the board of directors to classify a portion of retained earnings as unavailable for dividends.

Segment of a business A component of a business. The activities of the component represent a major line of business or class of customer.

Statement of retained earnings A basic financial statement showing the change in retained earnings during the year.

Stock dividend A distribution of additional shares to common shareholders in proportion to their holdings.

Stock split An increase in the number of shares outstanding. The additional shares are distributed proportionately to all common shareholders. Purpose is to reduce market price per share and encourage wider public ownership of the company's stock. A 2 for 1 stock split will give each shareholder twice as many shares as previously owned.

Treasury stock Shares of a corporation's stock that have been issued and then acquired, but not cancelled by the corporation.

DEMONSTRATION PROBLEM FOR YOUR REVIEW

The shareholders' equity of Sutton Corporation at December 31, 1988, follows:

Shareholders' equity:
Common stock, no-par, unlimited shares authorized,
  40,000 shares issued and outstanding . . . . $ 600,000
Retained earnings 1,500,000
  Total shareholders' equity $2,100,000

Transactions affecting shareholders' equity during 1989 are as follows:

Mar. 31 The stock was split 5 for 4.

Apr.   1 The company purchased 2,000 shares of its common stock on the open market at $37 per share.

July   2 The company reissued 1,000 shares of treasury stock at $45 per share.

July   2 Issued for cash 20,000 shares of previously unissued common stock at a price of $45 per share.

Dec.   1 A cash dividend of $1 per share was declared, payable on December 30, to shareholders of record at December 14.

Dec. 22 A 10% stock dividend was declared; the dividend shares to be distributed on January 24, 1990. The market price of the stock on December 22 was $48 per share.

The net income for the year ended December 31, 1989, amounted to $177,000, after an extraordinary loss of $35,400 (net of related income tax effects of $23,600).

Instructions   **a** Prepare journal entries to record the transactions relating to shareholders' equity that took place during 1989.

b Prepare the lower section of the income statement for the year ended December 31, 1989, beginning with the income before extraordinary items and showing the extraordinary loss and the net income. Also illustrate the presentation of earnings per share in the income statement, assuming that earnings per share is determined on the basis of the weighted-average number of shares outstanding during the year.

c Prepare a statement of retained earnings for the year ended December 31, 1989.

SOLUTION TO DEMONSTRATION PROBLEM

a
GENERAL JOURNAL

Mar. 31	Memorandum: The stock was split 5 for 4. This action increased the number of shares of common stock outstanding from 40,000 to 50,000.		
Apr. 1	Treasury Stock	74,000	
	Cash		74,000
	Acquired 2,000 shares of treasury stock at $37 per share.		
July 2	Cash	45,000	
	Treasury Stock		37,000
	Contributed Capital from Treasury Stock		
	Transactions		8,000
	Sold 1,000 shares of treasury stock at $45 per share.		
2	Cash	900,000	
	Common Stock		900,000
	Issued 20,000 shares of previously unissued common stock for cash.		
Dec. 1	Retained Earnings	69,000	
	Dividends Payable		69,000
	To record declaration of cash dividend of $1 per share on 69,000 shares of common stock outstanding (1,000 shares in treasury are not entitled to receive dividends).		
22	Retained Earnings	331,200	
	Stock Dividends to be Distributed		331,200
	To record declaration of 10% stock dividend consisting of 6,900 shares of common stock to be distributed on Jan. 24, 1990, based on the market price of $48 (6,900 × $48 = $331,200).		
31	Income Summary	177,000	
	Retained Earnings		177,000
	To close Income Summary account.		

Note: Entry to record the payment of the cash dividend is not shown here since the action does not affect the shareholders' equity.

b

SUTTON CORPORATION
Partial Income Statement
For Year Ended December 31, 1989

Income before extraordinary items ($177,000 + $35,400)	$212,400
Extraordinary loss, net of income tax reduction of $23,600	(35,400)
Net income	$177,000

Earnings per share:*	
Income before extraordinary items	$3.60
Extraordinary loss, net of tax effects	(0.60)
Net income	$3.00

*On 59,000 weighted-average number of shares of common stock outstanding during 1989 determined as follows:

Jan. 1–Mar. 31: (40,000 + 10,000 shares issued pursuant to a 5 for 4 split) × ¼ of year	12,500
Apr. 1–June 30: (50,000 − 2,000 shares of treasury stock) × ¼ of year	12,000
July 2–Dec. 31: (50,000 + 20,000 shares of new stock − 1,000 shares of treasury stock) × ½ of year	34,500
Weighted-average number of shares outstanding	59,000

c

SUTTON CORPORATION
Statement of Retained Earnings
For the Year Ended December 31, 1989

Retained earnings, Jan. 1, 1989		$1,500,000
Net income		177,000
Subtotal		$1,677,000
Dividends:		
Cash, $1 per share	$ 69,000	
Stock, 10% (to be distributed Jan. 24, 1990)	331,200	400,200
Retained earnings, Dec. 31, 1989		$1,276,800

ASSIGNMENT MATERIAL

REVIEW QUESTIONS

1 What is the purpose of arranging an income statement to show a subtotal for Income before Extraordinary Items?

2 Define *extraordinary items*. Give three examples of losses that qualify as extraordinary items and three examples of losses that would not be classified as extraordinary, even though they are unusual and are disclosed separately.

3 Briefly describe how each of the following should be reported in the income statement for the current year:

a Write-off of a very large account receivable from a bankrupt customer

b Large loss from sale of a major segment of a business

c Large gain from sale of one of many investments in common stock held for resale

d Large write-off of obsolete inventory

e Large uninsured loss from earthquake

f Settlement of income taxes related to the reported net income of an earlier year

4 Briefly describe the nature and accounting treatment of each of the following:

a A change in an accounting policy

b A change in an accounting estimate

c A correction of an error in prior period financial statements

5 Explain how each of the following is computed:

a Price-earnings ratio

b Basic earnings per share

c Fully diluted earnings per share

6 Throughout the year, Gold Seal Co. had 4 million shares of common stock and 120,000 shares of convertible preferred stock outstanding. Each share of preferred is convertible into four shares of common. What number of shares should be used in the computation of (a) basic earnings per share, and (b) fully diluted earnings per share?

7 A financial analyst notes that Baxter Corporation's earnings per share have been rising steadily for the last five years. The analyst expects the company's net income to continue to increase at the same rate as in the past. In forecasting future basic earnings per share, what special risk should the analyst consider if Baxter's basic earnings are significantly larger than its fully diluted earnings?

8 Explain the significance of the following dates relating to dividends: date of declaration, date of record, date of payment, ex-dividend date.

9 Distinguish between a *stock split* and a *stock dividend.* Is there any reason for the difference in accounting treatment of these two events?

10 What are *prior period adjustments?* How are they presented in financial statements?

11 What is the purpose of an appropriation of retained earnings? What are the arguments for and against the use of such appropriations?

12 If a statement of retained earnings consisted of only four items, what would these four items most probably be?

13 What is the most effective method of disclosing in financial statements the fact that a portion of the retained earnings is restricted by the terms of a long-term debt agreement and therefore not available for payment of dividends or acquisition of treasury stock?

14 "In a long-established, successful corporation the Cash account would normally have a dollar balance equal to or larger than the Retained Earnings account." Do you agree with this quotation? Explain.

15 What is *treasury stock?* Why do corporations purchase their own shares? Is treasury stock an asset? How should it be reported in the balance sheet?

16 What is the purpose for the requirement that retained earnings be restricted for dividend purposes to the extent of the cost of treasury shares?

EXERCISES

Exercise 15-1
Accounting
terminology

Listed below are nine technical accounting terms introduced in this chapter:

Prior period adjustment	Fully diluted earnings	Basic earnings per share
Date of record	per share	P/e ratio
Stock split	Date of declaration	Stock dividend
	Extraordinary items	

Each of the following statements may (or may not) describe one of these technical terms. For each statement, indicate the accounting term described, or answer "None" if the statement does not correctly describe any of the terms.

a A gain or loss that is unusual in nature, not expected to recur in the foreseeable future, and not a recurring factor in evaluating ordinary operations.

b A hypothetical figure, showing the result that would have occurred if all of the securities convertible into common stock had been converted at the beginning of the current year.

c The dividend rate associated with a company's highest-grade preferred stock.

d The date upon which the declaration of a cash dividend is recorded in the accounting records.

e An adjustment to the beginning balance of retained earnings to settle a lawsuit related to an accident that occurred five years ago.

f A distribution of additional shares to shareholders that does not change total shareholders' equity.

g A statistic expressing a relationship between the current market value of a share of common stock and the underlying earnings per share.

Exercise 15-2
Reporting an
extraordinary item

For the year ended December 31, Union Chemical Corporation had net sales of $4,500,000, costs and other expenses (including income taxes) of $4,030,000, and an extraordinary loss (net of income taxes of $198,000) of $200,000. Prepare a condensed income statement (including earnings per share), assuming that 200,000 shares of common stock were outstanding throughout the year.

Exercise 15-3
Extraordinary items,
accounting changes,
and prior period
adjustments

Select the **best** answer for each of the following multiple-choice questions:

1 Accounting changes include

   a A change in accounting policy and in accounting estimate

   b A correction of error in a prior period

   c A prior period adjustment

   d a and b

   e a, b, and c

2 An extraordinary item reflects an event that is

   a Unusual, material, and beyond management's control

   b Not reasonably estimated, not related to economic events, but within management's control

   c Not typical, not regular, and not a recurring consideration in ordinary operation evaluation

   d Not typical, irregular, but a recurring factor for ordinary operation evaluation

   e An element of an accounting change

3 Changes in accounting policy encompass

   a Changes in the statement of changes in financial position

   b Changes in accounting principles and methods

   c Changes in accounting estimates

   d Corrections of errors in prior period financial statements

   e Extraordinary items and prior period adjustments

4 Changes in accounting estimates include

   a Revision of the amount of allowance for doubtful accounts

   b Revision of the useful life of a depreciable asset

   c Revision of the residual value of a depreciable asset

   d A change of depreciation method

   e **a**, **b**, and **c**

5 Retroactive application and restatement are required by

   a A change in accounting policy

   b A changing in accounting estimate

   c A correction of an error in a prior period

   d **a** and **c**

   e **a** and **c** and a prior period adjustment.

6 An accounting change requiring a current or current and prospective application is

   a A change in accounting estimate

   b A change in accounting policy and accounting estimate

   c A change in accounting policy and accounting estimate as well as a correction of a prior period error

   d An extraordinary item

   e A prior period adjustment

Exercise 15-4
Computing earnings per share: changes in number of shares outstanding

In the year just ended, Sunshine Citrus earned net income of $9,020,000. The company has issued only one class of capital stock, of which 1 million shares were outstanding at January 1. Compute the company's earnings per share under each of the following *independent* assumptions:

   a No change occurred during the year in the number of shares outstanding.

   b On October 1, the company issued an additional 100,000 shares of capital stock in exchange for cash.

   c On July 2, the company distributed an additional 100,000 shares of capital stock as a 10% stock dividend. (No additional shares are issued on October 1.)

Exercise 15-5
Computing earnings per share: effect of preferred stock

The net income of Carriage Trade Clothiers amounted to $3,750,000 for the current year. Compute the amount of earnings per share assuming that the shares of capital stock outstanding throughout the year consisted of:

a 300,000 shares of no-par value common stock and no preferred stock.

b 200,000 shares of $9, no-par value preferred stock and 300,000 shares of no-par value common stock.

Exercise 15-6
Format of income statement and statement of retained earnings

From the following list of financial statement captions and items, prepare for Ocean Transport Corp. (a) a condensed income statement, and (b) a statement of retained earnings for the year ended December 31, 19___.

Costs and expenses ...	$8,200,000	Retained earnings,	
Dividends	250,000	Jan. 1, 19___ (as	
Net sales	9,000,000	originally reported) ...	$2,600,000
A gain from an		Loss from sale of a	
expropriation of land		major segment of	
by government, net		operations, net of	
of income taxes of		income taxes of	
$180,000	240,000	$250,000	350,000
		Prior period adjustment	
		(debit)	(40,000)

In addition to the preceding captions, include any subtotals in your financial statements that you consider appropriate. Also include a proper heading for each statement. (Omit earnings-per-share statistics.)

Exercise 15-7
Recording cash dividends and stock dividends

Glass Corporation has 1 million shares of no-par value capital stock outstanding. You are to prepare the journal entries to record the following transactions:

June   1 Declared a cash dividend of 60 cents per share.

July   2 Paid the 60-cent cash dividend to shareholders.

Aug.   1 Declared a 5% stock dividend. Market price of stock was $19 per share.

Sept. 10 Issued 50,000 shares pursuant to the 5% stock dividend.

Exercise 15-8
Effect of stock dividends on stock price

Jiffy Tool Co. Ltd. has a total of 40,000 shares of common stock outstanding and no preferred stock. Total shareholders' equity at the end of the current year amounts to $3 million and the market value of the stock is $84 per share. At year-end, the company declares a stock dividend of one share for each five shares held. If all parties concerned clearly recognize the nature of the stock dividend, what should you expect the market price per share of the common stock to be on the ex-dividend date?

Exercise 15-9
Recording treasury stock transactions

Cable Transmissions engaged in the following transactions involving treasury stock:

Nov. 10 Purchased for cash 12,500 shares of treasury stock at a price of $30 per share.

Dec.   4 Reissued 5,000 shares of treasury stock at a price of $33 per share.

Dec. 22 Reissued 4,000 shares of treasury stock at a price of $29 per share.

Instructions   **a** Prepare general journal entries to record these transactions.

b Compute the amount of retained earnings that should be restricted because of the treasury stock still owned at December 31.

PROBLEMS

Group A

Problem 15A-1
Income statement
and earnings per
share

Summarized below are the operations of Multi-Media, Inc., for last year:

Net sales	$9,640,000
Cost and expenses (including applicable income tax effects)	8,650,000
Loss on disposal of a plant, net of income taxes of $200,000	300,000
Bad debts written off due to unusual factors	400,000

Instructions   Assuming that the company had an average of 200,000 shares of a single class of capital stock outstanding during the year, prepare a condensed income statement (including earnings per share).

Problem 15A-2
Income statement and
earnings per share: an
alternative problem

Coastal Airlines, Inc., had 300,000 shares of common stock and 80,000 shares of $10, no-par value, preferred stock outstanding throughout the year. Dividends were paid on the preferred stock only.

Net sales	$38,000,000
Costs and expenses (including applicable income taxes)	34,800,000
Gain on sale of motel operations, net of income taxes of $360,000 . . .	530,000
Expropriation loss, net of income taxes of $480,000	900,000

The extraordinary loss resulted from the expropriation of an airliner by a foreign government.

Instructions   Prepare a condensed income statement for the year. Include all appropriate earnings-per-share figures.

Problem 15A-3
Format of an income
statement and a
statement of retained
earnings

Katherine McCall, accountant for Ranger Corporation, was injured in a skiing accident at year-end, and a temporary employee was assigned responsibility for preparing the financial statements. The temporary employee had a limited knowledge of accounting and improperly prepared the income statement which appears at the top of page 642.

The lawsuit was initiated by a customer for defective products sold in 1988. At the beginning of 1989, the company's financial statements showed retained earnings of $2,920,000. The total income taxes and the tax effects relating to the tornado loss have been correctly estimated by an income tax advisor.

Instructions   **a** Prepare a corrected income statement using the single-step format. Show appropriate earnings-per-share figures in the income statement. Assume that the company had a weighted average of 200,000 shares of a single class of capital stock outstanding during the year.

b Prepare a statement of retained earnings. The starting point for your statement should be retained earnings at the beginning of 1989 as originally reported ($2,920,000).

RANGER CORPORATION
Income Statement
For the Year Ended December 31, 1989

Net sales		$ 9,000,00
Sale of treasury stock (cost, $110,000; proceeds $150,000)		40,00
Excess of proceeds over par value of common stock issued in 1989 . .		1,300,00
Total revenue		$10,340,00
Less:		
Settlement of a law suit, net of income taxes		
of $160,000	$ 200,000	
Cost of goods sold	5,000,000	
Selling expenses	800,000	
General and administrative expenses	1,400,000	
Loss from tornado (net of income taxes of $200,000) .	260,000	
Dividends declared on common stock	300,000	
Income taxes (excluding effects of extraordinary		
loss)	840,000	8,800,00
Net income		$1,540,00

Problem 15A-4
Accounting changes

The following comparative statement of retained earnings relates to Omega Corporation which began operations in 1987:

	DECEMBER 31	
	1989	**1988**
Retained earnings at beginning of year	$500,000	$380,00
Net income	160,000	120,00
Retained earnings at end of year	$660,000	$500,00

Omega decided on January 1, 1990, to change its depreciation method from declining-balance to straight-line. The information for the depreciation expense is as follows:

YEAR	DECLINING-BALANCE	STRAIGHT-LINE
1987	$50,000	$21,000
1988	37,500	21,000
1989	28,125	21,000

Instructions

a Compute the amount of cumulative effect on the beginning balance of retained earnings fo 1989, as a result of the change in depreciation method and indicate whether the effect is a increase or a decrease. (Disregard income tax considerations.)

b How would the income statements for 1988 and 1989 be affected by the change in depreciatic method? (Disregard income tax considerations.)

c Assuming that after the 1990 net income of $188,000 was recorded, the company discovere that it should have changed the useful life of the assets in 1990. This change would hav increased the depreciation expense by $6,000 for each of 1989, 1990, and 1991. Explai how this change would affect the net income and retained earnings for these three years (Disregard income tax considerations.)

Problem 15A-5
Effects of stock
dividends, stock
splits, and treasury
stock transactions

At the beginning of the year, Hydro-Spa Co. Ltd. has total shareholders' equity of $660,000 and 20,000 outstanding shares of a single class of capital stock. During the year, the corporation completes the following transactions affecting its shareholders' equity accounts:

Jan. 10 A 10% stock dividend is declared and distributed. (Market price, $40 per share.)

Mar. 15 The corporation acquires 1,000 shares of its own capital stock at a cost of $40.50 per share.

May 30 All 1,000 shares of the treasury stock are reissued at a price of $44.90 per share.

July 31 The capital stock is split, two shares for one.

Dec. 15 The board of directors declares a cash dividend of $1.10 per share, payable on January 15.

Dec. 31 Net income of $127,600 (equal to $2.90 per share) is reported for the year ended December 31.

Instructions

Compute the amount of total shareholders' equity, the number of shares of capital stock outstanding, and the book value per share following each successive transaction. Organize your solution as a three-column schedule with separate column headings for (1) Total Shareholders' Equity, (2) Number of Shares Outstanding, and (3) Book Value per Share.

Problem 15A-6
Recording stock
dividends and
treasury stock
transactions

At the beginning of the year, Marco Construction Limited showed the following amounts in the shareholders' equity section of its balance sheet:

Shareholders' equity:
Common stock, no-par value, unlimited shares authorized,
191,000 issued and outstanding $3,450,000
Retained earnings   986,000
Total shareholders' equity $4,436,000

The transactions relating to shareholders' equity accounts during the year are as follows:

Jan. 3 Declared a dividend of $1 per share to shareholders of record on January 31, payable on February 15.

Feb. 15 Paid the cash dividend declared on January 3.

Apr. 12 The corporation purchased 3,000 shares of its own common stock at a price of $32 per share.

May 9 Reissued 2,000 shares of the treasury stock at a price of $36 per share.

June 1 Declared a 5% stock dividend to shareholders of record at June 15, to be distributed on June 30. The market price of the stock at June 1 was $35 per share.

June 30 Distributed the stock dividend declared on June 1.

Aug. 4 Reissued 500 of the 1,000 remaining shares of treasury stock at a price of $30 per share.

Dec. 31 The Income Summary account, showing net income for the year of $613,500, was closed into the Retained Earnings account.

Instructions

a Prepare in general journal form the entries to record the preceding transactions.

b Prepare the shareholders' equity section of the balance sheet at December 31. Include a supporting schedule showing your computation of retained earnings at that date.

c Compute the maximum cash dividend per share which legally could be declared at December 31, without impairing the contributed capital of Marco Construction.

Problem 15A-7
Stock dividends, stock splits, and treasury stock transactions

The Mandella family decided early in 1988 to incorporate their family-owned vineyards under the name Mandella Corporation. The corporation was authorized to issue unlimited shares of a single class of no-par value capital stock. Presented below is the information necessary to prepare the shareholders' equity section of the company's balance sheet at the end of 1988 and at the end of 1989.

1988. In January the corporation issued to members of the Mandella family 85,000 shares of capital stock in exchange for cash and other assets used in the operation of the vineyards. The fair market value of these assets indicated an issue price of $30 per share. In December, Joe Mandella died, and the corporation purchased 5,000 shares of its own capital stock from his estate at $35 per share. Because of the large cash outlay to acquire this treasury stock, the directors decided not to declare cash dividends in 1988 and instead declared a 10% stock dividend to be distributed in January of 1989. The stock price at the declaration date was $35 per share. Net income for 1988 was $470,000.

1989. In January the corporation distributed the stock dividend declared in 1988, and in February, the 5,000 treasury shares were sold to Maria Mandella at $39 per share. In June, the capital stock was split, two shares for one. On December 15, the directors declared a cash dividend of $2 per share, payable in January of 1990. Net income for 1989 was $540,000.

Instructions

Prepare the shareholders' equity section of the balance sheet at

a December 31, 1988

b December 31, 1989

Show any necessary computations.

Group B

Problem 15B-1
Income statement and earnings per share

Last year's operations for Replacement Parts, Inc., are summarized as follows:

Net sales	$14,000,000
Costs and expenses (including applicable income taxes)	12,200,000
Loss on disposal of a long-term investment, net of income taxes of $380,000	460,000
Write-off of obsolete inventory	600,000

Instructions

Assuming that the company had an average of 400,000 shares of a single class of capital stock outstanding, prepare a condensed income statement (including earnings per share) for the December 31 year end.

Problem 15B-2
Income statement and earnings per share: an alternative problem

Sea Quest Corporation operated both a fleet of commercial vessels and a chain of six seafood restaurants. The restaurants continuously lost money and were sold during the year just ended. The company's operating results for the year ended December 31, 19___ were as follows:

Net sales	$23,000,000
Costs and expenses (including applicable income taxes)	20,100,000
Gain on sale of restaurants, net of income taxes of $320,000	460,000
Expropriation loss, net of income taxes of $500,000	720,000

The extraordinary loss resulted from the expropriation of a fishing vessel by a foreign government.

Sea Quest Corporation had 500,000 shares of common stock and 30,000 shares of $10, no-par value, preferred stock outstanding throughout the year.

Instructions   Prepare a condensed income statement including all appropriate earnings-per-share figures.

Problem 15B-3
Format of an income statement and a statement of retained earnings

A new employee of La Roche Electronics improperly prepared the following income statement for the current year:

LA ROCHE ELECTRONICS LIMITED
Income Statement
For the Year Ended December 31, 1989

Net sales		$5,400,000
Sales of treasury stock in 1989 (cost $650,000; proceeds, $800,000)		150,000
Excess of proceeds over par value of capital stock issued in 1989		960,000
Total revenue		$6,510,000
Less:		
Settlement of income taxes	$ 250,000	
Cost of goods sold	2,480,000	
Selling expenses	1,160,000	
General and administrative expenses	840,000	
Loss from earthquake (net of income taxes of $160,000)	230,000	
Dividends declared on capital stock	150,000	
Income taxes (excluding tax effects of extraordinary loss)	390,000	5,500,000
Net income		$1,010,000

The settlement of income taxes is related to a dispute for 1988 that was settled with Revenue Canada in 1989. At the beginning of the current year, the financial statements of La Roche Electronics showed retained earnings of $2,300,000. Income taxes and the tax savings resulting from the earthquake loss have been correctly estimated by an income tax advisor.

Instructions   **a** Prepare a corrected income statement using the single-step format. Include at the bottom of your income statement all appropriate earnings in per-share figures. La Roche Electronics had a weighted average of 50,000 shares of a single class of capital stock outstanding during the year.

b Prepare a statement of retained earnings. The starting point of this statement should be retained earnings at the beginning of the year as originally reported ($2,300,000).

Problem 15B-4
Accounting changes

The following is a comparative statement of retained earnings for Sunset Limited for the last two years.

	DECEMBER 31 1989	DECEMBER 31 1988
Retained earnings at beginning of year	$460,000	$280,000
Net income	220,000	180,000
Retained earnings at end of year	$680,000	$460,000

Sunset Limited was incorporated on January 2, 1987, and used a straight-line method of depreciation for its depreciable assets until January 1, 1990. At that time, Sunset changed its depreciation method from straight-line to double-declining. The net income for 1990, based on the new depreciation method, is $268,000. The information for depreciation expense is as follows:

YEAR	STRAIGHT-LINE	DOUBLE-DECLINING
1987	$54,000	$120,000
1988	54,000	72,000
1989	54,000	43,200

Instructions

a Prepare a comparative statement of retained earnings for 1989 and 1990. (Disregard income tax considerations.)

b How would the income statement for 1988 be affected by the change in depreciation method? Explain. (Disregard income tax considerations.)

c Assuming that after the net income of $268,000 for 1990 was recorded, an engineering report showed that Sunset should have changed the useful life of its depreciable assets in 1990. Such a change would have decreased the depreciation expense by $9,600 for 1989 and by $5,760 for 1990. Explain how this change would affect the net income and retained earnings for 1989, 1990, and 1991. (Disregard income tax considerations.)

Problem 15B-5
Effects of stock dividends, stock splits, and treasury stock transactions

On January 1, Electric Pump Limited has total shareholders' equity of $4,400,000 and 50,000 outstanding shares of a single class of capital stock. During the year, the corporation completes the following transactions affecting its shareholders' equity accounts:

Jan. 10 The board of directors declares a cash dividend of $4.20 per share, payable on February 15.

Apr. 30 The capital stock is split, two shares for one.

June 11 The corporation acquires 2,000 shares of its own capital stock at a cost of $56.60 per share.

July 21 All 2,000 shares of the treasury stock are reissued at a price of $61.60 per share.

Nov. 10 A 5% stock dividend is declared and distributed (market value $60 per share).

Dec. 31 Net income of $378,000 (equal to $3.60 per share) is reported for year.

Instructions

Compute the amount of total shareholders' equity, the number of shares of capital stock outstanding, and the book value per share following each successive transaction. Organize your solution as a three-column schedule with separate column headings for (1) Total Shareholders' Equity, (2) Number of Shares Outstanding, and (3) Book Value per Share.

Problem 15B-6
Recording stock dividends and treasury stock transactions

The shareholders' equity of Precious Metals Incorporated at January 1, 19___ is as follows:

Shareholders' equity:
Common stock, no-par value, unlimited shares authorized,
240,000 issued and outstanding $5,265,000
Retained earnings 1,610,000
Total shareholders' equity $6,875,000

During the year the following transactions relating to shareholders' equity occurred:

Jan. 15 Paid a $1 per share cash dividend declared in December of the preceding year. This dividend was properly recorded at the declaration date and was the only dividend declared during the preceding year.

June 10 Declared a 5% stock dividend to shareholders of record on June 30, to be distributed on July 15. At June 10, the market price of the stock was $35 per share.

July 15 Distributed the stock dividend declared on June 10.

Aug. 4 Purchased 4,200 shares of treasury stock at a price of $30 per share.

Oct. 15 Reissued 2,200 shares of treasury stock at a price of $32 per share.

Dec. 10 Reissued 1,000 shares of treasury stock at a price of $28.50 per share.

Dec. 15 Declared a cash dividend of $1 per share to be paid on January 15 to shareholders of record on December 31.

Dec. 31 The Income Summary account, showing a credit balance of $780,000, was closed into the Retained Earnings account.

Instructions

a Prepare in general journal form the entries necessary to record these transactions.

b Prepare the shareholders' equity section of the balance sheet at December 31, 19___. Include a note following your shareholders' equity section indicating any portion of retained earnings that is not available for dividends. Also include a supporting schedule showing your computation of the balance of retained earnings at year-end.

c Comment on whether Precious Metals increased or decreased the total amount of cash dividends declared during the year in comparison with dividends declared in the preceding year.

Problem 15B-7
Preparing the shareholders' equity section of a balance sheet

David Klein was a freelance engineer who developed and patented a highly efficient turbocharger for automotive engines. In 1988, Klein and Scott Harris organized Performance, Inc., to manufacture the turbocharger. The corporation was authorized to issue unlimited shares of no-par value capital stock. Following is the information necessary to prepare the shareholders' equity section of the company's balance sheet at the end of 1988 and at the end of 1989.

1988. On January 20, the corporation issued 80,000 shares of common stock to Harris and other investors for cash at $32 per share. In addition, 5,000 shares of common stock were issued on that date to Klein in exchange for his patents. In November, Klein was killed while auto racing in Europe. At the request of Klein's heirs, Performance, Inc., purchased the 5,000 shares of its stock from Klein's estate at $44 per share. Because of the unexpected cash outlay to acquire treasury stock, the directors decided against declaring any cash dividends in 1988.

Instead, they declared a 5% stock dividend that was distributed on December 31. The stock price at the declaration date was $42 per share. Net income for the year was $415,000.

1989. In March, the 5,000 treasury shares were reissued at a price of $52 per share. In August, the stock was split four shares for one. On December 20, the directors declared a cash dividend of 70 cents per share, payable in January of 1990. Net income for the year was $486,000.

Instructions   Prepare the shareholders' equity section of the balance sheet at:

a December 31, 1988

b December 31, 1989

Show any necessary supporting computations.

BUSINESS DECISION CASES

Case 15-1
Forecasting future
earnings

Midwestern Publishing, Inc., publishes two newspapers and until recently owned a professional baseball team. The baseball team had been losing money for several years and was sold at the end of 1988 to a group of investors who plan to move it to a larger city. Also in 1988, Midwestern suffered an extraordinary loss when its Raytown printing plant was damaged by a tornado. The damage has since been repaired. A condensed income statement is shown below:

MIDWESTERN PUBLISHING, INC.
Income Statement
For the Year Ended December 31, 1988

Net revenue		$42,500,000
Costs and expenses		39,300,000
Income before extraordinary items*		$3,200,000
Extraordinary items:		
Gain on sale of baseball team	$4,700,000	
Tornado damage to Raytown printing plant	600,000	4,100,000
Net income		$ 7,300,000

*Included revenue of $8,500,000, and cost and expenses of $9,800,000 from the baseball operations.

Instructions   On the basis of this information, answer the following questions. Show any necessary computations and explain your reasoning.

a What would Midwestern's net income have been for 1988 if it *had not* sold the baseball team?

b Assume that for 1989, you expect a 7% increase in the profitability of Midwestern's newspaper business, but had projected a $2,000,000 operating loss for the baseball team if Midwestern had continued to operate the team in 1989. What amount would you forecast as Midwestern's 1989 net income *if the company had continued to own and operate the baseball team?*

c Given your assumptions in part **b**, but given that Midwestern *did* sell the baseball team in 1988, what would you forecast as the company's estimated net income for 1989?

Case 15-2
Using earnings-per share-statistics

For many years Windsor Studios has produced television shows and operated several FM radio stations. Late in the current year, the radio stations were sold to Times Publishing, Inc. Also during the current year, Windsor Studios sustained an extraordinary loss when one of its camera trucks caused an accident in an international grand prix auto race. Throughout the current year, the company had 3 million shares of common stock and a large quantity of convertible preferred stock outstanding. Earnings per share reported for the current year were as follows:

	BASIC	FULLY DILUTED
Earnings before extraordinary item	$6.90	$5.50
Net earnings	$3.80	$2.40

Instructions

a Briefly explain why Windsor Studios reports fully diluted earnings-per-share amounts as well as earnings per share computed on a basic basis. What is the purpose of showing investors the fully diluted figures?

b What was the total dollar amount of the extraordinary loss sustained by Windsor Studios during the current year?

c Assume that the price-earnings ratio shown in the morning newspaper for Windsor Studios' common stock indicates that the stock is selling at a price equal to 10 times the reported earnings per share. What is the approximate market price of the stock?

d Assume that you expect both the revenue and expenses involved in producing television shows to increase by 10% during the coming year. What would you forecast as the company's net earnings per share (basic basis) for the coming year under each of the following independent assumptions? (Show your computations and explain your reasoning.)

(1) *None* of the convertible preferred stock is converted into common stock during the coming year.

(2) *All* of the convertible preferred stock is converted into common stock at the beginning of the coming year.

BONDS PAYABLE, LEASES, AND OTHER LIABILITIES

CHAPTER PREVIEW

This chapter describes various types of long-term debt. Large corporations borrow vast amounts of money; George Weston Limited, for example, has debts of about $2 billion. Emphasis is placed upon the issuance of bonds payable — a form of borrowing that enables large corporations to raise hundreds of millions of dollars from thousands of individual investors. Both the straight-line and effective interest methods of amortizing bond discount and premium are illustrated and explained. Other long-term liabilities covered in this chapter include mortgages, lease payment obligations, and pension plans. The chapter concludes with a discussion of contingent losses — footnote disclosures of events that may threaten the very survival of an apparently healthy business.

After studying this chapter you should be able to meet these Learning Objectives:

1 Describe the typical characteristics of corporate bonds.

2 Explain the advantage of raising capital by issuing bonds instead of stock.

3 Discuss the relationship between interest rates and bond prices.

4 Explain how bond discount or premium affects the cost of borrowing.

5 Amortize bond discount or premium by the straight-line and effective-interest methods.

6 Explain the accounting treatment of operating leases and of capital leases.

7 Define contingent losses and explain how they are presented in financial statements.

BONDS PAYABLE

Financially sound corporations may arrange some long-term loans by issuing a note payable to a bank or an insurance company. But to finance a large project, such as building a refinery or acquiring a fleet of jumbo jets, a corporation may need more capital than any single lender can supply. When a corporation needs to raise large amounts of long-term capital — perhaps 10, 50, or 100 million dollars or more — it generally sells additional shares of capital stock or issues **bonds payable.** [1]

What is a bond issue?

1 Describe the typical characteristics of corporate bonds.

The issuance of bonds payable is a technique of splitting a large loan into a great many units, called bonds. Each bond is a long-term interest-bearing note payable, usually in the face amount of $1,000. The bonds are sold to the investing public, thus allowing many different investors to participate in the loan. An example of a corporate bond issue is the 10.25% bond issue of Maritime Telegraph & Telephone Company, Limited, due August 1, 2006. With this bond issue, Maritime Telegraph & Telephone borrowed $50 million by issuing 50,000 bonds of $1,000 each.

Bonds payable differ from capital stock in several ways. First, bonds payable are a liability; thus, bondholders are **creditors** of the corporation, not owners. Bondholders generally do not have voting rights and do not participate in the earnings of the corporation beyond receiving contractual interest payments. Next, bond interest payments are **contractual obligations** of the corporation. Dividends, on the other hand, do not become legal obligations of the corporation until they have been formally declared by the board of directors. Finally, bonds have a specified **maturity date,** upon which the corporation must redeem the bonds at their face amount (for example, $1,000 each). Capital stock, on the other hand, does not have a maturity date and may remain outstanding indefinitely.

Authorization of a bond issue   Formal approval of the board of directors and the shareholders may be required before bonds can be issued. If the bonds are to be sold to the general public, certain requirements of the provincial securities commissions must be met, just as for an issue of capital stock offered to the public.

The issuing corporation also selects a **trustee** to represent the interests of the bondholders. This trustee generally is a large bank or trust company. A contract is drawn up indicating the terms of the bond issue and the assets (if any) that are pledged as collateral for the bonds. Sometimes this contract places limitations on the payment of dividends to shareholders during the life of the bonds. For example, dividends may be permitted only when working capital is above specified amounts. If the issuing corporation defaults on any of the terms of this contract, the trustee may foreclose upon the assets that secure the bonds or may take other legal action on behalf of the bondholders.

The role of the underwriter in marketing a bond issue   An investment dealer or underwriter is usually employed to market a bond issue, just as in the case of capital

---

[1] Bonds payable also are issued by the federal government and by many other governmental units such as provinces and municipalities. In this chapter, our discussion is limited to corporate bonds, although the concepts also apply to the bond issues of governmental agencies.

stock. The corporation turns the entire bond issue over to the underwriter at a specified price; the underwriter sells the bonds to the public at a slightly higher price. By this arrangement the corporation is assured of receiving the entire proceeds on a specified date.

Transferability of bonds   Corporate bonds, like capital stocks, are traded daily on organized securities exchanges. The holders of a 25-year bond issue need not wait 25 years to convert their investment into cash. By placing a telephone call to a broker, an investor may sell bonds within a matter of minutes at the going market price. This quality of *liquidity* is one of the most attractive features of an investment in corporate bonds.

Quoted market prices   The market price of stocks is quoted in terms of dollars per share. Bond prices, however, are quoted as a *percentage* of their face value or *maturity* value, which is usually $1,000. The maturity value is the amount the issuing company must pay to redeem the bond at the date it matures (becomes due). A bond quoted at *102* would therefore have a market price of $1,020 (102% of $1,000). Bond prices are quoted at the nearest one-eighth of a percentage point. The following line from the *Financial Post* summarizes certain information on one of Bell Canada's bonds:

WHAT IS THE MARKET VALUE OF THIS BOND?

BONDS	INTEREST RATE	MATURITY DATE	BID	YIELD
Bell Canada	12.650%	Nov. 15, 03	$111.60	11.10%

This line of condensed information indicates that Bell Canada's 12.650% bonds will be matured on November 15, 2003, the buyers were willing to pay $111.60 or $1,116 for a bond of $1,000 face value and the yield rate on the bid price is 11.1%.

The primary factors that determine the market value of a bond are (1) the relationship of the bond's interest rate to other investment opportunities, (2) the length of time until the bond matures, and (3) investors' confidence that the issuing company has the financial strength to make all future interest and principal payments promptly. Thus, a bond with a 12% interest rate will command a higher market price than a 10% bond with the same maturity date if the two companies issuing the bonds are of equal financial strength.

A bond selling at a market price greater than its maturity value is said to be selling at a *premium;* a bond selling at a price below its maturity value is selling at a *discount.* As a bond nears its maturity date, the market price of the bond moves toward the maturity value. At the maturity date the market value of the bond will be exactly equal to its maturity value, because the issuing corporation will redeem the bond for that amount.

Types of bonds   Bonds secured by the pledge of specific assets are called *mortgage bonds.* An unsecured bond is called a *debenture bond;* its value rests upon the general credit of the corporation. A debenture bond issued by a very large and strong corporation may have a higher investment rating than a secured bond issued by a corporation in less satisfactory financial condition.

Some bonds have a single fixed maturity date for the entire issue. Other bond issues, called *serial bonds,* provide for varying maturity dates to lessen the problem of accumulating cash for payment. For example, serial bonds in the amount of $20 million issued in 1980 might call for $2 million of bonds to mature in 1990, and an additional $2 million to become due in each of the succeeding nine years. Almost all bonds are *callable (redeemable)*, which means that the corporation has the right to pay off the bonds *in advance* of the scheduled maturity date. To compensate the bondholders for being forced to give up their investments, the call price is usually somewhat higher than the face value of the bonds.

Many corporation bonds issued in recent years have been *registered bonds;* that is, the name of the owner is registered with the issuing corporation. Payment of interest is generally made by semiannual cheques mailed to the registered owners. *Coupon bonds* were more popular some years ago and many are still outstanding. Coupon bonds have interest coupons attached; each six months during the life of the bond one of these coupons becomes due. The bondholder detaches the coupon and deposits it with a bank for collection. The names of the bondholders are not registered with the corporation.

As an additional attraction to investors, corporations sometimes include a conversion privilege in the bond indenture. A *convertible bond* is one which may be exchanged for common stock at the option of the bondholder. The advantages to the investor of the conversion feature in the event of increased earnings for the company were described in Chapter 14 with regard to converting preferred stock.

Tax advantage of bond financing

2 Explain the advantage of raising capital by issuing bonds instead of stock.

Interest payments on bonds payable are deductible as an expense by the issuing company in determining the income subject to corporation income tax, but dividends paid on capital stock are not. High tax rates on corporate earnings thus encourage the use of bonds rather than capital stock to obtain long-term capital.

To illustrate the advantage of tax deductible financing costs, assume that a corporation with 1 million shares of common stock outstanding needs $10 million to finance construction of a new plant. Before considering financing costs or income taxes, the new plan is expected to add $4 million to the annual earnings of the corporation. Management is considering whether to raise the $10 million by issuing 10% preferred stock or 10% bonds. From the viewpoint of the common shareholders, which financing plan is preferable? The schedule at the top of page 654 shows the expected increase in annual earnings per share of common stock under the two alternative financing plans.

At first glance, it appears that under either plan the annual financing cost is $1,000,000, whether this amount is paid out as interest or as dividends. Why, then, are the earnings applicable to common stock $400,000 greater each year if the new plant is financed by issuing bonds rather than preferred stock? The answer lies in the fact that interest payments are *deductible* in determining the income subject to income taxes, whereas dividend payments are not. Notice that the company will pay $400,000 *less income tax* each year if the new plant is financed by issuing bonds. In short, we might say that issuing bonds rather than stock reduces the annual *after-tax*

	IF 10% PREFERRED STOCK IS ISSUED	IF 10% BONDS ARE ISSUED
Increase in annual earnings before financing costs and income taxes	$4,000,000	$4,000,000
Less: Interest on bonds (10% × $10,000,000)	–0–	1,000,000
Increase in earnings subject to income taxes	$4,000,000	$3,000,000
Less: Income taxes (assume 40% rate)	1,600,000	1,200,000
Increase in net income	$2,400,000	$1,800,000
Less: Dividends on preferred stock (10% × $10,000,000)	1,000,000	–0–
Increase in earnings applicable to common stock	$1,400,000	$1,800,000
Number of shares of common stock outstanding	1,000,000	1,000,000
Increase in earnings per share of common stock	$1.40	$1.80

financing cost from $1,000,000 to $600,000. This $600,000 is a net amount, represented by the $1,000,000 increase in annual interest payments offset by the $400,000 reduction in annual income tax payments.

The use of borrowed capital to enhance earnings applicable to common stock is called *leverage;* this concept is discussed further in Chapter 20.

Accounting entries for a bond issue

Assume that Wells Corporation on January 1, 1988, after proper authorization by the board of directors and approval by the shareholders, issues $1,000,000 of 20-year, 12% bonds payable. All the bonds bear the January 1, 1988, date, and interest is computed from this date. Interest on the bonds is payable semiannually, each July 1 and January 1. If all the bonds are sold at par value (face value), the sale will be recorded by the following entry:

```
Jan. 1  Cash ....................................  1,000,000
             Bonds Payable ......................            1,000,000
        To record issuance of 12%, 20-year bonds at
        100 on the interest date.
```

The first semiannual interest payment of $60,000 would be due on July 1. The computation is ($1,000,000 × .12) ÷ 2 = $60,000. The interest payment would be recorded by the following entry:

```
July 1  Bond Interest Expense .........................  60,000
             Cash ......................................            60,000
        Paid semiannual interest on 12%, 20-year bonds
        with face amount of $1,000,000.
```

When the bonds mature 20 years later on January 1, 2008, the entry to record payment of the principal amount will be:

```
Jan. 1  Bonds Payable ..........................  1,000,000
            Cash ................................                1,000,000
        Paid face amount of bonds at maturity.
```

Recording the issuance of bonds between interest dates The semiannual interest dates (such as January 1 and July 1, or April 1 and October 1) are printed on the bond certificates. However, bonds are often issued between the specified interest dates. The investor is then required to pay the interest accrued to date of issuance in addition to the stated price of the bond. This practice enables the corporation to pay a full six months' interest on all bonds outstanding at the semiannual interest payment date. The accrued interest collected from investors purchasing bonds between interest payment dates is thus returned to them on the next interest payment date. To illustrate, let us modify our present example for Wells Corporation and assume that the $1,000,000 face value of 12% bonds were issued at 100 plus accrued interest, *two months after the interest date printed on the bonds*. The entry will be:

BONDS ISSUED BETWEEN
INTEREST DATES

```
Cash ........................................  1,020,000
        Bonds Payable .............................                1,000,000
        Bond Interest Payable ......................                   20,000
Issued $1,000,000 face value of 12%, 20-year bonds
at 100 plus accrued interest for two months.
```

Four months later on the regular semiannual interest payment date, a full six months' interest ($60 per each $1,000 bond) will be paid to all bondholders, regardless of when they purchased their bonds. The entry for the semiannual interest payment is illustrated as follows:

WHAT IS THE NET
INTEREST EXPENSE?

```
Bond Interest Payable .............................     20,000
Bond Interest Expense .............................     40,000
        Cash ......................................                  60,000
Paid semiannual interest on $1,000,000 face value of
12% bonds.
```

Now consider these interest transactions from the standpoint of the investors. They paid for two months' accrued interest at the time of purchasing the bonds, and they received cheques for six months' interest after holding the bonds for only four months. They have, therefore, been reimbursed for the use of their money for four months.

When bonds are subsequently sold by one investor to another, they sell at the quoted market price *plus accrued interest* since the last interest payment date. This practice enables the issuing corporation to pay all the interest for an interest period to the investor owning the bond at the interest date. Otherwise, the corporation would have to make partial payments to every investor who bought or sold the bond during the interest period. This would be costly and impractical.

The amount that investors will pay for bonds is the *present value* of the principal and interest payments they will receive. Before going further in our discussion of bonds payable, it will be helpful to review the concepts of present value and effective yield.

The concept of present value

The concept of present value is based upon the "time value" of money — the idea that receiving money today is preferable to receiving money at some later date. Assume, for example, that a bond will have a maturity value of $1,000 five years from today but will pay no interest in the meantime. Investors would not pay $1,000 for this bond today, because they would receive no return on their investment over the next five years. There are prices less than $1,000, however, at which investors would buy the bond. For example, if the bond could be purchased for $600, the investor could expect a return (interest) of $400 from the investment over the five-year period.

The *present value* of a future cash receipt is the amount that a knowledgeable investor will pay *today* for the right to receive that future payment. The exact amount of the present value depends upon (1) the amount of the future payment, (2) the length of time until the payment will be received, and (3) the rate of return required by the investor. However, the present value will always be *less* than the future amount. This is because money received today can be invested to earn interest and thereby becomes equivalent to a larger amount in the future.

The rate of interest that will cause a given present value to grow to a given future amount is called the discount rate or *effective interest rate.* The effective interest rate required by investors at any given time is regarded as the going *market rate* of interest. The procedures for computing the present value of a future amount are illustrated in an appendix following this chapter.

The present value concept and bond prices

3   Discuss the relationship between interest rates and bond prices.

The price at which bonds will sell is the present value to investors of the future principal and interest payments.[2] If the bonds sell at par, the effective interest rate is equal to the *contract interest rate* (or nominal rate) printed on the bonds. The higher the effective interest rate investors require, the less they will pay for bonds with a given contract rate of interest. For example, if investors insist upon a 10% return, they will pay less than $1,000 for a 9%, $1,000 bond. Thus, if investors require an effective interest rate *greater* than the contract rate of interest for the bonds, the bonds will sell at a *discount* (price less than face value). On the other hand, if investors require an effective interest rate of *less* than the contract rate, the bonds will sell at *premium* (price above face value).

A corporation wishing to borrow money by issuing bonds must pay the going market rate of interest. Since market rates of interest are fluctuating constantly, it must be expected that the contract rate of interest may vary somewhat from the market rate at the date the bonds are issued. Thus, bonds often are issued at either a discount or a premium.

Bond prices after issuance   As stated earlier, many corporate bonds are traded daily on organized securities exchanges at quoted market prices. After bonds are issued, their market prices vary *inversely* with changes in market interest rates. As interest

---

[2] The mechanics of determining the market price of a bond issue by using present value techniques are illustrated in the appendix following this chapter.

rates rise, investors will be willing to pay less money to own a bond that pays a given contract rate of interest. Conversely, as interest rates decline, the market prices of bonds rise.

 A few years ago, a large corporation sold to underwriters $500 million of $9^3/_8\%$ debenture bonds, due in 2004. The underwriters planned to sell the bonds to the public at a price of $99^5/_8$. Just as the bonds were offered for sale, however, a change in general business conditions and government policy started an upward surge in interest rates. The underwriters encountered great difficulty selling the bonds. Within one week, the market price of the bonds had fallen to $94^1/_2$. The underwriters dumped their unsold inventory at this price and sustained one of the largest underwriting losses in the history of the underwriting business.

During the months subsequent to issuance, interest rates soared to record levels. By the early part of the following year, the price of the bonds had fallen to $76^3/_8$. Thus, nearly one-fourth of the market value of these bonds evaporated in less than a year. The financial strength of the corporation was never in question; this dramatic loss in market value was caused entirely by rising interest rates.

In addition to the current level of interest rates, the market prices of bonds are strongly influenced by the *length of time remaining until the bonds mature* — that is, are redeemed at their maturity value (par value) by the issuing corporation. As a bond nears its maturity date, its market price normally will move closer and closer to the maturity value.

 A large corporation has outstanding two issues of $7^7/_8$ bonds; one issue maturing in 1989 and the other in 1992. In mid-1986, the bonds maturing in 1989 were selling at a quoted market price of 96, whereas the bonds maturing in 1992 were selling at a price of only $91^1/_2$. Both bonds pay the same amount of interest, were issued by the same corporation, and have identical credit ratings. Thus, the difference in the market prices is caused solely by differences in the bonds' maturity dates.

Bonds sold at a discount

To illustrate the sale of bonds at a discount, assume that a corporation plans to issue $1,000,000 face value of 9%, 10-year bonds, interest payable semiannually. At the issuance date, January 1, 1989, the going market rate of interest is slightly above 9% and the bonds sell at a price of only 98 ($980 for each $1,000 bond). The issuance of the bonds will be recorded by the following entry:

ISSUING BONDS AT DISCOUNT

Cash	980,000	
Discount on Bonds Payable	20,000	
Bonds Payable		1,000,000
Issued $1,000,000 face value of 9%, 10-year bonds at 98.		

If a balance sheet is prepared immediately after the issuance of the bonds, the liability for bonds payable will be shown as follows:

LIABILITY SHOWN NET
OF DISCOUNT

Long-term liabilities:		
9% bonds payable, due in 10 years	$1,000,000	
Less: Discount on bonds payable	20,000	$980,000

The amount of the discount is deducted from the face value of the bonds payable to show the *carrying value* or book value of the liability. At the date of issuance, the carrying value of bonds payable is equal to the amount for which the bonds were sold. In other words, the amount of the company's liability at the date of issuing the bonds is equal to the amount of money borrowed. Over the life of the bonds, however, we shall see that this carrying value gradually increases until it reaches the face value of the bonds at the maturity date.

4 **Explain how bond discount or premium affects the cost of borrowing.**

Bond discount as part of the cost of borrowing   In Chapter 8, we illustrated two ways in which interest charges can be specified in a note payable: the interest may be stated as an annual percentage rate of the face amount of the note, or it may be included in the face amount. Bonds issued at a discount include *both* types of interest charge. The $1,000,000 bond issue in our example calls for cash interest payments of $90,000 per year ($1,000,000 × 9% contract interest rate), payable semiannually. In addition to making the semiannual interest payments, the corporation must redeem the bond issue for $1 million on the maturity date. This maturity value is $20,000 greater than the $980,000 received when the bonds were issued. Thus, the $20,000 discount in the issue price may be regarded as an *interest charge included in the maturity value of the bonds.*

Although the interest charge represented by the discount will not be paid to bondholders until the bonds mature, the corporation benefits from this cost during the *entire period* that it has the *use of the bondholders' money* (that is, from the date of issue, which is not necessarily the date of the bonds, to the maturity date of the bonds). Therefore, the cost represented by the discount should be allocated over the life of the bond issue. For bonds issued between interest dates, the life of the bonds starts from the date that the bonds are sold. The process of allocating bond discount to interest expense is termed *amortization* of the discount.

In short, whenever bonds are issued at a discount, the total interest cost over the life of the bonds is equal to the total of the regular cash interest payments *plus the amount of the discount.* For the $1 million bond issue in our example, the total interest cost over the 10-year life of the bonds is $920,000, of which $900,000 represents the 20 semiannual cash interest payments and $20,000 represents the discount. The average annual interest expense, therefore, is $92,000 ($920,000 ÷ 10 years), consisting of $90,000 paid in cash and $2,000 amortization of the bond discount. This analysis is illustrated as follows:

Total cash interest payments to bondholders		
($1,000,000 × 9% × 10 years)		$900,000
Add: Interest charge included in face amount of bonds:		
Maturity value of bonds	$1,000,000	
Amount borrowed	980,000	20,000
Total cost of borrowing over life of bond issue		$920,000
Average annual interest expense ($920,000 ÷ 10 years)		$ 92,000

5 Amortize bond discount or premium by the straight-line and effective-interest methods.

Amortization of bond discount

The simplest method of amortizing bond discount is the **straight-line method,** which allocates an equal portion of the discount to Bond Interest Expense in each period.[3] In our example, the Discount on Bonds Payable account has a beginning debit balance of $20,000; each year one-tenth of this amount, or $2,000, will be amortized into Bond Interest Expense. Assuming that the interest payment dates are June 30 and December 31, the entries to be made each six months to record bond interest expense are as follows:

PAYMENT OF BOND INTEREST AND STRAIGHT-LINE AMORTIZATION OF BOND DISCOUNT

Bond Interest Expense	45,000	
Cash		45,000
Paid semiannual interest on $1,000,000 of 9%, 10-year bonds.		

Bond Interest Expense	1,000	
Discount on Bonds Payable		1,000
Amortized discount for six months on 10-year bond issue ($20,000 discount × 1/20).		

The two entries shown above to record the cash payment of bond interest and to record the amortization of bond discount can conveniently be combined into one compound entry, as follows:

Bond Interest Expense	46,000	
Cash		45,000
Discount on Bonds Payable		1,000
To record payment of semiannual interest on $1,000,000 of 9%, 10-year bonds ($1,000,000 × 9% × 1/2) and to amortize 1/20 of the discount on the 10-year bond issue.		

Regardless of whether the cash payment of interest and the amortization of bond discount are recorded in separate entries or combined in one entry, the amount recognized as Bond Interest Expense is the same — $46,000 each six months, or a total of $92,000 a year. An alternative accounting procedure that will produce the same results is to amortize the bond discount only at year-end rather than at each interest-payment date.

Note that the additional interest expense resulting from amortization of the discount does not require any additional cash payment. The credit portion of the entry is to the contra-liability account, Discount on Bonds Payable, rather than to the Cash account. Crediting this contra-liability account *increases the carrying value of bonds payable.* The original $20,000 discount will be completely written off by the end of the tenth year, and the net liability (carrying value) will be the full face value of the bonds.

It should also be noted that in this illustration the period of amortization of bond discount is 10 years because the date of the bonds and the date of issue coincide. However, if the bonds were issued two months after the date of the bonds (that is,

[3] An alternative method of amortization, called the **effective-interest method,** is illustrated later in this chapter. Although the effective-interest method is theoretically preferable to the straight-line method, the resulting differences generally are not material in dollar amount.

issuing bonds between interest dates), the period of amortization would be 9 years and 10 months rather than 10 years.

Bonds sold at a premium

Bonds will sell above par (face value) if the contract rate of interest specified on the bonds is higher than the current market rate for bonds of this grade. Let us now change our basic illustration by assuming that the $1 million issue of 9%, 10-year bonds is sold at a price of 102 ($1,020 for each $1,000 bond). The entry is shown in the following:

ISSUING BONDS AT
PREMIUM

Cash	1,020,000	
Bonds Payable		1,000,000
Premium on Bonds Payable		20,000
Issued $1,000,000 face value of 9%, 10-year bonds		
at price of 102.		

If a balance sheet is prepared immediately following the sale of the bonds, the liability will be shown as follows:

CARRYING VALUE
INCREASED BY
PREMIUM

Long-term liabilities:
   9% bonds payable, due in 10 years $1,000,000
   Add: Premium on bonds payable 20,000 $1,020,000

The amount of any unamortized premium is **added** to the maturity value of the bonds payable to show the current carrying value of the liability. Over the life of the bond issue, this carrying value will be reduced toward the maturity value of $1,000,000.

Bond premium as reduction in the cost of borrowing We have illustrated how issuing bonds at a discount increases the cost of borrowing above the amount of the regular cash interest payments. Issuing bonds at a premium, on the other hand, *reduces the cost of borrowing below the amount of the regular cash interest payments.*

The amount received from issuance of the bonds is $20,000 greater than the amount that must be repaid at maturity. This $20,000 premium is not a gain but is to be offset against the periodic interest payments in determining the net cost of borrowing. Whenever bonds are issued at a premium, the total interest cost over the life of the bonds is equal to the regular cash interest payments *minus the amount of the premium.* In our example, the total interest cost over the life of the bonds is computed as $900,000 of cash interest payments minus $20,000 of premium amortized, or a net borrowing cost of $880,000. The annual interest expense will be $88,000, consisting of $90,000 paid in cash less an offsetting $2,000 transferred from the Premium on Bonds Payable account to the credit side of the Bond Interest Expense account.

The semiannual entries on June 30 and December 31 to record the payment of bond interest and amortization of bond premium appear at the top of page 661.

As pointed out in the discussion on amortization of bond discount, the period of amortization of bond premium in this illustration is 10 years as the date of the bonds and the date of issue coincide. However, if these two dates do not coincide (that is, issuing bonds between interest dates), the amortization period will be less than 10 years.

PAYMENT OF BOND
INTEREST AND STRAIGHT-
LINE AMORTIZATION OF
BOND PREMIUM

Bond Interest Expense	45,000	
Cash		45,000

Paid semiannual interest on $1,000,000 of 9%, 10-year bonds.

Premium on Bonds Payable	1,000	
Bond Interest Expense		1,000

Amortized premium for six months on 10-year bond issue
($20,000 × $^1/_{20}$).

Year-end adjustments for bond interest expense

In the preceding illustration, it was assumed that one of the semiannual dates for payment of bond interest coincided with the end of the company's accounting year. In many cases, however, the semiannual interest payment dates will fall during an accounting period rather than on the last day of the year.

For purposes of illustration, assume that $1 million of 10%, 1G-year bonds are issued at a price of 97 on October 1, 1988. Interest payment dates are April 1 and October 1. The total discount to be amortized amounts to $30,000, or $1,500 in each six-month interest period. The company keeps its accounts on a calendar-year basis; consequently, the following adjusting entries will be necessary at December 31 for the accrued interest and the amortization of discount applicable to the three-month period since the bonds were issued.

Bond Interest Expense	25,750	
Bond Interest Payable		25,000
Discount on Bonds Payable		750

To adjust for accrued interest on bonds and to amortize discount for period from Oct. 1 to Dec. 31. Accrued interest: $1,000,000 × .10 × $^3/_{12}$ = $25,000. Amortization: $30,000 × $^3/_{120}$ = $750.

If the above bonds had been issued at a premium, similar entries would be made at the end of the period for any accrued interest and for amortization of premium for the fractional period from October 1 to December 31.

In the December 31 balance sheet, the $25,000 of accrued bond interest payable will appear as a current liability; the long-term liability for bonds payable will appear as follows:

Long-term liabilities:		
10% Bonds payable, due Oct. 1, 1998	$1,000,000	
Less: Discount on bonds payable	29,250	$970,750

When the bonds were issued on October 1, the net liability for bonds payable was $970,000. Notice that the carrying value of the bonds has **increased** over the three months by the amount of discount amortized. When the entire discount has been amortized, the carrying value of the bonds will be $1,000,000, which is equal to their maturity value.

At April 1, 1989, it is necessary to record interest expense and discount amortization only for the three-month period since year-end. Of the semiannual $50,000 cash payment to bondholders, one-half, or $25,000, represents payment of the liability for bond interest payable recorded on December 31, 1988. The entry on April 1 is:

Bond Interest Expense	25,750	
Bond Interest Payable	25,000	
Discount on Bonds Payable		750
Cash		50,000

To record bond interest expense and amortization of discount for three-month period since year-end and to record semiannual payment to bondholders.

Straight-line amortization: a theoretical shortcoming

Although the straight-line method of amortizing bond discount or premium recognizes the full cost of borrowing over the life of a bond issue, the method has one conceptual weakness: the same dollar amount of interest expense is recognized each year. Amortizing a discount, however, causes a gradual increase in the liability for bonds payable; amortizing a premium causes a gradual decrease in the liability. If the uniform annual interest expense is expressed as a *percentage* of either an increasing or a decreasing liability, it appears that the borrower's cost of capital is changing over the life of the bonds.

This problem can be avoided by using the *effective-interest method* of amortizing bond discount or premium. The effective-interest method recognizes annual interest expense equal to a *constant percentage of the carrying value of the related liability.* This percentage is the effective rate of interest incurred by the borrower. For this reason, the effective-interest method of amortization is considered theoretically preferable to the straight-line method. Whenever the two methods would produce *materially different* annual results, the use of the effective-interest method is preferable. In fact, the Financial Accounting Standards Board in the United States has taken such a position.

Over the life of the bonds, both amortization methods recognize the same total amount of interest expense. Even on an annual basis, the results produced by the two methods usually are very similar. Because of its simplicity, the straight-line method is widely used despite the theoretical arguments favouring the effective-interest method.

Effective-interest method of amortization

When bonds are sold at a discount, the effective interest rate incurred by the issuing corporation is *higher* than the contract rate printed on the bonds. Conversely, when bonds are sold at a premium, the effective rate of interest is *lower* than the contract rate.

When the effective-interest method is used, bond interest expense is determined by multiplying the *carrying value of the bonds* at the beginning of the period by the *effective rate of interest* for the bond issue. The amount of discount or premium to be amortized is the *difference* between the interest expense computed in this manner and the amount of interest paid (or payable) to bondholders for the period. The computation of effective interest expense and the amount of discount or premium amortization for the life of the bond issue is made in advance on a schedule called an *amortization table*.

Sale of bonds at a discount   To illustrate the effective-interest method, assume that on May 1 a corporation issues $1,000,000 face value, 9%, 10-year bonds with interest dates of November 1 and May 1. The bonds sell for $937,689, a price resulting in an effective interest rate of 10%.[4] An amortization table for this bond issue is illustrated below. (Amounts of interest expense have been rounded to the nearest dollar.)

Amortization Table for Bonds Sold at a Discount
($1,000,000, 10-year bonds, 9% interest payable semiannually,
sold at $937,689 to yield 10% compounded semiannually)

SIX-MONTH INTEREST PERIOD	(A) INTEREST PAID SEMIANNUALLY (4½% OF FACE VALUE)	(B) EFFECTIVE SEMIANNUAL INTEREST EXPENSE (5% OF BOND CARRYING VALUE)	(C) DISCOUNT AMORTI- ZATION (B − A)	(D) BOND DISCOUNT BALANCE	(E) CARRYING VALUE OF BONDS, END OF PERIOD ($1,000,000 − D)
Issue date				$62,311	$ 937,689
1	$45,000	$46,884	$1,884	60,427	939,573
2	45,000	46,979	1,979	58,448	941,552
3	45,000	47,078	2,078	56,370	943,630
4	45,000	47,182	2,182	54,188	945,812
5	45,000	47,291	2,291	51,897	948,103
6	45,000	47,405	2,405	49,492	950,508
7	45,000	47,525	2,525	46,967	953,033
8	45,000	47,652	2,652	44,315	955,685
9	45,000	47,784	2,784	41,531	958,469
10	45,000	47,923	2,923	38,608	961,392
11	45,000	48,070	3,070	35,538	964,462
12	45,000	48,223	3,223	32,315	967,685
13	45,000	48,384	3,384	28,931	971,069
14	45,000	48,553	3,553	25,378	974,622
15	45,000	48,731	3,731	21,647	978,353
16	45,000	48,918	3,918	17,729	982,271
17	45,000	49,114	4,114	13,615	986,385
18	45,000	49,319	4,319	9,296	990,704
19	45,000	49,535	4,535	4,761	995,239
20	45,000	49,761*	4,761	−0−	1,000,000

*In the last period, interest expense is equal to interest paid to bondholders plus the remaining balance on the bond discount. This compensates for the accumulated effects of rounding amounts.

[4] Computation of the exact effective interest rate involves mathematical techniques beyond the scope of this course. A very close estimate of the effective interest rate can be obtained by dividing the *average* annual interest expense by the *average* carrying value of the bonds. Computation of average annual interest expense was illustrated on page 658. The average carrying value of the bonds is found by adding the issue price and the maturity value of the bond issue and dividing this sum by 2. Applying these procedures to the bond issue in our example provides an estimated effective interest rate of 9.93%, computed [($900,000 interest + $62,311 discount) ÷ 10 years] divided by [($937,689 + $1,000,000) ÷ 2].

This amortization table can be used to illustrate the concepts underlying the effective-interest method of determining interest expense and discount amortization. Note that the "interest periods" in the table are the *semiannual* (six-month) interest periods. Thus, the interest payments (column A), interest expense (column B), and discount amortization (column C) are for six-month periods. Similarly, the balance of the Discount on Bonds Payable account (column D) and the carrying value of the liability (column E) are shown as of each semiannual interest payment date.

The original issuance price of the bonds ($937,689) is entered at the top of column E. This represents the carrying value of the liability throughout the first six-month interest period. The semiannual interest payment, shown in column A, is $4^{1}/_{2}\%$ (one-half of the original contract rate) of the $1,000,000 face value of the bond issue. The semiannual cash interest payment does not change over the life of the bonds. The interest expense shown in column B, however, *changes every period.* This expense is always a *constant percentage* of the carrying value of the liability as of the end of the preceding period. The "constant percentage" is the effective interest rate of the bond issue. The bonds have an effective annual interest rate of 10%, indicating a semiannual rate of 5%. Thus, the effective interest expense for the first six-month period is $46,884 (5% of $937,689). The discount amortization for period 1 is the difference between this effective interest expense and the contract rate of interest paid to bondholders.

After the discount is reduced by $1,884 at the end of period 1, the carrying value of the bonds in column E *increases* by $1,884 (from $937,689 to $939,573). In period 2, the effective interest expense is determined by multiplying the effective semiannual interest rate of 5% by this new carrying value of $939,573 (5% × $939,573 = $46,979).

Semiannual interest expense may be recorded every period directly from the data in the amortization table. For example, the entry to record bond interest expense at the end of the first six-month period is:

Bond Interest Expense	46,884	
Discount on Bonds Payable		1,884
Cash		45,000
To record semiannual interest payment and amortize		
discount for six months.		

Similarly, interest expense at the end of the *fifteenth* six-month period would be recorded by the journal entry that follows.

Bond Interest Expense	48,731	
Discount on Bonds Payable		3,731
Cash		45,000
To record semiannual interest payment and amortize		
discount for six months.		

When bond discount is amortized, the carrying value of the liability for bonds payable *increases* every period toward the maturity value. Since the effective interest expense in each period is a constant percentage of this increasing carrying value, the interest expense also increases from one period to the next. This is the basic difference between the effective-interest method and straight-line amortization.

Sale of bonds at a premium   Let us now change our illustration by assuming that the $1,000,000 issue of 9%, 10-year bonds is sold on May 1 at a price of $1,067,952, resulting in an effective interest rate of 8% annually (4% per six-month interest period). An amortization table for this bond issue follows:

Amortization Table for Bonds Sold at a Premium
($1,000,000, 10-year bonds, 9% interest payable semiannually,
sold at $1,067,952 to yield 8% compounded semiannually)

SIX-MONTH INTEREST PERIOD	(A) INTEREST PAID SEMIANNUALLY (4½% OF FACE VALUE)	(B) EFFECTIVE SEMIANNUAL INTEREST EXPENSE (4% OF BOND CARRYING VALUE)	(C) PREMIUM AMORTI-ZATION (A − B)	(D) BOND PREMIUM BALANCE	(E) CARRYING VALUE OF BONDS, END OF PERIOD ($1,000,000 + D)
Issue date				$67,952	$1,067,952
1	$45,000	$42,718	$2,282	65,670	1,065,670
2	45,000	42,627	2,373	63,297	1,063,297
3	45,000	42,532	2,468	60,829	1,060,829
4	45,000	42,433	2,567	58,262	1,058,262
5	45,000	42,330	2,670	55,592	1,055,592
6	45,000	42,224	2,776	52,816	1,052,816
7	45,000	42,113	2,887	49,929	1,049,929
8	45,000	41,997	3,003	46,926	1,046,926
9	45,000	41,877	3,123	43,803	1,043,803
10	45,000	41,752	3,248	40,555	1,040,555
11	45,000	41,622	3,378	37,177	1,037,177
12	45,000	41,487	3,513	33,664	1,033,664
13	45,000	41,347	3,653	30,011	1,030,011
14	45,000	41,200	3,800	26,211	1,026,211
15	45,000	41,048	3,952	22,259	1,022,259
16	45,000	40,890	4,110	18,149	1,018,149
17	45,000	40,726	4,274	13,875	1,013,875
18	45,000	40,555	4,445	9,430	1,009,430
19	45,000	40,377	4,623	4,807	1,004,807
20	45,000	40,193*	4,807	−0−	1,000,000

*In the last period, interest expense is equal to interest paid to bondholders minus the remaining balance of the bond premium. This compensates for the accumulated effects of rounding amounts.

In this amortization table, the interest expense for each six-month period is equal to 4% of the carrying value at the beginning of that period. This amount of interest expense is less than the amount of cash being paid to bondholders, illustrating that the effective interest rate is less than the contract rate.

Based upon this amortization table, the entry to record the interest payment and amortization of the premium for the first six months of the bond issue is:

AMORTIZATION OF
PREMIUM DECREASES
INTEREST EXPENSE

Bond Interest Expense	42,718	
Premium on Bonds Payable	2,282	
Cash		45,000

To record semiannual interest payment and amortization of premium.

As the carrying value of the liability declines, so does the amount recognized as bond interest expense.

Year-end adjusting entries   Since the amounts recognized as interest expense change from one period to the next, we must refer to the appropriate interest period in the amortization table to obtain the dollar amounts for use in year-end adjusting entries. To illustrate, consider our example of the bonds sold at a premium on May 1. The entry shown above records interest and amortization of the premium through November 1. If the company keeps its accounts on a calendar-year basis, two months' interest has accrued as of December 31, and the following adjusting entry is made at year-end:

YEAR-END ADJUSTMENT

Bond Interest Expense	14,209	
Premium on Bonds Payable	791	
Bond Interest Payable		15,000

To record two months' accrued interest and amortize one-third of the premium for the interest period.

This adjusting entry covers one-third (two months) of the second interest period. Consequently, the amounts shown as bond interest expense and amortization of premium are *one-third* of the amounts shown in the amortization table for the second interest period. Similar adjusting entries must be made at the end of every accounting period while the bonds are outstanding. The dollar amounts of these adjusting entries will vary, however, because the amounts of interest expense and premium amortization change in every interest period. The amounts applicable to any given adjusting entry will be the appropriate fraction of the amounts for the interest period then in progress.

Following the preceding year-end adjusting entry the interest expense and premium amortization on May 1 of the second year are recorded as follows:

INTEREST PAYMENT
FOLLOWING YEAR-END
ADJUSTMENT

Bond Interest Expense	28,418	
Bond Interest Payable	15,000	
Premium on Bonds Payable	1,582	
Cash		45,000

To record semiannual interest payment, a portion of which had been accrued, and amortize remainder of premium applicable to interest period.

Retirement of bonds payable

Bonds are sometimes retired before the maturity date. The principal reason for retiring bonds early is to relieve the issuing corporation of the obligation to make future interest payments. If interest rates decline to the point that a corporation can borrow at an interest rate below that being paid on a particular bond issue, the corporation may benefit from retiring those bonds and issuing new bonds at a lower interest rate.

Bond issues generally contain a call (redemption) provision, permitting the corporation to redeem the bonds by paying a specified price, usually a few points above par (face value). Even without a call provision, the corporation may retire its bonds before maturity by purchasing them in the open market. If the bonds can be purchased by the issuing corporation at less than their *carrying value,* a gain is realized on the retirement of the debt. If the bonds are acquired by the issuing corporation at a price in excess of their carrying value, a loss must be recognized. These gains and losses, if *material* in amount, should be shown separately in the income statement before extraordinary items.[5]

For example, assume that the Briggs Corporation has outstanding a $1 million bond issue with unamortized premium in the amount of $20,000. The bonds are callable at 105 and the company exercises the call provision on 100 of the bonds, or 10% of the issue. The entry would be as follows:

BONDS CALLED AT PRICE
ABOVE CARRYING
VALUE

Bonds Payable	100,000	
Premium on Bonds Payable	2,000	
Loss on Retirement of Bonds	3,000	
Cash		105,000

To record retirement of $100,000 face value of bonds called at 105.

The carrying value of each of the 100 called bonds was $1,020, whereas the call price was $1,050. For each bond called the company incurred a loss of $30, or a total loss of $3,000. Note that when 10% of the total issue was called, 10% of the unamortized premium was written off.

If bonds remain outstanding until the maturity date, the discount or premium will have been completely amortized and the accounting entry to retire the bonds (assuming that interest is paid separately) will consist of a debit to Bonds Payable and a credit to Cash.

One year before the maturity date, the bonds payable should be reclassified from long-term debt to a current liability in the balance sheet if payment is to be made from current assets rather than from a *bond sinking fund.*

Bond sinking fund

To make a bond issue attractive to investors, corporations may agree to create a sinking fund, exclusively for use in paying the bonds at maturity. A bond sinking fund is created by setting aside a specified amount of cash at regular intervals. The cash is usually deposited with a trustee, who invests it and adds the earnings to the amount of the sinking fund. The periodic deposits of cash plus the earnings on the sinking fund investments should cause the fund to equal approximately the amount of

---

[5] CICA, *CICA Handbook* (Toronto), paragraph 3480.11. Also see *Financial Reporting in Canada*, 17th ed. (Toronto, 1987), p. 187.

the bond issue by the maturity date. When the bond issue approaches maturity, the trustee sells all the securities in the fund and uses the cash proceeds to pay the holders of the bonds. Any excess cash remaining in the fund will be returned to the corporation by the trustee.

A bond sinking fund is not included in current assets because it is not available for payment of current liabilities. The cash and securities comprising the fund are usually shown as a single amount under a caption such as Long-Term Investments, which is placed just below the current asset section. Interest earned on sinking fund securities constitutes revenue to the corporation.

Conversion of bonds payable into common stock

Convertible bonds represent a popular form of financing, particularly during periods when common stock prices are rising. The conversion feature gives bondholders an opportunity to profit from a rise in the market price of the issuing company's common stock while still maintaining their status of creditors rather than share-holders. Because of this potential gain, convertible bonds generally carry lower interest rates than nonconvertible bonds.

The conversion ratio is typically set at a price above the current market price of the common stock at the date the bonds are authorized. For example, if common stock has a current market price of $42 a share, the **conversion price** might be set at $50 per share, thus enabling a holder of a $1,000 par value convertible bond to exchange the bond for 20 shares of common stock.[6] Let us assume that $5 million of such bonds are issued at par or face value, and that some time later when the common stock has risen in price to $60 per share, the holders of 100 bonds decide to convert their bonds into common stock. The conversion transaction would be recorded as follows:

CONVERSION OF BONDS
INTO COMMON STOCK

Convertible Bonds Payable	100,000	
Common Stock		100,000

To record the conversion of 100 bonds into 2,000 shares of common stock.

No gain or loss is recognized by the issuing corporation upon conversion of bonds; the carrying value of the bonds is simply assigned to the common stock issued in exchange. If the bonds had been issued at a price above or below face value, the unamortized premium or discount relating to the bonds would be written off at the time of conversion in order to assign the carrying value of the bonds to the common stock.

LEASES

6   Explain the accounting treatment of operating leases and of capital leases.

A company may purchase the assets needed in its business operations or, as an alternative, it may lease them. A **lease** is a contract in which the lessor gives the lessee the right to use an asset for a specified period of time in exchange for periodic rental payments. The **lessor** is the owner of the property; the **lessee** is a tenant or

[6] $1,000 ÷ $50 conversion price = 20 shares of common stock.

renter. Examples of assets frequently acquired by lease include automobiles, building space, computers, and equipment. Two types of lessee-operating and capital are presented in the remainder of this section.

Operating Leases

When the lessor gives the lessee the right to use leased property for a limited period of time, but retains the usual risks and rewards of ownership, the contract is known as an *operating lease.* An example of an operating lease is a contract leasing office space in an office building. If the building increases in value, the *lessor* can receive the benefits of this increase by either selling the building or increasing the rental rate once the lease term has expired. On the other hand, if the building declines in value, it is the lessor who bears the loss.

In accounting for an operating lease, the lessor views the monthly lease payments received as rental revenue, and the lessee regards these payments as rental expense. No asset or liability (other than a short-term liability for rent payable) relating to the lease appears in the lessee's balance sheet. Thus, operating leases are sometimes termed *off-balance-sheet financing.*

Capital leases

Some lease contracts are intended to provide financing to the lessee for the eventual purchase of the property, or provide the lessee with use of the property over most of its useful life. These lease contracts are called *capital leases* (or sales-type or direct financing leases). In contrast to an operating lease, a capital lease transfers most of the risks and rewards of ownership from the lessor to the *lessee.* Assume, for example, that City Realty leases a new automobile for a period of three years. Also assume that at the end of the lease, title to the automobile transfers to City Realty at no additional cost. Clearly, City Realty is not merely "renting" the use of the automobile; rather, it is using the lease agreement as a means of financing the purchase of the car.

From an accounting viewpoint, capital leases are regarded as *essentially equivalent to a sale* of the property by the lessor to the lessee, even though title to the leased property has not been transferred. Thus, a capital lease should be recorded by the lessor as a sale of property and by the lessee as a purchase. In such lease agreements, an appropriate interest charge usually is added to the regular sales prices of the property in determining the amount of the lease payments.

Some companies frequently use capital lease agreements as a means of financing the sale of their products to customers. In accounting for merchandise "sold" through a capital lease, the lessor debits Lease Payments Receivable and credits Sales for an amount equal to the *present value of the future lease payments.*[7] In most cases, the present value of these future payments is equal to the regular sales price of the merchandise. In addition, the lessor transfers the cost of the leased merchandise

---

[7] We have elected to record the present value of the future lease payments by a single debit entry to Lease Payments Receivable. An alternative is to debit Lease Payments Receivable for the total amount of the future payments and to credit Discount on Lease Payments Receivable, a contra-asset account, for the unearned finance charges included in the contractual amount. Either approach results in the lessor recording a net receivable equal to the present value of the future lease payments.

from the Inventory account to the Cost of Goods Sold account (assuming a perpetual inventory system is in use). When lease payments are received, the lessor should recognize an appropriate portion of the payment as representing interest revenue and the remainder as a reduction in Lease Payments Receivable.

When equipment is acquired through a capital lease, the lessee should debit an asset account, Leased Equipment, and credit a liability account, Lease Payment Obligation, for the present value of the future lease payments. Lease payments made by the lessee are allocated between Interest Expense and a reduction in the liability, Lease Payment Obligation. No rent expense is involved. The asset account, Leased Equipment, is depreciated over the life of the equipment rather than the life of the lease. (The journal entries used in accounting for a capital lease are illustrated on page 690 of the appendix to this chapter.)

Distinguishing between capital leases and operating leases   The *CICA Handbook* recommended the following distinction:[8]

1 A lease that transfers substantially all of the benefits and risks of ownership related to the leased property from the lessor to the lessee should be accounted for as a capital lease by the lessee and as a sales-type or direct financing lease by the lessor.
2 A lease where the benefits and risks of ownership related to the leased property are substantially retained by the lessor should be accounted for as an operating lease by the lessee and lessor.

OTHER LIABILITIES

Mortgage notes payable

Purchases of real estate and certain types of equipment often are financed by the issuance of mortgage notes payable. When a mortgage note is issued, the borrower pledges title to specific assets as collateral for the loan. If the borrower defaults on the note, the lender may foreclose upon these assets. Mortgage notes usually are payable in equal monthly instalments. These monthly instalments may continue until the loan is completely repaid, or the note may contain a "due date" at which the remaining unpaid balance of the loan must be repaid in a single, lump-sum payment.

A portion of each monthly payment represents interest on the unpaid balance of the loan and the remainder of the monthly payment reduces the amount of the liability (Mortgage Payable). Since the liability is being *reduced each month,* the portion of each successive payment representing interest will *decrease,* and the portion of the payment going toward repayment of the liability will *increase.* To illustrate, assume that on June 30 a company issues a $100,000 mortage note to finance the purchase of a warehouse. The note bears interest at the annual rate of 12% (or 1% per month) and will be paid in monthly instalments of $1,201 over a period of 15 years. The partial amortization table at the top of page 671 shows the allocation of the first three monthly payments between interest and principal (amounts are rounded to the nearest dollar).

---

[8] CICA, *CICA Handbook* (Toronto), paragraphs 3065.09 and 3065.10.

MONTHLY PAYMENTS ON
A MORTGAGE NOTE

PAYMENT DATE	(A) MONTHLY PAYMENT	(B) MONTHLY INTEREST EXPENSE (1% OF UNPAID BALANCE)	(C) REDUCTION IN MORTGAGE PAYABLE (A – B)	(D) BALANCE OF MORTGAGE PAYABLE
June 30 — Issue date				$100,000
July 31	$1,201	$1,000	$201	99,799
Aug. 31	1,201	998	203	99,596
Sept. 30	1,201	996	205	99,391

The entry to record the first monthly mortgage payment on July 31 would be:

PAYMENT IS ALLOCATED
BETWEEN INTEREST AND
PRINCIPAL

Interest Expense	1,000	
Mortgage Payable	201	
Cash		1,201

To record interest expense and reduction in principal included
in July 31 mortgage payment.

That portion of the mortgage that will be paid off within one year (the sum of
column C for the next 12 months) should be classified in the balance sheet as a
current liability. The caption used for this current liability may be "Current Portion
of Long-Term Debt." The remaining balance of the mortgage payable should appear
as a long-term liability.

Pension plans

A *pension plan* is a contract between a company and its employees under which the
company agrees to pay retirement benefits to eligible employees. An employer
company usually meets its obligations under a pension plan by making regular
payments to an insurance company or other outside agency. As pension obligations
accrue, the employer company records them by a debit to Pension Expense and a
credit to Cash. If all required payments are made promptly to the pension fund
trustee, no liability need appear on the employer company's financial statements.
When employees retire, their retirement benefits are paid by the insurance company.
This type of arrangement is called a *funded pension plan.* Pension plans are considered
in some detail in intermediate and advanced accounting courses.

Contingent loss

7   Define contingent
losses and explain how
they are presented in
financial statements.

In Chapter 8, we discussed the *contingent liability* that arises when notes receivable
are discounted at a bank. A contingent liability may be regarded as a *potential*
liability, which may develop into a full-fledged liability or may be eliminated entirely
by a future event. Contingent liabilities are also called *contingent losses.* "Contingent
losses," however, is a broader term, encompassing the possible impairment of assets
as well as the possible existence of liabilities.

A contingent loss may be defined as a possible loss, stemming from *past events,*
that will be resolved as to existence and amount by some future event. Central to the
definition of a contingent loss is the element of *uncertainty* — uncertainty as to the
amount of loss and, on occasion, uncertainty as to whether or not any loss actually

has been incurred. A common example of a contingent loss is the risk of loss from a lawsuit pending against a company. The lawsuit is based on past events, but until the suit is resolved, uncertainty exists as to the amount of the company's liability, if any.

Contingent losses are recorded in the accounting records at estimated amount only when both of the following criteria are met: (1) it is *likely* that a loss has been incurred, and (2) the amount of loss can be *reasonably estimated.*[9] Contingent losses that do not meet both of these criteria should be *disclosed in footnotes* to the financial statements whenever it is *likely* that a loss has been incurred. Pending lawsuits, for example, almost always are disclosed in footnotes, but the loss, if any, is not recorded in the accounting records until the lawsuit is settled.

When contingent losses are disclosed in footnotes to the financial statements, the footnote should describe the nature of the contingency and, if possible, provide an estimate of the amount of possible loss. If a reasonable estimate of the amount of possible loss cannot be made, the footnote should include the range of possible loss or a statement that an estimate cannot be made. The following footnote is typical of the dislosure of the contingent loss arising from pending litigation:

FOOTNOTE DISCLOSURE
OF A CONTINGENT LOSS

Note 8: Contingencies
    In October of the current year, the Company was named as defendant in a lawsuit alleging patent infringement and claiming damages of $408 million. The Company denies all charges in this case and is preparing its defenses against them. The Company is advised by legal counsel that it is not possible at this time to determine the ultimate legal or financial responsibility with respect to this litigation.

Users of financial statements should pay close attention to the footnote disclosure of contingent losses. Even though no loss has been recorded in the accounting records, some contingent losses may be so material in amount as to threaten the continued existence of the company.

Finally, notice that contingent losses relate only to possible losses from *past events.* The risk that losses might be incurred as a result of *future* events is *not* a contingent loss. The risk of *future* losses is *not* disclosed in financial statements for several reasons. For one, any disclosure of possible future losses based solely on future events would be sheer speculation. For another, it is not possible to foresee all the future events that might give rise to future losses.

END-OF-CHAPTER REVIEW

SUMMARY OF CHAPTER LEARNING OBJECTIVES

1 Describe the typical characteristics of corporate bonds.

Corporate bonds are transferrable long-term notes payable. Each bond usually has a face amount of $1,000 (or a multiple of $1,000), receives interest payments semiannually, and

[9] CICA, *CICA Handbook* (Toronto), paragraph 3290.12.

must be redeemed at its face amount at a specified maturity date. By issuing thousands of bonds at one time, the corporation is able to borrow millions of dollars from many different investors.

2 Explain the advantage of raising capital by issuing bonds instead of stock.

The principle advantage of issuing bonds rather than stock is that interest payments to bondholders are *deductible for income tax purposes,* whereas dividends to shareholders are not.

3 Discuss the relationship between interest rates and bond prices.

Bond prices vary inversely with interest rates. As interest rates rise, bond prices fall. Conversely, as interest rates fall, bond prices rise.

4 Explain how bond discount or premium affects the cost of borrowing.

When bonds are issued at a discount, the maturity value of the bonds will exceed the amount originally borrowed. Thus, the discount may be viewed as an interest charge included in the maturity value of the bonds. Amortization of this discount over the life of the bond issue *increases* periodic interest expense. When bonds are issued at a premium, the maturity value of the bonds will be less than the amount originally borrowed. Thus, amortization of bond premium *reduces* the periodic interest expense.

5 Amortize bond discount or premium by the straight-line and effective-interest methods.

When the straight-line method is used, an *equal portion* of discount or premium is amortized each period. When the effective-interest method is used, bond interest is computed by multiplying the carrying value of the bonds by the *effective interest rate.* The amount of discount or premium amortized is the *difference* between the interest expense computed in this manner and the amount of interest paid to bondholders.

6 Explain the accounting treatment of operating leases and of capital leases.

Operating leases are essentially rental agreements; the lessor recognizes rental revenue and the lessee recognizes rent expense. Capital leases, on the other hand, are treated by the lessor as a sale of the related asset and by the lessee as a purchase.

7 Define contingent losses and explain how they are presented in financial statements.

Contingent losses are possible losses, stemming from past events, that will be resolved as to existence and amount by some future event. Central to the concept of a contingent loss is the presence of uncertainty — uncertainty as to the amount of loss and whether, in fact, any loss has occurred. Most contingent losses are disclosed in notes to the financial statements.

KEY TERMS INTRODUCED OR EMPHASIZED IN CHAPTER 16

Amortization of discount or premium on bonds payable The process of systematically writing off a portion of bond discount to increase interest expense or writing off a portion of bond premium to decrease interest expense each period the bonds are outstanding.

Bond sinking fund Cash set aside by the corporation at regular intervals (usually with a trustee) to be used to pay the bonds at maturity.

Capital lease A lease contract that in essence, finances the eventual purchase by the lessee of leased property. The lessor accounts for a capital lease as a sale of property; the lessee records an asset and a liability equal to the present value of the future lease payments. Also called a *sales-type or direct financing lease.*

Contingent losses A situation involving uncertainty as to whether or not a loss has occurred. The uncertainty will be resolved by a future event. An example of a contingent loss is the possible loss related to a lawsuit pending against a company. Although contingent losses are sometimes recorded in the accounts, they are more frequently disclosed only in footnotes in the financial statements.

Contract interest rate The contractual rate of interest printed on bonds. The contract interest rate, applied to the face value of the bonds, determines the amount of the annual cash interest payments to bondholders. Also called the *nominal interest rate.*

Discount on bonds payable Amount by which the face amount of the bond exceeds the price received by the corporation at the date of issuance. Indicates that the contractual rate of interest is lower than the market rate of interest.

Effective-interest method of amortization A method of amortizing bond discount or premium that causes bond interest expense to be a constant percentage of the carrying value of the liability.

Effective interest rate The actual rate of interest expense to the borrowing corporation, taking into account the contractual cash interest payments and the discount or premium to be amortized.

Lessee The tenant, user, or renter of leased property.

Lessor The owner of property leased to a lessee.

Operating lease A lease contract that is in essence a rental agreement. The lessee has the use of the leased property, but the lessor retains the usual risks and rewards of ownership. The periodic lease payments are accounted for as rent expense by the lessee and as rental revenue by the lessor.

Premium on bonds payable Amount by which the issuance price of a bond exceeds the face value. Indicates that the contractual rate of interest is higher than the market rate.

Present value of a future amount The amount of money that an informed investor would pay today for the right to receive the future amount, based upon a specific rate of return required by the investor.

ASSIGNMENT MATERIAL

REVIEW QUESTIONS

1 Distinguish between the two terms in each of the following pairs:
  a Mortgage bond; debenture bond
  b Contract (or nominal) interest rate; effective interest rate
  c Fixed-maturity bond; serial bond
  d Coupon bond; registered bond

2 K Limited has decided to finance expansion by issuing $10 million of 20-year debenture bonds and will ask a number of underwriters to bid on the bond issue. Discuss the factors that will determine the amount bid by the underwriters for these bonds.

3 What is a *convertible bond?* Discuss the advantages and disadvantages of convertible bonds from the standpoint of (a) the investor and (b) the issuing corporation.

4 The Computer Sharing Co. Ltd., has contributed capital of $10 million and retained earnings of $3 million. The company has just issued $1 million in 20-year, 11% bonds.

is proposed that a policy be established of appropriating $50,000 of retained earnings each year to enable the company to retire the bonds at maturity. Evaluate the merits of this proposal in accomplishing the desired result.

5 The following excerpt is taken from an article in a leading business periodical: ''In the bond market high interest rates mean low prices. Bonds pay out a fixed percentage of their face value, usually $1,000; an 8% bond, for instance, will pay $80 a year. In order for its yield to rise to 10%, its price would have to drop to $800.'' Give a critical evaluation of this quotation.

6 Discuss the advantages and disadvantages of a *call (redemption) provision* in a bond contract from the viewpoint of (a) the bondholder and (b) the issuing corporation.

7 Some bonds now being bought and sold by investors on organized securities exchanges were issued when interest rates were much higher than they are today. Would you expect these bonds to be trading at prices above or below their face values? Explain.

8 The 6% bonds of Central Gas & Electric Ltd. are selling at a market price of 72, whereas the 6% bonds of Provincial Power Corporation are selling at a price of 97. Does this mean that Provincial Power has a better credit rating than Central Gas & Electric? Explain. (Assume current long-term interest rates are in the 11 to 13% range.)

9 Explain why the effective rate of interest differs from the contract rate when bonds are issued (a) at a discount and (b) at a premium.

10 When the effective interest method is used to amortize bond discount or premium, the amount of bond interest expense will differ in each period from that of the preceding period. Explain how the amount of bond interest expense changes from one period to another when the bonds are issued (a) at a discount and (b) at a premium.

11 Explain why the effective-interest method of amortizing bond discount or premium is considered to be theoretically preferable to the straight-line method.

12 Explain how the lessee accounts for an operating lease and a capital lease. Why is an operating lease sometimes called *off-balance-sheet financing?*

13 A friend of yours has just purchased a house and has incurred a $50,000, 11% mortgage, payable at $476.17 per month. After making the first monthly payment, he received a receipt from the bank stating that only $17.84 of the $476.17 had been applied to reducing the principle amount of the loan. Your friend computes that at the rate of $17.84 per month, it will take over 233 years to pay off the $50,000 mortgage. Do you agree with your friend's analysis? Explain.

14 Under what conditions are contingent losses recorded at estimated amounts in the accounting records?

15 A lawsuit has been filed against Telmar Corporation alleging patent violations and claiming damages totalling $1.2 billion. Telmar Corporation denies the charges and intends to contest the suit vigorously. Legal counsel advises the company that the litigation will last for many years and that a reasonable estimate of the final outcome cannot be made at this time.

  Should Telmar Corporation include in its current balance sheet a liability for the damages claimed in this lawsuit? Explain fully.

16 With reference to question 15, illustrate the disclosure of the pending lawsuit that should be included in the current financial statements of Telmar Corporation.

EXERCISES

Exercise 16-1
Accounting terminology

Listed below are nine technical accounting terms introduced in this chapter:

Amortization of bond discount	Amortization of bond premium	Effective-interest method of amortization
Capital lease	Contingent loss	Effective interest rate
Operating lease	Debenture	Contract interest rate

Each of the following statements may (or may not) describe one of these technical terms. For each statement, indicate the accounting term described, or answer "None" if the statement does not correctly describe any of the terms.

a The interest rate that determines the dollar amount of the semiannual payments to bondholders.

b A lease that requires the lessee to record both an asset and a long-term liability.

c The possibility that an operating loss might be incurred in some future year.

d The going market rate of interest at the time that bonds are issued.

e A bond in which past interest payments are in default.

f A lease agreement that does not require the lessee to include any long-term lease payment obligation in its balance sheet.

g An adjusting entry that reduces the amount of semiannual interest expense below the amount of the semiannual cash payment to bondholders.

h Amortizing bond discount or premium in a manner that the amount of interest expense remains the same in every period in which bonds are outstanding.

Exercise 16-2
Bond interest (bonds issued at par)

On March 31, Wayne Corporation received authorization to issue $50,000,000 of 12% 30-year debenture bonds. Interest payment dates were March 31 and September 30. The bonds were all issued at par on May 31, two months after the interest date printed on the bonds.

Instructions

a Prepare the journal entry at May 31, to record the sale of the bonds.

b Prepare the journal entry at September 30, to record the semiannual bond interest payment.

c Prepare the adjusting entry at December 31, to record bond interest accrued since September 30.

Exercise 16-3
Tax advantage of bond financing

Eastern Electric and Western Edison have the same amount of operating income (earnings before bond interest and income taxes) and the same number of outstanding shares of common stock. However, the two companies have different capital structures. Determine the earnings per share of common stock for each of the two companies and explain the source of any difference.

	EASTERN ELECTRIC	WESTERN EDISON
14% debenture bonds payable	$10,000,000	–0–
14% cumulative preferred stock, $10 par	–0–	$10,000,000
Common stock, no-par, 500,000 shares issued and outstanding	2,500,000	2,500,000
Operating income, before interest and income taxes (assume a 40% tax rate)	7,000,000	7,000,000

Exercise 16-4
Amortizing bond/
discount and premium:
straight-line method

North Limited issued $40 million of 11%, 10-year bonds on January 1. Interest is payable semi-annually on June 30 and December 31. The bonds were sold to an underwriting group at 105.

South Corporation issued $40 million of 10%, 10-year bonds on January 1. Interest is payable semiannually on June 30 and December 31. The bonds were sold to an underwriting group at 95.

Prepare journal entries to record all transactions during the year for (a) the North bond issue and (b) the South bond issue. Assume that both companies amortize bond discount or premium by the straight-line method at each interest payment date.

Exercise 16-5
Partial retirement of
a bond issue

The following liability appears on the balance sheet of the Sunrise Limited on December 31, 1988:

Long-term liabilities:
Bonds payable, 11%, due Dec. 31, 2002 . . . . $20,000,000
Premium on bonds payable 420,000 $20,420,000

On January 1, 1989, 25% of the bonds are retired at 98. Interest had been paid on December 31, 1988.

a Record the retirement of $5,000,000 of bonds on January 1, 1989.

b Record the interest payment for the six months ending December 31, 1989, and the amortization of the premium on December 31, 1989, assuming that amortization is recorded by the straight-line method only at the end of each year.

Exercise 16-6
Amortizing bond
discount: effective-
interest method

On April 1, Basin Corporation issued $1,000,000 of 10-year, 9% bonds payable and received proceeds of $937,689, resulting in an effective interest rate of 10%. Interest is payable on September 30 and March 31. The effective-interest method is used to amortize bond discount; an amortization table for this bond issue is illustrated in this chapter.

Instructions

Prepare the necessary journal entries (rounding all amounts to the nearest dollar) on:

a April 1, to record the issuance of the bonds

b September 30, to record the payment of interest and amortization of discount at the first semiannual interest payment date

c December 31, to accrue bond interest expense through year-end

d March 31, to record the payment of interest and amortization of bond discount at the second semiannual interest payment date

Exercise 16-7
Using an amortization
table

Crown Point Corporation issued on the authorization date $1,000,000 of 10-year, 9% bonds payable and received proceeds of $1,067,952, resulting in an effective interest rate of 8%. The premium is amortized by the effective-interest method; the amortization table for this bond issue is illustrated in this chapter. Interest is payable semiannually.

Instructions

a Show how the liability for the bonds would appear on a balance sheet prepared immediately after issuance of the bonds.

b Show how the liability for the bonds would appear on a balance sheet prepared after 14 semiannual interest periods (three years prior to maturity).

c Show the necessary calculations to determine interest expense by the effective-interest method for the *second* six-month period, the premium amortized at the end of that second period, and the cash interest payment. Your calculations should include use of the effective interest rate and also the contractual rate. Round all amounts to the nearest dollar.

Exercise 16-8
Conversion of bonds
into capital stock

Brand Corporation issued $5,000,000 of 7%, 10-year convertible bonds dated December 31, at a price of 98. Semiannual interest payment dates were June 30 and December 31. The conversion rate was 20 shares of no-par common stock for each $1,000 bond. Four years later on December 31, bondholders converted $2,000,000 face value of bonds into common stock. Assume that unamortized discount on this date amounted to $60,000 for the entire bond issue. Prepare a journal entry to record the conversion of the bonds.

PROBLEMS

Group A

Problem 16A-1
Bond interest (bonds issued at par)

Texa Bus & Tractor Co. Ltd. obtained authorization to issue $12,000,000 face value of 10% 20-year bonds, dated April 30, 1988. Interest payment dates were October 31 and April 30. Issuance of the bonds did not take place until July 31, 1988. On this date all the bonds were sold at a price of 100 plus three months' accrued interest.

Instructions

Prepare the necessary entries in general journal form on:

a July 31, 1988, to record the issuance of the bonds

b October 31, 1988, to record the first semiannual interest payment on the bond issue

c December 31, 1988, to accrue bond interest expense through year-end

d April 30, 1989, to record the second semiannual interest payment

Problem 16A-2
Amortizing bond discount and premium: straight-line method

On September 1, 1988, Americ Farm Equipment issued $9 million in 9% debenture bonds. Interest is payable semiannually on March 1 and September 1, and the bonds mature in 10 years. Company policy is to amortize bond discount or premium by the straight-line method at each interest payment date; the company's fiscal year ends at December 31.

Instructions

a Make the necessary adjusting entries at December 31, 1988, and the journal entry to record the payment of bond interest on March 1, 1989, under each of the following assumptions:
(1) The bonds were issued at 98.
(2) The bonds were issued at 103.

b Compute the net bond liability at December 31, 1988, under assumptions (1) and (2) above.

Problem 16A-3
Accrual and payment of interest, amortization of bond discount, and bond redemption

The items shown below appear in the balance sheet of Pilsner Breweries Limited at December 31, 1988:

Current liabilities:
    Bond interest payable (for three months from Sept. 30
       to Dec. 31) . . . . $ 180,00
Long-term debt:
    Bonds payable, 9%, due Sept. 30, 1993 . . . . $8,000,000
    Less: Discount on bonds payable   68,400   7,931,60

The bonds are redeemable on any interest date. On September 30, 1989, Pilsner Breweries redeemed $2 million of the bonds at 105.

Instructions

a Prepare journal entries to record the semiannual interest payment on March 31, 1989. Discount is amortized by the straight-line method at each interest payment date and was amortized to December 31, 1988.

b Prepare journal entries to record the amortization of bond discount and payment of bond interest at September 30, 1989, and also to record the redemption of $2,000,000 of the bonds at this date.

c Prepare a journal entry to record the accrual of interest at December 31, 1989. Include the amortization of bond discount to the year-end.

Problem 16A-4
Comprehensive problem: straight-line amortization

Country Recording Studios Limited obtained the necessary approvals to issue $6 million of 10%, 10-year bonds, dated March 1, 1988. Interest payment dates were September 1 and March 1. Issuance of the bonds did not occur until June 1, 1988. On this date, the entire bond issue was sold to an underwriter at a price that included three months' accrued interest. Country Recording Studios Limited follows the policy of amortizing bond discount or premium by the straight-line method at each interest date as well as for year-end adjusting entries at December 31.

Instructions

a Prepare all journal entries necessary to record the issuance of the bonds and bond interest expense during 1988, assuming that the sales price of the bonds on June 1 was $6,618,000, including accrued interest.

b Assume that the sales price of the bonds on June 1 had been $5,799,000, including accrued interest. Prepare journal entries for 1988 parallel to those in part **a** above.

c Show the proper balance sheet presentation of the liability for bonds payable (including accrued interest) in the balance sheet prepared at December 31, *1992,* assuming that the original sales price of the bonds (including accrued interest) had been:
(1) $6,618,000, as described in part **a**
(2) $5,799,000, as described in part **b**

Problem 16A-5
Effective-interest method: bonds issued at premium

On June 30, 1989, Laser Graphics issued $8,000,000 face value of 10-year, 9½% bonds payable at a price of 103¼, resulting in an effective annual rate of interest of 9%. The semiannual interest payment dates are June 30 and December 31, and the bonds mature on June 30, 1999. The company maintains its accounts on a calendar-year basis and amortizes bond premium by the effective-interest method.

Instructions

a Prepare the required journal entries (with explanations) on:
(1) June 30, 1989, to record the sale of the bonds.
(2) December 31, 1989, for payment of interest and amortization of premium on bonds. (Use one compound entry.)
(3) June 30, 1999, for payment of interest, amortization of the remaining premium, and to retire the bonds. Assume that the carrying value of the bonds at the beginning of this last six-month interest period is $8,019,138.

b Show how the accounts, Bonds Payable and Premium on Bonds Payable, would appear on the balance sheet at December 31, 1989.

Problem 16A-6
Preparing and using an amortization table

On December 31, 1988, Glenview Hospital sold a $10,000,000 face value, 10%, 10-year bond issue to an underwriter at a price of 94. This price results in an effective annual interest rate of 11%. Interest is payable semiannually on June 30 and December 31. Glenview Hospital amortizes bond discount by the effective-interest method.

Instructions

a Prepare an amortization table for the first two years (four interest periods) of this bond issue. Round all amounts to the nearest dollar and use the following column headings for your table:

SIX-MONTH INTEREST PERIOD	(A) INTEREST PAID SEMI-ANNUALLY ($10,000,000 × 5%)	(B) EFFECTIVE SEMI-ANNUAL INTEREST EXPENSE (CARRYING VALUE × 5½%)	(C) DISCOUNT AMORTI-ZATION (B − A)	(D) BOND DISCOUNT BALANCE	(E) CARRYING VALUE OF BONDS, END OF PERIOD ($10,000,000 − D)

b Using the information from your amortization table, prepare all journal entries necessary to record issuance of the bonds on December 31, 1988 and bond interest for 1989. (Use a compound entry for interest payment and amortization of bond discount at each semiannual interest payment date.)

c Show the proper balance sheet presentation of Bonds Payable and Discount on Bonds Payable at December 31, 1990.

Problem 16A-7
Comprehensive problem: effective-interest method

Crescent Bay Gas & Electric, on September 1, 1988, issued $9,000,000 par value, 8½%, 10-year bonds payable with interest dates of March 1 and September 1. The company maintains its accounts on a calendar-year basis and follows the policy of amortizing bond discount and bond premium by the effective-interest method at the semiannual interest payment dates as well as at the year-end adjusting of the accounts.

Instructions

a Prepare the necessary journal entries to record the following transactions, assuming that the bonds were sold for $8,700,000, a price resulting in an effective annual interest rate of 9%.
  (1) Sale of the bonds on September 1, 1988.
  (2) Adjustment of the accounts at December 31, 1988, for accrued interest and amortization of a discount.
  (3) Payment of bond interest and amortization of discount on March 1, 1989.

b Assume that the sales price of the bonds on September 1, 1988, had been $9,300,000, resulting in an effective annual interest rate of 8%. Prepare journal entries parallel to those called for in **a** above at the dates of September 1, 1988; December 31, 1988; and March 1, 1989.

c State the amounts of bond interest expense for 1988 and the *net* amount of the liability for the bonds payable at December 31, 1988, under the independent assumptions set forth in both **a** and **b** above. Show your computations.

Group B

Problem 16B-1
Bond interest (bonds issued at par)

Plaza Hotel obtained all necessary approvals to issue $10,000,000 face value of 9%, 20-year bonds dated March 31, 1989. Interest payment dates were September 30 and March 31. The bonds were not issued, however, until four months later, August 1, 1989. On this date the entire bond issue was sold to an underwriter at a price of 100 plus accrued interest.

Instructions

Prepare the required entries in general journal form on:

a August 1, to record the issuance of the bonds

b September 30, to record the first semiannual interest payment on the bonds

c December 31, to accrue bond interest expense through year-end

d March 31, 1990, to record the second semiannual interest payment

Problem 16B-2
Amortizing bond discount and premium: straight-line method

On October 31, 1989, Perfect Racquet Mfg. Co. Ltd. issued $12,000,000 face value of 11% debenture bonds, with interest payable on April 30 and October 31. The bonds mature 10 years from the date of issuance. Company policy is to amortize bond discount or premium by the straight-line method at each interest payment date; the company's fiscal year ends at December 31.

Instructions

a Make the necessary adjusting entries at December 31, 1989, and the journal entry to record the payment of bond interest on April 30, 1990, under each of the following assumptions:
  (1) The bonds were issued at 97.
  (2) The bonds were issued at 102.

b Compute the net bond liability at December 31, 1989, under assumptions (1) and (2) above.

Problem 16B-3

Accrual and payment of interest, amortization of bond discount, and bond redemption

The following items appear in the balance sheet of Napa Vineyards Limited at December 31, 1988:

Current liabilities:
Bond interest payable (for three months from
Sept. 30 to Dec. 31) . . . . $ 200,000
Long-term debt:
Bonds payable, 8%, due Mar. 31, 1999 . . . . $10,000,000
Less: Discount on bonds payable 196,800 9,803,200

The bonds are redeemable on any interest date. On September 30, 1989, Napa Vineyards redeemed $2,000,000 of the bonds at 103.

Instructions

a Prepare journal entries to record the semiannual payment on March 31, 1989. Discount is amortized by the straight-line method at each interest payment date and was amortized to December 31, 1988.

b Prepare journal entries to record the amortization of bond discount and payment of bond interest at September 30, 1989, and also to record the redemption of $2,000,000 of the bonds at this date.

c Prepare a journal entry to record the accrual of interest at December 31, 1989. Include the amortization of bond discount to the year-end.

Problem 16B-4

Comprehensive problem: straight-line amortization

Kent Coal Mines Corporation obtained authorization to issue $8,000,000 of 9%, 10-year bonds, dated May 1, 1989. Interest payment dates were May 1 and November 1. Issuance of the bonds did not take place until July 1, 1989. On this date, the entire bond issue was sold to an underwriter at a price that included the two months' accrued interest. Kent Coal Mines follows the policy of amortizing bond discount or premium by the straight-line method at each interest date as well as for year-end adjusting entries at December 31.

Instructions

a Prepare all journal entries necessary to record the issuance of the bonds and bond interest expense during 1989, assuming that the sales price of the bonds on July 1 was $8,415,000 including accrued interest.

b Assume that the sales price of the bonds on July 1 had been $7,907,600, including accrued interest. Prepare journal entries for 1989 parallel to those in part **a** above.

c Show the proper balance sheet presentation of the liability for bonds payable (including accrued interest) in the balance sheet prepared at December 31, *1994* assuming that the original sales price of the bonds (including accrued interest) had been:
(1) $8,415,000, as described in part **a**
(2) $7,907,600, as described in part **b**

Problem 16B-5

Effective-interest method: bonds issued at discount

Arcades R Fun maintains its accounts on a calendar-year basis. On June 30, 1989, the company issued $6,000,000 face value of 7.6% bonds at a price of 97¼, resulting in an effective rate of interest of 8%. Semiannual interest payment dates are June 30 and December 31. Bond discount is amortized by the effective-interest method. The bonds mature on June 30, 1999.

Instructions

a Prepare the required journal entries on:
(1) June 30, 1989, to record the sale of the bonds.
(2) December 31, 1989, to pay interest and amortize the discount using the effective-interest method.

(3) June 30, 1999, to pay interest, amortize the discount, and retire the bonds. Assume that at the beginning of this last interest period, the carrying value of the bonds is $5,988,462. (Use a separate journal entry to show the retirement of the bonds.)

b Show how the accounts, Bonds Payable and Discount on Bonds Payable, should appear on the balance sheet at December 31, 1989.

Problem 16B-6
Preparing and using an amortization table

On December 31, 1989, Roadside Inns sold an $8,000,000, 9½%, 12-year bond issue to an underwriter at a price of 103½. This price results in an effective annual interest rate of 9%. The bonds were dated December 31, and the interest payment dates were June 30 and December 31. Roadside Inns follows a policy of amortizing the bond premium by the effective-interest method at each semiannual payment date.

Instructions

a Prepare an amortization table for the first two years (four interest periods) of the life of this bond issue. Round all amounts to the nearest dollar and use the following column headings:

(A) SIX-MONTH INTEREST PERIOD	(B) INTEREST PAID SEMI-ANNUALLY ($8,000,000 × 4³/₄%)	(C) EFFECTIVE SEMI-ANNUAL INTEREST EXPENSE (CARRYING VALUE × 4¹/₂%)	(C) PREMIUM AMORTI-ZATION (A − B)	(D) BOND PREMIUM BALANCE	(E) CARRYING VALUE OF BONDS, END OF PERIOD ($8,000,000 + D)

b Using the information in your amortization table, prepare all journal entries necessary to record the bond issue on December, 1989, and the bond interest expense during 1990.

c Show the proper balance sheet presentation of the liability for bonds payable at December 31, 1991.

Problem 16B-7
Effective-interest method: bonds issued at discount

On November 1, 1989, Action Computers issued $11,900,000 face value of 8½% 10-year bonds with interest dates of May 1 and November 1. The bonds were purchased by an underwriter for $11,500,000, resulting in an effective interest rate to Action Computers of 9%. Company policy calls for amortizing bond discount by the effective-interest method at each interest payment date as well as for year-end adjustment of the accounts. The accounting records are maintained on a calendar-year basis.

Instructions

a Prepare the journal entries required to:
  (1) Record the sale of the bonds on November 1, 1989.
  (2) Adjust the accounts at December 31, 1989, for accrued bond interest and amortization of discount. (Use one compound entry.)
  (3) Record the semiannual payment of bond interest on May 1, 1990, and amortize the bond discount. (Use one compound entry.)

b State the amounts to be reported on the financial statements at the end of 1989 for:
  (1) Bonds payable (face amount)
  (2) Unamortized discount on bonds payable
  (3) Net amount of liability for bonds payable
  (4) Interest expense for 1989

BUSINESS DECISION CASES

Case 16-1
Financing alternatives

Marvelous Co. Ltd. currently earns $2,000,000 a year before income taxes and has 400,000 shares of capital stock outstanding. The company is planning to expand its plant facilities at a cost of $6,000,000. Management estimates that this expansion will increase annual income before income taxes by 24% of the cost of the new facilities. The company pays income taxes equal to 40% of its income before income taxes.

Two proposals are under consideration for raising the $6,000,000 for the new plant facilities:

Stock Financing   Issue 200,000 shares of capital stock at a price of $30 per share.

Bond Financing   Borrow $6,000,000 on a 20-year bond issue with interest at 14%.

Instructions

a Prepare a schedule showing the expected earnings per share of capital stock during the first year of operations following the completion of the $6,000,000 expansion under each of the two proposed means of financing.

b Evaluate the two proposed means of financing from the viewpoint of a major shareholder of Marvelous Co. Ltd.

Case 16-2
Contingent losses

Discuss each of the following situations, indicating whether the situation is a contingent loss that should be recorded or disclosed in the financial statements of Aztec Airlines. If the situation is not a contingent loss, explain how (if at all) it should be reported in the company's financial statements. (Assume that all dollar amounts are material.)

a Aztec estimates that $100,000 of its accounts receivable will prove to be uncollectible.

b The company's president is in poor heath and has previously suffered two heart attacks.

c As with any airline, Aztec faces the risk that a future airplane crash could cause considerable loss.

d Due to a mathematical error, depreciation expense was understated by $200,000 in last year's income statement.

e Aztec is being sued for $2 million for failing to adequately provide for passengers whose reservations were cancelled as a result of the airline overbooking certain flights. This suit will not be resolved for a year or more.

APPLICATIONS OF PRESENT VALUE

Several preceding chapters have included brief references to the concept of present value in discussions of the valuation of certain assets and liabilities. The purpose of this appendix is to discuss this concept more fully and also to demonstrate the use of present value tables as an aid to making present value computations. In addition, the appendix summarizes in one location the various applications of the present value concept that have been discussed throughout the book. These applications include the valuation of long-term notes receivable and payable, estimation of goodwill, computation of bond prices, and accounting for capital lease transactions.

After studying this appendix you should be able to meet these Learning Objectives:

1 **Explain the concept of present value.**

2 **Identify the three factors that affect the present value of a future amount.**

3 **Compute the present value of a future amount and of an annuity using present value tables.**

4 **Discuss accounting applications of the present value concept.**

---

1 Explain the concept of present value.

The concept of present value

The concept of present value has many applications in accounting, but it is most easily explained in the context of evaluating investment opportunities. In this context, the present value of an expected future cash receipt is the amount that a knowledgeable investor would pay *today* for the right to receive that future amount. The present value is always *less* than the future amount, because the investor will expect to earn a return on the investment. The amount by which the future cash receipt exceeds its present value represents the investor's profit; in short, this difference may be regarded as *interest revenue* included in the future amount.

2   Identify the three factors that affect the present value of a future amount.

The present value of a particular investment opportunity depends upon three factors: (1) the expected dollar amount to be received in the future, (2) the length of time until the future amount will be received, and (3) the rate of return (called the *discount rate*) required by the investor. The process of determining the present value of a future cash receipt or payment is called *discounting* the future amount.

To illustrate the present value concept, assume that a specific investment is expected to result in a $1,000 cash receipt at the end of one year. An investor requiring a 10% annual rate of return would be willing to pay $909 today (computed as $1,000 ÷ 1.10) for the right to receive this future amount. This computation may be verified as follows (amounts rounded to the nearest dollar):

Amount to be invested (present value)	$ 909
Required return on investment ($909 × 10%)	91
Amount to be received in one year (future value)	$1,000

If the $1,000 is to be received *two years* in the future, the investor would pay only $826 for the investment today [($1,000 ÷ 1.10) ÷ 1.10]. This computation may be verified as follows (amounts rounded to the nearest dollar):

Amount to be invested (present value)	$ 826
Required return on investment in first year ($826 × 10%)	83
Amount invested after one year	$909
Required return on investment in second year ($909 × 10%)	91
Amount to be received in two years (future value)	$1,000

The amount that our investor would pay today, $826, is the *present value* of $1,000 to be received two years later, discounted at an annual rate of 10%. The $174 difference between the $826 present value and the $1,000 future amount may be regarded as the return (interest revenue) to be earned by the investor over the two-year period.

Present value tables

Although we can compute the present value of future amounts by a series of divisions as in the preceding illustration, a more convenient method is available. We can use a *table of present values* to find the present value of $1 at a specified discount rate and then multiply that value by the future amount. For example, in Table 1 on the next page, the present value of $1 to be received in two years, discounted at an annual rate of 10%, is $0.826. If we multiply .826 by the expected future cash receipt of $1,000, we get an answer of $826, the same amount produced by the series of divisions in our previous illustration.

Selecting an appropriate discount rate

The *discount rate* may be viewed as the investor's required rate of return. All investments involve some degree of risk that actual future cash flows may turn out to be less than expected. Investors usually will expect a rate of return that justifies taking this risk. Under today's market conditions, investors require annual returns of between 6% and 9% on low-risk investments, such as government bonds and term deposits. For relatively high-risk investments, such as the introduction of a new product line, investors may expect to earn an annual return of perhaps 15% or more.

TABLE 1
Present Values of $1 Due in n Periods*

NUMBER OF PERIODS (n)	DISCOUNT RATE							
	1%	1½%	5%	6%	10%	12%	15%	20%
1	.990	.985	.952	.943	.909	.893	.870	.833
2	.980	.971	.907	.890	.826	.797	.756	.694
3	.971	.956	.864	.840	.751	.712	.658	.579
4	.961	.942	.823	.792	.683	.636	.572	.482
5	.951	.928	.784	.747	.621	.567	.497	.402
6	.942	.915	.746	.705	.564	.507	.432	.335
7	.933	.901	.711	.665	.513	.452	.376	.279
8	.923	.888	.677	.627	.467	.404	.327	.233
9	.914	.875	.645	.592	.424	.361	.284	.194
10	.905	.862	.614	.558	.386	.322	.247	.162
20	.820	.742	.377	.312	.149	.104	.061	.026
24	.788	.700	.310	.247	.102	.066	.035	.013

*The present value of $1 is computed by the formula $p = 1/(1 + i)^n$, where p is the present value of $1, i is the discount rate, and n is the number of periods until the future cash flow will occur. Amounts in this table have been rounded to three decimal places and are shown for a limited number of periods and discount rates.

In addition to the amount of risk involved, the "appropriate" discount rate for determining the present value of a specific investment depends upon the investor's cost of capital and the returns available from other investment opportunities. When a higher discount rate is used, the resulting present value will be lower and the investor, therefore, will be interested in the investment only at a lower price.

Discounting annual cash flows

3 Compute the present value of a future amount and of an annuity using present value tables.

Let us now assume that an investment is expected to produce an annual net cash flow of $10,000 for each of the next three years. If Camino Company expects a 12% return on this type of investment, it may compute the present value of these cash flows as follows:

YEAR	EXPECTED NET CASH FLOW	×	PRESENT VALUE OF $1 DISCOUNTED AT 12%	=	PRESENT VALUE OF NET CASH FLOWS
1	$10,000		.893		$ 8,930
2	10,000		.797		7,970
3	10,000		.712		7,120
Total present value of the investment					$24,020

This analysis indicates that the present value of the expected net cash flows from the investment, discounted at an annual rate of 12%, amounts to $24,020. This is the maximum amount that Camino Company could afford to pay for this investment and still expect to earn the 12% required rate of return.

In the preceding schedule, we multiplied each of the expected annual cash flows by the present value of $1 in the appropriate future period, discounted at 12% per year. The present values of the annual cash flows were then added to determine the total present value of the investment. Separately discounting each annual cash flow to its present value is necessary only when the cash flows vary in amount from one year to the next. Since the annual cash flows in our example are *uniform in amount,* there are two easier ways to compute the total present value.

One way is to add the three decimal figures representing the present value of $1 in the successive years (.893 + .797 + .712) and then to multiply this total (2.402) by the $10,000 annual cash flow. This approach produces the same result ($10,000 × 2.402 = $24,020) we obtained by determining the present value of each year's cash flow separately and adding the results.

An even easier approach to determining the present value of uniform annual cash flows is to refer to an *annuity table,* which shows the present value of *$1 to be received periodically* for a given number of periods. An annuity table is shown as follows:

TABLE 2
Present Value of $1 to Be Received Periodically for n Periods

NUMBER OF PERIODS (n)	DISCOUNT RATE							
	1%	1½%	5%	6%	10%	12%	15%	20%
1	0.990	0.985	0.952	0.943	0.909	0.893	0.870	0.833
2	1.970	1.956	1.859	1.833	1.736	1.690	1.626	1.528
3	2.941	2.912	2.723	2.673	2.487	2.402	2.283	2.106
4	3.902	3.854	3.546	3.465	3.170	3.037	2.855	2.589
5	4.853	4.783	4.329	4.212	3.791	3.605	3.352	2.991
6	5.795	5.697	5.076	4.917	4.355	4.111	3.784	3.326
7	6.728	6.598	5.786	5.582	4.868	4.564	4.160	3.605
8	7.652	7.486	6.463	6.210	5.335	4.968	4.487	3.837
9	8.566	8.361	7.108	6.802	5.759	5.328	4.772	4.031
10	9.471	9.222	7.722	7.360	6.145	5.650	5.019	4.192
20	18.046	17.169	12.462	11.470	8.514	7.469	6.259	4.870
24	21.243	20.030	13.799	12.550	8.985	7.784	6.434	4.937

Note that the present value of $1 to be received periodically (annually) for three years, discounted at 12% per year, is 2.402. Thus, $10,000 received annually for three years, discounted at 12%, is $24,020 ($10,000 × 2.402).

Discount periods of less than one year

The interval between regular periodic cash flows is termed the **discount period.** I our preceding examples we have assumed annual cash flows and, therefore, discou periods of one year. Often a note or a contract may call for cash payments on a mor frequent basis, such as monthly, quarterly, or semiannually. The illustrated preser value tables can be used with discount periods of any length, **but the discount ra must relate to the time interval of the discount period.** Thus, if we use the annuit table to find the present value of a series of monthly cash payments, the discount ra must be expressed as a monthly interest rate.

To illustrate, assume that StyleMart purchases merchandise from Western Fashions issuing in exchange a $9,600 note payable to be paid in 24 monthly instalments c $400 each. As discussed in earlier chapters, both companies should record this trans action at the present value of the note. If a reasonable **annual** interest rate for thi type of note is 12%, we should discount the monthly cash payments at the **monthl** rate of 1%. The annuity table shows the present value of $1 to be received (or paid for 24 monthly periods, discounted at 1% per month, is 21.243. Thus, the preser value of the instalment note issued by StyleMart is $8,497 ($400 × 21.243, rounde to the nearest dollar).

Accounting applications of the present value concept

Accounting applications of the concept of present value have been discussed appropriate points throughout this textbook. We will now demonstrate these applica tions with examples that make use of our present value tables.

4 Discuss accounting applications of the present value concept.

Valuation of long-term notes receivable and payable (Chapters 8 and 11)   When long-term note receivable or payable does not bear a realistic stated rate of interes a portion of the face amount of the note should be regarded as representing an intere: charge. The amount of this interest charge can be determined by discounting th note to its present value using as a discount rate a realistic rate of interest.

To illustrate, consider our preceding example in which StyleMart purchases mer chandise from Western Fashions by issuing an instalment note payable with a fac amount of $9,600 and no stated rate of interest. The present value of this note discounted at the realistic market interest rate of 1% per month, was $8,497. Th difference between the $9,600 face amount of the note and its present value c $8,497 is $1,103, which represents the interest charge included in the face amount StyleMart should use the present value of the note in determining the cost of th merchandise and the amount of the related net liability, as shown below:

Purchases	8,497	
Discount on Notes Payable	1,103	
Notes Payable		9,60

Purchased merchandise by issuing a 24-month instalment
note payable with a 1% monthly interest charge included in
the face amount.

Assuming that StyleMart uses the effective-interest method to amortize the discount on the note, the entry to record the first monthly payment and the related interest expense is as follows:

```
Notes Payable . . . . . . . . . . . . . . . . . . . . . . . . . . . . . . . . . . . . . . . . . .   400
Interest Expense . . . . . . . . . . . . . . . . . . . . . . . . . . . . . . . . . . . . . . . .    85
   Discount on Notes Payable . . . . . . . . . . . . . . . . . . . . . . . . . . . .              85
   Cash . . . . . . . . . . . . . . . . . . . . . . . . . . . . . . . . . . . . . . . . . . . . . .              400
To record first monthly payment on instalment note payable and
recognize one month's interest expense ($8,497 × 1%, rounded
to nearest dollar).
```

Estimating the value of goodwill (Chapter 10)   The asset goodwill may be defined as the present value of expected future earnings in excess of the normal return on net identifiable assets. One method of estimating goodwill is to estimate the annual amounts by which earnings are expected to exceed a normal return and then to discount these amounts to their present value.

For example, assume that Lorna Liew is negotiating to purchase a small but very successful business. In addition to paying the fair market value of the company's net identifiable assets, Liew is willing to pay an appropriate amount for goodwill. She believes that the business will probably earn at least $40,000 in excess of "normal earnings" in each of the next five years. If Liew requires a 20% annual return on purchased goodwill, she would be willing to pay $119,640 for this expected five-year $40,000 annuity, computed as follows: $40,000 × 2.991 (from Table 2) = $119,640.

Market prices of bonds (Chapter 16)   The market price of bonds may be regarded as the *present value* to bondholders of the future principal and interest payments. To illustrate, assume that a corporation issues $1,000,000 face value of 9%, 10-year bonds when the going market rate of interest is 10%. Since bond interest is paid semiannually, we must use 20 *semiannual* periods as the life of the bond issue and a 5% *semiannual* market rate of interest in our present value calculations. The expected issuance price of this bond issue may be computed as follows:

```
Present value of future principal payments:
   $1,000,000 due after 20 semiannual periods, discounted at
   5% per period: $1,000,000 × .377 (from Table 1, page 686) . . . . . . . .   $377,000
Present value of future interest payments:
   45,000 per period ($1,000,000 × 9% × ½) for 20 semiannual
   periods, discounted at 5%: $45,000 × 12.462 (from Table 2,
   page 687) . . . . . . . . . . . . . . . . . . . . . . . . . . . . . . . . . . . . . . . . . . .    560,790
Expected issuance price of bond issue* . . . . . . . . . . . . . . . . . . . . . . .   $937,790
```

*The terms of this bond issue correspond with those of the bond issue illustrated in the amortization table on page 663 in Chapter 16. In the amortization table, however, the issuance price of the bonds is $937,689, or $101 less than indicated by our computations above. The difference results from our rounding the present value of $1 to only three decimal places. Rounding to three decimal places may cause an error of up to $500 per $1 million.

Capital leases (Chapter 16)   A capital lease is regarded as a sale of the leased asset by the lessor to the lessee. At the date of this sale, the lessor recognizes sales revenue equal to the *present value* of the future lease payments receivable, discounted at a realistic rate of interest. The lessee also uses the present value of the future payments to determine the cost of the leased asset and the valuation of the related liability.

To illustrate, assume that on December 1, Kelly Grading Co. Ltd. enters into a capital lease contract to finance the purchase of a bulldozer from Midwest Tractor Sales. The terms of the lease call for 24 monthly payments of $7,000 each, beginning on December 31. These lease payments include an interest charge of 1¹/₂% per month. At the end of the 24-month lease, title to the bulldozer will pass to Kelly Grading.

The annuity table on page 687 shows that the present value of $1 to be received monthly for 24 months, discounted at 1¹/₂% per month, is 20.030. therefore, the present value of the 24 future lease payments is $7,000 × 20.030, or $140,210. Kelly Grading (the lessee) should use this present value in determining the cost of the bulldozer and the amount of the related liability, as shown in the following entry:

ENTRY BY LESSEE

Leased Equipment 140,210
    Lease Payment Obligation 140,210
To record acquisition of bulldozer from Midwest Tractor
Sales on a capital lease. Lease terms call for 24 monthly
payments of $7,000, which include a 1¹/₂% monthly
interest charge.

Note that the cost assigned to the leased equipment is only $140,210, even though Kelly Grading must actually pay $168,000 ($7,000 × 24 payments) over the life of the lease. The difference between these two amounts, $27,790, will be recognized by Kelly Grading as interest expense over the next 24 months.

Midwest Tractor Sales (the lessor) should also use the present value of the future lease payments in determining the sales price of the bulldozer and the amount of the related receivable. Assuming that the bulldozer was carried in the perpetual inventory records at a cost of $110,000, the entry to record the sale is:

ENTRY BY LESSOR

Lease Payments Receivable (net) 140,210
Cost of Goods Sold 110,000
    Inventory 110,000
    Sales 140,210
Financed sale of bulldozer to Kelly Grading Co. Ltd. using
a direct financing (capital) lease. Terms call for 24 monthly
payments of $7,000 including a 1¹/₂% monthly interest
charge. Gross amount of the receivable is $168,000, of
which $27,790 is unearned interest.

PROBLEMS

Problem 1
Using present value tables

Use Tables 1 and 2 in this appendix to determine the present value of the following cash flows:

a $10,000 to be paid annually for seven years, discounted at an annual rate of 12%.

b $6,300 to be received today, assuming that money can be invested to earn 15% annually.

c $600 to be paid monthly for 24 months, with an additional "balloon payment" of $15,000 due at the end of the twenty-fourth month, discounted at a monthly interest rate of 1½%.

d $40,000 to be received annually for the first three years, followed by $30,000 to be received annually for the next two years (total of five years in which payments are made), discounted at an annual rate of 15%.

Problem 2
Present value and bond prices

On June 30 of the current year, Rural Gas & Electric Co. Ltd. issued $50,000,000 face value, 11%, 10-year bonds payable, with interest dates of December 31 and June 30. The bonds were issued at a discount, resulting in an effective semiannual interest rate of 6%. The company maintains its accounts on a calendar-year basis and amortizes the bond discount by the effective-interest method.

Instructions

a Compute the issuance price for the bond issue that results in an effective semiannual interest rate of 6%.

b Prepare all journal entries necessary to record the issuance of the bonds and bond interest expense during the current year, assuming that the sales price of the bonds on June 30 was the amount you computed in part **a**.

Problem 3
Valuation of a note payable

On December 1, Showcase Interiors purchased a shipment of furniture from Colonial House by paying $15,000 cash and issuing an instalment note payable in the face amount of $36,000. The note is to be paid in 24 monthly instalments of $1,500 each. Although the note makes no mention of an interest charge, the rate of interest usually charged to Showcase Interiors in such transactions is 1½% per month.

Instructions

a Compute the present value of the note payable, using a discount rate of 1½% per month.

b Prepare the journal entries in the accounts of Showcase Interiors on:
   (1) December 1, to record the purchase of the furniture (debit Purchases).
   (2) December 31, to record the first $1,500 monthly payment on the note and to recognize interest expense for one month by the effective-interest method. (Round interest expense to the nearest dollar.)

c Show how the liability for this note would appear in the balance sheet at December 31. (Assume that the note is classified as a current liability.)

Problem 4
Discounting lease agreements to present value

Metropolitan Transit District (MTD) plans to acquire a large computer system by entering into a long-term lease agreement with the computer manufacturer. The manufacturer will provide the computer system under either of the following lease agreements:

Five-year lease MTD is to pay $2,500,000 at the beginning of the lease (delivery date) and $1,000,000 annually at the end of each of the next five years. At the end of the fifth year, MTD may take title to the system for an additional payment of $3,000,000.

Ten-year lease MTD is to pay $2,000,000 at the beginning of the lease and $900,000 annually at the end of each of the next 10 years. At the end of the tenth year, MTD may take title for an additional payment of $1,300,000.

Under either proposal, MTD will buy the computer at the end of the lease. MTD is a governmental agency that does not seek to earn a profit and is not evaluating alternative investment opportunities. However, MTD does attempt to minimize its costs and it must borrow the money to finance either lease agreement at an annual interest rate of 12%.

Instructions   **a** Determine which lease proposal results in the lower cost for the computer system when the future cash outlays are discounted at an annual interest rate of 12%.

b Prepare a journal entry to record the acquisition of the computer system under the lease agreement selected in part **a**. This journal entry will include the initial cash payment to the computer manufacturer required at the beginning of the lease.

Problem 5
Valuation of a note receivable with unrealistically low interest

On December 31, Richland Farms sold a tract of land, which had cost $310,000, to Skyline Developers in exchange for $50,000 cash and a five-year, 4%, note receivable for $300,000. Interest on the note is payable annually, and the principal amount is due in five years. The accountant for Richland Farms did not notice the unrealistically low interest rate on the note and made the following entry on December 31 to record this sale:

Cash	50,000	
Notes Receivable	300,000	
Land		310,000
Gain on Sale of Land		40,000
Sold land to Skyline Developers in exchange for cash and a five-year note with interest due annually.		

Instructions   **a** Compute the present value of the note receivable from Skyline Developers at the date of sale, assuming that a realistic rate of interest for this transaction is 15%.

b Prepare the journal entry on December 31 to record the sale of the land correctly. Show supporting computations for (1) the gain or loss on the sale, and (2) the discount on the note receivable.

c Explain what effects the error made by Richland Farms' accountant will have upon (1) the net income in the year of the sale, and (2) the combined net income of the next five years. Ignore income taxes.

INVESTMENTS IN CORPORATE SECURITIES

CHAPTER PREVIEW

In this chapter, we discuss investments in corporate securities (stocks and bonds) from the viewpoint of the investor. We first focus upon short-term investments in marketable securities — that is, highly liquid investments made primarily for the purpose of earning dividend or interest revenue. Next, we discuss long-term investments in common stock made for the purpose of exercising significant influence or control over the issuing corporation. We illustrate the equity method of accounting for these investments and explain how a parent company and its subsidiaries function as one economic entity. The chapter concludes with a discussion of consolidated financial statements.

After studying this chapter you should be able to meet these Learning Objectives:

1 Account for short-term investments in stocks and bonds.

2 Account for an investment in common stock by the equity method.

3 Explain how a parent company "controls" its subsidiaries.

4 Describe the distinctive feature of consolidated financial statements.

5 Explain why intercompany transactions must be eliminated as a step in preparing consolidated financial statements.

6 Prepare a consolidated balance sheet.

Securities exchanges

The stocks and bonds of most large corporations are listed on organized securities exchanges, such as the *Toronto Stock Exchange.* An investor may either buy or sell these listed securities through any brokerage house that is a member of the exchange. The brokerage company represents the investor and negotiates with other exchange members to buy or to sell the securities on behalf of its customer. The price at which the broker negotiates the transaction represents the current market value of the security and is immediately printed on the stock exchange ticker tape for reference by other investors. The financial pages of many newspapers report on a daily basis the highest, lowest, and closing (last) prices at which each listed security is exchanged.

At the time of issuance of stocks or bonds, the transaction is between the investor and the issuing corporation. The great daily volume of transactions in securities, however, consists of the sale of stocks and bonds by investors to other investors. On the Toronto Stock Exchange alone, more than 20 million shares of stock are exchanged almost every day. The stocks and bonds of many smaller companies are not listed on an organized securities exchange, but brokerage firms also arrange for the purchase and sale of these unlisted or *over-the-counter* securities.

Quoted market prices   The market price of stocks is quoted in terms of dollars per share. As illustrated in Chapter 16, corporate bond prices are quoted as a *percentage* of the bond's maturity value, which generally is $1,000. Thus, a bond quoted at 87 has a market value of $870 ($1,000 × 87%).

Listed corporations report to a million owners   When a corporation invites the public to purchase its stocks and bonds, it accepts an obligation to keep the public informed on its financial condition and the profitability of operations. This obligation of disclosure includes public distribution of financial statements. The provincial securities commissions are the government agencies responsible for seeing that corporations make adequate disclosure of their affairs so that investors have a basis for intelligent investment decisions. The flow of corporate accounting data distributed through newspapers and financial advisory services to millions of investors is a vital force in the functioning of our economy; in fact, the successful working of a profit-motivated economy rests upon the quality and dependability of the accounting information being reported.

Listed corporations are audited by public accountants   Corporations with securities listed on organized stock exchanges are required to have regular audits by independent public accountants. The financial statements distributed each year to shareholders are accompanied by a report by a firm of public accountants indicating that an audit has been made and expressing an opinion as to the fairness of the company's financial statements. It is the *independent status* of the public accounting firm that enables investors to place confidence in audited financial statements.

INVESTMENTS IN MARKETABLE SECURITIES

The term *marketable securities* refers primarily to government bonds and the bonds and stocks of large corporations. Because these securities can be quickly sold on securities exchanges, an investment in these securities is almost as liquid an asset as cash itself. In fact, investments in marketable securities are often called "secondary cash reserves." If cash is needed for any operating purpose, these securities may quickly be converted into cash; in the meantime, investments in marketable securities are preferable to cash because of the interest or dividend revenue that they produce. Most companies watch their cash balances very carefully and invest any cash not needed for current operations in high-grade marketable securities.

When an investor owns several different marketable securities, the group of securities is termed an investment *portfolio.* In deciding upon the securities to include in the portfolio, the investor seeks to maximize return while minimizing risk. Risk often can be reduced by *diversification,* that is, by including in the portfolio a variety of securities, especially securities of companies in different industries.

Marketable securities as current assets

A recent balance sheet of Federal Industries Ltd. shows the following items listed first in the current asset section.

Current assets:
Cash and short-term deposits . . . . $ 2,134,000
Marketable securities   50,289,000

The large investment by Federal Industries in marketable securities is in no way unusual; many corporations have large holdings of marketable securities. In the balance sheet, marketable securities are usually listed immediately after the asset Cash, because they are so liquid as to be almost the equivalent of cash.

A company may separate its marketable securities into two groups: (1) temporary investments classified as current assets, and (2) long-term investments classified as non-current assets. Those marketable securities that management intends to hold on a long-term basis may be listed in the balance sheet just below the current asset section under the caption Long-Term Investments. In most cases, however, management stands ready to sell marketable securities whenever company needs or stock market trends make such action advantageous. Consequently, marketable securities generally are viewed as current assets.

1 Account for short-term investments in stocks and bonds.

Accounting for investments in marketable securities

When securities are purchased, an account entitled Marketable Securities is debited for the entire purchase price, including any commissions to stockbrokers. A subsidiary ledger must also be maintained that shows for each security owned the acquisition date, total cost, number of shares (or bonds) owned, and cost per share (or bond). This subsidiary ledger provides the information necessary to determine the amount of gain or loss when an investment in a particular stock or bond is sold.

The principal distinction between the recording of an investment in bonds and an investment in stocks is that interest on bonds accrues from day to day. When bonds are purchased between interest dates, the purchaser pays the quoted market price for the bond *plus* the interest accrued since the last interest payment date. By this arrangement the new owner becomes entitled to receive in full the next semiannual interest payment. An account called Bond Interest Receivable should be debited for the amount of interest purchased. Dividends on stock, however, *do not accrue* and the entire purchase price paid by the investor in stocks is recorded in the Marketable Securities account.

Income on investments in bonds   To illustrate the accounting entries for an investment in bonds, assume that on August 1 an investor purchases ten 9%, $1,000 bonds that pay interest on June 1 and December 1. The investor buys the bonds on August 1 at a price of $98, plus a brokerage commission of $50 and two months' accrued interest of $150 ($10,000 × 9% × $^2/_{12}$ = $150). The entry on August 1 to record this investment is:

SEPARATE ACCOUNT FOR ACCRUED BOND INTEREST PURCHASED

Marketable Securities	9,850	
Bond Interest Receivable	150	
Cash		10,000

Purchased ten 9% bonds of Rider Co. Ltd. at 98 plus a brokerage commission of $50 and two months' accrued interest.

On December 1, the semiannual interest payment date, the investor will receive an interest cheque for $450, which will be recorded as follows:

NOTE PORTION OF INTEREST CHEQUE EARNED

Cash	450	
Bond Interest Receivable		150
Bond Interest Revenue		300

Received semiannual interest on Rider Co. Ltd. bonds.

The $300 credit to Bond Interest Revenue represents the amount actually earned during the four months the bonds were owned by the investor (9% × $10,000 × $^4/_{12}$ = $300).

If the investor's accounting records are maintained on a calendar-year basis, the following adjusting entry is required at December 31 to record bond interest earned since December 1:

Bond Interest Receivable	75	
Bond Interest Revenue		75

To accrue one month's interest earned (Dec. 1–Dec. 31) on Rider Co. Ltd. bonds ($10,000 × 9% × $^1/_{12}$ = $75).

Amortization of bond discount or premium from the investor's viewpoint   We have discussed the need for the corporation issuing bonds payable to amortize any bond discount or premium to measure correctly the bond interest expense. But what about the *purchaser* of the bonds? Should an investor in bonds amortize any difference between the cost of the investment and its future maturity value in order to measure investment income correctly? The answer to this question depends upon whether the investor considers the bonds to be a *short-term* or a *long-term* investment.[1]

---

[1] According to *Financial Reporting in Canada*, 17th ed., CICA (Toronto, 1987), p. 85, the term ``short-term investments'' is most widely used.

A short-term investment in bonds generally is carried in the investor's accounting records at *cost,* and a gain or a loss is recognized when the investment is sold. Short-term investments in bonds usually will be sold before the bonds mature and the sales price will be determined by the current state of the bond market. Under these conditions, there is no assurance that amortization of premium or discount would give any more accurate measurement of investment income than would be obtained by carrying the bonds at cost.

When bonds are owned for the long term, however, it becomes more probable that the market price of the investment will move toward the maturity value of the bonds. At the maturity date, of course, the market value will be the maturity value of the bonds. Thus, companies making long-term investments in bonds *should* amortize any difference between the cost of the investment and its maturity value over the life of the bonds. If the effective-interest method of amortization would produce results materially different from those obtained by the straight-line method, the effective-interest method should be used.

Amortization of the difference between cost and maturity value is recorded by direct adjustment to the Marketable Securities account. When a long-term investment in bonds is purchased at a discount, the amortization entries consist of a debit to Marketable Securities and a credit to Interest Revenue. When the bonds are purchased at a premium, amortization is recorded by debiting Interest Revenue and crediting Marketable Securities.

Income on investments in stock   When should a cash dividend be recorded as income to the investor? Should it be the date the dividend is declared, the date of record, the ex-dividend date, or the date the dividend is received? Most investors record cash dividends as income on the date the dividend cheque arrives. The entry to record receipt of a cash dividend consists of a debit to Cash and a credit to Dividend Revenue.

Additional shares of stock received in stock splits or stock dividends *are not income* to the shareholder, and only a *memorandum entry* is used to record the increase in the number of shares owned. The *cost basis per share* is decreased, however, because of the larger number of shares comprising the investment after receiving additional "free" shares from a stock split or a stock dividend. As an example, assume that an investor paid $72 a share for 100 shares of stock, a total cost of $7,200. Later the investor received 20 additional shares as a stock dividend. The cost per share is thereby reduced to $60 a share, computed by dividing the total cost of $7,200 by the 120 shares owned after the 20% stock dividend. The memorandum entry to be made in the general journal would be as follows:

July 10   Memorandum: Received 20 additional shares of Delta Co. Ltd. common stock as a result of 20% stock dividend. Now own 120 shares with a cost basis of $7,200, or $60 per share.

Gains and losses from sale of investments in securities

The sale of an investment in stocks is recorded by debiting Cash for the amount received and crediting the Marketable Securities account for the carrying value of the securities sold. Any difference between the proceeds of the sale and the carrying value of the investment is recorded by a debit to Loss on Sale of Marketable Securities or by a credit to Gain on Sale of Marketable Securities.

At the date of sale of an investment in bonds, any interest accrued since the last interest payment date should be recognized as interest revenue. For example, assume that 10 bonds of the Elk Corporation carried in the accounts of an investor at $9,600 are sold at a price of 94 and accrued interest of $90. The commission on the sale is $50. The following entry should be made:

INVESTMENT IN BONDS
SOLD AT A LOSS

Cash	9,440	
Loss on Sale of Marketable Securities	250	
Marketable Securities		9,600
Bond Interest Revenue		90
Sold 10 bonds of Elk Corporation at 94 and accrued interest of $90 less broker's commission of $50.		

Balance sheet valuation of marketable securities

The market values of securities such as bonds and stocks fluctuate from day to day. An investor who sells an investment in marketable securities at a price above or below cost will recognize a gain or loss on the sale. But what if the investor continues to hold securities after a significant change in their market value? In this case, should any gain or loss be recognized in the financial statements? The answer depends on whether the securities are short-term or long-term investments and whether the change in market value is temporary in nature.

Short-term marketable securities should be shown in the balance sheet at the *lower* of their aggregate cost and market value. The effect of the *lower-of-cost-and-market* (LCM) rule is to recognize losses from drops in market value without recognizing gains from rising prices.

Marketable securities classified as long-term investments are accounted for in the balance sheet by either the cost method or the equity method. The *cost method* is used for long-term *portfolio investments* where the investor is not able to exercise significant influence over the investee. The account title for this type of investment is commonly called Marketable Securities—Long-Term. The *equity method* is used for those long-term investments where *the investor is able to exercise significant influence over the investee.* The common account title for this type of investment is Investment in X Corporation. When there is a decline in the market value of these long-term investments that is other than a temporary decline, these investments should be shown in the balance sheet at their lower market value. Consequently, a lower market value is also used for long-term investments if the decline in market value is not temporary in nature.

Accountants traditionally have applied different criteria in recognizing gains and losses. One of the basic principles in accounting is that gains shall not be recognized until they are *realized,* and the usual test of realization is the sale of the asset in question. Losses, on the other hand, are recognized as soon as objective evidence indicates that a loss has been incurred.

Lower of cost and market (LCM)

In applying the lower-of-cost-and-market rule, the total cost of the marketable securities is compared with their current market value, and the lower of these two amounts is used as the balance sheet valuation. If the market value is below cost, an entry is made to reduce the cost of the marketable securities to current market value and to recognize a *loss* for the amount of the market decline. The write-down of an investment in marketable securities to a market value below cost is an end-of-period adjusting entry and should be based upon market prices at the balance sheet date.

To illustrate the lower-of-cost-and-market adjustment, assume the following facts for the investment of Eagle Corporation at December 31, 1989:

	COST	MARKET VALUE
Common stock of Adams Corporation	$100,000	$106,000
Common stock of Barnes Limited	60,000	52,000
Preferred stock of Parker Industries Limited	200,000	182,000
Other marketable securities	25,000	25,000
Totals	$385,000	$365,000

Since the total market value of the securities in our example is less than their cost to Eagle Corporation, the balance sheet valuation would be the lower amount of $365,000. This downward adjustment of $20,000 means that a loss of $20,000 will be included in the determination of the year's net income. Also, the $365,000 market value becomes the *carrying value* for these securities and is used as the "new cost" for future applications of the lower-of-cost-and-market rule. The balance sheet presentation would be:

Current assets:
  Marketable securities (at the lower of cost and market,
    cost—$385,000) $365,000

The significance of the carrying value deserves an explanation. Since the carrying value is considered to be the "new cost" for the marketable securities, if there is a further decline in market value, this carrying value will be adjusted to the lower market value.[2] However, if there is a recovery in market value, the recovery is not recognized because the market value is higher than the carrying value even though it is still lower than the original cost. For example, if the marketable securities of Eagle Corporation were held until December 31, 1990, and the market value were $380,000 (still $5,000 below the original cost of $385,000), these securities would be stated in the balance sheet at the carrying value of $365,000 because it is lower than the current market value of $380,000. Consequently, the recovery in market value of $15,000 was not recognized. This practice of not recognizing the recovery in the decline of market value below cost lacks logical support.

In the United States, the FASB recommended that for marketable equity securities such as common stock the recovery in the decline of market value below cost should

---

[2] CICA, *CICA Handbook*, (Toronto), paragraph 3010.06.

be recognized. The decline and recovery in market value are considered as **unrealized loss** and **unrealized gain**, so as to distinguish them from a loss or a gain by an actual sale of securities. Based on the Eagle Corporation example, the $20,000 decline in market value would be recorded as follows:

```
1989
Dec. 31   Unrealized Loss on Marketable Securities . . . . . . . . . .   20,000
                Valuation Allowance for Marketable Securities . . .              20,000
          To reduce the cost of the investment in marketable
          securities to the lower of cost and market.
```

The Valuation Allowance for Marketable Securities is a **contra-asset** account or **valuation** account. In the balance sheet, this valuation account is offset against the asset Marketable Securities in the same manner as the Allowance for Doubtful Accounts is offset against Accounts Receivable. The following partial balance sheet illustrates the use of the Valuation Allowance for Marketable Securities:

```
Current assets:
   Marketable securities: . . . . . . . . . . . . . . . . . . . . . . . . . . . . .   $385,000
   Less: Valuation allowance for marketable securities . . . . . .     20,000   365,000
```

At the end of every period, the balance of the valuation account is adjusted so that marketable equity securities will be shown in the balance sheet at the lower of cost and current market value. If the valuation allowance must be increased because of further declines in market value, the adjusting entry will recognize an additional unrealized loss. On the other hand, if market prices have gone up since the last balance sheet date, the adjusting entry will reduce or eliminate the valuation allowance and recognize an **unrealized gain.**

To illustrate the adjustment of the valuation account, let us assume that by the end of 1990 the market value of Eagle Corporation's investment has **increased** to an amount greater than cost. Since market value is no longer below cost, the valuation allowance, which has a credit balance of $20,000, is no longer needed. Thus, the following entry would be made to eliminate the balance of the valuation allowance:

UNREALIZED GAIN
CANNOT EXCEED THE
FORMER BALANCE OF THE
VALUATION ACCOUNT

```
1990
Dec. 31   Valuation Allowance for Marketable Securities . . . . . . .   20,000
                Unrealized Gain on Marketable Securities . . . . . . .           20,000
          To increase the carrying value of marketable
          securities to original cost following recovery
          of market value.
```

Note that the amount of unrealized gain recognized is limited to the amount in the valuation account. **Increases in market value above cost are not recognized in the accounting records.** In brief, when marketable securities have been written down to the lower of cost and market, they can be written back up only **to original cost** if the market prices recover.

Because the valuation allowance is based upon a comparison of **total** cost and market value, the allowance cannot be directly associated with individual investments.

The valuation allowance reduces the carrying value of the total investment but does not affect the individual carrying values of the investments. Lower-of-cost-and-market adjustments, therefore, have *no effect* upon the gain or loss recognized when an investment is sold. When specific securities are sold, the gain or loss realized from the sale is determined by comparing the *cost* of the securities (without regard to lower-of-cost-and-market adjustments) to their selling price.[3]

Presentation of marketable securities in financial statements

Gains and losses from the decline in market value of marketable investments or on the sale of marketable investments, as well as interest and dividend revenue, are types of nonoperating income. These items should be specifically identified in the income statement and shown after the determination of operating income.

Those marketable securities classified as current assets should be presented in the balance sheet at the lower of cost and market; those classified as long-term investments should be presented in the balance sheet at cost, unless the decline in market value is permanent, in which case the lower of cost and market should be used.

INVESTMENTS FOR PURPOSES OF SIGNIFICANT INFLUENCE OR CONTROL

An investor may acquire enough of a company's common stock to *significantly influence or control* that company's activities through the voting rights of the shares owned. Such large holdings of common stock create an important business relationship between the investor and the issuing company (called the *investee*). Since investments of this type cannot be sold without disrupting this relationship, they are not included in the marketable securities as current assets. These investments are shown in the balance sheet under the caption Long-Term Investments, which follows the current asset section.

If an investor is able to exercise significant influence over the investee's management, dividends paid by the investee may no longer be a good measure of the investor's income from the investment. This is because the investor may influence the investee's dividend policy. In such cases, dividends paid by the investee are likely to reflect the *investor's* cash needs and other considerations, rather than the profitability of the investment.

For example, assume that Sigma Corporation owns all the common stock of Davis Limited. For three years Davis Limited is very profitable but pays no dividends, because Sigma Corporation has no need for additional cash. In the fourth year, Davis Limited pays a large cash dividend to Sigma Corporation despite operating at a loss for that year. Clearly, it would be misleading for Sigma Corporation to report no investment income while the company it owns is operating profitably, and then to show large investment income in a year when Davis Limited incurred a net loss.

---

[3] The reader may notice that a decline in the market value of securities owned could be reported in the income statement on two separate occasions: first, as an unrealized loss in the period in which the price decline occurs; and second, as a realized loss in the period in which the securities are sold. However, after securities with market values below cost have been sold, the valuation allowance may be reduced or eliminated. The entry to reduce the valuation allowance involves the recognition of an unrealized gain that offsets the unrealized losses reported in earlier periods.

The investor does not have to own 30% or 40% of the common stock of the investee to exercise a significant degree of influence. An investor with much less than 30% or 40% of the voting stock may have significant influence, since the remaining shares are not likely to vote as an organized block. In the absence of other evidence (such as another large shareholder), ownership of *20% or more* of the investee's common stock is viewed as giving the investor significant influence over the investee's policies and operations. In such cases, the investor should account for the investment by using the *equity method.*[4]

The equity method

2   Account for an investment in common stock by the equity method.

When the equity method is used, an investment in common stock is first recorded at cost but later is adjusted each year for changes in the shareholders' equity in the investee. As the investee earns net income, the shareholders' equity in the company increases. An investor using the equity method recognizes its *proportionate share of the investee's net income* as an increase in the carrying value of its investment. A proportionate share of a net loss reported by the investee is recognized as a decrease in the investment.

When the investee pays dividends, the shareholders' equity in the company is reduced. The investor, therefore, treats dividends received from the investee as a conversion of the investment into cash, thus reducing the carrying value of the investment. In effect, the equity method causes the carrying value of the investment to rise and fall with changes in the book value of the shares.

Illustration of the equity method   Assume that Cove Corporation purchases 25% of the common stock of Bay Limited for $200,000, which corresponds to the underlying book value. During the following year, Bay Limited earns net income of $120,000 and pays dividends of $80,000. Cove Corporation would account for its investment as follows:

Investment in Bay Limited	200,000	
Cash		200,000
To record acquisition of 25% of the common stock of Bay Limited.		
Investment in Bay Limited	30,000	
Investment Income		30,000
To increase the investment for 25% share of net income earned by Bay Limited (25% × $120,000).		
Cash	20,000	
Investment in Bay Limited		20,000
To reduce investment for dividends received from Bay Limited (25% × $80,000).		

The net result of these entries by Cove Corporation is to increase the carrying value of the investment in Bay Limited account by $10,000. This corresponds

[4] CICA, *CICA Handbook* (Toronto), paragraph 3050.23.

to 25% of the increase reported by Bay Limited's retained earnings during the period [25% × ($120,000 − $80,000) = $10,000].

In this illustration of the equity method, we have made several simplifying assumptions: (1) Cove Corporation purchased the stock of Bay Limited at a price equal to the underlying book value; (2) Bay Limited had issued common stock only and the number of shares outstanding did not change during the year; and (3) there were no intercompany transactions between Cove Corporation and Bay Limited. If we were to change any of these assumptions, the computations in applying the equity method would become more complicated. Application of the equity method in more complex situations is discussed in intermediate and advanced accounting courses.

Parent and subsidiary companies

3 Explain how a parent company "controls" its subsidiaries.

A corporation that owns *all or a majority* of another corporation's capital stock is called a *parent* company, and the corporation that is wholly owned or majority-held is called a *subsidiary.*[5] Through the voting rights of the owned shares, the parent company can elect the board of directors of the subsidiary company and thereby control the subsidiary's resources and activities. In effect, the *affiliated companies* (the parent and its subsidiaries) function as a *single economic unit* controlled by the directors of the parent company. This relationship is illustrated below.

THREE CORPORATIONS BUT ONE BUSINESS ENTITY

**PARENT COMPANY
AND TWO SUBSIDIARIES**

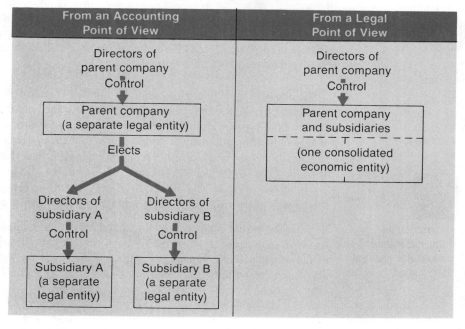

[5] Ownership of a majority of a company's voting stock means holding at least 50% plus one share.

For simplicity, our illustration shows a parent company with only two subsidiaries. It is not unusual, however, for a parent company to own and control a dozen or more subsidiaries.

There are a number of economic, legal, and income tax advantages that encourage large business organizations to operate through subsidiaries rather than through a single legal entity. Although we think of Canadian Pacific, Bell Canada Enterprises, or Provigo as single companies, each of these organizations is really a parent company with many subsidiaries. Since the parent company in each case controls the resources and activities of its subsidiaries, it is logical for us to consider an organization such as Canadian Pacific as one *economic* entity.

Growth through the acquisition of subsidiaries

A parent company may acquire another corporation as a subsidiary by purchasing more than 50% of the other corporation's voting stock. The purchase of one corporation by another may be termed a *merger,* a *business combination,* an *acquisition,* or a *takeover.* The acquisition of new subsidiaries is a fast and effective way for a company to grow, to diversify into new product lines, and to acquire new technology. In one recent year, the total price tag for the nine largest acquisitions or takeovers was over $14 billion, ranging from a low of a half-billion to a high of $5 billion.[6]

 Just a few well-known billion-dollar acquisitions: Campeau Corporation greatly increased its size and diversified its operations by acquiring Allied Stores Corporation in the United States for $5 billion. Hiram Walker-Gooderham & Worts, after a fierce battle to fight off a takeover, was acquired by Allied Lyons, a company in Britain, for $2.6 billion. Interprovincial Pipe Line expanded its scope of operations by acquiring Home Oil Limited for $1.1 billion.[7]

The acquisition of one corporation by another is, perhaps, the largest and most interesting of all business transactions. Such transactions may involve billions of dollars, bidding wars among prospective buyers, and dramatic increases in the value of a sought-after company's capital stock. Sometimes a company borrows vast amounts of money and acquires a corporation much larger than itself, thus doubling or tripling the size of the parent company overnight.

Financial statements for a consolidated economic entity

4   Describe the distinctive feature of consolidated financial statements.

Because the parent company and its subsidiaries are separate legal entities, separate financial statements are prepared for each company. In the *separate* financial statements of the parent company, the subsidiaries appear only as investments usually accounted for by the *equity method.* Since the affiliated companies function as a single economic unit, the parent company also prepares financial statements that

[6] This information is adapted from *The Financial Post 500,* Summer, 1987, p. 62. The nine acquisitions are related to 1986.

[7] Ibid.

show the financial position and operating results of the entire group of companies. Such statements are called *consolidated financial statements.*

In consolidated financial statements, the parent company and its subsidiaries are viewed as *one economic or business entity.* The distinctive feature of these statements is that the assets, liabilities, revenue, and expenses of *two or more separate legal entities* are combined in a single set of financial statements. For example, the amount shown as cash in a consolidated balance sheet is the total of the cash owned by all of the affiliated companies. Liabilities of the parent and subsidiary companies also are combined. Similarly, in a consolidated income statement, the revenue and expenses of the affiliated companies are combined to show the operating results of the consolidated economic entity.

Shareholders and creditors of the parent company have a vital interest in the financial results of all operations under the parent company's control, including those conducted by subsidiaries. Therefore, it is the consolidated financial statements that are included in the parent company's annual and quarterly reports to shareholders.

There are many interesting accounting issues involved in the preparation of consolidated financial statements. A brief introduction to some of these issues is provided in the following section of this chapter. However, no special problems are posed in reading a set of consolidated financial statements. The number of separate legal entities within the consolidated organization is an unimportant detail. For most purposes, consolidated financial statements may be interpreted *as if the parent companies and its subsidiaries were just one organization.*

CONSOLIDATED FINANCIAL STATEMENTS: CONCEPTS AND MECHANICS

Methods of consolidation

The purchase of an entire corporation usually is a very big investment. To accumulate the money necessary to buy another corporation, the parent company often needs to issue capital stock or bonds payable. If the parent company pays cash or issues debt securities to purchase the other corporation's capital stock, the business combination is accounted for by the *purchase method.*

A second method of accounting for a business combination is called a *pooling of interests.* The pooling method may be appropriate if the stock of a subsidiary is obtained in direct exchange for shares of the parent company's capital stock and neither company can be identified as the acquirer.[8] A key aspect of such a transaction is that the former shareholders of the subsidiary *become shareholders in the parent corporation.* The vast majority of business combinations are viewed as purchases, rather than poolings. In this textbook, we shall illustrate only the purchase method accounting for business combinations. The special case of a pooling-of-interests will be covered in more advanced accounting courses.

Consolidated financial statements are prepared by combining the amounts that appear in the separate financial statements of the parent and subsidiary companies.

---

[8] CICA, *CICA Handbook* (Toronto), paragraph 1580.08.

5   Explain why intercompany transactions must be eliminated as a step in preparing consolidated financial statements.

In the combining process, however, certain adjustments are made to *eliminate the effects of intercompany transactions* and thus to reflect the assets, liabilities, and shareholders' equity as those of a single economic entity.

Intercompany transactions   The term *intercompany transactions* refers to transactions between affiliated companies. These transactions may include, for example, the sale of merchandise, the leasing of property, and the making of loans. When the affiliated companies are viewed separately, these transactions may create assets and liabilities for the individual companies. However, when the affiliated companies are viewed as a single business entity, these assets and liabilities are merely the result of internal transfers within the business organization and should not appear in the consolidated financial statements.

For example, if a subsidiary borrows money from the parent company, a note payable will appear as a liability in the balance sheet of the subsidiary company and a note receivable will appear as an asset in the separate balance sheet of the parent. When the two companies are viewed as a single consolidated entity, however, this "loan" is nothing more than a transfer of cash from one part of the business to another. Transferring assets between two parts of a single business entity does not create either a receivable or a payable for that entity. Therefore, the parent company's note receivable and the subsidiary's note payable should not appear in the consolidated financial statements.

Preparing consolidated financial statements   Separate accounting records are maintained for each company in an affiliated group, but no accounting records are maintained for the consolidated entity. The amounts shown in consolidated financial statements *do not come from a ledger;* they are determined on a *working paper* by combining the amounts of like items on the financial statements of the affiliated companies. For example, the inventories of all the affiliated companies are combined into one amount for inventories. Entries to eliminate the effects of intercompany transactions are made *only* on this working paper. These elimination entries are *not recorded in the accounting records* of either the parent company or its subsidiaries.

Consolidation at the date of acquisition

6   Prepare a consolidated balance sheet.

To illustrate the basic principles of consolidation, we will now prepare a consolidated balance sheet. Assume that on January 1 Post Corporation purchases for cash 100% of the capital stock of Sun Limited at its book value of $300,000. (The shares are purchased from Sun Limited's former shareholders.) Also on this date, Post Corporation lends $40,000 cash to Sun Limited, receiving a note as evidence of the loan. Immediately after these two transactions, the separate balance sheet accounts of Post Corporation and Sun Limited are as shown in the working paper at the top of page 707.

Intercompany eliminations

Before the balance sheet amounts of Post Corporation and Sun Limited are combined, entries are made in the working paper to eliminate the effects of intercompany transactions. Intercompany eliminations may be classified into three basic types:

POST CORPORATION AND SUBSIDIARY
Working Paper — Consolidated Balance Sheet
January 1, 19___ (Date of Acquisition)

	POST CORPORATION	SUN LIMITED	INTERCOMPANY ELIMINATIONS		CONSOLIDATED BALANCE SHEET
			DEBIT	CREDIT	
Cash	60,000	45,000			105,000
Notes receivable	40,000			(b) 40,000	
Accounts receivable (net) . . .	70,000	50,000			120,000
Inventories	110,000	95,000			205,000
Investment in Sun Limited . .	300,000			(a) 300,000	
Plant & equipment (net)	210,000	180,000			390,000
Totals	790,000	370,000			820,000
Notes payable		40,000	(b) 40,000		
Accounts payable	125,000	30,000			155,000
Capital stock — Post Corporation	400,000				400,000
Capital stock — Sun Limited .		200,000	(a) 200,000		
Retained earnings — Post Corporation	265,000				265,000
Retained earnings — Sun Limited		100,000	(a) 100,000		
Totals	790,000	370,000	340,000	340,000	820,000

Explanation of elimination:
(a) To eliminate the Investment in Sun Limited against Sun Limited's shareholders' equity.
(b) To eliminate intercompany note receivable against related note payable.

1 Elimination of intercompany stock ownership
2 Elimination of intercompany debt
3 Elimination of intercompany revenue and expenses

The first two types of eliminations are illustrated in our example of Post Corporation and Sun Limited. The elimination of intercompany revenue and expenses will be discussed later in this chapter.

To understand the need for elimination entries, we must adopt the viewpoint of the consolidated entity, in which Post Corporation and Sun Limited are regarded as two departments within a single company.

Entry (a): Elimination of intercompany stock ownership   The purpose of entry (a) in the illustrated working paper is to eliminate from the consolidated balance sheet both the asset account and the shareholders' equity accounts representing the parent company's ownership of the subsidiary.

Post Corporation's ownership interest in Sun Limited appears in the *separate* balance sheets of both corporations. In the parent's balance sheet, this ownership interest is shown as the asset, Investment in Sun Limited. In the separate balance sheet of the subsidiary, the parent company's ownership interest is represented by the shareholders' equity accounts, Capital Stock and Retained Earnings. In the *consolidated* balance sheet, however, this "ownership interest" is neither an asset nor a part of shareholders' equity.

From the viewpoint of the single consolidated entity, *there are no shareholders in Sun Limited.* "Shareholders" are outside investors who have an ownership interest in the business. All of Sun Limited's capital stock is "internally owned" by another part of the consolidated entity. A company's "ownership" of its own stock does not create either an asset or shareholders' equity. Therefore the asset account, Investment in Sun Limited, and Sun Limited's related shareholders' equity accounts must be eliminated from the consolidated balance sheet.

Entry (b): Elimination of intercompany debt   When Post Corporation loaned $40,000 to Sun Limited, the parent company recorded a note receivable and the subsidiary recorded a note payable. This "receivable" and "payable" exist only when Post Corporation and Sun Limited are viewed as two separate entities. When both corporations are viewed as a single company, this "loan" is merely a transfer of cash from one part of the business to another. Such internal transfers of assets do not create either a receivable or a payable for the consolidated entity. Therefore, entry (b) is made to eliminate Post Corporation's note receivable and Sun Limited's note payable from the consolidated balance sheet.

After the necessary eliminations have been entered in the working paper, the remaining balance sheet amounts of Post Corporation and Sun Limited are combined to determine the assets, liabilities, and shareholders' equity of the consolidated entity. The consolidated balance sheet, which is shown below, is then prepared from the working paper.

NOTE SHAREHOLDERS'
EQUITY IS THAT OF THE
PARENT COMPANY

POST CORPORATION AND SUBSIDIARY
Consolidated Balance Sheet
January 1, 19___

ASSETS

Current assets:	
Cash	$105,000
Accounts receivable (net)	120,000
Inventories	205,000
Total current assets	$430,000
Plant & equipment (net)	390,000
Total assets	$820,000

LIABILITIES & SHAREHOLDERS' EQUITY

Current liabilities:		
Accounts payable		$155,000
Shareholders' equity:		
Capital stock	$400,000	
Retained earnings	265,000	
Total shareholders' equity		665,000
Total liabilities & shareholders' equity		$820,000

Acquisition of subsidiary's stock at a price above book value

When a parent company purchases a controlling interest in a subsidiary, it usually pays a price for the shares in excess of their book value.[9] We cannot ignore a difference between the cost of the parent company's investment and the underlying book value of these shares. In consolidation, the parent's investment is offset against the shareholders' equity accounts of the subsidiary, and if the two amounts are not equal, we must determine what the difference between them represents.

To illustrate, assume that C Limited purchases all of the outstanding shares of D Incorporated for $980,000. At the date of acquisition, D company's balance sheet shows total shareholders' equity of $700,000, consisting of capital stock of $300,000 and retained earnings of $400,000. In preparing the elimination entry on the working papers for a consolidated balance sheet, we must determine what to do with the $280,000 difference between the price paid, $980,000, and the shareholders' equity of D company, $700,000.

Why would C Limited pay a price in excess of book value for D Incorporated's stock? C Limited's management must believe that either (1) the fair market value of certain specific assets of D Incorporated (such as land or buildings) is in excess of book value, or (2) D Incorporated's future earnings prospects are so favourable as to justify paying $280,000 for D Incorporated's unrecorded *goodwill,* or both.

If we assume that the $280,000 represents unrecorded goodwill, the entry in the working papers to eliminate C Limited's investment account against the shareholders' equity accounts of D Incorporated would be:

ELIMINATION ENTRY
WHEN PRICE PAID FOR
SHARES OF SUBSIDIARY
EXCEEDS THEIR BOOK
VALUE

Capital Stock — D Incorporated	300,000	
Retained Earnings — D Incorporated	400,000	
Goodwill	280,000	
Investment in D Incorporated (C Limited's asset account) .		980,000

To eliminate the cost of C Limited's 100% interest in
D Incorporated against D's shareholders' equity accounts
and to recognize D Incorporated's unrecorded goodwill.

(Although we have shown this entry in general journal form, it actually would be made only in the Intercompany Eliminations columns of the working paper for a consolidated balance sheet.)

The $280,000 of goodwill will appear as an asset in the consolidated balance sheet.[10] This asset will be amortized to expense over its useful life, but not exceeding 40 years.[11]

Less than 100% ownership in subsidiary

If a parent company owns a majority interest in a subsidiary but less than 100% of the outstanding shares, a new kind of ownership equity known as the *minority*

---

[9] The parent company also might acquire the shares of the subsidiary at a price below book value. This situation will be discussed in an advanced accounting course.

[10] If specific assets of D company had been undervalued, the $280,000 would be allocated to increase the valuation of those assets in the consolidated working papers. The revaluation of specific assets is beyond the scope of our introductory discussion.

[11] CICA, *CICA Handbook* (Toronto), paragraph 1580.58.

interest will appear in the consolidated balance sheet. This minority interest represents the ownership interest in the subsidiary held by shareholders other than the parent company.

When there are minority shareholders, only the portion of the subsidiary's shareholders' equity owned by the parent company is eliminated. The remainder of the shareholders' equity of the subsidiary is included in the consolidated balance sheet under the caption Minority Interest.

To illustrate, assume that on December 31, Park Limited purchases 75% of the outstanding capital stock of Sims Limited for $150,000 cash, an amount equal to the book value of the stock acquired. The working paper to prepare a consolidated balance sheet on the date that control of Sims Limited is acquired follows.

PARK LIMITED AND SUBSIDIARY
Working Paper — Consolidated Balance Sheet
December 31, 19___ (Date of Acquisition)

	PARK LIMITED	SIMS LIMITED	INTERCOMPANY ELIMINATIONS		CONSOLIDATED BALANCE SHEET
			DEBIT	CREDIT	
Cash	200,000	50,000			250,000
Other assets	500,000	210,000			710,000
Investment in Sims Limited	150,000			(a) 150,000	
Totals	850,000	260,000			960,000
Liabilities	250,000	60,000			310,000
Capital stock — Park Limited	500,000				500,000
Capital stock — Sims Limited		120,000	{(a)　90,000 (b)　30,000		
Retained earnings — Park Limited	100,000				100,000
Retained earnings — Sims Limited		80,000	{(a)　60,000 (b)　20,000		
Minority interest (25% of $200,000)				(b)　50,000	50,000
Totals	850,000	260,000	200,000	(b) 200,000	960,000

Explanation of elimination:
(a) To eliminate Park Limited's investment in 75% of Sims Limited's shareholders' equity.
(b) To classify the remaining 25% of Sims Limited's shareholders' equity as a minority interest.

Entry (*a*) in this working paper offsets Park Limited's asset, Investment in Sims Limited, against 75% of Sims Limited's capital stock and retained earnings. The purpose of this entry is to eliminate intercompany stock ownership from the assets and shareholders' equity shown in the consolidated balance sheet. Entry (*b*) reclassifies the remaining 25% of Sims Limited's capital stock and retained earnings into a special account entitled Minority Interest. CICA has recommended that the minority interest appear *outside* the shareholders' equity section of the consolidated balance sheet.[12]

---

[12] CICA, *CICA Handbook* (Toronto), paragraph 1600.69.

Minority interest Why is the minority interest shown separately in the consolidated balance sheet instead of being included in the amounts shown for capital stock and retained earnings? The reason for this separate presentation is to distinguish between the ownership equity of the controlling shareholders and the equity of the minority shareholders.

The shareholders in the parent company own the controlling interest in the consolidated entity. Because these shareholders elect the directors of the parent company, they control the entire group of affiliated companies. The minority interest, however, has *no control* over any of the affiliated companies. Because they own shares only in a subsidiary, they cannot vote for the directors of the parent company. Also, they can never outvote the majority shareholder (the parent company) in electing the directors or establishing the policies of the subsidiary.

The minority shareholders receive 25% of the dividends declared by Sims company but do not participate in dividends declared by the parent company. The controlling shareholders, on the other hand, receive all the dividends declared by Park Limited but do not receive dividends declared by the subsidiary.

Consolidated income statement

A consolidated income statement is prepared by combining the revenue and expense accounts of the parent and subsidiary. Revenue and expenses arising from *intercompany transactions* are eliminated because they reflect transfers of assets from one affiliated company to another and do not change the net assets from a consolidated viewpoint.

Elimination of intercompany revenue and expenses Some of the more common examples of intercompany items that should be eliminated in preparing a consolidated income statement are:

1 Sales to affiliated companies
2 Cost of goods sold resulting from sales to affiliated companies
3 Interest expense on loans from affiliated companies
4 Interest revenue on loans made to affiliated companies
5 Rent or other revenue received for services rendered to affiliated companies
6 Rent or other expenses paid for services received from affiliated companies

In its separate accounting records, the parent company uses the *equity method* to account for its investment in a subsidiary. Under the equity method, the parent company recognizes as Investment Income its share of the subsidiary's earnings. Because the individual revenue and expenses of the subsidiary are included in a consolidated income statement, the parent company's Investment Income (from subsidiary) account must be eliminated to avoid double counting this portion of the subsidiary's earnings.

Because of the complexity of the intercompany eliminations, the preparation of a consolidated income statement and a consolidated statement of retained earnings are topics appropriately deferred to an advanced accounting course.

Unconsolidated subsidiaries

As a general rule, parent companies include in their consolidated financial statements the accounts of all subsidiaries in which the parent company owns a controlling

interest. Sometimes, however, it may ***not be appropriate*** to include the accounts o
a particular subsidiary in the consolidated statements. For example, a subsidiar
might not be consolidated if it is facing bankruptcy, or if the financial statement com
ponents of the subsidiary are so dissimilar from the other companies in the affiliate
group. In such cases, inclusion of the subsidiary's accounts in the consolidated finan
cial statements might create a confusing or misleading picture of the affiliated group'
financial position.

When consolidation is not considered appropriate, the ***unconsolidated subsidiar***
is shown in the financial statements as a long-term investment, usually accounted fo
by the cost or equity methods. The first footnote to consolidated financial statement
generally explains which subsidiaries were consolidated and which were not.

Accounting for investment in corporate securities: a summary

In this chapter, we have discussed investments in marketable securities, investment
accounted for by the equity method, and investments in subsidiaries which are show
in the financial statements on a consolidated basis. The accounting treatment of a
investment in stock depends primarily upon the ***degree of control*** that the investo
is able to exercise over the issuing corporation. These relationships are summarize
as follows:

DEGREE OF CONTROL OR INFLUENCE	GENERAL PRACTICE
1 Controlling interest (ownership of more than 50% of voting stock)	Consolidate, except in situations in whic consolidation might create a misleadin picture of the affiliated group. Any uncor solidated subsidiaries are shown as lonç term investments, usually accounted fo by the cost or equity method.
2 Influential but noncontrolling interest (usually ownership of between 20% and 50% of voting stock)	Show as a long-term investment, ac counted for by the equity method. A lowe market value is used if the decline i market value is not temporary in nature
3 Noninfluential interest (ownership of less than 20% of voting stock.)	Show as long-term portfolio investment Portfolio is valued at cost or lower of cos and market, when the decline in value i not temporary in nature.

END-OF-CHAPTER REVIEW

SUMMARY OF CHAPTER LEARNING OBJECTIVES

1 Account for short-term investments in stocks and bonds.

Investments in stocks and bonds are initially recorded at cost, and gains or losses from change
in the market value of the investments are recognized when the investments are sold. Intere

revenue from an investment in bonds is recognized each month as it accrues. Dividend revenue from stocks, however, does not accrue. Rather, it is recognized when the dividends are actually received. Short-term investments are valued at the lower of aggregate cost and market in the balance sheet.

2 Account for an investment in common stock by the equity method.

Under the equity method, the investor company recognizes as investment income its proportionate share of the investee's net income for the period. Dividends received from the investee are viewed as a conversion of the investment into cash. The equity method generally is used when the investor owns 20% or more of the investee's voting shares.

3 Explain how a parent company "controls" its subsidiaries.

A parent company controls a subsidiary by electing the subsidiary's board of directors, who, in turn, appoint the subsidiary's management personnel. From a practical point of view, a subsidiary is similar to a department within the parent company.

4 Describe the distinctive feature of consolidated financial statements.

Consolidated financial statements include the assets, liabilities, revenue, and expenses of two or more affiliated corporations, as if the affiliated companies were a single economic or business entity.

5 Explain why intercompany transactions must be eliminated as a step in preparing consolidated financial statements.

The term intercompany transactions refers to transactions between affiliated companies. When the affiliated companies are viewed as separate legal entities, these transactions may create assets (such as receivables) and liabilities (such as accounts payable) for the individual corporations. However, these "assets" and "liabilities" do not exist when the affiliated corporations are viewed as a single business entity.

6 Prepare a consolidated balance sheet.

A consolidated balance sheet is prepared by combining on a working paper the assets and liabilities of a parent company and all of its subsidiaries that are to be consolidated. It also is necessary, however, to eliminate the effects of intercompany transactions.

KEY TERMS INTRODUCED OR EMPHASIZED IN CHAPTER 17

Business combination The combining of two or more companies into a single economic or business entity. Also called a *merger, acquisition,* or *takeover.*

Consolidated financial statements A set of statements presenting the combined financial position and operating results of a consolidated entity consisting of a parent company and one or more subsidiaries.

Equity method The method of accounting used when the investment by one corporation in another is large enough to significantly influence the policies of the *investee.* The investor recognizes as investment income its proportionate share of the investee's net income, rather than considering dividends received as income.

Intercompany transactions Transactions between two affiliated companies. The effects in intercompany transactions, such as intercompany loans, are eliminated as a step in preparing consolidated financial statements.

Investee When an investor owns a sufficient amount (usually 20% or more) of the voting stock in a company to exercise a significant degree of influence over the company's policies, such a company is termed the investee. When the investor owns more than 50% of the investee's voting stock, the investee is called a *subsidiary.*

Lower of cost and market   The technique of valuing marketable securities in the balance sheet at the lower of cost and current market value. A write-down to a market value below cost involves recognition of a *loss.*

Marketable securities   A highly liquid type of investment that can be sold at any time without interfering with normal operation of the business. Usually classified as a current asset second only to cash in liquidity.

Minority interest   The shares of a subsidiary company owned by persons other than the parent corporation.

Parent company   A corporation that owns a controlling interest in another company.

Purchase method   The method used in preparing consolidated financial statements when the parent company has purchased the shares of its subsidiary by paying cash or issuing debt securities. The purchase method is not used for those special transactions which qualify as a *pooling of interests.*

Subsidiary   A corporation in which a controlling stock interest is held by another corporation (the parent).

ASSIGNMENT MATERIAL

REVIEW QUESTIONS

1 Why are investments in marketable securities usually regarded as current assets?

2 Why must an investor who owns numerous marketable securities maintain a marketable securities subsidiary ledger?

3 If an investor buys a bond between interest dates, he or she pays as a part of the purchase price the accrued interest since the last interest date. On the other hand, if the investor buys a share of common or preferred stock, no "accrued dividend" is added to the quoted price. Explain why this difference exists.

4 Should stock dividends received be considered revenue to an investor? Explain.

5 In the current asset section of its balance sheet, Delta Industries shows marketable securities (common and preferred stock) at a market value $120,000 below cost. If the market value of these securities rises by $190,000 during the next accounting period, how should Delta Industries' account for such an increase in its next income statement under the recommendations of the CICA and the FASB?

6 When should investors use the equity method to account for an investment in common stock?

7 Dividends on stock owned are usually recognized as income when they are received. Does an investor using the *equity method* to account for an investment in common stock follow this policy? Explain fully.

8 Alexander Corporation owns 80% of the outstanding stock of Benton Limited. Explain the basis for the assumption that these two companies constitute a single economic entity operating under unified control.

9 What are consolidated financial statements? Explain briefly how these statements are prepared.

10 List the three basic types of intercompany eliminations that should be made as a step in the preparation of consolidated financial statements.

11 Explain why the price paid to acquire a controlling interest in a subsidiary company may be different from the book value of the equity acquired.

12 The following items appear on a consolidated balance sheet: "Minority interest in subsidiary . . . $620,000." Explain the nature of this item, and where you would expect to find it on the consolidated balance sheet.

13 Briefly explain when a business combination is viewed as a *purchase* and when it might be viewed as a *pooling of interests.*

14 As a general rule, when are consolidated financial statements appropriate?

15 The annual report of Superior Manufacturing Limited and Subsidiaries included the following note: "Accounts of all subsidiaries in which the Company owns more than 50% of the voting stock are shown on a consolidated basis, with two exceptions: Western Casualty and Indemnity Limited, and Consumer Credit Corporation, which are accounted for by the equity method."

Explain the probable reasons for not consolidating these two subsidiaries. Also explain how the investments in these unconsolidated subsidiaries will be shown in the consolidated balance sheet.

16 What groups of persons are likely to be primarily interested in consolidated financial statements? Why?

EXERCISES

Exercise 17-1
Accounting
terminology

Listed below are nine technical accounting terms introduced in this chapter:

Consolidated financial statements	Lower of aggregate cost and market	Elimination of intercompany transactions
Parent company	Minority interest	Equity method
Marketable securities	Investee	Subsidiary

Each of the following statements may (or may not) describe one of these technical terms. For each statement, indicate the accounting term described, or answer "None" if the statement does not correctly describe any of the terms.

a Method used in the balance sheet valuation of marketable securities.

b A separate legal entity owned and controlled by another corporation.

c An accounting procedure that is a necessary step in preparing consolidated financial statements, but that does not involve making entries in the ledger accounts.

d A single set of financial statements showing the assets, liabilities, revenue, and expenses of all companies in a given industry.

e A corporation that owns at least 20% of the voting shares of another company, but which does not have controlling interest in that company.

f Procedures used to account for an investment that gives the investor significant influence over the policies of the other corporation.

g An investment that is too small to give the investor significant influence within the issuing company and that is almost as liquid an asset as cash.

Exercise 17-2
Investment in bonds

Yamato Corporation purchased as a short-term investment $50,000 face value of the 9% bonds of Lorenzo, Inc., on March 31 of the current year, at a total cost of $50,625, including interest accrued since January 1. Interest is paid by Lorenzo, Inc., on June 30 and December 31. On July 31, four months after the purchase, Yamato Corporation sold the bonds and interest accrued since July 1 for a total price of $50,525.

Prepare in general journal form all entries required in the accounting records of Yamato Corporation relating to the investment in Lorenzo, Inc., bonds. (Commissions are to be ignored.)

Exercise 17-3
Investment in stocks

Prepare the journal entries in the accounting records of Axel Masters, Inc., to record the following transactions. Include a memorandum entry on July 9 to show the change in the cost basis per share.

Jan. 7 Purchased as a short-term investment 1,000 shares of Reed Limited common stock at a price of $52 per share, plus a brokerage commission of $500.

Feb. 12 Received a cash dividend of $1 per share on the investment in Reed company stock.

July 9 Received an additional 50 shares of Reed Limited common stock as a result of a 5% stock divdend.

Aug. 14 Sold 500 shares of Reed Limited common stock at a price of $55 per share, less a brokerage commission of $290.

Exercise 17-4
Valuation at lower-of-cost-and-market

The cost and market value of Edgebrook Corporation's investment in marketable securities at the end of 1988 and 1989 follow. The marketable securities are viewed as a current asset.

	COST	MARKET VALUE
1988	$74,000	$61,000
1989 (carrying value $61,800)	74,000	78,000

Show how the investment would appear in the balance sheet at the end of 1988 and at the end of 1989 based on the recommendations of the CICA and the FASB. If appropriate, use a valuation account in your presentation.

Exercise 17-5
The equity method

On January 1, 1989, City Broadcasting Corporation purchases 30% of the common stock of News Service, Inc., for $250,000, which corresponds to the underlying book value. News Service, Inc., has issued common stock only. At December 31, News Service, Inc., reported net income for the year of $140,000 and paid cash dividends of $60,000. City Broadcasting uses the equity method to account for this investment.

Instructions

a Prepare all journal entries in the accounting records of City Broadcasting Corporation relating to the investment during 1989.

b During 1990, News Service, Inc., reports a net loss of $110,000 and pays no dividends. Compute the carrying value of City Broadcasting Corporation's investment in News Service, Inc., at the end of 1990.

Exercise 17-6
Eliminating intercompany stock ownership; recording goodwill

Midtown Cafeteria has purchased all the outstanding shares of Ballpark Caterers for $280,000. At the date of acquisition, Ballpark Caterers' balance sheet showed total shareholders' equity of $235,000, consisting of $200,000 capital stock and $35,000 retained earnings. The excess of this purchase price over the book value of Ballpark Caterers' shares is regarded as payment for Ballpark Caterers' unrecorded goodwill.

In general journal entry form, prepare the eliminating entry necessary on the working paper to consolidate the balance sheets of these two companies.

Exercise 17-7
Computing consolidated amounts

Selected account balances from the separate balance sheets of Adams Limited and its wholly owned subsidiary, Baker Limited, are shown as follows.

	ADAMS LIMITED	BAKER LIMITED	CONSOLIDATED
Accounts receivable	$ 300,000	$ 170,000	$
Rent receivable—Adams Limited		6,000	
Investment in Baker Limited	1,160,000		
Accounts payable	310,000	150,000	
Accrued expenses payable	11,000		
Bonds payable	1,400,000	900,000	
Capital stock	2,000,000	1,000,000	
Retained earnings	1,220,000	740,000	

Adams owes Baker $6,000 in accrued rent payable and Baker owes Adams $30,000 on account for services rendered. Show the amount that should appear in the consolidated balance sheet for each of these selected accounts. If the account would not appear in the consolidated balance sheet, indicate "None" as the consolidated account balance.

Exercise 17-8
Preparing a consolidated balance sheet; minority interest

On June 30, P Limited purchased 70% of the stock of S Limited for $420,000 in cash. The separate condensed balance sheets immediately after the purchase are shown.

	P LIMITED	S LIMITED
Cash	$ 130,000	$ 90,000
Investment in S Limited	420,000	
Other assets	2,250,000	710,000
	$2,800,000	$800,000
Liabilities	$ 600,000	$200,000
Capital stock	1,200,000	400,000
Retained earnings	1,000,000	200,000
	$2,800,000	$800,000

Instructions

Prepare a consolidated balance sheet immediately after P Limited acquired control of S Limited.

PROBLEMS

Group A

Problem 17A-1
Investments in bonds (includes amortization of premium)

On March 1, 1989, Imperial Motors purchased $50,000 face value of the 12% bonds of Tiger Trucking at a price of 104 plus accrued interest. The bonds pay interest seminannually on June 30 and December 31, and mature on June 30, 1992 (40 months from the date of purchase). Imperial Motors views these bonds as a long-term investment and follows the policy of amortizing the difference between the cost of the bonds and their maturity value by the straight line method at the end of each year.

Instructions   **a** Prepare the journal entries to record the following transactions in 1989:
   (1) Purchase of the bonds on March 1
   (2) Receipt of semiannual bond interest on June 30
   (3) Receipt of semiannual bond interest on December 31 and amortization of the difference between cost of the bonds and their maturity value for 10 months.

b Assume that an unexpected need for cash forces Imperial Motors to sell the entire investment in Tiger Trucking bonds for $51,800 plus accrued interest on January 31, 1990. Prepare the journal entries to:
   (1) Accrue bond interest receivable at January 31, 1989, and to amortize the difference between cost and maturity value for the one month since year-end.
   (2) Record the sale of the bonds on January 31.

Problem 17A-2
Investments in
marketable securities

During the current year, Overnight Air Freight (OAF) engaged in the following transactions relating to marketable securities:

Feb. 28 Purchased 1,000 shares of National Products common stock for $54.50 per share plus a broker's commission of $500.

Mar. 15 National Products paid a cash dividend of 50 cents per share, which had been declared on February 20 payable on March 15 to shareholders of record on March 6.

May 31 National Products distributed a 10% stock dividend.

Nov. 15 National Products distributed additional shares as the result of a 2 for 1 stock split.

Dec. 5 OAF sold 600 shares of its National Products stock at $27 per share, less a broker commission of $150.

Dec. 10 National Products paid a cash dividend of 25 cents per share. Dividend was declared November 20 payable December 10 to shareholders of record on November 30.

As of December 31, National Products common stock had a market value of $23 per share. OAF classifies its National Products stock as a current asset and owns no other marketable securities.

Instructions Prepare journal entries to account for this investment in OAF's accounting records. Include memorandum entries when appropriate to show changes in the cost basis per share. For journal entries involving computations, the explanation portion of the entry should include the computation. Also show how the investment should appear in the balance sheet at December 31.

Problem 17A-3
Accounting for
marketable securities:
a comprehensive
problem

The marketable securities owned by Sanford Communications at the beginning of the current year follow. Management considers all investments in marketable securities to be current assets.

$60,000 maturity value of Micro Computer Co. Ltd. 12% bonds due
   Apr. 30, 1999. Interest is payable on Apr. 30 and Oct. 31 of each
   year. Cost basis $990 per bond $59,400
2,000 shares of Ryan Corporation common stock. Cost basis
   $42 per share 84,000

Transactions relating to marketable securities during the current year were as follows:

Jan. 21 Received semiannual cash dividend of $1.10 per share on the 2,000 shares of Ryan Corporation common stock.

Feb. 8 Purchased 1,000 shares of Gramm Co. Ltd. common stock at $39³/₄ per share. Brokerage commissions amounted to $250.

Mar. 15 Received an additional 1,000 shares of Gramm Co. Ltd. common stock as a result of a 2 for 1 split.

Apr. 30 Received semiannual interest on Micro Computer Co. Ltd. 12% bonds. Accrued interest of $1,200 had been recorded on December 31 of last year in the Bond Interest Receivable account.

May 31 Sold $40,000 face value of Micro Computer Co. Ltd. 12% bonds at a price of 103, plus one month's accrued interest, less a brokerage commission of $200.

July 21 Received cash dividend on 2,000 shares of Ryan Corporation common stock. Amount of dividend has increased to $1.20 per share.

Oct. 18 Received an additional 100 shares of Ryan Corporation common stock as a result of a 5% stock dividend.

Oct. 19 Sold 600 shares of Ryan Corporation common stock at $37 per share, less a brokerage commission of $150.

Oct. 31 Received semiannual interest payment on remaining $20,000 face value of Micro Computer Co. Ltd. 12% bonds.

At December 31 of the current year, the quoted market prices of the marketable securities owned by Sanford Communications were as follows: Ryan Corporation, $33 per share; Gramm Co. Ltd., $21.50 per share; Micro Computer Co. Ltd., $970 per bond.

Instructions **a** Prepare journal entries to record the transactions listed above. Include an adjusting entry to record the accrued interest on the remaining Micro Computer Co. Ltd. bonds through December 31.

b Prepare a schedule showing the cost and market value of the marketable securities owned by Sanford Communications at December 31.

c Show how the marketable securities should appear in the balance sheet at December 31.

Problem 17A-4
Accounting for
marketable securities
nd applying the equity
method

Carolina Mills was organized on January 1, 1989, to manufacture carpeting. On this date, the corporation issued 400,000 shares of common stock at a price of $20 per share; 80,000 of these shares were issued to Discount Carpet Sales, Inc.

Discount Carpet Sales regards its investment in Carolina Mills as long-term. Following are the net income (or loss) earned and dividends paid by Carolina Mills during 1989 and 1990.

	NET INCOME (LOSS)	DIVIDENDS PAID (AT DEC. 31)
1989	$(230,000)	None
1990	900,000	$440,000*

*$1.10 per share.

Instructions **a** Assume that Discount Carpet Sales cannot exercise significant influence over Carolina Mills and regards this investment as a long-term investment in marketable securities. Prepare all journal entries relating to this investment in the accounting records of Discount Carpet Sales for the years 1989 and 1990.

b Now assume that Discount Carpet Sales *does* have significant influence over the policies and activities of Carolina Mills. Prepare all journal entries relating to this investment in 1989 and 1990 assuming that Discount Carpet Sales uses the *equity method* to account for its 20% ownership interest in Carolina Mills. Entries to recognize investment income c loss are made at year-end.

c For each ledger account used in parts **a** and **b**, explain briefly the nature of the account an where it will appear in the financial statements. Assume that the company prepares multiple-step income statement. Prepare a separate explanation for each account, b explain each account only once. You may omit an explanation of the Cash account.

An example of the type of explanation desired follows: "Marketable Securities — Long Term: This is an asset account that appears in the balance sheet under the caption Long-Ter Investments."

Problem 17A-5
Preparing a
consolidated balance
sheet

On June 30, 19___, Marina Restaurants paid $1 million cash to acquire all the outstandin capital stock of Pelican Pier. Immediately *before* this acquisition, the condensed separa balance sheets of the two companies were as follows. (As these balance sheets were prepare immediately *before* the acquisition, the current assets of Marina Restaurants still include th $1 million in cash which will be paid to acquire Pelican Pier.)

ASSETS	MARINA RESTAURANTS	PELICAN PIER
Current assets	$1,980,000	$ 320,00
Plant and equipment	1,620,000	900,00
Total assets	$3,600,000	$1,220,00

LIABILITIES & SHAREHOLDERS' EQUITY		
Current liabilities	$ 540,000	$ 180,00
Long-term debt	1,300,000	200,00
Capital stock	600,000	300,00
Retained earnings	1,160,000	540,00
Total liabilities & shareholders' equity	$3,600,000	$1,220,00

The excess of the $1 million purchase price over the book value of Pelican Pier's shares regarded as payment for Pelican Pier's unrecorded goodwill.

Instructions

Prepare a consolidated balance sheet for Marina Restaurants and its newly acquired subsidia (Pelican Pier) on June 30, 19___, the date of acquisition.

Problem 17A-6
Working papers for a
consolidated balance
sheet; includes
minority interest

The balance sheet accounts for Entertainment Tonight and Charlie's Pub at December 31 a shown at the top of page 721.

Additional information

(1) Entertainment Tonight owns 70% of the capital stock of Charlie's Pub, which was pu chased for cash at a price equal to its book value.

(2) Charlie's Pub owes Entertainment Tonight $6,000 in accrued rent payable. This amou is included in the accounts payable of the subsidiary and the accounts receivable of th parent company.

Instructions

Prepare a working paper for a consolidated balance sheet at December 31, 19___. Use th form illustrated in this chapter. Include at the bottom of the working paper explanations of th elimination entries.

ASSETS	ENTERTAINMENT TONIGHT	CHARLIE'S PUB
Cash	$ 55,000	$ 20,000
Accounts receivable	85,000	5,000
Inventories	60,000	45,000
Investment in Charlie's Pub stock (equity method) . . .	133,000	
Plant and equipment	274,000	195,000
Accumulated depreciation	(50,000)	(35,000)
Total assets	$557,000	$230,000

LIABILITIES & SHAREHOLDERS' EQUITY

	ENTERTAINMENT TONIGHT	CHARLIE'S PUB
Accounts payable	$ 65,000	$ 40,000
Common stock, no-par value	300,000	100,000
Retained earnings	192,000	90,000
Total liabilities & shareholders' equity	$557,000	$230,000

Group B

Problem 17B-1
Investments in bonds
(includes amortization of discount)

On May 1, 1989, Crest Theatres purchased $50,000 face value of the 9% bonds of Southern Gas Co. Ltd at a price of 95, plus accrued interest. The bonds pay interest semiannually on June 30 and December 31, and mature on June 30, 1993, (50 months from the date of purchase). Crest Theatres views these bonds as a long-term investment and follows the policy of amortizing the difference between the cost of the bonds and their maturity value by the straight-line method at the end of each year.

Instructions

a Prepare the journal entries to record the following transactions in 1989:

(1) Purchase of the bonds on May 1

(2) Receipt of semiannual bond interest on June 30

(3) Receipt of semiannual bond interest on December 31 and amortization of the difference between cost of the bonds and their maturity value for 8 months.

b Assume that an unexpected need for cash forces Crest Theatres to sell the entire investment in Southern Gas Co. Ltd. bonds for $47,750 plus accrued interest on January 31, 1990. Prepare the journal entries to:

(1) Accrue bond interest receivable at January 31, 1990, and to amortize the difference between cost and maturity value for the one month since year-end.

(2) Record the sale of the bonds on January 31.

Problem 17B-2
Investments in marketable securities

On January 31, Movie World purchased as a temporary investment 1,000 shares of Torch Limited common stock at $62.50 per share plus broker's commission of $500. Torch Limited declared a cash dividend of $1.20 per share on February 15, payable on March 31 to shareholders of record on March 15.

On June 30, Torch Limited distributed a 5% stock divdend. On July 31, the shares were split 2 for 1 and the additional shares distributed to shareholders. On August 25, a cash dividend of $1 per share was declared, payable on September 30 to shareholders of record on September 15. Movie World sold 1,000 shares of Torch Limited stock at $37 a share on December 31. Commission charges on the sale amounted to $200.

Instructions

Prepare journal entries to record the above events in Movie World's accounts. Include memorandum entries when appropriate, even though ledger accounts are not affected. For journal entries involving computations, the explanation portion of the entry should include the computations.

Problem 17B-3
Accounting for marketable securities: a comprehensive problem

The marketable securities owned by Bar Harbour Corporation at January 1 consisted of the three securities listed. All marketable securities are classified as current assets.

$50,000 maturity value Copper Products Co. Ltd. 9% bonds due April 30, 2002. Interest is payable on Apr. 30 and Oct. 31 of each year. Cost basis $990 per bond	49,500
1,500 shares of Aztec Corporation common stock. Cost basis $38.50 per share	57,750
800 shares of Donner-Pass, Inc., $6.00 cumulative preferred stock. Cost basis $55 per share	44,000

Jan. 10 Acquired 500 shares of Rhodes Ltd. common stock at $71¹/₂ per share. Brokerage commissions paid amounted to $250.

Jan. 21 Received quarterly dividend of $1.50 per share on 800 shares of Donner-Pass, Inc. preferred stock.

Mar. 5 Sold all 800 shares of Donner-Pass, Inc., preferred stock at $58 per share less a brokerage commission of $200.

Apr. 1 Received additional 1,000 shares of Rhodes Ltd. common stock as a result of a 3 for 1 split.

Apr. 30 Received semiannual interest on Copper Products Co. Ltd. 9% bonds. Accrued interest of $750 had been recorded on December 31 of last year in the Bond Interest Receivable account.

June 30 Sold $25,000 face value of Copper Products Co. Ltd. 9% bonds at 93, plus two months' accrued interest, less a commission of $125.

July 10 Received additional 150 shares of Aztec Corporation common stock as a result of 10% stock dividend.

Sept. 24 Sold 650 shares of Aztec Corporation common stock at $40 per share, less a brokerage commission of $150.

Oct. 31 Received semiannual interest payment on remaining $25,000 face value of Copper Products Co. Ltd. 9% bonds.

At December 31, 19___, the quoted market prices of the marketable securities owned by Sanford Communications were as follows: Aztec Corporation common stock, $37; Rhodes Ltd common stock, $18; and Copper Products Co. Ltd. bonds, $980 per bond.

Instructions

a Prepare journal entries to record the preceding transactions. Include an adjusting entry to record accrued interest on the remaining Copper Products Co. Ltd. bonds through December 31.

b Prepare a schedule showing the cost and market value of the marketable securities owned by Bar Harbour Corporation at December 31.

c Show how the marketable securities should be presented in the balance sheet at December 31.

Problem 17B-4
Comparison of accounting for marketable securities to the equity method.

Gremlin Village was organized on January 4, 1989, to operate an amusement park. On this date, the corporation issued 200,000 shares of common stock at a price of $25 per share; 40,000 of these shares were issued to Video Productions, Inc.

Video Productions regards its investment in Gremlin Village as long term. Following are the net income (or loss) earned and dividends paid by Gremlin Village during its first two years of operation.

	NET INCOME (LOSS)	DIVIDENDS PAID (AT DEC. 31)
1989	$420,000	$120,000*
1990	(270,000)	None

*60 cents per share.

Instructions

a Assume that Video Productions *cannot* exercise significant influence over Gremlin Village and therefore accounts for this investment as an investment in long-term marketable securities. Prepare all journal entries relating to the investment in 1989 and 1990 in the accounting records of Video Productions.

b Now assume that Video Productions *does* have significant influence over the operations of Gremlin Village. Prepare all journal entries relating to this investment in 1989 and 1990 assuming that Video Productions, Inc., uses the *equity method* to account for its 20% ownership interest in Gremlin Village. Entries to recognize investment income or loss are made at year-end.

c For each ledger account used in parts **a** and **b**, explain briefly the nature of the account and where it will appear in the financial statements. Assume that the company prepares a multiple-step income statement. Prepare a separate explanation for each account, but explain each account only once. You may omit an explanation of the Cash account.

An example of the type of explanation desired follows: "Marketable Securities—Long-Term: This is an asset account that appears in the balance sheet under the caption Long-Term Investments."

Problem 17B-5
Preparing a consolidated balance sheet

Just before Boone Corporation purchased Phillips Limited on December 31, 19___, the condensed balance sheets of the two companies were as follows:

ASSETS	BOONE CORPORATION	PHILLIPS LIMITED
Current assets	$1,520,000	$240,000
Other assets	1,980,000	660,000
Total assets	$3,500,000	$900,000

LIABILITIES & SHAREHOLDERS' EQUITY		
Current liabilities	$ 630,000	$120,000
Long-term debt	900,000	184,000
Capital stock	1,000,000	200,000
Retained earnings	970,000	396,000
Total liabilities & shareholders' equity	$3,500,000	$900,000

Instructions

Assume that on December 31, 19___, Boone Corporation purchased (using current assets) all the outstanding capital stock of Phillips Limited for $800,000. The excess of this purchase price over the book value of Phillips Limited's shares is regarded as payment for Phillips Limited's unrecorded goodwill. Prepare a consolidated balance sheet for Boone Corporation and its new subsidiary (Phillips Limited) at the date of acquisition.

Problem 17B-6
Working paper for a consolidated balance sheet

Osborne Electronics purchased 80% of the stock of Technical Instruments for cash. Following are the separate balance sheets of the two companies at the end of the current year:

ASSETS	OSBORNE ELECTRONICS	TECHNICAL INSTRUMENTS
Cash	$ 35,000	$ 28,000
Note receivable from Technical Instruments	50,000	
Accounts receivable	90,000	65,000
Inventories	100,000	130,000
Investment in Technical Instruments (equity method)	485,000	
Plant and equipment	340,000	405,000
Accumulated depreciation	(140,000)	(98,000)
Total assets	$960,000	$530,000

LIABILITIES & SHAREHOLDERS' EQUITY		
Notes payable	$100,000	$ 50,000
Accounts payable	150,000	80,000
Common stock, no-par value	400,000	150,000
Retained earnings	310,000	250,000
Total liabilities & shareholders' equity	$960,000	$530,000

Other information

(1) Osborne Electronics' asset account, Investment in Technical Instruments, represents ownership of 80% of Technical Instruments shareholders' equity, which has a book value of $320,000 [80% × ($150,000 + $250,000) = $320,000]. The remainder of the Investment account balance represents the purchase of Technical Instruments' unrecorded goodwill. Amortization of this goodwill has already been recorded through December 31.

(2) During the current year, Technical Instruments borrowed $50,000 from Osborne Electronics by issuing a one-year note payable. (Ignore interest.)

(3) The accounts payable of Osborne Electronics include $12,000 owed to Technical Instruments for services rendered during the current year. This amount also is included in the accounts receivable of Technical Instruments.

Instructions

Prepare a working paper for a consolidated balance sheet at December 31 of the current year. Use the form illustrated in this chapter. Include at the bottom of the working paper explanations of the elimination entries.

BUSINESS DECISION CASES

Case 17-1
Off to the stacks!

This case has two purposes: first, to tie the chapter coverage of business acquisitions or combinations into current business events, and second, to acquaint students with business periodicals and publications such as *Canadian Business, The Financial Post, The Financial Post 500* and the *Financial Times*, as well as with the business environment.

Instructions   Identify two recent business acquisitions or combinations involving well-known corporations *other than the examples cited in this chapter* (page 704) and briefly explain the specific reasons for each business acquisition or combination.

Case 17-2
Deciding whether or
not to consolidate a
subsidiary

Ten years ago, Milton Paper Co. Ltd. acquired 58% of the capital stock in Travis Book Limited for $5 million — a price equal to the book value of the purchased shares. The balance sheet of Travis Book Limited at the end of the current year includes the following:

	DECEMBER 31
Current assets	$14,800,000
Current liabilities	10,000,000
Other assets	15,000,000
Long-term liabilities	2,800,000
Capital stock, no-par value, 600,000 shares issued	3,000,000
Retained earnings	14,000,000

The balance sheet of the Milton Paper Co. Ltd. at December 31 of the current year follows:

MILTON PAPER CO. LTD.
Balance Sheet
December 31, 19___

ASSETS

Current assets	$19,000,000
Investment in Travis Book Limited (equity method)	9,860,000
Other assets	26,140,000
Total assets	$55,000,000

LIABILITIES & SHAREHOLDERS' EQUITY

Current liabilities		$10,000,000
Bonds payable		20,000,000
Total liabilities		$30,000,000
Shareholders' equity:		
Capital stock, no-par	$ 7,500,000	
Retained earnings	17,500,000	
Total shareholders' equity		25,000,000
Total liabilities & shareholders' equity		$55,000,000

The accounts receivable of Milton Paper include $8,500,000 due from Travis Book company. The accounts of the two companies have never been consolidated because one manufactures a variety of paper products and the other publishes children's books.

Susan Brent, a director of Milton Paper, suggests that a consolidated balance sheet be prepared for the two companies in order to show a more meaningful financial position. "Through our ownership of 58% of Travis's voting stock, we control the resources and activities of Travis just as if it were a division of Milton Paper."

Louis Joseph, another director of Milton Paper, objects to Brent's suggestion because of the relatively weak financial position of Travis Book and the low percentage of stock held in Travis Book. "We have almost twice as much working capital as Travis, and our current ratio is nearly 2 to 1, while theirs is not even $1^1/_2$ to 1. Why would we hide our highly solvent position by preparing consolidated financial statements with a weaker company? We own only 58% of the stock in Travis. Besides, Travis is not in our kind of business, and I don't think we should include its earnings in our income statement because we haven't realized that profit. To recognize income from this investment before we receive cash dividends violates the accounting principle of conservatism.''

Instructions   Carefully evaluate the points made by Louis Joseph and give your recommendation whether or not the preparation of consolidated statements for the two companies would be appropriate. Your answer should discuss the following points:

(a) Does Milton Paper Co. Ltd. control Travis Book Limited and do the two companies engage in similar or unrelated types of business activity?

(b) Would a consolidated balance sheet indicate a less solvent position than does the separate balance sheet of Milton Paper Co. Ltd? In support of your answer, prepare a schedule showing the working capital and current ratio of Milton Paper, Travis Book, and the consolidated entity.

(c) Should Milton Paper Co. Ltd. recognize as income its share of the annual earnings of Travis Book Limited?

6

SPECIAL REPORTS AND USES OF ACCOUNTING INFORMATION

This part consists of three chapters and two appendices. In the first chapter, we show how individuals and corporations use accounting information to measure taxable income and to determine the amount of income tax owed. In the second chapter, we illustrate and explain a new major financial statement — the statement of changes in financial position. The appendix presents the T account method of developing such a statement. In the third chapter, we describe some of the techniques by which investors analyze financial statements. The appendix allows students to apply these analytical techniques to the financial statements of a large corporation.

INCOME TAXES
AND
BUSINESS DECISIONS

CHAPTER PREVIEW

For many college and university students, this chapter may be their only academic exposure to the truly remarkable system known as income taxes. The early part of the chapter presents a brief history, rationale, and basic structure of the federal tax structure, including the tax reform of 1987. This introduction also stresses the pervasive influence of income taxes upon economic activity. The next section portrays the basic process of determining taxable income and the tax liability for individual taxpayers. The income tax computations for a corporation are also explained and illustrated. The final section of the chapter gives students an understanding of the important role that tax planning can play in the affairs of individuals and also in the decision-making of a business entity.

After studying this chapter you should be able to meet these Learning Objectives:

1 Describe the history of the federal income tax, the highlights of the tax reform of 1987, and the basic structure of the tax system.

2 Explain the formula for determining the taxable income and tax liability of an individual taxpayer.

3 Explain the income tax treatment of dividends received by individuals.

4 Determine the tax liability of an individual.

5 Determine the taxable income and income tax of a corporation.

6 Determine the amount of capital cost allowance.

7 Discuss the concept of interperiod income tax allocation.

8 Explain how tax planning is used in choosing the form of business organization, timing and nature of transactions, and the capital structure.

1 Describe the history of the federal income tax, the highlights of the tax reform of 1987, and the basic structure of the tax system.

The federal income tax: history and objectives

The federal income tax legislation, the **Income Tax Act**, has undergone many changes since its inception as the **Income War Tax Act** in 1917. The most significant changes occurred in the years 1948, 1952, and 1972. Similarly, the objectives of income tax legislation also have been changed and expanded over the years. The administration and enforcement of the **Income Tax Act** rest with the Department of National Revenue for Taxation, commonly known as Revenue Canada, Taxation.

Originally, the objective of the federal income tax was simply to obtain revenue to help meet Canada's growing war expenditures. It was intended as a temporary measure and the tax rates were quite low. Today, the objectives are many and the tax rates are significantly higher.

The objectives of federal income tax today include a number of goals in addition to raising revenue. Among these goals are to combat inflation, to influence the rate of economic growth, to encourage full employment, to provide incentive for small businesses, and to redistribute national income on a more equal basis.

Tax reform of 1987

In 1987, the federal government introduced **_proposed_** new income tax legislation that would bring sweeping changes in income tax rules and rates.[1] Although annual changes in the income tax law have become normal practice, the changes in this new legislation represent some of the most drastic in the history of the federal income tax. Annual changes, however, will continue. In fact, this new legislation prescribes changes in rules and rates to become effective in 1988, further changes in 1989, and still more changes in 1990. In other words, some of the changes created by the new legislation are to be phased in over a period of years. In this textbook we have utilized as fully as possible the changes brought into being by the new tax legislation, emphasizing those which would become effective in 1988. The five most striking characteristics of the new tax legislation are the broadening of the tax base, the lowering of tax rates, the reduction of the number of tax brackets, the replacement of various exemptions and deductions with tax credits, and a shifting of the tax burden from individuals to corporations and to sales tax.

Provincial income tax

All ten provinces as well as the Northwest and Yukon Territories levy income tax. The federal government collects the income tax of individuals and corporations except for the Provinces of Ontario, Alberta, and Quebec; Ontario and Alberta collect their corporate income tax and Quebec collects its income tax on both individuals and corporations. The rate of income tax varies among the jurisdictions; for example, in 1987, it was from 46.5% for Alberta to 60% for Newfoundland for individuals (plus a surtax or flat tax in some provinces) and from 0–15% for Alberta to 10–16% for Newfoundland for corporations (the lower rate applies to small businesses). The tax rate for individuals is expressed as a percentage of the individual's basic federal tax. The tax rate for corporations, on the other hand, applies to the corporation's taxable income. The computations of provincial income tax will be illustrated later.

---

[1] Hereafter, we will use "new income tax legislation" to mean "proposed new income tax legislation."

Tax planning versus tax evasion

Individuals and corporations who plan their business and financial affairs in a manner that will result in the lowest possible income taxes are engaged in tax planning. The goals of tax planning are to minimize and to postpone income taxes on a rational and legal basis.

Almost every business or financial decision requires a choice among alternative courses of action with different tax consequences. For example: Should business automobiles be leased or purchased? Should needed capital be financed by issuing bonds or preferred stock? Should a business be incorporated? Some of these alternatives will lead to much lower income taxes than others. Tax planning, therefore, means *determining in advance the income tax effect* of every proposed business action and then making business decisions that will lead to the smallest income tax liability. Tax practice is an important element of the services furnished to clients by public accounting firms. This service includes not only the preparation of tax returns but also tax planning.

Tax planning must begin early. Unfortunately, some wait until the end of the year and then, faced with the prospect of paying a large amount of income tax, ask their accountants what can be done to reduce the tax liability. If we are to arrange transactions in a manner that will lead to the minimum income tax liability, the tax planning must be carried out *before* the date of a transaction, not after it is an accomplished fact. Because it is important for everyone to recognize areas in which tax savings may be substantial, a few of the major opportunities for tax planning are discussed in the final section of this chapter.

Newspaper stories tell us each year of some taxpayers who have deliberately understated their taxable income by failing to report a portion of income received or by claiming fictitious expenses or tax credits. Such purposeful understatement of taxable income is called *tax evasion* and is, of course, illegal. On the other hand, *tax planning* (the arranging of business and financial affairs in a manner that will minimize tax liability) is legal.

The critical importance of income taxes

Taxes levied by federal and provincial governments are a significant part of the cost of operating a typical household, as well as a business enterprise. Every manager who makes business decisions, and every individual who makes personal investments, urgently needs some knowledge of income taxes. A general knowledge of income taxes will help any business manager or owner to benefit more fully from the advice of the professional tax accountant.

Some understanding of income taxes will also aid the individual citizen in voting intelligently, because a great many of the issues decided in every election have tax implications. Such issues as pollution, inflation, foreign policy, and employment are quite closely linked with income taxes. For example, the offering of special tax incentives to encourage businesses to launch massive programs to reduce pollution is one approach to protection of the environment.

In terms of revenue generated, income taxes constitute one of the most important sources of revenue in Canada. Income taxes also exert a pervasive influence on all types of business decisions and affect millions of individuals. For example, tax returns filed annually in recent years were in excess of 16 million for individuals and about 800,000 for corporations. The annual tax revenue from individuals and corporations in recent years was well over $60 billion. For this reason we shall limit our discussion to the basic federal and provincial income tax rules applicable to individuals and corporations.

Income taxes are usually determined from information contained in accounting records. The amount of income tax is computed by applying the appropriate tax rates to *taxable income.* As explained later in this chapter, *taxable income* is not necessarily the same as *accounting income* even though both are derived from the accounting records. Business managers can influence the amount of taxes they pay by their choice of form of business organization, methods of financing, and timing of transactions. Thus income taxes are inevitably an important factor in reaching business decisions.

Classes of taxpayers and liability for tax

In the eyes of the income tax law, the classes of taxpayers are: individuals, corporations, and trusts. Since trusts are taxed as individuals, there are in essence two classes of taxpayers.

Proprietorships and partnerships are not taxed as business units; their income is taxed directly to the individual proprietor or partners, *whether or not actually withdrawn from the business.* A proprietor reports his or her business income on an individual tax return; the members of a partnership include on their individual tax returns their respective shares of the partnership net income. An individual taxpayer's income tax return must include not only any business income from a proprietorship or partnership, but also any salary or income from other sources and any deductions affecting the tax liability.

A corporation is a separate taxable entity; it must file an income tax return and pay a tax on its annual taxable income. In addition, individual shareholders must report dividends received as part of their personal taxable income. This is sometimes called "double taxation" of corporate income — once to the corporation and again when it is distributed as dividends to shareholders. However, this double taxation is minimized by the "dividend tax credit" claimed by the shareholders.

The income tax law stipulates that income tax is payable on the taxable income for each taxation year of every person resident in Canada. Moreover, income tax is payable on the taxable income earned in Canada by a nonresident person. The word "person" may include an individual or a corporation.

INCOME TAXES: INDIVIDUALS

Cash basis of accounting for individual tax returns

Most of the individual tax returns are prepared on the cash basis of measuring income. The cash basis is advantageous for the individual taxpayer for several reasons. It is simple and requires a minimum of record keeping. Moreover, the income of most individuals comes in the form of salaries, interest, and dividends. At the end of each year, employers are required to inform each employee (and Revenue Canada, Taxation) of the salary earned and the income tax withheld during the year. The report (a T-4 form, illustrated in Chapter 11) must be prepared on the cash basis without any accrual of unpaid wages. Companies paying interest and dividends also use the cash basis in reporting the amounts paid during the year. Thus, most individuals are provided with reports prepared on a cash basis for use in preparing their individual tax returns. However, businesses and professional practices, with rare exceptions such as a farming business, are not allowed to use the cash basis for tax purposes.

Tax rates for individuals

All taxes may be characterized as progressive, proportional, or regressive with respect to any given base. A *progressive* tax becomes a larger portion of the base as that base increases. A *proportional* tax remains a constant percentage of the base no matter how that base changes. For example, a 6% sales tax remains a constant percentage of sales regardless of changes in the dollar amount of sales. A *regressive* tax becomes a smaller percentage of the base as the base increases. Regressive taxes, however, are extremely rare.

Federal income tax is *progressive* with respect to income, since a higher tax *rate* applies as the amount of taxable income increases. Since provincial income tax is expressed as a percentage of "basic federal tax," it is also progressive with respect to income. The 1987 federal and provincial tax rates for individuals are as follows:

FEDERAL TAX RATES FOR INDIVIDUALS — 1987

TAXABLE INCOME	MARGINAL TAX RATE
0–$ 1,318	6%
$ 1,319– 2,638	16%
2,639– 5,278	17%
5,279– 7,917	18%
7,918– 13,196	19%
13,197– 18,475	20%
18,476– 23,754	23%
23,755– 36,591	25%
36,592– 63,346	30%
63,347– over	34%

PROVINCIAL TAX RATES FOR INDIVIDUALS — 1987

Alberta	46.5%*
British Columbia	51.5%
Manitoba	54%*
New Brunswick	58%
Newfoundland	60%
Nova Scotia	56.5%
Ontario	50%*
Prince Edward Island	55%
Saskatchewan	50%*

*There was a surtax or flat tax or both for these provinces.

(The province of Quebec collects its own individual income tax. The 1987 rate ranges from 13% to 28%, and the rate applies to taxable income as computed under the Quebec Taxation Act.)

As mentioned earlier, two of the most striking characteristics of the new tax legislation are the reduction of the number of tax brackets and the lowering of tax rates. In contrast to the 10 tax brackets and marginal tax rates ranging from 6% to 34% for 1987, the new tax legislation provides for only 3 tax brackets and 3 marginal tax rates ranging from 17% to 29% for 1988.

FEDERAL TAX RATES FOR INDIVIDUALS — 1988

TAXABLE INCOME	MARGINAL TAX RATE
0–$27,500	17%
$27,501– 55,000	26%
55,001 and over	29%

To minimize the impact of severe inflation, the new tax legislation provides for the indexing, starting in 1989, of the three tax brackets and tax credits relating to "personal exemptions" by any annual increase in the Consumers Price Index in excess of 3%. Also, the 3% federal surtax (based on basic federal tax) will remain in force until the federal sales tax reform is in place.

Income tax formula for individuals

2   Explain the formula for determining the taxable income and tax liability of an individual taxpayer.

The federal government supplies a standard income tax form (T1 General) on which individual taxpayers are guided to a proper computation of their taxable income and the amount of the tax. It is helpful to visualize the computation in terms of an income tax formula. Moreover, it is easier to understand the structure and logic of income tax and to analyze tax rules and their effect by referring to a tax formula. The general income tax formula, based on the standard income tax form for individuals, is outlined on page 735. The items in the formula are explained in more detail in the following paragraphs.

Total income

The total income of an individual taxpayer is his or her world income from all sources except those explicitly excluded by the income tax law. If an amount received by an individual is income and not a return of capital and it is not explicitly excluded by the tax law, then it should be included as income. To identify whether an amount is excluded as income for tax purposes, it is necessary to refer to the income tax law, regulations, and court decisions.

The major categories of income for tax purposes are:

1 **Income from an office or employment** This category includes salaries, wages, directors' fees, and other remuneration and taxable fringe benefits such as bonuses, tips, honoraria, and certain allowances for personal or living expenses.
2 **Income from a business or property** This category includes net income from a proprietorship, partnership, or a professional business, as well as rental, royalty, interest, and dividend income. Also, income from a business of an illegal nature is to be included in income for tax purposes.
3 **Capital gains** This category includes gains from selling capital assets such as stocks, bonds, and depreciable properties used in the business. For 1988 and 1989

General Income Tax Formula for Individuals

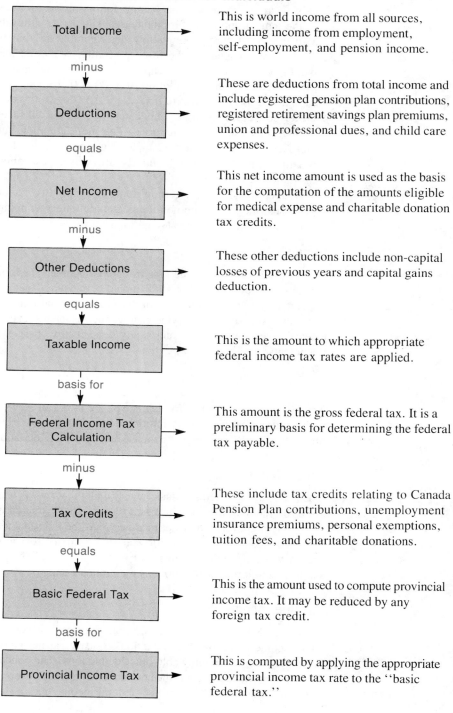

Total Income — This is world income from all sources, including income from employment, self-employment, and pension income.

minus

Deductions — These are deductions from total income and include registered pension plan contributions, registered retirement savings plan premiums, union and professional dues, and child care expenses.

equals

Net Income — This net income amount is used as the basis for the computation of the amounts eligible for medical expense and charitable donation tax credits.

minus

Other Deductions — These other deductions include non-capital losses of previous years and capital gains deduction.

equals

Taxable Income — This is the amount to which appropriate federal income tax rates are applied.

basis for

Federal Income Tax Calculation — This amount is the gross federal tax. It is a preliminary basis for determining the federal tax payable.

minus

Tax Credits — These include tax credits relating to Canada Pension Plan contributions, unemployment insurance premiums, personal exemptions, tuition fees, and charitable donations.

equals

Basic Federal Tax — This is the amount used to compute provincial income tax. It may be reduced by any foreign tax credit.

basis for

Provincial Income Tax — This is computed by applying the appropriate provincial income tax rate to the "basic federal tax."

two-thirds (for 1990, *three-quarters*) of capital gains, known as ''taxable capital gains,'' are to be included as income for tax purposes. These gains may be offset by the same proportion of capital losses, known as ''allowable capital losses,'' for a given year. Any remaining allowance capital losses may be carried back against taxable capital gains of the three preceding years and may be carried forward indefinitely against taxable capital gains in future years. However, there is a lifetime capital gains exemption of $100,000. In other words, $100,000 of the capital gain is not subject to tax.

4 Other sources of income This category includes all income items not covered by the preceding three categories. The more common items are: benefits from Old Age Security Pension, Canada or Quebec Pension Plan, and other pensions or superannuation; taxable family allowance payments; and unemployment insurance benefits.

As mentioned earlier, certain items are explicitly excluded as income for tax purposes; the more common items include lottery winnings, war disability pensions, and income from personal injury awards.

Deductions

There are a number of deductions from total income. The more common ones under the new tax legislation for 1988 include: registered pension plan contributions, registered retirement savings plan premiums, annual union and professional dues, child care expenses, and carrying charges such as interest expense on money borrowed to earn investment income and safety deposit box charges for storing investment documents.

Net income

The net income of an individual taxpayer is his or her total income minus the deductions. This amount is important because it is the basis for computing the amounts eligible for medical expense and charitable donation tax credits.

Other deductions

There are very few items in this category under the new tax legislation. The deductions for 1988 include: non-capital losses of previous years and capital gain deductions. For many taxpayers, their net income would be the same as taxable income unless they had business losses in prior years to be carried forward to the current year, or they have capital gains eligible for exemption from tax this year (the lifetime capital gains exemption of $100,000 was mentioned earlier).

Taxable income

This is the amount subject to federal income tax. It is computed by deducting from total income the allowable deductions to arrive at net income and then deducting from net income the allowable other deductions. The concept of taxable income is most important because it is the amount to which the appropriate tax rate is applied to determine the amount of ''gross'' federal income tax.

Federal income tax calculation

This is the amount of "gross" federal income tax. It is not the amount of tax payable because there are a number of tax credits to be deducted from it to determine the basic federal tax and the federal tax payable.

Tax credits

As mentioned earlier, one of the most striking characteristics of the new tax legislation is the replacement of various deductions and exemptions with tax credits. Deductions such as Canada Pension Plan contributions, unemployment insurance premiums, tuition fees, education deductions, medical expenses in excess of 3% of net income, and charitable donations are substituted by tax credits for 1988. Similarly, all the personal exemptions — basic, married, dependent children, and age — are replaced by tax credits for 1988. Also, under the new tax legislation, a dependant of the age of 18 or older is not eligible for a tax credit unless he or she is infirm. Thus, a taxpayer cannot claim an 18-year-old son or daughter as a dependant unless he or she is infirm. While some of the tax credits may be transferred to a spouse or a parent, any unused tax credits are not refundable. The more common tax credits and the amounts for 1988 under the new legislation are:

1 **Personal tax credits**
   - **(a)** basic (for the taxpayer) $1,020
   - **(b)** married (for the taxpayer's spouse)*   850
   - **(c)** dependants under 18*   65
   - **(d)** infirm dependants aged 18 and over   250
   - **(e)** age (65 and over)   550

*A spouse and dependant can earn a net income of $500 and $2500 respectively without reduction in the amount of tax credits. The tax credit will be reduced by 17% of net income in excess of these limits. Also, the tax credit for the third and subsequent dependent children is $130 each.

2 **Deduction tax credits** based on 17% of the amount of the allowable deductions.
   - **(a)** Canada Pension Plan contributions
   - **(b)** Unemployment insurance premiums
   - **(c)** Tuition fees
   - **(d)** Medical expenses in excess of 3% of net income (this excess is commonly called "allowable medical expenses")
   - **(e)** Charitable donations (the 17% is for the first $250 in donations and 29% for the amount in excess of $250, up to a maximum of 20% of net income)

3 **Education deduction** of $10 for each month in full-time attendance at a designated educational institution and enrolled in a qualifying educational program.

It should be mentioned that under the new tax legislation two common deductions — the employment expense deduction and the interest and dividend income deduction — were eliminated rather than replaced by tax credits. Such an elimination is an example of the broadening of the tax base, one the most striking characteristics of this new legislation that was mentioned earlier.

Basic federal tax

The amount of basic federal tax is "gross" federal income tax (federal income tax calculation) minus tax credits. It is the basis for computing the provincial income tax. This amount plus the 3% federal surtax and minus any foreign tax credit becomes the amount of federal tax payable.

Provincial income tax

The amount of provincial income tax is determined by applying the appropriate provincial tax rate to the amount of basic federal tax. Since the tax rate varies among provinces, an average rate of 55% will be used as a provincial tax rate for illustration purposes and for the assignment materials.

Federal dividend tax credit for individuals

3 Explain the income tax treatment of dividends received by individuals.

To minimize the impact of double taxation on corporate income upon its subsequent distribution as dividends to individual shareholders, income tax law allows a special deduction from tax called "federal dividend tax credit." However, an individual taxpayer must first include in his or her income the dividends from taxable Canadian corporations at 125% for 1988 under the new tax legislation (known as the "gross-up" or "taxable" amount of dividends). This "gross-up" amount is taxed at the normal rate of the taxpayer. The federal income tax is then reduced by the dividend tax credit at $13^1/_3\%$ of the "gross-up" amount of dividends. Since income tax is progressive, the dividend tax credit provides more tax benefit to taxpayers with lower income. To illustrate, let us assume that the federal tax rates for three individuals are 17%, 26%, and 29% and each has $8,000 of dividends from taxable Canadian corporations.

		17%	26%	29%
Tax Rate				
Dividends	(a)	$ 8,000	$ 8,000	$ 8,000
Add: "gross-up" of 25%		2,000	2,000	2,000
Taxable (gross-up) amount of dividends (125% of dividends received)		$10,000	$10,000	$10,000
Federal income tax on taxable amount of dividends		$ 1,700	$ 2,600	$ 2,900
Less: dividend tax credit of $13^1/_3\%$ on taxable (gross-up) amount of dividends ($13^1/_3\%$ × $10,000)		1,333	1,333	1,333
Federal tax on dividends	(b)	$ 367	$ 1,267	$ 1,567
Effective rate of federal tax on dividends (b) ÷ (a)		4.6%	15.8%	19.6%

It is clear from the preceding illustration that the difference in the effective tax rate on the dividend income between the lowest and the highest tax brackets is very substantial — a 15% difference. The 15% difference is greater than the 12% (29% − 17%) difference between the tax rates for these two tax brackets. This is, of course, in keeping with the progressive nature or the "ability to pay" philosophy of our current income tax system.

Instalment payment of estimate tax for individuals

For self-employed persons such as public accountants, doctors, dentists, and owners of unincorporated businesses, there is, of course, no salary and no tax withholding. Other examples of income on which no withholding occurs are rental income, dividends, and interest income. In these cases, instalment tax is required if tax is not withheld from at least three-quarters of a taxpayer's net income and if the taxpayer's tax in the year or in the preceding year is $1,000 or more. The amount of instalment payments, due on or before March 31, June 30, September 30, and December 31, is based either on a reasonable estimate or on the tax applicable to the taxable income of the preceding year, whichever is lower. Any additional tax is due on or before April 30 of the following year.

Tax returns, tax refunds, and payment of the tax

All individuals with tax owing must file an income tax return on or before April 30 for the preceding calendar year; otherwise, late filing penalties and interest will be charged. The payment of income taxes is on a "pay as you go" basis. The procedure by which employers withhold income taxes from the salaries of employees has been discussed previously in Chapter 11. The amounts withheld from an employee's salary for income taxes can be considered as payment on account. If the amount of income taxes as computed by preparing a tax return is less than the amount withheld during the year, the taxpayer is entitled to a refund. On the other hand, if the tax computed is more than the amount withheld, the balance should be paid with the filing of the tax return. Individuals who are entitled to a refund will have to file a tax return to obtain a refund.

Computation of individual income tax illustrated

4 Determine the tax liability of an individual.

The computation of the 1988 federal and provincial income tax for John Kaiser is illustrated on the next page. The illustration highlights some of the main features of the new tax legislation and is based on the following assumed data:

1 Mr. John Kaiser is married and has a sixteen-year-old son who has $380 net income from various part-time jobs. Also, Mrs. Kaiser has a net income of $500.

2 Mr. Kaiser's income, withholdings, and disbursements include:

Income:

Salary from employment (before tax withholding)	$60,000
Taxable family allowance payments	388
Dividends from taxable Canadian corporations	8,000
Interest from Canada Savings Bonds	1,800
Gain on sale of shares of Canadian Ltd.	1,200

Withholdings:

Income taxes	18,400
Canada Pension Plan contributions	480
Unemployment insurance premiums	700
Contribution to a registered pension plan*	3,500
Union membership dues	530

*Maximum amount for 1988. The determination of the maximum amount can be very complex, depending on the types of pension plan and such elements as pensionable earnings, years of services, etc.

Disbursements:
Medical expenses   900
Charitable donations   1,600
Professional membership dues   490

3 Provincial tax rate is 55%

JOHN KAISER
Illustrative Federal and Provincial Income Tax Computation
For the Year 1988

Total income:
Salary	$60,000
Taxable family allowance payments	388
Dividends ($8,000 plus 25% gross-up)	10,000
Interest	1,800
Taxable capital gain ($2/3$ of the $1,200 gain)	800
	$72,988

Deductions
Registered pension plan contributions	$3,500	
Union and professional dues	1,020	4,520
Net income		$68,468

Other deductions
Capital gains deduction ($2/3$ of the $1,200 gain)	800
Taxable income	$67,668

Federal income tax calculation:
$27,500 at 17%	$ 4,675
$27,500 at 26%	7,150
$12,668 at 29%	3,674
$67,668	$15,499

Tax credits:
Canada Pension Plan contributions credit	$ 82	
Unemployment insurance premiums credit	119	
Basic personal credit	1,020	
Spousal credit	850	
Dependant credit (16 years old)	65	
Charitable donations credit		
($250 at 17% and $1,350 at 29%)	434	
Dividend credit ($13^1/3$% of the gross-up amount		
of $10,000)	1,333	3,903
Basic federal tax		$11,596
3% federal surtax		348
Federal tax payable		$11,944
Provincial tax—55% of "basic federal tax"		6,378
Total tax payable		$18,322
Less: income taxes withheld		18,400
Amount of refund		$ 78

Note: Since the amount of medical expenses of $900 is less than 3% of net income, there is no tax credit for medical expenses.

INCOME TAXES: CORPORATIONS

Taxation and tax rates

A corporation is a separate taxable entity. Every corporation, unless specifically exempt from taxation, must file an income tax return (Form T2) within six months from the end of its taxation year, whether or not it has taxable income or owes any tax. Also, corporations are required to pay their income taxes on a monthly instalment basis. Our discussion is focussed on the ordinary business public corporations, with only brief references to certain other types of corporations for which special tax treatment applies.

As with individuals, the federal income tax rate applies to the corporation's taxable income. Under the new tax legislation, the tax rates effective on July 1, 1988 are as shown below:

TYPE OF BUSINESS	TAX RATE
General business	28%
Manufacturing business	26%
Small business	12%

However, the 3% surtax on federal corporate income tax will remain until the sales tax reform is implemented.

In addition to federal tax, all provinces levy income tax on corporations. The provincial tax rate for 1987 for general business public corporations ranges from 5.9% to 17%. Also, provincial rates are lower for certain businesses, such as manufacturing and processing and small businesses.

Computation of taxable income of corporations

While the taxable income of corporations is computed in much the same way as for individuals there are a number of differences. The major ones include:

1 **Tax credits of a personal nature** Corporations are not allowed tax credits of a personal nature, such as basic personal, married, dependent tax credits and medical expenses tax credits, which are allowed for individuals.
2 **Dividends received** The dividends received by a corporation from other taxable Canadian corporations are *not* included in the corporation's taxable income. Since these dividends are not taxable, the dividend tax credit for individuals does not apply to corporations. However, certain private corporations pay a special refundable tax on certain dividends received, which will be refunded when the corporation subsequently pays a taxable dividend to its shareholders.
3 **Capital gains and losses** Corporations, like individuals, may deduct the *allowable* capital losses *only* to the extent of *taxable* capital gains. Also, corporations may carry back and forward the remaining allowable capital losses against taxable capital gains in the same manner as for individuals, as discussed earlier. However, the lifetime capital gains exemption of $100,000 for individuals is *not* available for corporations.

Computation of taxable income and federal income tax for corporation illustrated

5 Determine the taxable income and income tax of a corporation.

To highlight some of the main features of the new tax legislation as it applies to corporations, the computation of federal tax for Stone Corporation, a general business operation, for the 1988 taxation year follows. Remember this illustration is not an income statement and does not show items in the sequence of an income statement.

NOTICE THE DIFFERENCE BETWEEN INCOME PER ACCOUNTING RECORDS ($184,000) AND TAXABLE INCOME ($176,000)

STONE CORPORATION
Illustrative Federal Tax Computation
(In thousands of dollars)

Revenue:		
Sales		$800,000
Dividends received from taxable Canadian corporations		20,000
Total revenue		$820,000
Expenses:		
Cost of goods sold	$536,000	
Other expenses (includes capital loss of $12,000)	$100,000	636,000
Income per accounting records		$184,000
Add back:		
Capital loss deducted as part of operating expenses		12,000
Subtotal		$196,000
Deduct (item not subject to tax)		
Dividends received from taxable Canadian corporations		20,000
Taxable income		$176,000
Federal tax computation:		
28%* on $176,000		$ 49,280
Deduct: Monthly instalment payments		49,000
Balance of federal tax payable		$ 280

*To simplify the illustration, the new tax rate of 28% is used for the whole year rather than for the period starting July 1, 1988, the effective date.

Accounting income versus taxable income

In the determination of *accounting income,* the objective is to measure business operating results as accurately as possible in accordance with generally accepted accounting principles. *Taxable income,* on the other hand, is a legal concept governed by statute and subject to frequent change by Parliament. In setting the rules for determining taxable income, Parliament is interested not only in meeting the revenue needs of government but also in achieving certain public policy objectives. Since accounting income and taxable income are determined with different purposes in mind, it is not surprising that they often differ by material amounts.

The following are some of the major areas of difference between accounting income and taxable income:

1 Certain income and expense items included in computing accounting income are either excluded or partly excluded from computing taxable income. For example,

dividends received by a taxable Canadian corporation from other taxable Canadian corporations are included in accounting income but are excluded from taxable income; goodwill and organization costs incurred after 1971 may be amortized for accounting purposes, but only one-half of them can be amortized for tax purposes.

2 Capital gains and losses are fully included in computing accounting income, but only a portion of these gains and losses is included in computing taxable income.

3 Methods used for computing accounting income may differ from those used for computing taxable income. For example, lifo method of inventory may be used for accounting purposes, but is not allowed for tax purposes; straight-line or sum-of-the-years'-digits method of depreciation may be used for computing accounting income, but a declining balance method based on tax regulations is used to compute depreciation, called "capital cost allowance," for tax purposes.

Capital cost allowances

6 Determine the amount of capital cost allowance.

There are special tax regulations for recognizing a portion of a depreciable asset as an expense each year. This expense is called *capital cost allowance* rather than depreciation. The recognition of capital cost allowance for tax purposes differs significantly from depreciation for accounting purposes. The main features of capital cost allowance are:

1 Depreciable assets of a similar nature are grouped into a particular class or pool.

2 Costs of additions are added to, and proceeds of disposals (up to the original cost of the asset) and capital cost allowances are deducted from, the balance of the class or pool.

3 When a class or pool has a credit balance at the end of a taxation year, the credit balance, known as "recaptured capital cost allowance," is to be included in income for tax purposes.

4 A stipulated rate is applied to the balance of each class or pool to obtain the amount of capital cost allowance for the year. However, in the year where there is net addition of assets (i.e., total addition exceeds total disposal), only one-half of such net addition is eligible for capital cost allowance.

Some of the more common classes of depreciable assets and their stipulated rates are:

CLASS		MAXIMUM RATE
3	Brick, stone, cement buildings, and most buildings (other than those in Classes 6, 31, or 32)	5%*
8	Machinery, equipment, and furniture	20%
10	Automobiles, trucks, and tractors	30%

*For buildings acquired in 1988 and subsequent years, the maximum rate is 4% under the new tax legislation. The 5% applies to buildings acquired prior to 1988.

Taxpayers may claim an amount of capital cost allowance in each taxation year up to the maximum amount allowed for each class. The example below illustrates the application of the main features of capital cost allowance.

X Ltd. has a number of trucks (Class 10) used in its business operations. The beginning balance is $100,000. During the year, two trucks costing $48,000 were purchased and one old truck, with an original cost of $12,000, was sold for $8,000.

The capital cost allowance for the year is computed as follows:

Beginning balance	$100,000
Add: purchase of two trucks	48,000
	$148,000
Deduct: proceeds of disposal of one truck	8,000
Ending balance	$140,000
Capital cost allowance: 30% on beginning balance of $100,000	$ 30,000
30% on ¹/₂ of net asset addition of $40,000	
[($48,000 − $8,000) × ¹/₂ × 30%]	6,000
	$ 36,000

X Ltd. may claim a capital cost allowance for class 10 of up to a maximum of $36,000 for the year.

Interperiod income tax allocation

7 Discuss the concept of interperiod income tax allocation.

We have seen that differences between generally accepted accounting principles and income tax rules can be material. Some businesses might consider it more convenient to maintain their accounting records in conformity with the tax rules, but the result would be to distort financial statements. It is clearly preferable to maintain accounting records by the principles that produce relevant information about business operations. The data in the records can then be adjusted by use of work sheets to arrive at taxable income.

When a corporation follows one method in its accounting records and financial statements but uses a different method for its income tax return, a financial reporting problem arises. The difference in method will usually have the effect of postponing the recognition of income on the tax return (either because an expense deduction is accelerated or because revenue recognition is postponed). The question is whether the income tax expense should be accrued when the income is recognized in the accounting records or when it is actually subject to taxation.

To illustrate the problem, let us consider a very simple case. Suppose the Pryor Corporation has before-tax accounting income of $600,000 in each of two years. However, the company takes as a tax deduction in Year 1 an expense of $200,000 that is reported for accounting purposes in Year 2. The company's accounting and taxable income and the actual income taxes due (assuming an average federal and provincial tax rate of 43%) are as follows:

	YEAR 1	YEAR 2
Accounting income (before income taxes)	$600,000	$600,000
Taxable income	400,000	800,000
Actual income taxes due each year, at assumed rate		
of 43% of taxable income	172,000	344,000

Let us assume Pryor Corporation reports in its income statement in each year the amount of income taxes due for that year as computed on the company's income tax returns. The effect on reported net income as shown in the company's financial statements would be:

	YEAR 1	YEAR 2
Accounting income (before income taxes)	$600,000	$600,000
Income taxes expense (amount actually due)	172,000	344,000
Net income	$428,000	$256,000

The readers of Pryor Corporation's income statement might well wonder why the same $600,000 accounting income before income taxes in the two years produced such widely varying amounts of tax expense and net income.

To deal with this distortion between pre-tax income and after-tax income, an accounting policy known as *interperiod income tax allocation* is required for financial reporting purposes.[2] Briefly, the objective of income tax allocation is to accrue income taxes in relation to accounting income whenever differences between accounting and taxable income are caused by differences in the *timing* of revenue or expenses. In the Pryor Corporation example, this means we would report in the Year 1 income statement a tax expense based on $600,000 of accounting income even though a portion of this income ($200,000) will not be subject to income tax until Year 2. The effect of this accounting procedure is demonstrated by the following journal entries to record the income tax expense in each of the two years:

Year 1	Income Taxes Expense	258,000	
	Income Tax Payable		172,000
	Deferred Income Tax		86,000
	To record current and deferred income taxes at 43% of accounting income of $600,000.		

Year 2	Income Taxes Expense	258,000	
	Deferred Income Tax	86,000	
	Income Tax Payable		344,000
	To record income taxes of 43% of accounting income of $600,000 and to record actual income taxes due.		

Using tax allocation procedures, Pryor Corporation's financial statements would report net income during the two-year period as follows:

Income before income taxes	$600,000	$600,000
Income taxes expense (tax allocation basis)	258,000	258,000
Net income	$342,000	$342,000

In this example, the difference between taxable income and accounting income (caused by the accelerated deduction of an expense) was fully offset in a period of

---

[2] For a more complete discussion of tax allocation procedures, see *CICA Handbook*, Section 3470, on "Corporate income taxes."

two years. In practice, differences between accounting and taxable income may persist over extended time periods and deferred tax liabilities may accumulate to significant amounts. For example, in a recent balance sheet of Petro-Canada, deferred income taxes of over $1 billion were reported as a result of the differences in depletion, capital cost allowance, and other costs for accounting and tax purposes.

TAX PLANNING OPPORTUNITIES

Income tax laws have become so complex that detailed tax planning has become a way of life for most business firms. Almost all companies today engage professional tax specialists to review the tax aspects of major business decisions and to develop plans for legally minimizing income taxes. We will now consider some areas in which tax planning may offer substantial benefits.

Form of business organization

8 Explain how tax planning is used in choosing the form of business organization, timing and nature of transactions, and the capital structure.

Tax factors should be carefully considered at the time a business is organized. As a sole proprietor or partner, a business owner will pay taxes at individual rates on the business income earned in any year *whether or not it is withdrawn from the business*. On the other hand, corporations deduct salaries paid to owners for services but cannot deduct dividends paid to shareholders. Both *salaries and dividends* are taxable income to the persons receiving them. However, the tax on dividends is reduced by a dividend tax credit.

These and other factors must be weighed in deciding in any given situation whether the corporate or noncorporate form of business organization is preferable. There is no simple rule of thumb, even considering only these basic differences. To illustrate, suppose that Able, a married man, starts a small business that he expects will produce, before any compensation to himself and before income taxes, an average annual income of $80,000. Able plans to recognize a salary of $20,000 and to withdraw all income from the business. The combined corporate and individual taxes (based on 1988 tax rates) under the corporate and sole proprietorship form of business organization are summarized at the top of the next page.

Under these assumptions, the formation of a corporation is not favourable from an income tax viewpoint. However, the tax difference between the corporation and sole proprietorship of $435 is very small. Another factor to be considered is that, with the corporation, Able can postpone the amount of tax payable by retaining the income in the corporation rather than paying it out as dividends. Of course, factors other than income tax (such as limited liability) must be considered in deciding whether to incorporate the business.

Planning business transactions to minimize or postpone income taxes

Business transactions may often be arranged in such a way as to produce favourable tax treatment. For example, timing of disposal of investments in securities can postpone income taxes because capital losses from securities can be offset against capital gains.

Sometimes sellers try to arrange a transaction one way to their tax benefit and buyers try to shape it another way to produce tax savings for them. Income tax

	CORPORATION	SOLE PROPRIETORSHIP
Business income	$80,000	$80,000
Salary to Able	20,000	
	$60,000	$80,000
Corporate taxes (on the $60,000 taxable income of a small business)		
Federal 12%* $7,200		
Provincial 10%** 6,000	13,200	
Amount to Able (the $46,800 as dividends)	$46,800	$80,000
Combined corporate and individual tax:		
Corporate tax on $60,000 taxable income	$13,200	
Individual tax* (assume a total deduction of $8,500 and total tax credits of $10,060, including dividend tax credit of $7,800)		
On Able's $20,000 salary and $46,800 dividends*	9,478	
On Able's $80,000 share of business income*		$22,243
Total income tax on business income	$22,678	$22,243

*Surtax is ignored to simplify computations.
**Assumed 1988 rate.

effects thus become a part of price negotiation. For example, in buying business property, the purchasers will try to allocate as much of the cost of the property to the building and as little to the land as possible, since building costs can be depreciated for tax purposes. Similarly, in buying a business, the buyers will want as much as possible of the total purchase price to be attributed to inventories or to depreciable assets rather than goodwill. The cost of goods sold and depreciation are deductible against income, whereas only one-half of goodwill can be amortized for tax purposes. Thus, the main point is: *any failure to consider tax effects on major business transactions can be costly.*

Tax planning in the choice of financial structure

In deciding upon the best means of raising capital to start or expand a business, consideration should be given to income taxes. Different forms of business financing produce different amounts of tax expense. Interest on debt, for example, is *fully deductible,* but dividends on preferred or common stock are not. This factor operates as a strong incentive to finance expansion by borrowing.

Let us suppose that a company subject to a 44% marginal tax rate needs $100,000 to invest in productive assets on which it can earn a 20% annual return. If the company obtains the needed money by issuing $100,000 in 16% preferred stock, it will earn *after taxes* only $11,200, which is not even enough to cover the $16,000 preferred dividend. (This after-tax amount is computed as $20,000 income less taxes at 44% of $20,000.)

Now let us assume, on the other hand, that the company borrowed $100,000 at 16% interest. The additional gross income would be $20,000 but interest expense of

$16,000 would be deducted, leaving taxable income of $4,000. The tax on the $4,000 at 44% would be $1,760, leaving after-tax income of $2,240. Analysis along these lines is also needed in choosing between debt financing and financing by issuing common stock.

END-OF-CHAPTER REVIEW

SUMMARY OF CHAPTER LEARNING OBJECTIVES

1 Describe the history of the federal income tax, the highlights of the tax reform of 1987, and the basic structure of the tax system.

The federal income tax legislation owes its origin to the Income War Tax Act of 1917, intended as a "temporary measure" to obtain revenue to finance Canada's growing war expenditures. This objective of raising revenue has been broadened to such other objectives as combating inflation, influencing the rate of economic growth, encouraging full employment, providing incentive for small business, and redistributing national income on a more equal basis. The tax reform of 1987 contains some of the most drastic changes in the history of the federal income tax. The five most striking characteristics of the new tax legislation are the broadening of the tax base, the lowering of tax rates, the reduction of the number of tax brackets, the replacement of various exemptions and deductions with tax credits, and a shifting of the tax burden from individuals to corporations and to sales tax. The basic structure of the tax system includes such elements as classes of taxpayers, the progressive nature of income tax, and the federal and provincial tax rates.

2 Explain the formula for determining the taxable income and tax liability of an individual taxpayer.

The formula consists of the following steps: (a) total income minus deductions equals net income, (b) net income minus other deductions equals taxable income, (c) taxable income is the basis for calculating "gross" federal income tax, (d) "gross" federal income tax minus tax credits equals basic federal tax, (e) basic federal tax plus federal surtax and minus foreign tax credit equals federal tax payable (f) provincial tax is calculated as a percentage of basic federal tax.

3 Explain the income tax treatment of dividends received by individuals.

To minimize the impact of double taxation on corporate income upon its subsequent distribution as dividends to shareholders, an individual taxpayer can claim a special deduction from tax called "federal dividend tax credit." The dividends received are grossed up by 25% and the gross-up amount is included in computing taxable income and income tax. The income tax thus computed is reduced by the federal dividend tax credit. The effective federal tax rates on dividends under the new tax legislation range from 4.6% to 19.6%, which are much lower than the federal tax rates on taxable income, which range from 17% to 29%.

4 Determine the tax liability of an individual.

The illustrative example shows the type of income (salary, family allowances, dividends, interest, and capital gain) to be included, the deductions used (registered pension plan contributions, union and professional dues) to arrive at the amount of net income, and the other deduction used (capital gain deduction) to obtain the taxable income amount. Then the gross federal income tax is computed. A number of tax credits (basic personal, married, dependent, charitable donation, and dividend) are deducted from the gross federal tax to yield the basic federal tax. This basic federal tax plus the 3% federal surtax produces the total federal tax payable. The provincial tax is obtained by multiplying the basic federal tax with a percentage.

5 Determine the taxable income and income tax of a corporation.

The illustrative example shows the determination of taxable income from accounting income by adding back a capital loss to, and deducting dividends income from, accounting income. Then the taxable income is multiplied by the federal tax rate to determine the amount of federal income tax.

6 Determine the amount of capital cost allowance.

Capital cost allowance is determined by applying a percentage to the declining balance of a class or pool of similar depreciable assets. The percentage or rate for each class is stipulated by tax law. Costs of additions are added to, and proceeds of disposals (up to the original cost) and capital cost allowance are deducted from, the balance of the asset pool. Only half of the net additions (additions minus disposals) is eligible for computing capital cost allowance in the year of the additions.

7 Discuss the concept of interperiod income tax allocation.

The purpose of income tax allocation is to accrue income tax expense in the income statement in relation to the accounting income shown in that statement. Without income tax allocation, the differences between GAAP and income tax rules would often cause the income tax expense for a given year to be unrelated to the accounting income of that year.

8 Explain how tax planning is used in choosing the form of business organization, timing and nature of transactions, and the capital structure.

An important decision in tax planning is whether a business will achieve tax benefits by incorporating rather than operating as a sole proprietorship or partnership. The decision will vary from case to case depending on such factors as the tax bracket of the owners as individual taxpayers, and the intent of the owners to withdraw earnings from the corporation in the form of dividends as opposed to retaining earnings in the corporation to facilitate growth of the business.

Timing of disposal of certain assets such as investments can yield a lower amount of tax payable for the current year. Allocating the amount of a transaction between depreciable and undepreciable assets, or between goodwill and tangible assets, produces different tax effects for the buyer and the seller.

In deciding on a capital structure, the owners of a business should be aware that interest on debt such as bonds and notes payable is deductible in arriving at taxable income, but dividends paid on common or preferred stock are not.

KEY TERMS INTRODUCED OR EMPHASIZED IN CHAPTER 18

Basic federal tax The gross amount of federal minus tax credits. The basic federal tax is the basis for computing provincial tax.

Capital cost allowance The amount of expense for depreciable assets for tax purposes.

Capital gain or loss The difference between the cost or adjusted-cost base of a capital asset and the amount received from its sale.

Dividend tax credit This credit is intended to minimize the impact of "double taxation" on corporate income. It is computed by applying 13⅓% to the taxable (gross-up) amount of dividends and is deducted from federal income tax.

Gross federal tax Taxable income times federal tax rate equals gross federal tax.

Interperiod tax allocation Allocation of income tax expense among accounting periods because of timing differences between accounting income and taxable income. Causes income tax expense reported in financial statements to be in logical relation to accounting income.

Marginal tax rate The tax rate to which a taxpayer is subject on the additional dollar of income received.

Tax credit An amount to be subtracted from gross federal income tax to arrive at basic federal tax, including credits for Canada Pension Plan contributions, unemployment insurance premiums, basic personal, married, dependent, tuition fees, and charitable donations.

Tax planning A systematic process of legally minimizing income taxes by considering in advance the tax consequences of alternative business or investment actions.

Taxable income The computed amount to which the appropriate tax rate is to be applied to arrive at the gross amount of federal tax.

Total income An individual's world income from all sources, including income from employment, self-employment, and pension.

ASSIGNMENT MATERIAL

REVIEW QUESTIONS

1 What are some objectives of the federal income tax legislation other than providing revenue for the government?

2 List the five most striking characteristics of the new tax legislation.

3 List three examples of tax credits under the new tax legislation.

4 What is meant by the expression "tax planning"?

5 What are the major classes of taxpayers under the federal income tax law?

6 It has been claimed that corporate income is subject to "double taxation." Explain the meaning of this expression, and indicate whether there is provision in the tax law to minimize it.

7 Taxes are characterized as either *progressive, proportional,* or *regressive* with respect to any given base. Describe an income tax rate structure that would fit each of these characterizations.

8 State whether you agree with the following statement and explain your reasoning: A person in a very high tax bracket who makes a cash contribution to a charitable organization will reduce his or her federal income tax liability by more than the amount of the donation.

9 State the federal income tax formula for individuals, beginning with total income and ending with basic federal tax.

10 From an individual taxpayer's viewpoint, it is better to have a $10,000 capital gain than $10,000 of ordinary income. Explain.

11 Cite an example to illustrate the broadening of the tax base under the new tax legislation.

12 Even when a corporation uses the accrual method of accounting, taxable income may differ from accounting income. Give four *examples* of differences between the tax treatment and accounting treatment of items that are included in the determination of income.

13 Under what circumstances is the accounting procedure known as *income tax allocation* appropriate? Explain the purpose of this procedure.

14 The depreciation expense computed by Zane Corporation as the capital cost allowance (permitted by the income tax law) appeared in the tax return as $150,000. In the accounting records and financial statements, Zane's depreciation was computed on the straight-line basis and amounted to $100,000. Under interperiod tax allocation procedures, would Zane's balance sheet show deferred income taxes as a debit or credit? Explain.

15 List some tax factors to be considered in deciding whether to organize a new business as a corporation or as a partnership.

16 Explain how the corporate income tax makes debt financing in general more attractive than financing through the issuance of preferred stock.

17 Some of the decisions that business owners must make in the organization and operation of a business will affect the amount of income taxes to be paid. List some of these decisions that affect the amount of income taxes legally payable.

EXERCISES

Exercise 18-1
Accounting and
tax terminology

Listed below are nine technical accounting and tax terms introduced in this chapter:

Basic federal tax	Capital gain	Gross federal tax
Cash basis of accounting	Tax credit	Tax planning
Capital cost allowance	Taxable income	Interperiod tax allocation

Each of the following statements may (or may not) describe one of these technical terms. For each statement, indicate the term described, or answer ''None'' if the statement does not correctly describe any of the terms.

a Profit from disposal of such assets as stock and bonds acquired as long-term investments.

b Revenue recorded when received in cash and expenses recorded in period payment is made.

c Income tax recognized each period as a constant percentage of net sales.

d Causes income tax expense reported in financial statements to be in logical relationship to accounting income.

e An amount to be subtracted from gross federal tax.

f Depreciation calculated according to tax law and regulations.

g Net income minus other deductions, which serves as a basis to compute gross federal tax.

h Taxable income multiplied by an appropriate federal tax rate.

i Gross federal tax minus tax credits.

Exercise 18-2
Inclusion or exclusion?

Some of the following items should be included in income; others on the list should be excluded. For each item listed, write the identifying letter and the word *included* or *excluded* to show whether the item belongs in income on the income tax return of an individual.

a Kickbacks received by automobile salespeople from insurance brokers to whom they referred customers.

b Money received from lottery winnings.

c Tips received by waiter.

d Interest received on investment bonds.

e Gain on sale of shares of Canadian Ltd. common stock.

f Gift from relative.

g Dividends from investment in a taxable Canadian corporation.

h Compensation received for damages suffered in automobile accident.

Exercise 18-3
Deductible or
nondeductible?

George Scrimger has a total income of $68,000 and a net income of $54,000. For each item listed, write the identifying letter and the word *deductible* or *nondeductible*.

a	Interest paid on instalment contract on automobile	$ 180
b	Gift to an unemployed relative	300
c	Professional dues	360
d	Contribution to Red Cross	225
e	Cost of commuting between home and work	800
f	Canada Pension Plan contributions	480
g	Unemployment insurance premiums	700
h	Registered pension plan contributions	3,500
i	Medical expenses (not covered by insurance)	500
j	Interest paid on a bank loan for investment purposes	450
k	Safety deposit box fee (to keep investment certificates)	35
l	Cash stolen in a burglary	80

Exercise 18-4
Determine total, net,
and taxable income,
and federal tax for
an individual.

Angela Lambert has the following information for her first tax return, one year after graduation from a top university.

Salary	$88,000
Taxable family allowance payments	388
Canada Pension Plan contributions	480
Unemployment insurance premiums	700
Professional dues	800
Registered pension plan contributions	3,500
Basic personal and dependent tax credits	1,085
Dental expenses	2,980
Charitable donations	2,600

Compute (a) total income, (b) net income, (c) taxable income, (d) gross federal tax, and (e) basic federal tax for Angela Lambert. The federal tax rates are assumed to be: 17% the first $27,500, 26% on the second $27,500, and 29% on the remaining taxable income.

Exercise 18-5
Determine taxable
income for an
individual

Gloria Chan has the following sources of income for 1988:

Interest from Canada Savings Bonds	$ 1,000
Dividends from taxable Canadian corporations	12,000
Gains on sales of shares in Canadian National Ltd.	3,000

Compute the *net* amount that should be included as taxable income, assuming no capital gain was reported in prior years.

Exercise 18-6
Determine taxable income and federal tax liability for a corporation

Windsor Corporation reports the following income during Year 1:

Operating income (after deducting depreciation of $100,000) $600,000
Capital gains 180,000
Dividends received from taxable Canadian corporations 60,000
Capital cost allowances 120,000

Compute the taxable income and *federal* income tax liability for Windsor Corporation for Year 1. Assume a 28% federal tax rate and ignore any surtax.

Exercise 18-7
Interperiod tax allocation

Mission Bay Corporation deducted on its tax return for 1988 an expense of $100,000 that was not recognized as an expense for accounting purposes until 1989. The corporation's accounting income before income taxes in each of the two years was $425,000. The company uses tax allocation procedures.

a Prepare the journal entries required at the end of 1988 and 1989 to record income tax expense, assuming a combined federal and provincial tax rate of 44%.

b Prepare a two-column schedule showing the net income to appear on the financial statements for 1988 and 1989, assuming tax allocation procedures are used. Also prepare a similar schedule on the assumption that tax allocation procedures are not used.

PROBLEMS

Group A

Problem 18A-1
Inclusion in or exclusion from income?

State whether each item listed below should be included in or excluded from an individual's income for federal income tax purposes. Add explanatory comments if they are necessary.

(1) Trip to Hawaii given by employer as reward for outstanding service.

(2) Taxpayer owed $1,500 on a note payable. During the current year the taxpayer painted a building owned by the creditor, and in turn the creditor cancelled the note.

(3) Gain on sale of taxable Canadian Ltd. capital stock.

(4) Salary received from a corporation by a shareholder who owns directly or indirectly all the shares of the corporation's outstanding stock.

(5) Amount received as damages in a libel lawsuit.

(6) Share of income from partnership in excess of drawings.

(7) An honorarium of $100 for a speech to charitable organizations.

(8) Interest received on Canada Savings Bonds.

(9) Value of a colour TV set won as a prize in a quiz contest.

(10) Cash dividends received from Canadian Oil Ltd.

(11) Unemployment insurance benefits.

(12) Inheritance received on death of a rich uncle.

Problem 18A-2
Deductible or not deductible from income?

State whether each item listed below is deductible or not deductible by an individual for federal income tax purposes.

(1) Interest paid on mortgage covering personal residence.

(2) Capital loss on the sale of securities.

(3) Life insurance premium paid by a taxpayer.

(4) Professional membership fee.

(5) Interest on a loan that was used to invest in a taxable Canadian corporation.

(6) Fees for preparation of personal income tax return.

(7) Lawyer's fee for appealing an assessment by Revenue Canada, Taxation.

(8) Registered pension plan contributions.

(9) Child care expenses.

(10) Tuition fees.

(11) Lottery losses.

(12) Expenses incurred in moving from Windsor to Halifax to accept a new position with a different company, not reimbursed by employer.

Problem 18A-3
Determine income tax for an individual

The following information is related to Joan French, a resident of a province with a tax rate of 55%.

Income:
Salary from employment	$68,000
Taxable family allowance payments	760
Dividends from taxable Canadian corporations	6,000
Interest from savings account with Bank of Nova Scotia	600
Gain on sale of shares of Halifax Ltd.	1,800

Withholdings:
Income taxes	22,000
Canada Pension Plan contributions	482
Unemployment insurance premiums	700
Contribution to a registered pension plan	3,500

Disbursements:
Charitable donations	1,200
Professional membership fees	820

Others:
Loss on sale of shares of Sydney Mines Ltd.	600
Lottery winnings	10,000
Tax credits relating to the taxpayer and her children	1,150

Instructions

Compute French's federal and provincial income tax for the year by using the following federal tax rates: 17% on the first $27,500, 26% on the second $27,500, and 29% on the remaining amount. Assume that French had not reported any capital gains or losses in prior years and that there is a 3% federal surtax.

Problem 18A-4
Determine capital cost allowance, federal tax, and deferred tax

Beazley Corporation has the following operation results for the current year:

Operating income (after depreciation of $170,000 and before capital gains and losses and dividends)	$600,000
Net capital gains from sale of securities (capital gains of $30,000 less capital losses of $18,000)	12,000
Dividends received from taxable Canadian corporations	30,000

The only depreciation assets of Beazley Corporation are machinery, equipment, and furniture. The ending balance from last year's tax return was $800,000. During the current year, the company added equipment and furniture at a cost of $450,000 and sold a machine (original cost $66,000) for $50,000. The capital cost allowance rate for tax purposes is 20%.

Instructions

a Compute the amount of capital cost allowance for the current year.

b Compute the federal income tax for the current year, based on 28% tax rate.

c Compute the amount of federal income tax deferred by claiming the maximum capital cost allowance rather than the amount of depreciation for accounting purposes.

Problem 18A-5
Determine accounting and taxable income, income tax and deferred tax, and tax advantage of financing method

The following information appears in the records of Plummer Corporation for the current year:

Net sales	$978,000
Cost of goods sold	697,200
Operating expenses (including depreciation of $80,000)	150,800
Dividends received from taxable Canadian corporations	20,000
Net capital losses from sale of securities (capital losses of $35,000 less capital gains of $19,000)	16,000
Capital cost allowance	180,000

Plummer Corporation is considering whether it should issue bonds or cumulative preferred stock to finance its expanded operations. The amount needed would be $600,000. Both the interest and dividend rates would be at 12%.

Instructions

a Compute the accounting income for the current year.

b Compute the taxable income for the current year.

c Compute the federal and provincial income taxes for the current year, based on the respective rates of 28% and 14%.

d Prepare the journal entry to record the current and deferred income taxes for the year.

e Explain which method of financing the $600,000 expansion is more beneficial to the company from an income tax viewpoint.

Group B

Problem 18B-1
Inclusion in or exclusion from income?

State whether each item listed below should be included in or excluded from an individual's income for federal income tax purposes. Add explanatory comments if needed.

(1) Cash dividends received on stock of Canadian Ltd.

(2) Lottery winnings.

(3) Income from personal injury awards.

(4) Interest received on a savings account in Y bank.

(5) Gain on sale of Dominion Ltd. shares of common stock.

(6) Unemployment insurance benefits.

(7) Drawing received from a proprietorship in excess of its income.

(8) Painted a building owned by the creditor in return for the cancellation of a note payable of $1,000.

(9) Las Vegas vacation paid by employer as reward for outstanding service.

(10) Proceeds of life insurance policy received on death of a taxpayer.

(11) Tips received by a doorman at a luxury hotel.

(12) Income from a business of an illegal nature.

Problem 18B-2
Deductible or not deductible from income?

State whether each of the following items is deductible or not deductible by an individual for federal income tax purposes.

(1) Cost of commuting between home and place of employment.

(2) Registered retirement savings plan premiums for a spouse.

(3) Unemployment insurance premiums.

(4) Gambling losses.

(5) Loss on sale of investment in securities.

(6) Tuition fees.

(7) Fee paid to chartered accountant for services in contesting assessment of additional income taxes by Revenue Canada, Taxation.

(8) Expenses incurred in moving across country to accept a position with different employer. Not reimbursed.

(9) Registered pension plan contributions.

(10) Union dues.

(11) Child care expenses.

(12) Interest paid on mortgage on personal residence.

Problem 18B-3
Determine income tax for an individual

Gloria Hoysum, a resident of a province with a 55% tax rate, asks you to prepare her tax return for the current year. She provides you with the following information:

Income:

Salary from employment	$60,000
Dividends from taxable Canadian corporations	3,000
Interest from Canada Savings Bonds	1,200
Gains on sale of shares of B.C. Ltd.'s common stock	2,000
Rental income (net)	8,000

Withholdings:

Income taxes	20,200
Canada Pension Plan contributions	480
Unemployment insurance premiums	706
Registered pension plan contributions	3,500

Disbursements:

Medical expenses	600
Charitable donations	2,500
Professional membership fees	800

Others:

Loss on sale of shares in Victoria Mines Ltd.	5,000
Lottery losses	300
Basic personal tax credit	1,020

Instructions   Compute Hoysum's federal and provincial income taxes for the year by using the following federal tax rates: 17% on the first $27,500, 26% on the second $27,500, and 29% on the balance. There is also a 3% federal surtax.

Problem 18B-4
Determine capital cost allowance, federal tax, and deferred tax

The following information is related to Ancaster Corporation for the current year:

Operating income (before depreciation, dividends, capital gains, and capital losses)	$800,000
Depreciation (automobiles and trucks, straight-line basis)	120,000
Dividends received from taxable Canadian corporations	80,000
Capital gains from sale of securities	20,000
Capital losses from sale of securities	50,000
Automobiles and trucks (class 10, maximum rate 30%):	
Beginning balance	600,000
Additions during the last month of the year	300,000
Proceeds from disposal of trucks (original cost $460,000) during the year	200,000

Instructions   **a** Compute the amount of capital cost allowance for the current year.

b Compute the federal income tax for the current year, based on a 28% tax rate.

c Compute the amount of federal income tax deferred by claiming the maximum capital cost allowance rather than the amount of depreciation for accounting purposes.

Problem 18B-5
Determine accounting and taxable income, income tax and deferred tax, and tax advantage of financing method

The accounting records of Macri Corporation included the following information for the current year:

Net sales	$7,500,000
Cost of goods sold	5,000,000
Dividends received from a taxable Canadian corporation	50,000
Operating expenses (including depreciation of $200,000)	1,600,000
Capital gains from sales of securities	28,000
Capital losses from sales of securities	10,000
Capital cost allowance	310,000

Macri is considering expanding its facilities as a result of increased sales, financed either by issuing $500,000, 10% bonds or 10% cumulative preferred stock.

Instructions

a Compute the accounting income for the current year.

b Compute the taxable income for the current year.

c Compute the federal and provincial income taxes for the current year. Assume that the federal rate is 28% and provincial rate is 14%.

d Prepare the journal entry to record the current and deferred income taxes for the year.

e Explain which method of financing the $500,000 expansion is more beneficial to the company from an income tax viewpoint.

BUSINESS DECISION CASES

Case 18-1
Investors choose
between debt and
equity

Bill and Hannah Bailey own a successful small company, Bailey Corporation. The outstanding capital stock consists of 1,000 shares, of which 400 shares are owned by Bill and 600 by Hannah. In order to finance a new branch operation, the corporation needs an additional $100,000 in cash. Bill and Hannah have this amount on deposit with a bank and intend to put these personal funds into the corporation in order to establish the new branch. They will either arrange for the corporation to issue to them an additional 1,000 shares of stock, or they will make a loan to the corporation at an interest rate of 12%.

Income before taxes of the corporation has been consistently averaging $150,000 a year, and annual dividends of $64,000 have been paid regularly on the $100,000 of capital stock. It is expected that the new branch will cause *income before taxes* to increase by $30,000. If new common stock is issued to finance the expansion, the total annual dividend of $64,000 will be continued unchanged. If a loan of $100,000 is arranged, the dividend will be reduced by $12,000, the amount of annual interest on the loan.

Instructions

a From the income tax standpoint of Bill and Hannah Bailey (with a marginal tax rate of 29%), would there be any savings as between the stock issuance and the loan? Explain.

b From the standpoint of getting their money out of the corporation (assuming that the new branch is profitable), should Bill and Hannah choose capital stock or a loan for the infusion of new funds to the corporation?

c Prepare a two-column schedule, with one column headed If New Stock Is Used and the other headed If Loan Is Used. For each of these proposed methods of financing, show (1) the present corporate income *before taxes;* (2) the corporate income *before taxes* after the expansion; (3) the corporate income taxes (12% tax rate) after the expansion; and (4) the corporate net income after the expansion.

Case 18-2
Tax advantage: sole
proprietorship
versus corporation

Paul Cormier is in the process of organizing a business that is expected to produce, before any compensation to him and before income taxes, an income of $98,000 per year. In deciding whether to operate as a sole proprietorship or as a corporation, he is willing to make the choice on the basis of the relative income tax advantage under either form of organization.

If the business is organized as a sole proprietorship, Cormier plans to withdraw the entire income of $98,000 each year.

If the business is organized as a corporation, Cormier will own all the shares and will pay himself a salary of $32,000. He will distribute the remaining after-tax income as dividends.

It may be assumed that the accounting income and the taxable income for the corporation would be the same and that the corporation would be qualified as a small business for income tax purposes.

Cormier is a resident of a province where the tax rate for individuals is 55% and has a total deduction of $6,000, and a total tax credit (not including any dividend tax credit) of $1,600.

Instructions   Determine the relative income tax advantage to Paul Cormier of operating the business as a sole proprietorship or as a corporation, and make a recommendation as to the form of organization he should adopt. Would it be beneficial to Cormier, from an income tax viewpoint, to keep the remaining after-tax income in the corporation rather than distribute it as dividend? Assume a combined federal and provincial tax rate of 20% for a corporation qualified as a small business and that the federal income tax rates for individuals are: 17% for the first $27,500, 26% for the second $27,500, and 29% for the amount in excess of $55,000.

STATEMENT OF CHANGES IN FINANCIAL POSITION

CHAPTER PREVIEW

In this chapter we introduce a new major financial statement — a statement of changes in financial position. First, we differentiate this statement from the balance sheet and the income statement. Second, we explain the nature and objective of, as well as the disclosure and presentation requirements for, a statement of changes in financial position. Third, we identify the principal sources and uses of cash. Fourth, we show step-by-step how a statement of changes in financial position can be developed, using both a simple and a comprehensive case. Finally, we demonstrate how a statement of changes in a financial position may be analyzed and interpreted.

After studying this chapter you should be able to meet these Learning Objectives:

1   Differentiate a statement of changes in financial position from an income statement and a balance sheet.

2   Explain the nature and objective of the statement of changes in financial position.

3   Explain the disclosure and presentation requirements for a statement of changes in financial position.

4   Identify the principal sources and uses of cash.

5   Develop a statement of changes in financial position — a simple and a comprehensive illustration.

6   Analyze and interpret a statement of changes in financial position.

Differentiate a statement of changes in financial position from an income statement and a balance sheet.

In Chapter 1, we introduced two key financial objectives of every business organization: *operating profitably* and *staying solvent.* Operating profitably means increasing the amount of the owners' equity through the activities of the business; in short, providing the owners with a satisfactory return on their investment. Staying solvent means being able to pay the debts and obligations of the business as they come due.

An income statement is designed to measure the success or failure of the business in achieving its objective of profitable operations. To some extent, a balance sheet shows whether or not the business is solvent. It shows, for example, the nature and amounts of current assets and current liabilities. From this information, users of the financial statements may compute such measures of solvency as the current ratio and the amount of working capital.

However, assessing the ability of a business to remain solvent involves more than just evaluating the liquid resources on hand at the balance sheet date. In this chapter we introduce a new major financial statement, the *statement of changes in financial position,* which provides *additional* information on the solvency and liquidity of a business. Liquidity means the ability to generate and maintain an adequate amount of the most liquid financial resources—cash and cash equivalents. Thus, this statement complements the balance sheet and the income statement.

STATEMENT OF CHANGES IN FINANCIAL POSITION
Nature and Objective

Explain the nature and objective of the statement of changes in financial position.

A statement of changes in financial position summarizes the operating, financing, and investing activities of a business for a period on a *cash basis* (i.e., cash and cash equivalents).[1] Thus, it explains how and why the cash position of a business has changed during a period. The objective of this statement is to provide information to financial statement users to assess the liquidity and solvency of a business, that is, its ability to generate cash from internal and external sources to finance its operations and investments.[2] With this information on how cash has flowed into the business and how cash has been used, we can begin to answer such important questions as: Do the normal operations of the business generate sufficient cash to enable the company to continue paying dividends? Did the company have to borrow to finance the acquisition of new plant assets, or was it able to generate the cash from current operations? Is the business becoming more or less solvent? And perhaps the most puzzling question: How can a *profitable* business be running low on cash? Even though a business operates profitably, its cash may decline and the business may even become insolvent.

The statement of changes in financial position gives us answers to these questions, because it shows in detail the amount of cash received from each source and the amount of cash used for each purpose throughout the year. In fact, this statement is also called a "cash flow statement," a "statement of changes in cash resources," and a "statement of operating, financing, and investing activities." However, the

---

[1] CICA, *CICA Handbook,* (Toronto), paragraphs 1540.01, 1540.02, and 1540.03.

[2] The terms "operations" and "operating activities" are used interchangeably.

most commonly used title for this statement is the ***statement of changes in financial position***.[3]

Prior to 1985, the statement of changes in financial position was prepared on a working capital (current assets less current liabilities) basis, that is, it focussed on the sources and uses of working capital. In September, 1985, the Accounting Standards Committee, through Section 1540 of the *CICA Handbook*, recommended that the statement of changes in financial position should be prepared on a basis of cash rather than of working capital. The reason for this change is to accommodate the financial statement users' increasing interest and preference for information on cash flows. Many corporations with a year-end date subsequent to the date of the CICA pronouncement followed this recommendation by publishing their statements of changes in financial position on a cash basis.

Cash Defined

Section 1540 of the *CICA Handbook* recommends that the statement of changes in financial position "should report the changes in ***cash and cash equivalents*** resulting from the activities of the enterprise during the period." (Emphasis added.) Thus, this statement shows the changes not only for cash but also for cash equivalents. Cash and cash equivalents are described in Section 1540 as follows: "Cash and cash equivalents would normally include cash, net of short-term borrowings, and temporary investments and may, in some cases, include ***certain other elements of working capital when they are equivalent to cash***." (Emphasis added.) It should be noted that it is the short-term ***borrowings*** (such as bank loans), not short-term debts (such as accounts payable), that are included in the calculation of cash and cash equivalents.

Unfortunately, Section 1540 neither identifies these "other elements" nor explains the conditions under which these elements are considered as equivalent to cash. It has been suggested that these elements would include such working capital items as "receivables, inventories, and payables when they are equivalent to cash."[4]

3   Explain the disclosure and presentation requirements for a statement of changes in financial position.

Disclosure and presentation

While the exact format of the statement of changes in financial position may vary from company to company, Section 1540 stipulates the items that should be disclosed and the manner in which these items should be presented. To ensure that the statement of changes in financial position is as informative as possible, Section 1540 recommends that it contain separate disclosures of at least the following items:

1 Cash from operations: the amount of cash from operations should be reconciled to the income statement, or the components of cash from operations should be disclosed.[5]

2 Cash flows resulting from extraordinary items.

3 Outlays for acquisition and proceeds on disposal of assets, by major category, not included in **1** or **2** above.

4 The issue, assumption, redemption, and repayment of debt not included in **1** or **2** above.

---

[3] According to the CICA's *Financial Reporting in Canada*, 17th ed. (Toronto), 1987, p. 208, of the 299 companies surveyed, 228 used this title.

[4] Sam Marinucci, "Changes to Statement of Changes," *CA Magazine*, October, 1985, p. 68.

[5] *Financial Reporting in Canada*, p. 210. Of the 271 companies surveyed, 263 reconcile the amount of cash from operations to net income in the income statement. This approach is used here in Chapter 19.

5 The issue, redemption, and acquisition of share capital.

6 The payment of dividends, identifying separately dividends paid by subsidiaries to minority interests.

Furthermore, it recommends that the above items be classified into three categories: *operating, financing*, and *investing.* Cash flows from *operating activities* relate to cash from operations and would include net income before extraordinary items and changes in noncash current accounts. Cash flows from *financing activities* refer to those items affecting the size and composition of a company's long-term debt and equity capital structure and would include items **4** and **5** above. Cash flows from *investing activities* pertain to those items affecting the noncurrent assets such as long-term investments, plant, and equipment implied in item **3** above.

Certain financing and investing activities such as the acquisition of plant assets by issuing long-term debt or capital stock, or the conversion of long-term debt to equity, even though they do not involve cash, are to be disclosed, since the effect of these activities is "similar to a cash inflow followed immediately by a cash outflow, or vice versa."[6] These activities are often referred to as *exchange transactions.*

The rationale for the recommended disclosure and presentation is to provide information to financial statement users to assess a company's ability to generate cash from internal and external sources to finance its operating and investing activities, as well as to show the changes in the structure of a company's long-term assets, long-term debts, and equity capital. Consequently, these users are better able to evaluate the company's liquidity and solvency position, and its cash policies on operating, financing, and investing activities.

The cash flow from operations is of critical importance because in the long run, a business must generate positive cash flows from operations if the business is to survive. A business with negative cash flows from operations will not be able to raise cash from other sources indefinitely. In fact, the ability of a business to raise cash through financing activities is highly dependent upon its ability to generate cash from operations. Creditors and shareholders are reluctant to invest in a company that does not generate enough cash from operations to assure prompt payment of maturing liabilities, interest, and dividends.

A statement of changes in financial position of a large Canadian company that followed the recommended disclosure and presentation is shown on page 764.

SOURCES AND USES OF CASH

4 Identify the principal sources and uses of cash.

Cash may be provided by a number of sources. Any transaction that increases the amount of cash is a *source of cash.* The sales of merchandise for cash, the collection on accounts receivable, and the issuance of debt or equity instruments for cash are examples of sources of cash, as they cause cash to increase. Also, cash may be used in many ways. Any transaction that decreases the amount of cash is a *use of cash.* The purchase of merchandise for cash, the payment of accounts payable or expenses, and the payment for redemption or retirement of long-term debt are examples of uses of cash, as they lead to a decrease in cash.

[6] CICA, *CICA Handbook*, paragraph 1540.20.

Spar Aerospace Limited

CONSOLIDATED STATEMENT OF CHANGES IN FINANCIAL POSITION

($000s) for the year ended December 31, 1986

	1986	1985
Operating activities		
Net income from operations	$ 4,394	$13,070
Items not affecting cash (note 13)	3,146	7,613
	7,540	20,683
Net increase (decrease) in cash invested in working capital related to operations (note 13)	14,761	(29,369)
Other	193	747
Net cash from (used in) operating activities	22,494	(7,939)
Financing activities		
Issue of subordinate voting shares	19,512	14,078
Conversion of subordinated debentures to share capital	(14,987)	(7,838)
Employee share purchase plan term loans	(32)	(119)
Long term debt repayments and provision for current instalments	(5,381)	(1,493)
Increase in long term debt	–	736
Dividends	(4,845)	(4,342)
Net cash from (used in) financing activities	(5,733)	1,022
Investment activities		
Additions to fixed assets	(9,397)	(8,660)
Long term investment	(678)	(2,600)
Deferred costs	(4,070)	(1,349)
Purchase of technology	(555)	(300)
Net cash used in investment activities	(14,700)	(12,909)
Increase (decrease) in cash	2,061	(19,826)
Cash, beginning of year	3,924	23,750
Cash, end of year	$ 5,985	$ 3,924

"Cash" consists of marketable securities less bank indebtedness.

NOTES TO CONSOLIDATED FINANCIAL STATEMENTS (continued)

(tabular amounts are in thousands of dollars)

December 31, 1986

13. Statement of changes in financial position

Items not affecting cash

The components of net income which did not affect cash consist of the following:

	($000s)	
	1986	1985
Depreciation and amortization	$ 6,612	$ 5,650
Deferred income taxes	257	4,072
Amortization of goodwill	485	426
Accrued incentive revenue	(4,208)	(2,535)
	$ 3,146	$ 7,613

Net increase (decrease) in cash invested in working capital related to operations

The net increase in cash invested in working capital related to operations results from the following increases (decreases) in working capital components:

	($000s)	
	1986	1985
Accounts receivable	$25,804	$ 9,753
Income tax recoverable	717	4,298
Inventories	(20,449)	16,166
Prepaid expenses and other	3,233	2,851
Accounts payable and accrued charges	(7,991)	(4,073)
Payroll and other taxes payable	(1,517)	(1,255)
Dividend payable	93	(291)
Customer advance payments	(14,651)	1,920
Net increase (decrease) in working capital related to operations	$(14,761)	$29,369

On the other hand, transactions affecting only the cash and cash equivalent accounts *equally* do not change the amount of cash and cash equivalents. For example, the purchase of temporary investments such as marketable securities with cash (which decreases cash and increases temporary investments equally) changes the components but does not change the total amount of cash and cash equivalents. Similarly, short-term borrowings such as bank loans (which increase cash and increase short-term borrowings equally) change the components but do not change the total amount of cash and cash equivalents. Of course, if a transaction affects both cash and cash equivalent accounts and the effect on the cash account is different from the effect on the cash equivalent accounts, there will be an increase or decrease in the total amount of cash and cash equivalents. Selling temporary investments at a gain, for example, will increase the amount of cash and cash equivalents and the increase is included in net income from operating activities. Obtaining a short-term bank loan at a discount (i.e., with prepaid interest deducted from the loan) or selling temporary investments at a loss will decrease the amount of cash and cash equivalents and the decrease is included in net income from operating activities.

The principal sources and uses of cash are listed as follows:

Sources of cash

1 **Current operations** If the inflow of cash from sales and collection of accounts receivable exceeds the outflow of cash to cover the cost of merchandise purchases and expenses of doing business, current operations will provide a *net source of cash.* If the inflow of cash from sales and collection of accounts receivable is less than the outflow of cash, operations will result in a *net use of cash.* Thus, the net source or use of cash from operations accounts for the portion of the change in cash (cash and cash equivalents) resulting from the changes in *all other current asset accounts and all current liability accounts that are related to the income statement.* Certain current liability accounts, such as dividends payable, and the current portion of long-term debts are not related to the income statement and therefore have no effect on the net source or use of cash from operations.

Since the timing of recognizing cash inflows and cash outflows is different from recognizing revenue and its related costs and expenses, the amount of cash provided by operations is *not* the same as the amount of net income earned during the period. Other differences between the amount of cash provided by operations or operating activities and the amount of net income will be discussed later in the chapter.

2 **Long-term borrowing** Long-term borrowing, such as issuing bonds payable for cash, results in an increase in cash. Thus, the proceeds from this transaction are a source of cash.

3 **Sale of additional shares of stock** The sale or issuance of capital stock for cash results in an inflow of cash. Thus, this transaction is a source of cash. In a similar manner, additional investments of cash by owners represent sources of cash to sole proprietorships and partnerships. The issuance of capital stock in conjunction with a stock dividend or a stock split, however, does not bring any new resources into the company and is not a source of cash.

4 Sale of noncurrent assets A business may obtain cash by selling noncurrent assets, such as plant and equipment or long-term investments, in exchange for cash. As long as cash is received, the sale is a source of cash *regardless of whether the noncurrent assets are sold at a gain or a loss.* For example, assume that a company sells land that cost $80,000 for $60,000 in cash. Although the land was sold at a loss, the company has increased its cash by $60,000. Thus, the transaction is a source of cash.

Item **1** above is classified under operating activities, items **2** and **3** under financing activities, and item **4** under investing activities.

Uses of Cash

1 Payment of cash dividends The payment of cash dividend results in a decrease in cash and is therefore a use of cash. Notice that it is the payment of the dividend rather than the declaration of the dividend, which is the use of cash. Stock dividends that do not involve any distribution of cash or any option to distribute cash are not a use of cash.

2 Repayment of long-term debt Cash is decreased when it is used to repay long-term debt. Thus, such a repayment is a use of cash.

3 Repurchase or retirement of outstanding stock When cash is paid out to repurchase or to retire outstanding shares of stock, cash is reduced. Thus, the transaction is a use of cash.

4 Purchase of noncurrent assets Purchases of noncurrent (long-term) assets such as plant and equipment with cash represent a use of cash. Special situations in which noncurrent assets are acquired in exchange for other noncurrent assets or long-term liabilities are shown as both a source and a use of cash.

Items **1**, **2**, and **3** are classified under financing activities and item **4** under investing activities.

DEVELOP A STATEMENT OF CHANGES IN FINANCIAL POSITION

Cash flow: a simple illustration

5 Develop a statement of changes in financial position — a simple and a comprehensive illustration.

Assume that John Claire started a business, Claire Company, as a sole proprietorship on April 30 by investing $40,000 cash; the company rented a building on May 1 and completed the following transactions during the month of May:

(1) Claire invested an additional $27,000 cash in the business.
(2) Purchased merchandise costing $40,000 on credit and sold three-fourths of this also on credit, for $58,000.
(3) Collected $45,000 on receivables; paid $31,000 on accounts payable.
(4) Incurred $20,500 of operating expenses, of which $18,500 was paid, $2,000 was accrued.
(5) Purchased land for the construction of a store by issuing a six-year mortgage note for $17,000.
(6) Paid $30,000 for equipment purchased on May 31.
(7) Paid $1,000 for a one-year insurance policy which begins on June 1.
(8) Withdrew $2,000 cash from the business for personal use.

The company's income statement and balance sheet at May 31 follow:

CLAIRE COMPANY
Income Statement
For the Month Ended May 31

Sales		$58,000
Cost of goods sold:		
Purchases	$40,000	
Less: Ending inventory (one-fourth of purchases)	10,000	30,000
Gross profit on Sales		$28,000
Operating expenses		20,500
Net income		$7,500

CLAIR COMPANY
Comparative Balance Sheet

ASSETS	MAY 31	APR. 30
Cash	$ 29,500	$40,000
Accounts receivable	13,000	
Inventory	10,000	
Unexpired insurance	1,000	
Land	17,000	
Equipment	30,000	
Total assets	$100,500	$40,000

LIABILITIES & OWNER'S EQUITY		
Accounts payable	$ 9,000	
Accrued liabilities	2,000	
Mortgage payable (due in six years)	17,000	
John Claire, capital	72,500	$40,000
Total liabilities & owner's equity	$100,500	$40,000

The cash account amounted to $40,000 on April 30 but was only $29,500 on May 31, a decrease of $10,500. In analyzing the transactions completed during the month of May, we see that cash was increased and decreased as follows:

Transactions increasing cash:		
Additional investment by owner		$27,000
Collection of accounts receivable		45,000
Total increases in cash		$72,000
Transactions decreasing cash:		
Payment of accounts payable	$31,000	
Payment of operating expenses	18,500	
Payment for purchase of equipment	30,000	
Payment for unexpired insurance	1,000	
Withdrawal of cash by owner	2,000	
Total decrease in cash		82,500
Decrease in cash during May		$10,500

A complete list of transactions for a fiscal period may not be readily available, and even if it were, analysis of such a list would be a laborious process. In practice, a statement of changes in financial position is prepared by analyzing the changes that occurred *in the noncash accounts* (that is, all accounts other than the accounts for cash, temporary investment, and short-term borrowing such as bank loans) during the fiscal period. An analysis of the comparative balance sheet for Claire Company indicates the following changes in the noncash accounts:

(1) Increase in accounts receivable, $13,000.
(2) Increase in inventory, $10,000.
(3) Increase in unexpired insurance, $1,000.
(4) Increase in land, $17,000.
(5) Increase in equipment, $30,000.
(6) Increase in accounts payable, $9,000.
(7) Increase in accrued liabilities, $2,000.
(8) Increase in mortgage payable, $17,000.
(9) Increase in Claire's capital, $32,500, resulting from additional cash investment of $27,000, net income of $7,500, and a withdrawal of cash of $2,000.

Based on this analysis, we can prepare the following statement of changes in financial position for the month of May to account for the $10,500 decrease in cash.

A SIMPLE STATEMENT OF
CHANGES IN FINANCIAL
POSITION

CLAIRE COMPANY
Statement of Changes in Financial Position
For Month of May

Operating activities:		
Net income		$ 7,500
Deduct: Increase in accounts receivable	$(13,000)	
Increase in inventory	(10,000)	
Increase in unexpired insurance	(1,000)	(24,000)
Add: Increase in accounts payable	$9,000	
Increase in accrued liabilities	2,000	11,000
Cash used by operating activities		$ (5,500)
Financing activities:		
Additional investment by owner	$27,000	
Withdrawal by owner	(2,000)	
Issuance of mortgage note for land	17,000	
Cash provided by financing activities		42,000
Investing activities:		
Purchase of land in exchange for a mortgage note	$(17,000)	
Purchase of equipment	(30,000)	
Cash used in investing activities		(47,000)
Decrease in cash		$(10,500)

The difference between net income and net cash flow should be carefully noted i this example. Although Claire Company's net income for May was $7,500, experienced a *cash deficiency* of $5,500 from operating activities and its cas account *decreased* by $10,500. This is not unusual for a company just beginning i business. However, a company will experience financial difficulty if there is a continuing cash deficiency from its operations and a continuing decline in its most liquid asset — cash.

The preceding statement illustrates the recommendation of Section 1540 of the *CICA Handbook* that requires a reconciliation of the amount of cash provided or used by operations with the net income from the income statement. This reconciliation is in essence a conversion of the net income figure from an accrual basis to a cash basis. Thus, changes in the noncash current asset and liability accounts such as accounts receivable, inventory, unexpired insurance, accounts payable, and accrued liabilities, which have a different effect on net income on an accrual basis than on net income on a cash basis, must be taken into account in the conversion process.[7] Let us now explain why the increase or decrease of these noncash current items is added to or deducted from accrual basis net income to arrive at cash provided or used by operating activities (cash basis net income or net loss.)

To explain why an *increase* in accounts receivable is *deducted* from accrual basis net income to obtain cash provided or used by operating activities, we must understand the relationship between the amount of cash collected from customers and the sales reported in the income statement. If accounts receivable have increased during the period, we know that credit sales are being made faster than the cash is being collected. In other words, an increase in accounts receivable means a *higher* amount of sales is being reported, causing a *higher* net income to be shown on an accrual than a cash basis.

In the Claire Company example, the increase in accounts receivable of $13,000 means that sales and net income in the income statements on an accrual basis are $13,000 *higher* than on a cash basis. Consequently, this *increase* must be *deducted* from the net income of $7,500 in computing the cash provided or used by operating activities.

Net income per income statement	$ 7,500
Deduct: Increase in accounts receivable	(13,000)

Alternatively, we can deduct this increase of accounts receivable from sales to produce the same result — reducing the revenue and thus the net income by $13,000, as shown below (with *sales on a cash basis*):

Sales	$58,000
Less: Increase in accounts receivable	13,000
Sales on a cash collected basis	$45,000

While the Claire Company example shows an increase in accounts receivable, the amount of accounts receivable can be either an increase or a decrease in a given

---

[7] The cash basis of accounting was explained in Chapter 3. Under the cash basis, revenue is not recorded until cash is collected from the customer; purchases of merchandise and expenses are recorded in the period in which payment is made. Under the accrual basis, on the other hand, revenue is recognized at the date of sale and expenses are recorded when the related goods or services are used.

situation. If accounts receivable have decreased, cash is being collected faster than credit sales are being made. Thus, a decrease in accounts receivable means a *lower* amount of sales is being reported, causing a *lower* net income to be shown on an accrual than on a cash basis. Consequently, a *decrease* in accounts receivable must be *added* to the sales or net income on an accrual basis in computing the cash provided or used by operating activities.

Since inventory and accounts payable are interrelated, it is necessary to combine the two in our discussion. An *increase in inventory is deducted* from, and *an increase in accounts payable is added* to the net income on an accrual basis to obtain the cash provided or used by operating activities. To explain why, we must understand the relationship between these two items and the cost of goods sold on an accrual basis on the one hand, and their relationship with cash payments for purchases on a cash basis on the other. An increase in inventory means more goods are purchased on credit than are sold, causing the cost of goods *purchased* to be larger than the cost of goods sold during the period. This in turn causes a corresponding increase in accounts payable for purchases. If the increase in accounts payable is equal to the increase in inventory, the amount of cash payments for purchases is the same as the amount of cost of goods sold. However, an increase in accounts payable can be reduced by payments; the amount of this increase that is reduced by payments represents the extent of the cash payments for purchases in excess of the cost of goods sold. In other words, when the increase in inventory is more than the increase in accounts payable for purchases, the cash payments for purchases are greater than the cost of goods sold. The result is that the net income on an accrual basis is *higher* than that on a cash basis. Accordingly, the amount of the increase in inventory over the increase in accounts payable must be *deducted* from the net income reported in the income statement to arrive at the cash provided or used by operating activities. This has the same effect as *deducting the increase in inventory from, and adding the increase in accounts payable to, accrual basis net income to produce cash provided or used by operating activities.*

Referring to the Claire Company example, we can see that the company increased its inventory by $10,000 and that its accounts payable for purchases increased by $9,000. The increase in inventory is deducted from and the increase in accounts payable is added to the net income in the income statement to obtain the cash provided or used by operating activities.

Net income per income statement	$ 7,50
Deduct: Increase in inventory*	(10,00
Add: Increase in accounts payable*	9,00

*This has the same effect as deducting the difference between the increase in inventory and the increase in accounts payable from net income: $7,500 − (10,000 − 9,000).

Alternatively, we can use the above information to convert the cost of goods sold to cash payments for purchases to produce the same result — increasing the cost of goods sold of $30,000 to cash payments for purchases of $31,000 and thereby reducing the net income by $1,000:

Cost of goods sold	$30,000
Add: Increase in inventory	10,000
Purchases (accrual basis)	$40,000
Less: Increase in accounts payable for purchases	9,000
Cash payments for purchases (cash basis)	31,000*

*As mentioned earlier, if the increase in accounts payable equals the increase in inventory, cash payments for purchases would be the same as cost of goods sold — both would be $30,000.

While the amount of cash payments for purchases of $31,000 is already provided in the Claire Company example for illustration purposes, it is usually not readily available. Therefore, it is important to understand the elements involved in converting the cost of goods sold to cash payments for purchases.

So far we have discussed the case where there is an increase in inventory and an increase in accounts payable. What happens if there is a decrease in inventory and a decrease in accounts payable? The answer should be quite obvious — *the decrease in inventory* should be *added back to*, and *the decrease in accounts payable deducted from*, the accrual basis net income to arrive at the cash provided or used by operating activities. The reason for such an answer is that when both inventory and accounts payable are decreased, and the decrease in inventory is *greater* than in accounts payable, the cash payments for purchases are smaller than the cost of goods sold. On the other hand, if the decrease in inventory is *smaller* than the decrease in accounts payable, the cash payments for purchases are larger than the cost of goods sold. Thus, a decrease in inventory is added to, and a decrease in accounts payable is deducted from, accrual basis net income to obtain the cash provided or used by operating activities.

Why is the increase in a short-term prepayment such as unexpired insurance deducted from the accrual basis net income to obtain the cash provided or used by operating activities? The answer is that the increase represents the amount of cash payments for operating expenses during the period that is *not* recognized in computing accrual basis net income but *is* recognized in computing cash provided or used by operating activities. Thus, in converting the accrual basis net income to the cash provided or used by operating activities, the *increase* in a short-term prepayment such as unexpired insurance must be *deducted* from the accrual basis net income.

Referring to the Claire Company example, the increase in unexpired insurance of $1,000 is not recognized in computing the accrual basis net income of $7,500 but is recognized in computing the cash provided or used by operating activities. Therefore, this $1,000 *increase* in unexpired insurance must be *deducted* from the accrual basis net income of $7,500 to arrive at the cash provided or used by operating activities.

Net income per income statement	$7,500
Deduct: Increase in unexpired insurance	1,000

Alternatively, we can convert the operating expenses of $20,500 to cash payments for expenses of $21,500 to produce the same result — reducing the accrual basis net income by $1,000, as follows:

Operating expenses	$20,500
Add: Increase in unexpired insurance	1,000
Cash payments for operating expenses	$21,500*

*If the increase in accrued liabilities is deducted, as discussed later, the cash payments for operating expenses will be $19,500 ($20,500 − 2,000 + 1,000).

How should a decrease in a short-term prepayment be handled? A *decrease* in a short-term prepayment is *added* to the accrual basis net income to determine cash provided or used by operating activities because it represents the amount of operating expenses recognized by the accrual basis in excess of the amount of cash payments for operating expenses during the period.

An understanding of the relationship between operating expenses and cash payments for these expenses helps to explain why an increase in accrued liabilities is added to the accrual basis net income to obtain the cash provided or used by operating activities. On an accrual basis, all operating expenses incurred during the period are recognized in the income statement; on a cash basis, only cash payments for expenses are recognized. Therefore, when there is an increase in accrued liabilities during the period, we know that more operating expenses are incurred than cash payments for these expenses. That is, an increase in accrued liabilities means a *larger* amount of operating expenses is being reported, causing a *lower* net income to be shown on an accrual basis than on a cash basis. Thus, in converting accrual basis net income to cash provided or used by operating activities, an *increase* in accrued liabilities is *added* to net income.

In the Claire Company example, the increase in accrued liabilities of $2,000 means that the income statement shows $2,000 more operating expenses than cash payments for expenses and $2,000 less in net income on an accrual basis than on a cash basis. Consequently, this increase must be *added* to the net income of $7,500 in computing the cash provided or used by operating activities.

Net income per income statement	$7,500
Add: Increase in accrued liabilities	2,000

Alternatively, we can deduct this increase of $2,000 from operating expenses to produce the same result — increasing net income by $2,000.

Operating expenses	$20,500
Deduct: Increase in accrued liabilities	2,000
Cash payments for operating expenses	$18,500

As explained above, since an *increase* in accrued liabilities is *added* to accrual basis net income, it follows that a *decrease* in accrued liabilities should be *deducted* from accrual basis net income to obtain cash provided or used by operating activities. A decrease in accrued liabilities means that the expenses reported on an accrual basis are *less* than the cash payments for expenses and for accrued liabilities, causing the accrual basis net income to be *more* than the cash provided or used by operating activities. Thus, the *decrease* in accrued liabilities must be *deducted* from accrual basis net income.

We have now explained in detail the reasons underlying each of the items involved in the conversion of net income to cash provided or used by operating activities. We may summarize the relationship between income and cash provided or used by operating activities as follows:

Net income

+ {
decrease in accounts receivable
decrease in inventory
decrease in short-term prepayments
increase in accounts payable
increase in accrued liabilities
}

or

− {
increase in accounts receivable
increase in inventory
increase in short-term prepayments
decrease in accounts payable
decrease in accrued liabilities
}

= cash provided or used by operating activities

Applying the above formula to the Claire Company example, we will achieve the same result as shown on page 768.

Net income		$ 7,500
Deduct: Increase in accounts receivable	$(13,000)	
Increase in inventory	(10,000)	
Increase in unexpired insurance	(1,000)	(24,000)
Add: Increase in accounts payable	$ 9,000	
Increase in accrued liabilities	2,000	11,000
Cash used by operating activities		$ (5,500)

If all the items in the income statement are converted to a cash basis, the relationship between the accrual and cash basis for each statement item may be stated as set out below:

Net sales {
+ decrease in accounts receivable
or
− increase in accounts receivable
} = cash receipts from customers

Cost of goods sold {
+ increase in inventory
or
− decrease in inventory
and
+ decrease in accounts payable
or
− increase in accounts payable
} = cash payments for purchases

Expenses {
+ decrease in accrued liabilities
+ increase in short-term prepayments
or
− increase in accrued liabilities
− decrease in short-term prepayments
} = cash payments for expenses

Applying the above formula to the Claire Company example, we have the following:

Net sales	$58,000
Less: Increase in accounts receivable	13,000
Cash receipts from customers	$45,000
Cost of goods sold	$30,000
Add: Increase in inventory	10,000
	$40,000
Deduct: Increase in accounts payable	9,000
Cash payments for purchases	$31,000
Operating expenses	$20,500
Deduct: Increase in accrued liabilities	2,000
	$18,500
Add: Increase in unexpired insurance (short-term prepayment)	1,000
Cash payments for operating expenses	$19,500

Thus, the income statement on a cash basis is

Cash receipts from customers	$45,000
Cash payments for purchases	31,000
	$14,000
Cash payments for operating expenses	19,500
Cash used by operating activities	$ 5,500

Note that in using either formula, we come to the same result, an amount of cash used by operating activities or net cash loss of $5,500.

As far as the items relating to financing and investing activities are concerned they can be readily determined from the analysis of the noncurrent accounts and the additional information provided in the Claire Company illustration.

One item in the Claire Company's statement of changes in financial position relating to the financing and investing activities that deserves special attention is the presentation of the mortgage note. This mortgage note was issued for the purchase of land. This transaction did not involve cash but it is still shown in the statement of changes in financial position. Why? The issuance of the $17,000 mortgage note for land is considered an **exchange transaction.** As discussed earlier in the chapter, the effect of an exchange transaction is similar to two related transactions involving a cash inflow followed immediately by a cash outflow, or vice versa. Thus, the exchange of a mortgage note for land is treated as if it consists of two parts: (1) the issuance of a mortgage note for $17,000 cash, and (2) the use of this $17,000 to purchase land. Accordingly, this transaction is shown as **both a source of cash** (issuance of mortgage note) from financing activities, **and a use of cash** (purchase of land) in investing activities, together with proper disclosure on the nature of the relationship of these two items. The objective of this treatment is to disclose **all** financing and investing activities affecting the long-term debt and equity capital and long-term asset structure of business.[8]

---

[8] CICA, *CICA Handbook*, paragraph 1540.20.

Other examples of exchange transactions that have no direct effect upon cash but are required by Section 1540 of the *CICA Handbook* to be shown as both a source and a use of cash include the acquisition of plant assets by issuing capital stock, the conversion of bonds payable or preferred stock into common stock, and the issuance of stock dividends where shareholders have an ***option of receiving cash or shares of capital stock*** (optional stock dividends). Most transactions affecting ***only long-term (noncurrent) accounts*** are exchange transactions. Four exceptions, however, are: (1) stock dividends where shareholders can only receive shares of capital (non-optional stock dividends); (2) stock splits; (3) transfers to and from reserve accounts; and (4) appraisal adjustments.[9] These exceptions do not involve an exchange and ***are not*** regarded as financing and investing activities. For this reason, they are not shown in a statement of changes in financial position.

Cash provided by operations — additional matters

Cash provided by operations is the net increase or decrease in cash resulting from the normal business activities of collecting revenue and paying expenses. There are similarities between the providing of cash by operations and the earning of net income. For example, earning revenue increases net income, and the related inflow of cash increases the amount of cash from operations. However, there are also significant differences between net income and the amount of cash provided by operations. In addition to differences identified as reconciliation items in the Claire Company example in the preceding section, there are others.

Some expenses do not reduce cash   Some expenses, such as depreciation, amortization of intangible assets, and amortization of discount on bonds payable, reduce net income but have no immediate effect on the amount of cash provided by normal operations.

To illustrate, assume that on December 31, 1988, City Delivery Service buys two trucks for cash at a cost of $30,000. As of January 1, 1989, the company has no assets other than the trucks and has no liabilities. During 1989 the company does business on a cash basis, collecting revenue of $40,000 and paying expenses of $22,000, thus showing an $18,000 increase in cash. The company then records depreciation expense of $6,000 on its trucks, resulting in a $12,000 net income for 1989. What is the amount of cash provided by operations in 1989? The recording of depreciation expense reduces net income, ***but it does not reduce cash;*** cash provided by operations remains at $18,000. The $12,000 net income figure therefore ***understates*** the amount of cash provided by operations by the amount of depreciation expense recorded during the period.

One objective of the statement of changes in financial position is to explain any differences between net income and the amount of cash provided by operations. If we are to convert the $12,000 net income of City Delivery Service to the amount of cash provided by operations, we must ***add back*** the depreciation expense of $6,000. The computation of cash provided by operations in the statement of changes in financial position of City Delivery for 1989 is shown at the top of page 776.

[9] CICA, *CICA Handbook*, paragraph 1540.21.

Operating activities
Net income $12,00C
Add: Expenses not requiring the use of cash—depreciation 6,00C
Cash provided by operating activities $18,00C

Depreciation is not a source of cash   The addition of depreciation expense to the net income figure has led some people to view depreciation expense as a source of cash. It is important for the user of financial statements to understand that depreciation is neither a source nor a use of cash. *No cash flows into a business as a result of recording depreciation expense.* It is shown in the statement of changes in financial position merely to explain one of the differences between the concept of net income and the concept of cash provided by operations.

Some items that increase income do not increase cash   We have seen that some expenses do not reduce cash. Similarly, some items in the income statement increase net income without increasing cash; such items must be *deducted* from net income in arriving at cash provided by operations. An example of such an item is the amortization of premium on bonds payable, which causes annual interest expense to be less than the cash payments of interest to bondholders.[10]

Extraordinary gains and losses   Extraordinary gains and losses should be excluded from net income in order to show cash provided by "normal" operations. For example, assume that a new and undepreciated plant costing $600,000 is sold at a net gain of $50,000. In the statement of changes in financial position, the entire $650,000 in proceeds from the sale should be reported as cash provided by the sale of a plant. The $50,000 extraordinary gain, however, is included in the net income for the period. In determining the amount of cash provided by operations, this $50,000 extraordinary gain must be *deducted* from the net income figure because the entire proceeds from the sale of the plant are reported elsewhere in the statement of changes in financial position.

As a separate example, assume that the same plant is sold for $570,000; then the extraordinary loss of $30,000 should be *added back* to net income to arrive at cash provided by operations, and the cash provided through sale of the plant should be reported at $570,000.

Summary   The foregoing discussion relating to the measurement of cash provided by operations or operating activities can be summarized by the following formula

$$\begin{matrix} \text{Cash provided} \\ \text{by} \\ \text{operating activities} \end{matrix} = \text{Net income} + \left\{ \begin{matrix} \text{Depreciation} \\ \text{Amortization of} \\ \text{intangibles} \\ \text{Amortization of} \\ \text{discount on} \\ \text{bonds payable} \\ \text{Extraordinary} \\ \text{losses} \end{matrix} \right\} - \left\{ \begin{matrix} \text{Amortization of} \\ \text{premium on} \\ \text{bonds payable} \\ \text{Extraordinary} \\ \text{gains} \end{matrix} \right\}$$

[10] The treatment of this item in the working paper and in the statement of changes in financial position is illustrated in the Demonstration Problem on pages 789–790.

An overall summary of computation of cash provided by operating activities   The preceding formula can now be combined with the formula described on page 773, relating to the Claire Company example.

IMPACT OF OPERATIONS ON CASH

Computation of Cash Provided by Operating Activities

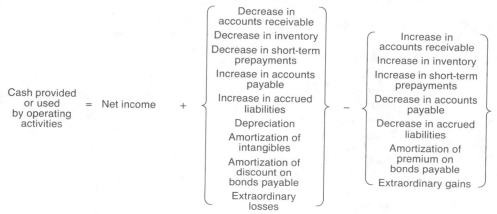

Cash provided or used by operating activities = Net income +

{
Decrease in accounts receivable
Decrease in inventory
Decrease in short-term prepayments
Increase in accounts payable
Increase in accrued liabilities
Depreciation
Amortization of intangibles
Amortization of discount on bonds payable
Extraordinary losses
}

−

{
Increase in accounts receivable
Increase in inventory
Increase in short-term prepayments
Decrease in accounts payable
Decrease in accrued liabilities
Amortization of premium on bonds payable
Extraordinary gains
}

A few observations may be noted from the above formula. First, decreases in noncash current asset accounts are added to net income because they cause a lower accrual basis net income to be reported. Second, increases in noncash current asset accounts are deducted from net income because they cause a higher accrual basis net income to be reported. Third, increases in current liability accounts (other than short-term borrowings, such as bank loans, which are included in the computation of cash and cash equivalents) are added because they cause a lower accrual basis net income to be reported. Fourth, decreases in current liability accounts are deducted because they cause a higher accrual basis net income to be reported.

Cash flow: a comprehensive illustration

To illustrate the points just discussed, we shall prepare a statement of changes in financial position for the Allison Corporation from the comparative balance sheet and the condensed income statement that appear on page 778. A summary of the transactions completed by Allison Corporation that resulted in a change in *noncash accounts* during 1989 follows:

1 Changes in noncash current accounts:
  a Increase in accounts receivable, $20,000
  b Increase in inventory, $80,000
  c Increase in short-term prepayments, $13,000
  d Increase in accounts payable, $55,000
  e Decrease in accrued liabilities, $19,500

2 Changes in noncurrent assets:
  a A plant costing $50,000 was sold for $70,000 cash. This plant was acquired in 1988 and was not used in operation due to technical problems. Thus, no depreciation was recorded.

b A parcel of land was acquired for $150,000 by issuing a long-term note payable for the entire purchase price.

c Equipment was purchased for $90,000; the invoice was paid within 10 days.

d Depreciation of $67,500 was recorded.

ANALYSIS OF THESE
FINANCIAL STATEMENTS
WILL EXPLAIN THE
SOURCES AND USES OF
CASH

ALLISON CORPORATION
Comparative Balance Sheet
At December 31

ASSETS	1989	1988
Current assets:		
Cash	$ 12,000	$ 35,000
Marketable securities	23,000	–0–
Accounts receivable (net)	105,000	85,000
Inventory	200,000	120,000
Short-term prepayments	25,000	12,000
Total current assets	$365,000	$252,000
Land	300,000	150,000
Plant	–0–	50,000
Equipment	470,000	380,000
Less: Accumulated depreciation	(192,500)	(125,000)
Total assets	$942,500	$707,000

LIABILITIES & SHAREHOLDERS' EQUITY		
Current liabilities:		
Bank loan	$ 20,000	$ –0–
Accounts payable (for purchases)	145,000	90,000
Accrued liabilities	22,500	42,000
Total current liabilities	$187,500	$132,000
Notes payable, long-term	170,000	20,000
Bonds payable, due June 30, 2005	110,000	185,000
Capital stock, no-par	255,000	160,000
Retained earnings	220,000	210,000
Total liabilities & shareholders' equity	$942,500	$707,000

ALLISON CORPORATION
Condensed Income Statement
For Year Ended December 31, 1989

Sales (net)	$900,00
Cost of goods sold	500,00
Gross profit on sales	$400,00
Operating expenses and income taxes	340,00
Income before extraordinary item	$ 60,00
Extraordinary item: Gain on sale of plant	20,00
Net income	$ 80,00

3 Changes in noncurrent liabilities:

  a As stated in transaction **2b**, a $150,000 long-term note payable was issued in exchange for land.

  b Bonds payable of $75,000 were retired at a price equal to face value.

4 Changes in shareholders' equity accounts:

  a A stock dividend (non-optional) was declared in January, requiring a transfer of $30,000 from the Retained Earnings account to the Capital Stock account.

  b In February, 2,000 shares of no-par value stock were issued for $65,000 cash.

  c Cash dividends of $40,000 were declared and paid, causing a reduction in retained earnings.

  d The net income for the year, $80,000 (including the $20,000 extraordinary gain on sale of a plant), was transferred to the Retained Earnings account.

From the comparative balance sheets, the income statement, and the summary of transactions affecting noncash accounts, we can prepare a statement of changes in financial position by completing the following three steps:

1 Compute the change in cash (i.e., cash and cash equivalents) during the period.

2 Prepare a working paper for analysis of changes in noncash accounts.

3 Prepare the statement of changes in financial position.

Computation of increase in cash during the period   The first step in preparing a statement of changes in financial position is to determine the net increase or decrease in cash during the period covered by the statement.

Cash of the Allison Corporation decreased by $20,000 during 1989, determined as follows:

USES OF CASH EXCEED SOURCES BY $20,000

ALLISON CORPORATION
Computation of Decrease in Cash during 1989

	DEC. 31 1989	DEC. 31 1988
Cash and cash equivalents (cash and marketable securities)	$35,000	$35,000
Less: Short-term borrowing (bank loan)	20,000	–0–
Cash and cash equivalents	$15,000	$35,000
Decrease in cash during 1989 ($15,000 – $35,000)	20,000	
	$35,000	$35,000

The purpose of the statement of changes in financial position is to explain the *reasons* for the change in cash. This is accomplished by listing the specific sources and uses of cash during the period. Since cash for the Allison Corporation decreases by $20,000, the uses of cash during 1989 exceeded the sources by this amount. But before a statement of changes in financial position can be prepared, we must analyze the changes that took place during the year in the noncash accounts.

Preparation of working paper for analysis of changes in noncash accounts   A working paper showing the analysis of changes in noncash accounts for Allison Corporation is illustrated on pages 780–781. The amount of cash and the balances in noncash

ALLISON CORPORATION
Working Paper for Statement of Changes in Financial Position
For Year Ended December 31, 1989

DEBITS	ACCOUNT BALANCES, END OF 1988	ANALYSIS OF TRANSACTIONS FOR 1989 DEBIT	ANALYSIS OF TRANSACTIONS FOR 1989 CREDIT	ACCOUNT BALANCES, END OF 1989
Cash and marketable securities, net of bank loan	35,000		(x) 20,000	15,000
Accounts receivable (net)	85,000	(6) 20,000		105,000
Inventory	120,000	(7) 80,000		200,000
Short-term prepayments	12,000	(8) 13,000		25,000
Land	150,000	(11) 150,000		300,000
Plant	50,000		(4) 50,000	–0–
Equipment	380,000	(12) 90,000		470,000
Total	832,000			1,115,000
CREDITS				
Accumulated Depreciation	125,000		(5) 67,500	192,500
Accounts payable	90,000		(9) 55,000	145,000
Accrued liabilities	42,000	(10) 19,500		22,500
Notes payable, long-term	20,000		(11) 150,000	170,000
Bonds payable, due June 30, 2005 . . .	185,000	(13) 75,000		110,000
Capital stock, no-par	160,000		(3) 30,000 } (14) 65,000 }	255,000
Retained earnings	210,000	(2) 40,000 (3) 30,000	(1) 80,000 }	220,000
Total	832,000	517,500	517,500	1,115,000

		SOURCES	USES	
Operating activities:				
Net income		(1) 80,000		Net income
Deduct: Gain on sale of plant			(4) 20,000	before extra-
Increase in accounts receivable			(6) 20,000	ordinary item
Increase in inventory			(7) 80,000	$60,000; cash
Increase in short-term prepayments			(8) 13,000	provided by
Decrease in accrued liability			(10) 19,500	operating
Add: Depreciation		(5) 67,500		activities,
Increase in accounts payable		(9) 55,000		$50,000
Financing Activities:				
Cash dividends			(2) 40,000	Cash provided
Issuance of long-term note payable for land		(11) 150,000		by financing
Retirement of bonds payable			(13) 75,000	activities
Issuance of capital stock		(14) 65,000		$100,000
Investing activities:				
Sale of plant, including an extraordinary gain of $20,000		(4) 70,000		Cash used in investing
Purchase of land in exchange for long-term note payable			(11) 150,000	activities $170,000
Purchase of equipment			(12) 90,000	
Total sources and uses of cash		487,500	507,500	
Decrease in cash during the year		(x) 20,000		
		507,500	507,500	

Explanation of transactions for 1989:

(1) Net income, $80,000 (including extraordinary gain of $20,000 on sale of plant), is transferred to Retained Earnings and is classified as a tentative source of cash [to be adjusted by entries (4) through (10) below].

(2) Cash dividends paid, $40,000, reduce retained earnings and cash, and this is a use of cash.

(3) A stock dividend has no effect on cash.

(4) Sale of plant for $70,000. Explains a $50,000 credit change in the Plant account. The $20,000 extraordinary gain on the sale is reclassified within the sources of cash from the "operating activities" section to the "investing activities" section.

(5) Depreciation, $67,500, is added to net income in arriving at cash provided by operating activities.

(6) Increase in accounts receivable of $20,000 is deducted from net income in arriving at cash provided by operating activities.

(7) Increase in inventory of $80,000 is deducted from net income in arriving at cash provided by operating activities.

(8) Increase in short-term prepayments of $13,000 is deducted from net income in arriving at cash provided by operating activities.

(9) Increase in accounts payable of $55,000 is added to net income in arriving at cash provided by operating activities.

(10) Decrease in accrued liabilities of $19,500 is deducted from net income in arriving at cash provided by operating activities.

(11) A $150,000 long-term note payable was issued (a source of cash) to acquire land (a use of cash).

(12) Cash of $90,000 was used to purchase equipment, an investing activity.

(13) Cash of $75,000 was used to retire bonds payable, a financing activity.

(14) Issued capital stock, increasing cash by $65,000, a financing activity.

(x) Balancing figure — decreases in cash during the year.

---

accounts at the beginning of the period are listed in the first column of the working paper; balances at the end of the year are listed in the last (right-hand) column. The two middle columns are used to *explain the changes* in each *noncash* account during the year and to indicate whether each change represents a source or a use of cash. Transactions for the year (in summary form) are recorded in these middle columns, and an offsetting entry is made in the lower section of the working paper indicating the effect of each transaction upon cash.

Explanation of entries in the middle columns By studying the changes in the noncash accounts during 1989, we are able to find the specific reasons for the $20,000 decrease in cash. The noncash accounts may be analyzed in any sequence; however, we recommend the following approach.

1 Explain all transactions affecting the Retained Earnings account.

2 Explain the adjustment and reclassification of extraordinary items.

3 Explain the expense items that have no effect on cash.

4 Explain the changes in the *noncash current* accounts.

5 Explain any remaining changes in *noncurrent* accounts.

6 Make an entry explaining the net change in cash. This entry should bring both the upper and lower sets of middle columns into balance.

Using this approach, the entries in our illustrated working paper are explained as follows:

Entry

STEP 1:
EXPLAIN THE CHANGES
IN RETAINED EARNINGS

(1) Allison Corporation's net income explains an $80,000 credit change in the Retained Earnings account. In the bottom portion of the working papers, an offsetting entry is made identifying net income as a source of cash, which is shown in the "operating activities" section.

(2) Cash dividends of $40,000 declared and paid during 1989 caused a debit change in the Retained Earnings account and were a use of cash which is shown in the "financing activities" section.

(3) The stock dividend (non-optional) caused a $30,000 debit change in the Retained Earnings account and a $30,000 credit change in the Capital Stock account. Notice that both the debit and credit portions of this entry appear in the *top portion* of the working papers. As previously stated, non-optional stock dividends (and stock splits) are an exception to the general rule that changes in noncurrent accounts represent either sources or uses of cash. Non-optional stock dividends have *no effect* upon cash.

With these first three entries, we have explained how the Retained Earnings account increased during 1989 from $210,000 to its ending balance of $220,000.

(4) To compute the cash provided by operating activities, we must remove from net income the $20,000 extraordinary gain arising from the sale of a plant to show the amount of net income before extraordinary item. Entry (4) removes the $20,000 gain from the "operating activities" section and shows the entire $70,000 proceeds from the sale as a source of cash in the "investing activities" section in the bottom portion of the working paper. In the top portion of the working paper, entry (4) shows that the sale of this plant caused a $50,000 credit change in the Plant account.

(5) The $80,000 net income figure appearing in the bottom portion of the working paper is only a tentative measure of the cash provided by operating activities. Depreciation expense, for example, must be added back to this figure, because the recording of depreciation expense reduced net income but did not reduce cash. Entry (5) shows that depreciation expense explains the $67,500 credit change in the Accumulated Depreciation account and adds this amount to net income as a step in determining cash provided by operating activities.

(6) To complete the computation of cash provided by operating activities, we must convert the net income of $80,000 from an accrual to a cash basis by also taking into consideration the changes in these noncash current accounts that are related to the income statement. The rationale for involving the changes of these accounts in the conversion has been explained earlier in the Claire Company example. The changes in the noncash current accounts of Allison Corporation are considered in entries (6) through (10) in the working paper.

The increase in accounts receivable of $20,000 means that credit sales were being made faster than the cash was being collected, causing a corresponding higher sales and net income to be shown on an accrual than on a cash basis. Thus entry (6) shows the increase of $20,000 as a deduction from net income in the "operating activities" section in arriving at cash provided by operating activities, and as a debit change in accounts receivable in the top portion of the working paper.

(7) & (9) To explain the reason for deducting the increase in inventory from, and adding the increase in accounts payable to, net income in arriving at cash

provided by operating activities, we must remember that cost of goods sold is used for accrual basis, and cash payments for purchases are used for cash basis. An increase in inventory means more goods are purchased on credit than are sold, causing the cost of goods *purchased* to be larger than the cost of goods *sold.* This in turn causes a corresponding increase in accounts payable for purchases. Such an increase in accounts payable can be reduced by payments; the amount of this increase that is reduced by payments represents the extent of the cash payments for purchases in excess of the cost of goods sold. When the increase in inventory is more than the increase in accounts payable for purchases, the cash payments for purchases are greater than the cost of goods sold. The result of this is that the net income, on an accrual basis, is higher than on a cash basis. Accordingly, the amount of the increase in inventory of $80,000 over the increase in accounts payable of $55,000 must be deducted from the net income of $80,000. Deducting this excess of $25,000 from the net income has the same effect as deducting the $80,000 from and adding the $55,000 to the net income. Therefore, the increase in inventory should be deducted from and the increase in accounts payable should be added to accrual basis net income to convert it to a cash basis. Thus, entry (7) shows the increase in inventory as a deduction from net income in the "operating activities" section in arriving at cash provided by operating activities, and as a debit change in inventory in the top portion of the working paper. Entry (9) shows the increase in accounts payable as an addition to net income in the "operating activities" section in arriving at cash provided by operating activities, and as a credit change in accounts payable in the top portion of the working paper.

(8)   An increase in short-term prepayments represents the amount of cash payments that is *not* recognized in computing accrual basis net income but *is* recognized in computing cash provided by operating activities. Thus, in converting accrual basis net income to cash provided by operating activities, the increase in short-term prepayments of $13,000 is deducted from the net income of $80,000. Accordingly, entry (8) shows the increase as a deduction from net income in the "operating activities" section in arriving at cash provided by operating activities and as a debit change in short-term prepayments in the top portion of the working paper.

(10) On an accrual basis, all operating expenses incurred are recognized; on a cash basis, only cash payments are recognized. Therefore, when there is a decrease in accrued liabilities, less operating expenses are incurred than cash payments for these expenses. That is, a decrease in accrued liabilities means a smaller amount of operating expense is being reported, causing a higher net income to be shown on an accrual basis than on a cash basis. Thus, in converting accrual basis net income to cash provided by operating activities, the decrease in accrued liabilities of $19,500 is deducted from the net income of $80,000. Accordingly, entry (10) shows the decrease as a deduction from net income in the "operating activities" section in arriving at cash provided by operating activities, and as a debit change in accrued liabilities in the top portion of the working paper.

We have now determined that cash of $50,000 was provided by operating activities, and net income before extraordinary item was $60,000.

STEP 5:
EXPLAIN ANY REMAINING
CHANGES IN NON-
CURRENT ACCOUNTS.

(11) The issuance of a $150,000 long-term note payable in exchange for land is an exchange transaction, representing both a source and a use of cash. First, an entry is made in the top portion of the working paper explaining the $150,000 increase in the Notes Payable account and an offsetting entry is made in the "financing activities" section below showing a $150,000 source of cash. Next, a debit entry is made in the upper portion of the working paper explaining the $150,000 increase in the Land account, and an offsetting entry is made in the following "investing activities" section showing this $150,000 use of cash.

(12) The purchase of equipment explains the $90,000 debit change in the Equipment account and is a use of cash for investigating activities.

(13) During the year, Allison Corporation retired $75,000 of bonds payable at par. A reduction in long-term debt is a use of cash. This transaction is recorded in the working paper by a debit to the Bonds Payable account and an offsetting entry describing the use of cash for financing activities.

(14) The issuance of capital stock in February for $65,000 is recorded in the upper section of the working paper by credits to Capital Stock. The issuance of capital stock is a source of cash; therefore, the offsetting entry in the lower section of the working papers is entered in the "financing activities" section as a source of cash.

At this point we should check carefully to determine that our entries in the Debit and Credit columns correctly explain the difference between the beginning and ending balances of each noncash account. If the top section of the working paper explains the change in every noncash account, the bottom section should include all of the sources and uses of cash for the year.

STEP 6:
RECORD THE NET
CHANGE IN CASH.

(x) We now total the Sources column ($487,500) and the Uses column ($507,500) in the bottom section of the working paper. The $20,000 difference between these column totals represents the net change in cash during the year. Since cash decreased, this $20,000 is entered as a credit to cash on the top line of the working paper and as the balancing figure in the Sources column at the bottom of the working paper.

Totals can now be determined for the Debit and Credit columns in the top section of the working paper. If these totals agree, we know that our analysis is correct, at least so far as the mechanics are concerned.

Preparation of statement of changes in financial position   The preceding working paper analysis explained all changes in noncash accounts that took place during 1989. In making this analysis, we listed the sources and uses of cash in the lower section of the working paper on pages 780-781. The decrease of $20,000 in cash has been confirmed and a statement of changes in financial position including a schedule showing the change in cash, can now be prepared as follows:

ALLISON CORPORATION
Statement of Changes in Financial Position
For Year Ended December 31, 1989

Operating activities:		
Net income before extraordinary item		$ 60,000
Deduct: Increase in accounts receivable	$ (20,000)	
Increase in inventory	(80,000)	
Increase in short-term prepayments	(13,000)	
Decrease in accrued liabilities	(19,500)	(132,500)
Add: Expenses not requiring the use of cash —		
depreciation	$ 67,500	
Increase in accounts payable	55,000	122,500
Cash provided by operating activities		$ 50,000
Financing activities:		
Cash dividends	$(40,000)	
Issuance of long-term note payable for land	150,000	
Retirement of bonds payable	(75,000)	
Issuance of capital stock	65,000	
Cash provided by financing activities		100,000
Investing activities:		
Sale of plant, including extraordinary gain of $20,000	$ 70,000	
Purchase of land in exchange for long-term note payable	(150,000)	
Purchase of equipment	(90,000)	
Cash used in investing activities		(170,000)
Decrease in cash and cash equivalents		$ (20,000)

Schedule of Changes in Cash and Cash Equivalents

	DECEMBER 31	
	1989	**1988**
Cash	$ 12,000	$35,000
Marketable securities	23,000	–0–
	$ 35,000	$35,000
Deduct: Bank loan (short-term)	20,000	–0–
Cash and cash equivalents	$ 15,000	$35,000
	(35,000)	
Decrease in cash and cash equivalents	$(20,000)	

The preceding statement of changes in financial position illustrates the disclosure and presentation requirements of Section 1540 of the *CICA Handbook* in a clear and understandable manner. The schedule of changes in cash and cash equivalents is included here to enhance understanding of the ''cash and cash equivalents'' definition for cash. In published financial statements, such a schedule is seldom presented because the change can be easily determined from the few items involved. Instead, the items included as ''cash and cash equivalents'' are simply described in a note below the statement or in the last heading in the statement.

Cash dividends paid are shown in the "financing activities" section because dividends are an important factor in attracting equity capital. Thus, the amount of dividends affects the market price of a company's stock and its ability to raise equity capital. Accordingly, it is more logical to treat dividends as a financing activity. Section 1540 of the *CICA Handbook* does not take a position on the presentation of dividends but indicates that dividends may be presented as a financing activity, as an operating activity, or as an activity apart from both financing and operating. In published financial statements, the amount of cash dividends paid is generally presented as a financing activity.[11]

In published financial statements, the changes in noncash current accounts are usually presented in the statement of changes in financial position as one lump sum amount entitled "Changes in noncash working capital components" or "Changes in noncash working capital." This amount is sometimes supported by a schedule or a footnote showing the changes in the individual noncash current or working capital accounts.

ANALYSIS AND INTERPRETATION OF A STATEMENT OF CHANGES IN FINANCIAL POSITION

6   Analyze and interpret a statement of changes in financial position.

As discussed in the early part of this chapter, the statement of changes in financial position provides information on the liquidity and solvency position of a business, as well as the cash policies on its operating, financing, and investing activities. The amount of cash and cash equivalents together with the changes in noncash current account in the statement will provide insights into the liquidity position and the cash policy on operating activities. The changes in the noncurrent accounts shown in the financing and investing activities sections of the statement will provide information on the cash policies regarding the extent of financing and investing activities. Thus, a careful analysis and interpretation of this statement will enable management and other users to logically assess the soundness of the business's liquidity position and its cash policies on operating, financing, and investing activities.

The following analysis and interpretation of a statement of changes in financial position is based on the Allison Corporation example.

The Allison Corporation's liquidity position is deteriorating; its cash and cash equivalents at the end of 1989 are less than half that in 1988, as shown in the Schedule of Changes in Cash and Cash Equivalents on page 785. Moreover, the amount of cash and cash equivalents of $15,000 seems to be inadequate to meet the need for paying the $167,500 of accounts payable and accrued liabilities, especially if the company continues its existing policy on collection from customers, which is explained later.

The company does not appear to have a well-coordinated and satisfactory cash policy on operating activities. The increase in accounts receivable means that credit sales are being made faster than the cash is being collected. Since the increase in inventory exceeds the increase in accounts payable, more goods are being purchased on credit than are being sold and payments are less than the credit purchases. The

---

[11] *Financial Reporting in Canada*, p. 210. Of the 224 companies surveyed, 129 presented dividends as a financing activity.

increase in short-term prepayments indicates that more expenses are being prepaid than are being incurred. Similarly, the decrease in accrued liabilities means that payments are being made faster than the expenses are being incurred. These analyses show that the company seems to be slow in collecting its accounts receivable and in paying its suppliers but too quick in paying its other expenses. Consequently, the company should evaluate its credit, collection, and payment policies for their soundness and coordination. The fact that the cash provided from operating activities is much less than the amount of depreciation indicates that the company will have to borrow more, or issue additional capital stock, in order to maintain its present operating capacity, unless this is a temporary situation. However, this had already occurred in 1989 as the company had to issue long-term notes payable and capital stock to finance its purchase of land and equipment.

The company's cash policy on financing activities seems unsound. The retirement of $75,000 bonds payable, in spite of an unsatisfactory cash position, was ill-advised. The cash dividends of about two-thirds of net income before extraordinary item and 80% of the amount of cash from operations were unusually large and caused a further strain on the cash resources. Consequently, the company should amend its policy in each of these areas. It should also be noted that, by presenting the information on financing activities in one place, it is easier for users to analyze and interpret the extent and reasonableness of these activities.

The company's cash policy on investing activities reflects the desire to finance its investments through long-term debt and capital stock. The heavier emphasis on debt than equity financing appeared to be logical in view of the relationship between the amount of long-term debts and the amount of long-term assets on the one hand, and the amount of long-term debts and the amount of shareholders' equity on the other. However, since the total amount of debts is about 50% of the total assets, the company may find borrowing increasingly difficult and risky in the future, unless there is a substantial increase in shareholders' equity. Since the investing activities are presented in one place, it is easier for users to analyse and interpret the extent and reasonableness of these activities.

END-OF-CHAPTER REVIEW

SUMMARY OF CHAPTER LEARNING OBJECTIVES

1 Differentiate a statement of changes in financial position from an income statement and a balance sheet.

A statement of changes in financial position provides additional information on the solvency and liquidity of a business. The income statement shows profitability and the balance sheet shows only to some extent the solvency of a business.

2 Explain the nature and objective of the statement of changes in financial position.

A statement of changes in financial position summarizes the operating, financing, and investing activities for a period on a cash basis and explains how and why the cash position has changed during a period. The objective of this statement is to provide information to financial statement users to assess the liquidity and solvency of a business.

3 Explain the disclosure and presentation requirements for a statement of changes in financial position.

To ensure that the statement of changes in financial position is sufficiently informative, separate disclosures are required of (1) cash from operation, (2) cash flows from extraordinary items, (3) outlays for acquisition and proceeds on disposal of long-term assets, (4) cash inflows and outflows from long-term debt and equity capital transactions, and (5) payment of dividends. These items are classified into three categories: operating activities (item 1), financing activities (items 4 and 5) and investing activities (items 2 and 3).

4 Identify the principal sources and uses of cash.

The principal sources of cash are (1) operations, (2) long-term borrowing, (3) sale of additional shares of capital stock, and (4) sale of non-current assets. Item (1) is classified under operating activities, items (2) and (3) under financing activities, and item (4) under investing activities. The principal uses of cash are related to (1) payment of cash dividends, (2) repayment of long-term debt, (3) repurchase or retirement of outstanding capital stock, and (4) purchase of noncurrent (long-term) assets. Items (1), (2), and (3) are classified under financing activities and item (4) under investing activities.

5 Develop a statement of changes in financial position — a simple and a comprehensive illustration.

A statement of changes in financial position is developed by illustrating how the information for operating, financing, and investing activities is derived and presented together with the underlying reasons. Cash flows from operating activities can be derived from the income statement and the changes in those noncash current accounts that are related to the income statement. Cash flows from financing and investing activities can be determined by examining the changes in the noncurrent accounts. In converting net income to cash provided or used by operating activities, increases in noncash current asset accounts are deducted from, and decreases are added to, accrual basis net income. On the other hand, increases in noncash current liability accounts (other than short-term borrowings) are added to, and decreases are deducted from, accrual basis net income.

6 Analyze and interpret a statement of changes in financial position.

A statement of changes in financial position should be analyzed to gain insights into the liquidity position and the cash policies on operating, financing, and investing activities. Such insights can then be interpreted to determine the soundness of the liquidity position and the cash policies.

KEY TERMS INTRODUCED OR EMPHASIZED IN CHAPTER 19

Accrual basis A method of summarizing operating results in terms of revenue earned and expenses incurred, rather than cash receipts or cash payments.

Cash basis A method of summarizing operating results in terms of cash receipts and cash payments rather than revenue earned and expenses incurred.

Cash and cash equivalents Cash and cash equivalents encompass cash, net of short-term borrowings, and temporary investments. In some cases, cash and cash equivalents may include certain other elements of working capital when they are equivalent to cash.

Cash flows from financing activities Cash flows that affect the size and composition of a company's long-term debt and equity capital structure.

Cash flows from investing activities Cash flows that affect the noncurrent assets such as plant and equipment.

Cash flows from operating activities Cash flows from operations, including net income before extraordinary items and changes in noncash current accounts.

Exchange transaction In the context of a statement of changes in financial position, exchange transactions are financing or investing activities that do not directly affect cash. An example of such a transaction is the purchase of plant assets by issuing common stock. Such transactions should be shown in a statement of changes in financial position as both a source and a use of cash.

Noncash current accounts All current asset and current liability accounts other than cash or cash equivalents. Also referred to as noncash working capital accounts.

Noncurrent account Any balance sheet account *other than* a current asset or a current liability. Noncurrent accounts include long-term investments, plant assets, intangible assets, long-term liabilities, and shareholders' equity accounts.

Noncurrent assets All long-term assets such as long-term investments, plant, and equipment; they are part of the noncurrent accounts.

Non-optional stock dividends Stock dividends where shareholders can only receive shares of capital stock.

Optional stock dividends Stock dividends where shareholders have an option of receiving cash or shares of capital stock.

Statement of changes in financial position A financial statement showing the sources and uses of cash from operating, financing, and investing activities during the accounting period. In addition, this statement shows financing and investing activities, such as exchange transactions, that do not directly affect cash.

Working capital Current assets minus current liabilities. Working capital represents the net amount of liquid resources available to a business.

DEMONSTRATION PROBLEM FOR YOUR REVIEW

Comparative financial data for Liquid Gas Limited for the last two years are shown on page 790.

Other Data

(1) During 1989, the board of directors of the company authorized a transfer of $15,000 from retained earnings to reflect a stock dividend on the common stock. (This a non-optional stock dividend because common stock is increased by the same amount.)

(2) Cash dividends of $6,000 were declared and paid on the preferred stock, and cash dividends of $50,000 were declared and paid on the common stock.

(3) Three hundred shares of preferred stock were retired for $30,000 cash.

(4) The only entries recorded in the Retained Earnings account were for dividends and to close the Income Summary account, which had a credit balance of $66,000 after the loss on the sale of the land.

(5) There were no sales or retirements of building and equipment during the year; land was sold for $8,000, resulting in a loss of $2,000. The loss was considered as an extraordinary item.

DEBITS	DECEMBER 31 1989	1988
Cash	$ 39,220	$ 15,800
Marketable securities	20,000	28,000
Receivables (net of allowance for doubtful accounts)	41,400	24,000
Inventories, lower of cost and market	27,600	36,800
Short-term prepayments	4,180	4,400
Land	9,000	19,000
Buildings	270,000	250,000
Equipment	478,600	450,000
Total debits	$890,000	$828,000

CREDITS		
Accumulated depreciation: buildings	$ 95,000	$ 77,000
Accumulated depreciation: equipment	153,000	120,000
Bank loan	12,000	23,000
Accounts payable	67,200	35,000
Accrued liabilities	20,000	10,000
Bonds payable	90,000	90,000
Premium on bonds payable	2,800	3,000
Preferred stock (no-par)	70,000	100,000
Common stock (no-par)	305,000	290,000
Retained earnings	75,000	80,000
Total credits	$890,000	$828,000

Instructions   **a** Compute the change in cash and cash equivalents during 1989.

b Prepare a working paper for a statement of changes in financial position for 1989.

c Prepare a statement of changes in financial position for 1989, without showing the schedule of change in cash.

SOLUTION TO DEMONSTRATION PROBLEM

a Computation of change in cash and cash equivalents:

	DECEMBER 31 1989	1988
Cash	$39,200	$15,80
Marketable securities	20,000	28,00
	$59,220	$43,80
Less: Bank loan	12,000	23,00
Cash and cash equivalents	$47,220	$20,80
Increase in cash during 1989		26,42
	$47,220	$47,22

b The solution to this part of the problem is presented on pages 792–793.

c

LIQUID GAS LIMITED
Statement of Changes in Financial Position
For Year Ended December 31, 1989

Operating activities:

Net income before extraordinary item		$ 68,000
Deduct: Increase in accounts receivable	$(17,400)	
Expense reduction which increased income but with no effect on cash — amortization of premium on bonds payable	(200)	(17,600)
Add: Expenses not requiring the use of cash — depreciation	$ 51,000	
Decrease in inventory	9,200	
Decrease in short-term prepayments	220	
Increase in accounts payable	32,200	
Increase in accrued liabilities	10,000	102,620
Cash provided by operating activities		$153,020

Financing activities:

Cash dividends	$(56,000)	
Retirement of preferred stock	(30,000)	
Cash used in financing activities		(86,000)

Investing activities:

Sale of land, including an extraordinary loss of $2,000 ...	$ 8,000	
Purchase of building	(20,000)	
Purchase of equipment	(28,600)	
Cash used in investing activities		(40,600)
Increase in cash and cash equivalents		$ 26,420

LIQUID GAS LIMITED
Working Paper for Statement of Changes in Financial Position
For Year Ended December 31, 1989

DEBITS	ACCOUNT BALANCES, END OF 1988	ANALYSIS OF TRANSACTIONS FOR 1989		ACCOUNT BALANCES, END OF 1989
		DEBIT	CREDIT	
Cash and marketable securities, net of bank loan	20,800	(x) 26,420		47,220
Accounts receivable (net)	24,000	(6) 17,400		41,400
Inventories	36,800		(7) 9,200	27,600
Short-term prepayments	4,400		(8) 220	4,180
Land	19,000		(4) 10,000	9,000
Buildings	250,000	(11) 20,000		270,000
Equipment	450,000	(12) 28,600		478,600
Total	805,000			878,000
CREDITS				
Accumulated depreciation: buildings .	77,000		(5) 18,000	95,000
Accumulated depreciation: equipment	120,000		(5) 33,000	153,000
Accounts payable	35,000		(9) 32,200	67,200
Accrued liabilities	10,000		(10) 10,000	20,000
Bonds payable	90,000			90,000
Premium on bonds	3,000	(13) 200		2,800
Preferred stock, no-par	100,000	(14) 30,000		70,000
Common stock, no-par	290,000		(2) 15,000	305,000
Retained earnings	80,000	(2) 15,000	(1) 66,000 }	75,000
		(3) 56,000		
Total	805,000	193,620	193,620	878,000

		SOURCES	USES	
Operating activities:				
Net income		(1) 66,000		Net income before extra-ordinary item, $68,000; cash provided by operating activities, $153,020.
Add: Loss on sale of land		(4) 2,000		
Deduct: Increase in accounts receivable			(6) 17,400	
Amortization of premium on bonds payable			(13) 200	
Add: Depreciation		(5) 51,000		
Decrease in inventories		(7) 9,200		
Decrease in short-term prepayments		(8) 220		
Increase in accounts payable		(9) 32,200		
Increase in accrued liabilities		(10) 10,000		
Financing activities:				
Cash dividends			(3) 56,000 }	Cash used in financing activities, $86,000.
Retirement of preferred stock			(14) 30,000	
Investing activities:				
Sale of land, including an extraordinary loss of $2,000		(4) 8,000		Cash used in investing activities, $40,600.
Purchase of building			(11) 20,000	
Purchase of equipment			(12) 28,600	
Total sources and uses of cash		178,620	152,200	
Increase in cash during the year			(x) 26,420	
		178,620	178,620	

Explanation of transactions for 1989:

(1) Net income, $66,000, including an extraordinary loss of $2,000 on sale of land, transferred to Retained Earnings account.

(2) Entry to record stock dividend; no effect on cash.

(3) Cash dividends declared, $56,000 (preferred stock, $6,000, and common, $50,000).

(4) To record sale of land for $8,000; the $2,000 extraordinary loss is reclassified from the "operating activities" section to "investing activities" section.

(5) Depreciation, $51,000, is added to net income because it is an expense that did not reduce cash.

(6) Increase in accounts receivable of $17,400 is deducted from net income in arriving at cash provided by operating activities.

(7) Decrease in inventory of $9,200 is added to net income in arriving at cash provided by operating activities.

(8) Decrease in short-term prepayment of $220 is added to net income in arriving at cash provided by operating activities.

(9) Increase in accounts payable of $32,200 is added to net income in arriving at cash provided by operating activities.

(10) Increase in accrued liabilities of $10,000 is added to net income in arriving at cash provided by operating activities.

(11) To record cash used for purchase of building.

(12) To record cash used for purchase of equipment.

(13) Amortization of premium on bonds payable decreased expense and thus increased net income but had no effect on cash.

(14) To record cash used for retirement of preferred stock.

(x) Balancing figure — increase in cash during the year.

T ACCOUNT METHOD FOR THE PREPARATION OF STATEMENT OF CHANGES IN FINANCIAL POSITION

The "T account method," as the name suggests, utilizes T accounts to summarize the same information as the working paper method illustrated in the chapter. First, all the accounts required for the preparation of the statement of changes in financial position are set up in the T account format rather than in the working paper format. Second, the changes between the beginning and ending balances for these accounts are noted in the T accounts. (With the working paper method, the beginning and ending balances of a period rather than their changes are noted.) Third, these changes are accounted for by reconstructing the entries posted to these accounts during the period. (With the working paper method, the beginning and ending balances of a period are reconciled by reconstructing the entries posted to these accounts.) The examples on page 795, selected from the demonstration problem — Liquid Gas Limited — delineate these three basic differences.

A careful study of these examples shows clearly that both the working paper and the T accounts contain the same information needed for the preparation of the statement of changes in financial position. The essential difference is really the format in which the information is presented. In the example shown on page 795, the two items in the credit column in the use of cash section of the working paper — purchase of building, $20,000, and retirement of preferred stock, $30,000 — are the same as the two items in the credit column of the financing and investing activities accounts. Similar parallels can be made for all the other accounts in the Liquid Gas Limited demonstration problem. It is suggested that the T account method may be more efficient, particularly for solving relatively simple problems.

The T account method generally involves the following steps:

1 Open a T account for "Cash" (that is, cash and cash equivalents) and debit or credit the account with the increase or decrease (change) in cash. Double underline this amount.

2 Open a T account for each noncash account with the change between the beginning and ending balances and debit or credit the change to these accounts. Double underline the amount in each of these accounts.

Working Paper Method				
DEBITS	ACCOUNT BALANCES, END OF 1988	ANALYSIS OF TRANSACTIONS FOR 1989		ACCOUNT BALANCES, END OF 1989
		DEBIT	CREDIT	
Buildings	250,000	(11) 20,000		270,000
CREDITS				
Preferred stock, no-par	100,000	(14) 30,000		70,000
		SOURCES	USES	
Financing activities: Retirement of preferred stocks			(14) 30,000	
Investing activities: Purchase of building			(11) 20,000	

T Account Method
BUILDINGS

Change 20,000	
(11) Purchase of building 20,000	

PREFERRED STOCK, NO-PAR

Change 30,000	
(14) Retirement of Preferred Stock 30,000	

FINANCING ACTIVITIES

	(14) Retirement of Preferred Stock 30,000

INVESTING ACTIVITIES

	(11) Purchase of building 20,000

3 Add the debits and credits of the T account for cash and for the noncash accounts. The equality of the debit and credit totals proves that the amounts have been correctly noted on these accounts (unless there are exact offsetting errors, which are usually unlikely).

4 Open a T account for "Operating Activities" for the reconstruction of the posting of entries related to cash from operations such as net income, extraordinary

items, items included in the income statement but not providing cash or requiring the use of cash (e.g., amortization of premium on bonds payable or depreciation), and changes in noncash current accounts. This account shows the details of cash provided or used by operating activities.

5 Open a T account for "Financing Activities" for the reconstruction of the postings of entries related to cash flows on such activities as the issuance, redemption, and retirement of long-term debt and capital stock. This account shows the details of cash provided by or used in financing activities.

6 Open a T account for "Investing Activities" for the reconstruction of the postings of entries related to cash flows on such activities as the acquisition and disposal of long-term assets such as plant and equipment. This account shows the details of cash provided by or used in investing activities.

7 Analyze all available information, and reconstruct the postings to account for the changes in the T accounts set up thus far.

8 Check that the changes in each noncash T account have been accounted for.

9 Add the Operating Activities, Financing Activities, and Investing Activities T accounts and transfer the balances (these are the amounts of cash provided by or used in operating, financing and investing activities) to the Cash T account.

10 Check that the total amount of the balances transferred from step 9 is the same amount and on the same side of the T account as that already noted in the cash T account.

11 Review all the noncurrent T accounts to ensure that exchange transactions have been accounted for.

12 Prepare the statement of changes in financial position from
   i The Operating Activities T account, which provides all the details on cash provided or used by operations.
   ii The Financing Activities T account, which provides all the details on cash provided by or used in financing activities.
   iii The Investing Activities T account, which provides all the details on cash provided by or used in investing activities.

These twelve steps are used to illustrate the T account method using the information of the Liquid Gas Limited demonstration problem.

a The information contained in the T accounts after steps 1 to 6 is as follows [the total of debits ($127,620) equals the total of credits ($127,620)]:

CASH*		ACCOUNTS RECEIVABLE	
26,420		17,400	

INVENTORIES		SHORT-TERM PREPAYMENTS	
	9,200		220

*Cash and cash equivalents

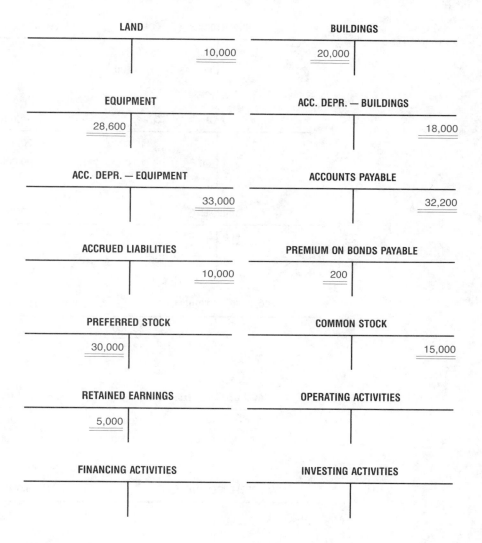

LAND		BUILDINGS	
	10,000	20,000	

EQUIPMENT		ACC. DEPR. — BUILDINGS	
28,600			18,000

ACC. DEPR. — EQUIPMENT		ACCOUNTS PAYABLE	
	33,000		32,200

ACCRUED LIABILITIES		PREMIUM ON BONDS PAYABLE	
	10,000	200	

PREFERRED STOCK		COMMON STOCK	
30,000			15,000

RETAINED EARNINGS		OPERATING ACTIVITIES	
5,000			

FINANCING ACTIVITIES		INVESTING ACTIVITIES	

b After analyzing all available information and reconstructing the postings to account for the differences in the T accounts as required by step 7, the T accounts are as follows. (Comparing the numbered items in these T accounts with the numbered items in the middle columns of the working paper on page 792 will show that the information is identical in both places.)

CASH		ACCOUNTS RECEIVABLE	
26,420		17,400	
		(6) 17,400	

	INVENTORIES			SHORT-TERM PREPAYMENTS	
		9,200			220
(7)		9,200	(8)		220

	LAND			BUILDINGS	
		10,000		20,000	
(4)		10,000	(11)	20,000	

	EQUIPMENT			ACC. DEPR. — BUILDINGS	
	28,600				18,000
(12)	28,600		(5)		18,000

	ACC. DEPR. — EQUIPMENT			ACCOUNTS PAYABLE	
		33,000			32,200
(5)		33,000	(9)		32,200

	ACCRUED LIABILITIES			PREMIUM ON BONDS PAYABLE	
		10,000		200	
(10)		10,000	(13)	200	

	PREFERRED STOCK			COMMON STOCK	
	30,000				15,000
(14)	30,000		(2)		15,000

	RETAINED EARNINGS		
	5,000		
(2)	15,000	(1)	66,000
(3)	56,000		
	71,000		
	5,000		

(Check that the difference in each noncash T account has been accounted for.)

OPERATING ACTIVITIES

(1) Net income	66,000	(6) Increase in accounts	
(4) Loss on sale of land	2,000	receivable	17,400
Net income before		(13) Amortization of premium	
extraordinary item	68,000	on bonds payable	200
(5) Depreciation	51,000		
(7) Decrease in inventories ...	9,200		
(8) Decrease in short-term			
prepayments	220		
(9) Increase in accounts			
payable	32,200		
(10) Increase in accrued			
liability	10,000		

FINANCING ACTIVITIES

(3) Cash dividends	56,000
(14) Retirement of preferred	
stock	30,000

INVESTING ACTIVITIES

(4) Sale of land, including		(11) Purchase of building	20,000
an extraordinary loss		(12) Purchase of equipment	28,600
of $2,000	8,000		

c Add the Operating Activities, Financing Activities, and Investing Activities T accounts and transfer the balances to the Cash T account. Check that the total amount of the balances transferred to and the amount already noted in the Cash T account are in agreement. These are required by steps 9 and 10. These four accounts, after the two steps have been performed, are as follows:

OPERATING ACTIVITIES

(1) Net income	66,000	(6) Increase in accounts	
(4) Loss on sale of land	2,000	receivable	17,400
Net income before		(13) Amortization of premium	
extraordinary item	68,000	on bonds payable	200
(5) Depreciation	51,000		
(7) Decrease in inventories ...	9,200		
(8) Decrease in short-term			
prepayments	220		
(9) Increase in accounts			
payable	32,200		
(10) Increase in accrued			
liability	10,000		
	170,620		17,600
		(x) Transfer to cash T acct ...	153,020
	170,620		170,620

FINANCING ACTIVITIES

		(3) Cash dividends	56,000
		(14) Retirement of preferred	
		stock	30,000
(x) Transfer to cash			
T account	86,000		86,000

INVESTING ACTIVITIES

(4) Sale of land, including an		(11) Purchase of building	20,000
extraordinary loss of $2,000	8,000	(12) Purchase of equipment	28,600
	8,000		48,600
(x) Transfer to cash T account . . .	40,600		
	48,600		48,600

CASH

	26,420		
(x) Transfer from operating		(x) Transfer from:	
activities	153,020	Financing activities	86,000
		Investing activities	40,600
	126,600		126,600
	26,420		

d Review all the noncurrent T accounts to ensure that exchange transactions have been accounted for.

e Use the information in the Operating Activities, Financing Activities, and Investing Activities T accounts to prepare the statement of changes in financial position. This statement is the same as that on page 791.

ASSIGNMENT MATERIAL

REVIEW QUESTIONS

1 Explain why an adequate amount of cash is essential to the successful operation of a business.

2 What is the nature and objective of the statement of changes in financial position?

3 What information can a reader gain from a statement of changes in financial position that is not apparent from reading an income statement?

4 How is "cash and cash equivalents" defined by Section 1540 of the *CICA Handbook*?

5 List the items required to be separately disclosed in a statement of changes in financial position by Section 1540 of the *CICA Handbook*.

6 How should the items in 5 be classified?

7 Briefly describe the meaning of: cash flows from operating activities; cash flows from financing activities; cash flows from investing activities.

8 Explain the rationale of Section 1540 of the *CICA Handbook* for the recommended disclosure and presentation for the statement of changes in financial position.

9 What are the primary ways in which a firm generates cash and the primary ways in which a firm uses cash?

10 List six items that are added to or deducted from net income in computing cash provided or used by operating activities.

11 List four items that are included in computing cash provided by or used in financing activities.

12 List four items that are included in computing cash provided by or used in investing activities.

13 How should an increase and a decrease in accounts receivable be handled in converting accrual basis net income to cash provided or used by operating activities? Why?

14 How should an increase and a decrease in inventory and in accounts payable be handled in converting accrual basis net income to cash provided or used by operating activities? Why?

15 How should an increase and a decrease in short-term prepayments be handled in converting accrual basis net income to cash provided or used by operating activities? Why?

16 How should an increase and a decrease in accrued liabilities be handled in converting accrual basis net income to cash provided or used by operating activities? Why?

17 In converting accrual basis net income to cash provided or used by operating activities, are all

(a) increases in noncash current asset accounts handled in the same manner? Explain.

(b) decreases in noncash current asset accounts handled in the same manner? Explain.

18 In converting accrual basis net income to cash provided or used by operating activities, are all

(a) increases in current liability accounts other than bank loans handled in the same manner? Explain.

(b) decreases in current liability accounts other than bank loans handled in the same manner? Explain.

19 What is an "exchange transaction"? List two examples and explain how they are handled in a statement of changes in financial position.

20 List four transactions that are neither a source nor a use of cash and are not disclosed in a statement of changes in financial position.

21 Sources of cash include long-term borrowing, sale of noncurrent assets, operations, and sale of capital stock. Which of these possible sources of cash do you consider to be most important to the long-run survival of a business?

22 Give examples of expenses, other than depreciation expense, that reduce net income but do not result in the use of cash during the period.

23 Give an example of an increase in net income that does not result in an increase in cash during the period.

24 The following quotation appeared in the annual report of a large corporation: "Depreciation, depletion, and amortization charges provide cash that causes our cash provided by operating activities to consistently exceed our net income." Evaluate this quotation.

25 Although extraordinary gains and losses may be included in net income, what reason can you give for excluding such gains and losses in computing the cash provided by operating activities? Use the following facts to illustrate your point: Net income including gain on sale of plant, $100,000; sale of plant, with a book value of $70,000, for $150,000 cash.

26 Miller Corporation acquired a building for $300,000, paying $60,000 cash and issuing a long-term note payable for the balance. What is the effect of this transaction upon the cash of Miller Corporation? How should the transaction be shown in a statement of changes in financial position?

27 During the year, holders of $4 million of Dall Limited convertible bonds converted their bonds into shares of Dall common stock. The president of Dall Limited made the following statement: "By issuing common stock to retire these bonds, the company has saved $4 million in cash. Our statement of changes in financial position will not have to show the retirement of bonds among the uses of cash." Do you agree with this statement? Explain.

28 An outside member of the board of directors of a small corporation made the following comment after studying the comparative financial statements for the past two years: "I have trouble understanding why our cash has increased steadily during the past two years, yet our profits have been negligible; we have paid no dividends; and inventories, receivables, payables, cost of plant and equipment, long-term debt, and capital stock have remained essentially unchanged." Write a brief statement explaining how this situation might occur.

EXERCISES

Exercise 19-1
Accounting
terminology

Listed below are nine technical accounting terms introduced in this chapter:

Statement of changes in financial position	Operating activities	Working capital
Income statement	Investing activities	Accrual basis
Cash equivalents	Financing activities	Cash basis

Each of the following statements may (or may not) describe one of these technical terms. For each statement, indicate the accounting term described, or answer "None" if the statement does not correctly describe any of the terms.

a The financial statement that best describes the profitability of a business that receives most of its revenue in cash.

b Transactions involving the issuance and repayment of debt, investments by owners, and distributions to owners.

c A method of accounting that summarizes operating results in terms of cash receipts and cash payments.

d The financial statement that shows the financial position of the business at a particular date.

e An asset consisting of investments in marketable securities.

f The section of a statement of changes in financial position summarizing the cash effects of most transactions that enter into the determination of net income.

g The section of a statement of changes in financial position summarizing the acquisition and disposal of plant and equipment.

Exercise 19-2
Computing cash equivalents

Compute the amount of the increase or decrease in cash and cash equivalents during 1990 from the following information:

	DECEMBER 31	
	1990	1989
Cash	$ 16,000	$ 20,000
Marketable securities	32,000	18,000
Accounts receivable (net)	81,000	79,000
Unexpired insurance	3,000	1,500
Bank loans	20,000	28,000
Accounts payable	50,000	73,000
Mortgage payable	100,000	100,000

Exercise 19-3
Effect of transactions on cash and cash equivalents

Indicate the amount of the increase or decrease (if any) in cash and cash equivalents as a result of each of the following situations:

a During the first year of operations, cash sales were $120,000, credit sales were $300,000, and accounts receivable at the end of the year were $60,000.

b Land costing $18,000 was sold for $26,000; the purchaser paid $12,000 and issued a mortgage note for $14,000.

c Issued $500,000 of bonds payable for an office building.

d Issued capital stock to investors for $600,000 cash.

e Purchased equipment costing $400,000 for $100,000 cash and $300,000 mortgage payable.

f Declared cash dividends of $80,000.

g Obtained a short-term bank loan of $150,000.

h Purchased temporary investments for $90,000 cash.

Exercise 19-4
Items to be reported in the statement of changes in financial position

Briefly explain how each of the following situations should be reported in the statement of changes in financial position for 1989.

a Depreciation of $100,000 was recorded for the year.

b In July, the 10,000 shares of no-par value capital stock of $500,000 were split 3 for 6, and in November, a 10% stock dividend in common stock was distributed to shareholders.

c Cash of $50,000 was paid and capital stock with a market value of $450,000 was issued to acquire land worth $500,000.

d Classified a portion of long-term debt as current liabilities, $280,000.

e Sold a plant for $2,000,000 cash, resulting in an extraordinary gain of $160,000 which was reported in the income statement.

Exercise 19-5
Conversion of accrual to cash basis

Indicate whether each of the following changes during the year should be added or deducted in converting accrual basis net income to cash provided or used by operating activities:

a Increase in accounts receivable.

b Decrease in inventory.

c Decrease in short-term prepayments.

d Increase in accounts payable.

e Decrease in accrued liabilities.

Exercise 19-6
Classification of items
in the statement of
changes in financial
position

Indicate in which of the three categories of activities in the statement of changes in financial position each of the following items should be presented:

a Depreciation expense.

b Increase in inventory.

c Decrease in accrued liabilities.

d Purchased a building costing $60,000 by issuing capital stock.

e Issued bonds payable for cash.

f Redeemed preferred stock.

g Purchased equipment for cash.

h Sold land for cash.

i Paid cash dividends of $800,000.

Exercise 19-7
Determine cash from
operations

The Tri Corporation reported a net loss of $80,000 on its income statement. In arriving at this figure, the following items, among others, were included:

Amortization of patents	$16,000
Amortization of premium on bonds payable	10,000
Gain on sale of a plant (an extraordinary item)	40,000
Depreciation expense	50,000
Uninsured fire damage to building	88,400

In addition, the changes in noncash current accounts were:

Increase in accounts receivable	$ 8,000
Decrease in inventory	11,000
Increase in short-term prepayments	1,200
Increase in accounts payable	12,000
Decrease in accrued liabilities	1,000

From the information above, compute the amount of cash provided or used by operating activities.

Exercise 19-8
Converting net income
to cash from operations

The following data are taken from the records of the Ferraro Company:

	END OF YEAR	BEGINNING OF YEAR
Accounts receivable	$ 20,200	$ 10,200
Inventories	32,000	40,000
Short-term prepayments	2,300	1,500
Accounts payable (merchandise creditors)	28,000	25,000
Accrued expenses payable	1,000	1,200
Net sales	300,000	
Cost of goods sold	180,000	
Operating expenses (includes depreciation of $10,000)	80,000	

From the foregoing information, convert the accrual basis net income to the amount of cash provided or used by operating activities.

Exercise 19-9
Converting income statement items to a cash basis

From the information provided in Exercise 19-8, compute the following:

a Cash collected from customers during the year.

b Cash paid to merchandise creditors during the year.

c Cash paid for operating expenses during the year.

d Cash provided or used by operating activities during the year.

Exercise 19-10
Preparing a statement of changes in financial position

A summary of the comparative financial position for Landscape Consultants, Inc., for the current year appears as follows:

	END OF CURRENT YEAR	BEGINNING OF CURRENT YEAR
Cash (cash and cash equivalents)	$ 16,000	$ 12,000
Accounts receivable (net)	100,000	90,000
Inventory	54,000	63,000
Land	90,000	50,000
Buildings	160,000	100,000
Less: Accumulated depreciation	(40,000)	(35,000)
Totals	$380,000	$280,000
Accounts payable (for purchases)	$ 42,000	$ 31,000
Accrued liabilities	8,000	9,000
Notes payable, due in five years	70,000	–0–
Capital stock, no-par value	210,000	200,000
Retained earnings	50,000	40,000
Totals	$380,000	$280,000

The net income was $17,000 and included no extraordinary gains or losses. Depreciation expense for the current year was $5,000. A cash dividend of $7,000 was paid at the end of the current year.

Prepare a statement of changes in financial position for the current year without using a working paper.

PROBLEMS

Group A

Problem 19A-1
Effect of transactions on cash and cash equivalents and on net income conversion, and identifying exchange transactions

For each of the following business transactions and adjustments, you are to indicate the effect, first, on cash and cash equivalents, and second, on accrual basis net income in its conversion to cash provided or used by operating activities. In each case, the possible effects are an increase, decrease, or no change.

(1) A plant sold for cash at a price below its carrying value.

(2) Declaration of a cash dividend.

(3) Payment of a previously declared cash dividend.

(4) One-year fire insurance policy paid in advance at year-end date.

(5) Inventory destroyed by earthquake; one-half of its carrying value covered by insurance and paid by the insurance company.

(6) Charging the portion of unexpired insurance expense that expired during the current year.

(7) Purchase of patent, which gives 200 shares of the company's common stock in exchange.

(8) Marketable securities (temporary investments) sold for cash at a price above cost.

(9) Amortization of premium on bonds payable.

(10) Temporary investments in marketable securities sold for cash at cost, i.e., its carrying value.

Instructions **a** List the numbers 1 to 10 on your answer sheet, and set up two columns headed "Effect on cash and cash equivalents" and "Effect on net income conversion." For each item, write the words *increase, decrease,* or *no change* in the appropriate column to indicate the effect of the item on cash and cash equivalents, and on net income conversion.

b Are any of the items listed above considered "exchange transactions," which would be listed as both a source and use of cash in a statement of changes in financial position? Explain.

Problem 19A-2
Prepare and comment
on a statement of
changes in financial
position

The information which is illustrated below is taken from the annual report of El Toro Corporation:

	1989	1988
Cash	$ 65,000	$ 80,000
Temporary investments	35,000	20,000
Accounts receivable (net)	160,000	105,000
Inventories	140,000	170,000
Short-term prepayments	10,000	5,000
Long-term investments	80,000	100,000
Equipment	600,000	420,000
Less: Accumulated depreciation	(190,000)	(110,000)
Bank loan	75,000	55,000
Accounts payable	110,000	135,000
Accrued liabilities	15,000	10,000
Capital stock	250,000	200,000
Retained earnings	450,000	390,000

Depreciation for 1989 amounted to $80,000; no equipment items were sold; long-term investments were sold at a gain of $10,000; capital stock was issued for $50,000; and net income (including the $10,000 extraordinary gain) was $135,000. Cash dividends of $75,000 were declared and paid.

Instructions **a** Compute the amount of increase or decrease in cash and cash equivalents for 1989.

b Prepare a statement of changes in financial position for 1989, without using working papers.

c Briefly comment on the company's liquidity position and cash policies on operating, financing, and investing activities for 1989.

Problem 19A-3
Working paper

Using the information provided in Problem 19A-2, prepare a working paper for a statement of changes in financial position. (If you have already worked Problem 19A-2, determine that your solutions to both problems are in agreement.)

Problem 19A-4
Show how the increase in cash and cash equivalents is determined and prepare a statement of changes in financial position

During the year, Wildcat Tractor Limited showed the following changes in amount for the following groups of accounts. For example, cash and cash equivalents increased by $8,000 during the year, and this amount therefore appears in the Debit change column.

	CHANGES DURING THE YEAR	
	DEBIT	CREDIT
Cash and cash equivalents	$ 8,000	
Accounts receivable	27,000	
Inventories		$ 5,000
Building	100,000	
Equipment	60,000	
Accumulated depreciation		40,000
Accounts payable	60,000	
Accrued liabilities		2,000
Capital stock, no-par		160,000
Retained earnings		48,000
Totals	$255,000	$255,000

During the year the company sold 12,800 shares of capital stock and applied the proceeds to the purchase of building and equipment. There were no retirements of building and equipment during the year. Net income was $142,000 and cash dividends declared and paid during the year amounted to $94,000.

Instructions

a Show how the $8,000 increase in cash and cash equivalents may be determined by using some necessary *assumed* amounts.

b Prepare a statement of changes in financial position without using working papers.

Problem 19A-5
Prepare schedule of cash and cash equivalents, and working paper, and statement of changes in financial position

Comparative balance sheets for Sierra Hot Tub Co. Ltd. at the end of 1988 and 1989 are shown below:

	1989	1988
Cash	$ 35,000	$ 60,000
Marketable securities	30,000	28,000
Accounts receivable (net)	90,000	105,000
Inventory	195,000	150,000
Prepaid rent	10,000	8,000
Land for future expansion	75,000	
Plant and equipment (See accumulated depreciation below)	500,000	375,000
Patents (net of amortization)	55,000	60,000
Totals	$990,000	$786,000
Accumulated depreciation	$157,500	$120,000
Bank loan	26,000	20,000
Accounts payable (suppliers)	61,500	45,000
Accrued salaries	14,000	16,000
Dividends payable	6,000	
Notes payable due in 1992	45,000	
Capital stock, no-par	650,000	525,000
Retained earnings	30,000	60,000
Totals	$990,000	$786,000

Additional data   (1) The net loss for 1989 amounted to $24,000.

(2) Cash dividends of $6,000 were declared.

(3) The company incurred the following expenses, which did not require the use of cash: depreciation, $37,500; and amortization of patents, $5,000.

(4) Land for future expansion was acquired at a cost of $75,000. This acquisition was financed by paying $30,000 cash and issuing a 10% note payable due in three years for the balance of the purchase price.

(5) The company issued 12,500 shares of its capital stock for cash. The market value of the stock was $10 per share. The proceeds were used to purchase equipment.

Instructions   **a** Prepare a schedule of cash and cash equivalents for 1989.

b Prepare a working paper for a statement of changes in financial position for 1989.

c Prepare a statement of changes in financial position for 1989.

Problem 19A-6
Prepare schedule of cash and cash equivalents, and working paper and statement of changes in financial position

Comparative after-closing trial balances for Emerging Technologies, Inc., at the ends of 1989 and 1990 follow:

	1990	1989
DEBITS		
Cash	$ 160,000	$ 120,000
Marketable securities	200,000	170,000
Accounts receivable (net)	350,000	280,000
Inventories	650,000	815,000
Prepaid expenses	20,000	35,000
Land	600,000	750,000
Buildings & equipment	1,600,000	1,135,000
Goodwill	388,000	400,000
Discount on bonds payable	13,000	15,000
Totals	$3,981,000	$3,720,000

CREDITS		
Bank loan (short-term)	$ 20,000	$ 205,000
Accounts payable	515,000	495,000
Accrued liabilities	8,000	20,000
Accumulated depreciation	628,000	520,000
Long-term notes payable	150,000	
Bonds payable	1,000,000	1,000,000
11% preferred stock, $100 par		300,000
Common stock, no-par	1,005,000	630,000
Retained earnings	655,000	550,000
Totals	$3,981,000	$3,720,000

Additional data   (1) Net income for 1990 was $280,000.

(2) Land with a cost of $150,000 was sold for $170,000 cash. This is considered as an extraordinary item.

(3) The company incurred, among others, the following expenses: depreciation, amortization of goodwill, and amortization of discount on bonds payable.

(4) Equipment was purchased for $465,000 by paying $315,000 in cash and issuing a 12% long-term note payable for the remaining $150,000.

(5) The company issued 10,000 shares of common stock at a price of $20 per share. The proceeds, along with some additional cash, were used to retire the entire issue of 11% preferred stock at its par value.

(6) Stock dividends of $175,000 in common stock were issued where shareholders were given a choice of receiving cash or common stock.

Instructions

a Prepare a schedule of change in cash and cash equivalents during 1990.

b Prepare a working paper for a statement of changes in financial position for 1990.

c Prepare a statement of changes in financial position for 1990.

Problem 19A-7
Convert income statement from accrual to cash basis, prepare and comment on the statement of changes in financial position

When the controller of Trans-Canada Corporation presented the following condensed comparative financial statements to the board of directors, the reaction of the board members was very favourable.

TRANS-CANADA CORPORATION
Comparative Financial Position
As of December 31
(in thousands of dollars)

	1990	1989
Current assets	$ 410	$ 395
Less: Current liabilities	200	225
Working capital	$ 210	$ 170
Long-term investments	–0–	150
Patents (net of amortization)	8	10
Plant and equipment (net)	962	660
Total assets minus current liabilities	$1,180	$ 990
Long-term liabilities	$ 250	$ –0–
Preferred stock (non-cumulative)	–0–	170
Common stock	500	500
Retained earnings	430	320
Total long-term debt and capital	$1,180	$ 990

TRANS-CANADA CORPORATION
Comparative Income Statements
(in thousands of dollars)

	1990	1989
Net sales	$1,000	$ 680
Cost of goods sold	590	480
Gross profit on sales	$ 410	$ 200
Operating expenses, including depreciation of $80 in 1990 and $60 in 1989	(180)	(140)
Extraordinary loss on sale of long-term investments	(30)	–0–
Income taxes	(90)	(25)
Net income	$ 110	$ 35

Noting that net income rose from $3.50 per share of capital stock to $11 per share, one member of the board proposed that a substantial cash dividend be paid. "Our working capital is up by $40,000; we should be able to make a distribution to shareholders," he commented. The controller replied that the company's cash position was precarious and pointed out that at the end of 1990 a cash balance of only $15,000 was on hand, a decline from $145,000 at the end of 1989. The controller also reminded the board that the company bought some new equipment during 1990. When a board member asked for an explanation of the increase of $40,000 in working capital, the controller presented the following schedule (in thousands of dollars):

		EFFECT ON WORKING CAPITAL
Increase in working capital:		
Accounts receivable increased by		$ 83
Inventories increased by		72
Accounts payable reduced by		62
Accrued expenses payable reduced by		28
Total increases in working capital		$245
Decreases in working capital:		
Cash decreased by	$130	
Prepaid expenses reduced by	10	
Income tax liability increased by	65	205
Increase in working capital during 1990		$ 40

After examining this schedule, the board member shook his head and said, "I still don't understand how our cash position can be so tight in the face of a tripling of net income and a substantial increase in working capital! Also, I am not sure what our cash policies in the operating, financing, and investing areas are. The information provided by the controller really does not help me at all."

Instructions

a Prepare a statement converting Trans-Canada Corporation's income statement to a cash basis, determining the cash generated by operations during 1990.

b From the information and the comparative statement of financial position provided above, prepare a statement of changes in financial position for 1990, explaining the $130,000 decrease in the cash balance. (Check that the cash from operating activities is the same in both a and b.)

c Comment on the issues raised by the board member.

GROUP B

Problem 19B-1

Effect of transactions on cash and cash equivalents and on net income conversion, and identifying exchange transactions

A list of business transactions and adjustments follows. For each item you are to indicate the effect, first, on cash and cash equivalents, and second, on accrual basis net income in its conversion to cash provided or used by operating activities. In each case, the possible effects are an increase, a decrease, or no change.

(1) Payment of an account payable.

(2) Depreciation recorded for the period.

(3) Sale of long-term investment at a price above its carrying value, resulting in an extraordinary gain.

(4) Payment of last year's income tax liability, which was previously recorded in the accounting records.

(5) Shares of common stock issued in exchange for convertible bonds converted by bondholders.

(6) Empty warehouse destroyed by fire; one-half of its carrying value covered by insurance and paid by the insurance company.

(7) Amortization of discount on bonds payable.

(8) Premium paid for a one-year insurance policy (debit to Unexpired Insurance) at year-end date.

(9) Short-term loan from bank.

(10) Temporary investments sold for cash at a price below cost.

Instructions **a** List the numbers 1 to 10 on your answer sheet, and set up two columns headed "Effect on cash and cash equivalents" and "Effect on net income conversion." For each item write the words *increase, decrease,* or *no change* in the appropriate column to indicate the effect of the item on cash and cash equivalents, and on net income conversion.

b Are any of the items listed above considered "exchange transactions," which would be listed as both a source and a use of cash in a statement of changes in financial position? Explain.

Problem 19B-2
Prepare and comment on a statement of changes in financial position

The following information is taken from the 1989 annual report of Nightwatch, Inc.:

	END OF 1989	END OF 1988
Cash	$ 32,000	$ 20,000
Temporary investments	31,000	12,000
Accounts receivable	67,000	58,000
Inventories	93,000	107,000
Short-term prepayments	2,000	3,000
Long-term investments	48,000	60,000
Equipment	440,000	280,000
Less: Accumulated depreciation	(120,000)	(70,000)
Bank Loan	26,000	10,000
Accounts payable	74,000	72,000
Accrued liabilities	–0–	8,000
Bonds payable	60,000	–0–
Capital stock	150,000	150,000
Retained earnings	283,000	230,000

Depreciation for 1989 amounted to $50,000; no equipment items were sold; long-term investments were sold at a gain of $6,000; bonds were issued for $60,000 cash; and net income (including the $6,000 extraordinary gain) was $93,000. Cash dividends of $40,000 were declared and paid.

Instructions **a** Compute the amount of increase or decrease in cash and cash equivalents for 1989.

b Prepare a statement of changes in financial position for 1989, without using working papers.

c Briefly comment on the company's liquidity position and cash policies on operating, financing, and investing activities.

Problem 19B-3
Working paper

Using the information provided in Problem 19B-2, prepare a working paper for a statement of changes in financial position. (If you have already worked Problem 19B-2, determine that your solutions to both problems are in agreement.)

Problem 19B-4
Show how the increase in cash and cash equivalents is determined and prepare a statement of changes in financial position

During the year Paperback Publishers showed the following *changes* in amount for the following groups of accounts. For example, cash and cash equivalents increased by $12,000 during the year, and this amount therefore appears in the Debit change column.

	CHANGES DURING THE YEAR	
	DEBIT	CREDIT
Cash and cash equivalents	$ 12,000	
Accounts receivable		$ 8,000
Inventories	70,000	
Prepaid equipment rental	6,000	
Land	100,000	
Buildings	440,000	
Accumulated depreciation		230,000
Accounts payable		106,000
Accrued salaries	10,000	
Capital stock, no-par		162,000
Retained earnings		132,000
Totals	$638,000	$638,000

During the year the company issued 9,000 shares of capital stock at a price of $18 per share. There were no retirements of land and buildings during the year. Net income was $252,000, and cash dividends declared and paid during the year amounted to $120,000.

Instructions

a Show how the $12,000 increase in cash and cash equivalents maybe determined by using some *assumed* amounts.

b Prepare a statement of changes in financial position for the year without using working papers.

Problem 19B-5
Prepare a schedule of cash and cash equivalents, and working paper and statement of changes in financial position

Comparative after-closing trial balances for Home Port, Inc., follow:

DEBITS	DECEMBER 31,	
	1990	1989
Cash	$ 72,000	$ 78,000
Marketable securities		96,000
Accounts receivable	162,000	160,000
Inventories	132,000	180,000
Prepaid expenses	36,000	24,000
Land	120,000	
Buildings	500,000	
Patents (net of amortization)	58,000	68,000
Totals	$1,080,000	$606,000

CREDITS	DECEMBER 31,	
	1990	1989
Allowance for doubtful accounts	$ 6,000	$ 12,000
Bank loans	30,000	10,000
Accounts payable	138,000	92,000
Accrued liabilities	72,000	78,000
Long-term notes payable	300,000	60,000
Capital stock	396,000	246,000
Retained earnings	138,000	108,000
Totals	$1,080,000	$606,000

During 1989, Home Port, Inc., operated in rented space. Early in 1990 the company acquired suitable land and made arrangements to borrow funds on long-term notes to finance the construction of new buildings. The company also sold additional stock for $150,000 and all its marketable securities at a gain of $2,000. Construction of the buildings was not completed until the end of 1990; therefore, no depreciation expense was recorded in 1990. Net income was $78,000; cash dividends declared and paid amounted to $48,000.

Instructions   **a** Prepare a schedule of change in cash and cash equivalents.

b Prepare a working paper for a statement of changes in financial position.

c Prepare a statement of changes in financial position for 1990.

Problem 19B-6
Prepare schedule of cash and cash equivalents, and working paper and statement of changes in financial position

Comparative account balances for Long Island Corporation at the end of 1989 and 1990 follow:

DEBIT	1990	1989
Cash	$ 110,000	$ 190,000
Marketable securities		20,000
Accounts receivable (net)	150,000	175,000
Inventory	350,000	250,000
Land for future expansion	100,000	
Plant and equipment		
(see accumulated depreciation below)	1,750,000	1,625,000
Patents (net of amortization)	90,000	100,000
Totals	$2,550,000	$2,360,000

CREDIT	1990	1989
Accumulated depreciation	$ 162,500	$ 200,000
Bank loan	20,000	
Accounts payable	132,500	100,000
Dividends payable	10,000	
Notes payable due in three years	125,000	
Bonds payable	1,000,000	1,000,000
Premium on bonds payable	50,000	60,000
Capital stock	1,000,000	850,000
Retained earnings	50,000	150,000
Totals	$2,550,000	$2,360,000

Additional data

(1) The net loss for 1990 amounted to $40,000.

(2) Cash dividends of $10,000 were declared.

(3) The company incurred the following expenses, among others: depreciation, amortization of patents, and amortization of premium on bonds payable.

(4) The company issued 10,000 shares of its common stock in exchange for land to be held for future expansion. The land was appraised at $100,000.

(5) The abandonment of an obsolete and fully depreciated plant with an original cost of $100,000 resulted in a cash penalty assessed by government. This penalty of $25,000 was considered as an extraordinary loss.

(6) Equipment was purchased for $225,000. The company paid $100,000 of this amount in cash and issued a 12%, three-year note payable for the balance.

(7) Capital stock of $50,000 was issued for stock dividends.

Instructions

a Prepare a schedule of change in cash and cash equivalents during 1990.

b Prepare working papers for a statement of changes in financial position for 1990.

c Prepare a statement of changes in financial position for 1990.

Problem 19B-7
Prepare statement of changes in financial position from accrual and cash basis income statement and other information, comment on cash policies and relevancy of information

In an attempt to provide the most relevant information on cash flows to the members of the board of directors, the controller of Ancaster Corporation presented the following:

ANCASTER CORPORATION
Income Statement on an Accrual and Cash Basis
For the Year Ended December 31, 1990
(in thousands of dollars)

	ACCRUAL BASIS	ADD OR (DEDUCT)	CASH BASIS
Net Sales	$800		
Add: Decrease in accounts receivable		$28	$828
Cost of goods sold	510		
Add: Increase in inventories		46	
Less: Increase in accounts payable		(93)	463
Gross profit on sales	$290		$365
Operating expenses	$180		
Less: Depreciation expenses		(35)	
Increase in accrued liabilities		(16)	$129
Income taxes	36		
Less: Increase in income tax liability		(12)	24
Extraordinary gain	(22)		
Total expenses less extraordinary gain	$194		$153
Net income	$96		
Cash provided by operating activities			$212

In his presentation to the board, the controller also mentioned:

(1) Disposal of an old plant for $30,000 cash, resulting in an extraordinary gain of $22,000.

(2) Purchase of a large tract of land for a new plant for $325,000 cash.

(3) Issuance of common stock for $500,000 cash.

(4) Issuance of 10-year bonds payable, $1,000,000.

(5) Net income before extraordinary item and cash from operating activities have been stable over the past two-year period and cash from operating activities in 1991 would be similar to that of 1990.

(6) Cash dividends of $150,000 were declared and paid.

(7) Cash balance at December 31, 1990, was $1,500,000. There were no cash equivalents such as temporary investments or short-term borrowings.

"Ladies and gentlemen," concluded the controller, "you can see that our cash position is improving and our profitability is stable. Our future looks good, as we will substantially increase our production capacity when our new plant is completed next year. The cost of construction and equipment will be $2 million and we have agreed to pay it off during next year."

However, some board members were not quite sure whether the company would have sufficient cash to finance its operations, the $150,000 annual dividends, and immediate plant expansion in 1991, since the board had decided not to incur any long-term debt or issue any capital stock. They also complained that the information provided by the controller was too fragmentary to help them to assess the cash policies on operating, financing, and investing activities.

Instructions   **a** From the information provided by the controller, prepare a statement of changes in financial position for 1990.

b Comment on the issues raised by the board members.

BUSINESS DECISION CASES

Case 19-1
Can we make it?
Olympic Sportwear Limited has a cash balance of $6,150,000 at the beginning of 1989. Restrictions contained in bank loans require that the cash balance not fall below $6,000,000. The following projected information is available for 1989.

(1) Budgeted net income (including the gain on sale of plant assets, an extraordinary item) is $7,500,000. The following items are included in estimating net income: depreciation, $2,100,000; amortization of premium on bonds payable, $150,000. Also, accounts receivable and inventory are expected to increase by $3,200,000 and $3,600,000 respectively. Accounts payable are expected to increase by $6,800,000. The company's sales are expected to be similar to 1988.

(2) Sale of plant assets with a carrying value of $1,200,000 is expected to bring $1,500,000 cash.

(3) Additional plant assets costing $15,000,000 will be acquired. Payment will be as follows: 40% cash, and 60% through issuance of capital stock.

(4) Long-term investment will be sold at cost, $300,000 cash.

(5) Bonds payable in the amount of $1,500,000, bearing interest at 11%, will be redeemed at 105, approximately 10 years prior to maturity in order to eliminate the high interest expense of $165,000 per year. The elimination of this interest and the gain or loss on the retirement of bonds payable were taken into account in estimating net income for 1989. These bonds had been issued at par.

(6) Tentative planned cash dividend, $4,500,000.

Instructions   **a** Consider all the information that has been given and prepare a projected statement of changes in financial position in order to determine the estimated increase or decrease in cash for 1989.

b The planned cash dividend of $4,500,000 represents the same dividend per share as paid last year. The company would like to maintain dividends at this level. Does it appear likely that the past dividend policy can be maintained in 1989? What factors other than cash position should be considered in determining the level of cash dividends declared by the board of directors?

c Comment on the company's cash policy on operating activities.

Case 19-2
On target or not?
Lancaster Corporation is assessing its three-year plan on plant modernization and expansion. The company is in a capital-intensive industry where plant and equipment can become obsolete in a few years. This plan is as follows:

1988 Modernization by replacing obsolete equipment.

1989 Commencing the expansion by constructing a new plant and by purchasing equipment, financed partly by selling the remaining long-term investments of $32 million.

1990 Completing the expansion and starting the operating of the new plant at the beginning of 1991. Of the total cost of $190 million incurred in 1990 ($52 million for plant and $138 million for equipment), $170 million will be financed equally by issuing bonds payable and capital stock.

To enhance the attractiveness of its capital stock issue, the company wants to continue its long-established dividend policy of about 8% on capital, which will require a cash dividend of

LANCASTER CORPORATION
Comparative Statements of Changes in Financial Position
For 1989 and 1988
(In millions of dollars)

	1989	1988
Operating activities:		
Net income	$ 12	$ 16
Add: Expenses not requiring the use of cash — Depreciation	8	6
Decrease in accounts receivable	5	2
Decrease in inventories	2	2
Increase in accounts payable	10	3
Increase in accrued liabilities	2	1
Cash provided by operating activities	$ 39	$ 30
Financing activities:		
Sale of long-term investments	$ 32	$ 62
Issuance of bonds payable	116	
Cash dividends	(30)	(30)
Cash provided by financing activities	$ 118	$ 32
Investing activities:		
Construction of plant	$ (90)	
Purchase of equipment	(36)	$ (60)
Cash used in investing activities	$(126)	$ (60)
Increase in cash	$ 31	$ 2
Cash Balance	$ 41	$ 10

$38 million in 1990. Also, the company will have more than half of its assets financed by debts after issuing the bonds payable in 1990. The new and old bond indentures (bonds were also issued prior to 1988) will require the company to maintain a minimum cash balance of $30 million for 1990 and subsequent years. It is expected that the net income for 1990 will be similar to that for 1989.

The comparative statements of changes in financial position for 1988 and 1989 are presented on page 816.

Instructions

a Assess the company's liquidity position for 1989.

b Comment on the company's cash policies on operating, financing, and investing activities in 1989.

c Will the company be able to finance its activities in 1990 as planned? If yes, explain. If not, explain and suggest alternatives.

ANALYSIS AND INTERPRETATION OF FINANCIAL STATEMENTS

20

CHAPTER PREVIEW

In many of the preceding chapters we have been concerned with preparing a set of financial statements. In Chapter 19, the statement of changes in financial position was analyzed and interpreted. In this chapter we start with the other financial statements (balance sheet, income statement, and statement of retained earnings) and concentrate on methods of analyzing and interpreting the information they contain. Our goal is to determine whether a company is gaining or losing ground in the unending struggle for profitability and solvency. We explore the techniques for comparing a company's present financial position with its position a year ago and for comparing this year's earnings with last year's earnings. We also compare a company's performance with that of other companies in the industry. Various types of analysis are presented to meet the special needs of common shareholders, long-term creditors, preferred shareholders, and short-term creditors.

After studying this chapter you should be able to meet these Learning Objectives:

1 Put the dollar amount of a company's net income into perspective by relating it to the company's sales, assets, and shareholders' equity.

2 Describe several sources of financial information about a business.

3 Explain the uses of dollar and percentage changes, trend percentages, component percentages, and ratios.

4 Discuss the "quality" of a company's earnings, assets, and working capital.

5 Analyze financial statements from the viewpoints of common shareholders, creditors, and others.

6 Compute the ratios widely used in financial statement analysis and explain the significance of each.

Financial statements are the instrument panel of a business enterprise. They constitute a report on managerial performance, attesting to managerial success or failure and flashing warning signals of impending difficulties. To read a complex instrument panel, one must understand the gauges and their calibration to make sense out of the array of data they convey. Similarly, one must understand the inner workings of the accounting system and the significance of various financial relationships to interpret the data appearing in financial statements. To a reader with a knowledge of accounting, a set of financial statements tells a great deal about a business enterprise.

The financial affairs of a business may be of interest to a number of different groups; management, creditors, investors, politicians, union officials, and government agencies. Each of these groups has somewhat different needs, and, accordingly, each tends to concentrate on particular aspects of a company's financial picture.

1 Put the dollar amount of a company's net income into perspective by relating it to the company's sales, assets, and shareholders' equity.

What is your opinion of the level of corporate earnings?

As a college student who has completed (or almost completed) a course in accounting, you have a much better understanding of corporate earnings than do people who have never studied accounting. The level of earnings of large corporations is a controversial topic, a favourite topic in many political speeches and at cocktail parties. Many of the statements one reads or hears from these sources are emotional rather than rational, and fiction rather than fact. Public opinion polls show that the public believes the average manufacturing company has an after-tax net income of about 30% of sales, when in fact such net income has been *about 5% of sales* in recent years. A widespread public belief that net income is six times the actual rate may lead to some unwise decisions.

An in-depth knowledge of accounting does not enable you to say at what level corporate earnings *should be;* however, a knowledge of accounting does enable you to read audited financial statements that show what the level of corporate earnings *actually is.* Moreover, you are aware that the information in published financial statements of corporations has been audited by public accounting firms. Consequently, you know that the earnings reported in these published financial statements are reasonably reliable; they have been determined in accordance with generally accepted accounting principles and verified by independent experts.

When such troublesome problems as severe unemployment and rising prices for consumer goods and services affect so many people, it is not surprising that some political leaders look for a scapegoat to hold responsible. Very often, the blame has been laid on corporate earnings, which sometimes have been labelled as "excessive," "outrageous," and even "obscene." Usually the speaker who uses these emotional adjectives cites an absolute dollar amount of earnings without relating it in any way to the volume of sales or the amount of assets necessary to produce the quoted figure.

There are many ways of appraising the adequacy of corporate earnings. Certainly, earnings should be compared with total assets and with invested capital as well as with sales. In this chapter we shall look at a number of ways of evaluating corporate earnings and solvency.

2   Describe several sources of financial information about a business.

Sources of financial information

For the most part, our discussion will be limited to the kind of analysis that can be made by "outsiders" who do not have access to internal accounting records. Investors must rely to a considerable extent on financial statements in published annual and quarterly reports. Financial information about most large corporations is also published by the *Financial Post*, Dun & Bradstreet of Canada, Moody's Investors Service, Standard & Poor's Corporation, and stock brokerage firms.

Bankers are usually able to secure more detailed information by requesting it as a condition for granting a loan. Trade creditors may obtain financial information for businesses from credit-rating agencies such as Dun & Bradstreet.

Comparative financial statements

Significant changes in financial data are easy to see when financial statement amounts for two or more years are placed side by side in adjacent columns. Such a statement is called a *comparative financial statement*. The amounts for the most recent years are usually placed in the left-hand money column. Both the balance sheet and the income statement are often prepared in the form of comparative statements. A highly condensed comparative income statement covering three years follows.

CONDENSED
THREE-YEAR INCOME
STATEMENT

BENSON CORPORATION
Comparative Income Statement
For the Years Ended December 31, 1989, 1988, and 1987
(in thousands of dollars)

	1989	1988	1987
Net sales	$600	$500	$400
Cost of goods sold	370	300	235
Gross profit	$230	$200	$165
Expenses	194	160	115
Net income	$ 36	$ 40	$ 50

3   Explain the uses of dollar and percentage changes, trend percentages, component percentages, and ratios.

Tools of analysis

Few figures in a financial statement are highly significant in and of themselves. It is their relationship to other quantities or the amount and direction of change since a previous date that is important. Analysis is largely a matter of establishing significant relationships and pointing up changes and trends. Four widely used analytical techniques are (1) dollar and percentage changes, (2) trend percentages, (3) component percentages, and (4) ratios.

Dollar and percentage changes

The dollar amount of change from year to year is significant, but expressing the change in percentage terms adds perspective. For example, if sales this year have increased by $100,000, the fact that this is an increase of 10% over last year's sales of $1 million puts it in a different perspective than if it represented a 1% increase over sales of $10 million for the prior year.

The dollar amount of any change is the difference between the amount for a *comparison* year and for a *base* year. The percentage change is computed by dividing the amount of the change between years by the amount for the base year. This is illustrated in the following tabulation, using data from the preceding comparative income statement.

DOLLAR AND PERCENTAGE CHANGES

| | IN THOUSANDS | | | INCREASE OR (DECREASE) | | | |
| | | | | 1989 OVER 1988 | | 1988 OVER 1987 | |
	YEAR 1989	YEAR 1988	YEAR 1987	AMOUNT	%	AMOUNT	%
Net sales	$600	$500	$400	$100	20%	$100	25%
Net income	36	40	50	(4)	(10%)	(10)	(20%)

Although net sales increased $100,000 in both 1988 and 1989, the percentage of change differs because of the shift in the base from 1987 to 1988. These calculations present no problems when the figures for the base year are positive amounts. If a negative amount or a zero amount appears in the base year, however, a percentage change cannot be computed. Thus if Benson Corporation had incurred a net loss in 1988, the percentage change in net income from 1988 to 1989 could not have been calculated.

Evaluating percentage changes in sales and earnings   Computing the percentage changes in sales, gross profit, and net income from one year to the next gives insight into a company's rate of growth. If a company is experiencing growth in its economic activities, sales and earnings should increase at *more than the rate of inflation.* Assume, for example, that a company's sales increase by 6% while the general price level rises by 10%. It is probable that the entire increase in sales may be explained by inflation, rather than by an increase in sales volume. In fact, the company may well have sold fewer goods than in the preceding year.

In measuring the dollar or percentage change in *quarterly* sales or earnings, it is customary to compare the results of the current quarter with those of the *same quarter in the preceding year.* Use of the same quarter of the preceding year as the base period prevents our analysis from being distorted by seasonal fluctuations in business activity.

Percentages become misleading when the base is small   Percentage changes may create a misleading impression when the dollar amount used as a base is unusually small. Occasionally we hear a television newscaster say that a company's net income has increased by a very large percentage, such as 900%. The initial impression created by such a statement is that the company's net income must now be excessively large. But assume, for example, that a company had net income of $100,000 in its first year; that in the second year net income drops to $10,000, and that in the third year, net income returns to the $100,000 level. In this third year, net income has increased by $90,000, representing a 900% increase over the net income of the second year. What needs to be added is that this 900% increase in net income in the third year *exactly offsets* the 90% decline in net income in the second year. Not too many people realize that a 90% decline in earnings must be followed by a 900% increase just to get back to the starting point.

Trend percentages

The changes in financial statement items from a base year to following years are often expressed as *trend percentages* to show the extent and direction of change. Two steps are necessary to compute trend percentages. First, a base year is selected and each item in the financial statements for the base year is given a weight of 100%. The second step is to express each item in the financial statements for following years as a percentage of its base-year amount. This computation consists of dividing an item such as Sales in each of the years after the base year by the amount of Sales in the base year.

For example, assume that 1985 is selected as the base year and that Sales in the base year amounted to $300,000 as shown in the following illustration. The trend percentages for Sales are computed by dividing the Sales amount of each following year by $300,000. Also shown are the yearly amounts of net income. The trend percentages for net income are computed by dividing the Net Income amount for each following year by the base-year amount of $15,000.

	1990	1989	1988	1987	1986	1985
Sales	$450,000	$360,000	$330,000	$320,000	$312,000	$300,000
Net income .	22,950	14,550	21,450	19,200	15,600	15,000

When the computations described above have been made, the trend percentages will appear as follows.

	1990	1989	1988	1987	1986	1985
Sales	150%	120%	110%	107%	104%	100%
Net income	153%	97%	143%	128%	104%	100%

The above trend percentages indicate a very modest growth in sales in the early years and accelerated growth in 1989 and 1990. Net income also shows an increasing growth trend with the exception of the year 1989, when net income declined despite a solid increases in sales. This variation could have resulted from an unfavourable change in the gross profit margin or from unusual expenses. However, the problem was overcome in 1990 with a sharp rise in net income. Overall the trend percentages give a picture of a profitable growing enterprise.

As another example, assume that sales are increasing each year, but that the cost of goods sold is increasing at a faster rate. This means that the gross profit margin is shrinking. Perhaps the increases in sales are being achieved through excessive price cutting. The company's net income may be declining even though sales are rising.

Component percentages

Component percentages indicate the *relative size* of each item included in a total. For example, each item on a balance sheet could be expressed as a percentage of total assets. This shows quickly the relative importance of current and noncurrent assets as well as the relative amount of financing obtained from current creditors, long-term creditors, and shareholders. By computing component percentages for several successive balance sheets, we can see which items are increasing in importance and which are becoming less significant.

Common size income statement   Another application of component percentages is to express all items on an income statement as a percentage of net sales. Such a statement is sometimes called a common size income statement. Following is a condensed income statement in dollars and in common size form.

ARE THE YEAR-TO-YEAR CHANGES FAVOURABLE?

Income Statement

	DOLLARS		COMPONENT PERCENTAGES	
	1989	1988	1989	1988
Net sales	$1,000,000	$600,000	100.0%	100.0%
Cost of goods sold	700,000	360,000	70.0	60.0
Gross profit on sales	$ 300,000	$240,000	30.0%	40.0%
Expenses (including income taxes) ..	200,000	150,000	20.0	25.0
Net income	$ 100,000	$ 90,000	10.0%	15.0%

Looking only at the component percentages, we see that the decline in the gross profit rate from 40% to 30% was only partially offset by the decrease in expenses as a percentage of net sales, causing net income to decrease from 15% to 10% of net sales. The dollar amounts in the first pair of columns, however, present an entirely different picture. It is true that net sales increased faster than net income, but the dollar amount of net income did increase in 1989, a fact not apparent from a review of component percentages alone. This points out an important limitation in the use of component percentages. Changes in the component percentage may result from a change in the component, in the total, or in both. It is important to recognize that 10% of a large total may be a greater amount than 15% of a smaller total.

Ratios

A ratio is a simple mathematical expression of the relationship of one item to another. Ratios may be stated several ways. To illustrate, let us consider the current ratio, which expresses the relationship between current assets and current liabilities. If current assets are $100,000 and current liabilities are $50,000, we may say either that the current ratio is 2 to 1 (which is written as 2:1), or that current assets are

CANADA PACKERS INC.
10-Year Summary of Consolidated Financial Data
($ millions, except per common share data)

FISCAL YEARS

	1987	1986	1985	1984	1983	1982	1981	1980	1979	1978
SALES AND EARNINGS										
Net sales	$3,080.9	$3,108.6	$3,051.0	$3,176.0	$3,001.4	$2,943.1	$2,842.4	$2,711.2	$2,330.5	$1,878.4
Taxes on income	21.7	25.0	12.0	15.0	9.8	17.3	17.5	15.1	12.6	11.4
Depreciation	28.1	25.9	24.3	21.8	19.7	19.1	17.8	15.3	15.0	14.0
Net income	38.6	38.1	25.0	25.3	21.0	30.0	26.1	25.6*	20.9	18.1
As a % of net sales	1.3%	1.2%	0.8%	0.8%	0.7%	1.0%	0.9%	1.0%	0.9%	1.0%
PER SHARE										
Net income	$1.04	$1.04	$ .69	$ .70	$ .58	$ .83	$ .73	$ .71*	$ .58	$ .50
Dividends	.38	.31	.31	.29	.27	.27	.26	.21	.37	.16
Shareholders' investment (Book value)	10.10	9.37	8.61	8.26	7.83	7.51	6.94	6.48	5.69	5.48
FINANCIAL POSITION										
Working capital	$160.0	$155.6	$163.0	$155.5	$134.2	$160.1	$167.9	$158.2	$135.5	$113.9
Capital expenditures	48.4	41.3	26.5	35.8	40.2	36.2	37.0	35.3	24.3	23.6
Land, plant, and equipment — net	278.3	245.2	224.7	219.9	203.7	177.6	156.6	136.2	121.4	112.9
Shareholders' investment	377.2	344.7	311.1	297.4	281.8	270.4	250.0	233.2	204.9	197.4

*Before extraordinary item

200% of current liabilities. Either statement correctly summarizes the relationship—that is, that current assets are twice as large as current liabilities.

In order to compute a meaningful ratio, there must be a *significant relationship* between the two figures. A ratio focusses attention on a relationship that is significant, but a full interpretation of the ratio usually requires further investigation of the underlying data. Ratios are an aid to analysis and interpretation; they are not a substitute for sound thinking.

Comparative data in annual reports of major corporations

The annual reports of major corporations usually contain a comparative balance sheet and a comparative income statement for two years. Supplementary schedules showing sales, net income, and other key amounts are often presented for periods of 5 to 10 years. Shown on the facing page is a 10-year summary by Canada Packers Inc. showing the trend of selected operating and financial data.

Standards of comparison

In using dollar and percentage changes, trend percentages, component percentages, and ratios, financial analysts constantly search for some standard of comparison against which to judge whether the relationships that they have found are favourable or unfavourable. Two such standards are (1) the past performance of the company and (2) the performance of other companies in the same industry.

Past performance of the company   Comparing analytical data for a current period with similar computations for prior years affords some basis for judging whether the position of the business is improving or worsening. This comparison of data over time is sometimes called *horizontal* or *trend* analysis, to express the idea of reviewing data for a number of consecutive periods. It is distinguished from *vertical* or *static* analysis, which refers to the review of the financial information for only one accounting period.

In addition to determining whether the situation is improving or becoming worse, horizontal analysis may aid in making estimates of future prospects. Since changes may reverse their direction at any time, however, projecting past trends into the future is always a somewhat risky statistical pastime.

A weakness of horizontal analysis is that comparison with the past does not afford any basis for evaluation in absolute terms. The fact that net income was 2% of sales last year and is 3% of sales this year indicates improvement, but if there is evidence that net income *should be* 7% of sales, the record for both years is unfavourable.

Industry standards   The limitations of horizontal analysis may be overcome to some extent by finding some other standard of performance as a yardstick against which to measure the record of any particular firm. The yardstick may be a comparable company, the average record of several companies in the same industry, or some predetermined standard.

Suppose that Y company suffers a 5% drop in its sales during the current year. The discovery that the sales of all companies in the same industry fell an average of 20% would indicate that this was a favourable rather than an unfavourable performance.

Assume further that Y company's net income is 2% of net sales. Based on comparison with other companies in the industry, this would be substandard performance if Y company were a manufacturer of commercial aircraft, but it would be a satisfactory record if Y company were a grocery chain.

When we compare a given company with its competitors or with industry averages our conclusions will be valid only if the companies in question are reasonably comparable. Because of the large number of diversified companies formed in recent years, the term *industry* is difficult to define, and companies that fall roughly within the same industry may not be comparable in many respects. For example, one company may engage only in the marketing of oil products; another may be a fully integrated producer from the well to the gas pump, yet both are said to be in the "oil industry."

Differences in accounting methods may lessen the comparability of financial data for two companies. For example, companies may employ different depreciation methods or estimates of the useful life of substantially similar assets; inventories may be valued by different methods; and the timing of revenue recognition may differ significantly among companies engaged in certain industries. Despite these limitations, studying comparative performances is a useful method of analysis if carefully and intelligently done.

Quality of earnings

4   Discuss the "quality" of a company's earnings, assets, and working capital.

Earnings are the lifeblood of a business entity. No entity can survive for long and accomplish its other goals unless it is profitable. On the other hand, continuous losses will drain assets from the business, consume owners' equity, and leave the company at the mercy of creditors. In assessing the prospects of a company, we are interested not only in the total *amount* of earnings but also in the *rate* of earnings on sales, on total assets, and on owners' equity. In addition, we must look at the *stability* and *source* of earnings. An erratic earnings performance over a period of years, for example, is less desirable than a steady level of earnings. A history of increasing earnings is preferable to a "flat" earnings record.

A breakdown of sales and earnings by *major product lines* is useful in evaluating the future performance of a company. Publicly owned companies include with their financial statements supplementary schedules showing sales and profits by product line and by geographical area. These schedules assist financial analysts in forecasting the effect upon the company of changes in consumer demand for particular types of products.

Financial analysts often express the opinion that the earnings of one company are of higher quality than earnings of other similar companies. This concept of *quality of earnings* arises because each company management can choose from a variety of accounting principles and methods, all of which are considered generally acceptable. A company's management often is under heavy pressure to report rising earnings, and accounting policies may be tailored toward this objective. We have already pointed out the impact on current reported earnings of the choice between the lifo and fifo methods of inventory valuation and the choice of depreciation policies. In judging the quality of earnings, the financial analyst should consider whether the accounting principles and methods selected by management lead to a conservative measurement of earnings or tend to inflate reported earnings.

Quality of assets and the relative amount of debt

Although a satisfactory level of earnings may be a good indication of the company's long-run ability to pay its debts and dividends, we must also look at the composition of assets, their condition and liquidity, the relationship between current assets and current liabilities, and the total amount of debt outstanding. A company may be profitable and yet be unable to pay its liabilities on time; sales and earnings may be satisfactory but plant and equipment may be deteriorating because of poor maintenance policies; valuable patents may be expiring; substantial losses may be in prospect from slow-moving inventories and past-due receivables. Companies with large amounts of debt often are vulnerable to increases in interest rates.

 The home building industry is especially vulnerable to increases in interest rates. When interest rates rise, people stop buying new homes. In addition, most construction companies have large amounts of debt, upon which the interest charges are adjusted monthly to reflect current interest rates. Thus, when interest rates rise, these companies face large increases in their interest expense as well as declining revenue. The sustained period of high interest rates in the early 1980s caused the bankruptcy of many construction companies. In the later 1980s, a spectacular decline in interest rates was accompanied by a boom in home building.

Impact of inflation

During a period of significant inflation, financial statements that are prepared in terms of historical costs do not reflect fully the economic resources or the *real income* (in terms of purchasing power) of a business enterprise. We discussed in Chapter 13 the requirements of Section 4510 of the *CICA Handbook* for large corporations to diclose current cost and general price level data in their annual reports. Financial analysts should therefore attempt to evaluate the impact of inflation on the financial position and operating results of the company being studied. They should raise such questions as: How much of the net income can be attributed to the increase in the general price level? Will the company lose or gain from inflation because of its holdings of monetary assets and liabilities? Will the company be able to keep its "physical capital" intact by paying the higher prices necessary to replace plant assets as they wear out? The topics of developing and interpreting accounting information designed to measure the impact of inflation were discussed in Chapter 13.

Illustrative analysis for Seacliff Limited

Keep in mind the preceding discussion of analytical principles as you study the illustrative financial analysis that appears on pages 828 and 841. The basic information for our analysis is contained in a set of condensed two-year comparative financial statements for Seacliff Limited shown on the following pages. Summarized statement data, together with computations of dollar increases and decreases, and component percentages where applicable, have been compiled. For convenience in this illustration, relatively small dollar amounts have been used in the Seacliff Limited financial statements.

SEACLIFF LIMITED
Condensed Comparative Balance Sheet*
December 31, 1989 and December 31, 1988

	1989	1988	INCREASE OR (DECREASE)		PERCENTAGE OF TOTAL ASSETS	
			DOLLARS	%	1989	1988
ASSETS						
Current assets	$390,000	$288,000	$102,000	35.4	41.1	33.5
Plant and equipment (net)	500,000	467,000	33,000	7.1	52.6	54.3
Other assets (loans to officers)	60,000	105,000	(45,000)	(42.9)	6.3	12.2
Total assets	$950,000	$860,000	$ 90,000	10.5	100.0	100.0
LIABILITIES & SHAREHOLDERS' EQUITY						
Liabilities:						
Current liabilities	$112,000	$ 94,000	$ 18,000	(19.1)	11.8	10.9
12% long-term note payable	200,000	250,000	(50,000)	(20.0)	21.1	29.
Total liabilities	$312,000	$344,000	$ (32,000)	(9.3)	32.9	40.0
Shareholders' equity:						
$9 preferred stock, no-par, callable at						
105, 1,000 shares	$100,000	$100,000			10.5	11.0
Common stock, 1989, 5,000 shares;						
1988, 4,000 shares	320,000	240,000	$ 80,000	33.3	33.7	27.9
Retained earnings	218,000	176,000	42,000	23.9	22.9	20.5
Total shareholders' equity	$638,000	$516,000	$122,000	23.6	67.1	60.0
Total liabilities & shareholders' equity	$950,000	$860,000	$ 90,000	10.5	100.0	100.0

*In order to focus attention on important subtotals, this statement is highly condensed and does not show individual asse and liability items. These details will be introduced as needed in the text discussion. For example, a list of Seacli Limited's current assets and current liabilities appears on page 837.

Using the information in these statements, let us consider the kind of analysis tha might be of particular interest to (1) common shareholders, (2) long-term creditors (3) preferred shareholders, and (4) short-term creditors.

Analysis by common shareholders

5 Analyze financial statements from the viewpoints of common shareholders, creditors, and others.

Common shareholders and potential investors in common stock look first at company's earnings record. Their investment is in shares of stock, so *earnings pe share and dividends per share* are of particular interest.

Earnings per share of common stock   As indicated in Chapter 15, earnings per shar of common stock are computed by dividing the income applicable to the commo stock by the weighted average number of shares of common stock outstanding durin the year. Any preferred dividend requirements must be subtracted from net incom to determine income applicable to common stock, as shown in the computations fo Seacliff Limited at the bottom of page 829.

SEACLIFF LIMITED
Comparative Income Statement
For the Years Ended December 31, 1989 and December 31, 1988

	1989	1988	INCREASE OR (DECREASE)		PERCENTAGE OF NET SALES	
			DOLLARS	%	1989	1988
Net sales	$900,000	$750,000	$150,000	20.0	100.0	100.0
Cost of goods sold	530,000	420,000	110,000	26.2	58.9	56.0
Gross profit on sales	$370,000	$330,000	$ 40,000	12.1	41.1	44.0
Operating expenses:						
Selling expenses	$117,000	$ 75,000	$ 42,000	56.0	13.0	10.0
Administrative expenses	126,000	95,000	31,000	32.6	14.0	12.7
Total operating expenses	$243,000	$170,000	$ 73,000	42.9	27.0	22.7
Operating income	$127,000	$160,000	$ (33,000)	(20.6)	14.1	21.3
Interest expense	24,000	30,000	(6,000)	(20.0)	2.7	4.0
Income before income taxes	$103,000	$130,000	$ (27,000)	(20.8)	11.4	17.3
Income taxes	28,000	40,000	(12,000)	(30.0)	3.1	5.3
Net income	$ 75,000	$ 90,000	$ (15,000)	(16.7)	8.3	12.0
Earnings per share of common stock (see the bottom of page 829)	$13.20	$20.25	$(7.05)	(34.8)		

SEACLIFF LIMITED
Statement of Retained Earnings
For the Years Ended December 31, 1989 and December 31, 1988

	1989	1988	INCREASE OR (DECREASE)	
			DOLLARS	%
Retained earnings, beginning of year	$176,000	$115,000	$61,000	53.0
Net income	75,000	90,000	(15,000)	(16.7)
	$251,000	$205,000	$46,000	22.4
Less: Dividends on common stock	$ 24,000	$ 20,000	$ 4,000	20.0
Dividends on preferred stock	9,000	9,000		
	$ 33,000	$ 29,000	$ 4,000	13.8
Retained earnings, end of year	$218,000	$176,000	$42,000	23.9

EARNINGS RELATED TO NUMBER OF COMMON SHARES OUTSTANDING

Earnings per Share of Common Stock

		1989	1988
Net income		$75,000	$90,000
Less: Preferred dividend requirements		9,000	9,000
Income applicable to common stock	(a)	$66,000	$81,000
Shares of common stock outstanding, during the year	(b)	5,000	4,000
Earnings per share of common stock (a ÷ b)		$13.20	$20.25

Dividend yield and price-earnings ratio   Dividends are of prime importance to some shareholders, but a secondary factor to others. In other words, some shareholders invest primarily to receive regular cash income, while others invest in stocks principally with the hope of securing capital gains through rising market prices. If a corporation is profitable and retains its earnings for expansion of the business, the expanded operations should produce an increase in the net income of the company and thus tend to make each share of stock more valuable.

In comparing the merits of alternative investment opportunities, we should relate earnings and dividends per share to the *market value* of the stock. Dividends per share divided by market price per share determines the *yield* rate of a company's stock. Dividend yield is especially important to those investors whose objective is to maximize the dividend revenue from their investments.

Earnings performance of common stock is often expressed as a *price-earnings ratio* by dividing the market price per share by the annual earnings per share. Thus, a stock selling for $60 per share and earning $5 per share in the year just ended may be said to have a price-earnings ratio of 12 times earnings ($60 ÷ $5). The price-earnings ratio of the 300 stocks included in the TSE 300 Composite (Toronto Stock Exchange) has varied widely in recent years, ranging from a low of about 8 for the group to a high of about 21.

Assume that the 1,000 additional shares of common stock issued by Seacliff Limited on January 1, 1989 received the full dividend of $4.80 paid in 1989. When these new shares were issued, Seacliff Limited announced that it planned to continue indefinitely the $4.80 dividend per common share currently being paid. With this assumption and the use of assumed market prices of the common stock at December 31, 1988 and December 31, 1989, earnings per share and dividend yield may be summarized as follows:

EARNINGS AND DIVIDENDS RELATED TO MARKET PRICE OF COMMON STOCK

Earnings and Dividends per Share of Common Stock

DATE	ASSUMED MARKET VALUE PER SHARE	EARNINGS PER SHARE	PRICE-EARNINGS RATIO	DIVIDENDS PER SHARE	DIVIDEND YIELD, %
Dec. 31, 1988	$125	$20.25	6	$5.00	4.0
Dec. 31, 1989	100	13.20	8	4.80	4.8

The decline in market value during 1989 presumably reflects the decrease in earnings per share. Investors appraising this stock at December 31, 1989, would consider whether a price-earnings ratio of 8 and a dividend yield of 4.8% represented a satisfactory situation in the light of alternative investment opportunities. They would also place considerable weight on estimates of the company's prospective future earnings and the probable effect of such estimated earnings on the market price of the stock and on dividend payments.

Book value per share of common stock   The procedures for computing book value per share were fully described in Chapter 14 and will not be repeated here. We will, however, determine the book value per share of common stock for Seacliff Limited:

WHY DID BOOK VALUE
PER SHARE DECREASE?

Book Value per Share of Common Stock

		1989	1988
Total shareholders' equity		$638,000	$516,000
Less: Equity of preferred shareholders			
(1,000 shares at call price of $105)		105,000	105,000
Equity of common shareholders	(a)	$533,000	$411,000
Shares of common stock outstanding	(b)	5,000	4,000
Book value per share of common stock (a ÷ b)		$106.60	$102.75

Book value indicates the net assets represented by each share of stock. This statistic is often helpful in estimating a reasonable price for a company's stock, especially for small corporations whose shares are not publicly traded.[1] However, if a company's future earnings prospects are unusually good or unusually poor, or the market value of the company's assets is different from their carrying (book) value, the market price of its shares may differ significantly from their book value.

A recent study on Canada's top 100 public corporations (in terms of the market value of their listed shares) compared the market values with book values of the common stock of these corporations and computed a "premium market/book value" statistic. For example, a premium market/book value of plus 100% means that the market value of common stock is twice the book value. The percentages of the premium market/book value of these top 100 public corporations range from a negative 18% for Canadian Imperial Bank of Commerce and Falconbridge to a plus 887% for Cadillac Fairview.

Revenue and expense analysis   The trend of earnings of Seacliff Limited is unfavourable and shareholders will want to know the reasons for the decline in net income. The comparative income statement shows that despite a 20% increase in net sales, net income fell from $90,000 in 1988 to $75,000 in 1989, a decline of 16.7%. As a percentage of net sales, net income fell from 12% to only 8.3%. The primary causes of this decline were the increases in selling expenses (56.0%), in general and administrative expenses (32.6%), and in the cost of goods sold (26.2%), all of which exceeded the 20% increase in net sales.

Let us assume that further investigation reveals Seacliff Limited decided in 1989 to reduce its sales prices in an effort to generate greater sales volume. This would explain the decrease in gross profit rate from 44% to 41.1% of net sales. Since the dollar amount of gross profit increased $40,000 in 1989 the strategy of reducing sales prices to increase volume would have been successful if there had been little or no increase in operating expenses. However, operating expenses rose by $73,000, resulting in a $33,000 decrease in operating income.

The next step is to find which expenses increased and why. An investor may be handicapped here, because detailed operating expenses are not usually shown in

---

[1] As pointed out in Chapter 14, book value per share is regularly reported in such financial news media as the *Financial Post* and the *Financial Times*, and also in the annual reports of large corporations such as Dofasco Inc., Federal Industries Ltd., and Nova, An Alberta Corporation.

published financial statements. Some conclusions, however, can be reached on the basis of even the condensed information available in the comparative income statement for Seacliff Limited.

The substantial increase in selling expenses presumably reflects greater selling effort during 1989 in an attempt to improve sales volume. However, the fact that selling expenses increased $42,000 while gross profit increased only $40,000 indicates that the cost of this increased sales effort was not justified in terms of results. Even more disturbing is the increase in general and administrative expenses. Some growth in administrative expenses might be expected to accompany increased sales volume, but because some of the expenses are fixed, the growth generally should be *less than proportional* to any increase in sales. The increase in general and administrative expenses from 12.7% to 14% of sales would be of serious concern to informed investors.

Management generally has greater control over operating expenses than over revenue. The *operating expense ratio* is often used as a measure of management's ability to control its operating expenses. The unfavourable trend in this ratio for Seacliff Limited is shown in the following illustration.

DOES A HIGHER OPERATING EXPENSE RATIO INDICATE HIGHER NET INCOME?

Operating Expense Ratio

		1989	1988
Operating expenses	(a)	$243,000	$170,000
Net sales	(b)	$900,000	$750,000
Operating expense ratio (a ÷ b)		27.0%	22.7%

If management were able to increase the sales volume while at the same time increasing the gross profit rate and decreasing the operating expense ratio, the effect on net income could be quite dramatic. For example, if in 1990 Seacliff Limited can increase its sales by 11% to $1,000,000, increase its gross profit rate from 41.1% to 44%, and reduce the operating expense ratio from 27% to 24%, its operating income will increase from $127,000 to $200,000 ($1,000,000 − $560,000 − $240,000), an increase of over 57%.

Return on investment (ROI)

The rate of return on investment (often called ROI) is a test of management's efficiency in using available resources. Regardless of the size of the organization capital is a scarce resource and must be used efficiently. In judging the performance of branch managers or of company-wide management, it is reasonable to raise the question: What rate of return have you earned on the resources under your control? The concept of return on investment can be applied to a number of situations: for example, evaluating a branch, a total business, a product line, or an individual investment. A number of different ratios have been developed for the ROI concept each well suited to a particular situation. We shall consider the return on total asset and the return on common shareholders' equity as examples of the return on investment concept.

Return on assets   An important test of management's ability to earn a return on funds supplied from all sources is the rate of return on total assets.

The income figure used in computing this ratio should be *operating income,* since interest expense and income taxes are determined by factors other than the efficient use of resources. Operating income is earned throughout the year and therefore should be related to the *average* investment in assets during the year. Following is the computation of this ratio for Seacliff Limited (the beginning balance of total assets is assumed to be $820,000):

ARNINGS RELATED TO
NVESTMENT IN ASSETS

Percentage Return on Assets

		1989	1988
Operating income	(a)	$127,000	$160,000
Total assets, beginning of year	(b)	$860,000	$820,000
Total assets, end of year	(c)	$950,000	$860,000
Average investment in assets [(b + c) ÷ 2]	(d)	$905,000	$840,000
Return on total assets (a ÷ d)		14%	19%

This ratio shows that earnings per dollar of assets have fallen off in 1989. Before drawing conclusions as to the effectiveness of Seacliff Limited's management, however, we should consider the trend in the return on assets earned by other companies of similar kind and size.

Return on common shareholders' equity   Because interest and dividends paid to creditors and preferred shareholders are fixed in amount, a company may earn a greater or smaller return on the common shareholders' equity than on its total assets. The computation of return on shareholders' equity for Seacliff Limited is as follows:

OES THE USE
F LEVERAGE
ENEFIT COMMON
HAREHOLDERS?

Return on Common Shareholders' Equity

		1989	1988
Net income		$ 75,000	$ 90,000
Less: Preferred dividend requirements		9,000	9,000
Net income applicable to common stock	(a)	$ 66,000	$ 81,000
Common shareholders' equity, beginning of year	(b)	$416,000	$355,000
Common shareholders' equity, end of year	(c)	$538,000	$416,000
Average common shareholders' equity [(b + c) ÷ 2]	(d)	$477,000	$385,500
Return on common shareholders' equity (a ÷ d)		13.8%	21.0%

In both years, the rate of return on common shareholders' equity was higher than the rate of interest paid to long-term creditors or the dividend rate paid to preferred shareholders. This result was achieved through the favourable use of leverage.

Leverage

When the return on total assets is higher than the average cost of borrowed capital, as was the case in Seacliff Limited, the common shareholders may benefit from the use of leverage. *Leverage* (or *trading on the equity*) refers to buying assets with money raised by borrowing or by issuing preferred stock. If the borrowed capital can be invested to earn a return *greater* than the cost of borrowing, then the net income and the return on common shareholders' equity will *increase.* In other words, if you can borrow money at 12% and use it to earn 20%, you will benefit by doing so.

However, leverage can act as a "double-edged sword"; the effects may be favourab⬧ or unfavourable to the holders of common stock. If the return on total assets shou⬧ fall *below* the average cost of borrowed capital, leverage will *reduce* net income ar⬧ the return on common shareholders' equity. When this unfavourable situation occur⬧ one possible solution would be to pay off the loans that carry high interest rate⬧ However, most companies do not have sufficient amounts of cash to retire long-ter⬧ debt or preferred stock on short notice. Therefore, the common shareholders ma⬧ become "locked in" for a long period of time to the unfavourable effects of leverag⬧

When the return on assets exceeds the cost of borrowed capital, the extensive u⬧ of leverage can increase dramatically the return on common shareholders' equit⬧ However, extensive leverage also increases the *risk* to common shareholders th⬧ their return may be reduced dramatically in future years. Furthermore, if a busine⬧ incurs so much debt that it becomes unable to meet the required interest and princip⬧ payments, creditors may force liquidation or reorganization of the business, to t⬧ detriment of shareholders.

In deciding how much leverage is appropriate, the common shareholders shou⬧ consider the *stability* of the company's return on assets, as well as the relationship⬧ this return to the average cost of borrowed capital. Also, they should consider t⬧ amount of risk that they are willing to accept in the effort to increase the return ⬧ their investment.

Leverage most frequently is achieved through debt financing, including bo⬧ current and long-term liabilities. One advantage of debt financing is that intere⬧ payments are deductible in determining taxable income. Leverage also can be achiev⬧ through the issuance of preferred stock. Since preferred stock dividends are *n*⬧ deductible for income tax purposes, however, the advantage gained in this respe⬧ will be much smaller than in the case of debt financing.

Equity ratio   One indicator of the amount of leverage used by a business is t⬧ equity ratio. This ratio measures the proportion of the total assets financed ⬧ shareholders, as distinguished from creditors. It is computed by dividing to⬧ shareholders' equity by total assets. A *low* equity ratio indicates an extensive use⬧ leverage, that is, a large proportion of financing provided by creditors. A high equi⬧ ratio, on the other hand, indicates that the business is making little use of leverag⬧

The equity ratio at year-end for Seacliff Limited is determined as follows:

PROPORTION OF ASSETS
FINANCED BY
SHAREHOLDERS

Equity Ratio

		1989	1988
Total shareholders' equity	(a)	$638,000	$516,0⬧
Total assets (or total liabilities & shareholders' equity)	(b)	$950,000	$860,0⬧
Equity ratio (a ÷ b)		67.2%	60.0%⬧

Seacliff Limited has a higher equity ratio in 1989 than in 1988. Is this favourable⬧ unfavourable?

From the viewpoint of the common shareholder, a low equity ratio will prod⬧ maximum benefits if management is able to earn a rate of return on assets grea⬧

than the rate of interest paid to creditors. However, a low equity ratio can be very unfavourable if the return on assets falls below the rate of interest paid to creditors. Since the return on total assets earned by Seacliff Limited has declined from 19% in 1988 to a relatively low 14% in 1989, the common shareholders probably would *not* want to risk a low equity ratio. The action by management in 1989 of retiring $50,000 in long-term liabilities will help to protect the common shareholders from the unfavourable effects of leverage should the return on assets continue to decline.

Analysis by long-term creditors

Bondholders and other long-term creditors are primarily interested in three factors: (1) the rate of return on their investment, (2) the firm's ability to meet its interest requirements, and (3) the firm's ability to repay the principal of the debt when it falls due.

Yield rate on bonds   The yield rate on bonds or other long-term indebtedness cannot be computed in the same manner as the yield rate on shares of stock, because bonds, unlike stocks, have a definite maturity date and amount. The ownership of a 12%, 10-year $1,000 bond represents the right to receive $1,000 at the end of 10 years and the right to receive $120 per year during each of the next 10 years. If the market price of this bond is $950, the yield rate on an investment in the bond is the rate of interest that will make the present value of these two contractual rights equal to $950. *The yield rate varies inversely with changes in the market price of the bond.* If interest rates rise, the market price of existing bonds will fall; if interest rates decline, the price of bonds will rise. If the price of a bond is above maturity value, the yield rate is less than the bond interest rate; if the price of a bond is below maturity value, the yield rate is higher than the bond interest rate.

Number of times interest earned   Long-term creditors have learned from experience that one of the best indications of the safety of their investment is the fact that, over the life of the debt, the company has sufficient income to cover its interest requirements by a wide margin. A failure to cover interest requirements may have serious repercussions on the stability and solvency of the firm.

  A common measure of debt safety is the ratio of income available for the payment of interest to the annual interest expense, called *number of times interest earned.* This computation for Seacliff Limited would be

JNG-TERM CREDITORS
ATCH THIS RATIO

Number of Times Interest Earned

		1989	1988
Operating income (before interest and income taxes) ..	(a)	$127,000	$160,000
Annual interest expense	(b)	$ 24,000	$ 30,000
Times interest earned (a ÷ b)		5.3	5.3

The ratio remained unchanged at a satisfactory level during 1989. A ratio of 5.3 times interest earned would be considered strong in many industries. In the electric utilities industry, for example, the interest coverage ratio for the leading companies generally averages about 3, with the ratios of individual companies varying from 2 to 6.

Debt ratio   Long-term creditors are interested in the amount of debt outstanding in relation to the amount of capital contributed by shareholders. The *debt ratio* is computed by dividing total liabilities by total assets, shown in the following example for Seacliff Limited.

WHAT PORTION OF TOTAL
ASSETS IS FINANCED BY
DEBT?

Debt Ratio

		1989	1988
Total liabilities	(a)	$312,000	$344,000
Total assets (or total liabilities & shareholders' equity) . .	(b)	$950,000	$860,000
Debt ratio (a ÷ b)		32.8%	40.0%

From a creditor's viewpoint, the lower the debt ratio (or the higher the equity ratio) the better, since this means that shareholders have contributed the bulk of the funds to the business, and therefore the margin of protection to creditors against shrinkage of the assets is high.

Analysis by preferred shareholders

Some preferred stocks are convertible into common stock at the option of the holder. However, many preferred stocks do not have the conversion privilege. If a preferred stock is convertible, the interests of the preferred shareholders are similar to those of common shareholders. If a preferred stock is not convertible, the interests of the preferred shareholders are more like those of long-term creditors.

Preferred shareholders are interested in the yield on their investment. The yield is computed by dividing the dividend per share by the market value per share. The dividend per share of Seacliff Limited preferred stock is $9. If we assume that the market value at December 31, 1989, is $60 per share, the yield rate at that time would be 15% ($9 ÷ $60).

The primary measurement of the safety of an investment in preferred stock is the ability of the firm to meet its preferred dividend requirements. The best test of this ability is the ratio of the net income available to pay the preferred dividend to the amount of the annual dividend, as follows:

IS THE PREFERRED
DIVIDEND SAFE?

Times Preferred Dividends Earned

		1989	1988
Net income available to pay preferred dividends	(a)	$75,000	$90,000
Annual preferred dividend requirements	(b)	$ 9,000	$ 9,000
Times dividends earned (a ÷ b)		8.3	10

Although the margin of protection declined in 1989, the annual preferred dividend requirement still appears well protected.

As previously discussed in Chapter 14 the market price of a preferred stock tends to vary inversely with interest rates. When interest rates are moving up, preferred stock prices tend to decline; when interest rates are dropping, preferred stock prices rise.

Analysis by short-term creditors

Bankers and other short-term creditors share the interest of shareholders and bondholders in the profitability and long-run stability of a business. Their primary interest, however, is in the current position of the firm — its ability to generate sufficient cash and working capital to meet current operating needs and to pay current debts promptly. Thus the analysis of financial statements by a banker considering a short-term loan, or by a trade creditor investigating the credit status of a customer, is likely to centre on the working capital position of the prospective debtor. (Cash position and cash flows were discussed in the statement of changes in financial position in Chapter 19).

Amount of working capital   The details of the working capital of Seacliff Limited are shown in the following illustration:

SEACLIFF LIMITED
Comparative Schedule of Working Capital
As of December, 31, 1989 and December 31, 1988

	1989	1988	INCREASE OR (DECREASE) DOLLARS	%	PERCENTAGE OF TOTAL CURRENT ITEMS 1989	1988
Current assets:						
Cash	$ 38,000	$ 40,000	$ (2,000)	(5.0)	9.7	13.9
Receivables (net)	117,000	86,000	31,000	36.0	30.0	29.9
Inventories	180,000	120,000	60,000	50.0	46.2	41.6
Prepaid expenses	55,000	42,000	13,000	31.0	14.1	14.6
Total current assets	$390,000	$288,000	$102,000	35.4	100.0	100.0
Current liabilities:						
Notes payable to creditors	$ 14,600	$ 10,000	$ 4,600	46.0	13.1	10.7
Accounts payable	66,000	30,000	36,000	120.0	58.9	31.9
Accrued liabilities	31,400	54,000	(22,600)	(41.9)	28.0	57.4
Total current liabilities	$112,000	$ 94,000	$ 18,000	19.1	100.0	100.0
Working capital	$278,000	$194,000	$ 84,000	43.3		

The amount of working capital is measured by the *excess of current assets over current liabilities.* Thus, working capital represents the amount of cash, near-cash items, and cash substitutes (prepayments) on hand after providing for payment of all current liabilities.

This schedule shows that current assets increased $102,000, while current liabilities rose by only $18,000, with the result that working capital increased $84,000.

Quality of working capital   In evaluating the debt-paying ability of a business, short-term creditors should consider the quality of working capital as well as the total dollar amount. The principal factors affecting the quality of working capital are (1) the nature of the current assets comprising the working capital and (2) the length of time required to convert these assets into cash.

The preceding schedule shows an unfavourable shift in the composition of Seacliff Limited's working capital during 1989; cash decreased from 13.9% to 9.7% of current assets, while inventory rose from 41.6% to 46.2%. Inventory is a less liquid resource than cash. Therefore, the quality of working capital is not as liquid as in 1988. *Turnover ratios* may be used to assist short-term creditors in estimating the time required to turn assets such as inventories and receivables into cash.

Inventory turnover   The cost of goods sold figure on the income statement represents the total cost of all goods that have been transferred out of inventories during any given period. Therefore the relationship between cost of goods sold and the average balance of inventories maintained throughout the year indicates the number of times that inventories "turn over" and are replaced each year.

Ideally we should total the inventories at the end of each month and divide it by 12 to obtain an average inventory. This information is not always available, however, and the nearest substitute is a simple average of the inventory at the beginning and at the end of the year. This tends to overstate the turnover rate, since many companies choose an accounting year that ends when inventories are at a minimum.

Assuming that only beginning and ending inventories are available, the computation of inventory turnover for Seacliff Limited may be illustrated as follows:

Inventory Turnover

WHAT DOES INVENTORY
TURNOVER MEAN?

		1989	1988
Cost of goods sold	(a)	$530,000	$420,000
Inventory, beginning of year		$120,000	$100,000
Inventory, end of year		$180,000	$120,000
Average inventory	(b)	$150,000	$110,000
Average inventory turnover per year (a ÷ b)		3.5 times	3.8 times
Average number of days to sell inventory (divide 365 days by inventory turnover)		104 days	96 days

The trend indicated by this analysis is unfavourable, since the length of time required for Seacliff Limited to turn over (sell) its inventory is increasing. Furthermore, the inventory status *at the end of the year* has changed even more: At the end of 1988 there were 104 days' sales represented in the ending inventory ($120,000/ $420,000 × 365 days) compared with 124 days' sales contained in the ending inventory at the end of 1989 ($180,000/$530,000 × 365 days).

The relation between inventory turnover and gross profit per dollar of sales may be significant. A high inventory turnover and a low gross profit rate frequently go hand in hand. This, however, is merely another way of saying that if the gross profit rate is low, a high volume of business is necessary to produce a satisfactory return on total assets. Short-term creditors generally regard a high inventory turnover as a good sign, indicating that the inventory is readily marketable.

Accounts receivable turnover   The turnover of accounts receivable is computed by dividing net credit sales by the average balance of accounts receivable. Ideally, a monthly average of receivables should be used, and only sales on credit should be included in the sales figure. For illustrative purposes, we shall assume that Seacliff Limited sells entirely on credit and that only the beginning and ending balances of receivables are available.

ARE CUSTOMERS PAYING PROMPTLY?

Accounts Receivable Turnover

		1989	1988
Net sales on credit	(a)	$900,000	$750,000
Receivables, beginning of year		$ 86,000	$ 80,000
Receivables, end of year		$117,000	$ 86,000
Average receivables	(b)	$101,500	$ 83,000
Receivable turnover per year (a ÷ b)		8.9 times	9.0 times
Average number of days to collect receivables (divide 365 days by receivable turnover)		41 days	41 days

There has been no significant change in the average time required to collect receivables. The interpretation of the average age of receivables would depend upon the company's credit terms and the seasonal activity immediately before year-end. If the company grants 30-day credit terms to its customers, for example, the above analysis indicates that accounts receivable collections are lagging. If the terms were for 60 days, however, there is evidence that collections are being made ahead of schedule.

In Chapter 5 we defined the term *operating cycle* as the average time period between the purchase of merchandise and the conversion of this merchandise back into cash. In other words, the merchandise acquired for inventory is gradually converted into accounts receivable by selling goods to customers on credit, and these receivables are converted into cash through the process of collection. The word *cycle* refers to the circular flow of capital from cash to inventory to receivables to cash again.

The *operating cycle* in 1989 was approximately 145 days, computed by adding the 104 days required to turn over inventory and the average 41 days required to collect receivables. This compares to an operating cycle of only 137 days in 1988, computed as 96 days to dispose of the inventory plus 41 days to collect the resulting receivables. From the viewpoint of short-term creditors, the shorter the operating cycle, the higher the quality of the borrower's working capital. Therefore, these creditors would regard the lengthening of Seacliff Limited's operating cycle as an unfavourable trend.

Current ratio   The current ratio (current assets divided by current liabilities) is another widely used method of expressing the relationship between current assets and current liabilities. The current ratio for Seacliff Limited is computed as follows:

DOES THIS INDICATE SATISFACTORY DEBT-PAYING ABILITY?

Current Ratio

		1989	1988
Total current assets	(a)	$390,000	$288,000
Total current liabilities	(b)	$112,000	$ 94,000
Current ratio (a ÷ b)		3.5	3.1

A widely used rule of thumb is that a current ratio of 2 to 1 or better is satisfactory. By this standard, Seacliff Limited's current ratio appears quite strong. As with all rules of thumb, however, this is an arbitrary standard and is subject to numerous exceptions and qualifications.

In interpreting the current ratio, a number of factors should be kept in mind:

1 Creditors tend to feel that the higher the current ratio the better, although from a managerial view there is an upper limit. Too high a current ratio may indicate that capital is not being used productively in the business.

2 Because creditors tend to stress the current ratio as an indication of short-term solvency, some firms may take conscious steps to improve this ratio just before statements are prepared at the end of a fiscal period for submission to bankers or other creditors. This may be done by postponing purchases, and by paying current liabilities.

3 The current ratio computed at the end of a fiscal year may not be representative of the current position of the company throughout the year. Since many firms arrange their fiscal year to end during a low point in the seasonal swing of business activity, the current ratio at year-end is likely to be more favourable than at any other time during the year.

Use of both the current ratio and the amount of working capital helps to place debt-paying ability in its proper perspective. For example, if Company X has current assets of $200,000 and current liabilities of $100,000 and Company Y has current assets of $2,000,000 and current liabilities of $1,900,000, each company has $100,000 of working capital, but the current position of Company X is clearly superior to that of Company Y. The current ratio for Company X is quite satisfactory at 2 to 1, but Company Y's current ratio is very low — only slightly above 1 to 1.

As another example, assume that Company A and Company B both have current ratios of 3 to 1. However, Company A has working capital of $20,000 and Company B has working capital of $200,000. Although both companies appear to be good credit risks, Company B would no doubt be able to qualify for a much *larger* bank loan than would Company A.

Adjustment for undervalued inventories   The cost of inventory is a major factor in the computation of the current ratio or the amount of working capital. If a company uses the *lifo* inventory method, the cost of inventory appearing in the balance sheet may be unrealistically low in terms of current costs. In such cases, many financial analysts substitute the *current cost* of inventories for the historical cost figure in computing the current ratio or amount of working capital. As explained in earlier chapters, the CICA requires large corporations to disclose the current cost of their inventories and other items as supplementary information in their financial statements.

Quick ratio   Because inventories and prepaid expenses are further removed from conversion into cash than other current assets, a statistic known as the *quick ratio* is sometimes computed as a supplement to the current ratio. The quick ratio compares the highly liquid current assets (cash, marketable securities, and receivables) with current liabilities. Seacliff Limited has no marketable securities; its quick ratio is computed as follows:

A MEASURE OF LIQUIDITY

Quick Ratio

		1989	1988
Quick assets (cash and receivables)	(a)	$155,000	$126,000
Current liabilities	(b)	$112,000	$ 94,000
Quick ratio (a ÷ b)		1.4	1.3

Here again the analysis reveals a favourable trend and a strong position. If the credit periods extended to customers and granted by creditors are roughly equal, a quick ratio of 1.0 or better is considered satisfactory.

Summary of analytical measurements

6   Compute the ratios widely used in financial statement analysis and explain the significance of each.

The basic ratios and other measurements discussed in this chapter and their significance are summarized in the following illustration.

The student should keep in mind the fact that the full significance of any of these ratios or other measurements depends on the *direction of its trend* and its *relationship to some predetermined standard* or industry average.

RATIO OR OTHER MEASUREMENT	METHOD OF COMPUTATION	SIGNIFICANCE
1 Earnings per share of common stock	$\dfrac{\text{Net income} - \text{preferred dividends}}{\text{Shares of common outstanding}}$	Gives the amount of earnings applicable to a share of common stock.
2 Dividend yield	$\dfrac{\text{Dividend per share}}{\text{Market price per share}}$	Shows the rate of earnings distributed to shareholders based on current price for a share of stock.
3 Price-earnings ratio	$\dfrac{\text{Market price per share}}{\text{Earnings per share}}$	Indicates if price of stock is in line with earnings.
4 Book value per share of common stock	$\dfrac{\text{Common shareholders' equity}}{\text{Shares of common outstanding}}$	Measures the recorded value of net assets behind each share of common stock.
5 Operating expense ratio	$\dfrac{\text{Operating expenses}}{\text{Net sales}}$	Indicates management's ability to control expenses.
6 Return on assets.	$\dfrac{\text{Operating Income}}{\text{Average investment in assets}}$	Measures the productivity of assets regardless of capital structures.
7 Return on common shareholders' equity	$\dfrac{\text{Net income} - \text{preferred dividends}}{\text{Average common shareholders' equity}}$	Indicates the earning power of common stock equity.

RATIO OR OTHER MEASUREMENT	METHOD OF COMPUTATION	SIGNIFICANCE
8 Equity ratio	$$\frac{\text{Total shareholders' equity}}{\text{Total assets}}$$	Shows the protection to creditors and the extent of leverage being used.
9 Number of times interest earned	$$\frac{\text{Operating income}}{\text{Annual interest expense}}$$	Measures the coverage of interest requirements, particularly on long-term debt.
10 Debt ratio	$$\frac{\text{Total liabilities}}{\text{Total assets}}$$	Indicates the pecentage of assets financed through borrowing; it shows the extent of leverage being used.
11 Times preferred dividends earned	$$\frac{\text{Net income}}{\text{Annual preferred dividends}}$$	Shows the adequacy of current earnings to pay dividends on preferred stock.
12 Working capital	Current assets − current liabilities	Measures short-run debt-paying ability.
13 Inventory turnover	$$\frac{\text{Cost of goods sold}}{\text{Average inventory}}$$	Indicates marketability of inventory and reasonableness of quantity on hand.
14 Accounts receivable turnover	$$\frac{\text{Net sales on credit}}{\text{Average receivables}}$$	Indicates reasonableness of accounts receivable balance and effectiveness of collections.
15 Current ratio	$$\frac{\text{Current assets}}{\text{Current liabilities}}$$	Measures short-run debt-paying ability.
16 Quick ratio	$$\frac{\text{Quick assets}}{\text{Current liabilities}}$$	Measures the short-term liquidity of a firm.

END-OF-CHAPTER REVIEW

SUMMARY OF CHAPTER LEARNING OBJECTIVES

1 Put the dollar amount of a company's net income into perspective by relating it to the company's sales, assets, and shareholders' equity.

To judge the adequacy of a corporation's net income, we need to relate the dollar amount of net income to the company's annual sales, to the amount of its assets, and to the shareholders' equity. A net income of $1,000,000 may represent very good earnings or very poor earnings depending upon the size of operations and amounts invested.

2 Describe several sources of financial information about a business.

Sources of information about a listed corporation include the company's published annual report, quarterly reports, data available from stock brokerage firms, financial periodicals published by Financial Post, Dun & Bradstreet, Moody's Investor Service, Standard & Poor's Corporation, and investment advisory services.

3 Explain the uses of dollar and percentage changes, trend percentages, component percentages, and ratios.

Analysis of financial statements should indicate whether a company's earnings and solvency are on the upgrade or are deteriorating. The dollar change in any item is the difference between the amount for a *comparison* year and for a *base* year. The percentage change is computed by dividing the change between years by the amount for the base year. Trend percentages are useful to compare performance in each of a series of years with a selected base year. Thus, the rate of growth in sales is revealed by trend percentages. Component percentages indicate the relative size of each item included in a total. Thus, each item on a balance sheet may be expressed as a percentage of total assets. Each item on an income statement may be expressed as a percentage of net sales. A ratio is a simple mathematical expression of the relationship of one item to another. In order to compute a meaningful ratio, there must be a significant relationship between the two figures.

4 Discuss the "quality" of a company's earnings, assets, and working capital.

The concept of "quality" of earnings exists because each company management can choose from a variety of accounting principles and methods, all of which are considered generally accepted. For example, the choice between straight-line depreciation and accelerated depreciation leads to different reported earnings. In judging the quality of earnings, the financial analyst considers whether the accounting principles and methods selected by management lead to a conservative measurement of earnings or tend to inflate earnings. The trend of earnings, their stability, and source are also significant in judging quality of earnings. The quality of assets and of working capital may reflect a well-maintained plant, long-run patents, a strong current position, and liquidity of working capital.

5 Analyze financial statements from the viewpoints of common shareholders, creditors, and others.

Investors in *common stocks* are interested in earnings per share, price-earnings ratios, and dividend yields. These items help an investor to determine whether the current market price per share is excessive or undervalued. *Long-term creditors* are interested in the rate of return and the ability of the company to meet its obligations both as to interest on debt and repayment of principal. *Short-term creditors* are primarily interested in a company's ability to pay its current debts promptly. This quality of short-run solvency is measured by the current ratio, quick ratio, and the amount and liquidity of working capital. *Management* is interested in all the ratios mentioned above, and also has a strong interest in the efficiency of operations as measured by the return on investment (ROI) and the use of leverage.

6 Compute the ratios widely used in financial statement analysis and explain the significance of each.

The ratios widely used in financial statement analysis, the methods of computation, and the significance of each ratio are summarized in the table on page 841–842.

KEY TERMS INTRODUCED OR EMPHASIZED IN CHAPTER 20

Comparative financial statements Financial statement data for two or more successive years placed side by side in adjacent columns to facilitate study of changes.

Component percentage The percentage relationship of any financial statement item to a total including that item. For example, each type of asset as a percentage of total assets.

Horizontal analysis Comparison of the change in a financial statement item such as inventories during two or more accounting periods.

Leverage Refers to the practice of financing assets with borrowed capital. Extensive leverage creates the possibility for the rate of return on common shareholders' equity to be substantially above or below the rate of return on total assets. When the rate of return on total assets exceeds the average cost of borrowed capital, leverage increases net income and the return on common shareholders' equity. However, when the return on total assets is less than the average cost of borrowed capital, leverage reduces net income and the return on common shareholders' equity. Leverage is also called *trading on the equity.*

Quality of assets The concept that some companies have assets of better quality than others, such as well-balanced composition of assets, well-maintained plant and equipment, and receivables that are all current. A lower quality of assets might be indicated by poor maintenance of plant and equipment, slow-moving inventories with high danger of obsolescence, past-due receivables, and patents approaching an expiration date.

Quality of earnings Earnings are said to be of high quality if they are stable, the source seems assured, and the methods used in measuring income are conservative. The existence of this concept suggests that the range of alternative but acceptable accounting principles may still be too wide to produce financial statements that are comparable.

Rate of return on investment (ROI) The overall test of management's ability to earn a satisfactory return on the assets under its control. Numerous variations of the ROI concept are used such as return on total assets, return on total equities, etc.

Ratios See pages 841 and 842 for list of ratios, methods of computation, and significance.

Trend percentages The purpose of computing trend percentages is to measure the increase or decrease in financial items (such as sales, net income, cash, etc.) from a selected base year to a series of following years. For example, the dollar amount of net income each year is divided by the base year net income to determine the trend percentage.

Vertical analysis Comparison of a particular financial statement item to a total including that item, such as inventories as a percentage of current assets, or operating expenses in relation to net sales.

DEMONSTRATION PROBLEM FOR YOUR REVIEW

The accounting records of King Corporation showed the following balances at the end of 1988 and 1989:

	1989	1988
Cash	$ 35,000	$ 25,000
Accounts receivable (net)	91,000	90,000
Inventory	160,000	140,000
Short-term prepayments	4,000	5,000
Investment in land	90,000	100,000
Equipment	880,000	640,000
Less: Accumulated depreciation	(260,000)	(200,000)
	$1,000,000	$ 800,000

Accounts payable	$ 105,000	$ 46,000
Income taxes payable and other accrued liabilities	40,000	25,000
Bonds payable — 8%	280,000	280,000
Premium on bonds payable	3,600	4,000
Capital stock, (1989, 33,000 shares;		
1988, 22,000 shares)	165,000	110,000
Retained earnings	406,400	335,000
	$1,000,000	$ 800,000

Sales (net of discounts and allowances)	$2,200,000	$1,600,000
Cost of goods sold	1,606,000	1,120,000
Gross profit on sales	$ 594,000	$ 480,000
Expenses (including $22,400 interest expense)	(330,000)	(352,000)
Income taxes	(91,000)	(48,000)
Extraordinary loss	(6,600)	–0–
Net income	$ 166,400	$ 80,000

Cash dividends of $40,000 were paid and a 50% stock dividend was distributed early in 1989. All sales were made on credit at a relatively uniform rate during the year. Inventory and receivables did not fluctuate materially. The market price of the company's stock on December 31, 1989, was $86 per share; on December 31, 1988, it was $43.50 (before the 50% stock dividend distributed in 1989).

Instructions   Compute the following for 1989 and 1988.
(1) Quick ratio
(2) Current ratio
(3) Equity ratio
(4) Debt ratio
(5) Book value per share of capital stock (based on shares outstanding after 50% stock dividend in 1989)
(6) Earnings per share of capital stock (after extraordinary loss)
(7) Price-earnings ratio
(8) Gross profit percentage
(9) Operating expense ratio
(10) Income *before extraordinary loss* as a percentage of net sales
(11) Inventory turnover (Assume an average inventory of $150,000 for both years.)
(12) Accounts receivable turnover (Assume average accounts receivable of $90,000 for 1988.)
(13) Times bond interest earned (before interest expense and income taxes)

SOLUTION TO DEMONSTRATION PROBLEM

	1989	1988
(1) Quick ratio:		
$126,000 ÷ $145,000	.9 to 1	
$115,000 ÷ $71,000		1.6 to 1
(2) Current ratio:		
$290,000 ÷ $145,000	2 to 1	
$260,000 ÷ $71,000		3.7 to 1

(3) Equity ratio:

$571,400 ÷ $1,000,000 . . . .   57%

$445,000 ÷ $800,000 . . . .   56%

(4) Debt ratio:

$428,600 ÷ $1,000,000 . . . .   43%

$355,000 ÷ $800,000 . . . .   44%

(5) Book value per share of capital stock:

$571,400 ÷ 33,000 shares $17.32

$445,000 ÷ 33,000* shares $13.48

(6) Earnings per share of capital stock (including
   extraordinary loss of $0.20 per share in 1989):

$166,400 ÷ 33,000 shares $5.04

$80,000 ÷ 33,000* shares $2.42

(7) Price-earnings ratio:

$86 ÷ $5.04 . . . .   17 times

$43.50 ÷ 1.5* = $29, adjusted market price:

$29 ÷ $2.42 . . . .   12 times

(8) Gross profit percentage:

$594,000 ÷ $2,200,000 . . . .   27%

$480,000 ÷ $1,600,000 . . . .   30%

(9) Operating expense ratio:

($330,000 − $22,400) ÷ $2,200,000 . . . .   14%

($352,000 − $22,400) ÷ $1,600,000 . . . .   20.6%

(10) Income before extraordinary loss as a
    percentage of net sales:

$173,000 ÷ $2,200,000 . . . .   7.9%

$80,000 ÷ $1,600,000 . . . .   5%

(11) Inventory turnover:

$1,606,000 ÷ $150,000 . . . .   10.7 times

$1,120,000 ÷ $150,000 . . . .   7.5 times

(12) Accounts receivable turnover:

$2,200,000 ÷ $90,500 . . . .   24.3 times

$1,600,000 ÷ $90,000 . . . .   17.8 times

(13) Times bond interest earned:

($166,400 + $22,400 + $91,000) ÷ $22,400 . . . . . .   12.5 times

($80,000 + $22,400 + $48,000) ÷ $22,400 . . . .   6.7 times

*Adjusted retroactively for 50% stock dividend.

ASSIGNMENT MATERIAL

REVIEW QUESTIONS

1 a What groups are interested in the financial affairs of publicly owned corporations?

b List some of the more important sources of financial information for investors.

2 In financial statement analysis, what is the basic objective of observing trends in data and ratios? Suggest some other standards of comparison.

3 In financial statement analysis, what information is produced by computing a ratio that is not available in a simple observation of the underlying data?

4 Distinguish between *trend percentages* and *component percentages.* Which would be better suited to analyzing the change in sales over a term of several years?

5 "Although net income declined this year as compared with last year, it increased from 3% to 5% of net sales." Are sales increasing or decreasing?

6 Differentiate between *horizontal* and *vertical* analysis.

7 Assume that Chemco Corporation is engaged in the manufacture and distribution of a variety of chemicals. In analyzing the financial statements of this corporation, why would you want to refer to the ratios and other measurements of companies in the chemical industry? In comparing the financial results of Chemco Corporation with another chemical company, why would you be interested in the accounting procedures used by the two companies?

8 Explain how the following accounting practices will tend to raise or lower the quality of a company's earnings. (Assume the continuance of inflation.)

a Adoption of an accelerated depreciation method rather than straight-line depreciation.
b Adoption of fifo rather than lifo for the valuation of inventories.
c Adoption of a 7-year life rather than a 10-year life for the depreciation of equipment.

9 What single ratio do you think should be of greatest interest to:

a a banker considering a short-term loan?
b a common shareholder?
c an insurance company considering a long-term mortgage loan?

10 Modern Limited earned a 16% return on its total assets. Current liabilities are 10% of total assets. Long-term bonds carrying a 13% coupon rate are equal to 30% of total assets. There is no preferred stock. Is this application of leverage favourable or unfavourable from the viewpoint of Modern Limited's shareholders?

11 In deciding whether a company's equity ratio is favourable or unfavourable, creditors and shareholders may have different views. Why?

12 Company A has a current ratio of 3 to 1. Company B has a current ratio of 2 to 1. Does this mean that A's operating cycle is longer than B's? Why?

13 An investor states, "I bought this stock for $50 several years ago and it now sells for $100. It paid $5 per share in dividends last year so I'm earning 10% on my investment." Criticize this statement.

14 Company C experiences a considerable seasonal variation in its business. The high point in the year's activity comes in November, the low point in July. During which month would you expect the company's current ratio to be higher? If the company were choosing a fiscal year for accounting purposes, how would you advise them?

15 Both the inventory turnover and accounts receivable turnover increased from 10 times to 15 times from Year 1 to Year 2, but net income decreased. Can you offer some possible reasons for this?

16 Is the rate of return on investment (ROI) intended primarily to measure liquidity, solvency, or some other aspect of business operations? Explain.

17 Mention three financial amounts to which corporate earnings can logically be compared in judging their adequacy or reasonableness.

18 Under what circumstances would you consider a corporate net income of $1,000,000 for the year as being unreasonably low? Under what circumstances would you consider a corporate net income of $1,000,000 as being unreasonably high?

EXERCISES

Exercise 20-1
Accounting terminology

Listed below are nine technical accounting terms introduced in this chapter.

Trend percentages	Leverage	Inventory turnover
Vertical analysis	Yield	Operating cycle
Return on assets	Quick ratio	Book value per share

Each of the following statements may (or may not) describe one of these technical terms. For each statement, indicate the accounting term described, or answer ''None'' if the statement does not correctly describe any of the terms.

a Buying assets with money raised by borrowing or by issuing preferred stock.

b The proportion of total assets financed by shareholders, as distinguished from creditors.

c Net assets represented by each share of stock.

d Changes in financial statement items from a base year to following years expressed as a percentage of the base year amount and designed to show the extent and direction of change.

e Dividends per share divided by market price per share.

f Average time period between the purchase of merchandise and the conversion of this merchandise back into cash.

g Comparison of a particular financial statement item to a total including that item.

h Net sales divided by average inventory.

i Comparison of highly liquid current assets (cash, marketable securities, and receivables) with current liabilities.

Exercise 20-2
Trend percentages

Compute *trend percentages* for the following items taken from the financial statements of Raybar, Inc. over a five-year period. Treat 1985 as the base year. State whether the trends are favourable or unfavourable.

	1989	1988	1987	1986	1985
Sales	$440,000	$380,000	$310,000	$300,000	$250,000
Cost of Goods Sold	$308,000	$247,000	$198,000	$186,000	$150,000

Exercise 20-3
Percentage changes

At the top of page 849 are some financial items taken from the annual reports of Coast Lands, Inc., for two successive years. Compute the percentage of change from 1988 to 1989 whenever possible.

	1989	1988
a Sales	$960,000	$800,000
b Accounts receivable	132,000	120,000
c Notes receivable	52,200	60,000
d Retained earnings (deficit)	20,000	(40,000)
e Notes payable	50,000	–0–
f Marketable securities	–0–	20,000

Exercise 20-4
Common-size income statements

Prepare *common size* income statements for Bell Company, a sole proprietorship, for the two years shown in the following illustration by converting the dollar amounts into percentages. For each year, sales will appear as 100% and other items will be expressed as a percentage of sales. (Income taxes are not involved as the business is not incorporated.) Comment on whether the changes from 1988 to 1989 are favourable or unfavourable.

	1989	1988
Sales	$600,000	$500,000
Cost of goods sold	384,000	325,000
Gross profit	$216,000	$175,000
Operating expenses	168,000	145,000
Net income	$ 48,000	$ 30,000

Exercise 20-5
Computing ratios

A condensed balance sheet for Magnet Corporation prepared at the end of the year appears as follows:

ASSETS		LIABILITIES & SHAREHOLDERS' EQUITY	
Cash	$ 26,000	Notes payable	$ 60,000
Accounts receivable	90,000	Accounts payable	100,000
Inventory	200,000	Long-term liabilities	140,000
Prepaid expenses	10,000	Capital stock,	
Plant & equipment (net)	399,000	20,000 shares issued	200,000
Other assets	25,000	Retained earnings	250,000
Total	$750,000	Total	$750,000

During the year the company earned a gross profit of $324,000 on sales of $1,080,000. Accounts receivable, inventory, and plant assets remained almost constant in amount throughout the year. From this information, compute the following:

a Current ratio

b Quick ratio

c Working capital

d Equity ratio

e Accounts receivable turnover (all sales were on credit)

f Inventory turnover

g Book value per share of capital stock.

Exercise 20-6
Ratios for a retail store

Selected financial data for Silverwoods, a retail store, appear at the top of page 850. Since monthly figures are not available, the average amounts for inventories and for accounts receivable should be based on the amounts shown for the beginning and end of 1989.

	1989	1988
Sales (terms 2/10, n/30)	$420,000	$300,000
Cost of goods sold	315,000	225,000
Inventory at end of year	54,000	60,000
Accounts receivable at end of year	62,000	47,000

Compute the following for 1989:

a Gross profit percentage

b Inventory turnover

c Accounts receivable turnover

Exercise 20-7
Current ratio, debt
ratio, and earnings
per share

Selected financial data from Rustic Products, Inc., follow.

	1989	1988
Total assets (40% of which are current)	$500,000	$340,000
Current liabilities	$ 90,000	$100,000
Bonds payable, 12%	150,000	65,000
Capital stock, 15,000 shares issued	150,000	150,000
Retained earnings	110,000	25,000
Total liabilities & shareholders' equity	$500,000	$340,000

The average income tax rate is 40% and dividends of $10,000 were declared and paid in 1989. Compute the following:

a Current ratio for 1989 and 1988

b Debt ratio for 1989 and 1988

c Earnings per share for 1989

Exercise 20-8
Ratio analysis for
two similar companies

Selected data from the financial statements of X Limited and Y Limited for the year just ended are shown below. Assume that for both companies dividends declared were equal in amount to net earnings during the year and therefore shareholders' equity did not change. The two companies are in the same line of business.

	X LIMITED	Y LIMITED
Total liabilities	$ 400,000	$ 200,000
Total assets	1,600,000	800,000
Sales (all on credit)	3,200,000	2,400,000
Average inventory	480,000	280,000
Average receivables	400,000	200,000
Gross profit as a percentage of sales	40%	30%
Operating expenses as a percentage of sales	38%	26%
Net income as a percentage of sales	2%	4%

Compute the following for each company:

a Net income

b Net income as a percentage of shareholders' equity

c Accounts receivable turnover

d Inventory turnover

PROBLEMS

Problem 20A-1
Common size income statement; comparison with industry averages

Group A

Harvest King manufactures and distributes farm equipment. Shown below are the income statement for the company and a common size summary for the industry in which the company operates. (Note: Notice that the percentages in the right-hand column are *not* for Harvest King, but are average percentages for the industry.)

	HARVEST KING	INDUSTRY AVERAGE
Sales (net)	$8,000,000	100%
Cost of goods sold	5,040,000	58%
Gross profit on sales	$2,960,000	42%
Operating expenses:		
Selling	$ 960,000	10%
General and administrative	1,120,000	15%
Total operating expenses	$2,080,000	25%
Operating income	$ 880,000	17%
Income taxes	420,000	8%
Net income	$ 460,000	9%
Return on shareholders' equity	10%	18%

Instructions

a Prepare a two-column common size income statement. The first column should show for Harvest King all items expressed as a percentage of net sales. (Round all figures to the nearest whole percent.) The second column should show as an industry average the percentage data given in the problem. The purpose of this common size statement is to compare the operating results of Harvest King with the average for the industry.

b Comment specifically on differences between Harvest King and the industry average with respect to gross profit on sales, selling expenses, general and administrative expenses, operating income, income taxes, net income, and return on shareholders' equity. Suggest possible reasons for the more important disparities.

Problem 20A-2
Ratios based on balance sheet and income statement data

Cyclone Corporation has issued common stock only. The company has been successful and has a gross profit rate of 25%. The following information was derived from the company's financial statements.

Beginning inventory	$ 700,000
Purchases	3,100,000
Ending inventory	?
Average accounts receivable	250,000
Average common shareholders' equity	1,800,000
Sales (80% on credit)	4,000,000
Net income	225,000

Instructions

On the basis of the above information, compute the following:

a Accounts receivable turnover and the average number of days required to collect the accounts receivable.

b The inventory turnover and the average number of days required to turn over the inventory.

c Return on common shareholders' equity.

Problem 20A-3
Percentage relationships on the income statement

The information set out below was developed from the financial statements of Quarry Tile, Inc. At the beginning of 1989, the company began buying its merchandise from a new supplier.

	1989	1988
Gross profit on sales	$405,000	$320,000
Income before income taxes	45,000	60,000
Net income	36,000	48,000
Net income as a percentage of net sales	4%	6%

Instructions

a Compute the net sales for each year.

b Compute the cost of goods sold in dollars and as a percentage of net sales for each year.

c Compute the operating expenses in dollars and as a percentage of net sales for each year.

d Prepare a condensed comparative income statement for 1988 and 1989. Include the following items: Net sales, cost of goods sold, gross profit, operating expenses, income before income taxes, income taxes expense, and net income. Omit earnings per share statistics.

e Comment on any significant favourable trends and unfavourable trends in the performance of Quarry Tile, Inc.

Problem 20A-4
Ratios; consider advisability of incurring long-term debt

At the end of the year, the following information was obtained from the accounting records of Santa Fe Boot Co. Ltd.

Sales (all on credit)	$800,000
Cost of goods sold	480,000
Average inventory (fifo method)	120,000
Average accounts receivable	80,000
Interest expense	6,000
Income taxes	8,000
Net income for the year	36,000
Average investment in assets	500,000
Average shareholders' equity	400,000

The company declared no dividends of any kind during the year and did not issue or retire any capital stock.

Instructions

From the information given, compute the following for the year.

a Inventory turnover.

b Accounts receivable turnover.

c Total operating expenses. (Interest expense is a nonoperating expense.)

d Gross profit percentage.

e Return on average shareholders' equity.

f Return on average assets.

g Santa Fe Boot Co. Ltd. has an opportunity to obtain a long-term loan at an annual interest rate of 12% and could use this additional capital at the same rate of profitability as indicated above. Would obtaining the loan be desirable from the viewpoint of the shareholders? Explain.

Problem 20A-5
Ratios; evaluation of two companies

Following are selected financial data for Another World and Imports, Inc., at the end of the current year:

	ANOTHER WORLD	IMPORTS, INC.
Net credit sales	$675,000	$560,000
Cost of goods sold	504,000	480,000
Cash	51,000	20,000
Accounts receivable (net)	75,000	70,000
Inventory	84,000	160,000
Current liabilities	105,000	100,000

Assume that the year-end balances for accounts receivable and for inventory also represent the average balances for these items throughout the year.

Instructions

a For each of the two companies, compute the following:

(1) Working capital.
(2) Current ratio.
(3) Quick ratio.
(4) Number of times inventory turned over during the year and the average number of days required to turn over the inventory. (Round computation to the nearest day.)
(5) Number of times accounts receivable turned over during the year and the average number of days required to collect accounts receivable. (Round computation to the nearest day.)
(6) Operating cycle.

b From the viewpoint of a short-term creditor, comment upon the relative *quality* of each company's working capital. To which company you would prefer to sell $20,000 in merchandise on a 30-day open account?

Problem 20A-6
Constructing a balance sheet from various ratios and miscellaneous data

Given below are selected balance sheet items and ratios for the Metro Corporation at June 30.

Total shareholders' equity (includes 100,000 shares of no-par value capital stock issued at $5 per share, also retained earnings)	$ 800,000
Plant and equipment (net)	590,000
Long-term debt	400,000
Net sales (all on credit)	6,600,000
Inventory turnover rate per year	6 times
Average accounts receivable collection period (assuming a 360-day year)	30 days
Gross profit percentage	30%
Equity ratio	40%
Quick ratio	0.8 to 1

Assume that balance sheet figures did not change significantly during the year and that all sales are made on account.

Instructions

From the foregoing information, construct a balance sheet for the Metro Corporation at June 30, in as much detail as the data permit. It is suggested that you prepare the liabilities and shareholder's equity side of the balance sheet first. The following sequence of steps affords one convenient approach:

(1) List the capital stock (as given in the problem) in the shareholders' equity section.

(2) Compute the amount of retained earnings on the assumption that there are only two items comprising shareholders' equity.

(3) Compute total assets. You will then be able to fill in the balance sheet totals for assets, liabilities, and liabilities and shareholders' equity. Complete the liabilities section by indicating the amounts of current liabilities and of long-term debt.

(4) Compute accounts receivable by relating the average collection period (given as 30 days) to the year's sales. Remember to assume a 360-day year.

(5) Compute inventory by two steps:

(a) Compute cost of goods sold.

(b) Use cost of goods sold and inventory turnover rate to compute inventory.

(6) Determine cash as a balancing amount (a plug figure).

Problem 20A-7
Analysis and interpretation from viewpoint of common shareholders and of bondholders

The following financial information for Continental Transfer Ltd. and National Van Lines Ltd. (except market price per share of stock) is stated in ***thousands of dollars.*** The figures are as of the end of the current year. The two companies are in the same industry and are quite similar as to operations, facilities, and accounting methods. Assume that both companies pay income taxes equal to 50% of income before income taxes.

ASSETS	CONTINENTAL TRANSFER LTD.	NATIONAL VAN LINES LTD.
Current assets	$ 97,450	$132,320
Plant and equipment	397,550	495,680
Less: Accumulated depreciation	(55,000)	(78,000)
Total assets	$440,000	$550,000

LIABILITIES & SHAREHOLDERS' EQUITY		
Current liabilities	$ 34,000	$ 65,000
Bonds payable, 12%, due in 15 years	120,000	100,000
Capital stock, no-par	150,000	200,000
Retained earnings	136,000	185,000
Total liabilities & shareholders' equity	$440,000	$550,000

Analysis of retained earnings:		
Balance, beginning of year	$125,200	$167,200
Net income for the year	19,800	37,400
Dividends	(9,000)	(19,600)
Balance, end of year	$136,000	$185,000

Market price of capital stock, per share	$30	$61
Number of shares of capital stock outstanding	6 million	8 million

Instructions   **a** Compute for each company:

(1) The number of times bond interest was earned during the current year.

(2) The debt ratio.

b In the light of the information developed in **a** above, write a paragraph indicating which company's bonds you think would trade in the market at the higher price. Which would probably provide the higher yield? Explain how the ratios developed influence your answer. (It may be assumed that the bonds were issued several years ago and are traded on an organized securities exchange.)

c For each company compute the dividend yield, the price-earnings ratio, and the book value per share. (Show supporting computations to determine dividends per share. Remember that dollar amounts in the problem are in thousands of dollars, that is, three zeros omitted.)

d Express an opinion, based on the data developed in **c** above, as to which company's stock is a better investment at the present market price.

Group B

Problem 20B-1
Comparing operating results with average performance in the industry

Sub Zero, Inc., manufactures camping equipment. Shown below for the current year are the income statement for the company and a common size summary for the industry in which the company operates. (Notice that the percentages in the right-hand column are *not* for Sub Zero, Inc., but are average percentages for the industry.)

	SUB ZERO, INC.	INDUSTRY AVERAGE
Sales (net)	$20,000,000	100%
Cost of goods sold	9,800,000	57
Gross profit on sales	$10,200,000	43%
Operating expenses:		
Selling	$ 4,200,000	16%
General and administrative	3,400,000	20
Total operating expenses	$ 7,600,000	36%
Operating income	$ 2,600,000	7%
Income taxes	1,200,000	3
Net income	$ 1,400,000	4%
Return on shareholders' equity	23%	14%

Instructions

a Prepare a two-column common size income statement. The first column should show for Sub Zero, Inc., all items expressed as a percentage of net sales. The second column should show as an industry average the percentage data given in the problem. The purpose of this common size statement is to compare the operating results of Sub Zero, Inc., with the average for the industry.

b Comment specifically on differences between Sub Zero, Inc., and the industry average with respect to gross profit on sales, selling expenses, general and administrative expenses, operating income, net income, and return on shareholders' equity. Suggest possible reasons for the more important disparities.

Problem 20B-2
Analysis to identify favourable and unfavourable trends

The information which you will find set out at the top of page 856 was developed from the financial statements of Pioneer Waterbeds. At the beginning of 1989, the company's former supplier went bankrupt, and at that time the company began buying merchandise from another supplier.

	1989	1988
Gross profit on sales	$280,000	$315,000
Income before income taxes	64,000	70,000
Net income	48,000	52,500
Net income as a percentage of net sales	6.0%	7.5%

Instructions

a Compute the net sales for each year.

b Compute the cost of goods sold in dollars and as a percentage of net sales for each year.

c Compute operating expenses in dollars and as a percentage of net sales for each year. (Income taxes expense is not an operating expense.)

d Prepare a condensed comparative income staement for 1988 and 1989. Include the following items: Net sales, cost of goods sold, gross profit, operating expenses, income before income taxes, income taxes expense, and net income. Omit earnings per share statistics.

e Identify the significant favourable trends and unfavourable trends in the performance of Pioneer Waterbeds. Comment on any unusual changes.

**Problem 20B-3
Ratios; consider advisability of incurring long-term debt**

At the end of the year, the following information was obtained from the accounting records of Craftsman Clocks.

Sales (all on credit)	$900,000
Cost of goods sold	585,000
Average inventory (fifo method)	117,000
Average accounts receivable	100,000
Interest expense	15,000
Income taxes	28,000
Net income	53,000
Average investment in assets	600,000
Average shareholders' equity	265,000

Instructions

From the information given, compute the following:

a Inventory turnover.

b Accounts receivable turnover.

c Total operating expenses. (Interest expense and income taxes are nonoperating expenses.)

d Gross profit percentage.

e Return on average shareholders' equity.

f Return on average assets.

g Craftsman Clocks has an opportunity to obtain a long-term loan at an annual interest rate of 11% and could use this additional capital at the same rate of profitability as indicated above. Would obtaining the loan be desirable from the viewpoint of the shareholders? Explain.

**Problem 20B-4
Analysis and interpretation from viewpoint of short-term creditor**

The top of page 857 shows selected financial data for Hill Corporation and Valley Limited at the end of the current year. Assume that the year-end balances shown for accounts receivable and for inventory also represent the average balances of these accounts throughout the year.

Instructions

a For each company, compute the following:

(1) Working capital.

(2) Current ratio.

	HILL CORPORATION	VALLEY LIMITED
Net credit sales	$480,000	$595,000
Cost of goods sold	420,000	412,500
Cash	12,000	35,000
Accounts receivable (net)	60,000	70,000
Inventory	168,000	82,500
Current liabilities	80,000	75,000

(3) Quick ratio.

(4) Number of times inventory turned over during the year and the average number of days required to turn over inventory.

(5) Number of times accounts receivable turned over during the year and the average number of days required to collect accounts receivable. (Round to the nearest day.)

(6) Operating cycle.

b From the viewpoint of a short-term creditor, comment upon the relative *quality* of each company's working capital. To which company would you prefer to sell $15,000 in merchandise on a 30-day open account?

Problem 20B-5
Effects of transactions
on various ratios

Listed in the left-hand column below is a series of twelve business transactions and events relating to the activities of Potomac Mills. Opposite each transaction is listed a particular ratio used in financial analysis:

TRANSACTION	RATIO
(1) Purchased inventory on open account.	Quick ratio
(2) A larger physical volume of goods was sold at smaller unit prices.	Gross profit percentage
(3) Corporation declared a cash dividend.	Current ratio
(4) An uncollectible account receivable was written off against the allowance account.	Current ratio
(5) Issued additional shares of common stock and used proceeds to retire long-term debt.	Debt ratio
(6) Paid stock dividend on common stock, in common stock.	Earnings per share
(7) Conversion of a portion of bonds payable into common stock. (Ignore income taxes.)	Times interest charges earned
(8) Appropriated retained earnings.	Rate of return on shareholders' equity.
(9) During period of rising prices, company changes from fifo to lifo method of inventory pricing.	Inventory turnover
(10) Paid a previously declared cash dividend.	Debt ratio
(11) Purchased factory supplies on open account.	Current ratio (assume that ratio is greater than 1:1)
(12) Issued shares of capital stock in exchange for patents.	Equity ratio

Instructions

What effect would each transaction or event have on the ratio listed opposite to it; that is, as a result of this event would the ratio increase, decrease, or remain unchanged? Your answer for each of the twelve transactions should include a brief explanation.

Problem 20B-6
Evaluating short-term
debt-paying ability

Following is the working capital information for the Oakridge Corporation at the beginning of the year.

Cash	$225,000
Temporary investments in marketable securities	120,000
Notes receivable—current	180,000
Accounts receivable	300,000
Allowance for doubtful accounts	15,000
Inventory	240,000
Prepaid expenses	30,000
Notes payable within one year	90,000
Accounts payable	247,500
Accrued liabilities	22,500

The following transactions are completed during the year:
- **(0)** Sold inventory costing $36,000 for $30,000.
- **(1)** Declared a cash dividend, $120,000.
- **(2)** Declared a 10% stock dividend.
- **(3)** Paid accounts payable, $60,000.
- **(4)** Purchased goods on account, $45,000.
- **(5)** Collected cash on accounts receivable, $90,000.
- **(6)** Borrowed cash on short-term note, $150,000.
- **(7)** Issued additional shares of capital stock for cash, $450,000.
- **(8)** Sold temporary investments costing $30,000 for $27,000 cash.
- **(9)** Acquired temporary investments, $52,500. Paid cash.
- **(10)** Wrote off uncollectible accounts, $9,000.
- **(11)** Sold inventory costing $37,500 for $48,000.
- **(12)** Acquired plant and equipment for cash, $240,000.

Instructions

a Compute the amount of quick assets, current assets, and current liabilities at the beginning of the year as shown by the preceding account balances.

b Use the data compiled in part **a** to compute: (1) current ratio, (2) quick ratio, and (3) working capital.

c Indicate the effect (increase, decrease, none) of each transaction listed on the current ratio, quick ratio, and working capital. Use the following four-column format (item **0** is given as an example):

	EFFECT ON		
ITEM	CURRENT RATIO	QUICK RATIO	WORKING CAPITAL
0	Decrease	Increase	Decrease

Problem 20B-7
Building financial
statements from
limited information,
including ratios

John Gale, the accountant for Southbay Corporation, prepared the year-end financial statements, including all ratios, and agreed to bring them along on a hunting trip with the executives of the corporation. To his embarrassment, he found that only certain fragmentary information had been placed in his briefcase and the completed statements had been left in his office. One hour before Gale was to present the financial statements to the executives, he was able to come up with the following information:

SOUTHBAY CORPORATION
Balance Sheet
December 31, 19___
(in thousands of dollars)

ASSETS			LIABILITIES & SHAREHOLDERS' EQUITY		
Current assets:			Current liabilities		$?
Cash		$?	Long-term debt, 8% interest . . .		?
Accounts receivable (net)		?	Total liabilities		$?
Inventory		?	Shareholders' equity:		
Total current assets		$?	Capital stock, no-par .	$300	
Plant assets:			Retained earnings . . .	100	
Machinery and			Total shareholders'		
equipment	$580		equity		400
Less: Accumulated					
depreciation	80	500	Total liabilities &		
Total assets		$?	shareholders' equity		$?

SOUTHBAY CORPORATION
Income Statement
For the Year Ended December 31, 19___
(in thousands of dollars)

Net sales	$?
Cost of goods sold	?
Gross profit on sales (25% of net sales)	$?
Operating expenses	?
Operating income (10% of net sales)	$?
Interest expense	28
Income before income taxes	$?
Income taxes — 40% of income before income taxes	?
Net income	$60

Additional information   **(1)** The equity ratio was 40%; the debt ratio was 60%.
(2) The only interest expense was on the long-term debt.
(3) The beginning inventory was $150,000; the inventory turnover was 4.8 times.
(4) The current ratio was 2 to 1; the quick ratio was 1 to 1.
(5) The beginning balance in accounts receivable was $80,000; the accounts receivable turn-over for the year was 12.8 times. All sales were made on account.

Instructions   The accountant asks you to help complete the financial statements for the Southbay Corporation, using only the information available. Present supporting computations and explanations for all amounts appearing in the balance sheet and the income statement.

BUSINESS DECISION CASES

**Case 20-1
Telling it like it
never was**   Holiday Greeting Cards is a local company organized late in July of 1988. The company's net income for each of its first six calendar quarters of operations is summarized at the top of page 860. The amounts are stated in thousands of dollars.

	1989	1988
First quarter (January through March)	$ 253	—
Second quarter (April through June)	308	—
Third quarter (July through September)	100	$ 50
Fourth quarter (October through December)	450	500
Total for the calendar year	$1,111	$550

Glen Wallace reports the business and economic news for a local radio station. On the day that Holiday Greeting Cards released the preceding financial information, you heard Wallace make the following statement during his broadcast: "Holiday Greeting Cards enjoyed a 350% increase in its profits for the fourth quarter, and profits for the entire year were up by over 100%."

Instructions   **a** Show the computations that Wallace probably made in arriving at his statistics. (Hint: Wallace did not make his computations in the manner recommended in this chapter. His figures, however, can be developed from the financial data above.)

b Do you believe that Wallace's percentage changes present a realistic impression of Holiday Greeting Cards' rate of growth in 1989? Explain.

c What figure would you use to express the percentage change in Holiday Greeting Cards' fourth-quarter profits in 1989? Explain why you would compute the change in this manner.

Case 20-2
Evaluation of capital
structure and liquidity:
two companies

At the top of page 861 is certain financial information relating to two companies, London Conspiracy and Coventry Clothiers, as of the end of the current year. All figures (except market price per share of stock) are in ***thousands of dollars.***

Instructions   London Conspiracy and Coventry Clothiers are generally comparable in the nature of their operations, products, and accounting procedures used. Write a short answer to each of the following questions, using whatever analytical computations you feel will best support your answer. Show the amounts used in calculating all ratios and percentages. Carry per-share computations to the nearest cent and percentages one place beyond the decimal point, for example, 9.8%.

a What is the book value per share of stock for each company?

b Prepare a four-column schedule showing for each company the component percentages represented by current liabilities, by long-term liabilities, and by shareholders' equity. Use the first two columns for London Conspiracy, showing dollar amounts in the first column and component percentages in the second column. Use the last two columns in the same way for Coventry Clothiers. On the basis of this analysis, express an opinion as to which company has a more conservative capital structure.

c Compute the price-earnings ratio and the dividend yield for each company. Use a work sheet with five money columns. Use the headings Market Price per Share, Earnings per Share, Price-Earnings Ratio, Dividends per Share, and Dividend Yield, %. Show all computations as supporting schedules.

d Compute (1) quick assets, (2) total current assets, and (3) working capital. Then compute the quick ratio and the current ratio. Finally, write a brief statement as to which company has the more liquid financial position. Base your answer on the above measurements.

ASSETS	LONDON CONSPIRACY	COVENTRY CLOTHIERS
Cash	$ 126.0	$ 180.0
Marketable securities, at lower-of-cost-and-market	129.0	453.0
Accounts receivable, net	145.0	167.0
Inventories	755.6	384.3
Prepaid expenses	24.4	15.7
Plant and equipment, net	1,680.0	1,570.0
Intangibles and other assets	140.0	30.0
Total assets	$3,000.0	$2,800.0

LIABILITIES & SHAREHOLDERS' EQUITY

	LONDON CONSPIRACY	COVENTRY CLOTHIERS
Accounts payable	$ 344.6	$ 304.1
Accrued liabilities, including income taxes	155.4	95.9
Bonds payable, 7%, due in 10 years	200.0	500.0
Capital stock (London, 100,000 shares; Coventry, 60,000 shares)	1,450.0	1,350.0
Retained earnings	910.0	550.0
Treasury stock (1,000 shares, at cost)	(60.0)	–0–
Total liabilities & shareholders' equity	$3,000.0	$2,800.0
Analysis of retained earnings:		
Balance, beginning of year	$ 712.0	$ 430.0
Add: Net income	297.0	240.0
Less: Dividends	(99.0)	(120.0)
Balance, end of year	$ 910.0	$ 550.0
Market price per share of stock, end of year	$50	$40

FINANCIAL STATEMENTS OF A LARGE COMPANY: A CASE STUDY

The purpose of this Appendix is to acquaint you with the financial statements of a large company. The financial statements of Canada Packers Inc. were selected because they illustrate many of the financial reporting issues discussed in this textbook. Notice that several pages of explanatory notes are included with the basic financial statements. These explanatory notes supplement the condensed information in the financial statements and are designed to carry out the disclosure principle discussed in Chapter 13.

The form and content of published financial statements varies somewhat from one company to another. In addition, the presentation of specific items in the financial statements of any given company may vary in some respects from the illustrations contained in this textbook.

Consolidated Statement of Income

For the year ended March 28, 1987
(with comparative figures for 1986)

**Canada
Packers Inc.**
*(Incorporated under
the laws of Canada)*

	1987	1986
	(thousands of dollars)	
Sales	$3,205,281	$3,233,494
Less freight and delivery costs	124,388	124,851
Net sales	3,080,893	3,108,643
Cost of products sold	2,761,139	2,804,633
Selling, research and administrative expenses	216,376	208,511
Depreciation of fixed assets	28,115	25,860
Interest *(Note 4)*	4,661	9,245
	3,010,291	3,048,249
Income from operations before income taxes	70,602	60,394
Income taxes *(Note 9)*	27,768	24,762
Income from operations	42,834	35,632
Other income (expense)		
Income from investments *(Note 3)*	907	498
Profits and losses from disposals of fixed assets and investments	327	2,457
Provision for closing operations *(Note 10)*	(10,750)	
	(9,516)	2,955
Income taxes *(Note 9)*	(6,099)	263
Total other income (expense)	(3,417)	2,692
Income before minority interests	39,417	38,324
Minority interests in net income of subsidiary companies	830	268
Net income	$ 38,587	$ 38,056
Income before minority interests as % of net sales	1.28%	1.23%
Income from operations per share	$1.15	$ .98
Net income per share	$1.04	$1.04

(see accompanying notes)

Consolidated Balance Sheet

Canada Packers Inc.

March 28, 1987
(with comparative figures at March 29, 1986)

Assets	1987	1986
	(thousands of dollars)	
Current:		
Short term deposits – at cost	$ 12,957	$ 2,038
Trade accounts receivable	150,949	158,498
Inventories	212,221	205,040
Prepaid expenses	4,484	3,497
Sundry receivables	10,299	4,834
Total current assets	390,910	373,907
Investments *(Note 3)*	5,765	3,772
Fixed assets at cost:		
Land and buildings	175,407	158,460
Machinery and equipment	338,380	305,414
Construction in progress	20,283	15,410
	534,070	479,284
Less accumulated depreciation	255,777	234,076
	278,293	245,208
	$674,968	$622,887

(see accompanying notes)

Auditors' Report

To the Shareholders of Canada Packers Inc.:

We have examined the consolidated balance sheet of Canada Packers Inc. as at March 28, 1987 and the consolidated statements of income, reinvested earnings and changes in financial position for the year then ended. Our examination was made in accordance with generally accepted auditing standards, and accordingly included such tests and other procedures as we considered necessary in the circumstances.

In our opinion, these consolidated financial statements present fairly the financial position of the company as at March 28, 1987 and the results of its operations and the changes in its financial position for the year then ended in accordance with generally accepted accounting principles applied on a basis consistent with that of the preceding year.

Clarkson Gordon

Chartered Accountants

Toronto, Canada
May 12, 1987

Liabilities and Shareholders' Investment	1987	1986
	(thousands of dollars)	
Current:		
Borrowings	$ 60,307	$ 67,477
Accounts payable and accrued charges	148,128	130,754
Income and other taxes payable	8,965	15,925
Dividend payable April 1	3,547	2,816
Current portion of notes payable	10,000	1,300
Total current liabilities	230,947	218,272
Notes payable *(Note 4)*	17,622	11,300
Deferred income taxes	44,585	44,745
Minority interests in subsidiary companies	4,664	3,886
Shareholders' investment:		
Capital stock *(Note 6)*	23,137	15,657
Earnings reinvested in the business	351,657	327,150
Unrealized foreign currency adjustment	2,356	1,877
Total shareholders' investment	377,150	344,684
	$674,968	$622,887

On behalf of the Board:

Director

Director

Consolidated Statement of Reinvested Earnings

For the year ended March 28, 1987
(with comparative figures for 1986)

	1987	1986
	(thousands of dollars)	
Balance at beginning of year	**$327,150**	$300,484
Net income for the year	**38,587**	38,056
	365,737	338,540
Less dividends of 38¢ per share (30.7¢ in 1986)	**14,080**	11,206
Less excess of cost over stated capital of shares purchased	**—**	184
Balance at end of year	**$351,657**	$327,150

Consolidated Statement of Changes in Financial Position

For the year ended March 28, 1987
(with comparative figures for 1986)

	1987	1986
	(thousands of dollars)	
Cash provided by (used in) operating activities		
Income from operations	**$ 42,834**	$ 35,632
Adjustments for non-cash items		
Depreciation	**28,115**	25,860
Deferred income tax	**3,740**	3,619
Unrealized foreign currency adjustment	**(946)**	(2,478)
Net change in non-cash working capital balances related to operations	**9,212**	20,499
	82,955	83,132
Cash provided by (used in) investment activities		
Additions to fixed assets	**(48,368)**	(41,293)
Acquisitions *(Note 8)*	**(21,781)**	(3,776)
Proceeds on sale of fixed assets	**870**	5,096
Closing operations	**(3,404)**	
Investments	**(1,325)**	(1,118)
Income from investments	**257**	228
	(73,751)	(40,863)
Cash provided by (used in) financing activities		
Additions to (repayments of) notes payable, net	**15,022**	(26,446)
Issue of common shares	**7,309**	4,654
Dividends	**(13,349)**	(11,159)
Dividends to minority shareholders in subsidiary companies	**(97)**	—
	8,885	(32,951)
Decrease in borrowings and short term deposits during the year	**18,089**	9,318
Borrowings and short term deposits at beginning of year	**(65,439)**	(74,757)
Borrowings and short term deposits at end of year*	**$(47,350)**	$(65,439)

(see accompanying notes) *The comparative figures have been adjusted to reflect the reclassification of cheques issued as borrowings.*

Notes to Consolidated Financial Statements

For the year ended March 28, 1987

1. Accounting Policies

a) Principles of Consolidation

The consolidated statements include the accounts of the company and all its subsidiaries and the company's proportionate share of the assets, liabilities, revenues and expenses of joint ventures. Certain investments in which the company has significant influence are accounted for on the equity method.

b) Industry Segments

Sales by industry segments include sales to other segments at approximately equivalent commercial selling prices.

c) Translation of Foreign Currencies

The accounts of foreign subsidiaries are translated to Canadian dollars using the current-rate method. Under this method, assets and liabilities are translated at the exchange rate in effect at the year-end and revenues and expenses at the average rate for the year. Exchange gains or losses on translation are deferred and included as a separate component in shareholders' investment.

d) Inventories

Inventories are valued at the lower of cost and net realizable value with cost being determined substantially on a first-in, first-out basis.

e) Fixed Assets and Depreciation

Fixed assets are shown at acquisition cost, including costs of transportation and installation. Interest costs on significant projects are capitalized during the construction period. Cost of fixed assets acquired through purchase of subsidiaries includes the excess, if any, of purchase price over the vendors' book values attributable to such fixed assets.

Depreciation is based on the estimated productive life of the asset calculated on the straightline method. Estimates generally used are:
Buildings – 30 years
Machinery and Equipment – 10 years
Leaseholds – the shorter of term of the lease or estimated life

f) Research and Development

Research and development costs are expensed as incurred. The amount for 1987 was $6,800,000 (1986 $6,400,000).

g) Retirement Plan Costs

Retirement plan costs related to current service are accrued on a current basis. Retirement plan costs related to any improvement in past service benefits are amortized over 6 years.

2. Retirement Plan

As at March 28, 1987, the retirement plans were fully funded.

3. Investments

	1987	1986
	(thousands of dollars)	
At cost	$2,044	$ 544
Market value approximates cost		
At equity	3,721	3,228
	$5,765	$3,772
Income from investments:		
Dividend and interest	$ 109	$ 143
Equity investments	798	355
	$ 907	$ 498

4. Notes Payable

	1987	1986
	(thousands of dollars)	
Canada Packers Inc. Term borrowings due 1991, interest 12½%	$17,622	—
Note payable, due 1988 interest rate, 14%	10,000	$12,600
	27,622	12,600
Less current portion	10,000	1,300
	$17,622	$11,300
Interest expense for the year	$ 3,535	$ 5,621

Requirements for payment within the next 5 years are:

1988 $10,000,000   1991 $17,622,000

Term borrowings, due 1991, are under an agreement which provides a 7-year unsecured revolving credit facility of $20,000,000. The borrowings may consist at any time of bankers' acceptances, commercial paper or term loans at current competitive rates of interest. In a related transaction the company entered into an interest rate conversion agreement which has the effect of fixing the interest cost of borrowings under this credit facility at 12½%.

5. Purchase of Fixed Assets

Purchases of fixed assets have been reduced by related investment tax credits and government assistance grants received during the year in the amount of approximately $3,900,000 (1986 $3,300,000).

6. Capital Stock

The capital consists of an unlimited number of common shares without nominal or par value. On July 4, 1986 the common shares were subdivided on a 3 for 1 basis. Share data has been adjusted retroactively to reflect this subdivision. Changes in capital stock during the year were as follows:

	1987 Shares Issued	Amount	1986 Shares Issued	Amount
		000's		*000's*
Beginning of year	36,766,650	$15,657	36,117,000	$10,819
Issued on exercise of options	64,000	460	294,000	1,630
Issued under employee share purchase plan	506,900	6,844	355,650	3,023
Issued as stock dividends	11,463	177	17,400	192
Less purchased for cancellation	(1,050)	(1)	(17,400)	(7)
End of year	37,347,963	$23,137	36,766,650	$15,657

As at March 28, 1987 725,000 common shares have been set aside for issue under the terms of an employee share option plan. Outstanding options as at March 28, 1987 are:

Number of Shares	Exercise Price per Share	Option Expiry Date
140,000	$ 6.555	April 14, 1988
54,000	$ 8.639	June 22, 1989
39,000	$11.056	February 18, 1991

No dilution of earnings per share would have resulted had these stock options been exercised.

Net income per share and income from operations per share are calculated on the basis of the weighted average number of shares outstanding during the year.

7. Industry Segment and Geographic Area Information

(millions of dollars)

	Meat Products		Processed Foods		Non-Food Products		Total Company		Operations outside Canada	
	1987	1986	1987	1986	1987	1986	1987	1986	1987	1986
Sales to customers	$2,221.7	$2,190.2	$339.0	$362.3	$520.2	$556.1	$3,080.9	$3,108.6	$466.0	$419.3
Sales to other segments	23.4	28.6	123.8	113.2	50.7	49.5				
	$2,245.1	$2,218.8	$462.8	$475.5	$570.9	$605.6				
Segment operating income	34.0	31.8	23.8	19.2	17.5	18.6	75.3	69.6	10.7	4.5
Interest							4.7	9.2		
Income from operations before income taxes							70.6	60.4		
Identifiable assets	366.2	341.8	112.7	101.5	190.9	176.4	669.8	619.7	104.1	89.9
Corporate assets							5.2	3.2		
Total assets							675.0	622.9		
Capital expenditures	21.9	19.4	16.2	13.0	10.3	8.9	48.4	41.3		
Depreciation	$ 15.1	$ 13.9	$ 4.7	$ 4.4	$ 8.3	$ 7.6	$ 28.1	$ 25.9		

Meat Products – includes fresh meats, processed and cooked meats, canned meats and poultry.

Processed Foods – includes edible oil products (margarine, shortening, salad oils, and refined oils), lard, canned and frozen foods, cheese and other dairy products, and peanut butter and nut products.

Non-Food Products – predominantly animal feeds and feed ingredients. Also included are fine chemicals and pharmaceuticals, gelatine, soaps and detergents, jute and cotton bags, leather products, inedible tallow, and crude vegetable oils.

Export sales of Canadian operations amounted to $211.3 (1986 $222.3).

8. Acquisitions

During the year the company purchased a poultry processing plant at Aurora, Ontario, a livestock feed mill at Stevensville, Ontario and a Canola seed crushing plant at Fort Saskatchewan, Alberta. These businesses were purchased for a total cash consideration of $21,781,000 and consisted of fixed assets at their fair values of $14,648,000, and other assets net, $7,133,000.

9. Income Taxes

The company's effective income tax rate on income from operations is made up as follows:

	1987 %	1986 %
Combined Canadian federal and provincial rate	50.4	49.6
Increase (decrease) in the income tax rate resulting from:		
Manufacturing and processing deduction	(4.1)	(4.6)
Inventory allowance	—	(3.9)
Foreign higher (lower) rates	(1.5)	(.1)
Realization of acquired tax benefits	(5.1)	—
Other items	(.4)	—
Effective income tax rate	39.3	41.0

Income taxes on other income (expense) are lower than the basic combined Canadian federal and provincial rate by $1,300,000 ($1,200,000 in 1986), due to transactions subject to capital gains rate and transactions not subject to tax.

10. Provision for Closing Operations

During the year, a decision was made to close the Beardmore leather operations at Acton, Ontario, and discontinue the cattle and hog slaughtering operations at Winnipeg, Manitoba, and the processed meats manufacturing operations at Vancouver, British Columbia. As a result, a charge of $10,750,000 has been made against net income for the year. This includes a write-down of fixed assets of $1,300,000, costs incurred during the year and a provision for costs which will be incurred following the year end. The total net after tax cost amounts to $4,800,000.

11. Joint Ventures

The company's proportionate share in the assets, liabilities, revenues, and expenses of its joint ventures is as follows:

	1987	1986
	(thousands of dollars)	
Assets	$ 42,132	$33,661
Liabilities	24,011	19,572
Net investment	$ 18,121	$14,089
Revenues	$117,491	$94,594
Expenses	113,496	92,706
Net income	$ 3,995	$ 1,888

12. Commitments and Contingent Liabilities

Approved capital projects at March 28, 1987 on completion, will result in additions of approximately $20,000,000 (1986 $34,000,000) to fixed assets.

Annual lease costs are approximately $13,000,000. Generally the lease terms do not exceed five years.

The class action, brought in 1980 by the Alberta Pork Producers Marketing Board and others against the company and 11 other defendants for damages, claimed to have resulted from an alleged conspiracy to reduce the price of hogs, is proceeding but is currently inactive. Six of the original corporate defendants settled the class action against them by paying a total of $1,076,000. The company refused to settle and is vigorously defending this action.

In 1984 the Attorney-General of Canada preferred an indictment against the company on charges laid in 1982 under section 32(1) (c) of the Competition Act, (formerly the Combines Investigation Act) against five of the corporate defendants in the class action referred to above, including the company, despite the fact that a significant portion of the charges against the company were dismissed at the conclusion of the preliminary inquiry. Three of the other corporate defendants settled the proceedings before the conclusion of the preliminary inquiry, by pleading guilty and paying fines totalling $375,000. The trial commenced in January, 1986 and shortly thereafter the only other codefendant pleaded guilty, but sentencing is reserved until the conclusion of the trial. The company is vigorously defending all charges.

In July 1976, the trustees of the company's Retirement Plan Trusts invested in secured debentures issued under a deed of trust and mortgage between Abacus Cities Ltd. and Guaranty Trust Company of Canada as trustee. In May 1979, the Bank of Montreal appointed a receiver and manager of the assets of Abacus Cities Ltd. Guaranty Trust appointed the same receiver and manager to enforce the security for the debentures. The debenture holders, including the trustees of the Retirement Plan Trusts, are liable to indemnify Guaranty Trust on a pro rata basis against any liabilities it might incur by reason of the enforcement of the security. The company, in turn, is obligated under its agreement with the trustees of the Retirement Plan Trusts to indemnify them against any liabilities they may properly incur in the administration of the trusts.

Actions against Guaranty Trust, the Bank of Montreal and others, claiming damages arising out of the appointment of a receiver and manager by Guaranty Trust and the Bank of Montreal, are pending in British Columbia and in Alberta. Both actions have been dismissed on preliminary motions and appeals are pending. Guaranty Trust is also defending a claim for indemnity by its co-defendants in the British Columbia action. Counsel for Guaranty Trust is opposing both appeals and advises that, if the appeals are successful and the actions proceed, Guaranty Trust has a good defense to all actions including the claim for indemnity.

PROBLEM

Problem 1
Introduction to
published financial
statements

Published financial statements include not only the statements themselves, but also notes and an auditors' report. The purpose of this problem is to acquaint you with the form and content of these materials. After answering each of the following questions, briefly explain where in the statements, notes, or auditors' report you located the information used in your answer.

a Are these financial statements prepared for a single legal entity or for a parent corporation and its subsidiaries?

b Write out the total dollar amount of the company's net sales in 1987 using words rather than numbers.

c The comparative financial statements include the balance sheets, income statements, and statement of changes in financial position for two years. Were all of these financial statements audited by a firm of public accountants? Name the firm that audited some or all of these statements.

d What was the amount of gross profit for 1987?

e What was the total amount of dividends declared by the company in 1986? In 1987?

f In the valuation of inventories, did the company use lifo, fifo, average cost, or other methods?

g Is the company a defendant in any lawsuits? If so, are these lawsuits expected to have a material adverse effect upon the company's financial position?

h In the notes to the financial statements, the company's net sales are classified into "industry segments." Identify the three "industry segments" into which sales are classified. What percentage of 1987 net sales falls into the each classification?

i Did the company acquire new business entities and close certain of its operations? What were the amounts involved, if any?

BUSINESS DECISION CASES

Case 1
Evaluating solvency

Assume that in mid-1987 you are the credit manager of a company that sells cattle and other farm products. Canada Packers wants to make credit purchases from your company of between $5 million and $10 million per month, with payment due in 60 days.

Instructions

a As part of your credit investigation, compute the following from Canada Packers' financial statements:

(1) Current ratio at March 28, 1987. (Express as a decimal and round to one decimal place; e.g., 2.1 to 1.)

(2) Quick ratio at March 28, 1987 (Round as in part 1.)

(3) Working capital at March 28, 1987, and the amount of increase from 1986, if any. (Express in thousands of dollars.)

(4) The increase (or decrease) in cash and cash equivalents in 1986 and 1987.

(5) Inventory turnover in 1987 (rounded to one decimal place), and the average number of days required to sell the inventory (rounded to the nearest day, using your turnover figure, which was rounded to one decimal place).

(6) Accounts receivable turnover in 1987 and the average number of days required to collect accounts receivable. (Assume that all net sales are made on account; round as in part 5.)

(7) The company's operating cycle, stated in days.

b Your company assigns each customer one of the four credit ratings listed below. Assign a credit rating to Canada Packers and write a memorandum explaining your decision. (In your memorandum, you may use any of your computations in part **a**, and may refer to other information in Canada Packers' financial statements.)

Possible Credit Ratings

A Outstanding. Little or no risk of inability to pay. For customers in this category, we fill any reasonable order, without imposing a credit limit. The customer's credit is re-evaluated annually.

B Good. Customer has good debt paying ability, but is assigned a credit limit that is reviewed every six months. Orders above the established credit limit are accepted only on a cash basis.

C Marginal. Customer appears sound, but credit should be extended only on a 30-day basis with a relatively low credit limit. Credit status and credit limit are re-evaluated every 90 days.

D Unacceptable. Customer does not qualify for credit.

Case 2
Evaluating the
company from a share-
holder's perspective

Assume that you are an investment advisor who publishes a monthly newsletter with recommendations on buying and selling common stocks. One of the common stocks you will evaluate this month is Canada Packers Inc. It is now mid-1987, and the price of the company's stock is $16 per share.

Instructions

a As a starting point in your investigation, compute the following. (Follow the company's practice of stating all dollar amounts in thousands, except for per-share amounts. Round percentage computations to 1/10 of 1%.)

(1) Price-earnings ratio. (Use 1987 earnings and the current market price of $16 per share.)

(2) Dividend yield on the common stock.

(3) Return on average total assets in 1987. (Use Income from operations before income taxes and add back interest of $4,661 as "operating income" in this computation.)

(4) Return on average total shareholder's equity in 1987.

(5) Equity ratio.

(6) Prepare trend percentages for (a) net sales, (b) net income, and (c) net earnings per share for 1986 and 1987 using 1986 as the base year at 100%.

b Write a brief memorandum on the topic of leverage as it relates to Canada Packers. Does the company make extensive use of long-term debt financing? Assuming that long-term interest rates are about 9%, would the use of long-term debt as a means of financing future growth be desirable from the viewpoint of common shareholders?

c Write a brief memorandum on the "quality" of the company's earnings. As a basis for this memorandum, review trends in the comparative income statements and in the major product lines shown in note 7.

d Write a statement for your newsletter in which you recommend that your clients take one of the following actions with respect to Canada Packers' common stock:

BUY (Your most positive recommendation; you think the market price of the stock will go up.)

SELL (Your most negative recommendation; you feel that the stock is overpriced and will fall in value.)

HOLD (A relatively neutral position; you feel that the stock is priced at a fair value with good but not exceptional prospects.)

Explain the reasoning behind your recommendation.

In addition to the information developed in other parts of this problem, your recommendation should consider the following about the economic environment in late 1987:

(1) The stock market is in the midst of a rally after a very big drop.

(2) Interest rates are at a relatively low level.

e Look up the current price of Canada Packers' common stock in the financial pages of a newspaper. How did your recommendation work out?

7

MANAGERIAL ACCOUNTING: COST ACCOUNTING SYSTEMS

In the remaining chapters, we shift our emphasis from financial accounting to the field of managerial accounting. Managerial accounting serves the information needs of internal decision makers at all levels — from supervisors to chief executives. In the next three chapters, we will show how accounting systems can measure the performance of each department in a business and determine the per-unit cost of manufacturing a product or performing a service.

21 RESPONSIBILITY ACCOUNTING: DEPARTMENTS AND BRANCHES

22 ACCOUNTING FOR MANUFACTURING OPERATIONS

23 COST ACCOUNTING SYSTEMS

RESPONSIBILITY ACCOUNTING: DEPARTMENTS AND BRANCHES

CHAPTER PREVIEW

Chapter 21 is the first of six chapters emphasizing the specialized use of accounting information by managers. In the opening pages, managerial accounting is contrasted with financial accounting. The major objective of this chapter, however, is to explain how and why accounting information is developed for the individual parts of a business entity — namely, for each department within the company. The concept of a responsibility accounting system is explained and illustrated. We emphasize the importance of distinguishing between direct and indirect expenses, and of using appropriate methods to allocate expenses among departments. The decision of whether or not to discontinue an ''unprofitable'' department is used to illustrate many of the chapter's key concepts. The chapter concludes with a discussion of centralized and decentralized systems of accounting for business conducted at branch locations.

After studying this chapter you should be able to meet these Learning Objectives:

1 **Distinguish between the fields of managerial accounting and financial accounting.**

2 **Explain the need for departmental information and describe a responsibility accounting system.**

3 **Distinguish between direct and indirect expenses.**

4 **Allocate expenses among the departments of a business and discuss the appropriate bases for these allocations.**

5 **Prepare departmental income statements showing operating income and contribution to indirect expenses.**

6 **Determine whether it appears profitable to close a department.**

7 **Describe centralized and decentralized systems of accounting for a branch operation.**

1 Distinguish between the fields of managerial accounting and financial accounting.

INTRODUCTION TO MANAGERIAL ACCOUNTING

In preceding chapters we have emphasized the topic of financial accounting. The term *financial accounting* refers to the preparation and interpretation of accounting information describing the financial position and operating results of a business entity. Financial accounting serves as the basis for the preparation of both financial statements and income tax returns. Because financial statements are used by outsiders such as creditors, shareholders, and potential investors, the information in these statements is presented in conformity with *generally accepted accounting principles*. Although income tax rules differ somewhat from generally accepted accounting principles, there are many similarities between these two sets of reporting standards.

Beginning with this chapter, we shall shift our emphasis toward the field of managerial accounting. *Managerial accounting* involves the preparation and interpretation of accounting information designed to assist managers in planning and controlling the operations of the business. In short, managerial accounting information is used by *insiders* rather than outsiders. Since managerial accounting reports are used exclusively by management, the content of these reports is *not* governed by generally accepted accounting principles or by income tax rules. Rather, managerial accounting information is organized in whatever manner *best suits the needs of management.* One of the greatest challenges of managerial accounting is to organize accounting information in the manner most relevant to a particular business decision.

Both managerial and financial accounting reports use information that is accumulated by a central accounting system. This system collects various types of accounting information from all parts of the business. The basic features of managerial and financial accounting are summarized on page 877.

Overlap of managerial and financial accounting

Before we begin our discussion of managerial accounting concepts, it is important to recognize that managerial and financial accounting are *not* two entirely separate disciplines. Financial accounting information is widely used in many managerial decisions. For example, managers daily use information about sales, expenses, and income taxes in many business decisions. However, managers also require additional information, such as revenue and expense broken down by department or by product line. Thus, much managerial accounting information is actually financial accounting information, rearranged to suit a particular managerial purpose.

As you progress through the remaining chapters, you should encounter many familiar accounting terms and concepts. However, you will also encounter new terms and concepts, as well as new ways of interpreting familiar accounting information.

Departments: centres of managerial responsibility

Most businesses are organized into a number of separate departments, which perform different business functions. For example, an automobile dealership may have separate departments for new car sales, used car sales, and repair service. Th

ACCOUNTING SYSTEM

Identifies, measures, records, classifies, and summarizes accounting information used for both financial and managerial purposes.

MANAGERIAL ACCOUNTING

Purpose

To provide managers with information useful in planning and controlling business activities. Managerial accounting information is often tailored to assist in specific managerial decisions.

Types of Reports

Special reports to management. May resemble financial statements, but this is not a requirement. Many reports include estimates of future operating results.

Standards for Presentation

No specific rules; whatever method of presentation is most relevant to the decisions made by management.

Business Entity

Usually a subdivision of the company, such as a department, a branch, or a product line.

FINANCIAL ACCOUNTING

Purpose

To present the financial position, operating results, and changes in financial position for a business viewed as a whole. Also used in income tax returns.

Types of Reports

Financial statements, income tax returns, and reports to regulatory agencies. Reports emphasize the current accounting period.

Standards for Presentation

Generally accepted accounting principles, income tax regulations, and requirements of regulatory agencies.

Business Entity

Usually the entire company, viewed as a whole.

Users of the Information

Management. Managerial accounting information generally is not distributed to outsiders.

Users of the Information

Outsiders as well as managers. Outsiders include shareholders, creditors, prospective investors, regulatory agencies, labour unions, and the general public.

formation of departments enables company personnel to specialize in specific areas of business activity. Companies use many different names to describe their internal units, including departments, divisions, product lines, regions, stores, and branches. In our discussions, we generally use the term *department* to describe a specialized subunit of a business.

A manager is put in charge of each department. Top management holds the department manager responsible for the department's overall performance. Thus, a department may be viewed as an *area of responsibility* for a given manager, and sometimes is called a *responsibility centre*. At this stage of our discussion, we should point out that large departments often are further subdivided into smaller responsibility centres. Consider, for example, a retail store within a chain such as Zellers or Sears. A store is a responsibility centre under the control of the store manager. However, each store is further divided into many separate sales departments, such as appliances, shoes, and sporting goods. Each sales department is a responsibility centre under the control of a department manager. The managers of the sales departments report to, and are supervised by, the store manager.

Each department is assigned resources to enable it to carry out its functions. In addition, the department manager may draw upon the general resources and staff talent of the business for such services as accounting, legal advice, hiring, and maintenance. Departments that provide services to other departments, but that do not sell goods or services directly to customers, are called *service departments*.

The subdivision of a business into departments creates a need for internal information about the operating results of each department. Departmental information enables top management to answer such questions as: Is the level of costs incurred by the accounting department reasonable? Is store No. 6 operating profitably? Has the performance of the sporting goods department improved or weakened over the past year?

Departmental accounting information provides a basis for intelligent planning and control, as well as for evaluating the performance of departments and department managers. To serve these managerial needs, accountants must refine their measurement process. In addition to determining the revenue and expenses of the business as a whole, accountants face the challenge of measuring the revenue and expenses of each responsibility centre.

2 Explain the need for departmental information and describe a responsibility accounting system.

Cost centres and profit centres　The departments within a business may be organized either as cost centres or profit centres. A *cost centre* is a unit of the business that incurs expenses (or costs) but that does not directly generate revenue. Examples of cost centres include the service departments, such as accounting, personnel, maintenance, and security. A *profit centre,* on the other hand, is a department that not only incurs expenses, but also *generates revenue.* Examples of profit centres include a retail store, the sales departments in a retail store, a branch office of a bank, and the Chevrolet Division of General Motors.

The managers of cost centres are evaluated in terms of their departments' ability to provide adequate services within the budgeted level of costs and expenses. The managers of profit centres are evaluated in terms of their departments' ability to generate profits.

Uses of departmental information

The details of departmental revenue and expenses usually are not made available to the public, on the grounds that such information is too detailed to be useful to investors but would be of considerable aid to competitors.[1] Departmental accounting information is designed to serve the needs of internal management. For example, departmental information is useful to management in:

1 **Planning and allocating resources** Management wants to know how well various departments are performing in order to have a guide in planning future activities and in allocating resources to those areas that have the greatest profit potential. If one department is producing larger profits than another, this may indicate that greater effort should be made to expand and develop the activities of the more profitable department.

2 **Controlling operations** Departmental information throws a spotlight on problem areas within the business. When revenue lags or when costs become excessive, departmental information focusses management's attention upon the departments responsible for the poor performance.

3 **Evaluating performance** Top management's ability to evaluate the performance of specific departments and of department managers depends in large part upon an accounting system that can separately measure the operating results of each responsibility centre.

RESPONSIBILITY ACCOUNTING SYSTEMS

An accounting system designed to separately measure the performance of each responsibility centre within a business is termed a *responsibility accounting system.* Measuring performance along lines of managerial responsibility is an important managerial tool. A responsibility accounting system holds individual managers accountable for the performance of the business units *under their control.* In addition, such systems provide top management with information identifying the individuals responsible for both strong and weak performance throughout the organization.

The use of a responsibility accounting system involves three basic steps. First, *budgets* are prepared for each responsibility centre. These budgets serve as targets, against which the department's actual performance will be measured. All departmental managers should participate in the budgeting process. It is important that each manager understand in advance the level of performance expected of his or her department. Second, the accounting system *separately measures the performance of each responsibility centre.* Third, timely *performance reports* are prepared, comparing the actual revenue and expenses of each responsibility centre with the budgeted amounts. Frequent performance reports help department managers in keeping their departments' performance ''on target'' and also assist top management in evaluating the performance of department managers.

In the following sections of this chapter, we will emphasize the second step in the operation of a responsibility accounting system — measuring the performance of individual responsibility centres. Budgeting and performance reports will be discussed in Chapter 25.

---

[1] Both the *CICA Handbook* and the Canadian Business Corporations Act require publicly owned corporations to disclose in notes to their financial statements certain information about major *industry segments* of the business. The definition of an ''industry segment'' is much broader than that of a ''department.'' Segment reporting requirements are discussed in intermediate accounting courses.

Responsibility accounting: an illustration

A responsibility accounting system requires a sufficiently detailed chart of accounts *to measure separately the performance of each responsibility centre.* The recording of revenue and expenses should begin at the *lowest level* of managerial responsibility.

To illustrate, assume that PriceBusters, Inc., has both a manufacturing division and a retail sales division. The retail sales division consists of 20 stores. Each retail store has several sales departments, one of which sells major appliances (stoves, refrigerators, etc.). The following diagram shows in condensed form how the monthly performance of the sales departments, retail stores, and retail division is measured and reported in a responsibility accounting system.

WHICH RESPONSIBILITY CENTRES HAVE PROBLEMS?

Condensed View of a Responsibility Accounting System

RESPONSIBLE MANAGER	REVENUE AND EXPENSES UNDER MANAGER'S CONTROL	ACTUAL	BUDGET
Manager of Appliance Dept. →	Sales (Appliance Dept.)	$ 410,000	$ 400,000
	Expenses applicable to the department	315,000	320,000
	Profit (Appliance Dept.)	$ 95,000	$ 80,000
	Profit (Appliance Dept.)	$ 95,000	$ 80,000
	Profit (other depts.)	460,000	500,000
	Expenses not controllable by department managers	(290,000)	(280,000)
Store Manager →	Profit (Store no. 1)	$ 265,000	$ 300,000
	Profit (Store no. 1)	$ 265,000	$ 300,000
	Profit (other stores)	4,600,000	4,500,000
	Expenses not controllable by store managers	(2,600,000)	(2,650,000)
Vice-President, Retail Sales Division →	Profit (Retail Division)	$2,265,000	$2,150,000

Assigning revenue and expenses to responsibility centres   Notice that sales and expenses are recorded separately for each sales department — the lowest level of managerial responsibility.[2] This enables both the department managers and the store manager to evaluate the performance of specific sales departments.

The next level of managerial responsibility is the store. The store manager is responsible not only for the performance of all the departments within the store, but also for certain "storewide" expenses that are *not under the control of the sales*

---

[2] It is possible to extend the concept of a responsibility accounting system to an even lower level of responsibility, such as recording separately the sales of each salesperson within the department. In addition, sales data may be accumulated separately for each type of product. This type of detailed recording is easily done in computer-based accounting systems. In such cases, departmental sales may be determined by adding the sales recorded for each salesperson in the department or for each type of product sold by the department.

department managers. Examples of expenses controlled by the store manager, but not by the sales department managers, include store security, utilities, and janitorial service.

The final level of managerial responsibility shown in our diagram is the entire retail sales division. Notice that the vice-president of this division is charged with certain "division" expenses that are not controllable by the individual store managers. Such expenses might include national advertising and the operation of national *service departments* for accounting, legal services, and site acquisition.

In summary, revenue and expense should be assigned to the department *which has control* over that revenue or expense. This practice holds each department accountable for the revenue that it generates and the costs that it incurs.

The sales department of a large manufacturing company used to request many "Rush" orders from the production department. To fill these rush orders, the production department had to work overtime, which caused the production department to incur labour costs well in excess of budgeted amounts. The company's controller modified the responsibility accounting system to charge the sales department with the extra labour cost of processing rush orders. After this change was made, the sales department made a greater effort to give the production department adequate notice of all sales orders. As a result, the number of costly "Rush" orders was substantially reduced.

Using a responsibility accounting system   Notice how our diagram on page 880 allows us to evaluate quickly the performance of individual responsibility centres. The appliance department in store No. 1 did well, exceeding its budgeted level of sales and keeping departmental expenses below the budgeted amounts. Store No. 1, however, fell $35,000 short of its budgeted profit objective. Part of this problem is attributable to "store-wide" expenses running $10,000 in excess of the budgeted amount. These expenses are under the direct control of the store manager. The remainder of the problem stems from various sales departments that failed to meet their profit objectives. By reviewing the detailed performance report of each department, the store manager will be able to identify the departments that are not performing up to expectation. The store manager will then work with the managers of these departments to see that appropriate corrective action is taken.

Despite the poor profit performance of store No. 1, the retail sales division of PriceBusters had a good month. Total store profits were in excess of the budgeted amounts, and "division" expenses were held below the budgeted amounts. However, the vice-president is now aware of the problem at store No. 1 and will watch that store carefully to see that performance improves.

Nonfinancial objectives and information

Profitability over the long run is an important objective of almost any business enterprise. In addition, many firms specify nonfinancial objectives that they consider important to their basic goals. Thus, a responsibility accounting system also may gather much nonfinancial information about each responsibility centre.

 Among the factors used by McDonald's Restaurants to evaluate a restaurant manager is the manager's performance on the company's QSC standards. "QSC" stands for "quality, service, and cleanliness." Each restaurant manager periodically is rated on these standards by a member of McDonald's supervisory staff. Among the many items listed on McDonald's QSC rating forms are:

Quality: Temperature, appearance, quantity, and taste of food servings.

Service: Appearance and general conduct of employees; use of proper procedures in greeting customers.

Cleanliness: Cleanliness in all areas in the kitchen, front counter, tables, and restrooms. Appearance of building exterior and parking lot.

Collecting information on departmental revenue and expenses

Two basic approaches may be used in developing departmental information:

1 **Maintain separate departmental accounts for various types of revenue and expense** This method is easily adapted for accounts such as sales, purchases, and inventories. For example, a business having three departments would use a separate sales account, a separate purchases account, and a separate inventory account for each department.

2 **Maintain only one general ledger account for each type of revenue and expense and allocate the total amount among the various departments at the end of the accounting period** When this approach is used, the total amount of the revenue or expense is allocated among the departments on a work sheet at the end of the accounting period rather than in the ledger accounts. For example, rent expense might be recorded in a single general ledger account and then allocated among the departments. A departmental expense allocation work sheet is illustrated on page 885.

Many companies use a combination of these methods. For example, separate departmental accounts may be used to record revenue and to determine the cost of goods sold. The same company, however, may record each type of operating expense in a single ledger account and allocate the total among the departments at the end of the period.

Computer-based systems

Departmental information regarding sales and the cost of goods sold is easily obtained when electronic cash registers are in use. The registers now in use in large stores are connected to the store's computer. When a code number identifying the merchandise is entered into the register, the computer will display the proper sales price, record the transaction in the departmental sales accounts, and update the accounts receivable subsidiary ledger for sales on account. In addition, the computer can transfer the cost of the merchandise from the departmental inventory account to the departmental cost of goods sold account. Daily, weekly, or monthly summaries of departmental sales and gross profit are printed by the computer for use by management.

Manual systems

Departmental information about sales and the cost of goods sold also may be accumulated in a manual system. To illustrate, assume that Day Corporation maintains in its general ledger separate departmental sales accounts. As a convenient means of accumulating departmental revenue data, special columns may be added to the various journals. For example, Day Corporation's sales journal for a typical month might appear as follows:

Sales Journal

DATE	INVOICE NO.	ACCOUNT DEBITED	LP	ACCOUNTS RECEIVABLE DR	SALES	
					DEPT. A CR	DEPT. B CR
19__						
Aug. 1	4100	Abar Co.	✓	1,700	1,700	
	4101	Tilden Industries	✓	2,180	1,470	710
31		Totals		165,100	102,600	62,500
				(5)	(200)	(300)

The amounts debited to customers' accounts are entered in the Accounts Receivable column and are posted daily to the accounts receivable subsidiary ledger. The total of this column ($165,100) is posted to the Accounts Receivable controlling account at the end of each month. Also, the totals of the departmental sales columns are posted to the departmental sales accounts at each month-end.

In addition to departmental sales accounts, Day Corporation must also maintain separate departmental accounts for sales returns and allowances and for sales discounts. The net sales of each department can then be determined directly from the balances of these accounts.

Departmental cost of goods sold We will assume that Day Corporation uses the periodic inventory system and keeps separate departmental accounts for each element of cost of goods sold.[3] Inventories, purchases, and purchase returns are readily identified by department. Purchase discounts and transportation-in must also be classified by department to determine the cost of goods sold by each department. This classification may be made at the time of each transaction, or the total purchase discounts and total transportation-in may be allocated to individual departments at the end of the accounting period. The cost of goods sold by departments for the current year is shown in the income statement illustrated in the following section.

---

[3] When a perpetual inventory system is in use, separate Inventory and Cost of Goods Sold accounts are maintained for each department.

Income statement showing departmental gross profit

Following is an income statement departmentalized only through the gross profit on sales:

DAY CORPORATION
Departmental Income Statement
For the Year Ended December 31, 19___

	TOTAL	DEPT. A	DEPT. B
Sales	$2,500,000	$1,600,000	$ 900,000
Less: Sales returns and allowances ...	(25,000)	(11,500)	(13,500)
Sales discounts	(40,000)	(30,000)	(10,000)
Net sales	$2,435,000	$1,558,500	$ 876,500
Cost of goods sold:			
Beginning inventory	$ 350,000	$ 140,000	$ 210,000
Purchases	1,800,000	1,026,000	774,000
Transportation-in	85,000	24,000	61,000
Purchase returns	(50,000)	(28,500)	(21,500)
Purchase discounts	(30,500)	(15,000)	(15,500)
Cost of goods available for sale	$2,154,500	$1,146,500	$1,008,000
Less: Ending Inventory	450,000	180,000	270,000
Cost of goods sold	$1,704,500	$ 966,500	$ 738,000
Gross profit on sales	$ 730,500	$ 592,000	$ 138,500
Operating expenses (details omitted) ..	627,500		
Income from operations	$ 103,000		
Income taxes	33,000		
Net income	$ 70,000		

It is evident that Department A earns a far larger gross profit than Department B. By studying the reasons for this difference, management may be led to make changes in buying policies, selling prices, or the personnel of Department B in an effort to improve its performance. Whether Department A contributes more than B to the net income of the business, however, depends on the amount of operating expenses attributable to each department.

Only departments organized as profit centres earn revenue and have a cost of goods sold. Therefore, a departmental income statement usually has separate departmental columns *only for departments organized as profit centres*. The costs and expenses of departments organized as *cost centres* are included among the operating expenses of the business. As departmental income statements are intended only for use by management, earnings per share figures generally are omitted.

Allocating operating expenses to departments

3 Distinguish between direct and indirect expenses.

Many companies allocate their operating expenses among the various departments thus making it possible to prepare an income statement showing departmental operating income. Two steps are generally involved in allocating operating expenses to departments: First, identify the expenses that are considered *direct* expenses of certain departments, and second, identify the expenses that are considered *indirect* departmental expenses and allocate these to the respective departments on some basis that will recognize the benefits received by each department.

Direct expenses are those that may be *clearly identified by department,* in the sense that if the department did not exist, *the expense would not be incurred.* For example, the cost of advertising a particular product is a direct expense of the department in which that product is sold. *Indirect expenses* are incurred *for the benefit of the business as a whole;* they cannot be identified readily with the activities of a given department. Indirect expenses would, for the most part, continue even though a particular department were discontinued. The cost of advertising the name and location of the business, rather than particular products, is an example of an indirect expense.

4 Allocate expenses among the departments of a business and discuss the appropriate bases for these allocations.

Some direct expenses may be charged to separate departmental expense accounts at the time they are incurred. Other expenses, even though they are direct in nature, may more conveniently be charged to a single ledger account and allocated to departments at the end of the accounting period.

Indirect expenses, by their very nature, can be assigned to departments only by a process of *allocation.* For example, the salary of the president of the company is an expense not directly related to the activities of any particular department. If the president's salary is to be divided among the departments, some method of allocation is necessary to charge each department with the approximate cost of the benefits it received.

Operating expense may be allocated to departments through the use of a *departmental expense allocation sheet* similar to the following illustration for Day Corporation:

DAY CORPORATION
Departmental Expense Allocation Sheet
For the Year Ended December 31, 19___

	TOTAL OPERATING EXPENSES	DEPARTMENT A	DEPARTMENT B
Direct expenses:			
Sales salaries expense	$135,000	$ 84,500	$ 50,500
Advertising expense	40,000	25,000	15,000
Buying expense	109,000	70,000	39,000
Delivery expense	10,000	–0–	10,000
Administration expense	28,500	15,500	13,000
Total direct expenses	$322,500	$195,000	$127,500
Indirect expenses:			
Advertising expense	$ 50,000	$ 31,250	$ 18,750
Buying expense	25,000	14,250	10,750
Delivery expense	50,000	15,000	35,000
Administrative expense	100,000	64,000	36,000
Occupancy expense	80,000	48,000	32,000
Total indirect expenses	$305,000	$172,500	$132,500
Total operating expenses (direct and indirect)	$627,500	$367,500	$260,000

In order to keep this example relatively short, we have grouped Day Corporation's operating expenses into broad, functional categories. For example, building expense includes all costs associated with occupancy of the building, including depreciation, property taxes, utilities, and maintenance. Delivery expense includes the depreciation on the delivery trucks, wages of the drivers, gasoline, and all other costs relating to shipping merchandise to customers. The allocation of operating expenses shown in Day Corporation's expense allocation sheet is explained in the following sections:

1 **Sales salaries expense** Day Corporation's salespeople work *exclusively* in either Department A or Department B. Thus, sales salaries is an example of a *direct expense* that can be clearly identified with specific departments. The company's payroll records indicate that sales salaries expense is $84,500 for Department A and $50,500 for Department B.

2 **Advertising expense** Day Corporation advertises primarily through newspapers, with occasional spot advertisements on radio and television. *Direct* advertising expense amounts to $40,000 and represents the cost of newspaper space and time purchased to advertise specific products identified with each department. *Indirect* advertising expense amounts to $50,000 and includes the cost of administering the advertising program, plus advertising applicable to the business as a whole.

Day Corporation follows the policy of allocating indirect advertising expense to the departments in proportion to the direct advertising expense incurred by the departments. This computation is shown as follows:

	DIRECT ADVERTISING EXPENSE	PERCENTAGE OF TOTAL	INDIRECT ADVERTISING EXPENSE	TOTAL DIRECT AND INDIRECT
Department A	$25,000	62.5[a]	$31,250[c]	$56,250
Department B	15,000	37.5[b]	18,750[d]	33,750
Total	$40,000	100.0	$50,000	$90,000

[a]$25,000 ÷ $40,000 = 62.5%   [c]$50,000 × 62.5% = $31,250
[b]$15,000 ÷ $40,000 = 37.5%   [d]$50,000 × 37.5% = $18,750

3 **Buying expense** This expense includes the salaries of the company's buyers and all of their travel expenses in purchasing merchandise for the company. However, buying expense does *not* include the cost of merchandise purchased.

Buying expenses that can be associated directly with specific departments amount to $109,000 and are allocated as follows: Department A, $70,000; Department B, $39,000. Indirect buying expense, such as the cost of a trip on which a buyer made purchases for both departments, are allocated on the basis of total departmental purchases. As shown in the departmental income statement on page 884, purchases amount to $1,026,000 for Department A and $774,000 for Department B, for a total of $1,800,000. The allocation of indirect buying expense on the basis of departmental purchases is shown below:

Department A ($1,026,000/$1,800,000 × $25,000)	$14,250
Department B ($774,000/$1,800,000 × $25,000)	10,750
Total	$25,000

4 Delivery expense Department B shipped certain merchandise by common carriers at a cost of $10,000, a direct expense of this department. The $50,000 balance of the cost of maintaining a delivery service applies to both departments. A study covering several months of typical operation showed that on the average 70% of all delivery requests originated in Department B; therefore 30% ($15,000) of the indirect delivery expense is charged to Department A, 70% ($35,000) is charged to Department B.

5 Administrative expense Two direct expenses were included in the administrative expense category; the remainder were indirect:

	TOTAL	DEPARTMENT A	DEPARTMENT B
Direct administrative expense:			
Uncollectible accounts expense	$ 18,500	$11,500	$ 7,000
Insurance on inventories	10,000	4,000	6,000
Total direct expenses	$ 28,500	$15,500	$13,000
Indirect administrative expense (allocated on basis of gross sales)	100,000	64,000	36,000
Total administrative expense	$128,500	$79,500	$49,000

The division of the $18,500 uncollectible accounts expense is made on the basis of an analysis of accounts charged off during the period. Insurance expense of $10,000 on inventories is charged to the departments on the basis of the average inventory in each department ($160,000 and $240,000, respectively), or a 40:60 ratio. (The beginning and ending inventory for each department appears in the departmental income statement illustrated on page 884. Average inventory is found by adding the beginning and ending inventory figures and dividing this total by 2).

Indirect administrative expenses, such as the salaries of office workers and of the company president, is allocated on the basis of gross sales, as follows:

Department A, $1,600,000/$2,500,000 × $100,000 .... $ 64,000
Department B, $900,000/$2,500,000 × $100,000 36,000
   Total $100,000

6 Occupancy expense This expense includes all costs relating to occupancy of the building, including depreciation, property taxes, and maintenance. These costs would continue even if one of the two departments were closed. Therefore, Day Corporation's occupancy costs are viewed as *indirect* expenses to the departments.

Day Corporation allocates the building expense on the basis of square metres occupied by each department, 60% by Department A and 40% by Department B. Thus $48,000 (60% of $80,000) was allocated to Department A and $32,000 (40% of $80,000) was allocated to Department B. If the value of the floor space varies (as, for example, between the first floor and the second floor) then the allocation should be made on the basis of the *relative value* of the space rather than square metres.

5 Prepare departmental income statements showing operating income and contribution to indirect expenses.

NOTICE THAT
DEPARTMENT B
SHOWS A NET LOSS

Departmental operating income

The expense allocation sheet for Day Corporation allows us to prepare an income statement showing the operating income earned by each profit centre. In the following income statement, the amount of operating expense charged to each department is determined by combining both the direct and indirect expenses shown in the expense allocation sheet. For example, the $56,250 in advertising expense charged to Department A consists of $25,000 in direct advertising expense and $31,250 in indirect advertising.

DAY CORPORATION
Departmental Income Statement
For the Year Ended December 31, 19___

	TOTAL	DEPARTMENT A	DEPARTMENT B
Net sales	$2,435,000	$1,558,500	$ 876,500
Cost of goods sold	1,704,500	966,500	738,000
Gross profit on sales	$ 730,500	$ 592,000	$ 138,500
Operating expenses (from departmental expense allocation sheet on page 885):			
Sales salaries expense	$ 135,000	$ 84,500	50,500
Advertising expense	90,000	56,250	33,750
Buying expense	134,000	84,250	49,750
Delivery expense	60,000	15,000	45,000
Administrative expense	128,500	79,500	49,000
Occupancy expense	80,000	48,000	32,000
Total operating expenses	$ 627,500	$ 367,500	$ 260,000
Income (or loss) from operations	$ 103,000	$ 224,500	$(121,500)
Income taxes	33,000		
Net income (or loss)	70,000		

We have carried the departmental operating results only through income from operations (or operating income). Income taxes expense is based upon the total taxable income of the entire business, not upon the earnings of individual departments.

Departmental contribution to indirect expenses

Some accountants argue that departmental operating income is not the most appropriate basis for evaluating departmental performance. They point out that the indirect expenses charged against a department generally are *beyond the control* of the departmental manager. In fact, many indirect expenses would continue at current levels even if a particular department were eliminated entirely.

Critics of the departmental income approach view indirect expenses as *expenses of the entire organization*, not as expenses of individual departments. This viewpoint leads to an alternative format for a departmental income statement that shows each department's *contribution to the indirect expenses of the business*. A department's contribution to indirect expenses (also called contribution to overhead) is the amount by which departmental revenue exceeds direct costs and expenses. Following is a departmental income statement for Day Corporation showing each department's contribution to indirect expenses.

NOTICE THAT
DEPARTMENT B
CONTRIBUTES TO
INDIRECT EXPENSES

DAY CORPORATION
Departmental Income Statement Showing Contribution to Indirect Expenses
For the Year Ended December 31, 19___

	TOTAL	DEPARTMENT A	DEPARTMENT B
Net sales	$2,435,000	$1,558,500	$876,500
Cost of goods sold	1,704,500	966,500	738,000
Gross profit on sales	$ 730,500	$ 592,000	$138,500
Direct departmental expenses (see page 885)			
Sales salaries expense	$ 135,000	$ 84,500	$ 50,500
Advertising expense	40,000	25,000	15,000
Buying expense	109,000	70,000	39,000
Delivery expense	10,000		10,000
Administrative expense	28,500	15,500	13,000
Total direct expenses	$ 322,500	$ 195,000	$127,500
Contribution to indirect expenses	$ 408,000	$ 397,000	$ 11,000
Indirect expenses (see page 885)			
Advertising expense	$ 50,000		
Buying expense	25,000		
Delivery expense	50,000		
Administrative expense	100,000		
Occupancy expense	80,000		
Total indirect expenses	$ 305,000		
Income from operations	$ 103,000		
Income taxes	33,000		
Net income	$ 70,000		

When is a department "unprofitable"?

6   Determine whether it appears profitable to close a department.

To illustrate the usefulness of an income statement showing contributions to indirect expenses, let us consider the question of whether Day Corporation could increase its operating income by closing Department B. If we look only at the income statement on page 888, we see that Department B incurred an operating loss of $121,500 for the current year. In seeing this large loss, our first reaction might be that income from operations will rise substantially if Department B is eliminated. This conclusion, however, could be very much in error, because it ignores the nature of indirect expenses.

In the determination of departmental operating income, *all* operating expenses are allocated between the two departments. But just because an expense is allocated to a department *does not mean that the expense will disappear* if the department is eliminated. Most *direct* expenses can be eliminated; however, many indirect expenses continue at their present levels even after a department is closed. For example, consider the $32,000 of indirect building expense allocated to Department B. Building expense includes such costs as depreciation, property taxes, and utilities. Most of these expenses will continue whether Department B is closed or not. If Department B is closed, these expenses will merely have to be allocated to Department A.

The income statement showing departmental contributions to indirect expenses (page 889) sheds more light on the profitability of Department B. This income statement shows that Department B contributes $11,000 toward the indirect expenses of Day Corporation. If Department B is closed, this contribution will be lost. Thus, closing Department B will *reduce* Day Corporation's operating income *unless management is also able to reduce the company's indirect expenses by at least $11,000.*

Elimination of a department when indirect expenses do not change   Assume that closing Department B will eliminate all of the direct expenses charged to that department, but *none* of the indirect expenses. The expected operating income of Day Corporation after the elimination of Department B may be computed as follows:

Contribution to indirect expenses (from Department A only)	$397,000
Less: Indirect expenses (unchanged)	305,000
Income from operations	$ 92,000

If no indirect expenses can be eliminated, we should expect the elimination of Department B to *decrease* Day Corporation's operating income from the current level of $103,000 to $92,000. The amount of this decrease, $11,000, is equal to the contribution of Department B to indirect expenses. This contribution will be lost, of course, if the department is closed.

Elimination of a department when indirect expenses can be reduced   The assumption that indirect expenses will not change may be realistic when the department being closed is very small, such as the key shop or the candy counter in a large department store. Usually, however, closing a department does enable management to eliminate *some* of the indirect expenses formerly charged to the department. For example, some of the indirect delivery expenses charged to Department B, such as gasoline and truck maintenance, should be eliminated if the department is closed.

As an illustration, let us now assume that careful analysis indicates that closing Department B will eliminate all of the direct expenses and $16,000 of the indirect expenses currently being charged to that department. The expected effect upon the operating income of Day Corporation may be determined as follows:

Increases in operating income:	
Reduction in direct expenses of Department B	$ 127,500
Reduction in indirect expenses allocated to Department B	16,000
Total expected increases in operating income	$ 143,500
Decreases in operating income:	
Elimination of gross profit generated by Department B	(138,500)
Net increase in operating income expected from closing	
Department B	$ 5,000

Notice that in this situation, it appears profitable to close Department B. Let us repeat our main point: the elimination of Department B will only increase operating income if management is able to eliminate indirect expenses *in excess of the department's contribution to indirect expenses.* In the preceding illustration, the reduction in indirect expenses ($16,000) *did* exceed the department's contribution to indirect expenses ($11,000) by $5,000.

Of course, management should consider many other factors in deciding whether to close a department. For example:

1 What is the trend of Department B's performance? Is it improving or getting worse?

2 What effect would closing Department B have upon the sales of Department A?

3 What alternative use can be made of the facilities now used by Department B? Can Department A be expanded? A new, profitable department opened? Or the facilities rented to another business?

4 What would be the effect of closing Department B upon employee morale?

Such considerations will be discussed further in Chapter 26.

ACCOUNTING SYSTEMS FOR BRANCH OPERATIONS

Merchandising companies often do business in more than one location by opening *branches.* As a business grows it may open branches in order to market its products over a larger territory and thus increase its earnings. A branch typically is located some distance from the *home office* and generally carries a stock of merchandise, sells the merchandise, makes collection on receivables, and pays some of its operating expenses. A branch is not a separate legal entity; it is simply a subdivision of the business organization. From an accounting standpoint, a branch is a clearly identifiable *profit centre* and offers an opportunity to implement the principles of responsibility accounting discussed earlier in this chapter.

An accounting system for a branch should generate information needed to measure the profitability of the branch and to ensure strong control over branch assets. Management needs information to answer questions such as: Is the branch earning a satisfactory rate of return on its assets? Should the branch be expanded or closed? How much of a bonus should the branch manager receive? How much merchandise does the branch have in stock? Branch accounting systems are either *centralized* in the home office or *decentralized* at the branches.

Centralized accounting systems

7 Describe centralized and decentralized systems of accounting for a branch operation.

In a *centralized* accounting system, most accounting records for branch operations are maintained at the home office. Separate records are maintained of the assets, liabilities, revenue, and expenses of each branch. In this way, the financial position and operating results of each branch can be readily determined. A centralized accounting system is especially appropriate when customers of the business often conduct business through different branches. For example, banks with branch locations generally need centralized accounting systems.

Often transactions are recorded in the centralized accounting records through computer terminals located at the branches. However, a centralized accounting system also may be operated on a manual basis. In this case, business documents (sales slips, deposit slips, invoices, etc.) are sent from the branch to the home office. These documents are then processed and recorded by accounting personnel in the home office.

In a centralized system, each branch usually is provided with a small *working fund*, similar to a petty cash fund. This fund is used by the branch to pay for small items of expense and to make necessary cash disbursements to customers. Major expenditures are made through the home office. Cash received by the branch usually is deposited directly into a bank account controlled by the home office.

Decentralized accounting systems

As an alternative to the centralized system, a branch may maintain its own accounting records. In such *decentralized* accounting systems, the accounting department of the branch usually will prepare monthly financial statements and forward them to the home office. These statements are then combined with the statements of the other branches and of the home office to prepare financial statements for the entire organization.

Although decentralized accounting records are *maintained* at the branch, the entire accounting system (including accounting policies, internal controls, and business documents) usually is *designed* by the home office. Decentralized systems are most frequently used when each branch operates *somewhat independently* of the home office and the other branches. Examples include the branch locations of chains of motels, restaurants, and retail stores.

Branch operations: an illustration   In order to illustrate the basic features of a decentralized branch accounting system, assume that on March 1, Pat's Skis & Boots opens a branch in Banff, Alberta. The company rents a fully equipped store and transfers cash of $40,000 and store supplies of $1,500 to the branch. The entries in the accounts of the Banff Branch and the home office to record this transfer, along with other *branch* transactions during March, are summarized on the facing page.

Only transactions (1), (4) and (8) are recorded in the home office accounting records, because these three transactions involve both the branch and the home office and thus require the use of the *reciprocal* accounts as shown below:

Branch Accounting Records		Home Office Accounting Records	
HOME OFFICE		**BANFF BRANCH**	
20,000	41,500 ← Assets sent to branch → 41,500		20,000
	300 ← Expense allocated to branch → 300		
	Remittance of cash to home office		

These accounts are called *reciprocal accounts* because they are used to record the *same transactions* from two opposite points of view. Note that the credit balance in

SUMMARY OF TRANSACTIONS FOR MARCH

Transaction	BRANCH ACCOUNTING RECORDS			HOME OFFICE ACCOUNTING RECORDS		
(1) Home office opened Banff Branch and transferred cash and store supplies to the branch.	Cash	40,000		Banff Branch	41,500	
	Store Supplies	1,500		Cash		40,000
	Home Office		41,500	Store Supplies		1,500
(2) Merchandise purchased by branch. Branch uses a perpetual inventory system. *	Inventory	70,000		No entry		
	Accounts Payable		70,000			
(3) Expenses incurred by branch.	Selling Expense	10,000		No entry		
	General Expense	7,700				
	Cash		13,200			
	Accounts Payable		4,000			
	Store Supplies		500			
(4) General expense incurred by home office allocated to branch.	General Expense	300		Banff Branch	300	
	Home Office		300	General Expense		300
(5) Sales made by branch.	Cash	12,000		No entry		
	Accounts Receivable	68,000				
	Sales		80,000			
(6) Collections by branch on accounts receivable.	Cash	50,000		No entry		
	Accounts receivable		50,000			
(7) Payments by branch to merchandise creditors.	Accounts Payable	55,000		No entry		
	Cash		55,000			
(8) Branch remits cash to home office at end of month.	Home Office	20,000		Cash	20,000	
	Cash		20,000	Banff Branch		20,000
(9) To record the cost of goods sold by branch during the month.	Cost of Goods Sold	48,000		No entry		
	Inventory		48,000			

*See Chapter 9 for a description of a perpetual inventory system.

the Home Office account, $21,800, is equal to the debit balance in the Banff Branch account, 21,800.

Branch records   The *Home Office account* in the branch accounting records may be viewed as a "proprietorship" account, which shows the net investment in the branch made by the home office. It is credited for assets transferred to the branch and for expenses allocated to the branch by the home office; it is debited when cash or other assets are remitted to the home office by the branch. At the end of the accounting period when the branch closes its accounts, the branch income or loss is closed into the Home Office account. Branch net income is debited to the Income Summary account and credited to the Home Office account; a loss reported by the branch would be debited to the Home Office account and credited to Income Summary.

Home office records   In the accounting records of the home office, the *Banff Branch account* is viewed as an asset representing the net investment in the branch. This account is debited when assets are transferred to the branch or when expenses incurred at the home office are allocated to the branch; it is credited when cash or other assets are received from the branch. Income reported by the branch is debited to the Banff Branch account and credited to Income — Banff Branch; branch losses would be debited to Loss — Banff Branch and credited to the Banff Branch account.

Statements for the ranch   After the transactions illustrated on page 893 are recorded and summarized, the accountant for the Banff Branch submits the following statements to the home office:

<table>
<tr><td colspan="3" align="center">BANFF BRANCH
Income Statement
For the Month Ended March 31, 19___</td><td colspan="2" align="center">BANFF BRANCH
Balance Sheet
March 31, 19___</td></tr>
<tr><td>Sales ....</td><td></td><td>$80,000</td><td>Cash ....</td><td>$13,800</td></tr>
<tr><td>Cost of goods sold ....</td><td></td><td>48,000</td><td>Accounts receivable ....</td><td>18,000</td></tr>
<tr><td>Gross profit on sales ....</td><td></td><td>$32,000</td><td>Inventory ....</td><td>22,000</td></tr>
<tr><td>Less: Selling</td><td></td><td></td><td>Store supplies ....</td><td>1,000</td></tr>
<tr><td>expense ..</td><td>$10,000</td><td></td><td>Total ....</td><td>$54,800</td></tr>
<tr><td>General</td><td></td><td></td><td>Accounts payable ....</td><td>$19,000</td></tr>
<tr><td>expense ..</td><td>8,000</td><td>18,000</td><td>Home office ($21,800 +</td><td></td></tr>
<tr><td>Net income ....</td><td></td><td>$14,000</td><td> net income of $14,000) ....</td><td>35,800</td></tr>
<tr><td></td><td></td><td></td><td>Total ....</td><td>$54,800</td></tr>
</table>

Working papers for combined statements for home office and branch   When the accountants for the home office receive the branch staements for March, they can prepare *combined statements* through the use of working papers similar to those in the illustration at the top of page 895. The branch figures are taken from the statements submitted by the branch, and the home office figures are assumed.

The figures in the Combined column are used to prepare the income statement and the balance sheet for Pat's Skis & Boots. Because there is nothing unusual about these statements, they will not be illustrated.

PAT'S SKIS & BOOTS
Working Papers for Combined Statements
For Month Ended March 31, 19___

| | ADJUSTED TRIAL BALANCES | | ELIMINATIONS | | |
	HOME OFFICE	BRANCH	DEBIT	CREDIT	COMBINED
Debit balances:					
Cash	24,200	13,800			38,000
Accounts receivable	53,000	18,000			71,000
Inventory	78,000	22,000			100,000
Store supplies	3,000	1,000			4,000
Land	110,000				110,000
Buildings and equipment	230,000				230,000
Banff Branch	21,800			(a) 21,800	
Cost of goods sold	150,000	48,000			198,000
Selling expense	21,000	10,000			31,000
General expense	17,000	8,000			25,000
Interest expense	2,000				2,000
Total debits	710,000	120,800			809,000
Credit balances:					
Notes payable	170,000				170,000
Accounts payable	56,000	19,000			75,000
Accrued liabilities	6,000				6,000
Home office		21,800	(a) 21,800		
Pat Morris, capital	225,000				225,000
Sales	250,000	80,000			330,000
Purchase discounts	3,000				3,000
Total credits	710,000	120,800	21,800	21,800	809,000

Explanation of elimination:
(a) Reciprocal accounts maintained by the home office and branch are eliminated. These accounts have no significance since the home office and the branch are a single entity. This elimination entry is made only on the working papers; it is not recorded in the accounting records of either the home office or the branch.

Closing entries   At the end of the accounting period, the revenue and expense accounts at the branch are closed and the income of $14,000 is transferred to the Home Office account. The home office records the branch income in the Income — Banff Branch account; the balance in this account is then closed to Income Summary when the home office accounts are closed. These entries are illustrated at the top of page 896.

Branch Accounting Records		
Sales	80,000	
Cost of Goods Sold		48,000
Selling Expense		10,000
General Expense		8,000
Income Summary		14,000
To close revenue and expense accounts.		
Income Summary	14,000	
Home Office		14,000
To transfer balance in Income Summary account to Home Office account.		

Home Office Accounting Records		
Banff Branch	14,000	
Income — Banff Branch		14,000
To record branch income.		
Income — Banff Branch	14,000	
Income Summary		14,000
To close branch income to Income Summary.		

Interdepartmental and interbranch pricing policies

In order to obtain a better measure of departmental or branch profit performance, some companies bill the merchandise transferred to departments or branches at prices above cost. Of course, a company does not "make a profit" by simply transferring merchandise to one of its departments or branches; a profit on such transfers can only be realized when the merchandise is sold to customers. When end-of-period statements for the company as a whole are prepared, the *unrealized profits* on intracompany transfers of merchandise are eliminated.

END-OF-CHAPTER REVIEW

SUMMARY OF CHAPTER LEARNING OBJECTIVES

1 Distinguish between the fields of managerial accounting and financial accounting.

Managerial accounting refers to the preparation and interpretation of accounting information designed to assist managers in planning and controlling the operations of a business. Financial accounting refers to the preparation and interpretation of information designed primarily to describe the financial position and operating results of a business to outsiders, such as shareholders, creditors, and the public.

2 Explain the need for departmental information and describe a responsibility accounting system.

Departmental information measures the performance of individual departments. This information is useful to management in planning, allocating resources, controlling business operations, and evaluating the performance of departmental managers. A responsibility accounting system separately measures the performance of each area of business activity for which a given manager is responsible.

3 Distinguish between direct and indirect expenses.

Direct expenses are incurred for the benefit of a particular department only. Indirect expenses are incurred for the benefit of the business as a whole and cannot be readily identified with the activities of a given department.

4 Allocate expenses among the departments of a business and discuss the appropriate bases for these allocations.

Direct expenses are charged to departments on a basis of direct benefit. Indirect expenses can be assigned to departments only by a process of allocation. The basis used to allocate an indirect expense should coincide as closely as possible with benefit derived by each department.

5 Prepare departmental income statements showing operating income and contribution to indirect expenses.

In an income statement showing departmental operating income, net sales, the cost of goods sold, and all operating expenses are allocated to departments. If the statement shows departmental contribution to indirect expenses, the indirect operating expenses are viewed as expenses of the business and are not allocated to departments. Examples of these two forms of departmental income statements appear on pages 888 and 889.

6 Determine whether it appears profitable to close a department.

As a starting point, we may say that it is not profitable to close a department unless indirect expenses can be reduced by at least as much as the department's contribution to indirect expenses. In addition, management should consider such factors as the effect closing the department may have upon the sales of other departments, employee morale, and the alternative use that may be made of the facilities.

7 Describe centralized and decentralized systems of accounting for a branch operation.

In a centralized system, most accounting records are maintained in the home office. In a decentralized system, each branch maintains its own accounting records. These records are then combined with those in the home office to develop financial statements for the entire business organization.

KEY TERMS INTRODUCED OR EMPHASIZED IN CHAPTER 21

Centralized accounting system A system in which the branches of a company send information on daily transactions to the home office, which maintains the accounting records for the entire company.

Contribution to indirect expenses (overhead) The amount by which a department's revenue exceeds the direct costs and expenses allocated to the department.

Cost centre A unit of a business that incurs expenses or costs but does not directly generate revenue; for example, the personnel department.

Decentralized accounting system A system in which each branch of a company maintains its own complete set of accounting records.

Departmental income statement An income statement showing the revenue, expenses, and net income of the business and of each profit centre.

Direct expense An expense that can be associated directly with the activities of a specific department, in the sense that if the department did not exist, the expense would not be incurred.

Indirect expense Expenses incurred for the benefit of several departments or for the business as a whole. By their nature, indirect expenses cannot be directly associated with individual departments; they are, however, often allocated to departments on a subjective basis.

Profit centre A unit of a business that produces revenue that can be identified with the unit; for example, the meat department of a supermarket.

Reciprocal accounts Offsetting accounts maintained by the home office and a branch. The home office maintains an asset account (with a debit balance) summarizing its investment in the branch. The branch maintains a Home Office account (with a credit balance) similar to an owner's capital account. Both of these accounts are eliminated (offset against each other) when combined financial statements are prepared for the home office and its branches.

Responsibility accounting A system designed to measure performance of each segment of a business for which a manager is responsible.

Responsibility centre An area of business activity over which a particular manager is in charge and for which he or she is held responsible.

ASSIGNMENT MATERIAL

REVIEW QUESTIONS

1 Briefly distinguish between managerial and financial accounting information in terms of (a) the intended users of the information, and (b) the purpose of the information.

2 Are financial accounting and managerial accounting two entirely separate disciplines? Explain.

3 Is managerial accounting information developed in conformity with generally accepted accounting principles or some other set of prescribed standards? Explain.

4 What is a *responsibility accounting system?*

5 Distinguish between a *cost centre* and a *profit centre.*

6 What are some uses that management may make of departmental accounting information?

7 The College Bookstore has employed Kay Barton as its new manager. In the past the income statement of the bookstore has shown only total revenue and operating expenses. The new manager wants to introduce procedures for measuring gross profits for each of three departmental areas: texbooks, general books, and other merchandise. Explain what changes in the accounting system will be required and what benefits Barton may expect to gain from the departmental information.

8 Explain how a responsibility accounting system can assist management in controlling the costs of a large business organization.

9 Briefly describe two approaches that may be used to develop departmental information from revenue and expenses recorded in the general ledger.

10 Explain how electronic cash registers that are connected to a central computer may simplify the task of preparing departmental gross profit information in a large department store.

11 Give three examples of items representing indirect expenses to the departments within a large department store, such as Zellers or Sears. For each example of an indirect expense, indicate a reasonable basis for use in allocating this expense among the various departments.

12 Explain the distinction between direct expenses and indirect expenses as these terms are used in relation to expense allocation among departments.

13 Atwood Hardware has three operating departments. In its departmental income statement, building occupancy expenses are allocated among departments on the basis of sales. Explain why you do or do not agree that this procedure will produce useful information for management.

14 In a retail department store with 21 departments, which can be determined with greater objectivity — the operating income of a department or the operating income of the entire store? Explain the reasoning behind your answer.

15 Criticize the following statement: "In our business we maximize total income from operations by closing any department that incurs an operating loss, no matter how small that loss might be."

16 Porterfield's is a retail store with nine sales departments. For the current year, the departmental income statement shows that Department No. 4 incurred an operating loss of $34,000. Would you expect Porterfield's total operating income to have been $34,000 greater if Department No. 4 had been closed at the beginning of the year? Explain.

17 What is meant by the term *contribution to indirect expenses?* Explain why management may find information about the contribution to indirect expenses of each department more useful than departmental net income figures.

18 Differentiate between a *centralized* and a *decentralized* accounting system for branch operations.

19 Describe the nature of the Home Office account that appears in the records of the branch and the Branch account that appears in the records of the home office. Why are these two accounts referred to as *reciprocal* accounts?

20 What is the reason for preparing working papers for combined statements of the home office and branch?

EXERCISES

**Exercise 21-1
Accounting
terminology**

Listed below are nine technical accounting terms introduced or emphasized in this chapter:

Responsibility
  accounting system
	Decentralized
	  accounting system
		Centralized
		  accounting system

Direct expense	Profit centre	Operating income
Indirect expense	Cost centre	Contribution to indirect expenses

Each of the following statements may (or may not) describe one of these technical terms. For each statement, indicate the accounting term described, or answer "None" if the statement does not correctly describe any of the terms.

a An accounting system in which branch locations use computer terminals of record transactions executed by the branch in an accounting system maintained by the home office.

b A segment of a business that provides support services to other departments, but does not directly generate revenue.

c The gross profit of a department, less the direct expenses charged to the department.

d An expense that benefits the business as a whole, rather than benefiting a particular department.

e An accounting system that separately measures and reports the amounts of revenue and expense under the control of individual managers.

f An expense that probably would be eliminated if a particular department were closed.

g A measure of departmental performance after indirect expenses have been allocated to the departments.

Exercise 21-2
Allocation of indirect expense

Confidence Insurance Company sells health, homeowners', and automobile insurance. The direct advertising expense incurred during the current year for each of these types of insurance is shown as follows:

Health insurance	$200,000
Homeowners' insurance	250,000
Automobile insurance	50,000
Total direct advertising	$500,000

In addition, the company incurred indirect advertising expense of $220,000.

Prepare a schedule showing the allocation of indirect advertising expense *in proportion to the direct advertising expense* incurred for each type of insurance. Also show the total advertising expense charged to each type of insurance.

Exercise 21-3
Allocation of indirect expenses: reasonable or not?

Community Music School allocates indirect operating expenses to its Vocal Music Department and Instrumental Music Department on the basis of the total tuition revenue in each department. Last year, the following allocation was made:

	TOTAL	VOCAL MUSIC DEPARTMENT	INSTRUMENTAL MUSIC DEPARTMENT
Tuition revenue	$70,000	$40,000	$30,000
Indirect operating expenses	19,600	11,200	8,400

Assume that in the current year the number of students enrolled in each department remains the same. Moreover, the tuition revenue in the Vocal Music Department remains at $40,000. However, as a result of a one-third increase in the tuition per instrumental-music student, tuition revenue in the Instrumental Music Department increases to $40,000. If indirect operating expenses for the current year remain at $19,600, what portion of these expenses will be allocated to each department? Is this result logical? Explain.

Exercise 21-4
Profitability of a service

The president of Niagara Bus Tours is considering the elimination of the company's winery tour. Last year revenue for this tour amounted to $6,200, but operating expenses were $11,300, resulting in an operating loss of $5,100. The operating expense consisted of $9,200 in direct tour expenses and $2,100 in indirect expenses. Discontinuing the tour will eliminate all the direct expenses but none of the indirect expenses. Moreover, eliminating the winery tour is not expected to have any impact on the company's other bus tours. What would be the effect on the company's operating income if the winery tour were discontinued?

Exercise 21-5
Profitability of a sales department

The president of Dunbar Limited wants to eliminate Department B "because it's losing money." The operating results for the latest year appear at the top of page 901.

What advice would you give the president, assuming that the indirect operating expenses of $324,000 (40% of $810,000) would remain unchanged if Department B is eliminated?

	TOTAL	DEPT. A	DEPT. B
Sales	$900,000	$600,000	$ 300,000
Operating expenses (40% of which are indirect expenses and remain constant at all levels of sales)	810,000	360,000	450,000
Operating income	$ 90,000	$240,000	$(150,000)

Exercise 21-6
Accounting for branch operations

Quality Home Furnishings Company operates a branch store in Baltimore. Given below are the reciprocal accounts as of December 31:

BALTIMORE BRANCH RECORDS
Home office

DATE	TRANSACTION	DR	CR	BALANCE
Dec. 1	Balance			101,700
Dec. 15	Cash remitted to home office	29,000		72,700
Dec. 22	Equipment received from home office		19,000	91,700
Dec. 29	Cash remitted to home office	1,700		90,000
Dec. 31	Net income		11,300	101,300

HOME OFFICE RECORDS
Baltimore Branch

DATE	TRANSACTION	DR	CR	BALANCE
Dec. 1	Balance			101,700
Dec. 17	Cash received from branch		29,000	72,700
Dec. 19	Equipment sent to branch	19,000		91,700
Dec. 30	Merchandise shipped to branch	4,200		95,900

Prepare the entries required in (**a**) the Baltimore branch records and (**b**) the home office records to bring each set of accounts up to date as of December 31. (Assume use of a perpetual inventory system.)

Exercise 21-7
Branch and home office reciprocal accounts

Refer to Exercise 21-6:

a What is the *correct* balance in each reciprocal account as of December 31?

b Show the elimination entry that would be required on the working papers on December 31 in order to prepare combined statements for the home office and the Baltimore branch. (Show this entry in general journal form even though it would be made only on the working papers.)

PROBLEMS

Problem 21A-1
Evaluating the profitability of a department

Group A

Computer World sells personal computers, computer software, and video game cartridges. Overall the business is quite profitable, but the departmental income statement for the current year shows the following results for the Video Games Department:

Gross profit on sales		$ 32,500
Direct expenses	$27,200	
Indirect expenses	19,600	46,800
Operating income (loss)		$(14,300)

The store manager is considering eliminating the Video Games Department. Closing this department would eliminate all the direct costs and $3,200 of the indirect costs currently being charged to the department.

Instructions

a Compute the expected effect of closing the Video Games Department upon the annual operating income of Computer World.

b Briefly identify other factors that you believe the manager should consider in deciding whether to eliminate this department.

Problem 21A-2
Basis for allocating
an expense

Surfside Hotel classifies all the costs associated with the occupancy and maintenance of the hotel building as occupancy expense. During the current year, this occupancy expense amounted to $102,300. The hotel includes 11,000 square metres of usable space, 9,900 of which are used by the Rooms Department and 1,100 of which are used by the Food and Beverage Department.

In allocating the occupancy expense between the two departments, the hotel's accountant computed the annual cost per square metre at $9.30 ($102,300 ÷ 11,000 square metres). Therefore, the Rooms Department was charged with $92,070 of occupancy expense (9,900 square metres × $9.30), and the Food and Beverage Department was charged with $10,230 (1,100 square metres × $9.30).

Meg Johnston, the manager of the Food and Beverage Department, feels that this allocation is unreasonable. She has pointed out that the Surfside Hotel has some guest rooms and one private dining room that have ocean views. Other guest rooms, the front desk area, the main dining room, and the kitchen do not have ocean views. The distribution of space in the hotel is as follows:

	SQUARE METRES OF SPACE WITH OCEAN VIEW	SQUARE METRES OF SPACE WITHOUT OCEAN VIEW
Rooms Department	5,400	4,500
Food and Beverage Department	100	1,000
Total	5,500	5,500

Based on information received from the local association of realtors, Johnston estimates that the space in the hotel with an ocean view is twice as valuable as the space without a view. She based this conclusion on the following rental prices for commercial building space in the area:

	AVERAGE ANNUAL RENTAL PRICE PER SQUARE METRE FOR SPACE IN COMMERCIAL BUILDINGS
Space with ocean view	16.00
Space without ocean view	8.00

On the basis of this information, Johnston argues that the charges to her department should be on the basis of the ***relative value*** of the space occupied by each department.

Instructions **a** Comment on the validity of Johnston's position.

b On the basis of Johnston's analysis, how much annual occupancy expense should be charged to each department? Show computations.

Problem 21A-3
Evaluating the
profitability of a
department

Solana Sand & Gravel Co. is a sole proprietorship with four operating departments. At the end of the current year the controller has computed departmental results in three ways, showing income by departments, the departmental contribution to indirect expenses, and the gross profit on sales for each department, as follows:

	TOTAL	DEPT. ONE	DEPT. TWO	DEPT. THREE	DEPT. FOUR
Departmental net sales	$800,000	$320,000	$180,000	$220,000	$80,000
Departmental net income	21,200	68,300	(4,000)	(13,100)	(30,000)
Departmental contribution to indirect expenses	88,800	98,000	14,000	(2,200)	(21,000)
Departmental gross profit on sales	184,000	128,000	36,000	22,000	(2,000)
Gross profit as a percentage of sales	23%	40%	20%	10%	(2½%)

Note: Parentheses indicate a loss.

Instructions **a** On the basis of the above information, prepare a departmental income statement showing for each department gross profit, contribution to indirect expenses, and net income. It will be necessary to compute the following amounts: cost of goods sold, direct expenses, and indirect expenses. (Since the company is a sole proprietorship, there are no income taxes to be considered.)

b What conclusions would you reach about the operations of Departments One, Two, Three, and Four on the basis of the statement prepared in **a**? Should any of these departments be discontinued? Explain your reasoning.

Problem 21A-4
Allocating indirect
expenses; departmental
income statements

Turner & Cole, a retailing partnership, maintains departmental accounts for net sales and cost of goods sold. Operating expenses are allocated between the two departments of the business at the end of each quarter. The operating results for the quarter ended March 31 are summarized below:

	TOTAL	DEPT. A	DEPT. B
Net sales	$900,000	$540,000	$360,000
Cost of goods sold	540,000	297,000	243,000
Gross profit	$360,000	$243,000	$117,000
Operating expenses (not yet allocated)	289,600		
Net income*	$ 70,400		

*No income taxes expense appears because the business is organized as a partnership.

An analysis of the operating expenses indicates that the following amounts in each class of expense are directly chargeable to the departments. (The allocation basis of the ***indirect*** portion of each class of expense is shown in brackets.)

	DIRECT EXPENSES		INDIRECT EXPENSES
	DEPT. A	DEPT. B	
Administrative expense (on basis of direct administrative expense)	$28,000	$19,000	$56,400
Advertising expense (on basis of net sales)	11,000	7,000	18,000
Buying expense (on basis of cost of goods sold) ...	21,900	16,500	21,600
Occupancy expense (equally)	4,500	9,000	11,500
Selling expense (on basis of net sales)	25,400	11,600	28,200

Instructions

a Prepare a departmental expense allocation sheet for the quarter ended March 31, 19___. Use the form illustrated in this chapter.

b Prepare a departmental income statement showing contribution to indirect expenses. Use the form illustrated in this chapter.

c Prepare a condensed income statement for the quarter, assuming that both direct and indirect expenses are allocated to the departments. Show a single figure for operating expenses. Based on the income statements prepared in parts **b** and **c,** do you believe that Department B should be eliminated? Explain.

Problem 21A-5
Accounting for
branch operations

Auto Tune, Inc., operates several sales and service outlets (branches) throughout the metropolitan area of a large city. A decentralized accounting system is used by each branch. At the end of October, the following reciprocal accounts appear in the accounting records of the Central branch and the home office:

BRANCH RECORDS		HOME OFFICE RECORDS	
Home Office (credit balance)	$19,640	Central Branch (debit balance)	$18,810

The reason for the discrepancy in the amounts shown in the two accounts is that the branch net income for October, $1,950, and a cash deposit made by the branch to the account of the home office, $1,120, have not been recorded by the home office. Both the branch and the home office use a perpetual inventory system.

During November, the following transactions affected the two accounts:

Nov. 6 Home office shipped merchandise to branch, $7,530.

Nov. 12 Branch transferred $5,140 from its bank account to the bank account of the home office.

Nov. 19 Branch returned shop supplies costing $830 to the home office. Shop supplies are carried in the Shop Supplies account in both sets of accounts.

Nov. 30 Home office notified branch that operating expenses of $1,300 that had been recorded in the accounts of the home office in the Operating Expense account were chargeable to the Central branch.

Nov. 30 The Income Summary account in the accounts of the branch showed a debit balance of $680 at the end of November.

Instructions

a Record the transactions listed above in the accounts of the Central branch. (Explanations may be omitted for all journal entries in this problem.)

b Record the two transactions relating to the month of October and all transactions for November in the accounts of the home office.

c Determine the balances in the Home Office account and the Central Branch account at the end of November.

Group B

Problem 21B-1
Evaluating the profitability of a department

Mercury Air is a small commuter airline that flies several routes in Ontario and Quebec. Several years ago, Mercury Air added a local rent-a-car business at Pearson International Airport. All customer transactions for the rent-a-car business are handled by the personnel at the airline's ticket counter in the airport. John Davis, the president of Mercury Air, has been disappointed with the performance of the rental car business. He just received the following report showing the current year's operating results for the rent-a-car business:

Rental revenue		$178,400
Direct expenses	$134,400	
Indirect expenses	48,600	183,000
Operating income (loss)		$ (4,600)

Davis is considering the elimination of the rent-a-car business. Discontinuing the operation would eliminate all the direct costs and $19,200 of the indirect costs currently being charged to the rent-a-car business.

Instructions

a Compute the expected effect of closing down the rent-a-car business on the annual operating income of Mercury Air.

b Briefly identify other factors that you believe Davis should consider in deciding whether to eliminate the rent-a-car operation.

Problem 21B-2
Basis for allocating an expense

Parkway Mall operates a retail business in a two-story building. Each floor has usable space of 2,000 square metres. The occupancy cost for the building per year averages $276,000. There are a number of separate departments in the store, and departmental income statements are prepared each year. Department No. 4 occupies 200 square metres of space on the first floor. Department No. 8 occupies 350 square metres of space on the second floor.

In allocating occupancy cost among the various departments, the accountant has determined that the average annual occupancy cost per square metre is 69 ($276,000 ÷ 4,000); therefore Department No. 4 has been charged with $13,800 of occupancy cost and Department No. 8 with $24,150, on the basis of space occupied.

Ellen Ward, the manager of Department No. 8, feels that this allocation is unreasonable. She has made a study of rental prices being charged for similar property in the area and finds the following:

**Average Yearly Rental
per Square Metre**

First-floor space	$100
Second-floor space	50

On the basis of this evidence, Ward argues that the charge to her department should be made on the ***relative value*** of space of each floor.

Instructions **a** Comment on the validity of Ward's position.

b On the basis of Ward's findings, how much occupancy cost per year should be charged to Department No. 4 and to Department No. 8? Show computations.

Problem 21B-3
Contribution margin
and product-line
income statements

Joe Miller owns an apple orchard, from which he harvested and sold during the current year 200,000 kilograms of apples. The price received varied in accordance with the grade of apple, as shown in the following table:

	KILOGRAMS	PRICE PER KILOGRAM	RECEIPTS
Superior	50,000	$0.352	$17,600
Medium	110,000	0.20	22,000
Cooking	40,000	0.11	4,400
	200,000		$44,000

Miller's expenses for the year, as taken from his accounting records, are shown below:

	DOLLARS	PER KILOGRAM
Indirect expenses:		
Growing expenses	$16,000	$.08
Harvesting expenses	12,000	.06
Direct expenses:		
Packing and Shipping:		
Superior (50,000 kilograms)	$2,500	.05
Medium (110,000 kilograms)	3,300	.03
Cooking (40,000 kilograms)	1,600 7,400	.04
Total expenses	$35,400	

Miller asked a friend, who was taking an accounting course at a nearby university, to determine his income from each grade of apple. The friend prepared the following schedule:

	TOTAL	SUPERIOR	MEDIUM	COOKING
Sales	$44,000	$17,600	$22,000	$ 4,400
Expenses:				
Growing*	$16,000	$ 4,000	$ 8,800	$ 3,200
Harvesting*	12,000	3,000	6,600	2,400
Packing and shipping	7,400	2,500	3,300	1,600
Total expenses	$35,400	$ 9,500	$18,700	$ 7,200
Net income (or loss)	$ 8,600	$ 8,100	$ 3,300	$(2,800)

*Allocated to each grade on the basis of the number of kilograms sold.

After studying this statement, Miller remarked to a neighbour, ''I made a lot of money on my superiors and a little bit on the mediums, but I should have dumped the cooking apples in the river; they cost me more than I got for them!''

Instructions **a** Prepare an income statement in a form that will show the contribution of each grade of apple to overhead (indirect expenses of growing and harvesting). Packing and shipping expenses should be considered direct expenses. Use separate columns for Total, Superior, Medium, and Cooking.

b Do you agree with Miller's remark to his neighbour? Discuss. Comment on the conclusion to be drawn as to the contribution of the cooking apples.

c Prepare an income statement showing *net income* for each grade of apple by allocating growing and harvesting expenses on the basis of the *relative sales value* of each grade.

Problem 21B-4
Allocating indirect
expenses; evaluating
a department

The Computer Store is a partnership that sells home computing equipment, software, and video games. The business maintains departmental accounts for net sales and cost of goods sold for the Computer Department and the Games Department. Operating expenses are allocated between the two departments at the end of the year. The operating results for the year ended December 31, 19___ are summarized below:

	TOTAL	COMPUTER DEPT.	GAMES DEPT.
Net sales	$816,000	$510,000	$306,000
Cost of goods sold	460,000	276,000	184,000
Gross profit	$356,000	$234,000	$122,000
Operating expenses (not yet allocated)	317,640		
Net income*	$38,360		

*No income taxes expense appears because the business is organized as a partnership.

An analysis of the operating expenses indicates that the following amounts in each class of expense are directly chargeable to the departments. (The allocation basis of the *indirect* portion of each class of expense is shown in parentheses.)

	DIRECT EXPENSES		
	COMPUTER DEPT.	GAMES DEPT.	INDIRECT EXPENSES
Administrative expense (on basis of direct administrative expense)	$15,000	$ 4,000	$38,000
Advertising expense (on basis of net sales)	20,000	14,000	20,000
Buying expense (on basis of cost of goods sold) . .	18,000	18,800	22,400
Occupancy expense (equally)	1,400	1,500	61,000
Selling expense (on basis of net sales)	34,300	19,400	29,840

Instructions

a Prepare a departmental expense allocation sheet for the year. Use the format illustrated in this chapter. Below the Departmental Expense Allocation Sheet, show the calculations upon which the allocations are based.

b Prepare a departmental income statement showing contribution to indirect expenses. Use the form illustrated in this chapter.

c Prepare a condensed income statement, assuming that both direct and indirect expenses are allocated to the departments. Show a single figure for operating expenses. Based on the income statements prepared in parts **b** and **c,** do you believe that the Games Department should be eliminated? Explain.

Problem 21B-5
Accounting for
branch operations

For many years the Colonial Furniture Company has operated a store in Oxtongue Lake. Early this year the company decided to open a branch store in Springfield and to use a decentralized accounting system for the branch. Both the branch and the home office use a perpetual inventory system. During the month of February the transactions shown at the top of page 908 (given in summary form) were completed by the branch.

Feb. 1 The home office sent $10,000 cash to the branch to be used as a working fund and authorized the branch manager to sign a lease on a store.

Feb. 2 The branch manager paid store rent for February, $2,000 (store rent is an operating expense in branch records).

Feb. 3 Received merchandise from home office, $14,400.

Feb. 5 Purchased merchandise on credit from local factory, $13,600.

Feb. 12 Borrowed $6,000 from local bank and deposited in branch chequing account.

Feb. 28 Sales during February: cash, $8,400; credit, $24,200.

Feb. 28 Payments to merchandise creditors, $8,000.

Feb. 28 Collections on accounts receivable, $11,500.

Feb. 28 Paid operating expenses, $3,300.

Feb. 28 Sent cash of $9,000 to home office. Also sent to the home office inventory items costing $350; these items will become part of the inventory at the home office.

Feb. 28 Home office notified branch that operating expenses allocated to the branch for the month of February amounted to $840. This included advertising and other expenses paid by the home office. These expenses were originally recorded by the home office in the Operating Expense account.

Feb. 28 Cost of goods sold by the Springfield Branch during February amounted to $22,400.

Instructions **a** Record the foregoing transactions in journal entry form in the records of the branch. (Explanations may be omitted from all journal entries in this problem.) Also prepare closing entries. Compute the balance at February 28 in the Home Office account that appears in the accounts of the branch.

b Select the transactions which should be recorded in the records of the home office (including entry to record branch net income) and prepare entries to record them. Ignore closing entries. Compute the balance in the Springfield Branch account at February 28 that appears in the accounts of the home office.

BUSINESS DECISION CASES

Case 21-1
The perfect product:
low fat, low cost

Bloom Ridge Dairy prepares income statements that show the operating income of each of the company's major product lines — butter, ice cream, and milk. Depreciation on all plant assets is viewed as an indirect expense. Indirect expenses are allocated to the various product lines based upon the amount of butterfat included in the product. Butter and ice cream are the highest in butterfat. This practice developed because the sales value of dairy products traditionally has varied with the amount of butterfat in the product. Thus, allocating expenses by butterfat content gave results similar to those achieved by allocating indirect expenses on a basis of net sales.

Last year, however, the company added a new product line — dehydrated milk. The manufacture of dehydrated milk requires large amounts of expensive equipment, but dehydrated milk contains almost no butterfat. After reviewing recent income statements, the company president stated, "The profitability of our butter and ice cream lines has really fallen off. It's a good thing that we started manufacturing dehydrated milk when we did, because that has become our most profitable product. It looks to me as if we should cut back our production of butter and ice cream, and expand our production of dehydrated milk."

Instructions The manner in which Bloom Ridge Dairy's accounting department classifies and allocates expenses may be influencing the president's thinking. Identify any problems that you see in the company's allocation of depreciation expense and explain how these problems might cause the president to reach improper conclusions. Include in your answer recommendations for improving the company's allocation of depreciation expense.

Case 21-2
Closing a department: a more comprehensive analysis

Bay Marina, located in Halifax, Nova Scotia, is subdivided into three departments. These departments are listed along with a description of their operations:

Bay Rentals (rents small boats and berths on the marina's dock).
Mariner Shop (sells a variety of marine equipment on a retail basis).
Hungry Fisherman Snack Bar (sells sandwiches, soft drinks, and light snacks).

Fred Lee, the proprietor of the marina, is considering the advisability of eliminating the retail sales and snack bar operations in order to concentrate on the rental business. During the past year, the revenue and cost of goods sold for the three departments were as follows:

	TOTAL	BAY RENTALS	MARINER SHOP	HUNGRY FISHERMAN SNACK BAR
Revenue (net)	$342,000	$207,000	$89,000	$46,000
Cost of goods (service) sold	163,700	60,000	66,500	37,200

Lee has studied trade association publications summarizing the reports of other marina operators who have had similar decisions. They report that after dropping snack bar operations, marina rental revenue declined an average of 10%, and sales of marine equipment fell 8%. Reports from marina operators who discontinued equipment sales but continued to operate a snack bar indicate that rental revenue fell by an average of 3% and snack bar sales declined by 5%. If the marina discontinued its equipment sales operation, it could lease the surplus space in the marina's building for $2,500 per month to another business, which would use it as a storage facility.

At the present time Lee employs six employees. One employee earns $10,200 per year and runs the Hungry Fisherman Snack Bar. The other five employees, who earn a combined salary of $70,000, operate both the Bay Rentals office and the Mariner Shop. These five employees spend about 10% of their total time in the Mariner Shop. The snack bar employee spends about a quarter of his time assisting in the Mariner shop, since the snack bar has periods of slack business. If the snack bar employee were no longer available to help, Lee estimates that the sales revenue of the Mariner Shop would decline an additional 2% (of present sales revenue) as a result of inconvenience to customers.

The employees of the rental operations do not have time to take over the snack bar. However, Lee believes that he could replace the snack bar employee by hiring seasonal student help at a cost of $5,300 per year if the Mariner Shop were discontinued. He also believes that the effect on indirect operating expenses as a result of dropping either the equipment sales or snack bar operations would be negligible. Lee feels that five employees would still be necessary to run the Bay Rentals operation even if the Mariner Shop were discontinued.

Instructions **a** Determine the departmental contribution to indirect expenses during the past year.

b Prepare an analysis of the estimated change that might be expected to result in the firm's total operating income if Lee discontinued only the Hungry Fisherman Snack Bar. Prepare a similar analysis assuming discontinuance of only the Mariner Shop. What would be your advice to Lee?

CHAPTER

22

ACCOUNTING FOR MANUFACTURING OPERATIONS

CHAPTER PREVIEW

In this chapter we emphasize how the accounting requirements of a manufacturing company differ from those of a merchandising company. The basic cost elements of manufacturing a product are the costs of raw materials, direct labour, and factory overhead. By relating these costs to the volume of output, we introduce the concept of cost per unit of product. Other important concepts considered are the distinction between product costs and period costs, and the application of factory overhead rates. Finally, we illustrate a work sheet for a manufacturing company and the year-end entries to close the accounts.

After studying this chapter you should be able to meet these Learning Objectives:

1   Explain the differences in accounting for inventories in manufacturing companies and merchandising companies.

2   Describe the three basic types of manufacturing cost.

3   Distinguish between direct and indirect manufacturing costs.

4   Distinguish between product costs and period costs and explain how product costs are offset against revenue.

5   Prepare a schedule of cost of finished goods manufactured.

6   Explain how to determine the cost of work in process inventory and the cost of finished goods inventory.

7   Prepare closing entries for a manufacturing company.

Assume that Starr Products sells 100 personal computers to Eastern University for a total of $120,000. What is Starr's gross profit on this transaction? The answer, of course, depends upon the *cost* of these computers to Starr Products. If Starr *purchased* the computers, the cost appeared on the supplier's invoice and was recorded in Starr's accounting records by a debit to the Purchases account. But what if Starr *manufactured* the computers? In this chapter, we shall see how manufacturing companies measure the cost of the goods they produce, value their inventories, and determine their cost of goods sold.

1   Explain the differences in accounting for inventories in manufacturing companies and merchandising companies.

Comparison of merchandising and manufacturing concerns

Merchandising companies and manufacturers are similar in many respects. Both businesses earn their revenue by selling products. There is, however, one important difference. The merchandising concern *buys* its goods in a ready-to-sell condition. Thus, the merchant's cost of goods sold is based upon the *cost of purchasing* the merchandise. The manufacturer, on the other hand, *produces* the goods it sells. Therefore, its cost of goods sold is based upon *manufacturing costs*.

This basic difference may be seen by comparing the partial income statement of a merchandising company with that of a manufacturing company. (The treatment of selling expenses, general and administrative expenses, and income taxes would be the same in both income statements.)

APEX MERCHANDISING LIMITED
Partial Income Statement
For the Year Ended December 31, 19___

Sales		$1,300,000
Cost of goods sold:		
Beginning inventory of merchandise	$150,000	
Net purchases	800,000	
Cost of goods available for sale	$950,000	
Less: Ending inventory of merchandise	170,000	
Cost of goods sold		780,000
Gross profit on sales		$ 520,000

ALLIED MANUFACTURING CORPORATION
Partial Income Statement
For the Year Ended December 31, 19___

Sales		$1,300,000
Cost of goods sold:		
Beginning inventory of finished goods	$150,000	
Cost of finished goods manufactured (see supporting schedule)	800,000	
Cost of goods available for sale	$950,000	
Less: Ending inventory of finished goods	170,000	
Cost of goods sold		780,000
Gross profit on sales		$ 520,000

Notice that in Allied Manufacturing's income statement the "Cost of finished goods manufactured. . . . $800,000" replaces the "Net purchases" shown in the income statement of the merchandising company. The *cost of finished goods manufactured* represents all the the manufacturing costs incurred by Allied Manufacturing that are applicable to units of product completed during the year. Notice also that the reader of the income statement is referred to a supplementary schedule to see how the cost of finished goods manufactured was computed. This supplementary schedule, illustrated on page 919, will be discussed later in this chapter.

Before we describe how the cost of finished goods manufactured is computed, let us first consider the *types of costs* that a manufacturer is likely to incur in producing a finished product.

Manufacturing costs

2   Describe the three basic types of manufacturing cost.

A typical manufacturing firm buys raw materials and converts them into a finished product. The raw materials purchased by an aircraft manufacturer, for example, include sheet aluminum, steel, jet engines, and a variety of electronic instruments. The completed airplanes assembled from these components are the finished goods of an aircraft manufacturer. The terms *raw materials* and *finished goods* are defined from the viewpoint of each manufacturing firm. For example, electronic instruments are raw materials to an aircraft manufacturer, but they are finished goods to an electronics manufacturer.

An illustration of the various types of manufacturing costs incurred by a manufacturer appears on page 913. In converting raw materials into finished goods, a manufacturer incurs *direct labour* costs as well as many other costs of operating a factory, such as supervisors' salaries, depreciation on buildings and machinery, and electrical power.[1] All manufacturing costs other than raw materials and direct factory labour are called *factory overhead*. Thus, we have three basic types of manufacturing costs: (1) raw materials used, (2) direct labour, and (3) factory overhead.

Raw materials used   Parts and materials used in producing finished goods are called raw materials. Raw materials become a manufacturing cost when they are *used* rather than when they are purchased. Unused raw materials on hand at the end of the period should be listed in the balance sheet as an asset, entitled *raw material inventory.* The cost of raw materials used during the period is computed as follows:

COMPUTING THE COST
OF RAW MATERIALS USED

Raw materials used:	
Beginning raw materials inventory	$ 25,000
Purchases of raw materials	140,000
Transportation-in (raw materials)	5,000
Cost of raw materials available for use	$170,000
Less: Ending raw materials inventory	20,000
Cost of raw materials used	$150,000

Notice the similarities between the way that a manufacturing business computes the cost of raw materials used and the way that a merchandising company computes the cost of goods sold.

---

[1] Items entering into the computation of the cost of finished goods manufactured, such as raw materials used, direct labour, and factory overhead, are described as *costs* and not as *expenses.*

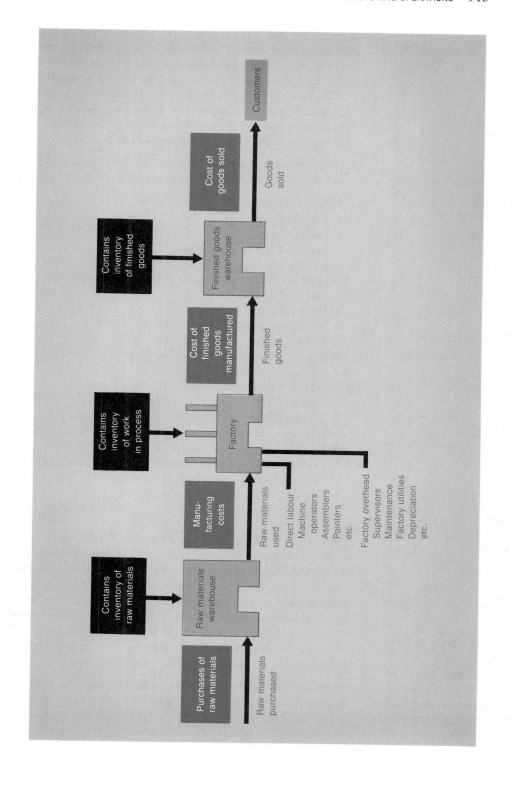

Direct labour cost   The second basic element of manufacturing costs is called *direct labour* and represents the wages paid to factory employees *who work directly on the products being manufactured.* Direct labour includes the costs of machine operators, assemblers, and others who work on the goods by hand or with tools.

Many factory employees *do not* work directly upon the goods being manufactured. Examples of these *indirect* workers include supervisors, timekeepers, janitors, and plant security guards. The wages and salaries of indirect workers are considered part of factory overhead rather than direct labour cost.

Factory overhead   Factory overhead includes all manufacturing costs other than the costs of raw materials and direct labour. Examples of factory overhead include:

1 **Indirect labour**
   a Supervision
   b Timekeeping
   c Janitorial and maintenance
   d Factory medical personnel
   e Plant security service
2 **Factory occupancy costs**
   a Depreciation of buildings
   b Insurance on buildings
   c Property taxes on land and buildings
   d Repairs and maintenance of buildings
   e Electricity, water, and other factory utilities
3 **Machinery and equipment costs**
   a Depreciation of machinery and equipment
   b Property taxes and insurance on machinery and equipment
   c Repairs and maintenance of machinery and equipment
   d Factory supplies and small tools used in the factory
4 **Cost of compliance with federal, provincial, and local regulations**
   a Meeting factory safety requirements
   b Disposal of hazardous waste materials
   c Control over factory emissions (clean air standards)

These are only examples; it is not possible to compile a complete list of all factory overhead costs. For this reason, factory overhead is defined as *all costs incurred in the manufacturing process other than raw materials and direct labour.*

Selling expenses, general and administrative expenses, and income taxes do not relate to the manufacturing process and are *not* included in factory overhead. Certain costs, such as insurance, property taxes, and salaries of executives, may be applicable in part to factory operations and in part to administrative and selling functions. In such cases these costs should be apportioned among factory overhead, general and administrative expense, and selling expense accounts.

3   Distinguish between direct and indirect manufacturing costs.

Direct and indirect manufacturing costs   Factory overhead costs *cannot be traced directly to specific units of product* as can the costs of raw materials and direct labour. In a factory manufacturing both dishwashers and washing machines, it is relatively easy to measure the costs of raw materials and direct labour applicable to each product. Factory overhead costs (such as property taxes, fire insurance, and plant security) relate to factory operations *as a whole,* rather than to specific products. For this reason, factory overhead is considered an *indirect* manufacturing cost, whereas raw materials and direct labour are regarded as *direct* manufacturing costs.

Product costs contrasted with period costs

4 Distinguish between product costs and period costs and explain how product costs are offset against revenue.

Why is it important to associate such costs as factory wages and repairs of factory equipment with the cost of finished goods manufactured? Why not treat these costs as expenses of the current period? The answer to these questions is that manufacturing costs are *product costs* rather than *period costs.*

Product costs are *not viewed as expenses;* rather, they are the cost of *creating inventory.* Thus, product costs are considered an asset until the related goods are sold, at which time they are deducted from revenue as the *cost of goods sold.* In theory, product costs include all manufacturing costs—this is, all costs relating to the manufacturing process.

Costs that are charged to expense in the period in which they are incurred are called *period costs.* Such costs are *not* related to the production and flow of manufactured goods but are deducted from revenue on the assumption that the associated benefits are received in the same period as the cost is incurred. Period costs include all general and administrative expenses, selling expenses, and income taxes expense. Some specific examples are the salaries of the treasurer and controller and their staffs, commissions to salespeople, and advertising.

The flows of period costs and product costs through the financial statements are illustrated as follows:

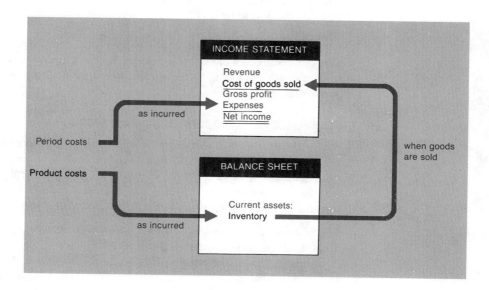

Depreciation on a raw materials warehouse is a product cost, because this cost relates to the manufacturing process. Depreciation on a finished goods warehouse, on the other hand, is a period cost because finished goods are goods that have been completed and are ready for sale.

The exact dividing line between product and period costs is not always clear. Traditionally, expenditures relating to the manufacturing function are considered product costs, and those relating to the selling and administrative functions are considered period costs. In some cases it is difficult to determine whether a particular cost relates to manufacturing or administrative functions. For example, the cost of maintaining a cost accounting department, or a personnel department, or a security service may be treated by some companies as factory overhead (product costs) and by other firms as administrative expense (period cost). These variations in accounting practice, however, stem from differences of interpretation rather than from theoretical distinctions.

Product costs and the matching concept: an illustration

To illustrate the relationship between product costs and the generation of revenue, consider a real estate developer who starts construction on a tract of 10 homes in 1989. During the year, the developer spends $90,000 on each house ($900,000 total) in materials, construction wages, and overhead. At the end of the year, all 10 houses are finished but none has yet been sold. How much of the $900,000 in construction costs should the developer recognize as expense in 1989?

The answer is *none*. These costs are not related to any revenue earned by the developer in 1989, but they are related to the revenue that will be earned in the period in which the houses are sold. Therefore, at the end of 1989, the $900,000 of product costs should appear in the developer's balance sheet as inventory. As each house is sold, $90,000 will be deducted from the sales revenue as the cost of goods sold. In this way, the developer's 1990 income statement will reflect properly both the revenue and the cost of each sale.

If any of the houses are still unsold at the end of 1990, their cost should remain in an Inventory account on the balance sheet. By this time, however, the developer may need to consider making an adjustment to reduce the carrying value of this slow moving inventory to a market value below cost.

Inventories for a manufacturing business

At any given moment, a manufacturer may have on hand three separate inventories: a stock of raw materials; partially completed products in various stages of manufacture; and finished goods awaiting sale. In place of the single inventory account found on the balance sheet of a retail or wholesale business, a manufacturing concern has three separate inventory accounts, all of which are current assets.

1 **Raw materials inventory** This account represents the unused portion of the raw materials on hand at the end of the year.
2 **Goods in process inventory** This inventory consists of the *partially completed* goods on hand in the factory at year-end. The cost of these partially manufactured goods is determined by *estimating* the costs of the raw materials, direct labour and factory overhead associated with these units.
3 **Finished goods inventory** This account shows the cost of finished goods on hand and awaiting sale to customers as of the end of the year. The cost of these finished

units is composed of the manufacturing costs (raw material, direct labour, and factory overhead) incurred in producing these goods.

Computing the cost of finished goods manufactured

In the partial income statement illustrated at the beginning, we saw that a manufacturing company uses the cost of finished goods manufactured in determining the cost of goods sold. Let us now see how a manufacturer would compute the cost of finished goods manufactured during the year.

Assume that Allied Manufacturing Corporation incurred the following manufacturing costs during 1989:

Raw materials used in production	$150,000
Direct labour	300,000
Factory overhead (detail omitted)	360,000
Total manufacturing costs	$810,000

In addition to the manufacturing costs incurred in the current period, the cost of finished goods manufactured is affected by any costs assigned to the *inventory of goods in process* at either the beginning or end of the period. To illustrate, we will now compute the cost of finished goods manufactured by Allied Manufacturing Corporation during the year under three alternative assumptions.

Case 1:   First, let us assume that Allied has no inventory of goods in process at either the beginning or the end of the year. In this case, all the manufacturing costs incurred are applicable to goods started and completed in the year. The cost of finished goods manufactured, therefore, is $810,000, the sum of the manufacturing costs incurred during the year.

Case 2:   Now assume that there was an inventory of goods in process of $30,000 at the beginning of the year, but no goods in process at the end of the year. This $30,000 beginning inventory of goods in process represents manufacturing costs incurred in 1988 relating to goods still in process at the end of that year. Since the manufacture of these goods was *completed* in 1989, this $30,000 is part of the cost of goods *finished* in 1989. Thus, the cost of finished goods manufactured during 1989 is $840,000 ($30,000 beginning inventory of goods in process, plus $810,000 manufacturing costs incurred in 1989).

Case 3:   Finally, assume that Allied begins the year with a $30,000 inventory of goods in process and ends the year with a $40,000 inventory of partially completed goods. The $40,000 ending inventory of goods in process represents the portion of 1989 manufacturing costs that are applicable to *partially* completed goods rather than to finished goods. In this case, the cost of *finished* goods manufactured during the year is computed as follows:

Goods in process inventory, beginning of year	$ 30,000
Total manufacturing costs incurred during year	810,000
Total cost of goods in process during year	$840,000
Less: Goods in process inventory, end of year	40,000
Cost of finished goods manufactured	$800,000

This third case is the normal situation; that is, most manufacturers have an inventory of partially completed goods at both the beginning and the end of each accounting period. Therefore, the cost of finished goods manufactured generally is computed as shown in the preceding illustration.

It is important to distinguish between the terms *cost of finished goods manufactured* and *total manufacturing costs.* Cost of finished goods manufactured means the cost of the units of finished product *completed* during the period. Total manufacturing costs, on the other hand, include the cost of raw materials used, direct labour, and factory overhead for the period, whether the units worked on have been completed or are still in process at the end of the period. As an extreme example, consider a shipyard engaged in the construction of an aircraft carrier. During the first year of work on the ship, the manufacturing costs are as follows:

COMPARE "TOTAL
MANUFACTURING COSTS"
WITH "COST OF FINISHED
GOODS MANUFACTURED"

Cost of raw materials used	$ 64,000,000
Direct labour	20,000,000
Factory overhead	40,000,000
Total manufacturing costs	$124,000,000
Less: Goods in process inventory, ending	124,000,000
Cost of finished goods manufactured	$ –0–

The cost of finished goods manufactured is zero in this illustration because no products (aircraft carriers) were *completed* during the year.

Schedule of cost of finished goods manufactured

5   Prepare a schedule of cost of finished goods manufactured.

Manufacturing companies often show their computation of the cost of finished goods manufactured in a supplementary schedule that accompanies the income statement. A Schedule of Cost of Finished Goods Manufactured for Allied Manufacturing Corporation is illustrated at the top of page 919. This schedule follows the same format as our computation in Case 3 (page 917) except that it is expanded to show the computation of the cost of raw materials used and the detail of factory overhead.

The income statement for Allied Manufacturing Corporation appears on page 919. Note that the final amount of $800,000 computed in the schedule of cost of finished goods manufactured is carried forward to this income statement and is used in determining the cost of goods sold. Also note that *no manufacturing costs are included in the operating expense section* of the income statement. The item "Cost of goods sold . . . $780,000" represents the manufacturing cost of the goods actually *sold* in 1989.

Valuation of inventories in a manufacturing business

6   Explain how to determine the cost of work in process inventory and the cost of finished goods inventory.

Under the periodic inventory system, a manufacturer determines the inventory quantities on the basis of a *physical count* of raw materials, goods in process, and finished goods at the end of each period. (The use of a perpetual inventory system in a manufacturing business is discussed in Chapter 23.) When the physical quantity of raw materials on hand has been established, the cost of the raw materials inventory is determined in the same manner as for an inventory of merchandise in a trading company. Cost is readily determinable by reference to purchase invoices.

ALLIED MANUFACTURING CORPORATION
Schedule of Cost of Finished Goods Manufactured
For the Year Ended December 31, 1989

Goods in process inventory, beginning of year		$ 30,000
Raw materials used:		
Beginning raw materials inventory	$ 25,000	
Purchases of raw materials (net)	140,000	
Transportation-in (raw materials)	5,000	
Cost of raw materials available for use	$170,000	
Less: Ending raw materials inventory	20,000	
Cost of raw materials used	$150,000	
Direct labour	300,000	
Factory overhead:		
Indirect labour	$145,000	
Occupancy costs	95,000	
Other factory overhead costs	120,000	
Total factory overhead	360,000	
Total manufacturing costs		810,000
Total cost of goods in process during the year		$840,000
Less: Goods in process inventory, end of year		40,000
Cost of finished goods manufactured		$800,000

ALLIED MANUFACTURING CORPORATION
Income Statement
For the Year Ended December 31, 1989

Sales		$1,300,000
Cost of goods sold:		
Beginning inventory of finished goods	$150,000	
Cost of finished goods manufactured		
(see supporting schedule)	800,000	
Cost of goods available for sale	$950,000	
Less: Ending inventory of finished goods	170,000	
Cost of goods sold		780,000
Gross profit on sales		$ 520,000
Operating expenses:		
Selling expenses	$135,000	
General and administrative expenses	265,000	
Total operating expenses		400,000
Income from operations		$ 120,000
Less: Interest expense		20,000
Income before income taxes		$ 100,000
Income taxes expenses		30,000
Net income		$ 70,000

Determining the cost of an inventory of goods in process and an inventory of finished goods is usually a more difficult process. Cost cannot be determined merely by pulling a purchase invoice out of the files. If a manufacturing plant produces only a single product, the *cost per unit* for the finished goods inventory can be computed by dividing the *cost of finished goods manufactured* by the *number of units produced.* For example, if the cost of finished goods manufactured were $100,000 in a given year, during which the factory turned out 1,000 identical units, the cost per unit would be $100.

Most factories, however, produce more than one product. In this case, the company's accounting records must be designed to show separately the raw materials and direct labour costs applicable to each product line. (Factory overhead is an indirect cost and generally cannot be identified with specific products.) The cost per unit of the goods in process at year-end can then be estimated by the following steps:

1 Estimate the per unit cost of the raw materials contained in the goods.
2 Add the estimated direct labour cost incurred per unit.
3 Add an appropriate amount of factory overhead cost per unit.

This same procedure of computing a total cost per unit by combining the three elements of manufacturing cost is followed in pricing the finished goods inventory.

The raw material cost included in a unit of goods in process or a unit of finished goods may be established by reference to the engineering specifications for the product. The cost of the direct labour applicable to each unit may be determined on the basis of time studies or by supervisors' estimates. Thus, both raw material costs and direct labour costs can be associated *directly* with units of product.

Overhead application rate As previously mentioned, factory overhead is an *indirect* manufacturing cost. It relates to factory operations viewed as a whole but cannot be traced to individual units of product. Therefore, the manufacturer must develop a method of *allocating an appropriate portion* of total factory overhead to the ending inventories of work in process and finished goods. One widely used method is to express total factory overhead as a *percentage* of total direct labour costs. This percentage is called the *overhead application rate.* The factory overhead cost per

NOTE THE THREE
COST ELEMENTS IN
ENDING INVENTORIES

ALLIED MANUFACTURING CORPORATION
Valuation of Ending Inventories
December 31, 1989

COMPONENTS OF UNIT COST

INVENTORY	DIRECT COSTS		FACTORY OVERHEAD (120% OF DIRECT LABOUR)	TOTAL UNIT COST	UNITS IN INVENTORY	TOTAL COST OF INVENTORY
	RAW MATERIALS	DIRECT LABOUR				
Goods in process:						
Product D-3 ..	$8	$10	$12	$30	900	$ 27,000
Product D-4 ..	2	5	6	13	1,000	13,000
Total						$ 40,000
Finished goods:						
Product D-3 ..	$10	$20	$24	$54	1,000	$ 54,000
Product D-4 ..	7	15	18	40	2,900	116,000
Total						$170,000

unit can then be estimated by multiplying the direct labour cost per unit by this overhead application rate. This technique assumes that the *same ratio* of factory overhead to direct labour is appropriate for all units of a particular product produced during the period.

For example, the schedule of cost of finished goods manufactured for Allied Manufacturing Corporation shows total factory overhead costs of $360,000 and direct labour of $300,000, indicating an overhead application rate of 120% ($360,000 ÷ $300,000). In other words, for every $1 of direct labour costs, the company incurred $1.20 of factory overhead. We would therefore estimate the factory overhead per unit to be equal to 120% of the direct labour cost per unit, as shown in the schedule at the bottom of page 920.

Additional ledger accounts needed by a manufacturing business

The accounting records of a manufacturer are likely to include more accounts than those of a merchandising or service business. Accounts relating to sales, selling expenses, administrative expenses, liabilities, and shareholders' equity are handled in the same manner by manufacturers as by other companies. However, manufacturing requires some additional asset accounts and a number of new accounts for recording manufacturing costs.

Inventory accounts and manufacturing cost accounts   As previously discussed, a manufacturing company uses three inventory accounts (raw materials, goods in process, and finished goods) in place of the single inventory account found in the balance sheet of a wholesale or retail business. In addition, the ledger of a manufacturing business must include accounts for recording each type of manufacturing cost. In recording factory overhead a separate account must be created for each type of overhead cost (Depreciation of Machinery, Repairs, Timekeeping, etc.). If there are a great many of these factory overhead accounts, it is convenient to transfer them to a subsidiary ledger that will be controlled by a general ledger account entitled Factory Overhead.

Plant and equipment accounts   Manufacturing companies typically own large amounts of plant and equipment, including factory buildings, warehouses, and many different kinds of manufacturing equipment. Because of this great variety of plant assets, most manufacturing companies maintain a subsidiary plant and equipment ledger as described in Chapter 10.

The Manufacturing Summary account   Perhaps the most distinctive account used by a manufacturing business is the Manufacturing Summary account. This account is used during the end-of-period closing procedures to bring together the various elements of manufacturing cost and to determine the cost of finished goods manufactured. The role of the Manufacturing Summary account in the closing process will be explained in detail after the following discussion of a manufacturing company's work sheet.

Work sheet for a manufacturing business

The work sheet for a merchandising business illustrated in Chapter 5 can be adapted for use in a manufacturing company merely by adding a pair of columns for the data

ALLIED MANUFACTURING CORPORATION
Work Sheet
For the Year Ended December 31, 1989

	ADJUSTED TRIAL BALANCE DR	ADJUSTED TRIAL BALANCE CR	MANUFACTURING DR	MANUFACTURING CR	INCOME STATEMENT DR	INCOME STATEMENT CR	BALANCE SHEET DR	BALANCE SHEET CR
Cash	62,000						62,000	
Accounts receivable (net)	190,000						190,000	
Inventories, beginning								
Raw materials	25,000		25,000					
Goods in process	30,000		30,000					
Finished goods	150,000				150,000			
Plant and equipment	535,000						535,000	
Accum. depr.: plant and equip.		175,000						175,000
Accounts payable		108,000						108,000
Accrued factory payroll		12,000						12,000
Income taxes payable		30,000						30,000
Note payable, 12%, due 1995		200,000						200,000
Capital stock		250,000						250,000
Retained earnings, beginning		172,000						172,000
Sales		1,300,000				1,300,000		
Purchases of raw materials	140,000		140,000					
Transportation-in (materials)	5,000		5,000					
Direct labour	300,000		300,000					
Indirect labour	145,000		145,000					
Occupancy costs	95,000		95,000					
Other factory overhead costs	120,000		120,000					
Selling expenses	135,000				135,000			
General and administrative expense	265,000				265,000			
Interest expense	20,000				20,000			
Income taxes expense	30,000				30,000			
	2,247,000	2,247,000						
Inventories, ending								
Raw materials				20,000			20,000	
Goods in process				40,000			40,000	
Finished goods						170,000	170,000	
Cost of finished goods manufactured				800,000	800,000			
			860,000	860,000	1,400,000	1,470,000		
Net income					70,000			70,000
					1,470,000	1,470,000	1,017,000	1,017,000

that will appear in the schedule of cost of finished goods manufactured. An illustrative work sheet for Allied Manufacturing Corporation is presented on the previous page. To emphasize the portions of this work sheet that are unique to a manufacturing business, we have omitted the columns containing the trail balance and adjustments and have begun the illustration with the Adjusted Trial Balance columns. Adjusting entries for a manufacturing business are similar to those previously described for a merchandising business.

Treatment of inventories in the work sheet   Since the Manufacturing columns are the distinctive feature of this work sheet, they require close study, especially the handling of the inventory accounts.

1 The beginning inventory of raw materials and the beginning inventory of goods in process have become part of the cost of finished goods manufactured and are, therefore, carried from the Adjusted Trial Balance debit column to the Manufacturing debit column.

2 The ending inventories of raw materials and of goods in process must be recorded as assets and must be shown as deductions in determining the cost of finished goods manufactured. This step requires the listing of these two inventories as debits in the Balance Sheet columns and as credits in the Manufacturing columns.

The nature of the Manufacturing columns may be clarified by a brief summary of the items placed in each column. The debit column includes the beginning inventories of raw materials and goods in process, plus all the manufacturing costs of the period. The credit column contains credits for the ending inventories of raw materials and goods in process. The total of the amounts in the debit column exceeds the total of the credit column by $800,000. This debit balance represents the cost of finished goods manufactured and is extended as a debit to the Income Statement columns.

The beginning and ending inventories of *finished goods* appear in the Income Statement columns but *not in the Manufacturing columns*. A review of the schedule at the top of page 919 shows that the inventory of finished goods is *not a factor* in computing the cost of finished goods manufactured during the period.

Closing the accounts at the end of the period

7   Prepare closing entries for a manufacturing company.

The new feature found in the closing entries of a manufacturing business is the Manufacturing Summary account. This account is used to bring together the balances of all of the accounts relating to manufacturing costs and serves three related purposes:

1 The balances of the manufacturing cost accounts are returned to zero so that these accounts are ready for use in measuring the manufacturing costs of the next accounting period.

2 The ending inventories of raw materials and goods in process are recorded as assets to be shown in the balance sheet.

3 The cost of finished goods manufactured is determined for the period.

The closing entries for Allied Manufacturing Corporation at December 31 appear at the top of page 924. These entries are based upon the amounts of expense and manufacturing costs shown in the work sheet.

Manufacturing Summary	860,000	
Raw Materials Inventory (beginning)		25,000
Goods in Process Inventory (beginning)		30,000
Purchases of Raw Materials		140,000
Transportation-in (raw materials)		5,000
Direct Labour		300,000
Indirect Labour		145,000
Occupancy Costs		95,000
Other Factory Overhead Costs		120,000
To close manufacturing cost accounts to Manufacturing Summary.		

Raw Materials Inventory (ending)	20,000	
Goods in Process Inventory (ending)	40,000	
Manufacturing Summary		60,000
To record ending inventories of goods in process and raw materials.		

Income Summary	1,400,000	
Finished Goods Inventory (beginning)		150,000
Selling Expenses		135,000
General and Administrative Expenses		265,000
Interest Expense		20,000
Income Taxes Expense		30,000
Manufacturing Summary		800,000
To close beginning inventory of finished goods, all expense accounts, and Manufacturing account to Income Summary.		

Sales (net)	1,300,000	
Finished Goods Inventory (ending)	170,000	
Income Summary		1,470,000
To close Sales account and to record ending finished goods inventory.		

Income Summary	70,000	
Retained Earnings		70,000
To transfer balance in Income Summary (net income) to Retained Earnings.		

Explanation of Allied's closing entries   The entries to close Allied's accouns can be taken directly from the work sheet. The first closing entry debits the Manufacturing Summary account for the $860,000 total of all the amounts listed in the Manufacturing debit column on the work sheet. The beginning inventories of raw material and of goods in process, the Purchase of Raw Materials and the related Transportation-in account, and all of the manufacturing cost accounts are returned to zero (closed) as a result of this entry. This entry also serves to debit the Manufacturing Summary for all the costs that contribute to the cost of finished goods manufactured during the period.

The second closing entry credits the Manufacturing Summary with the $60,000 total of the two amounts listed in the Manufacturing credit column on the work sheet. This entry records the ending balances of the inventories of raw materials and of goods in process. In addition, it removes from the Manufacturing Summary those manufacturing costs that were *not converted into finished goods* during the period.

As a result of the first two closing entries, the Manufacturing Summary account now has a debit balance of $800,000, which is equal to the cost of finished goods manufactured during the year. The third closing entry now transfers this cost from the Manufacturing Summary account to the Income Summary. This entry usually is combined with the entry that closes the beginning inventory of finished goods and the expense accounts into the Income Summary.

The fourth closing entry transfers the balances of the revenue accounts into the Income Summary and records the ending inventory of finished goods. This entry is the same as that which would be made to close the revenue accounts of a merchandising company. Finally, the balance of the Income Summary account (representing the net income for the year) is closed into Retained Earnings.

Illustration of the Manufacturing Summary account   During the closing process, three dollar amounts are posted to the Manufacturing Summary account. The costs represented by these three amounts are summarized in the following diagram:

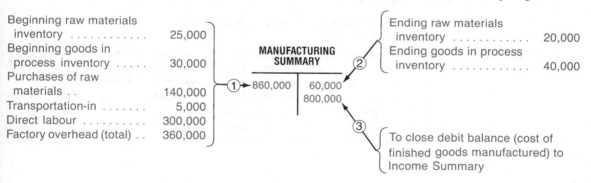

Beginning raw materials inventory 25,000
Beginning goods in process inventory 30,000
Purchases of raw materials .. 140,000
Transportation-in 5,000
Direct labour 300,000
Factory overhead (total) .. 360,000

MANUFACTURING SUMMARY
① ► 860,000 | 60,000
800,000

Ending raw materials inventory 20,000
Ending goods in process inventory 40,000

③ To close debit balance (cost of finished goods manufactured) to Income Summary

Cost accounting and perpetual inventory

Our discussion in this chapter assumes use of the periodic inventory method, although the concepts presented also apply to manufacturing companies that use perpetual inventory records. Many small manufacturers use the periodic inventory method, but it has several shortcomings for a manufacturing company, including the following:

1 Taking and pricing inventories is so time-consuming that it usually is done only once a year. Consequently, monthly financial statements and operating reports to management must be based upon estimates of inventory levels.

2 Cost data are averaged over all units produced during the period, so the system does not disclose changes in the unit cost of production occurring within the period.

3 The estimates used in computing the inventories of goods in process and finished goods are rough and inexact. Any error in pricing the inventories causes a corresponding error in net income for the period.

The greater the number of products being manufactured, the more critical these deficiencies become. For these reasons, many manufacturing businesses use *cost accounting systems* designed to provide a steady flow of reports summarizing *current* production costs on a per unit basis. Cost accounting is a specialized field of accounting, with the objective of providing management with a means of planning and controlling manufacturing operations. A cost accounting system is characterized by the maintenance of *perpetual* inventory records and by the development of cost figures for *each unit* manufactured. An introduction to cost accounting is presented in the following chapter.

END-OF-CHAPTER REVIEW

SUMMARY OF CHAPTER LEARNING OBJECTIVES

1 Explain the differences in accounting for inventories in manufacturing companies and merchandising companies.

A merchandising company buys goods for resale; these goods are in ready-to-sell condition and are not modified or processed before sale. Thus, only one inventory account is needed. The balance of this account is based upon the purchase cost of the inventory.

A manufacturing company, on the other hand, *produces* the goods it sells. Three inventory accounts may be used: (1) Raw Materials Inventory, (2) Work in Process Inventory, and (3) Finished Goods Inventory. The raw materials inventory is valued at its acquisition cost. The inventories of work in process and of finished goods are valued at the cost of manufacturing these goods.

2 Describe the three basic types of manufacturing cost.

Raw materials used consist of the parts and materials that become part of the finished products. Direct labour cost consists of the wages paid to factory employees who work directly on the products being manufactured. Factory overhead includes all manufacturing costs *other than* the cost of raw materials and direct labour. Examples of factory overhead include depreciation of machinery and the plant security service.

3 Distinguish between direct and indirect manufacturing costs.

The direct manufacturing costs of raw materials and direct labour can be identified with specific products. Indirect manufacturing costs are the many elements of factory overhead that apply to factory operations as a whole, and cannot be traced to specific products.

4 Distinguish between product costs and period costs and explain how product costs are offset against revenue.

Product costs are the cost of *creating* inventory. They are treated as assets until the related goods are sold, at which time the product costs are deducted from revenue as the cost of goods sold. Thus, goods manufactured this year but not sold until next year are deducted from next year's revenue.

Period costs are charged to expense in the accounting period in which they are incurred. Period costs are not related to production of goods; consequently, they are deducted from revenue on the assumption that the benefits obtained from the expenditures are received in the same period as the costs are incurred. Period costs include general and administrative expense, selling expense, and income taxes expense.

5 Prepare a schedule of cost of finished goods manufactured.

An important amount appearing in the income statement of a manufacturing company is the cost of finished goods manufactured. This amount is computed in a separate supporting schedule called the *schedule of cost of finished goods manufactured.* To prepare this supporting schedule, we start by listing the work in process inventory at the beginning of the year. To this amount we add the raw materials used during the year, the direct labour, and the factory overhead. By adding these items, we compute the total cost of goods in process during the year. A final step is to deduct the work in process inventory at the end of the year. This gives us the cost of finished goods manufactured, which is the amount to be carried to the income statement as part of the cost of goods sold section.

6 Explain how to determine the cost of work in process inventory and the cost of finished goods inventory.

Determining the cost of work in process inventory and of finished goods inventory is a more difficult process than computing the raw materials inventory or a merchandise inventory. Cost cannot be determined merely by pulling purchase invoices from the files. To determine the cost of the work in process and finished goods inventories, we first estimate the per unit cost of raw materials and direct labour included in the product. We then add an appropriate amount of factory overhead per unit. The factory overhead generally is applied by using an overhead application rate that expresses overhead as a percentage of the direct labour cost.

7 Prepare closing entries for a manufacturing company.

If we compare the closing entries for a manufacturing company with those for a merchandising business, the new feature is the Manufacturing Summary account. The first step is to close all manufacturing cost accounts by transferring their balances to the debit side of the Manufacturing Summary account. The next entry is to record the ending inventories of work in process and raw materials; the credit is to Manufacturing Summary. As a third entry, we close the Manufacturing Summary account by transferring its debit balance to Income Summary along with the balances of other expense accounts. The debit balance developed in the Manufacturing Summary account represents the cost of finished goods manufactured during the year. We then close the Sales account and record the ending Finished Goods Inventory; the offsetting credit is to Income Summary. The final closing entry (as in the case of a merchandising business) is to transfer the balance of the Income Summary account to Retained Earnings.

KEY TERMS INTRODUCED OR EMPHASIZED IN CHAPTER 22

Cost of finished goods manufactured Cost of units of finished product completed during the period. Beginning inventory of goods in process, plus cost of raw materials used plus direct labour and factory overhead and minus ending inventory of goods in process, equals cost of finished goods manufactured during the period.

Direct labour Wages paid to factory employees who work directly on the products being manufactured.

Direct manufacturing cost A cost that can be traced directly into specific units of finished product. Examples include the costs of raw materials used and direct labour.

Factory overhead All costs incurred in the manufacturing process other than the cost of raw materials and direct labour (for example, insurance, depreciation of machinery, and supervisors' salaries).

Finished goods inventory The completed units that have emerged from the manufacturing process and are on hand ready for sale to customers.

Goods in process inventory The inventory of partially completed goods in the process of manufacture as determined by a physical count at the balance sheet date.

Indirect labour Wages of employees in manufacturing operations who do not work directly with the product. Examples are wages of security guards and maintenance employees.

Indirect manufacturing cost A cost that cannot be traced directly into specific units of finished product. Examples include factory property taxes, plant security costs, and other types of factory overhead.

Manufacturing costs The costs of manufacturing goods that will be sold to customers. The basic types of manufacturing costs are raw materials used, direct labour, and factory overhead.

Manufacturing Summary account A summary account used in closing the accounts of a manufacturing business. All costs used in computing the cost of goods manufactured are transferred into the account, which is then closed to the Income Summary.

Overhead application rate Total factory overhead costs for the period expressed as a percentage of the total direct labour costs for the period. This rate is used in determining the amount of factory overhead applicable to each unit in the inventories of goods in process and finished goods. The application rate may be based on factors other than direct labour cost, e.g., direct labour hours, machine hours, etc.

Period costs Costs that are charged to expense in the period in which they are incurred. Generally include costs associated with selling and administrative functions.

Product costs Costs which become part of the inventory value of goods in process and finished goods. Deductible from revenue in the period the products in which they are included are sold.

Raw (direct) materials inventory The raw materials on hand and ready to be placed in production. Eventually these raw materials become part of the cost of the finished units.

Schedule of cost of finished goods manufactured A supplementary schedule accompanying the income statement of a manufacturing company. Shows the various costs assigned to the finished goods manufactured during the period.

ASSIGNMENT MATERIAL

REVIEW QUESTIONS

1 Explain how the content of the income statement of a manufacturing company differs from the items usually found in the income statement of a merchandising company.

2 A manufacturing company has more than one kind of inventory. Do all the types of inventories of a manufacturing company appear on its income statement? Explain.

3 What are the three basic types of manufacturing costs?

4 A manufacturing firm has three inventory control accounts. Name each of the accounts, and describe briefly what the balance in each at the end of any accounting period represents.

5 Into which of the three elements of manufacturing cost would each of the following be classified?

   a Gold bullion used by a jewelry manufacturer

   b Wages of assembly-line workers who package frozen food

   c Salary of plant superintendent

   d Electricity used in factory operations

   e Salary of a nurse in a factory first-aid station

   f Briar used in manufacturing pipes

   g Wages paid by an automobile manufacturer to employees who test-drive completed automobiles

   h Property taxes on machinery

6 During the current year the net cost of raw materials purchased by a manufacturing firm was $340,000, and the raw material inventory increased by $20,000. What was the cost of raw materials used during the year?

7 Explain the distinction between a *direct* manufacturing cost and an *indirect* manufacturing cost. Provide two examples of each type of cost.

8 Explain the distinction between *product costs* and *period costs*. Why is this distinction important?

9 Distinguish between *total manufacturing costs* and the *cost of finished goods manufactured*.

10 What is meant by the term *overhead application rate?*

11 Explain how the cost of the ending inventory of goods in process is determined at the end of the period under the periodic inventory system.

12 What does the balance in the Manufacturing Summary account represent, before the account is closed?

13 As part of the closing process for a manufacturing company, the Inventory of Raw Materials and Inventory of Goods in Process accounts are debited for their ending balances. Explain why the offsetting credit is to the Manufacturing Summary account.

14 What are the major shortcomings of the periodic inventory system when used by a manufacturing company?

EXERCISES

Exercise 22-1
Accounting
Terminology

Listed below are nine technical accounting terms introduced in this chapter:

Goods in process inventory	Schedule of Cost of Finished Goods Manufactured	Cost of finished goods manufactured
Direct labour	Overhead application rate	Product costs
Factory overhead	Manufacturing Summary	Period costs

Each of the following statements may (or may not) describe one of these technical terms. For each statement, indicate the accounting term described, or answer "None" if the statement does not correctly describe any of the terms.

a Costs that are charged to expense when incurred, including general and administrative expenses, selling expenses, and income taxes expense.

b The cost of the units of finished goods completed during the period.

c The cost of finished goods on hand and awaiting sale to customers at the end of the period.

d Partially completed goods on hand in the factory at year-end.

e All wages paid to factory employees.

f Manufacturing costs that become part of the inventory value of goods in process and finished goods. Deductible from revenue in the period during which the products in which they are included are sold.

g An account used in closing the accounts of a manufacturing company at the end of the period. All costs used in computing the cost of goods manufactured are transferred into the account, which is then closed to the Income Summary.

h Total factory overhead expressed as a percentage of total direct labour cost.

i A basic type of manufacturing costs, which includes indirect labour, depreciation of machinery, and insurance on factory buildings.

Exercise 22-2
Computing the cost of
finished goods
manufactured

From the information listed below, compute the cost of finished goods manufactured:

	DEC. 31	JAN. 1
Inventory of raw materials	$ 20,000	$24,000
Inventory of goods in process	12,000	8,000
Inventory of finished goods	90,000	80,000
Purchases of raw materials	210,000	
Direct labour	120,000	
Factory overhead	180,000	
Selling expenses	170,000	
General and administrative expenses	140,000	

Exercise 22-3
Computing the goods
in process inventory

The information at the top of page 931 is taken from the financial statements of Craftsman Products at the end of the current year. Compute the cost of the goods in process inventory at the *beginning* of the current year.

Goods in process inventory, ending	$ 50,000
Cost of raw materials used	260,000
Direct labour	100,000
Factory overhead	250,000
Cost of finished goods manufactured	602,000

Exercise 22-4
Closing the manufacturing accounts at year's end

From the following account balances, prepare the entries required to close the manufacturing accounts at the end of the year. Include an entry to close the Manufacturing Summary account to the Income Summary account.

	END OF YEAR	BEGINNING OF YEAR
Raw materials inventory	$ 45,000	$52,500
Goods in process inventory	70,500	57,600
Purchases of raw materials (net)	240,000	
Direct labour	116,000	
Factory overhead (detail omitted)	349,400	

Exercise 22-5
Product costs and period costs

Indicate whether each of the following should be considered a *product cost* or a *period cost*. If you identify the item as a product cost, also indicate whether it is a *direct* or *indirect* cost. For example, the answer to item **0** is "indirect product cost." Begin with item **a.**

0 Property taxes on factory building
a Salaries of office workers in the credit department
b Depreciation on raw materials warehouse
c Income taxes on a profitable manufacturing company
d Cost of disposal of hazardous waste materials to a chemical plant
e Amounts paid by a mobile home manufacturer to a subcontractor who installs plumbing in each mobile home
f Depreciation on sales showroom fixtures
g Salaries of security guards in administrative office building
h Salaries of factory security guards

Exercise 22-6
Determining the overhead application rate

From the following account balances for the Dell Products Corporation, determine the *overhead application rate* based on direct labour cost:

Raw materials used	$480,000
Direct labour	100,000
Indirect labour	88,000
Factory occupancy costs	182,000
Depreciation on machinery	39,000
Other factory overhead costs	51,000
Selling expenses (balance in controlling account)	200,000
General expenses (balance in controlling account)	300,000
Income taxes expense	60,000

Exercise 22-7
Computing year-end inventory of goods in process and finished goods

Monroe Company produces a single product. At the end of the current year, the inventories of goods in process and finished goods are summarized as follows:

	UNITS	RAW MATERIALS PER UNIT	DIRECT LABOUR PER UNIT
Goods in process	500	$6	$3
Finished goods	6,000	8	4

Factory overhead is applied to units produced at the rate of 210% of direct labour cost. Compute the cost of the ending inventory of goods in process and of finished goods.

PROBLEMS

Group A

Problem 22A-1
Inventories: goods in process and finished goods

Wonderbus, Inc., began operations early in the current year building luxury motor homes. During the year the company started and completed 20 motor homes at a cost of $24,000 per unit. Sixteen of these completed motor homes were sold for $40,000 each. In addition, the company has five partially completed motor homes in progress at year-end. Costs incurred during the year on these partially completed motor homes have totalled $14,000 per unit.

Instructions

Compute for the current year:

a Ending inventories of (1) goods in process and (2) finished goods

b Cost of finished goods manufactured

c Total manufacturing costs

d Cost of goods sold

e Gross profit on sales

Problem 22A-2
Schedule of cost of finished goods manufactured

The accounting records of Concord Manufacturing Co. Ltd. show the following costs and expenses for the year ended December 31:

Purchases of raw materials	$251,000
Transportation-in on raw materials	5,600
Indirect factory labour	92,600
Direct factory labour	230,000
Selling expenses (control)	177,200
Factory occupancy costs	85,400
General and administrative expenses (control)	203,600
Income taxes expense	90,000
Miscellaneous factory overhead	38,200

Inventories at the beginning and end of the year were as follows:

	END OF YEAR	BEGINNING OF YEAR
Raw materials	$ 44,300	$ 48,700
Goods in process	14,700	21,500
Finished goods	102,400	195,600

Instructions

a Prepare a schedule of cost of finished goods manufactured during the year.

b Prepare a partial income statement showing the cost of goods sold for the year.

Problem 22A-3
Schedule of cost of finished goods manufactured; closing entries; overhead application rate

The amounts appearing in the Manufacturing and the Income Statement columns of the work sheet of Genie Industries for the year ended December 31 are shown below:

	MANUFACTURING		INCOME STATEMENT	
Inventories, Jan. 1:				
Raw materials	51,000			
Goods in process	13,000			
Finished goods			95,000	
Sales				859,000
Purchases of raw materials	230,000			
Direct labour	140,000			
Indirect labour	55,000			
Factory occupancy costs	43,000			
Other factory overhead	77,000			
Selling expenses (control)			78,000	
General and administrative expenses (control)			202,000	
Income taxes expense			8,250	
Inventories, Dec. 31:				
Raw materials		56,000		
Goods in process		9,000		
Finished goods				110,000
	609,000	65,000		
Cost of finished goods manufactured		544,000	544,000	
	609,000	609,000	927,250	969,000
Net income			41,750	
			969,000	969,000

Instructions

From the data shown in the partial work sheet:

a Prepare a schedule of cost of finished goods manufactured during the year.

b Prepare closing entries for the year.

c Compute the overhead application rate (factory overhead expressed as a percentage of direct labour) that Genie Industries used in allocating factory overhead to its ending inventories of goods in process and finished goods.

Problem 22A-4
Valuation of inventories; multiproducts

The manufacturing costs of Auto Alarms, Inc., during the six-month period ended June 30, 19___, are summarized as follows:

Raw materials	$192,300
Direct labour costs	310,000
Factory overhead	248,000
Total manufacturing costs	$750,300

Inventories of goods in process and finished goods at the beginning of this period were as follows:

Inventories, Jan. 1, 19___:
Goods in process .... $ 32,400
Finished goods 134,000

An engineer in the production department has provided the following information relating to the cost of the inventories of goods in process and finished goods at June 30, 19___:

	UNITS IN INVENTORY	ESTIMATED COSTS PER UNIT	
		RAW MATERIALS	DIRECT LABOUR
Goods in process:			
Product #1	500	$4.00	$10.00
Product #2	1,000	6.00	5.00
Finished goods:			
Product #1	2,000	9.00	15.00
Product #2	2,610	8.40	12.00

Instructions

a Prepare a schedule determining the cost of the June 30 inventories of goods in process and finished goods. Use the form illustrated in the chapter. Determine the factory overhead cost per unit by using an overhead application rate based on direct labour costs.

b Compute the cost of finished goods manufactured during the six months ended June 30, 19___.

c Compute the cost of goods sold for the six months ended June 30, 19___.

Problem 22A-5
Effect on income statement of errors in handling manufacturing costs

William Nelson, the chief accountant of West Guitar Corporation, was injured in an automobile accident shortly before the end of the company's first year of operations. At year-end, a clerk with a very limited understanding of accounting prepared the following income statement, which is unsatisfactory in several respects:

WEST GUITAR CORPORATION
Income Statement
For the Year Ended December 31, 19___

Sales (net) $960,000
Cost of goods sold:
Purchases of raw materials $260,000
Transportation-in 12,000
Direct labour 125,000
Indirect labour 90,000
Depreciation on machinery — factory 30,000
Rent 24,000
Insurance 6,000
Utilities 18,000
Miscellaneous factory overhead 227,600
Other operating expenses 165,800
Dividends declared on common stock 36,000
Cost of goods sold 994,400
Loss for year .... $ (34,400)

You are asked to help management prepare a corrected income statement for the first year of operations. Management informs you that 60% of rent, insurance, and utilities is applicable to the factory and that correct ending inventories consist of the following: raw materials, $38,000; goods in process, $10,000; and finished goods, $110,400. (Since this is the first year of operations, there are no beginning inventories.)

Instructions   **a** Identify the shortcomings and errors in the above income statement. Based upon the shortcomings you have identified, explain whether you would expect the company's actual net income for the first year of operations to be higher or lower than the amount shown.

b Prepare a schedule of cost of finished goods manufactured during the year.

c Prepare a corrected income statement for the year. Assume that income taxes expense amounts to 30% of taxable income. (Omit earnings per share figures.)

Problem 22A-6
work sheet and
closing entries

Following is the adjusted trial balance of Green Bay Corporation at June 30, the end of the company's fiscal year:

GREEN BAY CORPORATION
Adjusted Trial Balance
June 30, 19___

Cash	$ 51,000	
Accounts receivable	311,000	
Raw materials inventory, beginning	38,200	
Goods in process inventory, beginning	34,500	
Finished goods inventory, beginning	218,000	
Prepaid expenses	8,000	
Plant and equipment	998,000	
Accumulated depreciation: plant and equipment		$ 300,500
Accounts payable		76,500
Accrued expenses payable		54,200
Income taxes payable		116,000
Notes payable (long-term)		150,000
Capital stock		525,000
Retained earnings, beginning of year		250,700
Sales		2,000,000
Purchases of raw materials	424,000	
Transportation-in (raw materials)	29,500	
Direct labour	200,500	
Factory overhead (control)	703,700	
Selling expenses (control)	180,000	
Administrative expenses (control)	160,500	
Income taxes expense	116,000	
	$3,472,900	$3,472,900

Ending inventories at June 30 are as follows:

Raw materials inventory	$ 40,200
Goods in process inventory	36,200
Finished goods inventory	200,500

Instructions   Prepare:

a An eight-column work sheet for the year ended June 30. (Follow the format illustrated in this chapter, begin with the adjusted trial balance and include a pair of columns for Manufacturing, Income Statement, and Balance Sheet.)

b Closing entries for the year ended June 30. (Use a Manufacturing Summary account to determine the cost of finished goods manufactured as part of your closing procedures.)

Group B

Problem 22B-1
Product costs and the matching concept

During the current year, Apex Construction Co. Ltd. started work on two residential housing developments. The status of each development at year-end is described. Apex had no projects in process at the beginning of the current year.

Indian Hills Condominiums A project of 80 two-bedroom condominiums completed in August of the current year at a cost of $60,000 per unit. As of year-end, 70 units have been sold at prices averaging $72,000 per unit.

Seaview Estates A project of 20 homes, each of which is approximately 60% complete at year-end. Costs incurred during the year have totalled $85,000 per house. None of the houses has yet been sold.

Instructions   Compute for the current year the:

a Ending inventories of (1) goods in process and (2) finished goods

b Cost of finished goods manufactured

c Total manufacturing costs

d Cost of goods sold

e Gross profit on sales

Problem 22B-2
Preparing a schedule of cost of finished goods manufactured from closing entries

Medallion Company prepared journal entries to close its accounts at December 31. Following are two of these year-end closing entries:

Manufacturing Summary	515,750	
Raw Materials Inventory (beginning)		51,500
Goods in Process Inventory (beginning)		27,250
Purchases of Raw Materials		225,500
Transportation-in		5,750
Direct Labour		96,500
Indirect Labour		53,500
Factory Occupancy Costs		30,750
Miscellaneous Factory Overhead		25,000
To close manufacturing cost accounts.		
Raw Materials Inventory (ending)	56,250	
Goods in Process Inventory (ending)	24,500	
Manufacturing Summary		80,750
To record ending inventories of raw materials and goods in process.		

Instructions   Prepare a schedule of cost of finished goods manufactured for the year.

Problem 22B-3
Computing cost per unit: single product

The accounting records of Scott Mfg. Co. include the following information relating to the current year. The company manufactures a single product; during the current year, 45,000 units were manufactured and 40,000 units were sold.

	DEC. 31	JAN. 1
Raw materials inventory	$120,000	$ 95,000
Goods in process inventory	37,500	40,000
Finished goods inventory, Jan. 1 (10,000 units)	?	190,000
Purchases of raw materials during year	285,000	
Direct labour cost during year	195,000	
Factory overhead costs during year	442,500	

Instructions

a Prepare a schedule of cost of finished goods manufactured for the current year.

b Compute the cost of producing a single unit during the current year.

c Compute the cost of goods sold during the year, assuming that the first-in, first-out method of inventory costing is used.

d Compute the cost of the inventory of finished goods at December 31 of the current year, assuming that the first-in, first-out method of inventory costing is used.

Problem 22B-4
Schedule of cost of finished goods manufactured; closing entries, overhead applications rate

Shirthouse West produces T-shirts and other apparel custom imprinted with company logos or other designs. Data from the Manufacturing and Income Statement columns of the company's work sheet for the year ended December 31 follow:

	MANUFACTURING		INCOME STATEMENT	
Inventories, Jan. 1:				
Raw materials	16,400			
Goods in process	2,300			
Finished goods			17,500	
Sales				967,000
Purchases of raw materials	217,600			
Direct labour	84,000			
Indirect labour	45,700			
Factory occupancy costs	23,400			
Other factory overhead	19,100			
Selling expenses (control)			271,000	
General and administrative expenses (control)			178,000	
Income taxes expense			29,300	
Inventories, Dec. 31:				
Raw materials		11,000		
Goods in process		3,500		
Finished goods				13,500
	408,500	14,500		
Cost of finished goods manufactured		394,000	394,000	
	408,500	408,500	889,800	980,500
Net income			90,700	
			980,500	980,500

Instructions   From the data shown in the partial work sheet:

a Prepare a schedule of cost of finished goods manufactured during the year.

b Prepare closing entries for the year.

c Compute the overhead application rate (factory overhead expressed as a percentage of direct labour) that Shirthouse West used in the valuation of its ending inventories of goods in process and finished goods.

Problem 22B-5
Valuation of
inventories;
multiproducts

Marathon Motors manufactures three different models of outboard motors. The beginning inventories and manufacturing costs for the first quarter (January 1 through March 31) of the year were as follows:

Inventories, Jan. 1	
Raw materials	$ 629,500
Goods in process	165,500
Finished goods	919,000
Purchases of raw materials	1,860,000
Direct labour	2,660,000
Factory overhead	2,128,000

At March 31, the following unit costs are applicable to the inventories of goods in process and finished goods:

	UNITS IN INVENTORY	COST PER UNIT	
		RAW MATERIALS	DIRECT LABOUR
Goods in process:			
Model 100	1,000	$45	$ 37.50
Model 200	750	50	50.00
Model 300	500	60	62.50
Finished goods:			
Model 100	2,500	45	75.00
Model 200	3,000	65	100.00
Model 300	2,000	85	125.00

The March 31 inventory of raw materials amounted to $613,000.

Instructions   **a** Prepare a schedule showing the cost of the inventories of goods in process and finished goods at March 31. Use the form illustrated in the chapter. Factory overhead is allocated to products on the basis of its relation to direct labour costs.

b Compute the cost of finished goods manufactured during the first quarter of the year.

c Compute the cost of goods sold for the first quarter of the year.

Problem 22B-6
Preparing work sheet
and closing entries

At December 31 the following adjusted trial balance was prepared for Bridgeport Manufacturing Co. Ltd.

BRIDGEPORT MANUFACTURING CO. LTD.
Adjusted Trial Balance
December 31, 19__

Cash	$ 92,000	
Accounts receivable	325,000	
Allowance for doubtful accounts		$ 12,000
Raw materials inventory, Jan. 1	61,200	
Goods in process inventory, Jan. 1	55,200	
Finished goods inventory, Jan. 1	130,000	
Prepaid expenses	13,000	
Plant and equipment	1,541,000	
Accumulated depreciation: plant and equipment		480,600
Patents	56,600	
Accounts payable		122,400
Accrued liabilities		94,000
Income taxes payable		130,500
Capital stock		1,000,000
Retained earnings, Jan. 1		252,000
Sales (net)		3,000,000
Purchases of raw materials	678,800	
Transportation-in (raw materials)	40,200	
Direct labour	441,000	
Factory overhead (control).......................	986,000	
Selling expenses (control)	284,600	
Administrative expenses (control)	256,400	
Income taxes expense	130,500	
	$5,091,500	$5,091,500

Inventories at December 31 are shown below:

Raw materials inventory	$ 64,400
Goods in process inventory	58,000
Finished goods inventory	126,500

Instructions Prepare the following:

a An eight-column work sheet, following the format illustrated in the chapter, for the year ended December 31. (Begin with the adjusted trial balance and include a pair of columns for Manufacturing, Income Statement, and Balance Sheet.)

b Closing entries for the year ended December 31. (Use a Manufacturing Summary account to determine the cost of finished goods manufactured as part of your closing procedures.)

BUSINESS DECISION CASES

Case 22-1
"I don't need an accountant. . . ."
Early in the year, John Raymond founded Raymond Engineering Co. Ltd. for the purpose of manufacturing a special flow control valve that he had designed. Shortly after year-end, the company's accountant was injured in a skiing accident, and no year-end financial statements

have been prepared. However, the accountant had assembled the following information about the December 31 inventories of goods in process and finished goods:

	UNITS IN INVENTORY	COST PER UNIT	
		RAW MATERIALS	DIRECT LABOUR
Goods in process	1,500	$ 7	$ 8
Finished goods	3,000	11	12

Raw materials on hand at December 31 amounted to $46,000. (Since this was the first year of operations, there were no beginning inventories.)

While the accountant was in the hospital, Raymond prepared the following schedule from the balances in the company's ledger accounts:

Sales		$603,100
Cost of goods sold:		
Purchases of raw materials	$181,000	
Direct labour costs	160,000	
Factory overhead	120,000	
Selling expenses	70,600	
Administrative expenses	132,000	
Total costs		663,600
Net loss for year		$ (60,500)

Raymond was very disappointed in these operating results. He states, "Not only did we lose more than $60,000 this year, but look at our unit production costs. We sold 10,000 units this year at a cost of $663,600; that amounts to a cost of $66.36 per unit. I know some of our competitors are able to manufacture similar valves for about $35 per unit. I don't need an accountant to know that this business is a failure."

Instructions
a Prepare a schedule showing the cost of the inventories of goods in process and finished goods at December 31. Determine the factory overhead cost per unit by using an overhead application rate based on direct labour costs.

b Compute the cost of finished goods manufactured during the year. After completing this computation, determine the average cost per finished unit manufactured. (This cost may differ from the cost per unit of the finished goods inventory, because it is an average unit cost of all finished goods produced throughout the year.)

c Prepare an income statement for the year. If the company has earned any operating income, assume an income tax rate of 30%. (Omit earnings per share figures.)

d Explain whether you agree or disagree with Raymond's remarks that the business is unprofitable and that its unit cost of production ($66.36, according to Raymond) is much higher than that of competitors (around $35). If you disagree with Raymond, explain any errors or shortcomings in his analysis.

Case 22-2
Units, units everywhere;
the old shell game

Prescott Manufacturing operates several plants, each of which produces a different product. Early in the current year, John Walker was hired as the new manager of the Meadowbrooke plant. At year-end, all the plant managers are asked to summarize the operations of their plants at a meeting of the company's board of directors. John Walker displayed the following information on a chart as he made his presentation:

	CURRENT YEAR	LAST YEAR
Inventories of finished goods:		
Beginning of the year (30,000 units in the current year and 10,000 units last year)	$255,000	$ 85,000
End of the year (20,000 units in the current year and 30,000 last year)	202,000	255,000
Cost of finished goods manufactured	909,000	1,020,000

Walker made the following statements to the board: "As you know, sales volume has remained constant for the Meadowbrooke plant. Both this year and last, our sales amounted to 100,000 units. We have made real gains, however, in controlling our manufacturing costs. Through efficient plant operations, we have reduced our cost of finished goods manufactured by over $100,000 from last year's levels. These economies are reflected in a reduction of the manufacturing cost per unit sold from $10.20 last year ($1,020,000 ÷ 100,000 units) to $9.09 in the current year ($909,000 ÷ 100,000 units)."

Father Alan Carter is president of St. Mary's University and is a member of Prescott Manufacturing's board of directors. However, Father Carter has little background in the accounting practices of manufacturing companies, and he asks you for assistance in evaluating Walker's statements.

Instructions   **a** As a preliminary step to your analysis, compute the following for the Meadowbrooke plant in each of the two years:

(1) Cost of goods sold
(2) Number of finished units manufactured
(3) Average cost per unit manufactured
(4) Average cost per unit sold

b Evaluate the statements made by Walker. Comment specifically upon whether it appears that the reduction in the cost of finished goods sold was achieved through more efficient operations and upon Walker's computation of the manufacturing cost of units sold.

23

COST ACCOUNTING SYSTEMS

CHAPTER PREVIEW

In the preceding chapter we saw how manufacturing companies using the periodic inventory system determine the cost of finished goods manufactured. The major limitation in this approach is that unit cost information is available only as frequently as physical inventory counts are taken. In this chapter we introduce cost accounting systems, which make use of perpetual inventory records. Both job order systems and process cost systems are explained and illustrated. These systems enable manufacturers to determine their per unit manufacturing costs on a monthly basis or, in some cases, as soon as production is completed on each batch of finished goods. In addition, cost accounting systems can measure separately the unit cost of performing each major step in the manufacturing process.

After studying this chapter you should be able to meet these Learning Objectives:

1 Explain the purpose of a cost accounting system.

2 Describe how manufacturing costs "flow" through perpetual inventory accounts.

3 Explain the characteristics of a job order cost accounting system.

4 Describe the purpose and the content of a job cost sheet.

5 Explain the characteristics of a process cost accounting system.

6 Define and compute "equivalent full units" of production.

7 Prepare a cost report for a production department using a process cost system.

1 Explain the purpose of a cost accounting system.

What is a cost accounting system?

A cost accounting system is a method of developing cost information about specific products or business activities within the framework of general ledger accounts. Because cost accounting systems are most widely used in manufacturing companies, we shall focus our discussion on the use of these systems to measure the cost of manufactured products. However, the concepts of cost accounting are applicable to a wide range of business situations. For example, banks, accounting firms, and governmental agencies all use cost accounting systems to determine the cost of performing various service functions.

Cost accounting serves two important managerial objectives: (1) to determine the *unit costs* of production, and (2) to provide management with information useful in *planning* future operations and *controlling* the costs of business operations. *Unit costs* of production are determined by relating prices paid for raw materials, direct labour, and factory overhead to some unit of output, such as tonnes of steel produced. Unit cost information provides the basis for inventory valuation and measurement of the cost of goods sold. It also provides information useful in pricing decisions, bidding on production contracts, and evaluating the efficiency of operations.

The phrase *controlling costs* means keeping costs down to reasonable levels. When a cost accounting system provides timely information about unit costs, managers are able to react quickly should costs begin rising to unacceptable levels. By comparing the current unit costs with budgets, past performance, and other yardsticks, managers are able to identify those areas in which corrective actions are most needed. Without a cost accounting system, however, managers may not realize that costs are excessive until year-end when inventory is counted and the cost of finished goods manufactured is determined.

2 Describe how manufacturing costs "flow" through perpetual inventory accounts.

Cost accounting systems — costs "flow" through perpetual inventory records

A basic feature of all cost accounting systems is the use of *perpetual* inventory records. As explained in Chapter 9, perpetual inventory records show continuously the cost of the inventories on hand. To accomplish this objective in a manufacturing business, manufacturing costs must be assigned to the Goods in Process Inventory account as the manufacturing costs are incurred. When the goods are completed, their cost is then transferred from the Goods in Process Inventory account to the Finished Goods Inventory account. Finally, when the goods are sold, their cost is transferred from the Finished Goods Inventory account to Cost of Goods Sold. Since the inventory accounts are kept continuously up to date, the average *unit cost* may be determined by dividing the balance of the inventory account by the number of units on hand.

Three perpetual inventory accounts are used in tracing the flow of manufacturing costs through a manufacturing business:

1 Raw Materials Inventory
2 Goods in Process Inventory (product in the process of manufacture)
3 Finished Goods Inventory (completed product)

To visualize basic cost flows, look at the following diagram. The arrows show the flow of costs through the perpetual inventory accounts; arrows connecting two items indicate the two sides of an accounting entry. Thus the use of raw materials reduces the Raw Materials Inventory account and increases the Goods in Process Inventory.

ARROWS SHOW FLOW
OF COSTS

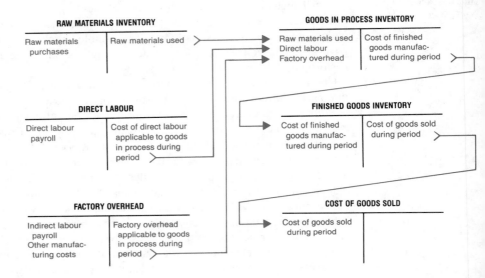

Notice that the Goods in Process Inventory account also is debited for the costs of direct labour and factory overhead applicable to goods worked on during the period. Direct labour and factory overhead often are termed *processing costs* or conversion costs, because these are the costs of converting raw materials into finished goods. Once the production process is complete, the cost of the goods is transferred from the Goods in Process Inventory account to the Finished Goods Inventory account. After all of the indicated entries have been made, the balances in the Raw Materials Inventory, Goods in Process Inventory, and Finished Goods Inventory accounts represent the *ending* (current) balances for these inventories.

Even when perpetual inventory records are maintained, however, *it is still essential to take a physical inventory* at least once a year. This physical inventory may disclose losses due to theft, waste, or breakage that were not recorded in the accounts.

Two basic types of cost accounting systems

There are two distinct types of cost accounting systems: a job order cost system and a process cost system. In both systems the end product is the average unit cost of physical output.

Under a *job order cost system,* the key point of costing is a particular quantity of finished products that are *manufactured together* as a single *job* or *lot.* The cost of raw materials, direct labour, and factory overhead applicable to each job is compiled and divided by the number of finished units in the job to arrive at average unit cost.

Under a *process cost system,* the key points in costing are the various *departments or processes* in the production cycle. First the cost of raw materials, direct labour, and factory overhead applicable to each department or process for a *given period of time* is compiled. The average cost of running a unit of product through each department then is determined by dividing the total departmental cost by the number of units processed in the department during the period. When a product moves through *two or more separate processes,* the unit costs incurred for each process are *combined* to determine the total unit cost of the finished products.

Each kind of cost accounting system (job order and process) has advantages in particular manufacturing situations. Both are widely used. In fact, a given manufacturing company may use a job order cost system to account for some of its products and a process cost system to account for others. In the sections that follow we shall examine briefly the basic structure of these two cost accounting systems.

JOB ORDER COST SYSTEM

3 Explain the characteristics of a job order cost accounting system.

In general, a job order cost system is applicable when each product or batch of product is *significantly different.* A job order cost system is used in the construction industry, for example, since each construction project has unique characteristics. Job order cost systems are also used in the aerospace, motion picture, and shipbuilding industries for similar reasons.

4 Describe the purpose and the content of a job cost sheet.

An essential requirement of a job order cost system is that *each product or batch of products can be identified* in each step of the manufacturing operation. The cost of raw materials, direct labour, and factory overhead applicable to each job is recorded on a *job cost sheet,* so that when the job is finished the total and the average unit cost of the job can be computed, as shown in the following illustration:

Job Cost Sheet

JOB NUMBER: 1407   **DATE STARTED:** Mar. 10, 1989
PRODUCT: MODEL 90 HAND DRILL   **DATE COMPLETED:** Apr. 15, 1989
UNITS COMPLETED: 2,000

Raw materials used	$ 7,500
Direct labour cost applicable to this job	10,000
Factory overhead applicable to this job, 125% of direct labour cost	12,500
Total cost of job No. 1407	$30,000
Average cost per unit ($30,000 ÷ 2,000)	$15

Flow of costs in a job order cost system

A flow chart showing the accounts used in a simple job order cost system, together with lines indicating the flow of costs from one account to another, appears on pages 946 and 947.

The flow chart contains figures representing one month's operations for the Job Manufacturing Company. The company makes three products, identified as product A, product B, and product C. Two kinds of raw materials (materials Y and Z) are used. Each of the three perpetual inventory accounts (Raw Materials Inventory, Goods in Process Inventory, and Finished Goods Inventory) is supported by subsidiary ledger records in which the details of the flow of costs are recorded.

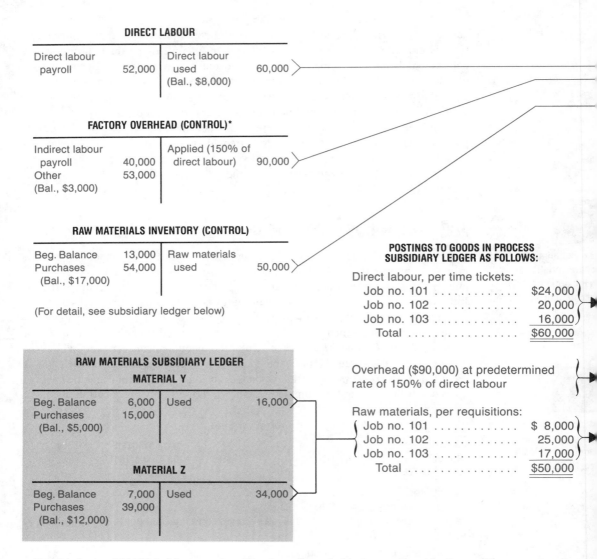

DIRECT LABOUR

| Direct labour payroll | 52,000 | Direct labour used (Bal., $8,000) | 60,000 |

FACTORY OVERHEAD (CONTROL)*

Indirect labour payroll	40,000	Applied (150% of direct labour)	90,000
Other	53,000		
(Bal., $3,000)			

RAW MATERIALS INVENTORY (CONTROL)

Beg. Balance	13,000	Raw materials used	50,000
Purchases	54,000		
(Bal., $17,000)			

(For detail, see subsidiary ledger below)

POSTINGS TO GOODS IN PROCESS SUBSIDIARY LEDGER AS FOLLOWS:

Direct labour, per time tickets:
Job no. 101 . . . . $24,000
Job no. 102   20,000
Job no. 103   16,000
      Total $60,000

RAW MATERIALS SUBSIDIARY LEDGER

MATERIAL Y

Beg. Balance	6,000	Used	16,000
Purchases	15,000		
(Bal., $5,000)			

MATERIAL Z

Beg. Balance	7,000	Used	34,000
Purchases	39,000		
(Bal., $12,000)			

Overhead ($90,000) at predetermined rate of 150% of direct labour

Raw materials, per requisitions:
Job no. 101 . . . . $ 8,000
Job no. 102   25,000
Job no. 103   17,000
      Total $50,000

*Debit balance of $3,000 in this account represents underapplied factory overhead for the month.

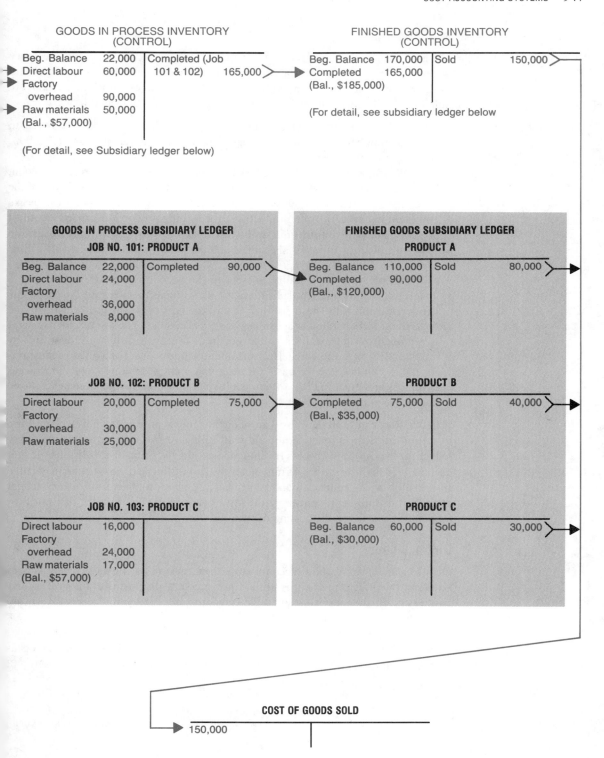

GOODS IN PROCESS INVENTORY (CONTROL)

Beg. Balance	22,000	Completed (Job	
Direct labour	60,000	101 & 102)	165,000
Factory overhead	90,000		
Raw materials	50,000		
(Bal., $57,000)			

(For detail, see Subsidiary ledger below)

FINISHED GOODS INVENTORY (CONTROL)

Beg. Balance	170,000	Sold	150,000
Completed	165,000		
(Bal., $185,000)			

(For detail, see subsidiary ledger below

GOODS IN PROCESS SUBSIDIARY LEDGER

JOB NO. 101: PRODUCT A

Beg. Balance	22,000	Completed	90,000
Direct labour	24,000		
Factory overhead	36,000		
Raw materials	8,000		

JOB NO. 102: PRODUCT B

Direct labour	20,000	Completed	75,000
Factory overhead	30,000		
Raw materials	25,000		

JOB NO. 103: PRODUCT C

Direct labour	16,000		
Factory overhead	24,000		
Raw materials	17,000		
(Bal., $57,000)			

FINISHED GOODS SUBSIDIARY LEDGER

PRODUCT A

Beg. Balance	110,000	Sold	80,000
Completed	90,000		
(Bal., $120,000)			

PRODUCT B

| Completed | 75,000 | Sold | 40,000 |
| (Bal., $35,000) | | | |

PRODUCT C

| Beg. Balance | 60,000 | Sold | 30,000 |
| (Bal., $30,000) | | | |

COST OF GOODS SOLD

| 150,000 | |

Raw materials

When perpetual inventory records are maintained, the Raw Materials Inventory account is debited when materials are purchased and credited when the materials are used. The summary entries in the Raw Materials Inventory controlling account are supported by detailed entries in the subsidiary ledger accounts as follows:

1 The $13,000 beginning balance in the Raw Materials Inventory account is equal to the beginning balances in the subsidiary ledger accounts for Material Y, $6,000, and Material Z, $7,000.
2 The cost of materials purchased, $54,000, was posted to the controlling account from the voucher register. Detailed entries showing the quantity and cost of the materials are posted to the subsidiary ledger accounts from the suppliers' invoices.
3 To obtain materials for the production process, the production department must present a *materials requisition* to the raw materials warehouse. This requisition shows the quantity of materials needed and the job on which the materials will be used.

Copies of these requisitions are sent to the accounting department, where a materials clerk refers to the subsidiary ledger accounts to determine the cost of the items requisitioned. The clerk then enters the cost of the materials used on the requisition form and in the subsidiary ledger accounts. (The use of raw materials is recorded by debit entries in the goods in process subsidiary ledger and by credit entries in the raw materials subsidiary ledger.) The completed requisitions for the month become the basis for a summary entry debiting Goods in Process Inventory and crediting Raw Materials Inventory for the cost of all materials used during the period ($50,000).

In our flow chart, all the subsidiary ledger accounts are shown in T-account form to conserve space. In practice, the individual *job cost sheets* serve as the subsidiary ledger for the Goods in Process Inventory controlling account. The subsidiary ledger accounts for the inventories of raw materials and of finished goods contain detailed information as to quantities and unit costs. A more complete subsidiary ledger account for Material Y appears at the top of page 949. (The first-in, first-out flow assumption is used in the costing of material used.)

Direct labour

Debits to the Direct Labour account arise from making payments to direct factory workers; the offsetting credit is to the Cash account.[1] Payments to *indirect* factory workers (such as supervisors and security guards) are debited to Factory Overhead, not to the Direct Labour account.

The Direct Labour account is credited as direct labour is *used* — that is, as employees work on specific jobs. A number of mechanical and computerized means have been developed for determining the direct labour cost applicable to each job.

---

[1] To the extent that amounts are withheld from employees' pay for such purposes as income taxes and other deductions, the offsetting credits are to various current liability accounts. Accounting for payrolls was discussed in Chapter 11.

Raw Materials Subsidiary Ledger
Material Y

REF.*	PURCHASED			USED			BALANCE		
	QUANTITY, KILOGRAMS	UNIT COST	AMOUNT	QUANTITY, KILOGRAMS	UNIT COST†	AMOUNT	QUANTITY, KILOGRAMS	UNIT COST†	AMOUNT
Balance beginning of month							6,000	$1.00	$6,000
Invoice No. 57	7,500	$1,20	$9,000				6,000	1.00	6,000
							7,500	1.20	9,000
Requisition No. 34				6,000	$1.00	$6,000			
				3,000	1.20	3,600	4,500	1.20	5,400
Invoice No. 98	4,800	1.25	6,000				4,500	1.20	5,400
							4,800	1.25	6,000
Requisition No. 61				4,500	1.20	5,400			
				800	1.25	1,000	4,000	1.25	5,000

*Identifying number of invoice or requisition from which data were taken.
†Fifo basis.

One common method is to prepare *time cards* for each employee, showing the number of hours worked on each job, the employee's rate of pay, and the direct labour cost chargeable to each job. These time cards become the basis for preparing factory payrolls and also for posting direct labour costs to the goods in process subsidiary ledger accounts (job cost sheets). At the end of each month, a summary entry is made debiting the Goods in Process Inventory account and crediting Direct Labour for all of the direct labour assigned to jobs in process during the month.

Notice that the direct labour account is debited when employees are *paid,* but is credited as *work is performed* on jobs. Work is performed on a daily basis, but employees are paid only at periodic intervals, such as every two weeks. Thus, the direct labour cost paid during the period does not necessarily equal the amount charged to jobs in process. In our example, $60,000 of direct labour was assigned to the three jobs in process, but payments to employees totalled only $52,000. Thus, the $8,000 credit balance of the Direct Labour account at month-end represents a liability for accrued factory wages payable.

Factory overhead

Factory overhead includes *all manufacturing costs other than the costs of raw materials and direct labour.* The Factory Overhead account is a controlling account; the details of individual overhead costs are kept in a subsidiary ledger. Charges to the Factory Overhead account come from several sources. Indirect labour costs, for example, are developed from payroll records; payments of utility bills are posted from the cash payments journal; and depreciation of plant assets is based upon end-of-period adjusting entries.

Factory overhead is an *indirect cost* and cannot be traced directly into specific jobs or units. Thus, an *overhead application rate* is used to assign a reasonable portion of factory overhead costs to each job. An overhead application rate expresses the relationship of total factory overhead to some other factor that *can* be traced directly to specific units of output. Factory overhead is then assigned to jobs *in proportion to this other factor.*

From a computational viewpoint, overhead costs can be assigned to production in proportion to any measurement that can be traced into specific units. However, a strong relationship often exists between the amount of direct labour used in a job and the overhead costs likely to be incurred. Jobs that require more direct labour generally require more indirect labour (supervision and timekeeping), more wear and tear on machinery (depreciation), and greater use of electrical power. Thus, overhead application rates often express the relationship between factory overhead costs and the amount of direct labour involved in the production process. This objective may be accomplished by charging factory overhead to jobs in proportion to *direct labour cost* (as illustrated in Chapter 22), *direct labour hours,* or *machine-hours.*

Predetermined overhead application rates   Many overhead costs tend to remain relatively fixed (constant) from month to month. Thus, total monthly overhead does *not vary in direct proportion* to seasonal or cyclical variations in factory output. Examples of *fixed costs* are property taxes and insurance on plant assets, and the monthly salary of the plant superintendent. *Variable costs* are those that *change in direct proportion* to the level of output. If we allocate actual overhead costs incurred each month to the output of that month, the unit cost of production is likely to vary widely from month to month. In months of high output, unit overhead costs would be low; in months of low output, unit overhead costs would be high. This tendency is illustrated as follows for a company with a capacity to produce 10,000 units per month:

OVERHEAD UNIT COSTS
INCREASE AS VOLUME
DECREASES

Overhead Costs per Unit at Different Levels of Output

	LEVEL OF OUTPUT			
	100% OF CAPACITY	75% OF CAPACITY	50% OF CAPACITY	25% OF CAPACITY
Fixed overhead costs (constant at all levels)	$ 60,000	$ 60,000	$ 60,000	$60,000
Variable overhead costs	100,000	75,000	50,000	25,000
Total overhead costs	$160,000	$135,000	$110,000	$85,000
Number of units produced	10,000	7,500	5,000	2,500
Overhead cost per unit	$16	$18	$22	$34

Note that the *overhead cost per unit increases as the level of output decreases* and that the variable cost remains constant at $10 per unit. For most business purposes, it would be confusing to have product cost figures that vary widely in response to short-run fluctuations in the volume of output. Management needs product cost information for long-range product pricing decisions, income determination, and inventory valuation. For these purposes it is more useful to use what might be called "normal" costs than to have unit cost figures that reflect short-run variations in volume. For example, if we were determining the cost of two identical units of product in the finished goods inventory, it would not seem reasonable to say that one unit cost $30 because it was produced in a low-volume month and the other cost $20 because it was produced in a high-volume month.

This problem can be solved by developing a **predetermined** overhead application rate for use during the entire year. To determine the overhead application rate in advance, we first make an estimate of the expected total factory overhead for the year. This estimated amount is called **budgeted overhead.** We then estimate the direct labour costs, direct labour hours, or machine-hours, whichever is to be used as the basis for applying overhead costs to production. The predetermined overhead application rate is equal to the budgeted overhead divided by the application base. For example, assume that factory overhead is to be applied to jobs in proportion to direct labour costs. Factory overhead is budgeted at $900,000 and direct labour at $600,000. The overhead application rate would be determined as follows:

PREDETERMINED
OVERHEAD APPLICATION
RATE

Budgeted factory overhead for year	$900,000
Budgeted direct labour cost for year	600,000
Overhead application rate ($900,000 ÷ $600,000)	150%

The use of predetermined overhead rate has another advantage. Because the rate is estimated at the beginning of the year, "normal" product costs can be determined as various jobs are completed. *It is not necessary to wait until the end of the period to know the factory overhead chargeable to goods produced.*

Factory overhead, expressed as a percentage of direct labour costs, varies greatly from one business to the next. Highly automated businesses tend to have very high overhead application rates, perhaps several hundred percent of their direct labour costs. Less automated, more labour intensive businesses, may have much lower overhead application rates.

Assume that we are using direct labour cost as the overhead application base and that the predetermined application rate is 150% of direct labour cost. The actual overhead cost for any given period will be accumulated in the Factory Overhead control account. As production takes place and the direct labour cost is charged against jobs, overhead will also be applied to jobs at the predetermined rate of 150% of direct labour cost. As soon as a job is completed, we can determine the total cost and the unit cost of that job order. In the accounting records, the total amount of overhead applied to jobs during the period will be debited to Goods in Process and credited to Factory Overhead.

In our illustration, for example, the total direct labour charged against the three jobs worked on during the month was $60,000, and 150% of this amount, or $90,000, was applied as the overhead cost applicable to these three jobs.

Overapplied or underapplied overhead   We should not expect that applied overhead will ever exactly equal actual overhead, since the predetermined overhead application rate was based on estimates. A debit balance in the Factory Overhead account at the end of a period indicates that overhead applied to jobs was *less* than the actual overhead costs incurred (*underapplied overhead*). A credit balance in the account shows that overhead applied to jobs *exceeded* the overhead costs actually incurred (*overapplied overhead*).

Normally the amount of overapplied or underapplied overhead is *not material* in dollar amount, and it is closed into the Cost of Goods Sold, on the grounds that most of the error is applicable to goods sold during the period. If the overapplied or underapplied overhead *is* material in dollar amount, it is apportioned among the Goods in Process Inventory, the Finished Goods Inventory, and the Cost of Goods Sold accounts.

Goods in process inventory The Goods in Process Inventory account is charged with the cost of raw materials used, direct labour, and an estimate of the factory overhead costs applicable to all jobs. The supporting subsidiary ledger records for this controlling account are the job cost sheets relating to each job in process during the period. In the illustrated flow chart, note that the balance in the goods in process inventory at the beginning of the month, $22,000, represents the cost incurred on job No. 101 during the previous month. During the current month additional costs of $200,000 were incurred. The flow of costs through subsidiary cost sheets and the Goods in Process Inventory controlling account is shown in the following illustration:

FLOW OF COSTS THROUGH JOB ORDER COST SHEETS AND CONTROL ACCOUNT

	JOB 101	JOB 102	JOB 103	TOTAL (CONTROLLING ACCOUNT)
Goods in process inventory, beginning of month	$ 22,000			$ 22,000
Direct labour	24,000	$ 20,000	$16,000	60,000
Raw materials used	8,000	25,000	17,000	50,000
Factory overhead	36,000	30,000	24,000	90,000
Total costs incurred	$ 90,000	$ 75,000	$57,000	$ 222,000
Less: Cost of jobs completed — transferred to Finished Goods Inventory account	(90,000)	(75,000)	–0–	(165,000)
Goods in process inventory, end of month	$ –0–	$ –0–	$57,000	$ 57,000

Note that the only job in process at the end of the month is job 103, and the cost of this job to date, $57,000, is equal to the balance in the controlling account, Goods in Process Inventory. The Goods in Process Inventory account includes all the information needed to prepare a schedule of cost of finished goods manufactured at the end of an accounting period.

Finished goods inventory When a job is completed, the information on the job cost sheet is summarized and the *total cost* of that job becomes the basis for an entry crediting Goods in Process Inventory and debiting Finished Goods Inventory. Subsidiary ledger records are maintained for each type of finished product. When finished product is sold, Cash (or Accounts Receivable) is debited and Sales is credited. In addition, information in the stock ledger records becomes the basis for removing the cost of these products from the Finished Goods Inventory account and charging the

Cost of Goods Sold account. Once more some flow assumption (such as fifo or lifo) is required.

The relation between entries in the Finished Goods Inventory controlling account and the subsidiary finished goods ledger, as shown on the illustrated flow chart, is summarized in the following schedule:

STOCK LEDGER SUPPORTS ENTRIES IN CONTROL ACCOUNT

FINISHED GOODS INVENTORY, CONTROL ACCOUNT		SUBSIDIARY FINISHED GOODS LEDGER		
Beginning balance	$170,000	Product A	$110,000	
		Product C	60,000	$170,000
Completed during period . .	165,000	Product A (job 101)	$ 90,000	
		Product B (job 102)	75,000	165,000
Total goods available for sale	$335,000			$335,000
Less: Cost of goods sold during the period	(150,000)	Product A	$ 80,000	
		Product B	40,000	
		Product C	30,000	(150,000)
Balance on hand at end of period	$185,000	Product A	$120,000	
		Product B	35,000	
		Product C	30,000	$185,000

PROCESS COST SYSTEM

Job order cost systems are appropriate when each batch of production is manufactured to different specifications. Many companies, however, produce a standardized product that flows on a relatively continuous basis through a series of production steps called *processes*. The natural focus of cost measurement in these situations is a *cost centre* such as a manufacturing operation, department, or process. A process cost system is a method of accumulating cost information for such cost centres.

Characteristics of a process cost system

5   Explain the characteristics of a process cost accounting system.

In a process cost system, no attempt is made to determine the cost of particular lots of product as they move through the factory. Instead, the costs of materials, labour, and factory overhead during the period are charged to the various manufacturing processes or departments. The costs incurred in each process are accumulated in separate Goods in Process Inventory accounts, and a record is kept of the number of units passing through each process. The *average unit cost* of performing each process is then determined by dividing the departmental costs by the number of units processed during the period. The cost of a finished unit consists of the *sum* of the unit costs of performing each process involved in the unit's manufacture.

Process cost systems are particularly suitable for mass-production operations of all types. They are used in such industries as automobiles, electronics, breweries, steel, and refining of petroleum products. The process cost approach also may be used in the analysis of nonmanufacturing costs. Marketing activities, for example, may be divided into such functions as advertising, field calls by sales personnel, warehouse operations, and delivery of goods to customers. The cost per unit sold may then be computed for each of these marketing functions.

Flow of costs in a process cost system

To illustrate the basic features of a process cost system, assume that the Process Cost Company manufactures a standard-model tennis racquet. The company has two processing departments: In the Framing Department, wood strips are cut, shaped, and laminated together to form the racquet frame; in the Stringing Department, the racquet head is strung with nylon and a vinyl grip is placed on the handle. Finished racquets are stored in a warehouse and shipped to customers as orders are received.

The cost flow diagram on the next page shows the basic process cost accounts and a summary of the manufacturing costs for the month of July. A careful study of the diagram will show that the Goods in Process account for each department contains all the information necessary to prepare a departmental schedule of the cost of goods manufactured.[2] Each cost flow in our illustration will now be examined to demonstrate the operation of a process cost system.

Raw materials   There was a $4,000 balance in the Raw Materials Inventory control account at the beginning of July. During the month of July purchases of raw materials were charged to the Raw Materials Inventory account in the amount of $26,000. At the end of July the following entry is made to summarize the raw materials requisitioned during the month by each department:

<table>
<tr><td>END-OF-MONTH ENTRY:
MATERIALS USED</td><td>Goods in Process: Framing Department . . . .</td><td>18,800</td><td></td></tr>
<tr><td></td><td>Goods in Process: Stringing Department . . . .</td><td>7,790</td><td></td></tr>
<tr><td></td><td>   Raw Materials Inventory . . . .</td><td></td><td>26,590</td></tr>
<tr><td></td><td>To record raw materials used in July.</td><td></td><td></td></tr>
</table>

Direct labour   During July paycheques issued to direct factory workers totalled $17,900. This factory payroll was recorded by a debit to Direct Labour and a credit to Cash. The cost of direct labour used by each department during July was determined from employees' time cards. The entry summarizing the direct labour costs chargeable to each department appears below:

<table>
<tr><td>END-OF-MONTH ENTRY:
FACTORY PAYROLL</td><td>Goods in Process: Framing Department . . . .</td><td>12,000</td><td></td></tr>
<tr><td></td><td>Goods in Process: Stringing Department . . . .</td><td>9,500</td><td></td></tr>
<tr><td></td><td>   Direct Labour . . . .</td><td></td><td>21,500</td></tr>
<tr><td></td><td>To record direct labour used in July.</td><td></td><td></td></tr>
</table>

Notice that direct labour costs charged to the two departments totalled $21,500 while payments to employees during the month amounted to only $17,900. The

---

[2] When a perpetual inventory system is used, it is unnecessary to show the beginning and ending inventories and purchases of materials in the schedule of cost of goods manufactured; only the cost of materials used in production need be shown.

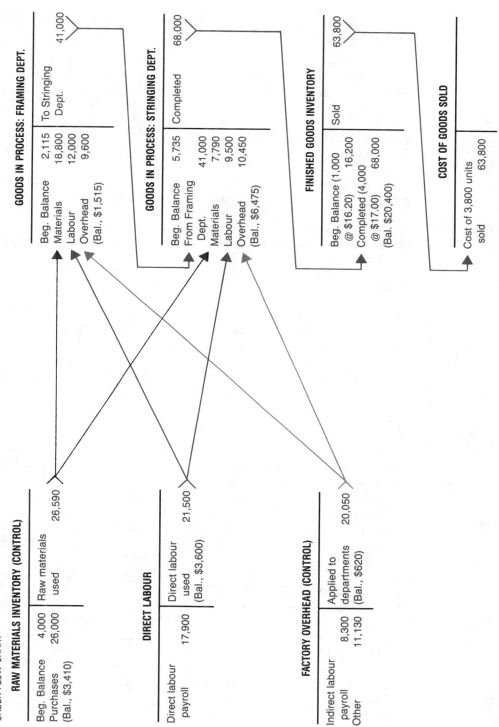

COST FLOW DIAGRAM
FOR PROCESS COSTING—
COMPARE WITH JOB
ORDER FLOW CHART

RAW MATERIALS INVENTORY (CONTROL)

Beg. Balance	4,000	Raw materials	
Purchases	26,000	used	26,590
(Bal., $3,410)			

DIRECT LABOUR

Direct labour		Direct labour	
payroll	17,900	used	21,500
		(Bal., $3,600)	

FACTORY OVERHEAD (CONTROL)

Indirect labour		Applied to	
payroll	8,300	departments	20,050
Other	11,130	(Bal., $620)	

GOODS IN PROCESS: FRAMING DEPT.

Beg. Balance	2,115	To Stringing	
Materials	18,800	Dept.	41,000
Labour	12,000		
Overhead	9,600		
(Bal., $1,515)			

GOODS IN PROCESS: STRINGING DEPT.

Beg. Balance	5,735	Completed	
From Framing			68,000
Dept.	41,000		
Materials	7,790		
Labour	9,500		
Overhead	10,450		
(Bal., $6,475)			

FINISHED GOODS INVENTORY

Beg. Balance (1,000		Sold	
@ $16.20)	16,200		63,800
Completed (4,000			
@ $17.00)	68,000		
(Bal. $20,400)			

COST OF GOODS SOLD

| Cost of 3,800 units | | | |
| sold | 63,800 | | |

$3,600 credit balance in the Direct Labour account represents the company's liability for wages payable at the end of July.

Factory overhead   Process Cost Company prepares a departmental factory overhead budget at the beginning of each year, and factory overhead is applied to departmental goods in process accounts on the basis of departmental direct labour cost at the following rates:

Framing Department	80% of direct labour cost
Stringing Department	110% of direct labour cost

The entry charging the departmental goods in process accounts for their share of factory overhead, at these predetermined rates, may be summarized as follows:

Goods in Process: Framing Department (80% of $12,000)	9,600	
Goods in Process: Stringing Department (110% of $9,500)	10,450	
Factory Overhead		20,050
To record factory overhead applied to production on basis of direct labour cost.		

Actual overhead for July totalled $19,430, leaving a credit balance of $620 in the Factory Overhead account, representing **overapplied overhead** for the month. This amount would be carried forward month to month, and any balance at the end of the year would be apportioned between ending inventories of goods in process and finished goods and the cost of goods sold during the year, or, if not material, simply closed out to the Cost of Goods Sold account.

Equivalent full units — the key to determining unit cost

A basic objective of a process cost system is to determine the unit cost of materials, labour, and factory overhead for each manufacturing process or department. These unit costs become the basis for valuing inventories and for tracing the flow of costs through the departmental goods in process accounts and finally to Finished Goods Inventory and to Cost of Goods Sold.

If all units of product in a given department are **completely processed** (started and finished) during the period, computing unit costs is a simple matter of dividing the departmental costs by the number of units processed. In most cases, however, there are unfinished units of product on hand at the beginning as well as at the end of the accounting period. When some of the units on hand are unfinished, we cannot compute unit costs merely by dividing total costs by the number of units worked on, for this would assign the same unit cost to finished and unfinished goods. If completed and partially completed units of product are expressed in **equivalent full units** of completed product, however, this difficulty is overcome. Meaningful unit costs can then be determined by dividing the total cost by the equivalent full units produced. This computation is illustrated as follows for raw materials costs:

$$\text{MATERIALS COST PER UNIT} = \frac{\text{TOTAL COST OF RAW MATERIALS USED DURING MONTH}}{\text{EQUIVALENT FULL UNITS PRODUCED DURING MONTH}}$$

6 Define and compute "equivalent full units" of production.

What are "equivalent full units"?   Equivalent full units are a measure of the *work done* in a given accounting period. The concept of an equivalent full unit is based on the assumption that creating two units, each of which is 50% complete, represents the *same amount of work* as does producing one finished unit. Similarly, producing 1,000 units that are 25% complete is viewed as equivalent to 250 full units of production.

The work accomplished by a manufacturing department during a given accounting period may include (1) completing units that were already in process at the beginning of the period, (2) working on units started and completed during the current period, and (3) working on units that are still in process at the end of the current period. If we are to measure the work accomplished by the department, we must determine the equivalent full units of production represented *by each of these three types of work effort.* The following illustration shows the computation of equivalent full units of production for a hypothetical company during the month of March:

EQUIVALENT FULL UNITS — AN INDEX OF PRODUCTIVE EFFORT FOR A PERIOD

Computation of Equivalent Full Units

	UNITS	×	PORTION COMPLETED DURING MARCH	=	EQUIVALENT FULL UNITS COMPLETED (ALL COSTS)
Beginning inventory in process (Mar. 1): 80% completed in February but finished in March	20,000	×	20%	=	4,000
Units started & completed in March ..	50,000	×	100%	=	50,000
Units completed and transferred to storage	70,000				
Ending inventory in process (Mar. 31), 40% completed in March	25,000	×	40%	=	10,000
Equivalent full units of production during March					64,000

Although 70,000 units were completed and transferred to storage in our example, the actual amount of *work* accomplished during March was equivalent to producing only 64,000 full units. The work performed in March consists of 4,000 equivalent full units of work (20% of 20,000) to complete the beginning inventory of goods in process, 50,000 equivalent full units to start and complete additional units during March, and 10,000 equivalent full units (40% of 25,000) on the goods still in process at the end of the month.

When raw materials costs and processing costs (direct labour and factory overhead) are applied at a *uniform rate* throughout the production process, the equivalent units of work done will be identical for all three cost elements. If the materials are placed in process at various stages (such as 100% at the beginning of production, or 80% at the beginning and 20% when most of the processing has been completed), the equivalent unit figure for raw materials will differ from that for processing costs. In such situations, the equivalent-unit computation for raw materials must be done separately from that for processing costs.

Determination of unit costs and valuation of inventories: an example

We will now return to our example of the Process Cost Company to illustrate the computation of unit costs and the assignment of departmental costs to goods completed and goods in process at the end of the period. The costs incurred in the two processing departments during July appear in the departmental goods in process accounts, illustrated on page 955. The following production report shows the number of units processed in each department and provides information about the beginning and ending inventories of goods in process:

PRODUCTION REPORT
SHOWS UNITS ONLY

Production Report for July

	FRAMING DEPT.	STRINGING DEPT.
Units in process on July 1	500[a]	400[c]
Add: Units placed in production during July	3,900	4,100
Total units worked on during July	4,400	4,500
Less: Units in process on July 31	300[b]	500[d]
Units completed during July	4,100	4,000

[a]50% complete as to materials and processing costs on July 1.
[b]50% complete as to materials and processing costs on July 31.
[c]100% complete as to materials and 75% complete as to processing costs on July 1.
[d]100% complete as to materials and 20% complete as to processing costs on July 31.

Using this information, we can now determine the unit costs in each of the two departments.

7   Prepare a cost report for a production department using a process cost system.

Framing Department   From the information contained on the debit side of the departmental goods in process account (page 955) and in the preceding production report, a *cost report* for the Framing Department for July may be prepared as shown at the top of page 959. The purposes of the cost report are (1) to summarize the units and cost charged to the department during the month, (2) to compute the unit costs of production during the month, and (3) to allocate the costs charged to the department between completed units and the ending inventory of goods in process.

The first section of the cost report (labelled Inputs) shows that total costs charged to the Framing Department during July amounted to $42,515, including the cost of $2,115 applicable to the beginning goods in process inventory that was carried forward from June. This total cost of $42,515 was incurred on the 4,400 units worked on during July. We could not, however, divide the total cost by 4,400 units to determine the manufacturing cost per unit for the month. Not all of these units were entirely processed in July; 500 units were already 50% complete at the beginning of the month, while another 300 units were only 50% complete at month-end. Therefore, we must compute the equivalent full units of production for July as a preliminary step toward determining unit cost.

In the Framing Department, raw materials and processing costs (labour and overhead) are applied to units of product at a uniform rate; that is, a unit that has received 50% of the required raw materials has also received 50% of the processing costs required to complete the unit. Therefore, the equivalent full units of production

FRAMING DEPARTMENT
Cost Report for July

	TOTAL UNITS	TOTAL COSTS	÷ EQUIVALENT FULL UNITS*	= UNIT COST
Inputs:				
Units in process at beginning of month (50% completed in June) .	500	$ 2,115		
Units placed in production during July	3,900			
Raw materials		18,800	4,000	$ 4.70
Direct labour		12,000	4,000	3.00
Factory overhead		9,600	4,000	2.40
Total inputs—units and costs	4,400	$42,515		
Unit cost of work done in July				$10.10
Outputs:				
Units in process at end of month, 50% complete (300 units × 50% × $10.10)	300	$ 1,515		
Units completed and transferred to Stringing Dept. ($42,515 – $1,515)	4,100	41,000		$10.00
Total outputs—units and costs	4,400	$42,515		

*COMPUTATION OF EQUIVALENT FULL UNITS:	UNITS ×	PORTION COMPLETED DURING JULY	= EQUIVALENT FULL UNITS PRODUCED
Units in process at beginning of month (50% completed in June)	500	50%	250
Units started and completed in July	3,600†	100%	3,600
Units completed and transferred to Stringing Dept.	4,100		
Units in process at end of month (50% complete)	300	50%	150
Equivalent full units of production during July			4,000

†The number of units started and completed during July is found by subtracting the 300 units in process at July 31 from the 3,900 units placed in production during July.

are the same for all three cost elements and may be determined by a single computation as shown as the bottom of the cost report. This computation shows that the work done in the Framing Department during July was equivalent to producing 4,000 full units.

We are now ready to determine the ***average unit cost*** of producing racquet frames during July. In the Inputs section of the cost report, the cost of materials used in July ($18,800) is divided by the equivalent full units of production (4,000) to give us a unit cost for raw materials of $4.70. The direct labour and factory overhead costs per unit are computed in a similar manner. The total of these three cost elements gives an average unit cost of *$10.10* for the work performed by the Framing Department during July.

Once the unit manufacturing costs have been determined, the total costs charged to the department during July ($42,515) can be allocated between units completed and transferred to the Stringing Department in July and units still in process in the Framing Department at July 31. The easiest method of allocating these costs is to value the ending inventory of goods in process using the current unit cost figure, and then to assign the *remainder* of the costs to the units completed during the month.[3] This approach is illustrated in the Outputs section of the cost report.

Although 300 units are in process in the Framing Department at July 31, each unit is only 50% complete; therefore, the ending inventory of goods in process is assigned a cost of $1,515 (300 units × $10.10 × 50%). The remaining $41,000 ($42,515 − $1,515) represents the cost of the 4,100 units completed and transferred to the Stringing Department during July. The entry to transfer the cost of units completed in the Framing Department to the Stringing Department is illustrated as follows:

TRANSFER OF COST TO
NEXT DEPARTMENT

Goods in Process: Stringing Department   41,000
    Goods in Process: Framing Department   41,000
To transfer cost of 4,100 completed racquet frames from
Framing Department to Stringing Department.
Average unit cost = $10.00.

Note that the average unit cost of racquet frames *completed* in July is only $10.00, while the average unit cost of *work done* in July is $10.10. The reason for this difference is that some of the units completed in July received part of their processing during June. The cost of units *completed* in July, therefore, is a combination of manufacturing costs incurred in both June and July.[4]

Stringing Department   The July report of the Stringing Department is illustrated on the following page. In most respects, this report parallels that of the Framing Department. A few new features, however, appear in the cost report of the Stringing Department; these features will now be explained.

First, note that the cost inputs section of the report includes the cost of the *racquet frames transferred* into the Stringing Department from the Framing Department

---

[3] Using the current month's unit cost to value ending inventory conforms to the *first-in, first-out* method of inventory valuation. The use of other inventory methods (such as weighted average) in a process cost system is discussed in cost accounting courses.

[4] The $2,115 cost of goods in process at July 1 is the cost of 250 equivalent units of work performed in June (500 units, each 50% complete), indicating a June cost per unit of $8.46 ($2,115 ÷ 250). While 4,100 units were completed during July, 250 equivalent units of work were done on these units in June and the remaining 3,850 equivalent units of work were done in July. Thus, the cost of these units includes the following "layers":

Costs brought forward from June: 250 equivalent units @ $8.46 .... $ 2,115
Costs incurred in July: 3,850 equivalent units @ $10.10   38,885
Total cost of 4,100 units completed in July $41,000

Average unit cost ($41,000 ÷ 4,100) .... $ 10.00

STRINGING DEPARTMENT
Cost Report for July

	TOTAL UNITS	TOTAL COSTS	÷ EQUIVALENT FULL UNITS*	= UNIT COST
Inputs				
Units in process at beginning of month (100% complete as to materials and 75% as to processing costs)	400	$ 5,735		
Units transferred in from Framing Department	4,100	41,000	4,100	$10.00
Raw materials added		7,790	4,100	1.90
Direct labour		9,500	3,800	2.50
Factory overhead		10,450	3,800	2.75
Total inputs — units and costs	4,500	$74,475		
Unit cost of work done in July				$17.15
Outputs:				
Units in process at end of month (100% complete as to materials and 20% as to processing):				
Units transferred in from Framing Department (500 frames × $10.00)	500	$ 5,000		
Raw Materials added (500 × $1.90 × 100%)		950		
Direct labour (500 × $2.50 × 20%)		250		
Factory overhead (500 × $2.75 × 20%)		275		
Cost of units in process, July 31		$ 6,475		
Units completed and transferred to Finished Goods Warehouse ($74,475 − $6,475)	4,000	68,000		$17.00
Total output — units and costs	4,500	$74,475		

*COMPUTATION OF EQUIVALENT FULL UNITS:	UNITS ×	PORTION COMPLETED DURING JULY	= EQUIVALENT FULL UNITS PRODUCED
Raw Materials:			
Units in process at beginning of month (100% completed as to raw materials in June)	400	-0-	-0-
Units started and completed in July	3,600	100%	3,600
Units completed and transferred to Finished Goods Warehouse	4,000		
Units in process at end of month (100% complete as to materials)	500	100%	500
Equivalent full units of production — raw materials			4,100
Processing costs (direct labour and overhead):			
Units in process at beginning of month (75% complete as to processing costs in June)	400	25%	100
Units started and completed in July	3,600†	100%	3,600
Units completed and transferred to Finished Goods Warehouse	4,000		
Units in process at end of month (20% complete as to processing costs) .	500	20%	100
Equivalent full units of production — processing costs			3,800

†The number of units started and completed in July is found by subtracting the 500 units still in process at July 31 from the 4,100 units transferred in from the Framing Department during July.

during July. From the viewpoint of the Stringing Department, these racquet frames are a form of "raw material" that will be processed into finished tennis racquets. (The $7,790 cost identified as "Raw materials added" represents only the nylon strings and vinyl grips attached to the racquet frames in the Stringing Department.) Obviously, the cost of finished tennis racquets would be understated if we did not include the cost of the racquet frames.

Second, notice that the equivalent full units of production figures are computed *separately* for raw materials and for processing costs. In our example involving the Framing Department, both raw materials and processing costs were applied to units of product uniformly throughout the production process, which meant that the equivalent full units of production was the same for each cost element. In the Stringing Department, however, 100% of the materials needed to complete each unit are placed in process at the beginning of production, while processing costs are applied uniformly throughout the production process. Since raw materials costs and processing costs are applied to units of product at *different rates,* the equivalent units figure for raw materials must be computed separately from that for processing costs.

The computations at the bottom of the cost report show that enough raw materials were used during July to produce 4,100 full units. Thus, the raw materials cost per unit is found by dividing the total raw materials cost, $7,790, by 4,100 equivalent full units of production. In terms of direct labour and overhead, however, the work accomplished during July was equivalent to fully processing only 3,800 units. Therefore, the 3,800 equivalent unit figure is used in determining the unit costs for direct labour and factory overhead. Note that the $17.15 unit cost of work performed in July *includes the $10.00 unit cost* of the racquet frames transferred in from the Framing Department.

A third new feature in the Stringing Department cost report is the itemizing of the various cost elements included in the ending inventory of units in process. Since these units are 100% complete as to materials but only 20% complete as to processing costs, the amount of each manufacturing cost included in the units must be computed separately. Also note that the cost of the racquet frames ($10.00 per unit) is included in the cost of the 500 units in process at July 31.

All of the $74,475 in costs charged to the Stringing Department during July are applicable either to the goods in process at July 31 or to units completed during the month. Since we have assigned $6,475 of these costs to the ending inventory of goods in process, the remaining $68,000 ($74,475 − $6,475) represents the cost of the 4,000 tennis racquets completed during July. The entry to transfer the cost of goods completed in the Stringing Department during July to the Finished Goods Inventory account follows:

TRANSFER OF COST TO
FINISHED GOODS
INVENTORY

| Finished Goods Inventory | 68,000 | |
| Goods in Process: Stringing Department | | 68,000 |

To transfer cost of 4,000 tennis racquets completed in Stringing Department during July to Finished Goods Inventory. Unit cost = $17.00.

The entries to record the sales of goods for $84,000 by Process Manufacturing Company during July appear at the top of page 963.

Accounts Receivable	84,000	
Sales		84,000

To record sales on account during July.

Cost of Goods Sold	63,800	
Finished Goods Inventory		63,800

To record cost of 3,800 tennis racquets sold during July,
computed on a Fifo basis: 1,000 units @ $16.20 + 2,800
units @ $17.00.

Summary of job order and process cost systems

Several simplifying assumptions have been made in developing the illustrations of job order and process cost systems; nevertheless, the essential features of the two types of cost systems were included. Both the job order and the process cost systems are essentially devices for collecting cost information. A job order cost system produces information about the cost of manufacturing a particular product or a batch of a given product; a process cost system produces information about the *average cost* of putting a homogeneous unit of product through various manufacturing operations for a given time period. A job order cost system usually involves more detailed cost accounting work and in return gives more specific cost information. A process cost system involves less detailed accounting work and accumulates costs in terms of major production processes or departmental cost centres. Both systems provide the information required to prepare a schedule of cost of finished goods manufactured, to arrive at unit costs, and to formulate business decisions.

END-OF-CHAPTER REVIEW

SUMMARY OF CHAPTER LEARNING OBJECTIVES

1 Explain the purpose of a cost accounting system.

The purpose of a cost accounting system is to provide current information about the total cost and the per-unit cost of manufacturing a product or performing a service. This information is used by financial accountants to value inventories and the cost of goods sold, and by managerial accountants for controlling costs and planning future operations.

2 Describe how manufacturing costs "flow" through perpetual inventory accounts.

As manufacturing costs are incurred, they are assigned to the Goods in Process Inventory account. When the goods are completed, their cost is then transferred from the Goods in Process Inventory account to the Finished Goods Inventory account. Finally, when the goods are sold, their cost is transferred from Finished Goods Inventory to the Cost of Goods Sold account.

3 Explain the characteristics of a job order cost accounting system.

A job order cost system measures the total cost and the per-unit cost of each "job," — that is, each specific batch of production. All the manufacturing costs relating to the job are accumulated on a job cost sheet. Once the job is complete, unit cost is determined by dividing the total cost of the job by the number of units produced.

4 Describe the purpose and the content of a job cost sheet.

The purpose of a job cost sheet is to keep track of all manufacturing costs relating to a particular job. Each job cost sheet shows the cost of all the materials, direct labour, and factory overhead charged to the job. The job cost sheets of all jobs in process serve as a subsidiary ledger supporting the balance of the Goods in Process Inventory controlling account.

5 Explain the characteristics of a process cost accounting system.

A process cost system measures the manufacturing costs incurred by each manufacturing process or department during the accounting period. The unit cost of each process then is determined by dividing the manufacturing costs assigned to the department by the equivalent full units of production. The cost of a finished unit is the sum of the unit costs of performing each process in the unit's manufacture.

6 Define and compute "equivalent full units" of production.

Equivalent full units of production is a measure of the work done by a production department during the accounting period. The concept of an "equivalent full unit" is based upon the idea that creating two units, each of which is 50% complete, represents the same amount of "work" as does completing one finished unit. The equivalent full units of production for a department are computed by considering the amount of work performed on (1) units already in process at the beginning of the period, (2) units started and completed during the period, and (3) units still in process at the end of the period.

7 Prepare a cost report for a production department using a process cost system.

A separate cost report is prepared for each manufacturing process or each production department. These reports (1) summarize the manufacturing costs charged to a department during the accounting period, (2) compute the unit cost of performing the production process during the period, and (3) allocate the manufacturing costs charged to the department between completed units and the ending inventory of goods in process.

KEY TERMS INTRODUCED OR EMPHASIZED IN CHAPTER 23

Cost report A schedule prepared for each production process or department in a process cost system. Shows the costs charged to the department during the period and the computation of unit manufacturing costs, and allocates the departmental costs between units completed during the period and the ending inventory of goods in process.

Equivalent full units of production A measure of the work done during an accounting period. Includes work done on beginning and ending inventories of goods in process as well as work on units completely processed during the period.

Job cost sheet A record used in a job order cost system to summarize the manufacturing costs (materials, labour, and overhead) applicable to each job, or batch or production. Job cost sheets may be viewed as a subsidiary ledger supporting the balance of the Goods in Process Inventory control account.

Job order cost system A cost accounting system under which the focal point of costing is a quantity of product known as a *job* or *lot*. Costs of raw materials, direct labour, and factory overhead applicable to each job are compiled to arrive at average unit cost.

Overapplied or underapplied overhead The difference between the actual factory overhead incurred during the period and the amount applied to goods in process by use of a pre-determined factory overhead rate. A physical measure of production activity.

Predetermined overhead rate A rate estimated at the beginning of the year as the probable relationship of factory overhead expenses to a correlated factor such as direct labour cost, direct labour hours, or machine-hours. This predetermined rate is used to allocate factory overhead to goods in process, thus making it possible to determine the approximate complete cost of finished units as quickly as possible.

Process cost system A cost accounting system used mostly in industries such as petroleum or chemicals characterized by continuous mass production. Costs are not assigned to specific units but to a manufacturing process or department.

Processing costs The cost of processing raw materials into a finished product; includes both direct labour costs and factory overhead costs.

DEMONSTRATION PROBLEM FOR YOUR REVIEW

The Diversified Mfg. Company started operations early in January with two production departments, Foundry and Blending. The Foundry Department produces special castings to customer specifications and the Blending Department produces an industrial compound that is sold by the kilogram. The company uses a job order cost system in the Foundry and a process cost system in the Blending Department.

The following schedule summarizes the operations for January:

	TOTAL COSTS INCURRED	FOUNDRY	BLENDING	INVENTORY AT JAN. 31
Raw Materials	$40,000	$13,000	$23,000	$4,000
Direct labour	56,800	20,000	36,800	
Factory overhead	43,600	16,000	27,600	

Following is the schedule of the jobs in process in the Foundry Department at January 31:

	RAW MATERIALS	DIRECT LABOUR
Job No. 9	$600	$400
Job No. 10	580	500

All other jobs were shipped to customers at a billed price of $60,000. The factory overhead in the Foundry is applied on the basis of direct labour cost.

The January production report for the Blending Department shows the following:

	KILOGRAMS
Placed in production	95,000
Completed	80,000
In process at Jan. 31, 80% complete as to raw materials and processing costs	15,000

Of the units completed, 70,000 were sold for $92,500 and the other 10,000 are stored in the warehouse.

Instructions   **a** Prepare the journal entries to record (1) raw materials purchases and the requisitions for the Foundry and Blending Departments, (2) payments for direct labour and overhead costs (assume credit is to Cash), and (3) the allocation of direct labour used and of factory overhead to the two departments.

b Determine the cost of the jobs in process in the Foundry Department at the end of January and prepare journal entries (1) to transfer the cost of jobs completed to Finished Goods Inventory and (2) to record the sales and cost of goods sold for the month.

c Prepare a cost report for the Blending Department and prepare journal entries (1) to transfer the cost of the finished products to the Finished Goods Inventory account and (2) to record the sales and cost of goods sold for the month.

SOLUTION TO DEMONSTRATION PROBLEM

a (1) Raw Materials Inventory 40,000
           Accounts Payable   40,000
        To record purchase of raw materials.

      Goods in Process: Foundry Department 13,000
      Goods in Process: Blending Department 23,000
           Raw Materials Inventory   36,000
        To record requisitions of raw materials.

   (2) Direct Labour 56,800
       Factory Overhead 43,600
           Cash   100,400
        To record payments for direct labour and overhead
        costs.

   (3) Goods in Process: Foundry Department 36,000
       Goods in Process: Blending Department 64,400
           Direct Labour   56,800
           Factory Overhead   43,600
        To allocate direct labour and overhead costs to
        productive departments.

b Cost of jobs in process in Foundry Department at January 31:

	TOTAL	JOB NO. 9	JOB NO. 10
Raw materials	$1,180	$ 600	$ 580
Direct labour	900	400	500
Factory overhead, 80% of direct labour	720	320	400
	$2,800	$1,320	$1,480

   (1) Finished Goods Inventory 46,200
           Goods in Process: Foundry Department   46,200
        To record cost of jobs completed: Total costs charged
        to Foundry Dept., $49,000, less cost of jobs in process,
        $2,800 = $46,200.

(2) Accounts Receivable   60,000
      Sales   60,000
    To record sale of goods completed in Foundry
    Department.

Cost of Goods Sold   46,200
      Finished Goods Inventory   46,200
    To record cost of goods sold from Foundry
    Department.

c

BLENDING DEPARTMENT
Cost Report for January

	TOTAL UNITS	TOTAL COSTS	÷ EQUIVALENT FULL UNITS*	= UNIT COST
Inputs:				
Raw materials	95,000	$23,000	92,000	$0.25
Direct labour		36,800	92,000	0.40
Factory overhead		27,600	92,000	0.30
Total inputs — units and costs	95,000	$87,400		
Unit cost for January				$0.95
Outputs:				
Units in process at end of month, 80% complete (15,000 × $0.95 × 80%)	15,000	$11,400		
Transferred to Finished Goods Inventory ($87,400 − $11,400)	80,000	76,000		$0.95
Total outputs — units and costs . . .	95,000	$87,400		

*Computation of equivalent full units:

Beginning inventory of goods in process . . . .   -0-
Units started and completed during January   80,000
Add: Full units of work done in January on ending inventory in process
(15,000 × 80%)   12,000
Equivalent full units of production in January   92,000

(1) Finished Goods Inventory   76,000
      Goods in Process: Blending Department   76,000
    To record cost of finished product.

(2) Accounts Receivable   92,500
      Sales   92,500
    To record sales from Blending Department.

Cost of Goods Sold   66,500
      Finished Goods Inventory   66,500
    To record cost of goods sold from Blending Department,
    70,000 units @ $0.95 per unit.

ASSIGNMENT MATERIAL

REVIEW QUESTIONS

1 What is a cost accounting system?

2 What are the two major objectives of cost accounting?

3 What are the major advantages to a manufacturing company of using a cost accounting system instead of using the periodic inventory method to determine the cost of finished goods manufactured?

4 Rodeo Drive Jewelers makes custom jewelry for celebrities. Would you expect the company to use a job order or a process cost accounting system? Explain.

5 What factors should be taken into account in deciding whether to use a job order cost system or a process cost system in any given manufacturing situation?

6 Describe the three kinds of charges on a job cost sheet. For what general ledger control account do job cost sheets constitute supporting detail?

7 Distinguish between fixed and variable overhead costs. Explain what happens to total overhead costs per unit when the level of production rises, assuming that some overhead costs are fixed.

8 Explain why it is advantageous to use predetermined overhead rates in associating factory overhead with output.

9 What is meant by underapplied overhead? By overapplied overhead?

10 Gerox Company applies factory overhead on the basis of machine-hours, using a predetermined overhead rate. At the end of the current year the factory overhead account has a credit balance. What are the possible explanations for this? What disposition should be made of this balance?

11 What are the characteristics of a process cost system?

12 Silex Mfg. has two processing departments: Assembly and Packaging. Identify the four accounts most likely to be *credited* as costs are charged to the Goods in Process account of the Packaging Department.

13 What is meant by the term *equivalent full units?* How is this concept used in computing average unit costs?

14 When must the equivalent full units of production figure for raw materials be computed separately from that for processing costs? Explain.

15 If a department has no beginning inventory of goods in process but has 10,000 units in process at month-end, will the equivalent full units of work performed be greater or smaller than the number of units completed during the month? Explain.

16 Briefly describe the purposes of a cost report in a process cost system.

17 In a process cost system, is the average unit cost of *work performed* during the month always exactly equal to the average unit cost of *goods completed* in the month? Explain.

EXERCISES

Exercise 23-1
Accounting
terminology Listed below are nine technical accounting terms introduced in this chapter:

Job order cost system	Process costs system	Equivalent full units of production
Cost report	Variable costs	Overapplied overhead
Job cost sheet	Fixed costs	Underapplied overhead

Each of the following statements may (or may not) describe one of these technical terms. For each statement, indicate the accounting term described, or answer "None" if the statement does not correctly describe any of the terms.

a A debit balance remaining in the Factory Overhead account at the end of an accounting period.

b Manufacturing costs that do not vary based upon the level of production.

c The type of cost accounting system likely to be used by a construction company that is building several different projects at one time.

d Manufacturing costs that change in direct proportion to the level of production (for example, raw materials used).

e The number of units completed during the period and transferred from the Goods in Process Inventory account to Finished Goods Inventory.

f The schedule used to accumulate the total manufacturing costs and to determine the unit cost of a particular batch production.

g A measure of the amount of work performed by a production department during a given accounting period.

Exercise 23-2
Flow of costs in a cost
accounting system For each of the following four accounts prepare an example of a journal entry that would cause the account to be (1) debited, and (2) credited. Assume perpetual inventory records are maintained. Include written explanations with your journal entries and use "XXX" in place of dollar amounts.

a Raw Materials Inventory

b Direct Labour

c Factory Overhead

d Finished Goods Inventory

Exercise 23-3
Flow of costs in a
job order cost system The following information is taken from the job cost sheets of Gate Company:

JOB NUMBER	MANUFACTURING COSTS AS OF JUNE 30	MANUFACTURING COSTS IN JULY
101	$4,200	
102	3,240	
103	900	$1,950
104	2,250	3,900
105		5,700
106		3,630

During July, jobs No. 103 and 104 were completed, and jobs No. 101, 102, and 103 were delivered to customers. From this information, compute the following:

a The goods in process inventory at June 30

b The finished goods inventory at June 30

c The cost of goods sold during July

d The goods in process inventory at July 31

e The finished goods inventory at July 31

Exercise 23-4
Preparing journal entries in a job order cost system

Snowplow Company, which uses a job order cost system, completed the following transactions during the month of November:

a Direct labour, $30,000, was transferred from the Direct Labour account to the appropriate inventory account.

b Factory overhead costs of $57,500 were incurred on credit.

c Factory overhead costs were applied to goods in process at the rate of 180% of direct labour cost.

d Raw materials used on specific jobs amounted to $164,000.

e Jobs with total accumulated costs of $230,000 were finished.

f The cost of units sold during the month amounted to $236,000; the sales price of units sold is $400,000. All sales were made on account.

Prepare journal entries to record the foregoing transactions. Explanations may be omitted.

Exercise 23-5
Computing the equivalent full units of production

The following relates to the Assembly Department of Lawncraft Mowers during the month of May:

Units in process at May 1 (80% completed in April)	2,000
Additional units placed in production during May	20,000
Units in process at May 31 (60% completed)	5,000

Determine the equivalent full units of production during the month of May, assuming that all costs are incurred uniformly as the units move through the production line.

Exercise 23-6
Preparing journal entries in a process cost system

Shamrock Industries uses a process cost system. Products are processed successively by Department A and Department B, and are then transferred to the finished goods warehouse. Following is cost information for Department B during the month of June:

Cost of goods in process at June 1		$ 21,000
Cost of units transferred in from Department A during June		73,500
Manufacturing costs incurred in June:		
Materials added	$34,000	
Direct labour	6,100	
Factory overhead	17,400	57,500
Total costs charged to Department B in June		$152,000

The cost of goods in process in Department B at June 30 has been determined to be $23,700.

Prepare journal entries to record for the month of June (1) the transfer of production from Department A to Department B, (2) the manufacturing costs incurred by Department B, and (3) the transfer of completed units from Department B to the finished goods warehouse.

Exercise 23-7
Computing unit costs

Following are the production data for Department No. 1 for the first month of operation:

Inputs to department:

Raw materials	$12,000
Direct labour	4,750
Factory overhead	28,500
Total	$45,250

During this first month, 1,000 units were placed into production; 800 units were completed and the remaining 200 units are 100% completed as to material and 75% completed as to direct labour and factory overhead.

You are to determine:

a Unit cost of material used

b Equivalent full units of production for direct labour and factory overhead

c Unit cost of direct labour

d Unit cost of factory overhead

e Total cost of 200 units in process at end of month

f Total cost of 800 units completed

PROBLEMS

Group A

Problem 23A-1
Job order cost
system: a short
problem

Riverside Engineers is a machine shop that uses a job order cost accounting system. Overhead is applied to individual jobs at a predetermined rate based on direct labour costs. The job cost sheet for job No. 321 appears as follows:

Job Cost Sheet

JOB NUMBER: 321   **DATE STARTED:** MAY 10

PRODUCT: 2" BRASS CHECK VALVES   **DATE COMPLETED:** MAY 21

UNITS COMPLETED: 4,000

Raw materials used	$17,500
Direct labour	3,000
Factory overhead (applied as a percentage of direct labour)	5,100
Total cost of job No. 321	$25,600

Instructions

a Compute (1) the predetermined overhead application rate used by the company, and (2) the average unit cost of the valves manufactured in job No. 321.

b Prepare general journal entries to:

(1) Summarize the manufacturing costs charged to job No. 321.

(2) Record the completion of job No. 321.

(3) Record the credit sale of 2,100 units from job No. 321 at a unit sales price of $10. Record in a separate entry the related cost of goods sold.

Problem 23A-2
Apply factory overhead

Georgia Woods, Inc., manufactures furniture to customers' specifications and uses a job order cost system. A predetermined overhead rate is used in applying factory overhead to individual jobs. In Department One, overhead is applied on the basis of direct labour hours, and in Department Two, on the basis of machine-hours. At the beginning of the current year, management made the following budget estimates to assist in determining the overhead application rate:

	DEPARTMENT ONE	DEPARTMENT TWO
Direct labour cost	$300,000	$225,000
Direct labour hours	20,000	15,000
Factory overhead	$500,000	$450,000
Machine-hours	12,000	7,500

Production of a batch of custom furniture ordered by City Furniture (job. No. 58) was started early in the year and completed three weeks later on January 29. The records for this job show the following cost information:

	DEPARTMENT ONE	DEPARTMENT TWO
Job order for City Furniture (job No. 58):		
Raw materials cost	$10,100	$ 7,600
Direct labour cost	$16,500	$11,100
Direct labour hours	1,100	740
Machine-hours	750	500

Selected additional information for January is given below:

	DEPARTMENT ONE	DEPARTMENT TWO
Direct labour hours — month of January	1,600	1,200
Machine-hours — month of January	1,100	600
Factory overhead incurred in January	$38,450	$36,970

Instructions   **a** Compute the predetermined overhead rate for each department.

b What is the total cost of the furniture produced for City Furniture?

c Prepare the entries required to record the sale (on account) of the furniture to City Furniture. The sales price of the order was $170,000.

d Determine the overapplied or underapplied overhead for each department at the end of January.

Problem 23A-3
Process cost system:
a short but
comprehensive
problem

One of the primary products of Oshima Company is the Shutterbug, an instant camera that is processed successively in the Assembly Department and the Lens Department, and then transferred to the company's sales warehouse. After having been shut down for three weeks as a result of a material shortage, the company resumed production of Shutterbugs on May 1. The flow of product through the departments during May, *stated in units,* was as follows:

ASSEMBLY DEPARTMENT GOODS IN PROCESS		LENS DEPARTMENT GOODS IN PROCESS	
Started in process — 30,000 units	To Lens Dept. — 25,000 units	From Assembly Dept. — 25,000 units	To warehouse — 21,000 units

Departmental manufacturing costs applicable to Shutterbug production for the month of May were as follows:

	ASSEMBLY DEPARTMENT	LENS DEPARTMENT
Units transferred from Assembly Department		?
Raw materials	$145,000	$72,600
Direct labour	101,500	48,400
Factory overhead	159,500	96,800
Total manufacturing costs	$406,000	$?

Unfinished goods in each department at the end of May were on the average 80% complete, with respect to both raw materials and processing costs.

Instructions   **a** Prepare a production report for the Shutterbug for the month of May. Your production report should indicate for each of the two processing departments the number of units placed in production, in process at May 31, and completed during May.

b Determine the equivalent full units of production in each department during May.

c Compute unit production costs in each department during May.

d Prepare the necessary journal entries to record the transfer of product out of the Assembly Department and the Lens Department during May.

Problem 23A-4
Process costs: cost report and journal entries

Aladdin Electric manufactures several products, including an electric garage door opener called the Door Tender. Door Tenders are completely processed in one department and are then transferred to the finished goods warehouse. All manufacturing costs are applied to Door Tender units at a uniform rate throughout the production process. The following information is available for July:

Inputs during July:	
Beginning inventory of goods in process	$ 25,030
Manufacturing costs incurred in July:	
Raw materials used	53,700
Direct labour	32,220
Factory overhead	57,280
Total costs to be accounted for	$168,230

The beginning inventory consisted of 400 units that had been 80% completed during June. In addition to completing these units, the department started and completed another 1,500 units during July and started work on 300 more units that were 70% completed at July 31.

Instructions   **a** Compute the equivalent full units of production in July.

b Prepare a cost report for the department for the month of July, as illustrated in this chapter. Use the July unit cost figures to determine the cost of the ending inventory of goods in process.

c Prepare journal entries to record (1) the manufacturing costs charged to the department during July, and (2) the transfer of 1,900 completed units to the finished goods warehouse.

Problem 23A-5
Process costs: cost
report and journal
entries

Saf-T-File, Inc., manufactures metal filing cabinets and uses a process cost system. The filing cabinets pass through a series of production departments, one of which is the Lock Assembly Department. The production report and a summary of the costs charged to the Lock Assembly Department during the month of April follow:

Production Report for April

Units in process at Apr. 1 (100% completed as to materials, 80% completed as to processing costs in March)	500
Add: Units transferred in from Drawer Assembly Dept. during April (of which 1,600 were completed by April 30)	2,000
Total units worked on during April	2,500
Less: Units in process at Apr. 30 (100% complete as to materials, 50% complete as to processing costs)	400
Units completed and transferred to Painting Dept. during April	2,100

Summary of Costs Charged to Lock Assembly Department

Costs brought forward from March (beginning inventory of goods in process)	$ 29,840
Costs transferred in from Drawer Assembly Dept.	104,000
Raw materials added	8,200
Direct labour added	3,800
Factory overhead (applied at 150% of direct labour cost)	5,700
Total costs to be accounted for	$151,540

Instructions

a Compute separately the equivalent full units of production during April for (1) materials and (2) processing costs (direct labour and factory overhead).

b Prepare a cost report for April, as illustrated in the chapter. Use April unit cost figures to determine the cost of goods in process at April 30; the remaining cost inputs apply to units transferred from the Lock Assembly Department to the Painting Department during April.

c Prepare journal entries to record:

(1) Transfer of the 2,000 units from the Drawer Assembly Department into the Lock Assembly Department.

(2) Manufacturing costs charged to the Lock Assembly Department during April.

(3) Transfer of 2,100 completed units from the Lock Assembly Department to the Painting Department.

Group B

Problem 23B-1
Job order cost
system: a short
problem

Chesapeake Sailmakers uses a job order cost accounting system. Factory overhead is charged to individual jobs through the use of a predetermined overhead rate based on direct labour costs. The following information appears in the company's Goods in Process Inventory account for the month of June:

Debits to account:

Balance, June 1	$ 8,300
Raw materials	12,000
Direct labour	9,000
Factory overhead (applied to jobs as a percentage of direct labour cost)	11,700
Total debits to account	$41,000

Credits to account:

Transferred to Finished Goods Inventory account	32,000
Balance, June 30	$ 9,000

Instructions

a Compute the predetermined overhead application rate used by the company.

b Assuming that the direct labour charged to the jobs still in process at June 30 amounts to $2,400, compute the amount of factory overhead and the amount of raw materials which have been charged to these jobs as of June 30.

c Prepare general journal entries to summarize:

(1) The manufacturing costs (materials, labour, and overhead) charged to production during June.

(2) The transfer of production completed during June to the Finished Goods Inventory account.

(3) The cash sale of 90% of the merchandise completed during June at a total sales price of $46,500. Show the related cost of goods sold in a separate journal entry.

Problem 23B-2
Job order cost system:
a comprehensive
problem

Precision Instruments, Inc., uses a job order cost system and applies factory overhead to individual jobs by using predetermined overhead rates. In Department C overhead is applied on the basis of machine-hours, and in Department D on the basis of direct labour hours. At the beginning of the current year, management made the following budget estimates as a step toward determining the overhead application rates:

	DEPARTMENT C	DEPARTMENT D
Direct labour	$420,000	$300,000
Factory overhead	$540,000	$412,500
Machine-hours	18,000	1,900
Direct labour hours	28,000	25,000

Production of 4,000 tachometers (job No. 399) was started in the middle of January and completed two weeks later. The cost records for this job show the following information:

	DEPARTMENT C	DEPARTMENT D
Job No. 399 (4,000 units of product):		
Cost of materials used on job	$6,800	$4,500
Direct labour cost	$8,100	$7,200
Direct labour hours	540	600
Machine-hours	250	100

Instructions   a Determine the overhead rate that should be used for each department in applying overhead costs to job No. 399.

b What is the total cost of job No. 399, and the unit cost of the product manufactured on this production order?

c Prepare the journal entries required to record the sale (on account) of 1,000 of the tachometers to SkiCraft Boats. The total sales price was $19,500.

d Assume that actual overhead costs for the year were $517,000 in Department C and $424,400 in Department D. Actual machine-hours in Department C were 17,000, and actual direct labour hours in Department D were 26,000 during the year. On the basis of this information, determine the overapplied or underapplied overhead in each department for the year.

Problem 23B-3
Process costs: journal
entries

After having been shut down for two months during a strike, Magic Touch resumed operations on August 1. One of the company's products is a dishwasher that is successively processed by the Tub Department and the Motor Department before being transferred to the finished goods warehouse. Following are the production reports and cost data for the two departments:

Production Report for August

	TUB DEPARTMENT	MOTOR DEPARTMENT
Units placed in production	1,700	900
Less: Goods in process, Aug. 31	800	400
Units completed during August	900	500

Departmental Cost Summary

	TUB DEPARTMENT	MOTOR DEPARTMENT
Transferred in from Tub Department		?
Raw materials used	$54,000	$57,600
Direct labour	30,000	10,400
Factory Overhead	46,500	14,400

Due to the strike, there were no goods in process at August 1 in either department. The units in process in both departments at August 31 are 75% complete with respect to both materials and processing costs.

Instructions   a Compute the equivalent full units of production in August for each department.

b Compute the unit production costs for August in each department. (Include in the production costs of the Motor Department the cost of the 900 units transferred in from the Tub Department.)

c Use the August unit cost figures to determine the cost of the ending inventory of goods in process in each department at August 31.

d Prepare the journal entries required to record the transfer of completed units out of each of the two departments during August.

Problem 23B-4
Process costs: cost
report and journal
entries

Shown at the top of page 977 are the production report and a summary of the costs charged to a production department of Gourmet Appliances for the month of July:

Summary of Costs

Costs brought forward from June (beginning inventory of goods in process)	$ 25,400
Raw materials used in July	137,400
Direct labour	56,000
Factory overhead (applied at 180% of direct labour cost)	100,800
Total costs to be accounted for	$319,600

Production Report for July

Units in process at July 1 (completed 40% as to materials and 60% as to processing costs in June)	2,000
Add: Units placed in production during July (of which 8,000 were completed during July)	11,000
Total units worked on during July	13,000
Less: Units in process at July 31 (75% complete as to materials and 80% complete as to processing costs)	3,000
Units completed and transferred to Finished Goods warehouse during July	10,000

Instructions

a Compute separately the equivalent full units of production during July for (1) raw materials and (2) processing costs.

b Prepare a cost report for July, as illustrated in this chapter. Use the July unit cost figures in determining the cost of the ending inventory of goods in process and assign the remaining costs to units completed during July (a *fifo* assumption).

c Prepare journal entries for (1) manufacturing costs charged to the department in July, and (2) transfer of completed units to the Finished Goods warehouse.

Problem 23B-5
Process costs: cost report and journal entries

Bond Mfg. Co. Ltd. manufactures an epoxy sealer, called Permacoat, in four sequential processes. The Fourth Process is the last step before the product is transferred to the warehouse as finished inventory.

All material needed to complete Permacoat is added at the beginning of the Fourth Process. The company accumulated the following cost information for the Fourth Process during the month of April:

Cost inputs to the Fourth Process during April:	
Costs brought forward from March (40,000 units which were 100% completed as to materials and 75% completed as to processing costs in March)	$ 387,000
Cost of 140,000 units transferred in from the Third Process during April (90,000 of these units were completed by Apr. 30)	700,000
Manufacturing costs incurred in April:	
Raw materials added	280,000
Direct labour	125,000
Factory overhead	375,000
Total costs to be accounted for	$1,867,000

During April, the 40,000 units in process at April 1 and 90,000 of the units transferred in from the Third Process were completed and transferred to the warehouse. The remaining 50,000 units transferred in from the Third Process were still in process at April 30 and were 100% complete as to materials and 50% complete as to direct labour and factory overhead.

Instructions

a Compute the equivalent full units of production during April. (Separate computations are required for raw materials and processing costs.)

b Prepare a cost report for the month of April. Use April unit cost figures to determine the cost of the goods in process at April 30; the remaining cost inputs apply to units completed during April (*fifo* method of inventory valuation).

c Prepare journal entries to record:

(1) Transfer of the 140,000 units from the Third Process into the Fourth Process.

(2) Manufacturing costs charged to the Fourth Process during April.

(3) Transfer of 130,000 completed units from the Fourth Process to the finished goods warehouse.

BUSINESS DECISION CASES

Case 23-1
Too much
overhead?

Olde Towne Printers and Laser Technology are two large print shops located in Quebec City. The two companies are similar in size in terms of their total sales. Both businesses have job order cost accounting systems and assign factory overhead costs to jobs using a predetermined overhead application rate based upon direct labour costs. For Olde Towne Printers, the overhead application rate is 150%; for Laser Technology, the rate is 550%.

a Suggest factors that might be responsible for the wide difference between the companies' overhead application rates.

b Does the lower overhead application rate at Olde Towne Printers indicate more efficient management? Explain.

Case 23-2
Factory overhead and
fluctuations in
production volume

John Park is the founder and president of Park West Engineering. One of the company's principal products is sold exclusively to BigMart, a national chain of retail stores. BigMart buys a large quantity of the product in the first quarter of each year, but buys successively smaller quantities in the second, third, and fourth quarters. Park West cannot produce in advance to meet the big first-quarter sales requirement, because BigMart frequently makes minor changes in the specifications for the product. Therefore, Park West must adjust its production schedules to fit BigMart's buying pattern.

In Park West's cost accounting system, unit costs are computed quarterly on the basis of actual material, labour, and factory overhead costs charged to goods in process at the end of each quarter. At the close of the current year, Park received the following cost report (shown on the next page), by quarters, for the year. (Fixed factory overhead represents items of manufacturing costs that remain relatively constant month by month; variable factory overhead includes those costs that tend to move up and down in proportion to changes in the volume of production.)

Park is concerned about the steadily rising unit costs. He states, "We have a contract to produce 50,000 units for BigMart next quarter at a unit sales price of $8.50. If this sales price won't even cover our unit production costs, I'll have to cancel the contract. But before I take such drastic action, I'd like you to study our method of computing unit costs to see if we might be doing something wrong."

	FIRST QUARTER	SECOND QUARTER	THIRD QUARTER	FOURTH QUARTER
Raw materials	$ 78,000	$ 60,000	$ 42,000	$22,000
Direct labour	80,000	60,000	40,000	20,000
Fixed factory overhead	30,000	30,000	30,000	30,000
Variable factory overhead	48,000	39,000	29,000	14,000
Total manufacturing cost	$236,000	$189,000	$141,000	$86,000
Equivalent full units produced	40,000	30,000	20,000	10,000
Unit production cost	$ 5.90	$ 6.30	$ 7.05	$ 8.60

Instructions

a As the first step in your study, determine the **unit cost** of each cost element (materials, labour, fixed factory overhead, and variable factory overhead) in the first quarter and in the fourth quarter of the current year.

b Based on your computation in part **a**, which cost element is primarily responsible for the increase in unit production costs? Explain why you think the unit cost for this cost element has been rising throughout the year.

c Compute an overhead application rate for Park West Engineering that expresses total factory overhead for the year (including both fixed and variable overhead) as a percentage of direct labour costs.

d Redetermine the unit production cost for each quarter using the overhead application rate to apply factory overhead costs.

e Determine the expected unit cost of producing 50,000 units next quarter. (Assume that unit costs for materials and direct labour remain the same as in the fourth quarter and use the overhead application rate to determine the unit cost of applied overhead.)

f Explain to Park how Park West might improve its procedures for determining unit production costs. Also explain whether Park West reasonably can expect to recover its production costs next quarter if it sells 50,000 units to BigMart at a unit sales price of $8.50.

MANAGERIAL ACCOUNTING: PLANNING AND CONTROL

Managers are responsible for planning and controlling the activities of the business. The functions of planning and control are closely related. Planning is the process of setting financial and operational goals for the business and deciding upon the strategies and actions for achieving these goals. Exercising control means monitoring actual operating results, comparing those results to the plan, and taking corrective action when actual results fall below expectation.

COST-VOLUME-PROFIT ANALYSIS

CHAPTER PREVIEW

This chapter has two major objectives. Our first is to explain how various costs respond to changes in the level of business activity. An understanding of these relationships is essential to developing successful business strategies and to planning future operations. Our second objective is to show how managers may use cost-volume-profit analysis in a wide variety of business decisions. We illustrate and explain the use of a "break-even" graph—a basic tool of cost-volume-profit analysis. Also, we discuss the concept of "contribution margin." In tailoring this important concept to specific managerial decisions, we show how contribution margin may be expressed on a per unit basis, as a percentage of sales, and in relation to available units of a scarce resource.

After studying this chapter you should be able to meet these Learning Objectives:

1 **Explain how fixed, variable, and semivariable costs respond to changes in sales volume.**

2 **Prepare a cost-volume-profit (break-even) graph.**

3 **Explain the meaning of contribution margin and compute contribution margin per unit and contribution rate.**

4 **Compute the sales volume required to earn a desired level of operating income.**

5 **Use the contribution rate to estimate the effect upon operating income of changes in sales volume.**

6 **Use cost-volume-profit relationships in evaluating various marketing strategies.**

7 **Determine the sales mix that will maximize the contribution margin per unit of a scarce resource.**

One of the most important analytical tools used by many managers is cost-volume-profit analysis. *Cost-volume-profit analysis* is a means of learning how costs and profits behave in response to changes in the level of business activity. An understanding of these relationships is essential in developing plans and budgets for future business operations. In addition, cost-volume-profit analysis assists managers in predicting the effects of various decisions and strategies upon the operating income of the business.

Cost-volume-profit analysis may be used by managers to answer questions such as the following:

1 What level of sales must be reached to cover all expenses, that is, to break even?
2 How many units of a product must be sold to earn a given operating income?
3 What will happen to our profitability if we expand capacity?
4 What will be the effect of changing compensation of sales personnel from fixed monthly salaries to a straight commission of 10% on sales?
5 If we increase our spending on advertising to $100,000 per month, what increase in sales volume will be required to maintain our current level of income from operations?

Cost-volume-profit relationships are useful not only to management but also to creditors and investors. The ability of a business to pay its debts and to increase its dividend payments, for example, depends largely upon its ability to generate earnings. Assume that a company's sales volume is expected to increase by 10% during the next year. What will be the effect of this increase in sales volume upon the company's net income? The answer depends upon how the company's costs behave in response to this increase in the level of business activity.

The concepts of cost-volume-profit analysis may be applied to the business as a whole, to individual segments of the business such as a division, a branch, a department, or to a particular product line.

Cost-volume relationships

1 Explain how fixed, variable, and semi-variable costs respond to changes in sales volume.

To illustrate the relationships between costs and the level of activity, we shall first consider cost behaviour in a simple and familiar setting, the cost of operating a personal automobile. Suppose that someone tells you that the average annual cost of owning and operating an automobile is $2,700. Obviously, each individual driver does not incur an annual cost of exactly $2,700. In large part, the annual cost of owning an automobile depends upon how much you drive.

The volume index   In studying cost behaviour, we first look for some measurable concept of volume or activity that has a strong influence on the amount of cost incurred, and we then try to find out how costs change in response to changes in volume. The unit of measure used to define ''volume'' is called the *volume index.* A volume index may be based upon production inputs, such as tonnes of peaches processed, direct labour hours used, or machine-hours worked; or it may be based upon outputs, such as equivalent full units of product manufactured, units sold, or the dollar value of sales revenue generated. Semester or quarter credit hours is a significant volume index in analyzing educational costs; passenger kilometres flown is a useful volume index in airline operations; dollar sales is an important volume measure for a department store.

In our example, we shall use **kilometres driven** as the volume index of operating a personal automobile. Once an appropriate volume index has been found, we can classify all costs into three general categories:

Variable costs   A *variable* cost increases and decreases directly and proportionately with changes in volume. If, for example, volume increases 10%, a variable cost will also increase by approximately 10%. Gasoline is an example of a variable automobile cost, since fuel consumption is directly related to kilometres driven.

Fixed costs   Costs that remain *unchanged* despite changes in volume are called *fixed* or *nonvariable*. Usually such costs are incurred as a function of some other factor such as time. For example, the annual insurance premium and license fee on an automobile are fixed costs since they are independent of the number of kilometres driven.

Semivariable (or mixed) costs   Semivariable costs are also called *mixed costs* because *part of the cost is fixed* and *part is variable*. As a result, semivariable costs change in response to a change in volume, but they change by less than a proportionate amount. A 10% increase in volume, for example, may result in a 6% increase in a semivariable cost.

In our example involving the automobile, depreciation is a semivariable cost. Some depreciation will occur simply from the passage of time, without regard to the kilometres driven. This represents the fixed portion of depreciation. However, the more kilometres an automobile is driven a year, the faster it depreciates. Thus, part of the total depreciation cost for the year is a variable cost.

In our discussions of cost-volume-profit relationships, the term ''cost'' is used to describe both costs and expenses.

Automobile costs — graphic analysis   To illustrate automobile cost-volume behaviour, we shall assume the following somewhat simplified data to describe the cost of owning and operating a typical automobile:

THREE CLASSES OF
AUTOMOBILE COSTS

TYPE OF COST	AMOUNT
Variable costs:	
Gasoline, oil, and servicing	8 cents per kilometre
Semivariable costs:	
Depreciation	$1,000 per year plus 4 cents per kilometre
Fixed costs:	
Insurance	$450 per year
License fee	$50 per year

We can express these cost-volume relationships graphically. The relation between volume (kilometres driven per year) and the three types of cost both separately and combined is shown in the diagrams at the top of page 986.

We can read from the total costs graph the estimated annual automobile cost for any assumed kilometres driven. For example, an owner who expects to drive 10,000 kilometres in a given year may estimate the total cost at $2,700, or 27.0 cents per kilometre. By combining all the fixed and variable elements of cost, we can generalize the cost-volume relationship and state simply that the cost of owning an automobile is $1,500 per year plus 12 cents per kilometre driven during the year.

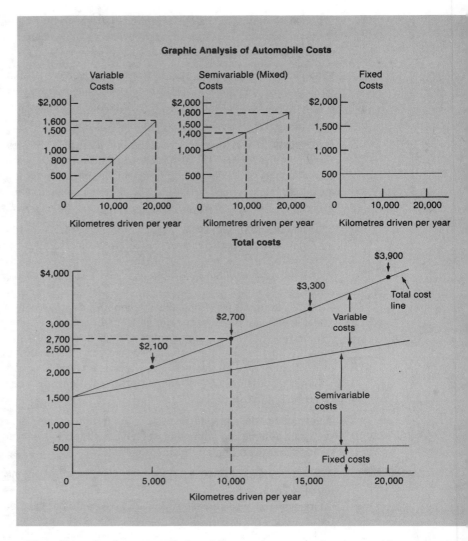

The effect of volume on unit (per-kilometre) costs can be observed by converting total cost figures to average unit costs as follows:

NOTE DECREASE IN COST
PER KILOMETRE AS
USE INCREASES

COST PER KILOMETRE OF OWNING AND USING AN AUTOMOBILE

	5,000	10,000	15,000	20,000
Kilometres driven	5,000	10,000	15,000	20,000
Costs:				
Fully variable (8 cents per kilometre)	$ 400	$ 800	$1,200	$1,600
Semivariable:				
Variable portion (4 cents per kilometre)	200	400	600	800
Fixed portion	1,000	1,000	1,000	1,000
Completely fixed ($450 + $50)	500	500	500	500
Total costs	$2,100	$2,700	$3,300	$3,900
Cost per kilometre	$ 0.42	$ 0.27	$ 0.22	$0.195

It should be noted that the variable portion of the costs incurred in operating an automobile increases in total as kilometres driven increase but **remains constant on a per-kilometre basis** (12 cents per kilometre). In contrast, total fixed costs remain the same regardless of the number of kilometres driven but **decrease on a per-kilometre basis** as kilometres driven increase. The average unit-cost behaviour of operating an automobile may be presented graphically as shown in the following illustration:

AVERAGE COST PER
KILOMETRE FOR DRIVING
A CAR

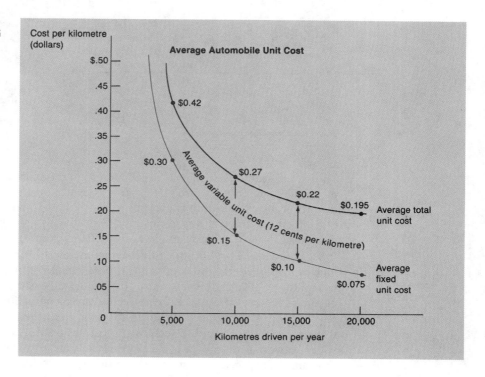

Cost behaviour in business

Cost relationships in a business are seldom as simple as those in our automobile example. Given a suitable index of volume (or activity), however, the operating costs of all businesses exhibit variable, semivariable, and fixed characteristics.

Some business costs increase in lump-sum steps rather than continuous increments, as shown in graph (**a**) at the top of page 988. For example, when production reaches a point where another supervisor and crew must be added, a lump-sum addition to labour costs occurs at this point. Other costs may vary along a curve rather than a straight line, as in graph (**b**). For example, when overtime must be worked to increase production, the labour cost per unit may rise more rapidly than volume because of the necessity of paying overtime premium to employees.

Taking all the possible variations of cost behaviour into account would add greatly to the complexity of cost-volume analysis. How far from reality are the assumed straight-line relationships? Fortunately, there are two factors that make straight-line approximations of cost behaviour useful for analytical purposes.

"STAIR-STEP:" AND
CURVILINEAR COSTS

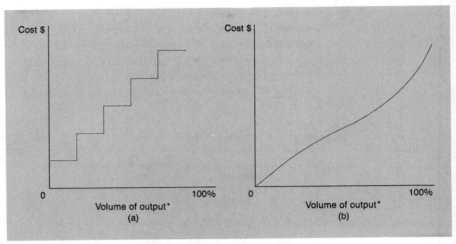

*Stated as a percentage of plant capacity.

First, unusual patterns of cost behaviour tend to offset one another. If we were to plot actual total costs incurred by a business over a time period in which volume changes occurred, the result might appear as in the cost-volume graph (**a**) on the next page. Total cost often moves in close approximation to a straight-line pattern when the various "stair-step" and curvilinear cost patterns of individual costs are combined.

Second, unusual patterns of cost behaviour are most likely to occur at extremely high or extremely low levels of volume. For example, if output were increased to near 100% of plant capacity, variable costs would curve sharply upward because of payments for overtime. An extreme decline in volume, on the other hand, might require shutting down plants and extensive layoffs, thereby reducing some expenditures that are usually considered fixed costs. Most businesses, however, operate somewhere between perhaps 45% and 80% of capacity and try to avoid large fluctuations in volume. For a given business, the probability that volume will vary outside of a fairly narrow range is usually remote. The range over which output may reasonably by expected to vary is called the ***relevant range,*** as shown in graph (**b**) at the top of page 989. Within this relevant range, the assumption that total costs vary in straight-line relation to changes in volume is reasonably realistic for most companies.

Profit-volume relationships

Business managers continually study the effect of internal decisions and external conditions on revenue, expenses, and ultimately on net income. Revenue is affected by the actions of competitors, by a firm's pricing policies, and by changes in the market demand for a firm's products or services. Expenses are affected by the prices paid for inputs, the volume of production or business activity, and the efficiency with which a firm translates input factors into salable output.

An important aspect of planning to meet given profit objectives is the analysis of the effect of volume changes on net income. The study of business profit-volume relationships is sometimes called ***break-even analysis,*** in honour of the point at which a business moves from a loss to a profit position.

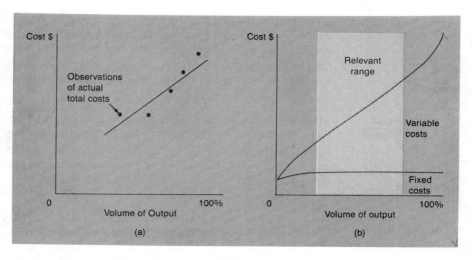

Cost-volume-profit analysis: an illustration

A simple business situation will be used to illustrate the kinds of information that can be derived from cost-volume-profit analysis. Hannigan's Ice Cream Limited has a chain of stores located throughout a large city, selling an exclusive brand of ice cream in various flavours. Although the company sells to customers in packages of different size, we shall assume that volume of business is measured in litres of ice cream sold. The company buys its ice cream from a dairy that produces this exclusive brand for Hannigan's at a price of $2.20 per litre. Retail sales prices vary depending on the quantity purchased by a customer, but revenue per litre of ice cream sold *averages* $4 per litre and does not vary significantly from store to store or from period to period. Monthly operating statistics for a typical store are shown below:

NOTE VARIABLE AND FIXED EXPENSE ELEMENTS

HANNIGAN'S ICE CREAM LIMITED
Monthly Operating Data — Typical Retail Store

		VARIABLE COSTS PER LITRE	VARIABLE COSTS AS PERCENTAGE OF SALES PRICE
Average selling price		$4.00	100%
Cost of ice cream		$2.20	55.0%
	FIXED COSTS		
Monthly operating expenses:			
Manager's salary	$2,200		
Wages	4,200 +	.14	3.5
Store rent	1,600		
Utilities	180 +	.04	1.0
Miscellaneous	820 +	.02	.5
Total expenses (except for income taxes)	$9,000 +	$2.40	60.0%
Contribution margin per unit and contribution rate (discussed later)		$1.60	40.0%

2 Prepare a cost-volume-profit (break-even) graph.

Notice that income taxes expense is not included among the monthly operating expenses of Hannigan's Ice Cream Limited. Income taxes are neither a fixed nor a variable cost, because they depend upon the amount of income before taxes, rather than being fixed in amount or based upon sales volume. Income taxes generally are ignored in cost-volume-profit analysis and "profit" is defined as *operating income* (or income before income taxes).[1]

Graphic analysis   A *cost-volume-profit* (or *break-even*) graph for the typical retail store of Hannigan's Ice Cream Limited, based on the preceding data, is shown below. The horizontal scale represents volume in thousands of litres of ice cream per month. Since none of the company's stores sells more than 10,000 litres per month, this is assumed to be the upper limit of the relevant volume range. The vertical scale

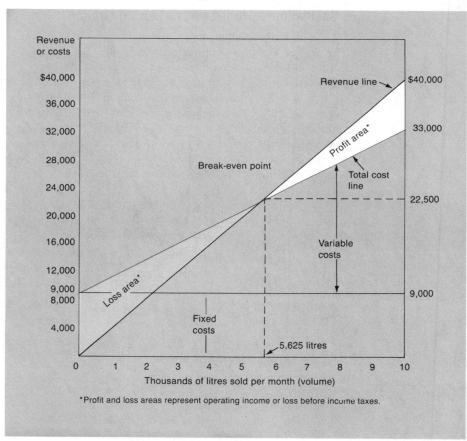

HANNIGAN'S ICE CREAM LIMITED
Monthly Cost-Volume-Profit Graph
Typical Retail Store

*Profit and loss areas represent operating income or loss before income taxes.

---

[1] Determination of the income tax expense applicable to a corporation's pretax income is discussed in Chapter 18.

is in dollars of revenue or costs (expenses). The steps in plotting this cost-volume graph are as follows:

1 First the revenue line is plotted, running from $0 at zero volume of sales to $40,000, representing 10,000 litres of sales per month at $4 per litre.

2 The fixed (nonvariable) monthly operating expenses are plotted as a horizontal line at the level of $9,000 per month.

3 Starting at the $9,000 fixed cost line, the variable costs of $2.40 per litre are plotted. Note that this line also becomes the total cost line since it is added on top of the fixed cost line.

The operating profit or loss expected at any sales level may be read from the cost-volume-graph. For example, the break-even point (zero profit) is 5,625 litres per month, or $22,500 of sales per month. Sales below 5,625 litres per month will result in a loss, and sales above 5,625 litres per month will result in operating income.

3 Explain the meaning of contribution margin and compute contribution margin per unit and contribution rate.

Contribution margin: a key relationship in cost-volume-profit analysis Variable costs vary in direct proportion to revenue. Thus, the generation of an additional dollar of revenue also generates some amount of variable costs. The operating data for our Hannigan's ice cream stores indicate that variable costs (such as the cost of ice cream) account for 60% of the company's sales revenue. Thus, if the company earns $100 in revenue, it may expect to pay out $60 of this amount to cover the related variable costs. The remaining $40 is called the *contribution margin*.

The contribution margin is the *amount of revenue in excess of variable costs.* This portion of the revenue is available to cover the company's fixed costs and, after all fixed costs have been covered, provide an operating income. The allocation of the average revenue dollar between the variable costs relating to the sale and the contribution margin is illustrated below for a typical Hannigan's store:

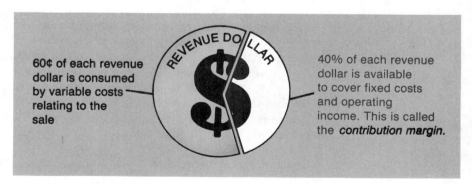

Contribution margin may be expressed in *total dollars* (sales revenue — total variable costs), on a *per unit basis* (sales price per unit minus variable costs per unit), or as a *percentage of sales.* When the contribution margin is expressed as a percentage of sales, it is called the contribution margin ratio or *contribution rate* and is computed as follows:

$$\text{CONTRIBUTION RATE} = \frac{\text{SALES PRICE PER UNIT} - \text{VARIABLE COSTS PER UNIT}}{\text{SALES PRICE PER UNIT}}$$

The data illustrated on page 989 indicate that the contribution rate at a typical Hannigan's ice cream store is 40%, computed:

$$\text{CONTRIBUTION RATE} = \frac{\$4.00 - \$2.40}{\$4.00} = 40\%$$

A contribution rate of 40% means that 40% of the revenue earned in a Hannigan's store is available to cover fixed costs and to contribute toward operating income. The remaining 60% is consumed by the variable costs.

4   Compute the sales volume required to earn a desired level of operating income.

Finding required sales volume (in units)

We may use the concept of contribution margin as a quick means of finding the *unit sales volume* required for a business to break even or to achieve any desired level of operating income. Break-even sales volume can be of vital importance, especially to companies deciding whether to introduce a new product line, build a new plant, or, in some cases, remain in business.

Chrysler Corp. in the United States, widely believed to be heading for bankruptcy during the early 1980s, undertook a severe cost cutting program and altered marketing strategies in an effort to lower the company's break-even point. In 1981, Chrysler had a break-even point of 1,413,000 vehicles; sales amounted to 1,282,000 vehicles and the company incurred substantial losses. For 1982, the company was able to reduce its break-even point to 1,244,000 vehicles. Chrysler surprised many people in the financial community by returning to profitable operations in 1982 with sales of approximately 1,400,000 vehicles. This "turnaround year" may well have saved Chrysler Corp. Notice, however, that the 1982 sales volume would have resulted in a net loss had Chrysler not been able to lower its break-even point.

To illustrate the relationship between sales volume and contribution margin, assume that we want to know how many litres of ice cream a Hannigan's store must sell to break even. At the break-even point, the store must earn a contribution margin large enough to cover all fixed costs. The illustrated data show that the monthly fixed costs amount to $9,000, and that the contribution margin per litre of ice cream is $1.60 ($4.00 sales price minus $2.40 variable costs). If the sale of each litre covers $1.60 of fixed costs, how many litres must be sold to cover fixed costs of $9,000? The answer is 5,625 litres, as shown below:

$$\text{SALES VOLUME (IN UNITS)} = \frac{\$9,000}{\$1.60 \text{ PER LITRE}} = 5,625 \text{ LITRES PER MONTH}$$

Notice that this answer corresponds to the sales volume shown earlier in the cost-volume-profit graph.

The reasoning in our above analysis may be summarized by the following formula:

$$\text{SALES VOLUME (IN UNITS)} = \frac{\text{FIXED COSTS} + \text{OPERATING INCOME}}{\text{CONTRIBUTION MARGIN PER UNIT}}$$

With this formula, we may find not only the break-even sales volume (at which operating income is zero), but also the unit sales volume needed to achieve *any desired level of operating income.* For example, how many litres of ice cream must be sold for a Hannigan's store to earn a monthly operating income of $4,000?

$$\text{SALES VOLUME (IN UNITS)} = \frac{\$9,000 + \$4,000}{\$1.60} = 8,125 \text{ LITRES PER MONTH}$$

Finding required dollar sales volume   To find the *dollar sales volume* needed to earn a given level of operating income, we could first compute the required unit sales and then multiply our answer by the unit sales price. Using the data from our preceding example, a Hannigan's store expecting to earn a monthly operating income of $4,000 would need sales revenue of $32,500 (8,125 litres × $4 per litre).

As a more direct approach, we may compute the required dollar sales volume by substituting the **contribution rate** for the contribution margin per unit in our sales volume formula. The formula then becomes

$$\text{SALES VOLUME (IN DOLLARS)} = \frac{\text{FIXED COSTS} + \text{OPERATING INCOME}}{\text{CONTRIBUTION RATE}}$$

To illustrate, let us again compute the sales volume required for a Hannigan's store to earn a monthly operating income of $4,000:

$$\text{SALES VOLUME (IN DOLLARS)} = \frac{\$9,000 + \$4,000}{.40} = \$32,500 \text{ PER MONTH}$$

Margin of safety   The amount by which actual sales volume *exceeds* the break-even sales volume is called the margin of safety. This is the amount by which sales could *decline* before the company will incur an operating loss. A typical Hannigan's store has a break-even sales volume of $22,500. Therefore, a store with actual sales of $32,500 has a **margin of safety** of $10,000; a store with sales of $35,000 has a margin of safety of $12,500 ($35,000 − $22,500).

The margin of safety provides us with a quick means of estimating operating income at any sales volume above the break-even point, as shown below:

$$\text{OPERATING INCOME} = \text{MARGIN OF SAFETY} \times \text{CONTRIBUTION RATE}$$

The rationale for this formula stems from the fact that the margin of safety represents sales in excess of the break-even point. Therefore, fixed costs have already been covered and the entire contribution margin from these sales enlarges operating income.

To illustrate this concept, let us estimate the operating income of a Hannigan's store with a sales volume of $32,500, which is $10,000 above the break-even point. The estimated operating income is $4,000 ($10,000 × 40%). (Notice that this answer is consistent with our earlier computations.)

5 Use the contribution rate to estimate the effect upon operating income of changes in sales volume.

Changes in operating income   The contribution rate in our example is 40%, which means that 40 cents out of every revenue dollar goes toward covering fixed costs (which reduces an operating loss) or toward increasing operating income. Thus, every additional dollar of sales improves Hannigan's profit picture by 40 cents. Conversely, a $1 sales decline lowers profitability by 40 cents. This relationship may be summarized as follows:

$$\text{CHANGE IN OPERATING INCOME} = \text{CHANGE IN SALES VOLUME} \times \text{CONTRIBUTION RATE}$$

To illustrate, let us assume that the sales volume at a given ice cream store increases from $22,500 (the break-even point) to $32,500, an increase of $10,000. According to the above equation, the operation income of the store should increase by $4,000 ($10,000 × 40%). This increase may be verified by reference to our earlier calculations. On page 990, we determined that a sales volume of $22,500 is the break-even point for a Hannigan's store; operating income at this sales volume, therefore, is zero. On page 993, we determined that the sales volume required to earn an operating income of $4,000 is $32,500.

Using cost-volume-profit relationships

6   Use cost-volume-profit relationships in evaluating various marketing strategies.

Cost-volume-profit relationships are widely used during the budgeting process to set sales targets, and to estimate costs and expenses. In addition, these relationships can provide information that is useful in a wide variety of planning decisions. To illustrate, let us consider several ways in which cost-volume-profit relationships might be used by the management of Hannigan's Ice Cream Limited in planning marketing strategies:

1 *Question:* To increase volume, management is considering a policy of giving greater discounts on litre packages of ice cream. It is estimated that the effect of this pricing policy would be to reduce the average selling price per litre by 16 cents (that is, from $4 per litre to $3.84) Management is interested in knowing the effect of such a price reduction on the number of litres of ice cream a store must sell to break even.

Analysis: The proposed change in average sales price changes the contribution margin per litre of ice cream from $1.60 to $1.44, as shown below:

SALES PRICE PER UNIT, $3.84, MINUS VARIABLE COSTS PER UNIT, $2.40 = $1.44

The fixed operating expenses remain unchanged by this pricing decision. Therefore, the unit sales volume to break even under the new pricing situation would be:

$$\text{SALES VOLUME (IN UNITS)} = \frac{\$9,000 + \$0}{\$1.44} = 6,250 \text{ LITRES PER MONTH}$$

This new break-even point, 6,250 litres, is more than 11% higher than the present 5,625 litre break-even volume. Thus management should be advised that the proposed pricing policy is desirable only if the unit sales volume per store can be expected to increase more than 11% per month as a result of the lower sales prices on litre packages.

2 *Question:* Management is considering a change in the method of compensating store managers. Instead of a fixed salary of $2,200 per month, it is proposed that managers be put on a salary of $680 per month plus a commission of 24 cents per litre of sales. The present average monthly operating income per store is $3,400 on sales of $31,000 (Proof: $31,000 × 40% − $9,000 = $3,400). What sales revenue per store will be necessary to produce the same monthly income under the proposed incentive compensation arrangement?

Analysis: This proposal involves a change in both the contribution rate and the fixed monthly operating expenses. Adding 24 cents per litre to variable costs raises the total variable cost to $2.64 per litre and reduces the contribution rate to 34%, as computed below:

$$\frac{\$4.00 - \$2.64}{\$4.00} = 34\%$$

Cutting the manager's salary from $2,200 to $680 per month will reduce monthly fixed costs from $9,000 to $7,480. The sales volume required to produce a monthly operating income of $3,400 may be computed as follows:

$$\frac{\$7,480 + \$3,400}{.34} = \$32,000 \text{ PER MONTH}$$

To produce the same $3,400 per month net income under the new compensation plan, sales volume per store would have to be increased by $1,000 (or 250 litres) over the current monthly sales volume of $31,000. The issue thus boils down to whether the incentive compensation arrangement will induce store managers to increase volume by more than 250 litres per month. Cost-volume-profit analysis does not answer this question, but it provides the information that enables management to exercise its judgment intelligently.

3 *Question:* Hannigan's Ice Cream stores are now open 12 hours each day (from 9 A.M. to 9 P.M.). Management is considering a proposal to decrease store hours by opening 2 hours later each morning. It is estimated that this policy would reduce sales volume by an average of 500 litres per month and would cut fixed costs (utilities and wages) by $1,000 per month. Would it pay the company to change its store hours?

Analysis: The loss of 500 litres of sales per month would decrease revenue by $2,000 (500 × $4). This would result in the loss of contribution margin of $800 ($2,000 × 40%). Therefore, whether the reduction in store hours would increase net income per store may be determined as follows:

Reduction in fixed costs	$1,000
Less: Loss of contribution margin ($2,000 × 40%)	800
Prospective increase in monthly operating income per store	$ 200

Importance of sales mix in cost-volume-profit analysis

7 Determine the sales mix that will maximize the contribution margin per unit of a scarce resource.

In our example of Hannigan's Ice Cream Limited, we assumed that the contribution rate *averaged* 40% of sales expressed in dollars and that the *average* selling price was $4 per litre of ice cream sold. Let us now change our example and assume that a detailed analysis indicated that ice cream is actually sold in three packages as shown at the top of page 996.

Earlier in this chapter we stated that Hannigan's Ice Cream is now selling a certain *mix* of the three sizes and that a sales volume of $22,500 is required to break even ($9,000 ÷ *average* contribution rate of 40%). If ice cream were sold exclusively in quarter-litres, sales of $30,000 would be required to break even; if only half-litre packages were sold, the break-even sales volume would be $20,000, if only litre packages were sold, the break-even sales volume would be $18,000. The reason the

	QUARTER-LITRE	HALF-LITRE	LITRE
Sales price per package	$1.20	$2.00	$3.60
Less: Variable expense per package	0.84	1.10	1.80
Contribution margin per package	$0.36	$0.90	$1.80
Contribution rate (contribution margin ÷ sales price)	30%	45%	50%
Break-even sales volume, assuming that only the one size package was sold (fixed expenses, $9,000, divided by contribution rate) . . .	$30,000	$20,000	$18,000

break-even sales volume differs for each size is because each size yields a different contribution margin per dollar of sales (contribution rate). *The higher the contribution rate, the lower the sales volume that is required to cover a given amount of fixed expenses.*

The amount of operating income earned by a business unit depends not only on the volume of sales and the ability to control expenses, but also on the *quality* of sales. At any given sales volume, selling products with high contribution rates is more profitable than selling products with low contribution rates. Thus, sales with high contribution rates are said to be *high-quality sales.* A shift from low-margin sales to high-margin sales can increase net income even though total sales volume may decline. On the other hand, a shift from high-margin to low-margin sales can cause profits to fall even though total sales may increase.

Contribution margin per unit of scarce resource

The contribution margin approach is useful to management in deciding what products to manufacture (or purchase for resale) and what products to eliminate when certain factors of production are available only in limited quantity. One of the important functions of management is to develop the most profitable uses of such scarce resources as raw materials, skilled labour, high-cost equipment, and factory floor space.

Assume that you are offered two equally satisfactory jobs, one paying $6 per hour and one paying $9 per hour. Since your time is scarce and you wish to maximize the pay that you receive for an hour of your time, you would naturally choose the job paying $9 per hour. For the same reason, if a company has the capacity to utilize only 100,000 direct labour hours per year, management would want to use this capacity in such a way as *to produce the maximum contribution margin per hour of direct*

MAXIMUS CORPORATION
Contribution Margin per Hour of Direct Labour

PRODUCT	SALES PRICE PER UNIT	−	VARIABLE COSTS PER UNIT	=	CONTRIBUTION MARGIN PER UNIT	÷	DIRECT LABOUR HOURS REQUIRED TO PRODUCE ONE UNIT	=	CONTRIBUTION MARGIN PER HOUR OF DIRECT LABOUR
A	$100		$60		$40		10		$ 4
B	80		50		30		5		6
C . . .	60		40		20		2		10

labour. To illustrate this concept, assume that the Maximus Corporation is considering the production of three products. The contribution margin per direct labour hour required to produce each of the three products is estimated as illustrated at the bottom of page 996.

Even though a unit of product A yields the highest contribution margin ($40) and the highest contribution rate (40%), it is *the least profitable product in terms of contribution margin per hour of direct labour.* If sales of products B and C do not depend on the sales of product A and there are no operational problems involved in varying the production mix of the three products, the production of product A should be kept to a minimum. This would be particularly appropriate if the Maximus Corporation could not meet the demand for all three products because of inability to expand plant capacity beyond 100,000 direct labour hours.

We can see that a unit of product A requires 10 hours of direct labour and generates $40 in contribution margin; a unit of product B requires only 5 hours of direct labour and yields $30 in contribution margin; and a unit of product C requires only 2 hours of direct labour and yields $20 in contribution margin. In summary, 10 hours of effort on product A yields $40 in contribution margin while 10 hours of effort on product B yields $60 in contribution margin, and 10 hours of effort on product C generates $100 in contribution margin. If the entire capacity of 100,000 direct labour hours were used to produce *only a single product,* the following total contribution margin would result:

WHY SHOULD WE
CONTINUE TO PRODUCE
PRODUCT A?

PRODUCT	TOTAL CAPACITY (HOURS)	×	CONTRIBUTION MARGIN PER HOUR OF DIRECT LABOUR	=	TOTAL CONTRIBUTION MARGIN IF ONLY ONE PRODUCT IS MANUFACTURED
A	100,000		$ 4		$ 400,000
B	100,000		6		600,000
C	100,000		10		1,000,000

This schedule does not mean that the production of product A can be discontinued. While product C is clearly the most profitable, perhaps the demand for it is not enough to keep the plant working at full capacity; or the sales of product C may to some extent depend on sales of products A and B. For these reasons a company may not be in a position to manufacture only the product that yields the highest contribution margin. A company should, however, try to sell as much of the high-margin products as possible in order to maximize its net income.

Assumptions underlying cost-volume-profit analysis

In cost-volume-profit analysis, accountants assume the following:

1 Sales price per unit remains constant.
2 If more than one product is sold, the proportion of the various products sold (sales mix) is assumed to be constant.
3 Fixed costs remain constant at all levels of sales within the assumed relevant range of activity.
4 Variable costs remain constant as a percentage of sales revenue.

5 For a business engaged in manufacturing, the number of units produced is assumed to be equal to the number of units sold.

These assumptions simplify cost-volume-profit analysis. In actual practice, however, some of these assumptions may not hold true. However, cost-volume-profit analysis is still a useful planning tool for management. As changes take place in selling prices, sales mix, expenses, and production levels, management should update and revise its analysis.

Summary of basic cost-volume-profit relationships

In this chapter, we have demonstrated a number of mathematical relationships that are useful in cost-volume-profit analysis. For your convenience, these relationships are summarized as follows:

MEASUREMENT	METHOD OF COMPUTATION
Contribution margin	Sales revenue − Total variable costs
Contribution margin per unit	Unit sales price − Variable costs per unit
Contribution rate	$\dfrac{\text{Sales price per unit} - \text{Variable costs per unit}}{\text{Sales price per unit}}$
Sales volume (in units)	$\dfrac{\text{Fixed costs} + \text{Operating income}}{\text{Contribution margin per unit}}$
Sales volume (in dollars)	$\dfrac{\text{Fixed costs} + \text{Operating income}}{\text{Contribution rate}}$
Margin of safety	Actual sales volume − Break-even sales volume
Operating income	Margin of safety × Contribution rate
Change in operating income	Changes in sales volume × Contribution rate

END-OF-CHAPTER REVIEW

SUMMARY OF CHAPTER LEARNING OBJECTIVES

1 Explain how fixed, variable, and semivariable costs respond to changes in sales volume

Fixed costs remain unchanged despite changes in sales volume, while variable costs change in direct proportion to changes in sales volume. With a semivariable cost, part of the cost is fixed and part is variable. Semivariable costs change in response to a change in sales volume, but they change by less than a proportionate amount.

2 Prepare a cost-volume-profit (break-even) graph.

The vertical axis on a break-even graph is dollars of revenue or costs, and the horizontal axis is unit sales. Lines are plotted on the graph showing revenue and total costs. The vertical distance between these lines represents the amount of operating income (or loss). The lines intersect at the "break-even" point.

3 Explain the meaning of contribution margin and compute contribution margin per unit and contribution rate.

Contribution margin is the excess of revenue over variable costs. Thus, it represents the amount of revenue available to cover fixed costs and to provide an operating profit. Contribution margin may be expressed in total dollars, on a per unit basis (sales price per unit minus variable costs per unit), or as a percentage of unit selling price or total sales. Contribution margin stated as a percentage of unit selling price or total sales is called the *contribution rate*.

4 Compute the sales volume required to earn a desired level of operating income.

The unit sales volume required to earn a given level of operating income is equal to the sum of the fixed costs plus the desired operating income, divided by the contribution margin per unit. To find the sales volume stated in dollars, the sum of the fixed costs plus the desired operating income is divided by the contribution rate.

5 Use the contribution rate to estimate the effect upon operating income of changes in sales volume.

Multiplying the expected change in sales volume by the contribution rate indicates the expected change in operating income.

6 Use cost-volume-profit relationships in evaluating various marketing strategies.

Through cost-volume-profit analysis, we may estimate the effects upon operating income of changes in sales price, unit sales volume, and the level of expenses to evaluate various marketing strategies.

7 Determine the sales mix that will maximize the contribution margin per unit of a scarce resource.

The quantity of goods or services that a business can produce often is limited by the scarcity of a particular resource, such as direct labour hours or machine hours. In these cases, the company can maximize its profits by producing those products with the highest contribution margin per unit of the scarce resource.

KEY TERMS INTRODUCED OR EMPHASIZED IN CHAPTER 24

Break-even point The level of sales at which a company neither earns an operating income nor incurs a loss. Revenue exactly covers costs and expenses.

Contribution margin Sales minus variable expenses. The portion of sales revenue that is not consumed by variable expenses and, therefore, is available to cover fixed costs and contribute to operating income.

Contribution rate The contribution margin expressed as a percentage of sales price. Represents the percentage of each revenue dollar that is available to cover fixed costs or to provide an operating income.

Fixed (or nonvariable) costs Costs that remain unchanged despite changes in volume of output.

Margin of safety Amount by which actual sales exceed the break-even point.

Relevant volume range The span or range of output over which output is likely to vary and assumptions about cost behaviour are generally valid. Excludes extreme volume variations.

Semivariable costs Costs that respond to change in volume of output by less than a proportionate amount.

Variable costs Costs that vary directly and proportionately with changes in volume.

DEMONSTRATION PROBLEM FOR YOUR REVIEW

The management of the Fresno Processing Company has engaged you to assist in the development of information to be used for managerial decisions.

The company has the capacity to process 20,000 tonnes of cottonseed per year. The yield from a tonne of cottonseed is as shown below.

PRODUCT	AVERAGE YIELD PER TONNE* OF COTTONSEED	AVERAGE SELLING PRICE	TOTAL REVENUE
Oil	200 kilograms	$ 0.50 per kilogram	$100
Meal	300 kilograms	160.00 per tonne	48
Hulls	400 kilograms	100.00 per tonne	40
Lint	100 kilograms	0.12 per kilogram	12
Totals	1,000 kilograms		$200

*There are 1,000 kilograms in a tonne.

A special marketing study revealed that the company can expect to sell its entire output for the coming year at the average selling prices listed above.

You have determined the company's cost structure to be as follows:

Cost of cottonseed:	$80 per tonne
Processing costs:	
Variable:	$26 per tonne of cottonseed processed
Fixed:	$340,000 per year at all levels of production
Marketing costs:	All variable, $44 per tonne of all products sold
Administrative costs:	All fixed, $300,000 per year at all levels of production and sales activity

Instructions

a Compute per tonne of cottonseed (1) the contribution margin and (2) the contribution rate.

b Compute the break-even sales volume in (1) dollars and (2) tonnes of cottonseed.

c Assume that the company's budget calls for an operating income of $240,000. Compute the sales volume required to reach this profit objective, stated (1) in dollars and (2) in tonnes of cottonseed.

d Compute the maximum amount that the company can afford to pay per tonne of raw cottonseed and still break even by processing and selling 16,000 tonnes during the current year.

SOLUTION TO DEMONSTRATION PROBLEM

a (1) Total revenue per tonne of cottonseed $200
     Less: Variable costs:
        Cottonseed $80
        Processing 26
        Marketing 44   150
     Contribution margin per tonne .... $ 50

   (2) Contribution rate ($50 ÷ $200) 25%

b (1) Break-even sales volume (in dollars):

Fixed costs ($340,000 + $300,000)	$ 640,000
Contribution margin rate (part **a**)	25%
Break-even sales volume ($640,000 ÷ .25)	$2,560,000

(2) Break-even sales volume (in tonnes):

Fixed costs (per above)	$ 640,000
Contribution margin per tonne (part **a**)	$ 50
Break-even sales volume stated in tonnes of cottonseed products ($640,000 ÷ $50)	12,800

(Alternative computation: break-even sales volume in dollars, $2,560,000, divided by sales price per tonne, $200, equals 12,800 tonnes.)

c (1) Sales volume (in dollars):

Fixed costs	$ 640,000
Add: Desired operating income	240,000
Required contribution margin	$ 880,000
Contribution margin rate (part **a**)	25%
Sales volume ($880,000 ÷ 25%)	$3,520,000

(2) Sales volume (in units):

Sales volume in dollars (above)	$3,520,000
Sales price per tonne	$ 200
Sales volume in tonnes of cottonseed products ($3,520,000 ÷ $200)	17,600

d Total revenue per tonne of cottonseed $200

Less: Per unit costs other than cottonseed:

Processing	$26	
Marketing	44	
Fixed costs ($640,000 ÷ 16,000 tonnes)	40	110

Maximum amount that can be paid per tonne of cottonseed while allowing company to break even at 16,000 tonne volume . . . . $ 90

ASSIGNMENT MATERIAL

REVIEW QUESTIONS

1 Why is it important for management to understand cost-volume-profit relationships?

2 What is a *volume index* and why is it important in analyzing cost behaviour?

3 A is a variable cost; B is a fixed cost; and C is a semivariable cost. How would you expect each of these total dollar costs to vary with changes in production volume? How would they vary with changes in production if they were expressed in **dollars per unit** of production?

4 The simplifying assumption that costs and volume vary in straight-line relationships makes the analysis of cost behaviour much easier. What factors make this a reasonable and useful assumption in many cases?

5 What important relationships are shown on a cost-volume-profit (break-even) graph?

6 Kris Company has an average contribution margin of 35%. What dollar sales volume per month is necessary to produce a monthly operating income of $22,000, if fixed expenses are $118,000 per month?

7 Define the **relevant range** of activity.

8 Define (**a**) contribution margin and (**b**) contribution rate.

9 Explain how the contribution margin per unit can be used to determine the unit sales required to break even.

10 Reed Company has variable costs of $11 per unit and a contribution rate of 45%. Compute the selling price per unit.

11 Define **margin of safety.**

12 Explain the probable effect upon operating income of a $10,000 increase in sales volume by a company with variable costs of $50 per unit and a contribution rate of 35%.

13 An executive of a large steel company put the blame for lower net income for a recent fiscal period on the "shift in product mix to higher proportion of export sales." Sales for the period increased slightly while net income declined by 28%. Explain how a change in product (sales) mix to a higher proportion in export sales would result in a lower level of net income.

14 Why is it helpful to know the approximate amount of contribution margin generated from the use of a scarce resource such as a machine-hour or an hour of direct labour?

15 The president of an airline blamed a profit squeeze on "unwise and unjustifiable promotional fares." He pointed out that 50% of the company's revenue came from "discount fares." Explain why discount fares tend to reduce net income and point out circumstances in which a discount from the regular price of a plane fare could possibly increase net income.

EXERCISES

Exercise 24-1
Accounting
terminology

Listed below are nine technical accounting terms introduced in this chapter.

Fixed costs	Contribution margin	Break-even point
Variable costs	Margin of safety	Relevant range
Semivariable costs	Contribution rate	Sales mix

Each of the following statements may (or may not) describe one of these technical terms. For each statement, indicate the accounting term described, or answer "None" if the statement does not correctly describe any of the terms.

a The span over which output is likely to vary and assumptions about cost behaviour generally remain valid.

b Contribution margin per unit expressed as a percentage of unit sales price.

c Costs that respond to changes in sales volume by less than a proportionate amount.

d Operating income less variable costs.

e The level of sales at which revenue exactly equals costs and expenses.

f Costs that remain unchanged despite changes in sales volume.

g Revenue less variable expenses.

h The amount by which sales exceed the break-even point.

Exercise 24-2
Computing required sales volume

Bendix Co. has fixed costs of $330,000, variable costs of $12 per unit, and a contribution rate of 40%. Compute the dollar sales volume required for Bendix Co. to earn an operating income of $150,000.

Exercise 24-3
Computing contribution rate and margin of safety

The information show below relates to the only product sold by Portland Company:

Sales price per unit	$ 20
Variable cost per unit	15
Fixed costs per year	200,000

a Compute the contribution rate and the dollar sales volume required to break even.

b Assuming that the company sells 70,000 units during the current year, compute the margin of safety sales volume.

Exercise 24-4
Computing required sales volume

Information concerning a product manufactured by Ames Brothers appears below:

Sales price per unit	$ 140
Variable cost per unit	86
Total fixed production and operating costs	540,000

Determine the following:

a The contribution margin per unit.

b The number of units that must be sold to break even.

c The unit sales level that must be reached in order to earn an operating income of $270,000.

Exercise 24-5
Relating contribution rate to sales price

Firebird Mfg. Co. Ltd. has a contribution rate of 30% and must sell 20,000 units at a price of $100 each in order to break even. Compute:

a Total fixed costs.

b Variable costs per unit.

Exercise 24-6
Computing the break-even point

Malibu Corporation has fixed expenses of $36,000 per month. It sells two products as follows:

	SALES PRICE	VARIABLE EXPENSE	CONTRIBUTION MARGIN
Product No. 1	$10	$4	$6
Product No. 2	10	7	3

a What monthly dollar sales volume is required to break even if two units of product No. 1 are sold with one unit of product No. 2?

b What monthly dollar sales volume is required to break even if one unit of product No. 1 is sold with two units of product No. 2?

For each of the six independent situations below, compute the missing amounts:

a Only one product is manufactured:

	SALES	VARIABLE EXPENSES	CONTRIBUTION MARGIN PER UNIT	FIXED EXPENSES	OPERATING INCOME	UNITS SOLD
(1)	$_____	$120,000	$20	$_____	$25,000	4,000
(2)	180,000	_____	—	45,000	30,000	5,000
(3)	600,000	_____	30	150,000	90,000	_____

b Many products are manufactured:

	SALES	VARIABLE EXPENSES	CONTRIBUTION RATE	FIXED EXPENSES	OPERATING INCOME
(1)	$900,000	$720,000	___%	$_____	$95,000
(2)	600,000	_____	40%	_____	75,000
(3)	_____	_____	30%	90,000	60,000

PROBLEMS

Group A

MURDER TO GO! writes and manufactures murder mystery parlour games that it sells to retail stores. Shown below is per unit information relating to the manufacture and sale of this product:

Selling price per unit	$	10
Variable cost per unit		4
Fixed costs per year		360,000

Determine the following, showing as part of your answer the formula that you used in your computation. For example, the formula used to determine the contribution rate (part **a**) is:

$$\text{Contribution rate} = \frac{\text{Sales price per unit} - \text{Variable costs per unit}}{\text{Sales price per unit}}$$

a Contribution rate.

b Sales volume (in dollars) required to break even.

c Sales volume (in dollars) required to earn an annual operating income of $150,000.

d The margin of safety sales volume if annual sales total 75,000 units.

e Operating income if annual sales total 75,000 units.

Problem 24A-2
Setting sales price
and computing the
break-even point

Thermal Tent, Inc., is a newly organized manufacturing business that has plans to manufacture and sell 200,000 units per year of a new product. The estimates have been made of the company's costs and expenses (other than income taxes), which are illustrated at the top of page 1005.

	FIXED	VARIABLE PER UNIT
Manufacturing costs:		
Raw materials		$ 7
Direct labour		2
Factory overhead	$340,000	4
Period expenses:		
Selling expenses		1
Administrative expenses	200,000	
Totals	$540,000	$14

Instructions

a What should the company establish as the sales price per unit if it sets a budgeted operating income of $260,000 by producing and selling 200,000 units during the first year of operations?

b At the unit sales price computed in part **a**, how many units must the company produce and sell to break even? (Assume all units produced are sold.)

c What will be the margin of safety if the company produces and sells 200,000 units at the sales price computed in part **a**?

**Problem 24A-3
Drawing a cost-
volume-profit graph**

Rainbow Paints operates a chain of retail paint stores. Although the paint is sold under the Rainbow label, it is purchased from an independent paint manufacturer. Guy Walker, president of Rainbow Paints, is studying the advisability of opening another store. His estimates of monthly costs for the proposed location are:

Fixed costs:	
Occupancy costs	$3,160
Salaries	3,640
Other	1,200
Variable costs (including cost of paint)	$6 per litre

Although Rainbow stores sell several different types of paint, monthly sales revenue consistently averages $10 per litre sold.

Instructions

a Compute the contribution rate and the break-even point in dollar sales and in litres sold for the proposed store.

b Draw a monthly cost-volume-profit graph for the proposed store, assuming 3,000 litres per month as the maximum sales potential.

c Walker thinks that the proposed store will sell between 2,200 and 2,600 litres of paint per month. Compute the amount of operating income that would be earned per month at each of these sales volumes.

**Problem 24A-4
Determining optimal
sales mix**

Landry Knife Company manufactures three different products. The estimated demand for the products for the current year is such that production will not be able to keep pace with incoming orders. Some pertinent data for each product are listed below. Direct labour costs an average of $8 per hour.

PRODUCT	ESTIMATED UNIT SALES	SALES PRICE	RAW MATERIAL COST	DIRECT LABOUR COST	VARIABLE FACTORY OVERHEAD
A	16,000	$18	$3	$8	$1
B	8,000	11	1	4	1
C	2,400	15	2	8	1

Instructions   **a** Prepare a schedule showing the contribution margin per one unit of each product and also the contribution margin per one hour of direct labour applied to the production of each class of product.

b If you were able to reduce the production of one of the products in order to meet the demand for the others, what would that product be? Why? Assume that available direct labour hours represent the scarce resource that limits total output.

c Assume that the 16,000 hours of direct labour now used to produce product A are used to produce additional units of product B. What would be the effect on total contribution margin?

Problem 24A-5
Analyzing the effects
of changes in costs

Precision Systems manufactures tape decks and currently sells 18,500 units annually to producers of sound reproduction systems. Jay Wilson, president of the company, anticipates a 15% increase in the cost per unit of direct labour on January 1 of next year. He expects all other costs and expenses to remain unchanged. Wilson has asked you to assist him in developing the information he needs to formulate a reasonable product strategy for next year.

You are satisfied that volume is the primary factor affecting costs and expenses and have separated the semivariable costs into their fixed and variable segments. Beginning and ending inventories remain at a level of 1,000 units.

Following are the current-year data assembled for your analysis:

Sales price per unit		$100
Variable costs per unit:		
Raw materials	$10	
Direct labour	20	
Factory overhead and selling and administrative expenses	30	60
Contribution margin per unit (40%)		$ 40
Fixed costs		$400,000

Instructions   **a** What increase in the selling price is necessary to cover the 15% increase in direct labour cost and still maintain the current contribution rate of 40%?

b How many tape decks must be sold to maintain the current operating income of $340,000 if the sales price remains at $100 and the 15% wage increase goes into effect?

c Wilson believes that an additional $600,000 of machinery (to be depreciated at 20% annually) will increase present capacity (20,000 units) by 40%. If all tape decks produced can be sold at the present price of $100 per unit and the wage increase goes into effect, how would the estimated operating income before capacity is increased compare with the estimated operating income after capacity is increased? Prepare schedules of estimated operating income at full capacity *before* and *after* the expansion.

Group B

Problem 24B-1
Introduction to cost-
volume-profit formulas

Shown below is information relating to the only product sold by Pinapple Pak, Inc.:

Sales price per unit	$	40
Variable cost per unit		28
Fixed costs per year		210,000

Instructions   Determine the following, showing as part of your answer the formula or relationships you used in your computations. For example, the formula used to determine the contribution rate (part **a**) is

$$\text{Contribution rate} = \frac{\text{Sales price per unit} - \text{Variable costs per unit}}{\text{Sales price per unit}}$$

a Contribution rate.

b Dollar sales volume required to break even.

c Dollar sales volume required to earn an annual operating income of $75,000.

d The margin of safety if annual sales total 25,000 units.

e Operating income if annual sales total 25,000 units.

Problem 24B-2
Estimating costs and
profits

Charlie Miller Company manufactures fishing rods. For the coming year, the company has budgeted the following costs for the production and sale of 20,000 rods:

	BUDGETED COSTS	BUDGETED COSTS PER UNIT	PERCENTAGE OF COSTS CONSIDERED VARIABLE
Raw materials	$200,000	$10	100%
Direct labour	160,000	8	100
Factory overhead (fixed and variable)	280,000	14	40
Selling and administrative expenses	240,000	12	20
Totals	$880,000	$44	

Instructions

a Compute the sales price per unit that would result in a budgeted operating income of $200,000, assuming that the company produces and sells 20,000 fishing rods.

b Assuming that the company decides to sell the rods at a unit price of $56, compute the following:

(1) Total fixed costs budgeted for the year.

(2) Variable costs per unit.

(3) The contribution margin per unit.

(4) The number of units that must be produced and sold annually to break even at a sales price of $56 per unit.

Problem 24B-3
Preparing a
"break-even"
graph

Stop-n-Shop operates a parking lot containing 800 parking spaces. The lot is open 2,500 hours per year. The parking charge per car is 40 cents per hour; the average customer parks two hours. Stop-n-Shop rents the lot for $4,750 per month. The lot supervisor is paid $16,000 per year. Five employees who handle the parking of cars are paid $250 per week for 50 weeks, plus $500 each for the two-week vacation period. Employees rotate vacations during the slow months when four employees can handle the reduced load of traffic. Lot maintenance, payroll taxes, and other costs of operating the parking lot include fixed costs of $2,000 per month and variable costs of 4 cents per parking-space hour.

Instructions

a Draw a cost-volume-profit graph for Stop-n-Shop on an annual basis. Use thousands of parking-space hours as the measure of volume of activity. Stop-n-Shop has an annual capacity of 2 million parking space hours (800 spaces × 2,500 hours per year).

b What is the contribution rate? What is the annual break-even point in dollars of parking revenue?

c Suppose that the five employees were taken off the hourly wage basis and paid 24 cents per car parked, with the same vacation pay as before. (1) How would this change the contribution rate and total fixed costs? (2) What annual sales revenue would be necessary to produce operating income of $44,500 under these circumstances?

Problem 24B-4
Determining the most profitable product given scarce resources

Optical Instruments produces two models of binoculars. Information for each model is as follows:

	MODEL 100	MODEL 101
Sales price per unit	$180	$125
Costs and expenses per unit:		
Raw materials	$51	$39
Direct labour	33	22
Factory overhead (applied at the rate of $18 per machine-hour, $1/3$ of which is fixed and $2/3$ variable)	36	18
Variable selling expenses	30	25
Total costs and expenses per unit	150	104
Profit per unit	$ 30	$ 21
Machine-hours required to produce one unit	2	1

Total factory overhead amounts to $180,000 per month, one-third of which is fixed. The demand for either product is sufficient to keep the plant operating at full capacity of 10,000 machine-hours per month. Assume that *only one product is to be produced in the future.*

Instructions

a Prepare a schedule showing the contribution margin per machine-hour for each product.

b Explain your recommendation as to which of the two products should be discontinued.

Problem 24B-5
Cost-volume-profit analysis; preparing a graph

James Denny is considering investing in a vending machine operation involving 25 vending machines located in various plants around the city. The machine manufacturer reports that similar vending machine routes have produced a sales volume ranging from 1,000 to 2,000 units per machine per month. The following information is made available to Denny in evaluating the possible profitability of the operation.

(1) An investment of $50,000 will be required, $14,000 for merchandise and $36,000 for the 25 machines.

(2) The machines have a service life of five years and no salvage value at the end of that period. Depreciation will be computed on the straight-line basis.

(3) The merchandise (candy and soft drinks) retails for an average of 30 cents per unit and will cost Denny an average of 15 cents per unit.

(4) Owners of the buildings in which the machines are located are paid a commission of 3 cents per unit of candy and soft drinks sold.

(5) One man will be hired to service the machines. He will be paid $1,400 per month.

(6) Other expenses are estimated at $400 per month. These expenses do not vary with the number of units sold.

Instructions

a Determine contribution margin per unit and the break-even volume in units and in dollars per month.

b Draw a monthly cost-volume-profit graph for sales volume up to 2,000 units per machine per month.

c What sales volume in units and in dollars per month will be necessary to produce an operating income equal to a 30% annual return on Denny's investment during his *first year* of operation? (Round to the nearest unit.)

d Denny is considering offering the building owners a flat rental of $30 per machine per month in lieu of the commission of 3 cents per unit sold. What effect would this change in commission arrangement have on his *monthly* break-even volume in terms of units?

BUSINESS DECISION CASES

Case 24-1
Iacocca's dilemma

Assume that you are part of the new management team that has taken over the management of a large diversified automobile manufacturer that is in serious financial condition. Despite several years of large losses, the company's previous management has made practically no changes in the company's operations. The automobiles manufactured by the company are satisfactory in terms of size, style, and fuel economy.

a Suggest some actions you might consider in an effort to reduce
  (1) Fixed costs
  (2) Variable costs per automobile

b Suggest some ways other than cost reductions by which the company may be able to lower its break-even point.

Case 24-2
Evaluating marketing
strategies

Purple Cow Drive-Ins operates a chain of drive-ins selling only an exclusive brand of top-quality ice cream products. The following information is taken from the records of a typical drive-in now operated by the company:

Average selling price of ice cream per litre	$	6.80
Number of litres sold per month		6,000
Variable costs per litre:		
Ice cream	$2.60	
Supplies (cups, cones, toppings, etc.)	1.20	
Total variable expenses per litre	$	3.80
Fixed costs per month:		
Rent on building and parking lot		$1,200.00
Utilities and upkeep		760.00
Wages, including payroll taxes		4,540.00
Manager's salary, including payroll taxes but excluding any bonus . .		1,800.00
Other fixed expenses		700.00
Total fixed costs per month		$9,000.00

Based on these data, the monthly break-even sales volume is determined as follows:

$$\frac{\$9,000 \text{ (fixed costs)}}{\$3.00 \text{ (contribution margin per unit)}} = 3,000 \text{ litres (or } \$20,400\text{)}$$

Instructions

a Assuming that the manager has a contract calling for a bonus of 50 cents per litre for each litre sold *beyond* the break-even point, compute the number of litres of ice cream that must be sold per month in order to earn a monthly operating income of $5,000.

b In order to increase operating income, the company is considering the following two alternatives:

  (1) Reduce the selling price to $5.80 per litre. This action is expected to increase the number of litres sold by 20%. The manager would be paid a salary of $1,800 per month without a bonus.

  (2) Spend $3,000 per month on advertising without any change in selling price. This action is expected to increase the number of litres sold by 10%. The manager would be paid a salary of $1,800 per month without a bonus.

  Which of these two alternatives would be more profitable for a typical drive-in store now selling 6,000 litres? How many litres must be sold per month under each alternative in order to break even? Give complete schedules in support of your answers and indicate to management which of the two alternatives it should adopt.

BUDGETING
AND
STANDARD
COSTS

CHAPTER PREVIEW

Budgeting — preparing a written plan — provides the very foundation for the managerial functions of planning and control. In this chapter we discuss the uses of budgets and the importance of setting budgeted amounts at realistic levels. Next, we illustrate the mechanics of preparing a master budget for a manufacturing business. The concept of "flexible budgets" also is explained and illustrated. Another major topic in the chapter is the use of standard costs — an important tool in achieving control over business operations. We show how standard costs may be incorporated into a cost accounting system to continually inform management of how well actual business performance is "measuring up" to the budget. This chapter builds upon your understanding of responsibility accounting, cost accounting systems, and cost-volume-profit relationships.

After studying this chapter you should be able to meet these Learning Objectives:

1 **Discuss the benefits that a company may derive from a formal budgeting process.**

2 **Explain why budgeted amounts should be set at realistic and achievable levels.**

3 **Describe the elements of a master budget.**

4 **Prepare any of the budgets or supporting schedules included in a master budget.**

5 **Prepare a flexible budget and explain its usefulness.**

6 **Explain how standard costs assist managers in controlling the costs of a business.**

7 **Compute the materials, labour, and overhead variances and explain the meaning of each cost variance.**

BUDGETING: THE BASIS FOR PLANNING AND CONTROL

A budget is a comprehensive *financial plan* setting forth the expected route for achieving the financial and operational goals of an organization. Budgeting is an essential step in effective financial planning. Even the smallest business will benefit from preparing a formal written plan for its future operations, including the expected levels of sales, expenses, net income, cash receipts, and cash outlays.

Virtually all economic entities—businesses, governmental agencies, universities, churches, and individuals — engage in some form of budgeting. For example, a college student with limited financial resources may prepare a list of expected monthly cash payments to see that they do not exceed expected monthly cash receipts. This list is a simple form of cash budget. Business managers must plan (budget) to achieve profit objectives as well as to meet the financial obligations of the business as they become due. Administrators of nonprofit organizations and governmental agencies must plan to accomplish the objectives of the organization with the available resources.

While all businesses engage in some degree of planning, the extent to which plans are formalized in written budgets varies from one business to another. Large well-managed companies generally have carefully developed budgets for every aspect of their operations. Inadequate or sloppy budgeting is a characteristic of companies with weak or inexperienced management.

Benefits derived from budgeting

1 Discuss the benefits that a company may derive from a formal budgeting process.

A budget is a forecast of future events. In fact, the process of budgeting is often called *financial forecasting.* Careful planning and preparation of a formal budget benefit a company in many ways, including:

1 **Enhanced managerial perspective** On a day-to-day basis, much of managers' attention is focussed upon the routine problems of running the business. In preparing a budget, however, managers are forced to make estimates of future economic conditions, including costs, interest rates, demand for the company's products, and the level of competition. Thus, budgeting increases management's awareness of the company's external economic environment.

2 **Advance warning of problems** Since the budget shows the expected results of future operations, management is forewarned of financial problems. If, for example, the budget shows that the company will run short of cash during the summer months, management has advance warning of the need to hold down expenditures or to obtain additional financing.

3 **Coordination of activities** Preparation of a budget provides management with an opportunity to coordinate the activities of the various departments within the business. For example, the production department should be budgeted to produce approximately the same quantity of goods as the sales department is budgeted to sell. A written budget shows departmental managers in quantitative terms exactly what is expected of their departments during the upcoming period.

4 **Performance evaluation** Budgets show the expected costs and expenses for each department as well as the expected output, such as revenue to be earned or units to

be produced. Thus, the budgets provide a yardstick against which each department's actual performance may be compared.

Establishing budgeted amounts

2 Explain why budgeted amounts should be set at realistic and achievable levels.

Departmental managers often are evaluated on the basis of whether their departments exceed or fall short of the budgeted level of performance. If the budget is to provide a fair basis for evaluating a manager's performance, *budgeted amounts should be set at realistic and achievable levels.* Consider, for example, the level of costs budgeted for the production department. If this level is set too high in relation to output, it will be easily achieved and inefficient operations will not be brought to management's attention. On the other hand, if the budgeted costs are too low, an excess of actual costs over budgeted costs becomes a normal condition, rather than an indication of inefficiency.

Differences of opinion often arise as to the dollar amounts used in the budget. Departmental managers naturally want high levels of expenditures and low levels of output budgeted for their departments. This would increase the resources available to the departmental manager and make it easier to meet the budgeted level of performance. Top management, on the other hand, wants the budget to promote high levels of output and low levels of expenditure by each department manager.

The delicate task of human relations is an important part of effective budgeting. A budget is most effective when the people whose performance is being evaluated recognize the budgeted amounts as realistic standards for performance. This recognition is best achieved when managers at all levels of the business are invited to participate in the preparation of the budget.

Once budgeted amounts have been established, they should not be regarded as "carved in stone." The budget should be *reviewed and revised* whenever significant changes occur in the economy, the extent of competition, production methods, or the costs of materials or labour.

The budget period

As a general rule, the period covered by a budget should be long enough to show the effect of managerial policies but short enough so that estimates can be made with reasonable accuracy. This suggests that different types of budgets should be made for different time spans.

A *master budget* is an overall financial and operating plan for a forthcoming fiscal period. It is usually prepared on a quarterly or an annual basis. Long-range budgets, called *capital expenditures budgets,* which summarize plans for major investments in plant and equipment or the addition of product lines, might be prepared to cover plans for as long as 5 to 10 years. *Responsibility budgets,* which are segments of the master budget relating to the responsibilities of a particular manager, are often prepared monthly. *Cash budgets* often are prepared on both a monthly as well as an annual basis. Some companies follow a *continuous budgeting* plan whereby budgets are constantly reviewed and updated. The updating is accomplished, for example, by extending the annual budget one additional month at the end of each month.

3   Describe the elements of a master budget.

Preparing a master budget

The master budget actually includes a number of budgets that together summarize all of the planned activities of the business. The format of the master budget depends upon the size and nature of the business. However, a typical master budget for a manufacturing business includes:

1 Operating budgets
   a Sales forecast
   b Production schedule (stated in number of units to be produced)
   c Manufacturing cost budget
   d Operating expense budget
   e Budgeted income statement
2 Capital expenditures budget
3 Financial budgets
   a Cash budget
   b Budgeted balance sheet

In addition to these separate budgets and schedules, the master budget may include breakdowns of budgeted totals on the basis of departments or managerial responsibility centres.

Some parts of the master budget should not be prepared until other parts have been completed. For example, the budgeted financial statements are not prepared until the sales, manufacturing, and operating expense budgets are available. A logical sequence of steps for preparing a master budget follows:

1 **Prepare a sales forecast** The sales forecast is based upon estimates of general business and economic conditions and upon expected levels of competition. The sales forecast is the starting point in preparing a master budget because production levels, materials purchases, and operating expenses depend upon sales volume.
2 **Prepare budgets for production, manufacturing costs, operating expenses** These forecasts depend in part upon the sales forecast and also upon the relationships between costs and the volume of activity.
3 **Prepare a budgeted income statement** The budgeted income statement is based upon the sales forecast and estimates of the cost of goods sold and operating expenses. It does not require estimates of the timing of cash receipts and cash payments.
4 **Prepare a cash budget** This is one of the largest tasks in the preparation of a master budget. Cash receipts depend upon the sales forecast and the company's experience in collecting amounts receivable from customers. Cash payments depend upon the budgeted levels of materials purchases, capital expenditures, and operating expenses, as well as the credit terms offered by suppliers. Anticipated borrowing, debt repayment, cash dividends, and issuances of capital stock also are reflected in the cash budget.
5 **Prepare a budgeted balance sheet** A projected balance sheet cannot be prepared until the effects of cash transactions upon the various asset, liability, and owners' equity accounts have been determined.

4   Prepare any of the budgets or supporting schedules included in a master budget.

Master budget illustrated

Master budgets are the end product of the entire planning process. To illustrate the preparation of a master budget, assume that Berg Corporation makes and sells a single product. The balance sheet for Berg Corporation as of January 1 is shown below. Management has asked for a master budget that will provide an estimate of net income for the first and second quarters of the coming year and a projected balance sheet at the end of each of the first two quarters. The company has notes payable of $160,000 due in quarterly instalments of $40,000, starting on March 31 of the current year. Sales of the company's product are seasonal; sales during the second quarter are expected to exceed first-quarter sales by 50%. However, the economies of a stable level of production have led management to schedule production of 120,000 units in both the first and second quarters.

BERG CORPORATION
Balance Sheet
January 1, 19___

ASSETS

Current assets:		
Cash		$ 75,000
Receivables		82,000
Inventories:		
Raw materials	$ 25,000	
Finished goods (fifo method)	52,000	77,000
Prepayments		21,000
Total current assets		$255,000
Plant and equipment:		
Buildings and equipment	$970,000	
Less: Accumulated depreciation	420,000	
Total plant and equipment		550,000
Total assets		$805,000

LIABILITIES & SHAREHOLDERS' EQUITY

Current liabilities:		
Notes payable, 16% ($40,000 payable quarterly)		$160,000
Other current payables		78,000
Income taxes payable		25,000
Total current liabilities		$263,000
Shareholders' equity:		
Capital stock, no-par, 100,000 shares issued		
and outstanding	$350,000	
Retained earnings	192,000	542,000
Total liabilities & shareholders' equity		$805,000

Operating budget estimates   The various operating budgets (except for the budgeted income statement) for each of the first two quarters are illustrated on the facing page.

BERG CORPORATION
Operating Budget Estimates
First and Second Quarters of the Current Year

SCHEDULE		1ST QUARTER	2ND QUARTER
A1	Sales forecast:		
	Selling price per unit	$ 3.00	$ 3.00
	Budgeted sales (in units)	100,000	150,000
	Budgeted sales (in dollars)	$300,000	$450,000
A2	Production schedule (in units):		
	Budgeted sales (A1)	100,000	150,000
	Add: Ending inventory of finished goods	50,000	20,000
	Units budgeted to be available for sale	150,000	170,000
	Less: Beginning inventory of finished goods ..	30,000	50,000
	Planned production of finished goods	120,000	120,000

		PER QUARTER
A3	Manufacturing cost estimates:	
	Variable costs:	
	Per unit manufactured:	
	Raw materials	$ 0.50
	Direct labour	0.60
	Variable factory overhead	0.30
	Fixed costs (per quarter):	
	Factory overhead	$ 42,000
A4	Manufacturing budget (for 120,000 units):	
	Raw materials used ($0.50 per unit)	$ 60,000
	Direct labour ($0.60 per unit)	72,000
	Variable factory overhead ($0.30 per unit)	36,000
	Fixed factory overhead	42,000
	Total cost of finished goods manufactured	$210,000
	Cost per unit ($210,000 ÷ 120,000 units)	$1.75

		1ST QUARTER	2ND QUARTER
A5	Ending finished goods inventory:		
	50,000 units at $1.75 (A4)	$ 87,500	
	20,000 units at $1.75 (A4)		$ 35,000
A6	Operating expense budget:		
	Variable expenses ($0.30 × units sold)	$ 30,000	$ 45,000
	Fixed expenses	70,000	70,000
	Total selling and administrative expense	$100,000	$115,000

Estimates of unit sales and sales prices per unit (Schedule A1) are based upon future marketing plans and forecasts of future economic conditions. The production schedule (Schedule A2) reflects both the decision to stabilize production and a decision to reduce the inventory of finished goods from its January 1 level of 30,000 to 20,000 units at the end of the second quarter. (Notice that the inventory of finished goods must rise to 50,000 units at the end of the first quarter in order to meet the budgeted sales and ending inventory of the second quarter.)

The cost estimates in Schedule A3 provide the basis for budgeting manufacturing costs. Schedule A4, the manufacturing budget, indicates the budgeted cost of producing 120,000 finished units in each quarter.

Schedule A5 shows the dollar value of the ending inventories of finished goods that will be on hand if the targets in the sales budget and the manufacturing budget are met. Schedule A6, the operating expense budget, summarizes numerous estimates made by departmental managers in light of the budgeted sales volume.

Budgeted income statement   The budgeted income statements for each quarter shown below are based upon the estimates in Schedules A1 through A6. In addition, these income statements include budgeted amounts for interest expense and income taxes expense. Interest on the $160,000 bank loan is estimated on the assumption that the $40,000 instalments will be paid at the end of each quarter. Interest at 16% per year, or 4% per quarter, is computed on the outstanding balance of $160,000 during the first quarter and on $120,000 during the second quarter. Income tax expense is budgeted at 50% of income before income taxes.

<table>
<tr><td>HERE IS WHAT
QUARTERLY INCOME
SHOULD BE</td><td colspan="3" style="text-align:center">BERG CORPORATION
Budgeted Income Statements
First Two Quarters of Current Year</td></tr>
<tr><td></td><td></td><td>1ST QUARTER</td><td>2ND QUARTER</td></tr>
<tr><td>Sales (A1) ....</td><td></td><td>$300,000</td><td>$450,000</td></tr>
<tr><td>Cost of goods sold:</td><td></td><td></td><td></td></tr>
<tr><td>Finished goods, beginning inventory ....</td><td></td><td>$ 52,000</td><td>$ 87,500</td></tr>
<tr><td>Cost of finished goods manufactured (A4) ....</td><td></td><td>210,000</td><td>210,000</td></tr>
<tr><td>Cost of goods available for sale ....</td><td></td><td>$262,000</td><td>$297,500</td></tr>
<tr><td>Less: Finished goods, ending inventory (A5) ....</td><td></td><td>87,500</td><td>35,000</td></tr>
<tr><td>Cost of goods sold ....</td><td></td><td>$174,500</td><td>$262,500</td></tr>
<tr><td>Gross profit on sales ....</td><td></td><td>$125,500</td><td>$187,500</td></tr>
<tr><td>Expenses:</td><td></td><td></td><td></td></tr>
<tr><td>Selling and administrative expenses (A6) ....</td><td></td><td>$100,000</td><td>$115,000</td></tr>
<tr><td>Interest expense ....</td><td></td><td>6,400</td><td>4,800</td></tr>
<tr><td>Total expenses ....</td><td></td><td>$106,400</td><td>$119,800</td></tr>
<tr><td>Income before income taxes ....</td><td></td><td>$ 19,100</td><td>$ 67,700</td></tr>
<tr><td>Income taxes (50% of income before income taxes) ....</td><td></td><td>9,550</td><td>33,850</td></tr>
<tr><td>Net income ....</td><td></td><td>$ 9,550</td><td>$ 33,850</td></tr>
</table>

The budgeted income statement shows the effects that our budgeted activities are expected to have upon revenue, expense, and net income. We are now ready to estimate the cash flows required by implementing our operating budgets and also to determine the effects of the budgeted activities upon balance sheet accounts.

Financial budget estimates The estimates and data necessary to prepare a cash budget and budgeted balance sheet for each quarter follow. (The amounts used in the preparation of the cash budget are highlighted in black.)

BERG CORPORATION
Financial Budget Estimates
First and Second Quarters of Current Year

SCHEDULE		1ST QUARTER	2ND QUARTER
B1	Budgeted raw materials purchases and inventory:		
	Raw materials used (A4)	$ 60,000	$ 60,000
	Desired ending inventory	40,000	40,000
	Raw materials available for use	$100,000	$100,000
	Less: Inventory at beginning of quarter	25,000	40,000
	Budgeted raw materials purchases	$ 75,000	$ 60,000

B2 Means of financing costs and expenses:

	TOTAL	CURRENT PAYABLES	EXPIRATION OF PREPAYMENTS	DEPRE-CIATION
First quarter:				
Raw material purchases (B1) ...	$ 75,000	$ 75,000		
Direct labour (A4) ...	72,000	72,000		
Factory overhead (A4)	78,000	64,000	$4,400	$ 9,600
Selling and adminis-trative expense (A6)	100,000	94,600	3,000	2,400
Total	$325,000	$305,600	$7,400	$12,000
Second quarter:				
Raw material purchases (B1) ...	$ 60,000	$ 60,000		
Direct labour (A4) ...	72,000	72,000		
Factory overhead (A4)	78,000	64,400	$4,000	$ 9,600
Selling and adminis-trative expense (A6)	115,000	109,500	3,100	2,400
Total	$325,000	$305,900	$7,100	$12,000

SCHEDULE		1ST QUARTER	2ND QUARTER
B3	Payments on current payables:		
	Balance at beginning of quarter	$ 78,000	$101,500
	Increase in payables during quarter (B2)	305,600	305,900
	Total payables during quarter	$383,600	$407,400
	Estimated balance at end of quarter (given) ...	101,500	85,000
	Payments on current payables during quarter	$282,100	$322,400

		1ST QUARTER	2ND QUARTER
B4	Prepayments budget:		
	Balance at beginning of quarter	$ 21,000	$ 15,600
	Estimated cash expenditure during quarter . . .	2,000	12,000
	Total prepayments	$ 23,000	$ 27,600
	Expiration of prepayments (B2)	7,400	7,100
	Prepayments at end of quarter	$ 15,600	$ 20,500
B5	Debt service budget:		
	Liability to bank at beginning of quarter	$160,000	$120,000
	Interest expense for the quarter	6,400	4,800
	Total principal plus accrued interest	$166,400	$124,800
	Cash payments (principal and interest)	46,400	44,800
	Liability to bank at end of quarter	$120,000	$ 80,000
B6	Budgeted income taxes:		
	Income tax liability at beginning of quarter	$ 25,000	$ 9,550
	Estimated income taxes for the quarter		
	(per budgeted income statement)	9,550	33,850
	Total accrued income tax liability	$ 34,550	$ 43,400
	Cash outlay (tax liability at beginning		
	of quarter)	25,000	9,550
	Income tax liability at end of quarter	$ 9,550	$ 33,850
B7	Estimated cash collections on receivables:		
	Balance of receivables at beginning of year . . .	$ 82,000	
	Collections on first-quarter sales of		
	$300,000 ($2/3$ in first quarter and $1/3$		
	in second)	200,000	$100,000
	Collections on second-quarter sales of		
	$450,000 ($2/3$ in second quarter)		300,000
	Total cash collections by quarter	$282,000	$400,000
B8	Budgeted accounts receivable:		
	Balance at the beginning of the quarter	$ 82,000	$100,000
	Sales on open account during quarter (A1) . . .	300,000	450,000
	Total accounts receivable	$382,000	$550,000
	Less: Estimated collections on accounts		
	receivable (B7)	282,000	400,000
	Estimated accounts receivable balance		
	at end of quarter	$100,000	$150,000

Let us now briefly discuss each of these schedules:

Schedule B1 In our manufacturing budget (A4), we estimated the cost of raw materials expected to be *used* in our manufacturing process at $60,000. In preparing a cash budget, however, we need to know the cost of raw materials to be *purchased* each quarter, rather than used. In budgeting purchases of raw materials, we must consider both the expected use of raw materials and the desired raw materials inventory at the end of each quarter.

Let us assume that the production supervisor feels that the January 1 inventory of raw materials of $25,000 is too low. The supervisor recommends that the raw materials inventory be increased to $40,000 and maintained at that level. Schedule B1 calculates the purchases of raw materials required to achieve this desired inventory level while allowing for the use of $60,000 of raw materials each quarter.

Schedule B2 The next step in preparing a cash budget is to estimate the portion of our budgeted costs and expenses that must be *paid in cash* in the near future. Costs and expenses may be financed in any of three ways: through (1) current payables (including accounts payable, accrued expenses payable, and immediate cash payments), (2) expiration of prepaid expenses, and (3) depreciation of plant assets.

Schedule B2 shows how the budgeted costs and expenses of Berg Corporation are expected to be financed. The column headed "Current Payables" indicates the portion of the costs and expenses to be paid in cash or financed by current liabilities. Examples of these items include purchases of raw materials (whether for cash or on account), factory payrolls, and utilities bills. The column headed "Expiration of Prepayments" includes costs and expenses stemming from the expiration of short-term prepayments, such as unexpired insurance and prepaid rent.

The budgeted manner of financing the costs and expenses listed in Schedule B2 is based upon an analysis of the prepaid expenses at the beginning of the first quarter and upon computations of depreciation on plant assets. All costs and expenses other than those resulting from depreciation or the expiration of prepayments require future cash outlays and, therefore, are listed as current payables.

Schedule B3 The purpose of this schedule is to estimate the cash outlays required in each quarter for the costs and expenses classified as current payables in Schedule B2. The starting point in Schedule B3 is the balance of the current payables at the beginning of the first quarter ($78,000), which is taken from the January 1 balance sheet presented earlier. To this amount, we add the $305,600 shown in Schedule B2 as the total current payables budgeted to arise during the first quarter. From this subtotal ($383,600), we subtract the estimated balance of current payables at the end of the quarter to determine the cash payments to be made during the first quarter. The $101,500 balance of current payables at the end of the first quarter was estimated by Berg Corporation's treasurer after an analysis of suppliers' credit terms.

Similar computations are made for the second quarter. The beginning balance of current payables for the second quarter is the ending balance from the first quarter. Again, the amount payable at the end of the second quarter ($85,000) was estimated by the treasurer.

Schedule B4 This schedule budgets the expected cash outlays for prepaid expenses during the period. These outlays were estimated by the treasurer after considering the amount of prepaid expenses at January 1 and the expiration of these items indicated in Schedule B2.

Schedule B5 This schedule summarizes the cash outlays required on Berg Corporation's bank loan during the budget period. The loan agreement calls for quarterly payments of $40,000 plus the interest accrued during the quarter. Interest is computed at an annual rate of 16%, or 4% per quarter. Thus, the interest amounts to $6,400 for the first quarter ($160,000 loan × 4%) and $4,800 in the second ($120,000 outstanding balance × 4%).

Schedule B6 The budgeted cash payments for income tax expense are summarized in Schedule *B6*. It is assumed that each quarter, Berg Corporation makes income tax payments equal to its income tax liability at the beginning of that quarter.

Schedule B7 All of Berg Corporation's sales are made on account. Therefore, the sole source of the company's cash receipts is the collection of accounts receivable. The credit manager estimates that two-thirds of the sales in any quarter will be collected in that quarter, and that the remaining one-third will be collected in the following quarter. Schedule *B7* indicates the budgeted cash collections under these assumptions. (Losses from uncollectible accounts are ignored in our example.)

Schedule B8 This schedule indicates the effect that credit sales (from the sales budget) and collections from customers (Schedule *B7*) are expected to have upon the balance of accounts receivable. The balances shown for accounts receivable at the end of each quarter are carried forward to the *budgeted* balance sheets.

Cash budget The information derived from the financial budget schedules is the basis for the following quarterly cash budget:

PROJECTED CASH FLOW AND ENDING CASH BALANCE

BERG CORPORATION
Cash Budget
First Two Quarters of Current Year

	1ST QUARTER	2ND QUARTER
Cash balance at beginning of quarter	$ 75,000	$ 1,500
Receipts:		
Collections on receivables (B7)	282,000	400,000
Total cash available	$357,000	$401,500
Disbursements:		
Payment of current payables (B3)	$282,100	$322,400
Prepayments (B4)	2,000	12,000
Payments on notes, including interest (B5)	46,400	44,800
Income tax payments (B6)	25,000	9,550
Total disbursements	$355,500	$388,750
Cash balance at end of the quarter	$ 1,500	$ 12,750

The cash budget is an important tool for forecasting whether the company will be able to meet its obligations as they mature. Often the cash budget may indicate a need for short-term borrowing or other measures to generate or conserve cash in order to keep the company solvent. Remember that one of the principal reasons for preparing budgets is to give advance warning of potential problems such as cash shortages.

Budgeted balance sheet We now have the necessary information to forecast the financial position of Berg Corporation at the end of each of the next two quarters. The budgeted balance sheets are illustrated at the top of page 1021. Budget schedules from which various figures on the balance sheets have been derived are indicated parenthetically.

BERG CORPORATION
Budgeted Balance Sheets
As of the End of First Two Quarters of Current Year

	1ST QUARTER	2ND QUARTER
ASSETS		
Current assets:		
Cash (per cash budget)	$ 1,500	$ 12,750
Receivables (B8)	100,000	150,000
Inventories:		
Raw materials (B1)	40,000	40,000
Finished goods (A5)	87,500	35,000
Prepayments (B4)	15,600	20,500
Total current assets	$244,600	$258,250
Plant and equipment:		
Buildings and equipment	$970,000	$970,000
Less: Accumulated depreciation (B2)	(432,000)	(444,000)
Total plant and equipment	$538,000	$526,000
Total assets	$782,600	$784,250
LIABILITIES & SHAREHOLDERS' EQUITY		
Current liabilities:		
Notes payable, 16% (B5)	$120,000	$ 80,000
Other current payables (B3)	101,500	85,000
Income taxes payable (B6)	9,550	33,850
Total current liabilities	$231,050	$198,850
Shareholders' equity:		
Capital stock, no-par, 100,000 shares issued and		
outstanding	$350,000	$350,000
Retained earnings, beginning of quarter	192,000	201,550
Net income for the quarter (per budgeted		
income statements)	9,550	33,850
Total shareholders' equity	$551,550	$585,400
Total liabilities & shareholders' equity	$782,600	$784,250

Using budgets effectively

Earlier in this chapter, we noted several ways in which budgeting benefits an organization. One benefit, an increased awareness by managers of the company's operations and its business environment, may be received even if the completed budget is promptly filed and forgotten. In preparing a budget, managers are forced to consider carefully all aspects of the company's activities. This study and analysis should, in itself, enable managers to do a better job of managing.

The primary benefits of budgeting, however, stem from the uses made of the budgeted information. Among these benefits are (1) advance warning of conditions that require advance corrective action, (2) coordination of the activities of all of the departments within the organization, and (3) the creation of standards for evaluating the performance of company personnel. Let us consider how the master budget for Berg Corporation might serve these functions.

An advance warning of potential trouble   One of the major concerns of the management of Berg Corporation was the ability of the company to meet the quarterly payments on its loan obligations. The cash budget for the first two quarters of the year indicates that the cash position of the company at the end of each quarter will be precariously low. A cash balance of $1,500 is forecast at the end of the first quarter, and a balance of $12,750 at the end of the second quarter. If all goes well the payments *can* be met, but there is little margin for error in the estimates.

When confronted with such a forecast, management should take steps in advance to prevent the cash balance from dropping as low as the budgeted amounts. It may be possible to obtain longer credit terms from suppliers and thus reduce payments on accounts payable during the first two quarters. The company may decide to let inventories fall below scheduled levels in order to postpone cash outlays. An extension of the terms of the note payable might be sought, or the possibility of long-term financing might be considered. If any or all of these steps were taken, it would be necessary to revise the budget estimates accordingly. The fact that management is *forewarned* of this condition several months before it happens, however, illustrates one of the prime values of budgeting.

Coordination of the activities of departments   The budget provides a comprehensive plan for all the departments to work together in a coordinated manner. For example, the production department knows the quantity of goods that must be produced to meet the expected needs of the sales department. The purchasing department knows the quantities of raw materials that must be ordered to meet the requirements of the production department.

If all the departments meet their individual budget objectives. Berg will meet its overall profit goals as set forth in the budgeted income statement. The responsibility for securing the sales revenue budgeted in each quarter rests with the sales department. The problem of scheduling the production of 120,000 units each quarter and of seeing that production costs do not exceed budget estimates is the responsibility of the manufacturing department. General management is responsible for maintaining control over administrative expenses.

In order to focus responsibility for achieving budgeted amounts upon individual managers, it is desirable to divide the overall master budget into a series of *responsibility budgets*. A responsibility budget covers only that portion of the business that is *under the control of a particular manager.* For example, the sales forecast in the master budget might be divided into responsibility budgets for each sales territory. The manufacturing budget might be divided into responsibility budgets for each manufacturing process.

Dividing the total budget into responsibility segments ensures that each manager knows the goals and his or her part in achieving the budgeted goals. The use of responsibility budgets requires a carefully designed *responsibility accounting system* in order that the results of each responsibility centre can be measured and compared with the budget.[1]

---

[1] Responsibility accounting systems are discussed in Chapter 21.

A yardstick for evaluating managerial performance   Comparison of actual results with budgeted amounts is a common means of evaluating the performance of departmental managers. The evaluation of performance should be based only upon those costs and revenues that are under the control of the person being evaluated. For example, Mike Jones, the supervisor of a manufacturing department, can influence labour costs in his department through his control over idle time, overtime hours, and the number of employees to be hired. He may also exert some control over such overhead costs as equipment maintenance, supplies used, and power expenses. On the other hand, Jones probably has no influence on either the salary of the plant manager or the amount of building depreciation, some portion of which might be charged to his department.

The idea that an individual such as a manager should ***not be charged with costs over which he or she has no control*** is widely used in modern budgeting practice. Thus, responsibility budgets often include only ***controllable costs***.

A second point is that even controllable costs may be affected by factors over which a manager has little influence. An example is the effect of significant differences between the volume of production originally budgeted and the volume actually attained. The fact that actual volume varied from budgeted volume might cause many departmental costs to differ significantly from the budgeted amounts. Some method must be devised for evaluating the department manager's performance ***given the level of production that was actually attained.*** This can be done through the use of ***flexible budgets.***

Flexible budget — a more effective control tool

5   Prepare a flexible budget and explain its usefulness.

Suppose, for example, that Harold Stone, production manager of Berg Corporation, is presented with the following ***performance report*** comparing budgeted and actual results at the end of the first quarter's operations:

IS THIS A GOOD OR A
BAD PERFORMANCE?

BERG CORPORATION
Performance Report for Production Department
For the Quarter Ended March 31, 19___

	BUDGETED	ACTUAL	OVER OR (UNDER) BUDGET
Production costs:			
Raw materials used	$ 60,000	$ 63,800	$ 3,800
Direct labour	72,000	76,500	4,500
Variable factory overhead	36,000	38,000	2,000
Fixed factory overhead	42,000	42,400	400
Total production costs	$210,000	$220,700	$10,700

At first glance it appears that the production manager's cost control performance is poor, since his production costs are $10,700 in excess of budget. However, one piece of information has been deliberately omitted from the above schedule. Instead of the ***120,000*** units of production planned for the first quarter, ***130,000 units*** were actually manufactured.

Under these circumstances, the above comparison of budgeted and actual costs becomes meaningless as a measure of the production manager's performance. There is no point in comparing actual costs for one level of output with budgeted cost for a different level of output.

One solution is to base performance evaluation on a *flexible budget.* A flexible budget consists of advance estimates of costs and expenses for *each of several possible levels of activity,* such as 100,000 units, 120,000 units, and 130,000 units. Production costs at various levels of production may be determined from the cost estimates in Schedule A3. For example, the schedule shows raw materials cost at $0.50 per unit. Therefore, at a production level of 130,000 units, the budgeted materials cost would be $65,000.

As the year progresses, the actual level of production will become known. The *budgeted costs* then may be compared with the *actual costs* to determine how well management has performed. Such a comparison is illustrated in the following *performance report:*

BERG CORPORATION
Performance Report for Production Department
For the Quarter Ended March 31, 19___

	ORIGINALLY BUDGETED	FLEXIBLE BUDGET	ACTUAL COSTS	ACTUAL COSTS OVER OR (UNDER) FLEXIBLE BUDGET
Units of production	120,000	130,000	130,000	
Production costs:				
Raw materials used	$ 60,000	$ 65,000	$ 63,800	$(1,200)
Direct labour	72,000	78,000	76,500	(1,500)
Variable factory overhead . .	36,000	39,000	38,000	(1,000)
Fixed factory overhead	42,000	42,000	42,400	400
Total production costs	$210,000	$224,000	$220,700	$(3,300)

This comparison gives quite a different picture of the production manager's cost performance. On the basis of actual volume, Stone has done better than budgeted costs in all categories except fixed factory overhead, most of which is probably outside his control.

Computer-based budgeting

At first glance, the preparation of a ''series'' of budgets for different levels of business activity seems to be an enormous task. However, the mechanical computations involved in the preparation of a budget can be performed quickly and inexpensively by computer. Management need only enter the appropriate cost-volume-profit relationships into a computerized budgeting program. The computer, guided by an appropriate program, can then perform the computations and printing necessary to generate a complete master budget for any level of business activity.

STANDARD COSTS FOR PRODUCT COSTING AND CONTROL

In Chapter 23 we saw how cost accounting systems are used to determine the actual cost to produce products or perform specific manufacturing processes. A cost accounting system becomes even more useful when it includes the budgeted amounts for raw

6 Explain how standard costs assist managers in controlling the costs of a business.

materials, direct labour, and factory overhead to serve as standards for comparison with the actual costs. The budgeted amounts used in a cost accounting system are called *standard costs*. Standard costs may be used in both job order and process cost accounting systems.

The standard cost is the cost that *should be* incurred to produce a product *under normal conditions*. Thus, comparison of actual costs to the predetermined standard alerts managers to those areas in which the actual costs appear excessive. Assume, for example, that the standard (budgeted) cost of producing a product is $10 per unit. If job No. 430, which makes 1,000 units of the product, has an average unit cost of $12.50, management should investigate immediately to determine why actual costs exceeded the standard by such a large margin (25%).

Cost accountants often speak of the "standard" raw material cost and the "standard" labour cost: Remember that these "standard" costs are actually *budgeted* costs.

Establishing and revising standards

Standard costs are established during the budgeting process. Along with the budget, standard costs should be reviewed periodically and revised if significant changes occur in production methods or the prices paid for raw materials, direct labour, or factory overhead. When actual costs exceed standard costs because of waste or inefficiency, however, the standard costs should *not* be revised upward. A standard cost for raw materials, for example, would not be changed if 10% of raw material placed in production has been spoiled because of carelessness by employees. The standard cost for raw material would be changed, however, if the price for raw materials is increased by suppliers. Similarly, the standard cost for direct labour would not be changed if too many hours of direct labour are wasted; but it would be changed if laboursaving equipment is installed or if new contracts with labour unions call for increased wage rates.

Cost variances

Even though standard costs may be carefully set and revised as conditions change, actual costs will still vary from standard costs. The differences between standard costs and actual costs are known as *cost variances*. Cost variances for raw materials, direct labour, and factory overhead result from a wide variety of causes that must be carefully measured and analyzed. As might be expected, different individuals within an organization are responsible for different cost variances.

It is possible to use standard costs only for cost control purposes and for the preparation of various internal reports for management's use. In most cases, however, standard costs and cost variances actually are recorded in the accounts. Under standard cost procedures, the costs charged to Goods in Process, Finished Goods, and Cost of Goods Sold are the *standard costs* of raw materials, direct labour, and factory overhead, not the actual costs. Any differences between the actual costs and the standard costs of goods produced are accumulated in a number of *variance accounts*.

A cost variance is said to be *unfavourable* when actual costs exceed standard costs. When actual costs are less than standard costs, the cost variance is said to be *favourable*.

Illustration of the use of standard costs

To illustrate the use of standard costs and the computation of cost variances, assume that Standard Manufacturing Company has a normal monthly capacity to work 10,000 direct labour hours and to produce 10,000 units of product M. The standard cost for a unit of product M is shown below:

Raw materials, one kilogram at $5 per kilogram		$ 5
Direct labour, one hour at $10 per hour		10
Factory overhead:		
Fixed ($40,000 ÷ 10,000 units monthly capacity)	$4	
Variable ($20,000 ÷ 10,000 units monthly capacity)	2	6
Standard cost per unit of product M		$21

During the month of March, the following actual costs were incurred in producing 9,500 units of product M. There was no work in process either at the beginning or at the end of March.

Raw materials, 9,400 kilograms at $5.20 per kilogram		$ 48,880
Direct labour, 9,600 hours at $10.40 per hour		99,840
Factory overhead:		
Fixed	$40,000	
Variable	22,980	62,980
Total actual costs incurred in March		$211,700

By comparing these actual costs to the standard cost of product M, we can determine the net cost variance for March:

Total actual costs (see above)	$211,700
Total standard costs for units produced, 9,500 units at $21 per unit	199,500
Net unfavourable cost variance (excess of actual over standard costs)	$ 12,200

In planning corrective action, management will want to know the specific causes of this $12,200 net unfavourable cost variance. By comparing each element of manufacturing cost (materials, labour, and overhead) to the related standard costs, we can explain the net cost variance for March in greater detail. Let us begin by determining the portion of this variance that is attributable to the price and the quantity of materials used in March.

7 Compute the materials, labour, and overhead variances and explain the meaning of each cost variance.

Materials price and materials quantity variances[2]   In establishing the standard raw materials cost for each unit of product, two factors were considered: (1) the *quantity* of raw materials that should have been used in making a unit of finished product, and (2) the *prices* that should have been paid in acquiring this quantity of raw materials. Therefore, the total materials cost variance may result from differences between standard and actual materials usage, or between standard and actual prices paid for raw materials, or from a combination of these two factors. This can be illustrated by the diagram at the top of page 1027.

---

[2] The terms "material price variance" and "raw material price variance," as well as "material quantity variance" and "raw material quantity variance" are interchangeable.

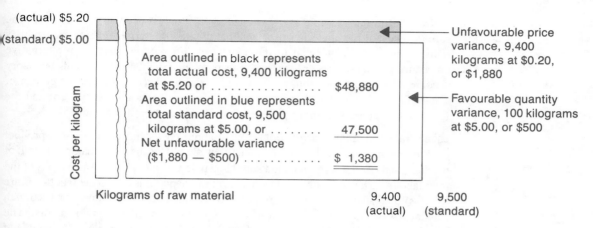

WHY WAS ACTUAL
MATERIALS COST HIGHER
THAN STANDARD?

The variances for raw materials and the journal entry required to record the cost of raw materials incurred by the Standard Manufacturing Company in the month of March may be summarized as shown below:

MATERIALS PRICE AND QUANTITY VARIANCES

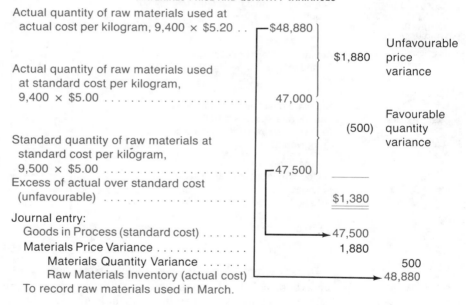

The excess of actual cost of raw materials over standard cost was caused by two factors: The unfavourable ***materials price variance*** of $1,880 resulted from the fact that each kilogram of raw material used cost 20 cents more than the standard price of $5; this portion of the total material variance is the responsibility of the person placing orders for raw materials. The favourable ***materials quantity variance*** of $500 resulted from using 100 fewer kilograms of raw materials than the standard allowed; this variance indicates that the shop supervisors are doing a good job because they are responsible for seeing that raw materials are not wasted or spoiled.

Note that in the example above the Goods in Process account is debited for the *standard cost* of raw materials used and that the Raw Materials Inventory account is reduced by an amount equal to the actual cost of materials used. An alternative procedure would be to record raw materials purchased in the Raw Materials Inventory account at standard cost, thus recording the price variance at the time of purchase. The unfavourable materials price variance is recorded as a debit (a loss) and the favourable materials quantity variance is recorded as a credit (a gain).

Labour rate and labour usage variances[3]   Labour cost standards are also a product of two factors: (1) the hours of labour that should be used in making a unit of product, and (2) the wage rate that should be paid for that labour. An analysis of the total labour variance will indicate whether the variance was due to the fact that more (or less) than standard time was required in production, or that more (or less) than standard wage rates were paid, or some combination of these two factors. The computation of the labour variances for the Standard Manufacturing Company and the journal entry required to record the direct labour cost for March are as follows:

DIRECT LABOUR COST
EXCEEDED STANDARD
BECAUSE OF A WAGE
INCREASE AND BECAUSE
100 HOURS OF DIRECT
LABOUR WERE WASTED

LABOUR RATE AND USAGE VARIANCES

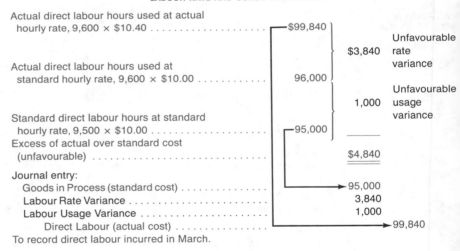

In our example, both the *labour rate variance* and the *labour usage variance* are unfavourable. The causes of these variances should be carefully investigated. If the rate increase of 40 cents per direct labour hour resulted from a new union contract, the $10 per hour standard cost figure should be revised. However, if the increase resulted from using highly paid employees to perform lower pay-scale jobs or from unnecessary overtime work, corrective action on the part of the department supervisor may be in order. The supervisor should also be asked to explain the reason why 100 hours of direct labour in excess of standard were used during the month.

---

[3] The terms "labour rate variance" and "direct labour rate variance," as well as "labour usage variance" and "direct labour usage variance" are interchangeable.

Factory overhead variances   The difference between actual factory overhead costs incurred and the standard factory overhead costs charged to the units produced during the period is called the *overhead variance.* Two factors can contribute to the overhead variance. First, *expenditures* for factory overhead may differ from the standard amounts. Secondly, fixed factory overhead per unit will vary inversely with the *number of units produced.* Since fixed factory overhead remains relatively constant in dollar amount, the fewer units produced during the period, the higher the amount of fixed overhead per unit.

In computing the standard cost of fixed overhead per unit ($4 in our example), it was necessary to assume some normal volume of production. *Normal volume* is the expected average utilization of plant capacity over many years. In the computation of the standard cost of product M, a normal volume of 10,000 units per month was used in determining the standard cost of fixed overhead. It follows that whenever actual production is less than 10,000 units per month, an unfavourable cost variance will result; when actual production exceeds 10,000 units per month, there will be a favourable cost variance. The portion of the overhead variance that results from a difference between actual and normal volume is called the *volume variance.*

Production managers generally are not responsible for the volume variance, because production volume depends upon such factors as sales demand and inventory levels. On the other hand, they can exercise considerable control over the level of expenditures for variable overhead. Therefore, the portion of the overhead variance caused by variations in the dollar amount of overhead expenditures is called the *controllable variance.*

The computation of the two elements of the overhead variance for the Standard Manufacturing Company and the journal entry to record factory overhead for March are shown below:

ACTUAL FACTORY OVERHEAD EXCEEDED STANDARD. CAN YOU EXPLAIN WHY THIS HAPPENED?

FACTORY OVERHEAD VARIANCES

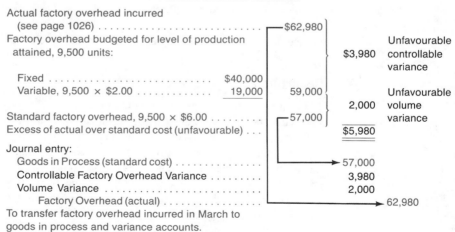

Actual factory overhead incurred (see page 1026)		$62,980		
Factory overhead budgeted for level of production attained, 9,500 units:			$3,980	Unfavourable controllable variance
Fixed	$40,000			
Variable, 9,500 × $2.00	19,000	59,000		Unfavourable volume variance
Standard factory overhead, 9,500 × $6.00		57,000	2,000	
Excess of actual over standard cost (unfavourable)			$5,980	

Journal entry:
Goods in Process (standard cost)	57,000	
Controllable Factory Overhead Variance	3,980	
Volume Variance	2,000	
Factory Overhead (actual)		62,980

To transfer factory overhead incurred in March to goods in process and variance accounts.

The controllable variance is the difference between actual expenditures for factory overhead and the factory overhead **budgeted** for the actual volume of production.

The reason for this $3,980 unfavourable variance is that expenditures for variable factory overhead amounted to $22,980 in March compared to standard variable overhead of $19,000 (9,500 units × $2) at the 9,500-unit production level. This unfavourable controllable variance should alert management to the need to exercise greater control over variable factory overhead.

The unfavourable volume variance occurred because the actual level of production was less than the normal production level used in estimating the standard unit cost. Budgeted fixed overhead for March was $40,000. The standard unit cost figure is based on a normal volume of 10,000 units, and therefore includes fixed overhead of $4 per unit. Since the actual volume was 9,500 units, only $38,000 of fixed overhead (9,500 units × $4 per unit) was charged to the Goods in Process account. The remaining $2,000 of fixed overhead is therefore recorded as an unfavourable volume variance.

An unfavourable volume variance *necessarily* occurs when actual production is *less* than normal volume (10,000 units). Similarly, a favourable volume variance necessarily results when actual volume exceeds normal volume. As mentioned earlier, the scheduled volume of production depends on many factors, such as inventory levels and sales demands. Therefore, production managers generally are *not* responsible for volume variances. An unfavourable volume variance may be viewed as an *idle capacity loss* — the cost of maintaining a plant with a capacity greater than current production levels.

Transfer of cost of units completed to finished goods inventory   At the end of March, the entry to record the transfer of cost of goods completed from the Goods in Process account to the Finished Goods Inventory account is shown as follows:

ENTRY TO RECORD
GOODS COMPLETED

Finished Goods Inventory (at standard cost)	199,500	
Goods in Process (at standard cost)		199,500

To record transfer of completed goods to finished goods inventory at standard cost (9,500 units × $21 = $199,500).

Notice that the finished goods are valued at standard cost.

Disposition of variance accounts

Under a standard cost system, monthly inventories of goods in process and finished goods may be priced at standard cost. Cost variances are allowed to accumulate from month to month; hopefully, only a small total variance will remain because unfavourable variances in one month are offset by favourable variances in other months. At the end of the fiscal year, a small net unfavourable cost variance would be added to Cost of Goods Sold, as illustrated at the top of page 1031. A small net favourable cost variance would be deducted from the balance of the Cost of Goods Sold account at the end of the fiscal year.

However, if the total cost variance (either favourable or unfavourable) for the year is *material in dollar amount,* it should be allocated among Goods in Process, Finished Goods, and Cost of Goods Sold in order to restate these accounts to *actual cost.*

UNFAVOURABLE COST
VARIANCE IS ADDED TO
COST OF GOODS SOLD

RAQUEL MFG. LIMITED
Partial Income Statement
Year 1

Sales (net)		$4,500,000
Cost of goods sold, at standard	$3,000,000	
Add: Net unfavourable cost variance	21,000	
Cost of goods sold		3,021,000
Gross profit on sales		$1,479,000

END-OF-CHAPTER REVIEW

SUMMARY OF CHAPTER LEARNING OBJECTIVES

1 Discuss the benefits that a company may derive from a formal budgeting process.

The benefits of budgeting are simply the benefits that come from "thinking ahead." Budgeting helps to coordinate the activities of the different departments, provides a basis for evaluating departmental performance, and often provides managers with advance warning of possible problems. In addition, budgeting forces management to estimate future economic conditions, including costs of materials, demand for the company's products, and interest rates.

2 Explain why budgeted amounts should be set at realistic and achievable levels.

A budget should provide a fair basis for evaluating the performance of each departmental manager. Therefore, the budgeted amounts should be set at realistic and achievable levels. If the budget calls for a level of performance that cannot realistically be achieved, failure to "meet the budget" becomes a normal condition rather than an indication of inefficiency.

3 Describe the elements of a master budget.

A "master budget" actually is a group of related budgets and forecasts that together summarize all the planned activities of the business. For example, a master budget usually includes a sales forecast, production schedule, manufacturing costs budget, operating expense budget, cash budget, capital expenditures budget, and projected financial statements. The number and type of individual budgets and schedules that make up the master budget depend upon the size and nature of the business.

4 Prepare any of the budgets or supporting schedules included in a master budget.

Preparation of any budget (or supporting schedule) involves two basic considerations. First, the budgeted levels of performance should be reasonable and achievable. Second, the activity summarized in the budget should be coordinated with the related activities budgeted for other departments. For example, a production schedule should be realistic in terms of plant capacity and available labour and materials. However, it also should be coordinated with the company's sales forecast and the budgeted level of production costs.

5 Prepare a flexible budget and explain its usefulness.

A flexible budget shows budgeted revenue, costs, and profits for different levels of business activity. Thus, a flexible budget can be used to evaluate the efficiency of departments throughout the business even if the actual level of business activity differs from management's original estimates. The amounts included in a flexible budget at any given level of activity are based upon cost-volume-profit relationships.

6 Explain how standard costs assist managers in controlling the costs of a business.

Standard costs are the "expected" (or budgeted) costs per unit. When standard costs are used in a cost accounting system, differences between actual costs and budgeted costs are immediately recorded in the accounting records as cost variances. Thus, any "cost overruns" or other variations from the budget are promptly brought to management's attention.

7 Compute the materials, labour, and overhead variances and explain the meaning of each cost variance.

Cost variances are computed by comparing actual costs to standard costs and explaining the reasons for any differences. Differences in the cost of raw materials used may be caused either by variations in the price paid to purchase raw materials or in the quantity of raw materials used. Differences in the cost of direct labour may be caused by variations in wage rates or in the number of hours worked. Variances from budgeted levels of factory overhead may be caused by differences in outlays for controllable overhead expenditures or in the actual and budgeted levels of production.

KEY TERMS INTRODUCED OR EMPHASIZED IN CHAPTER 25

Budget A comprehensive financial plan setting forth the expected route for achieving the financial and operational goals of an organization.

Cash budget A forecast of expected cash receipts, payments, and periodic balances.

Controllable cost A cost over which a manager has significant short-run influence (ability to change).

Controllable factory overhead variance The difference between actual factory overhead and the budgeted factory overhead for the level of output achieved.

Favourable cost variance The amount by which actual costs are *less* than standard costs. Recorded by a credit entry to the variance account.

Flexible budget A series of budgets for different levels of production. Facilitates evaluation of performance.

Idle capacity loss An unfavourable volume variance—the portion of fixed overhead costs that are not assigned to units of production as a result of actual production volume being less than normal volume. Fixed overhead costs not charged to production may be viewed as the cost of maintaining idle plant capacity.

Labour rate variance The difference between the standard direct labour rate and actual rate multiplied by the actual hours.

Labour usage variance The difference between standard direct labour hours and actual direct labour hours used multiplied by the standard hourly rate.

Master budget An overall financial and operating plan, including a sales budget, budgets for production, manufacturing cost, inventory, and operating expenses, and budgeted financial statements.

Materials price variance The difference between the standard price and actual price of raw materials used multiplied by the standard quantity.

Materials quantity variance The difference between standard quantity and actual quantity of raw materials used multiplied by the standard price of the raw materials.

Performance report A schedule comparing the actual and budgeted performances for a particular responsibility centre (or department) within the business.

Responsibility budgets Budgets organized to show those revenues, expenses, costs, and cash flows that are the responsibility of a particular manager.

Standard costs The budgeted costs that should be incurred to produce a product under normal conditions.

Volume variance The portion of the overhead variance that results from a difference between actual production and the normal production level that was assumed in computing standard unit cost.

ASSIGNMENT MATERIAL

REVIEW QUESTIONS

1 Explain the relationship between the managerial functions of *planning* and *controlling costs*.

2 Briefly explain at least three ways in which a business may expect to benefit from preparing a formal budget.

3 Criticize the following quotation:
   "At our company, budgeted revenue is set so high and budgeted expenses so low that no department can ever meet the budget. This way, department managers can never relax; they are motivated to keep working harder no matter how well they are already doing."

4 Identify at least five budgets or schedules that are often included in the master budget of a manufacturing business.

5 Describe the major steps in the preparation of a master budget.

6 Why is the preparation of a sales budget or forecast one of the earliest steps in preparing a master budget?

7 What are *responsibility budgets?* What responsibility segments would serve as the basis for preparing responsibility sales budgets in a large retail store, such as Zellers or Sears?

8 What is a *flexible budget?* Explain how a flexible budget increases the usefulness of budgeting as a means of evaluating performance.

9 It has been suggested that approximately one-third of the total federal budget is considered "controllable." What is meant by a budgeted expenditure being controllable? Give two examples of government expenditures that may be considered "noncontrollable."

10 Define *standard costs* and briefly indicate how they may be used by management in planning and control.

11 What is wrong with the following statement: "There are three basic kinds of cost accounting systems: job order, process, and standard."

12 Once standard costs are established, what conditions would require that standards be revised?

13 List the variances from standard cost that are generally computed for raw materials, direct labour, and factory overhead.

14 What is meant by a favourable labour usage variance? How is the labour usage variance computed?

15 Define each of the following terms: ***normal volume, fixed costs,*** and ***idle capacity loss.***

16 Explain the cause of an unfavourable and of a favourable overhead volume variance.

17 Why is an unfavourable overhead volume variance sometimes called an idle capacity loss?

18 Would a production supervisor be equally responsible for an unfavourable materials price variance and an unfavourable materials quantity variance? Explain.

EXERCISES

Exercise 25-1
Accounting
terminology

Listed below are nine technical accounting terms introduced in this chapter:

Materials quantity variance	Controllable factory overhead variance	Materials price variance
Standard costs	Labour rate variance	Master budget
Idle capacity loss	Labour usage variance	Flexible budget

Each of the following statements may (or may not) describe one of these technical terms. For each statement, indicate the accounting term described, or answer "None" if the statement does not correctly describe any of the terms.

a An unfavourable volume variance.

b The difference between actual factory overhead and the level of overhead budgeted for the level of output actually achieved.

c A budget that shows alternative levels of budgeted amounts at different possible levels of output.

d The difference between the actual and standard unit cost of materials used, multiplied by the actual quantity of materials used.

e The cost or savings resulting from the actual number of required hours of direct labour differing from standard.

f A budget showing cost levels that departmental managers may not exceed without written permission from top management.

g The budgeted costs of producing a product under normal conditions.

h An overall financial plan for the operation of a business, which includes separate budgets or supporting schedules for each aspect of business operations.

Exercise 25-2
Budgeting purchases
and cash payments

The following information is taken from the manufacturing budget and budgeted financial statements of Weiss Mfg. Co. Ltd.:

Raw materials inventory, Jan. 1	$ 62,000
Raw materials inventory, Dec. 31	75,000
Raw materials budgeted for use during the year	220,000
Accounts payable to suppliers of raw materials, Jan. 1	48,000
Accounts payable to suppliers of raw materials, Dec. 31	60,000

Compute the budgeted amounts for:

a Purchases of raw materials during the year.

b Cash payments during the year to suppliers of raw materials.

Exercise 25-3
Budgeting cash receipts

Sales on account for the first two months of the current year are budgeted as follows:

January	$500,000
February	600,000

All sales are made on terms of 2/10, n/30; collections on accounts receivable are typically made as follows:

In month of sale:	
Within discount period	50%
After discount period	20%
In month following sale:	
Within discount period	15%
After discount period	10%
Returns, allowances, and uncollectibles	5%
Total	100%

Compute the estimated cash collections on accounts receivable for the month of *February.*

Exercise 25-4
Preparing a flexible budget

The flexible budget at the 70% and 80% levels of activity is shown below:

	AT 70%	AT 80%	AT 90%
Sales	$700,000	$800,000	$
Cost of goods sold	420,000	480,000	
Gross profit on sales	$280,000	$320,000	$
Operating expenses ($45,000 fixed)	185,000	205,000	
Operating income	$ 95,000	$115,000	$
Income taxes, 30%	28,500	34,500	
Net income	$ 66,500	$ 80,500	$

Complete the flexible budget at the 90% level of activity. Assume that the cost of goods sold and variable operating expenses vary directly with sales and that income taxes remain at 30% of operating income.

Exercise 25-5
More on flexible budgeting

The cost accountant for Modern Molding Co. Ltd. prepared the following monthly report relating to the Grinding Department:

	BUDGET (1,000 HOURS)	ACTUAL (1,100 HOURS)	VARIANCES UNFAVOURABLE	VARIANCES FAVOURABLE
Raw materials used	$30,000	$32,000	$2,000	
Direct labour	10,000	11,500	1,500	
Variable factory overhead	25,000	27,150	2,150	
Fixed factory overhead	15,000	14,950		$50

Prepare a revised report of production costs in which the variances are computed by comparing the actual costs incurred with estimated costs *using a flexible budget* for 1,100 hours. Assume that raw materials used, direct labour, and variable factory overhead would all be 10% higher when 1,100 hours are worked than when only 1,000 hours are worked.

Exercise 25-6
Computing cost variances: materials

The standard for materials in manufacturing item Z is one kilogram at $4.00. During the current month, 5,000 units of item Z were produced and 5,200 kilograms of materials costing $21,320 were used. Analyze the $1,320 variance between actual cost and standard cost in such a way as to show how much of it was attributed to price change and how much to excess quantity of raw materials used. Indicate whether the variances are favourable or unfavourable.

Exercise 25-7
Computing cost variances: overhead

From the following information for Fitch Corporation, compute the controllable factory overhead variance and the volume variance and indicate whether the variances are favourable or unfavourable.

Standard factory overhead based on normal monthly volume:

Fixed ($120,000 ÷ 10,000 units)	$12.00	
Variable ($80,000 ÷ 10,000 units)	8.00	$20.00
Units actually produced in current month		9,000 units
Actual factory overhead costs incurred (including $120,000 fixed)		$186,200

PROBLEMS

Group A

Problem 25A-1
Budgeting factory overhead

Roto Tool Co. Ltd. produces a machine part that is processed successively by Department X and Department Y. Factory overhead is applied to units of production at the following standard costs:

	FACTORY OVERHEAD PER UNIT		
	FIXED	VARIABLE	TOTAL
Department X	$20.00	$6.50	$26.50
Department Y	14.00	5.00	19.00

These standard overhead costs per unit are based on a normal volume of production of 1,000 units per month. In January, variable factory overhead is expected to be 10% above standard because of scheduled repairs to equipment. The company plans to produce 800 units during January.

Instructions

Prepare a budget for factory overhead costs in January. Use column headings as follows: Total, Department X, and Department Y.

Problem 25A-2
Short budgeting problem

Olympic Cameras manufactures and sells a single product. In preparing the budget for the current year, the company's cost accountant has assembled the following information:

	UNITS	DOLLARS
Sales (budgeted)	150,000	$2,400,000
Finished goods inventory, Jan. 1 (actual)	30,000	270,000
Finished goods inventory, Dec. 31 (budgeted)	20,000	?
Cost of finished goods manufactured (budgeted manufacturing cost is $10 per unit)	?	?

The company uses the first-in, first-out method of pricing its inventory of finished goods.

Instructions   Compute the following budgeted quantities or dollar amounts:

a Planned production of finished goods (in units).

b Cost of finished goods manufactured.

c Finished goods inventory, December 31. (Remember to use the first-in, first-out method in pricing the inventory.)

d Cost of goods sold.

Problem 25A-3
Preparing a cash
budget

Barnes Company wants a projection of cash receipts and disbursements for the month of November. On November 28, a note will be payable in the amount of $46,350, including interest. The cash balance on November 1 is $23,900. Accounts payable to merchandise creditors at the end of October were $77,500.

The company's experience indicates that 60% of sales will be collected during the month of sale, 30% in the month following the sale, and 8% in the second month following the sale; 2% will be uncollectible. The company sells various products at an average price of $8 per unit. Selected sales figures are shown below:

	UNITS
September — actual	20,000
October — actual	30,000
November—estimated	40,000
December—estimated	25,000
Total estimated for the current year	400,000

Because purchases are payable within 15 days, approximately 50% of the purchases in a given month are paid in the following month. The average cost of units purchased is $5 per unit. Inventories at the end of each month are maintained at a level of 1,000 units plus 10% of the number of units that will be sold in the following month. The inventory on October 1 amounted to 4,000 units.

Budgeted operating expenses for November are $85,000. Of this amount, $30,000 is considered fixed (including depreciation of $12,000). All operating expenses, other than depreciation, are paid in the month in which they are incurred.

The company expects to sell fully depreciated equipment in November for $9,500 cash.

Instructions   Prepare a cash budget for the month of November, supported by schedules of cash collections on accounts receivable and cash disbursements for purchases of merchandise.

Problem 25A-4
Preparing and using
a flexible budget

Three Sisters is a retail department store. The following cost-volume relationships were used in developing a flexible budget for the company for the current year:

	YEARLY FIXED EXPENSES	VARIABLE EXPENSES PER SALES DOLLAR
Cost of merchandise sold		$0.600
Selling and promotion expense	$ 70,000	0.082
Building occupancy expense	62,000	0.022
Buying expense	50,000	0.040
Delivery expense	37,000	0.010
Credit and collection expense	24,000	0.002
Administrative expense	177,000	0.003
Totals	$420,000	$0.759

Management expected to attain a sales level of $4 million during the current year. At the end of the year the actual results achieved by the company were as follows:

Net sales	$3,500,000
Cost of goods sold	2,060,000
Selling and promotion expense	340,000
Building occupancy expense	140,000
Buying expense	198,000
Delivery expense	61,000
Credit and collection expense	30,000
Administrative expense	188,000

Instructions

a Prepare a schedule comparing the actual results with flexible budget amounts developed for the actual sales volume of $3,500,000. Organize your schedule as a partial multiple-step income statement, ending with operating income. Include separate columns for (1) flexible budget amounts, (2) actual amounts, and (3) any amount over or (under) budget. Use the cost-volume relationships given in the problem to compute the flexible budget amounts.

b Write a statement evaluating the company's performance in relation to the plan reflected in the flexible budget.

Problem 25A-5
Computing cost
variances

The accountants for Polyglaze, Inc., have developed the following information regarding the standard cost and the actual cost of a product manufactured in June:

	STANDARD COST	ACTUAL COST
Raw materials:		
Standard: 10 grams at $0.30 per gram	$3.00	
Actual: 11 grams at $0.29 per gram		$3.19
Direct labour:		
Standard: .50 hour at $10.00 per hour	5.00	
Actual: .45 hour at $10.40 per hour		4.68
Factory overhead:		
Standard: $9,000 fixed cost and $5,000 variable cost		
for 10,000 units normal monthly volume	1.40	
Actual: $9,000 fixed cost and $4,600 variable cost		
for 8,000 units actually produced in June		1.70
Total unit cost	$9.40	$9.57

The normal volume is 10,000 units per month, but only 8,000 units were manufactured in June.

Instructions

Compute the following cost variances for the month of June and indicate whether each variance is favourable or unfavourable:

a Materials price variance and materials quantity variance

b Labour rate variance and labour usage variance

c Controllable factory overhead variance and volume variance

Problem 25A-6
Using standard costs

Death Trap, Inc., manufactures an insecticide and uses standard costs in its job cost system. The insecticide is processed in 400-kilogram batches. You are engaged to explain any differences between standard and actual costs incurred in producing 100 batches during the first month of operation. The following additional information is available:

(1) The standard costs for a 400-kilogram batch are as follows:

	QUANTITY	PRICE	TOTAL COST
Raw materials:			
Various chemicals	400 kilograms	$0.60	$240
Direct labour:			
Preparation, blending, etc.	20 hours	5.00	100
Factory overhead:			
Variable costs	20 hours	3.00	60
Fixed costs	20 hours	1.00	20
Total standard cost per 400-kilogram batch			$420

(2) During the first month, 41,000 kilograms of chemicals were purchased for $23,370, an average cost of 57 cents per kilogram. All the chemical was used during the month, resulting in a price variance of $1,230 and a quantity variance of $600.

(3) Average wage paid for 1,900 hours of direct labour was $4.80 per hour and amounted to $9,120. The labour rate variance was $380 and the labour usage variance was $500.

(4) The standards were established for a normal production volume of 125 batches per month. At this level of production, variable factory overhead was budgeted at $7,500 per month and fixed factory overhead was budgeted at $2,500 per month. During the first month, actual factory overhead amounted to $8,800, including $2,500 fixed costs. The controllable factory overhead variance was $300 and the volume variance was $500.

Instructions   **a** Prepare schedules showing how the variances from standard for materials, labour, and factory overhead were computed. Indicate whether the variances are favourable or unfavourable.

b Prepare journal entries to record the variances and costs incurred (at standard) in the Goods in Process account for (1) raw materials, (2) direct labour, and (3) factory overhead.

Group B

Problem 25B-1
Budgeting labour costs

Farm Fresh Nuts manufactures a product that is first dry roasted and then packed for shipment to customers. The standard direct labour cost per kilogram of product in each process follows:

PROCESS	DIRECT LABOUR HOURS PER KILOGRAM	STANDARD DIRECT LABOUR COST PER HOUR
Dry roasting	.02	$9.00
Packing	.01	6.80

The budget for October calls for the production of 100,000 kilograms of product. The expected labour cost in the dry roasting department is expected to be 7% above standard for the month of October as a result of higher wage rates and inefficiencies in the scheduling of work. The expected cost of direct labour in the packing room is expected to be 5% below standard because of a new arrangement of equipment.

Instructions   Prepare a budget for direct labour costs for October. Use column headings as follows: Total, Dry Roasting, and Packing.

Problem 25B-2
Budgeting production,
inventories, and the
cost of sales

Digital Technology manufactures and sells a single product. In preparing the budget for the current year, the company's controller has assembled the following information:

	UNITS	DOLLARS
Sales (budgeted)	200,000	$7,000,000
Finished goods inventory, beginning of the year	52,000	992,000
Finished goods inventory, end of the year	40,000	?
Cost of finished goods manufactured (budgeted manufacturing cost is $20 per unit)	?	?

The company uses the weighted-average method of pricing its inventory of finished goods.

Instructions   Compute the following budgeted quantities or dollar amounts:

a Planned production of finished goods (in units).

b Cost of finished goods manufactured.

c Finished goods inventory, end of the year.

d Cost of goods sold.

Problem 25B-3
Flexible budgeting

Rimfire Rifle Corporation uses departmental budgets and performance reports in planning and controlling its manufacturing operations. The following annual performance report for the production department for the year was presented to the president of the company.

	BUDGETED COSTS FOR 10,000 UNITS		ACTUAL COSTS INCURRED	OVER OR (UNDER) BUDGET
	PER UNIT	TOTAL		
Variable manufacturing costs:				
Raw materials	$15.00	$150,000	$171,500	$21,500
Direct labour	24.00	240,000	264,000	24,000
Indirect labour	7.50	75,000	97,500	22,500
Indirect materials, supplies, etc.	4.50	45,000	49,500	4,500
Total variable manufacturing costs	$51.00	$510,000	$582,500	$72,500
Fixed manufacturing costs:				
Lease rental	$ 4.50	$ 45,000	$ 45,000	None
Salaries of supervisors	12.00	120,000	125,000	$ 5,000
Depreciation and other	7.50	75,000	77,500	2,500
Total fixed manufacturing costs ..	$24.00	$240,000	$247,500	$ 7,500
Total manufacturing costs	$75.00	$750,000	$830,000	$80,000

Although a production volume of 10,000 guns was originally budgeted for the year, the actual volume of production achieved for the year was 12,000 guns. The company does not use standard costs; raw materials and direct labour are charged to production at actual cost. Factory overhead is applied to production at the predetermined rate of 150% of the actual direct labour cost.

After a quick glance at the performance report showing an unfavourable manufacturing cost variance of $80,000, the president said to the accountant: "Fix this thing so it makes sense. It looks as though our production people really blew the budget. Remember that we exceeded our budgeted production schedule by a significant margin. I want this performance report to show a better picture of our ability to control costs."

Instructions

a Prepare a revised performance report for the year on a flexible budget basis. Use the same format as the production report above, but revise the budgeted cost figures to reflect the actual production level of 12,000 guns.

b In a few sentences compare the original performance report with the revised report.

c What is the amount of overapplied or underapplied factory overhead for the year? (Note that a standard cost system is not used.)

Problem 25B-4
Preparing a cash budget

Helen Rogers, owner of the Rogers Company, is negotiating with the bank for a $100,000, 12%, 90-day loan effective July 2 of the current year. If the bank grants the loan, the proceeds will be $97,000, which Rogers intends to use on July 2 as follows: pay accounts payable, $75,000; purchase equipment, $8,000; add to bank balance, $14,000.

The current working capital position of the Rogers Company, according to financial statements as of June 30, is as follows:

Cash in bank	$ 10,000
Receivables (net of allowance for doubtful accounts)	80,000
Merchandise inventory	45,000
Total current assets	$135,000
Accounts payable (including accrued operating expenses)	75,000
Working capital	$ 60,000

The bank loan officer asks Rogers to prepare a forecast of her cash receipts and disbursements for the next three months to demonstrate that the loan can be repaid at the end of September.

Rogers has made the following estimates, which are to be used in preparing a three-month cash budget: Sales (all on open account) for July, $150,000; August, $180,000; September, $135,000; and October, $100,000. Past experience indicates that 80% of the receivables generated in any month will be collected in the month following the sale, 19% in the second month following the sale, and 1% will prove uncollectible. Barnes expects to collect $60,000 of the June 30 receivables in July, and the remaining $20,000 in August.

Cost of goods sold has averaged consistently about 65% of sales. Operating expenses are budgeted at $18,000 per month plus 8% of sales. With the exception of $2,200 per month depreciation expense, all operating expenses and purchases are on open account and are paid in the month following their incurrence.

Merchandise inventory at the end of each month should be sufficient to cover the following month's sales.

Instructions

a Prepare a monthly cash budget showing estimated cash receipts and disbursements for July, August, and September, and the cash balance at the end of each month. Supporting schedules should be prepared for estimated collections on receivables, estimated merchandise purchases, and estimated payments for operating expenses and of accounts payable for merchandise purchases.

b On the basis of this cash forecast, write a brief report to Rogers explaining whether she will be able to pay the $100,000 loan at the bank at the end of September.

Problem 25B-5
Computing cost
variances

Wall Systems Corporation uses standard costs in its cost accounting system. The standard cost for a certain product at a normal volume of 1,000 units per month is as follows:

Lumber, 100 metres at $300 per 1,000 metres		$30.00
Direct labour, 5 hours at $8.00 per hour		40.00
Factory overhead (applied at $22.00 per unit produced):		
Fixed ($15,000 ÷ 1,000 units)	$15.00	
Variable	7.00	22.00
Total standard unit cost		$92.00

The actual unit cost for a given month in which 800 units were produced is as follows:

Lumber, 110 metres at $280 per 1,000 metres	$30.80
Direct labour, 5¹/₂ hours at $7.80 per hour	42.90
Factory overhead, $20,080 ÷ 800 units	25.10
Total actual unit cost	$98.80

Instructions

Compute the following cost variances for the month and indicate whether each variance is favourable or unfavourable:

a Material price variance and material quantity variance.

b Labour rate variance and labour usage variance.

c Controllable factory overhead variance and volume variance.

Problem 25B-6
Using standard
costs

Safari Outfitters uses standard costs in a process cost system. At the end of the current month, the following information is prepared by the company's cost accountant:

	RAW MATERIALS	DIRECT LABOUR	FACTORY OVERHEAD
Actual costs incurred	$96,000	$82,500	$123,240
Standard costs	90,000	84,000	115,500
Material price variance (favourable)	2,400		
Material quantity varience (unfavourable) . .	8,400		
Labour rate variance (favourable)		3,000	
Labour usage variance (unfavourable)		1,500	
Controllable factory overhead variance			
(unfavourable)			3,240
Volume variance (unfavourable)			4,500

The total standard cost per unit of finished product is $30. During the current month, 9,000 units were completed and transferred to the finished goods inventory and 8,800 units were sold. The inventory of goods in process at the end of the month consists of 1,000 units which are 65% completed. There was no inventory in process at the beginning of the month.

Instructions

a Prepare journal entries to record all variances and the costs incurred (at standard) in the Goods in Process account. Prepare separate compound entries for (1) raw materials, (2) direct labour, and (3) factory overhead.

b Prepare journal entries to record (1) the transfer of units finished to the Finished Goods Inventory account and (2) the cost of goods sold (at standard) for the month.

c Assuming that the company operated at 90% of its normal capacity during the current month, what is the amount of the fixed factory overhead per month?

BUSINESS DECISION CASES

Case 25-1
It's not my fault

Cabinets, Cabinets, Inc., is a large manufacturer of modular kitchen cabinets, sold primarily to builders and developers. The company uses standard costs in a responsibility accounting system. Standard production costs have been developed for each type of cabinet; these costs, and any cost variances, are charged to the production department. A budget also has been developed for the sales department. The sales department is credited with the gross profit on sales (measured at standard costs) and is charged with selling expenses and any variations between budgeted and actual selling expenses.

In early April, the manager of the sales department asked the production department to fill a "rush" order of kitchen cabinets for a tract of 120 homes. The sales manager stated that the entire order must be completed by May 31. The manager of the production department argued that an order of this size would take 12 weeks to produce. The sales manager answered, "The customer needs it on May 31, or we don't get the business. Do you want to be responsible for our losing a customer who makes orders of this size?"

Of course, the production manager did not want to take that responsibility. Therefore, he gave in and processed the rush order by having production personnel work overtime through April and May. As a result of the overtime, the performance reports for the production department in those months showed large, unfavourable labour rate variances. The production manager, who in the past had prided himself on "coming in under budget," now has very ill feelings toward the sales manager. He also has stated that the production department will never again accept a "rush" order.

Instructions

a Identify any problem that you see in the company's standard cost system or in the manner in which cost variances are assigned to the responsible managers.

b Make recommendations for changing the cost accounting system to reduce or eliminate any problems that you have identified.

Case 25-2
Revising standard costs?

Armstrong Chemical began operations in January. The company manufactures an acrylic floor wax called Tough-Coat. The following standard cost esimates were developed several months before the company began its actual operations:

	ESTIMATED STANDARD COST PER UNIT
Raw material X-1 (one gram)	$1.00
Raw material X-2 (one kilogram)	.50
Direct labour	.80
Factory overhead	1.40
Total estimated cost per unit	$3.70

The estimated factory overhead cost per unit was determined by dividing budgeted factory overhead for the year by the 1,000,000 units scheduled to be produced.

During the year, 1,000,000 units of Tough-Coat were actually produced and 900,000 units were sold. Actual costs incurred during the year were:

Material X-1 purchased, 1,200,000 grams @ $0.70	$ 840,000
Material X-2 purchased, 1,150,000 kilograms @ $0.50	575,000
Direct labour	880,000
Factory overhead	1,400,000
Total production costs incurred during the year	$3,695,000

At the end of the year, the following variance accounts appeared in the company's accounting records:

Favourable price variance on all material X-1 purchased, 1,200,000 grams (credit)	$(360,000)
Unfavourable materials quantity variance, 50,000 kilograms of material X-2 spoiled in production (debit)	25,000
Unfavourable direct labour rate variance because of 10% wage increase early in the year (debit)	80,000
Net favourable cost variance	$(255,000)

The company's inventories at the end of the year, stated at standard cost, were as follows:

Raw materials:		
Material X-1, 200,000 grams @ $1.00	$200,000	
Material X-2, 100,000 kilograms @ $0.50	50,000	$250,000
Finished goods:		
Tough-Coat, 100,000 units @ $3.70		370,000
Total inventory at Dec. 31		$620,000

The independent public accountant, who has been engaged to audit the company's financial statements, wants to adjust this inventory to "a revised standard cost," which would take into account the favourable price variance on material X-1 ($0.30 per gram) and the 10% wage increase early in the year. The president of the company objects on the following grounds: "Such a revision is not necessary because the cost of material X-1 already shows signs of going up and the wage increase was not warranted because the productivity of workers did not increase one bit. Furthermore, if we revise our inventory figure of $620,000, our operating income will be reduced from the current level of $100,000." You are called in by the president to help resolve the controversy.

Instructions   Do you agree with the president? Assuming that you conclude that the standards for July should be revised, what value should be assigned to the inventory at the end of the year? What effect would this revaluation of inventory have upon the company's $100,000 operating income?

26

RELEVANT INFORMATION, INCREMENTAL ANALYSIS, AND CAPITAL BUDGETING

CHAPTER PREVIEW

In this chapter, we discuss several analytical techniques that aid managers in making a wide variety of business decisions. First, we explain the nature of ''relevant'' financial information and identify the information relevant to several common types of business decisions. We show how relevant information can be evaluated by a technique called incremental analysis. Next, we illustrate and explain variable costing—a special method of accounting for manufacturing costs that makes the income statement more suitable for cost-volume-profit analysis. Our third major topic is capital budgeting—the process of planning and evaluating proposals for investments in plant assets. We illustrate and explain the widely used capital budgeting techniques of payback period, return on average investment, and discounting future cash flows.

After studying this chapter you should be able to meet these Learning Objectives:

1 **Identify the financial information that is relevant to a particular business decision.**

2 **Use incremental analysis to evaluate alternative courses of action.**

3 **Discuss the relevance of opportunity costs, sunk costs, and out-of-pocket costs in making business decisions.**

4 **Determine the effect upon operating income of discontinuing a product line.**

5 **Explain the difference between full costing and variable costing.**

6 **Evaluate capital budgeting proposals using (a) the payback period, (b) return on average investment, and (c) discounted future cash flows.**

The concept of relevant information

Many types of information may be relevant to a given business decision. For example, information as to the number of jobs to be created, the expected effect of a decision upon public opinion, or the political consequences of a decision may be quite relevant. Our discussion, however, will be limited to relevant *financial* information — namely, costs and revenue.

All business decisions involve a choice among alternative courses of action. The only information relevant to a decision is that information which *varies among the alternative courses of action being considered.* Costs or revenue that *do not vary* among alternative courses of action *are not relevant* to the decision.

To illustrate the concept of relevant information, assume that the sawmill of Sierra Lumber is closed because of a labour strike expected to last for several months. During the strike, Sierra Lumber is incurring costs at the mill of $7,500 per week. (These costs include depreciation, interest expense, and salaries to nonstriking employees.) Assume also that a film company has offered to rent the mill for one week at a price of $5,000 in order to shoot scenes for a new James Bond movie. If the mill is rented to the company, Sierra's management estimates that clean-up costs will amount to approximately $500 after shooting is completed. Based solely upon this information, would it be profitable to rent the closed sawmill to the film company?

If the mill is rented to the film company, the profitability of the mill during that week may be measured as follows:

Revenue		$ 5,000
Costs and expenses:		
Weekly sawmill expenses	$7,500	
Clean-up cost	500	8,000
Operating income (loss)		$(3,000)

However, not all the information in this analysis is relevant to the decision at hand. The $7,500 in weekly sawmill expenses will continue *whether or not* the mill is rented to the film company.

The relevant factors in this decision are the *differences* between the costs incurred and revenue earned under the alternative courses of action (renting or not renting). These differences are often called the *incremental* costs and revenue. An incremental analysis of the Sierra Lumber decision is shown as follows:

	REJECT OFFER	ACCEPT OFFER	INCREMENTAL ANALYSIS
Revenue	$ 0	$ 5,000	$5,000
Costs and expenses:			
Weekly sawmill expenses	(7,500)	(7,500)	
Clean-up costs	0	(500)	(500)
Operating income (loss)	$(7,500)	$(3,000)	$4,500

The incremental analysis shows that accepting the film company's offer results in $5,000 of incremental revenue, but only $500 in incremental costs. Thus, renting the sawmill to the company will benefit Sierra by reducing its operating loss for the week by $4,500.

Accepting special orders

A more commonplace example of the need to identify relevant information is the decision of whether or not to accept an order for an additional volume of business at special terms. Assume, for example, that Sports Supply Company has scheduled the production of 200,000 dozen golf balls during the coming year, although its plant has the capacity to produce considerably more. At the scheduled level of production, budgeted manufacturing costs amount to $10.50 per dozen. Now assume that the company receives a special order from a foreign company for 50,000 dozen balls bearing a special imprint. Sports Supply Company normally sells golf balls for $12 per dozen, but the foreign company's offer is only $8 per dozen. If this special order is accepted, Sports Supply must spend $15,000 in cash to design and set up the special imprint on the balls. A summary of the estimated results for the coming year is presented as follows:

A SPECIAL ORDER IS PROFITABLE IF INCREMENTAL REVENUE EXCEEDS INCREMENTAL COSTS

	PLANNED OUTPUT (200,000 DOZEN)	WITH SPECIAL ORDER (250,000 DOZEN)	INCREMENTAL ANALYSIS
Sales: $12 per dozen	$2,400,000	$2,400,000	
$8 per dozen		400,000	$400,000
Variable costs:			
$6 per dozen	(1,200,000)	(1,500,000)	(300,000)
Fixed costs	(900,000)	(900,000)	
Special imprint costs		(15,000)	(15,000)
Estimated operating income	$ 300,000	$ 385,000	$ 85,000

Note that the average cost of producing golf balls without the special order is $10.50 per dozen [($1,200,000 + $900,000) ÷ 200,000 dozen]. If a decision were made based on this average cost, the special order would probably be rejected. Incremental analysis, however, shows that *incremental revenue* from accepting the special order amounts to $400,000, while the *incremental cost* is only $315,000. Thus, accepting the special order will increase Sports Supply Company's operating income by $85,000.

The relevant factors in this type of decision are the incremental revenue that will be earned and the additional (incremental) cost that will be incurred by accepting the special order. *The average cost of production is not relevant to the decision.*

In evaluating the merits of a special order such as the one received by the Sports Supply Company, we must consider the effect that such an order may have on the company's regular sales volume and selling prices. Obviously, it would not be wise for Sports Supply Company to sell 50,000 dozen golf balls at $8 a dozen to a domestic company that might try to sell the golf balls to the regular customers of Sport Supply Company for, say, $10 per dozen.

Make or buy decisions

In many manufacturing situations, a company faces decisions whether (1) to produce a certain component part required in the assembly of its finished products or (2) to buy the part from outside suppliers. If a company produces a part that can be purchased at a lower cost, it may be more profitable for the company to buy the part and utilize its productive resources for other purposes.

For example, if a company can buy for $5 per unit a part that costs the company $6 per unit to produce, the choice seems to be clearly in favour of buying. But the astute reader will quickly raise the question, "What is included in the cost of $6 per unit?" Assume that the $6 unit cost of producing 10,000 units was determined as follows:

	COST OF PART
Raw materials	$ 8,000
Direct labour	12,500
Variable factory overhead	10,000
Fixed factory overhead	29,500
Total costs	$60,000
Cost per unit ($60,000 ÷ 10,000 units)	$6

A careful review of operations indicates that if the production of this part were discontinued, all the cost of raw materials and direct labour and $9,000 of the variable factory overhead would be eliminated. In addition, $2,500 of the fixed factory overhead can be eliminated. These, then, are the relevant costs in producing the 10,000 parts, and we can summarize them as follows:

IS IT CHEAPER TO
MAKE OR TO BUY?

	MAKE THE PART	BUY THE PART	INCREMENTAL ANALYSIS
Manufacturing costs for 10,000 units:			
Raw materials	$ 8,000		$ 8,000
Direct labour	12,500		12,500
Variable factory overhead	10,000	$ 1,000	9,000
Fixed factory overhead	29,500	27,000	2,500
Purchase price of part, $5 per unit		50,000	(50,000)
Total cost to acquire part	$60,000	$78,000	$(18,000)

Our analysis shows that making the part will cost $60,000 per year, while buying the part will cost $78,000. Thus, the company will save $18,000 per year by continuing to make the part.

In our example, we assumed that only part ($9,000) of the variable factory overhead incurred in producing the part would be eliminated if the part were purchased. We also assumed that $2,500 of the fixed factory overhead could be eliminated if the part were purchased. The purpose of these assumptions was to show that not all variable costs are incremental, and that some fixed costs may be incremental in a given situation.

Opportunity costs

3   Discuss the relevance of opportunity costs, sunk costs, and out-of-pocket costs in making business decisions.

At this stage of our discussion, it is appropriate to introduce the topic of opportunity costs. An *opportunity cost* is the benefit that could have been obtained *by following another course of action.* For example, assume that you pass up a summer job which pays $2,400 in order to attend summer school. The $2,400 may be viewed as an opportunity cost of attending summer school.

Opportunity costs are not recorded in the accounting records, but they are an important factor in many business decisions. Ignoring opportunity costs is a common source of error in cost analyses. In our preceding example, we determined that the company could save $18,000 per year by continuing to manufacture a particular part, rather than buying it from an outside supplier. Assume, however, that the production facilities used to make the part could instead be used to manufacture a product that would increase the company's profitability by $25,000. Obviously, the company should not forgo a $25,000 profit in order to save $18,000. When this $25,000 opportunity cost is considered, it becomes evident that the company should buy the part and use its productive facilities to produce the other product.

Sunk costs versus out-of-pocket costs

The only costs relevant to a decision are those costs that vary among the alternative courses of action being considered. A *sunk cost* is one which has *already been incurred* by past actions. Sunk costs are *not relevant* to decisions because they *cannot be changed* regardless of what decision is made. The term *out-of-pocket cost* is often used to describe costs that have *not yet* been incurred and that *may vary* among the alternative courses of action. Out-of-pocket costs, therefore, are relevant in making decisions.

Scrap or rebuild defective units

To illustrate the irrelevance of sunk costs, assume that 500 television sets that cost $80,000 to manufacture are found to be defective and that management must decide what to do with them. These sets may be sold "as is" for $30,000, or be rebuilt and placed in good condition at an additional out-of-pocket cost of $60,000. If the sets are rebuilt, they can be sold for the regular price of $100,000. Should the sets be sold as is or rebuilt?

Regardless of whether the sets are sold or rebuilt, the $80,000 sunk cost has already been incurred. The relevant considerations in the decision to sell the sets as is or rebuild are the *incremental revenue* and the *incremental cost*. By rebuilding the sets, the company will realize $70,000 more revenue than if the sets are sold as is. The incremental cost necessary to obtain this incremental revenue is the $60,000 cost of rebuilding the sets. Thus, the company will be $10,000 ($70,000 − $60,000) better off if it rebuilds the sets.

Whether to discontinue an unprofitable product line

4 Determine the effect upon operating income of discontinuing a product line.

Management often must decide whether a company's overall profitability can be improved by discontinuing one or more product lines. To illustrate this type of decision, assume that Suncraft Corporation manufactures electric mixers in three models: deluxe, standard, and economy. A partial income statement showing the profitability of each product line is shown at the top of page 1050.

If we look only at the subtotals for operating income, we might expect that dropping both the deluxe and economy models would cause income from operations to rise to $68,000 per year — a striking improvement. This analysis is erroneous, however, because it assumes that discontinuing a product will cause all the costs and expenses allocated to that product to disappear. In reality, most variable costs (such as raw materials, direct labour, and sales commissions) can be eliminated when a

SUNCRAFT CORPORATION
Partial Income Statement
For the Current Year

	TOTAL	DELUXE MODEL	STANDARD MODEL	ECONOMY MODEL
Sales (units)	34,000	4,000	20,000	10,000
Sales revenue	$960,000	$160,000	$600,000	$200,000
Manufacturing costs	730,000	138,000	412,000	180,000
Gross profit on sales	$230,000	$ 22,000	$188,000	$ 20,000
Operating expenses	213,200	36,200	120,000	57,000
Income or (loss) from operations . .	$ 16,800	$ (14,200)	$ 68,000	$ (37,000)

product is discontinued. Many fixed costs (such as property taxes and depreciation on the factory) *cannot be eliminated* and end up being charged against the remaining products.

Our product line income statement becomes more useful if it is reorganized to show the contribution margin of each product. As explained in Chapter 24, *contribution margin* is sales revenue minus the related variable costs — or, in short, the amount that a product contributes toward covering fixed costs and providing operating income. A partial income statement showing the contribution margin for each of Suncraft Corporation's products is shown below:

SUNCRAFT CORPORATION
Partial Income Statement
For the Current Year

		TOTAL	DELUXE MODEL	STANDARD MODEL	ECONOMY MODEL
Sales (units)	(a)	34,000	4,000	20,000	10,000
Sales revenue		$960,000	$160,000	$600,000	$200,000
Less: Variable costs and					
expenses		774,000	144,000	440,000	190,000
Contribution margin	(b)	$186,000	$ 16,000	$160,000	$ 10,000
Less: Fixed costs and					
expenses		169,200	30,200	92,000	47,000
Income or (loss) from					
operations		$ 16,800	$ (14,200)	$ 68,000	$ (37,000)
Contribution margin per					
unit (b ÷ a)			$4	$8	$1

This analysis shows that each of the three products makes a positive contribution toward the fixed costs and operating income of the company. Assume, for a moment, that discontinuing a product line *will not eliminate any fixed costs or affect the sales of other products.* Under these assumptions, dropping the economy model will reduce revenue by $200,000 and expenses by only $190,000, thus causing operating income to decline by $10,000. Dropping the deluxe model will reduce revenue by

$160,000, expenses by $144,000, and operating income by $16,000. In short, discontinuing either product will reduce operating income *by the amount of that product's contribution margin.*

Shifts in sales and elimination of fixed costs   In our preceding analysis, we assumed that dropping one product would not affect the sales of other products or eliminate any fixed costs. In some cases, these assumptions are reasonably valid, and an analysis based solely upon contribution margins is sound. In other cases, however, it is appropriate to consider the effects of dropping a product line upon fixed costs and sales of other products.

To illustrate, assume that discontinuing the economy mixer is expected to eliminate $7,000 of fixed costs and also to increase annual sales of the standard mixer by 3,500 units. (As shown earlier, the contribution margin for the standard mixer is $8 per unit.) An analysis of the effect of discontinuing the economy mixer upon the operating income of Suncraft appears below:

COMPLETE ANALYSIS
OF DECISION VARIABLES

SUNCRAFT CORPORATION
Estimate of Change in Operating Income from Dropping Economy Model

Increases in operating income from dropping economy model:
Estimated reduction in fixed costs	$ 7,000
Additional contribution margin resulting from increased sales of standard model (3,500 units × $8 per unit)	28,000
Total increases in operating income	$35,000
Less: Reductions in operating income from dropping economy model:	
Lost contribution margin from current sales of economy model	$10,000
Estimated net increase in operating income if economy model is dropped	$25,000

Opportunity costs are an important part of a decision whether or not to discontinue a product line. For example, the $28,000 in contribution margin expected to result from additional sales of standard mixers is an opportunity cost of continuing to sell economy mixers. In addition, Suncraft may be able to use the plant facilities now committed to economy mixers to manufacture a food processor or other product. The contribution margin expected from this alternative product is another opportunity cost of continuing to manufacture economy mixers.

Variable costing

5   Explain the difference between full costing and variable costing.

Our preceding decision and many of the cost-volume-profit relationships discussed in Chapter 24 are based upon the concept of contribution margin — sales revenue minus the related variable costs. Through a technique called *variable costing,* a cost accounting system may be modified to show contribution margin and other cost-volume-profit relationships.

In conventional cost accounting systems, such as those described in Chapter 23, *all* manufacturing costs are charged to the Goods in Process account. From this account, the costs flow into the Finished Goods Inventory account and into the Cost of Goods Sold. *Notice that no distinction is made between fixed and variable manufacturing costs.* Since all manufacturing costs are "absorbed" into the cost of finished goods manufactured, this traditional costing approach is termed absorption costing or *full costing.*

Variable costing is an alternative to full costing. Under variable costing, *fixed manufacturing costs are treated as expenses of the current period.* Thus, only *variable* manufacturing costs are assigned to the goods manufactured. The flow of costs under variable and full costing is illustrated at the top of page 1053.

Before we illustrate variable costing, we must point out that this technique is *not acceptable* for use in published financial statements. It is used only as a tool for managerial analysis. A company that uses variable costing must make adjusting entries at year-end to convert its accounting records to a full costing basis before preparing its published financial statements.

Illustration of variable costing

The differences between variable costing and full costing may be illustrated by preparing an income statement under each method, using the following information for the Hamilton Corporation. During the first year of operations, 40,000 units were produced, of which 30,000 were sold.

	TOTAL	NUMBER OF UNITS	PER UNIT
Sales	$1,500,000	30,000	$50
Manufacturing costs:			
Variable	800,000	40,000	$20
Fixed	240,000	40,000	6
Total	$1,040,000		$26
Selling and administrative expenses:			
Variable	$ 150,000		
Fixed	320,000		
Total	$ 470,000		

A partial income statement based upon this information using the traditional *full costing* assumption is shown as follows:

FIXED FACTORY OVERHEAD COSTS INCLUDED IN INVENTORY AND COST OF GOODS SOLD

HAMILTON CORPORATION
Partial Income Statement — Full Costing
For the Current Year

Sales (30,000 units @ $50)	$1,500,000
Cost of goods sold*	780,000
Gross profit on sales	$ 720,000
Selling and administrative expenses (fixed and variable)	470,000
Income from operations	$ 250,000

*Computation of cost of goods sold:

Variable manufacturing costs (40,000 units @ $20)	$ 800,000
Fixed manufacturing costs	240,000
Cost of finished goods manufactured (40,000 units × $26)	$1,040,000
Less: Ending inventory of finished goods (10,000 units @ $26)	260,000
Cost of goods sold (30,000 units × $26)	$ 780,000

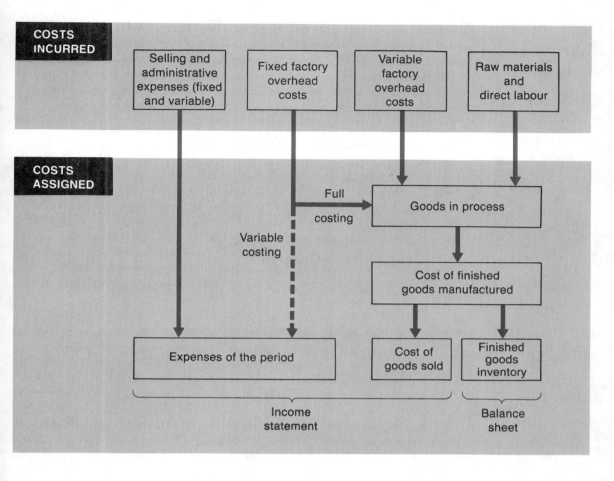

A partial income statement using the same data following the *variable costing* approach appears below:

FIXED FACTORY
OVERHEAD COSTS
TREATED AS EXPENSE
OF THE PERIOD

HAMILTON CORPORATION
Partial Income Statement — Variable Costing
For the Current Year

Sales (30,000 units @ $50)		$1,500,000
Cost of goods sold (30,000 units @ $20 variable manufacturing costs)		600,000
Manufacturing margin		$ 900,000
Variable selling and administrative expenses		150,000
Contribution margin		$ 750,000
Fixed costs:		
Manufacturing	$240,000	
Selling and administrative expenses	320,000	560,000
Income from operations		$ 190,000

(Ending inventory of finished goods, 10,000 units at $20 = $200,000)

In the income statement using variable costing, the variable manufacturing costs of the units sold are subtracted from sales to arrive at a subtotal called ***manufacturing margin.*** When variable selling and administrative expenses are deducted from this manufacturing margin we have the ***contribution margin,*** which is available to cover fixed costs and to contribute toward operating income. Income from operations is then determined by subtracting all fixed costs from the contribution margin.

Using a variable costing income statement   Notice how the variable costing income statement lends itself to cost-volume-profit analysis. For example, we may easily determine the contribution margin per unit by dividing the total contribution margin by the number of units sold ($750,000 ÷ 30,000 units = $25). The contribution margin per unit may then be used to compute Hamilton Corporation's break-even point, as follows:

$$\text{BREAK-EVEN SALES VOLUME} = \frac{\text{FIXED COSTS}}{\text{CONTRIBUTION MARGIN PER UNIT}}$$

$$= \frac{\$560,000}{\$25} = \underline{\underline{22,400 \text{ UNITS}}}$$

Effects of variable costing upon income and inventory   Comparing the two partial income statements shows that the income from operations using full costing exceeds by $60,000 the income using variable costing. This difference is explained by analyzing the disposition of fixed manufacturing costs under the two costing methods. Under variable costing, all $240,000 of the fixed manufacturing costs are recognized as expenses in the current period. Under full costing, however, the fixed manufacturing costs are apportioned between the ending inventory of finished goods and the cost of goods sold. Since only 75% of units produced were sold, only $180,000 of the $240,000 fixed manufacturing costs are included in the cost of goods sold. The remaining $60,000 in fixed costs are included in valuation of ending inventory.

Remember that variable costing is ***not acceptable*** for external financial reporting purposes. A company that uses variable costing must make adjusting entries at the end of the accounting period to convert from variable costing to full costing. In our example, notice that variable costing has caused Hamilton Corporation to understate its inventory of finished goods by $60,000 (25% of the fixed manufacturing costs) and its cost of goods sold by $180,000 (75% of the fixed manufacturing costs). Therefore, the year-end adjusting entry required to convert Hamilton Corporation's accounting records from variable costing to full costing would be as is illustrated below:

Finished Goods Inventory	60,000	
Cost of Goods Sold	180,000	
Fixed Manufacturing Costs (control account)		240,000

To convert from variable to full costing by allocating
fixed manufacturing costs to units produced.

6 Evaluate capital budgeting proposals using (a) the payback period, (b) return on average investment, and (c) discounted future cash flows.

CAPITAL BUDGETING

In terms of dollar amounts, some of the most significant decisions made by management involve expenditures to acquire plant assets. The process of planning and evaluating proposals for investment in plant assets is called *capital budgeting.* Capital budgeting decisions are complicated by the fact that the decision must be made from estimates of future operating results, which by their nature involve a considerable degree of uncertainty. Yet these decisions are crucial to the long-run financial health of a business enterprise. Not only are large amounts of money committed for long periods of time, but many capital budgeting decisions are difficult or impossible to reverse once the funds have been committed and the project has begun. Thus, companies may benefit from good capital budgeting decisions and suffer from poor ones for many years.

Many nonfinancial factors are considered in making capital budgeting decisions. For example, many companies give high priority to creating new jobs and avoiding layoffs. However, it is also essential that investments in plant assets earn a satisfactory return on the funds invested. Without this return, investors will not be willing to make funds available to finance the project and the company will not be able to generate sufficient funds for future investment projects.

Capital budgeting is a broad field, involving many sophisticated techniques for evaluating the financial and nonfinancial considerations. We shall limit our discussion in this area to three of the most common techniques of evaluating investment opportunities: payback period, return on average investment, and discounted cash flow analysis.

To illustrate these techniques, let us assume that Tanner Corporation is considering several alternative investments, including the purchase of equipment to produce a new product. The equipment costs $45,000, has a 10-year service life, and an estimated salvage value of $5,000. Tanner Corporation estimates that production and sale of the new product will increase the company's net income by $5,000 per year, computed as follows:

Estimated sales of new product		$40,000
Deduct estimates expenses:		
Depreciation on new equipment		
[($45,000 − $5,000) ÷ 10 years]	$ 4,000	
Manufacturing costs other than depreciation	20,000	
Additional selling and general expenses	6,000	30,000
Estimated increase in income before tax		$10,000
Less: Additional income taxes (50%)		5,000
Estimated increase in net income		$ 5,000

Most capital budgeting techniques involve analysis of the estimated annual net cash flows pertaining to the investment. Annual net cash flow is the excess of cash receipts over cash payments in a given year. In our example, assume that all revenue is received in cash and all expenses other than depreciation are paid in cash. Tanner

Corporation should expect an annual *net cash flow of $9,000* ($40,000 − $20,000 − $6,000 − $5,000) from sales of the new product. Note that annual net cash flow exceeds estimated net income ($5,000) by the amount of the depreciation expense ($4,000). This is because none of the cash received as revenue is paid out as depreciation expense. Other differences that may exist between net income and net cash flow were discussed in Chapter 19.

Payback period

The *payback period* is the length of time necessary to recover the entire cost of an investment from the resulting annual net cash flow. In our example, the payback period is computed as follows:

$$\frac{\text{AMOUNT TO BE INVESTED}}{\text{ESTIMATED ANNUAL NET CASH FLOW}} = \frac{\$45,000}{\$9,000} = 5 \text{ YEARS}$$

In selecting among alternative investment opportunities, a short payback period is considered desirable because the sooner the amount of the investment is recovered, the sooner the funds may be put to other use. A short payback period also reduces the risk that changes in economic conditions will prevent full recovery of the investment. Before an investment can be considered profitable, the life of the investment must exceed the payback period. However, the payback period ignores the total life and, therefore, the total profitability of the investment. For this reason, the payback period should never be the only factor considered in a major capital budgeting decision.

Return on average investment

The *rate of return on average investment* is the average annual net income from an investment expressed as a percentage of the *average* amount invested. Tanner Corporation will have to invest $45,000 in the new equipment, but each year depreciation will reduce the carrying value of this asset by $4,000. Since the annual cash flow will exceed net income by this amount, we may view depreciation expense as providing for the recovery of the amount originally invested. Thus, the amount invested in the equipment at any given time is represented by the carrying value (cost less accumulated depreciation) of the asset.

When straight-line depreciation is used, the carrying value of an asset decreases uniformly over the asset's life. Thus, the average carrying value is equal to an amount halfway between the asset's original cost and its salvage value. (When the expected salvage value is zero, the average investment is simply one-half of the original investment.) Mathematically, the average amount invested over the life of an asset may be determined as follows:

$$\text{AVERAGE INVESTMENT} = \frac{\text{ORIGINAL COST} + \text{SALVAGE VALUE}}{2}$$

Thus, Tanner Corporation will have an average investment in the new equipment of ($45,000 + $5,000) ÷ 2, or $25,000. We may compute the expected rate of return on this average investment as follows:

$$\frac{\text{AVERAGE ESTIMATED NET INCOME}}{\text{AVERAGE INVESTMENT}} = \frac{\$5,000}{\$25,000} = 20\%$$

In deciding whether 20% is a satisfactory rate of return, Tanner Corporation should consider such factors as the rate of return available from alternative investment opportunities, the risk involved in actually realizing the expected rate of return, the corporation's cost of capital, and the nonfinancial factors relating to the investment. In comparing alternative investment opportunities, management usually prefers the investment with the lowest risk, highest rate of return, and shortest payback period. Of course, the same investment is seldom superior to all others in every respect. Thus, managers must consider many subjective factors in making their decisions.

A weakness in the concept of return on average investment is the failure to consider the *timing* of the future cash flows. Computing the average annual net income, for example, ignores the question of whether the cash receipts will occur early or late in the life of the investment. Also, computing the average investment in the equipment fails to consider whether the purchase price of the equipment must be paid in advance or in instalments stretching over a period of years. A technique that does take into account the timing of cash flows is called *discounting* future cash flows.

Discounting future cash flows

As explained in Chapter 16, the present value of a future cash flow is the amount that a knowledgeable investor would pay today for the right to receive that future amount. The exact amount of the present value depends upon (1) the amount of the future payment, (2) the length of time until the future amount will be received, and (3) the rate of return required by the investor. *Discounting* is the process of determining the present value of cash flows.

The use of present value tables to discount future cash flows was demonstrated in Appendix A, entitled Applications of Present Value, at the end of Chapter 16. (Readers who are not familiar with the concept of present value and with the use of present value tables should review that appendix before continuing with this chapter.) The two present value tables presented in the appendix are repeated on page 1058 for your convenience.

Table 1 shows the present value of a single lump-sum payment of $1 to be received *n* periods (years) in the future. *Table 2* shows the present value of a $1 annuity — that is, $1 to be received each year for *n* consecutive years. For illustrative purposes, both tables have been kept short and include only selected discount rates and extend for a limited number of periods. However, the tables contain the appropriate rates and periods for all problem material in this chapter.

The discount rate may be viewed as the investor's required rate of return. The present value of the future cash flows is the maximum amount that the investor may pay for the investment and still expect to earn the required rate of return. Therefore, an investment is considered desirable when its cost is less than the present value of the expected future cash flows. Conversely, an investment is undesirable when its cost is greater than the present value of expected future cash flows.

The higher the discount rate being used, the lower will be the resulting present value. Therefore the investor will be interested in the investment only at a lower

TABLE 1
Present value of $1 Due in n Periods

NUMBER OF PERIODS (n)	DISCOUNT RATE							
	1%	1½%	5%	6%	10%	12%	15%	20%
1	.990	.985	.952	.943	.909	.893	.870	.833
2	.980	.971	.907	.890	.826	.797	.756	.694
3	.971	.956	.864	.840	.751	.712	.658	.579
4	.961	.942	.823	.792	.683	.636	.572	.482
5	.951	.928	.784	.747	.621	.567	.497	.402
6	.942	.915	.746	.705	.564	.507	.432	.335
7	.933	.901	.711	.665	.513	.452	.376	.279
8	.923	.888	.677	.627	.467	.404	.327	.233
9	.914	.875	.645	.592	.424	.361	.284	.194
10	.905	.862	.614	.558	.386	.322	.247	.162
20	.820	.742	.377	.312	.149	.104	.061	.026
24	.788	.700	.310	.247	.102	.066	.035	.013

TABLE 2
Present value of $1 to Be Received Periodically for n Periods

NUMBER OF PERIODS (n)	DISCOUNT RATE							
	1%	1½%	5%	6%	10%	12%	15%	20%
1	0.990	0.985	0.952	0.943	0.909	0.893	0.870	0.833
2	1.970	1.956	1.859	1.833	1.736	1.690	1.626	1.528
3	2.941	2.912	2.723	2.673	2.487	2.402	2.283	2.106
4	3.902	3.854	3.546	3.465	3.170	3.037	2.855	2.589
5	4.853	4.783	4.329	4.212	3.791	3.605	3.352	2.991
6	5.795	5.697	5.076	4.917	4.355	4.111	3.784	3.326
7	6.728	6.598	5.786	5.582	4.868	4.564	4.160	3.605
8	7.652	7.486	6.463	6.210	5.335	4.968	4.487	3.837
9	8.566	8.361	7.108	6.802	5.759	5.328	4.772	4.031
10	9.471	9.222	7.722	7.360	6.145	5.650	5.019	4.192
20	18.046	17.169	12.462	11.470	8.514	7.469	6.259	4.870
24	21.243	20.030	13.799	12.550	8.985	7.784	6.434	4.937

price. The "appropriate" discount rate for determining the present value of a specific investment depends upon the nature of that investment, the alternative investment opportunities available, and the investor's cost of capital.

Let us now apply the concept of discounting cash flows to our continuing example of the Tanner Corporation. We shall assume that Tanner Corporation requires a 15% annual rate of return on investments in new plant assets. The $45,000 investment in equipment is expected to produce annual net cash flows of $9,000 for 10 years. Table 2 on the preceding page shows that the present value of $1 to be received annually for 10 years, discounted at an annual rate of 15%, is 5.019. Therefore, the present value of $9,000 received annually for 10 years is $9,000 × 5.019, or $45,171.

In addition to the annual cash flows, Tanner Corporation expects to receive $5,000 in salvage value for the equipment at the end of the tenth year. Referring to Table 1 on the preceding page, we see that the present value of $1 due in 10 years, discounted at 15% per year, is .247. Thus, the present value of $5,000 to be received 10 years hence is $5,000 × .247, or $1,235. We may now analyze the proposal to invest in the equipment as follows:

Present value of expected annual cash flows ($9,000 × 5.019)	$45,171
Present value of proceeds from disposal of equipment ($5,000 × .247) . .	1,235
Total present value of future cash flows	$46,406
Amount to be invested (payable in advance)	45,000
Net present value of proposed investment	$ 1,406

This analysis indicates that the present value of the expected net cash flows from the investment, discounted at an annual rate of 15%, amounts to $46,406. This is the maximum amount that Tanner Corporation could afford to invest in the project and still expect to earn the required 15% annual rate of return. Since the actual cost of the investment is only $45,000 Tanner Corporation can expect to earn more than 15%.

The **net present value** of the proposal is the difference between the total present value of the net cash flows and the cost of the investment. When the net present value is equal to zero, the investment provides a rate of return exactly equal to the rate used in discounting the cash flows. A **positive** net present value means that the investment provides a rate of return **greater than the discount rate;** a **negative** net present value means that the investment yields a return of **less** than the discount rate. Since the discount rate is usually the minimum rate of return required by the investor, proposals with a positive net present value are considered acceptable and those with a negative net present value are viewed as unacceptable.

Replacement of old equipment

A problem often facing management is whether it should buy new and more efficient equipment or whether it should continue to use existing equipment. Assume, for example, that Ardmore Limited is meeting increasing competition in the sale of product Q. The sales manager believes the source of the trouble is that competitors have installed more efficient equipment, which has enabled them to reduce prices. The issue raised therefore is whether Ardmore Limited should (1) buy new equipment at a cost of $120,000, or (2) continue using its present equipment. We will make the simplifying assumption that both the new and present equipment have a remaining useful life of five years and neither will have any residual value. The new equipment will produce substantial savings in direct labour, raw materials, and factory overhead costs. The company does not believe the use of new equipment will have any effect on sales volume, so the decision rests entirely on whether cost savings are possible.

The old equipment has a book value of $100,000 but can be sold for only $20,000 if it is replaced. At first glance, the resulting $80,000 loss on disposal appears to be a good reason for not replacing the old equipment. However, the cost of the old equipment is a *sunk cost* and is not relevant to the decision. If the old machinery is sold, its book value contributes to the amount of the loss; if the old machinery is retained, its book value will be recognized as expense through future charges to depreciation. Thus, this cost cannot be avoided by Ardmore Limited regardless of which decision is made. From a present value standpoint, there is some benefit to recognizing this sunk cost as a loss in the current period inasmuch as the related tax reduction will occur this year rather than over the remaining life of the equipment.

In deciding whether to replace the old equipment, Ardmore Limited should determine the *present value of the incremental net cash flows* resulting from replacement of the old machinery. This present value may then be compared with the cost of the new equipment to determine whether the investment will provide the required rate of return. To compute the incremental annual net cash flow from replacing the old equipment, management must consider both the annual cash savings in manufacturing costs and the difference in annual income taxes. Income taxes will differ under the alternative courses of action because of differences in (1) variable manufacturing costs and (2) annual depreciation expense.

Let us assume that the new machinery will result in a $34,000 annual cash savings in variable manufacturing costs. However, annual depreciation on the new equipment will be $24,000 ($120,000 ÷ 5 years), whereas annual depreciation on the old equipment is $20,000 ($100,000 ÷ 5 years).[1] This $4,000 increase in depreciation expense means that purchase of the new equipment will *increase* taxable income by $30,000 ($34,000 cost savings less $4,000 additional depreciation). Assuming a tax rate of 40%, purchase of the new equipment will increase annual income tax expense by $12,000 ($30,000 × .40). The incremental annual net cash flow from owning the new machinery, therefore, amounts to $22,000 ($34,000 cost savings less $12,000 additional income tax expense).

We shall assume that Ardmore Limited requires a 12% return on investments in plant assets. Referring to the annuity table on page 1058, we see that the present value of $1 received annually for five years is 3.605. Therefore, $22,000 received annually for five years, discounted at an annual rate of 12%, has a present value of $79,310 ($22,000 × 3.605). In addition to the present value of the annual net cash flows, however, we must consider two other factors: (1) the proceeds from sale of the old equipment and (2) the tax savings resulting from the loss on disposal.

The $20,000 proceeds from sale of the old equipment will be received immediately and, therefore, have a present value of $20,000. The $80,000 loss on disposal is assumed, for tax purposes, to result in a $32,000 reduction ($80,000 × .4) in income taxes payable at the end of the first year. The present value of $32,000 one

---

[1] In order to focus on the essential issues and to simplify the calculations, it is assumed that the depreciation expenses are the same for income tax purposes.

year hence discounted at 12% is $28,576 ($32,000 × .893), as determined from a present value table.

We may now determine the net present value of the proposal to replace the old equipment with new as follows:

Present value of incremental annual cash flows ($22,000 × 3.605)	$ 79,310
Present value of proceeds from sale of old equipment	20,000
Present value of tax savings from loss on disposal ($32,000 × .893)	28,576
Total present value	$127,886
Amount to be invested	120,000
Net present value	$ 7,886

Since the total present value of all future cash flows from acquiring the new equipment exceeds the cost of the investment, Ardmore Limited should replace the old equipment with new.

Concluding comments

We have merely scratched the surface in discussing the possible kinds of analyses that might be prepared in making decisions. The brief treatment in this chapter, however, has been sufficient to establish the basic principles that lie behind such analyses. The most profitable course of action is determined by studying the costs and revenue that are *incremental* to the particular alternatives under consideration. The relevant information generally involves making *estimates* about the future. As a result, such information is subject to some degree of error. Of course it is important to remember that many nonfinancial factors may be brought into the decision picture after the quantitative analysis has been made.

END-OF-CHAPTER REVIEW

SUMMARY OF CHAPTER LEARNING OBJECTIVES

1 Identify the financial information that is relevant to a particular business decision.

Only that information which *varies* among the alternative courses of action being considered is relevant to the decision. Costs or revenue that do not vary among the alternative courses of action are not relevant to the decision.

2 Use incremental analysis to evaluate alternative courses of action.

Incremental analysis is the technique of comparing one course of action to another by determining the *differences* expected to arise in revenue and in costs.

3 Discuss the relevance of opportunity costs, sunk costs, and out-of-pocket costs in making business decisions.

An *opportunity cost* is the benefit that could have been obtained by pursuing another course of action. Opportunity costs often are subjective, but they are important considerations in any business decision. *Sunk costs,* on the other hand, have already been incurred as a result of past actions. These costs cannot be changed regardless of the action taken and are not relevant to the decision at hand. *Out-of-pocket costs* will be incurred in the future and are relevant if they will vary among the possible courses of action.

4 Determine the effect upon operating income of discontinuing a product line.

To determine the effects of discontinuing a product line, we must look at both the increases and decreases that may result in the level of operating income. In addition to the lost contribution margin from the discontinued line, factors to be considered include the effects upon sales of other products, opportunity costs, and possible reductions in "fixed" costs.

5 Explain the difference between full costing and variable costing.

Under full costing, fixed manufacturing costs are viewed as product costs and are included in the cost of finished goods manufactured. Under variable costing, fixed manufacturing costs are treated as period expenses. An income statement prepared on a variable costing basis is useful for cost-volume-profit analysis; however, variable costing is *not acceptable* for use in published financial statements.

6 Evaluate capital budgeting proposals using (a) the payback period, (b) return on average investment, and (c) discounted future cash flows.

The payback period is the length of time needed to recover the cost of an investment from the resulting net cash flows. However, this type of investment analysis fails to consider the total life and overall profitability of the investment.

   Return on average investment expresses the average estimated net income from the investment as a percentage of the average investment. This percentage represents the "rate of return" earned on the investment. A shortcoming is that "average" estimated net income ignores the timing of future cash flows. Therefore, no consideration is given to the "time value" of money.

   Discounting future cash flows determines the *net present value* of an investment proposal. Proposals with a positive net present value usually are considered acceptable, while proposals with a negative present value are considered unacceptable. This technique considers both the life of the investment and the timing of future cash flows.

KEY TERMS INTRODUCED OR EMPHASIZED IN CHAPTER 26

Capital budgeting The process of planning and evaluating proposals for investments in plant assets.

Discount rate The required rate of return used by an investor to discount future cash flows to their present value.

Discounted cash flows The present value of expected future cash flows.

Full (absorption) costing The traditional method of product costing in which both fixed and variable manufacturing costs are treated as product costs and charged to goods produced.

Incremental (or differential) cost The difference between the total cost of alternative courses of action.

Net present value The excess of the present value of the net cash flows expected from an investment over the amount to be invested. Net present value is one method of ranking alternative investment opportunities.

Opportunity cost The benefit foregone by not pursuing an alternative course of action. Opportunity costs are not recorded in the accounting records, but are important in making many types of business decisions.

Payback period The length of time necessary to recover the cost of an investment through the cash flows generated by that investment. Payback period is one criterion used in making capital budgeting decisions.

Present value The amount of money today that is considered equivalent to a cash inflow or outflow expected to take place in the future. The present value of money is always less than the future amount, since money on hand today can be invested to become the equivalent of a larger amount in the future.

Relevant information Information that should be given consideration in making a specific decision and that varies among the alternative courses of action being considered.

Return on average investment The average annual net income from an investment expressed as a percentage of the average amount invested. Return on average investment is one method of ranking alternative investment opportunities according to their relative profitability.

Sunk cost A cost that has irrevocably been incurred by past actions. Sunk costs are irrelevant to decisions regarding future actions.

Variable costing The technique of product costing in which variable manufacturing costs are charged to goods produced and fixed manufacturing costs are treated as period expenses.

ASSIGNMENT MATERIAL

REVIEW QUESTIONS

1 Comment on the following position taken by a business executive: "Since relevant quantitative information is difficult to obtain and is subject to some degree of error, I'd rather make decisions on the basis of subjective factors and my many years of business experience."

2 What is the difference between a *sunk cost* and an *out-of-pocket cost?*

3 Define *opportunity costs* and explain why they represent a common source of error in making cost analyses.

4 Briefly discuss the type of information you would want before deciding to discontinue the production of a major line of products.

5 Explain why the book value of existing equipment is not relevant in deciding whether the equipment should be scrapped (without realizing any proceeds) or continued in use.

6 The Inglis Corporation produces a large number of products. The costs per unit for one product, a fishing reel, are shown below:

Direct manufacturing costs (raw materials and direct labour)	$7.00
Variable factory overhead	4.00
Fixed factory overhead	2.00

The company recently decided to buy 10,000 fishing reels from another manufacturer for $12.50 per unit because "it was cheaper than our cost of $13.00 per unit." Evaluate the decision only on the basis of the cost data given.

7 A company regularly sells 100,000 washing machines at an average price of $250. The average cost of producing these machines is $180. Under what circumstances might the company accept an order for 20,000 washing machines at $175 per machine?

8 Distinguish between *variable costing* and *full costing*. Which method is used in published financial statements?

9 Explain why a variable costing income statement provides a better basis for cost-volume-profit analysis than does a full costing income statement.

10 The Liuku Company reports an amount labelled *manufacturing margin* in its income statement. The income statement is stamped "for management's use only." Explain what is meant by "manufacturing margin" and why the income statement containing this term is not issued to outsiders.

11 What is *capital budgeting?* Why are capital budgeting decisions crucial to the long-run financial health of a business enterprise?

12 A company invests $100,000 in plant assets with an estimated 20-year service life and no salvage value. These assets contribute $10,000 to annual net income when depreciation is computed on a straight-line basis. Compute the payback period and explain your computation.

13 What is the major shortcoming of using the payback period as the only criterion in making capital budgeting decisions?

14 What factors should an investor consider in appraising the adequacy of the rate of return from a specific investment proposal?

15 Discounting a future cash flow at 15% results in a lower present value than does discounting the same cash flow at 10%. Explain why.

16 What factors determine the present value of a future cash flow?

17 Discounting cash flows takes into consideration one characteristic of the earnings stream that is ignored in the computation of return on average investment. What is this characteristic and why is it important?

EXERCISES

Exercise 26-1
Accounting
terminology

Listed below are nine technical accounting terms emphasized in this chapter:

Sunk cost	Out-of-pocket cost	Opportunity cost
Full costing	Incremental analysis	Net present value
Variable costing	Relevant information	Capital budgeting

Each of the following statements may (or may not) describe one of these technical terms. For each statement, indicate the accounting term described, or answer "None" if the statement does not correctly describe any of the terms.

a The benefit foregone by not pursuing an alternative course of action.

b The process of planning and evaluating proposals for investment in plant assets.

c The average annual net income from an investment expressed as a percentage of the average amount invested.

d An accounting technique in which fixed manufacturing costs are viewed as expenses of the period, rather than as product costs.

e A cost that will occur in the future and that may vary depending upon future decisions.

f The method of assigning manufacturing costs to inventories and to the cost of goods sold that is in compliance with generally accepted accounting principles.

g A cost incurred in the past that cannot be changed as a result of future actions.

h Costs and revenue that are expected to vary, depending upon the course of action decided upon.

Exercise 26-2
Incremental analysis:
make or buy decision

The cost to Ellis Company of manufacturing 10,000 units of item X is $230,000, including $80,000 of fixed costs and $150,000 of variable costs. The company can buy the part from an outside supplier for $18.00 per unit, but the fixed factory overhead now allocated to the part will remain unchanged. Should the company buy the part or continue to manufacture it? Prepare a comparative schedule in the format illustrated in this chapter.

Exercise 26-3
Relevant information:
scrap or rework
decision

Auto Parts Company has 20,000 units of a defective product on hand that cost $43,200 to manufacture. The company can either sell this product as scrap for $1.18 per unit or it can sell the product for $4.20 per unit by reworking the units and correcting the defects at a cost of $26,400. What should the company do? Prepare a schedule in support of your recommendation.

Exercise 26-4
Eliminating a product
line

Following is the typical monthly operating data of Arrow Hardware Store:

	HARDWARE	SPORTING GOODS	TOTAL
Sales	$120,000	$ 6,000	$126,000
Cost of goods sold:			
Variable	(42,000)	(3,500)	(45,500)
Fixed	(12,000)	(1,200)	(13,200)
Gross profit on sales	$ 66,000	$ 1,300	$ 67,300
Operating expenses:			
Variable	(30,000)	(1,800)	(31,800)
Fixed	(18,000)	(2,500)	(20,500)
Operating income (before taxes)	$ 18,000	$(3,000)	$ 15,000

The store manager is considering discontinuing the sale of sporting goods in order to improve the profitability of the store. Prepare a schedule showing the effect upon monthly operating income of eliminating the sale of sporting goods. Assume that no fixed costs will be eliminated and that hardware sales will not change as a result of discontinuing sporting goods sales.

Exercise 26-5
Full costing and
variable costing

Following are the production and sales data for Aluminum Products Limited at the end of its first year of operations:

Sales (6,000 units × $76)	$456,000
Production costs (10,000 units):	
Variable	350,000
Fixed	210,000
Selling and administrative expenses (all fixed)	70,000

Compute income from operations for the year using (**a**) full costing and (**b**) variable costing.

Exercise 26-6
Discounting cash flows

Using the tables in the chapter, determine the present value of the following cash flows, discounted at an annual rate of 15%:

a $25,000 to be received 20 years from today

b $14,000 to be received annually for 5 years

c $45,000 to be received annually for 7 years, with an additional $30,000 salvage value due at the end of the seventh year.

d $30,000 to be received annually for the first 3 years, followed by $20,000 received annually for the next 2 years (total of 5 years in which cash is received).

Exercise 26-7
Capital budgeting

Bowman Corporation is considering an investment in special-purpose equipment to enable the company to obtain a four-year government contract for the manufacture of a special item. The equipment costs $300,000 and would have no salvage value when its use is discontinued at the end of the four years. Estimated annual operating results of the project are:

Revenue from contract sales		$325,000
Expenses other than depreciation	$225,000	
Depreciation (straight-line basis)	75,000	300,000
Increase in net income from contract work		$ 25,000

All revenue and all expenses other than depreciation will be received or paid in cash in the same period as recognized for accounting purposes. Compute, for the proposal to undertake the contract work, the following:

a Payback period.

b Return on average investment.

c Net present value of proposal to undertake contract work, discounted at an annual rate of 12%.

PROBLEMS

Group A

Problem 26A-1
Evaluating a special order

D. Lawrance designs and manufactures fashionable men's clothing. For the coming year, the company has scheduled production of 30,000 ultra-suede jackets. The budgeted costs for this product are as follows:

	UNIT COSTS (30,000 UNITS)	TOTAL
Variable manufacturing costs	$51	$1,530,000
Variable selling expenses	15	450,000
Fixed manufacturing costs	8	240,000
Fixed operating expenses	6	180,000
Total costs and expenses	$80	$2,400,000

The management of D. Lawrance is considering a special order from Discount House for an additional 10,000 jackets. These jackets would carry the Discount House label, rather than that of D. Lawrance. In all other respects, they would be identical to the regular D. Lawrance jackets.

Although D. Lawrance sells its regular jackets to retail stores at a price of $120 each, Discount House has offered to pay only $69 per jacket. However, no sales commissions are involved on this special order, so D. Lawrance would incur variable selling expenses of only $3 per unit on these jackets, rather than the regular $15. Accepting the order would cause no change in D. Lawrance's fixed costs or fixed operating expenses. D. Lawrance has enough plant capacity to produce 45,000 jackets per year.

Instructions **a** Using incremental revenue and incremental costs, compute the expected effect of accepting this special order upon D. Lawrance's operating income.

b Briefly discuss any other factors that you believe D. Lawrance's management should consider in deciding whether to accept this special order. You may include nonfinancial as well as financial considerations.

Problem 26A-2
Make or buy decision

Guaranteed Tools manufactures an electric motor that it uses in several of its products. Management is considering whether to continue manufacturing the motors, or whether to buy them from an outside source. The following information is available:

(1) The company needs 10,000 motors per year. The motors can be purchased from an outside supplier at a cost of $20 per unit.

(2) The cost of manufacturing the motors is $25 per unit, computed as follows:

Raw materials	$ 65,000
Direct labour	55,000
Factory overhead:	
Variable	70,000
Fixed	60,000
Total manufacturing costs	$250,000
Cost per unit ($250,000 ÷ 10,000 units)	$25

(3) Discontinuing the manufacture of motors will eliminate all of the raw materials and direct labour costs, but will eliminate only 60% of the variable factory overhead costs.

(4) If the motors are purchased from an outside source, certain machinery used in the production of motors will be sold at its book value. The sale of this machinery will reduce fixed factory overhead costs by $3,600 for depreciation and $400 for property taxes. No other reductions in fixed factory overhead will result from discontinuing production of the motors.

Instructions **a** Prepare a schedule in the format illustrated in this chapter to determine the incremental cost or benefit of buying the motors from the outside supplier. Based on this schedule, would you recommend that the company manufacture the motors or buy them from the outside source?

b Assume that if the motors are purchased from the outside source, the factory space previously used to produce motors can be used to manufacture an additional 7,000 power trimmers per year. Power trimmers have an estimated contribution margin of $8 per unit. The manufacture of the additional power trimmers would have no effect upon fixed factory overhead. Would this new assumption change your recommendation as to whether to make or buy the motors? In support of your conclusion, prepare a schedule showing the incremental cost or benefit of buying the motors from the outside source and using the factory space to produce additional power trimmers.

Problem 26A-3
Variable costing

At the beginning of the current year, Audio Corporation opened its Windville Plant to manufacture a new model stereo speaker. During the year, 100,000 speakers were manufactured, of which 80,000 were sold at a unit sales price of $90. Variable manufacturing costs for the year amounted to $3,600,000, and fixed manufacturing costs totalled $1,100,000. Variable operating expenses were $720,000, and fixed operating expenses were $970,000.

Instructions **a** Prepare a schedule showing variable, fixed, and total manufacturing costs per unit.

b Prepare partial income statements (ending with income from operations) for the Windville Plant for the current year using:
(1) Full costing
(2) Variable costing

c Briefly explain the difference in the amount of income from operations reported in the two partial income statements.

d Using the data contained in the variable costing income statement, compute (1) the contribution margin per unit sold, and (2) the number of speakers that must be manufactured and sold annually for the Windville Plant to cover its fixed manufacturing costs and fixed operating expenses — that is, to break even.

Problem 26A-4
Capital budgeting

Micro Technology is considering two alternative proposals for modernizing its production facilities. To provide a basis for selection, the cost accounting department has developed the following data regarding the expected annual operating results for the two proposals:

	PROPOSAL 1	PROPOSAL 2
Required investment in equipment	$360,000	$350,000
Estimated service life of equipment	8 years	7 years
Estimated salvage value	–0–	$ 14,000
Estimated annual cost savings (net cash flow)	$ 75,000	$ 76,000
Depreciation on equipment (straight-line basis)	$ 45,000	$ 48,000
Estimated increase in annual net income	$ 30,000	$ 28,000

Instructions **a** For each proposal, compute the (1) payback period, (2) return on average investment, and (3) net present value, discounted at an annual rate of 12%. (Round the payback period to the nearest tenth of a year and the return on investment to the nearest tenth of a percent.)

b Based on your analysis in part **a**, state which proposal you would recommend and explain the reasons for your choice.

Problem 26A-5
Another capital
budgeting problem

Rothmore Appliance Limited is planning to introduce a built-in blender to its line of small home appliances. Annual sales of the blender are estimated at 10,000 units at a price of $35 per unit. Variable manufacturing costs are estimated at $15 per unit, incremental fixed manufacturing costs (other than depreciation) at $40,000 annually, and incremental selling and general expenses relating to the blenders at $50,000 annually.

To build the blenders, the company must invest $240,000 in molds, patterns, and special equipment. Since the company expects to change the design of the blender every four years, this equipment will have a four-year service life with no salvage value. Depreciation will be computed on a straight-line basis. All revenue and expenses other than depreciation will be received or paid in cash. The company's income tax rate is 40%.

Instructions **a** Prepare a schedule showing the estimated annual net income from the proposal to manufacture and sell the blenders.

b Compute the annual net cash flow expected from the proposal.

c Compute for this proposal (1) payback period (round to the nearest tenth of a year), (2) return on average investment (round to the nearest tenth of a percent), and (3) net present value, discounted at an annual rate of 15%.

Group B

Problem 26B-1
Evaluating a special order

The Magic Game Company sells 600,000 game sets per year at $12.00 each. The current unit cost of the game sets is broken down as follows:

Raw materials	$2.50
Direct labour	2.70
Variable factory overhead	1.60
Fixed factory overhead	2.20
Total	$9.00

At the beginning of the current year the company receives a special order for 10,000 game sets per month *for one year only* at $8.00 per unit. A new machine with an estimated life of five years would have to be purchased for $30,000 to produce the additional units. Management thinks that it will not be able to use the new machine beyond one year and that it will have to be sold for approximately $20,000.

Instructions

Compute the estimated increase or decrease in annual operating income that will result from accepting this special order.

Problem 26B-2
Make or buy decision

Solar Systems manufactures a check valve that is used in several of its products. The vice president of production is considering whether to continue manufacturing these valves, or whether to buy them from an outside source at a cost of $8.50 per valve. Solar Systems uses 50,000 of the valves each year. The cost to manufacture the valves is $9.60 per unit, as shown below:

Raw materials	$150,000
Direct labour	140,000
Factory overhead:	
Variable	80,000
Fixed	110,000
Annual manufacturing costs for 50,000 valves	$480,000
Unit cost ($480,000 ÷ 50,000 units)	$9.60

If the valves are purchased, all of the raw materials and direct labour costs will be eliminated, and 80% of the variable overhead will be eliminated. In addition, some of the equipment used in the manufacture of the valves will be sold at its book value. The sale of this equipment will reduce fixed factory overhead costs by $7,900 for depreciation and $200 for property taxes. No other reduction in fixed factory overhead will result from discontinuing production of the valves.

Instructions

a Prepare a schedule in the format illustrated in this chapter to determine the incremental cost or benefit of buying the valves from the outside supplier. Based on this schedule, would you recommend that Solar Systems manufacture the valves or buy them from the outside source?

b Assume that if the valves are purchased from the outside source, the factory space previously used to manufacture valves can be used to manufacture an additional 2,000 solar collectors per year. Solar collectors have an estimated contribution margin of $70 per unit. Manufacturing the additional solar collectors would not increase fixed factory overhead. Would this new assumption change your recommendation as to whether to make or buy the check valves? In support of your conclusion, prepare a schedule showing the incremental cost or benefit of buying the valves from the outside supplier and using the factory space to produce more solar collectors.

Problem 26B-3
Variable costing and evaluating a special order

A partial income statement for the Bow River Company for the first year of its operations, prepared in conventional (full costing) form, is shown below. During the year 125,000 units were manufactured, of which 100,000 units were sold.

BOW RIVER COMPANY
Income Statement
For First Year of Operations (in thousands)

Sales (100,000 units at $100 per unit)		$10,000
Cost of goods sold:		
Raw material	$3,500	
Direct labour	2,750	
Variable factory overhead	250	
Fixed factory overhead	2,000	
Total manufacturing costs	$8,500	
Less: Ending finished goods inventory (25,000 units)	1,700	
Cost of goods sold ($68 per unit)		6,800
Gross profit on sales		$ 3,200
Less: Operating expenses:		
Variable	$1,000	
Fixed	1,200	
Total operating expenses		2,200
Income from operations		$ 1,000

Instructions

a Revise the statement using the variable (direct) costing approach. Briefly explain the difference in the income from operations reported in the two statements. (Note that income statement amounts are shown in thousands of dollars.)

b Prepare a schedule showing whether it would be profitable for the Bow River Company to accept an offer from a foreign customer to purchase 25,000 units for $60 per unit. This special order would have no effect on fixed factory overhead or on operating expenses.

Problem 26B-4
Capital budgeting

Banner Equipment Co. is evaluating two alternative investment opportunities. The controller of the company has prepared the following analysis of the two investment proposals:

	PROPOSAL A	PROPOSAL B
Required investment in equipment	$220,000	$240,000
Estimated service life of equipment	5 years	6 years
Estimated salvage value	$ 10,000	–0–
Estimated annual net cash flow	$ 60,000	$ 60,000
Depreciation on equipment (straight-line basis)	$ 42,000	$ 40,000
Estimated annual net income	$ 18,000	$ 20,000

Instructions

a For each proposed investment, compute the (1) payback period, (2) return on average investment, and (3) net present value, discounted at an annual rate of 12%. (Round the payback period to the nearest tenth of a year and the return on investment to the nearest tenth of a percent.)

b Based upon your computations in part **a**, which proposal do you consider to be the better investment? Explain.

Problem 26B-5
Evaluating changes in
operating income

Cornbelt Cereal Company is engaged in manufacturing a breakfast cereal. You are asked to advise management on sales policy for the coming year.

Two proposals are being considered by management that will (1) increase the volume of sales, (2) reduce the ratio of selling expense to sales, and (3) decrease manufacturing cost per unit. These proposals are as follows:

Proposal No. 1: Increase advertising expenditures by offering premium stamps

It is proposed that each box of cereal will contain premium stamps that will be redeemed for cash prizes. The estimated cost of this premium plan is estimated at $0.10 per box of cereal sold. The new advertising plan will take the place of all existing advertising expenditures and the current selling price of $1.00 per unit will be maintained.

Proposal No. 2: Reduce selling price of product

It is proposed that the selling price of the cereal be reduced to $0.95 per box, and that advertising expenditures be increased over those of the current year. This plan is an alternative to Proposal No. 1, and only one will be adopted by management.

Management has provided you with the following information as to the current year's operations:

Sales (5,000,000 boxes at $1.00 per box)	$5,000,000
Manufacturing costs (5,000,000 boxes at $0.60 per box)	3,000,000
Selling expenses, 20% of sales (one-fourth of which was for newspaper advertising)	1,000,000
Administrative expenses	420,000

Estimates for the coming year for each proposal are as follows:

	PROPOSAL NO. 1	PROPOSAL NO.2
Increase in unit sales volume	50%	30%
Decrease in manufacturing cost per unit	10%	5%
Newspaper advertising	None	10% of sales
Other selling expenses	8% of sales	8% of sales
Premium plan expense	$0.10 per box	None
Administrative expenses	$515,000	$475,000

Instructions

Which of the two proposals should management select? In support of your recommendation, prepare a statement comparing the income from operations for the current year with the anticipated income from operations for the coming year under Proposal No. 1 and under Proposal No. 2. In preparing the statement use the following three column headings: Current Year, Proposal No. 1, and Proposal No. 2.

BUSINESS DECISION CASES

Case 26-1
The case of the
costly laser

The management of Metro Printers is considering a proposal to replace some existing equipment with a new highly efficient laser printer. The existing equipment has a current book value of $2,200,000 and a remaining life (if not replaced) of 10 years. The laser printer has a cost of $1,300,000 and an expected useful life of 10 years. The laser printer would increase the company's annual cash flow by reducing operating costs and by increasing the company's ability to generate revenue. Susan Mills, controller of Metro Printers, has prepared the following estimates of the laser printer's effect upon annual earnings and cash flow:

Estimated increase in annual cash flow		
(before income taxes):		
Incremental revenue	$140,000	
Cost savings (other than depreciation)	110,000	$250,000
Reduction in annual depreciation expense:		
Depreciation on existing equipment	$220,000	
Depreciation on laser printer	130,000	90,000
Estimated increase in income before income taxes		$340,000
Increase in annual income taxes (40%)		136,000
Estimated increase in annual net income		$204,000
Estimated increase in annual net cash flow ($250,000 − $136,000)		$114,000

Don Adams, a director of Metro Printers, makes the following observation: "These estimates look fine, but won't we take a huge loss in the current year on the sale of our existing equipment? After the invention of the laser printer, I doubt that our old equipment can be sold for much at all." In response, Miller provides the following information about the expected loss on the sale of the existing equipment:

Book value of existing printing equipment	$2,200,000
Estimated current sales price, net of removal costs	200,000
Estimated loss on sale, before income taxes	$2,000,000
Reduction in current year's income taxes as a result of loss (40%)	800,000
Loss on sale of existing equipment, net of tax savings	$1,200,000

Adams replies, "Good grief, our loss would be almost as great as the cost of the laser printer. If we have to take a $1,200,000 loss and pay $1,300,000 for the laser printer, we'll be into the new equipment for $2,500,000. I'd go along with a cost of $1,300,000, but $2,500,000 is just too high a price to pay."

Instructions
a Compute the net present value of the proposal to sell the existing equipment and buy the laser printer, discounted at an annual rate of 15%. In your computation, make the following assumptions regarding the timing of cash flows:
 (1) The purchase price of the laser printer will be paid in cash immediately.
 (2) The $200,000 sales price of the existing equipment will be received in cash immediately.
 (3) The income tax benefit from selling the equipment will be realized one year from today.
 (4) The annual net cash flows may be regarded as received at year-end for each of the next ten years.

b Is the cost to Metro Printers of acquiring the laser printer $2,500,000, as Adams suggests? Explain fully.

Case 26-2
Congratulations!?
Advance Electronics opened its new Jefferson Plant at the beginning of the current year to manufacture a burglar alarm. During the year, the Jefferson Plant manufactured 60,000 burglar alarms, of which 50,000 were sold and 10,000 remain on hand as finished goods inventory.

There was no goods in process inventory at year-end. A partial income statement for the Jefferson Plant, prepared in conventional (full costing) form, is shown below:

JEFFERSON PLANT
Partial Income Statement
For First Year of Operations

Sales (50,000 units @ $60)		$3,000,000
Cost of goods sold:		
Manufacturing costs (60,000 units @ $42)	$2,520,000	
Less: Ending inventory (10,000 units @ $42)	420,000	2,100,000
Gross profit on sales		$ 900,000
Operating expenses:		
Variable ($8 per unit sold)	$ 400,000	
Fixed	425,000	825,000
Income from operations		$ 75,000

The $2,520,000 in total manufacturing costs consisted of the following cost elements:

Raw materials		$ 900,000
Direct labour		720,000
Factory overhead:		
Variable	$300,000	
Fixed	600,000	900,000
Total manufacturing costs		$2,520,000

The manager of the Jefferson Plant is proud of the $75,000 operating income reported for the first year of operations. However, the controller of Advance Electronics, an advocate of variable costing, makes the following statement: "The only reason that the Jefferson Plant shows a profit is that $100,000 of fixed costs are carried in the ending inventory figure. Actually, a sales volume of 50,000 units is below the break-even point."

Instructions

a Prepare a schedule showing each manufacturing cost on a per unit basis. As a subtotal in your schedule, show the variable manufacturing cost per unit. The final total in your schedule will be the total manufacturing cost per unit ($42).

b Prepare a revised partial income statement (concluding with Income from operations) for the Jefferson Plant using the variable costing approach.

c Briefly explain the difference in the amount of operating income reported in the two statements. Is the controller correct about the $420,000 ending inventory in the full costing statement including $100,000 of fixed manufacturing costs?

d Compute the contribution margin per unit sold.

e How many units must be produced and sold each year for the Jefferson Plant to break even — that is, to cover its fixed expenses? (In computing the break-even point, assume all units produced are sold.) Is the controller correct that the Jefferson Plant failed to achieve the break-even point in unit sales volume during its first year of operations?

INDEX

INDEX

NOTES

NOTES

NOTES

STUDENT REPLY CARD

In order to improve future editions, we are seeking your comments on
Accounting: The Basis for Business Decisions, Fifth Canadian Edition,
by Meigs, Meigs, and Lam.
After you have read this text, please answer the following questions and return
this form via Business Reply Mail. *Thanks in advance for your feedback!*

1. Name of your college or university: _____

2. Major program of study: _____

3. Your instructor for this course: _____

4. Are there any sections of this text which were not assigned as course reading?
    If so, please specify those chapters or portions:

5. How would you rate the overall accessibility of the content? Please
    feel free to comment on reading level, writing style, terminology, layout
    and design features, and such learning aids as chapter objectives,
    summaries, and appendices.

6. What did you like *best* about this book?

7. What did you like *least*?

If you would like to say more, we'd love to hear from you. Please write to us at
the address shown on the reverse of this card.

----------------------------------CUT HERE--------------------------------------

- -FOLD HERE -

(continued from inside front cover)

CHECKLIST OF KEY FIGURES

12B-5 (c) Bonus to existing partners, $60,000
12B-6 (d) Debit to Swartz, Capital, $26,250
12B-7 (b) Cash to Dell, $26,000
Case 12-1 No key figure
Case 12-2 No key figure

13A-1 No key figure
13A-2 No key figure
13A-3 (a) Profit under instalment method, 1989, $2 million
13A-4 (d) Decrease in purchasing power, $8,000
13A-5 Cost of goods sold, constant dollar basis, $425,000
13B-1 No key figure
13B-2 No key figure
13B-3 (a) Gross profit on boats under construction, $40,000
13B-4 (d) Increase in purchasing power, $14,000
13B-5 Cost of goods sold, constant dollar basis, $472,500
Case 13-1 No key figure
Case 13-2 (b) (1) Net income, same accounting, Year 9, $60,000; (2) Revised accounting, Year 9, $75,000.

14A-1 Shareholders' equity, (a) $363,000; (b) $6,320,000
14A-2 (b) Shareholders' equity, $881,500
14A-3 (b) Total assets, $1,008,200
14A-4 No key figure
14A-5 No key figure
14A-6 Shareholders' equity, (a) $895,000; (b) $1,983,000
14B-1 Shareholders' equity, (a) $189,000; (b) $1,390,000
14B-2 (d) Shareholders' equity, $730,300
14B-3 (b) Shareholders' equity, $990,000
14B-4 No key figure
14B-5 (c) Book value per share, $18
14B-6 Shareholders' equity, (a) $1,143,000; (b) $1,989,000
Case 14-1 No key figure
Case 14-2 No key figure

15A-1 Income before extraordinary item, $590,000
15A-2 Income before extraordinary items, $3,200,000
15A-3 (a) Net income, $700,000
15A-4 (a) Cumulative effect, $45,500

15A-5 Book value per share, July 31, $15.10
15A-6 (b) Shareholders' equity, $4,849,500
15A-7 (a) Total contributed capital, $2,830,000; (b) Retained earnings, $358,000
15B-1 Income before extraordinary item, $1,200,000
15B-2 Income before extraordinary items, $2,900,000
15B-3 (a) Net income, $300,000
15B-4 (a) Retained earnings, Dec. 31, 1989, $606,800
15B-5 Book value per share, July 21, $42
15B-6 (b) Shareholders' equity, $7,376,900
15B-7 (a) Shareholders' equity, $2,915,000; (b) Retained earnings, $483,800
Case 15-1 (b) Forecast net income, $2,815,000
Case 15-2 (d) Basic earnings per share, $7.59

16A-1 (c) Debit Bond Interest Expense, $200,000
16A-2 (b) Net bond liability, issued at 98, $8,826,000
16A-3 (b) Loss on retirement of bonds $114,400
16A-4 (c) (1) Premium on bonds payable, $248,000
16A-5 (b) Total long-term liability, $8,251,700
16A-6 (a) Carrying value of bonds, June 30, 1989, $9,417,000
16A-7 (c) Interest expense, issued at discount, $261,000; issued at premium, $248,000
16B-1 (c) Debit Bond Interest Expense, $225,000
16B-2 (b) Net bond liability, issued at 97, $11,646,000
16B-3 (b) Loss on retirement of bonds, $96,480
16B-4 (c) (1) Premium on bonds payable, $130,000
16B-5 (b) Net long-term liability, $5,840,400
16B-6 (a) Carrying value of bonds, June 30, 1990, $8,272,600
16B-7 (b) (4) Interest expense, $172,500
Case 16-1 No key figure
Case 16-2 No key figure

Appendix A
1 (c) Present value, $22,518
2 (b) Amortization of discount at June 30, $2,857,500
3 (c) Net liability, Dec. 31, $28,996
4 (a) Present value under five-year lease, $7,806,000
5 (b) Discount on Notes Receivable, $110,676

(continued on inside back cover)

This book is the property of the York Region
Board of Education and is on loan to:

Year	Name	Teacher
19 91	Conrad Chan	Mrs. Mooshuly
19		
19		
19		
19		
19		

Book No.	A reasonable sum will be charged if the book is lost or damaged.
88624	